HALSBURY'S
Laws of England

FIFTH EDITION
2015

Volume 36

This is volume 36 of the Fifth Edition of Halsbury's Laws of England, containing the second part of the title EDUCATION.

The title EDUCATION replaces the EDUCATION title contained in volumes 35 (2011), 36 (2011).

Volumes 35 (2011), 36 (2011) may now be archived.

For a full list of volumes comprised in a current set of Halsbury's Laws of England please see overleaf.

Fifth Edition volumes:

1 (2008), 2 (2008), 3 (2011), 4 (2011), 5 (2013), 6 (2011), 7 (2015), 8 (2015), 9 (2012), 10 (2012), 11 (2009), 12 (2009), 13 (2009), 14 (2009), 15 (2009), 16 (2011), 17 (2011), 18 (2009), 19 (2011), 20 (2014), 21 (2011), 22 (2012), 23 (2013), 24 (2010), 25 (2010), 26 (2010), 27 (2010), 28 (2010), 29 (2014), 30 (2012), 31 (2012), 32 (2012), 33 (2013), 34 (2011), 35 (2015), 36 (2015), 37 (2013), 38 (2013), 38A (2013), 39 (2014), 40 (2014), 41 (2014), 41A (2014), 42 (2011), 43 (2011), 44 (2011), 45 (2010), 46 (2010), 47 (2014), 47A (2014), 48 (2008), 49 (2008), 49 (2015), 50 (2008), 51 (2013), 52 (2014), 53 (2014), 54 (2008), 55 (2012), 56 (2011), 57 (2012), 58 (2014), 58A (2014), 59 (2014), 59A (2014), 60 (2011), 61 (2010), 62 (2012), 63 (2012), 64 (2012), 65 (2015), 66 (2015), 67 (2008), 68 (2008), 69 (2009), 70 (2012), 71 (2013), 72 (2015), 73 (2015), 74 (2011), 75 (2013), 76 (2013), 77 (2010), 78 (2010), 79 (2014), 80 (2013), 81 (2010), 82 (2010), 83 (2010), 84 (2013), 84A (2013), 85 (2012), 86 (2013), 87 (2012), 88 (2012), 88A (2013), 89 (2011), 90 (2011), 91 (2012), 92 (2010), 93 (2008), 94 (2008), 95 (2013), 96 (2012), 97 (2015), 97A (2014), 98 (2013), 99 (2012), 100 (2009), 101 (2009), 102 (2010), 103 (2010), 104 (2014)

Additional Materials:

Sentencing and Disposition of Offenders (Release and Recall of Prisoners) containing vol **92** (2010) paras 761–820

Consolidated Index and Tables:

2015 Consolidated Index (A–E), 2015 Consolidated Index (F–O), 2015 Consolidated Index (P–Z), 2016 Consolidated Table of Statutes, 2016 Consolidated Table of Statutory Instruments, etc, 2015 Consolidated Table of Cases (A–G), 2015 Consolidated Table of Cases (H–Q), 2015 Consolidated Table of Cases (R–Z, ECJ Cases)

Updating and ancillary materials:

2015 Annual Cumulative Supplement; Monthly Current Service; Annual Abridgments 1974–2014

September 2015

HALSBURY'S
Laws of England

Volume 36

2015

Members of the LexisNexis Group worldwide

United Kingdom	LexisNexis, a Division of Reed Elsevier (UK) Ltd, Lexis House, 30 Farringdon Street, LONDON, EC4A 4HH, and 9–10, St Andrew Square, EDINBURGH, EH2 2AF
Australia	Reed International Books Australia Pty Ltd trading as LexisNexis, Chatswood, New South Wales
Austria	LexisNexis Verlag ARD Orac GmbH & Co KG, Vienna
Benelux	LexisNexis Benelux, Amsterdam
Canada	LexisNexis Canada, Markham, Ontario
China	LexisNexis China, Beijing and Shanghai
France	LexisNexis SA, Paris
Germany	LexisNexis GmbH, Dusseldorf
Hong Kong	LexisNexis Hong Kong, Hong Kong
India	LexisNexis India, New Delhi
Italy	Giuffrè Editore, Milan
Japan	LexisNexis Japan, Tokyo
Malaysia	Malayan Law Journal Sdn Bhd, Kuala Lumpur
New Zealand	LexisNexis New Zealand Ltd, Wellington
Singapore	LexisNexis Singapore, Singapore
South Africa	LexisNexis, Durban
USA	LexisNexis, Dayton, Ohio

FIRST EDITION	*Published in 31 volumes between 1907 and 1917*
SECOND EDITION	*Published in 37 volumes between 1931 and 1942*
THIRD EDITION	*Published in 43 volumes between 1952 and 1964*
FOURTH EDITION	*Published in 56 volumes between 1973 and 1987, with reissues between 1988 and 2008*
FIFTH EDITION	*Published between 2008 and 2014, with reissues from 2014*

A CIP Catalogue record for this book is available from the British Library.

ISBN 13 (complete set, standard binding): 9781405734394

ISBN 13: 9781405798525

ISBN 978-1-4057-9852-5

9 781405 798525

Typeset by Letterpart Limited, Caterham on the Hill, Surrey CR3 5XL
Printed and bound by CPI Group (UK) Ltd, Croydon, CR0 4YY
Visit LexisNexis at www.lexisnexis.co.uk

EDUCATION

Consultant Editor
TANYA CALLMAN, MA (Cantab),
Barrister and Legal Trainer, EduLaw Chambers;
Member of the Honourable Society of the Middle Temple;
Ad Eundem Member of the Honourable Society of the Inner Temple;
Exhibitioner at Peterhouse, Cambridge;
Founder and Former Editor of Education, Public Law and the Individual

The law stated in this volume is in general that in force on 1 August 2015,
although subsequent changes have been included wherever possible.

Any future updating material will be found in the Current Service and annual
Cumulative Supplement to Halsbury's Laws of England.

TABLE OF CONTENTS

HOW TO USE HALSBURY'S LAWS OF ENGLAND

Volumes

Each text volume of Halsbury's Laws of England contains the law on the titles contained in it as at a date stated at the front of the volume (the operative date).

Information contained in Halsbury's Laws of England may be accessed in several ways.

First, by using the tables of contents.

Each volume contains both a general Table of Contents, and a specific Table of Contents for each title contained in it. From these tables you will be directed to the relevant part of the work.

Readers should note that the current arrangement of titles can be found in the Current Service.

Secondly, by using tables of statutes, statutory instruments, cases or other materials.

If you know the name of the Act, statutory instrument or case with which your research is concerned, you should consult the Consolidated Tables of statutes, cases and so on (published as separate volumes) which will direct you to the relevant volume and paragraph.

(Each individual text volume also includes tables of those materials used as authority in that volume.)

Thirdly, by using the indexes.

If you are uncertain of the general subject area of your research, you should go to the Consolidated Index (published as separate volumes) for reference to the relevant volume(s) and paragraph(s).

(Each individual text volume also includes an index to the material contained therein.)

Updating publications

The text volumes of Halsbury's Laws should be used in conjunction with the annual Cumulative Supplement and the monthly Noter-Up.

The annual Cumulative Supplement

The Supplement gives details of all changes between the operative date of the text volume and the operative date of the Supplement. It is arranged in the same volume, title and paragraph order as the text volumes. Developments affecting particular points of law are noted to the relevant paragraph(s) of the text volumes.

For narrative treatment of material noted in the Cumulative Supplement, go to the Annual Abridgment volume for the relevant year.

Destination Tables

In certain titles in the annual *Cumulative Supplement*, reference is made to Destination Tables showing the destination of consolidated legislation. Those Destination Tables are to be found either at the end of the titles within the annual *Cumulative Supplement*, or in a separate *Destination Tables* booklet provided from time to time with the *Cumulative Supplement*.

The Noter-Up

The Noter-Up is contained in the Current Service Noter-Up booklet, issued monthly and noting changes since the publication of the annual Cumulative Supplement. Also arranged in the same volume, title and paragraph order as the text volumes, the Noter-Up follows the style of the Cumulative Supplement.

For narrative treatment of material noted in the Noter-Up, go to the relevant Monthly Review.

REFERENCES AND ABBREVIATIONS

ACT	Australian Capital Territory
A-G	Attorney General
Admin	Administrative Court
Admlty	Admiralty Court
Adv-Gen	Advocate General
affd	affirmed
affg	affirming
Alta	Alberta
App	Appendix
art	article
Aust	Australia
B	Baron
BC	British Columbia
C	Command Paper (of a series published before 1900)
c	chapter number of an Act
CA	Court of Appeal
CAC	Central Arbitration Committee
CA in Ch	Court of Appeal in Chancery
CB	Chief Baron
CCA	Court of Criminal Appeal
CCR	County Court Rules 1981 (as subsequently amended)
CCR	Court for Crown Cases Reserved
CJEU	Court of Justice of the European Union
C-MAC	Courts-Martial Appeal Court
CO	Crown Office
COD	Crown Office Digest
CPR	Civil Procedure Rules
Can	Canada
Cd	Command Paper (of the series published 1900–18)
Cf	compare
Ch	Chancery Division
ch	chapter
cl	clause
Cm	Command Paper (of the series published 1986 to date)

Cmd	Command Paper (of the series published 1919–56)
Cmnd	Command Paper (of the series published 1956–86)
Comm	Commercial Court
Comr	Commissioner
Court Forms (2nd Edn)	Atkin's Encyclopaedia of Court Forms in Civil Proceedings, 2nd Edn. See note 2 post.
CrimPR	Criminal Procedure Rules
DC..	Divisional Court
DPP	Director of Public Prosecutions
EAT	Employment Appeal Tribunal
EC	European Community
ECJ.......................................	Court of Justice of the European Community (before the Treaty of Lisbon (OJ C306, 17.12.2007, p 1) came into force on 1 December 2009); European Court of Justice (after the Treaty of Lisbon (OJ C306, 17.12.2007, p 1) came into force on 1 December 2009)
EComHR...............................	European Commission of Human Rights
ECSC.....................................	European Coal and Steel Community
ECtHR Rules of Court...........	Rules of Court of the European Court of Human Rights
EEC.......................................	European Economic Community
EFTA	European Free Trade Association
EGC	European General Court
EWCA Civ	Official neutral citation for judgments of the Court of Appeal (Civil Division)
EWCA Crim..........................	Official neutral citation for judgments of the Court of Appeal (Criminal Division)
EWHC...................................	Official neutral citation for judgments of the High Court
Edn.......................................	Edition
Euratom	European Atomic Energy Community
EU	European Union
Ex Ch	Court of Exchequer Chamber
ex p	ex parte
Fam	Family Division
Fed	Federal
Forms & Precedents (5th Edn)...................................	Encyclopaedia of Forms and Precedents other than Court Forms, 5th Edn. See note 2 post.
GLC	Greater London Council
HC	High Court
HC	House of Commons

HK	Hong Kong
HL	House of Lords
IAT	Immigration Appeal Tribunal
ILM	International Legal Materials
INLR	Immigration and Nationality Law Reports
IRC	Inland Revenue Commissioners
Ind	India
Int Rels	International Relations
Ir	Ireland
J	Justice
JA	Judge of Appeal
Kan	Kansas
LA	Lord Advocate
LC	Lord Chancellor
LCC	London County Council
LCJ	Lord Chief Justice
LJ	Lord Justice of Appeal
LoN	League of Nations
MR	Master of the Rolls
Man	Manitoba
n	note
NB	New Brunswick
NI	Northern Ireland
NS	Nova Scotia
NSW	New South Wales
NY	New York
NZ	New Zealand
OHIM	Office for Harmonisation in the Internal Market
OJ	The Official Journal of the European Community published by the Office for Official Publications of the European Community
Ont	Ontario
P	President
PC	Judicial Committee of the Privy Council
PEI	Prince Edward Island
Pat	Patents Court
q	question
QB	Queen's Bench Division
QBD	Queen's Bench Division of the High Court
Qld	Queensland
Que	Quebec
r	rule

RDC...............................	Rural District Council
RPC...............................	Restrictive Practices Court
RSC...............................	Rules of the Supreme Court 1965 (as subsequently amended)
reg	regulation
Res	Resolution
revsd.............................	reversed
Rly................................	Railway
s..................................	section
SA................................	South Africa
S Aust............................	South Australia
SC................................	Supreme Court
SI.................................	Statutory Instruments published by authority
SR & O	Statutory Rules and Orders published by authority
SR & O Rev 1904	Revised Edition comprising all Public and General Statutory Rules and Orders in force on 31 December 1903
SR & O Rev 1948	Revised Edition comprising all Public and General Statutory Rules and Orders and Statutory Instruments in force on 31 December 1948
SRNI	Statutory Rules of Northern Ireland
STI...............................	Simon's Tax Intelligence (1973–1995); Simon's Weekly Tax Intelligence (1996-current)
Sask	Saskatchewan
Sch...............................	Schedule
Sess..............................	Session
Sing	Singapore
TCC	Technology and Construction Court
TS................................	Treaty Series
Tanz..............................	Tanzania
Tas...............................	Tasmania
UDC	Urban District Council
UKHL..............................	Official neutral citation for judgments of the House of Lords
UKPC	Official neutral citation for judgments of the Privy Council
UN	United Nations
V-C...............................	Vice-Chancellor
Vict..............................	Victoria
W Aust............................	Western Australia
Zimb	Zimbabwe

NOTE 1. A general list of the abbreviations of law reports and other sources used in this work can be found at the beginning of the Consolidated Table of Cases.

NOTE 2. Where references are made to other publications, the volume number precedes and the page number follows the name of the publication; eg the reference '12 Forms & Precedents (5th Edn) 44' refers to volume 12 of the Encyclopaedia of Forms and Precedents, page 44.

NOTE 3. An English statute is cited by short title or, where there is no short title, by regnal year and chapter number together with the name by which it is commonly known or a description of its subject matter and date. In the case of a foreign statute, the mode of citation generally follows the style of citation in use in the country concerned with the addition, where necessary, of the name of the country in parentheses.

NOTE 4. A statutory instrument is cited by short title, if any, followed by the year and number, or, if unnumbered, the date.

TABLE OF STATUTES

TABLE OF STATUTORY INSTRUMENTS

TABLE OF EUROPEAN
UNION LEGISLATION

TABLE OF CONVENTIONS ETC

TABLE OF CASES

PARA

R

PARA

PARA

PARA

Decisions of the European Court of Justice are listed below numerically. These decisions
are also included in the preceding alphabetical list.

EDUCATION

5. EDUCATION, TRAINING AND APPRENTICESHIPS

(1) ENTITLEMENT TO EDUCATION AND TRAINING

724.   Entitlement to education and training for persons aged 16 to 18.   As from a day to be appointed the following provisions have effect[1].

A person[2] over compulsory school age[3] but under 19 has the core entitlement[4].

'The core entitlement' is an entitlement to follow a course of study[5] in each of the core subjects chosen by the person who has the entitlement (the 'chosen core subjects')[6]. The core entitlement is satisfied in relation to a person if a course of study in each of the chosen core subjects is made available to the person at a school[7] or institution[8]. A person's entitlement to follow a course of study in one of the chosen core subjects ceases if a course of study in the subject is made available to the person[9], but the person does not begin the course of study before reaching the age of 19[10].

1   The Education Act 1996 ss 17A–17D are added by the Apprenticeships, Skills, Children and Learning Act 2009 s 45 as from a day to be appointed under s 269(4). At the date at which this volume states the law no such day had been appointed. The Education Act 1996 s 17B and s 17D are repealed from 15 January 2012 by virtue of the Education Act 2011 s 30(1), (4), (6).
2   As to the meaning of 'person' see PARA 7 note 6.
3   As to the meaning of 'compulsory school age' see PARA 19.
4   Education Act 1996 s 17C(A1) (s 17C as added (see note1); and s 17C(A1) added by the Education Act 2011 s 30(1), (5)(a)). As to the duty of a local authority in England to exercise its functions in such a way as to secure that the core entitlement is satisfied in relation to persons in its area who are over compulsory school age but under 19 see the Education Act 1996 s 17A(1), (6), (9); and PARA 35.
5   'Course of study' means a course of education or training leading to a qualification specified, or a qualification of a description specified, by the Secretary of State by order for these purposes: Education Act 1996 s 17C(5) (s 17C as added (see note 1); and s 17C(5) added by the Education Act 2011 s 30(1), (5)(c)). As to the Secretary of State see PARA 58. At the date at which this volume states the law no such order had been made.
6   Education Act 1996 s 17A(7), 17C(1) (both as added (see note 1); and s 17C(1) amended by the Education Act 2011 s 30(1), (5)(b)). The core subjects are mathematics, English, and information and communication technology: Education Act 1996 s 17C(2) (as so added).
7   As to the meaning of 'school' see PARA 91.
8   Education Act 1996 s 17C(3) (as added: see note 1).
9   Education Act 1996 s 17C(4)(a) (as added: see note 1).
10 Education Act 1996 s 17C(4)(b) (as added: see note 1).

(2) DUTY TO PARTICIPATE IN EDUCATION OR TRAINING

(i) Duty of Young Persons

725.   Duty to participate in education or training.   Any person[1] who is resident in England[2] and who has ceased to be of compulsory school age[3], has not reached the age of 18[4], and has not attained a level 3 qualification[5], must[6]:

(1)   be participating in appropriate full-time education or training[7];

(2)   be participating in training in accordance with a contract of apprenticeship or an apprenticeship agreement[8]; or

(3)   both be in full-time occupation[9], and participate in sufficient relevant training or education in each relevant period[10].

For these purposes, a person who is in full-time occupation is to be taken to be participating in sufficient relevant training or education at any particular time if: (a) arrangements have been made (whether by means of enrolment on a course or courses, or otherwise) for the person to receive sufficient relevant training or education during the current relevant period[11]; and (b) where the arrangements call for the person to be participating in training or education at the time, the person is so participating[12].

Regulations[13] may provide for any provision relating to the duty to participate in education or training[14] to apply with modifications[15] in cases where a person[16] (i) is employed under a contract of employment[17]; and (ii) is for the time being supplied by the employer to another person[18] ('the principal') to perform work in accordance with a contract made between the employer and the principal[19].

1   Ie a person to whom the Education and Skills Act 2008 Pt 1 (ss 1–67) applies: see s 1.
2   Regulations may provide for a person to be, or not to be, regarded as resident in England for the purposes of any provision of the Education and Skills Act 2008 Pt 1 (ss 1–67): s 66(2). 'Regulations' means regulations made under the Education and Skills Act 2008 by the Secretary of State: s 168(1). As to the Secretary of State see PARA 58. At the date at which this volume states the law no such regulations had been made under s 66(2). As to the meaning of 'England' see PARA 7 note 3.
3   Education and Skills Act 2008 s 1(a). As to the meaning of 'compulsory school age' see PARA 19.
4   Education and Skills Act 2008 s 1(b). As to the time at which a person attains a particular age see PARA 7 note 6.
5   Education and Skills Act 2008 s 1(c). 'Level 3 qualification' means a prescribed qualification, or a qualification of a prescribed description, at level 3: s 3(1) (amended by SI 2013/1242). For this purpose, 'level 3' is the level of attainment (in terms of breadth and depth) which, in the opinion of the Secretary of State, is demonstrated by the General Certificate of Education at the advanced level in two subjects: Education and Skills Act 2008 s 3(2). A qualification, or description of qualification, prescribed under s 3(1) may be prescribed by reference to an assessment made by the Office of Qualifications and Examinations Regulation (Ofqual) of the level of attainment demonstrated by a qualification; and for that purpose regulations under s 3(1) may confer a function (which may include the exercise of a discretion) on Ofqual: s 3(3) (amended by SI 2013/1242). The Secretary of State may by order amend the Education and Skills Act 2008 s 3(2) so as to substitute a different qualification for the qualification for the time being referred to: s 3(5). 'Prescribed' means prescribed by regulations: see s 168(1). As to regulations made for the purposes of the Education and Skills Act 2008 s 3(1), see the Duty to Participate in Education or Training (Miscellaneous Provisions) Regulations 2013, SI 2013/1205. As to the Office of Qualifications and Examinations Regulation (Ofqual) see PARA 825 et seq.
6   As to the enforcement of this duty see PARA 747 et seq.
7   Education and Skills Act 2008 s 2(1)(a). As to the meaning of 'appropriate full-time education or training' see PARA 726.
8   Education and Skills Act 2008 s 2(1)(b) (amended by the Apprenticeships, Skills, Children and Learning Act 2009 s 37(1), (2)). As to the meaning of 'apprenticeship agreement' see PARA 766 (definition applied by the Education and Skills Act 2008 s 66(1) (amended by the Apprenticeships, Skills, Children and Learning Act 2009 s 37(1), (3)(a))).
9   Education and Skills Act 2008 s 2(1)(c)(i). As to the meaning of 'full-time occupation' see PARA 727.
10 Education and Skills Act 2008 s 2(1)(c)(ii). As to the meanings of 'sufficient relevant training or education' and 'relevant period' see PARA 728. As to the position if a measure of the National Assembly for Wales includes provision that appears to the Secretary of State to correspond to provision made by s 2, see PARA 759. The Education and Skills Act 2008 s 2(1)(c)(ii), (2)(a) is modified in relation to a person serving as a member of the armed forces of the Crown: see the Duty to Participate in Education and Training (Miscellaneous Provisions) Regulations 2013, SI 2013/1205, reg 8.
11 Education and Skills Act 2008 s 2(2)(a). See note 10.
12 Education and Skills Act 2008 s 2(2)(b).
13 At the date at which this volume states the law no such regulations had been made.
14 Ie any provision of the Education and Skills Act 2008 Pt 1 (ss 1–67).
15 As to the meaning of 'modifications' see PARA 21 note 15 (definition applied by the Education and Skills Act 2008 s 168(2), (3)).

16   Ie a person to whom the Education and Skills Act 2008 Pt 1 (ss 1–67). As to such persons see s 1; and the text to notes 1–6.

17   Education and Skills Act 2008 s 61(2)(a). At the date at which this volume states the law do day had been appointed for the commencement of s 61. 'Contract of employment' means a contract of service, whether express or implied and (if it is express) whether oral or in writing, but does not include a contract of apprenticeship or an apprenticeship agreement: s 66(1) (definition amended by the Apprenticeships, Skills, Children and Learning Act 2009 s 37(1), (3)(b)). As to the meaning of 'writing' see PARA 76 note 8. As to contracts of employment see EMPLOYMENT vol 39 (2014) PARA 1 et seq.

18   As to the meaning of 'person' in this context see PARA 7 note 6.

19   Education and Skills Act 2008 s 61(2)(b). See note 17.

726. Meaning of 'appropriate full-time education or training'. 'Appropriate full-time education or training', in relation to a person, means full-time education or training which is suitable for the person, having regard:

(1)   to the person's age, ability and aptitude[1]; and

(2)   to any special educational needs[2] which the person may have[3],

and is provided at a school[4], at a college of further education[5], at an institution within the higher education sector[6] or otherwise[7].

Regulations[8] may provide that a particular description of education provided otherwise than at a school[9], or training[10], is, or is not, to be treated as being 'full-time' for these purposes[11].

1   Education and Skills Act 2008 s 4(1)(a).

2   As to the meaning of 'special educational needs' see PARA 943 (definition applied by the Education and Skills Act 2008 s 168(2), (3)). In regard to codes of practice see also PARA 978.

3   Education and Skills Act 2008 s 4(1)(b) (amended by the Children and Families Act 2014 Sch 3 paras 82, 83(a)).

4   As to the meaning of 'school' see PARA 91 (definition applied by the Education and Skills Act 2008 s 168(2), (3)).

5   As to the meaning of 'further education' see PARA 23 (definition applied by the Education and Skills Act 2008 s 168(2), (3)).

6   As to the meaning of 'institution within the higher education sector' see PARA 619 (definition applied by the Education and Skills Act 2008 s 168(2), (3)).

7   Education and Skills Act 2008 s 4(1).

8   'Regulations' means regulations made under the Education and Skills Act 2008 by the Secretary of State: s 168(1). As to the Secretary of State see PARA 58. As to regulations made for the purposes of s 4, see the Duty to Participate in Education or Training (Miscellaneous Provisions) Regulations 2013, SI 2013/1205.

9   Education and Skills Act 2008 s 4(2)(a).

10   Education and Skills Act 2008 s 4(2)(b).

11   Education and Skills Act 2008 s 4(2).

727. Meaning of 'full-time occupation'. A person is in 'full-time occupation' if he works for at least 20 hours per week:

(1)   under a contract of employment[1]; or

(2)   in any other way which may be prescribed[2],

otherwise than under a short-term contract or arrangement[3]. For these purposes, the number of hours for which a person works per week is the number of the person's normal weekly working hours[4], less the number of hours of actual guided learning[5] which constitute relevant training or education[6] and in which the young person participates each week during normal weekly working hours[7]. Where a person works otherwise than under a single contract of employment[8] or a single arrangement[9], the number of hours for which the person works per week is the aggregate of the amounts calculated as above[10] in relation to each of the contracts or arrangements under which the person works[11].

For the purposes of the above provisions[12]:

(a) Crown employment[13], and service as a member of the armed forces of the Crown[14], are each to be treated as working under a contract of employment[15]; and

(b) working as a relevant member of the House of Commons staff[16] is to be treated as working under a contract of employment[17].

Specified provisions of the Education and Skills Act 2008[18] apply in relation to employment under a contract of employment with the Corporate Officer of the House of Lords[19] as they apply in relation to other employment[20].

1 Education and Skills Act 2008 s 5(1)(a). As to the meaning of 'contract of employment' see PARA 725 note 17.

2 Education and Skills Act 2008 s 5(1)(b). The power conferred by s 5(1)(b) includes, in particular, power to prescribe the following ways of working: (1) as a self-employed person (s 5(2)(a)); (2) otherwise than for reward (s 5(2)(b)); or (3) as the holder of an office (s 5(2)(c)). Regulations may: (a) provide for who is to be treated as the employer for the purposes of Pt 1 (ss 1–67) in relation to any way of working prescribed by regulations under s 5(1)(b) (s 61(1)(a)), and (b) provide for any provision of Pt 1 to apply with modifications in relation to any such way of working (s 61(1)(b)). As to the meaning of 'modifications' see PARA 21 note 15 (definition applied by s 168(2), (3)). 'Prescribed' means prescribed by regulations; and 'regulations' means regulations made under the Education and Skills Act 2008 by the Secretary of State: s 168(1). As to the Secretary of State see PARA 58. See the Duty to Participate in Education or Training (Alternative Ways of Working) Regulations 2013, SI 2013/1243.

3 Education and Skills Act 2008 s 5(1). For these purposes: (1) a contract of employment is a short-term contract unless it has a fixed term of eight weeks or longer (s 5(8)(a)(i)), or does not have a fixed term but has been, or can reasonably be expected to be, in force for at least eight weeks (s 5(8)(a)(ii)); (2) an arrangement, in the case of a way of working prescribed under s 5(1)(b) (see head (2) in the text), is a short-term arrangement unless it has been, or can reasonably be expected to be, in force for at least eight weeks (s 5(8)(b)).

4 Education and Skills Act 2008 s 5(3)(a). 'Normal weekly working hours': (1) in relation to a person employed under a contract of employment, means the person's normal working hours in a week (s 5(4)(a)); and (2) in relation to a person working in a way prescribed under s 5(1)(b) (see head (2) in the text), has the prescribed meaning (s 5(4)(b)). The Employment Rights Act 1996 s 234 (construction of references to normal working hours where employee entitled to overtime pay: see EMPLOYMENT vol 39 (2014) PARA 142) applies for the purposes of the definition of 'normal weekly working hours' as it applies for the purposes of that Act: Education and Skills Act 2008 s 5(5). Regulations may make provision for a person to be, or not to be, treated as working for at least 20 hours per week in cases where the number of hours for which the person works per week (calculated under s 5(3)) varies from week to week: s 5(6). As to regulations made for the purposes of the Education and Skills Act 2008 s 5(4)(b), (6), see Duty to Participate in Education or Training (Miscellaneous Provisions) Regulations 2013, SI 2013/1205.

5 'Actual guided learning' has the meaning given by the Education and Skills Act 2008 s 8(3) (see PARA 728 note 4): s 5(4).

6 Education and Skills Act 2008 s 5(3)(b)(i). As to the meaning of 'relevant training or education' see PARA 728.

7 Education and Skills Act 2008 s 5(3)(b)(ii).

8 Education and Skills Act 2008 s 5(7)(a).

9 Ie in the case of a way of working prescribed under the Education and Skills Act 2008 s 5(1)(b) (see head (2) in the text): see s 5(7)(b).

10 Ie under the Education and Skills Act 2008 s 5(3): see the text to notes 4–7.

11 Education and Skills Act 2008 s 5(7).

12 Ie for the purposes of the Education and Skills Act 2008 s 5: see the text to notes 1–11.

13 Education and Skills Act 2008 s 62(1)(a). 'Crown employment' means employment under or for the purposes of a government department or any officer or body exercising on behalf of the Crown functions conferred by statutory provision (s 62(5)); however, Crown employment does not include service as a member of the armed forces of the Crown (s 62(6)(a)), but does include employment by an association established for the purposes of the Reserve Forces Act 1996 Pt XII (ss 110–119) (see ARMED FORCES vol 3 (2011) PARA 473) (Education and Skills Act 2008 s 62(6)(b)).

14 Education and Skills Act 2008 s 62(1)(b).

15 Education and Skills Act 2008 s 62(1). Regulations may provide for Ch 1 (ss 1–9) to have effect subject to modifications in relation to persons working in either of those ways: s 62(2). Chapter 3 (ss 19–39) (see PARA 735 et seq) applies in relation to Crown employment and persons in Crown employment as it applies in relation to other employment and other employees, but subject to s 62(4): s 62(3). For the purposes of the application of Ch 3 in relation to Crown employment and persons in Crown employment: (1) references to a contract of employment are to be construed, in relation to a person in Crown employment, as references to the terms and conditions under which the person works (s 62(4)(a)); and (2) references to an employee are to be construed as references to a person in Crown employment (s 62(4)(b)). At the date at which this volume states the law no such regulations had been made.

16 'Relevant member of the House of Commons staff' has the same meaning as in the Employment Rights Act 1996 s 195 (see EMPLOYMENT vol 39 (2014) PARA 165): Education and Skills Act 2008 s 64(5). The Employment Rights Act 1996 s 195(6), (7), (12) (person to be treated as employer of relevant member of House of Commons staff) apply (with any necessary modifications) for the purposes of the Education and Skills Act 2008 ss 19–21, 27–29 as applied by virtue of s 64(3) (see note 17): s 64(6).

17 Education and Skills Act 2008 s 64(1). Regulations may provide for Ch 1 (ss 1–9) to have effect subject to modifications in relation to persons working in that way: s 64(2). At the date at which this volume states the law no such regulations had been made. Sections 19–21 (see PARA 735), and ss 27–29 (see PARA 739) apply in relation to employment as a relevant member of the House of Commons staff as they apply in relation to other employment: s 64(3). For the purposes of the application of Ch 3 (ss 19–39) in relation to a relevant member of the House of Commons staff: (1) references to a contract of employment are to be construed as including references to the terms of employment of a relevant member of the House of Commons staff (s 64(4)(a)); and (2) references to an employee are to be construed as references to a relevant member of the House of Commons staff (s 64(4)(b)).

18 Ie the Education and Skills Act 2008 ss 19–21 (see PARA 735) and ss 27–29 (see PARA 739): see s 63(a), (b). At the date at which this volume states the law s 63 is not in force.

19 As to the corporate officer of the House of Lords see PARLIAMENT vol 78 (2010) PARA 990.

20 See the Education and Skills Act 2008 s 63. See note 18.

728. Meaning of 'sufficient relevant training or education'. 'Relevant training or education' means training or education towards a regulated qualification[1] provided by a course or courses[2].

Relevant training or education is 'sufficient' in relation to any relevant period[3] if it amounts in aggregate to: (1) at least 280 hours of guided learning[4], in the case of a relevant period which is one year[5]; (2) such number of hours of guided learning as is determined in accordance with regulations, in the case of any other relevant period[6].

1 'Regulated qualification' has the same meaning as in the Apprenticeships, Skills, Children and Learning Act 2009 Pt 7 (ss 127–174) (see s 130; and PARA 826 note 7): Education and Skills Act 2008 ss 6(2), 8(3) (s 6(2) substituted and definition in s 8(3) added by SI 2013/1242).

2 Education and Skills Act 2008 s 6(1) (amended by SI 2013/1242). The Education and Skills Act 2008 ss 6(1), (2), 7, 8 are modified in relation to a person serving as a member of the armed forces of the Crown: see the Duty to Participate in Education or Training (Miscellaneous Provisions) Regulations 2013, SI 2013/1205, reg 8.

3 'Relevant period', in relation to a person, means a period beginning with a start date and ending with the next end date: Education and Skills Act 2008 s 7(1). The following are start dates for this purpose: (1) a date on which s 7(4) starts to apply to the person (s 7(2)(a)); (2) the date immediately following the end of a relevant period (if on that date s 7(4) still applies to the person) (s 7(2)(b)). The following are end dates for this purpose: (a) a prescribed date (s 7(3)(a)); (b) a date on which s 7(4) ceases to apply to the person (s 7(3)(b)). Section 7(4) applies to a person at any time when Pt 1 (ss 1–67) applies to the person (see s 1; and PARA 725) (s 7(4)(a)), and the person is not participating in education or training in accordance with s 2(1)(a) or (b) (see PARA 725) (s 7(4)(b)). 'Prescribed' means prescribed by regulations; and 'regulations' means regulations made under the Education and Skills Act 2008 by the Secretary of State: s 168(1). As to the Secretary of State see PARA 58. As to regulations made for the purposes of s 7(3)(a) see the Duty to Participate in Education or Training (Miscellaneous Provisions) Regulations 2013, SI 2013/1205. See also note 2.

4   A person participates in a particular number of hours of guided learning by: (1) participating in actual guided learning for that number of hours (Education and Skills Act 2008 s 8(2)(a)); or (2) completing a course or courses which can reasonably be expected to be adequate to enable persons completing it or them to achieve any standard required to attain a form of a regulated qualification to which that number of hours of guided learning has been assigned (s 8(2)(b) (amended by SI 2013/1242)). 'Actual guided learning' in relation to a person, means time the person spends: (a) being taught or given instruction by a lecturer, tutor, supervisor or other appropriate provider of training or education (Education and Skills Act 2008 s 8(3)(a)); or (b) otherwise participating in education or training under the immediate guidance or supervision of such a person (s 8(3)(b)), but does not include time spent on unsupervised preparation or study, whether at home or otherwise (s 8(3)). 'Assigned' means assigned by a recognised body in accordance with the Apprenticeships, Skills, Children and Learning Act 2009 s 145 (see PARA 838): Education and Skills Act 2008 s 8(3) (definition substituted by SI 2013/1242). Regulations may make provision for attributing to any relevant period a number of hours of guided learning in which a person participates (or is treated by the regulations as participating) by virtue of the Education and Skills Act 2008 s 8(2)(b) (see head (2) above) in cases where courses do not begin and end during a single relevant period: s 8(4). As to regulations made for the purposes of s 8(4), see the Duty to Participate in Education or Training (Miscellaneous Provisions) Regulations 2013, SI 2013/1205. See also note 2.

5   Education and Skills Act 2008 s 8(1)(a). See note 2.

6   Education and Skills Act 2008 s 8(1)(b). As to regulations made for the purposes of s 8(1)(b), (4), see the Duty to Participate in Education or Training (Miscellaneous Provisions) Regulations 2013, SI 2013/1205. See also note 2.

(ii) Duties of Local Authorities and Educational Institutions etc

729.   Local authority to promote fulfilment of duty to participate.   A local authority[1] in England[2] must ensure that its functions[3] are (so far as they are capable of being so exercised) exercised so as to promote the effective participation in education or training of persons[4] belonging to its area[5] with a view to ensuring that those persons fulfil the duty imposed[6] on them to participate in education or training[7].

1   As to the meaning of 'local authority' see PARA 25 (definition applied by the Education and Skills Act 2008 s 168(2), (3)). In exercising its functions under s 10, a local authority must have regard to any guidance given by the Secretary of State: see s 18 (amended by SI 2010/1158). As to the publication of guidance see the Education Act 1996 s 571 (applied by the Education and Skills Act 2008 s 168(2), (3)); and PARA 60. As to the Secretary of State see PARA 58.

2   As to the meaning of 'England' see PARA 7 note 3.

3   As to the meaning of 'functions' see PARA 18 note 5 (definition applied by the Education and Skills Act 2008 s 168(2), (3)). As to the general functions and duties of local authorities in relation to education see PARA 25 et seq.

4   Ie persons to whom the Education and Skills Act 2008 Pt 1 (ss 1–67) applies. As to such persons see s 1; and PARA 725.

5   As to when a person is treated as belonging, or as not belonging, to the area of a local authority see PARA 27 note 6.

6   Ie by the Education and Skills Act 2008 s 2: see PARA 725.

7   See the Education and Skills Act 2008 s 10 (amended by SI 2010/1158).

730.   Educational institutions to promote good attendance.   The governing body[1] of:

(1)   a community, foundation or voluntary school[2];

(2)   a community or foundation special school[3];

(3)   a pupil referral unit[4]; or

(4)   an institution within the further education sector[5],

in England[6] must exercise its functions[7] (so far as they are capable of being so exercised) so as to promote the participation, through regular attendance, of persons subject to the duty to participate in education or training[8], and for whom the institution provides education or training, in that education or training[9].

1   For these purposes, 'governing body': (1) in relation to a pupil referral unit maintained by a local authority, means any management committee established for the unit by virtue of the Education Act 1996 Sch 1 para 15 (see PARA 434) or, if there is no such committee, the authority (Education and Skills Act 2008 s 11(3)(a) (amended by SI 2010/1158)); and (2) in relation to an institution within the further education sector has the meaning given by the Further and Higher Education Act 1992 s 90 (see PARA 560 note 6) (Education and Skills Act 2008 s 11(3)(b)). As to pupil referral units see PARA 427 et seq. As to the meaning of 'local authority' see PARA 25; and as to the meaning of 'institution within the further education sector' see PARA 555 (definitions applied by s 168(2), (3)). As to the governing bodies of maintained schools in England see PARA 150 et seq.

2   See the Education and Skills Act 2008 s 11(2)(a). As to the meaning of references to a community, foundation or voluntary school see PARA 106. These provisions potentially include academies: see PARAS 91, 99, 345 et seq.

3   See the Education and Skills Act 2008 s 11(2)(b). As to the meaning of references to a community or foundation special school see PARA 106.

4   See the Education and Skills Act 2008 s 11(2)(c).

5   See the Education and Skills Act 2008 s 11(2)(d).

6   As to the meaning of 'England' see PARA 7 note 3.

7   As to the meaning of 'functions' see PARA 18 note 5 (definition applied by the Education and Skills Act 2008 s 168(2), (3)).

8   Ie persons to whom the Education and Skills Act 2008 Pt 1 (ss 1–67) applies. As to such persons see s 1; and PARA 725.

9   Education and Skills Act 2008 s 11(1).

731. Identification of persons not fulfilling duty to participate. A local authority[1] in England[2] must make arrangements to enable it to establish (so far as it is possible to do so) the identities of persons[3] belonging to its area[4] but who are failing to fulfil the duty imposed[5] on them to participate in education or training[6].

Where:

(1)   arrangements have been made for a person to participate in education or training provided by an educational institution[7] in England[8];

(2)   the person is not participating in that education or training at a time when the arrangements call for the person to be so participating[9]; and

(3)   the responsible person[10] has reasonable cause to believe that in consequence of that failure to participate the person is failing to fulfil the duty imposed on him to participate in education or training[11],

the responsible person must give notice[12] to the appropriate service provider[13] of those circumstances[14].

1   As to the meaning of 'local authority' see PARA 25 (definition applied by the Education and Skills Act 2008 s 168(2), (3)). In exercising its functions under ss 12, 13, a local authority must have regard to any guidance given by the Secretary of State: see s 18 (amended by SI 2010/1158). As to the publication of guidance see the Education Act 1996 s 571 (applied by the Education and Skills Act 2008 s 168(2), (3)); and PARA 60. As to the Secretary of State see PARA 58.

2   As to the meaning of 'England' see PARA 7 note 3.

3   Ie persons to whom the Education and Skills Act 2008 Pt 1 (ss 1–67) applies. As to such persons see s 1; and PARA 725.

4   As to when a person is treated as belonging, or as not belonging, to the area of a local authority see PARA 27 note 6.

5   Ie by the Education and Skills Act 2008 s 2: see PARA 725.

6   Education and Skills Act 2008 s 12 (amended by SI 2010/1158). For the purposes of the Education and Skills Act 2008 Pt 1 (ss 1–67), a person is failing to fulfil the duty imposed by s 2 if the person: (1) is not participating in education or training in accordance with s 2(1)(a) or (b)

(see PARA 725) (s 66(4)(a)); and (2) is not in full-time occupation or is not participating in sufficient relevant training (s 66(4)(b)). A reasonable excuse for a failure to be in full-time occupation is not a reasonable excuse for a failure to fulfil the duty imposed by s 2 (unless it is also a reasonable excuse for any failure to participate as mentioned in s 66(4)): s 66(5). As to the meaning of 'full-time occupation' see PARA 727. As to the meaning of 'sufficient relevant training' see PARA 728.

7 'Educational institution' means: (1) a community, foundation or voluntary school; (2) a community or foundation special school; (3) a city technology college, a city college for the technology of the arts or an academy; (4) a pupil referral unit; (5) an institution within the further education sector; or (6) an institution (other than one within any of heads (1)–(5) above) in receipt of funding from a local authority, or the Secretary of State: Education and Skills Act 2008 s 13(5) (definition amended by SI 2010/1080; the Education Act 2011 Sch 16 paras 40, 41; and the Deregulation Act 2015 Sch 14 Pt 2 paras 60, 61). As to the meaning of references to a community, foundation or voluntary school or a community or foundation special school see PARA 106. As to city technology colleges and city colleges for the technology of the arts see PARA 345. As to the meaning of 'academy' see PARA 346; and as to the meaning of 'institution within the further education sector' see PARA 555 (definitions applied by the Education and Skills Act 2008 s 168(2), (3)). As to pupil referral units see PARA 427 et seq.

8 Education and Skills Act 2008 s 13(1)(a).
9 Education and Skills Act 2008 s 13(1)(b).
10 'Responsible person' means: (1) in relation to a community, foundation or voluntary school or a community or foundation special school, the governing body; (2) in relation to (a) a city technology college, a city college for the technology of the arts or an academy, or (b) an institution (other than one within any of heads (1)–(5) in note 7) in receipt of funding from a local authority or the Secretary of State, the proprietor; (3) in relation to a pupil referral unit, the local authority by which it is maintained; (4) in relation to an institution within the further education sector, the governing body within the meaning given by the Further and Higher Education Act 1992 s 90 (see PARA 560 note 6): see the Education and Skills Act 2008 s 13(5) (definition amended by SI 2010/1158). As to the governing bodies of maintained schools in England see PARA 150 et seq. As to the meaning of 'proprietor' see PARA 51 note 4 (definition applied by the Education and Skills Act 2008 s 168(2), (3)).
11 See the Education and Skills Act 2008 s 13(1)(c).
12 As to the service of notices and documents see the Education Act 1996 s 572 (applied by the Education and Skills Act 2008 s 168(2), (3)); and PARA 76.
13 'The appropriate service provider', in relation to an educational institution, means the service provider of the local authority in whose area the institution is situated; and 'service provider', in relation to a local authority, means: (1) where the authority itself provides services in exercise of its functions under the Education and Skills Act 2008 s 68(1) (see PARA 802), the authority; (2) where, in exercise of its functions under s 68(3)(b) (see PARA 802), the authority makes arrangements for the provision of services, the person providing those services: s 13(5) (definitions amended by SI 2010/1158). As to the meaning of 'person' see PARA 7 note 6.
14 Education and Skills Act 2008 s 13(1). Where a local authority itself provides services in exercise of its functions under s 68(1) (see PARA 802) (s 13(2)(a)), and receives a notice under s 13(1) relating to a person who belongs to the area of another local authority (s 13(2)(b) (amended by SI 2010/1158)), it must as soon as reasonably practicable give notice to the service provider for the other local authority of the circumstances notified to it under the Education and Skills Act 2008 s 13(1) (s 13(2) (amended by SI 2010/1158)). As to when a person is treated as belonging, or as not belonging, to the area of a local authority see PARA 27 note 6 (definition applied by the Education and Skills Act 2008 s 168(2), (3)).

Where, in exercise of its functions under s 68(3)(b) (see PARA 802), a local authority makes arrangements with another person ('the provider') for the provision of services (s 13(3) (amended by SI 2010/1158)), the arrangements must secure that, as soon as reasonably practicable after receiving a notice under the Education and Skills Act 2008 s 13(1) relating to a person who belongs to the area of another local authority, the provider gives notice to the service provider for the other local authority of the circumstances notified to the provider under s 13(1) (s 13(4) (amended by SI 2010/1158)).

732. Duty of educational institutions to provide information. Relevant information[1] about a pupil or student[2] who is attending an educational institution[3] in England[4] must, on request by a local authority[5] in England, be provided by the responsible person to the authority[6]. A local authority may request such information only for the purpose of enabling or assisting it to exercise its functions[7] relating to the participation of persons in education or training[8].

1   'Relevant information' means: (1) the name, address and date of birth of the pupil or student (Education and Skills Act 2008 s 14(3)(a)); (2) the name and address of a parent of the pupil or student (s 14(3)(b)); (3) information in the institution's possession about the pupil or student (s 14(3)(c)). Information within s 14(3)(c) (see head (3) above) must not be provided under s 14(1) if: (a) the pupil or student concerned, in the case of a pupil or student who has attained the age of 16 (s 14(4)(a)); or (b) a parent of the pupil or student concerned, in the case of a pupil or student who has not attained the age of 16 (s 14(4)(b)), has instructed the responsible person not to provide information of that kind under s 14 (s 14(4)). As to the meaning of 'pupil' see PARA 20 note 4; and as to the meaning of 'parent' see PARA 7 note 6 (definitions applied by s 168(2), (3)). As to the time at which a person attains a particular age see PARA 7 note 6. As to the meaning of 'responsible person' see PARA 731 note 10 (definition applied by s 14(5)).

2   Ie a pupil or student to whom the Education and Skills Act 2008 Pt 1 (ss 1–67) applies: see s 14(1)(b). As to the persons to whom Pt 1 applies see s 1; and PARA 725.

3   As to the meaning of 'educational institution' see PARA 731 note 7 (definition applied by the Education and Skills Act 2008 s 14(5)).

4   Education and Skills Act 2008 s 14(1)(a). As to the meaning of 'England' see PARA 7 note 3.

5   As to the meaning of 'local authority' see PARA 25 (definition applied by the Education and Skills Act 2008 s 168(2), (3)).

6   Education and Skills Act 2008 s 14(1) (amended by SI 2010/1158).

7   Ie under the Education and Skills Act 2008 Pt 1 (ss 1–67). As to the meaning of 'functions' see PARA 18 note 5 (definition applied by s 168(2), (3)).

8   Education and Skills Act 2008 s 14(2) (amended by SI 2010/1158). In exercising its functions under the Education and Skills Act 2008 Pt 1 (ss 1–67), a local authority must have regard to any guidance given by the Secretary of State: see s 18 (amended by SI 2010/1158). As to the publication of guidance see the Education Act 1996 s 571 (applied by the Education and Skills Act 2008 s 168(2), (3)); and PARA 60. As to the Secretary of State see PARA 58.

733. Supply of information by public bodies. Any of the following persons[1] or bodies may supply information about a person[2] to a local authority[3] in England[4] for the purpose of enabling or assisting the authority to exercise its functions[5] relating to the participation of persons in education or training[6]. Those persons and bodies are: (1) a local authority[7]; (2) a non-metropolitan district council for an area for which there is a county council[8]; (3) a clinical commissioning group[9]; (4) a chief officer of police[10]; (5) a provider of probation services[11]; (6) a local probation board[12]; and (7) a youth offending team[13].

1   As to the meaning of 'person' see PARA 7 note 6.

2   As to the persons to whom the Education and Skills Act 2008 Pt 1 (ss 1–67) applies see s 1; and PARA 725.

3   As to the meaning of 'local authority' see PARA 25 (definition applied by the Education and Skills Act 2008 s 168(2), (3)). In exercising its functions under Pt 1 (ss 1–67), a local authority must have regard to any guidance given by the Secretary of State: see s 18 (amended by SI 2010/1158). As to the publication of guidance see the Education Act 1996 s 571 (applied by the Education and Skills Act 2008 s 168(2), (3)); and PARA 60. As to the Secretary of State see PARA 58.

4   As to the meaning of 'England' see PARA 7 note 3.

5   Ie under the Education and Skills Act 2008 Pt 1 (ss 1–67). As to the meaning of 'functions' see PARA 18 note 5 (definition applied by s 168(2), (3)).

6   See the Education and Skills Act 2008 s 16(1) (amended by SI 2010/1158).

7   Education and Skills Act 2008 s 16(2)(a).

8   Education and Skills Act 2008 s 16(2)(aa) (added by SI 2010/1158). As to local government areas and authorities in England see LOCAL GOVERNMENT vol 69 (2009) PARA 22 et seq.

9   Education and Skills Act 2008 s 16(2)(da) (added by the Health and Social Care Act 2012 Sch 5 paras 168, 169(c). As to clinical commissioning groups see HEALTH SERVICES.

10   Education and Skills Act 2008 s 16(2)(e). As to chief officers of police see POLICE AND INVESTIGATORY POWERS vol 84 (2013) PARA 112 et seq.

11 Education and Skills Act 2008 s 16(2)(f). As to providers of probation services see SENTENCING AND DISPOSITION OF OFFENDERS vol 92 (2010) PARA 733 et seq.

12 Education and Skills Act 2008 s 16(2)(g). 'Local probation board' means a local probation board established under the Criminal Justice and Court Services Act 2000 s 4 (see SENTENCING AND DISPOSITION OF OFFENDERS vol 92 (2010) PARA 737 et seq): Education and Skills Act 2008 s 16(3).

13 Education and Skills Act 2008 s 16(2)(h). 'Youth offending team' means a team established under the Crime and Disorder Act 1998 s 39 (see CHILDREN AND YOUNG PERSONS vol 10 (2012) PARA 1193): Education and Skills Act 2008 s 16(3).

734. Sharing and use of information. A local authority[1] in England[2], and a service provider[3] of that authority[4] may: (1) provide relevant information[5] to each other[6]; (2) make arrangements for the holding by either of them of information provided, or which could be provided, under head (1) above[7].

Information so provided may only be used by the person to whom it is provided for a purpose which is a relevant purpose in relation to that person[8]. A local authority in England may use relevant information held by it for any relevant purpose[9]; and may provide relevant information to any other such authority for a purpose which is a relevant purpose in relation to that other authority[10]. A service provider of a local authority in England may provide relevant information to any other service provider of that or any other such authority for a purpose which is a relevant purpose in relation to that other service provider[11].

Nothing in the above provisions authorises the disclosure of any information in contravention of any provision of, or made under, the Education and Skills Act 2008 or any other Act (whenever passed or made) which prevents disclosure of the information[12].

1 As to the meaning of 'local authority' see PARA 25 (definition applied by the Education and Skills Act 2008 s 168(2), (3)). In exercising its functions under Pt 1 (ss 1–67), a local authority must have regard to any guidance given by the Secretary of State: see s 18 (amended by SI 2010/1158). As to the publication of guidance see the Education Act 1996 s 571 (applied by the Education and Skills Act 2008 s 168(2), (3)); and PARA 60. As to the Secretary of State see PARA 58.

2 See the Education and Skills Act 2008 s 17(1), (2)(a) (amended by SI 2010/1158). As to the meaning of 'England' see PARA 7 note 3.

3 'Service provider', in relation to a local authority in England, means: (1) where the authority itself provides services in exercise of its functions under the Education and Skills Act 2008 s 68(1) (see PARA 802), the authority; (2) where, in exercise of its functions under s 68(3)(b) (see PARA 802), the authority makes arrangements for the provision of services, the person providing those services: s 17(7) (definition amended by SI 2010/1158). As to the meaning of 'functions' see PARA 18 note 5 (definition applied by the Education and Skills Act 2008 s 168(2), (3)). As to the meaning of 'person' see PARA 7 note 6.

4 See the Education and Skills Act 2008 s 17(1), (2)(b).

5 'Relevant information', in relation to a person providing or holding information, means information which (1) is held by the person for a relevant purpose; and (2) is about a young person or a relevant young adult in England, but does not include information provided under the Welfare Reform and Pensions Act 1999 s 72 (see WELFARE BENEFITS AND STATE PENSIONS vol 104 (2014) PARA 551): Education and Skills Act 2008 s 17(7) (definition amended by the Apprenticeships, Skills, Children and Learning Act 2009 s 254(1), (3), (5)). 'Relevant purpose': (a) in relation to a local authority, means the purpose of, or a purpose connected with, the exercise of any function of the authority under the Education and Skills Act 2008 Pt 1 (ss 1–67), or under or by virtue of ss 68–78 (see PARA 802 et seq); (b) in relation to a service provider of a local authority (other than the authority in question), means the purpose of providing services of the kind mentioned in s 68(1) (see PARA 802): s 17(7) (definition amended by SI 2010/1158). 'Young person' means a person who has attained the age of 13 but not the age of 20: Education and Skills Act 2008 s 17(8)(a). 'Relevant young adult' means a person who has attained the age of 20 but not the age of 25, and has special educational needs: Education and Skills Act 2008 s 17(8)(b) (amended by SI 2010/1080; and the Children and Families Act 2014 Sch 3 paras 82,

84). As to the time at which a person attains a particular age see PARA 7 note 6. As to the meaning of 'special educational needs' see PARA 943 (definition applied by the Education and Skills Act 2008 s 168(2), (3)).

6   Education and Skills Act 2008 s 17(1)(a) (s 17(1)(a), (b) substituted by the Apprenticeships, Skills, Children and Learning Act 2009 s 254(1), (3), (4)).
7   Education and Skills Act 2008 s 17(1)(b) (as substituted: see note 6).
8   Education and Skills Act 2008 s 17(3).
9   Education and Skills Act 2008 s 17(4) (amended by SI 2010/1158).
10   Education and Skills Act 2008 s 17(5) (amended by SI 2010/1158).
11   Education and Skills Act 2008 s 17(6) (amended by SI 2010/1158).
12   Education and Skills Act 2008 s 17(8) (added by the Apprenticeships, Skills, Children and Learning Act 2009 s 254(1), (3), (6)). As to the protection of information under the Data Protection Act 1998 see CONFIDENCE AND INFORMATIONAL PRIVACY vol 19 (2011) PARA 95 et seq.

(iii) Duties of Employers

A. COMMENCEMENT OF EMPLOYMENT

735.   Appropriate arrangements to be in place before employment begins. As from a day to be appointed the following provisions have effect[1].

A person[2] must not, as employer, enter into a relevant contract of employment[3] with a person subject to the duty to participate in education or training[4] without being satisfied, having taken all such steps as are reasonable to ascertain, that the person has made appropriate arrangements for training or education[5]. In the case of a relevant contract of employment which provides for commencement of the employment to be conditional on the employee's having made such arrangements, the above provision does not apply[6], but the employer must not permit the employment to commence, at a time when the employee is a person subject to the duty to participate in education or training, without being satisfied, having taken all such steps as are reasonable to ascertain, that the employee has made appropriate arrangements for training or education[7].

Failure to comply with these provisions in relation to a contract of employment is not to be taken to affect the validity of the contract[8].

1   The Education and Skills Act 2008 ss 19–21 are to come into force as from a day to be appointed: see s 173(4). At the date at which this volume states the law no such day had been appointed. As to the application of ss 19–36 to Wales see s 67; and PARA 759. As to the meaning of 'Wales' see PARA 7 note 3.
2   As to the meaning of 'person' see PARA 7 note 6.
3   'Relevant contract of employment' means a contract of employment: (1) under which the employee is required to work for at least 20 hours per week (Education and Skills Act 2008 s 19(1)(a)); (2) which has a fixed term of eight weeks or longer (s 19(1)(b)(i)), or does not have a fixed term but can reasonably be expected to be, or has been, in force for at least eight weeks (s 19(1)(b)(ii)); and (3) under which the place of work, or one of the places where the employee may be required to work, is in England (s 19(1)(c)). But a contract is not a 'relevant contract of employment' if the employer has undertaken to provide the employee with sufficient relevant training or education in each relevant period (s 19(2)(a)), and by virtue of the contract, the employee is in full-time occupation (s 19(2)(b)). As to the meaning of 'contract of employment' see PARA 725 note 17. As to the meaning of 'England' see PARA 7 note 3. As to the meaning of 'sufficient relevant training or education' see PARA 728. As to the meaning of 'relevant period' see PARA 728 note 3. As to the meaning of 'full-time occupation' see PARA 727.
4   Ie a person to whom the Education and Skills Act 2008 Pt 1 (ss 1–67) applies. As to such persons see s 1; and PARA 725.
5   Education and Skills Act 2008 s 21(1). For the purposes of Pt 1 Ch 3 (ss 19–39), a person to whom Pt 1 (ss 1–67) applies has made 'appropriate arrangements for training or education' if: (1) the person has enrolled on a course or courses constituting relevant training or education (or arrangements have otherwise been made for the person to receive relevant training or education) (s 20(1)(a)); or (2) the person is participating in full-time education or training (s 20(1)(b)).

References in Pt 1 Ch 3 to 'appropriate arrangements' made by the person are to the arrangements (of whatever kind and whether or not made by the person) for the person to receive the training or education in question: s 20(2).
6 Education and Skills Act 2008 s 21(2)(a).
7 Education and Skills Act 2008 s 21(2)(b).
8 Education and Skills Act 2008 s 21(3).

736. Financial penalty for contravention of provisions in respect of duty as to appropriate arrangements. As from a day to be appointed the following provisions have effect[1].

Where a relevant local authority[2] is satisfied that a person[3] ('the employer') has contravened the statutory provisions[4] relating to the employment of persons subject to the duty to participate in education or training, the authority may by notice[5] (a 'penalty notice') require the employer to pay a financial penalty[6]. A penalty notice must state: (1) particulars of the contravention in respect of which the penalty is imposed[7]; (2) the amount of the penalty[8]; (3) how payment may be made[9]; (4) the period within which the penalty must be paid (which must be not less than four weeks beginning with the date on which the notice is given)[10]; (5) the steps that the employer may take if the employer objects to the giving of the penalty notice, including how the employer may appeal against it[11]; and (6) the consequences of non-payment[12].

A penalty payable by virtue of a penalty notice is payable to the local authority which issued the notice[13]. A penalty (and any interest or financial penalty for late payment) is recoverable, if the county court so orders, as if it were payable under an order of that court[14]. Where a person is required by a penalty notice to pay a financial penalty, and has given a notice of objection to the local authority[15], or has appealed[16] against the giving of the penalty notice[17], the penalty is not enforceable until the authority has given a determination notice[18] in relation to the penalty notice, or, as the case may be, the appeal has been determined[19].

1 The Education and Skills Act 2008 ss 22, 65 are to come into force as from a day to be appointed: see s 173(4). At the date at which this volume states the law no such day had been appointed. As to the application of ss 19–36 to Wales see s 67; and PARA 759. As to the meaning of 'Wales' see PARA 7 note 3.
2 A local authority is a 'relevant local authority' in relation to a contract of employment under which a person to whom the Education and Skills Act 2008 Pt 1 (ss 1–67) applies is employed if (s 22(4) (amended by SI 2010/1158)): (1) the person belongs to the authority's area (Education and Skills Act 2008 s 22(4)(a)); or (2) the person's place of work, or one of the places at which the person works, under the contract is in the authority's area (s 22(4)(b)). As to the meaning of 'local authority' see PARA 25 (definition applied by s 168(2), (3)). As to the meaning of 'contract of employment' see PARA 725 note 17. As to persons to whom Pt 1 (ss 1–67) applies see s 1; and PARA 725. As to when a person is treated as belonging, or as not belonging, to the area of a local authority see PARA 27 note 6 (applied by s 168(2), (3)).
3 As to the meaning of 'person' see PARA 7 note 6.
4 Ie the Education and Skills Act 2008 s 21: see PARA 735.
5 As to the service of notices and documents see the Education Act 1996 s 572 (applied by the Education and Skills Act 2008 s 168(2), (3)); and PARA 76.
6 Education and Skills Act 2008 s 22(1). The amount of the financial penalty is to be determined in accordance with regulations: s 22(2). Without prejudice to s 166(6) (general provision as to orders and regulations), regulations under s 22(2) may make provision for penalties of different amounts to be payable in different cases or circumstances (including provision for the penalty payable under a penalty notice to differ according to the time by which it is paid): s 22(5). 'Regulations' means regulations made under the Education and Skills Act 2008 by the Secretary of State: s 168(1). As to the Secretary of State see PARA 58. At the date at which this volume states the law no such regulations had been made.
7 Education and Skills Act 2008 s 22(3)(a).
8 Education and Skills Act 2008 s 22(3)(b).

9   Education and Skills Act 2008 s 22(3)(c).
10 Education and Skills Act 2008 s 22(3)(d).
11 Education and Skills Act 2008 s 22(3)(e). As to notice of objection see s 23; and PARA 737. As to appeals see s 24; and PARA 738.
12 Education and Skills Act 2008 s 22(3)(f).
13 See the Education and Skills Act 2008 s 65(1)(a) (s 65(1), (2) amended by SI 2010/1158). Any sums so received by a local authority may be used by the authority for the purposes of any of its functions which may be specified in regulations but, to the extent that they are not so used, must be paid in accordance with regulations to the Secretary of State: see the Education and Skills Act 2008 s 65(2) (as so amended). As to the meaning of 'functions' see PARA 18 note 5 (definition applied by s 168(2), (3)). At the date at which this volume states the law no such regulations had been made.
14 See the Education and Skills Act 2008 s 65(3) (amended by the Crime and Courts Act 2013 Sch 9 para 52(1)(b), (2)). As to county courts see COURTS AND TRIBUNALS vol 24 (2010) PARA 758 et seq.
15 See the Education and Skills Act 2008 s 65(4)(a) (amended by SI 2010/1158).
16 Ie under the Education and Skills Act 2008 s 24: see PARA 738.
17 See the Education and Skills Act 2008 s 65(4)(b).
18 Ie under the Education and Skills Act 2008 s 23: see PARA 737.
19 See the Education and Skills Act 2008 s 65(4).

737.   Withdrawal or variation of penalty notice following notice of objection.
As from a day to be appointed the following provisions have effect[1].

Where a penalty notice has been given[2] to a person[3] ('the employer') by a local authority[4], the employer may, by giving notice[5] (a 'notice of objection') to the authority, object to the giving of the penalty notice on either or both of the following grounds: (1) that the employer did not commit the contravention[6] stated in the penalty notice[7]; (2) that the amount of the penalty stated in the penalty notice is too high[8]. A notice of objection may be given to the authority only during the period of two weeks beginning with the day on which the penalty notice was given to the employer[9], and must state the grounds of the objection and the employer's reasons for objecting on those grounds[10].

A local authority must consider a notice of objection and, by giving notice (a 'determination notice') to the employer[11]: (a) withdraw the penalty notice[12]; (b) if the amount of the penalty determined[13] is smaller than the amount stated in the penalty notice, replace the penalty with the smaller amount[14]; or (c) confirm the penalty notice[15].

If a penalty notice is withdrawn, any sum already paid or recovered in respect of the penalty notice must be repaid to the employer with interest at the appropriate rate[16] running from the date when the sum was paid or recovered[17]. If the amount of a penalty is reduced, any sum already paid or recovered must, to the extent that it was paid or recovered in respect of any amount in excess of the reduced amount, be repaid to the employer with interest at the appropriate rate running from the date when the sum was paid or recovered[18].

1   The Education and Skills Act 2008 ss 23, 26 are to come into force as from a day to be appointed: see s 173(4). At the date at which this volume states the law no such day had been appointed. As to the application of ss 19–36 to Wales see s 67; and PARA 759. As to the meaning of 'Wales' see PARA 7 note 3.
2   Ie under the Education and Skills Act 2008 s 22: see PARA 736.
3   As to the meaning of 'person' see PARA 7 note 6.
4   Education and Skills Act 2008 s 23(1) (amended by SI 2010/1158). As to the meaning of 'local authority' see PARA 25 (definition applied by the Education and Skills Act 2008 s 168(2), (3)).
5   As to the service of notices and documents see the Education Act 1996 s 572 (definition applied by the Education and Skills Act 2008 s 168(2), (3)); and PARA 76.
6   Ie the contravention of the Education and Skills Act 2008 s 21: see PARA 735.
7   Education and Skills Act 2008 s 23(2)(a).
8   Education and Skills Act 2008 s 23(2)(b).

9   Education and Skills Act 2008 s 23(3)(a).
10 Education and Skills Act 2008 s 23(3)(b).
11 Education and Skills Act 2008 s 23(4) (amended by SI 2010/1158). The determination notice must be given within the prescribed period beginning with the day on which the notice of objection was given: Education and Skills Act 2008 s 23(5). 'Prescribed' means prescribed by regulations; and 'regulations' means regulations made under the Education and Skills Act 2008 by the Secretary of State: s 168(1). As to the Secretary of State see PARA 58. At the date at which this volume states the law no such regulations had been made.
12 Education and Skills Act 2008 s 23(4)(a).
13 Ie in accordance with regulations under the Education and Skills Act 2008 s 22(2): see PARA 736.
14 Education and Skills Act 2008 s 23(4)(b). Where, under s 23(4)(b), the amount of a penalty stated in a penalty notice is replaced with a smaller amount, the notice is to have effect as if it had originally stated the smaller amount: s 23(6).
15 Education and Skills Act 2008 s 23(4)(c).
16 'The appropriate rate' means the rate that, on the date the sum was paid or recovered, was specified in the Judgments Act 1838 s 17 (see CIVIL PROCEDURE vol 12 (2009) PARA 1149): Education and Skills Act 2008 s 26(3).
17 See the Education and Skills Act 2008 s 26(1).
18 Education and Skills Act 2008 s 26(2).

738. Appeal against penalty notice. As from a day to be appointed the following provisions have effect[1].
   Where a penalty notice has been given[2] to a person[3] ('the employer') and:
   (1)   the period during which a notice of objection[4] may be given in relation to the penalty notice has expired[5]; and
   (2)   if a notice of objection has been given in relation to the penalty notice, a determination notice[6] has been given in relation to the notice of objection[7],
the employer may appeal to the First-tier Tribunal[8] against the giving of the penalty notice[9]. The appeal may be made on one or more of the following grounds: (a) that the employer did not contravene the statutory provisions[10] relating to the employment of persons subject to the duty to participate in education or training in the way stated in the penalty notice[11]; (b) that the circumstances of the contravention stated in the penalty notice make the giving of the notice unreasonable[12]; (c) that the amount of the penalty stated in the penalty notice is too high[13].
   On such an appeal, the First-tier Tribunal may: (i) allow the appeal and cancel the penalty notice[14]; (ii) if the amount of the penalty determined in accordance with regulations[15] is smaller than the amount stated in the penalty notice, allow the appeal and replace the penalty with the smaller amount[16]; or (iii) dismiss the appeal[17].
   Where a penalty notice has been given to the employer by a local authority[18], and any appeal made[19] in respect of the penalty notice has not been determined[20], the authority may withdraw the penalty notice by giving notice[21] of the withdrawal to the employer[22]. If a penalty notice is so withdrawn, any sum already paid or recovered in respect of the penalty notice must be repaid to the employer with interest at the appropriate rate[23] running from the date when the sum was paid or recovered[24].

1   The Education and Skills Act 2008 ss 24–26 are to come into force as from a day to be appointed: see s 173(4). At the date at which this volume states the law no such day had been appointed. As to the application of ss 19–36 to Wales see s 67; and PARA 759. As to the meaning of 'Wales' see PARA 7 note 3.
2   Ie under the Education and Skills Act 2008 s 22: see PARA 736.
3   As to the meaning of 'person' see PARA 7 note 6.
4   As to notices of objection see PARA 737.

5 Education and Skills Act 2008 s 24(1)(a).
6 As to determination notices see PARA 737.
7 Education and Skills Act 2008 s 24(1)(b).
8 As to the First-tier Tribunal see COURTS AND TRIBUNALS vol 24 (2010) PARA 874 et seq.
9 See the Education and Skills Act 2008 s 24(2).
10 Ie the Education and Skills Act 2008 s 21: see PARA 735.
11 Education and Skills Act 2008 s 24(2)(a).
12 Education and Skills Act 2008 s 24(2)(b).
13 Education and Skills Act 2008 s 24(2)(c).
14 Education and Skills Act 2008 s 24(3)(a).
15 Ie regulations under the Education and Skills Act 2008 s 22(2): see PARA 736.
16 Education and Skills Act 2008 s 24(3)(b). Where, under s 24(3)(b), the amount of a penalty stated in a penalty notice is replaced with a smaller amount, the notice is to have effect as if it had originally stated the smaller amount: s 24(4).
17 Education and Skills Act 2008 s 24(3)(c).
18 See the Education and Skills Act 2008 s 25(1)(a) (amended by SI 2010/1158). As to the meaning of 'local authority' see PARA 25 (definition applied by the Education and Skills Act 2008 s 168(2), (3)).
19 Ie under the Education and Skills Act 2008 s 24: see the text to notes 1–17.
20 Education and Skills Act 2008 s 25(1)(b).
21 As to the service of notices and documents see the Education Act 1996 s 572 (applied by the Education and Skills Act 2008 s 168(2), (3)); and PARA 76.
22 Education and Skills Act 2008 s 25(2).
23 As to the meaning of 'appropriate rate' see PARA 737 note 16.
24 See the Education and Skills Act 2008 s 26(1).

B. ENABLING PARTICIPATION IN EDUCATION OR TRAINING

739. Duty to enable participation: initial arrangements. As from a day to be appointed the following provisions have effect[1].
Where:

(1)   a person subject to the duty to participate in education or training[2] is employed under a relevant contract of employment[3]; and

(2)   before commencement of the employment the person notified the employer[4] of appropriate arrangements which the person had made[5],

the employer must permit the employee to participate in training or education in accordance with those appropriate arrangements[6]. This obligation operates as a requirement, in relation to each of the times specified in the notice[7] which falls during normal working time[8], for the employer: (a) if the contract was entered into before the notice was given, to offer to vary the terms and conditions of the contract of employment so as to secure that that time does not fall during normal working time[9]; or (b) in any case, to permit the employee to take that time off[10].

An employee has the right not to be subjected to any detriment by any act, or any deliberate failure to act, by his employer done on the ground that he exercised, or proposed to exercise the right to participate in education or training under the above provisions[11]. Dismissal or redundancy on such grounds is also automatically unfair[12].

1 The Education and Skills Act 2008 ss 27, 29 are to come into force as from a day to be appointed: see s 173(4). At the date at which this volume states the law no such day had been appointed. As to the application of ss 19–36 to Wales see s 67; and PARA 759. As to the meaning of 'Wales' see PARA 7 note 3.
2 Ie a person to whom the Education and Skills Act 2008 Pt 1 (ss 1–67) applies. As to such persons see s 1; and PARA 725. Where (1) a person to whom Pt 1 applies is employed under a relevant contract of employment (s 29(1)(a)); (2) the person reaches the age of 18 (s 29(1)(b)); and (3) at that time the person is participating in a course of education or training for the purpose of fulfilling the duty imposed by s 2 (see PARA 725) (s 29(1)(c)), the person is to continue to be treated, for the purposes of ss 27, 30–36 (see PARAS 741–744) as a person to

whom Pt 1 applies until one of the following occurs: (a) the course of education or training concludes (s 29(2)(a)); (b) the person reaches the age of 19 (s 29(2)(b)); (c) the person ceases to be resident in England (s 29(2)(c)); (d) the person attains a level 3 qualification (s 29(2)(d)). As to the meaning of 'relevant contract of employment' see PARA 735 note 3. As to the time at which a person attains a particular age see PARA 7 note 6. As to the meaning of 'England' see PARA 7 note 3. As to when a person is to treated as resident in England, see s 66(2); and PARA 725 note 2. As to the meaning of 'level 3 qualification' see PARA 725 note 5.

3   Education and Skills Act 2008 s 27(1)(a).
4   Ie in accordance with the Education and Skills Act 2008 s 27(3): see s 27(1)(b). A person notifies an employer (or a prospective employer) of appropriate arrangements by giving a notice which: (1) specifies the arrangements (s 27(3)(a)); (2) states the times when the person would need to be not at work in order to participate in training or education in accordance with those arrangements (s 27(3)(b)); and (3) if so required under s 27(4), is given in writing (s 27(3)(c)). Such a notice need not be given in writing, but, if it is not, the employer may, on the occasion when the notice is given, require it to be given in writing; and, if the employer does so, the notice is not to be treated as having been given until given in writing: s 27(4). As to the service of notices and documents see the Education Act 1996 s 572 (applied by the Education and Skills Act 2008 s 168(2), (3)); and PARA 76. As to the meaning of 'appropriate arrangements' see PARA 735 note 5. As to the meaning of 'writing' see PARA 76 note 8.
5   Education and Skills Act 2008 s 27(1)(b). As to the provisions applicable where notification is given after the commencement of employment, see s 28; and PARA 740.
6   Education and Skills Act 2008 s 27(2). As to enforcement of this duty see s 30; and PARA 741.
7   Ie under the Education and Skills Act 2008 s 27(3)(b): see note 4.
8   'Normal working time', in relation to a contract of employment, means any time when, in accordance with the contract, the employee is required to be at work: Education and Skills Act 2008 s 27(6). As to the meaning of 'contract of employment' see PARA 725 note 17.
9   Education and Skills Act 2008 s 27(5)(a).
10 Education and Skills Act 2008 s 27(5)(b).
11 See the Employment Rights Act 1996 s 47AA; and EMPLOYMENT vol 40 (2014) PARA 618.
12 See the Employment Rights Act 1996 s 101B (EMPLOYMENT vol 41 (2014) PARA 789), s 105 (EMPLOYMENT vol 41 (2014) PARA 781).

740. Duty to enable participation: arrangements subsequently notified. As from a day to be appointed the following provisions have effect[1].

Where:

(1)   a person subject to the duty to participate in education or training[2] is employed under a relevant contract of employment[3]; and

(2)   after commencement of the employment the person notifies the employer[4] of appropriate arrangements which the person has made[5],

the employer must, so far as is reasonable having regard to the specified matters[6], permit the person to participate in training or education in accordance with those appropriate arrangements[7]. This obligation operates as a requirement, in relation to each of the times specified in the notice[8] which falls during normal working time[9], for the employer: (a) to offer to vary the terms and conditions of the contract of employment so as to secure that, so far as is reasonable having regard to the specified matters[10], that time does not fall during normal working time[11]; or (b) so far as is reasonable having regard to those matters, to permit the employee to take that time off[12].

An employee has the right not to be subjected to any detriment by any act, or any deliberate failure to act, by his employer done on the ground that he exercised, or proposed to exercise the right to participate in education or training under the above provisions[13]. Dismissal or redundancy on such grounds is also automatically unfair[14].

1   The Education and Skills Act 2008 ss 28, 29 are to come into force as from a day to be appointed: see s 173(4). At the date at which this volume states the law no such day had been appointed. As to the application of ss 19–36 to Wales see s 67; and PARA 759. As to the meaning of 'Wales' see PARA 7 note 3.

2   Ie a person to whom the Education and Skills Act 2008 Pt 1 (ss 1–67) applies. As to such persons see s 1; and PARA 725. Where (1) a person to whom Pt 1 applies is employed under a relevant contract of employment (s 29(1)(a)); (2) the person reaches the age of 18 (s 29(1)(b)); and (3) at that time the person is participating in a course of education or training for the purpose of fulfilling the duty imposed by s 2 (see PARA 725) (s 29(1)(c)), the person is to continue to be treated, for the purposes of ss 28, 30–36 (see PARAS 741–744) as a person to whom Pt 1 applies until one of the following occurs: (a) the course of education or training concludes (s 29(2)(a)); (b) the person reaches the age of 19 (s 29(2)(b)); (c) the person ceases to be resident in England (s 29(2)(c)); (d) the person attains a level 3 qualification (s 29(2)(d)). As to the meaning of 'relevant contract of employment' see PARA 735 note 3. As to the time at which a person attains a particular age see PARA 7 note 6. As to the meaning of 'England' see PARA 7 note 3. As to when a person is to treated as resident in England see s 66(2); and PARA 725 note 2. As to the meaning of 'level 3 qualification' see PARA 725 note 5.

3   Education and Skills Act 2008 s 28(1)(a).

4   Ie in accordance with the Education and Skills Act 2008 s 28(4): see s 28(1)(b). A person notifies an employer of appropriate arrangements by giving a notice which: (1) specifies the arrangements (s 28(4)(a)); (2) states the times when the employee needs to be not at work in order to participate in education or training in accordance with those arrangements (s 28(4)(b)); and (3) if so required under s 28(5), is given in writing (s 28(4)(c)). Such a notice need not be given in writing but, if it is not, the employer may, on the occasion when the notice is given, require it to be given in writing; and, if the employer does so, the notice is not to be treated as having been given until given in writing: s 28(5). As to the service of notices and documents see the Education Act 1996 s 572 (applied by the Education and Skills Act 2008 s 168(2), (3)); and PARA 76. As to the meaning of 'appropriate arrangements' see PARA 735 note 5. As to the meaning of 'writing' see PARA 76 note 8.

5   Education and Skills Act 2008 s 28(1)(b). As to the provisions applicable where notification is given before the commencement of employment see s 27; and PARA 739.

6   The specified matters are: (1) the needs of the person in order to fulfil the duty imposed by the Education and Skills Act 2008 s 2 (see PARA 725) (s 28(3)(a)); (2) the circumstances of the employer's business (s 28(3)(b)); (3) the effect of the person's absence from work on the running of that business (s 28(3)(c)).

7   Education and Skills Act 2008 s 28(2). As to enforcement of this duty see s 30; and PARA 741.

8   Ie the notice under the Education and Skills Act 2008 s 28(4)(b): see note 4.

9   'Normal working time', in relation to a contract of employment, means any time when, in accordance with the contract, the employee is required to be at work: Education and Skills Act 2008 s 28(7).

10   Ie the matters mentioned in the Education and Skills Act 2008 s 28(3): see note 6.

11   Education and Skills Act 2008 s 28(6)(a).

12   Education and Skills Act 2008 s 28(6)(b).

13   See the Employment Rights Act 1996 s 47AA; and EMPLOYMENT vol 40 (2014) PARA 618).

14   See the Employment Rights Act 1996 s 101B (see EMPLOYMENT vol 41 (2014) PARA 789), s 105 (see EMPLOYMENT vol 41 (2014) PARA 781).

741. Enforcement notice. As from a day to be appointed the following provisions have effect[1].

Where a person who is subject to the duty to participate in education or training[2] is employed under a relevant contract of employment[3], and a relevant local authority[4] in England[5] is satisfied that the employer has contravened its duty as regards enabling the participation of such persons in education or training[6], the authority may give the employer a notice (an 'enforcement notice')[7]. An enforcement notice is a notice requiring the employer to take such steps as are specified in the notice[8]. The steps that may be specified in the notice[9] are:

(1)   to offer to vary the terms and conditions of employment in the manner specified in the notice[10];

(2)   to permit the employee to take time off during normal working time at the times specified in the notice[11].

An enforcement notice must also specify particulars of the contravention[12] in respect of which the notice is given[13], and the consequences of failure to comply with any requirement imposed by it[14].

Where an enforcement notice requires the employer to offer to vary the terms and conditions of employment under head (1) above: (a) the employer must make the offer within the time specified in the notice[15]; (b) the employer's offer must not be made directly or indirectly conditional on the employee's agreeing to any other variation of the terms and conditions of employment[16]; and if the employee accepts the employer's offer to vary the terms and conditions of employment, those terms and conditions have effect subject to the variation (but subject to any subsequent variation that may be agreed between the employer and employee)[17]. Where an enforcement notice requires the employer, under head (2) above, to permit the employee to take time off at specified times during normal working time, the enforcement notice remains in force until: (i) the last of the times so specified[18]; or (ii) if earlier, the termination of the contract of employment[19].

1   The Education and Skills Act 2008 s 30 is to come into force as from a day to be appointed: see s 173(4). At the date at which this volume states the law no such day had been appointed. As to the application of ss 19–36 to Wales see s 67; and PARA 759. As to the meaning of 'Wales' see PARA 7 note 3.
2   Ie a person to whom the Education and Skills Act 2008 Pt 1 (ss 1–67) applies. As to such persons see s 1; and PARA 725.
3   Education and Skills Act 2008 s 30(1). As to the meaning of 'relevant contract of employment' see PARA 735 note 3.
4   A local authority is a 'relevant local authority' in relation to a contract of employment under which a person to whom the Education and Skills Act 2008 Pt 1 (ss 1–67) applies is employed if (s 30(9) (amended by SI 2010/1158)): (1) the person belongs to the authority's area (Education and Skills Act 2008 s 30(9)(a)); or (2) the person's place of work, or one of the places at which the person works, under the contract is in the authority's area (s 30(9)(b)). As to the meaning of 'local authority' see PARA 25 (definition applied by s 168(2), (3)). As to when a person is treated as belonging, or as not belonging, to the area of a local authority see PARA 27 note 6 (provision applied by s 168(2), (3)).
5   As to the meaning of 'England' see PARA 7 note 3.
6   Ie the duty under the Education and Skills Act 2008 s 27 (see PARA 739) or s 28 (see PARA 740).
7   Education and Skills Act 2008 s 30(2) (amended by SI 2010/1158). As to the service of notices and documents see the Education Act 1996 s 572 (applied by the Education and Skills Act 2008 s 168(2), (3)); and PARA 76. In exercising its functions under Pt 1 (ss 1–67), a local authority must have regard to any guidance given by the Secretary of State: see s 18 (amended by SI 2010/1158). As to the publication of guidance see the Education Act 1996 s 571 (applied by the Education and Skills Act 2008 s 168(2), (3)); and PARA 60. As to the Secretary of State see PARA 58.
8   Education and Skills Act 2008 s 30(3). As to the power to withdraw an enforcement notice see s 32; and PARA 743.
9   In the case of an enforcement notice given in respect of a contravention of the Education and Skills Act 2008 s 28 (see PARA 740), any steps specified in the notice must be steps which it would be reasonable for the employer to take having regard to the matters mentioned in s 28(3): s 30(5)(c).
10 Education and Skills Act 2008 s 30(4)(a). Any variation specified under s 30(4)(a) must be a variation only for the purpose of securing that normal working time does not include any time when, in order to be able to participate in education or training in accordance with appropriate arrangements notified to the employer under s 27(1)(b) (see PARA 739) or s 28(1)(b) (see PARA 740), the employee needs to be not at work: s 30(5)(a). 'Normal working time', in relation to a contract of employment, means any time when, in accordance with the contract, the employee is required to be at work: s 30(10).
11 Education and Skills Act 2008 s 30(4)(b). Any time specified under s 30(4)(b) must be a time when the employee needs to be not at work in order to participate in education or training in accordance with appropriate arrangements so notified to the employer: s 30(5)(b).
12 Ie of the Education and Skills Act 2008 s 27 (see PARA 739) or s 28 (see PARA 740).

13 Education and Skills Act 2008 s 30(6)(a).
14 Education and Skills Act 2008 s 30(6)(b). As to financial penalty for failure to comply with an enforcement notice see s 31; and PARA 742.
15 Education and Skills Act 2008 s 30(7)(a).
16 Education and Skills Act 2008 s 30(7)(b).
17 Education and Skills Act 2008 s 30(7)(c).
18 Education and Skills Act 2008 s 30(8)(a).
19 Education and Skills Act 2008 s 30(8)(b).

742. Financial penalty for non-compliance with enforcement notice. As from a day to be appointed the following provisions have effect[1].

Where a local authority[2] has given an enforcement notice[3] to an employer[4], and the local authority is satisfied:

(1) that the employer has failed to comply with the notice[5]; or

(2) in the case of an enforcement notice requiring the employer to offer to vary the terms and conditions of employment[6], the employee has agreed to the variation but the employer has failed to give effect to the variation[7],

the authority may by notice[8] (a 'penalty notice') require the employer to pay a financial penalty[9]. A penalty notice must state: (a) particulars of the failure by the employer in respect of which the penalty notice is given[10]; (b) the amount of the penalty[11]; (c) how payment may be made[12]; (d) the period within which the penalty must be paid (which must be not less than four weeks beginning with the date on which the notice is given)[13]; (e) the steps that the employer may take if the employer objects to the giving of the penalty notice, including how the employer may appeal against it[14]; and (f) the consequences of non-payment[15].

Where a penalty notice has been given to an employer by a local authority in respect of a failure of a kind mentioned head (1) or (2) above[16], the employer may, by giving notice (a 'notice of objection') to the authority, object to the giving of the penalty notice on one or more of the following grounds:

(i) that the employer did not contravene the statutory provisions[17] in the way stated in the enforcement notice[18];

(ii) that the requirements imposed by the enforcement notice were unreasonable[19];

(iii) that the employer did not fail in the way stated in the penalty notice[20];

(iv) that the amount of the penalty stated in the penalty notice is too high[21].

A notice of objection may be given to the authority only during the period of two weeks beginning with the day on which the penalty notice was given to the employer[22], and must set out the grounds of the objection and the employer's reasons for objecting on those grounds[23]. A local authority must consider a notice of objection given to it and, by giving notice (a 'determination notice') to the employer[24]: (A) withdraw the penalty notice[25]; (B) if the amount of the penalty determined in accordance with regulations[26] is smaller than the amount stated in the penalty notice, replace the penalty with the smaller amount[27]; or (C) confirm the penalty notice[28].

If a penalty notice is so withdrawn, any sum already paid or recovered in respect of the penalty notice must be repaid to the employer with interest at the appropriate rate[29] running from the date when the sum was paid or recovered[30]. If the amount of a penalty is reduced, any sum already paid or recovered must, to the extent that it was paid or recovered in respect of any amount in excess of the reduced amount, be repaid to the employer with interest at the appropriate rate running from the date when the sum was paid or recovered[31].

1   The Education and Skills Act 2008 ss 31, 33, 36, 65 are to come into force as from a day to be appointed: see s 173(4). At the date at which this volume states the law no such day had been appointed. As to the application of ss 19–36 to Wales see s 67; and PARA 759. As to the meaning of 'Wales' see PARA 7 note 3.

2   As to the meaning of 'local authority' see PARA 25 (definition applied by the Education and Skills Act 2008 s 168(2), (3)). In exercising its functions under Pt 1 (ss 1–67), a local authority must have regard to any guidance given by the Secretary of State: see s 18 (amended by SI 2010/1158). As to the publication of guidance see the Education Act 1996 s 571 (applied by the Education and Skills Act 2008 s 168(2), (3)); and PARA 60. As to the Secretary of State see PARA 58.

3   Ie under the Education and Skills Act 2008 s 30: see PARA 741.

4   Education and Skills Act 2008 s 31(1) (amended by SI 2010/1158).

5   Education and Skills Act 2008 s 31(2)(a).

6   Ie by virtue of the Education and Skills Act 2008 s 30(4)(a): see PARA 741.

7   Education and Skills Act 2008 s 31(2)(b).

8   As to the service of notices and documents see the Education Act 1996 s 572 (applied by the Education and Skills Act 2008 s 168(2), (3)); and PARA 76.

9   Education and Skills Act 2008 s 31(2) (amended by SI 2010/1158). The amount of the financial penalty is to be determined in accordance with regulations: Education and Skills Act 2008 s 31(3). Without prejudice to section 166(6) (general provision relating to orders and regulations), regulations under s 31(3) may make provision for penalties of different amounts to be payable in different cases or circumstances (including provision for the penalty payable under a penalty notice to differ according to the time by which it is paid): s 31(5). 'Regulations' means regulations made under the Education and Skills Act 2008 by the Secretary of State: s 168(1). At the date at which this volume states the law no such regulations had been made.

    A penalty payable by virtue of a penalty notice under s 31 is payable to the local authority which issued the notice: see s 65(1)(b) (s 65(1), (2) amended by SI 2010/1158). Any sums so received by a local authority may be used by the authority for the purposes of any of its functions which may be specified in regulations but, to the extent that they are not so used, must be paid in accordance with regulations to the Secretary of State: see the Education and Skills Act 2008 s 65(2) (as so amended). At the date at which this volume states the law no regulations had been made under s 65(2). As to the meaning of 'functions' see PARA 18 note 5 (definition applied by s 168(2), (3)). A penalty under s 31 (and any interest or financial penalty for late payment) is recoverable, if the county court so orders, as if it were payable under an order of that court: see s 65(3) (amended by the Crime and Courts Act 2013 Sch 9 para 52(1)(b), (2)). As to county courts see COURTS AND TRIBUNALS vol 24 (2010) PARA 758 et seq. Where a person is required by a penalty notice given under the Education and Skills Act 2008 s 31 to pay a financial penalty, and (1) has given a notice of objection to the local authority under s 33 (see the text to notes 16–23) (see s 65(4)(a) (amended by SI 2010/1158)); or (2) has appealed against the giving of the penalty notice under the Education and Skills Act 2008 s 34 (see PARA 744) (see s 65(4)(b)), the penalty is not enforceable until the authority has given a determination notice under s 33 (see the text to notes 24–28) in relation to the penalty notice, or, as the case may be, the appeal has been determined (see s 65(4)).

10   Education and Skills Act 2008 s 31(4)(a).

11   Education and Skills Act 2008 s 31(4)(b).

12   Education and Skills Act 2008 s 31(4)(c).

13   Education and Skills Act 2008 s 31(4)(d).

14   Education and Skills Act 2008 s 31(4)(e). As to appeals see s 34; and PARA 744.

15   Education and Skills Act 2008 s 31(4)(f).

16   Education and Skills Act 2008 s 33(1) (amended by SI 2010/1158).

17   Ie the Education and Skills Act 2008 s 27 (see PARA 739) or s 28 (see PARA 740).

18   Education and Skills Act 2008 s 33(2)(a).

19   Education and Skills Act 2008 s 33(2)(b).

20   Education and Skills Act 2008 s 33(2)(c).

21   Education and Skills Act 2008 s 33(2)(d).

22   Education and Skills Act 2008 s 33(3)(a).

23   Education and Skills Act 2008 s 33(3)(b).

24   Education and Skills Act 2008 s 33(4) (amended by SI 2010/1158). The determination notice must be given within the prescribed period beginning with the day on which the notice of objection was given: Education and Skills Act 2008 s 33(5). 'Prescribed' means prescribed by regulations: s 168(1). At the date at which this volume states the law no such regulations had been made.

25   Education and Skills Act 2008 s 33(4)(a).

26 Ie regulations under the Education and Skills Act 2008 s 31(3): see note 9.
27 Education and Skills Act 2008 s 33(4)(b). Where, under s 33(4)(b), the amount of a penalty stated in a penalty notice is replaced with a smaller amount, the notice is to have effect as if it had originally stated the smaller amount: s 33(6).
28 Education and Skills Act 2008 s 33(4)(c).
29 'The appropriate rate' means the rate that, on the date the sum was paid or recovered, was specified in the Judgments Act 1838 s 17 (see CIVIL PROCEDURE vol 12 (2009) PARA 1149): Education and Skills Act 2008 s 36(3).
30 See the Education and Skills Act 2008 s 36(1).
31 Education and Skills Act 2008 s 36(2).

743. Withdrawal of enforcement notice. As from a day to be appointed the following provisions have effect[1].

Where an enforcement notice has been given[2] to an employer by a local authority[3], and, if a penalty notice has been given in respect of the enforcement notice[4], any appeal made[5] in respect of the penalty notice has not been determined[6], the local authority may withdraw the enforcement notice by giving notice of the withdrawal to the employer[7]. After the withdrawal, no penalty notice may be given[8] in respect of:

(1) any failure to comply with the enforcement notice[9]; or

(2) any failure to give effect to any variation of terms and conditions of employment required by the enforcement notice to be offered[10],

which occurred before the enforcement notice was withdrawn[11].

Where an enforcement notice is withdrawn any penalty notice given[12] in respect of the enforcement notice ceases to have effect[13]; and any sum paid or recovered in respect of any such penalty notice must be repaid to the employer with interest at the appropriate rate[14] running from the date when the sum was paid or recovered[15].

1 The Education and Skills Act 2008 s 32 is to come into force as from a day to be appointed: see s 173(4). At the date at which this volume states the law no such day had been appointed. As to the application of ss 19–36 to Wales see s 67; and PARA 759. As to the meaning of 'Wales' see PARA 7 note 3.
2 Ie under the Education and Skills Act 2008 s 30: see PARA 741.
3 Education and Skills Act 2008 s 32(1)(a) (amended by SI 2010/1158). As to the meaning of 'local authority' see PARA 25 (definition applied by the Education and Skills Act 2008 s 168(2), (3)). In exercising its functions under Pt 1 (ss 1–67), a local authority must have regard to any guidance given by the Secretary of State: see s 18 (amended by SI 2010/1158). As to the publication of guidance see the Education Act 1996 s 571 (applied by the Education and Skills Act 2008 s 168(2), (3)); and PARA 60. As to the Secretary of State see PARA 58.
4 Ie under the Education and Skills Act 2008 s 31: see PARA 742.
5 Ie under the Education and Skills Act 2008 s 34: see PARA 744.
6 Education and Skills Act 2008 s 32(1)(b).
7 Education and Skills Act 2008 s 32(2) (amended by SI 2010/1158). A notice of withdrawal must state the effect of the withdrawal (but a failure to do so does not make the notice of withdrawal ineffective): Education and Skills Act 2008 s 33(6). As to the service of notices and documents see the Education Act 1996 s 572 (applied by the Education and Skills Act 2008 s 168(2), (3)); and PARA 76.
8 Ie under the Education and Skills Act 2008 s 31: see PARA 742.
9 Education and Skills Act 2008 s 32(3)(a).
10 Education and Skills Act 2008 s 32(3)(b).
11 Education and Skills Act 2008 s 32(3).
12 Ie under the Education and Skills Act 2008 s 31: see PARA 742.
13 Education and Skills Act 2008 s 32(4)(a).
14 'The appropriate rate' means the rate that, on the date the sum was paid or recovered, was specified in the Judgments Act 1838 s 17 (see CIVIL PROCEDURE vol 12 (2009) PARA 1149): Education and Skills Act 2008 s 32(5).
15 Education and Skills Act 2008 s 32(4)(b).

744.   Appeal against penalty notice. As from a day to be appointed the following provisions have effect[1].

Where a penalty notice has been given to an employer[2] in respect of a failure[3] to comply with an enforcement notice[4] and:

(1)   the period during which a notice of objection[5] may be given in relation to the penalty notice has expired[6]; and

(2)   if a notice of objection has been given in relation to the penalty notice, a determination notice[7] has been given in relation to the notice of objection[8],

the employer may appeal to the First-tier Tribunal[9] against the giving of the penalty notice on one or more of the following grounds:

(a)   that the employer did not contravene the statutory provisions[10] in the way stated in the enforcement notice[11];

(b)   that the circumstances of the contravention of those provisions stated in the enforcement notice make the giving of an enforcement notice[12] unreasonable[13];

(c)   that the requirements imposed by the enforcement notice were unreasonable[14];

(d)   that the employer did not fail in the way stated in the penalty notice[15];

(e)   that the circumstances of the failure stated in the penalty notice make the giving of the notice unreasonable[16];

(f)   that the amount of the penalty stated in the penalty notice is too high[17].

On such an appeal, the First-tier Tribunal may: (i) allow the appeal and cancel the penalty notice[18]; (ii) if the amount of the penalty determined in accordance with regulations[19] is smaller than the amount stated in the penalty notice, allow the appeal and replace the penalty with the smaller amount[20]; or (iii) dismiss the appeal[21].

Where a penalty notice has been given to an employer[22] by a local authority[23], and any appeal made under the above provisions in respect of the penalty notice has not been determined[24], the authority may withdraw the penalty notice by giving notice of the withdrawal[25] to the employer[26]. If a penalty notice is so withdrawn, any sum already paid or recovered in respect of the penalty notice must be repaid to the employer with interest at the appropriate rate[27] running from the date when the sum was paid or recovered[28].

1   The Education and Skills Act 2008 ss 34–36 are to come into force as from a day to be appointed: see s 173(4). At the date at which this volume states the law no such day had been appointed. As to the application of ss 19–36 to Wales see s 67; and PARA 759. As to the meaning of 'Wales' see PARA 7 note 3.
2   Ie under the Education and Skills Act 2008 s 31: see PARA 742.
3   Ie a failure of a kind mentioned in the Education and Skills Act 2008 s 31(2): see PARA 742.
4   See the Education and Skills Act 2008 s 34(1).
5   As to notices of objection see PARA 742.
6   Education and Skills Act 2008 s 34(1)(a).
7   As to determination notices see PARA 742.
8   Education and Skills Act 2008 s 34(1)(b).
9   As to the First-tier Tribunal see COURTS AND TRIBUNALS vol 24 (2010) PARA 874 et seq.
10 Ie the Education and Skills Act 2008 s 27 (see PARA 739) or s 28 (see PARA 740).
11 Education and Skills Act 2008 s 34(2)(a).
12 Ie under the Education and Skills Act 2008 s 30: see PARA 741.
13 Education and Skills Act 2008 s 34(2)(b).
14 Education and Skills Act 2008 s 34(2)(c).
15 Education and Skills Act 2008 s 34(2)(d).
16 Education and Skills Act 2008 s 34(2)(e).
17 Education and Skills Act 2008 s 34(2)(f).

18 Education and Skills Act 2008 s 34(3)(a).
19 Ie regulations under the Education and Skills Act 2008 s 31(3): see PARA 742.
20 Education and Skills Act 2008 s 34(3)(b). Where, under s 34(3)(b), the amount of a penalty stated in a penalty notice is replaced with a smaller amount, the notice is to have effect as if it had originally stated the smaller amount: s 34(4).
21 Education and Skills Act 2008 s 34(3)(c).
22 Ie under the Education and Skills Act 2008 s 31: see PARA 742.
23 Education and Skills Act 2008 s 35(1)(a) (amended by SI 2010/1158). As to the meaning of 'local authority' see PARA 25 (definition applied by the Education and Skills Act 2008 s 168(2), (3)). In exercising its functions under Pt 1 (ss 1–67), a local authority must have regard to any guidance given by the Secretary of State: see s 18 (amended by SI 2010/1158). As to the publication of guidance see the Education Act 1996 s 571 (applied by the Education and Skills Act 2008 s 168(2), (3)); and PARA 60. As to the Secretary of State see PARA 58.
24 Education and Skills Act 2008 s 35(1)(b).
25 As to the service of notices and documents see the Education Act 1996 s 572 (applied by the Education and Skills Act 2008 s 168(2), (3)); and PARA 76.
26 Education and Skills Act 2008 s 35(2).
27 As to the meaning of 'appropriate rate' see PARA 742 note 29.
28 See the Education and Skills Act 2008 s 36(1).

(iv) Parenting Contracts and Parenting Orders

745. Parenting contracts. As from a day to be appointed the following provisions have effect[1].

Where a person who is subject to the duty to participate in education or training[2] ('the young person') is failing to fulfil that duty[3], a local authority[4] in England may enter into a parenting contract with a parent of the young person[5], if the parent is resident in England[6] and the authority considers that entering into the parenting contract would be desirable in the interests of the young person's fulfilment of that duty[7].

A 'parenting contract' is a document which contains: (1) a statement by the parent that the parent agrees to comply with such requirements as may be specified in the document for such period as may be so specified[8]; and (2) a statement by the local authority that it agrees to provide support to the parent for the purpose of complying with those requirements[9]. The requirements may include (in particular) a requirement to attend a counselling or guidance programme[10]. A parenting contract must be signed by the parent and signed on behalf of the local authority[11]. A parenting contract does not create any obligations in respect of whose breach any liability arises in contract or in tort[12].

1 The Education and Skills Act 2008 ss 40, 44 are to come into force as from a day to be appointed: see s 173(4). At the date at which this volume states the law no such day had been appointed.
2 Ie a person to whom the Education and Skills Act 2008 Pt 1 (ss 1–67) applies. As to such persons see s 1; and PARA 725.
3 See the Education and Skills Act 2008 s 40(1). The duty referred to is that under s 2 (see PARA 725): see s 40(1). As to the meaning of 'failing to fulfil the duty imposed under s 2' see PARA 731 note 6.
4 As to the meaning of 'local authority' see PARA 25 (definition applied by the Education and Skills Act 2008 s 168(2), (3)). Local authorities in England must, in carrying out their functions in relation to parenting contracts under s 40, have regard to the extent to which any failure by, or anything done by, a parent of a person to whom Pt 1 (ss 1–67) applies is affecting, or is likely to affect, that person's fulfilment of the duty imposed by s 2 (see PARA 725): see s 44(1) (s 44 amended by SI 2010/1158). Regulations may make further provision about the exercise by local authorities in England of their functions relating to parenting contracts under the Education and Skills Act 2008 s 40 (s 44(2)(a) (as so amended)). The provision that may be made under s 44(2) includes: (1) provision limiting the power of a local authority to enter into a parenting contract in prescribed cases (see s 44(3)(a) (as so amended)); (2) provision requiring one local authority to consult with another before taking any prescribed step (s 44(3)(b) (as so amended));

(3) provision requiring the provision of information by one local authority in England to another (s 44(3)(c) (as so amended)); (4) provision as to how the costs associated with parenting contracts under s 40 (including the costs of providing counselling or guidance programmes) are to be met (see s 44(3)(d)). As to the meaning of 'England' see PARA 7 note 3. As to the meaning of 'functions' see PARA 18 note 5 (definition applied by s 168(2), (3)). 'Parent', in relation to a young person, is to be construed in accordance with the Education Act 1996 s 576 (see PARA 7 note 6), but does not include a person who is not an individual: Education and Skills Act 2008 s 44(4). 'Prescribed' means prescribed by regulations; and 'regulations' means regulations made under the Education and Skills Act 2008 by the Secretary of State: s 168(1). As to the Secretary of State see PARA 58. At the date at which this volume states the law no such regulations had been made.

In exercising its functions under Pt 1 (ss 1–67), a local authority must have regard to any guidance given by the Secretary of State: see s 18 (amended by SI 2010/1158). As to the publication of guidance see the Education Act 1996 s 571 (applied by the Education and Skills Act 2008 s 168(2), (3)); and PARA 60.

5 Education and Skills Act 2008 s 40(2) (amended by SI 2010/1158).
6 Education and Skills Act 2008 s 40(2)(a). As to when a person is to be regarded as resident in England see s 66(2); and PARA 725 note 2.
7 Education and Skills Act 2008 s 40(2)(b).
8 Education and Skills Act 2008 s 40(3)(a).
9 Education and Skills Act 2008 s 40(3)(b) (amended by SI 2010/1158).
10 Education and Skills Act 2008 s 40(4).
11 Education and Skills Act 2008 s 40(5) (amended by SI 2010/1158).
12 Education and Skills Act 2008 s 40(6).

746. Parenting orders. As from a day to be appointed the following provisions have effect[1].

Where a person who is subject to the duty to participate in education or training[2] ('the young person') is failing to fulfil that duty[3], a local authority[4] in England may apply to a magistrates' court[5] for a parenting order in respect of a parent of the young person, if the parent is resident in England[6]. A 'parenting order' is an order which requires the parent:

(1) to comply, for a period not exceeding 12 months[7], with such requirements as are specified in the order[8]; and

(2) to attend, for a concurrent period not exceeding three months, such counselling or guidance programme[9] as may be specified in directions given by the responsible officer[10].

If such an application is made, the court may make a parenting order in respect of the parent if it is satisfied that: (a) the young person is failing to fulfil the duty to participate in education or training[11]; and (b) the making of the order would be desirable in the interests of the young person's fulfilment of that duty[12]. In deciding whether to make a parenting order, a court must take into account (amongst other things)[13]: (i) any refusal by the parent to enter into a parenting contract[14] in respect of the young person[15]; or (ii) if the parent has entered into such a parenting contract, any failure by the parent to comply with the requirements specified in the contract[16].

An appeal lies to the Crown Court[17] against the making of a parenting order[18].

1 The Education and Skills Act 2008 ss 41–44 are to come into force as from a day to be appointed: see s 173(4). At the date at which this volume states the law no such day had been appointed.
2 Ie a person to whom the Education and Skills Act 2008 Pt 1 (ss 1–67) applies. As to such persons see s 1; and PARA 725.
3 See the Education and Skills Act 2008 s 41(1). The duty referred to is that under s 2 (see PARA 725): see s 41(1). As to the meaning of 'failing to fulfil the duty imposed under s 2' see PARA 731 note 6.

4 As to the meaning of 'local authority' see PARA 25 (definition applied by the Education and Skills Act 2008 s 168(2), (3)). Local authorities in England and responsible officers (see the text to note 10) must, in carrying out their functions in relation to parenting orders under s 41, have regard to the extent to which any failure by, or anything done by, a parent of a person to whom this Pt 1 (ss 1–67) applies is affecting, or is likely to affect, that person's fulfilment of the duty imposed by s 2 (see PARA 725): see s 44(1) (s 44 amended by SI 2010/1158). Regulations may make further provision about the exercise by local authorities in England of their functions relating to parenting orders under the Education and Skills Act 2008 s 41: s 44(2)(b) (as so amended). The provision that may be made under s 44(2) includes: (1) provision limiting the power of a local authority to apply for a parenting order, in prescribed cases (see s 44(3)(a) (as so amended)); (2) provision requiring one local authority to consult with another before taking any prescribed step (s 44(3)(b) (as so amended)); (3) provision requiring the provision of information by one local authority in England to another (s 44(3)(c) (as so amended)); (4) provision as to how the costs associated with parenting orders under s 41 (including in each case the costs of providing counselling or guidance programmes) are to be met (see s 44(3)(d) (as so amended)). As to the meaning of 'parent' see PARA 745 note 4. 'Responsible officer', in relation to a parenting order, means an officer of a local authority who is specified in the order: s 44(4) (as so amended). As to the meaning of 'functions' see PARA 18 note 5 (definition applied by s 168(2), (3)). As to the meaning of 'England' see PARA 7 note 3. 'Prescribed' means prescribed by regulations; and 'regulations' means regulations made under the Education and Skills Act 2008 by the Secretary of State: s 168(1). As to the Secretary of State see PARA 58. At the date at which this volume states the law no such regulations had been made.

In exercising its functions under Pt 1 (ss 1–67), a local authority must have regard to any guidance given by the Secretary of State: see s 18 (amended by SI 2010/1158). As to the publication of guidance see the Education Act 1996 s 571 (applied by the Education and Skills Act 2008 s 168(2), (3)); and PARA 60.

5 As to magistrates' courts see MAGISTRATES vol 71 (2013) PARA 470 et seq.

6 Education and Skills Act 2008 s 41(2). As to when a person is to be regarded as resident in England, see s 66(2); and PARA 725 note 2.

7 As to the meaning of 'month' see PARA 54 note 26.

8 Education and Skills Act 2008 s 41(4)(a).

9 A counselling or guidance programme which a parent is required to attend by virtue of the Education and Skills Act 2008 s 41(4)(b) may be or include a residential course but only if the court is satisfied that the following two conditions are fulfilled: s 41(6). The first condition is that the attendance of the parent at a residential course is likely to be more effective than attendance at a non-residential course in the interests of the young person's fulfilment of the duty imposed by s 2 (see PARA 725): s 41(7). The second condition is that any interference with family life which is likely to result from the attendance of the parent at a residential course is proportionate in all the circumstances: s 41(8).

10 Education and Skills Act 2008 s 41(4)(b). This provision is expressed to be subject to s 41(5): see s 41(4)(b). A parenting order may, but need not, include a requirement mentioned in s 41(4)(b) in any case where a parenting order under s 41 or any other enactment has been made in respect of the parent on a previous occasion: s 41(5). See also note 4.

11 See the Education and Skills Act 2008 s 41(3)(a).

12 Education and Skills Act 2008 s 41(3)(b).

13 Education and Skills Act 2008 s 42(1). The provisions of the Crime and Disorder Act 1998 s 9(3)–(7) (supplemental provisions about parenting orders: see CHILDREN AND YOUNG PERSONS vol 10 (2012) PARAS 1279, 1281) apply in relation to a parenting order under the Education and Skills Act 2008 s 41 as they apply in relation to a parenting order under the Crime and Disorder Act 1998 s 8: Education and Skills Act 2008 s 42(2).

14 Ie under the Education and Skills Act 2008 s 40: see PARA 745.

15 See the Education and Skills Act 2008 s 42(1)(a).

16 Education and Skills Act 2008 s 42(1)(b).

17 As to the Crown Court see COURTS AND TRIBUNALS vol 24 (2010) PARA 716 et seq.

18 Education and Skills Act 2008 s 43(1). The provisions of the Crime and Disorder Act 1998 s 10(2), (3) (appeals against parenting orders: see CHILDREN AND YOUNG PERSONS vol 10 (2012) PARA 1282) apply in relation to such an appeal as they apply in relation to an appeal under the Crime and Disorder Act 1998 s 10(1)(b): Education and Skills Act 2008 s 43(2).

(v) Attendance Notices

747. Initial steps. As from a day to be appointed the following provisions have effect[1].

Where it appears to a local authority[2] that a person who is subject to the duty to participate in education or training[3] and who belongs to the authority's area[4] is failing to fulfil that duty[5], the authority may give a written notice[6] to the person stating: (1) that it appears to the authority that the person is a person who is subject to the duty to participate in education or training[7], and is failing without reasonable excuse to fulfil that duty[8]; and (2) that if, after the date specified in the notice[9], the person appears to the authority to be failing, without reasonable excuse, to fulfil that duty, the authority may issue[10] an attendance notice[11], and explaining the effect of an attendance notice[12].

Where an authority proposes to give such a notice[13] to a person[14], the authority:

(a) must take all reasonable steps to secure that relevant support[15] is offered to the person[16], and may not give the notice unless satisfied that the person has been afforded an opportunity to take advantage of the support offered[17];

(b) must give the person an opportunity to make representations[18], and may not give the notice:

  (i) in a specified case[19], unless, having regard to any representations made, the person appears to the authority to have no reasonable excuse for the failure[20];

  (ii) in any other case, if, having regard to any representations made, the person appears to the authority to have a reasonable excuse for the failure[21].

1 The Education and Skills Act 2008 s 45 is to come into force as from a day to be appointed: see s 173(4). At the date at which this volume states the law no such day had been appointed. As to the review of the initial operation of Pt 1 Ch 5 (ss 45–60), see s 60; and PARA 758.

2 As to the meaning of 'local authority' see PARA 25 (definition applied by the Education and Skills Act 2008 s 168(2), (3)). In exercising its functions under Pt 1 (ss 1–67), a local authority must have regard to any guidance given by the Secretary of State: see s 18 (amended by SI 2010/1158). As to the publication of guidance see the Education Act 1996 s 571 (applied by the Education and Skills Act 2008 s 168(2), (3)); and PARA 60. As to the Secretary of State see PARA 58.

3 Ie a person to whom the Education and Skills Act 2008 Pt 1 (ss 1–67) applies. As to such persons see s 1; and PARA 725.

4 As to when a person is treated as belonging, or as not belonging, to the area of a local authority see PARA 27 note 6 (provision applied by the Education and Skills Act 2008 s 168(2), (3)).

5 See the Education and Skills Act 2008 s 45(1) (amended by SI 2010/1158). The duty referred to is that under the Education and Skills Act 2008 s 2 (see PARA 725): see s 41(1). As to the meaning of 'failing to fulfil the duty imposed under s 2' see PARA 731 note 6.

6 As to the meaning of 'written' see PARA 76 note 8. As to the service of notices and documents see the Education Act 1996 s 572 (applied by the Education and Skills Act 2008 s 168(2), (3)); and PARA 76.

7 Education and Skills Act 2008 s 45(2)(a)(i).

8 Education and Skills Act 2008 s 45(2)(a)(ii).

9 The date specified must not be less than 15 days after the date on which the notice is given: Education and Skills Act 2008 s 45(3).

10 Ie under the Education and Skills Act 2008 s 46: see PARA 748.

11 Education and Skills Act 2008 s 45(2)(b).

12 Education and Skills Act 2008 s 45(2).

13 Ie a notice under the Education and Skills Act 2008 s 45(2): see the text to notes 6–12.

14 See the Education and Skills Act 2008 s 45(4).

15 'Relevant support' means support provided by means of services made available by the local authority in exercise of its functions under the Education and Skills Act 2008 s 68 (see PARA 802): s 45(8) (amended by SI 2010/1158).
16 Education and Skills Act 2008 s 45(5)(a).
17 Education and Skills Act 2008 s 45(5)(b).
18 Education and Skills Act 2008 s 45(6)(a).
19 Ie a case within the Education and Skills Act 2008 s 45(7): see s 45(6)(b)(i). Section 45(7) applies where: (1) arrangements have been made for the person to participate during the current relevant period in a course or courses constituting relevant training or education (s 45(7)(a)); (2) the only failure by the person during that relevant period is that the relevant education and training to which the arrangements relate is not sufficient relevant education and training (s 45(7)(b)); (3) the course has not, or the courses have not all, concluded (s 45(7)(c)); and (4) further arrangements for relevant training or education after the conclusion of the course or courses could be made which would enable the person to participate in sufficient relevant training or education during the current relevant period (s 45(7)(d)). As to the meaning of 'relevant period' see PARA 728 note 3. As to the meanings of 'relevant training or education' and 'sufficient relevant training or education' see PARA 728.
20 Education and Skills Act 2008 s 45(6)(b)(i).
21 Education and Skills Act 2008 s 45(6)(b)(ii).

748. Attendance notices. As from a day to be appointed the following provisions have effect[1].
Where:

(1)   a local authority[2] has given a initial notice[3] to a person[4];
(2)   that person is still a person who is subject to the duty to participate in education or training[5]; and
(3)   at any time after the date specified in the notice[6], it appears to the local authority that the person is, without reasonable excuse, failing to fulfil that duty[7],

the local authority may, before the end of the period of six months[8] beginning with the day on which the notice was given to the person, give the person a further notice[9] (an 'attendance notice') requiring the person to participate in education or training specified in the notice[10].

Where the education or training specified is education or training provided by means of a course, the attendance notice must specify the school, college or other training or educational establishment at which the education or training is to be provided[11], and the name and description of the course[12]. Where the education or training specified is training provided in accordance with a contract of apprenticeship otherwise than by a course, the attendance notice must specify prescribed[13] details of the contract of apprenticeship[14]. An attendance notice given to a person:

(a)   must specify the place or places at which the person is required to attend[15], the time or times at which the person is required to attend[16], and the person or persons to whom the person must present himself or herself[17];
(b)   may specify other prescribed requirements relating to the description of education or training specified in the notice[18];
(c)   must state the period for which the notice has effect[19], the consequences of failing to comply with any requirement imposed by the notice[20], and such other matters as may be prescribed[21].

1 The Education and Skills Act 2008 ss 46, 47 are to come into force as from a day to be appointed: see s 173(4). At the date at which this volume states the law no such day had been appointed. As to the review of the initial operation of Pt 1 Ch 5 (ss 45–60) see s 60; and PARA 758.

2   As to the meaning of 'local authority' see PARA 25 (definition applied by the Education and
    Skills Act 2008 s 168(2), (3)). In exercising its functions under Pt 1 (ss 1–67), a local authority
    must have regard to any guidance given by the Secretary of State: see s 18 (amended by
    SI 2010/1158). As to the publication of guidance see the Education Act 1996 s 571 (applied by
    the Education and Skills Act 2008 s 168(2), (3)); and PARA 60. As to the Secretary of State see
    PARA 58.
3   Ie a notice under the Education and Skills Act 2008 s 45(2): see PARA 747.
4   See the Education and Skills Act 2008 s 46(1)(a) (amended by SI 2010/1158).
5   Ie the Education and Skills Act 2008 Pt 1 (ss 1–67) still applies to the person: see s 46(1)(b). As
    to such persons see s 1; and PARA 725.
6   Ie under the Education and Skills Act 2008 s 45(2)(b): see PARA 747.
7   See the Education and Skills Act 2008 s 46(1)(c) (amended by SI 2010/1158). The duty referred
    to is that imposed by the Education and Skills Act 2008 s 2 (see PARA 725): see s 46(1)(c) (as so
    amended).
8   As to the meaning of 'month' see PARA 54 note 26.
9   The Education and Skills Act 2008 s 45(6), (7) (see PARA 747) applies in relation to the giving of
    attendance notices as it applies in relation to the giving of notices under s 45(2): s 46(3). As to
    the service of notices and documents see the Education Act 1996 s 572 (applied by the
    Education and Skills Act 2008 s 168(2), (3)); and PARA 76.
10 Education and Skills Act 2008 s 46(2) (amended by SI 2010/1158). The education or training
    specified under the Education and Skills Act 2008 s 46(2) must satisfy s 47: s 46(4). The
    following provisions must be satisfied in relation to education or training specified in an
    attendance notice given to a person to whom Pt 1 (ss 1–67) applies by a local authority: s 47(1)
    (amended by SI 2010/1158). The education or training must be provided: (1) at a school, college
    or other training or educational establishment by means of a course (Education and Skills
    Act 2008 s 47(2)(a)); or (2) in accordance with a contract of apprenticeship (s 47(2)(b)). The
    education or training must be such that, by participating in it, the young person would fulfil the
    duty imposed by s 2 (see PARA 725) (s 47(3)); and for that purpose, account may be taken of any
    contract of employment of the person or other arrangement under which the person works
    (s 47(4)). The education or training must: (a) be appropriate full-time education or training
    (s 47(5)(a)); or (b) otherwise be suitable for the person, having regard to the person's age, ability
    and aptitude (s 47(5)(b)(i)), and to any special educational needs which the person may have
    (s 47(5)(b)(ii) (amended by the Children and Families Act 2014 Sch 3 paras 82, 85(a)). Where
    the education or training is to be provided by means of a course, the local authority: (i) must
    have consulted the governing body or proprietor of the school, college or other training or
    educational establishment at which the education or training is to be provided (Education and
    Skills Act 2008 s 47(7)(a) (s 47(7) amended by SI 2010/1158)); and (ii) must have made
    arrangements, or be satisfied that arrangements have been made, for the education or training to
    be provided there for the person (Education and Skills Act 2008 s 47(7)(b)). Where the
    education or training is training provided in accordance with a contract of apprenticeship, the
    local authority must have consulted the employer in relation to the contract of apprenticeship:
    s 47(8) (amended by SI 2010/1158). As to the meaning of 'school' see PARA 91; as to the
    meaning of 'proprietor' see PARA 51 note 4; and as to the meaning of 'special educational needs'
    see PARA 943 (definition applied by the Education and Skills Act 2008 s 168(2), (3)). As to the
    meaning of 'contract of employment' see PARA 725 note 17. As to the meaning of 'appropriate
    full-time education or training' see PARA 726. As to the governing bodies of maintained schools
    in England see PARA 150 et seq. As to the exercise of the duty to consult see JUDICIAL REVIEW
    vol 61 (2010) PARA 627.
11 Education and Skills Act 2008 s 46(5)(a).
12 Education and Skills Act 2008 s 46(5)(b).
13 'Prescribed' means prescribed by regulations; and 'regulations' means regulations made under
    the Education and Skills Act 2008 by the Secretary of State: s 168(1). At the date at which this
    volume states the law no such regulations had been made.
14 Education and Skills Act 2008 s 46(6).
15 Education and Skills Act 2008 s 46(7)(a).
16 Education and Skills Act 2008 s 46(7)(b).
17 Education and Skills Act 2008 s 46(7)(c).
18 Education and Skills Act 2008 s 46(7). At the date at which this volume states the law no
    regulations had been made for this purpose.
19 Education and Skills Act 2008 s 46(8)(a). An attendance notice given by a local authority to a
    person has effect for the period beginning with the day on which it is given and ending with: (1)
    the last day on which the person is a person to whom Pt 1 (ss 1–67) applies (s 46(9)(a) (s 46(9)

amended by SI 2010/1158)); or (2) if earlier, the day on which it is revoked (Education and Skills Act 2008 s 46(9)(b)). As to the variation and revocation of attendance notices see s 50; and PARA 751.

20 Education and Skills Act 2008 s 46(8)(b). As to failure to comply with an attendance notice, see ss 51–58; and PARAS 752–756. As to appeals against attendance notices see s 49; and PARA 750.

21 Education and Skills Act 2008 s 46(8)(c). At the date at which this volume states the law no regulations had been made for this purpose.

749. Attendance panel. As from a day to be appointed the following provisions have effect[1].

A local authority[2] in England[3] must establish a panel (an 'attendance panel'), constituted in accordance with regulations[4]. An attendance panel has the following functions[5]:

(1) functions conferred on it[6] in relation to appeals against attendance notices[7];

(2) functions conferred on it[8] in relation to the variation of attendance notices[9];

(3) functions conferred on it[10] in relation to the institution of proceedings for an offence of failure to comply with an attendance notice[11];

(4) functions conferred on it[12] in relation to appeals against fixed penalty notices[13].

1 The Education and Skills Act 2008 s 48 is to come into force as from a day to be appointed: see s 173(4). At the date at which this volume states the law no such day had been appointed. As to the review of the initial operation of Pt 1 Ch 5 (ss 45–60), see s 60; and PARA 758.

2 As to the meaning of 'local authority' see PARA 25 (definition applied by the Education and Skills Act 2008 s 168(2), (3)). In exercising its functions under Pt 1 (ss 1–67), a local authority must have regard to any guidance given by the Secretary of State: see s 18 (amended by SI 2010/1158). As to the publication of guidance see the Education Act 1996 s 571 (applied by the Education and Skills Act 2008 s 168(2), (3)); and PARA 60. As to the Secretary of State see PARA 58.

3 As to the meaning of 'England' see PARA 7 note 3.

4 Education and Skills Act 2008 s 48(1). Such regulations: (1) must require a local authority to secure that any person who chairs an attendance panel is not a member of the authority (s 48(3)(a) (s 48(3) amended by SI 2010/1158)); and (2) may make provision for the payment by the local authority of allowances to members of an appeal panel (Education and Skills Act 2008 s 48(3)(b) (as so amended)). Regulations made by virtue of s 48(3)(b) may provide for any of the provisions of the Local Government Act 1972 ss 173–174 (repealed) (allowances to members of local authorities and other bodies: see LOCAL GOVERNMENT vol 69 (2009) PARAS 171, 172, 175) or (in relation to Wales) the Local Government (Wales) Measure 2011 Pt 8 (ss 141–160) (payments and pensions: see LOCAL GOVERNMENT) to apply with prescribed modifications in relation to members of an attendance panel: Education and Skills Act 2008 s 48(4) (amended by the Local Government (Wales) Measure 2011 Sch 3 para 7). 'Prescribed' means prescribed by regulations; and 'regulations' means regulations made under the Education and Skills Act 2008 by the Secretary of State: s 168(1). At the date at which this volume states the law no such regulations had been made.

5 As to the meaning of 'functions' see PARA 18 note 5 (definition applied by the Education and Skills Act 2008 s 168(2), (3)).

6 Ie by virtue of the Education and Skills Act 2008 s 49: see PARA 750.

7 Education and Skills Act 2008 s 48(2)(a). As to attendance notices see s 46; and PARA 748.

8 Ie by virtue of the Education and Skills Act 2008 s 50(6)(b): see PARA 751.

9 Education and Skills Act 2008 s 48(2)(b).

10 Ie by the Education and Skills Act 2008 s 52(5), (6): see PARA 752.

11 Education and Skills Act 2008 s 48(2)(c).

12 Ie by virtue of the Education and Skills Act 2008 s 54: see PARA 754.

13 Education and Skills Act 2008 s 48(2)(d). As to fixed penalty notices see s 53; and PARA 753.

750. Appeal arrangements. As from a day to be appointed the following provisions have effect[1].

A local authority[2] in England[3] must make arrangements for enabling a young person to whom an attendance notice[4] is given by the authority to appeal against[5]:

(1)   the giving of the attendance notice[6];

(2)   the description of education or training specified in the attendance notice[7];

(3)   any variation[8] of the notice[9].

The arrangements must provide for any appeal under the arrangements to be to an attendance panel[10]. Regulations[11] may make provision about the making of appeals under the arrangements, including provision: (a) as to the procedure on such appeals[12]; and (b) as to the powers of the attendance panel in relation to such appeals[13].

1   The Education and Skills Act 2008 s 49 is to come into force as from a day to be appointed: see s 173(4). At the date at which this volume states the law no such day had been appointed. As to the review of the initial operation of Pt 1 Ch 5 (ss 45–60), see s 60; and PARA 758.

2   As to the meaning of 'local authority' see PARA 25 (definition applied by the Education and Skills Act 2008 s 168(2), (3)). In exercising its functions under Pt 1 (ss 1–67), a local authority must have regard to any guidance given by the Secretary of State: see s 18 (amended by SI 2010/1158). As to the publication of guidance see the Education Act 1996 s 571 (applied by the Education and Skills Act 2008 s 168(2), (3)); and PARA 60. As to the Secretary of State see PARA 58.

3   As to the meaning of 'England' see PARA 7 note 3.

4   As to attendance notices see PARA 748.

5   Education and Skills Act 2008 s 49(1) (amended by SI 2010/1158).

6   Education and Skills Act 2008 s 49(1)(a).

7   Education and Skills Act 2008 s 49(1)(b).

8   Ie under the Education and Skills Act 2008 s 50(2) (see PARA 751) (s 49(1)(c)(i)), or by virtue of s 50(5) or (6)(b) (see PARA 751) (s 49(1)(c)(ii)).

9   Education and Skills Act 2008 s 49(1)(c).

10   Education and Skills Act 2008 s 49(2). An attendance panel is one established under s 48 (see PARA 749): see s 49(2).

11   'Regulations' means regulations made under the Education and Skills Act 2008 by the Secretary of State: s 168(1). At the date at which this volume states the law no such regulations had been made.

12   Education and Skills Act 2008 s 49(3)(a).

13   Education and Skills Act 2008 s 49(3)(b).

751.   Variation and revocation of attendance notice. As from a day to be appointed the following provisions have effect[1].

Where a local authority[2] has given an attendance notice[3] to a person[4] who is subject to the duty to participate in education or training[5], if the attendance notice still has effect[6] when:

(1)   the education or training specified in the notice ends[7]; or

(2)   it becomes impracticable for the person to comply with the requirements specified in the notice because of a change of residence[8],

the local authority may by notice[9] to the person specify other education or training[10]. Where the local authority gives such a notice, the attendance notice has effect as if it specified the education or training specified in the notice[11].

Prescribed[12] matters specified in an attendance notice given by a local authority may be varied by the authority by notice given to the person to whom the attendance notice was given[13]. Regulations[14] may provide for other matters specified in an attendance notice given by a local authority to be varied[15] with the consent of the person to whom the notice was given[16], or with the consent of an attendance panel established[17] by the local authority[18].

An attendance notice given by a local authority may be revoked by the authority by notice given to the person to whom the attendance notice was given[19].

1   The Education and Skills Act 2008 s 50 is to come into force as from a day to be appointed: see s 173(4). At the date at which this volume states the law no such day had been appointed. As to the review of the initial operation of Pt 1 Ch 5 (ss 45–60), see s 60; and PARA 758.
2   As to the meaning of 'local authority' see PARA 25 (definition applied by the Education and Skills Act 2008 s 168(2), (3)). In exercising its functions under Pt 1 (ss 1–67), a local authority must have regard to any guidance given by the Secretary of State: see s 18 (amended by SI 2010/1158). As to the publication of guidance see the Education Act 1996 s 571 (applied by the Education and Skills Act 2008 s 168(2), (3)); and PARA 60. As to the Secretary of State see PARA 58.
3   Ie under the Education and Skills Act 2008 s 46: see PARA 748.
4   Ie a person to whom the Education and Skills Act 2008 Pt 1 (ss 1–67) applies. As to such persons see s 1; and PARA 725.
5   See the Education and Skills Act 2008 s 50(1) (amended by SI 2010/1158).
6   As to the period during which an attendance notice has effect see the Education and Skills Act 2008 s 46(9); and PARA 748 note 19.
7   Education and Skills Act 2008 s 50(2)(a).
8   Education and Skills Act 2008 s 50(2)(b). As to the determination of a person's residence see s 66(2); and PARA 725 note 2.
9   As to the service of notices and documents see the Education Act 1996 s 572 (applied by the Education and Skills Act 2008 s 168(2), (3)); and PARA 76.
10 Education and Skills Act 2008 s 50(2) (amended by SI 2010/1158). The provisions of the Education and Skills Act 2008 s 46(4)–(7), (8)(c) (see PARA 748) apply in relation to specifying education or training under s 50(2) as they apply in relation to the giving of an attendance notice: s 50(3).
11 Education and Skills Act 2008 s 50(4) (amended by SI 2010/1158).
12 'Prescribed' means prescribed by regulations; and 'regulations' means regulations made under the Education and Skills Act 2008 by the Secretary of State: s 168(1).
13 Education and Skills Act 2008 s 50(5) (amended by SI 2010/1158).
14 At the date at which this volume states the law no such regulations had been made.
15 Education and Skills Act 2008 s 50(6) (amended by SI 2010/1158).
16 Education and Skills Act 2008 s 50(6)(a).
17 Ie under the Education and Skills Act 2008 s 48: see PARA 749.
18 Education and Skills Act 2008 s 50(6)(b) (amended by SI 2010/1158). Regulations under the Education and Skills Act 2008 s 50(6)(b) may in particular make provision as to the procedure to be followed in relation to the giving of any consent under the regulations: s 50(7).
19 Education and Skills Act 2008 s 50(8) (amended by SI 2010/1158).

752.   Offence of failure to comply with attendance notice. As from a day to be appointed the following provisions have effect[1].

It is an offence for a person to whom an attendance notice[2] has been given to fail, without reasonable excuse, to comply with the requirements of the attendance notice[3]. It is a defence for a person charged with such an offence to show[4] that he or she is, and since the giving of the attendance notice has been, fulfilling the duty[5] to participate in education or training[6].

Proceedings for an alleged offence under the above provisions may not be instituted except by the local authority[7] which gave the attendance notice[8]. The proceedings may not be instituted:

(1)   if the attendance notice has been rescinded on an appeal[9], or revoked[10];

(2)   unless: (a) a penalty notice has been given[11] in respect of the alleged offence and has not been rescinded on an appeal[12], (b) the penalty imposed by the notice has not been paid in accordance with the notice[13], and (c) an attendance panel established by the local authority[14] has, on

being consulted by the local authority about the question whether the proceedings should be instituted, recommended to the authority that the proceedings should be instituted[15];

(3)   after the relevant statutory provisions[16] have ceased to apply[17] to the person alleged to have committed the offence[18].

1   The Education and Skills Act 2008 ss 51, 52 are to come into force as from a day to be appointed: see s 173(4). At the date at which this volume states the law no such day had been appointed. As to the review of the initial operation of Pt 1 Ch 5 (ss 45–60), see s 60; and PARA 758.
2   As to attendance notices see PARA 748.
3   Education and Skills Act 2008 s 51(1). A person guilty of such an offence is liable on summary conviction to a fine not exceeding level 1 on the standard scale: s 51(3). As to the standard scale see SENTENCING AND DISPOSITION OF OFFENDERS vol 92 (2010) PARA 142.
4   As to the standard of proof on the accused see CRIMINAL PROCEDURE vol 28 (2010) PARA 466.
5   Ie the duty imposed by the Education and Skills Act 2008 s 2: see PARA 725.
6   Education and Skills Act 2008 s 51(2).
7   As to the meaning of 'local authority' see PARA 25 (definition applied by the Education and Skills Act 2008 s 168(2), (3)). In exercising its functions under Pt 1 (ss 1–67), a local authority must have regard to any guidance given by the Secretary of State: see s 18 (amended by SI 2010/1158). As to the publication of guidance see the Education Act 1996 s 571 (applied by the Education and Skills Act 2008 s 168(2), (3)); and PARA 60. As to the Secretary of State see PARA 58.
8   See the Education and Skills Act 2008 s 52(1), (2) (amended by SI 2010/1158).
9   Education and Skills Act 2008 s 52(3)(a). The appeal referred to is one by virtue of s 49 (see PARA 750): see s 52(3)(a).
10 Ie under the Education and Skills Act 2008 s 50(8) (see PARA 751): s 52(3)(b).
11 Ie under the Education and Skills Act 2008 s 53: see PARA 753.
12 Education and Skills Act 2008 s 52(4)(a). The appeal referred to is one by virtue of s 54 (see PARA 754): see s 52(4)(a).
13 Education and Skills Act 2008 s 52(4)(b).
14 Ie under the Education and Skills Act 2008 s 48: see PARA 749.
15 Education and Skills Act 2008 s 52(4)(c) (amended by SI 2010/1158). Regulations (1) must make provision to secure that, before a recommendation under the Education and Skills Act 2008 s 52(4)(c) is made by an attendance panel in a person's case, the person has an opportunity to make representations to the panel (s 52(5)(a)); and (2) may make other provision as to the procedure to be followed in relation to the making of such recommendations (s 52(5)(b)). 'Regulations' means regulations made under the Education and Skills Act 2008 by the Secretary of State: s 168(1). At the date at which this volume states the law no such regulations had been made.
16 Ie the Education and Skills Act 2008 Pt 1 (ss 1–67).
17 As to the application of the Education and Skills Act 2008 Pt 1 (ss 1–67), see s 1; and PARA 725.
18 Education and Skills Act 2008 s 52(6). Section 52(6) does not affect proceedings for such an offence by a person which were instituted while Pt 1 (ss 1–67) applied to the person: s 52(7).

753.   Failure to comply with attendance notice: penalty notice. As from a day to be appointed the following provisions have effect[1].

Where a local authority[2] which has given an attendance notice to a person[3] has reason to believe that the person has committed an offence[4] relating to the notice, the authority may give the person a penalty notice in respect of the offence[5]. A 'penalty notice' is a notice offering a person the opportunity of discharging any liability to conviction in respect of the offence to which the notice relates by payment of a penalty in accordance with the notice[6].

Where a person is given a penalty notice proceedings for the offence to which the notice relates may not be instituted[7] before the end of such period as may be prescribed[8], and the person cannot be convicted of the offence to which the notice relates if a penalty is paid in accordance with the notice[9].

Regulations[10] may make:

(1)   provision as to the form and content of penalty notices[11];

(2)   provision as to the amount of any penalty and the time by which it is to be paid[12];

(3)   provision as to the methods by which penalties may be paid[13];

(4)   provision as to the records which are to be kept in relation to penalty notices[14];

(5)   provision for or in connection with the withdrawal of a penalty notice, or its ceasing to have effect, in prescribed circumstances, including (a) provision about repayment of any amount paid by way of penalty under a penalty notice which is withdrawn or ceases to have effect[15]; and (b) provision prohibiting the institution or continuation of proceedings for the offence to which such a notice relates[16];

(6)   provision for a certificate purporting to be signed by or on behalf of a prescribed person[17], and stating that payment of any amount paid by way of penalty was or, as the case may be, was not received on or before a date specified in the certificate[18], to be received in evidence of the matters so stated[19];

(7)   provision as to the action to be taken if a penalty is not paid in accordance with a penalty notice[20];

(8)   provision for or in connection with the preparation of codes of conduct in relation to the giving of penalty notices[21];

(9)   such other provision in relation to penalties under penalty notices or in relation to penalty notices as the Secretary of State thinks necessary or expedient[22].

A penalty payable by virtue of a penalty notice is payable to the local authority which issued the notice[23].

1   The Education and Skills Act 2008 ss 53, 65 are to come into force as from a day to be appointed: see s 173(4). At the date at which this volume states the law no such day had been appointed. As to the review of the initial operation of Pt 1 Ch 5 (ss 45–60), see s 60; and PARA 758.

2   As to the meaning of 'local authority' see PARA 25 (definition applied by the Education and Skills Act 2008 s 168(2), (3)).

3   Ie under the Education and Skills Act 2008 s 46: see PARA 748.

4   Ie under the Education and Skills Act 2008 s 51: see PARA 752.

5   Education and Skills Act 2008 s 53(1) (amended by SI 2010/1158). In exercising its functions under the Education and Skills Act 2008 Pt 1 (ss 1–67), a local authority must have regard to any guidance given by the Secretary of State: see s 18 (amended by SI 2010/1158). As to the publication of guidance see the Education Act 1996 s 571 (applied by the Education and Skills Act 2008 s 168(2), (3)); and PARA 60. As to the Secretary of State see PARA 58. As to the meaning of 'functions' see PARA 18 note 5 (definition applied by the Education and Skills Act 2008 s 168(2), (3)).

6   Education and Skills Act 2008 s 53(2). As to appeals against penalty notices see s 54; and PARA 754.

7   As to the institution of proceedings see PARA 752.

8   Education and Skills Act 2008 s 53(3)(a). 'Prescribed' means prescribed by regulations; and 'regulations' means regulations made under the Education and Skills Act 2008 by the Secretary of State: s 168(1). At the date at which this volume states the law no such regulations had been made.

9   Education and Skills Act 2008 s 53(3)(b).

10   At the date at which this volume states the law no such regulations had been made.

11   Education and Skills Act 2008 s 53(4)(a).

12   Education and Skills Act 2008 s 53(4)(b). The amount of any penalty payable by virtue of regulations under s 53(4)(b) must not exceed the amount for the time being specified as level 1 on the standard scale of fines for summary offences: s 53(6). Without prejudice to s 166(6) (general provision about orders and regulations), regulations under s 53(4)(b) may make provision for penalties of different amounts to be payable in different cases or circumstances

(including provision for the penalty payable under a penalty notice to differ according to the time by which it is paid): s 53(5). As to the standard scale see SENTENCING AND DISPOSITION OF OFFENDERS vol 92 (2010) PARA 142.

13 Education and Skills Act 2008 s 53(4)(c).
14 Education and Skills Act 2008 s 53(4)(d).
15 Education and Skills Act 2008 s 53(4)(e)(i).
16 Education and Skills Act 2008 s 53(4)(e)(ii).
17 Education and Skills Act 2008 s 53(4)(f)(i). As to the meaning of 'person' see PARA 7 note 6.
18 Education and Skills Act 2008 s 53(4)(f)(ii).
19 Education and Skills Act 2008 s 53(4)(f). As to the evidential effect of certificates admissible by statute see CIVIL PROCEDURE vol 11 (2009) PARA 897.
20 Education and Skills Act 2008 s 53(4)(g).
21 Education and Skills Act 2008 s 53(4)(h).
22 Education and Skills Act 2008 s 53(4)(i).
23 See the Education and Skills Act 2008 s 65(1)(c) (s 65(1), (2) amended by SI 2010/1158). Any such sums received by a local authority may be used by the authority for the purposes of any of its functions which may be specified in regulations but, to the extent that they are not so used, must be paid in accordance with regulations to the Secretary of State: Education and Skills Act 2008 s 65(2) (as so amended). At the date at which this volume states the law no such regulations had been made.

754. Penalty notices: appeal arrangements. As from a day to be appointed the following provisions have effect[1].

A local authority[2] in England[3] must make arrangements for enabling a young person to whom a penalty notice is given by the authority[4] to appeal against the notice[5]. The arrangements must provide for any appeal under the arrangements to be to an attendance panel established[6] by the authority[7]. Regulations[8] may make provision about the making of appeals under such arrangements, including provision as to the procedure on such appeals[9], and as to the powers of an attendance panel in relation to such appeals[10].

1 The Education and Skills Act 2008 s 54 is to come into force as from a day to be appointed: see s 173(4). At the date at which this volume states the law no such day had been appointed. As to the review of the initial operation of Pt 1 Ch 5 (ss 45–60), see s 60; and PARA 758.
2 As to the meaning of 'local authority' see PARA 25 (definition applied by the Education and Skills Act 2008 s 168(2), (3)). In exercising its functions under Pt 1 (ss 1–67), a local authority must have regard to any guidance given by the Secretary of State: see s 18 (amended by SI 2010/1158). As to the publication of guidance see the Education Act 1996 s 571 (applied by the Education and Skills Act 2008 s 168(2), (3)); and PARA 60. As to the Secretary of State see PARA 58.
3 As to the meaning of 'England' see PARA 7 note 3.
4 Ie under the Education and Skills Act 2008 s 53: see PARA 753.
5 Education and Skills Act 2008 s 54(1).
6 Ie under the Education and Skills Act 2008 s 48: see PARA 749.
7 See the Education and Skills Act 2008 s 54(2).
8 'Regulations' means regulations made under the Education and Skills Act 2008 by the Secretary of State: s 168(1). At the date at which this volume states the law no such regulations had been made.
9 Education and Skills Act 2008 s 54(3)(a).
10 Education and Skills Act 2008 s 54(3)(b).

755. Enforcement of non-participation fine: person reaching 18. As from a day to be appointed the following provisions have effect[1].
Where:

(1) a non-participation fine[2] has been imposed on a person aged under 18[3]; and

(2) the relevant sum[4], or any part of it, remains unpaid when the person reaches the age of 18[5],

then, when the person reaches the age of 18, the relevant sum ceases to be enforceable as a sum adjudged to be paid by a conviction of a magistrates' court[6]. Accordingly, after the person has reached the age of 18 the normal enforcement provisions[7] do not apply in relation to the relevant sum[8], and the normal enforcement powers[9] are not exercisable in relation to the relevant sum[10], except so far as necessary to permit current enforcement processes[11] to be concluded[12].

Any order or warrant made or issued in relation to the non-participation fine, with certain exceptions[13], ceases to have effect when the person reaches the age of 18[14]. A magistrates' court may, after the person has reached the age of 18, order that payment of so much of the relevant sum as remains unpaid may be enforced as if it were a sum due to the relevant local authority[15] in pursuance of a judgment or order of the county court[16]; but such an order may not be made unless the person appears to the court to have sufficient means to pay the sum forthwith[17], and any current enforcement processes have been concluded[18].

1 The Education and Skills Act 2008 ss 55, 56, 58 are to come into force as from a day to be appointed: see s 173(4). At the date at which this volume states the law no such day had been appointed. As to the review of the initial operation of Pt 1 Ch 5 (ss 45–60), see s 60; and PARA 758.

2 'Non-participation fine' means a fine imposed for an offence under the Education and Skills Act 2008 s 51 (see PARA 752), or in respect of a failure to comply with any sentence imposed for such an offence: s 55(1). References in ss 56–59 to a fine being imposed are, in the case of a fine varied or confirmed on appeal, references to its being varied or confirmed: s 55(2).

3 Education and Skills Act 2008 s 56(1)(a). As to the time at which a person attains a particular age see PARA 7 note 6.

4 'The relevant sum', in relation to a non-participation fine, means: (1) the non-participation fine; (2) any surcharge ordered under the Criminal Justice Act 2003 s 161A (surcharges: see SENTENCING AND DISPOSITION OF OFFENDERS vol 92 (2010) PARA 158) to be paid solely in relation to the offence; and (3) any costs ordered by a court to be paid by the person on whom the fine was imposed in connection with the offence or proceedings relating to the offence or any sentence imposed (including proceedings on appeal): Education and Skills Act 2008 s 55(1).

5 Education and Skills Act 2008 s 56(1)(b).

6 Education and Skills Act 2008 s 56(2). Section 56(2) does not affect the exercise of any power, or any order made, in respect of the offence before the person reached the age of 18: s 56(8). As to magistrates' courts see MAGISTRATES vol 71 (2013) PARA 470 et seq.

7 'The normal enforcement provisions' means: (1) the Magistrates' Courts Act 1980 Pt III (ss 75–96A) (satisfaction and enforcement: see MAGISTRATES vol 71 (2013) PARA 667 et seq); (2) ss 135 and 136 of that Act (committal and detention for short period: see SENTENCING AND DISPOSITION OF OFFENDERS vol 92 (2010) PARA 7; MAGISTRATES vol 71 (2013) PARA 681); (3) the Powers of Criminal Courts (Sentencing) Act 2000 s 108 (repealed with savings) (detention of persons aged at least 18 but under 21 for default or contempt: see SENTENCING AND DISPOSITION OF OFFENDERS vol 92 (2010) PARA 11); (4) the Courts Act 2003 Schs 5, 6 (collection of fines etc and discharge of fines by unpaid work: see MAGISTRATES vol 71 (2013) PARA 656 et seq); and (5) the Criminal Justice Act 2003 s 300 (power to impose unpaid work requirement or curfew requirement on fine defaulter): Education and Skills Act 2008 s 58(1). The Lord Chancellor may by order amend s 58(1) by: (a) adding a reference to any statutory provision which relates to enforcement of fines, costs or surcharges, or to any power to enforce payment of such sums (s 58(3)(a)); or (b) removing a reference to any provision or power for the time being listed in that section (s 58(3)(b)). As to the Lord Chancellor see CONSTITUTIONAL AND ADMINISTRATIVE LAW vol 20 (2014) PARA 255 et seq. At the date at which this volume states the law no such order had been made. Where (i) a sum is payable at a time or times specified by an order under the Magistrates' Courts Act 1980 s 75 (power to dispense with immediate payment: see MAGISTRATES vol 71 (2013) PARA 627), or orders under s 75 and s 85A (variation of instalments of sum adjudged to be paid by conviction: see MAGISTRATES vol 71 (2013) PARA 649); and (ii) the sum would (but for this provision) be treated by virtue of the Education and Skills Act 2008 s 56 or s 57 (see PARA 756) as due to a local authority in pursuance of a judgment or order of the county court, the sum is to be treated as so payable to that authority at the time or times referred to in head (i) above by virtue of an order of the county court under the County Courts Act 1984 s 71(1) (satisfaction of judgments and orders

for payment of money: see CIVIL PROCEDURE vol 12 (2009) PARA 1229): Education and Skills Act 2008 s 58(4) (amended by SI 2010/1158; and the Crime and Courts Act 2013 Sch 9 para 52(1)(b), (2)). As to the meaning of 'local authority' see PARA 25 (definition applied by the Education and Skills Act 2008 s 168(2), (3)).

8   Education and Skills Act 2008 s 56(3)(a).

9   'The normal enforcement powers', in relation to any sum, means: (1) any power of a magistrates' court or an officer of such a court to enforce payment of the sum, or which is exercisable in consequence of a default in payment of the sum or any part of it (Education and Skills Act 2008 s 58(2)(a)); (2) in the case of a fine imposed, varied or confirmed by a decision of any other court on an appeal, any power of that other court to enforce the decision (s 58(2)(b)). The Lord Chancellor may by order amend s 58(2) by: (a) adding a reference to any statutory provision which relates to enforcement of fines, costs or surcharges, or to any power to enforce payment of such sums (s 58(3)(a)); or (b) removing a reference to any provision or power for the time being listed in that section (s 58(3)(b)). At the date at which this volume states the law no such order had been made.

10   Education and Skills Act 2008 s 56(3)(b).

11   'Current enforcement process' means an order or warrant mentioned in head (1), (2) or (3) below and any reference to its conclusion is to be read in accordance with that head:

   (1)   a warrant of control issued under the Magistrates' Courts Act 1980 s 76 (warrants of control etc: see MAGISTRATES vol 71 (2013) PARA 667) for the purpose of recovering the relevant sum (or any part of it), and by virtue of which an enforcement agent has, before the person reaches the age of 18, taken control of any goods of the person under the Tribunals, Courts and Enforcement Act 2007 Sch 12 (taking control of goods: see CIVIL PROCEDURE vol 12 (2009) PARA 1386 et seq), is concluded when property in all goods of the person has, in accordance with Sch 12 para 6, ceased to be bound by virtue of the warrant (Education and Skills Act 2008 s 56(7)(a));

   (2)   an order in force when the person reaches the age of 18 under the Magistrates' Courts Act 1980 s 81(1)(b) (enforcement of fines imposed on young offenders: see MAGISTRATES vol 71 (2013) PARA 683), or the Powers of Criminal Courts (Sentencing) Act 2000 s 137(1) (power to order parent or guardian to pay fine, costs, compensation or surcharge: see SENTENCING AND DISPOSITION OF OFFENDERS vol 92 (2010) PARA 383), requiring that the relevant sum (or any part of it) be paid by a parent or guardian of the person is concluded when it is revoked (Education and Skills Act 2008 s 56(7)(b));

   (3)   an order in force when the person reaches the age of 18 under the Criminal Justice and Immigration Act 2008 s 39 (youth default orders) in respect of the relevant sum (or any part of it) is concluded when it is revoked (Education and Skills Act 2008 s 56(7)(c)).

   The Lord Chancellor may by order amend s 56(4) (see note 13) or (7) by: (a) adding to it provision about any warrant or order that may be issued or made, or step that may be taken, in relation to a non-participation fine before the person on whom it is imposed reaches the age of 18 (s 56(9)(a)); or (b) removing any such provision for the time being made by s 56(4), (7) (s 56(9)(b)). At the date at which this volume states the law no such order had been made.

12   Education and Skills Act 2008 s 56(3). As from a day to be appointed the following words are added at the end of s 56(3): 'or to preserve existing increases under the Magistrates' Courts Act 1980 s 75A (collection costs) or the Courts Act 2003 Sch 5 para 42A: Education and Skills Act 2008 s 56(3) (prospectively amended by the Crime and Courts Act 2013 s 26(8)). At the date at which this volume states the law no such day had been appointed.

13   Ie other than an order under the Magistrates' Courts Act 1980 s 75 (power to dispense with immediate payment: see MAGISTRATES vol 71 (2013) PARA 649) (Education and Skills Act 2008 s 56(4)(a)), an order under the Magistrates' Courts Act 1980 s 85A (variation of instalments of sum adjudged to be paid by conviction: see MAGISTRATES vol 71 (2013) PARA 649) (Education and Skills Act 2008 s 56(4)(b)), or a current enforcement process (Education and Skills Act 2008 s 56(4)(c)). See also s 56(9); and note 11.

14   Education and Skills Act 2008 s 56(4).

15   'Relevant local authority', in relation to a non-participation fine, means the local authority which issued the penalty notice under the Education and Skills Act 2008 s 53 (see PARA 753) in respect of the offence to which the fine relates: s 55(1) (definition amended by SI 2010/1158).

16   Education and Skills Act 2008 s 56(5) (amended by SI 2010/1158; and the Crime and Courts Act 2013 Sch 9 para 52(10(b), (2)). As to the summary recovery of civil debts see MAGISTRATES vol 71 (2013) PARA 625.

17   Education and Skills Act 2008 s 56(6)(a).

18   Education and Skills Act 2008 s 56(6)(b).

756. Enforcement of non-participation fine: fine imposed on person aged 18 or over. As from a day to be appointed the following provisions have effect[1].

Where a non-participation fine[2] is imposed on a person who has reached the age of 18[3], payment of the relevant sum[4] may be enforced as if it were a sum due to the relevant local authority[5] in pursuance of a judgment or order of the county court[6]. The relevant sum is not enforceable as a sum adjudged to be paid by a conviction of a magistrates' court[7]; and accordingly the normal enforcement provisions[8] do not apply in relation to the relevant sum[9], and the normal enforcement powers[10] are not exercisable in relation to the relevant sum[11]. However, these provisions[12] do not prevent a magistrates' court, on imposing the fine[13] from making certain orders[14].

1   The Education and Skills Act 2008 s 57 is to come into force as from a day to be appointed: see s 173(4). At the date at which this volume states the law no such day had been appointed. As to the review of the initial operation of Pt 1 Ch 5 (ss 45–60), see s 60; and PARA 758.
2   As to the meaning of 'non-participation fine' see PARA 755 note 2.
3   Education and Skills Act 2008 s 57(1). As to the time at which a person attains a particular age see PARA 7 note 6.
4   As to the meaning of 'the relevant sum' see PARA 755 note 4.
5   As to the meaning of 'relevant local authority' see PARA 755 note 15.
6   Education and Skills Act 2008 s 57(2) (amended by SI 2010/1158; and the Crime and Courts Act 2013 Sch 9 para 52(1)(b), (2)).
7   Education and Skills Act 2008 s 57(3).
8   As to the meaning of 'the normal enforcement provisions' see PARA 755 note 7.
9   Education and Skills Act 2008 s 57(4)(a).
10   As to the meaning of 'the normal enforcement powers' see PARA 755 note 9.
11   Education and Skills Act 2008 s 57(4)(b).
12   Ie the Education and Skills Act 2008 s 57(3), (4): see the text to notes 7–11.
13   As to the meaning of references to a fine being imposed see PARA 755 note 2.
14   See the Education and Skills Act 2008 s 57(5). The orders are: (1) an order under the Magistrates' Courts Act 1980 s 75 (power to dispense with immediate payment: see MAGISTRATES vol 71 (2013) PARA 649) (Education and Skills Act 2008 s 57(5)(a)); or (2) an order under the Magistrates' Courts Act 1980 s 80 (application of money found on defaulter to satisfy sum adjudged: see MAGISTRATES vol 71 (2013) PARA 654) for the person to be searched before leaving the precincts of the court-house; and s 80(2), (3) applies in relation to a search in pursuance of any such order (Education and Skills Act 2008 s 57(5)(b)).

757. Application of sums recovered by way of non-participation fines. As from a day to be appointed the following provisions have effect[1].

The Lord Chancellor[2] may by regulations[3] make provision as to the application of amounts recovered by local authorities[4] by virtue of the statutory provisions[5] relating to the enforcement of non-participation fines[6]. Any such regulations must make provision for securing that any such amount recovered, so far as not attributable to county court enforcement costs[7], or paid to a magistrates' court, or to an officer of such a court[8], is repaid to the person on whom the non-participation fine to which it relates was imposed (or other person who paid the amount)[9]. The regulations may make provision, in particular, as to: (1) the extent to which amounts recovered[10] are attributable to county court enforcement costs[11]; (2) further payments, or repayments, to be made in consequence of any appeal, or of any remission or variation of a non-participation fine or any other amount required to be paid[12].

1   The Education and Skills Act 2008 s 59 is to come into force as from a day to be appointed: see s 173(4). At the date at which this volume states the law no such day had been appointed. As to the review of the initial operation of Pt 1 Ch 5 (ss 45–60) see s 60; and PARA 758.
2   As to the Lord Chancellor see CONSTITUTIONAL AND ADMINISTRATIVE LAW vol 20 (2014) PARA 255 et seq.
3   At the date at which this volume states the law no such regulations had been made.

4   As to the meaning of 'local authority' see PARA 25 (definition applied by the Education and Skills Act 2008 s 168(2), (3)).
5   Ie the Education and Skills Act 2008 ss 56, 57: see PARAS 755, 756.
6   See the Education and Skills Act 2008 s 59(1) (amended by SI 2010/1158). As to the meaning of 'non-participation fine' see PARA 755 note 2.
7   Education and Skills Act 2008 s 59(2)(a). 'County court enforcement costs' in relation to a non-participation fine means costs incurred by a local authority in connection with the recovery of the relevant sum in the county court: s 59(4) (amended by SI 2010/1158; and the Crime and Courts Act 2013 Sch 9 para 52(1)(b), (2)). As to the meaning of 'the relevant sum' see PARA 755 note 4. As to county courts see COURTS AND TRIBUNALS vol 24 (2010) PARA 758 et seq.
8   Education and Skills Act 2008 s 59(2)(b). As to magistrates' courts see MAGISTRATES vol 71 (2013) PARA 470 et seq.
9   Education and Skills Act 2008 s 59(2).
10 Ie by virtue of the Education and Skills Act 2008 s 56 or s 57: see PARAS 755, 756.
11 Education and Skills Act 2008 s 59(3)(a).
12 Education and Skills Act 2008 s 59(3)(b).

(vi) Review and Application of Provisions

758. Review of initial operation of legislative provisions. As from a day to be appointed the following provisions have effect[1].

The Secretary of State[2] must appoint a person[3] to conduct a review of the initial operation of the statutory provisions[4] relating to attendance notices[5]. The person appointed must make a report to the Secretary of State on the review within a reasonable period after the school[6] leaving date for 2016[7]. The Secretary of State must lay a copy of the report before Parliament[8].

1   The Education and Skills Act 2008 s 60 is to come into force as from a day to be appointed: see s 173(4). At the date at which this volume states the law no such day had been appointed.
2   As to the Secretary of State see PARA 58.
3   As to the meaning of 'person' see PARA 7 note 6.
4   Ie the Education and Skills Act 2008 Pt 1 Ch 5 (ss 45–60): see PARA 747 et seq.
5   Education and Skills Act 2008 s 60(1). The Secretary of State may pay to the person appointed such remuneration and expenses as the Secretary of State may determine: s 60(4).
6   As to the meaning of 'school' see PARA 91 (definition applied by the Education and Skills Act 2008 s 168(2), (3)).
7   Education and Skills Act 2008 s 60(2). As to the fixing of dates for school terms and holidays see PARA 458.
8   Education and Skills Act 2008 s 60(3). As to the laying of documents before Parliament see STATUTES AND LEGISLATIVE PROCESS vol 96 (2012) PARA 1052.

759. Corresponding review provision for Wales. As from a day to be appointed the following provisions have effect[1].

If a measure of the National Assembly for Wales[2] includes provision that appears to the Secretary of State[3] to correspond to provision made by the Education and Skills Act 2008[4] in relation to the duty to participate in education or training[5], he may by order[6] make certain corresponding provision in relation to Wales[7].

1   The Education and Skills Act 2008 s 67 is to come into force as from a day to be appointed: see s 173(4). At the date at which this volume states the law no such day had been appointed.
2   As to the National Assembly for Wales and its legislative powers see CONSTITUTIONAL AND ADMINISTRATIVE LAW vol 20 (2014) PARA 351 et seq; STATUTES AND LEGISLATIVE PROCESS vol 96 (2012) PARA 986 et seq.
3   As to the Secretary of State see PARA 58.
4   Ie by the Education and Skills Act 2008 s 2: see PARA 725.
5   See the Education and Skills Act 2008 s 67(1).
6   At the date at which this volume states the law no such order had been made.
7   See the Education and Skills Act 2008 s 67(2). The provision which may be so made is such that corresponds to any provision made by ss 19–36 (see PARA 735 et seq): see s 67(2). Without

prejudice to s 166(6) (general provision as to orders and regulations), the power conferred by s 67 includes power to make provision in relation to Wales that corresponds to any of the following: (1) the Employment Rights Act 1996 s 47AA (see EMPLOYMENT vol 40 (2014) PARA 618), s 101B (see EMPLOYMENT vol 41 (2014) PARA 789) and the amendments made to that Act by the Education and Skills Act 2008 s 39 (see s 67(3)(a)); (2) ss 61 and 62 (see PARAS 725, 727) (s 67(3)(b), (c)); (3) s 65 so far as relating to financial penalties under s 22 and s 31 (see PARAS 736, 742) (s 67(3)(d)). Power conferred by s 67 to make provision in relation to Wales that corresponds to any other provision includes power: (a) to apply that other provision in relation to Wales, with or without modification (s 67(4)(a)); (b) to amend that other provision so that it applies in relation to Wales, with or without modification (s 67(4)(b)). As to the meaning of 'Wales' see PARA 7 note 3. As to the meaning of 'modification' see PARA 21 note 15 (definition applied by s 168(2), (3)).

(3) APPRENTICESHIPS

(i) Apprenticeships in England

760. Approved English apprenticeships, and completion. An 'approved English apprenticeship' is an arrangement which (1) takes place under an approved English apprenticeship agreement[1]; or (2) is an alternative English apprenticeship[2], and, in either case, satisfies any conditions specified in regulations made by the Secretary of State[3].

A person completes an approved English apprenticeship if the person achieves the approved apprenticeship standard while doing an approved English apprenticeship[4].

1   Apprenticeships, Skills, Children and Learning Act 2009 s A1(2)(a) (s A1 added by the Deregulation Act 2015 Sch 1 Pt 1 para 1). The Apprenticeships, Skills, Children and Learning Act 2009 s A1 applies for the purposes of Pt 1 Ch A1 (ss A1–A7): s A1(1) (as so added). As to the meaning of 'approved English apprenticeship agreement' see PARA 761.
2   Apprenticeships, Skills, Children and Learning Act 2009 s A1(2)(b) (as added: see note 1).
     An 'alternative English apprenticeship' is an arrangement, under which a person works, which is of a kind described in regulations made by the Secretary of State: s A1(4) (as so added). Regulations under s A1(4) may, for example, describe arrangements which relate to cases where a person (1) works otherwise than for another person; (2) works otherwise than for reward: s A1(5) (as so added). 'Regulations' means regulations made by the Secretary of State: s 264(1). At the date at which this volume states the law no regulations had been made under s A1.
3   Apprenticeships, Skills, Children and Learning Act 2009 s A1(2) (as added: see note 1). As to the Secretary of State see PARA 58. See note 2.
4   Apprenticeships, Skills, Children and Learning Act 2009 s A1(6) (as added: see note 1).

761. Approved English apprenticeship agreements. An 'approved English apprenticeship agreement' is an agreement which:

(1)   provides for a person[1] ('the apprentice') to work for another person for reward in a sector for which the Secretary of State[2] has published an approved apprenticeship standard[3];

(2)   provides for the apprentice to receive training in order to assist the apprentice to achieve the approved apprenticeship standard in the work done under the agreement[4]; and

(3)   satisfies any other conditions specified in regulations made by the Secretary of State[5].

1   As to the meaning of 'person' see PARA 7 note 6.
2   As to the Secretary of State see PARA 58.
3   Apprenticeships, Skills, Children and Learning Act 2009 s A1(3)(a) (ss A1, A5, A6, A7 added by the Deregulation Act 2015 Sch 1 Pt 1 para 1). The reference in the text is to an approved apprenticeship standard under the Apprenticeships, Skills, Children and Learning Act 2009 s A2: see PARA 762. The 'approved apprenticeship standard', in relation to an approved English

apprenticeship, means the standard which applies in relation to the work to be done under the apprenticeship (see s A2; and PARA 762): s A1(7) (as so added).

To the extent that it would otherwise be treated as being a contract of apprenticeship, an approved English apprenticeship agreement is to be treated as not being a contract of apprenticeship: s A5(1) (as so added). To the extent that it would not otherwise be treated as being a contract of service, an approved English apprenticeship agreement is to be treated as being a contract of service: s A5(2) (as so added). Section A5 applies for the purposes of any enactment or rule of law: s A5(3) (as so added).

If an agreement (1) contains provision which satisfies the conditions mentioned in s A1(3)(a)–(c) (see heads (a)–(c) in the text), but (2) also contains other provision which is inconsistent with those conditions, the other provision is to be treated as having no effect: s A6(1) (as so added). Before an agreement which satisfies the conditions mentioned in s A1(3)(a)–(c) is varied in such a way that it no longer satisfies one or more of those conditions, the person for whom the apprentice is working must give the apprentice a written notice: s A6(2) (as so added). The written notice must explain that, if the variation takes effect, the agreement will cease to be an approved English apprenticeship agreement: s A6(3) (as so added). If an agreement is varied in breach of the requirement under s A6(2), the variation has no effect: s A6(4) (as so added).

Section A1(3) (see heads (1)–(3) in the text) applies in relation to (a) an agreement under which a person undertakes Crown employment; (b) an agreement under which a person undertakes service as a member of the naval, military or air forces of the Crown; and (c) an agreement under which a person undertakes employment as a relevant member of the House of Lords staff, or a relevant member of the House of Commons staff, as it applies in relation to any other agreement under which a person is to work for another (and Pt 1 Ch A1 applies accordingly): s A7(1) (as so added). 'Crown employment' means employment under or for the purposes of a government department or an officer or body exercising on behalf of the Crown functions conferred by a statutory provision (but does not include service as a member of the naval, military or air forces of the Crown); 'relevant member of the House of Lords staff' has the meaning given by the Employment Rights Act 1996 s 194(6) (see EMPLOYMENT vol 39 (2014) PARA 164 note 3); and 'relevant member of the House of Commons staff' has the meaning given by s 195(5) (see EMPLOYMENT vol 39 (2014) PARA 165): Apprenticeships, Skills, Children and Learning Act 2009 s A7(6) (s so added).

Section A7(1) (see above) is subject to s A7(3) and to any modifications which may be prescribed under s A7(5): s A7(2) (as so added). Section A5(2) (see above) does not apply in relation to an approved English apprenticeship agreement that is an agreement within s A7(1) (a), (b) or (c) (see heads (a)–(c) above): s A7(3) (as so added).

Without prejudice to s 262(3) (general provision as to orders and regulations), the power conferred by s A1(3)(c) (see head (3) in the text) may be exercised, in particular, to make provision in relation to an agreement within any of s A7(1)(a), (b) and (c) that differs from provision made in relation to other agreements under which a person is to work for another: s A7(4) (as so added).

The Secretary of State may by regulations provide for any provision of Pt 1 Ch 1 to apply with modifications in relation to (i) an agreement within s A7(1)(a), (b) or (c); or (ii) a person working, or proposing to work, under such an agreement: s A7(5) (as so added).

4 Apprenticeships, Skills, Children and Learning Act 2009 s A1(3)(b) (as added: see note 3). See note 3.

5 Apprenticeships, Skills, Children and Learning Act 2009 s A1(3)(c) (as added: see note 3). See note 3.

762. Approved apprenticeship standards. The Secretary of State[1] must publish standards for such sectors of work as the Secretary of State thinks appropriate for the purposes of the relevant provisions ('the approved apprenticeship standards')[2].

Each standard must be (1) prepared by the Secretary of State; or (2) prepared by another person[3] and approved by the Secretary of State[4].

Each standard must (a) describe the sector of work to which it relates[5]; and (b) if there is more than one standard for that sector, describe the kind of work within that sector to which it relates[6].

Each standard must set out the outcomes that persons seeking to complete an approved English apprenticeship[7] are expected to achieve[8].

The Secretary of State may (i) publish a revised version of a standard[9]; or (ii) withdraw a standard (with or without publishing another in its place)[10].

Revisions of a standard may be (A) prepared by the Secretary of State[11]; or (B) prepared by another person[12] and approved by the Secretary of State[13].

1   As to the Secretary of State see PARA 58.
2   Apprenticeships, Skills, Children and Learning Act 2009 s A2(1) (s A2 added by the Deregulation Act 2015 Sch 1 Pt 1 para 1). The reference in the text to the relevant provisions is a reference to the Apprenticeships, Skills, Children and Learning Act 2009 Pt 1 Ch A1 (ss A1–A7). Such standards are 'approved apprenticeship standards': see PARA 761 note 3.
3   Apprenticeships, Skills, Children and Learning Act 2009 s A2(2)(a) (as added: see note 1).
4   As to the meaning of 'person' see PARA 7 note 6.
5   Apprenticeships, Skills, Children and Learning Act 2009 s A2(2)(b) (as added: see note 1).
6   Apprenticeships, Skills, Children and Learning Act 2009 s A2(3)(a) (as added: see note 1).
7   Apprenticeships, Skills, Children and Learning Act 2009 s A2(3)(b) (as added: see note 1).
8   As to the meaning of 'approved English apprenticeship' see PARA 760.
9   Apprenticeships, Skills, Children and Learning Act 2009 s A2(4) (as added: see note 1).
10 Apprenticeships, Skills, Children and Learning Act 2009 s A2(5)(a) (as added: see note 1).
11 Apprenticeships, Skills, Children and Learning Act 2009 s A2(5)(b) (as added: see note 1).
12 Apprenticeships, Skills, Children and Learning Act 2009 s A2(6)(a) (as added: see note 1).
13 Apprenticeships, Skills, Children and Learning Act 2009 s A2(6)(b) (as added: see note 1).

763. Power to issue apprenticeship certificate. The Secretary of State[1] may issue a certificate ('an apprenticeship certificate') to a person[2] who applies for it if it appears to the Secretary of State that the person has completed an approved English apprenticeship[3].

The Secretary of State may by regulations make provision about (1) the manner in which such applications[4] must be made[5]; (2) the supply by the Secretary of State of copies of apprenticeship certificates[6] to persons to whom they were issued[7].

The Secretary of State may charge a fee for issuing an apprenticeship certificate or supplying a copy only if, and to the extent that, the charging of the fee is authorised by regulations[8].

1   As to the Secretary of State see PARA 58.
2   As to the meaning of 'person' see PARA 7 note 6.
3   Apprenticeships, Skills, Children and Learning Act 2009 s A3(1) (s A3 added by the Deregulation Act 2015 Sch 1 Pt 1 para 1). As to the meaning of 'approved English apprenticeship' see PARA 761.
4   Ie applications under the Apprenticeships, Skills, Children and Learning Act 2009 s A3(1).
5   Apprenticeships, Skills, Children and Learning Act 2009 s A3(2)(a) (as added: see note 3). 'Regulations' means regulations made by the Secretary of State: s 264(1). At the date at which this volume states the law no regulations had been made under s A3.
6   Ie certificates issued under the Apprenticeships, Skills, Children and Learning Act 2009 s A3(1).
7   Apprenticeships, Skills, Children and Learning Act 2009 s A3(2)(b) (as added: see note 3).
8   Apprenticeships, Skills, Children and Learning Act 2009 s A3(3) (as added: see note 3).

764. Delegation of functions. Any function of the Secretary of State[1] under the relevant provisions[2] may be carried out by a person[3] designated by the Secretary of State[4]. This does not apply to any power of the Secretary of State to make regulations[5].

A person so designated[6] must (1) comply with directions given by the Secretary of State[7]; and (2) have regard to guidance given by the Secretary of State[8].

A designation[9] may be revoked[10].

1   As to the Secretary of State see PARA 58.
2   Ie the Apprenticeships, Skills, Children and Learning Act 2009 Pt 1 Ch A1 (ss A1–A7).

3   As to the meaning of 'person' see PARA 7 note 6.
4   Apprenticeships, Skills, Children and Learning Act 2009 s A4(1) (s A4 added by the Deregulation Act 2015 Sch 1 Pt 1 para 1).
5   Apprenticeships, Skills, Children and Learning Act 2009 s A4(2) (as added: see note 4). 'Regulations' means regulations made by the Secretary of State: s 264(1).
6   Ie designated under the Apprenticeships, Skills, Children and Learning Act 2009 s A4.
7   Apprenticeships, Skills, Children and Learning Act 2009 s A4(3)(a) (as added: see note 4).
8   Apprenticeships, Skills, Children and Learning Act 2009 s A4(3)(b) (as added: see note 4). As to the publication of such guidance see the Education Act 1996 s 571 (see PARA 60) applied by virtue of the Apprenticeships, Skills, Children and Learning Act 2009 s 264(2).
9   Ie a designation under the Apprenticeships, Skills, Children and Learning Act 2009 s A4.
10 Apprenticeships, Skills, Children and Learning Act 2009 s A4(4) (as added: see note 4).

(ii) Apprenticeships in Wales

A. APPRENTICESHIPS IN WALES GENERALLY

765. Apprenticeship sectors. The Welsh Ministers[1] must by order[2] specify sectors of skill, trade or occupation for the purposes of the provisions of the Apprenticeships, Skills, Children and Learning Act 2009[3] relating to apprenticeships[4]. The sectors so specified must in the opinion of the Welsh Ministers encompass the full range of skills, trades and occupations[5].

1   As to the Welsh Ministers see PARA 59.
2   As to the order made see the Apprenticeship Sectors (Specification) Order 2011, SI 2011/220.
3   Ie the Apprenticeships, Skills, Children and Learning Act 2009 Pt 1 Ch 1 (ss 2–39).
4   Apprenticeships, Skills, Children and Learning Act 2009 s 38(1) (amended by the Deregulation Act 2015 Sch 1Pt 2 paras 5, 15(a)).
5   Apprenticeships, Skills, Children and Learning Act 2009 s 38(2) (amended by the Deregulation Act 2015 Sch 1Pt 2 paras 5, 15(b)).

766. Apprenticeship agreements. 'Apprenticeship agreement' means[1] an agreement in relation to which each of the following conditions is satisfied[2]. The conditions are:
(1)   that a person (the 'apprentice') undertakes to work for another (the 'employer') under the agreement[3];
(2)   that the agreement is in the prescribed form[4];
(3)   that the agreement states that it is governed by the law of England and Wales[5];
(4)   that the agreement states that it is entered into in connection with a qualifying apprenticeship framework[6].
To the extent that provision included in an apprenticeship agreement conflicts with the prescribed apprenticeship provisions[7], it has no effect[8].

A variation to an apprenticeship agreement the nature of which is such that, were it to take effect, the agreement would cease to be an apprenticeship agreement[9], has effect only if, before it was made, the employer complied with the requirement[10] to give the apprentice written[11] notice stating that, if the variation takes effect, the agreement will cease to be an apprenticeship agreement[12].

For the purposes of any enactment or rule of law[13]: (a) to the extent that it would otherwise be treated as being a contract of apprenticeship, an apprenticeship agreement is to be treated as not being a contract of apprenticeship[14]; and (b) to the extent that it would not otherwise be treated as being a contract of service, an apprenticeship agreement is to be treated as being a contract of service[15].

The above provisions[16] apply in relation to:

(i)   an agreement under which a person undertakes Crown employment[17];

(ii)   an agreement under which a person undertakes service as a member of the naval, military or air forces of the Crown[18]; and

(iii)   an agreement under which a person undertakes employment as a relevant member of the House of Lords staff[19] or a relevant member of the House of Commons staff[20],

as they apply in relation to any other agreement under which a person undertakes to work for another[21].

1   Ie in the Apprenticeships, Skills, Children and Learning Act 2009 Pt 1 Ch 1 (ss 1–39).

2   Apprenticeships, Skills, Children and Learning Act 2009 s 32(1).

3   Apprenticeships, Skills, Children and Learning Act 2009 s 32(2)(a). References in Pt 1 Ch 1 (ss 1–39) to an 'employer' and an 'apprentice', in relation to an apprenticeship agreement, are to be construed in accordance with s 32: s 39(3).

4   Apprenticeships, Skills, Children and Learning Act 2009 s 32(2)(b). 'Prescribed' means prescribed by regulations; and 'regulations' means regulations made by the Secretary of State: s 264(1). The power conferred by s 32(2)(b) may be exercised, in particular: (1) to specify provisions that must be included in an apprenticeship agreement (s 32(3)(a)); (2) to specify provisions that must not be included in an apprenticeship agreement (s 32(3)(b)); (3) to specify all or part of the wording of provisions that must be included in an apprenticeship agreement (s 32(3)(c)). As to the Secretary of State see PARA 58. As to regulations made see the Apprenticeships (Form of Apprenticeship Agreement) Regulations 2012, SI 2012/844.

5   Apprenticeships, Skills, Children and Learning Act 2009 s 32(2)(c). As to the meanings of 'England' and 'Wales' see PARA 7 note 3.

6   Apprenticeships, Skills, Children and Learning Act 2009 s 32(2)(d). Where an agreement states that it is entered into in connection with an apprenticeship framework ('the relevant framework') that is not a qualifying apprenticeship framework, s 32(2)(d) is to be taken to be satisfied in relation to the agreement if: (1) at a time within the period of three years ending with the date of the agreement, the relevant framework was a qualifying apprenticeship framework (s 32(4)(a)); (2) at the date of the agreement, the apprentice has not completed the whole of a course of training for the competencies qualification identified in the relevant framework (s 32(4)(b)); (3) before the date of the agreement, the apprentice entered into an apprenticeship agreement ('the earlier agreement') which stated that it was entered into in connection with the relevant framework (s 32(4)(c)); and (4) at the date of the earlier agreement, the relevant framework was a qualifying apprenticeship framework (s 32(4)(d)). In s 32(4)(b) (see head (2) above), the reference to a course of training for the competencies qualification is to be read, in a case where the person follows two or more courses of training for the competencies qualification, as a reference to both or all of them: s 32(5). An apprenticeship framework is a 'qualifying apprenticeship framework', for these purposes, if it is a recognised Welsh framework (s 32(6)(b)). As to the meaning of 'recognised Welsh framework' see PARA 771 note 4. 'The competencies qualification', in relation to an apprenticeship framework, means the qualification identified in the framework as being the competencies qualification: s 39(1).

    In the Apprenticeships, Skills, Children and Learning Act 2009 Pt 1 Ch 1 (ss 2–39), 'apprenticeship framework' means a specification of requirements, for the purpose of the issue of apprenticeship certificates, that satisfies the following requirements: s 12(1). The requirements specified must: (a) be at a particular level stated in the specification (s 12(2)(a)); and (b) relate to a particular skill, trade or occupation included in an apprenticeship sector stated in the specification (s 12(2)(b)). For these purposes: (i) an apprenticeship framework is at the level of the requirements stated in it (s 12(5)(a)); (ii) an apprenticeship framework relates to the apprenticeship sector stated in it (s 12(5)(b)). References in Pt 1 Ch 1 to the level of an apprenticeship framework, or to the apprenticeship sector to which an apprenticeship framework relates, are to be construed in accordance with s 12(5): s 39(2).

7   The 'prescribed apprenticeship provisions', in relation to an apprenticeship agreement, means those provisions that are included in the agreement (Apprenticeships, Skills, Children and Learning Act 2009 s 33(2)(a)), and without the inclusion of which the agreement would not satisfy s 32(2)(b) (see head (2) in the text) (s 33(2)(b)).

8   Apprenticeships, Skills, Children and Learning Act 2009 s 33(1).

9   See the Apprenticeships, Skills, Children and Learning Act 2009 s 34(1), (2).

10 See the Apprenticeships, Skills, Children and Learning Act 2009 s 34(1).

11 As to the meaning of 'written' see PARA 76 note 8.

12 See the Apprenticeships, Skills, Children and Learning Act 2009 s 34(1), (3).

13 See the Apprenticeships, Skills, Children and Learning Act 2009 s 35(3).

14 Apprenticeships, Skills, Children and Learning Act 2009 s 35(1).

15 Apprenticeships, Skills, Children and Learning Act 2009 s 35(2). As to contracts of service see EMPLOYMENT vol 39 (2014) PARA 1.

16 Ie the Apprenticeships, Skills, Children and Learning Act 2009 ss 32–35: see the text to notes 1–15.

17 Apprenticeships, Skills, Children and Learning Act 2009 s 36(1)(a). 'Crown employment' means employment under or for the purposes of a government department or any officer or body exercising on behalf of the Crown functions conferred by a statutory provision (but does not include service as a member of the naval, military or air forces of the Crown): s 36(6).

18 Apprenticeships, Skills, Children and Learning Act 2009 s 36(1)(b).

19 Apprenticeships, Skills, Children and Learning Act 2009 s 36(1)(c)(i). 'Relevant member of the House of Lords staff' means any person who is employed under a contract of employment with the Corporate Officer of the House of Lords: Employment Rights Act 1996 s 194(6) (definition applied by the Apprenticeships, Skills, Children and Learning Act 2009 s 36(6)). As to the corporate officer of the House of Lords see PARLIAMENT vol 78 (2010) PARA 990.

20 Apprenticeships, Skills, Children and Learning Act 2009 s 36(1)(c)(ii). 'Relevant member of the House of Commons staff means any person who was appointed by the House of Commons Commission or is employed in the refreshment department, or who is a member of the Speaker's personal staff: Employment Rights Act 1996 s 195(5) (definition applied by the Apprenticeships, Skills, Children and Learning Act 2009 s 36(6)). As to the House of Commons Commission see PARLIAMENT vol 78 (2010) PARA 946. As to the Speaker see PARLIAMENT vol 78 (2010) PARA 931 et seq.

21 Apprenticeships, Skills, Children and Learning Act 2009 s 36(1). Section 36(1) is subject to s 36(3) and to any modifications which may be prescribed under s 36(5): s 36(2). Section 35(2) (see the text to note 15) does not apply in relation to an apprenticeship agreement that is an agreement within s 36(1)(a), (b) or (c) (see heads (i)–(iii) in the text): s 36(3). Regulations may provide for any provision of Pt 1 Ch 1 (ss 1–37) to apply with modifications in relation to: (1) an agreement within s 36(1)(a), (b) or (c) (s 36(5)(a) (s 36(5) amended by the Education Act 2011 Sch 18 paras 1, 3); or (2) a person working, or proposing to work, under such an agreement (Apprenticeships, Skills, Children and Learning Act 2009 s 36(5)(b)). Without prejudice to s 262(3) (general provision as to orders and regulations), the power conferred by s 32(2)(b) (see head (2) in the text) may be exercised, in particular, to make provision in relation to an apprenticeship agreement which is an agreement within any of s 36(1)(a)–(c) that differs from provision made in relation to other apprenticeship agreements: s 36(4). As to regulations made under s 36(4) see the Apprenticeships (Form of Apprenticeship Agreement) Regulations 2012, SI 2012/844.

B. APPRENTICESHIP CERTIFICATES

767. Meaning of 'completing a Welsh apprenticeship'. A person 'completes a Welsh[1] apprenticeship' in relation to an apprenticeship framework[2] if: (1) the standard Welsh completion conditions are met[3]; or (2) the alternative Welsh completion conditions are met[4].

The 'standard Welsh completion conditions' are:

(a)   that the person has entered into an apprenticeship agreement[5] in connection with the apprenticeship framework[6];

(b)   that at the date of that agreement the framework was a recognised Welsh framework[7];

(c)   that the person has completed a course of training for the competencies qualification[8] identified in the framework[9];

(d)   that, throughout the duration of the course, the person was working under the apprenticeship agreement[10]; and

(e)   that the person meets the requirements specified in the framework for the purpose of the issue of an apprenticeship certificate[11].

The 'alternative Welsh completion conditions' are conditions which apply in cases where a person works otherwise than under an apprenticeship agreement[12], and are specified in regulations made by the Welsh Ministers[13].

1   As to the meaning of 'Wales' see PARA 7 note 3.

2   Ie for the purposes of the Apprenticeships, Skills, Children and Learning Act 2009 Pt 1 Ch 1 (ss 1–39): see s 2(1). As to the meaning of 'apprenticeship framework' see PARA 766 note 6.

3   Apprenticeships, Skills, Children and Learning Act 2009 s 2(2)(a).

4   Apprenticeships, Skills, Children and Learning Act 2009 s 2(2)(b).

5   As to the meaning of 'apprenticeship agreement' see PARA 766.

6   Apprenticeships, Skills, Children and Learning Act 2009 s 2(3)(a).

7   Apprenticeships, Skills, Children and Learning Act 2009 s 2(3)(b). As to the meaning of 'recognised Welsh framework' see PARA 771 note 4.

8   As to the meaning of 'competencies qualification' see PARA 766 note 6.

9   Apprenticeships, Skills, Children and Learning Act 2009 s 2(3)(c).

10   Apprenticeships, Skills, Children and Learning Act 2009 s 2(3)(d). In s 2(3)(d): (1) the reference to the apprenticeship agreement mentioned in s 2(3)(a) (see head (a) in the text) includes a reference to any apprenticeship agreement which the person subsequently entered into in connection with the same apprenticeship framework (s 2(4)(a)); (2) the reference to the course of training for the competencies qualification is to be read, in a case where the person has followed two or more courses of training for the competencies qualification, as a reference to both or all of them (s 2(4)(b)).

11   Apprenticeships, Skills, Children and Learning Act 2009 s 2(3)(e). 'Apprenticeship certificate' means a certificate issued under s 7 or s 8 (see PARA 768): s 39(1) (definition amended by the Deregulation Act 2015 Sch 1 Pt 2 paras 5, 16(a)).

12   Apprenticeships, Skills, Children and Learning Act 2009 s 2(5)(a).

13   Apprenticeships, Skills, Children and Learning Act 2009 s 2(5)(b). The kinds of working in relation to which provision may be made under s 2(5) include: (1) working as a self-employed person (s 2(6)(a)); (2) working otherwise than for reward (s 2(6)(b)). As to the Welsh Ministers see PARA 59. As to regulations made under s 2(5) see the Apprenticeships (Alternative Welsh Completion Conditions) Regulations 2013, SI 2013/1468.

768. Issue of certificates. The Welsh certifying authority[1] must issue a certificate relating to an apprenticeship framework[2] to a person who applies to the authority in the prescribed manner[3] if;

(1)   it appears to the authority that the person has completed a Welsh apprenticeship[4] in relation to the apprenticeship framework[5];

(2)   in a case where the standard Welsh completion conditions are met[6], it appears to the authority that the specified condition[7] was met at the date of the person's application[8]; and

(3)   the person provides the authority with such information and evidence as the authority requires the person to provide[9], and pays any fee charged by the authority for the issue of the certificate[10].

The Welsh certifying authority may issue a certificate relating to an apprenticeship framework to a person who applies to the authority in the prescribed manner[11] if:

(a)   it appears to the authority that at the date of the application the person met the requirements specified in the framework for the purpose of the issue of an apprenticeship certificate[12];

(b)   the framework is, or has been, a recognised Welsh framework[13];

(c)   the person provides the authority with such information and evidence as the authority requires the person to provide[14], and pays any fee charged by the authority for the issue of the certificate[15].

The Welsh certifying authority may charge a fee for issuing an apprenticeship certificate only if, and to the extent that, it is authorised to do so by regulations made by the Welsh Ministers[16]. Regulations made by the Welsh Ministers may make provision about the supply of copies of apprenticeship certificates issued[17] by the authority[18].

1   The 'Welsh certifying authority', in relation to an apprenticeship certificate of any description, means: (1) the person (if any) designated under the Apprenticeships, Skills, Children and Learning Act 2009 s 10 to issue apprenticeship certificates of that description (s 10(1)(a)); (2) if there is no-one within head (1), the person (if any) designated under s 10 to issue apprenticeship certificates generally (s 10(1)(b)); (3) if there is no-one within heads (1) or (2), the Welsh Ministers (s 10(1)(c)). A person designated to issue apprenticeship certificates must, in exercising functions under Pt 1 Ch 1 (ss 1–39): (a) comply with directions given by the Welsh Ministers (s 10(2)(a)); and (b) have regard to guidance given by the Welsh Ministers (s 10(2)(b)). 'Designated' means designated by an order made by the Welsh Ministers: s 10(3). As to the meaning of 'apprenticeship certificate' see PARA 768. As to the meaning of 'person' see PARA 7 note 6. As to the Welsh Ministers see PARA 59. As to directions see s 263; and PARA 75. As to regulations made under s 10 see the Apprenticeships (Designation of Welsh Certifying Authority) Order 2013, SI 2013/1191.
2   As to the meaning of 'apprenticeship framework' see PARA 766 note 6. As to the contents of certificates see PARA 769.
3   The 'prescribed manner' is the manner prescribed by regulations made by the Welsh Ministers: Apprenticeships, Skills, Children and Learning Act 2009 s 7(2). As to regulations made under ss 7, 8, 9 see the Apprenticeships (Issue of Apprenticeship Certificates) (Wales) Regulations 2013, SI 2013/1190.
4   As to the meaning of 'completing a Welsh apprenticeship' see PARA 767.
5   Apprenticeships, Skills, Children and Learning Act 2009 s 7(1)(a).
6   Ie a case within the Apprenticeships, Skills, Children and Learning Act 2009 s 2(2)(a): see PARA 767.
7   Ie the condition in the Apprenticeships, Skills, Children and Learning Act 2009 s 2(3)(e): see PARA 767.
8   Apprenticeships, Skills, Children and Learning Act 2009 s 7(1)(b).
9   Apprenticeships, Skills, Children and Learning Act 2009 s 7(1)(c)(i).
10 Apprenticeships, Skills, Children and Learning Act 2009 s 7(1)(c)(ii).
11 The 'prescribed manner' is the manner prescribed by regulations made by the Welsh Ministers: Apprenticeships, Skills, Children and Learning Act 2009 s 8(2). As to regulations see note 3.
12 Apprenticeships, Skills, Children and Learning Act 2009 s 8(1)(a).
13 Apprenticeships, Skills, Children and Learning Act 2009 s 8(1)(b). As to the meaning of 'recognised Welsh framework' see PARA 771 note 4.
14 Apprenticeships, Skills, Children and Learning Act 2009 s 8(1)(c)(i).
15 Apprenticeships, Skills, Children and Learning Act 2009 s 8(1)(c)(ii).
16 Apprenticeships, Skills, Children and Learning Act 2009 s 9(1). As to regulations see note 3.
17 Ie under the Apprenticeships, Skills, Children and Learning Act 2009 s 7 or s 8: see the text to notes 1–15.
18 Apprenticeships, Skills, Children and Learning Act 2009 s 9(2). Regulations under s 9(2) may include provision authorising a person supplying a copy of an apprenticeship certificate to charge a fee for doing so: s 9(3). As to regulations see note 3. As to the meaning of 'person' in this context see PARA 7 note 6.

769.   Contents of certificates.   An apprenticeship certificate[1] must state:
(1)   the name of the person to whom it is issued[2];
(2)   the apprenticeship framework[3] to which it relates[4];
(3)   the level of that framework[5];
(4)   the apprenticeship sector to which that framework relates[6]; and
(5)   such other matters as the Welsh Ministers[7] may by regulations require to be stated in a certificate of that description[8].

1   As to the meaning of 'apprenticeship certificate' see PARA 768.
2   Apprenticeships, Skills, Children and Learning Act 2009 s 11(1)(a). As to the issue of certificates see PARA 768.
3   As to the meaning of 'apprenticeship framework' see PARA 766 note 6.
4   Apprenticeships, Skills, Children and Learning Act 2009 s 11(1)(b).

5   Apprenticeships, Skills, Children and Learning Act 2009 s 11(1)(c). As to the meaning of references to the level of a framework see PARA 766 note 6.
6   Apprenticeships, Skills, Children and Learning Act 2009 s 11(1)(d). As to the meaning of references to the apprenticeship sector to which an apprenticeship framework relates see PARA 766 note 6. As to apprenticeship sectors see PARA 765.
7   As to the Welsh Ministers see PARA 59.
8   Apprenticeships, Skills, Children and Learning Act 2009 s 11(2) (amended by the Deregulation Act 2015 Sch 1 Pt 2 paras 5, 9(a)). At the date at which this volume states the law no such regulations had been made.

C. APPRENTICESHIP FRAMEWORKS

770.   Welsh issuing authority. The Welsh Ministers[1] may designate a person[2] to issue apprenticeship frameworks[3] relating to a particular apprenticeship sector[4]. This power must be exercised so as to secure that, at any time, only one person is designated by the Welsh Ministers to issue apprenticeship frameworks relating to a particular apprenticeship sector[5]. A designated person is known as a 'Welsh issuing authority'[6]. A designation may be amended or revoked by the Welsh Ministers[7].

A designated person must, in exercising his functions[8], comply with directions given by the Welsh Ministers[9] and have regard to guidance given by the Welsh Ministers[10].

1   As to the Welsh Ministers see PARA 59.
2   As to the meaning of 'person' see PARA 7 note 6.
3   As to the meaning of 'apprenticeship framework' see PARA 766 note 6.
4   Apprenticeships, Skills, Children and Learning Act 2009 s 18(1). As to the meaning of references to the apprenticeship sector to which an apprenticeship framework relates see PARA 766 note 6. As to apprenticeship sectors see PARA 765.
5   Apprenticeships, Skills, Children and Learning Act 2009 s 18(2). As from a day to be appointed, the wording is replaced by the following: 'The power to designate conferred by this section may not be exercised in such a way that there is at any time more than one person designated to issue apprenticeship frameworks relating to a particular apprenticeship sector': s 18(2) (prospectively substituted by the Deregulation Act 2015 Sch 1 Pt 3 paras 24, 25(1), (2)). At the date at which this volume states the law no such day had been appointed.
6   In the Apprenticeships, Skills, Children and Learning Act 2009 Pt 1 Ch 1 (ss 2–39), the 'Welsh issuing authority', in relation to an apprenticeship framework, means the person designated under s 18 to issue frameworks of that description: s 18(5). As from a day to be appointed, the wording is replaced by the following: 'In Pt 1 Ch 1, the "Welsh issuing authority", in relation to an apprenticeship framework, means the person (if any) designated under this section to issue frameworks of that description; if there is no-one so designated, the Welsh Ministers: see s 18(5) (prospectively substituted by the Deregulation Act 2015 Sch 1 Pt 3 paras 24, 25(1), (3)). At the date at which this volume states the law no such day had been appointed.
7   Apprenticeships, Skills, Children and Learning Act 2009 s 18(4).
8   Ie his functions under the Apprenticeships, Skills, Children and Learning Act 2009 Pt 1 Ch 1 (ss 1–39).
9   Apprenticeships, Skills, Children and Learning Act 2009 s 18(3)(a). As to directions see s 263; and PARA 75.
10 Apprenticeships, Skills, Children and Learning Act 2009 s 18(3)(b).

771.   Issue of apprenticeship framework. The Welsh issuing authority[1] may issue an apprenticeship framework[2] only if the authority is satisfied that the framework meets the requirements specified, by the specification of apprenticeship standards for Wales[3], for recognised Welsh frameworks[4] of that description[5]. Recognition of a recognised Welsh framework may be withdrawn by the Welsh issuing authority[6], or if there is no Welsh issuing authority in relation to the framework, by the Welsh Ministers[7].

On issuing an apprenticeship framework, the Welsh issuing authority must publish the framework[8], and notify the Welsh Ministers of the issue of the framework[9]. A person[10] who withdraws recognition of an apprenticeship framework must publish a notice stating that recognition of the framework has been withdrawn[11], and in the case of withdrawal otherwise than by the Welsh Ministers, notify the Welsh Ministers of the withdrawal[12]. Publication of a framework or notice may be in such manner as the person on whom the duty of publication is imposed thinks fit[13].

1   As to the meaning of 'Welsh issuing authority' see PARA 770 note 6.
2   As to the meaning of 'apprenticeship framework' see PARA 766 note 6.
3   As to the meaning of 'the specification of apprenticeship standards for Wales' see PARA 773 note 6. As to the meaning of 'Wales' see PARA 7 note 3.
4   'Recognised Welsh framework' means an apprenticeship framework issued under the Apprenticeships, Skills, Children and Learning Act 2009 s 19(1) from which recognition has not been withdrawn under s 19(2) (see the text to notes 5–6): ss 12(4), 39(1).
5   Apprenticeships, Skills, Children and Learning Act 2009 s 19(1). As to the submission of draft frameworks for issue see PARA 772. The Welsh Ministers may by order provide for an existing vocational specification to be treated, for all purposes or for purposes specified in the order, as if it were an apprenticeship framework issued under s 19(1) that specified requirements for the purpose of the issue of apprenticeship certificates: s 22(1). For the purposes of its application in relation to an existing vocational specification that, by virtue of an order under s 22(1), is treated as an apprenticeship framework issued under s 19(1), Pt 1 Ch 1 (ss 1–39) has effect subject to any modifications specified in the order: s 22(2). An order under s 22(1) must: (1) specify a date on which the deemed framework is to be treated as being issued under s 19(1) (s 22(3)(a)); (2) specify a date on which recognition of the deemed framework is to be treated as having been withdrawn under s 19(2) (see the text to notes 6–7) (s 22(3)(b)); (3) specify a qualification that the deemed framework is to be treated as identifying as the competencies qualification (s 22(3)(c)); (4) specify the level and apprenticeship sector that are to be treated as being stated in the deemed framework (s 22(3)(d)). The date specified under s 22(3)(b) in an order under s 22(1) must be no later than the day after the day that is the school leaving date for 2013: s 22(4). 'The deemed framework', in relation to an order under s 22(1), means an existing vocational specification that, by virtue of the order, is treated as being an apprenticeship framework issued under s 19(1); and 'existing vocational specification' means a specification, prepared before the coming into force of s 19, of training, qualifications and skills appropriate for persons engaging in a particular trade, skill or occupation: s 22(5). Nothing in s 22 limits the powers conferred by s 262 (general provision as to orders and regulations): s 22(6). As to the meaning of 'apprenticeship certificate' see PARA 768. As to the meaning of 'competencies qualification' see PARA 766 note 6. As to the meaning of references to the level of a framework, and references to the apprenticeship sector to which an apprenticeship framework relates see PARA 766 note 6. As to apprenticeship sectors see PARA 765. As to the fixing of dates for school terms and holidays see PARA 458. As to regulations made under s 22 see the Apprenticeships (Transitional Provision for Existing Vocational Specifications) (Wales) Order 2013, SI 2013/1202.
6   Apprenticeships, Skills, Children and Learning Act 2009 s 19(2)(a). As from a day to be appointed, s 19(2) is revised by the insertion of the words 'by the Welsh issuing authority' after the word 'withdrawn' and by the omission of paras (a), (b): see s 19(2) (prospectively amended by the Deregulation Act 2015 Sch 1 Pt 3 paras 24, 26). At the date at which this volume states the law no such day had been appointed.
7   Apprenticeships, Skills, Children and Learning Act 2009 s 19(2)(b). See note 6. As to the Welsh Ministers see PARA 59.
8   Apprenticeships, Skills, Children and Learning Act 2009 s 20(1)(a).
9   Apprenticeships, Skills, Children and Learning Act 2009 s 20(1)(b). A notice given under s 20(1)(b) must be accompanied by a copy of the framework: s 20(2). As from a day to be appointed, s 20(1)(b) is revised by the insertion at the beginning of the words 'if the issuing authority is not the Welsh Ministers': s 20(1)(b) (prospectively amended by the Deregulation Act 2015 Sch 1 Pt 3 paras 24, 27(1), (2)). At the date at which this volume states the law no such day had been appointed.
10   As to the meaning of 'person' see PARA 7 note 6.
11   Apprenticeships, Skills, Children and Learning Act 2009 s 20(3)(a). As from a day to be appointed, the words 'A person who' is substituted by the words 'A Welsh issuing authority

which': s 20(3)(a) (prospectively amended by the Deregulation Act 2015 Sch 1 Pt 3 paras 24, 27(1), (3)(a)). At the date at which this volume states the law no such day had been appointed.

12 Apprenticeships, Skills, Children and Learning Act 2009 s 20(3)(b). As from a day to be appointed, the words 'in the case of withdrawal other than by the Welsh Ministers' is substituted by the words 'in the case where the issuing authority is not the Welsh Ministers': s 20(3)(b) (prospectively amended by the Deregulation Act 2015 Sch 1 Pt 3 paras 24, 27(1), (3)(b)). At the date at which this volume states the law no such day had been appointed.

13 See the Apprenticeships, Skills, Children and Learning Act 2009 s 20(4).

772. Submission of draft framework for issue. If a person[1] submits a draft of an apprenticeship framework[2] to the Welsh issuing authority[3], and requests that the authority issue a framework in the form of the draft[4], the authority may require the person to provide such information and evidence in connection with the draft as the authority thinks appropriate[5]. If the authority decides not to issue a framework in the form of the draft, it must give the person reasons for its decision[6].

1 As to the meaning of 'person' see PARA 7 note 6.
2 As to the meaning of 'apprenticeship framework' see PARA 766 note 6.
3 Apprenticeships, Skills, Children and Learning Act 2009 s 21(1)(a). As to the meaning of 'Welsh issuing authority' see PARA 770 note 6.
4 Apprenticeships, Skills, Children and Learning Act 2009 s 21(1)(b).
5 Apprenticeships, Skills, Children and Learning Act 2009 s 21(2).
6 Apprenticeships, Skills, Children and Learning Act 2009 s 21(3).

D. SPECIFICATION OF APPRENTICESHIP STANDARDS

773. Specification of apprenticeship standards for Wales. The Welsh Ministers[1] may prepare a draft specification of apprenticeship standards[2]. In preparing the draft, the Welsh Ministers must consult such persons[3] as they think appropriate[4]. Having prepared a draft, the Welsh Ministers may by order[5] provide that a specification of apprenticeship standards ('the specification of apprenticeship standards for Wales')[6] is to have effect: (1) in the form of the draft[7]; or (2) in that form with such modifications as the Welsh Ministers think appropriate[8]. This power is to be exercised so as to secure that at any time only one specification of apprenticeship standards has effect as the specification of apprenticeship standards for Wales[9].

The Welsh Ministers may not make such an order unless satisfied that the specification of apprenticeship standards given effect to by the order complies with the following requirements[10]. The specification of apprenticeship standards for Wales:

(a) must specify requirements to be met by recognised Welsh frameworks[11];
(b) may specify different requirements in relation to recognised Welsh frameworks at different levels[12].

The requirements specified by the specification of apprenticeship standards for Wales must include:

(i) requirements as to Welsh certificate requirements[13], including requirements as to standards of attainment to be required by them[14];
(ii) requirements for a recognised Welsh framework to include, as a Welsh certificate requirement, the requirement that an apprenticeship certificate relating to the framework may be issued to a person only if the person has received both on-the-job training[15] and off-the-job training[16]; and
(iii) requirements for a recognised Welsh framework to (A) include, as a

Welsh certificate requirement, the requirement that one or more qualifications be held[17]; (B) include, as a Welsh certificate requirement, the requirement that the qualification, or the qualifications taken together, demonstrate the relevant occupational competencies[18] and the relevant technical knowledge[19]; and (C) identify the qualification that demonstrates the relevant occupational competencies as the competencies qualification[20] in relation to the framework[21].

1   As to the Welsh Ministers see PARA 59.
2   Apprenticeships, Skills, Children and Learning Act 2009 s 28(1).
3   As to the meaning of 'person' see PARA 7 note 6.
4   Apprenticeships, Skills, Children and Learning Act 2009 s 28(2). Section 28(2) does not apply in relation to the first draft specification to be prepared by the Welsh Ministers after the commencement of s 28: s 28(4). As to the exercise of the duty to consult see JUDICIAL REVIEW vol 61 (2010) PARA 627.
5   As to the order made under the Apprenticeships, Skills, Children and Learning Act 2009 s 28 see the Apprenticeships (Specification of Apprenticeship Standards for Wales) Order 2013, SI 2013/1192, which brings the specification of apprenticeship standards for Wales into effect.
6   'The specification of apprenticeship standards for Wales' means the specification of apprenticeship standards having effect for the time being by virtue of an order made by the Welsh Ministers under the Apprenticeships, Skills, Children and Learning Act 2009 s 28 or s 29 (see PARA 774): s 39(1). As to the meaning of 'Wales' see PARA 7 note 3. See note 5.
7   Apprenticeships, Skills, Children and Learning Act 2009 s 28(3)(a). See note 5.
8   Apprenticeships, Skills, Children and Learning Act 2009 s 28(3)(b). See note 5.
9   Apprenticeships, Skills, Children and Learning Act 2009 s 28(6). As to the modification of the specification see PARA 774. As to the effect of modification or replacement see PARA 775.
10 See the Apprenticeships, Skills, Children and Learning Act 2009 s 28(5).
11 Apprenticeships, Skills, Children and Learning Act 2009 s 31(1)(a). As to the meaning of 'recognised Welsh framework' see PARA 771 note 4.
12 Apprenticeships, Skills, Children and Learning Act 2009 s 31(1)(b). As to the meaning of references to the level of a framework see PARA 766 note 6.
13 'Welsh certificate requirement' means a requirement specified in a recognised Welsh framework for the purpose of the issue of apprenticeship certificates relating to that framework by the Welsh certifying authority: Apprenticeships, Skills, Children and Learning Act 2009 s 31(4). As to the meaning of 'apprenticeship certificate' see PARA 768. As to the meaning of 'Welsh certifying authority' see PARA 768 note 1.
14 Apprenticeships, Skills, Children and Learning Act 2009 s 31(2)(a). Requirements as to standards of attainment may be specified by reference, in particular, to descriptions of qualifications or training: s 31(3).
15 'On-the-job training' in relation to a recognised Welsh framework, is training received in the course of carrying on the skill, trade or occupation to which the framework relates: Apprenticeships, Skills, Children and Learning Act 2009 s 31(4).
16 Apprenticeships, Skills, Children and Learning Act 2009 s 31(2)(b). 'Off-the-job training' in relation to a recognised Welsh framework, is training which is received for the purposes of the skill, trade or occupation to which the framework relates, and is not on-the-job training: s 31(4).
17 Apprenticeships, Skills, Children and Learning Act 2009 s 31(2)(c)(i).
18 'The relevant occupational competencies', in relation to a recognised Welsh framework, means the competencies required to perform the skill, trade or occupation to which the framework relates at the level required in the framework: Apprenticeships, Skills, Children and Learning Act 2009 s 31(4).
19 Apprenticeships, Skills, Children and Learning Act 2009 s 31(2)(c)(ii). 'The relevant technical knowledge', in relation to a recognised Welsh framework, means the technical knowledge required to perform the skill, trade or occupation to which the framework relates at the level required in the framework: s 31(4).
20 As to the meaning of 'competencies qualification' see PARA 766 note 6.
21 Apprenticeships, Skills, Children and Learning Act 2009 s 31(2)(c)(iii).

774.   Modification of specification. The Welsh Ministers[1] may by order[2] provide that the specification of apprenticeship standards for Wales[3] is to have effect subject to modifications specified in the order[4]. The Welsh Ministers may not make such an order unless satisfied that the specification, as so modified, complies with statutory provisions[5] relating to the contents of the specification[6].

1   As to the Welsh Ministers see PARA 59.
2   At the date at which this volume states the law no such order had been made.
3   As to the meaning of 'the specification of apprenticeship standards for Wales' see PARA 773 note 6.
4   Apprenticeships, Skills, Children and Learning Act 2009 s 29(1). As to the effect of modification see PARA 775.
5   Ie the Apprenticeships, Skills, Children and Learning Act 2009 s 31: see PARA 773.
6   Apprenticeships, Skills, Children and Learning Act 2009 s 29(2).

775.   Effect of replacement or modification of specification on recognised Welsh frameworks. A recognised Welsh framework[1] does not cease to be a recognised Welsh framework if, by virtue of an order[2], it ceases to meet the requirements specified for frameworks of its description by the specification of apprenticeship standards for Wales[3]. However, an order bringing a specification into effect[4] may provide for an apprenticeship framework which:

(1)   immediately before the making of the order is a recognised Welsh framework[5]; but

(2)   does not meet the requirements specified for frameworks of its description by the specification of apprenticeship standards for Wales to which the order gives effect[6],

to cease to have effect as a recognised Welsh framework[7].

1   As to the meaning of 'recognised Welsh framework' see PARA 771 note 4.
2   Ie under the Apprenticeships, Skills, Children and Learning Act 2009 s 28 (see PARA 773) or s 29 (see PARA 774).
3   Apprenticeships, Skills, Children and Learning Act 2009 s 30(1). As to the meaning of 'the specification of apprenticeship standards for Wales' see PARA 773 note 6. As to the meaning of 'Wales' see PARA 7 note 3.
4   Ie an order under the Apprenticeships, Skills, Children and Learning Act 2009 s 28: see PARA 773.
5   Apprenticeships, Skills, Children and Learning Act 2009 s 30(2)(a).
6   Apprenticeships, Skills, Children and Learning Act 2009 s 30(2)(b).
7   Apprenticeships, Skills, Children and Learning Act 2009 s 30(2).

(4) PROVISION OF FACILITIES, FINANCIAL RESOURCES AND SERVICES FOR APPRENTICESHIP TRAINING ETC

(i) Provision of Facilities etc in England

A. PROVISION OF FACILITIES FOR APPRENTICESHIP TRAINING

776.   Apprenticeship training for persons aged 16 to 18 and certain young adults. The Secretary of State[1] may secure the provision of facilities for suitable apprenticeship training[2] for persons who are over compulsory school age[3] but under 19[4], or who are aged 19 or over but under 25 for whom an EHC plan is maintained[5]. In deciding for these purposes whether apprenticeship training is suitable for persons for whom facilities are provided, the Secretary of State must have regard (in particular) to: (1) the persons' ages, abilities and aptitudes[6]; (2) any special educational needs[7] the persons may have[8]; (3) the quality of the training[9]; (4) the locations and times at which the training is provided[10].

In exercising this power, the Secretary of State must have regard (in particular) to the desirability of: (a) encouraging diversity of apprenticeship training available to persons[11]; (b) increasing opportunities for persons to exercise choice[12]; (c) enabling relevant persons[13] to fulfil the duty[14] to participate in education or training[15].

1   As to the Secretary of State see PARA 58. The functions of the Secretary of State under the Apprenticeships, Skills, Children and Learning Act 2009 Pt 4 (ss 83–121), other than the functions conferred by s 107 (see PARA 799), are exercisable in relation to England only: s 120A (added by the Deregulation Act 2015 Sch 14 paras 1, 26). As to the meaning of 'England' see PARA 7 note 3.
      The office of the Chief Executive of Skills Funding, which was established by the Apprenticeships, Skills, Children and Learning Act 2009 Pt 4, was abolished with effect from 26 May 2015: see the Deregulation Act 2015 s 64(1). Various amendments were made to the Apprenticeships, Skills, Children and Learning Act 2009 Pt 4 as a consequence of the abolition: see the Deregulation Act 2015 Sch 14. The property, rights and liabilities of the Chief Executive of Skills Funding were transferred to the Secretary of State: see s 64(2).
2   In the Apprenticeships, Skills, Children and Learning Act 2009 Pt 4 (ss 83–121) 'apprenticeship training' means training provided in connection with: (1) an approved English apprenticeship; or (2) any contract of service (other than an approved English apprenticeship agreement) or contract of apprenticeship: s 83(5) (amended by the Deregulation Act 2015 Sch 1 paras 5, 17). As to the meaning of 'approved English apprenticeship' see PARA 760 (definition applied by the Apprenticeships, Skills, Children and Learning Act 2009 s 121(1) (amended by the Deregulation Act 2015 Sch 1 paras 5, 22(b))).
3   As to the meaning of 'compulsory school age' see PARA 19.
4   Apprenticeships, Skills, Children and Learning Act 2009 s 83(1)(a) (s 83(1) amended by the Deregulation Act 2014 Sch 14 paras 1, 4). As to the time at which a person attains a particular age see PARA 7 note 6.
5   Apprenticeships, Skills, Children and Learning Act 2009 s 83(1)(b) (s 83(1), (2) amended by the Children and Families Act 2014 Sch 3 paras 88, 89(a)). As to persons for whom an EHC plan is maintained see PARA 441. As to EHC plans (ie education, health and care plans) generally see PARA 958 et seq.
6   Apprenticeships, Skills, Children and Learning Act 2009 s 83(2)(a) (s 83(2) amended by the Deregulation Act 2014 Sch 14 paras 1, 4).
7   As to the meaning of 'special educational needs' see PARA 943 (definition applied by the Apprenticeships, Skills, Children and Learning Act 2009 s 264(2), (3)).
8   Apprenticeships, Skills, Children and Learning Act 2009 s 83(2)(b) (as amended: see note 5).
9   Apprenticeships, Skills, Children and Learning Act 2009 s 83(2)(c).
10 Apprenticeships, Skills, Children and Learning Act 2009 s 83(2)(d).
11 Apprenticeships, Skills, Children and Learning Act 2009 s 83(3)(a) (s 83(3) amended by the Deregulation Act 2014 Sch 14 paras 1, 4).
12 Apprenticeships, Skills, Children and Learning Act 2009 s 83(3)(b).
13 Ie persons to whom the Education and Skills Act 2008 Pt 1 (ss 1–67) applies (see PARA 725).
14 Ie the duty imposed by the Education and Skills Act 2008 s 2 (see PARA 725).
15 Apprenticeships, Skills, Children and Learning Act 2009 s 83(3)(c).

777.   The apprenticeship offer.   The Secretary of State[1] must secure the provision of proper facilities for apprenticeship training[2] that is suitable to the requirements of persons[3] who fall within the specified provisions[4], and have an apprenticeship opportunity[5]; and this duty[6] is referred to for these purposes as 'the apprenticeship offer'[7]. An apprenticeship opportunity is an opportunity to enter into an approved English apprenticeship[8]. Facilities are proper if they are of a quantity sufficient to meet the reasonable needs of individuals, and of a quality adequate to meet those needs[9]. The Secretary of State may by order amend these provisions for the purpose of changing the descriptions of persons to whom the apprenticeship offer applies[10].

The Secretary of State is not required by the apprenticeship offer to secure the provision of facilities for apprenticeship training for the purpose of assisting a person to achieve a particular approved apprenticeship standard if the person (1) has already completed an approved English apprenticeship by achieving that standard[11]; (2) has already completed an approved English apprenticeship by achieving another standard and, in doing so, appears to the Secretary of State to have demonstrated a comparable level of achievement (whether or not in the same sector of work)[12]; or (3) has worked under another arrangement and, in doing so, appears to the Secretary of State to have demonstrated a comparable level of achievement (whether or not in the same sector of work)[13].

1   As to the Secretary of State see PARA 58.
2   As to the meaning of 'apprenticeship training' see PARA 776 note 2.
3   As to the meaning of 'person' see PARA 7 note 6.
4   Apprenticeships, Skills, Children and Learning Act 2009 s 83A(1)(a) (ss 83A, 83B added by the Education Act 2011 s 69(2); and the Apprenticeships, Skills, Children and Learning Act 2009 ss 83A(1), (9), 83B(1), (5) amended by the Deregulation Act 2015 Sch 14 paras 1, 5, 6). The provisions referred to in the text are the Apprenticeships, Skills, Children and Learning Act 2009 s 83A(4), (5) or s 83A(6): s 83A(1)(a) (as so added). A person within s 83A(4) is one who is over compulsory school age but under 19: s 83A(4) (as so added). A person within s 83A(5) is one who is not within s 83A(4) and: (1) is a person aged under 21 towards whom a local authority in England has the duties provided for in the Children Act 1989 s 23C (continuing functions in relation to certain formerly looked after children) (see CHILDREN AND YOUNG PERSONS vol 10 (2012) PARA 933); or (2) is a person to whom s 23CA applies (further assistance for certain formerly looked after children aged under 25) (see CHILDREN AND YOUNG PERSONS vol 10 (2012) PARA 934), in relation to whom a local authority in England is the responsible local authority (within the meaning of s 23CA): Apprenticeships, Skills, Children and Learning Act 2009 s 83A(5) (as so added). A person within s 83A(6) is one who: (a) is not within s 83A(4); and (b) is of a prescribed description: s 83A(6) (as so added). For the purposes of s 83A(6), a person is of a prescribed description if that person is aged 19 or over but under 25 and has a disability within the meaning of the Equality Act 2010 s 6(1) (see DISCRIMINATION vol 33 (2013) PARA 50): Apprenticeships (the Apprenticeship Offer) (Prescribed Persons) Regulations 2013, SI 2013/560, reg 2. If regulations under head (b) above describe a person by reference to an age or an age range, the age, or the upper age of the age range, must be less than 25: Apprenticeships, Skills, Children and Learning Act 2009 s 83A(7) (as so added). As to the meaning of 'compulsory school age' see PARA 19. As to the meaning of 'local authority in England' see PARA 25 (definition applied by s 264(2), (3)). As to the meaning of 'England' see PARA 7 note 3. As to the time at which a person attains a particular age see PARA 7 note 6.
5   Apprenticeships, Skills, Children and Learning Act 2009 s 83A(1)(b) (as added and amended: see note 4).
6   Ie the duty imposed by the Apprenticeships, Skills, Children and Learning Act 2009 s 83A(1) (see the text and notes 1–5). The duty imposed by s 83A(1) is subject to s 83B (limit on scope of apprenticeship offer: see the text and notes 11–13): s 83A(1) (as added: see note 4).
7   Apprenticeships, Skills, Children and Learning Act 2009 s 83A(2) (as added: see note 4). Section 83(2), (3) (see PARA 776) applies for the purposes of the apprenticeship offer: s 83A(9) (as so added).
8   Apprenticeships, Skills, Children and Learning Act 2009 s 83A(3) (as added (see note 4); and amended by the Deregulation Act 2015 Sch 1 paras 5, 18). As to the meaning of 'approved English apprenticeship' see PARA 760 (definition applied by the Apprenticeships, Skills, Children and Learning Act 2009 s 121(1) (amended by the Deregulation Act 2015 Sch 1 paras 5, 22(b)).
9   Apprenticeships, Skills, Children and Learning Act 2009 s 83A(8) (as added: see note 4).
10 Apprenticeships, Skills, Children and Learning Act 2009 s 83A(12) (as added: see note 4).
11 Apprenticeships, Skills, Children and Learning Act 2009 s 83B(1)(a) (as added (see note 4); and s 83B(1) amended by the Deregulation Act 2015 Sch 1 paras 5, 18(1), (2)). The Apprenticeships, Skills, Children and Learning Act 2009 s A1(6), (7) (see PARAS 760, 761) (which makes provision about when a person completes an approved English apprenticeship and about the meaning of 'approved apprenticeship standard') applies for the purposes of s 83(1): s 83B(1A) (added by the Deregulation Act 2015 Sch 1 paras 5, 19(1), (3)).
12 Apprenticeships, Skills, Children and Learning Act 2009 s 83B(1)(b) (as added and amended: see note 11).
13 Apprenticeships, Skills, Children and Learning Act 2009 s 83B(1)(b) (as added and amended: see note 11).

778. Education and training for persons aged 19 or over and others subject to adult detention. The Secretary of State[1] must secure the provision of such facilities[2] as the Secretary of State considers appropriate for[3]:

(1) education suitable to the requirements of persons who are aged 19 or over, other than persons aged under 25 for whom an EHC plan is maintained[4];

(2) education suitable to the requirements of persons who are subject to adult detention[5]; and

(3) training suitable to the requirements of persons within heads (1) and (2) above[6].

1 As to the Secretary of State see PARA 58.

2 For the purposes of the Apprenticeships, Skills, Children and Learning Act 2009 s 86, a reference to the provision of facilities for education or training (except so far as relating to facilities for persons subject to adult detention) includes a reference to the provision of facilities for organised leisure-time occupation in connection with education or (as the case may be) training: s 86(5). 'Education' includes full-time and part-time education; and 'training' includes (1) full-time and part-time training; (2) vocational, social, physical and recreational training; (3) apprenticeship training: s 86(6). As to the meaning of 'apprenticeship training' see PARA 776 note 2. Section 86 does not apply to the provision of facilities to the extent that s 83A (see PARA 777) or s 87 (see PARA 779) applies to the provision of those facilities: s 86(2) (amended by the Education Act 2011 Sch 18 para 7).

In the Apprenticeships, Skills, Children and Learning Act 2009 Pt 4 (ss 83–121), 'organised leisure-time occupation' means leisure-time occupation, in such organised cultural training and recreational activities as are suited to the requirements of persons who fall within s 86(1)(a) (see head (1) in the text) or s 86(1)(b) (see head (2) in the text), for any such persons who are able and willing to profit by facilities provided for that purpose: ss 86(7), 121(1). For the purposes of Pt 4 a person is subject to adult detention if the person is subject to a detention order and: (a) aged 19 or over, or (b) aged under 19 and detained in a young offender institution, or part of such an institution, that is used wholly or mainly for the detention of persons aged 18 and over, or a prison: s 121(4). As to when a person is subject to a detention order see PARA 46 note 8 (definition applied by s 264(2), (3)). As to the time at which a person attains a particular age see PARA 7 note 6.

3 Apprenticeships, Skills, Children and Learning Act 2009 s 86(1) (amended by the Deregulation Act 2015 Sch 14 paras 1, 8(1), (2)).

4 Apprenticeships, Skills, Children and Learning Act 2009 s 86(1)(a) (amended by the Children and Families Act 2014 Sch 3 paras 88, 90). As to persons for whom an EHC plan is maintained see PARA 441. As to EHC plans (ie education, health and care plans) generally see PARA 958 et seq.

5 Apprenticeships, Skills, Children and Learning Act 2009 s 86(1)(b).

6 Apprenticeships, Skills, Children and Learning Act 2009 s 86(1)(c).

779. Learning aims for persons aged 19 or over: provision of facilities. The Secretary of State[1] must secure the provision of such facilities as the Secretary of State considers appropriate for relevant education or training[2] for designated persons which is suitable to their requirements[3]. The designated persons are persons who:

(1) are aged 19 or over, and are not persons aged under 25 for whom an EHC plan is maintained[4];

(2) do not have the qualification in question or one (including one awarded by a person[5] outside England[6]) which appears to the Secretary of State to be at a comparable or higher level[7]; and

(3) satisfy such conditions as may be specified in regulations[8];

however, nothing in these provisions applies to the provision of facilities, or to courses of study, for persons subject to adult detention[9].

1 As to the Secretary of State see PARA 58.

2 For these purposes 'education' includes full-time and part-time education; and 'training' includes full-time and part-time training: Apprenticeships, Skills, Children and Learning Act 2009 s 87(6). 'Relevant education or training' is education or vocational training provided by means of a course of study for a qualification which is: (1) a specified qualification in literacy (see s 87(2), Sch 5 para 1(a)); (2) a specified qualification in numeracy (see s 87(2), Sch 5 para 1(b));

(3) a specified vocational qualification at level 2 (see s 87(2), Sch 5 para 1(c)). A reference to a specified qualification is to a regulated qualification which is specified, or which is of a description specified, in regulations: Sch 5 para 3(1). As to the meaning of 'regulated qualification' see PARA 826 note 7 (definition applied by Sch 5 para 3(4)). 'Regulations' means regulations made by the Secretary of State: s 264(1). The regulations may specify qualifications, or descriptions of qualifications, by reference to an assessment made by the Secretary of State of the level of attainment demonstrated by a qualification; and for that purpose the regulations may confer functions (which may include the exercise of a discretion) on the Secretary of State: Sch 5 para 3(2) (amended by the Deregulation Act 2015 Sch 14 paras 1, 30(a)). The regulations may make provision which applies subject to exceptions specified in the regulations: Apprenticeships, Skills, Children and Learning Act 2009 Sch 5 para 3(3). As to the meaning of 'functions' see PARA 18 note 5 (definition applied by s 264(2), (3)).

The level of attainment in literacy demonstrated by a specified qualification in literacy must be the level which, in the opinion of the Secretary of State, is the minimum required in that respect by persons aged 19 or over in order to be able to operate effectively in day-to-day life: Sch 5 para 4. The level of attainment in numeracy demonstrated by a specified qualification in numeracy must be the level which, in the opinion of the Secretary of State, is the minimum required in that respect by persons aged 19 or over in order to be able to operate effectively in day-to-day life: Sch 5 para 5. Level 2 is the level of attainment (in terms of breadth and depth) which, in the opinion of the Secretary of State, is demonstrated by the General Certificate of Secondary Education in five subjects, each at Grade C or above: Sch 5 para 6. In forming an opinion for the purposes of Sch 5, the Secretary of State may have regard, in particular, to advice or information relating to qualifications which is provided by the Office of Qualifications and Examinations Regulation (Sch 5 para 8(c)). As to the time at which a person attains a particular age see PARA 7 note 6. As to the Office of Qualifications and Examinations Regulation (Ofqual) see PARA 825 et seq.

The Secretary of State may by order amend Sch 5 so as to: (a) add a category of qualification to Pt 1 (paras 1–2) (Sch 5 para 9(1)(a)); (b) remove a category of qualification for the time being referred to in Pt 1 (Sch 5 para 9(1)(b)); (c) substitute a different qualification for a qualification for the time being referred to in Pt 2 (paras 3–9) (Sch 5 para 9(1((c)); (d) make consequential amendments (Sch 5 para 9(1)(d)). The power conferred by Sch 5 para 9(1)(b) includes power to remove every category of qualification to which a paragraph of Pt 1 for the time being applies: Sch 5 para 9(2). At the date at which this volume states the law no such order had been made.

As to the regulations made under ss 87, 89, Sch 5 see the Adult Skills (Specified Qualifications) Regulations 2010, SI 2010/733.

3   Apprenticeships, Skills, Children and Learning Act 2009 s 87(1) (amended by the Deregulation Act 2015 Sch 14 paras 1, 10(1)(2)).

4   Apprenticeships, Skills, Children and Learning Act 2009 s 87(3)(a) (amended by the Children and Families Act 2014 Sch 3 para 91). As to persons for whom an EHC plan is maintained see PARA 441. As to EHC plans (ie education, health and care plans) generally see PARA 958 et seq.

5   As to the meaning of 'person' see PARA 7 note 6.

6   As to the meaning of 'England' see PARA 7 note 3.

7   Apprenticeships, Skills, Children and Learning Act 2009 s 87(3)(b) (amended by the Deregulation Act 2015 Sch 14 paras 1, 10(1), (2)). Regulations may make provision as to circumstances in which: (1) despite having a specified qualification, a person is to be treated for the purposes of the Apprenticeships, Skills, Children and Learning Act 2009 s 87 as not having that qualification (s 89(1)(a)); (2) despite not having a specified qualification, a person is to be treated for any of those purposes as having that qualification (s 89(1)(b)). A reference to a specified qualification is to a qualification specified, or of a description specified, in the regulations: see s 89(3). As to the regulations made see note 2.

8   Apprenticeships, Skills, Children and Learning Act 2009 s 87(3)(c). A condition specified in regulations under s 87 may, in particular, relate to: (1) the possession, or lack, of a specified qualification (s 89(2)(a)); (2) the completion of, or failure to complete, a course for a specified qualification (s 89(2)(b)). A reference to a specified qualification is to a qualification specified, or of a description specified, in the regulations: see s 89(3).

9   See the Apprenticeships, Skills, Children and Learning Act 2009 s 89(5). As to when a person is subject to adult detention see PARA 778 note 2.

780. Learning aims for persons aged 19 or over: payment of tuition fees. The Secretary of State[1] must exercise his functions[2] so as to secure that a course of study for a qualification[3] is free[4] to a designated person if it is provided for the person by virtue of facilities whose provision is secured[5] by the Secretary of State[6]. A person is a designated person for these purposes if, at the time of starting the course in question, he:

(1)   is aged 19 or over[7];

(2)   does not have the qualification in question or one (including one awarded by a person outside England[8]) which appears to the Secretary of State to be at a comparable or higher level[9]; and

(3)   satisfies such conditions as may be specified in regulations[10].

The Secretary of State must also exercise his functions[11] so as to secure that a course of study for a specified qualification[12] is free to a designated person if it is provided for the person by virtue of facilities whose provision is secured[13] by the Secretary of State[14]. For these purposes, a person is a designated person if, at the time of starting the course in question, he:

(a)   is aged at least 19 but less than 24[15];

(b)   does not have the qualification in question or one (including one awarded by a person outside England) which appears to the Secretary of State to be at a comparable or higher level[16]; and

(c)   satisfies such conditions as may be specified in regulations[17].

Nothing in the above provisions applies to the provision of facilities, or to courses of study, for persons subject to adult detention[18].

1   As to the Secretary of State see PARA 58.

2   Ie his functions under the Apprenticeships, Skills, Children and Learning Act 2009 Pt 4 (ss 83–121). As to the meaning of 'functions' see PARA 18 note 5 (definition applied by s 264(2), (3)).

3   Ie a qualification to which the Apprenticeships, Skills, Children and Learning Act 2009 Sch 5 para 1(a) or para 1(b) (see PARA 779 note 2) applies.

4   For the purposes of the Apprenticeships, Skills, Children and Learning Act 2009 s 88, a course is free to a person if no tuition fees in respect of the provision of the course for the person are payable by a person other than the Secretary of State (s 88(6)(a) (s 88(1), (2), (2A), (3), (4), (6)(a) amended by the Deregulation Act 2015 Sch 14 paras 1, 11)), or a body specified by order by the Secretary of State for these purposes (Apprenticeships, Skills, Children and Learning Act 2009 s 88(6)(b)). 'Tuition fees', in relation to a course, means the fees charged in respect of the course by the person providing it (s 88(7)(a)), and such fees in respect of other matters relating to the course (such as undergoing a preliminary assessment or sitting an examination) as may be specified in regulations (s 88(7)(b)). As to the meaning of 'person' see PARA 7 note 6. 'Regulations' means regulations made by the Secretary of State: s 264(1). At the date at which this volume states the law no order had been made under s 88(6)(b). As to the regulations made under ss 88, 89 see the Adult Skills (Specified Qualifications) Regulations 2010, SI 2010/733.

5   Ie under the Apprenticeships, Skills, Children and Learning Act 2009 s 87 (see PARA 779).

6   See the Apprenticeships, Skills, Children and Learning Act 2009 s 88(1) (amended by the Education Act 2011 s 73(2)(a); and as further amended (see note 4).

7   Apprenticeships, Skills, Children and Learning Act 2009 s 88(2)(a). The Secretary of State may by order amend s 88(2)(a) by substituting a different age for the age for the time being referred to: s 88(5)(a). As to the time at which a person attains a particular age see PARA 7 note 6. At the date at which this volume states the law no such order had been made.

8   As to the meaning of 'England' see PARA 7 note 3.

9   Apprenticeships, Skills, Children and Learning Act 2009 s 88(2)(b) (as amended: see note 4). Regulations may make provision as to circumstances in which: (1) despite having a specified qualification, a person is to be treated for the purposes of s 88 as not having that qualification (s 89(1)(a)); (2) despite not having a specified qualification, a person is to be treated for any of those purposes as having that qualification (s 89(1)(b)). A reference to a specified qualification is to a qualification specified, or of a description specified, in the regulations: see s 89(3). As to the regulations made see note 4.

10 Apprenticeships, Skills, Children and Learning Act 2009 s 88(2)(c). A condition specified in regulations under s 88 may, in particular, relate to: (1) the possession, or lack, of a specified qualification (s 89(2)(a)); (2) the completion of, or failure to complete, a course for a specified qualification (s 89(2)(b)). A reference to a specified qualification is to a qualification specified,

or of a description specified, in the regulations: see s 89(3). Regulations under s 88 or s 89, may confer a function (which may relate to the administration of an assessment and may include the exercise of a discretion) on a person specified, or of a description specified, in the regulations: s 89(4). As to the regulations made see note 4.

11   Ie his functions under the Apprenticeships, Skills, Children and Learning Act 2009 Pt 4 (ss 83–121).

12   Ie a specified qualification at level 3: see the Apprenticeships, Skills, Children and Learning Act 2009 s 88(3), Sch 5 para 2. Level 3 is the level of attainment (in terms of breadth and depth) which, in the opinion of the Secretary of State, is demonstrated by the General Certificate of Education at the advanced level in two subjects: Sch 5 para 7. As to the power to specify qualifications, and the power to amend Sch 5, see Sch 5 Pt 2 (paras 3–9); and PARA 779 note 2.

13   Ie under the Apprenticeships, Skills, Children and Learning Act 2009 s 86 (see PARA 778).

14   See the Apprenticeships, Skills, Children and Learning Act 2009 s 88(3) (as amended: see note 4).

15   Apprenticeships, Skills, Children and Learning Act 2009 s 88(4)(a) (amended by the Education Act 2011 s 73(2)(c)). The Secretary of State may by order amend the Apprenticeships, Skills, Children and Learning Act 2009 s 88(4)(a) by substituting a different age for either of the ages for the time being referred to: s 88(5)(b). At the date at which this volume states the law no such order had been made. Functions under Pt 4 must be exercised by the Secretary of State so as to secure that a course of study for a qualification to which Sch 5 para 1(c) (see PARA 779) applies is free to a person falling within s 88(4) if it is provided for the person by virtue of facilities whose provision is secured under section 87 (see PARA 779): s 88(2A) (added by the Education Act 2011 s 73(2)(b); and the Apprenticeships, Skills, Children and Learning Act 2009 s 88(2A) (as amended: see note 4)).

16   Apprenticeships, Skills, Children and Learning Act 2009 s 88(4)(b) (as amended: see note 4). See also note 9.

17   Apprenticeships, Skills, Children and Learning Act 2009 s 88(4)(c). See also note 10.

18   See the Apprenticeships, Skills, Children and Learning Act 2009 s 89(5). As to when a person is subject to adult detention see PARA 778 note 2.

781. Encouragement of education and training for persons aged 19 or over and others subject to adult detention. The Secretary of State[1] must:

(1)   encourage participation by persons who are aged 19 or over[2] (other than persons aged under 25 for whom an EHC plan is maintained)[3] and persons who are subject to adult detention[4] in education and training within the Secretary of State's remit[5];

(2)   encourage employers to participate in the provision of education and training[6] within the Secretary of State's remit for persons[7] who are aged 19 or over (other than persons aged under 25 for whom an EHC plan is maintained)[8];

(3)   encourage employers to contribute to the costs of education and training within the Secretary of State's remit for such persons[9].

1   As to the Secretary of State see PARA 58.

2   As to the time at which a person attains a particular age see PARA 7 note 6.

3   Ie persons within the Apprenticeships, Skills, Children and Learning Act 2009 s 86(1)(a) (see PARA 778): see s 90(1)(a). As to persons for whom an EHC plan is maintained see PARA 441. As to EHC plans (ie education, health and care plans) generally see PARA 958 et seq.

4   Ie persons within the Apprenticeships, Skills, Children and Learning Act 2009 s 86(1)(b) (see PARA 778): see s 90(1)(a). As to when a person is subject to adult detention see PARA 778 note 2.

5   Apprenticeships, Skills, Children and Learning Act 2009 s 90(1)(a) (s 90(1) amended by the Deregulation Act 2015 Sch 14 paras 1, 12). The reference in the text is to the Secretary of State's remit under the Apprenticeships, Skills, Children and Learning Act 2009 Pt 4 (ss 83–121). In Pt 4 a reference to 'education within the Secretary of State's remit under Pt 4' is a reference to education falling within s 86(1)(a) or s 86(1)(b) (see PARA 778), and organised leisure-time occupation in connection with such education: s 121(2) (amended by the Deregulation Act 2015 Sch 14 paras 1, 27(1), (3)); and a reference to 'training within the Secretary of State's remit under [the Apprenticeships, Skills, Children and Learning Act 2009] Pt 4' is a reference to training falling within s 83(1) (see PARA 776), training falling within s 86(1)(c) (see PARA 778), and organised leisure-time occupation in connection with training falling within s 86(1)(c):

s 121(3) (amended by the Deregulation Act 2015 Sch 14 paras 1, 27(1), (3)). As to the meaning of 'organised leisure-time occupation' see PARA 778 note 2.

6 For these purposes, participating in the provision of training includes participating by entering into an approved English apprenticeship (Apprenticeships, Skills, Children and Learning Act 2009 s 90(2)(a) (s 90(2)(a), (b) substituted by the Deregulation Act 2015 Sch 1 paras 5, 20)), or any contract of employment (other than an approved English apprenticeship agreement) in connection with which training is provided (Apprenticeships, Skills, Children and Learning Act 2009 s 90(2)(b) (as so substituted)). As to the meaning of 'approved English apprenticeship' see PARA 760 (definition applied by the Apprenticeships, Skills, Children and Learning Act 2009 s 121(1) (amended by the Deregulation Act 2015 Sch 1 paras 5, 22(b)).

7 Ie persons within the Apprenticeships, Skills, Children and Learning Act 2009 s 86(1)(a) (see PARA 778).

8 Apprenticeships, Skills, Children and Learning Act 2009 s 90(1)(b) (as amended: see note 5).

9 Apprenticeships, Skills, Children and Learning Act 2009 s 90(1)(c) (as amended: see note 5).

782. Consideration to be given to the needs of persons with special educational needs and persons subject to adult detention. The Secretary of State[1] must, in performing the relevant functions[2], have regard to the needs of persons with special educational needs[3] who are persons aged 19 or over[4], other than persons aged under 25 for whom an EHC plan is maintained[5], or persons who are subject to adult detention[6]. The Secretary of State must also have regard to the needs of persons subject to adult detention[7].

1 As to the Secretary of State see PARA 58.
2 Ie functions under the Apprenticeships, Skills, Children and Learning Act 2009 Pt 4 (ss 83–121): see PARA 776 note 1.
3 See the Apprenticeships, Skills, Children and Learning Act 2009 s 115(1) (amended by the Children and Families Act 2014 Sch 3 para 93; and the Deregulation Act 2015 Sch 14 paras 1, 23). As to the meaning of 'special educational needs' see PARA 943 (definition applied by the Apprenticeships, Skills, Children and Learning Act 2009 s 264(2), (3)).
4 As to the time at which a person attains a particular age see PARA 7 note 6.
5 Apprenticeships, Skills, Children and Learning Act 2009 s 115(2)(a) (amended by the Children and Families Act 2014 Sch 3 para 93). As to persons for whom an EHC plan is maintained see PARA 441. As to EHC plans (ie education, health and care plans) generally see PARA 958 et seq.
6 Apprenticeships, Skills, Children and Learning Act 2009 s 115(2)(b). As to when a person is subject to adult detention see PARA 778 note 2.
7 Apprenticeships, Skills, Children and Learning Act 2009 s 116 (amended by the Deregulation Act 2015 Sch 14 paras 1, 24).

B. PROVISION OF FINANCIAL RESOURCES

783. Provision of financial resources by the Secretary of State. The Secretary of State[1] may secure the provision of financial resources[2] to:

(1) persons[3] providing or proposing to provide education or training within the Secretary of State's remit[4];

(2) persons providing or proposing to provide goods or services in connection with the provision by others of such education or training[5];

(3) persons receiving or proposing to receive such education or training[6];

(4) persons aged 18[7] receiving or proposing to receive education or training[8];

(5) persons making loans to others receiving or proposing to receive education or training[9];

(6) persons undertaking or proposing to undertake research relating to education or training[10];

(7) persons carrying out[11] means tests[12];

(8)   persons providing or proposing to provide information, advice or guidance about education or training or connected matters (including employment)[13].

The Secretary of State may secure the provision of financial resources to any person[14] (whether or not the resources could be secured as above[15]) (a) for the purpose of encouraging the provision of opportunities for individuals to complete approved English apprenticeships[16] or to undertake work following the completion of such apprenticeships[17]; or (b) otherwise in connection with approved English apprenticeships[18].

The Secretary of State may secure the provision of such financial resources[19] (i) by providing the resources[20]; (ii) by making arrangements for the provision of resources by another person[21]; (iii) by making arrangements for the provision of resources by persons jointly (whether or not including the Secretary of State)[22].

1   As to the Secretary of State see PARA 58.
2   Ie under the Apprenticeships, Skills, Children and Learning Act 2009 s 100(1). As to the imposition of conditions in relation to the provision of financial resources see PARA 784. As to the use of performance assessments and means tests in relation to the exercise of the power to provide financial resources see PARAS 785, 786.
3   As to the meaning of 'person' see PARA 7 note 6.
4   Apprenticeships, Skills, Children and Learning Act 2009 s 100(1)(a) (s 100(1) amended by the Deregulation Act 2014 Sch 14 paras 1, 13(1), (2)). The reference in the text is the Secretary of State's remit under the Apprenticeships, Skills, Children and Learning Act 2009 Pt 4 (ss 83–121). As to the meanings of 'education within the Secretary of State's remit under Pt 4' and 'training within the Secretary of State's remit' see PARA 781 note 5.
5   Apprenticeships, Skills, Children and Learning Act 2009 s 100(1)(b).
6   Apprenticeships, Skills, Children and Learning Act 2009 s 100(1)(c). The Secretary of State may under s 100(1)(c) or (1A) secure the provision of financial resources by reference to: (1) any fees or charges payable by the person receiving or proposing to receive the education or training (s 100(4)(a) (s 100(4) amended by the Deregulation Act 2014 Sch 1 para 2(1), (4), Sch 14 paras 1, 13(1), (5)); or (2) any other matter (such as transport or childcare) (Apprenticeships, Skills, Children and Learning Act 2009 s 100(4)(b)).
7   As to the time at which a person attains a particular age see PARA 7 note 6.
8   Apprenticeships, Skills, Children and Learning Act 2009 s 100(1)(d).
9   Apprenticeships, Skills, Children and Learning Act 2009 s 100(1)(e).
10 Apprenticeships, Skills, Children and Learning Act 2009 s 100(1)(g).
11 Ie under arrangements made under the Apprenticeships, Skills, Children and Learning Act 2009 s 103 (see PARA 786).
12 Apprenticeships, Skills, Children and Learning Act 2009 s 100(1)(h).
13 Apprenticeships, Skills, Children and Learning Act 2009 s 100(1)(j).
14 Ie under the Apprenticeships, Skills, Children and Learning Act 2009 s 100(1A).
15 Ie under the Apprenticeships, Skills, Children and Learning Act 2009 s 100(1).
16 As to the meaning of 'approved English apprenticeship' see PARA 760 (definition applied by the Apprenticeships, Skills, Children and Learning Act 2009 s 121(1) (amended by the Deregulation Act 2015 Sch 1 paras 5, 22(b)).
17 Apprenticeships, Skills, Children and Learning Act 2009 s 100(1A)(a) (s 100(1A) added by the Deregulation Act 2015 Sch 1 paras 2(1), (3)). See also the Apprenticeships, Skills, Children and Learning Act 2009 s 100(4); and note 6.
18 Apprenticeships, Skills, Children and Learning Act 2009 s 100(1A(b) (as added: see note 17).
19 Ie under the Apprenticeships, Skills, Children and Learning Act 2009 s 100(1) or (1A).
20 Apprenticeships, Skills, Children and Learning Act 2009 s 100(3)(a) (s 100(3) amended by the Deregulation Act 2015 Sch 1 para 2(1), (3), Sch 14 paras 1, 13(1), (3)).
21 Apprenticeships, Skills, Children and Learning Act 2009 s 100(3)(b).
22 Apprenticeships, Skills, Children and Learning Act 2009 s 100(3)(c) (as amended: see note 20).

784.   Conditions on the provision of financial resources by the Secretary of State. Financial resources provided by the Secretary of State[1] may be provided subject to conditions[2]. The conditions may (among other things) include:
(1)   information conditions[3], namely conditions which:

(a) require the Secretary of State, or a person[4] designated by the Secretary of State, to be given access to a person's accounts and documents and to be given rights in relation to a person's computers and associated apparatus and material[5]; or

(b) require a person to whom financial resources are provided to give to the Secretary of State such information as he may request for the purpose of carrying out the relevant functions[6];

(2) repayment conditions[7], namely conditions which:

(a) enable the Secretary of State to require the repayment (in whole or part) of sums paid by him if any of the conditions subject to which the sums were paid is not complied with[8];

(b) require the payment of interest in respect of any period in which a sum due to the Secretary of State in accordance with any condition is unpaid[9].

1 Ie by the Secretary of State under the Apprenticeships, Skills, Children and Learning Act 2009 s 100: see PARA 783. As to the Secretary of State see PARA 58.
2 Apprenticeships, Skills, Children and Learning Act 2009 s 101(1) (amended by the Deregulation Act 2015 Sch 14 paras 1, 14(1), (2)).
3 See the Apprenticeships, Skills, Children and Learning Act 2009 s 101(2)(a) (s 100(2) amended by the Deregulation Act 2015 Sch 1 para 3(1), (2)).
4 As to the meaning of 'person' see PARA 7 note 6.
5 Apprenticeships, Skills, Children and Learning Act 2009 s 101(3)(a) (amended by the Deregulation Act 2015 Sch 14 paras 1, 14(1), (3)(a)).
6 Apprenticeships, Skills, Children and Learning Act 2009 s 101(3)(b) (amended by the Deregulation Act 2015 Sch 14 paras 1, 14(1), (3)(b)). The reference in the text to 'relevant functions' is a reference to functions under the Apprenticeships, Skills, Children and Learning Act 2009 Pt 4 (ss 83–121): see PARA 776 note 1.
7 See the Apprenticeships, Skills, Children and Learning Act 2009 s 101(2)(c).
8 Apprenticeships, Skills, Children and Learning Act 2009 s 101(6)(a) (amended by the Deregulation Act 2015 Sch 14 paras 1, 14(1), (3)(b)).
9 Apprenticeships, Skills, Children and Learning Act 2009 s 101(6)(b) (amended by the Deregulation Act 2015 Sch 14 paras 1, 14(1), (3)(b)).

785. Performance assessments of persons providing education or training. The Secretary of State[1] may adopt or develop schemes for the assessment of the performance of persons[2] in providing education or training within the Secretary of State's remit[3]. The Secretary of State may take the assessments into account in deciding how to exercise his powers[4] to secure the provision of financial resources[5].

1 As to the Secretary of State see PARA 58.
2 As to the meaning of 'person' see PARA 7 note 6.
3 Apprenticeships, Skills, Children and Learning Act 2009 s 102(1) (amended by the Deregulation Act 2015 Sch 14 paras 1, 15(1), (2)). The reference in the text is the Secretary of State's remit under the Apprenticeships, Skills, Children and Learning Act 2009 Pt 4 (ss 83–121). As to the meanings of 'education within the Secretary of State's remit under Pt 4' and 'training within the Secretary of State's remit' see PARA 781 note 5.
4 Ie under the Apprenticeships, Skills, Children and Learning Act 2009 s 100 (see PARA 783).
5 Apprenticeships, Skills, Children and Learning Act 2009 s 102(2) (amended by the Deregulation Act 2015 Sch 14 paras 1, 15(1), (3)).

786. Means tests carried out by the Secretary of State. For the purpose of the exercise of certain powers[1], the Secretary of State[2] may carry out means tests[3], and arrange for other persons[4] to carry out means tests[5].

1 Ie for the purpose of the exercise of the exercise of the powers under the Apprenticeships, Skills, Children and Learning Act 2009 s 100(1)(c), (d) or (e) or s 100(1A): see PARA 783.
2 As to the Secretary of State see PARA 58.

3 Apprenticeships, Skills, Children and Learning Act 2009 s 103(1)(a) (s 102(1) amended by the Deregulation Act 2015 Sch 1 para 4, Sch 14 paras 1, 16(1), (2)).
4 As to the meaning of 'person' see PARA 7 note 6.
5 Apprenticeships, Skills, Children and Learning Act 2009 s 103(1)(b).

C. EFFICIENCY STUDIES

787. Secretary of State to arrange efficiency studies. The Secretary of State[1] may arrange for efficiency studies[2] to be promoted or carried out by any person[3] in respect of an institution in England[4] within the further education sector[5]. A person promoting or carrying out efficiency studies at the request of the Secretary of State may require the governing body[6] of the institution concerned to furnish the person, or any person authorised by him, with such information[7], and to make available to him, or any person so authorised, for inspection the governing body's accounts and such other documents[8], as the person may reasonably require for that purpose[9].

1 As to the Secretary of State see PARA 58.
2 As to the meaning of 'efficiency studies' see PARA 603 note 7.
3 As to the meaning of 'person' see PARA 7 note 6.
4 As to the meaning of 'England' see PARA 7 note 3.
5 See the Further and Higher Education Act 1992 s 83(1), (1B) (s 83(1) substituted by, and s 83(1B) added by, SI 2010/1080; and the Further and Higher Education Act 1992 s 83(1B) amended by the Deregulation Act 2015 Sch 14 paras 36, 40). As to the meaning of 'institution within the further education sector' see PARA 555. As from a day to be appointed the Further and Higher Education Act 1992 s 83(1B) is further amended: s 83(1B) (prospectively amended by the Higher Education (Wales) Act 2015 Schedule paras 1, 3). At the date at which this volume states the law no such day had been appointed. See generally PARA 721.
6 As to the meaning of 'governing body' see PARA 560 note 6.
7 Further and Higher Education Act 1992 s 83(2)(a) (amended by SI 2010/1080).
8 Further and Higher Education Act 1992 s 83(2)(b).
9 Further and Higher Education Act 1992 s 83(2).

D. INFORMATION SHARING

788. Sharing of information for education and training purposes. A specified person[1] may provide information to another such person, or to a local authority in England[2] or a person providing services to a local authority in England in connection with its education functions[3], for the purpose of enabling or facilitating the exercise of any relevant function[4]; and a local authority in England or a person providing services to a local authority in England in connection with its education functions may provide information to a specified person for the purpose of enabling or facilitating the exercise of any relevant function[5]. The specified persons are:

(1)   the Secretary of State[6];

(2)   a person providing services to the Secretary of State[7].

Nothing in these provisions affects any power to disclose information that otherwise[8] exists[9], or authorises the disclosure of any information in contravention of any provision made by or under any Act which prevents disclosure of the information[10].

1 As to the meaning of 'person' see PARA 7 note 6.
2 See the Apprenticeships, Skills, Children and Learning Act 2009 s 122(1), (4)(a) (amended by SI 2010/1158). As to the meaning of 'local authority in England' see PARA 25 (definition applied by the Apprenticeships, Skills, Children and Learning Act 2009 s 264(2), (3)).

3   See the Apprenticeships, Skills, Children and Learning Act 2009 s 122(1), (4)(b) (amended by SI 2010/1158). As to the meaning of 'education functions' see PARA 25 (definition applied by the Apprenticeships, Skills, Children and Learning Act 2009 s 264(2), (3)).

4   Apprenticeships, Skills, Children and Learning Act 2009 s 122(1). 'Relevant function' means: (1) any function of the Secretary of State relating to education or training (s 122(5)(b) (amended by the Education Act 2011 Sch 16 para 48(3))); or (2) any education function of a local authority in England (Apprenticeships, Skills, Children and Learning Act 2009 s 122(5)(c) (substituted by SI 2010/1158)), other than a function under the Apprenticeships, Skills, Children and Learning Act 2009 s 122 (s 122(5)). As to the meaning of 'function' see PARA 18 note 5 (definition applied by s 264(2), (3)). As to the Secretary of State see PARA 58.

5   See the Apprenticeships, Skills, Children and Learning Act 2009 s 122(2), (4) (amended by SI 2010/1158).

6   Apprenticeships, Skills, Children and Learning Act 2009 s 122(3)(b) (substituted by the Education Act 2011 Sch 16 para 48(2)).

7   Apprenticeships, Skills, Children and Learning Act 2009 s 122(3)(f) (amended by the Deregulation Act 2012 Sch 14 paras 1, 28(b)).

8   Ie apart from the Apprenticeships, Skills, Children and Learning Act 2009 s 122.

9   Apprenticeships, Skills, Children and Learning Act 2009 s 122(7)(a).

10 Apprenticeships, Skills, Children and Learning Act 2009 s 122(7)(b).

(ii) Provision of Facilities etc in Wales

A. PROVISION OF FACILITIES FOR EDUCATION AND TRAINING

789.   Education and training for persons aged 16 to 19, and for persons over 19. The Welsh Ministers[1] must secure the provision of proper facilities[2] for: (1) education[3], other than higher education[4], suitable to the requirements of persons who are above compulsory school age[5] but have not attained the age of 19[6]; (2) training[7] suitable to the requirements of such persons[8]; (3) organised leisure-time occupation connected with such education[9]; and (4) organised leisure-time occupation connected with such training[10].

The Welsh Ministers must also secure the provision of reasonable facilities for[11]: (a) education, other than higher education, suitable to the requirements of persons who have attained the age of 19[12]; (b) training suitable to the requirements of such persons[13]; (c) organised leisure-time occupation connected with such education[14]; and (d) organised leisure-time occupation connected with such training[15].

In performing these duties, the Welsh Ministers must[16]:

(i)   take account of the places where facilities are provided, the character of facilities and the way they are equipped[17];

(ii)   take account of the different abilities and aptitudes of different persons[18];

(iii)   take account of the education and training required in different sectors of employment for employees and potential employees[19];

(iv)   take account of facilities whose provision the Welsh Ministers think might reasonably be secured by other persons[20].

1   As to the Welsh Ministers see PARA 59. In exercising their functions under the Learning and Skills Act 2000 ss 31, 32 the Welsh Ministers must have regard to the needs of persons with learning difficulties: see s 41; and PARA 791.

2   Learning and Skills Act 2000 s 31(1) (amended by the Learning and Skills (Wales) Measure 2009 s 47, Schedule paras 1, 4(a); and SI 2005/3238). Facilities are proper if they are of a quantity sufficient to meet the reasonable needs of individuals (Learning and Skills Act 2000 s 31(2)(a)), of a quality adequate to meet those needs (s 31(2)(b)), and sufficient to satisfy the entitlements conferred under s 33F (see PARA 897) (s 31(2)(c) (added by the Learning and Skills (Wales) Measure 2009 s 21(1), (2)(c))).

3 For the purposes of the Learning and Skills Act 2000 ss 31, 32, education includes both full-time and part-time education: ss 31(5)(a), 32(5)(a).
4 For the purposes of the Learning and Skills Act 2000 ss 31, 32, 'higher education' is education provided by means of a course of any description mentioned in the Education Reform Act 1988 Sch 6 (see PARA 684): Learning and Skills Act 2000 ss 31(5)(d), 32(5)(d).
5 As to the meaning of 'compulsory school age' see PARA 19.
6 Learning and Skills Act 2000 s 31(1)(a). As to the time at which a person attains a particular age see PARA 7 note 6.
7 For the purposes of the Learning and Skills Act 2000 ss 31, 32, training includes both full-time and part-time training, and vocational, social, physical and recreational training: ss 31(5)(b), (c), 32(5)(b), (c).
8 Learning and Skills Act 2000 s 31(1)(b).
9 Learning and Skills Act 2000 s 31(1)(c).
10 Learning and Skills Act 2000 s 31(1)(d).
11 Learning and Skills Act 2000 s 32(1) (amended by the Learning and Skills (Wales) Measure 2009 s 47, Schedule paras 1, 3; and SI 2005/3238).
12 Learning and Skills Act 2000 s 32(1)(a).
13 Learning and Skills Act 2000 s 32(1)(b).
14 Learning and Skills Act 2000 s 32(1)(c).
15 Learning and Skills Act 2000 s 32(1)(d).
16 Learning and Skills Act 2000 ss 31(3), 32(3) (both amended by the Learning and Skills (Wales) Measure 2009 s 47, Schedule paras 1, 4, 5; and SI 2005/3238).
17 Learning and Skills Act 2000 ss 31(3)(a), 32(3)(a).
18 Learning and Skills Act 2000 ss 31(3)(b), 32(3)(b).
19 Learning and Skills Act 2000 ss 31(3)(c), 32(3)(c).
20 Learning and Skills Act 2000 ss 31(3)(d), 32(3)(d) (both amended by the Learning and Skills (Wales) Measure 2009 s 47, Schedule paras 1, 4, 5; and SI 2005/3238). As to the meaning of 'person' see PARA 7 note 6.

790. Encouragement of education and training. The Welsh Ministers must[1] encourage individuals to undergo post-16 education and training[2], encourage employers to participate in the provision of post-16 education and training[3], and encourage employers to contribute to the costs of post-16 education and training[4].

1 Learning and Skills Act 2000 s 33 (amended by the Learning and Skills (Wales) Measure 2009 s 47, Schedule paras 1, 3; and SI 2005/3238). As to the Welsh Ministers see PARA 59.
2 Learning and Skills Act 2000 s 33(a). References in Pt II (ss 31–41) to 'post-16 education' are to education falling within s 31(1)(a) or s 32(1)(a) (see PARA 789) (s 32(6)(a)), and organised leisure-time occupation connected with such education (s 32(6)(b)). References in Pt II to 'post-16 training' are to training falling within s 31(1)(b) or s 32(1)(b) (see PARA 789) (s 32(7)(a)), and organised leisure-time occupation connected with such training (s 32(7)(b)).
3 Learning and Skills Act 2000 s 33(b).
4 Learning and Skills Act 2000 s 33(c).

791. Persons with learning difficulties. In discharging their functions in relation to education and training for persons aged 16 to 19[1], education and training for persons over 19[2], and the provision of financial resources[3], the Welsh Ministers[4] must have regard[5] to the needs of persons with learning difficulties[6], and in particular, to any report of an assessment[7] relating to learning difficulties[8].

If the Welsh Ministers are satisfied that they cannot secure the provision of facilities for education or training which are sufficient in quantity and adequate in quality for a person with a learning difficulty who is over compulsory school age[9] but who has not attained the age of 19[10] unless they also secure the provision of boarding accommodation for him, they must secure the provision of boarding accommodation for him[11]. If the Welsh Ministers are satisfied that they cannot secure the provision of reasonable facilities for education or training for a person with a learning difficulty who has attained the age of 19 but not the age of 25 unless they also secure the provision of boarding accommodation for him, they must secure the provision of boarding accommodation for him[12]; and if the Welsh Ministers are satisfied that they cannot secure the provision of reasonable facilities for education or training for a person with a learning difficulty who has attained the age of 25 unless they also secure the provision of boarding accommodation for him, they may secure the provision of boarding accommodation for him[13].

1 Ie under the Learning and Skills Act 2000 s 31 (see PARA 789).
2 Ie under the Learning and Skills Act 2000 s 32 (see PARA 789).
3 Ie under the Learning and Skills Act 2000 s 34(1)(a)–(d), (g) (see PARA 792).
4 As to the Welsh Ministers see PARA 59.
5 Learning and Skills Act 2000 s 41(1) (amended by the Learning and Skills (Wales) Measure 2009 s 47, Schedule paras 1, 3; and SI 2005/3238).
6 Learning and Skills Act 2000 s 41(1)(a). A person has a learning difficulty if: (1) he has a significantly greater difficulty in learning than the majority of persons of his age (s 41(5)(a)); or (2) he has a disability which either prevents or hinders him from making use of facilities of a kind generally provided by institutions providing post-16 education or training (s 41(5)(b)). However, a person is not to be taken to have a learning difficulty solely because the language, or form of language, in which he is or will be taught is different from a language, or form of language, which has at any time been spoken in his home: s 41(6). As to the meanings of 'post-16 education' and 'post-16 training' see PARA 790 note 2. As to learning difficulties which call for special educational provision ('special educational needs') see PARA 989 et seq.
7 Ie conducted under the Learning and Skills Act 2000 s 140 (see PARA 998).
8 Learning and Skills Act 2000 s 41(1)(b) (amended by the Education and Skills Act 2008 s 169, Sch 1 Pt 2 paras 75, 76(d); and the Children and Families Act 2014 s 82, Sch 3 paras 71, 73.). See R (on the application of Hill) v Further Education Funding Council (18 December 2000, unreported), CA (decided under previous legislation in relation to a similar duty of the predecessor body).
9 As to the meaning of 'compulsory school age' see PARA 19.
10 As to the time at which a person attains a particular age see PARA 7 note 6.
11 Learning and Skills Act 2000 s 41(2) (amended by the Learning and Skills (Wales) Measure 2009 Schedule paras 1, 10; and SI 2005/3238).
12 Learning and Skills Act 2000 s 41(3) (amended by the Learning and Skills (Wales) Measure 2009 Schedule paras 1, 10; and SI 2005/3238;).
13 Learning and Skills Act 2000 s 41(4) (amended by the Learning and Skills (Wales) Measure 2009 Schedule paras 1, 10; and SI 2005/3238).

B. PROVISION OF FINANCIAL RESOURCES

792. Provision of financial resources for education and training. The Welsh Ministers[1] may secure the provision of financial resources to[2]:

(1) persons[3] providing or proposing to provide post-16 education or training[4];

(2) persons providing or proposing to provide goods or services in connection with the provision by others of post-16 education or training[5];

(3) persons receiving or proposing to receive post-16 education or training[6];

(4) persons providing or proposing to provide courses[7] in preparation for professional examinations at a higher level or providing education at a higher level[8];

(5) institutions within the further or higher education sector[9] which provide or propose to provide secondary education[10] (other than post-16 education)[11];

(6) persons undertaking or proposing to undertake research relating to education or training[12];

(7)   persons providing or proposing to provide facilities designed to form links between employers and persons who provide or receive education or training[13];

(8)   persons carrying out[14] means tests[15];

(9)   persons providing or proposing to provide information, advice or guidance about education or training or connected matters (including employment)[16].

The Welsh Ministers may secure the provision of financial resources under these provisions by providing resources themselves[17], by making arrangements for the provision of resources by another person[18], or by making arrangements for the provision of resources by persons jointly (whether or not including the Welsh Ministers)[19].

1   As to the Welsh Ministers see PARA 59.
2   Learning and Skills Act 2000 s 34(1) (amended by the Learning and Skills (Wales) Measure 2009 s 47, Schedule paras 1, 3; and SI 2005/3238).
3   As to the meaning of 'person' see PARA 7 note 6.
4   Learning and Skills Act 2000 s 34(1)(a). As to the meanings of 'post-16 education' and 'post-16 training' see PARA 790 note 2. In discharging their functions under s 34(1)(a), the Welsh Ministers must have regard to the needs of persons with learning difficulties: see s 41; and PARA 791.
5   Learning and Skills Act 2000 s 34(1)(b). In discharging their functions under s 34(1)(b), the Welsh Ministers must have regard to the needs of persons with learning difficulties: see s 41; and PARA 791.
6   Learning and Skills Act 2000 s 34(1)(c). In exercising their powers under s 34(1)(c), the Welsh Ministers may secure the provision of financial resources by reference to any fees or charges payable by the person receiving or proposing to receive the education or training or to any other matter, such as transport or childcare: s 34(3) (amended by the Learning and Skills (Wales) Measure 2009 Schedule paras 1, 3, 6; and SI 2005/3238). In discharging their functions under the Learning and Skills Act 2000 s 34(1)(c), the Welsh Ministers must have regard to the needs of persons with learning difficulties: see s 41; and PARA 791.
7   Ie courses falling within the Education Reform Act 1988 Sch 6 para 1(g) or para 1(h) (see PARA 684).
8   Learning and Skills Act 2000 s 34(1)(d). In discharging their functions under s 34(1)(d), the Welsh Ministers must have regard to the needs of persons with learning difficulties: see s 41; and PARA 791.
9   As to the meaning of 'institution within the further education sector' see PARA 555; and as to the meaning of 'institution within the higher education sector' see PARA 619 (definitions applied by the Learning and Skills Act 2000 s 34(1)(e)).
10 As to secondary education see PARA 21.
11 Learning and Skills Act 2000 s 34(1)(e).
12 Learning and Skills Act 2000 s 34(1)(f).
13 Learning and Skills Act 2000 s 34(1)(g). In discharging their functions under s 34(1)(g), the Welsh Ministers must have regard to the needs of persons with learning difficulties: see s 41; and PARA 791.
14 Ie under arrangements made under the Learning and Skills Act 2000 s 37 (see PARA 795).
15 Learning and Skills Act 2000 s 34(1)(h).
16 Learning and Skills Act 2000 s 34(1)(i).
17 Learning and Skills Act 2000 s 34(2)(a) (amended by the Learning and Skills (Wales) Measure 2009 Schedule paras 1, 6; and SI 2005/3238). As to the imposition of conditions for the provision of financial resources by the Welsh Ministers see PARA 793.
18 Learning and Skills Act 2000 s 34(2)(b).
19 Learning and Skills Act 2000 s 34(2)(c) (amended by the Learning and Skills (Wales) Measure 2009 Schedule paras 1, 3; and SI 2005/3238).

793.   Conditions for the provision of financial resources for education and training.   If the Welsh Ministers[1] themselves provide financial resources[2], they may impose conditions, which may include any of the following provisions[3].

The conditions may:

(1)   require the Welsh Ministers or a person[4] designated by them to be allowed access to a person's accounts and documents and to be given rights in relation to a person's computers and associated apparatus and material[5];

(2)   require a person to whom financial resources are provided to give to the Welsh Ministers information they request for the purpose of carrying out their functions[6] relating to further and sixth-form education[7].

The conditions may also require a person providing or proposing to provide education or training (the 'provider') to make arrangements providing for all or any of the following:

(a)   for the provider to charge fees by reference to specified criteria[8];

(b)   for the provider to make awards by reference to specified criteria[9];

(c)   for the provider to recover amounts from persons receiving education or training or from employers, or from both[10];

(d)   for amounts to be determined by reference to specified criteria where provision is made under head (c) above[11];

(e)   for specified exemptions to operate where provision is made under head (c) above[12];

(f)   for the provider to make provision specified in a report of an assessment[13] relating to learning difficulties[14].

The conditions may enable the Welsh Ministers to require the repayment (in whole or part) of sums paid by them if any of the conditions subject to which the sums were paid is not complied with[15]; and the conditions may require the payment of interest in respect of any period in which a sum due to the Welsh Ministers in accordance with any condition is unpaid[16].

1   As to the Welsh Ministers see PARA 59.
2   Ie under the Learning and Skills Act 2000 s 34: see PARA 792.
3   Learning and Skills Act 2000 s 35(1) (amended by the Learning and Skills (Wales) Measure 2009 s 47, Schedule paras 1, 7; and SI 2005/3238;).
4   As to the meaning of 'person' see PARA 7 note 6.
5   Learning and Skills Act 2000 s 35(2)(a) (amended by the Learning and Skills (Wales) Measure 2009 Schedule paras 1, 3, 7; and SI 2005/3238).
6   Ie under the Learning and Skills Act 2000 Pt II (ss 31–41).
7   Learning and Skills Act 2000 s 35(2)(b) (amended by the Learning and Skills (Wales) Measure 2009 Schedule paras 1, 3, 7; and SI 2005/3238).
8   Learning and Skills Act 2000 s 35(3)(a).
9   Learning and Skills Act 2000 s 35(3)(b).
10 Learning and Skills Act 2000 s 35(3)(c).
11 Learning and Skills Act 2000 s 35(3)(d).
12 Learning and Skills Act 2000 s 35(3)(e).
13 Ie an assessment conducted under the Learning and Skills Act 2000 s 140 (see PARA 998).
14 Learning and Skills Act 2000 s 35(3)(f) (amended by the Education and Skills Act 2008 s 169, Sch 1 Pt 2 paras 75, 76(c); and the Children and Families Act 2014 Sch 3 para 72).
15 Learning and Skills Act 2000 s 35(5)(a) (amended by the Learning and Skills (Wales) Measure 2009 Schedule paras 1, 3; and SI 2005/3238).
16 Learning and Skills Act 2000 s 35(5)(b) (amended by the Learning and Skills (Wales) Measure 2009 Schedule paras 1, 3; and SI 2005/3238).

794.   Funding of school sixth forms.   The Welsh Ministers[1] may make a grant to a local authority[2]:

(1)   on the condition that the grant be applied as part of the authority's schools budget[3] for a funding period[4]; and

(2)   with a view to the grant being used for the purposes of, or for purposes connected with, the provision by schools of education suitable to the requirements of persons above compulsory school age[5].

1 As to the Welsh Ministers see PARA 59.
2 Learning and Skills Act 2000 s 36(1) (amended by the Learning and Skills (Wales) Measure 2009 s 47, Schedule paras 1–3; SI 2005/3238; and SI 2010/1158). As to the meaning of 'local authority' see PARA 25 (definition applied by the Learning and Skills Act 2000 s 36(3) (substituted by the Education Act 2005 s 117, Sch 18 para 13(1), (3); and amended by SI 2010/1158)).
3 As to the meaning of 'schools budget' see PARA 315 (definition applied by the Learning and Skills Act 2000 s 36(3) (as substituted: see note 2)).
4 Learning and Skills Act 2000 s 36(1)(a) (amended by the Education Act 2002 Sch 21 para 125(1), (2); Education Act 2005 s 117, Sch 18 para 13(1), (2)). A grant made under the Learning and Skills Act 2000 s 36 may be made on conditions in addition to the condition mentioned in s 36(1)(a), including conditions of a kind which could be imposed under s 35 (see PARA 793): s 36(2). 'Funding period' means a financial year or, if some other period is prescribed in relation to Wales under the School Standards and Framework Act 1998 s 45(1B) (see PARA 315), that other period: s 36(3) (as substituted: see note 2).
5 Learning and Skills Act 2000 s 36(1)(b). As to the meaning of 'compulsory school age' see PARA 19.

795.   Assessments and means tests may determine provision of financial resources for education and training.   The Welsh Ministers[1] may develop schemes for the assessment of the performance of persons[2] in providing post-16 education and training[3]; and may take the assessments into account in deciding how to exercise their powers[4] in relation to the provision of financial resources[5].

The Welsh Ministers may[6] carry out means tests[7], or arrange for other persons to carry out means tests[8]; and may take the results of the tests into account in exercising their power[9] to provide financial resources to persons receiving or proposing to receive post-16 education or training[10].

1 As to the Welsh Ministers see PARA 59.
2 As to the meaning of 'person' see PARA 7 note 6.
3 Learning and Skills Act 2000 s 37(1) (amended by the Learning and Skills (Wales) Measure 2009 s 47, Schedule paras 1–3; and SI 2005/3238). As to the meanings of 'post-16 education' and 'post-16 training' see PARA 790 note 2.
4 Ie under the Learning and Skills Act 2000 s 34 (see PARA 792).
5 Learning and Skills Act 2000 s 37(2) (amended by the Learning and Skills (Wales) Measure 2009 Schedule paras 1–3, 8; and SI 2005/3238).
6 Learning and Skills Act 2000 s 37(3) (amended by the Learning and Skills (Wales) Measure 2009 Schedule paras 1–3; and SI 2005/3238).
7 Learning and Skills Act 2000 s 37(3)(a).
8 Learning and Skills Act 2000 s 37(3)(b).
9 Ie under the Learning and Skills Act 2000 s 34(1)(c) (see PARA 792).
10 See the Learning and Skills Act 2000 s 37(4) (amended by the Learning and Skills (Wales) Measure 2009 Schedule paras 1–3, 8; and SI 2005/3238).

796.   Qualifying accounts and arrangements.   The Welsh Ministers[1] may promote[2] the holding of qualifying accounts[3], and the making of qualifying arrangements[4].

1 As to the Welsh Ministers see PARA 59.
2 Learning and Skills Act 2000 s 38(1) (amended by the Learning and Skills (Wales) Measure 2009 s 47, Schedule paras 1–3; and SI 2005/3238).
3 Learning and Skills Act 2000 s 38(1)(a). The reference in the text to qualifying accounts is to those accounts which qualify under the Learning and Skills Act 2000 s 104 (see PARA 818).
4 Learning and Skills Act 2000 s 38(1)(b). The reference in the text to qualifying arrangements is to those arrangements which qualify under the Learning and Skills Act 2000 s 105 (see PARA 818).

C. INFORMATION AND STUDIES

797. Information about education and training. The Welsh Ministers[1] must establish systems for collecting information which is designed to secure that their decisions with regard to education and training are made on a sound basis[2].

The Welsh Ministers may secure the provision of facilities for providing information, advice or guidance about education or training or connected matters (including employment)[3].

1   As to the Welsh Ministers see PARA 59.
2   Learning and Skills Act 2000 s 40(5) (amended by the Learning and Skills (Wales) Measure 2009 s 47, Schedule paras 1–3, 9).
3   Learning and Skills Act 2000 s 40(6) (amended by the Learning and Skills (Wales) Measure 2009 Schedule paras 1–3).

798. Efficiency studies in respect of an institution in Wales. The Welsh Ministers[1] may arrange for efficiency studies[2] to be promoted or carried out by any person[3] in respect of an institution in Wales[4] within the further education sector[5]. A person promoting or carrying out efficiency studies at the request of the Welsh Ministers may require the governing body[6] of the institution concerned to furnish the person, or any person authorised by him, with such information[7], and to make available to him, or any person so authorised, for inspection the governing body's accounts and such other documents[8], as the person may reasonably require for that purpose[9].

1   As to the Welsh Ministers see PARA 59.
2   As to the meaning of 'efficiency studies' see PARA 603 note 8.
3   As to the meaning of 'person' see PARA 7 note 6.
4   As to the meaning of 'Wales' see PARA 7 note 3.
5   See the Further and Higher Education Act 1992 s 83(1), (1B) (s 83(1) substituted by, and s 83(1B) added by, SI 2010/1080; and the Further and Higher Education Act 1992 s 83(1B) amended by the Deregulation Act 2015 Sch 14 paras 36, 40). As to the meaning of 'institution within the further education sector' see PARA 555. As from a day to be appointed the Further and Higher Education Act 1992 s 83(1B) is further amended: s 83(1B) (prospectively amended by the Higher Education (Wales) Act 2015 Schedule paras 1, 3). At the date at which this volume states the law no such day had been appointed. See generally PARA 721.
6   As to the meaning of 'governing body' see PARA 560 note 6.
7   Further and Higher Education Act 1992 s 83(2)(a) (amended by SI 2010/1080).
8   Further and Higher Education Act 1992 s 83(2)(b).
9   Further and Higher Education Act 1992 s 83(2).

(iii) Provision of Services

799. Provision of services required in connection with the exercise of functions relating to education or training. The Secretary of State[1] may make arrangements with a permitted recipient[2] for the provision by the Secretary of State of services that are required by the permitted recipient in connection with the exercise of the recipient's functions relating to education or training[3]. The services that may be provided under such arrangements include: (1) providing accommodation and other facilities to a permitted recipient or managing such facilities on behalf of a permitted recipient[4]; (2) procuring, or assisting in procuring, goods and services for use by a permitted recipient[5]. The terms and conditions upon which the arrangements are made may include provision for making payments to the Secretary of State in respect of expenditure incurred by the Secretary of State in performing any function under the arrangements[6].

Before making arrangements under which he may provide services to a permitted recipient who falls within certain descriptions[7] in connection with the exercise of the recipient's functions relating to education or training provided in Wales, Scotland or Northern Ireland, the Secretary of State must obtain: (a) in relation to education or training provided in Wales, the consent of the Welsh Ministers[8]; (b) in relation to education or training provided in Scotland, the consent of the Scottish Ministers[9]; (c) in relation to education or training provided in Northern Ireland, the consent of the Minister for Employment and Learning in Northern Ireland[10]. Consent may be given[11] in relation to particular arrangements or arrangements of a particular description[12].

1   As to the Secretary of State see PARA 58.
2   'Permitted recipient' means the: (1) the Welsh Ministers (Apprenticeships, Skills, Children and Learning Act 2009 s 107(4)(b)); (2) the Scottish Ministers (s 107(4)(c)); (3) a Northern Ireland department (s 107(4)(d)); (4) a person, wholly or partly funded from public funds, who has functions relating to education or training (s 107(4)(f)); (5) any other person specified, or of a description specified, by order made by the appropriate national authority for these purposes (s 107(4)(g)). At the date at which this volume states the law no such order had been made. 'The appropriate national authority' means: (a) in relation to a person exercising functions relating only to education or training provided in Wales, the Welsh Ministers (s 107(8)(a)); (b) in relation to a person exercising functions relating only to education or training provided in Scotland, the Scottish Ministers (s 107(8)(b)); (c) in relation to a person exercising functions relating only to education or training provided in Northern Ireland, the Department for Employment and Learning in Northern Ireland (s 107(8)(c)); (d) in any other case, the Secretary of State (s 107(8)(d)). As to the Secretary of State see PARA 58. As to the Welsh Ministers see PARA 59. As to the Scottish Ministers, and as to devolved government in Northern Ireland, see CONSTITUTIONAL AND ADMINISTRATIVE LAW vol 20 (2014) PARAS 67, 83 et seq. As to the meaning of 'person' see PARA 7 note 6. As to the meaning of 'functions' see PARA 18 note 5 (definition applied by s 264(2), (3)). As to the meaning of 'Wales' see PARA 7 note 3.
3   Apprenticeships, Skills, Children and Learning Act 2009 s 107(1) (s 107(1), (3) amended by the Deregulation Act 2015 Sch 14 paras 1, 19(1), (2)).
4   Apprenticeships, Skills, Children and Learning Act 2009 s 107(2)(a).
5   Apprenticeships, Skills, Children and Learning Act 2009 s 107(2)(b).
6   Apprenticeships, Skills, Children and Learning Act 2009 s 107(3) (as amended: see note 3).
7   Ie a permitted recipient who falls within the Apprenticeships, Skills, Children and Learning Act 2009 s 107(4)(a), (e), (f) or (g) (see note 2).
8   Apprenticeships, Skills, Children and Learning Act 2009 s 107(6)(a) (s 10(6) amended by the Deregulation Act 2015 Sch 14 paras 1, 19(1), (6)).
9   Apprenticeships, Skills, Children and Learning Act 2009 s 107(6)(b).
10 Apprenticeships, Skills, Children and Learning Act 2009 s 107(6)(c).
11 Ie under the Apprenticeships, Skills, Children and Learning Act 2009 s 107(5) or (6) (see the text to notes 7–12).
12 Apprenticeships, Skills, Children and Learning Act 2009 s 107(7).

(iv) Joint Exercise of Functions

800. Joint exercise of functions. Any relevant authority[1] may exercise any of its functions[2] jointly with another relevant authority or the Secretary of State[3], where it appears to the persons who are to exercise functions jointly that to do so will be more efficient, or will enable them more effectively to discharge any of their functions[4].

A relevant authority must, if directed to do so[5], make provision jointly with another relevant authority or with the Secretary of State for the assessment by a person[6] appointed by them of matters relating to the arrangements made by each institution in Great Britain[7] which is within the higher education sector[8] for maintaining academic standards in the institution[9].

1   As to the meaning of 'relevant authority' see PARA 690 note 5.

2   As to the meaning of 'functions' see PARA 18 note 5 (definition applied by the Further and
    Higher Education Act 1992 s 90(5) (amended by the Education Act 1996 Sch 37 para 115(3);
    and the School Standards and Framework Act 1998 Sch 30 para 36(b)).
3   Ie to the extent that the Secretary of State is discharging functions under the Education Act 2002
    s 14 (see PARA 78). The Secretary of State may exercise functions under the Education Act 2002
    s 14 jointly with a relevant authority where it appears to the persons who are to discharge
    functions jointly that to do so will be more efficient, or will enable them more effectively to
    discharge any of their functions: Further and Higher Education Act 1992 s 82(1A), (1B)
    (s 82(1A), (1B) added by the Education Act 2011 Sch 12 paras 1, 36). As to the Secretary of
    State see PARA 58.
       The functions of the Secretary of State under the Further and Higher Education Act 1992
    s 82, so far as exercisable in relation to Wales, are only exercisable after consultation with the
    Welsh Minsters: see the National Assembly for Wales (Transfer of Functions) Order 1999,
    SI 1999/672, art 5, Sch 2; and the Government of Wales Act 2006 s 162(1), Sch 11 para 30. As
    to the Welsh Ministers see PARA 59. As to the meaning of 'Wales' see PARA 7 note 3.
       As to the transfer of functions of the Secretary of State, so far as exercisable in relation to
    Wales, to the National Assembly for Wales and then to the Welsh Ministers see the National
    Assembly for Wales (Transfer of Functions) Order 1999, SI 1999/672, art 2, Sch 1; and the
    Government of Wales Act 2006 s 162(1), Sch 11 para 30.
4   Further and Higher Education Act 1992 s 82(1), (1B) (s 82(1) substituted by the Education
    Act 2011 Sch 12 para 36); Further and Higher Education Act 1992 s 82(1B) (as added: see
    note 3).
5   As to directions see the Education Act 1996 s 570 (applied by the Further and Higher Education
    Act 1992 s 89(5)); and PARA 75.
6   As to the meaning of 'person' see PARA 7 note 6.
7   As to the meaning of 'Great Britain' see PARA 73 note 3.
8   References to institutions within the higher education sector include institutions within the
    higher education sector within the meaning of the Further and Higher Education (Scotland)
    Act 1992 Pt II: Further and Higher Education Act 1992 s 82(3)(b). As to the meaning of
    'institution within the higher education sector' generally see PARA 619.
9   Further and Higher Education Act 1992 s 82(2) (amended by the Education Act 2011 Sch 12
    paras 1, 36). The power of the Secretary of State to give directions under the Further and Higher
    Education Act 1992 s 82(2) must, as regards the Scottish Higher Education Funding Council, be
    treated as exercisable in or as regards Scotland and may be exercised separately: s 82(2A) (added
    by SI 1999/1756).

(v) Use of Information in connection with Assessment of Effectiveness of Education or Training

801. Use of information for assessment functions. Information[1] which:
(1)   is about an individual[2] and is held by the Secretary of State[3] for the
      purposes of any function of the Secretary of State relating to social
      security[4]; or
(2)   is about an individual[5], is held by the Secretary of State or a devolved
      authority[6], and relates to any training or course of education[7]
      undertaken by the individual[8],
may be (a) used in connection with the exercise of an assessment function[9] of the
Secretary of State or a devolved authority[10]; or (b) disclosed to a person for use
in connection with the exercise of an assessment function of the Secretary of
State or a devolved authority[11].

The Commissioners for Her Majesty's Revenue and Customs[12] may disclose
information relating to income tax or tax credits to a person for use in
connection with the exercise of an assessment function of the Secretary of State
or a devolved authority[13].

Information disclosed to a person in reliance on the above powers[14] may be
used by that person only in connection with the exercise of an assessment
function of the Secretary of State or a devolved authority[15]. Where information
about an individual is used in connection with the exercise of an assessment

function of the Secretary of State or a devolved authority[16], so far as is reasonably practicable, the information must not be used in such a way that the identity of the individual is disclosed to, or capable of being discovered by, a person carrying out an evaluation or assessment[17] in relation to that function[18].

A person commits an offence[19] if he discloses information[20] to another otherwise than in connection with the exercise of an assessment function of the Secretary of State or a devolved authority[21], and the information relates to a person whose identity is specified in or can be deduced from the disclosure[22]. It is a defence to prove[23] that a person charged with the offence reasonably believed that the disclosure was lawful[24], or that the information had already and lawfully been made available to the public[25]. A prosecution for such an offence may be instituted in England and Wales only with the consent of the Director of Public Prosecutions[26].

1   Nothing in the Education and Skills Act 2008 ss 87–90 affects the use or disclosure of information by virtue of the Social Security Act 1998 s 3 (see WELFARE BENEFITS AND STATE PENSIONS vol 104 (2014) PARA 546), or any other enactment or rule of law: s 91(2).
2   Education and Skills Act 2008 s 87(2)(a) (amended by the Small Business, Enterprise and Employment Act 2015 s 78(1), (2)(a)).
3   As to the Secretary of State see PARA 58. A reference to the Secretary of State includes a reference to a person providing services to the Secretary of State: Education and Skills Act 2008 s 91(4). As to the meaning of 'person' see PARA 7 note 6.
4   Education and Skills Act 2008 s 87(2)(b).
5   Education and Skills Act 2008 s 87(3)(a) (amended by the Small Business, Enterprise and Employment Act 2015 s 78(1), (2)(a)).
6   Education and Skills Act 2008 s 87(3)(b). The devolved authorities are the Scottish Ministers and the Welsh Ministers: s 91(3). A reference to a devolved authority includes a reference to a person providing services to the authority: s 91(5). As to the Scottish Ministers see CONSTITUTIONAL AND ADMINISTRATIVE LAW vol 20 (2014) PARA 67. As to the Welsh Ministers see PARA 59.
7   A reference to training or education does not include a reference to higher education (within the meaning of the Education Reform Act 1988 (see PARA 24) or the Further and Higher Education (Scotland) Act 1992 s 38): Education and Skills Act 2008 s 91(6).
8   Education and Skills Act 2008 s 87(3)(c) (amended by the Small Business, Enterprise and Employment Act 2015 s 78(1), (2)(b)).
9   'Assessment function' means any of the following functions: (1) evaluating the effectiveness of training or education (Education and Skills Act 2008 s 87(4)(a) (amended by the Small Business, Enterprise and Employment Act 2015 s 78(1), (2)(c))); (2) assessing policy in relation to the provision of training or education (Education and Skills Act 2008 s 87(4)(b) (amended by the Small Business, Enterprise and Employment Act 2015 s 78(1), (2)(d))); (3) assessing policy in relation to social security or employment as it affects the provision of or participation in training or education (Education and Skills Act 2008 s 87(4)(c) (amended by the Small Business, Enterprise and Employment Act 2015 s 78(1), (2)(d))).
10 Education and Skills Act 2008 s 87(1)(a).
11 Education and Skills Act 2008 s 87(1)(b).
12 The reference to the Commissioners for Her Majesty's Revenue and Customs includes a reference to a person authorised by the Commissioners: Education and Skills Act 2008 s 88(2). As to the Commissioners for Her Majesty's Revenue and Customs see INCOME TAXATION vol 58 (2014) PARA 33.
13 Education and Skills Act 2008 s 88(1).
14 Ie in reliance on the Education and Skills Act 2008 s 87(1)(b) or s 88 (see the text to notes 11–13).
15 Education and Skills Act 2008 s 89(1).
16 Ie in reliance on the Education and Skills Act 2008 s 87(1)(a) (see the text to notes 9–10) (s 89(2)(a)), or under s 89(1) (see the text to notes 14–15) (s 89(2)(b)).
17 Ie of a kind mentioned in the Education and Skills Act 2008 s 87(4)(a)–(c) (see note 9).
18 See the Education and Skills Act 2008 s 89(3).
19 A person guilty of such an offence is liable: (1) on conviction on indictment, to imprisonment for a term not exceeding two years or to a fine or to both (Education and Skills Act 2008 s 90(4)(a)); (2) on summary conviction, to imprisonment for a term not exceeding 12 months or

to a fine not exceeding the statutory maximum or to both (s 90(4)(b)). The reference in s 90(4)(b) to 12 months is to be read as a reference to six months in relation to an offence committed in England and Wales before the commencement of the Criminal Justice Act 2003 s 282 (not yet in force): Education and Skills Act 2008 s 90(6). As to the statutory maximum see SENTENCING AND DISPOSITION OF OFFENDERS vol 92 (2010) PARA 140. As to the meanings of 'England' and 'Wales' see PARA 7 note 3.

20 Ie information: (1) used in reliance on the Education and Skills Act 2008 s 87(1)(a) (see the text to notes 9–10) (s 90(1)(a)); or (2) disclosed in reliance on s 87(1)(b) or s 88 (see the text to notes 11–13) (s 90(1)(b)).

21 Education and Skills Act 2008 s 90(2)(a).

22 Education and Skills Act 2008 s 90(2)(b).

23 As to the standard of proof imposed on the accused see CRIMINAL PROCEDURE vol 28 (2010) PARA 466.

24 Education and Skills Act 2008 s 90(3)(a).

25 Education and Skills Act 2008 s 90(3)(b).

26 Education and Skills Act 2008 s 90(5). As to the Director of Public Prosecutions see CRIMINAL PROCEDURE vol 27 (2010) PARA 23.

(5) SUPPORT FOR PARTICIPATION IN EDUCATION OR TRAINING

(i) Provision of Services in England

A. SUPPORT SERVICES

802. Provision of support services by local authorities. A local authority in England[1] must make available to young persons[2] and relevant young adults[3] for whom it is responsible[4] such services[5] as it considers appropriate to encourage, enable or assist the effective participation of those persons in education or training[6]. However, nothing in this provision requires a local authority to make services available to a young person or relevant young adult for whom it is responsible[7] if another local authority in England is also responsible for the person[8], and services are being provided[9] to the person by, or under arrangements made by, the other authority[10].

In carrying out these functions, a local authority must[11] have regard to any guidance issued by the Secretary of State[12].

A local authority in England[13]:

(1) may provide, secure the provision of or participate in the provision of services under arrangements entered into by it with another local authority in pursuance of any function[14] of that other local authority[15]; and

(2) may otherwise[16] provide, secure the provision of or participate in the provision of services for encouraging, enabling or assisting the effective participation in education or training of young persons[17] or relevant young adults[18] (including such persons from other areas)[19].

Nothing in or done under these powers[20] is to be taken to prejudice any powers which a local authority otherwise[21] has with respect to the exercise of its functions[22].

1 As to the meaning of 'local authority in England' see PARA 25 (definition applied by the Education and Skills Act 2008 s 78(1) (amended by SI 2010/1158)).

2 'Young person' means a person who has attained the age of 13 but not the age of 20: Education and Skills Act 2008 s 78(1). As to the time at which a person attains a particular age see PARA 7 note 6.

3 'Relevant young adult' means a person who has attained the age of 20 but not the age of 25, and has special educational needs (within the meaning given by the Education Act 1996 s 579(1) (see

PARAS 943, 989): Education and Skills Act 2008 s 78(1) (definition amended by the Children and Families Act 2014 Sch 3 para 86; and SI 2010/1080).

4   For the purposes of the Education and Skills Act 2008 ss 68–77, a local authority is responsible for any young person or relevant young adult who is: (1) receiving education or training in its area; (2) normally resident in its area; or (3) otherwise within its area: s 78(2) (amended by SI 2010/1158). For the purposes of head (1), 'training' includes vocational, social, physical and recreational training: Education and Skills Act 2008 s 78(3).

5   A local authority makes services available if it provides them, or makes arrangements with another local authority or another person for their provision: Education and Skills Act 2008 s 68(3) (amended by the Education Act 2011 s 28(3)(a)(ii); and SI 2010/1158). As to the meaning of 'person' see PARA 7 note 6.

6   Education and Skills Act 2008 s 68(1) (amended by SI 2010/1158). Her Majesty's Chief Inspector of Education, Children's Services and Skills must, when requested to do so by the Secretary of State, inspect and report on the provision of services in pursuance of the Education and Skills Act 2008 s 68, and may undertake such other inspections of the provision of those services as the Chief Inspector thinks fit: see s 75; and PARA 1287. As to the Secretary of State see PARA 58.

7   Education and Skills Act 2008 s 68(5) (amended by SI 2010/1158).

8   Education and Skills Act 2008 s 68(5)(a) (amended by SI 2010/1158).

9   Ie in exercise of its functions under the Education and Skills Act 2008 s 68(1) (see the text to notes 1–6).

10 Education and Skills Act 2008 s 68(5)(b).

11 Education and Skills Act 2008 s 68(4) (amended by SI 2010/1158).

12 Education and Skills Act 2008 s 68(4)(b).

13 Education and Skills Act 2008 s 70(1) (amended by SI 2010/1158).

14 Ie under the Education and Skills Act 2008 s 68: see the text to notes 1–12.

15 Education and Skills Act 2008 s 70(1)(a) (amended by SI 2010/1158).

16 Ie otherwise than in accordance with the Education and Skills Act 2008 s 68 (see the text to notes 1–12) or s 70(1)(a) (see head (1) in the text).

17 Education and Skills Act 2008 s 70(1)(b)(i).

18 Education and Skills Act 2008 s 70(1)(b)(ii).

19 Education and Skills Act 2008 s 70(1)(b).

20 Ie the Education and Skills Act 2008 ss 68, 70 (see the text to notes 1–19).

21 Ie otherwise than under the Education and Skills Act 2008 ss 68, 70.

22 See the Education and Skills Act 2008 s 70(2) (amended by the Education Act 2011 s 28(3)(b); and SI 2010/1158).

803.   Provision of support on conditional basis.   Services provided[1] for young persons[2] may include the provision of support[3] on a conditional basis[4]. Where support is so provided for a young person on a conditional basis[5]:

(1)   the learning and support agreement must include provision (whether or not in the form of a learning and support condition) relating to the young person's participation in education or training[6];

(2)   the person[7] providing the support (the 'service provider') must consider that providing it on a conditional basis would be desirable in the interests of encouraging, enabling or assisting the young person (a) to fulfil the duty to participate in education or training[8] in a case where the young person is a person to whom[9] that duty applies[10], or (b) in any case, to participate effectively in education or training[11];

(3)   the learning and support conditions must be conditions (a) determined in consultation between the service provider and the young person, having regard to an assessment of the young person's needs conducted by the service provider and the young person for these purposes[12]; and (b) to which in the course of that consultation the young person has agreed[13], and the service provider must make arrangements for the learning and support conditions to be reviewed periodically[14].

Learning and support agreements made by virtue of these provisions do not create any obligations in respect of whose breach any liability arises in contract or in tort[15].

1 Ie in pursuance of the Education and Skills Act 2008 s 68 or s 70(1)(b) (see PARA 802).
2 As to the meaning of 'young person' see PARA 802 note 2.
3 'Support' provided for a person means any form of support and includes, in particular: (1) support in the form of medical or social care, including care provided otherwise than to that person (Education and Skills Act 2008 s 71(2)(a)(i)); (2) support in the form of incentives, including allowances and payments (s 71(2)(a)(ii)); and (3) other financial assistance (s 71(2)(a)(iii)).
4 Education and Skills Act 2008 s 71(1). Section 71(1) is subject to s 68(4) (see PARA 802): s 71(8) (amended by the Education Act 2011 s 28(3)(c)). Support is provided for a young person on a conditional basis if it is provided under arrangements (a 'learning and support agreement') under which its provision is subject to the young person's agreement to fulfil conditions ('learning and support conditions'): s 71(2)(b).
5 See the Education and Skills Act 2008 s 71(3).
6 Education and Skills Act 2008 s 71(4).
7 As to the meaning of 'person' see PARA 7 note 6.
8 Ie the duty imposed by the Education and Skills Act 2008 s 2 (see PARA 725).
9 Ie a person to whom the Education and Skills Act 2008 Pt 1 (ss 1–67) applies (see PARA 725).
10 Education and Skills Act 2008 s 71(5)(a).
11 Education and Skills Act 2008 s 71(5)(b).
12 Education and Skills Act 2008 s 71(6)(a).
13 Education and Skills Act 2008 s 71(6)(b).
14 Education and Skills Act 2008 s 71(6).
15 Education and Skills Act 2008 s 71(7).

804. Provision of information by educational institutions to persons involved in the provision of support services. Relevant information[1] about a pupil or student who is attending an educational institution in England[2] must be provided by the responsible person to a person involved in the provision of support services[3], on a request by that person[4]. Such a request by a person involved in the provision of support services[5] may be made only for the purposes of the provision of those services[6].

1 'Relevant information' means: (1) the name, address and date of birth of the pupil or student (Education and Skills Act 2008 s 72(3)(a)); (2) the name and address of a parent of the pupil or student (s 72(3)(b)); (3) information in the educational institution's possession about the pupil or student (see s 72(3)(c)). Information within head (3) must not be provided under s 72(1) if (a) the pupil or student concerned, in the case of a pupil or student who has attained the age of 16 (s 72(4)(a)); or (b) a parent of the pupil or student concerned, in the case of a pupil or student who has not attained the age of 16 (s 72(4)(b)), has instructed the responsible person not to provide information of that kind under s 72 (s 72(4)). As to the meaning of 'parent' see PARA 7 note 6 (definition applied by the Education and Skills Act 2008 s 78(1) (amended by SI 2010/1158)). As to the time at which a person attains a particular age see PARA 7 note 6.
  'Educational institution' means: (i) a community, foundation or voluntary school; (ii) a community or foundation special school; (iii) a city technology college, a city college for the technology of the arts or an academy; (iv) a pupil referral unit; (v) an institution within the further education sector; or (vi) an institution (other than one within any of heads (i)–(v)) in receipt of funding from a local authority, or the Secretary of State: Education and Skills Act 2008 s 72(5) (amended by SI 2010/1080; the Education Act 2011 Sch 16 para 42; and the Deregulation Act 2015 Sch 14 Pt 2 paras 60, 62). As to the meaning of references to a community, foundation or voluntary school or a community or foundation special school see PARA 106. As to city technology colleges and city colleges for the technology of the arts see PARA 345. As to academies see PARA 345 et seq. As to pupil referral units see PARA 427 et seq. As to the meaning of 'institution within the further education sector' see PARA 555. As to the meaning of 'local authority' see PARA 25 (definition applied by the Education and Skills Act 2008 s 78(1) (amended by SI 2010/1158)). As to the Secretary of State see PARA 58.
  'Responsible person' means: (A) in relation to a school within head (i) or (ii) of the definition of 'educational institution', the governing body; (B) in relation to an institution within head (iii)

or (vi) of that definition, the proprietor; (C) in relation to a pupil referral unit, the local authority by which it is maintained; (D) in relation to an institution within the further education sector, the governing body within the meaning given by the Further and Higher Education Act 1992 s 90 (see PARA 560 note 6): Education and Skills Act 2008 s 72(5) (amended by SI 2010/1158). 'Proprietor', in relation to a school or other institution, means the person or body of persons responsible for its management: Education and Skills Act 2008 s 78(1). As to the meaning of 'person' see PARA 7 note 6.

2   As to the meaning of 'England' see PARA 7 note 3.
3   Ie in pursuance of the Education and Skills Act 2008 s 68 or 70(1)(b) (see PARA 802).
4   Education and Skills Act 2008 s 72(1).
5   Ie in pursuance of the Education and Skills Act 2008 s 68 or 70(1)(b) (see PARA 802).
6   Education and Skills Act 2008 s 72(2).

805. Internet and telephone support services. The Secretary of State[1] may provide or secure the provision of services for encouraging, enabling or assisting the effective participation of young persons[2] and relevant young adults[3] in England[4] in education or training[5]. The services which may be so provided are services provided by means of: (1) the publication whether electronically or otherwise of information, advice and guidance[6]; (2) the provision, in response to requests by young persons and relevant young adults, of information, advice or guidance to those persons by telephone or other electronic means[7]. In securing the provision of those services the Secretary of State may, in particular, make arrangements with other persons[8] for the provision of services[9].

1   As to the Secretary of State see PARA 58.
2   As to the meaning of 'young person' see PARA 802 note 2.
3   As to the meaning of 'relevant young adult' see PARA 802 note 3.
4   For these purposes, a young person or relevant young adult is in England if he or she is a person for whom a local authority in England is responsible: Education and Skills Act 2008 s 74(5) (amended by SI 2010/1158). As to when a local authority is responsible for a young person or relevant young adult see PARA 802 note 4. As to the meaning of 'local authority in England' see PARA 25 (definition applied by the Education and Skills Act 2008 s 78(1) (amended by SI 2010/1158)).
5   Education and Skills Act 2008 s 74(1). Her Majesty's Chief Inspector of Education, Children's Services and Skills must, when requested to do so by the Secretary of State, inspect and report on the provision of services in pursuance of the Education and Skills Act 2008 s 74, and may undertake such other inspections of the provision of those services as the Chief Inspector thinks fit: see s 75; and PARA 1287.
6   Education and Skills Act 2008 s 74(2)(a).
7   Education and Skills Act 2008 s 74(2)(b).
8   As to the meaning of 'person' see PARA 7 note 6.
9   Education and Skills Act 2008 s 74(3). Arrangements under s 74(3) may include provision: (1) for grants, loans and other kinds of financial assistance to be provided by the Secretary of State (whether or not on conditions) (s 74(4)(a)); (2) requiring persons with whom arrangements are made to have regard to guidance issued by the Secretary of State (s 74(4)(b)).

806. Supply of social security information relating to young persons. The Secretary of State[1] may make arrangements with a person[2] for the supply of social security information[3] for the purposes of the provision of support services[4] for young persons[5]. Social security information may be supplied to the Secretary of State[6], or a person providing services[7] to the Secretary of State[8]. A person to whom social security information is so supplied may supply the information to a local authority[9] or other person involved in the provision of support services[10] for young persons or relevant young adults[11] for the purpose of the provision of those services[12].

Information supplied to a person[13] may be disclosed: (1) for the purpose of the provision[14] of support services[15]; (2) for the purpose of enabling or assisting the exercise of any function of a local authority in relation to the duty under the

Education and Skills Act 2008[16] to participate in education or training[17]; (3) in accordance with any provision of, or made under, any other Act[18]; (4) in accordance with an order of a court or tribunal[19]; (5) for the purpose of actual or contemplated proceedings before a court or tribunal[20]; (6) with consent given by or on behalf of the person to whom the information relates[21]; or (7) in such a way as to prevent the identification of the person to whom it relates[22].

It is an offence for a person to disclose restricted information[23] otherwise than in accordance with the above provisions[24]. It is a defence for a person charged with such an offence relating to a disclosure to prove that the person reasonably believed that the disclosure was lawful[25].

1   As to the Secretary of State see PARA 58.
2   As to the meaning of 'person' see PARA 7 note 6.
3   'Social security information' means personal information about a young person which is held for the purposes of functions relating to social security by the Secretary of State (Education and Skills Act 2008 s 76(2)(a)), or by a person providing services to the Secretary of State in connection with the provision of those services (s 76(2)(b)). For these purposes, 'personal information' in relation to a young person, means the person's name, address and date of birth: s 76(3) (substituted by the Apprenticeships, Skills, Children and Learning Act 2009 s 254(1), (7), (9)). As to the meaning of 'young person' see PARA 802 note 2.
4   Ie in pursuance of the Education and Skills Act 2008 s 68 or s 70(1)(b) (see PARA 802).
5   Education and Skills Act 2008 s 76(3A) (added by the Apprenticeships, Skills, Children and Learning Act 2009 s 254(1), (7), (9)).
6   Education and Skills Act 2008 s 76(3B)(a) (s 76(3B) added by the Apprenticeships, Skills, Children and Learning Act 2009 s 254(1), (7), (9)).
7   Ie under the Education and Skills Act 2008 s 76(3A) (see the text to notes 1–5).
8   Education and Skills Act 2008 s 76(3B)(b) (as added: see note 6).
9   As to the meaning of 'local authority' see PARA 25 (definition applied by the Education and Skills Act 2008 s 78(1) (amended by SI 2010/1158)).
10   See note 4.
11   As to the meaning of 'relevant young adult' see PARA 802 note 3.
12   Education and Skills Act 2008 s 76(3C) (s 76(3C), (3D) added by the Apprenticeships, Skills, Children and Learning Act 2009 s 254(1), (7), (9); Education and Skills Act 2008 s 76(3C) amended by SI 2010/1158). Information supplied to a person in reliance on the Education and Skills Act 2008 s 76(3C) or (3D) may be supplied in accordance with, or with arrangements made under, s 17(1) (see PARA 734): s 76(3D) (as so added).
13   Ie in reliance on the Education and Skills Act 2008 s 76(3B), (3C) or (3D) (see the text to notes 6–12).
14   See note 4.
15   Education and Skills Act 2008 s 76(3E)(a) (s 76(3E) added by the Apprenticeships, Skills, Children and Learning Act 2009 s 254(1), (7), (9)).
16   Ie under the Education and Skills Act 2008 Pt 1 (ss 1–67) (see PARA 725 et seq).
17   Education and Skills Act 2008 s 76(3E)(b) (as added (see note 15); and amended by SI 2010/1158).
18   Education and Skills Act 2008 s 76(3E)(c) (as added: see note 15).
19   Education and Skills Act 2008 s 76(3E)(d) (as added: see note 15).
20   Education and Skills Act 2008 s 76(3E)(e) (as added: see note 15).
21   Education and Skills Act 2008 s 76(3E)(f) (as added: see note 15).
22   Education and Skills Act 2008 s 76(3E)(g) (as added: see note 15).
23   'Restricted information', in relation to a person, means information that was disclosed to the person: (1) in reliance on the Education and Skills Act 2008 s 76(3B), (3C) or (3D) (see the text to notes 6–12) (s 76(4A)(a) (s 76(4A) added by the Apprenticeships, Skills, Children and Learning Act 2009 s 254(1), (7), (9))); or (2) in circumstances that constitute an offence under the Education and Skills Act 2008 76 (s 76(4A)(b) (as so added)).
24   Education and Skills Act 2008 s 76(4) (substituted by the Apprenticeships, Skills, Children and Learning Act 2009 s 254(1), (7), (9)). A person guilty of such an offence is liable: (1) on conviction on indictment, to imprisonment for a term not exceeding two years, to a fine or to both (Education and Skills Act 2008 s 76(6)(a)), or (2) on summary conviction, to imprisonment for a term not exceeding 12 months, to a fine not exceeding the statutory maximum, or to both (s 76(6)(b)). In head (2) the reference to 12 months is to be read in relation to an offence committed before the commencement of the Criminal Justice Act 2003 s 282 (not yet in force) as

a reference to six months: Education and Skills Act 2008 s 76(7). As to the statutory maximum see SENTENCING AND DISPOSITION OF OFFENDERS vol 92 (2010) PARA 140.

25 Education and Skills Act 2008 s 76(5). As to the standard of proof imposed on the accused see CRIMINAL PROCEDURE vol 28 (2010) PARA 466.

807. Supply of information by Secretary of State or person providing services. The Secretary of State[1] may make arrangements with any other person[2] for the holding and supply of relevant information[3] in connection with, or for the purposes of, the provision[4] of support services[5]. Relevant information may be supplied to the Secretary of State[6], or a person providing services[7] to the Secretary of State[8]. Information so supplied may be supplied to any person involved in the provision of support services[9] for the purposes of the provision of those services[10].

Nothing in the above provisions authorises the disclosure of any information in contravention of any provision of, or made under, the Education and Skills Act 2008 or any other Act (whenever passed or made) which prevents disclosure of the information[11].

1   As to the Secretary of State see PARA 58.
2   As to the meaning of 'person' see PARA 7 note 6.
3   The Education and Skills Act 2008 s 76A(1) refers to 'information'; however, it is submitted that this is intended to be a reference to 'relevant information'. In s 76A 'relevant information', in relation to a person by whom services are provided under s 68 or s 70(1)(b) (see PARA 802), means information which is obtained by a person involved in the provision of those services in, or in connection with, the provision of those services (s 76A(2)(a) (s 76A added by the Apprenticeships, Skills, Children and Learning Act 2009 s 255(1), (3))), and relates to a person for whom those services are provided (Education and Skills Act 2008 s 76A(2)(b) (as so added)); but does not include information provided under the Welfare Reform and Pensions Act 1999 s 72 (see WELFARE BENEFITS AND STATE PENSIONS vol 104 (2014) PARA 551) (s 76A(2) (as so added)).
4   Ie in pursuance of the Education and Skills Act 2008 s 68 or s 70(1)(b) (see PARA 802).
5   Education and Skills Act 2008 s 76A(1) (as added: see note 3).
6   Education and Skills Act 2008 s 76A(3)(a) (as added: see note 3).
7   Ie under the Education and Skills Act 2008 s 76A.
8   Education and Skills Act 2008 s 76A(3)(b) (as added: see note 3).
9   See note 4.
10 Education and Skills Act 2008 s 76A(4) (as added: see note 3).
11 Education and Skills Act 2008 s 76A(6) (as added: see note 3).

808. Supply of information by public bodies. Any of the following persons[1] or bodies may supply information about a young person[2] or relevant young adult[3] to any person or body involved in the provision of support services[4] for the purpose of the provision of those services[5]. The persons and bodies are: (1) a local authority[6]; (2) a non-metropolitan district council for an area for which there is a county council[7]; (3) the Secretary of State[8]; (4) a clinical commissioning group[9]; (5) a chief officer of police[10]; (6) a provider of probation services[11]; (7) a local probation board[12]; and (8) a youth offending team[13].

1   As to the meaning of 'person' see PARA 7 note 6.
2   As to the meaning of 'young person' see PARA 802 note 2.
3   As to the meaning of 'relevant young adult' see PARA 802 note 3.
4   Ie in pursuance of the Education and Skills Act 2008 s 68 or s 70(1)(b) (see PARA 802).
5   Education and Skills Act 2008 s 77(1).
6   Education and Skills Act 2008 s 77(2)(a). As to the meaning of 'local authority' see PARA 25 (definition applied by s 78(1) (amended by SI 2010/1158)).
7   Education and Skills Act 2008 s 77(2)(aa) (added by SI 2010/1158). As to local government areas and authorities see LOCAL GOVERNMENT vol 69 (2009) PARA 22 et seq.
8   Education and Skills Act 2008 s 77(2)(b) (substituted by SI 2010/1080; and amended by the Education Act 2011 Sch 16 para 43). As to the Secretary of State see PARA 58.

9   Education and Skills Act 2008 s 77(2)(da) (added by the Health and Social Care Act 2012 Sch 5 paras 168, 170(c)). As to clinical commissioning groups see HEALTH SERVICES vol 54 (2008) PARA 93B.
10 Education and Skills Act 2008 s 77(2)(e). As to chief officers of police see POLICE AND INVESTIGATORY POWERS vol 84 (2013) PARA 112 et seq.
11 Education and Skills Act 2008 s 77(2)(f). As to probation services see SENTENCING AND DISPOSITION OF OFFENDERS vol 92 (2010) PARA 733 et seq.
12 Education and Skills Act 2008 s 77(2)(g). 'Local probation board' means a local probation board established under the Criminal Justice and Court Services Act 2000 s 4 (see SENTENCING AND DISPOSITION OF OFFENDERS vol 92 (2010) PARA 737): Education and Skills Act 2008 s 77(3).
13 Education and Skills Act 2008 s 77(2)(h). 'Youth offending team' means a team established under the Crime and Disorder Act 1998 s 39 (see CHILDREN AND YOUNG PERSONS vol 10 (2012) PARA 1193): Education and Skills Act 2008 s 77(3).

809. Co-operation as regards provision of 14 to 19 education and training.
The arrangements made by a local authority in England[1] in relation to co-operation to improve the well-being of children[2] must include[3]:

(1)   arrangements to promote co-operation between the local authority[4], the authority's relevant partners[5], and the other persons[6] and bodies (of any nature) who exercise functions, or are engaged in activities, relevant to the provision of 14–19 education or training[7] in the authority's area[8]; or

(2)   arrangements made jointly by the local authority and one or more other local authorities in England to promote co-operation between[9] the authorities[10], the authorities' relevant partners[11], and the other persons and bodies (of any nature) who exercise functions, or are engaged in activities, relevant to the provision of 14–19 education or training in each of the authorities' areas[12].

1   'Local authority in England' means a county council in England, a metropolitan district council, a non-metropolitan district council for an area for which there is no county council, a London Borough council, the Common Council of the City of London (in its capacity as a local authority), and the Council of the Isles of Scilly: Children Act 2004 s 65(1) (definition added by SI 2010/1158) (definition applied by the Education and Skills Act 2008 s 85(5) (amended by SI 2010/1158)). As to the meaning of 'England' see PARA 7 note 3. As to local government areas and authorities in England see LOCAL GOVERNMENT vol 69 (2009) PARA 22 et seq.
2   Ie arrangements made under the Children Act 2004 s 10 (see CHILDREN AND YOUNG PERSONS vol 9 (2012) PARA 203).
3   See the Education and Skills Act 2008 s 85(1) (amended by SI 2010/1158). The Education and Skills Act 2008 s 85(1) is not to be read as affecting the generality of the duty imposed by the Children Act 2004 s 10(1) and (2) so far as relating to education and training: Education and Skills Act 2008 s 85(4).
4   Education and Skills Act 2008 s 85(2)(a) (amended by SI 2010/1158).
5   Education and Skills Act 2008 s 85(2)(b). 'Relevant partner', in relation to a local authority, has the meaning given by the Children Act 2004 s 10(4) (see CHILDREN AND YOUNG PERSONS vol 9 (2012) PARA 203): Education and Skills Act 2008 s 85(5) (definition amended by SI 2010/1158).
6   As to the meaning of 'person' see PARA 7 note 6.
7   '14–19 education' and '14–19 training' mean, respectively, education and training suitable to the requirements of persons during the period beginning with the start of the academic year in which they attain the age of 15 and ending when they attain the age of 19: Education and Skills Act 2008 s 85(5). For these purposes, 'education' means full-time or part-time education, but does not include higher education (namely, education provided by means of a course of any description mentioned in the Education Reform Act 1988 Sch 6 (see PARA 684)); 'training' means full-time or part-time training, and includes vocational, social, physical and recreational training; and 'academic year' means any period beginning with 1 August and ending with the next 31 July: Education and Skills Act 2008 s 85(6). As to the time at which a person attains a particular age see PARA 7 note 6.
8   Education and Skills Act 2008 s 85(2)(c).
9   Education and Skills Act 2008 s 85(3) (amended by SI 2010/1158).
10 Education and Skills Act 2008 s 85(3)(a).

11 Education and Skills Act 2008 s 85(3)(b).

12 Education and Skills Act 2008 s 85(3)(c).

B. TRANSPORT SERVICES

810. Provision of transport etc for certain adult learners. A local authority in England[1] must make such arrangements for the provision of transport and otherwise as it considers necessary, or as the Secretary of State[2] may direct[3], for the following purposes[4]:

(1) to facilitate the attendance of adults[5] receiving education at institutions maintained or assisted by the authority and providing further or higher education[6] (or both)[7], or within the further education sector[8];

(2) to facilitate the attendance of relevant young adults[9] receiving education or training at institutions outside both the further and higher education sectors[10], but only in cases where the local authority has secured for the adults in question[11] the provision of education or training at the institution in question[12] and the provision[13]of boarding accommodation[14].

Any transport so provided must be provided free of charge[15]. A local authority in England may pay all or part of the reasonable travelling expenses of an adult[16] receiving education or training at an institution mentioned in head (1) or (2) above[17], and for whose transport no arrangements[18] are made[19].

In considering what arrangements it is necessary to make in relation to relevant young adults, a local authority must have regard to what it is required to do under its relevant duty[20] in relation to those persons[21]. In considering whether they are required[22] to make arrangements in relation to a particular adult, a local authority must have regard (among other things) to the age of the adult and the nature of the route, or alternative routes, which the adult could reasonably be expected to take[23].

A local authority in England making arrangements, or proposing to pay travelling expenses, under the above provisions in relation to relevant young adults must consult[24]: (a) any other local authority that it considers it appropriate to consult[25]; (b) governing bodies[26] of institutions within the further education sector in the authority's area[27]; (c) proprietors of 16 to 19 academies[28] in the authority's area[29]; (d) persons in the local authority's area who will be relevant young adults when the arrangements or payments have effect, and their parents[30]; (e) the Secretary of State[31]; and (f) any other person[32] specified by the Secretary of State[33].

The authority must prepare for each academic year[34] a transport policy statement[35] which must: (i) specify any transport or other arrangements, and any payment of travelling expenses, made or to be made[36] in relation to the year in relation to relevant young adults[37]; and (ii) specify any travel concessions[38] which are to be provided under any scheme[39] to relevant young adults receiving education or training at an institution mentioned in head (1) or (2) above[40]. The authority must publish the statement by the end of May in the year in which the relevant academic year begins[41]. In preparing and publishing the statement, the authority must have regard (among other things) to the need to include in the statement sufficient information about the matters that the statement must specify[42], and publish the statement in time[43], to enable relevant young adults and their parents to take reasonable account of those matters when choosing between different institutions at which education or training is provided[44].

The publication of a statement in relation to an academic year does not prevent an authority from making additional arrangements or payments[45] in relation to the academic year[46], or providing additional travel concessions in relation to the academic year[47].

In making arrangements for the provision of transport[48] and preparing and publishing a transport policy statement[49], a local authority must have regard to any guidance issued by the Secretary of State[50].

1 As to the meaning of 'local authority in England' see PARA 25.
2 As to the Secretary of State see PARA 58.
3 As to directions see the Education Act 1996 s 570; and PARA 75.
4 Education Act 1996 s 508F(1) (ss 508F–508H added by the Apprenticeships, Skills, Children and Learning Act 2009, s 57(1), (2); Education Act 1996 s 508F(1) amended by SI 2010/1158).
5 'Adult' means a person who is neither a child nor a person of sixth form age: Education Act 1996 s 508F(9) (as added: see note 4). As to the meaning of 'child' see PARA 7 note 6. As to the meaning of 'sixth form age' see PARA 464 note 5 (definition applied by s 508F(9) (as so added)).
6 As to the meaning of 'further education' see PARA 23. As to the meaning of 'higher education' see PARA 24.
7 Education Act 1996 s 508F(2)(a) (as added: see note 4).
8 Education Act 1996 s 508F(2)(b) (as added: see note 4). As to the meaning of 'institution within the further education sector' see PARA 555.
9 'Relevant young adult' means an adult for whom an EHC plan is maintained: Education Act 1996 ss 508F(9), 508G(9) (both as added: see note 4; definition amended by the Children and Families Act 2014 Sch 3 para 46). As to the time at which a person attains a particular age see PARA 7 note 6. As to EHC plans see PARA 441.
10 As to the meaning of 'institution outside the further education sector' see PARA 555. As to the meaning of 'institution outside the higher education sector' see PARA 619.
11 Education Act 1996 s 508F(3) (as added (see note 4); and amended by SI 2010/1158).
12 Education Act 1996 s 508F(3)(a) (as added: see note 4).
13 Ie under the Education Act 1996 s 514A (see PARA 507).
14 Education Act 1996 s 508F(3)(b) (as added: see note 4). Arrangements made under the Education Act 1996 s 508F(1) (see the text to notes 1–4) by virtue of s 508F(3) to facilitate full-time education or training at an institution outside both the further and higher education sectors must be no less favourable than the arrangements made for relevant young adults of the same age for whom the authority secures the provision of education at another institution: s 508F(7) (as so added).
15 Education Act 1996 s 508F(4) (as added: see note 4).
16 Education Act 1996 s 508F(8) (as added (see note 4); and amended by SI 2010/1158).
17 Education Act 1996 s 508F(8)(a) (as added: see note 4).
18 Ie under the Education Act 1996 s 508F(1) (see the text to notes 1–4).
19 Education Act 1996 s 508F(8)(b) (as added: see note 4).
20 Ie under the Education Act 1996 s 15ZA(1) (see PARA 32).
21 Education Act 1996 s 508F(5) (as added (see note 4); and amended by SI 2010/1158).
22 Ie by the Education Act 1996 s 508F(1) (see the text to notes 1–4).
23 Education Act 1996 s 508F(6) (as added (see note 4); and amended by SI 2010/1158).
24 Education Act 1996 s 508G(1) (as added (see note 4); and amended by SI 2010/1158). As to the exercise of the duty to consult see JUDICIAL REVIEW vol 61 (2010) PARA 627.
25 Education Act 1996 s 508G(1)(a) (as added (see note 4); and amended by SI 2010/1158).
26 As to the meaning of 'governing body' see PARA 560 note 6 (definition applied by the Education Act 1996 s 508G(9) (as added: see note 4)).
27 Education Act 1996 s 508G(1)(b) (as added: see note 4).
28 As to the meaning of '16 to 19 academy' see PARA 346 note 13.
29 Education Act 1996 s 508G(1)(ba) (s 508G as added (see note 4);s 508G(1)(ba) added by the Education Act 2011 Sch 13 para 9(12)).
30 Education Act 1996 s 508G(1)(c) (as added (see note 4); and amended by SI 2010/1158). As to the meaning of 'parent' see PARA 7 note 6.
31 Education Act 1996 s 508G(1)(d) (as added: see note 4). As to the Secretary of State see PARA 58.
32 As to the meaning of 'person' see PARA 7 note 6.
33 Education Act 1996 s 508G(1)(e) (as added: see note 4).

34   As to the meaning of 'academic year' see PARA 464 note 3 (definition applied by the Education Act 1996 s 508G(9) (as added: see note 4)).

35   See the Education Act 1996 s 508G(2) (as added: see note 4). As to the revision of a transport policy statement following a complaint see s 508I; and PARA 811.

36   Ie under the Education Act 1996 s 508F (see the text to notes 1–23).

37   Education Act 1996 s 508G(3) (as added: see note 4).

38   Ie within the meaning of the Transport Act 1985 Pt V (ss 88–112) (see ROAD TRAFFIC vol 90 (2011) PARA 1025 et seq).

39   Ie established under the Transport Act 1985 s 93: (see ROAD TRAFFIC vol 90 (2011) PARA 1025).

40   Education Act 1996 s 508G(4) (as added: see note 4).

41   Education Act 1996 s 508G(5) (as added: see note 4). The Secretary of State may amend s 508G(5) by order to change the time by which the statement must be published: s 508G(8) (as so added). At the date at which this volume states the law no such order had been made.

42   Education Act 1996 s 508G(6)(a) (as added: see note 4).

43   Education Act 1996 s 508G(6)(b) (as added: see note 4).

44   Education Act 1996 s 508G(6) (as added: see note 4).

45   See note 36.

46   Education Act 1996 s 508G(7)(a) (as added: see note 4).

47   Education Act 1996 s 508G(7)(b) (as added: see note 4).

48   Ie arrangements under the Education Act 1996 s 508F: see the text to notes 1–23.

49   Ie under the Education Act 1996 s 508G: see the text to notes 34–47.

50   Education Act 1996 s 508H (as added (see note 4); and amended by SI 2010/1158). As to the publication of guidance see the Education Act 1996 s 571; and PARA 60.

811. Revision of transport policy statements following complaints. A local authority in England[1] may revise a transport policy statement[2] to change any matter specified in the statement[3] if, as a result of a relevant young adult transport complaint[4], it has come to consider the change necessary for a purpose[5] relevant to provision made in the statement[6]. A local authority must revise such a statement to change any matter specified in the statement[7] if, as a result of a relevant young adult transport complaint, the Secretary of State[8] has directed[9] it to do so[10]. An authority that so revises a statement[11] must publish the revised statement and a description of the revision as soon as practicable[12].

1   As to the meaning of 'local authority in England' see PARA 25.

2   Ie a statement prepared under the Education Act 1996 s 508G (see PARA 810).

3   Ie specified under the Education Act 1996 s 508G(3) (see PARA 810).

4   'Relevant young adult transport complaint' means a complaint that is about a local authority's exercise of, or failure to exercise, a function under the Education Act 1996 s 508F or s 508G (see PARA 810) in relation to relevant young adults (s 508I(5)(a) (s 508I added by the Apprenticeships, Skills, Children and Learning Act 2009 s 57(1), (2); Education Act 1996 s 508I(5)(a) amended by SI 2010/1158)), and made by a person who is, or will be, a relevant young adult when the matter complained of has effect, or by a parent of such a person (Education Act 1996 s 508I(5)(b) (as so added)). As to the meaning of 'relevant young adult' see PARA 810 note 9 (definition applied by s 508I(6) (as so added)). As to the meaning of 'function' see PARA 18 note 5. As to the meaning of 'parent' see PARA 7 note 6.

5   Ie a purpose mentioned in the Education Act 1996 s 508F(2) or (3) (see PARA 810).

6   See the Education Act 1996 s 508I(1) (as added (see note 4); and amended by SI 2010/1158).

7   Ie any matter specified under the Education Act 1996 s 508G(3) (see PARA 810).

8   As to the Secretary of State see PARA 58.

9   As to directions see the Education Act 1996 s 570; and PARA 75.

10   See the Education Act 1996 s 508I(2) (as added (see note 4); and amended by SI 2010/1158). The Secretary of State need not consider whether to exercise any power under ss 496, 497, 497A (powers to prevent unreasonable exercise of functions, etc: see PARAS 62, 64–65) or s 508I(2) in response to a matter that is, or could have been, the subject of a relevant young adult transport complaint made to him or her unless satisfied that the matter has been brought to the notice of the local authority concerned (s 508I(4)(a) (as so added; and amended by SI 2010/1158)), and the authority has had a reasonable opportunity to investigate the matter and respond (Education Act 1996 s 508I(4)(b) (as so added)).

11   Ie under the Education Act 1996 s 508I(1) or (2): see the text to notes 1–10.

12 Education Act 1996 s 508I(3) (as added: see note 4). For the purposes of s 508G(7) and s 508H
(see PARA 810), the revision of a statement under s 508I is to be treated as the preparation of a
statement under s 508G (see PARA 810): s 508I(6) (as so added). Where a local authority has
published in a single document a statement prepared under s 509AA (see PARA 464) and a
statement prepared under 508G, the requirement to publish a revised statement under s 508I(3)
is to be treated as a requirement to publish a version of the document that includes the revised
statement: s 508I(7) (as so added; and amended by SI 2010/1158).

(ii) Provision of Services in Wales

A. PROVISION OF SERVICES BY GOVERNING BODIES

812. Learner support services. The Welsh Ministers[1] may direct the governing
body of a maintained school in Wales[2], and the governing body of an institution
within the further education sector in Wales[3], to: (1) provide learner support
services[4]; (2) to secure the provision of learner support services[5]; (3) to
participate in the provision of learner support services[6]. A direction may:

(a) include provision for grants, loans and other kinds of financial
assistance to be provided by the Welsh Ministers (whether or not on
conditions)[7];

(b) require a governing body to have regard to guidance given by the Welsh
Ministers[8];

(c) require a governing body when making arrangements with other
persons[9] to require those persons to have regard to guidance given by
the Welsh Ministers[10];

(d) relate to a particular class of young person[11];

(e) make different provision for different classes of young person[12];

(f) be revoked or varied by a later direction[13].

Where a direction relates to the provision of a service in the form of advice or
information, it must be framed so that: (i) it relates only to information which is
presented in an impartial manner[14]; and (ii) it relates only to advice which is
given by a person who considers that it will promote the best interests of the
young person concerned[15], and which does not seek to promote, contrary to the
young person's best interests, the interests or aspirations of any school,
institution or other person[16].

A governing body of a maintained school or institution within the further
education sector must comply with any such direction given to it[17].

Where a person is involved in the provision of learner support services, an
educational institution must, for the purpose of the provision of those services,
provide certain information and facilities[18]. Learner support services are subject
to inspection by Her Majesty's Chief Inspector of Education and Training in
Wales[19].

1 As to the Welsh Ministers see PARA 59.
2 Learning and Skills (Wales) Measure 2009 s 40(2)(a). As to the meaning of 'maintained school'
see PARA 99 (definition applied by s 40(7)(c)). As to the governing bodies of maintained schools
in Wales see PARA 195. As to the meaning of 'Wales' see PARA 7 note 3.
3 Learning and Skills (Wales) Measure 2009 s 40(2)(b). As to the meaning of 'institution within
the further education sector' see PARA 555 (definition applied by s 40(7)(b)).
4 Learning and Skills (Wales) Measure 2009 s 40(1)(a). 'Learner support services' means services
which in the opinion of the Welsh Ministers will encourage, enable or assist young persons
(directly or indirectly): (1) to participate effectively in education or training (s 40(3)(a)); (2) to
take advantage of opportunities for employment (s 40(3)(b)); or (3) to participate effectively and

responsibly in the life of their communities (s 40(3)(c)). 'Young persons' means persons who
have attained the age of 11 but not the age of 26: s 40(7)(a). As to the time at which a person
attains a particular age see PARA 7 note 6.
5   Learning and Skills (Wales) Measure 2009 s 40(1)(b).
6   Learning and Skills (Wales) Measure 2009 s 40(1)(c).
7   Learning and Skills (Wales) Measure 2009 s 40(4)(a).
8   Learning and Skills (Wales) Measure 2009 s 40(4)(b).
9   As to the meaning of 'person' see PARA 7 note 6.
10 Learning and Skills (Wales) Measure 2009 s 40(4)(c).
11 Learning and Skills (Wales) Measure 2009 s 40(5)(a).
12 Learning and Skills (Wales) Measure 2009 s 40(5)(b).
13 Learning and Skills (Wales) Measure 2009 s 40(5)(c).
14 Learning and Skills (Wales) Measure 2009 s 40(6)(a).
15 Learning and Skills (Wales) Measure 2009 s 40(6)(b)(i).
16 Learning and Skills (Wales) Measure 2009 s 40(6)(b)(ii).
17 Learning and Skills (Wales) Measure 2009 s 41(1). Action which a governing body takes in
    pursuance of s 41(1) may relate to a particular class of young person: s 41(2).
18 See the Learning and Skills Act 2000 s 126; and PARA 816.
19 See the Learning and Skills Act 2000 s 127; and PARA 1288.

B. PROVISION OF SERVICES BY LOCAL AUTHORITIES

813.   Youth support services. The Welsh Ministers[1] may direct a local
authority[2]: (1) to provide youth support services[3]; (2) to secure the provision of
youth support services[4]; and (3) to participate in the provision of youth support
services[5]. However, this power does not relate to services which are provided or
to be provided outside Wales[6].
A direction may:
(a)   include provision for grants, loans and other kinds of financial
       assistance to be provided by the Welsh Ministers (whether or not on
       conditions)[7];
(b)   require local authorities to have regard to guidance issued by the Welsh
       Ministers[8];
(c)   require local authorities when making arrangements with other persons[9]
       to require those persons to have regard to guidance issued by the Welsh
       Ministers[10];
(d)   relate to a particular class of young person[11];
(e)   make different provision for different classes of young person[12];
(f)   be revoked or varied by a later direction[13].
Youth support services are subject to inspection by Her Majesty's Chief
Inspector of Education and Training in Wales[14].

1   As to the Welsh Ministers see PARA 59. The functions under the Learning and Skills Act 2000
    s 123 were formerly vested in the National Assembly for Wales and are now exercisable by the
    Welsh Ministers by virtue of the Government of Wales Act 2006 s 162(1), Sch 11 paras 30, 32.
2   'Local authority' means a county council or a county borough council: Learning and Skills
    Act 2000 s 129(1). As to local government areas and authorities in Wales see LOCAL
    GOVERNMENT vol 69 (2009) PARA 37 et seq. As to the duty of a local authority to consult
    various persons before complying with such a direction see s 125; and PARA 814. As to the duty
    of a local authority to comply with such a direction see s 124; and PARA 815.
3   Learning and Skills Act 2000 s 123(1)(a). 'Youth support services' means services which in the
    opinion of the Welsh Ministers will encourage, enable or assist young persons (directly or
    indirectly): (1) to participate effectively in education or training (ss 123(2)(a), 129(1)); (2) to
    take advantage of opportunities for employment (ss 123(2)(b), 129(1)); or (3) to participate
    effectively and responsibly in the life of their communities (ss 123(2)(c), 129(1)). 'Young
    persons' means persons who have attained the age of 11 but not the age of 26: ss 123(3), 129(1).
    As to the time at which a person attains a particular age see PARA 7 note 6.
4   Learning and Skills Act 2000 s 123(1)(b).

5   Learning and Skills Act 2000 s 123(1)(c).
6   Learning and Skills Act 2000 s 129(2). As to the meaning of 'Wales' see PARA 7 note 3.
7   Learning and Skills Act 2000 s 123(4)(a).
8   Learning and Skills Act 2000 s 123(4)(b).
9   As to the meaning of 'person' see PARA 7 note 6.
10 Learning and Skills Act 2000 s 123(4)(c).
11 Learning and Skills Act 2000 s 123(5)(a).
12 Learning and Skills Act 2000 s 123(5)(b).
13 Learning and Skills Act 2000 s 123(5)(c).
14 See the Learning and Skills Act 2000 s 127; and PARA 1288.

814. Consultation and co-ordination by local authority. Before complying with a direction of the Welsh Ministers[1] by providing, securing the provision of or participating in the provision of youth support services[2] for residents of a particular place or area, a local authority[3] must consult[4] each of the following with responsibility for all or part of the area: (1) a local health board[5]; (2) a chief officer of police[6]; (3) a police and crime commissioner[7]; (4) a probation committee[8]; (5) a provider of probation services[9]; and (6) a youth offending team[10]. The local authority must also:

(a)   consult any voluntary body which provides services for young persons[11] in the place or area concerned and which the local authority thinks it appropriate to consult[12];

(b)   consult any authority or person[13] with whom arrangements have been made[14] for the place or area concerned in relation to the provision of careers services[15];

(c)   consult any relevant organisation established for the purpose of enabling voluntary bodies to co-operate and co-ordinate their activities[16];

(d)   consult such other persons as the local authority thinks appropriate[17]; and

(e)   provide such opportunities as the local authority thinks appropriate for young persons in the place or area concerned to express their views[18].

Where a local authority provides or proposes to provide youth support services for the residents of a particular place or area[19], or secures or proposes to secure the provision of youth support services for the residents of a particular place or area[20], persons or bodies listed in heads (1) to (6) above with responsibility for all or part of that place or area must: (i) exercise their functions so as to support and assist the services provided, secured or proposed by the local authority[21]; and (ii) co-ordinate the exercise of their functions, so far as seems reasonable, with persons providing those services[22]. However, this does not require those persons or bodies to take action which would significantly interfere with the efficient or effective exercise of their functions[23].

1   Ie a direction under the Learning and Skills Act 2000 s 123(1) (see PARA 813). As to the Welsh Ministers see PARA 59. The functions under the Learning and Skills Act 2000 s 125 were formerly vested in the National Assembly for Wales and are now exercisable by the Welsh Ministers by virtue of the Government of Wales Act 2006 s 162(1), Sch 11 paras 30, 32.
2   As to the meaning of 'youth support services' see PARA 813 note 3.
3   As to the meaning of 'local authority' see PARA 813 note 2.
4   As to the exercise of the duty to consult see JUDICIAL REVIEW vol 61 (2010) PARA 627.
5   Learning and Skills Act 2000 s 125(1)(a) (amended by SI 2007/961). 'Local health board' has the meaning given by the National Health Service (Wales) Act 2006 s 11 (see HEALTH SERVICES vol 54 (2008) PARA 74): Learning and Skills Act 2000 s 129(1) (definition added by SI 2007/961).
6   Learning and Skills Act 2000 s 125(1)(b). As to chief officers of police see POLICE AND INVESTIGATORY POWERS vol 84 (2013) PARA 112 et seq.

7   Learning and Skills Act 2000 s 125(1)(c) (substituted by the Police Reform and Social Responsibility Act 2011 Sch 16 para 251). As to police and crime commissioners see POLICE AND INVESTIGATORY POWERS vol 84 (2013) PARA 55 et seq.

8   Learning and Skills Act 2000 s 125(1)(d). 'Probation committee' means a committee established under the Probation Service Act 1993 s 3 (repealed): Learning and Skills Act 2000 s 129(1).

9   Learning and Skills Act 2000 s 125(1)(da) (added by SI 2008/912). 'Provider of probation services' has the meaning given by the Offender Management Act 2007 s 3(6) (see SENTENCING AND DISPOSITION OF OFFENDERS vol 92 (2010) PARA 740): Interpretation Act 1978 s 5, Sch 1 (definition added by the Offender Management Act 2007 s 39, Sch 3 Pt 1 para 2).

10 Learning and Skills Act 2000 s 125(1)(e). 'Youth offending team' means a team established under the Crime and Disorder Act 1998 s 39 (see CHILDREN AND YOUNG PERSONS vol 10 (2012) PARA 1193): Learning and Skills Act 2000 s 129(1).

11 As to the meaning of 'young persons' see PARA 813 note 3.

12 Learning and Skills Act 2000 s 125(2)(a).

13 As to the meaning of 'person' see PARA 7 note 6.

14 Ie under the Employment and Training Act 1973 s 10(1) or (3)(a), (b) or (c) (see EMPLOYMENT vol 40 (2014) PARA 638).

15 See the Learning and Skills Act 2000 s 125(2)(c).

16 Learning and Skills Act 2000 s 125(2)(d).

17 Learning and Skills Act 2000 s 125(2)(e).

18 Learning and Skills Act 2000 s 125(2)(f).

19 Learning and Skills Act 2000 s 125(3)(a).

20 Learning and Skills Act 2000 s 125(3)(b).

21 Learning and Skills Act 2000 s 125(4)(a).

22 Learning and Skills Act 2000 s 125(4)(b).

23 Learning and Skills Act 2000 s 125(5).

815.   Duties and powers of local authorities. A local authority[1]: (1) must comply with a direction given to it by the Welsh Ministers[2] to provide, secure the provision of or participate in the provision of youth support services[3]; and (2) may provide, secure the provision of, or participate in the provision of, youth support services otherwise than in accordance with head (1) above[4]. For these purposes, a local authority may: (a) incur expenditure[5]; (b) employ officers[6]; (c) enter into agreements for the supply of goods or services[7]; and (d) do anything else (other than forming companies) which it considers necessary or expedient[8]. Action which a local authority takes in pursuance of heads (1) and (2) above may relate to a particular class of young persons[9], and may relate to services for a person from another area[10].

1   As to the meaning of 'local authority' see PARA 813 note 2.

2   Ie a direction given under the Learning and Skills Act 2000 s 123(1): see PARA 813. As to the Welsh Ministers see PARA 59. The functions under the Learning and Skills Act 2000 s 124 were formerly vested in the National Assembly for Wales and are now exercisable by the Welsh Ministers by virtue of the Government of Wales Act 2006 s 162(1), Sch 11 paras 30, 32.

3   See the Learning and Skills Act 2000 s 124(1)(a). In complying with a direction under s 123(1) a local authority must have regard to the expediency of co-operation with voluntary organisations: s 124(3). A local authority's power to provide services or incur expenditure is not prejudiced by anything in or done under s 123 (see PARA 813): s 124(5). As to the meaning of 'youth support services' see PARA 813 note 3.

4   Learning and Skills Act 2000 s 124(1)(b).

5   Learning and Skills Act 2000 s 124(4)(a).

6   Learning and Skills Act 2000 s 124(4)(b).

7   Learning and Skills Act 2000 s 124(4)(c).

8   Learning and Skills Act 2000 s 124(4)(d).

9   Learning and Skills Act 2000 s 124(2)(a). As to the meaning of 'young persons' see PARA 813 note 3.

10 Learning and Skills Act 2000 s 124(2)(b).

816.   Educational institutions' duty to provide information and access. Where a person[1] is involved in the provision of youth support services[2] or learner support services[3], any: (1) community, foundation and voluntary schools[4]; (2) community special schools (other than those established in hospitals)[5]; (3) city technology colleges and city colleges for the technology of the arts[6]; (4) pupil referral units[7]; (5) institutions within the further education sector[8]; and (6) institutions in receipt of funding[9] from the Welsh Ministers[10], must, for the purpose of the provision of those services[11]:

(a)   provide him on request with the name and address of a pupil or student[12];

(b)   provide him on request with the name and address of a parent[13] of a pupil or student[14];

(c)   provide him on request with information in its possession about a pupil or student[15];

(d)   permit him to have access to a pupil or student on the institution's premises at reasonable times[16];

(e)   make available to him, so far as is reasonably convenient, facilities on its premises for providing services to individual pupils or students or groups of pupils or students[17].

1   As to the meaning of 'person' see PARA 7 note 6.
2   Ie in pursuance of the Learning and Skills Act 2000 s 123(1)(a) or (b) (see PARA 813).
3   Ie in pursuance of the Learning and Skills (Wales) Measure 2009 s 40(1)(a) or (b) (see PARA 812).
4   Learning and Skills Act 2000 s 126(3)(a). As to the meaning of references to a community, foundation or voluntary school see PARA 106.
5   Learning and Skills Act 2000 s 126(3)(b) (amended by the School Standards and Organisation (Wales) Act 2013 Sch 5 para 20(5)). As to the meaning of references to a community or foundation special school see PARA 106.
6   Learning and Skills Act 2000 s 126(3)(c). As to city technology colleges and city colleges for the technology of the arts see PARA 345.
7   Learning and Skills Act 2000 s 126(3)(d). As to pupil referral units see PARA 427 et seq.
8   Learning and Skills Act 2000 s 126(3)(e). As to institutions within the further education sector see PARA 555.
9   Ie from the Welsh Ministers in the discharge of their functions under the Learning and Skills Act 2000 Pt 2 (ss 31–41) (see PARA 789 et seq). As to the Welsh Ministers see PARA 59.
10 Learning and Skills Act 2000 s 126(3)(f) (amended by SI 2005/3238).
11 Learning and Skills Act 2000 s 126(1) (amended by the Learning and Skills (Wales) Measure 2009 s 42(1), (2)).
12 Learning and Skills Act 2000 s 126(1)(a).
13 'Parent', in relation to a child, means a person who has parental responsibility for him within the meaning of the Children Act 1989 s 3 (see CHILDREN AND YOUNG PERSONS vol 9 (2012) PARA 151): Learning and Skills Act 2000 s 129(1).
14 Learning and Skills Act 2000 s 126(1)(b).
15 Learning and Skills Act 2000 s 126(1)(c). Information must not be provided under s 126(1)(c): (1) in the case of a pupil or student who has not attained the age of 16, if a parent of his has instructed the institution not to provide information of that kind under s 126 (s 126(2)(a)); or (2) in the case of a pupil or student who has attained the age of 16, if he has instructed the institution not to provide information of that kind under s 126 (s 126(2)(b)). As to the time at which a person attains a particular age see PARA 7 note 6.
16 Learning and Skills Act 2000 s 126(1)(d).
17 Learning and Skills Act 2000 s 126(1)(e).

817. Supply of information by public bodies. For the purpose of the provision in Wales[1] of youth support services[2], training and careers services[3], and services relating to careers in industry[4]: (1) a local authority[5]; (2) a local health board[6]; (3) the Welsh Ministers[7]; (4) a chief officer of police[8]; (5) a probation committee[9]; (6) a probation trust[10]; (7) a provider of probation services[11] (other than a probation trust or the Secretary of State[12]), in carrying out its statutory functions or activities of a public nature in pursuance of arrangements made[13] for the provision of probation services[14]; and (8) a youth offending team[15], may supply information about a young person to a local authority[16], and any other person[17] or body involved in the provision of the services[18].

1   As to the meaning of 'Wales' see PARA 7 note 3.
2   See the Learning and Skills Act 2000 s 138(1), (2)(a). Youth support services are services provided in pursuance of s 123 (see PARA 813).
3   See the Learning and Skills Act 2000 s 138(1), (2)(b). The services referred to are services provided in pursuance of the Employment and Training Act 1973 ss 2, 8, 9 and 10 (see PARA 819).
4   See the Learning and Skills Act 2000 s 138(1), (2)(c). The services referred to are services wholly or partly funded in pursuance of the Industrial Development Act 1982 s 12 (see TRADE AND INDUSTRY vol 97 (2015) PARA 1048).
5   Learning and Skills Act 2000 s 138(1), (3)(a).
6   Learning and Skills Act 2000 s 138(1), (3)(ba) (added by the National Health Service Reform and Health Care Professions Act 2002 s 6(2), Sch 5 para 47). As to local health boards see HEALTH SERVICES vol 54 (2008) PARA 74.
7   Learning and Skills Act 2000 s 138(1), (3)(c) (amended by SI 2005/3238). As to the Welsh Ministers see PARA 59.
8   Learning and Skills Act 2000 s 138(1), (3)(d). As to chief officers of police see POLICE AND INVESTIGATORY POWERS vol 84 (2013) PARA 112 et seq.
9   Learning and Skills Act 2000 s 138(1), (3)(e). As to probation services generally see SENTENCING AND DISPOSITION OF OFFENDERS vol 92 (2010) PARA 733.
10 Learning and Skills Act 2000 s 138(1), (3)(ea) (added by SI 2008/912). As to probation trusts see SENTENCING AND DISPOSITION OF OFFENDERS vol 92 (2010) PARA 740.
11 As to the meaning of 'provider of probation services' see PARA 814 note 9.
12 As to the Secretary of State see PARA 58.
13 Ie under the Offender Management Act 2007 s 3 (see SENTENCING AND DISPOSITION OF OFFENDERS vol 92 (2010) PARA 741).
14 Learning and Skills Act 2000 s 138(1), (3)(eb) (added by SI 2008/912).
15 Learning and Skills Act 2000 s 138(1), (3)(f). As to youth offending teams CHILDREN AND YOUNG PERSONS vol 10 (2012) PARA 1193.
16 Learning and Skills Act 2000 s 138(1)(a).
17 As to the meaning of 'person' see PARA 7 note 6.
18 Learning and Skills Act 2000 s 138(1)(b).

(6) GRANTS FOR EDUCATION AND TRAINING

818. Grants to or in respect of individuals in connection with their education or training. The appropriate national authority[1] may make regulations authorising grants to be paid to or in respect of individuals in connection with their education or training[2]. The regulations must provide that grants may be paid only to or in respect of individuals who:

(1)   hold qualifying accounts[3];
(2)   are parties to qualifying arrangements[4]; or
(3)   hold such accounts and are parties to such arrangements[5].

The regulations may provide that grants may not be paid unless other specified conditions are satisfied[6]. Conditions which may be included are conditions:

(a)   as to the way the qualifying accounts are operated (including conditions requiring them to contain a specified balance)[7];
(b)   as to the way the qualifying arrangements are conducted[8];
(c)   as to the employment or self-employment of individuals[9];
(d)   requiring individuals not to be receiving or to have received specified benefits[10];
(e)   as to the kinds of education or training which qualify[11].

The regulations may also provide:

(i)   that the amounts of grants, and when and how they are paid, are to be decided by the appropriate national authority[12];

(ii)   that grants may be paid on such terms as the appropriate national authority decides and that the terms may include terms requiring repayment in specified circumstances[13];

(iii)   that if grants are payable under the regulations they may be paid to persons providing education or training[14];

(iv)   that if grants are payable under the regulations they may be paid by the appropriate national authority or by other persons under arrangements made with it[15];

(v)   that if such arrangements are made the appropriate national authority may pay the persons concerned remuneration or amounts to meet their expenses[16].

The regulations may provide that a specification of the kinds of education or training which qualify may include a requirement for the education or training to be provided by persons for the time being approved by the appropriate national authority[17], or if the appropriate national authority so decides, by a person who, at the time of the approval, is designated by it[18].

1   Ie the Secretary of State or, in relation to Wales, the Welsh Ministers: see the Learning and Skills Act 2000 ss 108, 150(1). As to the Secretary of State see PARA 58. As to the Welsh Ministers see PARA 59. As to the meaning of 'Wales' see PARA 7 note 3. The functions under the Learning and Skills Act 2000 in relation to Wales were originally vested in the National Assembly for Wales and are now exercisable by the Welsh Ministers by virtue of the Government of Wales Act 2006 s 162(1), Sch 11 paras 30, 32.

2   Learning and Skills Act 2000 s 108(1). As to the regulations made under s 108 see the Individual Learning Accounts (England) Regulations 2000, SI 2000/2146; and the Individual Learning Accounts Wales Regulations 2003, SI 2003/918 (amended by SI 2005/1722; SI 2005/3238; and SI 2008/1879).

3   Learning and Skills Act 2000 s 108(2)(a). In order to be a 'qualifying account', the account must satisfy the conditions specified by the appropriate national authority in regulations made under s 104 (or satisfy them at the time concerned): see s 104(1)–(2). At the date at which this volume states the law, no such regulations had been made under s 104.

Conditions which may be included are conditions:

(1)   as to the description of individual who may hold an account (s 104(3)(a));
(2)   as to the description of institution with which an account may be held (s 104(3)(b));
(3)   requiring an account not to be a joint one, or not to be held on behalf of a person other than the holder, or not to be held with another account of a specified description, or not to be connected with another account (s 104(3)(c));
(4)   requiring an account to be identified by a specified name (s 104(3)(d)).

Conditions as to the description of institution with which an account may be held may themselves specify the description or may allow the appropriate national authority to specify it in a way it thinks fit: s 104(4). The regulations may provide that a specification of a description of institution with which an account may be held may include a requirement for institutions to have the benefit of approvals which have been given by the appropriate national authority and not withdrawn: s 104(5). The regulations may contain provision securing that an individual may not simultaneously hold more than one account which qualifies: s 104(6).

4   Learning and Skills Act 2000 s 108(2)(b). In order to be 'qualifying arrangements', the arrangements must satisfy the conditions specified by the appropriate national authority in regulations (or satisfy them at the time concerned): see s 105(1), (2). As to the regulations made see note 2.

Conditions which may be included are conditions:

(1)   as to the description of individual who may enter into arrangements (s 105(3)(a));
(2)   as to the description of body with which arrangements may be made (s 105(3)(b));
(3)   as to the nature of the arrangements and the way they are to be made (s 105(3)(c));
(4)   requiring the arrangements to be identified by a specified name (s 105(3)(d)).

Conditions as to the description of body with which arrangements may be made may themselves specify the description or may allow the appropriate national authority to specify it in a way it thinks fit: s 105(4). The regulations may provide that a specification of a description of body with which arrangements may be made may include a requirement for bodies to have the benefit of approvals which have been given by the appropriate national authority and not withdrawn: s 105(5). The regulations may contain provision securing that an individual may not simultaneously be a party to more than one set of arrangements which qualify under s 105, or be a party to arrangements which qualify under s 105 and to arrangements falling within s 105(7): s 105(6). Arrangements fall within s 105(7) if they are arrangements which qualify under such provision of the law of Scotland as in the opinion of the appropriate national authority corresponds to s 105, or arrangements which qualify under s 106 (qualifying arrangements: Northern Ireland): s 105(7).

The appropriate national authority, or a person designated by it, may make arrangements with a body in connection with the making by that body of qualifying arrangements (s 107(1)); and the appropriate national authority may pay to a person designated by it under s 107(1) remuneration or amounts to meet the person's expenses (s 107(4)(a)). These further arrangements may include provision for the remuneration of a body and the payment of its expenses: s 107(2). The arrangements may include provision for a person designated by the appropriate national authority to carry out on its behalf such of its functions under the arrangements as it specifies (s 107(3)); and the appropriate national authority may pay to a person designated by it under s 107(3) remuneration or amounts to meet the person's expenses (s 107(4)(b)). As to the meaning of 'person' see PARA 7 note 6.

5 Learning and Skills Act 2000 s 108(2)(c).
6 Learning and Skills Act 2000 s 108(3).
7 Learning and Skills Act 2000 s 108(4)(a).
8 Learning and Skills Act 2000 s 108(4)(b).
9 Learning and Skills Act 2000 s 108(4)(c).
10 Learning and Skills Act 2000 s 108(4)(d).
11 Learning and Skills Act 2000 s 108(4)(e). Conditions as to the kinds of education or training which qualify may include provision for the kinds to be specified by the appropriate national authority in a way it thinks fit, or if it so decides, by a person who, at the time of the specification, is designated by it and who specifies in a way it stipulates: s 108(6). As to the meaning of 'person' see PARA 7 note 6.
12 Learning and Skills Act 2000 s 108(5)(a). See *R (on the application of Amraf Training plc) v Department for Education and Employment* [2001] EWCA Civ 914, (2001) Times, 28 June, [2001] All ER (D) 276 (May) (grant withdrawn on the basis that course did not provide value for money).
13 Learning and Skills Act 2000 s 108(5)(b).
14 Learning and Skills Act 2000 s 108(5)(c).
15 Learning and Skills Act 2000 s 108(5)(d).
16 Learning and Skills Act 2000 s 108(5)(e).
17 Learning and Skills Act 2000 s 108(7)(a).
18 Learning and Skills Act 2000 s 108(7)(b).

(7) CAREERS EDUCATION AND GUIDANCE

819.   Provision of careers services for young persons in education.   The appropriate national authority[1] is under a duty to secure the provision of career services for: (1) assisting persons undergoing relevant education to decide what are suitable employments for them when they finish such education, and what training or education is or will be required and available in order to fit them for those employments; and (2) assisting persons finishing relevant education to obtain such employments, training and education[2]. The appropriate national authority also has power to arrange for the provision of careers services for other persons[3].

The appropriate national authority may perform this duty and exercise this power by: (a) making arrangements with local authorities, persons of any other description, or local authorities and persons of any other description acting jointly, under which they undertake to provide, or arrange for the provision of, services in accordance with the arrangements; and (b) giving directions to local authorities requiring them to provide, or arrange for the provision of, services in accordance with the directions[4]. The functions of a local authority include power to enter into agreements for the supply of certain goods or services with any person (other than an authority) who provides, or arranges for the provision of, such services and is a person with whom such arrangements may be made[5].

Her Majesty's Chief Inspector of Education, Children's Services and Skills[6] must, when requested to do so by the Secretary of State, inspect and report on the provision of services in England[7] by any person or institution, and may undertake such other inspections of the provision of those services by persons or institutions as he thinks fit[8].

1 Ie the Secretary of State or, in relation to Wales, the Welsh Ministers. As to the Secretary of State see PARA 58. As to the Welsh Ministers see PARA 59. As to the meaning of 'Wales' see PARA 7 note 3. The functions of the Secretary of State under the Employment and Training Act 1973 ss 8–10, so far as exercisable in relation to Wales, were transferred to the National Assembly for Wales (see the National Assembly for Wales (Transfer of Functions) Order 1999, SI 1999/672, art 2, Sch 1) and are now vested in the Welsh Ministers (see the Government of Wales Act 2006 s 162(1), Sch 11 para 30).
2 See the Employment and Training Act 1973 s 8; and EMPLOYMENT vol 40 (2014) PARA 638.
3 See the Employment and Training Act 1973 s 9; and EMPLOYMENT vol 40 (2014) PARA 639.
4 See the Employment and Training Act 1973 s 10; and EMPLOYMENT vol 40 (2014) PARA 640.
5 See the Employment and Training Act 1973 s 10A; and EMPLOYMENT vol 40 (2014) PARA 642.
6 As to Her Majesty's Chief Inspector of Education, Children's Services and Skills see PARA 1133.
7 Ie in pursuance of the Employment and Training Act 1973 s 8 or s 9.
8 See the Employment and Training Act 1973 s 10B; and EMPLOYMENT vol 40 (2014) PARA 641.

820. Provision of careers education in schools in England and Wales. The responsible authorities[1] for a school in England[2] which provides secondary education[3] and is one of the following: (1) a community, foundation or voluntary school[4]; (2) a community or foundation special school (other than one established in a hospital)[5]; (3) a pupil referral unit[6], must secure that all registered pupils[7] at the school are provided with independent careers guidance[8] during the relevant phase[9] of their education[10]. The responsible authorities must secure that careers guidance[11] provided[12] is presented in an impartial manner[13], includes information on options available in respect of 16 to 18 education or training[14], including apprenticeships[15] and is guidance that the person[16] giving it considers will promote the best interests of the pupils to whom it is given[17].

All registered pupils in Wales[18] at: (a) community, foundation and voluntary schools[19]; (b) community special schools (other than those established in hospitals)[20]; and (c) pupil referral units[21], must be provided, during the relevant phase[22] of their education, with a programme of careers education[23]. It is the duty of each of the following to secure that these requirements[24] are complied with, namely: (i) in the case of a school falling within head (a) or head (b) above, the governing body of the school and its head teacher[25]; and (ii) in the case of head (c) above, the local authority maintaining the unit and the teacher in charge of it[26].

The Secretary of State or, in relation to Wales, the Welsh Ministers may by regulations make provision for requiring the governing bodies of institutions within the further education sector[27], and the principals or other heads of such institutions[28], to secure that, in relation to England, careers guidance is provided for any specified[29] description of persons attending such institutions[30]; and, in relation to Wales, a programme of careers education is provided for any specified description of persons attending such institutions[31].

1 The responsible authorities for a school within the Education Act 1997 s 42A(2) are in the case of a school within head (1) or (2) in the text, its governing body; or in the case of a pupil referral

unit, the local authority that maintains it: s 42A(3) (s 42A added by the Education Act 2011 s 29(2)). As to the governing bodies of maintained schools in England see PARA 150 et seq. As to the meaning of 'local authority' see PARA 25.

2   As to the meaning of 'England' see PARA 7 note 3.

3   As to the meaning of 'secondary education' see PARA 21 (definition applied by the Education Act 1997 s 56(2)).

4   Education Act 1997 s 42A(2)(a) (as added: see note 1). As to the meaning of references to a community, foundation or voluntary school see PARA 106.

5   Education Act 1997 s 42A(2)(b) (as added: see note 1). As to the meaning of references to a community or foundation special school see PARA 106.

6   Education Act 1997 s 42A(2)(c) (as added: see note 1). As to pupil referral units see PARA 427 et seq.

7   As to the meaning of 'registered pupil' see PARA 437 (definition applied by the Education Act 1997 s 56(2)).

8   Careers guidance provided to pupils at a school is independent for the purposes of the Education Act 1997 s 42A if it is provided other than by a teacher employed or engaged at the school, or any other person employed at the school: s 42A(5) (as added: see note 1).

9   For these purposes, the relevant phase of a pupil's education is the period beginning at the same time as the school year in which the majority of pupils in the pupil's class attain the age of 14, and ending with the expiry of the school year in which the majority of pupils in the pupil's class attain the age of 16: Education Act 1997 s 42A(6) (as added: see note 1). The Secretary of State may by regulations extend the scope of operation of s 42A by substituting for the period specified in s 42A(6) such other period as is specified in the regulations: see s 46(1). In relation to England, s 42A has effect as if there were substituted for the period specified in s 42A(6) as the relevant phase of a pupil's education the period beginning at the same time as the school year in which the majority of pupils in the pupil's class attain the age of 13, and ending with the expiry of the school year in which the majority of pupils in the pupil's class attain the age of 18: see the Careers Guidance in Schools Regulations 2013, SI 2013/709, reg 2. However, the Education Act 1997 s 42A(4)(b) (see the text and note 15) does not apply in relation to any pupil over compulsory school age: see the Careers Guidance in Schools Regulations 2013, SI 2013/709, reg 3. 'Class', in relation to a pupil, means the teaching group in which the pupil is regularly taught, or, if the pupil is taught in different groups for different subjects, such one of those groups as is designated by the head teacher of the school or, in the case of a pupil at a pupil referral unit, by the teacher in charge of the unit: Education Act 1997 s 42A(7) (as so added), s 43(6) (amended by the Education Act 2011 s 29(1), (3)(f)(i)). As to the meaning of 'pupil' see PARA 20 note 4; and as to the meaning of 'school year' see PARA 19 note 12 (definitions applied by the Education Act 1997 s 56(2)). As to the meaning of 'head teacher' see PARA 86 note 4 (definition applied by s 56(2)). As to the meaning of 'compulsory school age' see PARA 19 (definition applied by s 56(2)). As to the time at which a person attains a particular age see PARA 7 note 6. As to the Secretary of State see PARA 58.

10 Education Act 1997 s 42A(1) (as added: see note 1). The persons responsible for discharging a duty under s 42A(1) in relation to a school in England falling within the Education Act 1997 s 42A(2) (see the text and notes 2–6) must, in discharging the duty, have regard to any guidance given from time to time by the Secretary of State: s 45A (added by the Education and Skills Act 2008 s 81(1), (4)). As to academies see PARA 345 et seq. As to independent schools see PARA 369 et seq.

11 'Careers guidance' means guidance about careers; and 'career' includes undertaking any training, education, employment or occupation: Education Act 1997 s 42A(7) (as added: see note 1). As to the duty of schools and other institutions to co-operate with careers advisors see PARA 822; and as to the provision of careers information see PARA 821.

12 Ie under the Education Act 1997 s 42A(1) (see the text and notes 1–10).

13 Education Act 1997 s 42A(4)(a) (as added: see note 1). The persons responsible for discharging a duty under s 42A(4) in relation to a school in England falling within the Education Act 1997 s 42A(2) (see the text and notes 2–6) must, in discharging the duty, have regard to any guidance given from time to time by the Secretary of State: s 45A (added by the Education and Skills Act 2008 s 81(1), (4)).

14 '16 to 18 education or training' means education or training suitable to the requirements of persons who have ceased to be of compulsory school age but have not attained the age of 18; and 'training' includes a voluntary or other placement apt to enable the development of any skill or competency (whether or not taking place at a time when the person concerned is still a registered pupil at a school in England): Education Act 1997 s 42A(7) (as added: see note 1).

15 Education Act 1997 s 42A(4)(b) (as added: see note 1). See note 13. In s 42A 'apprenticeship' includes employment and training leading to the issue of an apprenticeship certificate under the Apprenticeships, Skills, Children and Learning Act 2009 s 3 or s 4 (see PARA 761): Education Act 1997 s 42(7) (as so added).

16 As to the meaning of 'person' see PARA 7 note 6.

17 Education Act 1997 s 42A(4)(c) (as added: see note 1). See note 13.

18 As to the meaning 'Wales' see PARA 7 note 3.

19 Education Act 1997 s 43(2)(a) (substituted by the School Standards and Framework Act 1998 s 140(1), Sch 30 paras 207, 217(a)).

20 Education Act 1997 s 43(2)(c) (substituted by the School Standards and Framework Act 1998 Sch 30 paras 207, 217(c); and amended by the School Standards and Organisation (Wales) Act 2013 Sch 5 para 18(1), (3)).

21 Education Act 1997 s 43(2)(e).

22 The 'relevant phase' of a pupil's education is the period: (1) beginning at the same time as the school year in which the majority of pupils in his class attain the age of 14 (Education Act 1997 s 43(5)(a)); and (2) ending with the expiry of the school year in which the majority of pupils in his class attain the age of 16 (s 43(5)(b)).
    The Secretary of State or, in relation to Wales, the Welsh Ministers may by regulations extend the scope of operation of s 43 by substituting for the period specified in s 43(5) such other period as is specified in the regulations: see s 46(1) (as amended: see note 9). In relation to Wales, s 43 has effect as if there were substituted for the period specified in s 43(5) as the relevant phase of a pupil's education the period beginning at the same time as the school year in which the majority of pupils in his class attain the age of 14, and ending with the expiry of the school year in which the majority of pupils in his class attain the age of 19: see the Education (Extension of Careers Education) (Wales) Regulations 2001, SI 2001/1987, regs 1(2), 2.
    The functions of the Secretary of State under the Education Act 1997 ss 43, 46, so far as exercisable in relation to Wales, were transferred to the National Assembly for Wales (see the National Assembly for Wales (Transfer of Functions) Order 1999, SI 1999/672, art 2, Sch 1) and are now vested in the Welsh Ministers (see the Government of Wales Act 2006 s 162(1), Sch 11 para 30). As to the Welsh Ministers see PARA 59.

23 Education Act 1997 s 43(1) (amended by the Education Act 2011 s 29(1), (3)(a)). 'Careers education' means education designed to prepare persons for taking decisions about their careers and to help them implement such decisions: Education Act 1997 s 43(6). 'Career' includes the undertaking of any training, employment or occupation or any course of education: s 43(6)
    The Secretary of State or, in relation to Wales, the Welsh Ministers may by regulations make provision for extending the scope of operation of s 43 to primary schools or to any specified description of such schools: see s 46(2). As to the meaning of 'primary school' see PARA 91 (definition applied by s 56(2)). At the date at which this volume states the law no such regulations had been made.

24 Ie the Education Act 1997 s 43(1) (see the text to notes 18–22).

25 Education Act 1997 s 43(3)(a) (amended by the Education and Skills Act 2008 s 81(1), (2)(b); and the Education Act 2011 s 29(2), (3)(d)(i)). As to the governing bodies of maintained schools in in Wales see PARA 195.

26 Education Act 1997 s 43(3)(c) (amended by SI 2010/1158).

27 Education Act 1997 s 46(2A)(a), (3)(a) (s 46(2A) added and s 46(3) amended by the Education Act 2011 s 29(1), (8)(b), (c)). As to the meaning of 'institution within the further education sector' see PARA 555 (definition applied by the Education Act 1997 s 56(2)).

28 Education Act 1997 s 46(2A)(b), (3)(b) (as added and amended: see note 27).

29 'Specified' means specified in the regulations in question: Education Act 1997 s 46(5).

30 See the Education Act 1997 s 46(2A) (as added: see note 27), (5). At the date at which this volume states the law no such regulations had been made in relation to England.

31 See the Education Act 1997 s 46(3), (5). In relation to Wales, the governing bodies, and the principals or other heads, of institutions within the further education sector must secure that a programme of careers education is provided for persons attending those institutions (whether attending full-time or part-time) who have attained the age of 16 but who have not attained the age of 20: see the Education (Extension of Careers Education) (Wales) Regulations 2001, SI 2001/1987, regs 1(2), 3(1), (2). 'Careers' includes the undertaking of any training, employment or occupation or any course of education; and 'careers education' means education designed to prepare persons for taking decisions about their careers and to help them implement such decisions: reg 3(3).

821. Provision of careers information at schools in Wales and other institutions in England and Wales. Persons[1] attending: (1) community, foundation and voluntary schools in Wales[2]; (2) community special schools in Wales (other than those established in hospitals)[3]; and (3) institutions within the further education sector in England and Wales[4], must be provided with access to both guidance materials[5], and a wide range of up-to-date reference materials[6], relating to careers education[7] and career[8] opportunities[9].

It is the duty of each of the following to secure that these requirements[10] are complied with, namely[11]: (a) the governing body of the school[12] or institution[13]; and (b) its head teacher[14], principal or other head[15].

1   As to the meaning of 'person' see PARA 7 note 6.
2   See the Education Act 1997 s 45(1), (2)(a). As to the meaning of references to a community, foundation or voluntary school see PARA 106.
3   See the Education Act 1997 s 45(1), (2)(a). As to the meaning of references to a community special school see PARA 106.
4   Education Act 1997 s 45(1), (2)(b). As to the meaning of 'institution within the further education sector' see PARA 555.
5   Education Act 1997 s 45(1)(a).
6   Education Act 1997 s 45(1)(b).
7   As to the meaning of 'careers education' see PARA 820 note 11 (definition applied by the Education Act 1997 s 45(5) (amended by the Education and Skills Act 2008 s 81(1), (3)(d))).
8   As to the meaning of 'career' see PARA 820 note 11 (definition applied by the Education Act 1997 s 45(5)).
9   Education Act 1997 s 45(1). Nothing in s 45 applies to any primary school: s 45(6). However, the Secretary of State or, in relation to Wales, the Welsh Ministers may by regulations make provision for extending the scope of operation of s 45 to primary schools or to any specified description of such schools: see s 46(2). At the date at which this volume states the law no such regulations had been made. As to the meaning of 'primary school' see PARA 91 (definition applied by s 56(2)). As to the Secretary of State see PARA 58. As to the Welsh Ministers see PARA 59. As to the meaning of 'Wales' see PARA 7 note 3. The functions of the Secretary of State under the Education Act 1997 s 46, so far as exercisable in relation to Wales, were transferred to the National Assembly for Wales (see the National Assembly for Wales (Transfer of Functions) Order 1999, SI 1999/672, art 2, Sch 1) and are now vested in the Welsh Ministers (see the Government of Wales Act 2006 s 162(1), Sch 11 para 30). As to academies see PARA 345 et seq. As to independent schools see PARA 369 et seq.
10 Ie the Education Act 1997 s 45(1) (see the text to notes 1–9).
11 The persons who are responsible, under the Education Act 1997 s 45(3), for discharging that duty in relation to an institution must seek assistance with discharging it from a body providing services in pursuance of arrangements made or directions given under the Employment and Training Act 1973 s 10 (see EMPLOYMENT vol 40 (2014) PARA 640): Education Act 1997 s 45(4).
12 As to the governing bodies of maintained schools in England see PARA 150 et seq; and in Wales see PARA 195.
13 Education Act 1997 s 45(3)(a) (s 45(3) substituted by the Education Act 2011 s 29(1), (5)(d)).
14 As to the meaning of 'head teacher' see PARA 86 note 4 (definition applied by the Education Act 1997 s 56(2)).
15 Education Act 1997 s 45(3)(b) (as substituted: see note 13).

822. Schools and other institutions in Wales to co-operate with careers advisers. Where a careers adviser[1] has responsibilities in relation to persons attending: (1) community, foundation and voluntary schools in Wales[2]; (2) community special schools in Wales (other than those established in hospitals)[3]; and (3) institutions in Wales within the further education sector[4], he must on request[5] be provided with: (a) the name and address of every relevant pupil[6] or student[7] at the institution[8]; and (b) any information in the institution's possession about any such pupil or student which the careers adviser needs in order to be able to provide him with advice and guidance on decisions about his career[9] or with other information relevant to such decisions[10].

Such a careers adviser[11] must on request[12] be permitted to have, in the case of any relevant pupil or student specified by him, access to that person on the institution's premises[13], and at a reasonable time agreed by or on behalf of the head teacher, principal or other head of the institution[14], for the purpose of enabling him to provide that person with advice and guidance on decisions about his career and with any other information relevant to such decisions[15]. Such access includes an opportunity for the careers adviser to interview that person about his career, if he agrees to be so interviewed[16].

Such a careers adviser[17] must on request[18] be permitted to have, in the case of any group of relevant pupils or students specified by him, access to that group of persons in the manner specified[19] above[20] and to such of the institution's facilities as can conveniently be made available for his use[21], for the purpose of enabling him to provide those persons with group sessions on any matters relating to careers or to advice or guidance about careers[22].

It is the duty of each of the following to secure that the requirements described above[23] are complied with, namely: (i) the governing body of the school[24] or institution in Wales[25]; (ii) its head teacher, principal or other head[26].

1 'Careers adviser' means a person who is employed by a body providing services in pursuance of arrangements made or directions given under the Employment and Training Act 1973 s 10 (see EMPLOYMENT vol 40 (2014) PARA 640) and who is acting, in the course of his employment by that body, for the purposes of the provision of any such services: Education Act 1997 s 44(11)(a). A careers adviser has responsibilities for any persons if his employment by that body includes the provision of any such services for it: s 44(11)(b). The Secretary of State or, in relation to Wales, the Welsh Ministers may by regulations amend the definition of careers adviser in s 44(11)(a): see s 46(4). At the date at which this volume states the law no such regulations had been made. As to the Secretary of State see PARA 58. As to the Welsh Ministers see PARA 59. The functions of the Secretary of State under the Education Act 1997 ss 44, 46, so far as exercisable in relation to Wales, were transferred to the National Assembly for Wales (see the National Assembly for Wales (Transfer of Functions) Order 1999, SI 1999/672, art 2, Sch 1) and are now vested in the Welsh Ministers (see the Government of Wales Act 2006 s 162(1), Sch 11 para 30). As to the meaning of 'Wales' see PARA 7 note 3.

2 See the Education Act 1997 s 44(1), (8)(a) (s 44(8) amended by the Education Act 2011 s 29(1), (4)(a), (b)). As to the meaning of references to a community, foundation or voluntary school see PARA 106.

3 See the Education Act 1997 s 44(1), (8)(a) (as amended: see note 2). As to the meaning of references to a community special school see PARA 106.

4 See the Education Act 1997 s 44(1), (8)(b) (as amended: see note 2). As to the meaning of 'institution within the further education sector' see PARA 555.

5 Any request made under the Education Act 1997 s 44(1) must be made in writing to the head teacher, principal or other head of the institution in question: see s 44(7). As to the meaning of 'writing' see PARA 76 note 8. As to the meaning of 'head teacher' see PARA 86 note 4 (definition applied by s 56(2)).

6 A pupil at a school is a 'relevant pupil': (1) at any time during the period which is the relevant phase of his education for the purposes of the Education Act 1997 s 43 (see PARA 820) (s 44(10)(a)(i)); or (2) if he is over compulsory school age and receiving secondary education (s 44(10)(a)(ii)). As to the meaning of 'pupil' see PARA 20 note 4; and as to the meaning of 'secondary education' see PARA 21 (definitions applied by s 56(2)). As to the meaning of 'compulsory school age' see PARA 19. The Secretary of State or, in relation to Wales, the Welsh Ministers may by regulations extend the scope of operation of s 44 by substituting for the period specified in s 44(10)(a)(i) such other period as is specified: see s 46(1) (amended by the Education Act 2011 s 29(1), (8)(a)). The Education Act 1997 s 44 has effect as if there were substituted for the period specified in s 43(5) as the relevant phase of a pupil's education the period specified in the Education (Extension of Careers Education) (Wales) Regulations 2001, SI 2001/1987, reg 2 (PARA 820 note 22): see regs 1(2), 2.

7 A person is a 'relevant student' at an institution in Wales within the further education sector if he is receiving at the institution either full-time education, or part-time education of a description commonly undergone by persons in order to fit them for employment: Education Act 1997 s 44(10)(b) (amended by the Education Act 2011 s 29(1), (4)(e)).

8   Education Act 1997 s 44(1)(a). If the registered address of a parent of any such pupil is different from the pupil's registered address, s 44(1)(a) requires the parent's address to be provided as well: s 44(2). As to the meaning of 'registered' see PARA 437; and as to the meaning of 'parent' see PARA 7 note 6 (definitions applied by s 56(2)).
    However, the provisions of s 44(1)(a) or s 44(1)(b) (see the text to notes 10–11) do not apply to any pupil or student to the extent that (where he is under the age of 16) a parent of his or, (where he has attained that age) he himself, has indicated that any information falling within s 44(1)(a) or, as the case may be, s 44(1)(b) should not be provided to the careers adviser: s 44(3) (amended by the Learning and Skills Act 2000 Sch 9 paras 1, 72). As to the time at which a person attains a particular age see PARA 7 note 6.
9   As to the meaning of 'career' see PARA 820 note 11 (definition applied by the Education Act 1997 s 44(12)).
10 Education Act 1997 s 44(1)(b). See also note 8. The Welsh Ministers may by regulations make provision for extending the scope of operation of s 44 to primary schools or to any specified description of such schools: see s 46(2). As to the meaning of 'primary school' see PARA 91 (definition applied by s 56(2)). At the date at which this volume states the law no such regulations had been made.
11 Ie a careers adviser who has responsibilities in relation to persons attending an educational institution in Wales to which the Education Act 1997 s 44 applies (see heads (1)–(3) in the text).
12 Any request made under the Education Act 1997 s 44(4) must be made in writing to the head teacher, principal or other head of the institution in question: see s 44(7).
13 Education Act 1997 s 44(4)(a).
14 Education Act 1997 s 44(4)(b).
15 Education Act 1997 s 44(4).
16 Education Act 1997 s 44(5).
17 See note 11.
18 Any request made under the Education Act 1997 s 44(6) must be made in writing to the head teacher, principal or other head of the institution in question: see s 44(7).
19 Ie in the manner specified in the Education Act 1997 s 44(4)(a), (b) (see the text to notes 13–14).
20 Education Act 1997 s 44(6)(a).
21 Education Act 1997 s 44(6)(b).
22 Education Act 1997 s 44(6).
23 Ie the requirements of the Education Act 1997 s 44(1), (4), (6): see the text to notes 1–22.
24 As to the governing bodies of maintained schools Wales see PARA 195.
25 Education Act 1997 s 44(9)(a) (s 44(9) substituted by the Education Act 2011 s 29(1), (4)(c)).
26 Education Act 1997 s 44(9)(b) (as substituted: see note 25). The Education Act 1996 s 496 (power to prevent unreasonable exercise of functions: see PARA 64) and s 497 (general default powers: see PARA 65), in relation to the duty imposed by the Education Act 1997 s 44(9), have effect as if any reference to a body to which that provision applies included a reference to the proprietors of a school falling within head (3) in the text: s 43(4) (applied by s 44(9)). As to the meaning of 'proprietor' see PARA 51 note 4 (definition applied by s 56(2)).

823.   Provision of curriculum information in Wales. A service provider[1] may demand from the governing body[2] and head teacher[3] of a community, foundation or voluntary school[4] in Wales[5], and the governing body and principal of an institution within the further education sector[6] in Wales[7], such curriculum information[8] as is specified in the demand[9]. However, a service provider must not demand any curriculum information unless the provider reasonably considers that the information would assist it in providing its services[10]; and a service provider must not demand any curriculum information which identifies, or allows to be identified, any pupil or student[11].

The governing body and head teacher of a community, foundation or voluntary school in Wales, and the governing body and principal of an institution within the further education sector in Wales must comply with a demand by providing the service provider with the information demanded[12]. A service provider may publish in whatever form it sees fit any curriculum information so provided[13].

1   'Service provider' means a person providing services in pursuance of arrangements made with, or directions given by, the Welsh Ministers under the Employment and Training Act 1973 s 10

(see EMPLOYMENT vol 40 (2014) PARA 640); and 'services' must be construed accordingly: Education Act 1997 s 45B(7) (s 45B added by the Learning and Skills (Wales) Measure 2009 s 45). As to the meaning of 'person' see PARA 7 note 6. As to the Welsh Ministers see PARA 59.

2   As to the governing bodies of maintained schools in Wales see PARA 195.

3   As to the meaning of 'head teacher' see PARA 86 note 4 (definition applied by the Education Act 1997 s 56(2)).

4   As to the meaning of references to a community, foundation or voluntary school see PARA 106.

5   See the Education Act 1997 s 45B(1), (6)(a) (as added: see note 1). As to the meaning of 'Wales' see PARA 7 note 3.

6   As to the meaning of 'institution within the further education sector' see PARA 555 (definition applied by the Education Act 1997 s 56(2)).

7   See the Education Act 1997 s 45B(1), (6)(b) (as added: see note 1).

8   'Curriculum information' means: (1) in relation to a community, foundation or voluntary school, information about the curriculum for registered pupils at the school during the relevant phase of their education; and (2) in relation to an institution within the further education sector, information about the courses of study and other education and training available at the institution: Education Act 1997 s 45B(7) (as added: see note 1). 'Pupil' means, in relation to a community, foundation or voluntary school, a person receiving education at the school: s 45B(7) (as so added). As to the meaning of 'registered pupil' see PARA 437 (definition applied by s 56(2)). As to the meaning of 'relevant phase' see PARA 820 note 22 (definition applied by s 45B(7) (as so added)).

9   Education Act 1997 s 45B(1) (as added: see note 1).

10 Education Act 1997 s 45B(2) (as added: see note 1).

11 Education Act 1997 s 45B(3) (as added: see note 1). 'Student' means, in relation to an institution within the further education sector, a person receiving education at the institution: s 45B(7) (as so added).

12 Education Act 1997 s 45B(4) (as added: see note 1).

13 Education Act 1997 s 45B(5) (as added: see note 1).

6. CURRICULUM, ASSESSMENT AND EXTERNAL QUALIFICATIONS

(1) SUPERVISION OF CURRICULUM AND EXTERNAL QUALIFICATIONS

(i) Supervision of Curriculum and Qualifications in England

A. SUPERVISION IN ENGLAND

824. Responsibility for supervision in England. Previously the Qualifications and Curriculum Development Agency was the key body in England[1] in regard to matters relating to the curriculum, assessment and qualifications. The Agency was a body corporate[2], and there were provisions about its establishment, constitution and administration, and its functions, including in relation to qualifications, the curriculum and assessment, in the Apprenticeships, Skills, Children and Learning Act 2009[3]. However these provisions were mostly repealed as from 1 April 2012[4], with the effect that the Agency was abolished from that date[5].

The main supervisory body in England is now the Office of Qualifications and Examinations Regulation ('Ofqual')[6].

1   As to the meaning of 'England' see PARA 7 note 3.
2   The body corporate was originally established under the Education Act 1997 s 21 (repealed) as the Qualifications and Curriculum Authority and continued in existence but was known instead as the Qualifications and Curriculum Development Agency: see the Apprenticeships, Skills, Children and Learning Act 2009 s 175(1) (repealed); and notes 3, 4. As to bodies corporate see COMPANIES vol 14 (2009) PARA 2; CORPORATIONS vol 24 (2010) PARA 301 et seq.
3   Ie the Apprenticeships, Skills, Children and Learning Act 2009 Pt 8 (ss 175–192).
4   See the Education Act 2011 s 25 which specifically repealed the Apprenticeships, Skills, Children and Learning Act 2009 ss 175–191, Sch 11.
5   As to the transfer of staff, property, rights and liabilities from the Agency to other persons see the Education Act 2011 s 27, Sch 9.
6   See PARA 825 et seq. As to the role of the Secretary of State see PARA 856; and as to the Secretary of State generally see PARA 58. The Standards and Testing Agency, which is an executive agency of the Department for Education, is responsible for National Curriculum tests and assessment from early years to the end of key stage 2. See also the Education (National Curriculum) (Key Stages 1, 2, and 3 Assessment Arrangements) (England) Amendment Order 2011, SI 2011/2392; and PARA 863. As to the key stages of the curriculum see PARA 860.

B. THE OFFICE OF QUALIFICATIONS AND EXAMINATIONS REGULATION

(A) Constitution etc of the Office of Qualifications and Examinations Regulation

825. Establishment and constitution of the Office of Qualifications and Examinations Regulation. The Office of Qualifications and Examinations Regulation ('Ofqual')[1] is a body corporate[2] and is to perform its functions[3] on behalf of the Crown[4]. There are provisions as to the chief executive, the chair ('the chief regulator') and membership[5], staff[6], committees[7], procedure[8] and documents[9].

1   Ofqual is a non-ministerial government department which regulates qualifications, examinations and assessments in England and vocational qualifications in Northern Ireland. As to the functions of Ofqual see PARA 826 et seq.

2   See the Apprenticeships, Skills, Children and Learning Act 2009 s 127(1), (2). Ofqual was
    established on 1 April 2010: see the Apprenticeships, Skills, Children and Learning Act 2009
    (Commencement No 3 and Transitional and Transitory Provisions) and (Commencement No 2
    (Amendment)) Order 2010, SI 2010/1151, art 2, Sch 1.
3   As to the meaning of 'functions' see PARA 18 note 5 (definition applied by the Apprenticeships,
    Skills, Children and Learning Act 2009 s 264(2), (3)).
4   Apprenticeships, Skills, Children and Learning Act 2009 Sch 9 para 1.
5   See the Apprenticeships, Skills, Children and Learning Act 2009 Sch 9 paras 2, 3, 3A, 4, 5 (Sch 9
    para 2 amended by the Education Act 2011 Sch 7 paras 1, 2; the Apprenticeships, Skills,
    Children and Learning Act 2009 Sch 9 para 3 amended by the Education Act 2011 Sch 7
    paras 1, 3; the Apprenticeships, Skills, Children and Learning Act 2009 Sch 9 para 3A added by
    the Education Act 2011 Sch 7 paras 1, 4; the Apprenticeships, Skills, Children and Learning
    Act 2009 Sch 9 para 4 amended by the Education Act 2011 Sch 7 paras 1, 5; and the
    Apprenticeships, Skills, Children and Learning Act 2009 Sch 9 para 5 amended by the
    Education Act 2011 Sch 7 paras 1, 6, 7)
6   See the Apprenticeships, Skills, Children and Learning Act 2009 Sch 9 para 6(4), (5) (Sch 9
    para 6(4), (5) amended and Sch 9 para 6(1)–(3) repealed by the Education Act 2011 Sch 7
    paras 1, 9(1), (2), (3)).
7   See the Apprenticeships, Skills, Children and Learning Act 2009 Sch 9 paras 7, 8.
8   See the Apprenticeships, Skills, Children and Learning Act 2009 Sch 9 paras 9, 11.
9   See the Apprenticeships, Skills, Children and Learning Act 2009 Sch 9 paras 12, 13.

(B)   General Functions of the Office of Qualifications and Examinations

826.   Objectives.   The objectives of the Office of Qualifications and
Examinations Regulation[1] ('Ofqual') are:
   (1)   the qualifications standards objective[2];
   (2)   the assessments standards objective[3];
   (3)   the public confidence objective[4];
   (4)   the awareness objective[5]; and
   (5)   the efficiency objective[6].
The 'qualifications standards objective' is to secure that: (a) regulated
qualifications[7] give a reliable indication of knowledge, skills and understanding[8];
and (b) regulated qualifications indicate a consistent level of attainment
(including over time) between comparable regulated qualifications[9]; and a
consistent level of attainment (but not over time) between regulated
qualifications and comparable qualifications (including those awarded outside
the United Kingdom[10]) which are not qualifications to which these provisions[11]
apply[12].
The 'assessments standards objective' is to promote the development and
implementation of regulated assessment arrangements[13] which: (i) give a reliable
indication of achievement[14]; and (ii) indicate a consistent level of attainment
(including over time) between comparable assessments[15].
The 'public confidence objective' is to promote public confidence in regulated
qualifications and regulated assessment arrangements[16].
The 'awareness objective' is to promote awareness and understanding of: (A)
the range of regulated qualifications available[17]; (B) the benefits of regulated
qualifications to learners, employers and institutions within the higher education
sector[18]; and (C) the benefits of recognition[19] to bodies awarding or
authenticating qualifications[20].
The 'efficiency objective' is to secure that regulated qualifications are provided
efficiently and in particular that any relevant sums[21] payable to a body awarding
or authenticating a qualification in respect of which the body is recognised[22]
represent value for money[23].

1   As to the Office of Qualifications and Examinations Regulation generally see PARA 824.

2   Apprenticeships, Skills, Children and Learning Act 2009 s 128(1)(a).
3   Apprenticeships, Skills, Children and Learning Act 2009 s 128(1)(b).
4   Apprenticeships, Skills, Children and Learning Act 2009 s 128(1)(c).
5   Apprenticeships, Skills, Children and Learning Act 2009 s 128(1)(d).
6   Apprenticeships, Skills, Children and Learning Act 2009 s 128(1)(e).
7   A 'regulated qualification' means a qualification to which the Apprenticeships, Skills, Children and Learning Act 2009 Pt 7 (ss 127–174) applies which is awarded or authenticated by a body which is recognised under s 132 (see PARA 831) in respect of the qualification: s 130(1). Part 7 applies to any of the following qualifications which is not an excluded qualification: (1) an academic or vocational qualification awarded or authenticated in England (s 130(2)(a)); (2) a vocational qualification awarded or authenticated in Northern Ireland (s 130(2)(b)). An 'excluded qualification' is any of the following: (a) a foundation degree (s 130(3)(a)); (b) a first degree (s 130(3)(b)); (c) a degree at a higher level (s 130(3)(c)). For the purposes of s 130(2) a qualification is awarded or authenticated in England or Northern Ireland if there are, or may reasonably be expected to be, persons seeking to obtain the qualification who are, will be or may reasonably be expected to be assessed for those purposes wholly or mainly in England or Northern Ireland (as the case may be): s 130(4). The Secretary of State may by order repeal s 130(2)(b): s 130(5). An order under s 130(5) may make amendments and repeals to a provision of, or in an instrument made under, the Apprenticeships, Skills, Children and Learning Act 2009 or any other Act (including any Act passed after the Apprenticeships, Skills, Children and Learning Act 2009 (ie 12 November 2009)) in consequence of the repeal of s 130(2)(b): s 130(6). Before making an order under s 130(5) the Secretary of State must consult the Department for Employment and Learning in Northern Ireland: s 130(7). At the date at which this volume states the law no such order had been made. As to the meaning of 'England' see PARA 7 note 3. As to the Secretary of State see PARA 58. A reference in Pt 7 to the 'award or authentication of a qualification' includes a reference to (i) the award or authentication of credits in respect of components of a qualification; and (ii) the award or authentication of a qualification by a body either alone or jointly with others: s 172(2).
8   Apprenticeships, Skills, Children and Learning Act 2009 s 128(2)(a) (s 128(2) substituted by the Education Act 2011 s 22).
9   Apprenticeships, Skills, Children and Learning Act 2009 s 128(2)(b)(i) (as substituted: see note 8).
10   As to the meaning of 'United Kingdom' see PARA 73 note 3.
11   Ie the Apprenticeships, Skills, Children and Learning Act 2009 Pt 7 (ss 127–174).
12   Apprenticeships, Skills, Children and Learning Act 2009 s 128(2)(b)(ii) (as substituted: see note 8).
13   For the purposes of the Apprenticeships, Skills, Children and Learning Act 2009 Pt 7 (ss 127–174) (see s 131(1)), 'regulated assessment arrangements' means NC assessment arrangements (s 131(2)(a)), and EYFS assessment arrangements (s 131(2)(b)). 'NC assessment arrangements' means arrangements made under or by virtue of an order made under the Education Act 2002 s 87(3)(c) (see PARA 863) for assessing pupils in England in respect of each key stage for the specified purposes: s 131(3). In s 131(3), 'assessing' includes testing; and 'key stage' has the same meaning as in the Education Act 2002 Pt 6 (ss 76–96) (see PARA 860 note 1): Apprenticeships, Skills, Children and Learning Act 2009 s 131(4). 'EYFS assessment arrangements' means arrangements made under or by virtue of an order made under the Childcare Act 2006 s 39(1)(a) (see CHILDREN AND YOUNG PERSONS vol 10 (2012) PARA 1095) for assessing children in England for the specified purposes: Apprenticeships, Skills, Children and Learning Act 2009 s 131(5). 'The specified purposes' in relation to regulated assessment arrangements: (1) if the arrangements are NC assessment arrangements, has the same meaning as in the Education Act 2002 s 76(1) (see PARA 859) (Apprenticeships, Skills, Children and Learning Act 2009 s 131(6)(a)); (2) if the arrangements are EYFS assessment arrangements, has the same meaning as in the Childcare Act 2006 s 41(2)(c) (see CHILDREN AND YOUNG PERSONS vol 10 (2012) PARA 1095) (Apprenticeships, Skills, Children and Learning Act 2009 s 131(6)(b)).
14   Apprenticeships, Skills, Children and Learning Act 2009 s 128(3)(a).
15   Apprenticeships, Skills, Children and Learning Act 2009 s 128(3)(b). See *R (on the application of Lewisham London Borough) v Assessment and Qualifications Alliance* [2013] EWHC 211 (Admin), [2013] All ER (D) 228 (Feb) (judicial review seeking to have June exam papers assessed in accordance with January boundaries).
16   Apprenticeships, Skills, Children and Learning Act 2009 s 128(4).
17   Apprenticeships, Skills, Children and Learning Act 2009 s 128(5)(a).
18   Apprenticeships, Skills, Children and Learning Act 2009 s 128(5)(b). As to the meaning of 'institution within the higher education sector' see PARA 619 (definition applied by s 172(1)).

19 Ie under the Apprenticeships, Skills, Children and Learning Act 2009 s 132: see PARA 831.
20 Apprenticeships, Skills, Children and Learning Act 2009 s 128(5)(c). The qualifications referred to are those to which Pt 7 (ss 127–174) applies (see note 7): see s 128(5)(c).
21 For these purposes a sum is relevant if it is payable in respect of the award or authentication of the qualification in question: Apprenticeships, Skills, Children and Learning Act 2009 s 128(7).
22 Ie under the Apprenticeships, Skills, Children and Learning Act 2009 s 132: see PARA 831.
23 Apprenticeships, Skills, Children and Learning Act 2009 s 128(6).

827. General duties and powers. So far as reasonably practicable, in performing its functions[1] the Office of Qualifications and Examinations Regulation[2] ('Ofqual') must act in a way which is compatible with its objectives[3], and which it considers most appropriate for the purpose of meeting its objectives[4]. So far as relevant, in performing its functions Ofqual must have regard to:

(1)   the need to ensure that the number of regulated qualifications[5] available for award or authentication[6] is appropriate[7];

(2)   the other reasonable requirements of relevant learners[8], including persons with special educational needs[9];

(3)   the reasonable requirements of pupils[10] and children, including persons with special educational needs, in relation to regulated assessment arrangements[11];

(4)   the reasonable requirements of industry, commerce, finance, the professions and other employers regarding education and training (including required standards of practical competence)[12];

(5)   the reasonable requirements of institutions within the higher education sector[13];

(6)   information provided to Ofqual by[14] Her Majesty's Chief Inspector of Education, Children's Services and Skills[15], and such other relevant persons[16], or relevant persons of such a description, as the Secretary of State may direct[17];

(7)   the desirability of facilitating innovation in connection with the provision of regulated qualifications[18];

(8)   the specified purposes of regulated assessment arrangements[19].

In performing its functions Ofqual must also have regard to such aspects of government policy as the Secretary of State may direct[20]. Ofqual must perform its functions efficiently and effectively[21].

Ofqual may delegate any of its functions to: (a) a member of Ofqual[22] or Ofqual's staff[23]; (b) a committee established by Ofqual[24]; (c) a joint committee[25]. A function is so delegated to the extent and on the terms that Ofqual determines[26].

Ofqual may, subject to any statutory restrictions[27], do anything that it considers necessary or appropriate for the purposes of, or in connection with, its functions[28]. Ofqual may not lend money[29].

1   As to the meaning of 'functions' see PARA 18 note 5 (definition applied by the Apprenticeships, Skills, Children and Learning Act 2009 s 264(2), (3)).
2   As to the Office of Qualifications and Examinations Regulation generally see PARA 824.
3   Apprenticeships, Skills, Children and Learning Act 2009 s 129(1)(a). As to the objectives of Ofqual see PARA 826.
4   Apprenticeships, Skills, Children and Learning Act 2009 s 129(1)(b).
5   As to the meaning of 'regulated qualification' see PARA 826 note 7.
6   As to the meaning of references to award or authentication of a qualification see PARA 826 note 7.
7   Apprenticeships, Skills, Children and Learning Act 2009 s 129(2)(a). For the purposes of s 129(2)(a) the number of regulated qualifications available for award or authentication is

appropriate if the number is such that: (1) there is a reasonable level of choice for learners, in terms of both the number of different regulated qualifications and the number of different forms of such qualifications (s 129(3)(a)); but (2) the number of different regulated qualifications in similar subject areas or serving similar functions is not excessive (s 129(3)(b)).

8   'Relevant learner' means a person seeking to obtain, or who may reasonably be expected to seek to obtain, a regulated qualification: Apprenticeships, Skills, Children and Learning Act 2009 s 129(11).

9   Apprenticeships, Skills, Children and Learning Act 2009 s 129(2)(b) (s 129(2)(b), (c) amended by the Children and Families Act 2014 Sch 3 paras 88, 94(a)). As to the meaning of 'child' see PARA 7 note 6 (definition applied by the Apprenticeships, Skills, Children and Learning Act 2009 s 264(2), (3)). As to the meaning of 'special educational needs' see PARA 943 (definition applied by s 264(2), (3)).

10   As to the meaning of 'pupil' see PARA 20 note 4 (definition applied by the Apprenticeships, Skills, Children and Learning Act 2009 s 264(2), (3)).

11   Apprenticeships, Skills, Children and Learning Act 2009 s 129(2)(c) (as amended: see note 9). As to the meaning of 'regulated assessment arrangements' see PARA 826 note 13.

12   Apprenticeships, Skills, Children and Learning Act 2009 s 129(2)(d).

13   Apprenticeships, Skills, Children and Learning Act 2009 s 129(2)(e). As to the meaning of 'institution within the higher education sector' see PARA 619 (definition applied by s 172(1)).

14   See the Apprenticeships, Skills, Children and Learning Act 2009 s 129(2)(f).

15   Apprenticeships, Skills, Children and Learning Act 2009 s 129(4)(b). As to Her Majesty's Chief Inspector of Education, Children's Services and Skills see PARA 1133.

16   'Relevant person' means a person who appears to the Secretary of State to have knowledge of, or expertise in, requirements of a kind mentioned in the Apprenticeships, Skills, Children and Learning Act 2009 s 129(2)(d) (see the text to note 12): s 129(5). As to the meaning of 'person' see PARA 7 note 6. As to the Secretary of State see PARA 58.

17   Apprenticeships, Skills, Children and Learning Act 2009 s 129(4)(c). As to directions generally see PARA 75.

18   Apprenticeships, Skills, Children and Learning Act 2009 s 129(2)(g).

19   Apprenticeships, Skills, Children and Learning Act 2009 s 129(2)(h). As to the meaning of 'the specified purposes' in relation to regulated assessment arrangements see PARA 826 note 13.

20   Apprenticeships, Skills, Children and Learning Act 2009 s 129(6). The Secretary of State must publish a direction given under s 129(6): s 129(7).

21   Apprenticeships, Skills, Children and Learning Act 2009 s 129(8).

22   As to membership of Ofqual see PARA 824.

23   Apprenticeships, Skills, Children and Learning Act 2009 Sch 9 para 10(1)(a). As to Ofqual's staff see PARA 824.

24   Apprenticeships, Skills, Children and Learning Act 2009 Sch 9 para 10(1)(b). As to committees see PARA 824.

25   Apprenticeships, Skills, Children and Learning Act 2009 Sch 9 para 10(1)(c). As to joint committees see PARA 824.

26   Apprenticeships, Skills, Children and Learning Act 2009 Sch 9 para 10(2).

27   The power in the Apprenticeships, Skills, Children and Learning Act 2009 Sch 9 para 14(1) is subject to any restrictions imposed by or under any provision of any Act: Sch 9 para 14(2).

28   Apprenticeships, Skills, Children and Learning Act 2009 Sch 9 para 14(1).

29   Apprenticeships, Skills, Children and Learning Act 2009 Sch 9 para 14(3).

828.   Review of qualifications.   The Office of Qualifications and Examinations Regulation[1] ('Ofqual') may keep under review all aspects of the specified qualifications[2].

As from a day to be appointed the following provisions have effect[3].

Ofqual must keep under review any system used by the Secretary of State[4] for allocating values to those qualifications by reference to the level of attainment indicated by the qualifications[5]. Ofqual may at any time require the Secretary of State to provide it with any information which it considers it necessary or expedient to have for the purposes of, or in connection with, the performance by it of this duty[6].

1   As to the Office of Qualifications and Examinations Regulation generally see PARA 824.

2 See the Apprenticeships, Skills, Children and Learning Act 2009 s 154. The specified qualifications are those to which Pt 7 (ss 127–174) applies: see s 154. As to the meaning of 'qualifications to which Pt 7 applies' see PARA 826 note 7.

3 The Apprenticeships, Skills, Children and Learning Act 2009 s 155 comes into force on a day to be appointed under s 269(4). At the date at which this volume states the law no such day had been appointed.

4 As to the Secretary of State see PARA 58.

5 Apprenticeships, Skills, Children and Learning Act 2009 s 155(1). This duty applies only if the values are to be allocated for the purpose of a qualifications-based performance management system: s 155(2). A qualifications-based performance management system is a system for measuring the relative performance of schools by reference to the performance of pupils at the schools in qualifications to which Pt 7 (ss 127–174) applies: s 155(3). As to the meaning of 'school' see PARA 91; and as to the meaning of 'pupil' see PARA 20 note 4 (definitions applied by s 264(2), (3)).

6 Apprenticeships, Skills, Children and Learning Act 2009 s 155(4).

829. Co-operation and joint working. The Office of Qualifications and Examinations Regulation[1] ('Ofqual') may co-operate or work jointly with another public authority[2] where it is appropriate to do so for the efficient and effective performance of any of Ofqual's qualifications functions[3].

1 As to the Office of Qualifications and Examinations Regulation generally see PARA 824.

2 'Public authority' includes any person who performs functions (whether or not in the United Kingdom) which are of a public nature: Apprenticeships, Skills, Children and Learning Act 2009 s 156(2). As to the meaning of 'person' see PARA 7 note 6. As to the meaning of 'functions' see PARA 18 note 5 (definition applied by s 264(2), (3)). As to the meaning of 'United Kingdom' see PARA 73 note 3.

3 Apprenticeships, Skills, Children and Learning Act 2009 s 156(1). In Pt 7 Ch 2 (ss 132–158) 'qualifications functions' means functions in connection with qualifications to which Pt 7 (ss 127–174) applies: s 156(3). As to the meaning of 'qualifications to which Pt 7 applies' see PARA 826 note 7.

830. Power to provide information to qualifications regulators. The Office of Qualifications and Examinations Regulation[1] ('Ofqual') may provide information to a qualifications regulator[2] for the purpose of enabling or facilitating the performance of a relevant function[3] of the regulator[4]. Nothing in these provisions[5] affects any power to disclose information that exists apart therefrom[6], or authorises the disclosure of information in contravention of any provision made by or under any Act which prevents disclosure of the information[7].

1 As to the Office of Qualifications and Examinations Regulation see generally see PARA 824.

2 For these purposes, a 'qualifications regulator' is a person who has functions in any part of the United Kingdom which are similar to Ofqual's qualifications functions: Apprenticeships, Skills, Children and Learning Act 2009 s 157(2)(a). As to the meaning of 'person' see PARA 7 note 6. As to the meaning of 'functions' see PARA 18 note 5 (definition applied by s 264(2), (3)). As to the meaning of 'United Kingdom' see PARA 73 note 3. As to the meaning of 'qualifications functions' see PARA 829 note 3.

3 For these purposes, a function of a qualifications regulator is a 'relevant function' if it is similar to any of the qualifications functions of Ofqual: Apprenticeships, Skills, Children and Learning Act 2009 s 157(2)(b).

4 Apprenticeships, Skills, Children and Learning Act 2009 s 157(1).

5 Ie in the Apprenticeships, Skills, Children and Learning Act 2009 s 157.

6 Apprenticeships, Skills, Children and Learning Act 2009 s 157(3)(a).

7 Apprenticeships, Skills, Children and Learning Act 2009 s 157(3)(b).

(C) Functions in relation to Qualifications

(a) Recognition of Awarding Bodies

831.   Recognition of awarding bodies. The Office of Qualifications and
Examinations Regulation[1] ('Ofqual') must recognise an awarding body[2] in
respect of the award or authentication of a specified qualification, or description
of qualification[3], if:
- (1)   the awarding body has applied for recognition in the respect in
question[4]; and
- (2)   the body meets the applicable criteria for recognition most recently
published[5].

Ofqual may not recognise an awarding body if the requirements set out in heads
(1) and (2) above are not met by the body[6].
A recognition[7]:
- (a)   has effect from such date as Ofqual may specify[8];
- (b)   is subject to the general conditions[9];
- (c)   if in respect of a qualification subject to the accreditation requirement[10],
is subject to an accreditation condition[11]; and
- (d)   is subject to such other conditions that Ofqual may impose at the time
of recognition or later[12];

but Ofqual may, at the time of recognition or later, determine that a specified
recognition is not to be subject to a specified general condition[13]. Ofqual may
not charge an awarding body in respect of recognition[14]. If Ofqual refuses an
application for recognition it must provide the awarding body with a statement
setting out the reasons for its decision[15].

Ofqual must set and publish the criteria for recognition[16] of an awarding
body[17]. Different criteria may be set for: (i) recognition of different descriptions
of awarding bodies[18]; (ii) recognition in respect of different qualifications or
different descriptions of qualifications[19]; (iii) recognition in respect of credits in
respect of different components of qualifications or different descriptions of
components of qualifications[20]. Ofqual may revise the criteria[21]; and if it revises
the criteria it must publish them as revised[22]. Before setting or revising the
criteria Ofqual must consult such persons as it considers appropriate[23].

1   As to the Office of Qualifications and Examinations Regulation see generally see PARA 824. As
to the objectives and general duties of Ofqual see PARAS 826, 827.
2   In the Apprenticeships, Skills, Children and Learning Act 2009 Pt 7 Ch 2 (ss 132–158)
'awarding body' means a person who awards or authenticates, or who proposes to award or
authenticate, a qualification to which Pt 7 applies: ss 132(9), 158(1). As to the meaning of
'person' see PARA 7 note 6. As to the meaning of references to award or authentication of a
qualification see PARA 826 note 7. As to the meaning of 'qualification to which Pt 7 applies' see
PARA 826 note 7.
3   Ie a specified qualification, or description of qualification, to which the Apprenticeships, Skills,
Children and Learning Act 2009 Pt 7 applies: see s 132(1). In Pt 7 (ss 127–174) a reference to
recognition, or being recognised, in respect of a qualification is a reference to recognition, or
being recognised, under s 132 in respect of the award or authentication of the qualification or of
a description of qualification which applies to the qualification: s 172(3).
4   Apprenticeships, Skills, Children and Learning Act 2009 s 132(1)(a).
5   Apprenticeships, Skills, Children and Learning Act 2009 s 132(1)(b). The publication referred to
is that under s 133 (see the text to notes 16–23): see s 132(1)(b).
6   Apprenticeships, Skills, Children and Learning Act 2009 s 132(2).
7   In the Apprenticeships, Skills, Children and Learning Act 2009 Pt 7 Ch 2 (ss 132–158) a
'recognition' means a recognition under s 132: ss 132(9), 158(1).
8   Apprenticeships, Skills, Children and Learning Act 2009 s 132(3)(a).

9 Apprenticeships, Skills, Children and Learning Act 2009 s 132(3)(b). 'The general conditions', in respect of a recognition of an awarding body, means the general conditions for the time being in force under s 134 (see PARA 832) which are applicable to the recognition and the body: s 132(8).

10 As to the meaning of 'subject to the accreditation requirement' see PARA 835 note 3.

11 Apprenticeships, Skills, Children and Learning Act 2009 s 132(3)(c). An 'accreditation condition' in respect of a qualification subject to the accreditation requirement is a condition requiring that the recognised body may award or authenticate a particular form of the qualification only if, at the time of the award or authentication, that form of the qualification is accredited under s 139 (see PARA 836): s 132(5). In Pt 7 Ch 2 (ss 132–158) 'recognised body' means an awarding body recognised under s 132: ss 132(9), 158(1).

12 Apprenticeships, Skills, Children and Learning Act 2009 s 132(3)(d). As to the duty of Ofqual to publish a statement of how it intends to perform its functions under s 132(3)(d), see s 153; and PARA 845.

13 Apprenticeships, Skills, Children and Learning Act 2009 s 132(4).

14 Apprenticeships, Skills, Children and Learning Act 2009 s 132(6).

15 Apprenticeships, Skills, Children and Learning Act 2009 s 132(7).

16 Ie under the Apprenticeships, Skills, Children and Learning Act 2009 s 132: see the text to notes 1–15.

17 See the Apprenticeships, Skills, Children and Learning Act 2009 s 133(1). As to the duty of Ofqual to perform its functions under s 133 in relation to specified qualifications or descriptions of qualification in a way which secures that the minimum requirements in respect of the qualifications or descriptions of qualification are met, see s 143; and PARA 837.

18 Apprenticeships, Skills, Children and Learning Act 2009 s 133(2)(a).

19 Apprenticeships, Skills, Children and Learning Act 2009 s 133(2)(b).

20 Apprenticeships, Skills, Children and Learning Act 2009 s 133(2)(c).

21 Apprenticeships, Skills, Children and Learning Act 2009 s 133(3).

22 Apprenticeships, Skills, Children and Learning Act 2009 s 133(4).

23 Apprenticeships, Skills, Children and Learning Act 2009 s 133(5). As to the exercise of the duty to consult see JUDICIAL REVIEW vol 61 (2010) PARA 627.

832.   General conditions of recognition.   The Office of Qualifications and Examinations Regulation[1] ('Ofqual') must set and publish the general conditions to which a recognition[2] is to be subject[3]. Different general conditions may be set for: (1) recognition of different descriptions of awarding bodies[4]; (2) recognition in respect of different qualifications or different descriptions of qualifications[5]; (3) recognition in respect of credits in respect of different components of qualifications or different descriptions of components of qualifications[6]. Ofqual may revise the general conditions[7]; and if it does so it must publish them as revised[8]. Before setting or revising the general conditions Ofqual must consult such persons[9] as it considers appropriate[10].

The other conditions of recognition that Ofqual may impose[11] include in particular: (a) fee capping conditions[12]; (b) entry and inspection conditions[13].

'Fee capping conditions' are conditions limiting the amount of a fee chargeable by a recognised body[14] for the award or authentication[15] of a qualification in respect of which the body is recognised[16], or the provision of any other service in relation to such a qualification[17]. Ofqual may impose a fee capping condition limiting the amount of a particular fee only if satisfied that the limit is necessary in order to secure value for money[18]. Before imposing a fee capping condition in respect of a recognition Ofqual must give notice[19] to the recognised body of its intention to do so[20]. Ofqual must establish arrangements (the 'review arrangements') for the review, at the request of a recognised body, of a decision to impose a fee capping condition[21]. A decision to impose a fee capping condition must not take effect before the later of the expiry of the period during which a review can be requested under the review arrangements[22], and the completion of any review requested under those arrangements[23]. Ofqual must, in performing its functions[24] in relation to fee capping conditions, have regard to any guidance given by the Secretary of State[25].

'Entry and inspection conditions' are conditions requiring permission to enter premises[26] for the purposes of inspecting and copying documents so far as necessary for Ofqual to satisfy itself that the appropriate standards are being maintained by a recognised body in relation to the award or authentication of any qualification in respect of which the body is recognised[27], or to determine whether to impose a fee capping condition and, if so, what that condition should be[28]. An entry and inspection condition requires permission to enter premises to be given only if: (i) the premises in question are not used as a private dwelling[29]; (ii) the entry is to be by an authorised person[30]; (iii) reasonable notice has been given to the recognised body in question[31]; and (iv) the entry is to be at a reasonable time[32]. An entry and inspection condition may require an authorised person to be given permission to do anything that a person appropriately authorised[33] could do[34] in relation to the inspection of computer records[35].

1   As to the Office of Qualifications and Examinations Regulation generally see PARA 824. As to the objectives and general duties of Ofqual see PARAS 826, 827.
2   As to the meaning of 'recognition' see PARA 831 note 7.
3   Apprenticeships, Skills, Children and Learning Act 2009 s 134(1). As to the duty of Ofqual to perform its functions under s 134 in relation to specified qualifications or descriptions of qualification in a way which secures that the minimum requirements in respect of the qualifications or descriptions of qualification are met, see s 143; and PARA 837. As to the duty of Ofqual to publish a statement of how it intends to perform its functions under s 134, and to publish guidance regarding compliance with the general conditions, see s 153; and PARA 845.
4   Apprenticeships, Skills, Children and Learning Act 2009 s 134(2)(a). As to the meaning of 'awarding body' see PARA 831 note 2.
5   Apprenticeships, Skills, Children and Learning Act 2009 s 134(2)(b).
6   Apprenticeships, Skills, Children and Learning Act 2009 s 134(2)(c).
7   Apprenticeships, Skills, Children and Learning Act 2009 s 134(3).
8   See the Apprenticeships, Skills, Children and Learning Act 2009 s 134(4).
9   As to the meaning of 'person' see PARA 7 note 6.
10 Apprenticeships, Skills, Children and Learning Act 2009 s 134(5). As to the exercise of the duty to consult see JUDICIAL REVIEW vol 61 (2010) PARA 627.
11 Ie under the Apprenticeships, Skills, Children and Learning Act 2009 s 132(3)(d): see PARA 831.
12 Apprenticeships, Skills, Children and Learning Act 2009 s 135(1)(a).
13 Apprenticeships, Skills, Children and Learning Act 2009 s 135(1)(b). As to the duty of Ofqual to publish a statement of how it intends to perform its functions under an entry and inspection condition, see s 153; and PARA 845.
14 As to the meaning of 'recognised body' see PARA 831 note 11.
15 As to the meaning of references to award or authentication of a qualification see PARA 826 note 7.
16 Apprenticeships, Skills, Children and Learning Act 2009 s 135(2)(a).
17 Apprenticeships, Skills, Children and Learning Act 2009 s 135(2)(b).
18 Apprenticeships, Skills, Children and Learning Act 2009 s 136(1).
19 As to the service of notices and documents see the Education Act 1996 s 572 (applied by the Apprenticeships, Skills, Children and Learning Act 2009 s 264(2), (3)); and PARA 76.
20 Apprenticeships, Skills, Children and Learning Act 2009 s 136(2). The notice must: (1) set out Ofqual's reasons for proposing to impose the fee capping condition (s 136(3)(a)); and (2) specify the period during which, and the way in which, the recognised body may make representations about the proposal (s 136(3)(b)). Ofqual must have regard to any representations made by the recognised body during the period specified in the notice in deciding whether to impose the fee capping condition: s 136(4).
21 Apprenticeships, Skills, Children and Learning Act 2009 s 136(5). The review arrangements must require the decision on review to be made by a person (see s 136(6)) who appears to Ofqual to have skills likely to be relevant to decisions to impose fee capping conditions (s 136(7)(a)), and is independent of Ofqual (s 136(7)(b)). A person is independent of Ofqual for these purposes if the person is an individual who is not a member of Ofqual or Ofqual's staff (s 136(8)(a)), or a body none of whose members is a member of Ofqual or Ofqual's staff (s 136(8)(b)). As to membership of Ofqual see PARA 825. As to Ofqual's staff see PARA 825.

22 Apprenticeships, Skills, Children and Learning Act 2009 s 136(9)(a).
23 Apprenticeships, Skills, Children and Learning Act 2009 s 136(9)(b).
24 As to the meaning of 'functions' see PARA 18 note 5 (definition applied by the Apprenticeships, Skills, Children and Learning Act 2009 s 264(2), (3)).
25 Apprenticeships, Skills, Children and Learning Act 2009 s 136(10). The Secretary of State must publish any guidance given under s 136(10): s 136(11). As to the Secretary of State see PARA 58.
26 As to the meaning of 'premises' see PARA 62 note 19 (definition applied by the Apprenticeships, Skills, Children and Learning Act 2009 s 264(2), (3)).
27 Apprenticeships, Skills, Children and Learning Act 2009 s 135(3)(a).
28 Apprenticeships, Skills, Children and Learning Act 2009 s 135(3)(b).
29 Apprenticeships, Skills, Children and Learning Act 2009 s 137(1)(a).
30 Apprenticeships, Skills, Children and Learning Act 2009 s 137(1)(b). 'Authorised person' means a member of Ofqual's staff who is authorised (generally or specifically) for the purpose: s 137(2).
31 Apprenticeships, Skills, Children and Learning Act 2009 s 137(1)(c).
32 Apprenticeships, Skills, Children and Learning Act 2009 s 137(1)(d).
33 Ie authorised by a provision of the Education Act 2005 Pt 1 (ss 1–63) to inspect documents.
34 Ie by virtue of the Education Act 2005 s 58: see PARA 1152 note 7.
35 See the Apprenticeships, Skills, Children and Learning Act 2009 s 137(3).

833. Surrender of recognition. A recognised body[1] may give notice[2] to the Office of Qualifications and Examinations Regulation[3] ('Ofqual') that it wishes to cease to be recognised in respect of the award or authentication[4] of a specified qualification or description of qualification[5]. As soon as reasonably practicable after receipt of such a notice Ofqual must give notice to the recognised body of the date on which the body is to cease to be recognised in the respect in question ('the surrender date')[6]. At any time before the surrender date Ofqual may vary that date by giving further notice to the recognised body[7]. In deciding or varying the surrender date Ofqual must have regard to the need to avoid prejudicing persons who are seeking, or might reasonably be expected to seek, to obtain the qualification, or a qualification of the description, specified in the notice given by the recognised body[8]. Ofqual may make saving or transitional provision in connection with a recognised body ceasing to be recognised in any respect by virtue of these provisions[9].

1 As to the meaning of 'recognised body' see PARA 831 note 11.
2 As to the service of notices and documents see the Education Act 1996 s 572 (applied by the Apprenticeships, Skills, Children and Learning Act 2009 s 264(2), (3)); and PARA 76.
3 As to the Office of Qualifications and Examinations Regulation generally see PARA 824. As to the objectives and general duties of Ofqual see PARAS 826, 827.
4 As to the meaning of references to award or authentication of a qualification see PARA 826 note 7.
5 Apprenticeships, Skills, Children and Learning Act 2009 s 147(1).
6 Apprenticeships, Skills, Children and Learning Act 2009 s 147(2).
7 Apprenticeships, Skills, Children and Learning Act 2009 s 147(3).
8 See the Apprenticeships, Skills, Children and Learning Act 2009 s 147(4).
9 Apprenticeships, Skills, Children and Learning Act 2009 s 147(5).

834. Register. The Office of Qualifications and Examinations Regulation[1] ('Ofqual') must maintain and publish a register containing the following information in relation to each recognised body[2]:

(1) the qualifications in respect of which it is recognised[3];
(2) the forms of those qualifications which are awarded or authenticated by it[4], and
(3) as from a day to be appointed[5], if the recognised body has determined[6] that any of those qualifications is relevant for 2008 Act purposes[7], the

number of hours of guided learning[8] it has assigned to each form of the qualification awarded or authenticated by it[9].

The register may include such other information as Ofqual considers appropriate[10].

1   As to the Office of Qualifications and Examinations Regulation generally see PARA 824. As to the objectives and general duties of Ofqual see PARAS 826, 827.
2   As to the meaning of 'recognised body' see PARA 831 note 11.
3   Apprenticeships, Skills, Children and Learning Act 2009 s 148(1)(a). As to the meaning of a reference to recognition, or being recognised, in respect of a qualification see PARA 831 note 3.
4   Apprenticeships, Skills, Children and Learning Act 2009 s 148(1)(b). As to the meaning of references to award or authentication of a qualification see PARA 826 note 7.
5   The Apprenticeships, Skills, Children and Learning Act 2009 s 148(1)(c) comes into effect as from a day to be appointed under s 269(4). At the date at which this volume states the law no such day had been appointed.
6   Ie under the Apprenticeships, Skills, Children and Learning Act 2009 s 145: see PARA 838.
7   As to the meaning of 'relevant for 2008 Act purposes' see PARA 838 note 5.
8   As to the meaning of 'number of hours of guided learning' see PARA 838 note 7.
9   Apprenticeships, Skills, Children and Learning Act 2009 s 148(1)(c).
10 Apprenticeships, Skills, Children and Learning Act 2009 s 148(2).

(b) Accreditation of Certain Qualifications

835. Qualifications subject to the accreditation requirement. The Office of Qualifications and Examinations Regulation[1] ('Ofqual') may determine that a specified qualification, or description of qualification[2], is subject to the accreditation requirement[3]. Such a determination may provide that a qualification or description of qualification is subject to the accreditation requirement: (1) for all purposes[4]; or (2) for the purposes of award or authentication[5] by a specified awarding body[6]. Ofqual may revise a determination[7]. Ofqual must publish a determination falling within head (1) above[8], and if Ofqual revises a such determination it must publish the determination as revised[9].

Before making or revising a determination Ofqual must, if the determination falls within head (1) above, consult such persons[10] as it considers appropriate[11], and, if the determination falls within head (2) above, consult the awarding body in question[12].

1   As to the Office of Qualifications and Examinations Regulation generally see PARA 824. As to the objectives and general duties of Ofqual see PARAS 826, 827.
2   Ie a specified qualification, or description of qualification, to which the Apprenticeships, Skills, Children and Learning Act 2009 Pt 7 applies. As to the meaning of 'qualification to which Pt 7 applies' see PARA 826 note 7.
3   Apprenticeships, Skills, Children and Learning Act 2009 s 138(1). For the purposes of Pt 7 Ch 2 (ss 132–158) a qualification is subject to the accreditation requirement if a determination by Ofqual that the qualification, or a description of qualification which applies to the qualification, is to be subject to that requirement has effect under s 138: s 158(2). As to accreditation see s 139; and PARA 836. As to the duty of Ofqual to prepare and publish a statement of how it intends to perform its functions under s 138(1), see s 153; and PARA 845.
4   Apprenticeships, Skills, Children and Learning Act 2009 s 138(2)(a).
5   As to the meaning of references to award or authentication of a qualification see PARA 826 note 7.
6   Apprenticeships, Skills, Children and Learning Act 2009 s 138(2)(b). As to the meaning of 'awarding body' see PARA 831 note 2.
7   See the Apprenticeships, Skills, Children and Learning Act 2009 s 138(4).
8   See the Apprenticeships, Skills, Children and Learning Act 2009 s 138(3).
9   See the Apprenticeships, Skills, Children and Learning Act 2009 s 138(5).
10 As to the meaning of 'person' see PARA 7 note 6.

11 Apprenticeships, Skills, Children and Learning Act 2009 s 138(6)(a). As to the exercise of the duty to consult see JUDICIAL REVIEW vol 61 (2010) PARA 627.

12 Apprenticeships, Skills, Children and Learning Act 2009 s 138(6)(b).

836.   Accreditation. Where a qualification is subject to the accreditation requirement[1], the Office of Qualifications and Examinations Regulation[2] ('Ofqual') must accredit a particular form of the qualification if:

(1)   that form of the qualification has been submitted for accreditation by a recognised body[3] which is recognised in respect of the qualification[4]; and

(2)   that form of the qualification meets the applicable criteria for accreditation most recently published[5].

Ofqual may not accredit a form of a qualification if the requirements set out in heads (1) and (2) above are not met in respect of that form of the qualification[6]. An accreditation has effect from such date as Ofqual may specify[7]. Ofqual may not charge a recognised body in respect of accreditation[8]. If Ofqual refuses an application for accreditation it must provide the recognised body with a statement setting out the reasons for its decision[9].

Ofqual must set and publish the criteria for accreditation[10]. Different criteria may be set for the accreditation of different qualifications or different descriptions of qualifications[11]. Ofqual may revise the criteria[12], and if it does so it must publish them as revised[13]. Before setting or revising the criteria Ofqual must consult such persons[14] as it considers appropriate[15].

If Ofqual revises the criteria which are applicable to a form of a qualification which is accredited, the accreditation ceases to have effect on the date specified by Ofqual[16]. Ofqual may vary the date so specified at any time before the date[17]. Ofqual may make saving or transitional provision in connection with the accreditation of a form of a qualification ceasing[18] to have effect[19].

1   As to the meaning of references to a qualification subject to the accreditation requirement see PARA 835 note 3.

2   As to the Office of Qualifications and Examinations Regulation generally see PARA 824. As to the objectives and general duties of Ofqual see PARAS 826, 827.

3   As to the meaning of 'recognised body' see PARA 831 note 11.

4   Apprenticeships, Skills, Children and Learning Act 2009 s 139(1)(a). As to the meaning of 'recognised in respect of a qualification' see PARA 831 note 3.

5   Apprenticeships, Skills, Children and Learning Act 2009 s 139(1)(b). The publication referred to is that under s 140 (see the text to notes 10–19): see s 139(1)(b).

6   Apprenticeships, Skills, Children and Learning Act 2009 s 139(2).

7   Apprenticeships, Skills, Children and Learning Act 2009 s 139(3).

8   Apprenticeships, Skills, Children and Learning Act 2009 s 139(4).

9   Apprenticeships, Skills, Children and Learning Act 2009 s 139(5).

10   Apprenticeships, Skills, Children and Learning Act 2009 s 140(1). As to the duty of Ofqual to perform its functions under s 140 in relation to a qualification or description of qualification in a way which secures that the minimum requirements in respect of the qualification or description of qualification are met, see s 143; and PARA 837.

11   Apprenticeships, Skills, Children and Learning Act 2009 s 140(2).

12   Apprenticeships, Skills, Children and Learning Act 2009 s 140(3).

13   See the Apprenticeships, Skills, Children and Learning Act 2009 s 140(4).

14   As to the meaning of 'person' see PARA 7 note 6.

15   Apprenticeships, Skills, Children and Learning Act 2009 s 140(5). As to the exercise of the duty to consult see JUDICIAL REVIEW vol 61 (2010) PARA 627.

16   Apprenticeships, Skills, Children and Learning Act 2009 s 140(6). Ofqual may determine that s 140(6) does not apply in relation to a specified revision: s 140(8). Ofqual must publish such a determination: s 140(9).

17   Apprenticeships, Skills, Children and Learning Act 2009 s 140(7).

18 Ie under the Apprenticeships, Skills, Children and Learning Act 2009 s 140(6): see the text to note 16.

19 Apprenticeships, Skills, Children and Learning Act 2009 s 140(10).

837. Power of the Secretary of State to specify minimum requirements. The Secretary of State[1] may by order[2] specify minimum requirements in respect of a specified qualification, or description of qualification, to which these provisions apply[3]. But the Secretary of State may make such an order only if satisfied that it is necessary to do so for the purpose of ensuring that the curriculum studied by persons taking a course leading to the qualification, or a qualification of the description, is appropriate, having regard to the likely ages of those persons[4].

A 'minimum requirement' in respect of a qualification or description of qualification is a requirement which relates to the knowledge, skills or understanding which a person must demonstrate in order to obtain the qualification or a qualification of the description[5].

The Office of Qualifications and Examinations Regulation ('Ofqual') must perform various of its functions[6] in relation to a qualification or description of qualification in respect of which minimum requirements[7] have effect in a way which secures that the minimum requirements in respect of the qualification or description of qualification are met[8]. But Ofqual is not required to comply with this duty if it appears to Ofqual that complying with that duty would result in the level of attainment (in terms of depth of knowledge, skills or understanding) indicated by the qualification or description of qualification not being consistent with that indicated by comparable regulated qualifications[9].

If the Secretary of State has made an order[10] in respect of a qualification or description of qualification[11], and the qualification or description of qualification ceases to be one to which the appropriate provisions[12] apply[13], he may by order[14]: (1) revoke the order[15]; or (2) amend it for the purpose of removing the qualification or description of qualification from the application of the order[16]; but this does not affect the power of the Secretary of State to revoke or amend such an order in other circumstances[17].

1 As to the Secretary of State see PARA 58.

2 Before making an order under the Apprenticeships, Skills, Children and Learning Act 2009 s 141(1) the Secretary of State must consult the Office of Qualifications and Examinations Regulation ('Ofqual') and such other persons as he considers appropriate: s 142(1). For the purposes of consulting under s 142(1) the Secretary of State must publish a document setting out: (1) the grounds on which he is satisfied of the matter specified in s 141(2) (see the text to note 4) (s 142(2)(a)); (2) the proposed minimum requirements (s 142(2)(b)); and (3) his reasons for proposing those minimum requirements (s 142(2)(c)). The Secretary of State must provide a copy of the document to Ofqual and any other persons he proposes to consult under s 142(1): s 142(3). As to the Office of Qualifications and Examinations Regulation generally see PARA 824. As to the objectives and general duties of Ofqual see PARAS 826, 827. As to the meaning of 'person' see PARA 7 note 6. As to the exercise of the duty to consult see JUDICIAL REVIEW vol 61 (2010) PARA 627. At the date at which this volume states the law no order had been made under s 141(1).

3 See the Apprenticeships, Skills, Children and Learning Act 2009 s 141(1). Section 141 applies to a qualification, or description of qualification, if: (1) the qualification, or each qualification of the description, is one to which Pt 7 (ss 127–174) applies (s 141(3)(a)); and (2) the condition in s 141(4) is met in relation to the qualification or each qualification of the description (s 141(3)(b)). The condition is that: (a) one or more forms of the qualification is (or are) approved under the Learning and Skills Act 2000 s 98 (see PARA 935) (Apprenticeships, Skills, Children and Learning Act 2009 s 141(4)(a)); or (b) the Secretary of State reasonably expects approval under that section to be sought for one or more forms of the qualification (s 141(4)(b)). As to the meaning of 'qualification to which Pt 7 applies' see PARA 826 note 7.

4 Apprenticeships, Skills, Children and Learning Act 2009 s 141(2).

5 Apprenticeships, Skills, Children and Learning Act 2009 s 141(3).

6 Ie its functions under the Apprenticeships, Skills, Children and Learning Act 2009 s 133 (see PARA 831), s 134 (see PARA 832) and s 140 (see PARA 836). As to the meaning of 'functions' see PARA 18 note 5 (definition applied by s 264(2), (3)).

7 Ie specified in an order under the Apprenticeships, Skills, Children and Learning Act 2009 s 141(1): see the text to notes 1–3.

8 See the Apprenticeships, Skills, Children and Learning Act 2009 s 143(1), (2).

9 Apprenticeships, Skills, Children and Learning Act 2009 s 143(3). As to the meaning of 'regulated qualification' see PARA 826 note 7.

10 Ie under the Apprenticeships, Skills, Children and Learning Act 2009 s 141(1): see the text to notes 1–3.

11 Apprenticeships, Skills, Children and Learning Act 2009 s 144(1)(a).

12 Ie one to which the Apprenticeships, Skills, Children and Learning Act 2009 s 141 applies: see note 3.

13 Apprenticeships, Skills, Children and Learning Act 2009 s 144(1)(b).

14 The Apprenticeships, Skills, Children and Learning Act 2009s 141(2) (see the text to note 4) and s 142 (see note 2) do not apply to an order: (1) revoking an order under s 141(1) (s 144(4)(a)); or (2) amending an order under s 141(1) for the purpose only of removing a qualification or description of qualification from the application of the order (s 144(4)(b)). At the date at which this volume states the law no order had been made under s 144(2).

15 Apprenticeships, Skills, Children and Learning Act 2009 s 144(2)(a).

16 Apprenticeships, Skills, Children and Learning Act 2009 s 144(2)(b).

17 See the Apprenticeships, Skills, Children and Learning Act 2009 s 144(3).

(c) Guided Learning

838. Assignment of number of hours of guided learning. A recognised body[1] may only award or authenticate[2] a particular form of a qualification in respect of which it is recognised[3] if condition (1) or (2) is met[4]. Condition (1) is met if the recognised body determines that the qualification is not relevant for 2008 Act purposes[5]. Condition (2) is met if the recognised body determines that the qualification is relevant for 2008 Act purposes[6], and the body assigns to the particular form of the qualification a number of hours of guided learning[7]. A recognised body must apply the applicable criteria then in force[8] when determining: (a) whether or not a qualification is relevant for 2008 Act purposes[9]; and (b) in respect of a qualification which the body has determined is relevant for those purposes, a number of hours of guided learning to assign to a form of the qualification[10].

The Office of Qualifications and Examinations Regulation[11] ('Ofqual') may review any determination made by a recognised body under these provisions[12], and require the recognised body to revise any such determination in such respects as Ofqual may specify[13]. If Ofqual so requires a recognised body to revise a determination that a qualification is not relevant for 2008 Act purposes by specifying that the determination should provide that the qualification is so relevant, Ofqual may assign to a form of the qualification awarded or authenticated by the recognised body a number of hours of guided learning[14], and if it does so, the recognised body is to be treated as having determined to assign that number of hours of guided learning to that form of the qualification[15].

1 As to the meaning of 'recognised body' see PARA 831 note 11.

2 For the purposes of the Apprenticeships, Skills, Children and Learning Act 2009 s 145, a reference to the award or authentication of a qualification includes a reference to the award or authentication of a qualification by a body either alone or jointly with others: see ss 145(12), 172(2)(b).

3 As to the meaning of 'qualification in respect of which it is recognised' see PARA 831 note 3.

4 Apprenticeships, Skills, Children and Learning Act 2009 s 145(1).

5   Apprenticeships, Skills, Children and Learning Act 2009 s 145(2). For the purposes of Pt 7 Ch 2 (ss 132–158) a qualification is 'relevant for 2008 Act purposes' if there are, or may reasonably be expected to be, persons seeking to obtain the qualification for the purposes of discharging the duty under the Education and Skills Act 2008 s 2(1)(c) (duty to participate in education or training: see PARA 725): Apprenticeships, Skills, Children and Learning Act 2009 ss 145(9), 158(3).
6   Apprenticeships, Skills, Children and Learning Act 2009 s 145(3)(a).
7   Apprenticeships, Skills, Children and Learning Act 2009 s 145(3)(b). In Pt 7 Ch 2 (ss 132–158) a 'number of hours of guided learning', in relation to a form of a qualification, means a number of notional hours representing an estimate of the amount of actual guided learning which could reasonably be expected to be required in order for persons to achieve the standard required to obtain that form of the qualification: s 145(10). 'Actual guided learning' means time a person spends: (1) being taught or given instruction by a lecturer, tutor, supervisor or other appropriate provider of education or training (s 145(11)(a)); or (2) otherwise participating in education or training under the immediate guidance or supervision of such a person (s 145(11)(b)), but does not include time spent on unsupervised preparation or study, whether at home or otherwise (s 145(11)).
8   Ie under the Apprenticeships, Skills, Children and Learning Act 2009 s 146: see PARA 839. If revised criteria come into force under s 146, a recognised body must review any determination it has made under s 145: s 145(6).
9   Apprenticeships, Skills, Children and Learning Act 2009 s 145(5)(a).
10   Apprenticeships, Skills, Children and Learning Act 2009 s 145(5)(b).
11   As to the Office of Qualifications and Examinations Regulation generally see PARA 824. As to the objectives and general duties of Ofqual see PARAS 826, 827.
12   Apprenticeships, Skills, Children and Learning Act 2009 s 145(7)(a).
13   Apprenticeships, Skills, Children and Learning Act 2009 s 145(7)(b).
14   Apprenticeships, Skills, Children and Learning Act 2009 s 145(8)(a).
15   Apprenticeships, Skills, Children and Learning Act 2009 s 145(8)(b).

839.   Criteria for assignment of number of hours of guided learning. The Office of Qualifications and Examinations Regulation[1] ('Ofqual') must set and publish criteria for determining: (1) whether a qualification is relevant for 2008 Act purposes[2]; and (2) in respect of a qualification which a recognised body[3] has determined is relevant for those purposes, the number of hours of guided learning[4] that should be assigned to a form of the qualification[5]. Different criteria may be set for determinations in relation to different qualifications or different descriptions of qualifications[6]. Ofqual may revise the criteria[7], and if it does so must publish them as revised[8]. Before setting or revising the criteria Ofqual must consult such persons[9] as it considers appropriate[10].

1   As to the Office of Qualifications and Examinations Regulation generally see PARA 824. As to the objectives and general duties of Ofqual see PARAS 826, 827.
2   Apprenticeships, Skills, Children and Learning Act 2009 s 146(1)(a). As to the meaning of 'relevant for 2008 Act purposes' see PARA 838 note 5.
3   As to the meaning of 'recognised body' see PARA 1152 note 11.
4   As to the meaning of 'number of hours of guided learning' see PARA 838 note 7.
5   Apprenticeships, Skills, Children and Learning Act 2009 s 146(1)(b). As to the assignment of the number of hours of guided learning see PARA 838.
6   Apprenticeships, Skills, Children and Learning Act 2009 s 146(2).
7   Apprenticeships, Skills, Children and Learning Act 2009 s 146(3).
8   See the Apprenticeships, Skills, Children and Learning Act 2009 s 146(4).
9   As to the meaning of 'person' see PARA 7 note 6.
10   Apprenticeships, Skills, Children and Learning Act 2009 s 146(5). As to the exercise of the duty to consult see JUDICIAL REVIEW vol 61 (2010) PARA 627.

(d) Recognised Bodies: Monitoring and Enforcement

840.   Review of activities of recognised bodies and investigation of complaints. The Office of Qualifications and Examinations Regulation[1] ('Ofqual') may keep under review any connected activities of a recognised body[2].

An activity of a recognised body is a 'connected activity' if Ofqual considers that it is connected or otherwise relevant to: (1) the body's recognition[3] (including, in particular, the compliance by the body with the conditions to which the recognition is subject)[4]; or (2) the award or authentication[5] by the body of any qualification in respect of which it is recognised[6].

Ofqual may investigate, or make arrangements for the investigation of, complaints in relation to the award or authentication of a regulated qualification[7]. Such arrangements may in particular include arrangements for the referral of complaints to an independent party[8].

1 As to the Office of Qualifications and Examinations Regulation generally see PARA 824. As to the objectives and general duties of Ofqual see PARAS 826, 827.
2 Apprenticeships, Skills, Children and Learning Act 2009 s 149(1). As to the meaning of 'recognised body' see PARA 831 note 11. As to the duty of Ofqual to prepare and publish a statement of how it intends to perform its functions under s 149, see s 153; and PARA 845.
3 As to the meaning of a 'recognition' see PARA 831 note 7.
4 Apprenticeships, Skills, Children and Learning Act 2009 s 149(2)(a).
5 As to the meaning of references to award or authentication of a qualification see PARA 826 note 7.
6 Apprenticeships, Skills, Children and Learning Act 2009 s 149(2)(b). As to the meaning of 'qualification in respect of which it is recognised' see PARA 831 note 3.
7 Apprenticeships, Skills, Children and Learning Act 2009 s 150(1). As to the meaning of 'regulated qualification' see PARA 826 note 7. As to the duty of Ofqual to prepare and publish a statement of how it intends to perform its functions under s 150, see s 153; and PARA 845.
8 Apprenticeships, Skills, Children and Learning Act 2009 s 150(2). 'An independent party' means: (1) an individual who is not a member of Ofqual or Ofqual's staff (s 150(3)(a)); or (2) a body none of whose members is a member of Ofqual or Ofqual's staff (s 150(3)(b)). As to membership of Ofqual see PARA 825. As to Ofqual's staff see PARA 825. A description of the activities of an independent party must be included in Ofqual's annual report: see s 171; and PARA 852.

841. Power to give directions. If it appears to the Office of Qualifications and Examinations Regulation[1] ('Ofqual') that a recognised body[2] has failed or is likely to fail to comply with a condition to which the recognition[3] is subject[4], Ofqual may direct[5] the recognised body to take or refrain from taking specified steps with a view to securing compliance with the condition[6]. Before giving a recognised body such a direction Ofqual must give notice[7] to the body of its intention to do so[8]. The notice must set out Ofqual's reasons for proposing to give the direction[9], and specify the period during which, and the way in which, the recognised body may make representations about the proposal[10]. Ofqual must have regard to any representations made by the recognised body during the period specified in the notice in deciding whether to give a direction to the body[11].

A recognised body must comply with any such direction given to it[12]. A direction may be amended or revoked by Ofqual[13]. A direction is enforceable, on the application of Ofqual, by a mandatory order[14].

1 As to the Office of Qualifications and Examinations Regulation generally see PARA 824. As to the objectives and general duties of Ofqual see PARAS 826, 827.
2 As to the meaning of 'recognised body' see PARA 831 note 11.
3 As to the meaning of a 'recognition' see PARA 831 note 7.
4 Apprenticeships, Skills, Children and Learning Act 2009 s 151(1) (substituted by the Education Act 2011 s 23(1), (2)). As to the power to impose monetary penalties see the Apprenticeships, Skills, Children and Learning Act 2009 ss 151A–151D; and PARA 842. As to the recovery of costs incurred by Ofqual in relation to imposing a sanction under s 151, 151A or 152 see ss 152A–152C; and PARA 844.
5 As to directions generally see the Apprenticeships, Skills, Children and Learning Act 2009 s 263; and PARA 75.

6   Apprenticeships, Skills, Children and Learning Act 2009 s 151(2). As to the duty of Ofqual to prepare and publish a statement of how it intends to perform its functions under s 151, see s 153; and PARA 845.

7   As to the service of notices and documents see the Education Act 1996 s 572 (applied by the Apprenticeships, Skills, Children and Learning Act 2009 s 264(2), (3)); and PARA 76.

8   Apprenticeships, Skills, Children and Learning Act 2009 s 151(3).

9   Apprenticeships, Skills, Children and Learning Act 2009 s 151(4)(a).

10   Apprenticeships, Skills, Children and Learning Act 2009 s 151(4)(b).

11   Apprenticeships, Skills, Children and Learning Act 2009 s 151(5).

12   Apprenticeships, Skills, Children and Learning Act 2009 s 151(6).

13   Apprenticeships, Skills, Children and Learning Act 2009 s 151(8). The provisions of 151(3)–(5) (see the text to notes 7–11) apply to the amendment of a direction as they apply to the giving of a direction: see s 151(8).

14   Apprenticeships, Skills, Children and Learning Act 2009 s 151(7)(a). As to mandatory orders see JUDICIAL REVIEW vol 61 (2010) PARA 703 et seq.

842. Power to impose monetary penalties. If it appears to the Office of Qualifications and Examinations Regulation[1] ('Ofqual') that a recognised body[2] has failed to comply with a condition to which the recognition[3] is subject[4], Ofqual may impose a monetary penalty[5] on the recognised body[6].

Before imposing a monetary penalty on a recognised body, Ofqual must give notice to the body of its intention to do so[7]. The notice must (1) set out Ofqual's reasons for proposing to impose the penalty[8]; and (2) specify the period during which, and the way in which, the recognised body may make representations about the proposal[9].

Ofqual must have regard to any representations made by the recognised body during the period specified in the notice in deciding whether to impose a monetary penalty on the body[10]. If Ofqual decides to impose a monetary penalty on the body, it must give the body a notice containing information as to (a) the grounds for imposing the penalty[11]; (b) how payment may be made[12]; (c) the period within which payment is required to be made (which must not be less than 28 days)[13]; (d) rights of appeal[14]; (e) the period within which an appeal may be made[15]; and (f) the consequences of non-payment[16]. The amount of a monetary penalty imposed on a recognised body[17] must not exceed ten per cent of the body's turnover[18].

A recognised body may appeal to the First-tier Tribunal[19] against a decision to impose a monetary penalty on the body[20] and a decision as to the amount of the penalty[21]. An appeal[22] may be made on the grounds that the decision was based on an error of fact, that the decision was wrong in law, or that the decision was unreasonable[23]. The requirement to pay the penalty is suspended pending the determination of an appeal[24]. On such an appeal the Tribunal may (i) withdraw the requirement to pay the penalty[25]; (ii) confirm that requirement[26]; (iii) vary that requirement[27]; (iv) take such steps as Ofqual could take in relation to the failure to comply giving rise to the decision to impose the requirement[28]; (v) remit the decision whether to confirm the requirement to pay the penalty, or any matter relating to that decision, to Ofqual[29].

Certain provisions[30] apply if all or part of a monetary penalty imposed on a recognised body is unpaid at the end of the period ending on the applicable date[31]. The unpaid amount of the penalty for the time being carries interest[32]. Ofqual may recover from the body, as a civil debt due to it, the unpaid amount of the penalty and any unpaid interest[33].

1   As to the Office of Qualifications and Examinations Regulation generally see PARA 824. As to the objectives and general duties of Ofqual see PARAS 826, 827.

2   As to the meaning of 'recognised body' see PARA 831 note 11.

3 As to the meaning of a 'recognition' see PARA 831 note 7.
4 Apprenticeships, Skills, Children and Learning Act 2009 s 151A(1) (ss 151A–151D added by the
  Education Act 2011 s 23(1), (3)). As to the recovery of costs incurred by Ofqual in relation to
  imposing a sanction under the Apprenticeships, Skills, Children and Learning Act 2009 s 151,
  151A or 152 see ss 152A–152C; and PARA 844.
5 A 'monetary penalty' is a requirement to pay to Ofqual a penalty of an amount determined by
  Ofqual in accordance with the Apprenticeships, Skills, Children and Learning Act 2009 s 151B
  (see the text to note 18): s 151A(3) (as added: see note 4).
6 Apprenticeships, Skills, Children and Learning Act 2009 s 151A(2) (as added: see note 4).
7 Apprenticeships, Skills, Children and Learning Act 2009 s 151A(4) (as added: see note 4).
8 Apprenticeships, Skills, Children and Learning Act 2009 s 151A(5)(a) (as added: see note 4).
9 Apprenticeships, Skills, Children and Learning Act 2009 s 151A(5)(b) (as added: see note 4).
  The period specified under s 151A(5)(b) must not be less than 28 days beginning with the date
  on which the notice is received: s 151A(6) (as so added).
10 Apprenticeships, Skills, Children and Learning Act 2009 s 151A(7) (as added: see note 4).
11 Apprenticeships, Skills, Children and Learning Act 2009 s 151A(8)(a) (as added: see note 4).
12 Apprenticeships, Skills, Children and Learning Act 2009 s 151A(8)(b) (as added: see note 4).
13 Apprenticeships, Skills, Children and Learning Act 2009 s 151A(8)(c) (as added: see note 4).
14 Apprenticeships, Skills, Children and Learning Act 2009 s 151A(8)(d) (as added: see note 4).
15 Apprenticeships, Skills, Children and Learning Act 2009 s 151A(8)(e) (as added: see note 4).
16 Apprenticeships, Skills, Children and Learning Act 2009 s 151A(8)(f) (as added: see note 4).
17 Ie under the Apprenticeships, Skills, Children and Learning Act 2009 s 151A.
18 Apprenticeships, Skills, Children and Learning Act 2009 s 151B(1) (as added: see note 4). The
  turnover of a body for the purposes of s 151B(1) is to be determined in accordance with an
  order made by the Secretary of State: s 151B(2) (as so added). Subject to s 151B(1), the amount
  may be whatever Ofqual decides is appropriate in all the circumstances of the case: s 151B(3) (as
  so added). As to the order under s 151B(2) see the Office of Qualifications and Examinations
  Regulation (Determination of Turnover for Monetary Penalties) Order 2012, SI 2012/1768.
19 As to the First-tier Tribunal see COURTS AND TRIBUNALS vol 24 (2010) PARA 876 et seq.
20 Ie under the Apprenticeships, Skills, Children and Learning Act 2009 s 151A.
21 Apprenticeships, Skills, Children and Learning Act 2009 s 151C(1) (as added: see note 4).
22 Ie under the Apprenticeships, Skills, Children and Learning Act 2009 s 151C.
23 Apprenticeships, Skills, Children and Learning Act 2009 s 151C(2) (as added: see note 4).
24 Apprenticeships, Skills, Children and Learning Act 2009 s 151C(3) (as added: see note 4).
25 Apprenticeships, Skills, Children and Learning Act 2009 s 151C(4)(a) (as added: see note 4).
26 Apprenticeships, Skills, Children and Learning Act 2009 s 151C(4)(b) (as added: see note 4).
27 Apprenticeships, Skills, Children and Learning Act 2009 s 151C(4)(c) (as added: see note 4).
28 Apprenticeships, Skills, Children and Learning Act 2009 s 151C(4)(d) (as added: see note 4).
29 Apprenticeships, Skills, Children and Learning Act 2009 s 151C(4)(e) (as added: see note 4).
30 Ie the provisions of the Apprenticeships, Skills, Children and Learning Act 2009 s 151D.
31 Apprenticeships, Skills, Children and Learning Act 2009 s 151D(1) (as added: see note 4). The
  applicable date is (1) the last date on which the recognised body may make an appeal under
  s 151C in respect of the penalty, if no such appeal is made (s 151D(2)(a) (as so added)); (2) if an
  appeal under s 151C in respect of the penalty is made, the date on which the appeal is
  determined, or if the appeal is withdrawn before being determined, the date on which the appeal
  is withdrawn (s 151D(2)(b) (as so added)).
32 See the Apprenticeships, Skills, Children and Learning Act 2009 s 151D(3) (as added: see
  note 4). The interest is at the rate for the time being specified in the Judgments Act 1838 s 17
  (see CIVIL PROCEDURE vol 12 (2009) PARA 1149) (and does not also carry interest as a judgment
  debt under that provision): Apprenticeships, Skills, Children and Learning Act 2009 s 151D(3)
  (as so added). The total amount of interest imposed under s 151D(3) must not exceed the
  amount of the penalty: s 151D(4) (as so added).
33 Apprenticeships, Skills, Children and Learning Act 2009 s 151D(5) (as added: see note 4).

843. Power to withdraw recognition. If a recognised body[1] has failed to
comply with a condition to which the recognition[2] is subject[3], the Office of
Qualifications and Examinations Regulation[4] ('Ofqual') may withdraw
recognition from the recognised body in respect of the award or authentication[5]
of (1) a specified qualification[6] or description of qualification in respect of which
the body is recognised[7]; or (2) every qualification or description of qualification
in respect of which the body is recognised[8].

Before withdrawing recognition from a recognised body in any respect Ofqual must give notice[9] to the body of its intention to do so[10]. The notice must set out Ofqual's reasons for proposing to withdraw recognition from the recognised body in the respect in question[11], and specify the period during which, and the way in which, the recognised body may make representations about the proposal[12]. Ofqual must have regard to any representations made by the recognised body during the period specified in the notice in deciding whether to withdraw recognition from the body in the respect in question[13].

If Ofqual decides to withdraw recognition from a recognised body Ofqual must give notice to the body of its decision and of the date on which the withdrawal is to take effect[14], and may make saving or transitional provision[15]. At any time before a withdrawal takes effect Ofqual may vary the date on which it is to take effect by giving further notice to the recognised body[16].

Ofqual must establish arrangements for the review, at the request of a recognised body, of a decision to withdraw recognition[17]. The arrangements established must require the decision on review to be made by a person[18] who is independent of Ofqual[19].

1   As to the meaning of 'recognised body' see PARA 831 note 11.
2   As to the meaning of a 'recognition' see PARA 831 note 7.
3   Apprenticeships, Skills, Children and Learning Act 2009 s 152(1). As to the recovery of costs incurred by Ofqual in relation to imposing a sanction under s 151, 151A or 152 see ss 152A–152C; and PARA 844.
4   As to the Office of Qualifications and Examinations Regulation generally see PARA 824. As to the objectives and general duties of Ofqual see PARAS 826, 827.
5   As to the meaning of references to award or authentication of a qualification see PARA 826 note 7.
6   As to the meaning of references to recognition in respect of a qualification see PARA 831 note 3.
7   Apprenticeships, Skills, Children and Learning Act 2009 s 152(2)(a) (s 152(2) substituted by the Education Act 2011 s 23(1), (4)).
8   Apprenticeships, Skills, Children and Learning Act 2009 s 152(2)(b) (as substituted: see note 7).
9   As to the service of notices and documents see the Education Act 1996 s 572 (applied by the Apprenticeships, Skills, Children and Learning Act 2009 s 264(2), (3)); and PARA 76.
10 Apprenticeships, Skills, Children and Learning Act 2009 s 152(3).
11 Apprenticeships, Skills, Children and Learning Act 2009 s 152(4)(a).
12 Apprenticeships, Skills, Children and Learning Act 2009 s 152(4)(b).
13 Apprenticeships, Skills, Children and Learning Act 2009 s 152(5).
14 Apprenticeships, Skills, Children and Learning Act 2009 s 152(6)(a).
15 Apprenticeships, Skills, Children and Learning Act 2009 s 152(6)(b).
16 Apprenticeships, Skills, Children and Learning Act 2009 s 152(7).
17 Apprenticeships, Skills, Children and Learning Act 2009 s 152(8).
18 As to the meaning of 'person' see PARA 7 note 6.
19 Apprenticeships, Skills, Children and Learning Act 2009 s 152(9). A person is independent of Ofqual for these purposes if the person is: (1) an individual who is not a member of Ofqual or Ofqual's staff (s 152(10)(a)); or (2) a body none of whose members is a member of Ofqual or Ofqual's staff (s 152(10)(b)). As to membership of Ofqual see PARA 825. As to Ofqual's staff see PARA 825.

844.   Costs recovery.   The Office of Qualifications and Examinations Regulation[1] ('Ofqual') may, by notice, require a recognised body[2] on which a sanction has been imposed[3] to pay the costs[4] incurred by Ofqual in relation to imposing the sanction, up to the time it is imposed[5]. A notice given[6] to a recognised body must contain information as to (1) the amount required to be paid[7]; (2) how payment may be made[8]; (3) the period within which payment is required to be made (which must not be less than 28 days)[9]; (4) rights of appeal[10]; (5) the period within which an appeal may be made[11]; and (5) the consequences of non-payment[12]. The body may require Ofqual to provide a detailed breakdown of the amount specified in the notice[13].

A recognised body may appeal to the First-tier Tribunal[14] against a decision[15] to require the body to pay costs and a decision as to the amount of those costs[16]. An appeal[17] may be made on the grounds that the decision was based on an error of fact, that the decision was wrong in law, or that the decision was unreasonable[18]. The requirement to pay the costs is suspended pending the determination of an appeal[19]. On an appeal the Tribunal may (a) withdraw the requirement to pay the costs[20]; (b) confirm that requirement[21]; (c) vary that requirement[22]; (d) take such steps as Ofqual could take in relation to the failure to comply giving rise to the decision to impose the requirement[23]; (e) remit the decision whether to confirm the requirement to pay the costs, or any matter relating to that decision, to Ofqual[24].

Certain provisions[25] apply if all or part of an amount of costs that a recognised body is required to pay[26] is unpaid at the end of the period ending on the applicable date[27]. The unpaid amount of the costs for the time being carries interest[28]. Ofqual may recover from the body, as a civil debt due to it, the unpaid amount of the costs and any unpaid interest[29].

1   As to the Office of Qualifications and Examinations Regulation generally see PARA 824. As to the objectives and general duties of Ofqual see PARAS 826, 827.
2   As to the meaning of 'recognised body' see PARA 831 note 11.
3   The references in the Apprenticeships, Skills, Children and Learning Act 2009 s 152A(1) to imposing a sanction are to giving a direction under s 151 (see PARA 841), imposing a monetary penalty under s 151A (see PARA 842), or withdrawing recognition under s 152 (see PARA 843): s 152A(2) (ss 152A–152C added by the Education Act 2011 s 23(1), (5)).
4   'Costs' includes in particular investigation costs, administration costs, and costs of obtaining expert advice (including legal advice): Apprenticeships, Skills, Children and Learning Act 2009 s 152A(3) (as added: see note 3).
5   Apprenticeships, Skills, Children and Learning Act 2009 s 152A(1) (as added: see note 3).
6   Ie given under the Apprenticeships, Skills, Children and Learning Act 2009 s 152A(1).
7   Apprenticeships, Skills, Children and Learning Act 2009 s 152A(4)(a) (as added: see note 3).
8   Apprenticeships, Skills, Children and Learning Act 2009 s 152A(4)(b) (as added: see note 3).
9   Apprenticeships, Skills, Children and Learning Act 2009 s 152A(4)(c) (as added: see note 3).
10 Apprenticeships, Skills, Children and Learning Act 2009 s 152A(4)(d) (as added: see note 3).
11 Apprenticeships, Skills, Children and Learning Act 2009 s 152A(4)(e) (as added: see note 3).
12 Apprenticeships, Skills, Children and Learning Act 2009 s 152A(4)(f) (as added: see note 3).
13 Apprenticeships, Skills, Children and Learning Act 2009 s 152A(5) (as added: see note 3).
14 As to the First-tier Tribunal see COURTS AND TRIBUNALS vol 24 (2010) PARA 876 et seq.
15 Ie under the Apprenticeships, Skills, Children and Learning Act 2009 s 152A(1).
16 Apprenticeships, Skills, Children and Learning Act 2009 s 152B(1) (as added: see note 3).
17 Ie under the Apprenticeships, Skills, Children and Learning Act 2009 s 152B.
18 Apprenticeships, Skills, Children and Learning Act 2009 s 152B(2) (as added: see note 3).
19 Apprenticeships, Skills, Children and Learning Act 2009 s 152B(3) (as added: see note 3).
20 Apprenticeships, Skills, Children and Learning Act 2009 s 152B(4)(a) (as added: see note 3).
21 Apprenticeships, Skills, Children and Learning Act 2009 s 152B(4)(b) (as added: see note 3).
22 Apprenticeships, Skills, Children and Learning Act 2009 s 152B(4)(c) (as added: see note 3).
23 Apprenticeships, Skills, Children and Learning Act 2009 s 152B(4)(d) (as added: see note 3).
24 Apprenticeships, Skills, Children and Learning Act 2009 s 152B(4)(e) (as added: see note 3).
25 Ie the provisions of the Apprenticeships, Skills, Children and Learning Act 2009 s 152C.
26 See note 15.
27 Apprenticeships, Skills, Children and Learning Act 2009 s 152C(1) (as added: see note 3). The applicable date is (1) the last date on which the recognised body may make an appeal under s 152B in respect of the costs, if no such appeal is made (s 152C(2)(a) (as so added); (2) if an appeal under s 152B in respect of the costs is made the date on which the appeal is determined, or if the appeal is withdrawn before being determined, the date on which the appeal is withdrawn (s 152C(2)(b) (as so added)).
28 See the Apprenticeships, Skills, Children and Learning Act 2009 s 152C(3) (as added: see note 3). The interest is at the rate for the time being specified in the Judgments Act 1838 s 17

(see CIVIL PROCEDURE vol 12 (2009) PARA 1149) and does not also carry interest as a judgment debt under that provision): Apprenticeships, Skills, Children and Learning Act 2009 s 152C(3) (as so added). The total amount of interest imposed under s 152C(3) must not exceed the amount of the costs: s 152C(4) (s so added).

29 Apprenticeships, Skills, Children and Learning Act 2009 s 152C(5) (as added: see note 3).

845. Qualifications regulatory framework. The Office of Qualifications and Examinations Regulation[1] ('Ofqual') must prepare and publish:

(1)   a statement of how Ofqual intends to perform the monitoring and enforcement functions[2]; and

(2)   guidance to recognised bodies[3] in relation to the award and authentication[4] of qualifications in respect of which they are recognised[5];

the statement and guidance together being known as 'the qualifications regulatory framework'[6].

Guidance under head (2) above must include guidance for the purpose of helping to determine whether or not behaviour complies with the general conditions to which a recognition[7] is subject[8]. The guidance may in particular specify: (a) descriptions of behaviour which Ofqual considers complies with a general condition[9]; (b) descriptions of behaviour which Ofqual considers does not comply with a general condition[10]; (c) factors which Ofqual will take into account in determining whether or not a recognised body's behaviour complies with a general condition[11]. A recognised body must have regard to the guidance in awarding or authenticating a qualification in respect of which it is recognised[12].

Ofqual may revise the qualifications regulatory framework[13], and if it does so, must publish the revised version[14]. Before publishing the qualifications regulatory framework or a revised version of it, Ofqual must consult such persons[15] as it considers appropriate[16].

1   As to the Office of Qualifications and Examinations Regulation generally see PARA 824. As to the objectives and general duties of Ofqual see PARAS 826, 827.
2   Apprenticeships, Skills, Children and Learning Act 2009 s 153(1)(a). 'The monitoring and enforcement functions' means:
     (1)   Ofqual's power under s 132(3)(d) (power to impose other conditions: see PARA 831) (s 153(8)(a));
     (2)   Ofqual's functions under s 132(4) (see PARA 831) and s 134 (see PARA 832) (functions in relation to general conditions) (s 153(8)(b));
     (3)   Ofqual's functions under an entry and inspection condition to which a recognition is subject (see s 135; and PARA 832) (s 153(8)(c));
     (4)   Ofqual's functions under s 138(1) (power to determine that a qualification is subject to the accreditation requirement: see PARA 835) (s 153(8)(d));
     (5)   Ofqual's functions under ss 149–152C (see PARAS 840–844) (s 153(8)(e) (amended by the Education Act 2011 s 23(1), (6)).
     As to the meaning of 'functions' see PARA 18 note 5 (definition applied by the Apprenticeships, Skills, Children and Learning Act 2009 s 264(2), (3)).
3   As to the meaning of 'recognised body' see PARA 831 note 11.
4   As to the meaning of references to award or authentication of a qualification see PARA 826 note 7.
5   Apprenticeships, Skills, Children and Learning Act 2009 s 153(1)(b). As to the meaning of 'qualification in respect of which they are recognised' see PARA 831 note 3.
6   See the Apprenticeships, Skills, Children and Learning Act 2009 s 153(2).
7   As to the meaning of a 'recognition' see PARA 831 note 7.
8   Apprenticeships, Skills, Children and Learning Act 2009 s 153(3). As to the general conditions see s 134; and PARA 832.
9   Apprenticeships, Skills, Children and Learning Act 2009 s 153(4)(a).
10   Apprenticeships, Skills, Children and Learning Act 2009 s 153(4)(b).
11   Apprenticeships, Skills, Children and Learning Act 2009 s 153(4)(c).

12 Apprenticeships, Skills, Children and Learning Act 2009 s 153(7).
13 Apprenticeships, Skills, Children and Learning Act 2009 s 153(5)(a).
14 Apprenticeships, Skills, Children and Learning Act 2009 s 153(5)(b).
15 As to the meaning of 'person' see PARA 7 note 6.
16 Apprenticeships, Skills, Children and Learning Act 2009 s 153(6). As to the exercise of the duty
to consult see JUDICIAL REVIEW vol 61 (2010) PARA 627.

(D) Functions in relation to Assessment Arrangements

846. Review of regulated assessment arrangements. The Office of
Qualifications and Examinations Regulation[1] ('Ofqual') must keep under review
all aspects of assessment arrangements[2]. Ofqual may at any time require:

(1)   the Secretary of State[3];
(2)   a responsible body[4];
(3)   Her Majesty's Chief Inspector of Education, Children's Services and
        Skills[5];
(4)   any other person specified or of a description specified in regulations[6],
to provide it with any information which Ofqual considers it necessary or
expedient to have for the purposes of, or in connection with, the performance by
Ofqual of this function[7].

1   As to the Office of Qualifications and Examinations Regulation generally see PARA 824. As to
    the objectives and general duties of Ofqual see PARAS 826, 827.
2   See Apprenticeships, Skills, Children and Learning Act 2009 s 161(1), (2). The reference to
    'assessment arrangements' means NC assessment arrangements (see s 161(1)) and EYFS
    assessment arrangements (see s 161(2)). As to the meanings of 'NC assessment arrangements'
    and 'EYFS assessment arrangements' see PARA 826 note 13. As to the duty of Ofqual to prepare
    and publish a document setting out how it intends to perform its duties under s 161, see ss 164,
    165; and PARA 848.
3   See the Apprenticeships, Skills, Children and Learning Act 2009 s 162(2)(a), (4)(a). As to the
    Secretary of State see PARA 58.
4   See the Apprenticeships, Skills, Children and Learning Act 2009 s 162(2)(b), (4)(b). In the case
    of Ofqual's function under s 161(1) (see the text to notes 1–2) the responsible body is an NC
    responsible body (see s 162(2)(b)) and in the case of its function under s 161(2) (see the text to
    notes 1–2) the responsible body is an EYFS responsible body (see s 162(4)(b)). In Pt 7 Ch 3
    (ss 159–166): 'NC responsible body' means a person who under or by virtue of an order made
    under the Education Act 2002 s 87(3)(c) (see PARA 863) has functions in relation to the
    development, implementation or monitoring of NC assessment arrangements; and 'EYFS
    responsible body' means a person who under or by virtue of an order made under the Childcare
    Act 2006 s 39(1)(a) (see CHILDREN AND YOUNG PERSONS vol 10 (2012) PARA 1095) has
    functions in relation to the development, implementation or monitoring of EYFS assessment
    arrangements: Apprenticeships, Skills, Children and Learning Act 2009 s 162(5). As to the
    meaning of 'person' see PARA 7 note 6. As to the meaning of 'functions' see PARA 18 note 5
    (definition applied by s 264(2), (3)).
5   See the Apprenticeships, Skills, Children and Learning Act 2009 s 162(2)(c), (4)(c). As to Her
    Majesty's Chief Inspector of Education, Children's Services and Skills see PARA 1133.
6   See the Apprenticeships, Skills, Children and Learning Act 2009 s 162(2)(d), (4)(d).
    'Regulations' means regulations made by the Secretary of State: s 264(1). At the date at which
    this volume states the law no such regulations had been made.
7   See the Apprenticeships, Skills, Children and Learning Act 2009 s 162(1), (3).

847. Duty to notify significant failings. If it appears to the Office of
Qualifications and Examinations Regulation[1] ('Ofqual') that there is or is likely
to be a significant failing in assessment arrangements[2], Ofqual must notify: (1)
the Secretary of State[3]; and (2) any responsible body[4] whose act or omission
appears to Ofqual to have contributed to the significant failing[5].

1   As to the Office of Qualifications and Examinations Regulation generally see PARA 824. As to
    the objectives and general duties of Ofqual see PARAS 826, 827.

2 Ie in NC assessment arrangements (see the Apprenticeships, Skills, Children and Learning Act 2009 s 163(1)) or EYFS assessment arrangements (see s 163(2)). There is a significant failing in NC assessment arrangements or (as the case may be) EYFS assessment arrangements if, as a result of the way in which the arrangements are being developed or implemented, they fail in a significant way to achieve one or more of the specified purposes of the arrangements: s 163(3). As to the meanings of 'NC assessment arrangements' and 'EYFS assessment arrangements' see PARA 826 note 13.

3 See the Apprenticeships, Skills, Children and Learning Act 2009 s 163(1)(a), (2)(a).

4 Ie in the case of NC assessment arrangements, any NC responsible body (see the Apprenticeships, Skills, Children and Learning Act 2009 s 163(1)(b)), and in the case of any EYFS assessment arrangements, any EYFS responsible body (see s 163(2)(b)). As to the meanings of 'NC responsible body' and 'EYFS responsible body' see PARA 846 note 4.

5 See the Apprenticeships, Skills, Children and Learning Act 2009 s 163(1)(b), (2)(b).

848.   Regulatory frameworks. The Office of Qualifications and Examinations Regulation[1] ('Ofqual') must prepare and publish documents ('the NC assessments regulatory framework' and 'the EYFS assessments regulatory framework') which contain a description of how Ofqual intends to perform its functions[2] of keeping under review all aspects of assessment arrangements[3], and gives guidance to responsible bodies[4] about the performance of their functions in relation to assessment arrangements[5]. Ofqual may revise an assessments regulatory framework[6], and, if it does so, it must publish the revised version[7]. Before publishing a regulatory frameworks or a revised version of it, Ofqual must consult the Secretary of State[8] and such responsible bodies[9] and other persons[10] as it considers appropriate[11]. A responsible body must have regard to the appropriate assessments regulatory framework in performing its functions in relation to assessment arrangements[12].

1 As to the Office of Qualifications and Examinations Regulation generally see PARA 824. As to the objectives and general duties of Ofqual see PARAS 826, 827.

2 Ie under the Apprenticeships, Skills, Children and Learning Act 2009 s 161(1), (2): see PARA 846. As to the meaning of 'functions' see PARA 18 note 5 (definition applied by s 264(2), (3)).

3 See the Apprenticeships, Skills, Children and Learning Act 2009 ss 164(1)(a), 165(1)(a).

4 Ie in the case of NC assessment arrangements, NC responsible bodies (see the Apprenticeships, Skills, Children and Learning Act 2009 s 164(1)(b)), and in the case of EYFS assessment arrangements, EYFS responsible bodies (see s 165(1)(b)). As to the meanings of 'NC responsible body' and 'EYFS responsible body' see PARA 846 note 4. As to the meanings of 'NC assessment arrangements' and 'EYFS assessment arrangements' see PARA 826 note 13.

5 See the Apprenticeships, Skills, Children and Learning Act 2009 ss 164(1)(b), 165(1)(b).

6 See the Apprenticeships, Skills, Children and Learning Act 2009 ss 164(2)(a), 165(2)(a).

7 See the Apprenticeships, Skills, Children and Learning Act 2009 ss 164(2)(b), 165(2)(b).

8 See the Apprenticeships, Skills, Children and Learning Act 2009 ss 164(3)(a), 165(3)(a). As to the Secretary of State see PARA 58.

9 Ie in the case of the NC assessments regulatory framework, such NC responsible bodies (see the Apprenticeships, Skills, Children and Learning Act 2009 s 164(3)(b)), and in the case of the EYFS assessments regulatory framework, such EYFS responsible bodies (see s 165(3)(b)).

10 As to the meaning of 'person' see PARA 7 note 6.

11 See the Apprenticeships, Skills, Children and Learning Act 2009 ss 164(3)(b), 165(3)(b).

12 See the Apprenticeships, Skills, Children and Learning Act 2009 ss 164(4), 165(4).

(E)   Other Functions

849.   Provision of services, information or advice. The Office of Qualifications and Examinations Regulation[1] ('Ofqual') may, in connection with any of its functions[2], provide services to any person[3] (whether or not in the United Kingdom)[4], on such terms and subject to such conditions (if any) as Ofqual may determine[5]. Ofqual may charge a fee for, or in connection with, any such service[6].

If requested to do so by the Secretary of State[7], Ofqual must provide him with information or advice on such matters relating to any of its functions as may be specified in the request[8].

1   As to the Office of Qualifications and Examinations Regulation generally see PARA 824. As to the objectives and general duties of Ofqual see PARAS 826, 827.
2   As to the meaning of 'functions' see PARA 18 note 5 (definition applied by the Apprenticeships, Skills, Children and Learning Act 2009 s 264(2), (3)). As to Ofqual's functions see PARA 826 et seq.
3   As to the meaning of 'person' see PARA 7 note 6.
4   Apprenticeships, Skills, Children and Learning Act 2009 s 167(1). As to the meaning of 'United Kingdom' see PARA 73 note 3.
5   Apprenticeships, Skills, Children and Learning Act 2009 s 167(2).
6   Apprenticeships, Skills, Children and Learning Act 2009 s 167(3).
7   As to the Secretary of State see PARA 58.
8   Apprenticeships, Skills, Children and Learning Act 2009 s 168(1). Similarly, if requested to do so by the Department for Employment and Learning in Northern Ireland, Ofqual must provide the department with information or advice on such matters relating to any of its functions (so far as they relate to Northern Ireland) as may be specified in the request: s 168(2). As to devolved government in Northern Ireland see CONSTITUTIONAL AND ADMINISTRATIVE LAW vol 20 (2014) PARA 83 et seq.

850. Research and development. The Office of Qualifications and Examinations Regulation[1] ('Ofqual') may carry out programmes of research and development for purposes connected with qualifications[2], or regulated assessment arrangements[3]. Ofqual may commission, co-ordinate or facilitate the carrying out of programmes of research and development for those purposes[4].

1   As to the Office of Qualifications and Examinations Regulation generally see PARA 824. As to the objectives and general duties of Ofqual see PARAS 826, 827.
2   See the Apprenticeships, Skills, Children and Learning Act 2009 s 169(1)(a). The qualifications referred to are those to which Pt 7 (ss 127–174) applies: see s 169(1)(a). As to the meaning of 'qualification to which Pt 7 applies' see PARA 826 note 7.
3   Apprenticeships, Skills, Children and Learning Act 2009 s 169(1)(b). As to the meaning of 'regulated assessment arrangements' see PARA 826 note 13.
4   Apprenticeships, Skills, Children and Learning Act 2009 s 169(2).

851. Duty not to impose or maintain unnecessary burdens. The Office of Qualifications and Examinations Regulation[1] ('Ofqual') must keep its regulatory functions[2] under review[3]. Ofqual must secure that in performing any of its regulatory functions it does not impose burdens which it considers to be unnecessary[4], or maintain burdens which it considers to have become unnecessary[5]; but this does not require the removal of a burden which has become unnecessary where its removal would, having regard to all the circumstances, be impracticable or disproportionate[6].

Ofqual must publish a statement[7] setting out: (1) what it proposes to do pursuant to these duties[8] in the period to which the statement relates[9]; (2) (except in the case of the first statement to be published) what it has done pursuant thereto since the previous statement was published[10]; and (3) where a burden which has become unnecessary is maintained[11], the reasons why the removal of the burden would, having regard to all the circumstances, be impracticable or disproportionate[12]. Ofqual must, in performing any of its regulatory functions during a period for which a statement is in force, have regard to the statement[13].

1   As to the Office of Qualifications and Examinations Regulation generally see PARA 824. As to the objectives and general duties of Ofqual see PARAS 826, 827.

2   'Regulatory function' means: (1) a function under any enactment of imposing requirements, restrictions or conditions, or setting standards or giving guidance, in relation to any activity; or (2) a function which relates to the securing of compliance with, or the enforcement of, requirements, restrictions, conditions, standards or guidance which under or by virtue of any enactment relate to any activity: Legislative and Regulatory Reform Act 2006 s 32(2) (definition applied by the Apprenticeships, Skills, Children and Learning Act 2009 s 170(8)). For these purposes, the references to a function: (a) include a function exercisable by or on behalf of the Crown; (b) do not include any function exercisable by any body of, or any person holding office in, the Church of England, or any function of conducting criminal or civil proceedings: Legislative and Regulatory Reform Act 2006 s 32(2) (as so applied). The references in head (1) and (2) above to an activity include: (i) providing goods and services; and (ii) employing or offering employment to any person s 32(3) (as so applied). As to Ofqual's functions see PARA 826 et seq.

3   Apprenticeships, Skills, Children and Learning Act 2009 s 170(1).

4   Apprenticeships, Skills, Children and Learning Act 2009 s 170(2)(a).

5   Apprenticeships, Skills, Children and Learning Act 2009 s 170(2)(b).

6   Apprenticeships, Skills, Children and Learning Act 2009 s 170(3).

7   The first such statement must be published as soon as reasonably practicable after 1 April 2010 (ie the date of the commencement of the Apprenticeships, Skills, Children and Learning Act 2009 s 127: see PARA 825) (s 170(5)(a)), and is to be a statement for the period of 12 months beginning with the day of its publication (s 170(5)(b)). A subsequent statement must be published during the period to which the previous statement related or as soon as reasonably practicable after the end of that period (s 170(6)(a)), and must be a statement for the period of 12 months beginning with the end of the period to which the previous statement related (s 170(6)(b)). As to the meaning of 'month' see PARA 54 note 26.

8   Ie pursuant to the Apprenticeships, Skills, Children and Learning Act 2009 s 170(1), (2): see the text to notes 1–5.

9   Apprenticeships, Skills, Children and Learning Act 2009 s 170(4)(a).

10   Apprenticeships, Skills, Children and Learning Act 2009 s 170(4)(b).

11   Ie pursuant to the Apprenticeships, Skills, Children and Learning Act 2009 s 170(3): see the text to note 6.

12   Apprenticeships, Skills, Children and Learning Act 2009 s 170(4)(c).

13   Apprenticeships, Skills, Children and Learning Act 2009 s 170(7).

852.   Annual and other reports. As soon as reasonably practicable after the end of each reporting period[1] the Office of Qualifications and Examinations Regulation[2] ('Ofqual') must prepare and publish a report for the period ('the annual report')[3]. The annual report must include:

(1)   a statement of what Ofqual has done in performing its functions[4] in the reporting period[5];

(2)   an assessment of the extent to which Ofqual has met its objectives[6] in that period[7];

(3)   details of any information obtained by Ofqual in that period on the levels of attainment in relevant regulated qualifications[8];

(4)   if arrangements for referral of complaints to an independent party[9] were in place during the reporting period, a description of the activities of the independent party during the reporting period[10].

Ofqual may prepare and publish other reports on matters relating to its functions[11].

1   'Reporting period' means: (1) the period (being not longer than 12 months) beginning with 1 April 2010 (ie the day on which the Apprenticeships, Skills, Children and Learning Act 2009 s 127 (see PARA 825) came into force) and ending on such date as Ofqual decides (s 171(10)(a)); (2) each successive period of 12 months (s 171(10)(b)). As to the meaning of 'month' see PARA 54 note 26.

2   As to the Office of Qualifications and Examinations Regulation generally see PARA 824.

3   Apprenticeships, Skills, Children and Learning Act 2009 s 171(1). Ofqual may comply with s 171(1) by preparing and publishing a single document or separate documents in relation to England and to Northern Ireland: s 171(9). As to the meaning of 'England' see PARA 7 note 3.

Ofqual must lay a copy of each annual report before Parliament (s 171(6)(a)), and (so far as it relates to Northern Ireland) lay a copy of each annual report before the Northern Ireland Assembly (s 171(6)(b)). As to the laying of documents before Parliament see STATUTES AND LEGISLATIVE PROCESS vol 96 (2012) PARA 1052. As to devolved government in Northern Ireland see CONSTITUTIONAL AND ADMINISTRATIVE LAW vol 20 (2014) PARA 83 et seq.

4 As to Ofqual's functions see PARA 826 et seq.
5 Apprenticeships, Skills, Children and Learning Act 2009 s 171(2)(a).
6 As to Ofqual's objectives see PARA 826.
7 Apprenticeships, Skills, Children and Learning Act 2009 s 171(2)(b). An assessment under s 171(2)(b) in respect of the qualifications standards objective must in particular explain how, in making the assessment, Ofqual has taken account of any information within s 171(2)(c) (see head (3) in the text) obtained in the reporting period or an earlier reporting period: s 171(4). As to the qualifications standards objective see PARA 826.
8 Apprenticeships, Skills, Children and Learning Act 2009 s 171(2)(c). 'Relevant regulated qualifications' are regulated qualifications that are taken wholly or mainly by pupils at schools in England: s 171(3). As to the meaning of 'regulated qualification' see PARA 826 note 7. As to the meaning of 'pupil' see PARA 20 note 4; and as to the meaning of 'school' see PARA 91 (definitions applied by s 264(2), (3)).
9 Ie arrangements of the kind mentioned in the Apprenticeships, Skills, Children and Learning Act 2009 s 150(2): see PARA 840.
10 Apprenticeships, Skills, Children and Learning Act 2009 s 171(5).
11 Apprenticeships, Skills, Children and Learning Act 2009 s 171(7). If Ofqual prepares and publishes a report under s 171(7) it may lay a copy of the report before Parliament (s 171(8)(a)) and, so far as it relates to Northern Ireland, lay a copy of the report before the Northern Ireland Assembly (s 171(8)(b)).

(ii) Supervision of Curriculum and Qualifications in Wales

853. Establishment of Qualifications Wales as a new body with responsibilities in regard to qualifications in Wales. The Qualifications Wales Act 2015 establishes the body Qualifications Wales and transfers responsibility for regulation and quality assurance of qualifications awarded in Wales[1] from the Welsh Ministers[2] to this new body[3].

Qualifications Wales was established on 6 August 2015[4] as the independent regulatory body responsible for the recognition of awarding bodies and the review and approval of non-degree qualifications in Wales[5]. It is due to take over its responsibilities as from September 2015.

As from a day or days to be appointed, the provisions of the 2015 Act will supplement and replace certain provisions in the Education Act 1997 in regard to the functions of the Welsh Ministers to advance education and training and in relation to curriculum and assessment[6].

1 As to the meaning of 'Wales' see PARA 7 note 3.
2 As to the Welsh Ministers see PARA 59.
3 The Qualifications Wales Act 2015 received Royal Assent on 5 August 2015. As to the Qualifications Wales Act 2015 see further PARA 855.
4 See the Qualifications Wales Act 2015 s 2(1); and the Qualifications Wales Act 2015 (Commencement No 1) Order 2015, SI 2015/1591.
5 As to the status, constitution, procedure etc of Qualifications Wales see the Qualifications Wales Act 2015 s 2(2), Sch 1 Pt 1. As to the transfer of staff and property to Qualifications Wales see s 2(3), Sch 2. As to the principal aims of Qualifications Wales see s 3. See further PARA 855.
6 As to the functions of the Welsh Ministers in relation to the advancement of education and training and in relation to curriculum and assessment see PARA 854.

854. Functions of the Welsh Ministers to advance education and training, and in relation to curriculum and assessment. The functions[1] conferred on the Welsh Ministers[2] by the Education Act 1997[3] must be exercised by them for the purpose of advancing education and training in Wales[4]. The Welsh Ministers must exercise those functions with a view to promoting quality and coherence in education and training in relation to which they have those functions[5].

The functions of the Welsh Ministers with respect to: (1) pupils[6] at maintained schools[7] in Wales who have not ceased to be of compulsory school age[8]; (2) pupils at maintained nursery schools[9] in Wales[10]; and (3) children for whom funded nursery education[11] is provided in Wales otherwise than at a maintained school or maintained nursery school[12], are:

(a)   to keep under review all aspects of the curriculum for maintained schools or maintained nursery schools[13] and all aspects of school examinations and assessment[14];

(b)   to publish and disseminate, and assist in the publication and dissemination of, information relating to the curriculum for such schools or to school examinations and assessment[15];

(c)   to make arrangements with appropriate bodies for auditing the quality of assessments made in pursuance of assessment arrangements[16].

In carrying out such functions, the Welsh Ministers must[17], so far as relevant, have regard to: (i) the requirements[18] relating to general duties in respect of the curriculum[19]; (ii) the reasonable requirements of industry, commerce, finance and the professions regarding education and training, including required standards of practical competence[20]; and (iii) the reasonable requirements of persons with learning difficulties[21]. In carrying out those functions the Welsh Ministers must in addition have regard to information supplied to them by Her Majesty's Chief Inspector of Education and Training in Wales[22] or by any body designated by the Welsh Ministers for these purposes[23].

1   As to the meaning of 'functions' see PARA 18 note 5 (definition applied by the Education Act 1997 s 56(2)).
2   These functions in relation to Wales were originally vested in the National Assembly for Wales and are now exercisable by the Welsh Ministers by virtue of the Government of Wales Act 2006 s 162(1), Sch 11 paras 30, 32. As to the Welsh Ministers see PARA 59. As to the meaning of 'Wales' see PARA 7 note 3.
    As to the transfer of responsibility for regulation and quality assurance of qualifications awarded in Wales from the Welsh Ministers to Qualifications Wales see PARA 853.
3   Ie the Education Act 1997 Pt V (ss 28–32C).
4   Education Act 1997 s 28(1) (amended by SI 2005/3239).
5   Education Act 1997 s 28(2) (amended by SI 2005/3239).
6   As to the meaning of 'pupil' see PARA 20 note 4 (definition applied by the Education Act 1997 s 56(2)).
7   'Maintained school' means any community special school, within the meaning of the School Standards and Framework Act 1998 (see PARA 106): Education Act 1997 s 29(5), (6) (both amended by the School Standards and Organisation (Wales) Act 2013 Sch 5 para 18(1), (2)).
8   Education Act 1997 s 29(1)(a) (s 29(1) amended by the Education Act 2002 s 189, Sch 17 para 5(1), (2); and SI 2005/3239. As to the meaning of 'compulsory school age' see PARA 19.
9   As to the meaning of 'maintained nursery school' see PARA 99 note 4 (definition applied by the Education Act 1997 s 56(2)).
10   Education Act 1997 s 29(1)(b) (as amended: see note 8).
11   'Funded nursery education' has the meaning given by the Education Act 2002 s 98 (see PARA 870 note 6): Education Act 1997 s 29(5).
12   Education Act 1997 s 29(1)(c) (as amended: see note 8).
13   In the Education Act 1997 s 29(2), references to the curriculum for a maintained nursery school include references to the curriculum for any funded nursery education provided as mentioned in s 29(1)(c) (see head (3) in the text): s 29(2A) (added by the Education Act 2002 Sch 17 para 5(1), (4)).
14   Education Act 1997 s 29(2)(a) (amended by the Education Act 2002 Sch 17 para 5(1), (3)(a)). 'Assessment' includes examination and test: Education Act 1997 s 29(5). In s 29(2), references to assessment in schools include references to assessment in funded nursery education: s 29(2A) (as added: see note 13). As from a day to be appointed under the Qualifications Wales Act 2015 s 60, it is provided that in the Education Act 1997 s 29 references to 'school examinations and

'assessment' do not include examinations taken or assessments carried out for the purpose of the award of a qualification within the meaning of the Qualifications Wales Act 2015 s 56: see the Education Act 1997 s 29(7) (added by the Qualifications Wales Act 2015 s 58, Sch 4 para 2). At the date at which this volume states the law, no such day had been appointed.

15 Education Act 1997 s 29(2)(d).

16 Education Act 1997 s 29(2)(e). The Welsh Ministers have, in relation to Wales, the function of developing learning goals and related materials for children who are under compulsory school age: s 29(3) (amended by the School Standards and Framework Act 1998 s 140(1), Sch 30 para 215). The Welsh Ministers may exercise any function of a designated body in connection with baseline assessment schemes (within the meaning of the Education Act 1997 Pt IV Ch 1 (ss 15–18) (repealed)): see the Education Act 1997 s 29(4) (substituted by SI 2005/3239). As from a day to be appointed, the provisions of the Education Act 1997 s 29(3), (4) are repealed by the Education Act 2002 ss 189, 215(2), Sch 17 para 5(1), (5), Sch 22 Pt 2. At the date at which this volume states the law no such day had been appointed.

Provision is also made as to the functions of the Welsh Ministers in relation to certain academic or vocational qualifications awarded or authenticated in Wales: see the Education Act 1997 s 30 (amended by the Learning and Skills Act 2000 ss 103(1), (4)(c), 153, Sch 11; the Education and Skills Act 2008 s 162(1), (2), (5); the Apprenticeships, Skills, Children and Learning Act 2009 ss 174, 192, 266, Sch 12 paras 12, 15, Sch 16; and by SI 2005/3239). In relation to their qualifications functions, provision is made for the Welsh Ministers to co-operate or work jointly with a relevant authority: see the Education Act 1997 s 32ZA (added by the Apprenticeships, Skills, Children and Learning Act 2009 ss 174, 192, Sch 12, paras 12, 17).

Provision is also made as to the power of the Welsh Ministers to set the terms (including terms as to payment) and impose conditions as they may determine for the recognition of persons or accreditation of qualifications: see the Education Act 1997 s 32(3) (amended by the Education Act 2002 ss 189, 215(2), Sch 17 para 7(1), (2), Sch 22 Pt 2; SI 2005/3239; and the Education and Skills Act 2008 s 162(1), (6), (7)), the Education Act 1997 s 32(3A) (added by the Education Act 2002 Sch 17 para 7(1), (3); and amended by SI 2005/3239; and the Education and Skills Act 2008 s 162(1), (6), (8)), the Education Act 1997 s 32(4) (amended by the Education Act 2002 Sch 17 para 7; SI 2005/3239; the Education and Skills Act 2008 s 162(1), (6), (9); and the Apprenticeships, Skills, Children and Learning Act 2009 ss 174, 192, Sch 12 paras 12, 16(1), (3)). Welsh Minsters may give directions to secure compliance with any conditions it sets, and may withdraw recognition: see the Education Act 1997 s 32A (32A added by the Education Act 2002 s 189, Sch 17 para 8; substituted by the Education and Skills Act 2008 s 162(1), (10); and amended by the Education Act 2011 s 24); and the Education Act 1997 s 32B (added by the Apprenticeships, Skills, Children and Learning Act 2009 ss 174, 192, Sch 12 paras 12, 19; and amended by the Education Act 2011 s 24). As to the power of the Welsh Ministers to impose monetary penalties on recognised persons who award or authenticate qualifications see the Education Act 1997 ss 32AA–32AD (all added by the Education Act 2011 s 24(1), (4)). As to the order under the Education Act 1997 s 32AB(2) see the Recognised Persons (Monetary Penalties) (Determination of Turnover) (Wales) Order 2012, SI 2012/1248. As to costs recovery where a sanction has been imposed under the Education Act 1997 s 32A, 32AA or 32B see ss 32BA–32BC (all added by the Education Act 2011 s 24(1), (6)). Notice must be given if a person wishes to cease to be recognised in respect of the award or authentication of a qualification: see the Education Act 1997 s 32C (added by the Apprenticeships, Skills, Children and Learning Act 2009 ss 174, 192, Sch 12 paras 12, 19).

As from a day to be appointed under the Qualifications Wales Act 2015 s 60, the Education Act 1997 s 30, s 32(3), (3A), (4), ss 32ZA-32C are repealed by the Qualifications Wales Act 2015 s 58, Sch 4 para 2. At the date at which this volume states the law, no such day had been appointed.

17 See the Education Act 1997 s 32(1) (amended by SI 2005/3239).

18 Ie of the Education Act 2002 s 99: see PARA 870.

19 Education Act 1997 s 32(1)(c)(i) (amended by the Education Act 2002 s 215(1), Sch 21 para 70).

20 Education Act 1997 s 32(1)(c)(ii) (amended by the Apprenticeships, Skills, Children and Learning Act 2009 ss 174, 192, Sch 12 paras 12, 16(1), (2)(a)).

21 Education Act 1997 s 32(1)(c)(iii) (substituted by the Apprenticeships, Skills, Children and Learning Act 2009 ss 174, 192, Sch 12 para 16(1), (2)(b)). 'Persons with learning difficulties' means: (1) children with special educational needs (as defined in the Education Act 1996 s 312: see PARA 989) and (2) other persons who have a significantly greater difficulty in learning than the majority of persons of their age, or have a disability which either prevents or hinders them from making use of educational facilities of a kind generally provided for persons of their age: Education Act 1997 s 32(6) (s 32(6) substituted, s 32(7) added, by the Apprenticeships, Skills,

Children and Learning Act 2009 ss 174, 192, Sch 12 paras 12, 16(1), (5)). But a person is not to be taken to have a learning difficulty solely because the language (or form of language) in which the person is or will be taught is different from a language (or form of language) which has at any time been spoken in the person's home: Education Act 1997 s 32(7) (as so added).

22 As to Her Majesty's Chief Inspector of Education and Training in Wales see PARA 1148 et seq.
23 Education Act 1997 s 32(2) (amended by the Learning and Skills Act 2000 s 73(1), (3)(a); SI 2005/3239; and SI 2005/3239).

855. The Qualifications Wales Act 2015 generally. The Qualifications Wales Act 2015[1], which at the date at which this volume states the law was not fully in force[2], has nine parts.

Part 1[3] provides an overview of the main provisions of the Act[4]. Part 2[5] establishes Qualifications Wales and[6] makes provision about its membership and governance arrangements[7]; sets out the principal aims of Qualifications Wales[8], and requires Qualifications Wales, in exercising its functions, to act in a way that it considers appropriate for the purpose of achieving those aims[9]. Part 3[10] makes provision about the recognition by Qualifications Wales of bodies that award qualifications in Wales[11]. Part 4[12] makes provision about priority qualifications and the approval by Qualifications Wales of qualifications for award in Wales[13], and it requires Qualifications Wales and the Welsh Ministers to prepare a list of qualifications that are to be a priority for Qualifications Wales[14]; enables Qualifications Wales in certain circumstances to determine that the number of forms of those qualifications approved by it should be restricted (either to one or more than one)[15]; enables Qualifications Wales to enter into arrangements with a body for the development of a new form of qualification to be awarded in Wales, where it has made a determination as described above[16] in respect of the qualification concerned[17]; and enables Qualifications Wales to consider approving a qualification for award in Wales that is not included on the list referred above[18]. Part 5[19] enables Qualifications Wales to designate a qualification for the purpose of enabling a course leading to it to be funded by the Welsh Ministers or a local authority in Wales, or provided by or on behalf of a maintained school in Wales[20]. Part 6[21] provides that a course of education or training may be funded by the Welsh Ministers or a local authority in Wales, or provided by or on behalf of a maintained school in Wales, only if the form of the qualification to which it leads has been approved or designated by Qualifications Wales[22]; and makes provision restricting the effect of conditions imposed by the Office of Qualifications and Examinations Regulation ('Ofqual')[23], in respect of the award in Wales of a form of a qualification that has been approved by Qualifications Wales; and restricting the effect of conditions of recognition imposed by Qualifications Wales so that they do not apply in respect of the award of qualifications outside Wales[24]. Part 7[25] makes provision about steps that may be taken by Qualifications Wales if it considers that a body awarding qualifications in Wales has failed to comply with a condition to which its recognition, or the approval of a qualification awarded by it, is subject[26]. Part 8[27] makes provision about other functions of Qualifications Wales, including the power to provide consultancy and other services on a commercial basis[28]; the duty to prepare a policy statement[29]; how Qualifications Wales is to deal with complaints[30]; fees that may be charged by Qualifications Wales[31]; and the duty to have regard to certain principles in performing regulatory activities[32]. Part 9[33] makes general provision, including setting out an index of defined terms used in the Act[34].

In summary, the matters covered by the Qualifications Wales Act 2015 include:

(1)   establishment and principal aims of Qualifications Wales[35];

(2)   recognition of awarding bodies[36];

(3)   recognition criteria[37];

(4)   recognition of awarding bodies[38];

(5)   priority and other qualifications[39];

(6)   approval criteria[40];

(7)   power for Welsh Ministers to specify minimum requirements[41];

(8)   supplementary provision relevant to all approvals[42];

(9)   surrender and withdrawal of approval[43];

(10) designation of other qualifications[44];

(11) funding of certain courses[45];

(12) delineation of roles of Qualifications Wales and Ofqual[46];

(13) enforcement powers of Qualifications Wales[47];

(14) commercial activities[48];

(15) review and research[49];

(16) subsidiary functions[50]; and

(17) general matters[51].

1 As to Qualifications Wales and the Qualifications Wales Act 2015 see also PARA 853.
2 The Qualifications Wales Act 2015 received Royal Assent on 5 August 2015. In accordance with s 60(1) the following provisions came into force on Royal Assent: s 1 (overview), 2(3), Sch 2 (transfers of staff and property), ss 55–57 (regulations, interpretation), s 59 (power to make consequential and transitional provision etc), s 60 (commencement) and s 61 (short title and inclusion as one of the Education Acts) (as to definition of 'the Education Acts' see PARA 1 note 13). Under the Qualifications Wales Act 2015 s 60(2), (3) other provisions of the Act come into force on such day as the Welsh Ministers may appoint by order made by statutory instrument. Section 2(1) (establishment of Qualifications Wales), s 2(2) (further provision about Qualifications Wales), Sch 1 Pt 1 (status, constitution, procedure, etc, of Qualifications Wales), and Sch 1 Pt 2 para 37 (consequential amendment to the Freedom of Information Act 2000) were brought into force as from 6 August 2015: see the Qualifications Wales Act 2015 (Commencement No 1) Order 2015, SI 2015/1591. At the date at which this volume states the law, no other commencement orders had been made. As to the Welsh Ministers see PARA 59.
3 Ie the Qualifications Wales Act 2015 Pt 1 (s 1).
4 See the Qualifications Wales Act 2015 s 1(1).
5 Ie the Qualifications Wales Act 2015 Pt 2 (ss 2, 3, Schs 1, 2).
6 Ie at the Qualifications Wales Act 2015 Sch 1.
7 See the Qualifications Wales Act 2015 s 1(2)(a).
8 See the Qualifications Wales Act 2015 s 1(2)(b).
9 See the Qualifications Wales Act 2015 s 1(2)(c).
10 Ie the Qualifications Wales Act 2015 Pt 3 (ss 4–12, Sch 3).
11 See the Qualifications Wales Act 2015 s 1(3).
12 Ie the Qualifications Wales Act 2015 Pt 4 (ss 13–28).
13 As to the meaning of 'Wales' see PARA 7 note 3.
14 See the Qualifications Wales Act 2015 s 1(4)(a).
15 See the Qualifications Wales Act 2015 s 1(4)(b).
16 Ie in the Qualifications Wales Act 2015 s 1(4)(b).
17 See the Qualifications Wales Act 2015 s 1(4)(c).
18 See the Qualifications Wales Act 2015 s 1(4)(d). The list is the one referred to in s 1(4)(a).
19 Ie the Qualifications Wales Act 2015 Pt 5 (ss 29–33).
20 See the Qualifications Wales Act 2015 s 1(5).
21 Ie the Qualifications Wales Act 2015 Pt 6 (ss 34–36).
22 See the Qualifications Wales Act 2015 s 1(6)(a).
23 As to the Office of Qualifications and Examinations Regulation see PARA 824 et seq.
24 See the Qualifications Wales Act 2015 s 1(6)(b).
25 Ie the Qualifications Wales Act 2015 Pt 7 (ss 37–44).
26 See the Qualifications Wales Act 2015 s 1(7).
27 Ie the Qualifications Wales Act 2015 Pt 8 (ss 45–54).
28 See the Qualifications Wales Act 2015 s 1(8)(a).
29 See the Qualifications Wales Act 2015 s 1(8)(b).

30 See the Qualifications Wales Act 2015 s 1(8)(c).
31 See the Qualifications Wales Act 2015 s 1(8)(d).
32 See the Qualifications Wales Act 2015 s 1(8)(e).
33 Ie the Qualifications Wales Act 2015 Pt 9 (ss 55–61, Sch 4). In particular s 56 sets out the
    meaning of 'qualification' used in the Act.
34 See the Qualifications Wales Act 2015 s 1(9).
35 See the Qualifications Wales Act 2015 ss 2, 3, Schs 1, 2.
36 See the Qualifications Wales Act 2015 s 4.
37 See the Qualifications Wales Act 2015 ss 5–7.
38 See the Qualifications Wales Act 2015 ss 8–12, Sch 3.
39 See the Qualifications Wales Act 2015 ss 13–19.
40 See the Qualifications Wales Act 2015 s 20.
41 See the Qualifications Wales Act 2015 s 21.
42 See the Qualifications Wales Act 2015 ss 22–24.
43 See the Qualifications Wales Act 2015 ss 25–28.
44 See the Qualifications Wales Act 2015 ss 29–33.
45 See the Qualifications Wales Act 2015 s 34.
46 See the Qualifications Wales Act 2015 ss 35, 36.
47 See the Qualifications Wales Act 2015 ss 37–44.
48 See the Qualifications Wales Act 2015 s 45.
49 See the Qualifications Wales Act 2015 s 46.
50 See the Qualifications Wales Act 2015 ss 47–54.
51 See the Qualifications Wales Act 2015 ss 55–61, Sch 4.

(2) CURRICULUM

(i) The Curriculum in England

A. IN GENERAL

856.   General duties in respect of the curriculum in England. The Secretary of State[1] must exercise his functions[2] with a view to securing that the curriculum for every maintained school[3] or maintained nursery school[4], and every local authority in England must exercise its functions with a view to securing that the curriculum for every maintained school or maintained nursery school which it maintains[5], satisfies the requirements that it be a balanced and broadly based curriculum which: (1) promotes the spiritual, moral, cultural, mental and physical development of pupils[6] at the school and of society[7]; and (2) prepares pupils at the school for the opportunities, responsibilities and experiences of later life[8]. The governing body[9] and head teacher[10] of every maintained school or maintained nursery school must also exercise their functions with a view to securing that the curriculum for the school satisfies those requirements[11].

In exercising any function which may affect the provision of sex education[12] in maintained schools every local authority in England must have regard to the guidance issued[13] by the Secretary of State[14].

1 As to the Secretary of State see PARA 58.
2 The functions referred to in the Education Act 2002 s 79(1)–(3) (see the text to notes 3–11)
   include in particular: (1) functions conferred by Pt 6 (ss 76–96) in relation to the National
   Curriculum for England (s 79(4)(a)); and (2) except in relation to maintained nursery schools,
   functions relating to religious education and religious worship (s 79(4)(b) (amended by the
   Childcare Act 2006 ss 48, 103(2), Sch 1 para 6(1), (3), Sch 3 Pt 1)). As to the meaning of
   'functions' generally see PARA 18 note 5 (definition applied by the Education Act 2002
   s 212(2), (3)). As to the National Curriculum for England see PARA 857.
3 'Maintained school' means: (1) any community, foundation or voluntary school maintained by a
   local authority in England; or (2) except where otherwise stated, any community or foundation
   special school which is maintained by a local authority in England and is not established in a
   hospital: Education Act 2002 s 76(1) (definition amended by SI 2010/1158). As to the meaning

of references to a community, foundation or voluntary school or a community or foundation special school see PARA 106. As to the meaning of 'local authority' see PARA 25 (definition applied by the Education Act 2002 s 212(1)). As to the meaning of 'England' see PARA 7 note 3. Generally this is thought to include academies, as to which see PARA 345 et seq, in particular PARA 359.

4 See the Education Act 2002 s 79(1) (s 79(1), (2) substituted by the Childcare Act 2006 s 48, Sch 1 para 6(1), (2)). 'Maintained nursery school' means a nursery school which is maintained by a local authority in England and is not a special school: Education Act 2002 s 76(1) (definition amended by SI 2010/1158). As to the meaning of 'special school' see PARA 1041 (definition applied by the Education Act 2002 s 212(2), (3)).

5 See the Education Act 2002 s 79(2) (as substituted (see note 4); and amended by SI 2010/1158). See also note 2.

6 As to the meaning of 'pupil' see PARA 20 note 4 (definition applied by the Education Act 2002 s 212(2), (3)).

7 See the Education Act 2002 s 78(1)(a). As to how schools can demonstrate how they are meeting the requirements of s 78 in their provision of spiritual, moral, social and cultural values see the Department for Education's guidance at its website. See eg 'Promoting fundamental values through SMSC: Departmental advice on promoting basic important British values as part of pupils' spiritual, moral, social and cultural (SMSC) development' (27 November 2014). See also 'Protecting children from radicalisation: the prevent duty' (1 July 2015), under which the promotion of 'fundamental British values' is an important part. See also PARAS 8, 910 note 6.

8 See the Education Act 2002 s 78(1)(b).

9 As to the governing bodies of maintained schools in England see PARA 150 et seq.

10 As to the meaning of 'head teacher' see PARA 86 note 4 (definition applied by the Education Act 2002 s 212(2), (3)).

11 Education Act 2002 s 79(3). See also note 2.

12 As to the meaning of 'sex education' see PARA 857 note 10 (definition applied by the Education Act 2002 s 212(2), (3)).

13 Ie under Education Act 1996 s 403(1A): see PARA 905.

14 Education Act 2002 s 79(6) (amended by SI 2010/1158). Except to the extent provided, nothing in the Education Act 2002 s 79 is to be taken to impose duties on a local authority with regard to sex education: s 79(7) (amended by SI 2010/1158).

857. Basic curriculum for every maintained school in England. The curriculum for every maintained school[1] in England[2] must comprise a basic curriculum which includes:

(1) provision[3] for religious education for all registered pupils[4] at the school[5];

(2) a curriculum for all registered pupils at the school who have ceased to be young children[6] but are not over compulsory school age[7] (known as 'the National Curriculum for England')[8];

(3) in the case of a secondary school[9], provision for sex education[10] for all registered pupils at the school[11]; and

(4) in the case of a special school, provision for sex education for all registered pupils at the school who are provided with secondary education[12].

The Secretary of State may by order amend these provisions[13] so as to add further requirements, otherwise than in relation to religious education or sex education[14].

1 As to the meaning of 'maintained school' see PARA 856 note 3. As to academies see PARA 345 et seq. It is thought that academies must in practice follow the basic curriculum: see PARA 359.

2 As to the meaning of 'England' see PARA 7 note 3.

3 Ie in accordance with such of the provisions of the School Standards and Framework Act 1998 Sch 19 (see PARA 915 et seq) as apply in relation to the school.

4 As to the meaning of 'registered pupil' see PARA 437 (definition applied by the Education Act 2002 s 212(2), (3)).

5 Education Act 2002 s 80(1)(a). Section 80(1)(a) does not apply: (1) in relation to pupils who are under compulsory school age (s 80(2)(a) (amended by the Childcare Act 2006 s 48, Sch 1

para 7(1), (3))); or (2) in the case of a maintained special school (provision as to religious education in special schools being made by regulations under the School Standards and Framework Act 1998 s 71(7) (see PARA 924)) (Education Act 2002 s 80(2)(b)).

6 Ie for the purposes of the Childcare Act 2006 Pt 1 (ss 1–21): see CHILDREN AND YOUNG PERSONS vol 10 (2012) PARA 1077 et seq.

7 As to the meaning of 'compulsory school age' see PARA 19.

8 Education Act 2002 s 80(1)(b) (amended by the Childcare Act 2006 s 48, Sch 1 para 7(1), (2)). As to the National Curriculum for England see further PARA 859 et seq. The Secretary of State may by order amend s 80(1)(b) by substituting for the reference to compulsory school age (or to any age specified there by virtue of s 80(3)) a reference to such other age as may be specified in the order: s 80(3)(b). As to the Secretary of State see PARA 58. At the date at which this volume states the law no such order had been made.

9 As to the meaning of 'secondary education' see PARA 21 (definition applied by the Education Act 2002 s 212(2), (3)).

10 'Sex education' includes education about Acquired Immune Deficiency Syndrome and Human Immunodeficiency Virus and any other sexually transmitted disease: Education Act 1996 s 579(1) (definition added by the Education Act 2002 s 215(1), Sch 21 para 57(c)); definition applied by the Education Act 2002 s 212(2), (3)).

11 Education Act 2002 s 80(1)(c).

12 Education Act 2002 s 80(1)(d). As to the application of s 80(1)(d), with modifications, in relation to pupil referral units in England see the Education (Pupil Referral Units) (Application of Enactments) (England) Regulations 2007, SI 2007/2979, regs 1(3), 3, Sch 1 Pt 1 para 19. As to pupil referral units see PARA 427 et seq.

13 Ie the Education Act 2002 s 80(1).

14 Education Act 2002 s 80(3)(a). The Secretary of State may by order also amend any provision included in s 80(1) by virtue of s 80(3)(a): s 80(3)(c). At the date at which this volume states the law no such orders had been made.

858.   Careers education and guidance in England.   All registered pupils at community, foundation and voluntary schools, community or foundation special schools (other than those established in hospitals) and pupil referral units must be provided, during the relevant phase of their education, with a programme of careers guidance[1]. Persons attending educational institutions must be provided with access to both guidance materials, and a wide range of up to date reference materials, relating to careers education and career opportunities[2].

1   See the Education Act 1997 s 42A; and PARA 820.
2   See the Education Act 1997 s 45; and PARA 821.

B.   THE NATIONAL CURRICULUM FOR ENGLAND: IN GENERAL

859.   Constituents of the National Curriculum for England.   The National Curriculum for England[1] comprises the four key stages[2], and specifies:

(1)   'assessment arrangements', which, in relation to a key stage, means the arrangements for assessing[3] pupils[4] in respect of that stage for the specified purposes[5], namely: (a) the purpose of ascertaining what pupils have achieved in relation to the attainment targets for that stage, and (b) such other purposes as the Secretary of State[6] may by order specify[7];

(2)   'attainment targets', which, in relation to a key stage, means the knowledge, skills and understanding which pupils of different abilities and maturities are expected to have by the end of that stage[8];

(3)   'programmes of study', which, in relation to a key stage, means matters, skills and processes which are required to be taught to pupils of different abilities and maturities by the end of that stage[9].

Independent schools may choose to adopt the National Curriculum for England but are under no obligation to do so[10]. The position is similar with academies[11] and free schools[12].

Separate statutory provision is made in relation to early years provision, including education, for young children up to the age of five[13].

1   As to the National Curriculum for England see PARA 857.
2   As to the key stages see PARA 860.
3   'Assess' includes test, and related expressions must be construed accordingly: Education Act 2002 s 76(1) (definition amended by the Apprenticeships, Skills, Children and Learning Act 2009 ss 174, 192, 266, Sch 12 paras 31, 32(1), (3), Sch 16 Pt 4).
4   As to the meaning of 'pupil' see PARA 20 note 4 (definition applied by the Education Act 2002 s 212(2), (3)).
5   See the Education Act 2002 s 76(1) (definition substituted by the Childcare Act 2006 s 48, Sch 1 para 3(1), (2)).
6   As to the Secretary of State see PARA 58.
7   Education Act 2002 s 76(2) (added by the Apprenticeships, Skills, Children and Learning Act 2009 ss 174, 192, Sch 12 paras 31, 32(1), (5)). As to orders under the Education Act 2002 s 76(2) see the Education (National Curriculum) (Specified Purpose) (England) Order 2011, SI 2011/2751; and the Education (National Curriculum) (Specified Purpose) (England) Order 2015, SI 2015/901.
8   Education Act 2002 s 76(1).
9   Education Act 2002 s 76(1).
10 As to independent schools see PARA 369 et seq.
11 See PARA 359. As to academies generally see PARA 345 et seq.
12 As to free schools see PARA 368.
13 See the Childcare Act 2006 Pt 1 (ss 1–21); and CHILDREN AND YOUNG PERSONS vol 10 (2012) PARA 1077 et seq.

860. The key stages of the curriculum in England. There are four key stages in the National Curriculum for England[1]. The key stages in relation to a pupil[2] are:

(1)   the period beginning at the same time as the school year[3] in which he attains the age of six[4] and ending at the same time as the school year in which the majority of pupils in his class[5] attain the age of seven ('the first key stage')[6];

(2)   the period beginning at the same time as the school year in which the majority of pupils in his class attain the age of eight and ending at the same time as the school year in which the majority of pupils in his class attain the age of 11 ('the second key stage')[7];

(3)   the period beginning at the same time as the school year in which the majority of pupils in his class attain the age of 12 and ending at the same time as the school year in which the majority of pupils in his class attain the age of 14 ('the third key stage')[8]; and

(4)   the period beginning at the same time as the school year in which the majority of pupils in his class attain the age of 15 and ending with the expiry of the school year in which the majority of pupils in his class cease to be of compulsory school age[9] ('the fourth key stage')[10].

The head teacher of a school may elect, in relation to a particular pupil and a particular subject, that the definitions of the four key stages have effect as if any reference to the school year in which the majority of pupils in that pupil's class attain a particular age were a reference to the school year in which that pupil attains that age[11]. If at any time, in the case of a pupil of compulsory school age, the definitions of the four key stages[12] do not[13] apply to determine the period within which that time falls, heads (1) to (4) above have effect as if:

(a)   in the case of heads (1) to (3) above, any reference to the school year in which the majority of pupils in that pupil's class attain a particular age were a reference to the school year in which that pupil attains that age[14]; and

(b)   in the case of head (4) above, the period were a period beginning at the same time as the school year in which he attains the age of 15 and ending when he ceases to be of compulsory school age[15].

1   In the Education Act 2002 Pt 6 (ss 76–96), 'key stage', or references to a particular key stage, must be construed in accordance with s 82 (see the text to notes 2–15): s 76(1). As to the National Curriculum for England see PARA 857.
2   As to the meaning of 'pupil' see PARA 20 note 4 (definition applied by the Education Act 2002 s 212(2), (3)).
3   'School year', in relation to a school, means the period beginning with the first school term to begin after July and ending with the beginning of the first school term to begin after the following July: Education Act 2002 s 76(1) (definition amended by the Childcare Act 2006 ss 48, 103(2), Sch 1 para 3(1), (4), Sch 3 Pt 1). As to the meaning of 'school' see PARA 91 (definition applied by the Education Act 2002 s 212(2), (3)). As to the fixing of dates for school terms and holidays see PARA 458.
4   As to the time at which a person attains a particular age see PARA 7 note 6.
5   In the Education Act 2002 s 82, 'class', in relation to a particular pupil and a particular subject, means: (1) the teaching group in which he is regularly taught in that subject (s 82(5)(a)); or (2) where there are two or more such groups, such one of them as may be designated by the head teacher of the school (s 82(5)(b)). As to the meaning of 'head teacher' see PARA 86 note 4 (definition applied by s 212(2), (3)).
6   Education Act 2002 s 82(1)(a). The Secretary of State may by order: (1) provide that, in relation to any subject specified in the order, s 82(1) is to have effect as if for the ages of seven and eight there specified there were substituted such other ages (less than 11 and 12 respectively) as may be specified in the order (s 82(4)(a)); and (2) amend s 82(1)–(3) (s 82(4)(b)). As to the Secretary of State see PARA 58. As to the procedure for making orders under s 82(4) see PARA 865. At the date at which this volume states the law, no order had been made under s 82(4).
7   Education Act 2002 s 82(1)(b). See also note 6.
8   Education Act 2002 s 82(1)(c). See also note 6.
9   As to the meaning of 'compulsory school age' see PARA 19.
10   Education Act 2002 s 82(1)(d). See also note 6.
11   Education Act 2002 s 82(2). See also note 6.
12   Ie the Education Act 2002 s 82(1): see the text to notes 2–10.
13   Ie apart from the Education Act 2002 s 82(3): see the text to notes 14–15.
14   Education Act 2002 s 82(3)(a). See also note 6.
15   Education Act 2002 s 82(3)(b). See also note 6.

861. Curriculum requirements for the first, second and third key stages. For the first, second and third key stages[1], the National Curriculum for England[2] comprises the core subjects of mathematics[3], English[4] and science[5], and the other foundation subjects of design and technology[6], computing[7], physical education[8], history[9], geography[10], art and design[11], music[12], (in relation to the second key stage) a foreign language[13], and (in relation to the third key stage) citizenship[14] and a modern foreign language[15]. In relation to each of those subjects for each of those stages, the National Curriculum for England must specify attainment targets[16], programmes of study[17] and assessment arrangements[18].

1   As to the meaning of 'key stage' see PARA 860 note 1. As to first, second and third key stages see PARA 860.
2   As to the National Curriculum for England see PARA 857.
3   See the Education Act 2002 s 84(1), (2)(a). The Secretary of State may by order amend s 84(2)–(5): s 84(6). As to the procedure for making orders under s 84(6) see PARA 865. As to the Secretary of State see PARA 58. As to orders made under s 84(6) see the Education (Amendment of the Curriculum Requirements) (England) Order 2013, SI 2013/2092; and the Education (Amendment of the Curriculum Requirements for Second Key Stage) (England) Order 2013, SI 2013/2093.
4   See the Education Act 2002 s 84(1), (2)(b). See also note 3.
5   See the Education Act 2002 s 84(1), (2)(c). See also note 3.
6   See the Education Act 2002 s 84(1), (3)(a). See also note 3.
7   See the Education Act 2002 s 84(1), (3)(b) (substituted by SI 2013/2092). See also note 3.

8 See the Education Act 2002 s 84(1), (3)(c). See also note 3.
9 See the Education Act 2002 s 84(1), (3)(d). See also note 3.
10 See the Education Act 2002 s 84(1), (3)(e). See also note 3.
11 See the Education Act 2002 s 84(1), (3)(f). See also note 3.
12 See the Education Act 2002 s 84(1), (3)(g). See also note 3.
13 See the Education Act 2002 s 84(1), (3)(ga) (added by SI 2013/2093). See also note 3. In the Education Act 2002 s 84(3)(ga) 'foreign language' means (1) a foreign language specified in an order made by the Secretary of State for the purposes of the provision; or (2) if the order provides that any foreign language is a foreign language for the purposes of the provision, any foreign language: s 84(A4) (added by SI 2013/2093). An order under the Education Act 2002 s 84(A4) or (4) may: (a) specify circumstances in which a language is not to be treated as a foundation subject (s 84(5)(a) (s 84(5) amended by SI 2013/2093); and (b) provide for the determination under the order of any question arising as to whether a particular language is a foreign language or modern foreign language, as the case may be (Education Act 2002 s 84(5)(b) (amended by SI 2013/2093)). For the purposes of the Education Act 2002 s 84(A4) 'foreign language' means any foreign language: Education (National Curriculum) (Languages) (England) Order 2013, SI 2013/2230, art 2.
14 See the Education Act 2002 s 84(1), (3)(h)(i). See also note 3.
15 See the Education Act 2002 s 84(1), (3)(h)(ii). See also note 3. In s 84(3)(h)(ii) 'modern foreign language' means (1) a modern foreign language specified in an order made by the Secretary of State for the purposes of the provision (s 84(4)(a) (s 84(4) substituted by SI 2013/2093); or (2) if the order provides that any modern foreign language is a modern foreign language for the purposes of the provision, any modern foreign language: Education Act 2002 s 84(4)(b) (as so substituted). See also s 84(5); and note 13. For the purposes of s 84(4) 'modern foreign language' means any modern foreign language: Education (National Curriculum) (Languages) (England) Order 2013, SI 2013/2230, art 3.
16 As to the meaning of 'attainment targets' see PARA 859.
17 As to the meaning of 'programmes of study' see PARA 859.
18 See the Education Act 2002 s 84(1). As to the meaning of 'assessment arrangements' see PARA 859.

862. Curriculum requirements for the fourth key stage. Until a day to be appointed the following provisions have effect[1].

For the fourth key stage[2], the National Curriculum for England[3] comprises the core and other foundation subjects, the entitlement conferred on pupils[4] and the other elements[5] of the key stage[6]. The National Curriculum for England must specify programmes of study[7] in relation to each of the core and other foundation subjects for the fourth key stage[8].

The core subjects are mathematics[9], English[10] and science[11]; and the other foundation subjects of information and communication technology[12], physical education[13] and citizenship[14].

A pupil in the fourth key stage is entitled, if he so elects, to follow a course of study[15] in science which leads to such qualification or set of qualifications as the governing body[16] may choose from among those: (1) approved under the Learning and Skills Act 2000[17]; and (2) specified by the Secretary of State[18] by order for these purposes[19].

The elements for the fourth key stage[20] are in relation to any pupil who so elects, one subject from each of such one or more of the four 'entitlement areas' as the pupil may elect[21], namely: (a) arts, comprising art and design[22], music[23], dance[24], drama[25], and media arts[26]; (b) design and technology[27]; (c) humanities, comprising geography[28] and history[29]; and (d) modern foreign languages, comprising any modern foreign language specified in an order made by the Secretary of State[30] or, if the order so specifies, any modern foreign language[31].

The Secretary of State may by order amend any of the above provisions relating to requirements for the fourth key stage[32], or provide that, while the order remains in force, none of those provisions is to have effect[33].

As from a day to be appointed the following provisions have effect[34].

For the fourth key stage, the National Curriculum for England comprises the core and other foundation subjects[35], work-related learning[36], and, in relation to any pupil, such other courses of study as are necessary to satisfy the entitlements conferred[37] on him[38]. The National Curriculum for England must specify programmes of study in relation to each of the core and other foundation subjects for the fourth key stage[39].

The core subjects are mathematics[40], English[41], and science[42]; and the other foundation subjects are computing[43], physical education[44], and citizenship[45]. A pupil in the fourth key stage is entitled, if he so elects, to follow a course of study in science which leads to such qualification or set of qualifications as the governing body may choose from among those: (i) approved under the Learning and Skills Act 2000[46]; and (ii) specified by the Secretary of State by order for these purposes[47].

A pupil in the fourth key stage is also entitled to follow a course of study[48] in a subject within each of such one or more of the four entitlement areas specified[49] as he may choose[50]. The entitlement areas are arts, comprising art and design, music, dance, drama, and media arts[51]; design and technology (comprising only that subject)[52]; humanities, comprising geography[53] and history[54]; and modern foreign languages comprising any modern foreign language specified in an order made by the Secretary of State or, if the order so specifies, any modern foreign language[55]. The entitlement so conferred on a pupil is to be taken to be satisfied if a course of study within each of the entitlement areas specified[56] is made available to him by or on behalf of the school at which he is a registered pupil[57].

The Secretary of State may by order amend any of the above provisions[58] or provide that, while the order remains in force, those provisions are not to have effect[59].

1   The Education Act 2002 s 85 is substituted and s 85A is added by the Education and Inspections Act 2006 s 74(1) as from a day to be appointed under s 188(3). At the date at which this volume states the law no such day had been appointed.
2   As to the meaning of 'key stage' see PARA 860 note 1. As to the fourth key stage see PARA 860.
3   As to the National Curriculum for England see PARA 857.
4   Ie the entitlement conferred by the Education Act 2002 s 85(3A): see the text to notes 15–19. As to the meaning of 'pupil' see PARA 20 note 4 (definition applied by s 212(2), (3)).
5   Ie the elements referred to in the Education Act 2002 s 85(5): see the text to notes 20–21.
6   See the Education Act 2002 s 85(1) (s 85 substituted by SI 2003/2946; and the Education Act 2002 s 85(1) amended by the Education and Inspections Act 2006 s 74(4)(a)).
7   As to the meaning of 'programmes of study' see PARA 859.
8   Education Act 2002 s 85(2) (as substituted: see note 6).
9   Education Act 2002 s 85(3)(a) (as substituted: see note 6).
10   Education Act 2002 s 85(3)(b) (as substituted: see note 6).
11   Education Act 2002 s 85(3)(c) (as substituted: see note 6).
12   Education Act 2002 s 85(4)(a) (as substituted: see note 6).
13   Education Act 2002 s 85(4)(b) (as substituted: see note 6).
14   Education Act 2002 s 85(4)(c) (as substituted: see note 6).
15   'Course of study' means a course of education or training which leads to a qualification approved under the Learning and Skills Act 2000 s 98 (see PARA 935) for the purposes of s 96 of that Act: Education Act 2002 s 85(10) (as substituted: see note 6).
16   As to the governing bodies of maintained schools in England see PARA 150 et seq.
17   Ie approved under the Learning and Skills Act 2000 s 98 (see PARA 935) for the purposes of s 96 of that Act: Education Act 2002 s 85(3A)(a) (s 85 as substituted (see note 6); and s 85(3A) added by the Education and Inspections Act 2006 s 74(4)(b)).
18   As to the Secretary of State see PARA 58.
19   Education Act 2002 s 85(3A)(b) (as substituted and added: see note 17). Any such order made before the commencement of the Education and Inspections Act 2006 s 74(1) (which substitutes the Education Act 2002 s 85: see note 1) is to have effect from that commencement as if made

under s 85(5) (as substituted by the Education and Inspections Act 2006 s 74(1)) (see the text to notes 46–47): Education and Inspections Act 2006 s 74(5). As to the order made see the Education (National Curriculum) (Science at Key Stage 4) (England) Order 2007, SI 2007/2241.

20 Ie referred to in the Education Act 2002 s 85(1). In the exercise of functions under Pt 6 (ss 76–96) by virtue of s 85, a local authority, governing body or head teacher must have regard to any guidance relating to work-related learning or the entitlement areas (see the text to notes 21–31) which is issued from time to time by the Secretary of State: s 85(9) (as substituted (see note 6); and amended by SI 2010/1158; SI 2012/2056; and the Education Act 2011 Sch 8 paras 11, 12). As to the meaning of 'local authority' see PARA 25 (definition applied by the Education Act 2002 s 212(1)). As to the meaning of 'functions' see PARA 18 note 5; and as to the meaning of 'head teacher' see PARA 86 note 4 (definitions applied by s 212(2), (3)). As to the Qualifications and Curriculum Development Agency see PARA 824 et seq.

21 Education Act 2002 s 85(5) (as substituted (see note 6); and amended by SI 2012/2056)). A pupil in the fourth key stage is, if he so elects, entitled to follow a course of study in a subject within each of the four entitlement areas specified in the Education Act 2002 s 85(6) (see the text to notes 22–31); but this entitlement is satisfied where one subject within each of those entitlement areas is made available to him by or on behalf of the school at which he is a registered pupil: s 85(8) (as so substituted). As to the meaning of 'registered pupil' see PARA 437 (definition applied by s 212(2), (3)).

22 Education Act 2002 s 85(6)(a)(i) (as substituted: see note 6).

23 Education Act 2002 s 85(6)(a)(ii) (as substituted: see note 6).

24 Education Act 2002 s 85(6)(a)(iii) (as substituted: see note 6).

25 Education Act 2002 s 85(6)(a)(iv) (as substituted: see note 6).

26 Education Act 2002 s 85(6)(a)(v) (as substituted: see note 6).

27 Education Act 2002 s 85(6)(b) (as substituted: see note 6).

28 Education Act 2002 s 85(6)(c)(i) (as substituted: see note 6).

29 Education Act 2002 s 85(6)(c)(ii) (as substituted: see note 6).

30 An order made under the Education Act 2002 s 85(6)(d) may: (1) specify circumstances in which a language is not to be treated as falling within s 85(6)(d) (s 85(7)(a) (as substituted: see note 6)); and (2) provide for the determination under the order of any question arising as to whether a particular language is a modern foreign language (s 85(7)(b) (as so substituted)). At the date at which this volume states the law, no such order had been made.

31 Education Act 2002 s 85(6)(d) (as substituted: see note 6).

32 Ie the Education Act 2002 s 85: see the text to notes 2–31.

33 Education Act 2002 s 86. As to the order made see the Education (Amendment of the Curriculum Requirements for Fourth Key Stage) (England) Order 2003, SI 2003/2946.

34 See note 1.

35 Education Act 2002 s 85(1)(a) (as substituted: see note 1).

36 Education Act 2002 s 85(1)(b) (as substituted: see note 1). 'Work-related learning' means planned activity designed to use the context of work to develop knowledge, skills and understanding useful in work, including learning through the experience of work, learning about work and working practices and learning the skills for work: s 85(7) (as so substituted). In the exercise of their functions under Pt 6 (ss 76–96) so far as those functions relate by virtue of s 85 to work-related learning a local authority, governing body or head teacher must have regard to any guidance issued from time to time by the Secretary of State: s 85(6) (as so substituted; and amended by SI 2010/1158; and the Education Act 2011 Sch 8 paras 11, 12).

37 Ie by the Education Act 2002 s 85(5) and s 85A: see the text to notes 46–57.

38 Education Act 2002 s 85(1)(c) (as substituted: see note 1).

39 Education Act 2002 s 85(2) (as substituted: see note 1).

40 Education Act 2002 s 85(3)(a) (as substituted: see note 1).

41 Education Act 2002 s 85(3)(b) (as substituted: see note 1).

42 Education Act 2002 s 85(3)(c) (as substituted: see note 1).

43 Education Act 2002 s 85(4)(a) (as substituted (see note 1); and further substituted by SI 2013/2092).

44 Education Act 2002 s 85(4)(b) (as substituted: see note 1).

45 Education Act 2002 s 85(4)(c) (as substituted: see note 1).

46 Ie approved under the Learning and Skills Act 2000 s 98 (see PARA 935) for the purposes of s 96 of that Act: Education Act 2002 s 85(5)(a) (as substituted: see note 1).

47 Education Act 2002 s 85(5)(b) (as substituted: see note 1). At the date at which this volume states the law no such order had been made, but see also note 19.

48 'Course of study' means a course of education or training which leads to such qualification as the governing body may choose from among those approved under the Learning and Skills

Act 2000 s 98 (see PARA 935) for the purposes of s 96 of that Act: Education Act 2002 s 85A(6) (s 85A added (see note 1);and s 85A(6) amended by the Education Act 2011 s 31(1), (2)(e)).
49 Ie specified in the Education Act 2002 s 85A(2).
50 Education Act 2002 s 85A(1) (as added (see note 1); and amended by the Education Act 2011 s 31(1), (2)(a)). In the exercise of their functions by virtue of the Education Act 2002 Pt 6 (ss 76–96) in relation to courses of study falling within s 85A(1), a local authority, governing body or head teacher must have regard to any guidance issued from time to time by the Secretary of State or the Qualifications and Curriculum Development Agency: s 85A(5) (as so added; and amended by SI 2010/1158; the Apprenticeships, Skills, Children and Learning Act 2009 ss 174, 192, Sch 12 paras 31, 34; and the Education Act 2011 s 31(1), (2)(d)). As to the Qualifications and Curriculum Development Agency see PARA 824 et seq.
51 Education Act 2002 s 85A(2)(a)(i)–(v) (as added (see note 1); and s 85A(2) amended by the Education Act 2011 s 31(1), (2)(b)).
52 Education Act 2002 s 85A(2)(b) (as added: see note 1).
53 Education Act 2002 s 85A(2)(c)(i) (as added: see note 1).
54 Education Act 2002 s 85A(2)(c)(ii) (as added: see note 1).
55 Education Act 2002 s 85A(2)(d) (as added: see note 1). An order under s 85A(2)(d) may: (1) specify circumstances in which a language is not to be treated as falling within s 85A(2)(d) (s 85A(3)(a) (as so added)); and (2) provide for the determination under the order of any question arising as to whether a particular language is a modern foreign language (s 85A(3)(b) (as so added)). At the date at which this volume states the law no such order had been made.
56 Ie specified in the Education Act 2002 s 85A(2).
57 Education Act 2002 s 85A(4) (as added (see note 1); and amended by the Education Act 2011 s 31(1), (2)(c)).
58 Ie any provision of the Education Act 2002 s 85 and s 85A (see the text to notes 35–57): s 86(1)(a). As from a day to be appointed, s 86(1) is numbered as such and amended, and s 86(2) is added, by the Education and Inspections Act 2006 s 74(2). At the date at which this volume states the law no such day had been appointed. An order under the Education Act 2002 s 86 may make such amendments of the Education Act 2002 as appear to the Secretary of State to be necessary or expedient in connection with the provision made by virtue of s 86(1): s 86(2) (as so added). As to orders made see the Education (Amendment of the Curriculum Requirements for Fourth Key Stage) (England) Order 2012, SI 2012/2056; and the Education (Amendment of the Curriculum Requirements) (England) Order 2013, SI 2013/2092.
59 Education Act 2002 s 86(1)(b) (as renumbered and amended: see note 58). See also note 58.

863.   Establishment of the National Curriculum for England by order. The Secretary of State[1] must so exercise the following powers[2] as to revise the National Curriculum for England[3] whenever he considers it necessary or expedient to do so[4]. In respect of the first, second and third key stages[5] and[6] the fourth key stage, the Secretary of State may by order specify in relation to each of the foundation subjects[7] such attainment targets[8], such programmes of study[9], and such assessment arrangements[10], as he considers appropriate for that subject[11].

Such an order may not require[12]: (1) the allocation of any particular period or periods of time during any key stage to the teaching of any programme of study or any matter, skill or process forming part of it[13]; or (2) the making in school timetables of provision of any particular kind for the periods to be allocated to such teaching during any such stage[14]. Such an order may, instead of containing the provisions to be made, refer to provisions in a document published by a person, and in the manner, specified in the order and direct that those provisions are to have effect or, as the case may be, are to have effect as amended by the order[15].

1 As to the Secretary of State see PARA 58.
2 Ie the powers conferred by the Education Act 2002 s 87(3): see the text to notes 5–11.
3 As to the National Curriculum for England see PARA 857.
4 Education Act 2002 s 87(1) (substituted by the Childcare Act 2006 s 48, Sch 1 para 10(1), (2)).
5 As to the meaning of 'key stage' see PARA 860 note 1. As to the key stages see PARA 860.
6 Ie subject to the Education Act 2002 s 86: see PARA 862.

7   As to the foundation subjects in relation to the first, second and third key stages see PARA 861; and in relation to the fourth key stage see PARA 862.

8   Education Act 2002 s 87(3)(a). As to the meaning of 'attainment targets' see PARA 859. As to the procedure for making orders under s 87(3)(a) see s 96; and PARA 865.

9   Education Act 2002 s 87(3)(b). As to the meaning of 'programmes of study' see PARA 859. As to the procedure for making orders under s 87(3)(b) see s 96; and PARA 865.

10 Education Act 2002 s 87(3)(c). As to the meaning of 'assessment arrangements' see PARA 859. Before making an order under s 87(3)(c) the Secretary of State must consult the Office of Qualifications and Examinations Regulation, and may consult such other persons as he considers appropriate: s 87(6A) (added by the Apprenticeships, Skills, Children and Learning Act 2009 s 159(1), (2)). As to the Office of Qualifications and Examinations Regulation see PARA 824 et seq. As to the meaning of 'person' see PARA 7 note 6. As to the exercise of the duty to consult see JUDICIAL REVIEW vol 61 (2010) PARA 627.

An order under the Education Act 2002 s 87(3)(c) may confer or impose such functions on: (1) the governing body and head teacher (s 87(7)(a) (amended by the Apprenticeships, Skills, Children and Learning Act 2009 ss 174, 192, 266, Sch 12 paras 31, 35(1), (3)(a), Sch 16 Pt 4)); (2) the local authority (Education Act 2002 s 87(7)(b) (amended by SI 2010/1158)); and (3) any other person with whom the Secretary of State has made arrangements in connection with the development, implementation or monitoring of assessment arrangements, as appear to the Secretary of State to be required (Education Act 2002 s 87(7)(d) (s 87(7)(c), (d) added by the Apprenticeships, Skills, Children and Learning Act 2009 ss 174, 192, Sch 12 paras 31, 35(1), (3)(b); and the Education Act 2002 s 87(7)(c) repealed by the Education Act 2011 Sch 8 paras 11, 13)). As to the governing bodies of maintained schools in England see PARA 150 et seq. As to the meaning of 'functions' see PARA 18 note 5; and as to the meaning of 'head teacher' see PARA 86 note 4 (definitions applied by the Education Act 2002 s 212(2), (3)). As to the meaning of 'local authority' see PARA 25 (definition applied by s 212(1)). The duties that may be imposed by virtue of s 87(7)(a) or (b) (see heads (1) and (2) above) include, in relation to persons exercising any function in connection with the moderation or monitoring of assessment arrangements, the duty to permit them: (a) to enter premises of the school; (b) to observe implementation of the arrangements; and (c) to inspect, and take copies of, documents and other articles: s 87(10) (amended by the Childcare Act 2006 ss 48, 103(2), Sch 1 para 10(1), (8)(b), Sch 3 Pt 1; and the Apprenticeships, Skills, Children and Learning Act 2009 ss 174, 192, Sch 12 paras 31, 35(1), (5)). As to the meaning of 'premises' see PARA 62 note 19 (definition applied by the Education Act 2002 s 212(2), (3)).

An order under s 87(3)(c) may specify such assessment arrangements as may for the time being be made by a person specified in the order: s 87(8) (amended by the Childcare Act 2006 ss 48, 103(2), Sch 1 para 10(1), (7), Sch 3 Pt 1). An order under the Education Act 2002 s 87(3)(c) which includes provision made by virtue of s 87(8) must provide that before making or revising the assessment arrangements the person specified in the order must consult the Office of Qualifications and Examinations Regulation, and may consult such other persons as that person considers appropriate: s 87(8A) (added by the Apprenticeships, Skills, Children and Learning Act 2009 s 159(1), (3)). An order under the Education Act 2002 s 87(3)(c) may authorise a person specified in the order to make delegated supplementary provisions in relation to such matters as may be specified in the order: s 87(11) (s 87(11) substituted, 87(12) added, by the Apprenticeships, Skills, Children and Learning Act 2009 ss 174, 192, Sch 12 paras 31, 35(1), (6)). 'Delegated supplementary provisions means such provisions (other than provisions conferring or imposing functions as mentioned in the Education Act 2002 s 87(7)(a) or (b) (see heads (1) and (2) above)) as appear to the authorised person to be expedient for giving full effect to, or otherwise supplementing, the provisions made by the order: s 87(12) (as so added). An order under s 87(3)(c) which authorises a person to make delegated supplementary provisions must provide that before making, amending or revoking any such provisions the person so authorised must consult the Office of Qualifications and Examinations Regulation, and may consult such other persons as that person considers appropriate: s 87(12A) (added by the Apprenticeships, Skills, Children and Learning Act 2009 s 159(1), (4)). An order under the Education Act 2002 s 87(3)(c) authorising the making of delegated supplementary provisions may provide that such provisions may be made only with the approval of the Secretary of State: s 87(13) (s 87(13), (14) added by the Apprenticeships, Skills, Children and Learning Act 2009 ss 174, 192, Sch 12 paras 31, 35(1), (6)). Any delegated supplementary provisions, on being published as specified in the order under which they are made, have effect for the purposes of the Education Act 2002 Pt 6 (ss 76–96) as if made by the order: s 87(14) (as so added).

11 Education Act 2002 s 87(3). As to the orders made under s 87(3) see the Education (National Curriculum) (Key Stage 2 Assessment Arrangements) (England) Order 2003, SI 2003/1038 (amended by SI 2009/1585; SI 2010/290; SI 2011/2392; SI 2012/765; SI 2012/838;

SI 2013/1513; and SI 2015/900); the Education (National Curriculum) (Key Stage 3 Assessment Arrangements) (England) Order 2003, SI 2003/1039 (amended by SI 2008/3081; SI 2009/1585; SI 2011/2392; SI 2012/765; and SI 2015/900); the Education (National Curriculum) (Key Stage 1 Assessment Arrangements) (England) Order 2004, SI 2004/2783 (amended by SI 2011/2392; SI 2011/3057; SI 2012/765; SI 2013/1513; and SI 2015/900); the National Curriculum (Exceptions for First, Second, Third and Fourth Key Stages) (England) Regulations 2013, SI 2013/1487 (amended by SI 2014/1866; and SI 2014/3286); and the Education (National Curriculum) (Attainment Targets and Programmes of Study) (England) Order 2013, SI 2013/2232 (amended by SI 2014/1941; SI 2014/3285; and SI 2015/900).

12   Education Act 2002 s 87(4) (amended by the Childcare Act 2006 ss 48, 103(2), Sch 1 para 10(1), (4)(a), Sch 3 Pt 1).

13   Education Act 2002 s 87(4)(a) (amended by the Childcare Act 2006 ss 48, 103(2), Sch 1 para 10(1), (4)(b), Sch 3 Pt 1).

14   Education Act 2002 s 87(4)(b) (amended by the Childcare Act 2006 ss 48, 103(2), Sch 1 para 10(1), (4)(c), Sch 3 Pt 1).

15   Education Act 2002 s 87(5) (amended by the Childcare Act 2006 ss 48, 103(2), Sch 1 para 10(1), (5), Sch 3 Pt 1; and the Apprenticeships, Skills, Children and Learning Act 2009 ss 174, 192, Sch 12 paras 31, 35(1), (2)).

864. Duty to secure implementation of the National Curriculum for England. In relation to any maintained school[1] and any school year[2]:

(1)   the local authority[3] and the governing body[4] must exercise their functions[5] with a view to securing[6], and

(2)   the head teacher[7] must secure[8],

that the National Curriculum for England[9] as subsisting at the beginning of that year is implemented[10]. In relation to any maintained school:

(a)   the local authority and the governing body must exercise their functions with a view to securing[11], and

(b)   the head teacher must secure[12],

that the assessment arrangements specified for the time being in the National Curriculum for England are implemented[13].

1   As to the meaning of 'maintained school' see PARA 856 note 3. As to academies generally see PARA 345 et seq. As to the National Curriculum and academies see PARA 359.

2   As to the meaning of 'school year' see PARA 860 note 3.

3   As to the meaning of 'local authority' see PARA 25 (definition applied by the Education Act 2002 s 212(1)).

4   As to the governing bodies of maintained schools in England see PARA 150 et seq.

5   As to the meaning of 'functions' see PARA 18 note 5 (definition applied by the Education Act 2002 s 212(2), (3)).

6   Education Act 2002 s 88(1)(a) (s 88(1) numbered as such by the Education and Inspections Act 2006 s 74(3); and the Education Act 2002 s 88(1)(a) amended by SI 2010/1158).

7   As to the meaning of 'head teacher' see PARA 86 note 4 (definition applied by the Education Act 2002 s 212(2), (3)).

8   Education Act 2002 s 88(1)(b) (as renumbered: see note 6).

9   As to the National Curriculum for England see PARA 857.

10   Education Act 2002 s 88(1) (as renumbered: see note 6). Section 88(1) does not apply in relation to assessment arrangements: s 88(1) (as so renumbered; and amended by the Education and Skills Act 2008 s 156(1)). As to the meaning of 'assessment arrangements' see PARA 859. As to the duty of teachers to deliver the National Curriculum see *Wandsworth London Borough Council v National Association of Schoolmasters/Union of Women Teachers* [1994] ICR 81, [1994] ELR 170, (1993) 92 LGR 91, CA (decided under previous legislation).

11   Education Act 2002 s 88(1A)(a) (s 88(1A) added by the Education and Skills Act 2008 s 156(2); and the Education Act 2002 s 88(1A)(a) amended by SI 2010/1158).

12   Education Act 2002 s 88(1A)(b) (as added: see note 11).

13   Education Act 2002 s 88(1A) (as added: see note 11).

865. Procedure for making certain orders and regulations in relation to the National Curriculum for England. Where the Secretary of State[1] proposes to make certain orders[2] or certain regulations[3] in relation to the National

Curriculum for England[4], he must give notice[5] of the proposal to such of the following as appear to the Secretary of State to be concerned with the proposal: (1) associations of local authorities[6]; (2) bodies representing the interests of school governing bodies[7]; and (3) organisations representing school teachers[8]. The Secretary of State must also give notice of the proposal to any other persons[9] with whom consultation appears to the Secretary of State to be desirable[10].

The Secretary of State must give the bodies and other persons mentioned above[11] a reasonable opportunity of submitting evidence and representations as to the issues arising from the proposal[12]. After considering any evidence and representations submitted[13], the Secretary of State must publish, in such manner as, in the Secretary of State's opinion, is likely to bring them to the notice of persons with a special interest in education a draft of the proposed order or regulations and any associated document, and a summary of the views expressed during the consultation[14].

The Secretary of State must allow a period of at least one month[15] beginning with the publication of the draft of the proposed order or regulations for the submission of any further evidence and representations as to the issues arising[16]. When the period allowed has expired, the Secretary of State may make the order or regulations, with or without modifications[17].

1   As to the Secretary of State see PARA 58.
2   Ie an order under the Education Act 2002 s 82(4) (see PARA 860), s 84(6) (see PARA 861), s 87(3)(a) or (b) (see PARA 863).
3   Ie regulations under the Education Act 2002 s 91: see PARA 867.
4   See the Education Act 2002 s 96(1) (s 96 substituted by the Education Act 2011 Sch 8 paras 11, 15). As to the National Curriculum for England see PARA 857.
5   As to the service of notices and documents see the Education Act 1996 s 572 (applied by the Education Act 2002 s 212(2), (3)); and PARA 76.
6   Education Act 2002 s 96(2)(a) (as substituted: see note 4). As to the meaning of 'local authority' see PARA 25 (definition applied by s 212(2), (3)).
7   Education Act 2002 s 96(2)(b) (as substituted: see note 4). As to the governing bodies of maintained schools in England see PARA 150 et seq.
8   Education Act 2002 s 96(2)(c) (s substituted: see note 4).
9   As to the meaning of 'person' see PARA 7 note 6.
10 Education Act 2002 s 96(3) (as substituted: see note 4).
11 Ie mentioned in the Education Act 2002 s 96(2), (3).
12 Education Act 2002 s 96(4) (as substituted: see note 4).
13 Ie submitted in pursuance of the Education Act 2002 s 96(4).
14 Education Act 2002 s 96(5) (as substituted: see note 4).
15 As to the meaning of 'month' see PARA 54 note 26.
16 Education Act 2002 s 96(6) (as substituted: see note 4).
17 Education Act 2002 s 96(7) (as substituted: see note 4). As to the meaning of 'modifications' see PARA 21 note 15 (definition applied by s 212(2), (3)).

C. THE NATIONAL CURRICULUM FOR ENGLAND: SPECIAL CASES

866.   Curriculum: development work and experiments.   For the purpose of enabling development work or experiments to be carried out, the Secretary of State[1] may direct[2] in respect of a particular maintained school[3] that, for such period as may be specified in the direction, the National Curriculum for England[4] does not apply[5], or applies with such modifications[6] as may be specified in the direction[7]. Such a direction may apply either generally or in such cases as may be specified in the direction[8].

In the case of a community, voluntary controlled or community special school[9], a direction may not be given except on an application[10]:

(1)   by the governing body[11] with the agreement of the local authority[12]; or

(2)   by the local authority with the agreement of the governing body[13].

In the case of a foundation, voluntary aided or foundation special school[14], a direction must not be given except on an application by the governing body[15].

The Secretary of State may make it a condition of a direction that any person[16] by whom or with whose agreement the request for the direction was made should, when so directed or at specified intervals, report on any matters specified by the Secretary of State[17] to him[18] or a person designated for these purposes by the Secretary of State[19]. If required by the Secretary of State to do so a person designated for these purposes by the Secretary of State must keep under review development work or experiments carried out following the giving of a direction[20].

1   As to the Secretary of State see PARA 58.
2   The Secretary of State may by a direction under the Education Act 2002 s 90(6) vary or revoke a direction under s 90(1): s 90(6). As to directions generally see the Education Act 1996 s 570 (applied by the Education Act 2002 s 212(2), (3)); and PARA 75.
3   As to the meaning of 'maintained school' see PARA 856 note 3. As to academies see PARA 345 et seq.
4   Education Act 2002 s 90(1) (amended by the Childcare Act 2006 ss 48, 103(2), Sch 1 para 12(1), (2), Sch 3 Pt 1). As to the National Curriculum for England see PARA 857. As to the application of the Education Act 2002 s 90, with modifications, in relation to a proposed school in England see the School Governance (New Schools) (England) Regulations 2007, SI 2007/958, reg 30.
5   Education Act 2002 s 90(1)(a).
6   As to the meaning of 'modifications' see PARA 21 note 15 (definition applied by the Education Act 2002 s 212(2), (3)).
7   Education Act 2002 s 90(1)(b).
8   Education Act 2002 s 90(2).
9   As to community, voluntary and community special schools see PARA 106.
10 Education Act 2002 s 90(3) (amended by the Childcare Act 2006 ss 48, 103(2), Sch 1 para 12(1), (3), Sch 3 Pt 1).
11 As to the governing bodies of maintained schools in England see PARA 150 et seq.
12 Education Act 2002 s 90(3)(a) (amended by SI 2010/1158). As to the meaning of 'local authority' see PARA 25 (definition applied by the Education Act 2002 s 212(2), (3)).
13 Education Act 2002 s 90(3)(b) (amended by SI 2010/1158).
14 As to foundation and foundation special schools see PARA 106.
15 Education Act 2002 s 90(4) (amended by the Apprenticeships, Skills, Children and Learning Act 2009 ss 174, 192, Sch 12 paras 31, 36(1), (2); and the Education Act 2011 Sch 8 paras 11, 14(1), (3)).
16 As to the meaning of 'person' see PARA 7 note 6.
17 Education Act 2002 s 90(5) (amended by the Apprenticeships, Skills, Children and Learning Act 2009 ss 174, 192, Sch 12 paras 31, 36(1), (3)).
18 See the Education Act 2002 s 90(5)(a) (as amended: see note 17).
19 Education Act 2002 s 90(5)(b) (s 90(5) as amended (see note 17); and s 90(5)(b) substituted by the Education Act 2011 Sch 8 paras 11, 14(1), (4)). A designation under the Education Act 2002 s 90(5)(b) or s 90(5A) (see the text to note 20) may make different provision for different purposes: s 90(5C) (s 90(5A)–(5C) added by the Apprenticeships, Skills, Children and Learning Act 2009 ss 174, 192, Sch 12 paras 31, 36(1), (4); the Education Act 2002 s 90(5B) repealed by the Education Act 2011 Sch 8 paras 11, 14(1), (6); and the Education Act 2002 s 90(5C) amended by the Education Act 2011 Sch 8 paras 11, 14(1), (7))).
20 See the Education Act 2002 s 90(5A) (as added (see note 19); and amended by the Education Act 2011 Sch 8 paras 11, 14(1), (5)). See note 19.

867.   Curriculum: exceptions by regulations.   Regulations[1] may provide that the National Curriculum for England[2], or such of the provisions of the National Curriculum for England as may be specified in the regulations either do not apply[3], or apply with such modifications[4] as may be specified in the regulations[5], in such cases or circumstances as may be specified in the regulations[6].

1 'Regulations' means regulations made under the Education Act 2002 by the Secretary of State: s 212(1). As to the Secretary of State see PARA 58. As to the procedure for making regulations under s 91, see s 96; and PARA 865. As to the regulations made see the Education (National Curriculum) (Exceptions at Key Stage 4) (Revocation and Savings) (England) Regulations 2006, SI 2006/2495; and the National Curriculum (Exceptions for First, Second, Third and Fourth Key Stages) (England) Regulations 2013, SI 2013/1487 (amended by SI 2014/1866; and SI 2014/3286).

2 As to the National Curriculum for England see PARA 857.

3 Education Act 2002 s 91(a). See eg pupils with EHC plans at PARA 868, and temporary exceptions for individual pupils at PARA 869.

4 As to the meaning of 'modifications' see PARA 21 note 15 (definition applied by the Education Act 2002 s 212(2), (3)).

5 Education Act 2002 s 91(b).

6 Education Act 2002 s 91.

868. Pupils with EHC plans. The special educational provision[1] for any pupil[2] specified in an EHC plan[3] maintained for the pupil may include provision excluding the application of the National Curriculum for England[4], or applying the National Curriculum for England with such modifications[5] as may be specified in the plan[6].

1 As to the meaning of 'special educational provision' see PARA 943 (definition applied by the Education Act 2002 s 212(2), (3)).

2 As to the meaning of 'pupil' see PARA 20 note 4 (definition applied by the Education Act 2002 s 212(2), (3)).

3 As to the meaning of 'EHC plan' see PARA 958 (definition applied by the Education Act 2002 s 212(2), (3)). As to EHC plans (ie education, health and care plans) generally see PARA 958 et seq.

4 Education Act 2002 s 92(a) (s 92 amended by the Children and Families Act 2014 Sch 3 paras 76, 77(a), (b)). As to the National Curriculum for England see PARA 857.

5 As to the meaning of 'modifications' see PARA 21 note 15 (definition applied by the Education Act 2002 s 212(2), (3)).

6 Education Act 2002 s 92(b) (as amended: see note 4).

869. Temporary exceptions from the curriculum for individual pupils. Regulations[1] may enable the head teacher[2] of a maintained school[3], in such cases or circumstances and subject to such conditions as may be prescribed[4], to direct in respect of a registered pupil[5] at the school that, for such period as may be specified in the direction (the 'operative period' of the direction), the National Curriculum for England[6] does not apply[7], or applies with such modifications[8] as may be specified in the direction[9]. The conditions prescribed by the regulations must, in particular, limit the operative period that may be specified in a direction to a maximum period specified in the regulations[10]. The regulations may enable the head teacher of a maintained school, in such cases or circumstances and subject to such conditions as may be prescribed[11], to revoke any direction given by him under the regulations[12], and to vary such a direction, except so as to extend its operative period[13].

Where a head teacher gives or varies a direction under such regulations, he must, in such manner as may be prescribed, give the information mentioned in heads (1) to (3) below to the governing body[14], and to the local authority[15] by whom the school is maintained[16], and must take such steps as may be prescribed to give that information also to a parent[17] of the pupil concerned[18]. That information is:

(1) the fact that he has taken the action in question, its effect and his reasons for taking it[19];

(2) the provision that is being or is to be made for the pupil's education during the operative period of the direction[20]; and

(3)   either a description of the manner in which he proposes to secure the full implementation of the National Curriculum for England in relation to the pupil after the end of that period, or an indication that he has the opinion[21] that the pupil has or probably has special educational needs[22] and the responsible authority[23] ought to be required to secure an EHC needs assessment for the pupil[24] (or, if an EHC plan is maintained for the pupil, a re-assessment)[25].

Where the responsible authority receives information[26] which includes an indication that the head teacher has the opinion mentioned above[27], it must make a determination in respect of the pupil under the relevant provision[28] (or, if an EHC plan is maintained for the pupil under the relevant provision for that)[29].

Where a head teacher:

(a)   gives, revokes or varies a direction under regulations[30] made under the above provions[31];

(b)   refuses to give, revoke or vary such a direction in response to a request made, in such manner and circumstances as may be prescribed by the regulations, by the parent of a registered pupil at the school[32]; or

(c)   following the making of such a request, fails within such period as may be prescribed by the regulations to give, revoke or vary such a direction in accordance with the request[33],

the parent of the pupil concerned may appeal to the governing body[34]. On such an appeal, the governing body may confirm the head teacher's action[35], or direct the head teacher to take such action authorised by the regulations as it considers appropriate in the circumstances[36]. The head teacher must comply with any such directions of the governing body[37]. The governing body must notify[38] the appellant and the head teacher in writing[39] of its decision on such an appeal[40].

1   'Regulations' means regulations made under the Education Act 2002 by the Secretary of State: see s 212(1). Before making any regulations under s 93, the Secretary of State must consult with any persons with whom consultation appears to him to be desirable: s 93(6). As to the Secretary of State see PARA 58. As to the meaning of 'person' see PARA 7 note 6. As to the exercise of the duty to consult see JUDICIAL REVIEW vol 61 (2010) PARA 627. At the date at which this volume states the law, no regulations had been made under ss 93, 94 but, by virtue of the Interpretation Act 1978 s 17(2)(b), the Education (National Curriculum) (Temporary Exceptions for Individual Pupils) (England) Regulations 2000, SI 2000/2121, made under the Education Act 1996 ss 365–367 (repealed), have effect as if so made.
2   As to the meaning of 'head teacher' see PARA 86 note 4 (definition applied by the Education Act 2002 s 212(2), (3)).
3   As to the meaning of 'maintained school' see PARA 856 note 3. As to academies generally see PARA 345 et seq. As to the National Curriculum and academies see PARA 359. As to free schools see PARA 368.
4   'Prescribed' means prescribed by regulations: Education Act 2002 s 212(1).
5   As to the meaning of 'registered pupil' see PARA 437 (definition applied by the Education Act 2002 s 212(2), (3)).
6   Education Act 2002 s 93(1) (amended by the Childcare Act 2006 ss 48, 103(2), Sch 1 para 13, Sch 3 Pt 1). As to the National Curriculum for England see PARA 857.
7   Education Act 2002 s 93(1)(a).
8   As to the meaning of 'modifications' see PARA 21 note 15 (definition applied by the Education Act 2002 s 212(2), (3)).
9   Education Act 2002 s 93(1)(b).
10   Education Act 2002 s 93(2). Any maximum period specified (whether in relation to directions given under the regulations or in relation to directions given under the regulations in circumstances specified in the regulations) must be either: (1) a fixed period not exceeding six months (s 93(3)(a)); or (2) a period determinable (in such manner as may be specified in the regulations) not later than six months from its beginning (s 93(3)(b)). As to the meaning of 'month' see PARA 54 note 26. Any maximum period so specified may, without prejudice to the generality of s 210(7) (which provides that regulations under the Education Act 2002 may make

different provision for different cases or circumstances etc), differ according to whether or not the direction in question is given in respect of a period beginning: (a) immediately after the end of the operative period of a previous direction (s 93(4)(a)); or (b) within such period after the end of the operative period of a previous direction as may be specified in the regulations (s 93(4)(b)).

11 Education Act 2002 s 93(5) (amended by the Childcare Act 2006 ss 48, 103(2), Sch 1 para 13, Sch 3 Pt 1).

12 Education Act 2002 s 93(5)(a).

13 Education Act 2002 s 93(5)(b).

14 Education Act 2002 s 94(1)(a). As to the governing bodies of maintained schools in England see PARA 150 et seq.

15 As to the meaning of 'local authority' see PARA 25 (definition applied by the Education Act 2002 s 212(1)).

16 Education Act 2002 s 94(1)(b) (amended by SI 2010/1158).

17 As to the meaning of 'parent' see PARA 7 note 6 (definition applied by the Education Act 2002 s 212(2), (3)).

18 Education Act 2002 s 94(1).

19 Education Act 2002 s 94(2)(a).

20 Education Act 2002 s 94(2)(b).

21 See the Education Act 2002 s 94(2)(c).

22 As to the meaning of 'special educational needs' see PARA 943 (definition applied by the Education Act 2002 s 212(2), (3)).

23 'The responsible authority', in relation to a pupil, means the local authority responsible for him for the purposes of the Children and Families Act 2014 Pt 3 (ss 19–83) (see PARA 950 et seq) (see s 24) (see PARA 945): Education Act 2002 s 94(6) (amended by SI 2010/1158; and the Children and Families Act 2014 Sch 3 paras 76, 78(1), (4))).

24 Ie under the Children and Families Act 2014 s 36: see PARA 957.

25 Education Act 2002 s 94(3) (amended by the Children and Families Act 2014 Sch 3 paras 76, 78(1), (2)). The re-assessment referred to in the text is under s 44: see PARA 964. As to the meaning of 'EHC plan' see PARA 958 (definition applied by the Education Act 2002 s 212(2), (3)). As to EHC plans (ie education, health and care plans) generally see PARA 958 et seq.
   Where the head teacher of a maintained school includes an indication of any such opinion in information given under s 94(1) (see the text to notes 14–18) (s 94(4)(a) (amended by the Childcare Act 2006 ss 48, 103(2), Sch 1 para 14, Sch 3 Pt 1)); and the local authority by whom the school is maintained is not the responsible authority in relation to the pupil in question (Education Act 2002 s 94(4)(b) (amended by SI 2010/1158)), the head teacher must also give that information, in such manner as may be prescribed, to the responsible authority (Education Act 2002 s 94(4)).

26 Ie given to it under the Education Act 2002 s 94(1) (see the text to notes 14–18) or s 94(4) (see the text to note 25).

27 Ie the opinion mentioned in the Education Act 2002 s 94(3): see the text to notes 22–25.

28 Ie under the Children and Families Act 2014 s 36(3): see PARA 957.

29 Education Act 2002 s 94(5) (amended by the Children and Families Act 2014 Sch 3 paras 76, 78(1), (3)). The reference in the text to the relevant provision for that is a reference to s 36 as it applies to re-assessments by virtue of regulations under s 44(7): see PARA 964.

30 Ie regulations made under the Education Act 2002 s 93: see the text to notes 1–13.

31 Education Act 2002 s 95(1)(a).

32 Education Act 2002 s 95(1)(b).

33 Education Act 2002 s 95(1)(c).

34 Education Act 2002 s 95(1).

35 Education Act 2002 s 95(2)(a).

36 Education Act 2002 s 95(2)(b).

37 Education Act 2002 s 95(3).

38 As to the service of notices and documents see the Education Act 1996 s 572 (applied by the Education Act 2002 s 212(2), (3)); and PARA 76.

39 As to the meaning of 'writing' see PARA 76 note 8.

40 Education Act 2002 s 95(4).

(ii) The Curriculum in Wales

870.   General duties in respect of the curriculum in Wales.   The Welsh Ministers[1] must exercise their functions[2] with a view to securing[3] that the curriculum for every maintained school[4] or maintained nursery school[5], and for any funded nursery education[6] provided otherwise than at a maintained school or maintained nursery school[7], and every local authority in Wales must exercise its functions with a view to securing[8] that the curriculum for every maintained school or maintained nursery school which it maintains[9], and for any funded nursery education provided, under arrangements made by it, otherwise than at a maintained school or maintained nursery school[10], satisfies the requirements that it be a balanced and broadly based curriculum which: (1) promotes the spiritual, moral, cultural, mental and physical development of pupils[11] at the school and of society[12]; and (2) prepares pupils at the school for the opportunities, responsibilities and experiences of later life[13]. The governing body and head teacher[14] of every maintained school or maintained nursery school must also exercise their functions with a view to securing that the curriculum for the school satisfies those requirements[15]; and any person providing funded nursery education under the arrangements made with a local authority[16] must secure that the curriculum for that funded nursery education satisfies those requirements[17].

In exercising any function which may affect the provision of sex education[18] in maintained schools every local authority in Wales must have regard to the guidance issued[19] by the Welsh Ministers[20]. Except to that extent, nothing in these provisions[21] is to be taken to impose duties on a local authority with regard to sex education[22].

1   As to the Welsh Ministers see PARA 59.

2   The functions referred to in the Education Act 2002 s 100(1)–(3) include in particular: (1) functions conferred by Pt 7 (ss 97–118) in relation to the National Curriculum for Wales (s 100(4)(a) (amended by the Learning and Skills (Wales) Measure 2009 s 2(1), (2))); (2) except in relation to maintained nursery schools (see note 5) or the provision of funded nursery education (see note 6) otherwise than at a maintained school (see note 4) or maintained nursery school, functions relating to religious education and religious worship (Education Act 2002 s 100(4)(b)); and (3) functions conferred by Pt 7 in relation to the local curriculum or curricula for a local authority's area (s 100(4)(c) (added by the Learning and Skills (Wales) Measure 2009 s 2(1), (3))). As to the meaning of 'functions' generally see PARA 18 note 5 (definition applied by the Education Act 2002 s 212(2), (3)). As to the National Curriculum for Wales see PARA 871. As to the meanings of 'local curriculum' and 'local curricula' see PARA 885 note 3. As to the meaning of 'local authority' see PARA 25 (definition applied by the Education Act 2002 s 212(1)).

3   Education Act 2002 s 100(1) (amended by the Learning and Skills (Wales) Measure 2009 s 47, Schedule paras 11, 14).

4   'Maintained school' means: (1) any community, foundation or voluntary school maintained by a local authority in Wales; or (2) except where otherwise stated, any community special school which is maintained by a local authority in Wales and is not established in a hospital: Education Act 2002 s 97 (definition amended by SI 2010/1158; and the School Standards and Organisation (Wales) Act 2013 Sch 5 paras 21(1), (4)(a)). As to the meaning of references to a community, foundation or voluntary school or a community special school see PARA 106. As to the meaning of 'Wales' see PARA 7 note 3.

5   See the Education Act 2002 s 100(1)(a). 'Maintained nursery school' means a nursery school which is maintained by a local authority in Wales and is not a special school: s 97 (definition amended by SI 2010/1158). As to the meaning of 'nursery school' see PARA 91; and as to the meaning of 'special school' see PARA 1041 (definitions applied by the Education Act 2002 s 212(2), (3)).

6 'Nursery education' means full-time or part-time education suitable for children who have not attained compulsory school age (whether provided at schools or elsewhere): Education Act 2002 s 98(1). Nursery education is 'funded nursery education' in relation to a child if: (1) it is provided in a maintained school or a maintained nursery school (s 98(2)(a)); or (2) it is provided, by a person other than the governing body of any such school, under arrangements made with that person by a local authority in Wales in pursuance of the duty imposed on the authority by the School Standards and Framework Act 1998 s 118 (see PARA 96) and in consideration of financial assistance provided by the authority under those arrangements (s 98(2)(b) (amended by SI 2010/1158)). Funded nursery education provided in relation to a child otherwise than at a maintained school or maintained nursery school is to be taken to be provided by the person with whom the arrangements referred to in the Education Act 2002 s 98(2)(b) (see head (2) above) are made by the local authority: s 98(3) (amended by SI 2010/1158). As to the meaning of 'child' see PARA 7 note 6; and as to the meaning of 'school' see PARA 91 (definitions applied by the Education Act 2002 s 212(2), (3)). As to the meaning of 'compulsory school age' see PARA 19. As to the meaning of 'person' see PARA 7 note 6. As to the governing bodies of maintained schools in Wales see PARA 195.

7 See the Education Act 2002 s 100(1)(b).

8 See the Education Act 2002 s 100(2) (amended by SI 2010/1158). See also note 2.

9 See the Education Act 2002 s 100(2)(a).

10 See the Education Act 2002 s 100(2)(b).

11 'Pupil' includes a child for whom funded nursery education is provided: Education Act 2002 s 97. As to the meaning of 'pupil' generally see PARA 20 note 4 (definition applied by s 212(2), (3)).

12 Education Act 2002 s 99(1)(a).

13 Education Act 2002 s 99(1)(b).

14 As to the meaning of 'head teacher' see PARA 86 note 4 (definition applied by the Education Act 2002 s 212(2), (3)).

15 Education Act 2002 s 100(3). See also note 2.

16 Ie arrangements mentioned in the Education Act 2002 s 98(2)(b): see note 6.

17 Education Act 2002 s 100(5).

18 As to the meaning of 'sex education' see PARA 857 note 10 (definition applied by the Education Act 2002 s 212(2), (3)).

19 Ie under Education Act 1996 s 403(1A): see PARA 905.

20 Education Act 2002 s 100(6) (amended by the Learning and Skills (Wales) Measure 2009 s 47, Schedule paras 11–13; and SI 2010/1158).

21 Ie in the Education Act 2002 s 100.

22 Education Act 2002 s 100(7) (amended by SI 2010/1158).

871. Basic curriculum for every maintained school in Wales. The curriculum for every maintained school[1] in Wales[2] must comprise a basic curriculum which includes:

(1) provision for religious education[3] for all registered pupils[4] at the school[5];

(2) a curriculum for all registered pupils at the school who have attained the age of three[6] but are not over compulsory school age[7] (known as 'the National Curriculum for Wales')[8];

(3) provision for personal and social education for all registered pupils at the school who are of compulsory school age[9];

(4) provision for work-related education for all registered pupils at the school during the fourth key stage[10];

(5) in the case of a secondary school[11], provision for sex education[12] for all registered pupils at the school[13];

(6) in the case of a secondary school, provision for education which satisfies the entitlements of registered pupils[14] at the school[15]; and

(7) in the case of a special school, provision for sex education for all registered pupils at the school who are provided with secondary education[16].

The Welsh Ministers may by order amend these provisions[17] so as to add further requirements, otherwise than in relation to religious education or sex education[18].

1   As to the meaning of 'maintained school' see PARA 870 note 4.
2   As to the meaning of 'Wales' see PARA 7 note 3.
3   Ie in accordance with such of the provisions of the School Standards and Framework Act 1998 Sch 19 (see PARA 915 et seq) as apply in relation to the school.
4   As to the meaning of 'registered pupil' see PARA 437 (definition applied by the Education Act 2002 s 212(2), (3)).
5   Education Act 2002 s 101(1)(a). Section 101(1)(a) does not apply: (1) in relation to a nursery class in a primary school (s 101(2)(a)); or (2) in the case of a maintained special school (provision as to religious education in special schools being made by regulations under the School Standards and Framework Act 1998 s 71(7) (see PARA 924)) (Education Act 2002 s 101(2)(b)). As to the meaning of 'primary school' see PARA 91 (definition applied by s 212(2), (3)). As to compulsory collective worship see PARA 920 et seq.
6   As to the time at which a person attains a particular age see PARA 7 note 6.
7   As to the meaning of 'compulsory school age' see PARA 19.
8   Education Act 2002 s 101(1)(b). As to the National Curriculum for Wales see further PARA 873 et seq. The Welsh Ministers may by order amend the Education Act 2002 s 101(1)(b): (1) by substituting for the reference to the age of three (or to any age specified there by virtue of this provision) a reference to such other age as may be specified in the order (s 101(3)(b)(i) (s 101(3) amended by the Learning and Skills (Wales) Measure 2009 s 47, Schedule paras 11–13)); or (2) by substituting for the reference to compulsory school age (or to any age specified there by virtue of this provision) a reference to such other age as may be specified in the order (Education Act 2002 s 101(3)(b)(ii)). As to the Welsh Ministers see PARA 59. At the date at which this volume states the law, no order had been made under s 101(3)(b).
9   Education Act 2002 s 101(1)(ba) (added by SI 2003/932).
10 Education Act 2002 s 101(1)(bb) (added by SI 2003/932; and amended by SI 2008/1899). As to the meaning of 'key stage' see PARA 875 note 1.
11 As to the meaning of 'secondary school' see PARA 91 (definition applied by the Education Act 2002 s 212(2), (3)).
12 As to the meaning of 'sex education' see PARA 857 note 10 (definition applied by the Education Act 2002 s 212(2), (3)).
13 Education Act 2002 s 101(1)(c) (amended by the Learning and Skills (Wales) Measure 2009 s 3(1), (2)).
14 Ie under the Education Act 2002 s 116E: see PARA 888.
15 Education Act 2002 s 101(1)(ca) (added by the Learning and Skills (Wales) Measure 2009 s 3(1), (3)).
16 Education Act 2002 s 101(1)(d). As to the meaning of 'secondary education' see PARA 21 (definition applied by s 212(2), (3)). As to the application of s 101(1)(d) in relation to pupil referral units in Wales see the Education (Pupil Referral Units) (Application of Enactments) (Wales) Regulations 2007, SI 2007/1069, reg 3, Sch 1 Pt 1 para 10. As to pupil referral units see PARA 427 et seq.
17 Ie the Education Act 2002 s 101(1): see the text to notes 1–16.
18 Education Act 2002 s 101(3)(a) (s 101(3) amended by the Learning and Skills (Wales) Measure 2009 s 47, Schedule paras 11–13). The Welsh Ministers may by order also amend any provision included in the Education Act 2002 s 101(1) by virtue of s 101(3)(a): see s 101(3)(c) (as so amended). In exercising any function which may affect the provision in maintained schools of education of a kind required by virtue of an order under s 101(3)(a), a local authority in Wales or the governing body of a maintained school must have regard to any guidance from time to time given by the Welsh Ministers: s 100(8) (amended by the Learning and Skills (Wales) Measure 2009 s 47, Schedule paras 11–13; and SI 2010/1158). The Basic Curriculum for Wales (Amendment) Order 2003, SI 2003/932, and the School Curriculum in Wales (Miscellaneous Amendments) Order 2008, SI 2008/1899, have been made under the Education Act 2002 s 101(3)(a). As to the meaning of 'local authority' see PARA 25 (definition applied by the Education Act 2002 s 212(2), (3)). As to the governing bodies of maintained schools in Wales see PARA 195.

872.   Careers education and guidance. All registered pupils at community, foundation and voluntary schools, community or foundation special schools (other than those established in hospitals) and pupil referral units must be provided, during the relevant phase of their education, with a programme of careers geducation[1]. Educational institutions in Wales are required to co-operate with careers advisers[2], and persons attending such institutions must be provided with access to both guidance materials, and a wide range of up to date reference materials, relating to careers education and career opportunities[3].

1 See the Education Act 1997 s 43; and PARA 820.
2 See the Education Act 1997 s 44; and PARA 822.
3 See the Education Act 1997 s 45; and PARA 821.

B. THE NATIONAL CURRICULUM FOR WALES: IN GENERAL

873. Constituents of the National Curriculum for Wales. The National Curriculum for Wales[1] comprises the foundation phase[2] followed by four key stages[3], and specifies:

(1) 'assessment arrangements', which are arrangements for assessing[4] pupils[5] for the purpose of ascertaining what they have achieved in relation to the desirable outcomes[6] (in the case of the foundation phase) or (in the case of a key stage) in relation to the attainment targets for that stage[7];

(2) 'attainment targets', which, in relation to a key stage, means the knowledge, skills and understanding which pupils of different abilities and maturities are expected to have by the end of that stage[8];

(3) 'programmes of study', which, in relation to a key stage, means matters, skills and processes which are required to be taught to pupils of different abilities and maturities by the end of that stage[9].

The Welsh Ministers[10] may incur expenses in connection with the commissioning by them of such work, including programmes of research, development and dissemination, as they may require to be carried out for the purpose of facilitating the discharge of certain of their functions[11] in relation to the National Curriculum for Wales[12].

Independent schools may choose to adopt the National Curriculum for Wales but are under no obligation to do so[13].

1 As to the National Curriculum for Wales see PARA 871.
2 As to the foundation phase see PARA 874.
3 As to the meaning of 'key stage' see PARA 875 note 1. As to the key stages see PARA 875.
4 'Assess' includes examine and test; and related expressions must be construed accordingly: Education Act 2002 s 97.
5 As to the meaning of 'pupil' see PARA 870 note 11.
6 As to the meaning of 'desirable outcomes' see PARA 874.
7 See the Education Act 2002 s 97 (definition amended by the Education (Wales) Measure 2009 s 21(1), (2)(a)).
8 Education Act 2002 s 97.
9 Education Act 2002 s 97.
10 As to the Welsh Ministers see PARA 61.
11 Ie under the Education Act 2002 ss 102–108: see PARAS 874–878. As to the meaning of 'functions' see PARA 18 note 5 (definition applied by s 212(2), (3)).
12 See the Education Act 2002 s 118 (amended by the Learning and Skills (Wales) Measure 2009 Schedule, paras 11–13, 16, 20).
13 As to independent schools see PARA 369 et seq.

874. The National Curriculum for Wales for the foundation phase. The foundation phase in relation to a pupil[1] is such period as may be specified in an order made by the Welsh Ministers[2].

For the foundation phase, the National Curriculum for Wales[3] must specify 'areas of learning' and, in relation to each area of learning, may specify:

(1)   the knowledge, skills and understanding which pupils of different abilities and maturities are expected to have by the end of the foundation phase (known as 'desirable outcomes')[4];

(2)   the matters, skills and processes which are required to be taught to pupils of different abilities and maturities during the foundation phase (known as 'educational programmes')[5]; and

(3)   assessment arrangements[6].

1   As to the meaning of 'pupil' see PARA 870 note 11.

2   Education Act 2002 s 102 (amended by the Learning and Skills (Wales) Measure 2009 s 47, Schedule paras 11–13; and the Education (Wales) Measure 2009 s 21(1), (3)). As to the Welsh Ministers see PARA 59. The foundation phase in relation to a pupil is the period beginning with the relevant time and ending at the same time as the school year in which the majority of pupils in his or her class attain the age of seven: Education (National Curriculum) (Foundation Phase) (Wales) Order 2014, SI 2014/1996, art 3(1). 'The relevant time' means: (1) in the case of a child who is provided with funded nursery education before he or she attains the age of three, his or her third birthday; (2) in the case of a child who is provided with funded nursery education after he or she attains that age, the time when he or she is first provided with such education; and (3) in the case of a child who is not provided with any funded nursery education, the time when he or she first receives primary education other than nursery education: art 3(2). As to the meaning of 'child' see PARA 7 note 6; and as to the meaning of 'primary education' see PARA 20 (definitions applied by the Education Act 2002 s 212(2), (3)). As to the meanings of 'nursery education' and 'funded nursery education' see PARA 870 note 6. As to the time at which a person attains a particular age see PARA 7 note 6. 'School year', in relation to a school, means the period beginning with the first school term to begin after July and ending with the beginning of the first school term to begin after the following July; and has a corresponding meaning in relation to the provision of funded nursery education otherwise than at a school: s 97. As to the fixing of dates for school terms and holidays see PARA 458.

3   As to the National Curriculum for Wales see PARA 871.

4   Education Act 2002 s 104(a) (amended by the Education (Wales) Measure 2009 s 21(1), (5)).

5   Education Act 2002 s 104(b) (amended by the Education (Wales) Measure 2009 s 21(1), (5)).

6   Education Act 2002 s 104(c). As to the meaning of 'assessment arrangements' see PARA 873.

875.   The key stages of the curriculum in Wales.   There are now three key stages in the National Curriculum for Wales[1]. The key stages in relation to a pupil[2] are:

(1)   the period beginning at the same time as the school year[3] in which the majority of pupils in his class[4] attain the age of eight and ending at the same time as the school year in which the majority of pupils in his class attain the age of 11[5] ('the second key stage')[6];

(2)   the period beginning at the same time as the school year in which the majority of pupils in his class attain the age of 12 and ending at the same time as the school year in which the majority of pupils in his class attain the age of 14 ('the third key stage')[7]; and

(3)   the period beginning at the same time as the school year in which the majority of pupils in his class attain the age of 15 and ending at the same time as the school year in which the majority of pupils in his class cease to be of compulsory school age[8] ('the fourth key stage')[9].

The head teacher of a school may elect, in relation to a particular pupil and a particular subject, that the above provisions are to have effect as if any reference to the school year in which the majority of pupils in that pupil's class attain a particular age were a reference to the school year in which that pupil attains that age[10]. If at any time, in the case of a pupil of compulsory school age, the above provisions[11] do not[12] apply to determine the period within which that time falls, those provisions have effect as if:

(a)   in the case of heads (1) to (2), any reference to the school year in which the majority of pupils in that pupil's class attain a particular age were a reference to the school year in which that pupil attains that age[13]; and

(b)   in the case of head (3) above, the period were a period beginning at the same time as the school year in which he attains the age of 15 and ending when he ceases to be of compulsory school age[14].

1   'Key stage', or references to a particular key stage, must be construed in accordance with the Education Act 2002 s 103: s 97. As to the National Curriculum for Wales see PARA 871.
2   As to the meaning of 'pupil' see PARA 870 note 11.
3   As to the meaning of 'school year' see PARA 874 note 2.
4   'Class', in relation to a particular pupil and a particular subject, means: (1) the teaching group in which he is regularly taught in that subject(Education Act 2002 s 103(5)(a)); or (2) where there are two or more such groups, such one of them as may be designated by the head teacher of the school (s 103(5)(b)). As to the meaning of 'head teacher' see PARA 86 note 4 (definition applied by s 212(2), (3)).
5   As to the time at which a person attains a particular age see PARA 7 note 6.
6   Education Act 2002 s 103(1)(b) (and s 103(1)(a) repealed by the Education (Wales) Measure 2009 s 21(1), (4)). The Welsh Ministers may by order: (1) provide that, in relation to any subject specified in the order, the Education Act 2002 s 103(1) is to have effect as if for the ages of seven and eight there specified there were substituted such other ages (less than 11 and 12 respectively) as may be specified in the order (s 103(4)(a) (s 103(4) amended by the Learning and Skills (Wales) Measure 2009 s 47, Schedule paras 11–13)); and (2) amend the Education Act 2002 s 103(1)–(3) (s 103(4)(b) (as so amended)). As to the Welsh Ministers see PARA 59. As to the procedure for making orders under s 103(4) see PARA 880. At the date at which this volume states the law no such order had been made.
7   Education Act 2002 s 103(1)(c). See also note 6.
8   As to the meaning of 'compulsory school age' see PARA 19.
9   Education Act 2002 s 103(1)(d). See also note 6.
10 Education Act 2002 s 103(2). See also note 6.
11 Ie the Education Act 2002 s 103(1): see the text to notes 2–9.
12 Ie apart from the Education Act 2002 s 103(3).
13 Education Act 2002 s 103(3)(a). See also note 6.
14 Education Act 2002 s 103(3)(b). See also note 6.

876.   Curriculum requirements for the second and third key stages.   For the second and third key stages[1], the National Curriculum for Wales[2] comprises the core subjects of mathematics[3], English[4], science[5], and, in relation to Welsh-speaking schools, Welsh[6]; and the other foundation subjects of design and technology[7], information and communication technology[8], physical education[9], history[10], geography[11], art and design[12], music[13], Welsh (if the school is not a Welsh-speaking school)[14], and (in relation to the third key stage) a modern foreign language[15]. The National Curriculum for Wales must specify attainment targets[16], programmes of study[17] and assessment arrangements[18] in relation to each of the core and other foundation subjects for each stage[19].

1   As to the meaning of 'key stage' see PARA 875 note 1. As to the key stages see PARA 875.
2   As to the National Curriculum for Wales see PARA 871.
3   See the Education Act 2002 s 105(1), (2)(a) (s 105(1), (2), (3) amended by the Education (Wales) Measure 2009 s 21(1), (6)). The Welsh Ministers may by order amend the Education Act 2002 s 105(2)–(5): s 105(6). As to the Welsh Ministers see PARA 59. As to the procedure for making orders under s 105(6) see PARA 880. The School Curriculum in Wales (Miscellaneous Amendments) Order 2008, SI 2008/1899, has been made.
4   See the Education Act 2002 s 105(1), (2)(b) (s 105(1), (2) as amended: see note 3). See note 3.
5   See the Education Act 2002 s 105(1), (2)(c) (s 105(1), (2) as amended: see note 3). See note 3.

6   See the Education Act 2002 s 105(1), (2)(d) (s 105(1), (2) as amended: see note 3). See also
    note 3. For the purposes of s 105, a school is Welsh-speaking if more than one half of the
    following subjects are taught (wholly or partly) in Welsh: (1) religious education (s 105(7)(a));
    and (2) the subjects other than English and Welsh which are foundation subjects in relation to
    pupils at the school (s 105(7)(b)). For these purposes, 'school' includes part of a school:
    s 105(8). As to the meaning of 'school' see PARA 91 (definition applied by s 212(2), (3)). As to
    the meaning of 'pupil' see PARA 870 note 11.
7   See the Education Act 2002 s 105(1), (3)(a) (s 105(1), (3) (as amended (see note 3); and
    s 105(3)(a) also amended by SI 2008/1899). See also note 3.
8   See the Education Act 2002 s 105(1), (3)(aa) (s 105(1), (3) as amended (see note 3); and
    s 105(3)(aa) added by SI 2008/1899). See also note 3.
9   See the Education Act 2002 s 105(1), (3)(b) (s 105(1), (3) as amended: see note 3). See also
    note 3.
10 See the Education Act 2002 s 105(1), (3)(c) (s 105(1), (3) as amended: see note 3). See also
    note 3.
11 See the Education Act 2002 s 105(1), (3)(d) (s 105(1), (3) as amended: see note 3). See also
    note 3.
12 See the Education Act 2002 s 105(1), (3)(e) (s 105(1), (3) as amended (see note 3); and
    s 105(3)(e) also amended by SI 2008/1899). See also note 3.
13 See the Education Act 2002 s 105(1), (3)(f) (s 105(1), (3) as amended: see note 3). See also
    note 3.
14 See the Education Act 2002 s 105(1), (3)(g) (s 105(1), (3) as amended: see note 3). See also
    note 3.
15 See the Education Act 2002 s 105(1), (3)(h) (s 105(1), (3) as amended: see note 3). See also
    note 3. 'Modern foreign language' means a modern foreign language specified in an order made
    by the Welsh Ministers or, if the order so provides, any modern foreign language: s 105(4)
    (amended by the Learning and Skills (Wales) Measure 2009 s 47, Schedule paras 11–13). An
    order under the Education Act 2002 s 105(4) may: (1) specify circumstances in which a
    language is not to be treated as a foundation subject for the third key stage (s 105(5)(a)); and (2)
    provide for the determination under the order of any question arising as to whether a particular
    language is a modern foreign language (s 105(5)(b)). As to the order made see the Education
    (National Curriculum) (Modern Foreign Languages) (Wales) Order 2008, SI 2008/1408.
16 As to the meaning of 'attainment targets' see PARA 873.
17 As to the meaning of 'programmes of study' see PARA 873.
18 As to the meaning of 'assessment arrangements' see PARA 873.
19 Education Act 2002 s 105(1). See also note 2.

877.   Curriculum requirements for the fourth key stage. For the fourth key
stage[1], the National Curriculum for Wales[2] comprises the core subjects of
mathematics[3], English[4], science[5], and, in relation to Welsh-speaking schools,
Welsh[6]; and the other foundation subjects of physical education[7] and Welsh (if
the school is not a Welsh-speaking school)[8]. The National Curriculum for Wales
must specify attainment targets, programmes of study, and assessment
arrangements[9] in relation to each of the core and other foundation subjects[10].

1   As to the meaning of 'key stage' see PARA 875 note 1. As to the key stages see PARA 875.
2   As to the National Curriculum for Wales see PARA 871.
3   See the Education Act 2002 s 106(1), (2)(a). The Welsh Ministers may by order: (1) amend any
    provision of s 106 (s 107(1)(a) (s 107(1) numbered as such and amended by the Learning and
    Skills (Wales) Measure 2009 s 19(1), (2))); or (2) provide that, while the order remains in force,
    s 106 is not to have effect (Education Act 2002 s 107(1)(b) (as so numbered and amended)).
    Such an order may make such amendments of the Education Act 2002 as appear to the Welsh
    Ministers to be necessary or expedient in connection with the provision made under s 107(1):
    s 107(2) (added by the Learning and Skills (Wales) Measure 2009 s 19(1), (3)). At the date at
    which this volume states the law no such order had been made. As to the Welsh Ministers see
    PARA 59.
4   See the Education Act 2002 s 106(1), (2)(b). See also note 3.
5   See the Education Act 2002 s 106(1), (2)(c). See also note 3.
6   See the Education Act 2002 s 106(1), (2)(d). See also note 3. For the purposes of s 106, a school
    is Welsh-speaking if more than one half of the following subjects are taught (wholly or partly) in
    Welsh: (1) religious education (s 106(4)(a)); and (2) the subjects other than English and Welsh

which are foundation subjects in relation to pupils at the school (s 106(4)(b)). For the purposes of s 106, 'school' includes part of a school: s 106(5). As to the meaning of 'pupil' see PARA 870 note 11.

7   See the Education Act 2002 s 106(1), (3)(a). See also note 3.
8   See the Education Act 2002 s 106(1), (3)(b). See also note 3.
9   As to the meanings of 'attainment targets', 'programmes of study' and 'assessment arrangements' see PARA 873.
10 See the Education Act 2002 s 106(1). See also note 3.

878.   Establishment of the National Curriculum for Wales by order.   In respect of the foundation phase[1], the Welsh Ministers must by order specify the areas of learning[2], and may by order specify in relation to each of those areas such desirable outcomes[3], such educational programmes[4] and such assessment arrangements[5], as they consider appropriate for that area[6]. In respect of second and third key stages[7], and[8] in respect of the fourth key stage, the Welsh Ministers may by order specify in relation to each of the foundation subjects[9] such attainment targets[10], such programmes of study[11] and such assessment arrangements[12], as they consider appropriate for that subject[13].

An order[14] may not require: (1) the allocation of any particular period or periods of time during the foundation phase or any key stage to the teaching of any educational programme or programme of study or any matter, skill or process forming part of it[15]; or (2) the making in school timetables, or the timetables of any person providing funded nursery education, of provision of any particular kind for the periods to be allocated to such teaching during any such stage[16]. An order may, instead of containing the provisions to be made, refer to provisions in a document published as specified in the order and direct that those provisions are to have effect or, as the case may be, are to have effect as amended by the order[17].

The Welsh Ministers must exercise these powers conferred on them to make orders[18] so as to: (a) establish a complete National Curriculum for Wales[19] for the foundation phase as soon as is reasonably practicable[20]; and (b) revise the National Curriculum for Wales for the foundation phase and the key stages whenever they consider it necessary or expedient to do so[21].

1   As to the foundation phase see PARA 874.
2   Education Act 2002 s 108(2)(a) (s 108(1), (2), (4) amended by the Education (Wales) Measure 2009 s 21(1), (7)(a)). As to the areas of learning for the foundation phase see PARA 874. As to the Welsh Ministers see PARA 59.
3   Education Act 2002 s 108(2)(b)(i). As to the meaning of 'desirable outcomes' see PARA 874. See note 6.
4   Education Act 2002 s 108(2)(b)(ii). As to the meaning of 'educational programmes' see PARA 874. See note 6.
5   Education Act 2002 s 108(2)(b)(iii). As to the meaning of 'assessment arrangements' see PARA 873. An order under s 108(2)(b)(iii) may confer or impose such functions on: (1) the governing body and head teacher of a maintained school or a maintained nursery school (s 108(6)(a)); (2) a person providing funded nursery education under the arrangements mentioned in s 98(2)(b) (see PARA 870 note 6) (s 108(6)(b)); (3) an early years development and childcare partnership (s 108(6)(c)); and (4) a local authority (s 108(6)(d) (amended by SI 2010/1158)), as appear to the Welsh Ministers to be required (Education Act 2002 s 108(6) (amended by the Learning and Skills (Wales) Measure 2009 s 47, Schedule paras 11–13)). Such an order may also specify such assessment arrangements as may for the time being be made by a person specified in the order (see the Education Act 2002 s 108(8)); and may authorise the making of such provisions giving full effect to or otherwise supplementing the provisions made by the order, other than provision conferring or imposing functions as mentioned in s 108(6), as appear to the Welsh Ministers to be expedient; and any provisions made under such an order must, on being published as specified in the order, have effect for the purposes of Pt 7 (ss 97–118) as if made by the order (see s 108(11) (amended by the Learning and Skills (Wales) Measure 2009 s 47, Schedule paras 11–13)). Provision must be made for determining the extent to which any assessment

arrangements, and the implementation of the arrangements, achieve the purpose for which the arrangements are made; and any such provision may be made by or under the order specifying the arrangements or, where the order specifies the person making the arrangements, in the arrangements themselves: Education Act 2002 s 108(9). The duties that may be imposed by virtue of s 108(6) include, in relation to persons exercising any power in pursuance of provision made by virtue of s 108(9), the duty to permit them: (a) to enter premises of the school or, as the case may be, premises on which the funded nursery education is being provided (s 108(10)(a)); (b) to observe implementation of the arrangements (s 108(10)(b)); and (c) to inspect, and take copies of, documents and other articles (s 108(10)(c)). As the meaning of 'functions' see PARA 18 note 5; as to the meaning of 'head teacher' see PARA 86 note 4; and as to the meaning of 'premises' see PARA 62 note 20 (definitions applied by s 212(2), (3)). As to the governing bodies of maintained schools in Wales see PARA 195. As to the meaning of 'maintained school' see PARA 870 note 4. As to the meaning of 'maintained nursery school' see PARA 870 note 5. As to the meaning of 'person' see PARA 7 note 6. As to the meanings of 'nursery education' and 'funded nursery education' see PARA 870 note 6. As to early years development and childcare partnerships see PARA 97. As to the meaning of 'local authority' see PARA 25 (definition applied by s 212(1)). As to orders made see note 6.

 6   Education Act 2002 s 108(2) (amended by the Learning and Skills (Wales) Measure 2009 s 47, Schedule paras 11–13). As to the procedure for making orders under the Education Act 2002 s 108(2)(a), (b)(i), (b)(ii) see PARA 880. As to orders made see the Education (National Curriculum) (Assessment Arrangements for Reading and Numeracy) (Wales) Order 2013, SI 2013/433; the National Curriculum (Educational Programmes for the Foundation Phase and Programmes of Study for the Second and Third Key Stages) (Wales) Order 2013, SI 2013/434; the Education (National Curriculum) (Foundation Phase) (Wales) Order 2014, SI 2014/1996 (amended by SI 2015/1596); the National Curriculum (Assessment Arrangements for the Foundation Phase and the Second and Third Key Stages) (Wales) Order 2014, SI 2014/1999; and the National Curriculum (Desirable Outcomes, Educational Programmes and Baseline and End of Phase Assessment Arrangements for the Foundation Phase) (Wales) Order 2015, SI 2015/1596.

 7   As to the meaning of 'key stage' see PARA 875 note 1. As to the key stages see PARA 875.
 8   Ie subject to the Education Act 2002 s 107: see PARA 877.
 9   As to the foundation subjects in relation to the second and third key stages see PARA 876; and the fourth key stage see PARA 877.
10   Education Act 2002 s 108(3)(a) (s 108(3) amended by the Education (Wales) Measure 2009 s 21(1), (7)(b)). As to the meaning of 'attainment targets' see PARA 873. See note 13.
11   Education Act 2002 s 108(3)(b). As to the meaning of 'programmes of study' see PARA 873. See note 13.
12   Education Act 2002 s 108(3)(c). An order under s 108(3)(c) may confer or impose such functions on: (1) the governing body and head teacher (s 108(7)(a)); and (2) the local authority (s 108(7)(b) (amended by SI 2010/1158)), as appear to the Welsh Ministers to be required (Education Act 2002 s 108(7) (amended by the Learning and Skills (Wales) Measure 2009 s 47, Schedule paras 11–13)). Such an order may also specify such assessment arrangements as may for the time being be made by a person specified in the order (see the Education Act 2002 s 108(8)); and may authorise the making of such provisions giving full effect to or otherwise supplementing the provisions made by the order, other than provision conferring or imposing functions as mentioned in s 108(7), as appear to the Welsh Ministers to be expedient; and any provisions made under such an order must, on being published as specified in the order, have effect for the purposes of Pt 7 (ss 97–118) as if made by the order (s 108(11) (amended by the Learning and Skills (Wales) Measure 2009 s 47, Schedule paras 11–13)). Provision must be made for determining the extent to which any assessment arrangements, and the implementation of the arrangements, achieve the purpose for which the arrangements are made; and any such provision may be made by or under the order specifying the arrangements or, where the order specifies the person making the arrangements, in the arrangements themselves: Education Act 2002 s 108(9). The duties that may be imposed by virtue of s 108(7) include, in relation to persons exercising any power in pursuance of provision made by virtue of s 108(9), the duty to permit them: (a) to enter premises of the school or, as the case may be, premises on which the funded nursery education is being provided (s 108(10)(a)); (b) to observe implementation of the arrangements (s 108(10)(b)); and (c) to inspect, and take copies of, documents and other articles (s 108(10)(c)). As to an order made under s 108(3)(c), (7) see the National Curriculum (Moderation of Assessment Arrangements for the Second and Third Key Stages) (Wales) Order 2015, SI 2015/1309. See note 13.
13   Education Act 2002 s 108(3) (amended by the Learning and Skills (Wales) Measure 2009 s 47, Schedule paras 11, 15). As to the procedure for making orders under the Education Act 2002

s 108(3)(a), (b) see PARA 880. As to the orders made under s 108(3) see the National Curriculum (Key Stage 2 Assessment Arrangements) (Wales) Order 2004, SI 2004/2915 (amended by SI 2005/3239; and SI 2011/1937); the National Curriculum (Key Stage 3 Assessment Arrangements) (Wales) Order 2005, SI 2005/1394 (amended by SI 2005/3239; SI 2008/1899; and SI 2011/1937); the Education (National Curriculum) (Attainment Targets and Programmes of Study) (Wales) Order 2008, SI 2008/1409 (amended by SI 2008/1787); the School Curriculum in Wales (Miscellaneous Amendments) Order 2008, SI 2008/1899; the National Curriculum (Amendments to the Key Stage 2 and Key Stage 3 Assessment Arrangements) (Wales) Order 2011, SI 2011/1937; the National Curriculum (Assessment Arrangements on Entry to the Foundation Phase) (Wales) (Revocation) Order 2012, SI 2012/935; the Education (National Curriculum) (Assessment Arrangements for Reading and Numeracy) (Wales) Order 2013, SI 2013/433; the National Curriculum (Educational Programmes for the Foundation Phase and Programmes of Study for the Second and Third Key Stages) (Wales) Order 2013, SI 2013/434; the National Curriculum (Assessment Arrangements for the Foundation Phase and the Second and Third Key Stages) (Wales) Order 2014, SI 2014/1999; the National Curriculum (Moderation of Assessment Arrangements for the Second and Third Key Stages) (Wales) Order 2015, SI 2015/1309; and the National Curriculum (Desirable Outcomes, Educational Programmes and Baseline and End of Phase Assessment Arrangements for the Foundation Phase) (Wales) Order 2015, SI 2015/1596.

14 Ie an order under the Education Act 2002 s 108(2) or s 108(3): see the text to notes 1–13.
15 Education Act 2002 s 108(4)(a) (as amended: see note 2).
16 Education Act 2002 s 108(4)(b).
17 Education Act 2002 s 108(5).
18 Ie the powers conferred by the Education Act 2002 s 108(2) or s 108(3): see the text to notes 1–13.
19 As to the National Curriculum for Wales see PARA 871.
20 Education Act 2002 s 108(1)(a) (as amended: see note 2).
21 Education Act 2002 s 108(1)(b) (as amended (see note 2); and also amended by the Learning and Skills (Wales) Measure 2009 s 47, Schedule paras 11–13, 15).

879. Duty to secure implementation of the National Curriculum for Wales. In relation to any maintained school[1] and any school year[2]:

(1) the local authority[3] and the governing body[4] must exercise their functions[5] with a view to securing[6], and

(2) the head teacher[7] must secure[8],

that the National Curriculum for Wales[9] as subsisting at the beginning of that year is implemented[10].

In relation to any maintained nursery school[11] and any school year:

(a) the local authority and the governing body must exercise their functions with a view to securing[12], and

(b) the head teacher must secure[13],

that the National Curriculum for Wales as subsisting at the beginning of that year, so far as it relates to the foundation phase, is implemented[14]. In relation to any school year, any person[15] providing funded nursery education[16] must secure that the National Curriculum for Wales as subsisting at the beginning of that year is implemented, so far as it relates to the foundation phase, in respect of the pupils[17] for whom the funded nursery education is provided[18]. The local authority with whom the arrangements for providing funded nursery education are made[19] and the early years development and childcare partnership[20] for the area of the authority must each exercise its functions with a view to securing that any person, other than the governing body of a maintained school or maintained nursery school, who provides funded nursery education complies with the obligation[21] to secure that the National Curriculum for Wales is implemented[22].

1 As to the meaning of 'maintained school' see PARA 870 note 4.
2 As to the meaning of 'school year' see PARA 874 note 2.
3 As to the meaning of 'local authority' see PARA 25 (definition applied by the Education Act 2002 s 212(1)).

4   As to the governing bodies of maintained schools in Wales see PARA 195.
5   As to the meaning of 'functions' see PARA 18 note 5 (definition applied by the Education Act 2002 s 212(2), (3)).
6   Education Act 2002 s 109(a).
7   As to the meaning of 'head teacher' see PARA 86 note 4 (definition applied by the Education Act 2002 s 212(2), (3)).
8   Education Act 2002 s 109(b).
9   As to the National Curriculum for Wales see PARA 871.
10 Education Act 2002 s 109. As to the duty of teachers to deliver the National Curriculum see *Wandsworth London Borough Council v National Association of Schoolmasters/Union of Women Teachers* [1994] ICR 81, [1994] ELR 170, (1993) 92 LGR 91, CA (decided under previous legislation).
11 As to the meaning of 'maintained nursery school' see PARA 870 note 5.
12 Education Act 2002 s 110(1)(a) (amended by SI 2010/1158).
13 Education Act 2002 s 110(1)(b).
14 Education Act 2002 s 110(1) (amended by the Education (Wales) Measure 2009 s 21(1), (8)). As to the foundation phase see PARA 874.
15 As to the meaning of 'person' see PARA 7 note 6.
16 Ie under the arrangements mentioned in the Education Act 2002 s 98(2)(b): see PARA 870 note 6. As to the meanings of 'nursery education' and 'funded nursery education' see PARA 870 note 6.
17 As to the meaning of 'pupil' see PARA 870 note 11.
18 Education Act 2002 s 110(2) (amended by the Education (Wales) Measure 2009 s 21(1), (8)).
19 Ie the arrangements mentioned in the Education Act 2002 s 98(2)(b): see PARA 870 note 6.
20 As to early years development and childcare partnerships see PARA 97.
21 Ie the obligation imposed by the Education Act 2002 s 110(2): see the text to notes 15–18.
22 Education Act 2002 s 110(3).

880. Procedure for making certain orders and regulations in relation to the National Curriculum for Wales. Where the Welsh Ministers[1] propose to make certain orders[2] or regulations[3] in relation to the National Curriculum for Wales[4], they must make such arrangements for consultation about the proposals as they consider appropriate[5].

1   As to the Welsh Ministers see PARA 59.
2   Ie an order under the Education Act 2002 s 103(4) (see PARA 875), s 105(6) (see PARA 876), or s 108(2)(a), (b)(i), (b)(ii), (3)(a) or (3)(b) (see PARA 878).
3   Ie regulations under the Education Act 2002 s 112: see PARA 882.
4   As to the National Curriculum for Wales see PARA 871.
5   Education Act 2002 s 117 (amended by the Learning and Skills (Wales) Measure 2009 s 47, Schedule, paras 11, 19). As to the exercise of the duty to consult see JUDICIAL REVIEW vol 61 (2010) PARA 627.

C. THE NATIONAL CURRICULUM FOR WALES: SPECIAL CASES

881. Curriculum: development work and experiments. For the purpose of enabling development work or experiments to be carried out, the Welsh Ministers[1] may direct[2] in respect of a particular maintained school or maintained nursery school[3] that, for such period as may be specified in the direction, the National Curriculum for Wales[4] does not apply[5], or applies with such modifications[6] as may be specified in the direction[7]. Such a direction may apply either generally or in such cases as may be specified in the direction[8].

In the case of a community, voluntary controlled or community special school[9] or a maintained nursery school, such a direction must not be given except[10]:

(1)   on an application by the governing body[11] with the agreement of the local authority[12];

(2)   on an application by the local authority with the agreement of the governing body[13]; or

(3)   on a proposal by the Welsh Ministers with the agreement of both the local authority and the governing body[14].

In the case of a foundation or voluntary aided school[15], such a direction must not be given except on an application by the governing body or with the agreement of the governing body[16].

The Welsh Ministers may make it a condition of a direction that any person[17] by whom or with whose agreement the request for the direction was made should, when so directed or at specified intervals, report to the Welsh Ministers on any matters specified by them[18].

1   As to the Welsh Ministers see PARA 59.
2   The Welsh Ministers may by a direction under the Education Act 2002 s 111(6) vary or revoke a direction under s 111(1): s 111(6) (amended by the Learning and Skills (Wales) Measure 2009 s 47, Schedule paras 11–13). As to directions generally see the Education Act 1996 s 570 (applied by the Education Act 2002 s 212(2), (3)); and PARA 75.
3   As to the meaning of 'maintained school' see PARA 870 note 4. As to the meaning of 'maintained nursery school' see PARA 870 note 5.
4   Education Act 2002 s 111(1) (amended by the Learning and Skills (Wales) Measure 2009 s 47, Schedule paras 11–13). As to the National Curriculum for Wales see PARA 871.
5   Education Act 2002 s 111(1)(a).
6   As to the meaning of 'modifications' see PARA 21 note 15 (definition applied by the Education Act 2002 s 212(2), (3)).
7   Education Act 2002 s 111(1)(b).
8   Education Act 2002 s 111(2).
9   As to the meaning of references to a community, voluntary, or community special school see PARA 106.
10   Education Act 2002 s 111(3) (amended by SI 2005/3239).
11   As to the governing bodies of maintained schools in Wales see PARA 195.
12   Education Act 2002 s 111(3)(a) (amended by SI 2005/3239; SI 2010/1158). As to the meaning of 'local authority' see PARA 25 (definition applied by the Education Act 2002 s 212(1)).
13   Education Act 2002 s 111(3)(b) (amended by SI 2005/3239; and SI 2010/1158).
14   Education Act 2002 s 111(3)(c) (amended by SI 2005/3239; SI 2010/1158; and the Learning and Skills (Wales) Measure 2009 s 47, Schedule paras 11–13).
15   As to the meaning of references to a foundation school see PARA 106.
16   Education Act 2002 s 111(4) (amended by SI 2005/3239; and the School Standards and Organisation (Wales) Act 2013 s 21(1), (5)).
17   As to the meaning of 'person' see PARA 7 note 6.
18   Education Act 2002 s 111(5) (amended by the Learning and Skills (Wales) Measure 2009 s 47, Schedule paras 11–13, 16, 17).

882.   Curriculum: exceptions by regulations. Regulations[1] may provide that the National Curriculum for Wales[2], or such of the provisions of the National Curriculum for Wales as may be specified in the regulations either do not apply[3], or apply with such modifications[4] as may be specified in the regulations[5], in such cases or circumstances as may be specified in the regulations[6].

1   'Regulations' means regulations made by the Welsh Ministers: Education Act 2002 s 97 (definition added by the Learning and Skills (Wales) Measure 2009 s 1(1), (5)). As to the Welsh Ministers see PARA 59. As to the procedure for making regulations under the Education Act 2002 s 112, see s 117; and PARA 880. As to the regulations made under s 112 see the Education (Disapplication of the National Curriculum at Key Stage 1) (Wales) Regulations 2005, SI 2005/1511; the Education (National Curriculum for Wales) (Disapplication of Science at Key Stage 4) Regulations 2006, SI 2006/1335; and the Education (Disapplication of the National Curriculum for Wales at Key Stage 1) (Wales) Regulations 2008, SI 2008/1736. In addition, the following regulations, made under the Education Act 1996 s 363 (repealed), have effect, by virtue of the Interpretation Act 1978 s 17(2)(b), as if made under the Education Act 2002 s 112: the Education (National Curriculum) (Exceptions) (Wales) Regulations 1991, SI 1991/1657; the Education (National Curriculum) (Exceptions in Welsh at Key Stage 4) Regulations 1994, SI 1994/1270; and the Education (National Curriculum) (Exceptions) (Wales) Regulations 1995, SI 1995/1574.

2   As to the National Curriculum for Wales see PARA 871.
3   Education Act 2002 s 112(a).
4   As to the meaning of 'modifications' see PARA 21 note 15 (definition applied by the Education Act 2002 s 212(2), (3)).
5   Education Act 2002 s 112(b).
6   Education Act 2002 s 112.

883.   Pupils with statements of special educational needs. The special educational provision[1] for any pupil[2] specified in a statement of his special educational needs[3] may include provision excluding the application of the National Curriculum for Wales[4], or applying the National Curriculum for Wales with such modifications[5] as may be specified in the statement[6].

1   As to the meaning of 'special educational provision' see PARA 989 (definition applied by the Education Act 2002 s 212(2), (3)).
2   As to the meaning of 'pupil' see PARA 20 note 4.
3   Ie a statement under the Education Act 1996 s 324: see PARA 1002. As to the meaning of 'special educational needs' see PARA 989 (definition applied by the Education Act 2002 s 212(2), (3)).
4   Education Act 2002 s 113(a). As to the National Curriculum for Wales see PARA 871.
5   As to the meaning of 'modifications' see PARA 21 note 15 (definition applied by the Education Act 2002 s 212(2), (3)).
6   Education Act 2002 s 113(b).

884.   Temporary exceptions from the curriculum for individual pupils. Regulations[1] may enable the head teacher[2] of a maintained school[3] or maintained nursery school[4], in such cases or circumstances and subject to such conditions as may be prescribed[5], to direct in respect of a registered pupil[6] at the school that, for such period as may be specified in the direction (the 'operative period' of the direction), the National Curriculum for Wales[7] does not apply[8], or applies with such modifications[9] as may be specified in the direction[10].

The conditions prescribed by the regulations must, in particular, limit the operative period that may be specified in a direction to a maximum period specified in the regulations[11]. Any maximum period specified, whether in relation to directions given under the regulations or in relation to directions given under the regulations in circumstances specified in the regulations, must be either a fixed period not exceeding six months[12], or a period determinable, in such manner as may be specified in the regulations, not later than six months from its beginning[13]. Any maximum period so specified may[14] differ according to whether or not the direction in question is given in respect of a period beginning immediately after the end of the operative period of a previous direction[15], or within such period after the end of the operative period of a previous direction as may be specified in the regulations[16].

The regulations may enable the head teacher of a maintained school or maintained nursery school, in such cases or circumstances and subject to such conditions as may be prescribed, to revoke any direction given by him under the regulations[17], and to vary such a direction, except so as to extend its operative period[18].

Where a head teacher gives or varies a direction under such regulations[19], he must, in such manner as may be prescribed[20], give the information mentioned in heads (1) to (3) below to the governing body[21], and to the local authority[22] by whom the school is maintained[23], and must take such steps as may be prescribed to give that information also to a parent[24] of the pupil concerned[25]. That information is:

(1)   the fact that he has taken the action in question, its effect and his reasons for taking it[26];

(2) the provision that is being or is to be made for the pupil's education during the operative period of the direction[27]; and

(3) either a description of the manner in which he proposes to secure the full implementation of the National Curriculum for Wales in relation to the pupil after the end of that period, or an indication that he has the opinion[28] that the pupil has or probably has special educational needs[29] by virtue of which the responsible authority[30] would be required to determine the special educational provision[31] that should be made for him, whether initially or on a review of any statement of his special educational needs which the authority has for the time being required[32] to maintain[33].

Where the head teacher of a maintained school or maintained nursery school includes an indication of any such opinion in the information given[34], and the local authority by whom the school is maintained is not the responsible authority in relation to the pupil in question, the head teacher must also give that information, in such manner as may be prescribed, to the responsible authority[35]. Where the responsible authority receives information[36] which includes an indication that the head teacher has the opinion that the pupil has or probably has special educational needs[37], it must consider whether any action on its part is required[38] in the case of the pupil concerned[39].

Where a head teacher:

(a) gives, revokes or varies a direction under such regulations[40];

(b) refuses to give, revoke or vary such a direction in response to a request made, in such manner and circumstances as may be prescribed by the regulations, by the parent of a registered pupil at the school[41]; or

(c) following the making of such a request, fails within such period as may be prescribed by the regulations to give, revoke or vary such a direction in accordance with the request[42],

the parent of the pupil concerned may appeal to the governing body[43]. On such an appeal, the governing body may confirm the head teacher's action[44], or direct the head teacher to take such action authorised by the regulations as it considers appropriate in the circumstances[45]. The head teacher must comply with any such directions of the governing body[46]. The governing body must notify[47] the appellant and the head teacher in writing[48] of its decision on such an appeal[49].

1 'Regulations' means regulations made by the Welsh Ministers: Education Act 2002 s 97 (definition added by the Learning and Skills (Wales) Measure 2009 s 1(1), (5)). Before making any regulations under the Education Act 2002 s 114, the Welsh Ministers must consult with any persons with whom consultation appears to them to be desirable: s 114(6) (amended by the Learning and Skills (Wales) Measure 2009 s 47, Schedule, paras 11–13, 18). As to the Welsh Ministers see PARA 59. As to the meaning of 'person' see PARA 7 note 6. As to the exercise of the duty to consult see JUDICIAL REVIEW vol 61 (2010) PARA 627. At the date at which this volume states the law, no regulations had been made under the Education Act 2002 ss 114, 115 (see the text to note 19). However, the Education (National Curriculum) (Temporary Exceptions for Individual Pupils) (Wales) Regulations 1999, SI 1999/1815, made under the Education Act 1996 ss 365–367 (repealed), have effect, by virtue of the Interpretation Act 1978 s 17(2)(b), as if so made.

2 As to the meaning of 'head teacher' see PARA 86 note 4 (definition applied by the Education Act 2002 s 212(2), (3)).

3 As to the meaning of 'maintained school' see PARA 870 note 4.

4 As to the meaning of 'maintained nursery school' see PARA 870 note 5.

5 'Prescribed' means prescribed by regulations: Education Act 2002 s 212(1). As to the cases and circumstances in which directions may be given see the Education (National Curriculum) (Temporary Exceptions for Individual Pupils) (Wales) Regulations 1999, SI 1999/1815, reg 3.

6 As to the meaning of 'registered pupil' see PARA 437 (definition applied by the Education Act 2002 s 212(2), (3)). As to the meaning of 'pupil' see PARA 870 note 11.

7   As to the National Curriculum for Wales see PARA 871.

8   Education Act 2002 s 114(1)(a).

9   As to the meaning of 'modifications' see PARA 21 note 15 (definition applied by the Education Act 2002 s 212(2), (3)).

10   Education Act 2002 s 114(1)(b). As to the making of directions under s 114 see the Education (National Curriculum) (Temporary Exceptions for Individual Pupils) (Wales) Regulations 1999, SI 1999/1815, reg 4. As to the form and contents of directions under the Education Act 2002 s 114 see the Education (National Curriculum) (Temporary Exceptions for Individual Pupils) (Wales) Regulations 1999, SI 1999/1815, reg 5; and as to the requirement to keep records of relevant information see reg 6. As to further directions see regs 9–11. As to parental requests to the head teacher to give a direction or a further direction see regs 12–14.

11   Education Act 2002 s 114(2).

12   Education Act 2002 s 114(3)(a). As to the meaning of 'month' see PARA 54 note 26.

13   Education Act 2002 s 114(3)(b).

14   Ie without prejudice to the generality of the Education Act 2002 s 210(7) (which provides that regulations under the Education Act 2002 may make different provision for different cases or circumstances etc): see s 114(4).

15   Education Act 2002 s 114(4)(a).

16   Education Act 2002 s 114(4)(b).

17   Education Act 2002 s 114(5)(a). As to the revocation of directions see the Education (National Curriculum) (Temporary Exceptions for Individual Pupils) (Wales) Regulations 1999, SI 1999/1815, regs 7–8.

18   Education Act 2002 s 114(5)(b). As to the variation of directions see the Education (National Curriculum) (Temporary Exceptions for Individual Pupils) (Wales) Regulations 1999, SI 1999/1815, reg 7.

19   Ie under regulations made under the Education Act 2002 s 114: see the text to notes 1–18.

20   As to the regulations made see note 1.

21   Education Act 2002 s 115(1)(a). As to the governing bodies of maintained schools in Wales see PARA 195.

22   As to the meaning of 'local authority' see PARA 25 (definition applied by the Education Act 2002 s 212(1)).

23   Education Act 2002 s 115(1)(b) (amended by SI 2010/1158).

24   As to the meaning of 'parent' see PARA 7 note 6 (definition applied by the Education Act 2002 s 212(2), (3)).

25   Education Act 2002 s 115(1).

26   Education Act 2002 s 115(2)(a).

27   Education Act 2002 s 115(2)(b).

28   See the Education Act 2002 s 115(2)(c).

29   As to the meaning of 'special educational needs' see PARA 989 (definition applied by the Education Act 2002 s 212(2), (3)).

30   'The responsible authority', in relation to a pupil, means the local authority responsible for him for the purposes of the Education Act 1996 Pt IV (ss 311A–349) (see PARA 989 et seq): Education Act 2002 s 115(6) (amended by SI 2010/1158).

31   As to the meaning of 'special educational provision' see PARA 989 (definition applied by the Education Act 2002 s 212(2), (3)).

32   Ie under the Education Act 1996 s 324: see PARA 1002.

33   Education Act 2002 s 115(3).

34   Ie under the Education Act 2002 s 115(1): see the text to notes 19–25.

35   Education Act 2002 s 115(4) (amended by SI 2010/1158).

36   Ie given to it under the Education Act 2002 s 115(1) (see the text to notes 19–25) or s 115(4) (see the text to notes 34–35).

37   Ie the opinion mentioned in the Education Act 2002 s 115(3): see the text to notes 29–33.

38   Ie under the Education Act 1996 s 323 (assessment of special educational needs): see PARA 994.

39   Education Act 2002 s 115(5).

40   See the Education Act 2002 s 116(1)(a).

41   Education Act 2002 s 116(1)(b).

42   Education Act 2002 s 116(1)(c).

43   Education Act 2002 s 116(1). See also the Education (National Curriculum) (Temporary Exceptions for Individual Pupils) (Wales) Regulations 1999, SI 1999/1815, reg 14.

44   Education Act 2002 s 116(2)(a).

45   Education Act 2002 s 116(2)(b).

46   Education Act 2002 s 116(3).

47 As to the service of notices and documents see the Education Act 1996 s 572 (applied by the Education Act 2002 s 212(2), (3)); and PARA 76.

48 As to the meaning of 'writing' see PARA 76 note 8.

49 Education Act 2002 s 116(4).

D. FORMATION OF LOCAL CURRICULUM

(A) Local Curriculum for Pupils in the Fourth Key Stage

885. Formation of local curricula for pupils in the fourth key stage. Each local authority[1] in Wales[2] must form for its area one or more local curricula[3] for pupils in the fourth key stage[4]. A local curriculum must consist of suitable courses of study[5] each of which: (1) falls within a category of the learning domains[6]; and (2) is from time to time selected by a local authority to form part of that local curriculum[7]. The 'learning domains' are[8]: (a) mathematics, science and technology[9]; (b) business, administration and law[10]; (c) services for people[11]; (d) arts, media, culture and languages[12]; (e) humanities, social sciences and preparation for life and work[13].

Subject to any regulations[14], a local authority may form a local curriculum as it sees fit[15]. Regulations[16] may make provision as to the formation of a local curriculum, including in particular provision:

(i) requiring a minimum number of courses of study to be included within a local curriculum[17] or a particular learning domain of a local curriculum[18];

(ii) specifying a minimum proportion of vocational courses of study[19] (as compared with other courses of study) that must be included within a local curriculum[20], or a minimum number of vocational courses of study that must be included within a local curriculum[21];

(iii) preventing during a specified period any alteration to the contents of a local curriculum[22];

and may make different provision in relation to local curricula formed by different local authorities[23].

Where a local authority forms more than one local curriculum[24], in relation to each local curriculum, the local authority must designate the maintained secondary schools[25] whose registered pupils[26] are to be entitled to elect[27] to follow courses of study included within the curriculum[28].

1 As to the meaning of 'local authority' see PARA 25 (definition applied by the Education Act 2002 s 212(1)).

2 As to the meaning of 'Wales' see PARA 7 note 3.

3 'Local curriculum' and 'local curricula' are to be construed in accordance with the Education Act 2002 s 116A and, in relation to a pupil's school, 'local curriculum' means: (1) where the local authority by which the school is maintained has formed a single local curriculum under s 116A, that local curriculum; or (2) where the local authority by which the school is maintained has formed more than one local curriculum under s 116A, the local curriculum in respect of which the school is designated under s 116C(2) (see the text to notes 25–28): s 97 (definition added by the Learning and Skills (Wales) Measure 2009 s 1(1), (3); and amended by SI 2010/1148). As to the meaning of 'pupil' see PARA 870 note 11.

4 Education Act 2002 s 116A(1) (s 116A added by the Learning and Skills (Wales) Measure 2009 s 4; and amended by SI 2010/1148). As to the meaning of 'key stage' see PARA 875 note 1. As to the key stages see PARA 875. As to the curriculum requirements for the fourth key stage see PARA 877. As to local curricula in relation to the Welsh language see PARA 886. As to the application of the Education Act 2002 ss 116A–116K to other children see PARAS 893, 894.

5 'Course of study' means a course of education or training which leads to a qualification or set of qualifications approved under the Learning and Skills Act 2000 s 99 (see PARA 1139) for the purposes of s 96 of that Act: Education Act 2002 s 97 (definition added by the Learning and

Skills (Wales) Measure 2009 s 1(1), (2)). For the purposes of the Education Act 2002 s 116A, a course of study is suitable if it is designated as suitable for inclusion in local curricula by direction given by the Welsh Ministers: Education Act 2002 s 116A(6)(a) (as added: see note 4). Any such direction given by the Welsh Ministers may be varied or revoked by a further direction: see s 116O (added by the Learning and Skills (Wales) Measure 2009 s 18). As to the Welsh Ministers see PARA 59.

 6   See the Education Act 2002 s 116A(2)(a) (as added: see note 4). A course of study falls within a particular learning domain if a direction of the Welsh Ministers so provides: s 116A(6)(c) (as so added). Any such direction given by the Welsh Ministers may be varied or revoked by a further direction: see s 116O (as added: see note 5).

 7   Education Act 2002 s 116A(2)(b) (as added (see note 4); and amended by SI 2010/1148).

 8   The Welsh Ministers may by order: (1) amend or omit any paragraph of the Education Act 2002 s 116A(3); (2) add additional paragraphs to that subsection; (3) amend or omit such additional paragraphs: s 116L (added by the Learning and Skills (Wales) Measure 2009 s 15). At the date at which this volume states the law no such order had been made.

 9   Education Act 2002 s 116A(3)(a) (as added: see note 4).

10   Education Act 2002 s 116A(3)(b) (as added: see note 4).

11   Education Act 2002 s 116A(3)(c) (as added: see note 4).

12   Education Act 2002 s 116A(3)(d) (as added: see note 4).

13   Education Act 2002 s 116A(3)(e) (as added: see note 4).

14   Ie made under the Education Act 2002 s 116A(5): see the text to notes 16–22.

15   Education Act 2002 s 116A(4) (as added (see note 4); and amended by SI 2010/1148).

16   'Regulations' means regulations made by the Welsh Ministers: Education Act 2002 s 97 (definition added by the Learning and Skills (Wales) Measure 2009 s 1(1), (5)). As to the regulations made see the Education (Local Curriculum for Pupils in Key Stage 4) (Wales) Regulations 2009, SI 2009/3256 (amended by SI 2014/42).

17   Education Act 2002 s 116A(5)(a)(i) (as added: see note 4).

18   Education Act 2002 s 116A(5)(a)(ii) (as added: see note 4).

19   A 'vocational course of study' is a course of study designated as such by direction given by the Welsh Ministers: Education Act 2002 s 116A(6)(b) (as added: see note 4). Any such direction given by the Welsh Ministers may be varied or revoked by a further direction: see s 116O (as added: see note 5).

20   Education Act 2002 s 116A(5)(b)(i) (as added: see note 4).

21   Education Act 2002 s 116A(5)(b)(ii) (as added: see note 4).

22   Education Act 2002 s 116A(5)(c) (as added: see note 4).

23   See the Education Act 2002 s 116A(7) (as added (see note 4); and amended by SI 2010/1148).

24   See the Education Act 2002 s 116C(1) (s 116C added by the Learning and Skills (Wales) Measure 2009 s 6; and the Education Act 2002 s 116C(1) amended by SI 2010/1148).

25   'Maintained secondary school' means a maintained school which is a secondary school unless it is a community special school which is maintained by a local authority in Wales: Education Act 2002 s 97 (definition added by the Learning and Skills (Wales) Measure 2009 s 1(1), (4); and amended by SI 2010/1148; and the School Standards and Organisation (Wales) Act 2013 Sch 5 para 21(1), (4)(b)). As to the meaning of 'maintained school' see PARA 870 note 4. As to the meaning of 'secondary school' see PARA 91 (definition applied by the Education Act 2002 s 212(2), (3)). As to the meaning of references to a community special school see PARA 106.

26   As to the meaning of 'registered pupil' see PARA 437 (definition applied by the Education Act 2002 s 212(2), (3)).

27   Ie under the Education Act 2002 s 116D: see PARA 888.

28   Education Act 2002 s 116C(2) (as added: see note 24).

886. Local curricula: Welsh language. Each local authority[1] must exercise its functions[2] in relation to local curricula[3] so as to promote access to and availability of courses of study[4] which are taught through the medium of the Welsh language[5]. In the discharge of this duty, a local authority must have regard to any guidance given by the Welsh Ministers[6].

Within two months[7] of the end of each academic year[8], a local authority must, in accordance with any instructions given by the Welsh Ministers, provide the Welsh Ministers with a report which[9]:

(1)   describes the courses of study included within local curricula established
       by the authority for that academic year which were to be taught through
       the medium of Welsh[10];

(2)   describes how many pupils[11] elected to follow such courses[12] and how
       many pupils were entitled[13] to follow such courses[14];

(3)   explains what the authority plans to do in academic years following that
       to which the report relates so that registered pupils of schools
       maintained by the authority are given the opportunity to follow local
       curricula courses of study which are taught through the medium of
       Welsh[15].

1   As to the meaning of 'local authority' see PARA 25 (definition applied by the Education Act 2002
    s 212(2), (3)).
2   As to the meaning of 'functions' see PARA 18 note 5 (definition applied by the Education
    Act 2002 s 212(2), (3)).
3   As to the meanings of 'local curriculum' and 'local curricula' see PARA 885 note 3. As to the
    formation of local curricula see PARA 885.
4   As to the meaning of 'course of study' see PARA 885 note 5.
5   Education Act 2002 s 116B(1) (s 116B added by the Learning and Skills (Wales) Measure 2009
    s 5; and the Education Act 2002 s 116B(1), (2), (4) amended by SI 2010/1148). For provision
    relating to the Welsh Language see Welsh Language (Wales) Measure 2011; and
    CONSTITUTIONAL AND ADMINISTRATIVE LAW vol 20 (2014) PARA 406 et seq. As to Welsh in
    education strategic plans see PARA 887.
6   Education Act 2002 s 116B(2) (as added and amended: see note 5). Such guidance may be given
    to a particular authority, or to authorities of a particular class or to authorities generally:
    s 116B(3) (as so added). As to the Welsh Ministers see PARA 59. As to the publication of
    guidance see the Education Act 1996 s 571 (applied by the Education Act 2002 s 212(2), (3));
    and PARA 60.
7   As to the meaning of 'month' see PARA 54 note 26.
8   'Academic year' means the period of 12 months beginning on 1 September: Education Act 2002
    s 116B(5) (as added: see note 5).
9   Education Act 2002 s 116B(4) (as added and amended: see note 5).
10 Education Act 2002 s 116B(4)(a) (as added: see note 5).
11 As to the meaning of 'pupil' see PARA 870 note 11. As to the application of the Education
    Act 2002 ss 116A–116K to other children see PARAS 893, 894.
12 Ie under the Education Act 2002 s 116D: see PARA 888.
13 Ie under the Education Act 2002 s 116E: see PARA 888.
14 Education Act 2002 s 116B(4)(b) (as added: see note 5).
15 Education Act 2002 s 116B(4)(c) (as added: see note 5).

887.   **Welsh in education strategic plans.** A Welsh in education strategic plan
is a plan which contains (1) a local authority's[1] proposals on how it will carry
out its education functions to (a) improve the planning of the provision of
education through the medium of Welsh ('Welsh medium education') in its area;
(b) improve the standards of Welsh medium education and of the teaching of
Welsh in its area; (2) the local authority's targets for improving the planning of
the provision of Welsh medium education in its area and for improving the
standards of that education and of the teaching of Welsh in its area; (3) a report
on the progress made to meet the targets contained in the previous plan or
previous revised plan[2]. A local authority must prepare a Welsh in education
strategic plan for its area[3]. A local authority must keep its plan under review, and
if necessary, revise it[4].

In preparing a Welsh in education strategic plan or revised plan, a local
authority must consult (i) its neighbouring local authorities; (ii) the head teacher
of each school maintained by it; (iii) the governing body[5] of each school
maintained by it; (iv) each institution within the further education sector in its
area; (v) in relation to any foundation or voluntary school in its area the person

who appoints the foundation governors[6], and if the school has a religious character[7], the appropriate religious body[8]; (vi) other prescribed persons[9]. If a local authority carries out an assessment of the demand for Welsh medium education in accordance with regulations[10], it must take the results of that assessment into account when it next prepares or revises its Welsh in education strategic plan[11].

Provision is made for the approval, publication and implementation of Welsh in education strategic plans[12]. The Welsh Ministers may require a local authority, in accordance with regulations, to carry out an assessment of the demand among parents in its area for Welsh medium education for their children[13]. Further provision is made with respect to regulations and guidance[14].

1   As to the meaning of 'local authority' see the School Standards and Organisation (Wales) Act 2013 s 98(3).
2   See the School Standards and Organisation (Wales) Act 2013 s 84(1).
3   See the School Standards and Organisation (Wales) Act 2013 s 84(2).
4   See the School Standards and Organisation (Wales) Act 2013 s 84(3).
5   As to the governing bodies of maintained schools in Wales see PARA 195.
6   As to the meanings of 'foundation governor' and 'appropriate religious body' see the School Standards and Organisation (Wales) Act 2013 s 98(3).
7   As to references to a school which has a religious character see the School Standards and Organisation (Wales) Act 2013 s 98(5).
8   See note 6.
9   See the School Standards and Organisation (Wales) Act 2013 s 84(4).
10 Ie in accordance with regulations under the School Standards and Organisation (Wales) Act 2013 s 86: see the text to note 12.
11 See the School Standards and Organisation (Wales) Act 2013 s 84(5).
12 See the School Standards and Organisation (Wales) Act 2013 s 85.
13 See the School Standards and Organisation (Wales) Act 2013 s 86; and the Welsh in Education Strategic Plans and Assessing Demand for Welsh Medium Education (Wales) Regulations 2013, SI 2013/3048.
14 See the School Standards and Organisation (Wales) Act 2013 s 87; and the Welsh in Education Strategic Plans and Assessing Demand for Welsh Medium Education (Wales) Regulations 2013, SI 2013/3048.

888.   Pupils' choices of local curriculum courses.   A registered pupil[1] of a maintained secondary school[2] has the right to elect to follow, during the fourth key stage[3], a course or courses of study[4] included within the local curriculum[5] for the pupil's school[6]. But this is subject to regulations[7] which may make provision as to the making of elections, including in particular provision: (1) specifying the maximum number of courses of study of a particular type that a pupil has the right to elect to follow[8]; (2) identifying points to be allotted to courses of study and preventing a pupil from having the right to elect to follow a combination of courses of study if their aggregate points exceed a specified amount[9]; (3) as to the period during which elections are to be made[10].

During the fourth key stage, a pupil who has made an election[11] is entitled to follow the elected course of study unless:

(a)   the pupil ceases to be a registered pupil of the school at which he or she was registered when he or she elected to follow the course of study[12]; or

(b)   before the beginning of the fourth key stage, the head teacher[13] of the pupil's school has decided[14] that the pupil is not entitled to follow the course of study[15].

Where a pupil is so entitled to follow a course of study:

(i)   it is for the head teacher of the pupil's school to decide upon which date during the fourth key stage the course is to begin[16]; and

(ii) the governing body[17] of the pupil's school must ensure that during the
fourth key stage the course is made available to the pupil by or on
behalf of the governing body[18].

1 As to the meaning of 'registered pupil' see PARA 437 (definition applied by the Education
   Act 2002 s 212(2), (3)). As to the meaning of 'pupil' see PARA 870 note 11. As to the application
   of the Education Act 2002 ss 116A–116K to other children see PARAS 893, 894.
2 As to the meaning of 'maintained secondary school' see PARA 885 note 25.
3 As to the meaning of 'key stage' see PARA 875 note 1. As to the key stages see PARA 875.
4 As to the meaning of 'course of study' see PARA 885 note 5.
5 As to the meanings of 'local curriculum' and 'local curricula' see PARA 885 note 3. As to the
   formation of local curricula see PARA 885.
6 Education Act 2002 s 116D(1) (s 116D added by the Learning and Skills (Wales) Measure 2009
   s 7).
7 See the Education Act 2002 s 116D(1) (as added: see note 6). 'Regulations' means regulations
   made by the Welsh Ministers: s 97 (definition added by the Learning and Skills (Wales)
   Measure 2009 s 1(1), (5)). As to the Welsh Ministers see PARA 59. As to the regulations made see
   the Education (Local Curriculum for Pupils in Key Stage 4) (Wales) Regulations 2009,
   SI 2009/3256 (amended by SI 2014/42).
8 Education Act 2002 s 116D(2)(a) (as added: see note 6).
9 Education Act 2002 s 116D(2)(b) (as added: see note 6).
10 Education Act 2002 s 116D(2)(c) (as added: see note 6).
11 Ie under the Education Act 2002 s 116D(1): see the text to notes 1–7.
12 Education Act 2002 s 116E(1)(a) (s 116E added by the Learning and Skills (Wales)
   Measure 2009 s 8).
13 As to the meaning of 'head teacher' see PARA 86 note 4 (definition applied by the Education
   Act 2002 s 212(2), (3)).
14 Ie under the Education Act 2002 s 116F: see PARA 889.
15 Education Act 2002 s 116E(1)(b) (as added: see note 12).
16 See the Education Act 2002 s 116E(2) (as added: see note 12).
17 As to the governing bodies of maintained schools in Wales see PARA 195.
18 See the Education Act 2002 s 116G (added by the Learning and Skills (Wales) Measure 2009
   s 10).

889. Local curriculum: head teacher's decision as to entitlement. If the head
teacher[1] of a pupil's[2] school is satisfied that any of the following grounds apply,
the head teacher may decide that the pupil is not entitled to follow a course of
study[3] which the pupil has elected[4] to follow[5]. The grounds are that[6]:
(1) as a result of the pupil's level of educational attainment, the course of
      study is not suitable for him or her[7];
(2) as a result of other elections made by the pupil[8], it is not reasonably
      practicable for him or her to follow the course of study[9];
(3) the amount of time likely to be spent travelling to the place at which the
      course of study is likely to be delivered would be detrimental to the
      pupil's education[10];
(4) disproportionate expenditure would be incurred if the pupil were to
      follow the course of study[11];
(5) the pupil's or another person's health or safety would be placed
      unacceptably at risk if the pupil were to follow the course of study[12].
Regulations[13] may make provision connected with the making of such
decisions, including in particular provision: (a) as to the time or date by which
decisions are to be made[14]; (b) as to the procedure to be followed in connection
with the making of decisions[15]; (c) for appeals against decisions to be made to
the governing body[16] of a pupil's school or another person[17] specified in the
regulations[18]; (d) as to the time or date by which appeals are to be determined[19];
(e) as to the procedure to be followed in connection with the determination of an
appeal[20]. A head teacher and governing body or other person charged with

determining appeals under such regulations must have regard to any guidance[21] given from time to time by the Welsh Ministers as to the exercise of their functions[22] under these provisions[23].

1   As to the meaning of 'head teacher' see PARA 86 note 4 (definition applied by the Education Act 2002 s 212(2), (3)).
2   As to the meaning of 'pupil' see PARA 870 note 11. As to the application of the Education Act 2002 ss 116A–116K to other children see PARAS 893, 894.
3   As to the meaning of 'course of study' see PARA 885 note 5.
4   Ie under the Education Act 2002 s 116D(1): see PARA 888.
5   Education Act 2002 s 116F(1) (s 116F added by the Learning and Skills (Wales) Measure 2009 s 9).
6   The Welsh Ministers may by order: (1) amend or omit any paragraph of the Education Act 2002 s 116F(2); (2) add additional paragraphs to that subsection; (3) amend or omit such additional paragraphs: s 116F(5) (as added: see note 5). At the date at which this volume states the law no such order had been made.
7   Education Act 2002 s 116F(2)(a) (as added: see note 5).
8   Ie under the Education Act 2002 s 116D(1): see PARA 888.
9   Education Act 2002 s 116F(2)(b) (as added: see note 5).
10 Education Act 2002 s 116F(2)(c) (as added: see note 5).
11 Education Act 2002 s 116F(2)(d) (as added: see note 5).
12 Education Act 2002 s 116F(2)(e) (as added: see note 5).
13 'Regulations' means regulations made by the Welsh Ministers: Education Act 2002 s 97 (definition added by the Learning and Skills (Wales) Measure 2009 s 1(1), (5)). As to the Welsh Ministers see PARA 59. As to the regulations made see the Education (Local Curriculum for Pupils in Key Stage 4) (Wales) Regulations 2009, SI 2009/3256 (amended by SI 2014/42).
14 Education Act 2002 s 116F(3)(a) (as added: see note 5).
15 Education Act 2002 s 116F(3)(b) (as added: see note 5).
16 As to the governing bodies of maintained schools in Wales see PARA 195.
17 As to the meaning of 'person' see PARA 7 note 6.
18 Education Act 2002 s 116F(3)(c) (as added: see note 5).
19 Education Act 2002 s 116F(3)(d) (as added: see note 5).
20 Education Act 2002 s 116F(3)(e) (as added: see note 5).
21 As to the publication of guidance see the Education Act 1996 s 571 (applied by the Education Act 2002 s 212(2), (3)); and PARA 60.
22 Ie their functions under the Education Act 2002 s 116F. As to the meaning of 'functions' see PARA 18 note 5 (definition applied by s 212(2), (3)).
23 Education Act 2002 s 116F(4) (as added: see note 5).

890. Local curriculum: head teacher's decision to remove entitlement. If the head teacher[1] of a pupil's[2] school is satisfied that any of the following grounds apply, the head teacher may decide that a pupil is no longer entitled to follow a course of study[3] that the pupil was entitled[4] to follow[5]. The grounds are that[6]:

(1)   the pupil's or another person's health or safety would be placed unacceptably at risk if the pupil were to continue to follow the course of study[7];

(2)   disproportionate expenditure would be incurred if the pupil were to continue to follow the course of study[8].

Regulations[9] may make provision connected with the making of such decisions including in particular provision: (a) as to the procedure to be followed in connection with the making of decisions[10]; (b) for appeals against decisions to be made to the governing body[11] of a pupil's school or another person[12] specified in the regulations[13]; (c) as to the effect of a decision pending determination of an appeal[14]; (d) as to the procedure to be followed in connection with the determination of an appeal[15]. A head teacher and governing body or other person charged with determining appeals under such regulations must have regard to any guidance[16] given from time to time by the Welsh Ministers as to the exercise of their functions[17] under these provisions[18].

1   As to the meaning of 'head teacher' see PARA 86 note 4 (definition applied by the Education Act 2002 s 212(2), (3)).
2   As to the meaning of 'pupil' see PARA 870 note 11. As to the application of the Education Act 2002 ss 116A–116K to other children see PARAS 893, 894.
3   As to the meaning of 'course of study' see PARA 885 note 5.
4   Ie under the Education Act 2002 s 116E: see PARA 888.
5   Education Act 2002 s 116H(1) (s 116H added by the Learning and Skills (Wales) Measure 2009 s 11).
6   The Welsh Ministers may by order: (1) amend or omit any paragraph of the Education Act 2002 s 116H(2); (2) add additional paragraphs to that subsection; (3) amend or omit such additional paragraphs: s 116H(5) (as added: see note 5). As to the Welsh Ministers see PARA 59. At the date at which this volume states the law no such order had been made.
7   Education Act 2002 s 116H(2)(a) (as added: see note 5).
8   Education Act 2002 s 116H(2)(b) (as added: see note 5).
9   'Regulations' means regulations made by the Welsh Ministers: Education Act 2002 s 97 (definition added by the Learning and Skills (Wales) Measure 2009 s 1(1), (5)). As to the regulations made see the Education (Local Curriculum for Pupils in Key Stage 4) (Wales) Regulations 2009, SI 2009/3256 (amended by SI 2014/42).
10 Education Act 2002 s 116H(3)(a) (as added: see note 5).
11 As to the governing bodies of maintained schools in Wales see PARA 195.
12 As to the meaning of 'person' see PARA 7 note 6.
13 Education Act 2002 s 116H(3)(b) (as added: see note 5).
14 Education Act 2002 s 116H(3)(c) (as added: see note 5).
15 Education Act 2002 s 116H(3)(d) (as added: see note 5).
16 As to the publication of guidance see the Education Act 1996 s 571 (applied by the Education Act 2002 s 212(2), (3)); and PARA 60.
17 Ie under the Education Act 2002 s 116H. As to the meaning of 'functions' see PARA 18 note 5 (definition applied by s 212(2), (3)).
18 Education Act 2002 s 116H(4) (as added: see note 5).

891. Planning the local curriculum. The governing body[1] and head teacher[2] of any maintained secondary school[3] maintained by the local authority[4], and the governing body and principal or other head of an institution within the further education sector[5] in the authority's area[6], must assist that local authority in planning the local curriculum or curricula[7] for its area[8].

The relevant persons[9] must have regard to any guidance[10] given from time to time by the Welsh Ministers[11] as to the exercise of their functions[12]. The relevant persons[13] must also comply with any direction given by the Welsh Ministers as to the exercise of their functions[14].

1   As to the governing bodies of maintained schools in Wales see PARA 195.
2   As to the meaning of 'head teacher' see PARA 86 note 4 (definition applied by the Education Act 2002 s 212(2), (3)).
3   As to the meaning of 'maintained secondary school' see PARA 885 note 25.
4   Education Act 2002 s 116I(1)(a) (s 116I added by the Learning and Skills (Wales) Measure 2009 s 12; and the Education Act 2002 s 116I(1), (2) amended by SI 2010/1148). As to the meaning of 'local authority' see PARA 25 (definition applied by the Education Act 2002 s 212(1)).
5   As to the meaning of 'institution within the further education sector' see PARA 555.
6   Education Act 2002 s 116I(1)(b) (as added: see note 4).
7   'Planning the local curriculum or curricula' means the process by which a local authority decides under the Education Act 2002 s 116A (see PARA 885) which courses of study to include in the local curriculum or curricula for its area: s 116I(2) (as added and amended: see note 4). As to the meanings of 'local curriculum' and 'local curricula' see PARA 885 note 3. As to the meaning of 'course of study' see PARA 885 note 5.
8   Education Act 2002 s 116I(1) (as added and amended: see note 4).
9   Ie the persons mentioned in the Education Act 2002 s 16I(1)(a), (b). As to the meaning of 'person' see PARA 7 note 6.
10 As to the publication of guidance see the Education Act 1996 s 571 (applied by the Education Act 2002 s 212(2), (3)); and PARA 60.
11 As to the Welsh Ministers see PARA 59.

12 Education Act 2002 s 116I(3) (s 116I(3) substituted and s 116I(4) added by the Further and Higher Education (Governance and Information) (Wales) Act 2014 s 6(3)). The reference is to the exercise of functions under the Education Act 2002 s 116I(1): see the text to notes 1–8. As to the meaning of 'functions' see PARA 18 note 5 (definition applied by s 212(2), (3)).

13 Ie the persons mentioned in the Education Act 2002 s 16I(1)(a).

14 Education Act 2002 s 116I(4) (as added: see note 12). Any direction given by the Welsh Ministers under s 116I(4) may be varied or revoked by a further direction: see s 116O (added by the Learning and Skills (Wales) Measure 2009 s 18). The Education Act 2002 s 116O refers to any direction given under s 116I(3), but it is submitted that it should in fact refer to any direction given under s116I(4).

892. Delivery of local curriculum entitlements: joint working. In relation to the local curriculum or curricula[1] for the area of a local authority[2]:

(1)   the local authority[3];

(2)   the governing body[4] of a secondary school[5] maintained by the authority[6]; and

(3)   the governing body of an institution within the further education sector[7] which is situated within the area of the authority[8],

must take all reasonable steps in order to achieve the objective[9] of maximising the availability of courses of study[10] included in a local curriculum formed[11] by the local authority[12]. This duty includes, but is not limited to, a duty to seek to enter into cooperation arrangements[13] where, having considered whether it would further that objective to do so, those persons have concluded that entering into such arrangements would further that objective[14].

A local authority, a governing body of a maintained secondary school and the governing body of an institution within the further education sector in Wales must have regard to any guidance given from time to time by the Welsh Ministers[15] as to the discharge of their duties[16] under the above provisions[17]. A local authority and a governing body of a maintained secondary school must comply with any direction given by the Welsh Ministers as to the entering into of co-operation arrangements[18].

1   As to the meanings of 'local curriculum' and 'local curricula' see PARA 885 note 3. As to the formation of local curricula see PARA 885.

2   As to the meaning of 'local authority' see PARA 25 (definition applied by the Education Act 2002 s 212(1)).

3   Education Act 2002 s 116J(4)(a) (s 116J added by the Learning and Skills (Wales) Measure 2009 s 13; and the Education Act 2002 s 116J(2), (4), (6) amended by SI 2010/1148).

4   As to the governing bodies of maintained schools in Wales see PARA 195. As to the meaning of 'Wales' see PARA 7 note 3.

5   As to the meaning of 'secondary school' see PARA 91 (definition applied by the Education Act 2002 s 212(2), (3)).

6   Education Act 2002 s 116J(4)(b) (as added: see note 3).

7   As to the meaning of 'institution within the further education sector' see PARA 555.

8   Education Act 2002 s 116J(4)(c) (as added: see note 3).

9   See the Education Act 2002 s 116J(2) (as added and amended: see note 3).

10   As to the meaning of 'course of study' see PARA 885 note 5.

11   Ie under the Education Act 2002 s 116A: see PARA 885.

12   See the Education Act 2002 s 116J(1) (as added: see note 3).

13   'Co-operation arrangements' means: (1) arrangements under which any person provides, on behalf of the governing body of a maintained secondary school, a course of study included within the relevant local curriculum for the school (Education Act 2002 s 116J(5)(a) (as added: see note 3)); (2) arrangements made in exercise of the powers of collaboration described in the Education (Wales) Measure 2011 s 4 (see PARA 199) (Education Act 2002 s 116J(5)(aa) (s 116J(5)(aa) added and s 116J(5)(b), (c) repealed by the Education (Wales) Measure 2011 s 9(3)(b)). As to the meaning of 'person' see PARA 7 note 6. As to the meaning of 'maintained secondary school' see PARA 885 note 25. In relation to a maintained secondary school, 'relevant local curriculum' means: (a) where the local authority by which the school is maintained has

formed a single local curriculum for its area, that curriculum (Education Act 2002 s 116J(6)(a) (as added and amended: see note 3)); or (b) where the local authority by which the school is maintained has formed more than one local curriculum for its area, the curriculum in respect of which the school is designated under s 116C(2) (see PARA 885) (s 116J(6)(b) (as so added and amended)).

14 See the Education Act 2002 s 116J(3) (as added: see note 3).
15 As to the Welsh Ministers see PARA 59.
16 Ie under the Education Act 2002 s 116J: see the text to notes 1–14.
17 See the Education Act 2002 s 116K(1) (s 116K added by the Learning and Skills (Wales) Measure 2009 s 14; and the Education Act 2002 s 116K(1) amended by SI 2010/1148). Guidance given under the Education Act 2002 s 116K(1) may relate to the content of co-operation arrangements: s 116K(2) (as so added). As to the publication of guidance see the Education Act 1996 s 571 (applied by the Education Act 2002 s 212(2), (3)); and PARA 60.
18 See the Education Act 2002 s 116K(3) (as added (see note 17); and amended by the Further and Higher Education (Governance and Information) (Wales) Act 2014 s 6(4)). A direction: (1) may require persons to enter into specified arrangements (Education Act 2002 s 116K(4)(a) (as so added)); (2) may specify the terms upon which arrangements are to be entered into (whether generally or in respect of specified arrangements) (s 116K(4)(b) (as so added)); (3) in the case of a direction to enter into specified arrangements with a person who is not mentioned in s 116K(1) (see the text to notes 15–17), must not be given unless that person consents to the direction (s 116K(4)(c) (as so added)). Any direction given by the Welsh Ministers under s 116K(3) may be varied or revoked by a further direction: see s 116O (added by the Learning and Skills (Wales) Measure 2009, s 18).

893. Application of local curriculum provisions to children who are not registered pupils. Regulations[1] may apply the provisions relating to local curricula[2], and the provisions of any regulations in connection with the operation of local curricula[3], in respect of a person[4] who is of compulsory school age[5], is not a registered pupil[6] of a maintained school[7], and receives all, or the majority of, his or her education at, or under arrangements made by the governing body of, an institution within the further education sector[8] in Wales[9]. The regulations may apply those provisions with such modifications[10] as appear to the Welsh Ministers to be necessary or expedient[11].

1 'Regulations' means regulations made by the Welsh Ministers: Education Act 2002 s 97 (definition added by the Learning and Skills (Wales) Measure 2009 s 1(1), (5)). As to the Welsh Ministers see PARA 59. At the date at which this volume states the law no such regulations had been made.
2 Ie the provisions of the Education Act 2002 ss 116A–116K: see PARAS 885–892.
3 Ie regulations made under the Learning and Skills (Wales) Measure 2009 s 46: see PARA 903.
4 See the Education Act 2002 s 116M(1) (s 116M added by the Learning and Skills (Wales) Measure 2009 s 16).
5 Education Act 2002 s 116M(3)(a) (as added: see note 4). As to the meaning of 'compulsory school age' see PARA 19.
6 As to the meaning of 'registered pupil' see PARA 437 (definition applied by the Education Act 2002 s 212(2), (3)). As to the meaning of 'pupil' see PARA 870 note 11.
7 Education Act 2002 s 116M(3)(b) (as added: see note 4). As to the meaning of 'maintained school' see PARA 870 note 4.
8 As to the meaning of 'institution within the further education sector' see PARA 555.
9 Education Act 2002 s 116M(3)(c) (as added: see note 4). As to the meaning of 'Wales' see PARA 7 note 3.
10 As to the meaning of 'modifications' see PARA 21 note 15 (definition applied by the Education Act 2002 s 212(2), (3)).
11 Education Act 2002 s 116M(2) (as added: see note 4).

894. Application of local curriculum provisions to children who are registered pupils of special schools. Regulations[1] may apply the provisions relating to local curricula[2], and the provisions of any regulations in connection with the operation of local curricula[3], in respect of a person[4] who is of compulsory school age[5] and is a registered pupil[6] of a community special school[7] which is maintained by a local authority[8] in Wales[9] and is not established in a hospital[10]. The regulations may apply those provisions with such modifications[11] as appear to the Welsh Ministers to be necessary or expedient[12].

1 'Regulations' means regulations made by the Welsh Ministers: Education Act 2002 s 97 (definition added by the Learning and Skills (Wales) Measure 2009 s 1(1), (5)). As to the Welsh Ministers see PARA 59. At the date at which this volume states the law no such regulations had been made.
2 Ie the provisions of the Education Act 2002 ss 116A–116K: see PARAS 885–892.
3 Ie regulations made under the Learning and Skills (Wales) Measure 2009 s 46: see PARA 1102.
4 See the Education Act 2002 s 116N(1) (s 116N added by the Learning and Skills (Wales) Measure 2009 s 17).
5 Education Act 2002 s 116N(3)(a) (as added: see note 4).
6 As to the meaning of 'registered pupil' see PARA 437 (definition applied by the Education Act 2002 s 212(2), (3)). As to the meaning of 'pupil' see PARA 870 note 11.
7 As to the meaning of references to a community special school see PARA 106.
8 As to the meaning of 'local authority' see PARA 25 (definition applied by the Education Act 2002 s 212(2), (3)).
9 As to the meaning of 'Wales' see PARA 7 note 3.
10 Education Act 2002 s 116N(3)(b) (as added (see note 4); and amended by the School Standards and Organisation (Wales) Act 2013 Sch 5 para 21(1), (6)).
11 As to the meaning of 'modifications' see PARA 21 note 15 (definition applied by the Education Act 2002 s 212(2), (3)).
12 Education Act 2002 s 116N(2) (as added: see note 4).

(B) Local Curriculum for Students Aged 16 to 18

895. Formation of local curricula for students aged 16 to 18. The Welsh Ministers[1] must form for the area of each local authority in Wales[2] one or more local curricula[3] for students[4] who are above compulsory school age[5] but have not attained the age of 19[6]. Each local curriculum must consist of courses of study[7] each of which falls within a category of the learning domains[8], and is from time to time selected by the Welsh Ministers to form part of that local curriculum[9]. The 'learning domains' are[10]: (1) mathematics, science and technology[11]; (2) business, administration and law[12]; (3) services for people[13]; (4) arts, media, culture and languages[14]; (5) humanities, social sciences and preparation for life and work[15].

Where the Welsh Ministers form more than one local curriculum for the area of a local authority[16], in relation to each local curriculum, the Welsh Ministers must designate the maintained schools[17] or institutions[18] whose relevant students[19] are to be entitled to elect[20] to follow courses of study included within the curriculum[21].

The Welsh Ministers must exercise their functions[22] in relation to local curricula so as to promote access to and availability of courses of study which are taught through the medium of the Welsh language[23].

1 As to the Welsh Ministers see PARA 59.
2 As to the meaning of 'local authority' see PARA 25 (definition applied by the Learning and Skills Act 2000 s 33N(1), (2) (s 33N added by the Learning and Skills (Wales) Measure 2009 s 35; and the Learning and Skills Act 2000 s 33N(1) definition amended by SI 2010/1148)). As to the meaning of 'Wales' see PARA 7 note 3.
3 'Local curriculum' and 'local curricula' are to be construed in accordance with the Learning and Skills Act 2000 s 33A: s 33N(1) (as added: see note 2).
4 As to the meaning of 'student' see PARA 896 note 5.
5 As to the meaning of 'compulsory school age' see PARA 19.
6 Learning and Skills Act 2000 s 33A(1) (s 33A added by the Learning and Skills (Wales) Measure 2009 s 22). As to the time at which a person attains a particular age see PARA 7 note 6. As to the application of the Learning and Skills Act 2000 ss 33A–33L to other students and institutions see PARAS 901, 902.

7   'Course of study' means a course of education and training which leads to a qualification or set of qualifications approved under the Learning and Skills Act 2000 s 99 (see PARA 937) for the purposes of s 96: s 33N(1) (as added: see note 2).

8   Learning and Skills Act 2000 s 33A(2)(a) (as added: see note 6). A course of study falls within a particular learning domain if a direction of the Welsh Ministers so provides: s 33A(4) (as so added). Any such direction given by the Welsh Ministers may be varied or revoked by a further direction: see s 33O (added by the Learning and Skills (Wales) Measure 2009 s 36).

9   Learning and Skills Act 2000 s 33A(2)(b) (as added: see note 6).

10 The Welsh Ministers may by order: (1) amend or omit any paragraph of the Learning and Skills Act 2000 s 33A(3); (2) add additional paragraphs to that subsection; (3) amend or omit such additional paragraphs: s 33M (added by the Learning and Skills (Wales) Measure 2009 s 34). At the date at which this volume states the law no such order had been made.

11 Learning and Skills Act 2000 s 33A(3)(a) (as added: see note 6).

12 Learning and Skills Act 2000 s 33A(3)(b) (as added: see note 6).

13 Learning and Skills Act 2000 s 33A(3)(c) (as added: see note 6).

14 Learning and Skills Act 2000 s 33A(3)(d) (as added: see note 6).

15 Learning and Skills Act 2000 s 33A(3)(e) (as added: see note 6).

16 Learning and Skills Act 2000 s 33C(1) (added by the Learning and Skills (Wales) Measure 2009 s 24).

17 'Maintained school' means a community, foundation or voluntary school maintained by a local authority in Wales provided that it is also a secondary school: Learning and Skills Act 2000 s 33N(1) (as added: see note 2). As to community, foundation or voluntary schools see PARA 106. As to the meaning of 'secondary school' see PARA 91 (definition applied by s 33N(2) (as so added)).

18 'Institution' means an institution within the further education sector in Wales unless the institution provides education wholly or mainly for persons with a learning difficulty (within the meaning of the Learning and Skills Act 2000 s 41: see PARA 791): s 33N(1) (as added: see note 2). As to the meaning of 'institution within the further education sector' see PARA 729.

19 As to the meaning of 'relevant student' see PARA 896 note 5.

20 Ie under the Learning and Skills Act 2000 s 33E: see PARA 896.

21 Learning and Skills Act 2000 s 33C(2) (as added: see note 16).

22 As to the meaning of 'functions' see PARA 18 note 5 (definition applied by the Learning and Skills Act 2000 s 33N(2) (as added: see note 2)).

23 Learning and Skills Act 2000 s 33B (added by the Learning and Skills (Wales) Measure 2009 s 23).

896. Pupils' choices of local curriculum courses. Where, during the fourth key stage[1], a registered pupil[2] of a maintained school[3] requests that the school's head teacher[4] determines the pupil's relevant school or institution[5], the head teacher must comply with that request[6]. A pupil's 'relevant school or institution' is the maintained school or institution whose governing body[7] is, in the opinion of the head teacher, likely to be responsible for providing (or making arrangements for the provision of) the majority of the pupil's education once he or she has ceased to be of compulsory school age[8]. These provisions[9] do not require any person[10] to admit a pupil to a particular school or institution[11].

A registered pupil of a maintained school has the right to elect to follow, during the entitlement period, a course or courses of study[12] included within the relevant local curriculum[13] for that pupil[14]. The 'entitlement period' begins on the first day of the academic year[15] subsequent to the pupil having ceased to be of compulsory school age[16] and ends on the day on which he or she attains the age of 19[17]. Regulations[18] may make provision as to the making of such elections, including in particular provision: (1) specifying the maximum number of courses of study of a particular type that a pupil has the right to elect to follow[19]; (2) identifying points to be allotted to courses of study and preventing a pupil from having the right to elect to follow a combination of courses of study if their aggregate points exceed a specified amount[20]; (3) as to the period during which elections are to be made[21].

1   'Fourth key stage' is to be construed in accordance with the Education Act 2002 s 103 (see PARA 875): Learning and Skills Act 2000 s 33N(1) (s 33N added by the Learning and Skills (Wales) Measure 2009 s 35).

2   As to the meaning of 'registered pupil' see PARA 437 (definition applied by the Learning and Skills Act 2000 s 33N(2) (as added: see note 1)).

3   As to the meaning of 'maintained school' see PARA 895 note 17. As to the application of the Learning and Skills Act 2000 ss 33A–33L to other students and institutions see PARAS 901, 902.

4   As to the meaning of 'head teacher' see PARA 86 note 4 (definition applied by the Learning and Skills Act 2000 s 33N(2) (as added: see note 1)).

5   'Relevant school or institution', in relation to a person, is to be construed in accordance with the Learning and Skills Act 2000 s 33D: s 33N(1) (as added: see note 1). 'Relevant student', in relation to a maintained school or institution, means a student for whom the school or institution is his or her relevant school or institution: s 33N(1) (as so added). 'Student' means a person who has made an election under s 33E (see the text to notes 12–21): s 33N(1) (as so added). As to the meaning of 'institution' see PARA 895 note 18.

6   Learning and Skills Act 2000 s 33D(1) (s 33D added by the Learning and Skills (Wales) Measure 2009 s 25). But this is subject to regulations made under the Learning and Skills Act 2000 s 33D(3): s 33D(1) (as so added). Regulations may make provision as to the making of requests and determinations under s 33D, including in particular provision as to the date or time by which a request or determination is to be made: s 33D(3) (as so added). 'Regulations' means regulations made by the Welsh Ministers: s 33N(1) (as added: see note 1). As to the Welsh Ministers see PARA 59. As to the regulations made see the Education (Local Curriculum for Students Aged 16 to 18) (Wales) Regulations 2011, SI 2011/107.

7   As to the governing bodies of maintained schools in Wales see PARA 195.

8   Learning and Skills Act 2000 s 33D(2) (as added: see note 6). As to the meaning of 'compulsory school age' see PARA 19.

9   Ie the Learning and Skills Act 2000 s 33D: see the text to notes 1–8.

10 As to the meaning of 'person' see PARA 7 note 6.

11 Learning and Skills Act 2000 s 33D(4) (as added: see note 6).

12 As to the meaning of 'course of study' see PARA 895 note 7.

13 The 'relevant local curriculum', in relation to a pupil, means:

    (1)   where it has been determined under the Learning and Skills Act 2000 s 33D (see the text to notes 1–11) that a pupil's relevant school or institution is a school where the Welsh Ministers have formed under s 33A (see PARA 895) a single local curriculum for the area of the local authority by which the school is maintained, that local curriculum (s 33E(4)(a)(i) (s 33E added by the Learning and Skills (Wales) Measure 2009 s 26)); or where the Welsh Ministers have formed under the Learning and Skills Act 2000 s 33A more than one local curriculum for the area of the local authority by which the school is maintained, the local curriculum in respect of which the school is designated under s 33C(2) (see PARA 895) (s 33E(4)(a)(ii) (as so added));

    (2)   where it has been determined under s 33D that a pupil's relevant school or institution is an institution where the Welsh Ministers have formed under s 33A a single local curriculum for the local authority area in which the institution is situated, that local curriculum (s 33E(4)(b)(i) (as so added)); or where the Welsh Ministers have formed under s 33A more than one local curriculum for the local authority area in which the institution is situated, the local curriculum in respect of which the institution is designated under s 33C(2) (s 33E(4)(b)(ii) (as so added)).

As to the meanings of 'local curriculum' and 'local curricula' see PARA 895 note 3. As to the meaning of 'local authority' see PARA 25 (definition applied by s 33N(2) (as added: see note 1)).

14 Learning and Skills Act 2000 s 33E(1) (as added: see note 13). As to students' curriculum entitlements see further PARA 897.

15 'Academic year' means the period beginning on the fourth Monday of September in any year and ending on the first day of September in the following year: Learning and Skills Act 2000 s 33N(1) (as added (see note 1); and definition substituted by the Education (Wales) Measure 2009 s 22(1), (3)). As to the meaning of 'month' see PARA 54 note 26.

16 Learning and Skills Act 2000 s 33E(2)(a) (as added: see note 13).

17 Learning and Skills Act 2000 s 33E(2)(b) (as added: see note 3).

18 As to the regulations made see the Education (Local Curriculum for Students Aged 16 to 18) (Wales) Regulations 2011, SI 2011/107.

19 Learning and Skills Act 2000 s 33E(3)(a) (as added: see note 13).

20 Learning and Skills Act 2000 s 33E(3)(b) (as added: see note 13).

21 Learning and Skills Act 2000 s 33E(3)(c) (as added: see note 13).

897. Students' local curriculum entitlements. During the entitlement period[1], a student[2] who has made an election of local curriculum courses[3] is entitled to follow the elected course of study[4] unless:

(1) the governing body[5] of the student's relevant school or institution[6] was not at the beginning of the entitlement period, or subsequently ceases to be, responsible for providing (or making arrangements for the provision of) the majority of the student's education[7]; or

(2) before the beginning of the entitlement period, the head teacher[8] or principal[9] of the student's relevant school or institution has decided[10] that the student is not entitled to follow the course of study[11].

Where a person is entitled to follow a course of study, it is for the head teacher or principal of the relevant school or institution to decide upon which date during the entitlement period the course is to begin[12].

If the head teacher or principal of a student's relevant school or institution is satisfied that any of the following grounds apply, the head teacher or principal may decide that the student is not entitled to follow a course of study which the student has elected[13] to follow[14]. The grounds are that[15]:

(a) as a result of the student's level of educational attainment, the course of study is not suitable for him or her[16];

(b) as a result of other elections made by the student[17], it is not reasonably practicable for him or her to follow the course of study[18];

(c) the amount of time likely to be spent travelling to the place at which the course is likely to be delivered would be detrimental to the student's education[19];

(d) disproportionate expenditure would be incurred if the student were to follow the course of study[20];

(e) the student's or another person's health or safety would be placed unacceptably at risk if the student were to follow the course of study[21].

Regulations[22] may make provision connected with the making of such decisions, including in particular provision: (i) as to the time or date by which decisions are to be made[23]; (ii) as to the procedure to be followed in connection with the making of decisions[24]; (iii) for appeals against decisions to be made to the school or institution's governing body or another person[25] specified in the regulations[26]; (iv) as to the time or date by which appeals are to be determined[27]; (v) as to the procedure to be followed in connection with the determination of an appeal[28]. A head teacher or principal and governing body or other person charged with determining appeals under such regulations must have regard to any guidance given from time to time by the Welsh Ministers as to the exercise of their functions[29] under these provisions[30].

Where a student is entitled to follow a course of study[31], the governing body of the student's relevant school or institution must ensure that during the entitlement period the course is made available to the student by or on behalf of the governing body[32].

1 As to the meaning of 'entitlement period' see PARA 896.
2 As to the meaning of 'student' see PARA 896 note 5.
3 Ie under the Learning and Skills Act 2000 s 33E(1): see PARA 896. As to the meanings of 'local curriculum' and 'local curricula' see PARA 895 note 3. As to the formation of local curricula see PARA 895.
4 As to the meaning of 'course of study' see PARA 895 note 7.
5 As to the governing bodies of maintained schools in Wales see PARA 226 et seq.
6 As to the meaning of 'relevant school or institution' see PARA 896 note 5.

7   Learning and Skills Act 2000 s 33F(1)(a) (s 33F added by the Learning and Skills (Wales) Measure 2009 s 27; and the Learning and Skills Act 2000 s 33F(1)(a) amended by the Education (Wales) Measure 2009 s 22(1), (2)). As to the application of the Learning and Skills Act 2000 ss 33A–33L to other students and institutions see PARAS 901, 902.

8   As to the meaning of 'head teacher' see PARA 86 note 4 (definition applied by the Learning and Skills Act 2000 s 33N(2) (s 33N added by the Learning and Skills (Wales) Measure 2009 s 35)).

9   'Principal', in relation to an institution, means the principal or other head of the institution: Learning and Skills Act 2000 s 33N(1) (as added: see note 8). As to the meaning of 'institution' see PARA 895 note 18.

10 Ie under the Learning and Skills Act 2000 s 33G: see the text to notes 13–30.

11 Learning and Skills Act 2000 s 33F(1)(b) (as added: see note 7).

12 Learning and Skills Act 2000 s 33F(2) (as added: see note 7).

13 Ie under the Learning and Skills Act 2000 s 33E: see PARA 896.

14 Learning and Skills Act 2000 s 33G(1) (s 33G added by the Learning and Skills (Wales) Measure 2009 s 28).

15 The Welsh Ministers may by order: (1) amend or omit any paragraph of the Learning and Skills Act 2000 s 33G(2); (2) add additional paragraphs to that subsection; (3) amend or omit such additional paragraphs: s 33G(5) (as added: see note 14). As to the Welsh Ministers see PARA 59. At the date at which this volume states the law no such order had been made.

16 Learning and Skills Act 2000 s 33G(2)(a) (as added: see note 14).

17 Ie under the Learning and Skills Act 2000 s 33E(1): see PARA 896.

18 Learning and Skills Act 2000 s 33G(2)(b) (as added: see note 14).

19 Learning and Skills Act 2000 s 33G(2)(c) (as added: see note 14).

20 Learning and Skills Act 2000 s 33G(2)(d) (as added: see note 14).

21 Learning and Skills Act 2000 s 33G(2)(e) (as added: see note 14).

22 'Regulations' means regulations made by the Welsh Ministers: Learning and Skills Act 2000 s 33N(1) (as added: see note 8). As to the regulations made see the Education (Local Curriculum for Students Aged 16 to 18) (Wales) Regulations 2011, SI 2011/107.

23 Learning and Skills Act 2000 s 33G(3)(a) (as added: see note 14).

24 Learning and Skills Act 2000 s 33G(3)(b) (as added: see note 14).

25 As to the meaning of 'person' see PARA 7 note 6.

26 Learning and Skills Act 2000 s 33G(3)(c) (as added: see note 14).

27 Learning and Skills Act 2000 s 33G(3)(d) (as added: see note 14).

28 Learning and Skills Act 2000 s 33G(3)(e) (as added: see note 1).

29 Ie their functions under the Learning and Skills Act 2000 s 33G. As to the meaning of 'functions' see PARA 18 note 5 (definition applied by the Learning and Skills Act 2000 s 33N(2) (as added: see note 8)).

30 Learning and Skills Act 2000 s 33G(4) (as added: see note 14).

31 Ie under the Learning and Skills Act 2000 s 33F(1): see the text to notes 1–11.

32 Learning and Skills Act 2000 s 33H (added by the Learning and Skills (Wales) Measure 2009 s 29). As to the removal of entitlement see the Learning and Skills Act 2000 s 33I; and PARA 898.

898.   Head teacher's or principal's decision to remove entitlement. If the head teacher[1] or principal[2] of a student's[3] relevant school or institution[4] is satisfied that any of the following grounds apply, the head teacher or principal may decide that a student is no longer entitled to follow a course of study[5] that the student was entitled[6] to follow[7]. The grounds are that[8]:

(1)   the student's or another person's health or safety would be placed unacceptably at risk if the pupil were to continue to follow the course of study[9];

(2)   disproportionate expenditure would be incurred if the pupil were to continue to follow the course of study[10].

Regulations[11] may make provision connected with the making of such decisions including in particular provision: (a) as to the procedure to be followed in connection with the making of decisions[12]; (b) for appeals against decisions to be made to the school or institution's governing body[13] or another person[14] specified in the regulations[15]; (c) as to the effect of a decision pending determination of an appeal[16]; (d) as to the procedure to be followed in connection with the determination of an appeal[17]. A head teacher or principal and governing body or other person charged with determining appeals under such regulations must have regard to any guidance given from time to time by the Welsh Ministers as to the exercise of their functions[18] under these provisions[19].

1   As to the meaning of 'head teacher' see PARA 44 note 6 (definition applied by the Learning and Skills Act 2000 s 33N(2) (s 33N added by the Learning and Skills (Wales) Measure 2009 s 35)).
2   As to the meaning of 'principal' see PARA 897 note 9.
3   As to the meaning of 'student' see PARA 896 note 5.
4   As to the meaning of 'relevant school or institution' see PARA 896 note 5.
5   As to the meaning of 'course of study' see PARA 895 note 7.
6   Ie under the Learning and Skills Act 2000 s 33F: see PARA 897.
7   Learning and Skills Act 2000 s 33I(1) (s 33I added by the Learning and Skills (Wales) Measure 2009 s 30). As to the application of the Learning and Skills Act 2000 ss 33A–33L to other students and institutions see PARAS 901, 902.
8   The Welsh Ministers may by order: (1) amend or omit any paragraph of the Learning and Skills Act 2000 s 33I(2); (2) add additional paragraphs to that subsection; (3) amend or omit such additional paragraphs: s 33I(5) (as added: see note 7). As to the Welsh Ministers see PARA 59. At the date at which this volume states the law no such order had been made.
9   Learning and Skills Act 2000 s 33I(2)(a) (as added: see note 7).
10 Learning and Skills Act 2000 s 33I(2)(b) (as added: see note 7).
11 'Regulations' means regulations made by the Welsh Ministers: Learning and Skills Act 2000 s 33N(1) (as added: see note 1). As to the regulations made see the Education (Local Curriculum for Students Aged 16 to 18) (Wales) Regulations 2011, SI 2011/107.
12 Learning and Skills Act 2000 s 33I(3)(a) (as added: see note 7).
13 As to the governing bodies of maintained schools in Wales see PARA 195.
14 As to the meaning of 'person' see PARA 7 note 6.
15 Learning and Skills Act 2000 s 33I(3)(b) (as added: see note 7).
16 Learning and Skills Act 2000 s 33I(3)(c) (as added: see note 7).
17 Learning and Skills Act 2000 s 33I(3)(d) (as added: see note 7).
18 Ie their functions under the Learning and Skills Act 2000 s 33I. As to the meaning of 'functions' see PARA 18 note 5 (definition applied by s 33N(2) (as added: see note 1)).
19 Learning and Skills Act 2000 s 33I(4) (as added: see note 7).

899. Planning the local curriculum. The local authority[1], the governing body[2] and head teacher[3] of any maintained school[4] maintained by the authority[5], and the governing body and principal[6] of an institution[7] in the authority's area[8], must assist the Welsh Ministers[9] in planning the local curriculum or curricula[10] for the local authority's area[11]. Those persons[12] must have regard to any guidance given from time to time[13], and comply with any directions given[14], by the Welsh Ministers as to the exercise of their functions[15] under these provisions[16].

1   Learning and Skills Act 2000 s 33J(1)(a) (s 33J added by the Learning and Skills (Wales) Measure 2009 s 31; Learning and Skills Act 2000 s 33J(1)(a) amended by SI 2010/1148). As to the meaning of 'local authority' see PARA 25 (definition applied by the Learning and Skills Act 2000 s 33N(1), (2) (s 33N added by the Learning and Skills (Wales) Measure 2009 s 35; Learning and Skills Act 2000 s 33N(1) definition amended by SI 2010/1148).
2   As to the governing bodies of maintained schools in Wales see PARA 195.
3   As to the meaning of 'head teacher' see PARA 86 note 4 (definition applied by the Learning and Skills Act 2000 s 33N(2) (as added: see note 1)).
4   As to the meaning of 'maintained school' see PARA 895 note 17.
5   Learning and Skills Act 2000 s 33J(1)(b) (as added: see note 1).
6   As to the meaning of 'principal' see PARA 897 note 9.
7   As to the meaning of 'institution' see PARA 895 note 18.
8   Learning and Skills Act 2000 s 33J(1)(c) (as added: see note 1).
9   As to the Welsh Ministers see PARA 59.
10 'Planning the local curriculum or curricula' means the process by which the Welsh Ministers decide under the Learning and Skills Act 2000 s 33A (see PARA 895) which courses of study to include in the local curriculum or curricula: s 33J(2) (as added: see note 1). As to the meaning of 'course of study' see PARA 895 note 7. As to the meanings of 'local curriculum' and 'local curricula' see PARA 895 note 3.

11 Learning and Skills Act 2000 s 33J(1) (as added (see note 1); and amended by SI 2010/1148).

12 As to the meaning of 'person' see PARA 7 note 6.

13 Learning and Skills Act 2000 s 33J(3)(a) (as added: see note 1).

14 Learning and Skills Act 2000 s 33J(3)(b) (as added: see note 1). Any such direction given by the Welsh Ministers may be varied or revoked by a further direction: see s 33O (added by the Learning and Skills (Wales) Measure 2009 s 36).

15 Ie their functions under the Learning and Skills Act 2000 s 33J(1): see the text to notes 1–11. As to the meaning of 'functions' see PARA 18 note 5 (definition applied by s 33N(2) (as added: see note 1)).

16 Learning and Skills Act 2000 s 33J(3) (as added: see note 1).

900. Delivery of local curriculum entitlements: joint working. In relation to the local curriculum or curricula[1] for a local authority[2], the local authority[3], the governing body[4] of a secondary school[5] maintained by the authority[6], and the governing body of an institution within the further education sector[7] which is situated within the area of the authority[8], must take all reasonable steps in order to achieve the objective[9] of maximising the availability of courses of study[10] included in a local curriculum formed[11] by the Welsh Ministers[12]. This duty includes, but is not limited to, a duty to seek to enter into cooperation arrangements[13] where, having considered whether it would further the objective to do so, those persons have concluded that entering into such arrangements would further that objective[14].

A local authority, a governing body of a maintained school and the governing body of an institution must have regard to any guidance given from time to time by the Welsh Ministers as to the discharge of their duties[15] under the above provisions[16]. Such guidance may relate to the contents of co-operation arrangements[17]. A local authority and a governing body of a maintained school must also comply with any direction given by the Welsh Ministers as to the entering into of co-operation arrangements[18]. Such a direction: (1) may require persons to enter into specified arrangements[19]; (2) may specify the terms upon which arrangements are to be entered into (whether generally or in respect of specified arrangements)[20]; (3) in the case of a direction to enter into specified arrangements with a person who is not mentioned above[21], must not be given unless that person consents to the direction[22].

1 As to the meanings of 'local curriculum' and 'local curricula' see PARA 895 note 3.

2 As to the meaning of 'local authority' see PARA 25 (definition applied by the Learning and Skills Act 2000 s 33N(1), (2) (s 33N added by the Learning and Skills (Wales) Measure 2009 s 35; and the Learning and Skills Act 2000 s 33N(1) definition amended by SI 2010/1148).

3 Learning and Skills Act 2000 s 33K(4)(a) (s 33K added by the Learning and Skills (Wales) Measure 2009 s 32; and the Learning and Skills Act 2000 s 33K(4)(a) amended by SI 2010/1148).

4 As to the governing bodies of maintained schools in Wales see PARA 195.

5 As to the meaning of 'secondary school' see PARA 91 (definition applied by the Learning and Skills Act 2000 s 33N(2) (as added: see note 2)).

6 Learning and Skills Act 2000 s 33K(4)(b) (as added: see note 3).

7 As to the meaning of 'institution within the further education sector' see PARA 555.

8 Learning and Skills Act 2000 s 33K(4)(c) (as added: see note 3).

9 See the Learning and Skills Act 2000 s 33K(2) (as added (see note 3); and amended by SI 2010/1148).

10 As to the meaning of 'course of study' see PARA 895 note 7.

11 Ie under the Learning and Skills Act 2000 s 33A: see PARA 895.

12 See the Learning and Skills Act 2000 s 33K(1) (as added: see note 3). As to the Welsh Ministers see PARA 59. As to the application of ss 33A–33L to other students and institutions see PARAS 901, 902.

13 'Co-operation arrangements' means: (1) arrangements under which any person provides, on behalf of the governing body of a maintained school, a course of study included within the relevant local curriculum for the school (Learning and Skills Act 2000 s 33K(5)(a) (as added: see

note 3)); (2) arrangements under which any person provides, on behalf of the governing body of an institution, a course of study included within the relevant local curriculum for the institution (s 33K(5)(b) (as so added)); (3) arrangements made in exercise of the powers of collaboration described in the Education (Wales) Measure 2011 s 4 (see PARA 199): Learning and Skills Act 2000 s 33K(5)(ba) (s 33K(5)(ba) added and s 33K(5)(c), (d) repealed by the Education (Wales) Measure 2011 s 9(2)). As to the meaning of 'person' see PARA 7 note 6. 'Relevant local curriculum' means: (a) in relation to a maintained school, where the Welsh Ministers have formed a single local curriculum for the area of the local authority by which the school is maintained, that local curriculum; or where the Welsh Ministers have formed more than one local curriculum for the area of the local authority by which the school is maintained, the local curriculum in respect of which the school is designated under the Learning and Skills Act 2000 s 33C(2) (see PARA 895) (s 33K(6)(a) (as so added)); (b) in relation to an institution, where the Welsh Ministers have formed a single local curriculum for the local authority area in which the institution is situated, that curriculum; or where the Welsh Ministers have formed more than one local curriculum for the local authority area in which the institution is situated, the local curriculum in respect of which the institution is designated under s 33C(2) (s 33K(6)(b) (as so added)). As to the meaning of 'institution' see PARA 895 note 18.

14 Learning and Skills Act 2000 s 33K(3) (as added: see note 3).
15 Ie their duties under the Learning and Skills Act 2000 s 33K: see the text to notes 1–14.
16 Learning and Skills Act 2000 s 33L(1) (s 33L added by the Learning and Skills (Wales) Measure 2009 s 33; and the Learning and Skills Act 2000 s 33L(1) amended by SI 2010/1148).
17 Learning and Skills Act 2000 s 33L(2) (as added: see note 16).
18 Learning and Skills Act 2000 s 33L(3) (as added (see note 16); and amended by the Further and Higher Education (Governance and Information) (Wales) Act 2014 s 6(2)). Any direction given by the Welsh Ministers under the Learning and Skills Act 2000 s 33L(3) may be varied or revoked by a further direction: see s 33O (added by the Learning and Skills (Wales) Measure 2009 s 36).
19 Learning and Skills Act 2000 s 33L(4)(a) (as added: see note 16).
20 Learning and Skills Act 2000 s 33L(4)(b) (as added: see note 16).
21 Ie in the Learning and Skills Act 2000 s 33L(1): see the text to notes 15–16.
22 Learning and Skills Act 2000 s 33L(4)(c) (as added: see note 16).

901. Application of local curriculum provisions to students who are registered pupils of special schools or who have learning difficulties. Regulations[1] may apply the provisions relating to local curricula for students aged 16 to 18[2] (with such modifications[3] as appear to the Welsh Ministers to be necessary or expedient[4]) in respect of a person who falls, or is likely to fall, within a specified category[5]. A person falls within a specified category if he or she[6]:

(1) is above compulsory school age[7]; and
(2) either (a) a registered pupil[8] of a community special school[9] which is maintained by a local authority[10] in Wales[11] and is not established in a hospital[12]; or (b) receiving the majority of his or her education at an institution[13] which provides education wholly or mainly for persons with a learning difficulty[14].

1 'Regulations' means regulations made by the Welsh Ministers: Learning and Skills Act 2000 s 33N(1) (s 33N added by the Learning and Skills (Wales) Measure 2009 s 35). As to the Welsh Ministers see PARA 59. At the date at which this volume states the law no such regulations had been made.
2 Ie the provisions of the Learning and Skills Act 2000 ss 33A–33L, s 33N and s 33O (see PARAS 895–900) and the provisions of any regulations made under the Learning and Skills (Wales) Measure 2009 s 46 (see PARA 903).
3 As to the meaning of 'modifications' see PARA 21 note 15 (definition applied by the Learning and Skills Act 2000 s 33N(2) (as added: see note 1)).
4 See the Learning and Skills Act 2000 s 33P(2) (s 33P added by the Learning and Skills (Wales) Measure 2009 s 37).
5 See the Learning and Skills Act 2000 s 33P(1) (as added: see note 4).
6 See the Learning and Skills Act 2000 s 33P(3) (as added: see note 4).
7 Learning and Skills Act 2000 s 33P(3)(a) (as added: see note 4). As to the meaning of 'compulsory school age' see PARA 19.

8 As to the meaning of 'registered pupil' see PARA 437 (definition applied by the Learning and Skills Act 2000 s 33N(2) (as added: see note 1)).
9 As to community special schools see PARA 106.
10 As to the meaning of 'local authority' see PARA 25 (definition applied by the Learning and Skills Act 2000 s 33N(1), (2) (s 33N as added (see note 1); s 33N(1) amended by SI 2010/1148)).
11 As to the meaning of 'Wales' see PARA 7 note 3.
12 Learning and Skills Act 2000 s 33P(3)(b)(i) (as added (see note 4); and amended by SI 2010/1148; and the School Standards and Organisation (Wales) Act 2013 Sch 5 para 20(1), (2)).
13 As to the meaning of 'institution' see PARA 895 note 18.
14 Learning and Skills Act 2000 s 33P(3)(b)(ii) (as added: see note 4). 'Learning difficulty' has the meaning given by s 41 (see PARA 791): see s 33P(3)(b)(ii) (as so added).

902. Application of local curriculum provisions to institutions within the higher education sector. Regulations[1] may apply the provisions relating to local curricula for students aged 16 to 18[2] (with such modifications[3] as appear to the Welsh Ministers to be necessary or expedient[4]) in relation to an institution, or institutions, within the higher education sector[5] in Wales[6] as those provisions apply in relation to an institution within the further education sector[7] in Wales[8]. The regulations may also apply those provisions in relation to the principal or governing body of an institution within the higher education sector in Wales (or to persons[9] with functions[10] that are similar to those of a principal or governing body) as they apply in relation to the principal[11] or governing body of an institution within the further education sector in Wales[12].

1 'Regulations' means regulations made by the Welsh Ministers: Learning and Skills Act 2000 s 33N(1) (s 33N added by the Learning and Skills (Wales) Measure 2009 s 35). As to the Welsh Ministers see PARA 59. As to the regulations made see the Local Curriculum in Higher Education Institutions (Wales) Regulations 2011, SI 2011/270.
2 Ie the provisions of the Learning and Skills Act 2000 ss 33A–33L, s 33N and s 33O (see PARAS 895–900) and the provisions of any regulations made under the Learning and Skills (Wales) Measure 2009 s 46 (see PARA 903).
3 As to the meaning of 'modifications' see PARA 21 note 15 (definition applied by the Learning and Skills Act 2000 s 33N(2) (as added: see note 1)).
4 See the Learning and Skills Act 2000 s 33Q(2) (s 33Q added by the Learning and Skills (Wales) Measure 2009 s 38).
5 As to the meaning of 'institution within the higher education sector' see PARA 619 (definition applied by the Learning and Skills Act 2000 s 33N(2) (as added: see note 1)).
6 As to the meaning of 'Wales' see PARA 7 note 3.
7 As to the meaning of 'institution within the further education sector' see PARA 29 (definition applied by the Learning and Skills Act 2000 s 33N(2) (as added: see note 1)).
8 Learning and Skills Act 2000 s 33Q(1) (as added: see note 4).
9 As to the meaning of 'person' see PARA 7 note 6.
10 As to the meaning of 'functions' see PARA 18 note 5 (definition applied by the Learning and Skills Act 2000 s 33N(2) (as added: see note 1)).
11 As to the meaning of 'principal' in this context see PARA 897 note 9.
12 Learning and Skills Act 2000 s 33Q(2) (as added: see note 4).

(C) Regulations

903. Regulations in connection with the operation of the local curriculum. If the Welsh Ministers[1] are of the opinion that the provision is necessary, desirable or expedient in connection with the operation of the provisions[2] relating to local curricula[3], they may by regulations[4] make provision, for the specified purposes[5] of an enactment, as to the circumstances in which[6]:

(1)   a person[7] is, or is not, to be taken to be:
    (a)   a person for whom education is being provided at a school[8];

      (b)   a pupil or registered pupil of a school or a registered parent of a registered pupil[9];

      (c)   at a school[10];

      (d)   attending, attending at or in attendance at a school[11];

      (e)   receiving education at a school[12];

      (f)   studying, or intending to study at, a school[13];

      (g)   a person who is admitted to or has been refused admission to a school[14];

      (h)   applying for admission to a school, offering to admit a person to a school, accepting or refusing to accept an application for admission to a school or determining admissions to a school[15];

      (i)   a person who has made a decision as to the school at which education is to be provided for a child[16];

      (j)   a person in respect of whom charges may be made in respect of admission to a maintained school[17];

(2)   arrangements for the provision of education on behalf of a school are, or are not, to be taken to be admission arrangements[18];

(3)   arrangements for enabling preferences to be expressed as to the school at which the person expressing the preference wishes education to be provided for himself or herself or another person do, or do not, apply[19];

(4)   a person is, or is not, to be taken to be:

      (a)   receiving education or training at an institution within the further education sector[20];

      (b)   attending, or in attendance at, such an institution[21];

      (c)   a student of, or at, such an institution[22];

      (d)   studying, or intending to study, at such an institution[23];

      (e)   applying for admission to such an institution, offering to admit a person to such an institution, accepting or refusing to accept an application for admission to such an institution, selecting a person for admission to such an institution or determining admissions to such an institution[24];

      (f)   in relation to such an institution, a disabled person[25].

1 As to the Welsh Ministers see PARA 59.
2 Ie the amendments made to the Education Act 2002 and the Learning and Skills Act 2000 by the Learning and Skills (Wales) Measure 2009 Pt 1 (ss 1–20), Pt 2 (ss 21–39). As to such amendments see principally the Education Act 2002 ss 116A–116O (see PARAS 885–894); and the Learning and Skills Act 2000 ss 33A–33Q (see PARAS 895–902).
3 See the Learning and Skills (Wales) Measure 2009 s 46(2).
4 As to the regulations made see the Operation of the Local Curriculum (Wales) Regulations 2013, SI 2013/1793.
5 The purposes that may be specified under the Learning and Skills (Wales) Measure 2009 s 46(1) include those of making regulations or an order under an enactment: s 46(3). 'Enactment' includes an enactment contained in the Learning and Skills (Wales) Measure 2009 (s 46(4)(a)), or contained in an Act of Parliament or measure of the National Assembly for Wales passed after the passing of the Learning and Skills (Wales) Measure 2009 (ie 13 May 2009) (s 46(4)(b)). As to the measures of the National Assembly for Wales see CONSTITUTIONAL AND ADMINISTRATIVE LAW.
6 Learning and Skills (Wales) Measure 2009 s 46(1).
7 As to the meaning of 'person' see PARA 7 note 6.
8 Learning and Skills (Wales) Measure 2009 s 46(1)(a)(i).
9 Learning and Skills (Wales) Measure 2009 s 46(1)(a)(ii).
10 Learning and Skills (Wales) Measure 2009 s 46(1)(a)(iii).
11 Learning and Skills (Wales) Measure 2009 s 46(1)(a)(iv).
12 Learning and Skills (Wales) Measure 2009 s 46(1)(a)(v).
13 Learning and Skills (Wales) Measure 2009 s 46(1)(a)(vi).

14 Learning and Skills (Wales) Measure 2009 s 46(1)(a)(vii).
15 Learning and Skills (Wales) Measure 2009 s 46(1)(a)(viii).
16 Learning and Skills (Wales) Measure 2009 s 46(1)(a)(ix).
17 Learning and Skills (Wales) Measure 2009 s 46(1)(a)(x).
18 Learning and Skills (Wales) Measure 2009 s 46(1)(b).
19 Learning and Skills (Wales) Measure 2009 s 46(1)(c).
20 Learning and Skills (Wales) Measure 2009 s 46(1)(d)(i).
21 Learning and Skills (Wales) Measure 2009 s 46(1)(d)(ii).
22 Learning and Skills (Wales) Measure 2009 s 46(1)(d)(iii).
23 Learning and Skills (Wales) Measure 2009 s 46(1)(d)(iv).
24 Learning and Skills (Wales) Measure 2009 s 46(1)(d)(v).
25 Learning and Skills (Wales) Measure 2009 s 46(1)(d)(vi).

(D) Learning Pathways

904.   The learning pathway document. A relevant pupil[1] or a relevant student[2] is to be provided with a document which records his or her learning pathway (known as a 'learning pathway document')[3]. A pupil's or student's 'learning pathway' means: (1) the courses of study (if any) that the pupil or student is entitled[4] to follow[5]; and (2) the learner support services (if any) to be provided[6] to a pupil or student[7].

The learning pathway document: (a) must be provided within a reasonable period of time following an entitlement arising as described in head (1) above or a decision being taken to provide services as described in head (2) above[8]; and (b) must subsequently be amended or re-issued within a reasonable period of time following a variation in such an entitlement or decision[9], or such an entitlement arising or such a decision being taken[10].

In the case of a relevant pupil, the duty to provide, or to amend or re-issue, a learning pathway document is a duty of the head teacher of the pupil's maintained school when an event described in head (a) or head (b) above (as the case may be) occurs[11]. In the case of a relevant student, the duty to provide, or to amend or re-issue, a learning pathway document is a duty of the principal[12] of the student's institution when such an event occurs[13]. A head teacher of a maintained school and principal of an institution must have regard to any guidance given from time to time by the Welsh Ministers as to the exercise of their functions under these provisions[14].

1 'Relevant pupil' means a registered pupil of a maintained school; and 'registered pupil' has the same meaning as in the Education Act 1996 s 434 (see PARA 437): Learning and Skills (Wales) Measure 2009 s 44. 'Maintained school' means: (1) any community, foundation or voluntary school maintained by a local authority in Wales; or (2) any community special school which is maintained by a local authority in Wales and is not established in a hospital; and, in relation to a relevant pupil, means the maintained school of which he or she is a registered pupil: s 44 (definition amended by SI 2010/1148; and the School Standards and Organisation (Wales) Act 2013 Sch 5 para 26). As to community, foundation or voluntary schools and community special schools see PARA 106. 'Local authority in Wales' has the meaning given by the Education Act 1996 s 579(1) (see PARA 25): Learning and Skills (Wales) Measure 2009 s 44 (definition added by SI 2010/1148). As to the meaning of 'Wales' see PARA 7 note 3.
2 'Relevant student' means a person who receives the majority of his or her education at, or under arrangements made by the governing body of, an institution, and has not attained the age of 19 or such later age as may be prescribed in regulations made by the Welsh Ministers: Learning and Skills (Wales) Measure 2009 s 44. 'Institution' means an institution within the further education sector (within the meaning in the Education Act 1996: see PARA 555) in Wales, and, in relation to a relevant student, means the institution whose governing body is responsible for providing, or arranging for the provision of, all or the majority of his or her education: see the Learning and Skills (Wales) Measure 2009 s 44. As to the time at which a person attains a particular age see PARA 7 note 6. As to the Welsh Ministers see PARA 59. At the date at which this volume states the law no regulations had been made under s 44.

3　See the Learning and Skills (Wales) Measure 2009 s 43(1).
4　Ie under the Education Act 2002 s 116E(1) (see PARA 888) or the Learning and Skills Act 2000 s 33F(1) (see PARA 897).
5　Learning and Skills (Wales) Measure 2009 s 43(2)(a).
6　Ie by virtue of the Learning and Skills (Wales) Measure 2009 s 40: see PARA 812.
7　Learning and Skills (Wales) Measure 2009 s 43(2)(b).
8　Learning and Skills (Wales) Measure 2009 s 43(3)(a).
9　Learning and Skills (Wales) Measure 2009 s 43(2)(b)(i).
10　Learning and Skills (Wales) Measure 2009 s 43(2)(b)(ii).
11　See the Learning and Skills (Wales) Measure 2009 s 43(4)(a), (5)(a).
12　'Principal' means the principal or other head of an institution: Learning and Skills (Wales) Measure 2009 s 44.
13　See the Learning and Skills (Wales) Measure 2009 s 43(3)(b), (5)(b).
14　Learning and Skills (Wales) Measure 2009 s 434(6).

(iii) Sex Education

905. Sex education: manner of provision. The governing body[1] and head teacher[2] must take such steps as are reasonably practicable to secure that where sex education[3] is given to any registered pupils[4] at a maintained school[5], it is given in such a manner as to encourage those pupils to have due regard to moral considerations and the value of family life[6].

The appropriate national authority[7] must issue guidance[8] designed to secure that when sex education is given to registered pupils at maintained schools they: (1) learn the nature of marriage and its importance for family life and the bringing up of children[9]; and (2) are protected from teaching and materials which are inappropriate having regard to the age and the religious and cultural background of the pupils concerned[10]. The appropriate national authority may at any time revise such guidance[11]. Any such guidance must include guidance about any material which may be produced by NHS bodies[12] for use for the purposes of sex education in schools[13]. In discharging their functions[14] as regards the manner of provision of sex education, governing bodies and head teachers must have regard to the appropriate national authority's guidance[15].

1　As to the governing bodies of maintained schools in England see PARA 150 et seq; and in Wales see PARA 195.
2　As to the meaning of 'head teacher' see PARA 86 note 4.
3　As to the meaning of 'sex education' see PARA 857 note 10.
4　As to the meaning of 'registered pupil' see PARA 437.
5　'Maintained school' includes a community or foundation special school established in a hospital: Education Act 1996 s 403(2) (amended by the School Standards and Framework Act 1998 s 140(1), Sch 30 para 102; and the Learning and Skills Act 2000 s 148(1), (5)). As to the meaning of 'school' see PARA 91. As to maintained schools see PARA 99 et seq. As to the meaning of references to a community or foundation special school see PARA 106. As to academies generally see PARA 345 et seq. As to the National Curriculum and academies see PARA 359. As to academies generally see PARA 345 et seq. As to free schools see PARA 368.
6　Education Act 1996 s 403(1) (amended by the Learning and Skills Act 2000 ss 148(1), (3), 153, Sch 11).
7　Ie the Secretary of State or, in relation to Wales, the Welsh Ministers. As to the Secretary of State see PARA 58. As to the Welsh Ministers see PARA 59. As to the meaning of 'Wales' see PARA 7 note 3. The functions of the Secretary of State under the Education Act 1996 s 403, so far as exercisable in relation to Wales, were transferred to the National Assembly for Wales (see the National Assembly for Wales (Transfer of Functions) Order 1999, SI 1999/672, art 2, Sch 1) and are now vested in the Welsh Ministers (see the Government of Wales Act 2006 s 162(1), Sch 11 para 30).
8　As to the publication of guidance see the Education Act 1996 s 571; and PARA 60.
9　Education Act 1996 s 403(1A)(a) (s 403(1A)–(1D) added by the Learning and Skills Act 2000 s 148(1), (4)).
10　Education Act 1996 s 403(1A)(b) (as added: see note 9).

11 Education Act 1996 s 403(1D) (as added: see note 9).
12 'NHS body' has the same meaning as in the National Health Service Act 2006 (see s 275(1)) (see HEALTH SERVICES vol 54 (2008) PARA 8): Education Act 1996 s 403(2) (definition amended by the Learning and Skills Act 2000 s 148(5); and SI 2013/594).
13 Education Act 1996 s 403(1C) (as added: see note 9).
14 As to the meaning of 'functions' see PARA 18 note 5.
15 Education Act 1996 s 403(1B) (as added: see note 9).

906. Sex education: statements of policy. The governing body[1] of a maintained school[2] must make, and keep up to date, a separate written[3] statement of its policy with regard to the provision of sex education[4], and make copies of the statement available for inspection, at all reasonable times, by parents[5] of registered pupils[6] at the school and provide a copy of the statement free of charge to any such parent who asks for one[7]. The statement must include a statement of the effect of the statutory provision[8] which confers a right on a parent to withdraw a child from sex education[9].

1 As to the governing bodies of maintained schools in England see PARA 150 et seq; and in Wales see PARA 195. As to the meanings of 'England' and 'Wales' see PARA 7 note 3. As to the application of the Education Act 1996 s 404 in relation to the teacher in charge of a pupil referral unit in Wales, see the Education (Pupil Referral Units) (Application of Enactments) (Wales) Regulations 2007, SI 2007/1069, reg 3, Sch 1 Pt 1 para 1. As to the application of the Education Act 1996 s 404 in relation to management committees of pupil referral units in England, see the Education (Pupil Referral Units) (Application of Enactments) (England) Regulations 2007, SI 2007/2979, regs 1(3), 3, Sch 1 Pt 1 para 3. As to pupil referral units see PARA 427 et seq.
2 'Maintained school' includes, in relation to pupils who are provided with secondary education, a community or foundation special school established in a hospital: Education Act 1996 s 404(2) (amended by the School Standards and Framework Act 1998 s 140(1), Sch 30 paras 57, 103(a)). As to the meaning of 'pupil' see PARA 20 note 4. As to the meaning of 'secondary education' see PARA 21. As to the meaning of 'school' see PARA 91. As to maintained schools see PARA 99 et seq. As to the meaning of references to a community or foundation special school see PARA 106. As to the National Curriculum and academies see PARA 359. As to academies generally see PARA 345 et seq. As to free schools see PARA 368.
3 As to the meaning of 'written' see PARA 76 note 8.
4 Education Act 1996 s 404(1)(a). As to the meaning of 'sex education' see PARA 857 note 10. As to the manner of the provision of sex education see PARA 905.
5 As to the meaning of 'parent' see PARA 7 note 6.
6 As to the meaning of 'registered pupil' see PARA 437.
7 Education Act 1996 s 404(1)(b).
8 Ie the Education Act 1996 s 405: see PARA 907.
9 Education Act 1996 s 404(1A) (added by the Learning and Skills Act 2000 s 148(1), (6)).

907. Exemption from sex education. If the parent[1] of any pupil[2] in attendance at a maintained school[3] requests that he may be wholly or partly excused from receiving sex education[4] at the school, the pupil must, except so far as such education is comprised in the National Curriculum[5], be so excused accordingly until the request is withdrawn[6].

1 As to the meaning of 'parent' see PARA 7 note 6.
2 As to the meaning of 'pupil' see PARA 20 note 4.
3 As to the meaning of 'school' see PARA 91. As to maintained schools see PARA 99 et seq. As to the National Curriculum and academies see PARA 359. As to academies generally see PARA 345 et seq. As to free schools see PARA 368.
4 As to the meaning of 'sex education' see PARA 857 note 10. As to the manner of provision of sex education see PARA 905. As to statements of policy with regard to the provision of sex education see PARA 906.
5 'The National Curriculum' (without more) means, in relation to England, the National Curriculum for England; and, in relation to Wales, the National Curriculum for Wales: Education Act 1996 s 579(1) (definition added by the Education Act 2002 s 215(1), Sch 21

para 57(b)). As to the National Curriculum for England see PARA 859 et seq; and as to the National Curriculum for Wales see PARA 873 et seq. As to the meanings of 'England' and 'Wales' see PARA 7 note 3.

6 Education Act 1996 s 405. As to the application of s 405 in relation to pupil referral units in Wales, see the Education (Pupil Referral Units) (Application of Enactments) (Wales) Regulations 2007, SI 2007/1069, reg 3, Sch 1 Pt 1 para 2. As to the application of the Education Act 1996 s 405 in relation to pupil referral units in England, see the Education (Pupil Referral Units) (Application of Enactments) (England) Regulations 2007, SI 2007/2979, regs 1(3), 3, Sch 1 Pt 1 para 4. As to pupil referral units see PARA 427 et seq.

(iv) Politics

908. Political indoctrination. The local authority[1], governing body[2] and head teacher[3] must forbid[4]: (1) the pursuit of partisan political activities by any of those registered pupils[5] at a maintained school[6] who are junior pupils[7]; and (2) the promotion of partisan political views in the teaching of any subject in the school[8]. In the case of activities which take place otherwise than on the school premises[9], head (1) above applies only where arrangements for junior pupils to take part in the activities are made by any member of the school's staff, in his capacity as such[10], or anyone acting on behalf of the school or of a member of the school's staff, in his capacity as such[11].

1 As to the meaning of 'local authority' see PARA 25.
2 As to the governing bodies of maintained schools in England see PARA 150 et seq; and in Wales see PARA 195. As to the meanings of 'England' and 'Wales' see PARA 7 note 3.
3 As to the meaning of 'head teacher' see PARA 86 note 4.
4 Education Act 1996 s 406(1) (amended by SI 2010/1158). Any function of a local authority in England which is conferred by or under the Education Act 1996 s 406 may be exercised by, or by employees of, such person as may be authorised in that behalf by the local authority whose function it is: Contracting Out (Local Authority Education Functions) (England) Order 2002, SI 2002/928, art 3, Sch 1 para (y) (art 3 amended by SI 2010/1172). As to the meaning of 'person' see PARA 7 note 6.
5 As to the meaning of 'registered pupil' see PARA 437.
6 'Maintained school' includes a community or foundation special school established in a hospital: Education Act 1996 s 406(3) (amended by the School Standards and Framework Act 1998 s 140(1), Sch 30 paras 57, 104). As to the meaning of 'school' see PARA 91. As to maintained schools see PARA 99 et seq. As to the meaning of references to a community or foundation special school see PARA 106. As to the National Curriculum and academies see PARA 359. As to academies generally see PARA 345 et seq. As to free schools see PARA 368.
7 Education Act 1996 s 406(1)(a). As to the meaning of 'junior pupil' see PARA 20 note 4.
8 Education Act 1996 s 406(1)(b). The mere distribution by the Secretary of State of a film containing certain partisan political views, with accompanying guidance, did not, per se, amount to a promotion of those political views. 'Partisan' is not limited to party political views; and 'promotion' means more than mere presentation. What is forbidden by the statute is, as the side heading makes clear, 'political indoctrination': *R (on the application of Dimmock) v Secretary of State for Education and Skills* [2007] EWHC 2288 (Admin), [2008] 1 All ER 367, [2008] ELR 98.
9 As to the meaning of 'premises' see PARA 62 note 19.
10 Education Act 1996 s 406(2)(a).
11 Education Act 1996 s 406(2)(b).

909. Duty to secure balanced treatment of political issues. The local authority[1], governing body[2] and head teacher[3] must take such steps as are reasonably practicable to secure that where political issues are brought to the attention of pupils[4] while they are[5]:

(1) in attendance at a maintained school[6]; or
(2) taking part in extra-curricular activities which are provided or organised for registered pupils[7] at the school by or on behalf of the school[8],

they are offered a balanced presentation of opposing views[9].

1   As to the meaning of 'local authority' see PARA 25.
2   As to the governing bodies of maintained schools in England see PARA 150 et seq; and in Wales see PARA 195. As to the meanings of 'England' and 'Wales' see PARA 7 note 3.
3   As to the meaning of 'head teacher' see PARA 86 note 4.
4   As to the meaning of 'pupil' see PARA 20 note 4.
5   Education Act 1996 s 407(1) (amended by SI 2010/1158). Any function of a local authority in England which is conferred by or under the Education Act 1996 s 407 may be exercised by, or by employees of, such person as may be authorised in that behalf by the local authority whose function it is: Contracting Out (Local Authority Education Functions) (England) Order 2002, SI 2002/928, art 3, Sch 1 para (z) (art 3 amended by SI 2010/1172). As to the meaning of 'person' see PARA 7 note 6.
6   Education Act 1996 s 407(1)(a). For these purposes, 'maintained school' includes a community or foundation special school established in a hospital: s 407(2) (amended by the School Standards and Framework Act 1998 s 140(1), Sch 30 paras 57, 105). As to the meaning of 'school' see PARA 91. As to maintained schools see PARA 99 et seq. As to the meaning of references to a community or foundation special school see PARA 106. As to the National Curriculum and academies see PARA 359. As to academies generally see PARA 345 et seq. As to free schools see PARA 368.
7   As to the meaning of 'registered pupil' see PARA 437.
8   Education Act 1996 s 407(1)(b).
9   Education Act 1996 s 407(1). A balanced approach does not involve equality; 'balanced' means nothing more than fair and dispassionate: *R (on the application of Dimmock) v Secretary of State for Education and Skills* [2007] EWHC 2288 (Admin), [2008] 1 All ER 367, [2008] ELR 98. As to freedom of speech in universities and further and higher education establishments see PARA 6. As to promoting British values etc see PARA 910 note 6.

(v) Religious Education and Worship

A. AGREED SYLLABUSES

910.   Religion: agreed syllabuses.   Subject to the provisions relating to agreed syllabuses of religious education generally[1], any agreed syllabus[2] in force immediately before 1 November 1996[3] continues to have effect[4]. Every agreed syllabus must reflect the fact that the religious traditions in Great Britain[5] are in the main Christian whilst taking account of the teaching and practices of the other principal religions represented in Great Britain[6].

1   Ie subject to the Education Act 1996 Sch 31: see PARAS 911–913.
2   'Agreed syllabus' means a syllabus of religious education: (1) prepared before 1 November 1996 (ie the commencement date of the Education Act 1996: see s 583(2)) in accordance with the Education Act 1944 Sch 5 (repealed) or after 1 November 1996 in accordance with the Education Act 1996 Sch 31 (see PARAS 911–913) (s 375(2)(a)); and (2) adopted by a local authority under Sch 31 (s 375(2)(b) (amended by SI 2010/1158)), whether it is for use in all the schools maintained by it or for use in particular such schools or in relation to any particular class or description of pupils in such schools (Education Act 1996 s 375(2)). Any reference in the Education Act 1996 to an agreed syllabus adopted by a local authority includes a reference to an agreed syllabus deemed to be adopted by such an authority by virtue of the Education Act 1944 Sch 5 para 11 (repealed) or the Education Act 1996 Sch 31 para 14 (see PARA 913); and accordingly, in relation to an agreed syllabus deemed to be so adopted, any reference to the date on which an agreed syllabus was adopted is a reference to the date of deemed adoption specified by the Secretary of State or, in relation to Wales, the Welsh Ministers in a direction under Sch 31 para 14: s 375(4). As to the meaning of 'local authority' see PARA 25. As to the meaning of 'school' see PARA 91. As to the meaning of 'pupil' see PARA 20 note 4. As to the Secretary of State see PARA 58. As to the Welsh Ministers see PARA 59. As to the meaning of 'Wales' see PARA 7 note 3. The functions of the Secretary of State under the Education Act 1996 s 375, Sch 31, so far as exercisable in relation to Wales, were transferred to the National Assembly for Wales (see the National Assembly for Wales (Transfer of Functions) Order 1999, SI 1999/672, art 2, Sch 1) and are now vested in the Welsh Ministers (see the Government of Wales Act 2006 s 162(1), Sch 11 para 30).
3   Ie the commencement date of the Education Act 1996: see s 583(2).
4   Education Act 1996 s 375(1).

5 As to the meaning of 'Great Britain' see PARA 73 note 3.
6 Education Act 1996 s 375(3). Section 375(3) does not apply to any agreed syllabus adopted before 29 September 1988: s 375(5). Note should also be made of guidance published by the Department for Education on 27 November 2014 on promoting British values in schools to ensure young people leave school prepared for life in modern Britain. The guidance aims to help both independent and state-maintained schools understand their responsibilities in this area. According to the guidance, all have a duty to 'actively promote' the fundamental British values of democracy, the rule of law, individual liberty, and mutual respect and tolerance of those with different faiths and beliefs. These values were first set out by the government in the 'Prevent' strategy in 2011. See further 'Protecting children from radicalisation: the prevent duty' (1 July 2015), concerning (amongst other things) the promotion of 'fundamental British values'.

911. Duty to convene conference to reconsider agreed syllabus on religion. A local authority[1] must from time to time cause conferences to be convened for the purpose of reconsidering any agreed syllabus[2] for the time being adopted by it, whether adopted before, on or after 1 April 1994[3]. No such conference must be convened later than the end of the period of five years beginning with the date, falling after 31 March 1994, on which the authority adopted the syllabus[4], or the authority gave effect to a recommendation[5] that the syllabus should continue to be the agreed syllabus[6]. On receipt by a local authority of written[7] notification requiring the review of any agreed syllabus[8], the authority must cause a conference to be convened for the purpose of reconsidering any agreed syllabus to which the requirement relates[9].

1 As to the meaning of 'local authority' see PARA 25.
2 As to the meaning of 'agreed syllabus' see PARA 910 note 2.
3 Education Act 1996 Sch 31 para 2(1) (amended by SI 2010/1158). Where the agreed syllabus for the time being adopted by a local authority was adopted by it on or after 29 September 1988 but before 1 April 1994, the local authority was required, within the period of five years beginning with the date on which it adopted the syllabus, to convene a conference for the purpose of reconsidering the syllabus: see the Education Act 1996 Sch 31 para 1(1), (2) (Sch 31 para 1(1) amended by SI 2010/1158).
4 Education Act 1996 Sch 31 para 2(2)(a).
5 Ie under the Education Act 1996 Sch 31 para 10(2) (see PARA 913) or the Education Act 1944 Sch 5 para 13 (repealed).
6 Education Act 1996 Sch 31 para 2(2)(b).
7 As to the meaning of 'written' see PARA 76 note 8.
8 Ie notification of any such requirement as is mentioned in the Education Act 1996 s 391(3): see PARA 926.
9 Education Act 1996 Sch 31 para 3 (amended by SI 2010/1158).

912. Constitution of conference in regard to religion. A conference convened to reconsider the agreed syllabus[1] must consist of such groups of persons (called 'committees') appointed by the local authority[2] convening the conference as are required[3]. Those committees are:

(1) a committee of persons representing such Christian denominations and other religions and denominations of such religions as, in the opinion of the authority, will appropriately reflect the principal religious traditions in the area[4];

(2) except in the case of an area in Wales[5], a committee of persons representing the Church of England[6];

(3) a committee of persons representing such associations representing teachers as, in the opinion of the authority, ought to be represented, having regard to the circumstances of the area[7]; and

(4) a committee of persons representing the authority[8].

Where a committee is required to be appointed by virtue of head (2) above, the committee required to be appointed by virtue of head (1) above must not include persons appointed to represent the Church of England[9]. The number of persons appointed under head (1) above to represent each denomination or religion required to be represented must, so far as is consistent with the efficient discharge of the committee's functions[10], reflect broadly the proportionate strength of that denomination or religion in the area[11]. Any sub-committees appointed by the conference must each include at least one member of each of the committees constituting the conference[12]. On any question to be decided by the conference or by any sub-committee of the conference, a single vote must be given for each of the committees constituting the conference[13].

Before appointing a person to represent any religion, denomination or associations as a member of a committee, the local authority must take all reasonable steps to assure itself that he is representative of the religion, denomination or associations in question[14]. No proceedings[15] are invalidated on the ground that a member of a committee did not represent the religion, denomination or associations which he was appointed to represent, unless it is shown that the authority failed to take all reasonable steps to assure itself that he is representative of the religion, denomination or associations in question[16].

A person appointed as a member of a committee may resign his membership[17], or may be withdrawn from membership by the local authority if, in its opinion, he ceases to be representative of the religion, denomination or associations which he was appointed to represent or, as the case may be, of the authority[18]. Where a person resigns or is withdrawn from a committee, the local authority must appoint someone in his place in the same manner as that in which it made the original appointment[19].

1   Ie convened under the Education Act 1996 Sch 31. As to the duty to convene a conference see PARA 911. As to the meaning of 'agreed syllabus' see PARA 910 note 2.
2   As to the meaning of 'local authority' see PARA 25.
3   Education Act 1996 Sch 31 para 4(1) (amended by SI 2010/1158). As to access to meetings and documents of a conference and sub-committees appointed by it see PARA 930.
4   Education Act 1996 Sch 31 para 4(2)(a).
5   As to the meaning of 'Wales' see PARA 7 note 3.
6   Education Act 1996 Sch 31 para 4(2)(b).
7   Education Act 1996 Sch 31 para 4(2)(c).
8   Education Act 1996 Sch 31 para 4(2)(d).
9   Education Act 1996 Sch 31 para 4(3).
10 As to the meaning of 'functions' see PARA 18 note 5.
11 Education Act 1996 Sch 31 para 4(4).
12 Education Act 1996 Sch 31 para 5.
13 Education Act 1996 Sch 31 para 6.
14 Education Act 1996 Sch 31 para 7(1) (amended by SI 2010/1158).
15 Ie under the Education Act 1996 Sch 31.
16 Education Act 1996 Sch 31 para 7(2).
17 Education Act 1996 Sch 31 para 8(a).
18 Education Act 1996 Sch 31 para 8(b) (amended by SI 2010/1158).
19 Education Act 1996 Sch 31 para 9 (amended by SI 2010/1158).

913.   Religion: reconsideration of agreed syllabus and the preparation of a new syllabus by appointed body.   Where a local authority[1] causes a conference to be convened[2] for the purpose of reconsidering any agreed syllabus[3]:

(1)   if the conference unanimously recommends that the existing syllabus should continue to be the agreed syllabus[4], or unanimously recommends a new syllabus to be adopted in substitution for the existing syllabus[5]; and

(2)   it appears to the local authority that the syllabus or, as the case may be, the new syllabus, reflects the fact that the religious traditions in Great

Britain[6] are in the main Christian while taking account of the teaching and practices of the other principal religions represented in Great Britain[7],

the local authority may give effect to the recommendation[8].

If, however:

(a)   the authority reports to the appropriate national authority[9] that the conference is unable to reach unanimous agreement[10]; or

(b)   the conference unanimously recommends that the existing syllabus should continue to be the agreed syllabus but the local authority considers that head (2) above prevents it from giving effect to the recommendation[11]; or

(c)   it appears to the appropriate national authority that the authority has failed to exercise its power[12] to give effect to the unanimous recommendation of the conference[13],

the appropriate national authority must appoint a body of persons having experience in religious education to prepare a syllabus of religious education[14]. The appointed body must, so far as is practicable, be of a representative character which is the same as that required[15] in the case of a conference[16]. The appointed body must: (i) give the local authority, the conference and every committee constituting the conference an opportunity of making representations to it[17]; (ii) after considering any such representations made to it, prepare a syllabus of religious education[18]; and (iii) transmit a copy of that syllabus to the authority and to the appropriate national authority[19]. The syllabus prepared by the appointed body is deemed to be the agreed syllabus adopted for use in the schools[20] for which, or for the class or description of pupils[21] for which, it was prepared as from such date as the appropriate national authority may direct[22], and until a new syllabus is adopted[23] for use in those schools, or for pupils of that class or description[24].

1   As to the meaning of 'local authority' see PARA 25.
2   Ie under the Education Act 1996 Sch 31 paras 1–3: see PARA 911.
3   Education Act 1996 Sch 31 para 10(1) (amended by SI 2010/1158). As to the meaning of 'agreed syllabus' see PARA 910 note 2.
4   Education Act 1996 Sch 31 para 10(2)(a)(i).
5   Education Act 1996 Sch 31 para 10(2)(a)(ii).
6   As to the meaning of 'Great Britain' see PARA 73 note 3.
7   Education Act 1996 Sch 31 para 10(2)(b) (amended by SI 2010/1158).
8   Education Act 1996 Sch 31 para 10(2) (amended by SI 2010/1158).
9   Ie the Secretary of State or, in relation to Wales, the Welsh Ministers. As to the Secretary of State see PARA 58. As to the Welsh Ministers see PARA 59. As to the meaning of 'Wales' see PARA 7 note 3. The functions of the Secretary of State under the Education Act 1996 Sch 31, so far as exercisable in relation to Wales, were transferred to the National Assembly for Wales (see the National Assembly for Wales (Transfer of Functions) Order 1999, SI 1999/672, art 2, Sch 1) and are now vested in the Welsh Ministers (see the Government of Wales Act 2006 s 162(1), Sch 11 para 30).
10 Education Act 1996 Sch 31 para 10(3)(a).
11 Education Act 1996 Sch 31 para 10(3)(b) (amended by SI 2010/1158).
12 Ie under the Education Act 1996 Sch 31 para 10(2): see the text to notes 4–8.
13 Education Act 1996 Sch 31 para 10(3)(c).
14 See the Education Act 1996 Sch 31 paras 10(3), 12(1).
15 Ie required by the Education Act 1996 Sch 31 para 4: see PARA 912.
16 Education Act 1996 Sch 31 para 12(2).
17 Education Act 1996 Sch 31 para 13(1)(a) (amended by SI 2010/1158). Subject to the Education Act 1996 Sch 31 para 13(1)(a), the appointed body may conduct its proceedings in such manner as it thinks fit: Sch 31 para 13(2).
18 Education Act 1996 Sch 31 para 13(1)(b).
19 Education Act 1996 Sch 31 para 13(1)(c).

20 As to the meaning of 'school' see PARA 91.

21 As to the meaning of 'pupil' see PARA 20 note 4.

22 Education Act 1996 Sch 31 para 14(a). As to directions see s 570; and PARA 75.

23 Ie in accordance with the Education Act 1996 Sch 31.

24 Education Act 1996 Sch 31 para 14(b).

B. REQUIRED PROVISION FOR EDUCATION IN SCHOOLS

914.   Duty to secure due provision of religious education.   Subject to certain exceptions and special arrangements[1], in relation to any community, foundation or voluntary school[2] the local authority[3] and the governing body[4] must exercise their functions[5] with a view to securing[6], and the head teacher[7] must secure[8], that religious education is given in accordance with the provision for such education included[9] in the school's basic curriculum[10].

1   Ie subject to the School Standards and Framework Act 1998 s 71: see PARA 924.

2   As to the meaning of references to a community, foundation or voluntary school see PARA 106. As to the National Curriculum and academies see PARA 359. As to academies generally see PARA 345 et seq. As to free schools see PARA 368.

3   As to the meaning of 'local authority' see PARA 25 (definition applied by the School Standards and Framework Act 1998 s 142(8)). Any function of a local authority in England which is conferred by or under the School Standards and Framework Act 1998 s 69 may be exercised by, or by employees of, such person as may be authorised in that behalf by the local authority whose function it is: Contracting Out (Local Authority Education Functions) (England) Order 2002, SI 2002/928, art 3, Sch 2 para (r) (art 3 amended by SI 2010/1172). As to the meaning of 'England' see PARA 7 note 3. As to the meaning of 'person' see PARA 7 note 6.

4   As to the governing bodies of maintained schools in England see PARA 150 et seq; and in Wales see PARA 195.

5   As to the meaning of 'functions' see PARA 18 note 5 (definition applied by the School Standards and Framework Act 1998 s 142(8)).

6   School Standards and Framework Act 1998 s 69(1)(a).

7   As to the meaning of 'head teacher' see PARA 86 note 4 (definition applied by the School Standards and Framework Act 1998 s 142(8)).

8   School Standards and Framework Act 1998 s 69(1)(b).

9   Ie by virtue of the Education Act 2002 s 80(1)(a) (basic curriculum for every maintained school in England: see PARA 857) or s 101(1)(a) (basic curriculum for every maintained school in Wales: see PARA 871). As to the National Curriculum see PARA 856 et seq.

10 School Standards and Framework Act 1998 s 69(1) (amended by the Education Act 2002 s 215(1), Sch 21 para 104(1), (2); and SI 2010/1158). The School Standards and Framework Act 1998 Sch 19 (required provision for religious education: see PARAS 915–917) has effect for determining the provision for religious education which is required by the Education Act 2002 s 80(1)(a) or s 101(1)(a) to be included in the basic curriculum of schools within each of the following categories: (1) community schools and foundation and voluntary schools which do not have a religious character; (2) foundation and voluntary controlled schools which have a religious character; and (3) voluntary aided schools which have a religious character: School Standards and Framework Act 1998 s 69(2) (amended by the Education Act 2002 Sch 21 para 104(1), (3)). For the purposes of the School Standards and Framework Act 1998 Pt II (ss 20–83), a foundation or voluntary school has a religious character if it is designated as a school having such a character by an order made by the Secretary of State or, in relation to Wales, the Welsh Ministers: see s 69(3). An order under s 69(3) must state, in relation to each school designated by the order, the religion or religious denomination in accordance with whose tenets religious education is, or may be, required to be provided at the school in accordance with Sch 19, or, as the case may be, each such religion or religious denomination: s 69(4). The procedure to be followed in connection with the designation of a school in an order under s 69(3), and the inclusion in such an order, in relation to a school, of the statement required by s 69(4), is to be specified in regulations: s 69(5). As to schools and religious denominations see also PARA 146 note 12. As to the Secretary of State see PARA 58. As to the Welsh Ministers see PARA 59. As to the meaning of 'Wales' see PARA 7 note 3. The functions of the Secretary of State under s 69, so far as exercisable in relation to Wales, were transferred to the National Assembly

for Wales (see the National Assembly for Wales (Transfer of Functions) Order 1999, SI 1999/672, art 2, Sch 1) and are now vested in the Welsh Ministers (see the Government of Wales Act 2006 s 162(1), Sch 11 para 30).

Orders made under the School Standards and Framework Act 1998 s 69(3) designating specific schools are local in nature and are not recorded in this work. As to regulations made under s 69(5) see the Religious Character of Schools (Designation Procedure) Regulations 1998, SI 1998/2535 (amended by SI 1999/2243; SI 1999/2262; SI 2003/1558; SI 2005/2912; and SI 2007/958); and the Education (New Schools) (Wales) Regulations 1999, SI 1999/2243 (largely revoked by SI 2005/2912). The School Standards and Framework Act 1998 s 69(3)–(5) is applied, with modifications, in relation to an independent school with a religious character: see s 124B; and PARA 378.

915. Community schools and foundation and voluntary schools without a religious character. In relation to any community school[1], and in relation to any foundation or voluntary school[2] which does not have a religious character[3], the required provision for religious education[4] in the case of pupils at the school is provision for religious education in accordance with an agreed syllabus[5] adopted for the school or for those pupils[6]. Separate provision was made in relation to former grant-maintained schools[7].

If the school is a secondary school[8] so situated that arrangements cannot conveniently be made for the withdrawal of pupils from it to receive religious education elsewhere[9] and the local authority[10] is satisfied that:

(1) the parents[11] of any pupils at the school desire those pupils to receive religious education in the school in accordance with the tenets of a particular religion or religious denomination[12]; and

(2) satisfactory arrangements have been made for the provision of such education to those pupils in the school, and for securing that the cost of providing such education to those pupils in the school will not fall to be met from the school's budget share[13] or otherwise by the authority[14],

the authority must, unless it is satisfied that because of any special circumstances it would be unreasonable to do so, provide facilities for the carrying out of those arrangements[15]. No agreed syllabus may provide for religious education to be given to pupils at such a school by means of any catechism or formulary which is distinctive of a particular religious denomination, but this is not to be taken as prohibiting provision in such a syllabus for the study of such catechisms or formularies[16].

1 School Standards and Framework Act 1998 Sch 19 para 2(1)(a). As to the meaning of references to a community school see PARA 106.
2 As to the meaning of references to a foundation or voluntary school see PARA 106.
3 School Standards and Framework Act 1998 Sch 19 para 2(1)(b). As to the meaning of references to schools having a religious character see PARA 914 note 10.
4 'The required provision for religious education', in relation to a school, means the provision for pupils at the school which is required by the Education Act 2002 s 80(1)(a) (basic curriculum for every maintained school in England: see PARA 857) or s 101(1)(a) (basic curriculum for every maintained school in Wales: see PARA 871) to be included in the school's basic curriculum: School Standards and Framework Act 1998 Sch 19 para 1(1) (amended by the Education Act 2002 s 215(1), Sch 21 para 117(1), (2)(a)). As to the meaning of 'school' see PARA 91; and as to the meaning of 'pupil' see PARA 20 note 4 (definitions applied by the School Standards and Framework Act 1998 s 142(8)). As to the National Curriculum see PARA 856 et seq.
5 As to the meaning of 'agreed syllabus' see PARA 910 note 2 (definition applied by the School Standards and Framework Act 1998 Sch 19 para 1(2) (amended by the Education Act 2002 Sch 21 para 117(1), (2)(b)).
6 School Standards and Framework Act 1998 Sch 19 para 2(2).
7 If immediately before 1 September 1999 (ie the appointed day: see PARA 106 note 3) the school was a grant-maintained school (within the meaning of the Education Act 1996: see PARA 106 note 15), and in relation to the school or any pupils at the school the appropriate agreed

syllabus (as defined by s 382 (repealed)) was a syllabus falling within s 382(1)(c) (repealed), then until the end of such period as the Secretary of State may by order prescribe, or such earlier date as the governing body may determine, the required provision for religious education in the case of the school or, as the case may be, those pupils is provision for religious education in accordance with that syllabus: School Standards and Framework Act 1998 Sch 19 para 2(4). As to the Secretary of State see PARA 58. The prescribed period for the purposes of Sch 19 para 2(4) was five years commencing on 1 September 1999: see the Agreed Syllabus for Religious Education (Prescribed Period) Order 1999, SI 1999/1728, art 2.

8   As to the meaning of 'secondary school' see PARA 91 (definition applied by the School Standards and Framework Act 1998 s 142(8)).
9   Ie in accordance with the School Standards and Framework Act 1998 s 71: see PARA 924.
10 As to the meaning of 'local authority' see PARA 25 (definition applied by the School Standards and Framework Act 1998 s 142(8)).
11 As to the meaning of 'parent' see PARA 7 note 6 (definition applied by the School Standards and Framework Act 1998 s 142(8)).
12 School Standards and Framework Act 1998 Sch 19 para 2(3)(a).
13 As to the meaning of 'budget share' see PARA 315.
14 School Standards and Framework Act 1998 Sch 19 para 2(3)(b).
15 School Standards and Framework Act 1998 Sch 19 para 2(3) (amended by SI 2010/1158).
16 School Standards and Framework Act 1998 Sch 19 para 2(5).

916.   Foundation and voluntary controlled schools with a religious character. In relation to any foundation or voluntary controlled school[1] which has a religious character[2], the required provision for religious education[3] in the case of pupils[4] at the school is provision for religious education in accordance with any arrangements made by the foundation governors[5] under the provision described below[6], or subject to any such arrangements, provision in accordance with an agreed syllabus[7] adopted for the school or for those pupils[8]. Where the parents[9] of any pupils at the school request that they may receive religious education in accordance with any provisions of the trust deed[10] relating to the school[11] or, if provision for that purpose is not made by such a deed, in accordance with the tenets of the religion or religious denomination specified[12] in relation to the school[13], the foundation governors must, unless they are satisfied that because of any special circumstances it would be unreasonable to do so, make arrangements for securing that such religious education is given to those pupils in the school during not more than two periods in each week[14].

Separate provision was made in relation to former grant-maintained schools[15].

1   As to the meaning of references to a foundation or voluntary school see PARA 106.
2   School Standards and Framework Act 1998 Sch 19 para 3(1). As to references to schools having a religious character see PARA 914 note 10.
3   As to the meaning of 'the required provision for religious education' see PARA 915 note 4.
4   As to the meaning of 'pupil' see PARA 20 note 4 (definition applied by the School Standards and Framework Act 1998 s 142(8)).
5   As to the meaning of 'foundation governor' see PARA 108 note 6.
6   See the School Standards and Framework Act 1998 Sch 19 para 3(2)(a). The provisions referred to are those of Sch 19 para 3(3) (see the text to notes 9–14): see Sch 19 para 3(2)(a).
7   As to the meaning of 'agreed syllabus' see PARA 910 note 2 (definition applied by the School Standards and Framework Act 1998 Sch 19 para 1(2)).
8   School Standards and Framework Act 1998 Sch 19 para 3(2)(b).
9   As to the meaning of 'parent' see PARA 7 note 6 (definition applied by the School Standards and Framework Act 1998 s 142(8)).
10 As to the meaning of 'trust deed' see PARA 108 note 6 (definition applied by the School Standards and Framework Act 1998 s 142(8)).
11 School Standards and Framework Act 1998 Sch 19 para 3(3)(a).
12 Ie under the School Standards and Framework Act 1998 s 69(4): see PARA 914. As to the meaning of references to 'religion or religious denomination specified in relation to a school under s 69(4)' see PARA 146 note 12.

13　School Standards and Framework Act 1998 Sch 19 para 3(3)(b).

14　School Standards and Framework Act 1998 Sch 19 para 3(3).

15　If immediately before 1 September 1999 (ie the appointed day: see PARA 106 note 3) the school was a grant-maintained school (within the meaning of the Education Act 1996: see PARA 106 note 15), and in relation to the school or any pupils at the school the appropriate agreed syllabus (as defined by s 382 (repealed)) was a syllabus falling within s 382(1)(c) (repealed), then until the end of such period as the Secretary of State may by order prescribe, or such earlier date as the governing body may determine, that syllabus must be treated for the purpose of the School Standards and Framework Act 1998 Sch 19 para 3(2)(b) (see the text to notes 7–8) as an agreed syllabus adopted for the school or, as the case may be, those pupils: Sch 19 para 3(4). As to the Secretary of State see PARA 58. The prescribed period for the purposes of Sch 19 para 3(4) was five years commencing on 1 September 1999: see the Agreed Syllabus for Religious Education (Prescribed Period) Order 1999, SI 1999/1728, art 2.

917. Voluntary aided schools with a religious character. In relation to any voluntary aided school[1] which has a religious character[2], the required provision for religious education[3] in the case of pupils[4] at the school is provision for religious education in accordance with any provisions of the trust deed[5] relating to the school[6], or where provision for that purpose is not made by such a deed, in accordance with the tenets of the religion or religious denomination specified[7] in relation to the school[8], or in accordance with any arrangements made by the governing body under the provision described below[9]. Where the parents[10] of any pupils at the school desire them to receive religious education in accordance with any agreed syllabus[11] adopted by the local authority[12], and cannot with reasonable convenience cause those pupils to attend a school[13] at which that syllabus is in use[14], the governing body[15] must, unless it is satisfied that because of any special circumstances it would be unreasonable to do so, make arrangements for religious education in accordance with that syllabus to be given to those pupils in the school[16]. Religious education under any such arrangements must be given during the times set apart for the giving of religious education in the school in accordance with the provision for that purpose included[17] in the school's basic curriculum[18].

1　As to voluntary aided schools see PARA 106.

2　School Standards and Framework Act 1998 Sch 19 para 4(1). As to references to schools having a religious character see PARA 914 note 10.

3　As to the meaning of 'the required provision for religious education' see PARA 915 note 4.

4　As to the meaning of 'pupil' see PARA 20 note 4 (definition applied by the School Standards and Framework Act 1998 s 142(8)).

5　As to the meaning of 'trust deed' see PARA 108 note 6 (definition applied by the School Standards and Framework Act 1998 s 142(8)).

6　School Standards and Framework Act 1998 Sch 19 para 4(2)(a).

7　Ie under the School Standards and Framework Act 1998 s 69(4): see PARA 914. As to the meaning of references to 'religion or religious denomination specified in relation to the school under s 69(4)' see PARA 146 note 12.

8　School Standards and Framework Act 1998 Sch 19 para 4(2)(b).

9　School Standards and Framework Act 1998 Sch 19 para 4(2)(c). The arrangements referred to are those made under Sch 19 para 4(3) (see the text to notes 10–16): see Sch 19 para 4(2)(c).

10　As to the meaning of 'parent' see PARA 7 note 6 (definition applied by the School Standards and Framework Act 1998 s 142(8)).

11　As to the meaning of 'agreed syllabus' see PARA 910 note 2 (definition applied by the School Standards and Framework Act 1998 Sch 19 para 1(1)).

12　School Standards and Framework Act 1998 Sch 19 para 4(3)(a) (amended by SI 2010/1158). As to the meaning of 'local authority' see PARA 25 (definition applied by the School Standards and Framework Act 1998 s 142(8)).

13　As to the meaning of 'school' see PARA 91 (definition applied by the School Standards and Framework Act 1998 s 142(8)).

14　School Standards and Framework Act 1998 Sch 19 para 4(3)(b).

15 As to the governing bodies of maintained schools in England see PARA 150 et seq; and in Wales see PARA 195.
16 School Standards and Framework Act 1998 Sch 19 para 4(3). Any arrangements under Sch 19 para 4(3) must be made by the governing body, unless the local authority is satisfied that the governing body is unwilling to make them, in which case they must be made by the authority: Sch 19 para 4(5) (amended by SI 2010/1158). Subject to the School Standards and Framework Act 1998 Sch 19 para 4(3), the religious education given to pupils at the school is under the control of the governing body: Sch 19 para 4(6).
17 Ie by virtue of the Education Act 2002 s 80(1)(a) (basic curriculum for every maintained school in England: see PARA 857) or s 101(1)(a) (basic curriculum for every maintained school in Wales: see PARA 871).
18 School Standards and Framework Act 1998 Sch 19 para 4(4) (amended by the Education Act 2002 s 215(1), Sch 21 para 117(1), (3)).

918. Determination of question as to whether religious education is in accordance with trust deed. Where any trust deed[1] relating to a foundation or voluntary school[2] makes provision whereby a bishop or any other ecclesiastical or denominational authority has power to decide whether the religious education given in the school which purports to be in accordance with the provisions of the trust deed does or does not accord with those provisions, that question must be determined in accordance with the provisions of the trust deed[3].

1 As to the meaning of 'trust deed' see PARA 108 note 6.
2 As to the meaning of references to a foundation or voluntary school see PARA 106.
3 Education Act 1996 s 399 (amended by the School Standards and Framework Act 1998 s 140(1), Sch 30 paras 57, 100).

919. Religious education in approved special schools. Regulations[1] must make provision for securing that, so far as practicable, every pupil[2] attending an approved special school[3] in England: (1) receives religious education unless withdrawn from receiving such education in accordance with the wishes of the pupil's parent[4]; and (2) attends religious worship unless withdrawn from attendance at such worship, in the case of a sixth-form pupil[5], in accordance with the pupil's own wishes[6], and, in any other case, in accordance with the wishes of the pupil's parent[7].

Regulations[8] must make provision for securing that, so far as practicable, every pupil attending an approved special school[9] in Wales[10] receives religious education and attends religious worship[11], or is withdrawn from receiving such education or from attendance at such worship in accordance with the wishes of his parent[12].

The appropriate national authority[13] may by order make such modifications[14] of any trust deed[15] or other instrument relating to a school as, after consultation with the governing body or other proprietor[16] of the school, appear to it to be necessary to enable the governing body or proprietor to meet any requirement imposed by regulations[17] under the above provisions[18].

1 'Regulations' means regulations made by the Secretary of State: see the Education Act 1996 s 579(1). As to the Secretary of State see PARA 58. As to the regulations made see the Non-Maintained Special Schools (England) Regulations 2015, SI 2015/728. As to the meaning of 'England' see PARA 7 note 3.
2 As to the meaning of 'pupil' see PARA 20 note 4.
3 Ie a school approved under the Education Act 1996 s 342: see PARA 1042.
4 Education Act 1996 s 342(5A)(a) (s 342 substituted by the School Standards and Framework Act 1998 s 140(1), Sch 30 para 82; and the Education Act 1996 s 342(5A), (5B) added by the Education and Skills Act 2008 s 143(1), (2)). As to the meaning of 'parent' see PARA 7 note 6.

5 'A sixth-form pupil' means a pupil who has ceased to be of compulsory school age, and is receiving education suitable to the requirements of pupils over compulsory school age: Education Act 1996 s 342(5B) (as substituted and added: see note 4). As to the meaning of 'compulsory school age' see PARA 19.

6 Education Act 1996 s 342(5A)(b)(i) (as substituted and added: see note 4).

7 Education Act 1996 s 342(5A)(b)(ii) (as substituted and added: see note 4).

8 'Regulations' means regulations made by the Welsh Ministers: see the Education Act 1996 s 579(1). As to the Welsh Ministers see PARA 59. As to the meaning of 'Wales' see PARA 7 note 3. The functions of the Secretary of State under the Education Act 1996 s 342, so far as exercisable in relation to Wales, were transferred to the National Assembly for Wales (see the National Assembly for Wales (Transfer of Functions) Order 1999, SI 1999/672, art 2, Sch 1) and are now vested in the Welsh Ministers (see the Government of Wales Act 2006 s 162(1), Sch 11 para 30). As to the regulations made see the Education (Special Schools) Regulations 1994, SI 1994/652 (revoked in relation to England by SI 1999/2257) which, by virtue of the Education Act 1996 s 582(3), Sch 39 Pt I para 1 and the Interpretation Act 1978 s 17(2)(b) have effect as if made under the Education Act 1996 s 342(6).

9 Ie a school approved under the Education Act 1996 s 342: see PARA 1042.

10 Education Act 1996 s 342(6) (as substituted (see note 4); and amended by the Education and Skills Act 2008 s 143(1), (3)).

11 Education Act 1996 s 342(6)(a) (as substituted: see note 4).

12 Education Act 1996 s 342(6)(b) (as substituted: see note 4).

13 'Appropriate national authority' is not defined. It is submitted it means the Secretary of State or, in relation to Wales, the Welsh Ministers.

14 As to the meaning of 'modifications' see PARA 21 note 15.

15 As to the meaning of 'trust deed' see PARA 108 note 6.

16 As to the meaning of 'proprietor' see PARA 51 note 4.

17 Ie regulations under the Education Act 1996 s 342(5A), (6): see the text to notes 1–12.

18 See the Education Act 1996 s 349(1)(a) (amended by the Education and Skills Act 2008 ss 147(1), (2), 169(2), Sch 2; and the Academies Act 2010 s 14, Sch 2 paras 1, 3). Any modification made by such an order may be made to have permanent effect or to have effect for such period as may be specified in the order: Education Act 1996 s 349(2). Such orders, being of local effect, are not recorded in this work.

C. REQUIREMENT FOR COLLECTIVE WORSHIP

920. Requirements relating to collective worship. Subject to certain exceptions and special arrangements[1], each pupil[2] in attendance at a community, foundation or voluntary school[3] must on each school day[4] take part in an act of collective worship[5]. Subject to those exceptions and special arrangements, in relation to any community, foundation or voluntary school, the local authority[6] and the governing body[7] must exercise their functions[8] with a view to securing[9], and the head teacher[10] must secure[11], that each pupil in attendance at such a school takes part, on each school day, in an act of collective worship[12]. Further provision is made[13] with respect to the collective worship so required, including provision relating to the arrangements which are to be made in connection with such worship[14], and the nature of such worship[15].

1 Ie subject to the School Standards and Framework Act 1998 s 71: see PARA 924.

2 As to the meaning of 'pupil' see PARA 20 note 4 (definition applied by the School Standards and Framework Act 1998 s 142(8)).

3 As to the meaning of references to a community, foundation or voluntary school see PARA 106.

4 As to the meaning of 'school day' see PARA 229 note 6 (definition applied by the School Standards and Framework Act 1998 s 142(8)).

5 School Standards and Framework Act 1998 s 70(1). It has been held that ' ... when Parliament spoke of an 'act of collective worship', it was referring to the totality of events which happen on the occasion when pupils are assembled together for the purposes of collective worship rather than each of the successive incidents which take place during that assembly': *R v Secretary of State for Education, ex p R and D* [1994] ELR 495 at 499 per McCullough J. As to provision in the basic curriculum for religious education in relation to England see PARA 857; and as to provision in the basic curriculum for religious education in relation to Wales see PARA 871.

6   As to the meaning of 'local authority' see PARA 25 (definition applied by the School Standards and Framework Act 1998 s 142(8)). Any function of a local authority in England which is conferred by or under s 70 and Sch 20 (see PARAS 921–923) may be exercised by, or by employees of, such person as may be authorised in that behalf by the local authority whose function it is: Contracting Out (Local Authority Education Functions) (England) Order 2002, SI 2002/928, art 3, Sch 2 para (s) (art 3 amended by SI 2010/1172). As to the meaning of 'England' see PARA 7 note 3. As to the meaning of 'person' see PARA 7 note 6.

7   As to the governing bodies of maintained schools in England see PARA 150 et seq; and in Wales see PARA 195.

8   As to the meaning of 'functions' see PARA 18 note 5 (definition applied by the School Standards and Framework Act 1998 s 142(8)).

9   School Standards and Framework Act 1998 s 70(2)(a) (amended by SI 2010/1158).

10   As to the meaning of 'head teacher' see PARA 86 note 4 (definition applied by the School Standards and Framework Act 1998 s 142(8)).

11   School Standards and Framework Act 1998 s 70(2)(b).

12   School Standards and Framework Act 1998 s 70(2).

13   Ie by the School Standards and Framework Act 1998 Sch 20: see PARAS 921–923.

14   School Standards and Framework Act 1998 s 70(3)(a).

15   School Standards and Framework Act 1998 s 70(3)(b).

921.   Arrangements for collective worship. In relation to any community, foundation or voluntary school[1], the arrangements for the required collective worship[2] may, in respect of each school day[3], provide for a single act of worship for all pupils[4] or for separate acts of worship for pupils in different age groups or in different school groups[5]. The arrangements for the required collective worship must be made:

(1)   if the school is a community school or a foundation school which does not have a religious character[6], by the head teacher[7] after consulting the governing body[8];

(2)   if the school is a foundation school which has a religious character or a voluntary school, by the governing body after consulting the head teacher[9].

The required collective worship must take place on the school premises[10]. However, if the governing body of a community, foundation or voluntary school is of the opinion that it is desirable that any act of collective worship in the school[11] should, on a special occasion, take place elsewhere than on the school premises, it may, after consultation with the head teacher, make such arrangements for that purpose as it thinks appropriate[12].

1   School Standards and Framework Act 1998 Sch 20 para 2(1). As to the meaning of references to a community, foundation or voluntary school see PARA 106. As to the National Curriculum and academies see PARA 359. As to academies generally see PARA 345 et seq. As to free schools see PARA 368.

2   'The required collective worship', in relation to a school, means the collective worship in that school which is required by the School Standards and Framework Act 1998 s 70 (see PARA 920): Sch 20 para 1.

3   As to the meaning of 'school day' see PARA 229 note 6 (definition applied by the School Standards and Framework Act 1998 s 142(8)).

4   As to the meaning of 'pupil' see PARA 20 note 4 (definition applied by the School Standards and Framework Act 1998 s 142(8)).

5   School Standards and Framework Act 1998 Sch 20 para 2(2). A 'school group' is any group in which pupils are taught or take part in other school activities: Sch 20 para 2(3).

6   As to references to schools having a religious character see PARA 914 note 10.

7   As to the meaning of 'head teacher' see PARA 86 note 4 (definition applied by the School Standards and Framework Act 1998 s 142(8)).

8   School Standards and Framework Act 1998 Sch 20 para 2(4)(a). As to the governing bodies of maintained schools in England see PARA 150 et seq; and in Wales see PARA 195.

9   School Standards and Framework Act 1998 Sch 20 para 2(4)(b).

10 School Standards and Framework Act 1998 Sch 20 para 2(5). As to the meaning of 'premises' see PARA 62 note 19 (definition applied by s 142(8)).
11 Ie required by the School Standards and Framework Act 1998 s 70: see PARA 920.
12 School Standards and Framework Act 1998 Sch 20 para 2(6). The powers of a governing body under Sch 20 para 2(6) to arrange for an act of collective worship to take place elsewhere than on the school premises must not be exercised so as to derogate from the rule that the required collective worship must normally take place on the school premises: Sch 20 para 2(7).

922. Nature of collective worship in community schools and foundation schools without a religious character. In relation to any community school[1], and any foundation school[2] which does not have a religious character[3], the required collective worship[4] must be wholly or mainly of a broadly Christian character[5]. Not every act of collective worship[6] in the school[7] need be wholly or mainly of a broadly Christian character provided that, taking any school term as a whole, most such acts which take place in the school are[8]. However:

(1) the extent to which, if at all, any acts of collective worship[9] which are not wholly or mainly of a broadly Christian character[10] take place in the school[11];

(2) the extent to which any act of collective worship in the school which is wholly or mainly of a broadly Christian character[12] reflects the broad traditions of Christian belief[13]; and

(3) the ways in which those traditions are reflected in any such act of collective worship[14],

must be such as may be appropriate having regard to any relevant considerations relating to the pupils[15] concerned which fall to be taken into account[16]. Those considerations are any circumstances relating to the family backgrounds of the pupils which are relevant for determining the character of the collective worship which is appropriate in their case[17], and their ages and aptitudes[18].

While a determination by a standing advisory council on religious education[19] that it is not appropriate for the requirement[20] that collective worship to be wholly or mainly of a broadly Christian character in the case of any community school, or any foundation school which does not have a religious character, or in the case of any class or description of pupils at any such school, has effect[21]:

(a) that requirement for the collective worship to be wholly or mainly of a broadly Christian character does not apply in relation to such a school or, as the case may be, the pupils in question[22]; and

(b) the required collective worship[23] in the case of the school or pupils must not be distinctive of any particular Christian or other religious denomination[24].

1 School Standards and Framework Act 1998 Sch 20 para 3(1)(a). As to the meaning of references to a community school see PARA 106.
2 As to the meaning of references to a foundation school see PARA 106.
3 School Standards and Framework Act 1998 Sch 20 para 3(1)(b). As to references to schools having a religious character see PARA 914 note 10.
4 As to the meaning of 'the required collective worship' see PARA 921 note 2.
5 School Standards and Framework Act 1998 Sch 20 para 3(2). For the purposes of Sch 20 para 3(2), collective worship is of a broadly Christian character if it reflects the broad traditions of Christian belief without being distinctive of any particular Christian denomination: Sch 20 para 3(3). As to the nature of this requirement in the context of multi-faith worship or the inclusion of non-Christian elements see *R v Secretary of State for Education, ex p R and D* [1994] ELR 495 at 498–503 per McCullough J.
6 References to acts of collective worship in the school include such acts which by virtue of the School Standards and Framework Act 1998 Sch 20 para 2(6) (see PARA 921) take place

otherwise than on the school premises: Sch 20 para 3(7). As to the meaning of 'premises' see PARA 62 note 20 (definition applied by s 142(8)). As to an 'act of collective worship' see PARA 920 note 5.

7 Ie required by the School Standards and Framework Act 1998 s 70: see PARA 920.

8 School Standards and Framework Act 1998 Sch 20 para 3(4). As to the fixing of dates for school terms and holidays see PARA 458.

9 Ie required by the School Standards and Framework Act 1998 s 70: see PARA 920.

10 Ie which do not comply with the School Standards and Framework Act 1998 Sch 20 para 3(2): see the text to notes 4–5.

11 School Standards and Framework Act 1998 Sch 20 para 3(5)(a).

12 Ie which complies with the School Standards and Framework Act 1998 Sch 20 para 3(2): see the text to notes 4–5.

13 School Standards and Framework Act 1998 Sch 20 para 3(5)(b).

14 School Standards and Framework Act 1998 Sch 20 para 3(5)(c).

15 As to the meaning of 'pupil' see PARA 20 note 4.

16 School Standards and Framework Act 1998 Sch 20 para 3(5).

17 School Standards and Framework Act 1998 Sch 20 para 3(6)(a).

18 School Standards and Framework Act 1998 Sch 20 para 3(6)(b).

19 Ie under the Education Act 1996 s 394: see PARA 927.

20 Ie the requirement imposed by the School Standards and Framework Act 1998 Sch 20 para 3(2): see the text to notes 4–5.

21 School Standards and Framework Act 1998 Sch 20 para 4(1), (2).

22 School Standards and Framework Act 1998 Sch 20 para 4(2)(a).

23 Ie the collective worship required by the School Standards and Framework Act 1998 s 70: see PARA 920.

24 School Standards and Framework Act 1998 Sch 20 para 4(2)(b). Schedule 20 para 4(2)(b) must not be taken as preventing that worship from being distinctive of any particular faith: Sch 20 para 4(2).

923. Nature of collective worship in foundation schools with a religious character and voluntary schools. In the case of a foundation school[1] which has a religious character[2] or a voluntary school[3], the required collective worship[4] must be: (1) in accordance with any provisions of the trust deed[5] relating to the school[6]; or (2) where provision for that purpose is not made by such a deed[7], and the school has a religious character[8], in accordance with the tenets and practices of the religion or religious denomination specified[9] in relation to the school[10].

1 As to the meaning of references to a foundation school see PARA 106.

2 As to the meaning of references to schools having a religious character see PARA 914 note 10.

3 As to the meaning of references to a voluntary school see PARA 106.

4 As to the meaning of 'the required collective worship' see PARA 921 note 2.

5 As to the meaning of 'trust deed' see PARA 108 note 6 (definition applied by the School Standards and Framework Act 1998 s 142(8)).

6 School Standards and Framework Act 1998 Sch 20 para 5(a).

7 School Standards and Framework Act 1998 Sch 20 para 5(b)(i).

8 School Standards and Framework Act 1998 Sch 20 para 5(b)(ii).

9 Ie the religion or religious denomination specified in relation to the school under the School Standards and Framework Act 1998 s 69(4): see PARA 914. As to the meaning of references to 'religion or religious denomination specified in relation to the school under s 69(4)' see PARA 146 note 12.

10 School Standards and Framework Act 1998 Sch 20 para 5(b).

924. Collective worship: exceptions and special arrangements. If:

(1)   the parent[1] of a pupil[2] at a community, foundation or voluntary school[3] requests that he may be wholly or partly excused from receiving religious education given at the school in accordance with the school's basic curriculum[4], the pupil must be so excused until the request is withdrawn[5];

(2)   the parent of any pupil at a community, foundation or voluntary school

other than a sixth-form pupil[6] requests that he may be wholly or partly excused from attendance at religious worship at the school, the pupil must be so excused until the request is withdrawn[7];

(3)   a sixth-form pupil requests that he may be wholly or partly excused from attendance at religious worship at a community, foundation or voluntary school, the pupil must be so excused[8].

Where in accordance with head (1) or (2) above a pupil has been wholly or partly excused from receiving religious education or from attendance at religious worship and the local authority[9] is satisfied:

(a)   that the parent of the pupil desires him to receive religious education of a kind which is not provided in the school during the periods of time during which he is so excused[10];

(b)   that the pupil cannot with reasonable convenience be sent to another community, foundation or voluntary school where religious education of the kind desired by the parent is provided[11]; and

(c)   that arrangements have been made for him to receive religious education of that kind during school hours elsewhere[12],

the pupil may be withdrawn from the school during such periods of time as are reasonably necessary for the purpose of enabling him to receive religious education in accordance with the arrangements[13].

Where the parent of a pupil who is a boarder[14] at a community, foundation or voluntary school and is not a sixth-form pupil requests that the pupil be permitted to receive religious education in accordance with the tenets of a particular religion or religious denomination outside school hours[15], or to attend worship in accordance with such tenets on Sundays or other days exclusively set apart for religious observance by the religious body to which his parent belongs[16], the governing body[17] must make arrangements for giving the pupil reasonable opportunities for doing so[18]. Where a sixth-form pupil who is a boarder at a community, foundation or voluntary school requests that he be permitted to receive religious education in accordance with the tenets of a particular religion or religious denomination outside school hours[19], or to attend worship in accordance with such tenets on Sundays or other days exclusively set apart for religious observance by the religious body to which the pupil belongs[20], the governing body must make arrangements for giving the pupil reasonable opportunities for doing so[21]. Such arrangements[22] may provide for making facilities for such education or worship available on the school premises, but any expenditure entailed by the arrangements must not be met from the school's budget share[23] or otherwise by the local authority[24].

Regulations[25] must make provision for ensuring that, so far as practicable, every pupil attending a community or foundation special school[26]: (i) receives religious education unless withdrawn from receiving such education in accordance with the wishes of his parent[27]; and (ii) attends religious worship unless withdrawn from attendance at such worship, in the case of a sixth-form pupil, in accordance with his own wishes[28], and, in any other case, in accordance with the wishes of his parent[29].

1   As to the meaning of 'parent' see PARA 7 note 6 (definition applied by the School Standards and Framework Act 1998 s 142(8)).

2   As to the meaning of 'pupil' see PARA 20 note 4 (definition applied by the School Standards and Framework Act 1998 s 142(8)).

3   As to the meaning of references to a community, foundation or voluntary school see PARA 106. As to the National Curriculum and academies see PARA 359. As to academies generally see PARA 345 et seq. As to free schools see PARA 368.

4   In the School Standards and Framework Act 1998 s 71(1), (1A), (1B) (see heads (1)–(3) in the text) the reference to religious education given in accordance with the school's basic curriculum is a reference to such education given in accordance with the provision included in the school's basic curriculum by virtue of the Education Act 2002 s 80(1)(a) (basic curriculum for every maintained school in England: see PARA 857) or s 101(1)(a) (basic curriculum for every maintained school in Wales: see PARA 871): School Standards and Framework Act 1998 s 71(2)(a) (amended by the Education Act 2002 s 215(1), Sch 21 para 105; and the Education and Inspections Act 2006 s 55(1), (3)). The reference to religious worship in the school includes religious worship which by virtue of the School Standards and Framework Act 1998 Sch 20 para 2(6) (see PARA 921) takes place otherwise than on the school premises: s 71(2)(b). As to the meaning of 'premises' see PARA 62 note 19 (definition applied by s 142(8)).

5   School Standards and Framework Act 1998 s 71(1) (substituted by the Education and Inspections Act 2006 s 55(1), (2)). As to parents' rights to ensure that their children are educated in accordance with their wishes generally see PARA 7. As to school attendance generally see PARA 435 et seq. As to the right of parents to ensure education and teaching in conformity with their own religious and philosophical convictions under the Convention for the Protection of Human Rights and Fundamental Freedoms see PARA 3.

6   'Sixth-form pupil' means any pupil who has ceased to be of compulsory school age, and is receiving education suitable to the requirements of pupils over compulsory school age: School Standards and Framework Act 1998 s 71(8) (added by the Education and Inspections Act 2006 s 55(1), (9)). As to the meaning of 'compulsory school age' see PARA 19.

7   School Standards and Framework Act 1998 s 71(1A) (s 71(1A), (1B) added by the Education and Inspections Act 2006 s 55(1), (2)).

8   School Standards and Framework Act 1998 s 71(1B) (as added: see note 7).

9   As to the meaning of 'local authority' see PARA 25 (definition applied by the School Standards and Framework Act 1998 s 142(8)). Any function of a local authority in England which is conferred by or under s 71 may be exercised by, or by employees of, such person as may be authorised in that behalf by the local authority whose function it is: Contracting Out (Local Authority Education Functions) (England) Order 2002, SI 2002/928, art 3, Sch 2 para (t) (art 3 amended by SI 2010/1172). As to the meaning of 'England' see PARA 7 note 3. As to the meaning of 'person' see PARA 7 note 6.

10 School Standards and Framework Act 1998 s 71(3)(a).

11 School Standards and Framework Act 1998 s 71(3)(b).

12 School Standards and Framework Act 1998 s 71(3)(c).

13 School Standards and Framework Act 1998 s 71(3) (amended by SI 2010/1158). A pupil may not be withdrawn from school under the School Standards and Framework Act 1998 s 71(3) unless the local authority is satisfied that the arrangements there mentioned are such as will not interfere with the attendance of the pupil at school on any day except at the beginning or end of a school session (or, if there is only one, the school session) on that day: s 71(4) (amended by SI 2010/1158).

14 As to the meaning of 'boarder' see PARA 31 note 19.

15 School Standards and Framework Act 1998 s 71(5)(a).

16 School Standards and Framework Act 1998 s 71(5)(b).

17 As to the governing bodies of maintained schools in England see PARA 150 et seq; and in Wales see PARA 195.

18 School Standards and Framework Act 1998 s 71(5) (amended by the Education and Inspections Act 2006 s 55(1), (5)).

19 School Standards and Framework Act 1998 s 71(5A)(a) (s 71(5A) added by the Education and Inspections Act 2006 s 55(1), (6)).

20 School Standards and Framework Act 1998 s 71(5A)(b) (as added: see note 19).

21 School Standards and Framework Act 1998 s 71(5A) (as added: see note 19).

22 Ie under the School Standards and Framework Act 1998 s 71(5) or (5A): see the text to notes 14–21.

23 As to the meaning of 'budget share' see PARA 315.

24 School Standards and Framework Act 1998 s 71(6) (amended by the Education and Inspections Act 2006 s 55(1), (7); SI 2010/1158).

25 'Regulations' means regulations made by the Secretary of State or, in relation to Wales, the Welsh Ministers: see the School Standards and Framework Act 1998 s 142(1). As to the Secretary of State see PARA 58. As to the Welsh Ministers see PARA 59. As to the meaning of 'Wales' see PARA 7 note 3. The functions of the Secretary of State under s 71, so far as exercisable in relation to Wales, were transferred to the National Assembly for Wales (see the

National Assembly for Wales (Transfer of Functions) Order 1999, SI 1999/672, art 2, Sch 1) and are now vested in the Welsh Ministers (see the Government of Wales Act 2006 s 162(1), Sch 11 para 30).

As to the regulations made see the Education (Maintained Special Schools) (Wales) Regulations 1999, SI 1999/1780, reg 12 (substituted by SI 2009/48); and the Education (Special Educational Needs) (England) (Consolidation) Regulations 2001, SI 2001/3455, reg 5A (added by SI 2006/3346; and substituted by SI 2007/1860).

26 As to the meaning of references to a community or foundation special school see PARA 106.
27 School Standards and Framework Act 1998 s 71(7)(a) (s 71(7) (substituted by the Education and Inspections Act 2006 s 55(1), (8)).
28 School Standards and Framework Act 1998 s 71(7)(b)(i) (as substituted: see note 27).
29 School Standards and Framework Act 1998 s 71(7)(b)(ii) (as substituted: see note 27).

D. STANDING ADVISORY COUNCILS ON RELIGIOUS EDUCATION

925. Religion: constitution and membership of advisory councils. A local authority[1] must constitute a standing advisory council on religious education for the purposes of[2]:

(1) advising the local authority on such matters connected with religious worship in community schools[3] or in foundation schools[4] which do not have a religious character[5], and the religious education to be given in accordance with an agreed or other syllabus[6], as the authority may refer to the council or as the council may see fit[7]; and

(2) carrying out the functions conferred[8] on it[9].

The matters referred to in head (1) above include, in particular, methods of teaching, the choice of materials and the provision of training for teachers[10].

The council must consist of such groups of persons appointed by the authority as representative members (called 'representative groups') as are required[11]. The representative groups so required are:

(a) a group of persons to represent such Christian denominations and other religions and denominations of such religions as, in the opinion of the authority, will appropriately reflect the principal religious traditions in the area[12];

(b) except in the case of an area in Wales[13], a group of persons to represent the Church of England[14];

(c) a group of persons to represent such associations representing teachers as, in the opinion of the authority, ought to be represented, having regard to the circumstances of the area[15]; and

(d) a group of persons to represent the authority[16].

The council may also include co-opted members, that is persons co-opted as members of the council by members of the council who have not themselves been so co-opted[17]. Where a representative group is required by head (b) above, the representative group required by head (a) above must not include persons appointed to represent the Church of England[18]. The number of representative members appointed to any representative group under head (a) above to represent each denomination or religion required to be represented must, so far as consistent with the efficient discharge of the group's functions, reflect broadly the proportionate strength of that denomination or religion in the area[19]. On any question to be decided by the council only the representative groups on the council are entitled to vote, and each representative group has a single vote[20].

Before appointing a person to represent any religion, denomination or associations as a member of the council[21], the local authority must take all reasonable steps to assure itself that he is representative of the religion, denomination or associations in question[22]. A member of the council who was appointed by the authority may be removed from membership by the authority if, in its opinion, he ceases to be representative of the religion, denomination or associations which he was appointed to represent or, as the case may be, he ceases to be representative of the authority[23]. A person co-opted as a member of the council holds office on such terms as may be determined by the members co-opting him[24]. A member of the council may at any time resign his office[25].

Subject to the provision relating to voting[26], the council and, in relation to any question falling to be decided by members of the council of any particular category, the members of that category, may regulate their own proceedings[27]. The validity of proceedings of the council or of the members of the council of any particular category is not affected by a vacancy in the office of any member of the council[28], or on the ground that a member of the council appointed to represent any religion, denomination or associations does not at the time of the proceedings represent the religion, denomination or associations in question[29].

1   As to the meaning of 'local authority' see PARA 25. Any function of a local authority in England which is conferred by or under the Education Act 1996 s 390 or s 392 (see the text to notes 21–29) may be exercised by, or by employees of, such person as may be authorised in that behalf by the local authority whose function it is: Contracting Out (Local Authority Education Functions) (England) Order 2002, SI 2002/928, art 3, Sch 1 paras (w), (x) (art 3, Sch 1 para (w) amended by SI 2010/1172). As to the meaning of 'England' see PARA 7 note 3. As to the meaning of 'person' see PARA 7 note 6.
2   See the Education Act 1996 s 390(1) (amended by SI 2010/1158). Standard advisory councils on religious education are often abbreviated to 'SACREs'.
3   As to the meaning of references to a community school see PARA 106.
4   As to the meaning of references to a foundation school see PARA 106.
5   Education Act 1996 s 391(1)(a)(i) (s 391(1)(a) substituted by the School Standards and Framework Act 1998 s 140(1), Sch 30 para 94(1), (2)). As to the meaning of references to schools having a religious character see PARA 914 note 10 (definition applied by the Education Act 1996 s 391(1)(a) (as so substituted)).
6   Ie in accordance with the School Standards and Framework Act 1998 Sch 19 (see PARA 915 et seq): Education Act 1996 s 391(1)(a)(ii) (as substituted: see note 5).
7   Education Act 1996 s 391(1)(a) (as substituted (see note 5); and amended by SI 2010/1158).
8   Ie conferred by the Education Act 1996 s 394: see PARA 927. As to the meaning of 'functions' see PARA 18 note 5.
9   Education Act 1996 s 391(1)(b).
10 Education Act 1996 s 391(2).
11 Education Act 1996 s 390(2) (substituted by the School Standards and Framework Act 1998 Sch 30 para 93).
12 Education Act 1996 s 390(4)(a).
13 As to the meaning of 'Wales' see PARA 7 note 3.
14 Education Act 1996 s 390(4)(b). As to the Church of England see ECCLESIASTICAL LAW vol 34 (2011) PARA 50 et seq.
15 Education Act 1996 s 390(4)(c).
16 Education Act 1996 s 390(4)(d).
17 Education Act 1996 s 390(3).
18 Education Act 1996 s 390(5).
19 Education Act 1996 s 390(6).
20 Education Act 1996 s 390(7).
21 For these purposes, 'the council' means the standing advisory council on religious education constituted by a local authority under the Education Act 1996 s 390: s 392(1) (amended by SI 2010/1158). See the text to notes 1–20.
22 Education Act 1996 s 392(2). See also note 1.
23 Education Act 1996 s 392(3).
24 Education Act 1996 s 392(5).
25 Education Act 1996 s 392(6).
26 Ie subject to the Education Act 1996 s 390(7): see the text to note 20.
27 Education Act 1996 s 392(7).

28 Education Act 1996 s 392(8)(a).
29 Education Act 1996 s 392(8)(b).

926. Religion: functions of advisory councils. The representative groups[1] on the standing advisory council[2], other than the group consisting of persons appointed to represent the local authority[3], may at any time require a review of any agreed syllabus[4] for the time being adopted by the authority[5]. Each representative group concerned has a single vote on the question of whether to require such a review[6].

The council must in each year publish a report as to the exercise of its functions[7] and any action taken by representative groups on the council in relation to requiring a review of any agreed syllabus[8] during the last preceding year[9]. The council's report must in particular specify any matters in respect of which the council has given advice to the local authority[10], broadly describe the nature of the advice given[11], and, where any such matter was not referred to the council by the authority, it must give the council's reasons for offering advice on that matter[12]. A council for an area in Wales[13] must send a copy of each report so published by it to the Welsh Ministers[14].

1 Ie required by the Education Act 1996 s 390(4): see PARA 925.
2 As to standing advisory councils (often known as 'SACREs') see PARA 925.
3 As to the meaning of 'local authority' see PARA 25.
4 As to the meaning of 'agreed syllabus' see PARA 910 note 2.
5 Education Act 1996 s 391(3). As to access to meetings and documents of a council see PARA 930.
6 Education Act 1996 s 391(4). Schedule 31 para 3 (see PARA 911) has effect to require the authority, on receiving written notification of any such requirement, to cause a conference constituted in accordance with Sch 31 (see PARAS 911–913) to be convened for the purpose of reconsidering any agreed syllabus to which the requirement relates: s 391(5). As to the meaning of 'written' see PARA 76 note 8.
7 As to the meaning of 'functions' see PARA 18 note 5.
8 Ie under the Education Act 1996 s 391(3): see the text to notes 1–5.
9 Education Act 1996 s 391(6).
10 Education Act 1996 s 391(7)(a).
11 Education Act 1996 s 391(7)(b).
12 Education Act 1996 s 391(7)(c).
13 As to the meaning of 'Wales' see PARA 7 note 3.
14 Education Act 1996 s 391(10) (substituted by the Education Act 2011 Sch 8 paras 5, 6). As to the Welsh Ministers see PARA 59. The functions under the Education Act 1996 s 391(10) were originally vested in the National Assembly for Wales and are now exercisable by the Welsh Ministers by virtue of the Government of Wales Act 2006 s 162(1), Sch 11 paras 30, 32.

927. Determination of cases in which requirement for Christian collective worship is not to apply. The standing advisory council constituted by a local authority[1] must, on an application made by the head teacher[2] of:

(1) any community school maintained by the authority[3]; or

(2) any foundation school[4] which has not been designated[5] by the appropriate national authority[6] as having a religious character[7],

consider whether it is appropriate for the requirement for Christian collective worship[8] to apply in the case of the school or in the case of any class or description of pupils[9] at the school[10]. Where an application is made under head (1) above in respect of a community school which becomes a foundation school[11] before the application is determined, it must, unless withdrawn by the head teacher, continue as if made under head (2) above[12]. Before making an application under head (1) or head (2) above, the head teacher of a school must consult the governing body[13]; and on being consulted by the head teacher, the governing body may if it thinks fit take such steps as it considers appropriate for consulting all persons[14] appearing to it to be parents[15] of registered pupils[16] at the school[17]. An application must be made in such manner and form as the council may require[18].

In determining whether it is appropriate for that requirement to apply the council must have regard to any circumstances relating to the family backgrounds of the pupils at the school, or of the pupils of the particular class or description in question, which are relevant for determining the character of the collective worship appropriate in their case[19]. The council must give the head teacher written[20] notification of its decision on the application[21].

1   Ie under the Education Act 1996 s 390: see PARA 925. As to the meaning of 'local authority' see PARA 25.
2   As to the meaning of 'head teacher' see PARA 86 note 4.
3   Education Act 1996 s 394(1)(a) (amended by the School Standards and Framework Act 1998 s 140(1), Sch 30 para 97(1), (2)(a)). As to the meaning of references to a community school see PARA 106.
4   As to the meaning of references to a foundation school see PARA 106.
5   Ie under the School Standards and Framework Act 1998 s 69(3): see PARA 914.
6   Ie the Secretary of State or, in relation to Wales, the Welsh Ministers. As to the Secretary of State see PARA 58. As to the Welsh Ministers see PARA 59. As to the meaning of 'Wales' see PARA 7 note 3.
7   Education Act 1996 s 394(1)(b) (substituted by the School Standards and Framework Act 1998 Sch 30 para 97(1), (2)(b)).
8   Ie the requirement imposed by the School Standards and Framework Act 1998 Sch 20 para 3(2): see PARA 922.
9   As to the meaning of 'pupil' see PARA 20 note 4.
10 Education Act 1996 s 394(1) (amended by the School Standards and Framework Act 1998 Sch 30 para 97(1), (2)(c); and SI 2010/1158).
11 Ie by virtue of the relevant enactments. 'The relevant enactments' means, in relation to England, the Education and Inspections Act 2006 ss 18–24 (see PARAS 132–136): Education Act 1996 s 394(9) (added by the Education and Inspections Act 2006 s 30, Sch 3 para 9(1), (3); and amended by the School Standards and Organisation (Wales) Act 2013 Sch 5 para 17(1), (3)). As to the meaning of 'England' see PARA 7 note 3.
12 Education Act 1996 s 394(8) (amended by the School Standards and Framework Act 1998 Sch 30 para 97(1), (4); and the Education and Inspections Act 2006 s 30, Sch 3 para 9(1), (2)).
13 Education Act 1996 s 394(5). As to the governing bodies of maintained schools in England see PARA 150 et seq; and in Wales see PARA 195. As to the exercise of the duty to consult see JUDICIAL REVIEW vol 61 (2010) PARA 627.
14 As to the meaning of 'person' see PARA 7 note 6.
15 As to the meaning of 'parent' see PARA 7 note 6.
16 As to the meaning of 'registered pupil' see PARA 437.
17 Education Act 1996 s 394(6).
18 Education Act 1996 s 394(7).
19 Education Act 1996 s 394(2). As to the review of determinations see PARA 928. As to the power of the appropriate national authority to direct an advisory council to revoke a determination or discharge a duty see PARA 929.
20 As to the meaning of 'written' see PARA 76 note 8.
21 Education Act 1996 s 394(3). Where the council determines that it is not appropriate for the requirement to apply as mentioned in s 394(1) (see the text to notes 1–10), the determination takes effect for the purposes of the School Standards and Framework Act 1998 Sch 20 para 4 (disapplication of requirement for Christian collective worship: see PARA 922) on such date as may be specified in the notification of the council's decision under the Education Act 1996 s 394(3): s 394(4) (amended by the School Standards and Framework Act 1998 Sch 30 para 97(1), (3)).

928. Religion: review of determinations. Any determination by a standing advisory council[1] by virtue of which the requirement for Christian collective worship[2] does not for the time being apply in the case of a school or a class or description of pupils[3] at a school must be reviewed by the council[4]:

(1)   at any time on an application made by the head teacher[5]; and

(2)   in any event not later than the end of the period of five years beginning with the date on which the determination first took effect or, where it has since been reviewed, beginning with the effective date of the decision on the last review[6].

On any review under head (2) above the council must give the head teacher an opportunity of making representations as to the determination under review[7]. On any such review under head (1) and head (2) above, the council may confirm the determination, with or without variation[8], or revoke it[9]. The council must give the head teacher written[10] notification[11] of its decision, specifying the effective date of that decision for the purposes of head (2) above[12].

1   Ie any determination under the Education Act 1996 s 394: see PARA 927.
2   Ie the requirement imposed by the School Standards and Framework Act 1998 Sch 20 para 3(2): see PARA 922.
3   As to the meaning of 'pupil' see PARA 20 note 4.
4   Education Act 1996 s 395(1) (amended by the School Standards and Framework Act 1998 s 140(1), Sch 30 para 98).
5   Education Act 1996 s 395(1)(a). As to the meaning of 'head teacher' see PARA 86 note 4. An application under s 395(1)(a) must be made in such manner and form as the council may require: s 395(8). The head teacher of a school must consult the governing body before making an application under s 395(1)(a): s 395(6). On being consulted by the head teacher, the governing body may if it thinks fit take such steps as it considers appropriate for consulting all persons appearing to it to be parents of registered pupils at the school: s 395(7). As to the governing bodies of maintained schools in England see PARA 150 et seq; and in Wales see PARA 195. As to the meaning of 'person' see PARA 7 note 6. As to the meaning of 'parent' see PARA 7 note 6. As to the meaning of 'registered pupil' see PARA 437. As to the exercise of the duty to consult see JUDICIAL REVIEW vol 61 (2010) PARA 627.
6   Education Act 1996 s 395(1)(b). Any determination which is required to be reviewed under s 395(1)(b) ceases to have effect, if not confirmed on such a review, at the end of the period there mentioned: s 395(5).
7   Education Act 1996 s 395(2). The head teacher of a school must consult the governing body before making any such representations: s 395(6). On being consulted by the head teacher, the governing body may if it thinks fit take such steps as it considers appropriate for consulting all persons appearing to it to be parents of registered pupils at the school: s 395(7).
8   Education Act 1996 s 395(3)(a).
9   Education Act 1996 s 395(3)(b). Such revocation is without prejudice to any further determination under s 394 (see PARA 927): see s 395(3)(b).
10   As to the meaning of 'written' see PARA 76 note 8.
11   As to the service of notices and documents see the Education Act 1996 s 572; and PARA 76.
12   Education Act 1996 s 395(4). As to the power of the appropriate national authority to direct an advisory council to revoke a determination or discharge a duty see PARA 929.

929.   Religion: power to direct advisory council to revoke determination or discharge duty.   Where the appropriate national authority[1] is satisfied, either on complaint by any person[2] or otherwise, that any standing advisory council on religious education constituted by a local authority[3]:

(1)   has acted, or is proposing to act, unreasonably in determining[4] whether it is appropriate for the requirement for Christian collective worship[5] to apply in the case of any school or any class or description of pupils[6] at a school[7]; or

(2)   has failed to discharge any duty imposed[8] on it[9],

the appropriate national authority may give the council such directions[10] as to the revocation of the determination, or the withdrawal of the proposed determination or, as the case may be, the discharge of the duty as appears to it to be expedient, and the council must comply with the directions[11]. Such directions may provide for the making by the council of a new determination to take effect in place of the determination or proposed determination to be revoked or withdrawn by it[12].

1　Ie the Secretary of State or, in relation to Wales, the Welsh Ministers. As to the Secretary of State see PARA 58. As to the Welsh Ministers see PARA 59. As to the meaning of 'Wales' see PARA 7 note 3. The functions of the Secretary of State under the Education Act 1996 s 396, so far as exercisable in relation to Wales, were transferred to the National Assembly for Wales (see the National Assembly for Wales (Transfer of Functions) Order 1999, SI 1999/672, art 2, Sch 1) and are now vested in the Welsh Ministers (see the Government of Wales Act 2006 s 162(1), Sch 11 para 30).
2　As to the meaning of 'person' see PARA 7 note 6.
3　Ie constituted under the Education Act 1996 s 390: see PARA 925. As to the meaning of 'local authority' see PARA 25.
4　Ie for the purposes of the Education Act 1996 s 394 (see PARA 927) or s 395 (see PARA 928).
5　Ie the requirement imposed by the School Standards and Framework Act 1998 Sch 20 para 3(2): see PARA 922.
6　As to the meaning of 'pupil' see PARA 20 note 4.
7　Education Act 1996 s 396(1)(a) (amended by the School Standards and Framework Act 1998 s 140(1), Sch 30 para 99).
8　Ie under the Education Act 1996 s 394 (see PARA 927) or s 395 (see PARA 928).
9　Education Act 1996 s 396(1)(b).
10　As to directions generally see the Education Act 1996 s 570; and PARA 75.
11　Education Act 1996 s 396(1) (amended by SI 2010/1158).
12　Education Act 1996 s 396(2).

930. Religion: access to meetings and documents. In relation to any convened conference[1], and any standing advisory council on religious education[2], regulations[3] may make provision:

(1)　for meetings of conferences or councils to be open[4] to members of the public[5];

(2)　requiring conferences or councils to give notice, in such manner as may be prescribed, of the time and place of such meetings[6]; and

(3)　requiring conferences or councils, at such time or times as may be prescribed to make available for inspection[7], or to provide on payment of such fee as they think fit, not exceeding the cost of supply[8], copies of the agendas and reports for such meetings to members of the public[9].

Such regulations may apply to committees appointed[10] by local authorities[11], sub-committees appointed[12] by conferences[13], and representative groups[14] on councils[15], as they apply to conferences and councils[16].

1　Ie any conference convened under the Education Act 1996 Sch 31 paras 1–3 (see PARA 911): see s 397(1)(a).
2　Ie any standing advisory council on religious education constituted under the Education Act 1996 s 390 (see PARA 925): see s 397(1)(b).
3　'Regulations' means regulations made by the Secretary of State or, in relation to Wales, the Welsh Ministers: see the Education Act 1996 s 579(1). As to the Secretary of State see PARA 58. As to the Welsh Ministers see PARA 59. As to the meaning of 'Wales' see PARA 7 note 3. The functions of the Secretary of State under s 397, so far as exercisable in relation to Wales, were transferred to the National Assembly for Wales (see the National Assembly for Wales (Transfer of Functions) Order 1999, SI 1999/672, art 2, Sch 1) and are now vested in the Welsh Ministers (see the Government of Wales Act 2006 s 162(1), Sch 11 para 30). At the date at which this volume states the law, no regulations had been made under the Education Act 1996 s 397 but, by virtue of s 582(3), Sch 39 para 1, the Religious Education (Meetings of Local Conferences and Councils) Regulations 1994, SI 1994/1304, have effect as if so made.
4　Ie subject to prescribed exceptions. 'Prescribed' means prescribed by regulations: Education Act 1996 s 579(1).
5　Education Act 1996 s 397(2)(a). As to the requirement for meetings to be held in public see the Religious Education (Meetings of Local Conferences and Councils) Regulations 1994, SI 1994/1304, reg 3. As to the prescribed exceptions see regs 1–2, 9.

6   Education Act 1996 s 397(2)(b). As to the giving of notice of the time and place of such meetings see the Religious Education (Meetings of Local Conferences and Councils) Regulations 1994, SI 1994/1304, reg 4.
7   Education Act 1996 s 397(2)(c)(i).
8   Education Act 1996 s 397(2)(c)(ii).
9   Education Act 1996 s 397(2)(c). As to the inspection of agendas and reports of meetings and the provision of copies of agendas and reports see the Religious Education (Meetings of Local Conferences and Councils) Regulations 1994, SI 1994/1304, regs 5–10.
10 Ie under the Education Act 1996 Sch 31 para 4: see PARA 912.
11 Education Act 1996 s 397(3)(a) (amended by SI 2010/1158). As to the meaning of 'local authority' see PARA 25.
12 Ie under the Education Act 1996 Sch 31: see PARA 912.
13 Education Act 1996 s 397(3)(b).
14 Ie appointed under the Education Act 1996 s 390(4): see PARA 925.
15 Education Act 1996 s 397(3)(c).
16 Education Act 1996 s 397(3).

E. NO REQUIREMENT OF ATTENDANCE AT SUNDAY SCHOOL

931. No requirement of attendance at Sunday school etc. It must not be required, as a condition of a pupil[1] attending a maintained school[2], or a person attending such a school to receive further education[3] or any training for members of the school workforce[4], that he must attend or abstain from attending a Sunday school or a place of religious worship[5].

1   As to the meaning of 'pupil' see PARA 20 note 4.
2   Education Act 1996 s 398(1)(a) (s 398(1) renumbered by the Education Act 2005 s 98, Sch 14 para 16(1), (3)). As to the meaning of 'school' see PARA 91. As to maintained schools see PARA 99 et seq. As to academies see PARA 324 et seq.
3   As to the meaning of 'further education' see PARA 23.
4   Education Act 1996 s 398(1)(b) (s 398(1) as renumbered (see note 2); s 398(1)(b) amended by the Education Act 2005 Sch 14 para 16(1), (2)). For this purpose, the reference to training for members of the school workforce is to be read in accordance with the Education Act 2005 ss 96(1), 100 (references to training for teachers or other members of the school workforce: see PARA 1059 note 3): Education Act 1996 s 398(2) (added by the Education Act 2005 Sch 14 para 16(1), (3); and amended by the Education Act 2011 Sch 5 paras 10, 11).
5   Education Act 1996 s 398(1) (as renumbered: see note 2).

(3) EXTERNAL QUALIFICATIONS

932. Obligation to enter pupils for public examinations. The governing body[1] of a maintained school[2] must secure that each registered pupil[3] at the school is entered, at such time as it considers appropriate, for each prescribed public examination[4] for which he is being prepared at the school at the time in question in each syllabus for that examination for which he is being so prepared[5]. However, the governing body is not required to secure that a pupil is entered for any examination, or for an examination in any syllabus for that examination, if either:

(1)   it considers that there are educational reasons in the case of that particular pupil for not entering him for that examination or, as the case may be, for not entering him for that examination in that syllabus[6]; or

(2)   the parent[7] of the pupil requests in writing[8] that the pupil should not be entered for that examination or, as the case may be, for that examination in that syllabus[9];

but, these exceptions do not apply to an examination which is part of the assessment arrangements[10] for the fourth key stage[11] and which applies in the case of that pupil[12]. Nor is the governing body required to secure that a pupil is entered for any examination in any syllabus for that examination if it has secured his entry for another prescribed public examination in a corresponding syllabus[13]. A pupil excluded from a school for violence may be allowed to sit examinations as a visitor, rather than be reinstated[14].

As soon as practicable after determining whether or not to secure the entry of any pupil for a prescribed public examination in any syllabus for which he is being prepared at the school, the governing body must notify[15] the pupil's parent in writing of its determination in relation to each such syllabus[16].

1   As to the governing bodies of maintained schools in England see PARA 150 et seq; and in Wales see PARA 195. As to the meanings of 'England' and 'Wales' see PARA 7 note 3.

2   For these purposes, 'maintained school' includes a community or foundation special school established in a hospital: Education Act 1996 s 402(6)(a) (amended by the School Standards and Framework Act 1998 s 140(1), Sch 30 paras 57, 101). As to the meaning of 'school' see PARA 91. As to maintained schools generally see PARA 99 et seq. As to the meaning of references to a community or foundation special school see PARA 106. As to the National Curriculum and academies see PARA 359. As to academies generally see PARA 345 et seq. As to free schools see PARA 368. As to independent schools see PARA 369 et seq.

3   As to the meaning of 'registered pupil' see PARA 437.

4   For the purposes of the Education Act 1996 s 402, references to a 'prescribed public examination' are to be construed in accordance with s 462 (see PARA 335 note 6): s 402(6)(b). 'Prescribed' means prescribed by regulations; and 'regulations' means regulations made by the Secretary of State or, in relation to Wales, the Welsh Ministers: see the Education Act 1996 s 579(1). As to the Secretary of State see PARA 58. As to the Welsh Ministers see PARA 59. The functions of the Secretary of State under s 402, so far as exercisable in relation to Wales, were transferred to the National Assembly for Wales (see the National Assembly for Wales (Transfer of Functions) Order 1999, SI 1999/672, art 2, Sch 1) and are now vested in the Welsh Ministers (see the Government of Wales Act 2006 s 162(1), Sch 11 para 30).

    As to the regulations made see, in relation to England, the Education (Prescribed Public Examinations) (England) Regulations 2010, SI 2010/2327; and, in relation to Wales, the Education (Prescribed Public Examinations) Regulations 1989, SI 1989/377 (revoked in relation to England by SI 2010/2327) (which have effect as if made under the Education Act 1996 s 402 by virtue of s 582(3), Sch 39 para 1).

5   Education Act 1996 s 402(1).

6   Education Act 1996 s 402(2)(a).

7   As to the meaning of 'parent' see PARA 7 note 6.

8   As to the meaning of 'writing' see PARA 76 note 8.

9   Education Act 1996 s 402(2)(b).

10   For these purposes, 'assessment arrangements', in relation to a school maintained by a local authority in England, has the same meaning as in the Education Act 2002 Pt 6 (ss 76–96) (the curriculum in England: see PARA 859) and, in relation to a school maintained by a local authority in Wales, has the same meaning as in Pt 7 (ss 97–118) (the curriculum in Wales: see PARA 873): Education Act 1996 s 402(6)(aa) (added by the Education Act 2002 s 215(1), Sch 21 para 45; and amended by SI 2010/1158). As to the meaning of 'local authority' see PARA 25.

11   For these purposes, 'fourth key stage', in relation to a school maintained by a local authority in England, has the same meaning as in the Education Act 2002 Pt 6 (ss 76–96) (the curriculum in England: see PARA 860) and, in relation to a school maintained by a local authority in Wales, has the same meaning as in Pt 7 (ss 97–118) (the curriculum in Wales: see PARA 875): Education Act 1996 s 402(6)(aa) (as added and amended: see note 10).

12   Education Act 1996 s 402(2).

13   Education Act 1996 s 402(3). For the purposes of s 402(3), a syllabus for a prescribed public examination is to be regarded as corresponding to a syllabus for another prescribed public examination if the same course of study is provided at the school in preparation for both syllabuses: s 402(4).

14   *R (on the application of MB) v Independent Appeal Panel of S Metropolitan Borough Council* [2002] EWHC 1509 (Admin), [2002] ELR 676. As to the exclusion and reinstatement of pupils see PARA 517 et seq.

15   As to the service of notices and documents see the Education Act 1996 s 572; and PARA 76.

16   Education Act 1996 s 402(5).

933. National framework of qualifications. The Secretary of State[1] and the Welsh Ministers[2] are responsible for establishing a national framework of qualifications. This national framework comprises three main types of qualifications. These are:

(1) general qualifications, such as the General Certificate in Secondary Education ('GCSE')[3] and Advanced level ('A' level), which are about a particular subject;

(2) vocationally related qualifications, such as vocational A levels ('Advanced General National Vocational Qualifications', or 'Advanced GNVQs'), which give a broad introduction to a particular sector of the economy; and

(3) occupational qualifications, such as National Vocational Qualifications ('NVQs'), which test the skills and knowledge needed to do a specific job.

The Secretary of State and the Welsh Ministers are responsible for setting out the standards that such qualifications must meet, and determining which qualifications are included in the national framework according to these standards.

The Secretary of State and the Welsh Ministers are responsible for ensuring that such qualifications are assessed properly by the awarding bodies. There are three unitary awarding bodies[4] who are responsible for specification development, production of examination papers, centre approval, awarding qualifications and ensuring standardisation of marking. The Secretary of State and the Welsh Ministers are responsible for ensuring that the awarding bodies are capable of delivering qualifications effectively and that the qualifications are of good quality. If satisfied as to the awarding bodies' capability and the quality of the qualifications, the Secretary of State and the Welsh Ministers will accredit those qualifications which will then be included within the national framework.

The Secretary of State and the Welsh Ministers have power to approve external qualifications to be provided at schools, institutions and by employers[5]. In order for such external qualifications to be approved they must first have been accredited to the national framework.

1 As to the Secretary of State see PARA 58. Note that the Qualifications and Curriculum Development Agency was abolished in 2012: see PARA 824. Note also that National Curriculum assessments are now performed by the Standards and Testing Agency, an executive agency of the Department for Education: see further PARA 824 note 6. See also the Learning and Skills Act 2000 s 98; and PARA 935.

2 As to the Welsh Ministers see PARA 59.

3 As the final stage of GCSE reform the Department for Education announced on 16 June 2015 that pupils starting secondary school in September 2015 must study the key English Baccalaureate (EBacc) subjects at GCSE. From 2017, a new 9 to 1 GCSE grading scale is to replace the A to U system, level 5 being considered a 'good pass'. For more information see the Department for Education website. See in particular 'New reforms to raise standards and improve behaviour' (16 June 2015).

4 The former awarding bodies have been consolidated to form three unitary awarding bodies known as: (1) the Assessment and Qualifications Alliance; (2) the Edexcel Foundation; and (3) Oxford, Cambridge and RSA Examinations.

    The former awarding bodies (or examination boards) which are now part of the Assessment and Qualifications Alliance are the Associated Examining Board, the Joint Matriculation Board, the Northern Examinations and Assessment Board, the Northern Examining Association, the South East Regional Examinations Boards, the South Western Examinations Board, the Southern Examining Group, the Southern Regional Examinations Board, and the Southern Universities Joint Board.

The former awarding bodies which are now part of the Edexcel Foundation are the Business and Technical Education Council, the Business Education Council, the Technical Education Council, and the University of London Examinations and Assessment Council.

The former awarding bodies which are now part of Oxford, Cambridge and RSA Examinations are the East Midland Regional Examinations Board, the Midland Examining Group, the Oxford and Cambridge Schools Examination Board, the RSA Examinations Board, the University of Cambridge Local Examinations Syndicate, the University of Oxford Delegacy of Local Examinations and the West Midlands Examinations Board.

5 As to the approval of external qualifications see PARAS 935, 937.

934. Courses of education or training for persons under 19. In relation to a course[1] of education or training:

(1) which is provided, or proposed to be provided, by or on behalf of a school or institution or employer[2];

(2) which leads to a relevant qualification[3]; and

(3) which is provided, or proposed to be provided, for pupils who are of compulsory school age[4] or for pupils who are above that age but have not attained the age of 19[5],

unless the relevant qualification is approved[6], the course must not be funded by an authorised body[7], or provided by or on behalf of a maintained school[8].

1 The course may be one of two or more components leading to the same qualification: Learning and Skills Act 2000 s 96(4).
2 Learning and Skills Act 2000 s 96(1)(a).
3 Learning and Skills Act 2000 s 96(1)(b) (amended by the Apprenticeships, Skills, Children and Learning Act 2009 ss 174, 192, Sch 12 paras 26, 27(1), (2)). 'A relevant qualification': (1) in relation to England, means a qualification to which the Apprenticeships, Skills, Children and Learning Act 2009 Pt 7 (ss 127–174) (see PARA 825 et seq) applies; (2) in relation to Wales, has the same meaning as in the Education Act 1997 s 30 (see PARA 854 note 16): Learning and Skills Act 2000 s 96(5) (substituted by the Apprenticeships, Skills, Children and Learning Act 2009 ss 174, 192, Sch 12 paras 26, 27(1), (4)). As to the meanings of 'England' and 'Wales' see PARA 7 note 3. As from a day to be appointed, the definition is replaced to mean a qualification to which the Apprenticeships, Skills, Children and Learning Act 2009 Pt 7 (ss 127–174) applies: Learning and Skills Act 2000 s 96(5) (prospectively substituted by the Qualifications Wales Act 2015 Sch 4 para 3(1), (2)(b)). At the date at which this volume states the law no such day had been appointed.
4 As to the meaning of 'compulsory school age' see PARA 19.
5 Learning and Skills Act 2000 s 96(1)(c). As to the time at which a person attains a particular age see PARA 7 note 6.
6 Ie approved under the Learning and Skills Act 2000 s 98 in relation to England (see PARA 935) or s 99 in relation to Wales (see PARA 937). See note 7.
7 Learning and Skills Act 2000 s 96(2)(a). As from a day to be appointed, the reference to s 99 is omitted: s 96(2) (prospectively amended by the Qualifications Wales Act 2015 Sch 4 para 3(1), (2)(a)(i))). At the date at which this volume states the law no such day had been appointed. In application to England, the following are authorised bodies: (1) a local authority; (2) a body specified by order by the Secretary of State for these purposes: Learning and Skills Act 2000 s 100(1)(b), (c) (s 100(1) amended by the Apprenticeships, Skills, Children and Learning Act 2009 s 123(2), Sch 6 paras 14, 46; and SI 2010/1158). As from a day to be appointed, the reference to 'application to England' is repealed: Learning and Skills Act 2000 s 100(1) (prospectively amended by the Qualifications Wales Act 2015 Sch 4 para 3(1), (6)(a)). At the date at which this volume states the law no such day had been appointed. In application to Wales, the following are authorised bodies: (a) the Welsh Ministers; (b) a local authority; (c) a body specified by order by the Welsh Ministers for these purposes: Learning and Skills Act 2000 s 100(2)(a)–(c) (s 100(2) amended by SI 2005/3238; the Apprenticeships, Skills, Children and Learning Act 2009 s 123(2), Sch 6 paras 14, 46; and SI 2010/1158). As from a day to be appointed, the Learning and Skills Act 2000 s 100(2) is repealed by the Qualifications Wales Act 2015 Sch 4 para 3(1), (6)(b). At the date at which this volume states the law no such day had been appointed. At the date at which this volume states the law, no orders had been made under the Learning and Skills Act 2000 s 100. As to the meaning of 'local authority' see PARA 25 (definition applied by s 96(9) (added by SI 2010/1158)). As to the Secretary of State see PARA 58. As to the Welsh Ministers see PARA 59. As from a day to be appointed, the Learning

and Skills Act 2000 is revised to refer to ss 100 and 101 and for 'local authority' to have the
same meaning as 'local authority in England': s 96(9) (prospectively amended by the
Qualifications Wales Act 2015 Sch 4 para 3(1), (2)(c)). At the date at which this volume states
the law no such day had been appointed.

8   Learning and Skills Act 2000 s 96(2)(b). As from a day to be appointed, the words 'in England'
     are added to the end of this provision: s 96(2)(b) (prospectively amended by the Qualifications
     Wales Act 2015 Sch 4 para 3(1), (2)(a)(ii)). At the date at which this volume states the law no
     such day had been appointed. For these purposes, 'maintained school' means a community,
     foundation or voluntary school or a community or foundation special school: Learning and
     Skills Act 2000 s 96(8). As to the meaning of references to a community, foundation or
     voluntary school or a community or foundation special school see PARA 106. In relation to a
     maintained school, the local authority and the governing body must carry out their functions
     with a view to securing that s 96(2)(b) is not contravened: s 96(3) (amended by SI 2010/1158).
     As to the governing bodies of maintained schools in England see PARA 150 et seq; and in Wales
     see PARA 195. As to the enforcement of the Learning and Skills Act 2000 s 96 in relation to
     England see PARA 936; and in relation to Wales see PARA 938. As to academies see PARA 345 et
     seq.

935. Approved qualifications in England. In relation to England[1], a
qualification is approved at a given time if: (1) it is then approved by the
Secretary of State[2]; or (2) it is then approved by a body then designated by him
for these purposes[3]. A qualification may be approved only if the following
conditions are satisfied in relation to the qualification[4], or the Office of
Qualifications and Examinations Regulation[5] is consulted before the approval is
given[6]. The conditions are that: (a) the qualification is a regulated qualification[7];
and (b) if the qualification is subject to the accreditation requirement[8], it is
accredited[9]. Approval may be given generally or in relation to particular cases[10].

The Secretary of State may at any time revoke a designation[11], an approval
given by him[12], or an approval given by a designated body[13]; and a designated
body may at any time revoke an approval given by it[14].

1   The Learning and Skills Act 2000 s 98 has effect for the purposes of s 96 (see PARA 934) in its
     application to England: Learning and Skills Act 2000 s 98(1) (amended by the Apprenticeships,
     Skills, Children and Learning Act 2009 s 123(2), Sch 6 paras 14, 44(1), (2)). As to the meaning
     of 'England' see PARA 7 note 3. As from a day to be appointed, the words 'in its application to
     England' are repealed: Learning and Skills Act 2000 s 98(1) (prospectively amended by the
     Qualifications Wales Act 2015 Sch 4 para 3(1), (4)). At the date at which this volume states the
     law no such day had been appointed.
2   Learning and Skills Act 2000 s 98(2)(a). As to the Secretary of State see PARA 58.
3   Learning and Skills Act 2000 s 98(2)(b).
4   Learning and Skills Act 2000 s 98(2B)(a) (s 98(2B), (2C) added by the Apprenticeships, Skills,
     Children and Learning Act 2009 ss 174, 192, Sch 12 paras 26, 28(1), (2)).
5   As to the Office of Qualifications and Examinations Regulation see PARA 824 et seq.
6   Learning and Skills Act 2000 s 98(2B)(b) (as added: see note 4). As to the exercise of the duty to
     consult see JUDICIAL REVIEW vol 61 (2010) PARA 627.
7   Learning and Skills Act 2000 s 98(2C)(a) (as added: see note 4). A 'regulated qualification' is
     one within the meaning of the Apprenticeships, Skills, Children and Learning Act 2009 Pt 7
     (ss 127–174) (see PARA 826 note 7): see the Learning and Skills Act 2000 s 98(2C)(a) (as so
     added).
8   Ie within the meaning of the Apprenticeships, Skills, Children and Learning Act 2009 Pt 7 Ch 2
     (ss 132–158): see PARA 835 note 3.
9   Learning and Skills Act 2000 s 98(2C)(b) (as added: see note 4). The accreditation referred to is
     that under the Apprenticeships, Skills, Children and Learning Act 2009 s 139 (see PARA 836):
     see the Learning and Skills Act 2000 s 98(2C)(b) (as so added).
10   Learning and Skills Act 2000 s 98(3).
11   Learning and Skills Act 2000 s 98(5)(a).
12   Learning and Skills Act 2000 s 98(5)(b).
13   Learning and Skills Act 2000 s 98(5)(c).
14   Learning and Skills Act 2000 s 98(6).

936.   Enforcement in England.   In relation to England[1], if the Secretary of State[2] is satisfied that:

(1)   a local authority[3] or specified body[4] has failed to comply with the provision prohibiting it from funding a course where the relevant qualification has not been approved[5], or is proposing to do so[6]; or

(2)   a local authority or governing body[7] has failed to comply with the provision requiring it to carry out its functions with a view to securing that a course where the relevant qualification has not been approved is not provided by or on behalf of a maintained school[8], or is proposing to do so[9],

he may give such directions to the authority or body as he thinks fit[10]. An authority or body must comply with any such directions given to it[11].

1   The Learning and Skills Act 2000 s 101 has effect for the purposes of s 96 (see PARA 934) in its application to England: see s 101(1) (amended by the Apprenticeships, Skills, Children and Learning Act 2009 s 123(2), Sch 6 paras 14, 47(a)). As to the meaning of 'England' see PARA 7 note 3. As from a day to be appointed, the words 'in its application to England' are repealed: Learning and Skills Act 2000 s 101(1) (prospectively amended by the Qualifications Wales Act 2015 Sch 4 para 3(1), (7)). At the date at which this volume states the law no such day had been appointed.
2   As to the Secretary of State see PARA 58.
3   As to local authorities see PARA 25.
4   A specified body is a body specified under the Learning and Skills Act 2000 s 100(1)(c) (see PARA 934 note 7): s 101(4).
5   Ie has failed to comply with the Learning and Skills Act 2000 s 96(2)(a): see PARA 934.
6   Learning and Skills Act 2000 s 101(1)(a) (amended by the Apprenticeships, Skills, Children and Learning Act 2009 s 123(2), Sch 6 paras 14, 47(b); and SI 2010/1158).
7   As to the governing bodies of maintained schools in England see PARA 150 et seq. As to academies see PARA 345 et seq.
8   Ie has failed to comply with the Learning and Skills Act 2000 s 96(3): see PARA 934.
9   Learning and Skills Act 2000 s 101(1)(b) (amended by SI 2010/1158).
10   Learning and Skills Act 2000 s 101(2).
11   Learning and Skills Act 2000 s 101(3).

937.   Approved qualifications in Wales.   Until a day to be appointed, the following provisions have effect[1].

In relation to Wales[2], a qualification is approved at a given time if: (1) the specified conditions[3] are then satisfied in relation to the qualification[4]; (2) it is then otherwise approved by the Welsh Ministers[5]; or (3) it is then otherwise approved by a body then designated by the Welsh Ministers for these purposes[6]. Approval may be given generally or in relation to particular cases[7].

The Welsh Ministers may at any time revoke a designation[8], an approval given by them[9], or an approval given by a designated body[10]. A designated body may at any time revoke an approval given by it[11].

1   As from a day to be appointed, the Learning and Skills Act 2000 s 99 is repealed by the Qualifications Wales Act 2015 Sch 4 para 3(1), (5). At the date at which this volume no such day had been appointed.
2   The Learning and Skills Act 2000 s 99 has effect for the purposes of s 96 (see PARA 934) in its application to Wales: s 99(1) (amended by the Apprenticeships, Skills, Children and Learning Act 2009 s 123(2), Sch 6 paras 14, 45(1), (2)). As to the meaning of 'Wales' see PARA 7 note 3.
3   Ie the conditions mentioned in the Learning and Skills Act 2000 s 99(2ZA): see s 99(2)(za) (s 99(2)(za) added, 99(2)(a), (b) amended, by the Apprenticeships, Skills, Children and Learning Act 2009 ss 174, 192, Sch 12 paras 26, 29(1), (2)). The conditions are that: (1) the qualification is awarded or authenticated by a person recognised in that respect under the Education Act 1997 s 30(1)(e) (see PARA 854) (Learning and Skills Act 2000 s 99(2ZA)(a) (s 99(2ZA) added by the Apprenticeships, Skills, Children and Learning Act 2009 ss 174, 192, Sch 12 paras 26, 29(1), (3))); and (2) if the qualification is subject to a requirement of accreditation

pursuant to a determination made under the Education Act 1997 s 30(1)(f), it is accredited under s 30(1)(h) (see PARA 854) (Learning and Skills Act 2000 s 99(2ZA)(b) (as so added)).

4   Learning and Skills Act 2000 s 99(2)(za) (as added: see note 2).

5   Learning and Skills Act 2000 s 99(2)(a) (as amended: see note 2). The functions under s 99 were originally vested in the National Assembly for Wales and are now exercisable by the Welsh Ministers by virtue of the Government of Wales Act 2006 s 162(1), Sch 11 paras 30, 32. As to the Welsh Ministers see PARA 59.

6   Learning and Skills Act 2000 s 99(2)(b) (as amended: see note 2). An approval given by a designated body is ineffective unless the Welsh Ministers consent to the approval: s 99(4). As from a day to be appointed s 99(4) is repealed by the Education and Skills Act 2008 ss 160(1), (3), 169, Sch 2; see also note 1. At the date at which this volume states the law no such day had been appointed.

7   Learning and Skills Act 2000 s 99(3).

8   Learning and Skills Act 2000 s 99(5)(a).

9   Learning and Skills Act 2000 s 99(5)(b).

10 Learning and Skills Act 2000 s 99(5)(c).

11 Learning and Skills Act 2000 s 99(6).

938.   Enforcement in Wales. Until a day to be appointed, the following provisions have effect[1].

In relation to Wales[2], if the Welsh Ministers[3] are satisfied that:

(1)   a local authority[4] or specified body[5] has failed to comply with the provision prohibiting it from funding a course where the relevant qualification has not been approved[6], or is proposing to do so[7]; or

(2)   a local authority or governing body[8] has failed to comply with the provision requiring it to carry out its functions with a view to securing that a course where the relevant qualification has not been approved is not provided by or on behalf of a maintained school[9], or is proposing to do so[10],

the Welsh Ministers may give such directions to the authority or body as they think fit[11]. An authority or body must comply with any such directions given to it[12].

1   As from a day to be appointed, the Learning and Skills Act 2000 s 102 is repealed by the Qualifications Wales Act 2015 Sch 4 para 3(1), (8). At the date at which this volume states the law no such day had been appointed.

2   The Learning and Skills Act 2000 s 102 has effect for the purposes of s 96 (see PARA 934) in its application to Wales: see s 102(1) (amended by the Apprenticeships, Skills, Children and Learning Act 2009 s 123(2), Sch 6 paras 14, 48(a)). As to the meaning of 'Wales' see PARA 7 note 3.

3   The functions under the Learning and Skills Act 2000 s 102 were originally vested in the National Assembly for Wales and are now exercisable by the Welsh Ministers by virtue of the Government of Wales Act 2006 s 162(1), Sch 11 paras 30, 32. As to the Welsh Ministers see PARA 59.

4   As to local authorities see PARA 25.

5   A specified body is a body specified under the Learning and Skills Act 2000 s 100(2)(c) (see PARA 934 note 7): s 102(4).

6   Ie has failed to comply with the Learning and Skills Act 2000 s 96(2)(a): see PARA 934.

7   Learning and Skills Act 2000 s 102(1)(a) (amended by the Apprenticeships, Skills, Children and Learning Act 2009 s 123(2), Sch 6 paras 14, 48(b); and SI 2010/1158).

8   As to the governing bodies of maintained schools in Wales see PARA 195.

9   Ie has failed to comply with the Learning and Skills Act 2000 s 96(3): see PARA 934.

10 Learning and Skills Act 2000 s 102(1)(b) (amended by SI 2010/1158).

11 Learning and Skills Act 2000 s 102(2).

12 Learning and Skills Act 2000 s 102(3).

(4) SCHOOL PERFORMANCE TARGETS

939. School performance targets for performance of pupils. The appropriate national authority[1] may by regulations[2] make such provision as it considers appropriate for requiring the governing bodies of maintained schools[3] to secure that annual targets are set in respect of the performance of pupils[4]:

(1) in public examinations[5] or in assessments for the purposes of the National Curriculum[6], in the case of pupils of compulsory school age[7]; or

(2) in public examinations or in connection with the attainment of other external qualifications[8], in the case of pupils of any age over that age[9].

The regulations may require such targets[10], and the past performance of pupils in the particular examinations or assessments, or in connection with the attainment of the particular qualifications, to which such targets relate[11], to be published in such manner as is specified in the regulations[12].

1 Ie the Secretary of State or, in relation to Wales, the Welsh Ministers. As to the Secretary of State see PARA 58. As to the Welsh Ministers see PARA 59. As to the meaning of 'Wales' see PARA 7 note 3. The functions of the Secretary of State under the Education Act 1997 s 19, so far as exercisable in relation to Wales, were transferred to the National Assembly for Wales (see the National Assembly for Wales (Transfer of Functions) Order 1999, SI 1999/672, art 2, Sch 1) and are now vested in the Welsh Ministers (see the Government of Wales Act 2006 s 162(1), Sch 11 para 30). See note 4.

2 'Regulations' means regulations made by the Secretary of State or, in relation to Wales, the Welsh Ministers under the Education Act 1997: see s 56(1). As to the regulations made under s 19 see the School Performance and Absence Targets (Wales) Regulations 2011, SI 2011/1945; and the Education (School Development Plans) (Wales) Regulations 2014, SI 2014/2677.

3 For these purposes, 'maintained school' means a community, foundation or voluntary school, or a community or foundation special school, other than one established in a hospital: Education Act 1997 s 19(3) (substituted by the School Standards and Framework Act 1998 s 140(1), Sch 30 para 213). As to the meaning of references to a community, foundation or voluntary school or a community or foundation special school see PARA 106. As to the governing bodies of maintained schools in England see PARA 150 et seq; and in Wales see PARA 195. As to academies see PARA 345 et seq. As to independent schools see PARA 369 et seq. See note 4.

4 Education Act 1997 s 19(1). As to the meaning of 'pupil' see PARA 20 note 4 (definition applied by s 56(2)). As from a day to be appointed, s 19 ceases to have effect in relation to schools in England as a result of the Deregulation Act 2015 s 66(1). Accordingly, as from a day to be appointed, the Education Act 1997 s 19(1) is amended so as to refer to the Welsh Ministers and applies to Wales only: see s 19(1) (prospectively amended by the Deregulation Act 2015 s 66(2)). At the date at which this volume states the law no such day had been appointed.

5 As to the obligation to enter pupils for examinations see PARA 932.

6 As to the National Curriculum for England see PARA 859 et seq; and as to the National Curriculum for Wales see PARA 873 et seq.

7 Education Act 1997 s 19(1)(a). As to the meaning of 'compulsory school age' see PARA 19. See note 4.

8 As to external qualifications see PARA 932 et seq.

9 Education Act 1997 s 19(1)(b). As to the time at which a person attains a particular age see PARA 7 note 6. See note 4.

10 Education Act 1997 s 19(2)(a). See note 4.

11 Education Act 1997 s 19(2)(b). See note 4.

12 Education Act 1997 s 19(2). See note 4.

(5) PROVISION OF INFORMATION

940. Provision of information. Regulations[1] may require, in relation to every maintained school[2], the local authority[3], the governing body[4] or the head teacher[5] to make available either generally or to prescribed[6] persons, in such form and manner and at such times as may be prescribed such information[7] as may be prescribed[8]. This may include information as to:

(1)   the curriculum for maintained schools[9];

(2)   the educational provision made by the school for pupils[10] at the school and any syllabuses to be followed by those pupils[11];

(3)   the educational achievements of pupils at the school, including the results of any assessments of those pupils[12] for the purpose of ascertaining those achievements[13];

(4)   the educational achievements of such classes or descriptions of pupils as may be prescribed, including results of the kind mentioned in head (3) above[14]; and

(5)   arrangements relating to relevant qualifications[15] and courses leading to such qualifications[16].

The regulations must not require information as to the results of an individual pupil's assessment[17] to be made available to any persons other than[18]:

(a)   the parents[19] of the pupil concerned[20];

(b)   the pupil concerned[21];

(c)   in the case of a pupil who has transferred to a different school, the head teacher of that school[22];

(d)   the governing body of the school[23]; or

(e)   the local authority[24].

The regulations must not require such information to be made available to a governing body except where relevant for the purposes of the performance of any of its functions[25]; to a head teacher except where relevant for the purposes of the performance of any of the head teacher's functions[26]; to a local authority except where relevant for the purposes of the performance of any of its education functions[27]. The regulations may authorise local authorities, governing bodies and head teachers to make a charge, not exceeding the cost of supply, for any documents supplied by them in pursuance of the regulations[28].

Before making any regulations under these provisions, the appropriate national authority[29] must consult any persons with whom consultation appears to it to be desirable[30]. In relation to any maintained school, the local authority and the governing body must exercise their functions with a view to securing that the head teacher complies with any regulations so made[31].

Reference should also be made in particular regarding the provision of certain student information to the Secretary of State, the Welsh Ministers, an information collator; a prescribed person, or a person falling within a prescribed category[32].

1   'Regulations' means regulations made by the Secretary of State or, in relation to Wales, the Welsh Ministers: see the Education Act 1996 s 579(1). As to the Secretary of State see PARA 58. As to the Welsh Ministers see PARA 59. As to the meaning of 'Wales' see PARA 7 note 3. The functions of the Secretary of State under the Education Act 1996 s 408, so far as exercisable in relation to Wales, were transferred to the National Assembly for Wales (see the National Assembly for Wales (Transfer of Functions) Order 1999, SI 1999/672, art 2, Sch 1) and are now vested in the Welsh Ministers (see the Government of Wales Act 2006 s 162(1), Sch 11 para 30).

As to the regulations made under the Education Act 1996 s 408 see the Education (Pupil Information) (England) Regulations 2005, SI 2005/1437 (amended by SI 2007/3224; SI 2008/1747; SI 2012/765; SI 2012/979; SI 2012/1274; SI 2013/3212; and SI 2015/902); the Education (School Performance Information) (England) Regulations 2007, SI 2007/2324 (amended by SI 2007/2979; SI 2008/364; SI 2008/1727; SI 2009/646; SI 2012/765; SI 2012/1274; SI 2013/1759; SI 2013/3212; SI 2015/902; and SI 2015/1566); the Pupil Information (Wales) Regulations 2011, SI 2011/1942; the Head Teacher's Report to Parents and Adult Pupils (Wales) Regulations 2011, SI 2011/1943 (amended by SI 2013/437; and SI 2014/1998); the School Information (Wales) Regulations 2011, SI 2011/1944 (amended by

SI 2013/437); and the School Performance Information (Wales) Regulations 2011, SI 2011/1963 (amended by SI 2013/437). In addition, by virtue of the Education Act 1996 s 582(3), Sch 39 para 1, the following regulations have effect as if made under s 408: the Education (School Curriculum and Related Information) Regulations 1989, SI 1989/954 (amended by SI 1989/1136; SI 1990/1109; SI 1991/1278; SI 1991/1582; SI 1992/1089; SI 1992/1296; and SI 2003/2694); and the Education (Pupils' Attendance Records) Regulations 1991, SI 1991/1582.

2   For these purposes, 'maintained school' includes a maintained nursery school: Education Act 1996 s 408(9) (added by the Education Act 2002 s 215(1), Sch 21 para 46(1), (6)). As to the meaning of 'school' see PARA 91. As to the meaning of 'maintained nursery school' see PARA 99 note 4. As to maintained schools see PARA 99.

3   As to the meaning of 'local authority' see PARA 25. Any function of a local authority in England which is conferred by or under the Education Act 1996 s 408 may be exercised by, or by employees of, such person as may be authorised in that behalf by the local authority whose function it is: Contracting Out (Local Authority Education Functions) (England) Order 2002, SI 2002/928, art 3, Sch 1 para (aa) (art 3 amended by SI 2010/1172). As to the meaning of 'person' see PARA 7 note 6. As to the meaning of 'England' see PARA 7 note 3.

4   As to the governing bodies of maintained schools in England see PARA 150 et seq; and in Wales see PARA 195. As to the power of the Secretary of State or, in relation to Wales, the Welsh Ministers to require information from governing bodies and proprietors of schools see the Education Act 1996 s 537; and PARA 67.

5   As to the meaning of 'head teacher' see PARA 86 note 4.

6   'Prescribed' means prescribed by regulations: Education Act 1996 s 579(1). See note 1.

7   Ie including information as to the matters mentioned in the Education Act 1996 s 408(2) (see heads (1)–(5) in the text), relevant for the purposes of any of the relevant provisions of Pt V (ss 375–409) or the Education Act 1997 Pt V (ss 28–32C) (see PARA 854 et seq) or the Learning and Skills Act 2000 s 96 (relevant qualifications for persons under 19: see PARA 934) or the relevant provisions of the Education Act 2002 or the provisions of the Apprenticeships, Skills, Children and Learning Act 2009 Pt 7 (ss 127–174) (see PARA 825 et seq): Education Act 1996 s 408(1)(a) (amended by the Education Act 1997 s 57(1), Sch 7 para 30(a); the Learning and Skills Act 2000 s 149, Sch 9 paras 1, 57(1), (2); the Education Act 2002 s 215(1), Sch 21 para 46(1), (2); the Apprenticeships, Skills, Children and Learning Act 2009 ss 174, 192, Sch 12 paras 9, 11(1), (2); and the Education Act 2011 Sch 8 paras 5, 7). As from a day to be appointed, this provision is amended so as to refer also to the provisions of the Qualifications Wales Act 2015: Education Act 1996 s 408(1)(a) (as so amended; prospectively amended by the Qualifications Wales Act 2015 Sch 4 para 1(1), (2)(a)). At the date at which this volume states the law no such day had been appointed. The relevant provisions of the Education Act 1996 Pt V are: ss 390–392 (constitution of standing advisory councils on religious education: see PARA 925); ss 394–396 (determinations by standing advisory councils: see PARAS 927–929); s 398 (no requirement of attendance at Sunday School: see PARA 931); s 405 (exemption from sex education: see PARA 907); and s 409 (complaints and enforcement: see PARA 44): s 408(4) (amended by the Education Act 1997 s 57(1), (4), Sch 7 para 30(b), Sch 8; the School Standards and Framework Act 1998 s 140(1), (3), Sch 30 para 106(d), Sch 31; and the Education Act 2002 s 215, Sch 21 para 46(1), (3), Sch 22 Pt 3). As from a day to be appointed, there is added to that list in the Education Act 1996 s 408(4): 'in so far as s 408(1) applies in relation to Wales, ss 403, 404': s 408(4) (prospectively amended by the Violence against Women, Domestic Abuse and Sexual Violence (Wales) Act 2015 s 9(1), (3)). At the date at which this volume states the law no such day had been appointed. The relevant provisions of the Education Act 2002 are: Pt 6 (ss 76–96) (the curriculum in England: see PARA 856 et seq); and ss 97–117 (the curriculum in Wales: see PARA 870 et seq): Education Act 1996 s 408(4A) (added by the Education Act 2002 Sch 21 para 46(1), (4)).

8   Education Act 1996 s 408(1) (amended by the School Standards and Framework Act 1998 Sch 30 para 106(a), Sch 31; and SI 2010/1158).

As from a day to be appointed, a new provision is added to the effect that in exercising their functions under the Education Act 1996 s 408(1), the Welsh Ministers must have regard to the desirability of information being available to parents and others about whether, and if so how, any parts of the curriculum and any educational provision at maintained schools (other than maintained nursery schools) promote the purpose of the Violence against Women, Domestic Abuse and Sexual Violence (Wales) Act 2015 (see s 1): Education Act 1996 s 408(8A) (prospectively added by the Violence against Women, Domestic Abuse and Sexual Violence (Wales) Act 2015 s 9(1), (3)). At the date at which this volume states the law no such day had been appointed.

9 Education Act 1996 s 408(2)(a). As to general duties in respect of the curriculum in England see PARA 856.
10 As to the meaning of 'pupil' see PARA 20 note 4.
11 Education Act 1996 s 408(2)(b).
12 Ie whether under the Education Act 1996 Pt V (ss 375–409) or otherwise.
13 Education Act 1996 s 408(2)(c).
14 Education Act 1996 s 408(2)(d) (amended by the School Standards and Framework Act 1998 Sch 30 para 106(b)).
15 As to the meaning of 'relevant qualification' see PARA 934 note 3 (definition applied by the Education Act 1996 s 408(2)(e) (added by the Learning and Skills Act 2000 Sch 9 paras 1, 57(1), (3); and amended by the Apprenticeships, Skills, Children and Learning Act 2009 ss 174, 192, Sch 12 paras 9, 11(1), (3)(a))). See note 16.
16 Education Act 1996 s 408(2)(e) (as added and amended: see note 15). As from a day to be appointed, s 408(2)(e) is amended so as to remove the reference to the Learning and Skills Act 2000 s 99: Education Act 1996 s 408(2)(e) (as so added and amended; prospectively amended by the Qualifications Wales Act 2015 Sch 4 para 1(1), (2)(b)). At the date at which this volume states the law no such day had been appointed.
   As from a day to be appointed, the Education Act 1996 s 408(2)(f) is prospectively added by the Qualifications Wales Act 2015 Sch 4 paras 1(1), (2)(c), so that in addition to the matters listed in heads (1)–(5) in the text there is also mention of arrangements relating to qualifications within the meaning given in the Qualifications Wales Act 2015 s 56 which are approved under Pt 4 (ss 13–28) and to courses of education or training leading to such qualifications. At the date at which this volume states the law no such day had been appointed.
17 Ie whether under the Education Act 2002 Pt 6 (ss 76–96) (the curriculum in England: see PARA 856 et seq) or Pt 7 (ss 97–118) (the curriculum in Wales: see PARA 870 et seq) or otherwise: Education Act 1996 s 408(6) (amended by the Education Act 2002 Sch 21 para 46(1), (5)).
18 Education Act 1996 s 408(6) (as amended: see note 17).
19 As to the meaning of 'parent' see PARA 7 note 6.
   In practice much time is spent on the issue of what information pupils and parents are entitled to see. In this context it should be noted that there is also a statutory right of access to information held by public authorities under the Freedom of Information Act 2000 (see CONFIDENCE AND INFORMATIONAL PRIVACY vol 19 (2011) PARAS 7, 52; CONSTITUTIONAL AND ADMINISTRATIVE LAW vol 20 (2014) PARA 425 et seq) and parents may request access to their children's personal data under the Data Protection 1998 (see CONFIDENCE AND INFORMATIONAL PRIVACY vol 19 (2011) PARA 95 et seq). The latter is where the child cannot do so or gives permission.
20 Education Act 1996 s 408(6)(a).
21 Education Act 1996 s 408(6)(b). See note 19.
22 Education Act 1996 s 408(6)(c).
23 Education Act 1996 s 408(6)(d).
24 Education Act 1996 s 408(6)(e) (amended by SI 2010/1158).
25 Education Act 1996 s 408(6A)(a) (s 408(6A) added by SI 2010/1158). As to the meaning of 'functions' see PARA 18 note 5.
26 Education Act 1996 s 408(6A)(b) (as added: see note 25).
27 Education Act 1996 s 408(6A)(c) (as added: see note 25). As to the meaning of 'education functions' see PARA 25.
28 Education Act 1996 s 408(7) (amended by SI 2010/1158). See note 19.
29 Ie the Secretary of State or, in relation to Wales, the Welsh Ministers.
30 Education Act 1996 s 408(5). As to the exercise of the duty to consult see JUDICIAL REVIEW vol 61 (2010) PARA 627.
31 Education Act 1996 s 408(8) (amended by SI 2010/1158).
32 See the Apprenticeships, Skills, Children and Learning Act 2009 s 235A; and PARA 72.

7. SPECIAL EDUCATIONAL NEEDS AND DISABILITIES

(1) LEGISLATION RELATING TO SPECIAL EDUCATIONAL NEEDS AND DISABILITIES

941. The effect of the Children and Families Act 2014. As from 1 September 2014[1] the provisions in the Education Act 1996[2] relating to children with special educational needs ceased to apply in relation to children in the area of a local authority[3] in England[4], as a result of the Children and Families Act 2014[5]. For provisions relating to children and young persons[6] in England with special educational needs or disabilities reference should now thus be made to the provisions of Part 3 of the 2014 Act[7] which are considered below[8]. Accordingly, as from the above date the provisions of the Education Act 1996[9] apply only in relation to children in the area of a local authority in Wales[10] and are considered separately below[11].

1 See the Children and Families Act 2014 (Commencement No 2) Order 2014, SI 2014/889. As to transitional arrangements etc in regard to the coming into force of the Children and Families Act 2014 Pt 3 (ss 19–83) see the Children and Families Act 2014 (Transitional and Savings Provisions) (N0 2) Order 2014, SI 2014/2270 (amended by SI 2015/505; SI 2015/1619).
2 Ie the Education Act 1996 Pt IV Ch I (ss 311A–336A).
3 As to the meaning of 'local authority' see PARA 25 (definition applied by the Children and Families Act 2014 s 83(7)).
4 As to the meaning of 'England' see PARA 7 note 3.
5 See the Children and Families Act 2014 s 81.
6 As to the meaning of 'child' see PARA 7 note 6 (definition applied by the Children and Families Act 2014 s 83(7)). As to the meaning of 'young person' see PARA 950 note 4.
7 Ie the Children and Families Act 2014 Pt 3 (ss 19–83).
8 See PARA 950 et seq.
9 See note 2.
10 See the Education Act 1996 s 311A (added by the Children and Families Act 2014 Sch 3 paras 1, 10) which provides that the Education Act 1996 Pt IV Ch I applies only in relation to children in the area of a local authority in Wales. As to the meaning of 'Wales' see PARA 7 note 3.
11 See PARA 989 et seq.

942. Discrimination and the Equality Act 2010. In addition to the legislation dealing specifically with special educational needs and disabilities[1], consideration should also be given to the relevant provisions of the Equality Act 2010 and the duty not to discriminate in the provision of education[2].

1 See PARAS 941, 943 et seq.
2 See PARA 9 et seq; and DISCRIMINATION vol 33 (2013) PARA 166 et seq.

(2) CHILDREN AND YOUNG PEOPLE IN ENGLAND WITH SPECIAL EDUCATIONAL NEEDS AND DISABILITIES

(i) General Duties, Identification of Children and Young People with Special Needs and Disabilities etc

943. Meaning of 'special educational needs' etc. A child[1] or young person[2] has 'special educational needs' if he or she has a learning difficulty or disability[3] which calls for special educational[4] provision to be made for him or her[5].

A child of compulsory school age[6] or a young person has a learning difficulty or disability if he or she (1) has a significantly greater difficulty in learning than the majority of others of the same age[7]; or (2) has a disability which prevents or hinders him or her from making use of facilities of a kind generally provided for others of the same age in mainstream schools[8] or mainstream post-16 institutions[9]. A child under compulsory school age has a learning difficulty or disability if he or she is likely to be within the above provisions[10] when of compulsory school age (or would be likely, if no special educational provision were made)[11]. A child or young person does not have a learning difficulty or disability solely because the language (or form of language) in which he or she is or will be taught is different from a language (or form of language) which is or has been spoken at home[12].

'Special educational provision', for a child aged two or more or a young person, means educational or training provision that is additional to, or different from, that made generally for others of the same age in (a) mainstream schools in England[13]; (b) maintained nursery schools[14] in England[15]; (c) mainstream post-16 institutions in England[16]; or (d) places in England at which relevant early years education[17] is provided[18]. 'Special educational provision', for a child aged under two, means educational provision of any kind[19].

1 As to the meaning of 'child' see PARA 7 note 6 (definition applied by the Children and Families Act 2014 s 83(7)).
2 As to the meaning of 'young person' see PARA 950 note 4.
3 A child or young person has a disability for the purposes of the Children and Families Act 2014 Pt 3 (ss 19–83) if he or she has a disability for the purposes of the Equality Act 2010 (see DISCRIMINATION vol 33 (2013) PARA 50): Children and Families Act 2014 s 83(3).
4 As to references to 'education' see PARA 950 note 11.
5 Children and Families Act 2014 ss 20(1), 83(2), Education Act 1996 s 579(1) (definition added by the Children and Families Act 2014 Sch 1, 59(b)). The Education Act 1996 s 20 applies for the purposes of Pt 3 (ss 19–83): s 20(5).
6 As to the meaning of 'compulsory school age' see PARA 19.
7 Children and Families Act 2014 s 20(2)(a).
8 'Mainstream school' means a maintained school that is not a special school, or an academy school that is not a special school: Children and Families Act 2014 s 83(2). 'Maintained school' means (1) a community, foundation or voluntary school, or (2) a community or foundation special school not established in a hospital: s 83(2). A reference in Pt 3 (ss 19–83) to (a) a community, foundation or voluntary school; or (b) a community or foundation special school, is to such a school within the meaning of the School Standards and Framework Act 1998 (see PARA 106): Children and Families Act 2014 s 83(5). As to the meaning of 'academy school' see PARA 346 note 12 (definition applied by s 83(7)). As to the meaning of 'school' generally see PARA 91 (definition applied by s 83(7)).
9 Children and Families Act 2014 s 20(2)(b). 'Mainstream post-16 institution' means a post-16 institution that is not a special post-16 institution: s 83(2). 'Post-16 institution' means an institution which (1) provides education or training for those over compulsory school age; but (2) is not a school or other institution which is within the higher education sector or which provides only higher education: s 83(2). 'Special post-16 institution' means a post-16 institution that is specially organised to make special educational provision for students with special educational needs: s 83(2). 'Training' has the same meaning as in the Education Act 1996 s 15ZA (see PARA 32 note 4): Children and Families Act 2014 s 83(2).
10 Ie the Children and Families Act 2014 s 20(2).
11 Children and Families Act 2014 s 20(3).
12 Children and Families Act 2014 s 20(4).
13 Children and Families Act 2014 ss 21(1)(a), 83(2), Education Act 1996 s 579(1) (definition added by the Children and Families Act 2014 Sch 3 paras 1, 59(b)). As to the meaning of 'England' see PARA 7 note 3.
14 As to the meaning of 'maintained nursery school' see PARA 99 note 4 (definition applied by the Children and Families Act 2014 s 83(7)).
15 Children and Families Act 2014 ss 21(1)(b), 83(2), Education Act 1996 s 579(1) (definition as added: see note 13).
16 Children and Families Act 2014 ss 21(1)(c), 83(2), Education Act 1996 s 579(1) (definition as added: see note 13).

17 'Relevant early years education' has the meaning given by the School Standards and Framework Act 1998 s 123 (see PARA 1033 note 17): Children and Families Act 2014 s 83(2).

18 Children and Families Act 2014 ss 21(1)(d), 83(2), Education Act 1996 s 579(1) (definition as added: see note 13).

19 Children and Families Act 2014 ss 21(2), 83(2), Education Act 1996 s 579(1) (definition as added: see note 13).

944.   Identifying children and young people with special educational needs and disabilities.   A local authority[1] in England[2] must exercise its functions[3] with a view to securing that it identifies (1) all the children[4] and young people[5] in its area[6] who have or may have special educational needs[7]; and (2) all the children and young people in its area who have a disability[8].

The following provisions[9] apply where, in the course of exercising functions in relation to a child who is under compulsory school age[10], a clinical commissioning group, NHS trust or NHS foundation trust[11] form the opinion that the child has (or probably has) special educational needs or a disability[12]. The group or trust must (a) inform the child's parent[13] of their opinion and of their duty[14]; and (b) give the child's parent an opportunity to discuss their opinion with an officer of the group or trust[15]. The group or trust must then bring their opinion to the attention of the appropriate local authority in England[16]. If the group or trust think a particular voluntary organisation is likely to be able to give the parent advice or assistance in connection with any special educational needs or disability the child may have, they must inform the parent of that[17].

1   As to the meaning of 'local authority' see PARA 25 (definition applied by the Children and Families Act 2014 s 83(7)).

2   As to the meaning of 'England' see PARA 7 note 3.

3   As to the meaning of 'function' see PARA 18 note 5 (definition applied by the Children and Families Act 2014 s 83(7)).

4   As to the meaning of 'child' see PARA 7 note 6 (definition applied by the Children and Families Act 2014 s 83(7)).

5   As to the meaning of 'young person' see PARA 950 note 4.

6   A reference in the Children and Families Act 2014 Pt 3 (ss 19–83) to a child or young person who is 'in the area' of a local authority in England does not include a child or young person who is wholly or mainly resident in the area of a local authority in Wales: Children and Families Act 2014 s 83(6). As to the meaning of 'Wales' see PARA 7 note 3.

7   Children and Families Act 2014 s 22(1). As to the meaning of 'special educational needs' see PARA 943.

8   Children and Families Act 2014 s 22(2). As to the meaning of 'disability' see PARA 943 note 3.

9   Ie the provisions of the Children and Families Act 2014 s 23.

10 As to the meaning of 'compulsory school age' see PARA 19.

11 As to clinical commissioning group, NHS trusts or NHS foundation trusts see HEALTH SERVICES.

12 Children and Families Act 2014 s 23(1).

13 As to the meaning of 'parent' see PARA 7 note 6 (definition applied by the Children and Families Act 2014 s 83(7)).

14 Children and Families Act 2014 s 23(2)(a). The reference in the text is to their duty under s 23(3): see the text to note 16.

15 Children and Families Act 2014 s 23(2)(b).

16 Children and Families Act 2014 s 23(3).

17 Children and Families Act 2014 s 23(4).

945.   Children and young people for whom a local authority is responsible.   A local authority[1] in England[2] is responsible for a child[3] or young person[4] if he or she is in the authority's area[5] and has been (1) identified by the authority as someone who has or may have special educational needs[6]; or (2) brought to the authority's attention by any person as someone who has or may have special educational needs[7].

1 As to the meaning of 'local authority' see PARA 25 (definition applied by the Children and Families Act 2014 s 83(7)).
2 As to the meaning of 'England' see PARA 7 note 3.
3 As to the meaning of 'child' see PARA 7 note 6 (definition applied by the Children and Families Act 2014 s 83(7)).
4 As to the meaning of 'young person' see PARA 950 note 4.
5 As to being 'in the area' of a local authority see PARA 944 note 6.
6 Children and Families Act 2014 s 24(1)(a). As to the meaning of 'special educational needs' see PARA 943. Section 24 applies for the purposes of the Children and Families Act 2014 Pt 3 (ss 19–83): s 24(2).
7 Children and Families Act 2014 s 24(1)(b).

946. Education, health and care provision: promoting integration. A local authority[1] in England[2] must exercise its functions[3] under Part 3 of the Children and Families Act 2014[4] with a view to ensuring the integration of educational[5] provision and training[6] provision with health care provision[7] and social care provision[8], where it thinks that this would (1) promote the well-being of children[9] or young people[10] in its area[11] who have special educational needs[12] or a disability[13]; or (2) improve the quality of special educational provision[14] (a) made in its area for children or young people who have special educational needs[15]; or (b) made outside its area for children or young people for whom it is responsible who have special educational needs[16].

The reference above[17] to the well-being of children and young people is to their well-being so far as relating to (i) physical and mental health and emotional well-being[18]; (ii) protection from abuse and neglect[19]; (iii) control by them over their day-to-day lives[20]; (iv) participation in education, training or recreation[21]; (v) social and economic well-being[22]; (vi) domestic, family and personal relationships[23]; (vii) the contribution made by them to society[24].

1 As to the meaning of 'local authority' see PARA 25 (definition applied by the Children and Families Act 2014 s 83(7)).
2 As to the meaning of 'England' see PARA 7 note 3.
3 As to the meaning of 'function' see PARA 18 note 5 (definition applied by the Children and Families Act 2014 s 83(7)).
4 Ie the Children and Families Act 2014 Pt 3 (ss 19–83).
5 As to the meaning of 'educational' see PARA 950 note 11.
6 As to the meaning of 'training' see PARA 943 note 9.
7 'Health care provision' means the provision of health care services as part of the comprehensive health service in England continued under the National Health Service Act 2006 s 1(1) (see HEALTH SERVICES vol 54 (2008) PARA 10): Children and Families Act 2014 ss 21(3), 83(2). Health care provision or social care provision which educates or trains a child or young person is to be treated as special educational provision (instead of health care provision or social care provision): s 21(5). As to the meaning of 'special educational provision' see PARA 943.
8 'Social care provision' means the provision made by a local authority in the exercise of its social services functions: ss 21(4), 83(2). 'Social services functions' in relation to a local authority has the same meaning as in the Local Authority Social Services Act 1970 (see SOCIAL SERVICES AND COMMUNITY CARE vol 95 (2013) PARA 1): Children and Families Act 2014 s 83(2). See s 21(5); and note 7.
9 As to the meaning of 'child' see PARA 7 note 6 (definition applied by the Children and Families Act 2014 s 83(7)).
10 As to the meaning of 'young person' see PARA 950 note 4.
11 As to being 'in the area' of a local authority see PARA 944 note 6.
12 As to the meaning of 'special educational needs' see PARA 943.
13 Children and Families Act 2014 s 25(1)(a).
14 See note 7.
15 Children and Families Act 2014 s 25(1)(b)(i).
16 Children and Families Act 2014 s 25(1)(b)(ii).
17 Ie in the in the Children and Families Act 2014 s 25(1).
18 Children and Families Act 2014 s 25(2)(a).

19 Children and Families Act 2014 s 25(2)(b).
20 Children and Families Act 2014 s 25(2)(c).
21 Children and Families Act 2014 s 25(2)(d).
22 Children and Families Act 2014 s 25(2)(e).
23 Children and Families Act 2014 s 25(2)(f).
24 Children and Families Act 2014 s 25(2)(g).

947. Education, health and care provision: joint commissioning arrangements. A local authority[1] in England[2] and its partner commissioning bodies[3] must make arrangements ('joint commissioning arrangements') about the education, health and care provision[4] to be secured for (1) children[5] and young people[6] for whom the authority is responsible who have special educational needs[7]; and (2) children and young people in the authority's area[8] who have a disability[9].

Joint commissioning arrangements must include arrangements for considering and agreeing:

(a) the education, health and care provision reasonably required by (i) the learning difficulties and disabilities which result in the children and young people within head (1) above having special educational needs[10]; and (ii) the disabilities of the children and young people within head (2) above[11];

(b) what education, health and care provision is to be secured[12];

(c) by whom education, health and care provision is to be secured[13];

(d) what advice and information is to be provided about education, health and care provision[14];

(e) by whom, to whom and how such advice and information is to be provided[15];

(f) how complaints about education, health and care provision may be made and are to be dealt with[16];

(g) procedures for ensuring that disputes between the parties to the joint commissioning arrangements are resolved as quickly as possible[17].

Joint commissioning arrangements about securing education, health and care provision must in particular include arrangements for:

(i) securing EHC needs assessments[18];

(ii) securing the education, health and care provision specified in EHC plans[19];

(iii) agreeing [20]personal budgets[21].

Joint commissioning arrangements may also include other provision[22].

The parties to joint commissioning arrangements must (A) have regard to them in the exercise of their functions[23]; and (B) keep them under review[24].

1 As to the meaning of 'local authority' see PARA 25 (definition applied by the Children and Families Act 2014 s 83(7)).

2 As to the meaning of 'England' see PARA 7 note 3.

3 A local authority's 'partner commissioning bodies' are:
   (1) the National Health Service Commissioning Board, to the extent that it is under a duty under the National Health Service Act 2006 s 3B (see HEALTH SERVICES) to arrange for the provision of services or facilities for (a) any children and young people for whom the authority is responsible who have special educational needs; or (b) any children and young people in the authority's area who have a disability (Children and Families Act 2014 s 26(8)(a)); and
   (b) each clinical commissioning group that is under a duty under the National Health Service Act 2006 s 3 (see HEALTH SERVICES) to arrange for the provision of services or facilities for any children and young people within head (1) above (Children and Families Act 2014 s 26(8)(b)).

Regulations may prescribe circumstances in which a clinical commissioning group that would otherwise be a partner commissioning body of a local authority by virtue of s 26(8)(b) (see head (2) above) is to be treated as not being a partner commissioning body of the authority: s 26(9). At the date at which this volume states the law no such regulations have been made.

4 In the Children and Families Act 2014 Pt 3 (ss 19–83) 'education, health and care provision' means (1) special educational provision; (2) health care provision; (3) social care provision: ss 26(2), 83(2). As to the meaning of 'special educational provision' see PARA 943. As to the meaning of 'health care provision' see PARA 946 note 7. As to the meaning of 'social care provision' see PARA 946 note 8.

5 As to the meaning of 'child' see PARA 7 note 6 (definition applied by the Children and Families Act 2014 s 83(7)).

6 As to the meaning of 'young person' see PARA 950 note 4.

7 Children and Families Act 2014 s 26(1)(a). As to the meaning of 'special educational needs' see PARA 943.

The Local Government and Public Involvement in Health Act 2007 s 116B (duty to have regard to assessment of relevant needs and joint health and wellbeing strategy: see LOCAL GOVERNMENT vol 69 (2009) PARA 392) applies in relation to functions exercisable under the Children and Families Act 2014 s 26: s 26(7).

8 As to being 'in the area' of a local authority see PARA 944 note 6.

9 Children and Families Act 2014 s 26(1)(b). As to the meaning of 'disability' see PARA 943 note 3.

10 Children and Families Act 2014 s 26(3)(a)(i).

11 Children and Families Act 2014 s 26(3)(a)(ii).

12 Children and Families Act 2014 s 26(3)(b).

13 Children and Families Act 2014 s 26(3)(c).

14 Children and Families Act 2014 s 26(3)(d).

15 Children and Families Act 2014 s 26(3)(e).

16 Children and Families Act 2014 s 26(3)(f).

17 Children and Families Act 2014 s 26(3)(g).

18 Children and Families Act 2014 s 26(4)(a). As to the meaning of 'EHC needs assessment' see PARA 957 note 3.

19 Children and Families Act 2014 s 26(4)(b). As to the meaning of 'EHC plan' see PARA 958.

20 Ie under the Children and Families Act 2014 s 49: see PARA 966.

21 Children and Families Act 2014 s 26(4)(c).

22 Children and Families Act 2014 s 26(5).

23 Children and Families Act 2014 s 26(6)(a).

24 Children and Families Act 2014 s 26(6)(b).

948. Review of education and care provision. A local authority[1] in England[2] must keep under review (1) the educational[3] provision, training[4] provision and social care provision[5] made in its area[6] for children[7] and young people[8] who have special educational needs[9] or a disability[10]; and (2) the educational provision, training provision and social care provision made outside its area for children and young people for whom it is responsible who have special educational needs[11]; and children and young people in its area who have a disability[12].

The authority must consider the extent to which the provision referred to in head (1) and (2) above is sufficient to meet the educational needs, training needs and social care needs of the children and young people concerned[13].

In exercising its functions under these provisions[14], the authority must consult:

(a) children and young people in its area with special educational needs, and the parents[15] of children in its area with special educational needs[16];

(b) children and young people in its area who have a disability, and the parents of children in its area who have a disability[17];

(c) the governing bodies of maintained schools[18] and maintained nursery schools[19] in its area[20];

(d) the proprietors[21] of academies[22] in its area[23];

(e)   the governing bodies, proprietors or principals of post-16 institutions[24] in its area[25];

(f)   the governing bodies of non-maintained special schools[26] in its area[27];

(g)   the advisory boards of children's centres[28] in its area[29];

(h)   the providers of relevant early years education[30] in its area[31];

(i)   the governing bodies, proprietors or principals of other schools and post-16 institutions in England and Wales[32] that the authority thinks are or are likely to be attended by (i) children or young people for whom it is responsible[33]; or (ii) children or young people in its area who have a disability[34];

(j)   a youth offending team that the authority thinks has functions in relation to (i) children or young people for whom it is responsible[35]; or (ii) children or young people in its area who have a disability[36];

(k)   such other persons as the authority thinks appropriate[37].

1   As to the meaning of 'local authority' see PARA 25 (definition applied by the Children and Families Act 2014 s 83(7)).
2   As to the meaning of 'England' see PARA 7 note 3.
3   As to the meaning of 'educational' see PARA 950 note 11.
4   As to the meaning of 'training' see PARA 943 note 9.
5   As to the meaning of 'social care provision' see PARA 946 note 8.
6   As to being 'in the area' of a local authority see PARA 944 note 6.
7   As to the meaning of 'child' see PARA 7 note 6 (definition applied by the Children and Families Act 2014 s 83(7)).
8   As to the meaning of 'young person' see PARA 950 note 4.
9   As to the meaning of 'special educational needs' see PARA 943.
10 Children and Families Act 2014 s 27(1)(a). As to the meaning of 'disability' see PARA 943 note 3.
    The Local Government and Public Involvement in Health Act 2007 s 116B (duty to have regard to assessment of relevant needs and joint health and wellbeing strategy: see LOCAL GOVERNMENT vol 69 (2009) PARA 392) applies in relation to functions exercisable under the Children and Families Act 2014 s 27: s 27(4).
11 Children and Families Act 2014 s 27(1)(b)(i).
12 Children and Families Act 2014 s 27(1)(b)(ii).
13 Children and Families Act 2014 s 27(2).
14 Ie under the Children and Families Act 2014 s 27. As to the meaning of 'function' see PARA 18 note 5 (definition applied by s 83(7)).
15 As to the meaning of 'parent' see PARA 7 note 6 (definition applied by the Children and Families Act 2014 s 83(7)).
16 Children and Families Act 2014 s 27(3)(a).
17 Children and Families Act 2014 s 27(3)(b).
18 As to the governing bodies of maintained schools in England see PARA 150 et seq. As to the meaning of 'maintained school' see PARA 943 note 8.
19 As to the meaning of 'maintained nursery school' see PARA 99 note 4 (definition applied by the Children and Families Act 2014 s 83(7)).
20 Children and Families Act 2014 s 27(3)(c).
21 'Proprietor', in relation to an institution that is not a school, means the person or body of persons responsible for the management of the institution: Children and Families Act 2014 s 83(2). As to the meaning of 'person' see PARA 7 note 6.
22 As to the meaning of 'academy' see PARA 346 note 7 (definition applied by the Children and Families Act 2014 s 83(7)).
23 Children and Families Act 2014 s 27(3)(d).
24 As to the meaning of 'post-16 institution' see PARA 943 note 9.
25 Children and Families Act 2014 s 27(3)(e).
26 As to the meaning of 'non-maintained special school' see PARA 1042 (definition applied by the Children and Families Act 2014 s 83(7)).
27 Children and Families Act 2014 s 27(3)(f).
28 'Children's centre' has the meaning given by the Childcare Act 2006 s 5A(4) (see CHILDREN AND YOUNG PERSONS vol 10 (2012) PARA 1080): Children and Families Act 2014 s 27(5).
29 Children and Families Act 2014 s 27(3)(g).
30 As to the meaning of 'relevant early years education' see PARA 943 note 17.

31 Children and Families Act 2014 s 27(3)(h).
32 As to the meaning of 'Wales' see PARA 7 note 3.
33 Children and Families Act 2014 s 27(3)(i)(i).
34 Children and Families Act 2014 s 27(3)(i)(ii).
35 Children and Families Act 2014 s 27(3)(j)(i).
36 Children and Families Act 2014 s 27(3)(j)(ii).
37 Children and Families Act 2014 s 27(3)(k).

949. Co-operation and assistance. A local authority[1] in England[2] must co-operate with each of its local partners[3], and each local partner must co-operate with the authority, in the exercise of the authority's functions[4] under Part 3 of the Children and Families Act 2014[5]. A local authority in England must make arrangements for ensuring co-operation between (1) the officers of the authority who exercise the authority's functions relating to education or training[6]; (2) the officers of the authority who exercise the authority's social services functions[7] for children or young people with special educational needs[8]; and (3) the officers of the authority, so far as they are not officers within head (1) or (2) above, who exercise the authority's functions relating to provision which is within provision to assist in preparing children and young people for adulthood and independent living[9].

Where an appropriate authority[10] for a school or certain post-16 institutions[11] has functions under Part 3 of the 2014 Act[12], the appropriate authority must co-operate with each responsible local authority[13], and each responsible local authority must co-operate with the appropriate authority, in the exercise of those functions[14].

1   As to the meaning of 'local authority' see PARA 25 (definition applied by the Children and Families Act 2014 s 83(7)).
2   As to the meaning of 'England' see PARA 7 note 3.
3   Ie as listed in the Children and Families Act 2014 s 28(2). Each of the following is a 'local partner' of a local authority in England for this purpose:
    (1)   where the authority is a county council for an area for which there is also a district council, the district council (s 28(2)(a));
    (2)   the governing body of a maintained school or maintained nursery school that is maintained by the authority or provides education or training for children or young people for whom the authority is responsible (s 28(2)(b));
    (3)   the proprietor of an academy that is in the authority's area or provides education or training for children or young people for whom the authority is responsible (s 28(2)(c));
    (4)   the proprietor of a non-maintained special school that is in the authority's area or provides education or training for children or young people for whom the authority is responsible (s 28(2)(d));
    (5)   the governing body of an institution within the further education sector that is in the authority's area, or is attended, or likely to be attended, by children or young people for whom the authority is responsible (s 28(2)(e));
    (6)   the management committee of a pupil referral unit that is in the authority's area, or is in England and is or is likely to be attended by children or young people for whom the authority is responsible (s 28(2)(f));
    (7)   the proprietor of an institution approved by the Secretary of State under s 41 (independent special schools and special post-16 institutions: approval: see PARA 961) that is in the authority's area, or is attended, or likely to be attended, by children or young people for whom the authority is responsible (s 28(2)(g));
    (8)   any other person (other than a school or post-16 institution) that makes special educational provision for a child or young person for whom the authority is responsible (s 28(2)(h));
    (9)   a youth offending team that the authority thinks has functions in relation to children or young people for whom it is responsible (s 28(2)(i));
    (10)   a person in charge of relevant youth accommodation (a) in which there are detained persons aged 18 or under for whom the authority was responsible immediately before

the beginning of their detention (s 28(2)(j)(i)); or (b) that the authority thinks is accommodation in which such persons are likely to be detained (s 28(2)(j)(ii));

(11)   the National Health Service Commissioning Board (s 28(2)(k));

(12)   a clinical commissioning group (a) whose area coincides with, or falls wholly or partly within, the authority's area (s 28(2)(l)(i)); or (b) which is under a duty under the National Health Service Act 2006 s 3 (see HEALTH SERVICES vol 54 (2008) PARA 12) to arrange for the provision of services or facilities for any children and young people for whom the authority is responsible (Children and Families Act 2014 s 28(2)(l)(ii));

(13)   an NHS trust or NHS foundation trust which provides services in the authority's area, or which exercises functions in relation to children or young people for whom the authority is responsible (s 28(2)(m));

(14)   a local health board which exercises functions in relation to children or young people for whom the authority is responsible (s 28(2)(n)).

As to county councils and district councils see generally LOCAL GOVERNMENT. As to the governing bodies of maintained schools in England see PARA 150 et seq. As to the meaning of 'maintained school' see PARA 943 note 8. As to the meaning of 'maintained nursery school' see PARA 99 note 4 (definition applied by s 83(7)). As to the meaning of 'education' see PARA 950 note 11. As to the meaning of 'training' see PARA 943 note 9. As to the meaning of 'child' see PARA 7 note 6 (definition applied by s 83(7)). As to the meaning of 'young person' see PARA 950 note 4. As to the meaning of 'proprietor' see PARA 948 note 21. As to the meaning of 'non-maintained special school' see PARA 1042 (definition applied by s 83(7)). As to the meaning of 'academy' see PARA 346 note 7 (definition applied by s 83(7)). As to the meaning of 'further education' see PARA 23 (definition applied by s 83(7)). As to being 'in the area' of a local authority see PARA 944 note 6. As to pupil referral units generally see PARA 427 et seq. As to the Secretary of State see PARA 58. As to the meaning of 'person' see PARA 7 note 6. As to the meaning of 'school' generally see PARA 91 (definition applied by s 83(7)). As to the meaning of 'post-16 institution' see PARA 943 note 9. 'Relevant youth accommodation' has the same meaning as in the Education Act 1996 s 562(1A)(b) (see PARA 46 note 9) save that it does not include relevant youth accommodation which is not in England: Children and Families Act 2014 ss 70(5), 83(2). Generally as to persons detained in youth accommodation see PARA 547 et seq. As to the National Health Service Commissioning Board, clinical commissioning groups, NHS trusts, NHS foundation trusts and local health boards see HEALTH SERVICES.

Regulations may prescribe circumstances in which a clinical commissioning group that would otherwise be a local partner of a local authority by virtue of s 28(2)(l)(ii) (see head (12)(b) above) is to be treated as not being a local partner of the authority: s 28(4). At the date at which this volume states the law no such regulations had been made.

4   As to the meaning of 'function' see PARA 18 note 5 (definition applied by the Children and Families Act 2014 s 83(7)).

5   Children and Families Act 2014 s 28(1). The reference in the text is to Pt 3 (ss 19–83).

6   Children and Families Act 2014 s 28(3)(a). As to the meaning of 'training' see PARA 943 note 9.

7   As to the meaning of 'social services functions' see PARA 946 note 8.

8   Children and Families Act 2014 s 28(3)(b). As to the meaning of 'special educational needs' see PARA 943.

9   Children and Families Act 2014 s 28(3)(c). The reference in the text to provision to assist in preparing children and young people for adulthood and independent living is a reference to s 30(2)(e): see PARA 951 note 20.

10   The 'appropriate authority' for a school or post-16 institution is (1) in the case of a maintained school, maintained nursery school, or institution within the further education sector, the governing body; (2) in the case of an academy, the proprietor; (3) in the case of a pupil referral unit, the management committee: Children and Families Act 2014 s 29(5).

11   Ie a post-16 institution mentioned in the Children and Families Act 2014 s 29(2). The schools and post-16 institutions referred to in s 29(1) are:

(1)   mainstream schools (s 29(2)(a));

(2)   maintained nursery schools (s 29(2)(b));

(3)   16 to 19 academies (s 29(2)(c));

(4)   institutions within the further education sector (s 29(2)(d));

(5)   pupil referral units (s 29(2)(e));

(6)   alternative provision academies (s 29(2)(f)).

As to the meaning of '16 to 19 academy' see PARA 346 note 13 (definition applied by s 83(7)). As to the meaning of 'alternative provision academy' see PARA 346 note 14 (definition applied by s 83(7)).

12   Children and Families Act 2014 s 29(1).

13 A 'responsible local authority', in relation to an appropriate authority for a school or post-16
   institution mentioned in the Children and Families Act 2014 s 29(2) (see note 11), is a local
   authority in England that is responsible for any child or young person who is a registered pupil
   or a student at the school or post-16 institution: s 29(4). As to the meaning of 'registered pupil'
   see PARA 437 (definition applied by s 83(7)). As to the meaning of 'student' see PARA 67 note 8
   (definition applied by s 83(7)).
14 Children and Families Act 2014 s 29(3).

**950. Local authority functions: supporting and involving children and young
people.** In exercising a function[1] under Part 3 of the Children and Families
Act 2014[2] in the case of a child[3] or young person under 25[4], a local authority[5] in
England[6] must have regard to the following matters in particular:

(1)   the views, wishes and feelings of the child and his or her parent[7], or the
      young person[8];
(2)   the importance of the child and his or her parent, or the young person,
      participating as fully as possible in decisions relating to the exercise of
      the function concerned[9];
(3)   the importance of the child and his or her parent, or the young person,
      being provided with the information and support necessary to enable
      participation in those decisions[10];
(4)   the need to support the child and his or her parent, or the young person,
      in order to facilitate the development of the child or young person and
      to help him or her achieve the best possible educational[11] and other
      outcomes[12].

1 As to the meaning of 'function' see PARA 18 note 5 (definition applied by the Children and
   Families Act 2014 s 83(7)).
2 Ie the Children and Families Act 2014 Pt 3 (ss 19–83).
3 As to the meaning of 'child' see PARA 7 note 6 (definition applied by the Children and Families
   Act 2014 s 83(7)).
4 'Young person' means a person over compulsory school age but under 25: Children and Families
   Act 2014 s 83(2). As to the meaning of 'compulsory school age' see PARA 19.
5 As to the meaning of 'local authority' see PARA 25 (definition applied by the Children and
   Families Act 2014 s 83(7)).
6 As to the meaning of 'England' see PARA 7 note 3.
7 As to the meaning of 'parent' see PARA 7 note 6 (definition applied by the Children and Families
   Act 2014 s 83(7)).
8 Children and Families Act 2014 s 19(a).
9 Children and Families Act 2014 s 19(b).
10 Children and Families Act 2014 s 19(c).
11 A reference in the Children and Families Act 2014 Pt 3 (ss 19–83) to 'education' (1) includes a
   reference to full-time and part-time education, but (2) does not include a reference to higher
   education, and 'educational' and 'educate' (and other related terms) are to be read accordingly:
   s 83(4).
12 Children and Families Act 2014 s 19(d).

(ii) Information and Advice

951. Information and advice: local offers. A local authority[1] in England[2]
must publish information about (1) the provision[3] for children[4] and young
people[5] it expects to be available in its area[6] at the time of publication for
children and young people who have special educational needs[7] or a disability[8];
and (2) the provision[9] it expects to be available outside its area at that time for
children and young people for whom it is responsible[10]; and children and young
people in its area who have a disability[11].

The provision for children and young people referred to above[12] is:
(a) education, health and care provision[13]; (b) other educational provision[14];

(c) other training provision[15]; (d) arrangements for travel to and from schools[16] and post-16 institutions[17] and places at which relevant early years education[18] is provided[19]; and (e) provision to assist in preparing children and young people for adulthood and independent living[20].

Information required to be published by an authority as above[21] is to be known as its 'local offer'[22]. A local authority must keep its local offer under review and may from time to time revise it[23].

A local authority must from time to time publish:

(i)   comments about its local offer it has received from or on behalf of children and young people with special educational needs, and the parents[24] of children with special educational needs[25]; and children and young people who have a disability, and the parents of children who have a disability[26]; and

(ii)   the authority's response to those comments (including details of any action the authority intends to take)[27].

Regulations[28] may make provision about:

(A)   the information to be included in an authority's local offer[29];

(B)   how an authority's local offer is to be published[30];

(C)   who is to be consulted by an authority in preparing and reviewing its local offer[31];

(D)   how an authority is to involve children and young people with special educational needs, and the parents of children with special educational needs[32]; and children and young people who have a disability, and the parents of children who have a disability[33], in the preparation and review of its local offer[34];

(E)   the publication of comments on the local offer, and the local authority's response[35] (including circumstances in which comments are not required to be published)[36].

The regulations may in particular require an authority's local offer to include:

(aa)   information about how to obtain an EHC needs assessment[37];

(bb)   information about other sources of information, advice and support for children and young people with special educational needs and those who care for them[38]; and children and young people who have a disability and those who care for them[39];

(cc)   information about gaining access to provision additional to, or different from, the provision mentioned in heads (a) to (e) above[40];

(dd)   information about how to make a complaint about provision mentioned in heads (a) to (e) above[41].

1   As to the meaning of 'local authority' see PARA 25 (definition applied by the Children and Families Act 2014 s 83(7)).
2   As to the meaning of 'England' see PARA 7 note 3.
3   Ie within the Children and Families Act 2014 s 30(2).
4   As to the meaning of 'child' see PARA 7 note 6 (definition applied by the Children and Families Act 2014 s 83(7)).
5   As to the meaning of 'young person' see PARA 950 note 4.
6   As to being 'in the area' of a local authority see PARA 944 note 6.
7   As to the meaning of 'special educational needs' see PARA 943.
8   Children and Families Act 2014 s 30(1)(a). As to the meaning of 'disability' see PARA 943 note 3.
9   See note 3.
10 Children and Families Act 2014 s 30(1)(b)(i).
11 Children and Families Act 2014 s 30(1)(b)(ii).
12 Ie in the Children and Families Act 2014 s 30(1).
13 Children and Families Act 2014 s 30(2)(a). As to the meaning of 'education, health and care provision' see PARA 947 note 4.

14 Children and Families Act 2014 s 30(2)(b). As to the meaning of 'educational' see PARA 950 note 11.
15 Children and Families Act 2014 s 30(2)(c). As to the meaning of 'training' see PARA 943 note 9.
16 As to the meaning of 'school' generally see PARA 91 (definition applied by the Children and Families Act 2014 s 83(7)).
17 As to the meaning of 'post-16 institution' see PARA 943 note 9.
18 As to the meaning of 'relevant early years education' see PARA 943 note 17.
19 Children and Families Act 2014 s 30(2)(d).
20 Children and Families Act 2014 s 30(2)(e). For the purposes of s 30(2)(e) (see head (e) in the text), provision to assist in preparation for adulthood and independent living includes provision relating to finding employment; obtaining accommodation; and participation in society: s 30(3).
21 Ie under the Children and Families Act 2014 s 30.
22 Children and Families Act 2014 s 30(4).
23 Children and Families Act 2014 s 30(5).
24 As to the meaning of 'parent' see PARA 7 note 6 (definition applied by the Children and Families Act 2014 s 83(7)).
25 Children and Families Act 2014 s 30(6)(a)(i). Comments published under s (6)(a) must be published in a form that does not enable the person making them to be identified: s 30(7).
26 Children and Families Act 2014 s 30(6)(a)(ii). See note 25.
27 Children and Families Act 2014 s 30(6)(b).
28 As to regulations generally see the Children and Families Act 2014 s 135. As to regulations made under s 30(8), (9) see the Special Educational Needs and Disability Regulations 2014, SI 2014/1530 (amended by SI 2014/2096; and SI 2015/359).
29 Children and Families Act 2014 s 30(8)(a). See note 28.
30 Children and Families Act 2014 s 30(8)(b). See note 28.
31 Children and Families Act 2014 s 30(8)(c). See note 28.
32 Children and Families Act 2014 s 30(8)(d)(i). See note 28.
33 Children and Families Act 2014 s 30(8)(d)(ii). See note 28.
34 Children and Families Act 2014 s 30(8)(d). See note 28.
35 Ie under the Children and Families Act 2014 s 30(6): see the text to notes 24–27.
36 Children and Families Act 2014 s 30(8)(e). See note 28.
37 Children and Families Act 2014 s 30(9)(a). See note 28. As to the meaning of 'EHC needs assessment' see PARA 957 note 3.
38 Children and Families Act 2014 s 30(9)(b)(i). See note 28.
39 Children and Families Act 2014 s 30(9)(b)(ii). See note 28.
40 Children and Families Act 2014 s 30(9)(c). See note 28.
41 Children and Families Act 2014 s 30(9)(d). See note 28.

952. Co-operating in specific cases: local authority functions. Where a local authority[1] in England[2] requests the co-operation of any of the following persons[3] and bodies in the exercise of a function[4] under Part 3 of the Children and Families Act 2014[5] (1) another local authority[6]; (2) a youth offending team[7]; (3) the person in charge of any relevant youth accommodation[8]; (4) the National Health Service Commissioning Board[9]; (5) a clinical commissioning group[10]; (6) a local health board[11]; (7) an NHS trust or NHS foundation trust[12], the person or body must comply with the request, unless the person or body considers that doing so would be incompatible with the duties of the person or body[13]; or otherwise have an adverse effect on the exercise of the functions of the person or body[14].

A person or body that decides not to comply with a request as above[15] must give the authority that made the request written[16] reasons for the decision[17].

Regulations[18] may provide that, where a person or body is under a duty to comply with a request to co-operate with a local authority in securing an EHC needs assessment[19], a detained person's EHC needs assessment or the preparation of an EHC plan[20], the person or body must comply with the request within a prescribed period, unless a prescribed exception applies[21].

1 As to the meaning of 'local authority' see PARA 25 (definition applied by the Children and Families Act 2014 s 83(7)).

2 As to the meaning of 'England' see PARA 7 note 3.
3 As to the meaning of 'person' see PARA 7 note 6.
4 As to the meaning of 'function' see PARA 18 note 5 (definition applied by the Children and Families Act 2014 s 83(7)).
5 Ie the Children and Families Act 2014 Pt 3 (ss 19–83).
6 Children and Families Act 2014 s 31(1)(a).
7 Children and Families Act 2014 s 31(1)(b).
8 Children and Families Act 2014 s 31(1)(c). As to the meaning of 'relevant youth accommodation' see PARA 949 note 3.
9 Children and Families Act 2014 s 31(1)(d). As to the National Health Service Commissioning Board see HEALTH SERVICES.
10 Children and Families Act 2014 s 31(1)(e). As to clinical commissioning groups see HEALTH SERVICES.
11 Children and Families Act 2014 s 31(1)(f). As to local health boards see HEALTH SERVICES.
12 Children and Families Act 2014 s 31(1)(g). As to NHS trusts and NHS foundation trusts see HEALTH SERVICES.
13 Children and Families Act 2014 s 31(2)(a).
14 Children and Families Act 2014 s 31(2)(b).
15 Ie under the Children and Families Act 2014 s 31(1).
16 As to the meaning of 'written' see PARA 76 note 8.
17 Children and Families Act 2014 s 31(3).
18 As to regulations generally see the Children and Families Act 2014 s 135. As to regulations made under s 31(4) see the Special Educational Needs and Disability (Detained Persons) Regulations 2015, SI 2015/62.
19 As to the meaning of 'EHC needs assessment' see PARA 957 note 3.
20 As to the meaning of 'EHC plan' see PARA 958.
21 Children and Families Act 2014 s 31(4). See note 18.

953. Advice and information. A local authority[1] in England[2] must arrange for children[3] and young people[4] for whom it is responsible, and the parents[5] of children for whom it is responsible, to be provided with advice and information about matters relating to the special educational needs[6] of the children or young people concerned[7]. A local authority in England must arrange for children and young people in its area[8] with a disability[9], and the parents of children in its area with a disability, to be provided with advice and information about matters relating to the disabilities of the children or young people concerned[10].

The authority must take such steps as it thinks appropriate for making the services provided above[11] known to:

(1) the parents of children in its area[12];
(2) children in its area[13];
(3) young people in its area[14];
(4) the head teachers[15], proprietors[16] and principals of schools[17] and post-16 institutions[18] in its area[19].

The authority may also take such steps as it thinks appropriate for making the services provided above[20] known to such other persons as it thinks appropriate[21].

1 As to the meaning of 'local authority' see PARA 25 (definition applied by the Children and Families Act 2014 s 83(7)).
2 As to the meaning of 'England' see PARA 7 note 3.
3 As to the meaning of 'child' see PARA 7 note 6 (definition applied by the Children and Families Act 2014 s 83(7)).
4 As to the meaning of 'young person' see PARA 950 note 4.
5 As to the meaning of 'parent' see PARA 7 note 6 (definition applied by the Children and Families Act 2014 s 83(7)).
6 As to the meaning of 'special educational needs' see PARA 943.
7 Children and Families Act 2014 s 32(1).
8 As to being 'in the area' of a local authority see PARA 944 note 6.
9 As to the meaning of 'disability' see PARA 943 note 3.

10 Children and Families Act 2014 s 32(2).
11 Ie under the Children and Families Act 2014 s 32(1), (2).
12 Children and Families Act 2014 s 32(3)(a).
13 Children and Families Act 2014 s 32(3)(b).
14 Children and Families Act 2014 s 32(3)(c).
15 As to the meaning of 'head teacher' see PARA 86 note 4 (definition applied by the Children and
    Families Act 2014 s 83(7)).
16 As to the meaning of 'proprietor' see PARA 948 note 21.
17 As to the meaning of 'school' generally see PARA 91 (definition applied by the Children and
    Families Act 2014 s 83(7)).
18 As to the meaning of 'post-16 institution' see PARA 943 note 9.
19 Children and Families Act 2014 s 32(3)(d).
20 See note 11.
21 Children and Families Act 2014 s 32(4).

(iii) Presumption in Favour of Mainstream Education

954.   Children and young people with EHC plans. The following provisions[1]
apply where a local authority[2] is securing the preparation of an EHC plan[3] for a
child[4] or young person[5] who is to be educated[6] in a school[7] or post-16
institution[8]. In certain cases[9], the local authority must secure that the plan
provides for the child or young person to be educated in a maintained nursery
school[10], mainstream school[11] or mainstream post-16 institution[12], unless that is
incompatible with (1) the wishes of the child's parent[13] or the young person[14]; or
(2) the provision of efficient education for others[15].

A local authority may rely on the exception in head (2) above in relation to
maintained nursery schools, mainstream schools or mainstream post-16
institutions in its area[16] taken as a whole only if it shows that there are no
reasonable steps that it could take to prevent the incompatibility[17]. A local
authority may rely on the exception in head (2) above in relation to a particular
maintained nursery school, mainstream school or mainstream post-16 institution
only if it shows that there are no reasonable steps that it or the governing body[18],
proprietor[19] or principal could take to prevent the incompatibility[20]. The
governing body, proprietor or principal of a maintained nursery school,
mainstream school or mainstream post-16 institution may rely on the exception
in head (2) above only if they show that there are no reasonable steps that they
or the local authority could take to prevent the incompatibility[21].

The above provisions[22] do not prevent the child or young person from being
educated in an independent school[23], a non-maintained special school[24] or a
special post-16 institution[25], if the cost is not to be met by a local authority or
the Secretary of State[26].

1 Ie the provisions of the Children and Families Act 2014 s 33.
2 As to the meaning of 'local authority' see PARA 25 (definition applied by the Children and
   Families Act 2014 s 83(7)).
3 As to the meaning of 'EHC plan' see PARA 958.
4 As to the meaning of 'child' see PARA 7 note 6 (definition applied by the Children and Families
   Act 2014 s 83(7)).
5 As to the meaning of 'young person' see PARA 950 note 4.
6 As to the meanings of 'educate' and 'education' see PARA 950 note 11.
7 As to the meaning of 'school' generally see PARA 91 (definition applied by the Children and
   Families Act 2014 s 83(7)).
8 Children and Families Act 2014 s 33(1). As to the meaning of 'post-16 institution' see PARA 943
   note 9.
       Section 33 does not affect the operation of s 63 (fees payable by local authority for special
   educational provision at non-maintained schools and post-16 institutions: see PARA 967):
   s 34(10).

9   Ie in a case within the Children and Families Act 2014 s 39(5) or s 40(2): see PARA 960.
10 As to the meaning of 'maintained nursery school' see PARA 99 note 4 (definition applied by the Children and Families Act 2014 s 83(7)).
11 As to the meaning of 'mainstream school' see PARA 943 note 8.
12 As to the meaning of 'mainstream post-16 institution' see PARA 943 note 9.
13 As to the meaning of 'parent' see PARA 7 note 6 (definition applied by the Children and Families Act 2014 s 83(7)).
14 Children and Families Act 2014 s 33(2)(a).
15 Children and Families Act 2014 s 33(2)(b).
16 As to being 'in the area' of a local authority see PARA 944 note 6.
17 Children and Families Act 2014 s 33(3).
18 As to the governing bodies of maintained schools in England see PARA 150 et seq.
19 As to the meaning of 'proprietor' see PARA 948 note 21.
20 Children and Families Act 2014 s 33(4).
21 Children and Families Act 2014 s 33(5).
22 Ie the provisions of the Children and Families Act 2014 s 33(2).
23 As to the meaning of 'independent school' see PARA 369 (definition applied by the Children and Families Act 2014 s 83(7)).
24 As to the meaning of 'non-maintained special school' see PARA 1042 (definition applied by the Children and Families Act 2014 s 83(7)).
25 As to the meaning of 'special post-16 institution' see PARA 943 note 9.
26 Children and Families Act 2014 s 33(6). As to the Secretary of State see PARA 58. See also s 63 and footnote 8, i e that the child could (under an ECH plan) be placed in an independent school with costs paid for the local authority.

955.   Children and young people with special educational needs but no EHC plan. The following provisions[1] apply to a child[2] or young person[3] in England[4] who has special educational needs[5] but for whom no EHC plan[6] is maintained, if he or she is to be educated[7] in a school[8] or post-16 institution[9].

The child or young person must be educated in a maintained nursery school[10], mainstream school[11] or mainstream post-16 institution[12], subject to these conditions[13]. The child or young person may be educated in an independent school[14], a non-maintained special school[15] or a special post-16 institution[16], if the cost is not to be met by a local authority or the Secretary of State[17]. The child or young person may be educated in a special school[18] or special post-16 institution[19] during any period in which specified provision[20] applies[21].

1   Ie the provisions of the Children and Families Act 2014 s 34.
2   As to the meaning of 'child' see PARA 7 note 6 (definition applied by the Children and Families Act 2014 s 83(7)).
3   As to the meaning of 'young person' see PARA 950 note 4.
4   As to the meaning of 'England' see PARA 7 note 3.
5   As to the meaning of 'special educational needs' see PARA 943.
6   As to the meaning of 'EHC plan' see PARA 958.
7   As to the meaning of 'educate' see PARA 950 note 11.
8   As to the meaning of 'school' generally see PARA 91 (definition applied by the Children and Families Act 2014 s 83(7)).
9   Children and Families Act 2014 s 34(1). As to the meaning of 'post-16 institution' see PARA 943 note 9.
    Section 34 does not affect the operation of s 63 (fees payable by local authority for special educational provision at non-maintained schools and post-16 institutions: see PARA 967): s 34(10).
10 As to the meaning of 'maintained nursery school' see PARA 99 note 4 (definition applied by the Children and Families Act 2014 s 83(7)).
11 As to the meaning of 'mainstream school' see PARA 943 note 8.
12 As to the meaning of 'mainstream post-16 institution' see PARA 943 note 9.
13 Children and Families Act 2014 s 34(2). The conditions referred to in the text are those in the Children and Families Act 2014 s 34(3), (4): see the text to notes 14–21.
14 As to the meaning of 'independent school' see PARA 369 (definition applied by the Children and Families Act 2014 s 83(7)).

15 As to the meaning of 'non-maintained special school' see PARA 1042 (definition applied by the Children and Families Act 2014 s 83(7)).

16 As to the meaning of 'special post-16 institution' see PARA 943 note 9.

17 Children and Families Act 2014 s 34(3).

18 As to the meaning of 'special school' see PARA 1041 (definition applied by the Children and Families Act 2014 s 83(7)).

19 As to the meaning of 'special post-16 institution' see PARA 943 note 9.

20 Ie any of the Children and Families Act 2014 s 34(5)–(9).

Section 34(5) applies while the child or young person is admitted to a special school or special post-16 institution for the purposes of an EHC needs assessment, if all the following have agreed to his or her admission to the school or post-16 institution: (1) the local authority which is responsible for him or her (s 34(5)(a)); (2) the head teacher of the school or the principal of the academy or post-16 institution (s 34(5)(b)); (3) the child's parent or the young person (s 34(5)(c)); (4) anyone else whose advice is required to be obtained in connection with the assessment by virtue of regulations under s 36(11) (see PARA 957) (s 34(5)(d)). As to the meaning of 'EHC needs assessment' see PARA 957 note 3. As to the meaning of 'head teacher' see PARA 86 note 4 (definition applied by s 83(7)). As to the meaning of 'academy' see PARA 346 note 7 (definition applied by s 83(7)). As to the meaning of 'parent' see PARA 7 note 6 (definition applied by s 83(7)).

Section 34(6) applies while the child or young person remains admitted to a special school or special post-16 institution, in prescribed circumstances, following an EHC needs assessment at the school or post-16 institution: s 34(6).

Section 34(7) applies while the child or young person is admitted to a special school or special post-16 institution, following a change in his or her circumstances, if all the following have agreed to his or her admission to the school or post-16 institution: (a) the local authority which is responsible for him or her (s 34(7)(a)); (b) the head teacher of the school or the principal of the academy or post-16 institution (s 34(7)(b)); (c) the child's parent or the young person (s 34(7)(c)).

Section 34(8) applies while the child or young person is admitted to a special school which is established in a hospital and is (i) a community or foundation special school (s 34(8)(a)); or (ii) an academy school (s 34(8)(b)). As to references to community or foundations schools see PARA 943 note 8. As to the meaning of 'academy school' see PARA 346 note 12 (definition applied by s 83(7)).

Section 34(9) applies while the child is admitted to a special school or special post-16 institution that is an academy, if the academy arrangements made in respect of the school or post-16 institution permit it to admit children and young people with special educational needs for whom no EHC plan is maintained: s 34(9). As to the meaning of 'academy arrangements' see PARA 346 note 4 (definition applied by s 83(7)).

21 Children and Families Act 2014 s 34(4).

956. **Children with special educational needs in maintained nurseries and mainstream schools.** The following provisions[1] apply where a child[2] with special educational needs[3] is being educated[4] in a maintained nursery school[5] or a mainstream school[6]. Those concerned with making special educational provision[7] for the child must secure that the child engages in the activities of the school together with children who do not have special educational needs, subject to the condition below[8]. The above[9] applies only so far as is reasonably practicable and is compatible with (1) the child receiving the special educational provision called for by his or her special educational needs[10]; (2) the provision of efficient education for the children with whom he or she will be educated[11]; and (3) the efficient use of resources[12].

1 Ie the provisions of the Children and Families Act 2014 s 35.

2 As to the meaning of 'child' see PARA 7 note 6 (definition applied by the Children and Families Act 2014 s 83(7)).

3 As to the meaning of 'special educational needs' see PARA 943.

4 As to the meaning of 'educate' see PARA 950 note 11.

5 As to the meaning of 'maintained nursery school' see PARA 99 note 4 (definition applied by the Children and Families Act 2014 s 83(7)).

6 Children and Families Act 2014 s 35(1). As to the meaning of 'mainstream school' see PARA 943 note 8.

7 As to the meaning of 'special educational provision' see PARA 943.
8 Children and Families Act 2014 s 35(2). The condition referred to in the text is that in s 35(3): see the text and notes 9–12.
9 Ie the Children and Families Act 2014 s 35(2).
10 Children and Families Act 2014 s 35(3)(a).
11 Children and Families Act 2014 s 35(3)(b).
12 Children and Families Act 2014 s 35(3)(c).

(iv) Assessment of Educational, Health and Care Needs

957. Assessment of educational, health and care needs. A request for a local authority[1] in England[2] to secure an EHC needs assessment[3] for a child or young person may be made to the authority by the child's parent[4], the young person or a person acting on behalf of a school[5] or post-16 institution[6].

When such a request is made[7] to a local authority, or a local authority otherwise becomes responsible for a child or young person, the authority must determine whether it may be necessary for special educational provision[8] to be made for the child or young person in accordance with an EHC plan[9].

In making such a determination[10], the local authority must consult the child's parent or the young person[11]. Where the local authority determines that it is not necessary for special educational provision to be made for the child or young person in accordance with an EHC plan it must notify the child's parent or the young person (1) of the reasons for that determination[12]; and (2) that accordingly it has decided not to secure an EHC needs assessment for the child or young person[13].

Where (a) no EHC plan is maintained for the child or young person[14]; (b) the child or young person has not been assessed[15] during the previous six months[16]; and (c) the local authority determines that it may be necessary for special educational provision to be made for the child or young person in accordance with an EHC plan[17], the authority must notify the child's parent or the young person (i) that it is considering securing an EHC needs assessment for the child or young person[18]; and (ii) that the parent or young person has the right to express views to the authority (orally or in writing)[19], and submit evidence to the authority[20].

The local authority must secure an EHC needs assessment for the child or young person if, after having regard to any views expressed and evidence submitted[21], the authority is of the opinion that the child or young person has or may have special educational needs[22], and it may be necessary for special educational provision to be made for the child or young person in accordance with an EHC plan[23].

After an EHC needs assessment has been carried out, the local authority must notify the child's parent or the young person of (A) the outcome of the assessment[24]; (B) whether it proposes to secure that an EHC plan is prepared for the child or young person[25]; and (C) the reasons for that decision[26]. In making a determination or forming an opinion for these purposes[27] in relation to a young person aged over 18[28] a local authority must consider whether he or she requires additional time, in comparison to the majority of others of the same age who do not have special educational needs, to complete his or her education or training[29].

Regulations[30] may make provision about EHC needs assessments[31].

1 As to the meaning of 'local authority' see PARA 25 (definition applied by the Children and Families Act 2014 s 83(7)).
2 As to the meaning of 'England' see PARA 7 note 3.

3   An 'EHC needs assessment' is an assessment of the educational, health care and social care needs of a child or young person: Children and Families Act 2014 s 36(2). As to the meaning of 'educational' see PARA 950 note 11. As to the meaning of 'child' see PARA 7 note 6 (definition applied by s 83(7)). As to the meaning of 'young person' see PARA 950 note 4.

4   As to the meaning of 'parent' see PARA 7 note 6 (definition applied by the Children and Families Act 2014 s 83(7)).

5   As to the meaning of 'school' generally see PARA 91 (definition applied by the Children and Families Act 2014 s 83(7)).

6   Children and Families Act 2014 s 36(1). As to the meaning of 'post-16 institution' see PARA 943 note 9.

7   Ie under the Children and Families Act 2014 s 36(1).

8   As to the meaning of 'special educational provision' see PARA 943.

9   Children and Families Act 2014 s 36(3). As to the meaning of 'EHC plan' see PARA 958.

10 Ie a determination under the Children and Families Act 2014 s 36(3).

11 Children and Families Act 2014 s 36(4).

12 Children and Families Act 2014 s 36(5)(a).

13 Children and Families Act 2014 s 36(5)(b).

14 Children and Families Act 2014 s 36(6)(a).

15 Ie under the Children and Families Act 2014 s 36 or under s 71 (see PARA 971).

16 Children and Families Act 2014 s 36(6)(b).

17 Children and Families Act 2014 s 36(6)(c).

18 Children and Families Act 2014 s 36(7)(a).

19 As to the meaning of 'writing' see PARA 76 note 8.

20 Children and Families Act 2014 s 36(7)(b).

21 Ie under the Children and Families Act 2014 s 36(7).

22 As to the meaning of 'special educational needs' see PARA 943.

23 Children and Families Act 2014 s 36(8).

24 Children and Families Act 2014 s 36(9)(a).

25 Children and Families Act 2014 s 36(9)(b).

26 Children and Families Act 2014 s 36(9)(c).

27 Ie for the purposes of the Children and Families Act 2014 s 36.

28 As to the time at which a person attains a particular age see PARA 7 note 6.

29 Children and Families Act 2014 s 36(10). As to the meaning of 'training' see PARA 943 note 9.

30 As to regulations generally see the Children and Families Act 2014 s 135. As to regulations made under s 36(11) see the Special Educational Needs and Disability Regulations 2014, SI 2014/1530 (amended by SI 2014/2096; and SI 2015/359); and the Special Educational Needs and Disability (Detained Persons) Regulations 2015, SI 2015/62.

31 See the Children and Families Act 2014 s 36(11); and see note 30. In particular such regulations may make provision about EHC needs assessments:

    (1)   about requests under s 36(1) (see the text to notes 1–6) (s 36(11)(a));

    (2)   imposing time limits in relation to consultation under s 36(4) (see the text to notes 10, 11) (s 36(11)(b));

    (3)   about giving notice (s 36(11)(c));

    (4)   about expressing views and submitting evidence under s 36(7) (see the text to notes 18–20) (s 36(11)(d));

    (5)   about how assessments are to be conducted (s 36(11)(e));

    (6)   about advice to be obtained in connection with an assessment (s 36(11)(f));

    (7)   about combining an EHC needs assessment with other assessments (s 36(11)(g));

    (8)   about the use for the purposes of an EHC needs assessment of information obtained as a result of other assessments (s 36(11)(h));

    (9)   about the use of information obtained as a result of an EHC needs assessment, including the use of that information for the purposes of other assessments (s 36(11)(i));

    (10)   about the provision of information, advice and support in connection with an EHC needs assessment (s 36(11)(j)).

(v) Education, Health and Care ('EHC') Plans

958. Education, health and care plans generally. Where, in the light of an EHC needs assessment[1], it is necessary for special educational provision[2] to be made for a child[3] or young person[4] in accordance with an EHC plan (1) the local authority[5] must secure that an EHC plan is prepared for the child or young person[6]; and (2) once an EHC plan has been prepared, it must maintain the plan[7]. For the purposes of Part 3 of the Children and Families Act 2014[8], an 'EHC plan' is a plan specifying:

(a)   the child's or young person's special educational needs[9];

(b)   the outcomes sought for him or her[10];

(c)   the special educational provision required by him or her[11];

(d)   any health care provision[12] reasonably required by the learning difficulties and disabilities[13] which result in him or her having special educational needs[14];

(e)   in the case of a child or a young person aged under 18[15], any social care provision[16] which must be made for him or her by the local authority as a result of the Chronically Sick and Disabled Persons Act 1970[17];

(f)   any social care provision reasonably required by the learning difficulties and disabilities which result in the child or young person having special educational needs, to the extent that the provision is not already specified in the plan under head (e) above[18].

An EHC plan may also specify other health care and social care provision reasonably required by the child or young person[19]. Regulations may make provision about the preparation, content, maintenance, amendment and disclosure of EHC plans[20].

1   As to the meaning of 'EHC needs assessment' see PARA 957 note 3.
2   As to the meaning of 'special educational provision' see PARA 943.
3   As to the meaning of 'child' see PARA 7 note 6 (definition applied by the Children and Families Act 2014 s 83(7)).
4   As to the meaning of 'young person' see PARA 950 note 4.
5   As to the meaning of 'local authority' see PARA 25 (definition applied by the Children and Families Act 2014 s 83(7)).
6   Children and Families Act 2014 s 37(1)(a).
7   Children and Families Act 2014 s 37(1)(b).
8   Ie the Children and Families Act 2014 Pt 3 (ss 19–83).
9   Children and Families Act 2014 s 37(2)(a), Education Act 1996 s 579(1) (definition added by the Children and Families Act 2014 Sch 3 paras 1, 59(a)). As to the meaning of 'special educational needs' see PARA 943. See also PARA 947 note 7. As to reviews and re-assessments of EHC plans including timescales see PARA 964.
10   Children and Families Act 2014 s 37(2)(b), Education Act 1996 s 579(1) (definition as added: see note 9).
11   Children and Families Act 2014 s 37(2)(c), Education Act 1996 s 579(1) (definition as added: see note 9).
12   As to the meaning of 'health care provision' see PARA 946 note 7.
13   As to the meaning of 'disability' see PARA 943 note 3.
14   Children and Families Act 2014 s 37(2)(d), Education Act 1996 s 579(1) (definition as added: see note 9).
15   As to the time at which a person attains a particular age see PARA 7 note 6.
16   As to the meaning of 'social care provision' see PARA 946 note 8.
17   Children and Families Act 2014 s 37(2)(e), Education Act 1996 s 579(1) (definition as added: see note 9). The reference in the text to the Chronically Sick and Disabled Persons Act 1970 is a reference to s 2 (see SOCIAL SERVICES AND COMMUNITY CARE vol 95 (2013) PARA 6) (as it applies by virtue of s 28A: see SOCIAL SERVICES AND COMMUNITY CARE vol 95 (2013) PARA 6).
18   Children and Families Act 2014 s 37(2)(f), Education Act 1996 s 579(1) (definition as added: see note 9).
19   Children and Families Act 2014 s 37(3).
20   Children and Families Act 2014 s 37(4). Regulations under s 37(4) about amendments of EHC plans must include provision applying s 33 (mainstream education for children and young people with EHC plans: see PARA 954) to a case where an EHC plan is to be amended under those regulations: s 37(5). As to regulations made under s 37(4) see the Special Educational Needs and Disability Regulations 2014, SI 2014/1530 (amended by SI 2014/2096; and SI 2015/359); and the Special Educational Needs and Disability (Detained Persons) Regulations 2015, SI 2015/62.

959. Preparation of EHC plans: draft plan. Where a local authority[1] is required to secure that an EHC plan[2] is prepared for a child[3] or young person[4], it must consult the child's parent[5] or the young person about the content of the plan during the preparation of a draft of the plan[6].

The local authority must then (1) send the draft plan to the child's parent or the young person[7]; and (2) give the parent or young person notice of his or her right to (a) make representations about the content of the draft plan[8]; and (b) request the authority to secure that a particular school[9] or other institution[10] is named in the plan[11]. Such a notice[12] must specify a period before the end of which any representations or requests must be made[13].

The draft EHC plan sent to the child's parent or the young person must not (i) name a school or other institution[14]; or (ii) specify a type of school or other institution[15].

1 As to the meaning of 'local authority' see PARA 25 (definition applied by the Children and Families Act 2014 s 83(7)).
2 As to the meaning of 'EHC plan' see PARA 958.
3 As to the meaning of 'child' see PARA 7 note 6 (definition applied by the Children and Families Act 2014 s 83(7)).
4 As to the meaning of 'young person' see PARA 950 note 4.
5 As to the meaning of 'parent' see PARA 7 note 6 (definition applied by the Children and Families Act 2014 s 83(7)).
6 Children and Families Act 2014 s 38(1).
7 Children and Families Act 2014 s 38(2)(a).
8 Children and Families Act 2014 s 38(2)(b)(i).
9 As to the meaning of 'school' generally see PARA 91 (definition applied by the Children and Families Act 2014 s 83(7)). As to where the parent wishes an independent school to be involved which is not a special school see PARA 967.
10 Ie school or other institution within the Children and Families Act 2014 s 38(3) (see below). A school or other institution is within s 38(3) if it is:
  (1) a maintained school (s 38(3)(a));
  (2) a maintained nursery school (s 38(3)(b));
  (3) an academy (s 38(3)(c));
  (4) an institution within the further education sector in England (s 38(3)(d));
  (5) a non-maintained special school (s 38(3)(e));
  (6) an institution approved by the Secretary of State under s 41 (independent special schools and special post-16 institutions: approval: see PARA 961) (s 38(3)(f)).
  As to the meaning of 'maintained school' see PARA 943 note 8. As to the meaning of 'maintained nursery school' see PARA 99 note 4 (definition applied by s 83(7)). As to the meaning of 'academy' see PARA 346 note 7 (definition applied by s 83(7)). As to the meaning of 'further education' see PARA 23 (definition applied by s 83(7)). As to the meaning of 'England' see PARA 7 note 3. As to the meaning of 'non-maintained special school' see PARA 1042 (definition applied by s 83(7)). As to the Secretary of State see PARA 58.
11 Children and Families Act 2014 s 38(2)(b)(ii).
12 Ie a notice under the Children and Families Act 2014 s 38(2)(b).
13 Children and Families Act 2014 s 38(4). The parent or young person has 15 days in which to respond: see the Special Educational Needs and Disability Regulations 2014, SI 2014/1530, reg 13.
14 Children and Families Act 2014 s 38(5)(a).
15 Children and Families Act 2014 s 38(5)(b).

960. Finalising EHC plans. Where, before the end of the period specified in the relevant notice[1], a request is made to a local authority[2] to secure that a particular school[3] or other institution is named in an EHC plan[4], the local authority must consult:
  (1) the governing body[5], proprietor[6] or principal of the school or other institution[7];

(2)　the governing body, proprietor or principal of any other school or other institution the authority is considering having named in the plan[8]; and

(3)　if a school or other institution is within head (1) or (2) above and is maintained by another local authority, that authority[9].

The local authority must secure that the EHC plan names the school or other institution specified in the request, unless a certain provision[10] applies[11]. Where that provision[12] applies, the local authority must secure that the plan (a) names a school or other institution which the local authority thinks would be appropriate for the child or young person[13]; or (b) specifies the type of school or other institution which the local authority thinks would be appropriate for the child or young person[14].

Before securing that the plan names a school or other institution under head (a) above, the local authority must (if it has not already done so) consult the governing body, proprietor or principal of any school or other institution the authority is considering having named in the plan[15]; and if that school or other institution is maintained by another local authority, that authority[16].

The local authority must, at the end of the period specified in the notice[17], secure that any changes it thinks necessary are made to the draft EHC plan[18]. The local authority must send a copy of the finalised EHC plan to the child's parent[19] or the young person[20]; and the governing body, proprietor or principal of any school or other institution named in the plan[21].

Where no request is made to a local authority before the end of the period specified in the relevant notice[22] to secure that a particular school or other institution is named in an EHC plan[23], the local authority must secure that the plan (i) names a school or other institution which the local authority thinks would be appropriate for the child or young person concerned[24]; or (ii) specifies the type of school or other institution which the local authority thinks would be appropriate for the child or young person[25].

Before securing that the plan names a school or other institution under head (i) above, the local authority must consult the governing body, proprietor or principal of any school or other institution the authority is considering having named in the plan[26]; and if that school or other institution is maintained by another local authority, that authority[27].

The local authority must also secure that any changes it thinks necessary are made to the draft EHC plan[28]. The local authority must send a copy of the finalised EHC plan to the child's parent or the young person[29]; and the governing body, proprietor or principal of any school or other institution named in the plan[30].

1　Ie a notice under the Children and Families Act 2014 s 38(2)(b): see PARA 959. 20 weeks is the usual period (subject o exceptions) for the issuing of a finalised EHC plan: see the Special Educational Needs and Disability Regulations 2014, SI 2014/1530, regs 10(4), 13(3).
2　As to the meaning of 'local authority' see PARA 25 (definition applied by the Children and Families Act 2014 s 83(7)).
3　As to the meaning of 'school' generally see PARA 91 (definition applied by the Children and Families Act 2014 s 83(7)).
4　Children and Families Act 2014 s 39(1). As to the meaning of 'EHC plan' see PARA 958.
5　As to the governing bodies of maintained schools in England see PARA 150 et seq.
6　As to the meaning of 'proprietor' see PARA 948 note 21.
7　Children and Families Act 2014 s 39(2)(a).
8　Children and Families Act 2014 s 39(2)(b).
9　Children and Families Act 2014 s 39(2)(c).
10　Ie the Children and Families Act 2014 s 39(4). Section 39(4) applies where:
　　(1)　the school or other institution requested is unsuitable for the age, ability, aptitude or special educational needs of the child or young person concerned (s 39(4)(a)); or

(2)   the attendance of the child or young person at the requested school or other institution would be incompatible with (a) the provision of efficient education for others (s 39(4)(b)(i)); or (b) the efficient use of resources (s 39(4)(b)(ii)).

As to the meaning of 'special educational needs' see PARA 943. As to the meaning of 'child' see PARA 7 note 6 (definition applied by the Children and Families Act 2014 s 83(7)). As to the meaning of 'young person' see PARA 950 note 4.

11 Children and Families Act 2014 s 39(3).
12 Ie the Children and Families Act 2014 s 39(4): see note 10.
13 Children and Families Act 2014 s 39(5)(a).
14 Children and Families Act 2014 s 39(5)(b).
15 Children and Families Act 2014 s 39(6)(a).
16 Children and Families Act 2014 s 39(6)(b).
17 See note 1.
18 Children and Families Act 2014 s 39(7).
19 As to the meaning of 'parent' see PARA 7 note 6 (definition applied by the Children and Families Act 2014 s 83(7)).
20 Children and Families Act 2014 s 39(8)(a).
21 Children and Families Act 2014 s 39(8)(b).
22 See note 1.
23 Children and Families Act 2014 s 40(1).
24 Children and Families Act 2014 s 40(2)(a).
25 Children and Families Act 2014 s 40(2)(b).
26 Children and Families Act 2014 s 40(3)(a).
27 Children and Families Act 2014 s 40(3)(b).
28 Children and Families Act 2014 s 40(4).
29 Children and Families Act 2014 s 40(5)(a).
30 Children and Families Act 2014 s 40(5)(b).

961.   Approval of institution to be named in EHC plan. The Secretary of State[1] may approve certain institutions[2] for the purpose of enabling the institution to be the subject of a request for it to be named in an EHC plan[3].

The Secretary of State may so approve[4] an institution only if its proprietor[5] consents[6]. The Secretary of State may withdraw such approval[7].

Regulations[8] may make provision about giving and withdrawing approval[9], in particular:

(1)   about the types of special post-16 institutions which may be approved[10];
(2)   specifying criteria which an institution must meet before it can be approved[11];
(3)   about the matters which may or must be taken into account in deciding to give or withdraw approval[12];
(4)   about the publication of a list of all institutions who are approved[13].

1   As to the Secretary of State see PARA 58.
2   Ie an institution within the Children and Families Act 2014 s 41(2). An institution is within s 41(2) if it is:
    (1)   an independent educational institution (within the Education and Skills Act 2008 Pt 4 Ch 1 (ss 92–141): see PARA 382) (a) which has been entered on the register of independent educational institutions in England (kept under s 95: see PARA 384) (Children and Families Act 2014 s 41(2)(a)(i)); and (b) which is specially organised to make special educational provision for students with special educational needs (s 41(2)(a)(ii));
    (2)   an independent school (a) which has been entered on the register of independent schools in Wales (kept under the Education Act 2002 s 158: see PARA 417) (Children and Families Act 2014 s 41(2)(b)(i)); and (b) which is specially organised to make special educational provision for pupils with special educational needs (s 41(2)(b)(ii)); or
    (3)   a special post-16 institution which is not an institution within the further education sector or a 16 to 19 academy (s 41(2)(c)).
As to the meanings of 'special educational provision' and 'special educational needs' see PARA 943. As to the meaning of 'independent school' see PARA 369 (definition applied by s 83(7)). As

to the meaning of 'pupil' see PARA 20 note 4 (definition applied by s 83(7)). As to the meaning of 'special post-16 institution' see PARA 943 note 9. As to the meaning of 'further education' see PARA 23 (definition applied by s 83(7)). As to the meaning of '16 to 19 academy' see PARA 346 note 13 (definition applied by s 83(7)).

3   Children and Families Act 2014 s 41(1). As to the meaning of 'EHC plan' see PARA 958.
4   Ie under the Children and Families Act 2014 s 41(1).
5   As to the meaning of 'proprietor' see PARA 948 note 21.
6   Children and Families Act 2014 s 41(3).
7   Children and Families Act 2014 s 41(4). The approval is that given under s 41(1).
8   As to regulations generally see the Children and Families Act 2014 s 135. As to regulations made under s 41(5) see the Special Educational Needs and Disability Regulations 2014, SI 2014/1530 (amended by SI 2014/2096; and SI 2015/359).
9   The approval is under the Children and Families Act 2014 s 41(1).
10 Children and Families Act 2014 s 41(5)(a). See note 8.
11 Children and Families Act 2014 s 41(5)(b). See note 8.
12 Children and Families Act 2014 s 41(5)(c). See note 8.
13 Children and Families Act 2014 s 41(5)(d). See note 8.

962.   Duty to secure special educational and health care provision in accordance with EHC plan. Where a local authority[1] maintains an EHC plan[2] for a child[3] or young person[4], the local authority must secure the specified[5] special educational provision[6] for the child or young person[7].

If the plan specifies health care provision[8], the responsible commissioning body[9] must arrange the specified health care provision for the child or young person[10].

The above provisions[11] do not apply if the child's parent[12] or the young person has made suitable alternative arrangements[13].

1   As to the meaning of 'local authority' see PARA 25 (definition applied by the Children and Families Act 2014 s 83(7)).
2   As to the meaning of 'EHC plan' see PARA 958.
3   As to the meaning of 'child' see PARA 7 note 6 (definition applied by the Children and Families Act 2014 s 83(7)).
4   Children and Families Act 2014 s 42(1). As to the meaning of 'young person' see PARA 950 note 4.
5   'Specified', in relation to an EHC plan, means specified in the plan: Children and Families Act 2014 s 42(6).
6   As to the meaning of 'special educational provision' see PARA 943.
7   Children and Families Act 2014 s 42(2).
8   As to the meaning of 'health care provision' see PARA 946 note 7.
9   'The responsible commissioning body', in relation to any specified health care provision, means the body (or each body) that is under a duty to arrange health care provision of that kind in respect of the child or young person: Children and Families Act 2014 s 42(4).
10 Children and Families Act 2014 s 42(3).
11 Ie the provisions of the Children and Families Act 2014 s 42(2), (3).
12 As to the meaning of 'parent' see PARA 7 note 6 (definition applied by the Children and Families Act 2014 s 83(7)).
13 Children and Families Act 2014 s 42(5).

963.   Duty to admit for schools and other institutions named in EHC plan. If one of certain schools or other institutions[1] is named in an EHC plan[2], the governing body[3], proprietor[4] or principal of the school or other institution must admit the child[5] or young person[6] for whom the plan is maintained[7].

This does not affect any power to exclude a pupil or student from a school or other institution[8].

1   Ie one of the following:
    (1)   a maintained school (Children and Families Act 2014 s 43(1)(a));
    (2)   a maintained nursery school (s 43(1)(b));
    (3)   an academy (s 43(1)(c));

(4)   an institution within the further education sector in England (s 43(1)(d));
(5)   a non-maintained special school (s 43(1)(e));
(6)   an institution approved by the Secretary of State under s 41 (see PARA 961) (s 43(1)(f)).
As to the meaning of 'maintained school' see PARA 943 note 8. As to the meaning of 'maintained nursery school' see PARA 99 note 4 (definition applied by s 83(7)). As to the meaning of 'academy' see PARA 346 note 7 (definition applied by s 83(7)). As to the meaning of 'further education' see PARA 23 (definition applied by s 83(7)). As to the meaning of 'England' see PARA 7 note 3. As to the meaning of 'non-maintained special school' see PARA 1042 (definition applied by s 83(7)). As to the Secretary of State see PARA 58.
2   See the Children and Families Act 2014 s 43(1). As to the meaning of 'EHC plan' see PARA 958.
3   As to the governing bodies of maintained schools in England see PARA 150 et seq.
4   As to the meaning of 'proprietor' see PARA 948 note 21.
5   As to the meaning of 'child' see PARA 7 note 6 (definition applied by Children and Families Act 2014 s 83(7)).
6   As to the meaning of 'young person' see PARA 950 note 4.
7   Children and Families Act 2014 s 43(2). Section 43(2) has effect regardless of any duty imposed on the governing body of a school by the School Standards and Framework Act 1998 s 1(6) (see PARA 234): Children and Families Act 2014 s 43(3).
8   Children and Families Act 2014 s 43(4). As to exclusions see PARA 517 et seq.

964.   Reviews and re-assessments. A local authority[1] must review an EHC plan[2] that it maintains (1) in the period of 12 months[3] starting with the date on which the plan was first made[4]; and (2) in each subsequent period of 12 months starting with the date on which the plan was last reviewed[5].

A local authority must secure a re-assessment of the educational[6], health care and social care needs of a child[7] or young person[8] for whom it maintains an EHC plan if a request is made to it by (a) the child's parent[9] or the young person[10]; or (b) the governing body[11], proprietor[12] or principal of the school[13], post-16 institution[14] or other institution which the child or young person attends[15].

A local authority may also secure a re-assessment of those needs at any other time if it thinks it necessary[16].

In reviewing an EHC plan maintained for a young person aged over 18[17], or deciding whether to secure a re-assessment of the needs of such a young person, a local authority must have regard to whether the educational or training[18] outcomes specified in the plan have been achieved[19].

During a review or re-assessment, a local authority must consult the parent of the child, or the young person, for whom it maintains the EHC plan[20].

Regulations[21] may make provision about reviews and re-assessments[22], in particular:

(1)   about other circumstances in which a local authority must or may review an EHC plan or secure a re-assessment (including before the end of a specified phase of a child's or young person's education)[23];

(2)   about circumstances in which it is not necessary for a local authority to review an EHC plan or secure a re-assessment[24];

(3)   about amending or replacing an EHC plan following a review or re-assessment[25].

1   As to the meaning of 'local authority' see PARA 25 (definition applied by the Children and Families Act 2014 s 83(7)).
2   As to the meaning of 'EHC plan' see PARA 958.
3   As to the meaning of 'month' see PARA 54 note 26.
4   Children and Families Act 2014 s 44(1)(a). Section 44(1), (2) is subject to any contrary provision in regulations made under s 44(7)(b) (see the text to note 24): s 44(4).
5   Children and Families Act 2014 s 44(1)(b). The review is under s 44. See note 4.
6   As to the meaning of 'educational' see PARA 950 note 11.

7   As to the meaning of 'child' see PARA 7 note 6 (definition applied by the Children and Families Act 2014 s 83(7)).
8   As to the meaning of 'young person' see PARA 950 note 4.
9   As to the meaning of 'parent' see PARA 7 note 6 (definition applied by the Children and Families Act 2014 s 83(7)).
10   Children and Families Act 2014 s 44(2)(a). See note 4.
11   As to the governing bodies of maintained schools in England see PARA 150 et seq.
12   As to the meaning of 'proprietor' see PARA 948 note 21.
13   As to the meaning of 'school' generally see PARA 91 (definition applied by the Children and Families Act 2014 s 83(7)).
14   As to the meaning of 'post-16 institution' see PARA 943 note 9.
15   Children and Families Act 2014 s 44(2)(b). See note 4.
16   Children and Families Act 2014 s 44(3).
17   As to the time at which a person attains a particular age see PARA 7 note 6.
18   As to the meaning of 'training' see PARA 943 note 9.
19   Children and Families Act 2014 s 44(5).
20   Children and Families Act 2014 s 44(6).
21   As to regulations generally see the Children and Families Act 2014 s 135. As to regulations made under s 44(7) see the Special Educational Needs and Disability Regulations 2014, SI 2014/1530 (amended by SI 2014/2096; and SI 2015/359); and the Special Educational Needs and Disability (Detained Persons) Regulations 2015, SI 2015/62. As to reviews and re-assessments see in particular the Special Educational Needs and Disability Regulations 2014, SI 2014/1530, regs 18–28 (reg 20 amended by SI 2014/2096; and the Special Educational Needs and Disability Regulations 2014, SI 2014/1530, regs 21, 22, 25 amended by SI 2015/359), which include relevant timescales.
22   Regulations under the Children and Families Act 2014 s 44(7) about re-assessments may in particular apply provisions of or made under Pt 3 (ss 19–83) that are applicable to EHC needs assessments, with or without modifications: s 44(8). As to the meaning of 'EHC needs assessment' see PARA 957 note 3.
23   Children and Families Act 2014 s 44(7)(a).
24   Children and Families Act 2014 s 44(7)(b). See note 4.
25   Children and Families Act 2014 s 44(7)(c). Regulations under s 44(7)(c) must include provision applying s 33 (mainstream education for children and young people with EHC plans: see PARA 954) to a case where an EHC plan is to be amended following a review: s 44(9).

965. Maintaining and transferring EHC plans; ceasing to maintain EHC plans. A local authority[1] may cease to maintain an EHC plan[2] for a child[3] or young person[4] only if (1) the authority is no longer responsible for the child or young person[5]; or (2) the authority determines that it is no longer necessary for the plan to be maintained[6].

The circumstances in which it is no longer necessary for an EHC plan to be maintained for a child or young person include where the child or young person no longer requires the special educational provision[7] specified in the plan[8]. When determining whether a young person aged over 18[9] no longer requires the special educational provision specified in his or her EHC plan, a local authority must have regard to whether the educational[10] or training[11] outcomes specified in the plan have been achieved[12].

A local authority may not cease to maintain an EHC plan for a child or young person until (a) after the end of the period allowed for bringing an appeal[13] against its decision to cease to maintain the plan, where no such appeal is brought before the end of that period[14]; (b) after the appeal has been finally determined, where such an appeal is brought before the end of that period[15].

Regulations[16] may make provision about ceasing to maintain an EHC plan, in particular about:

(i)   other circumstances in which it is no longer necessary for an EHC plan to be maintained[17];

(ii)   circumstances in which a local authority may not determine that it is no longer necessary for an EHC plan to be maintained[18];

(iii) the procedure to be followed by a local authority when determining whether to cease to maintain an EHC plan[19].

A local authority may continue to maintain an EHC plan for a young person until the end of the academic year[20] during which the young person attains the age of 25[21].

Regulations[22] may make provision for an EHC plan maintained for a child or young person by one local authority to be transferred to another local authority in England, where the other authority becomes responsible for the child or young person[23]. The regulations may in particular:

(A) impose a duty on the other authority to maintain the plan[24];
(B) treat the plan as if originally prepared by the other authority[25];
(C) treat things done by the transferring authority in relation to the plan as done by the other authority[26].

Where (aa) a child or young person who has been subject to a detention order[27] is released[28]; (bb) on the release date, a local authority in England becomes responsible for him or her[29]; and (cc) an EHC plan was maintained for him or her immediately before the start of the detention[30]; or kept for him or her[31] during the detention[32], the local authority must maintain the plan[33]; and review the plan as soon as reasonably practicable after the release date[34].

1 As to the meaning of 'local authority' see PARA 25 (definition applied by the Children and Families Act 2014 s 83(7)).
2 As to the meaning of 'EHC plan' see PARA 958.
3 As to the meaning of 'child' see PARA 7 note 6 (definition applied by the Children and Families Act 2014 s 83(7)).
4 As to the meaning of 'young person' see PARA 950 note 4.
5 Children and Families Act 2014 s 45(1)(a).
6 Children and Families Act 2014 s 45(1)(b).
7 As to the meaning of 'special educational provision' see PARA 943.
8 Children and Families Act 2014 s 45(2).
9 As to the time at which a person attains a particular age see PARA 7 note 6.
10 As to the meaning of 'educational' see PARA 950 note 11.
11 As to the meaning of 'training' see PARA 943 note 9.
12 Children and Families Act 2014 s 45(3).
13 Ie and appeal under the Children and Families Act 2014 s 51: see PARA 980.
14 Children and Families Act 2014 s 45(4)(a).
15 Children and Families Act 2014 s 45(4)(b).
16 As to regulations generally see the Children and Families Act 2014 s 135. As to regulations made under s 45(5) see the Special Educational Needs and Disability Regulations 2014, SI 2014/1530 (amended by SI 2014/2096; and SI 2015/359).
17 Children and Families Act 2014 s 45(5)(a).
18 Children and Families Act 2014 s 45(5)(b).
19 Children and Families Act 2014 s 45(5)(c).
20 'Academic year' means the period of 12 months ending on the prescribed date: Children and Families Act 2014 s 46(2). As to the meaning of 'month' see PARA 54 note 26. As to regulations made under s 46(2) see the Special Educational Needs and Disability Regulations 2014, SI 2014/1530 (amended by SI 2014/2096; and SI 2015/359).
21 Children and Families Act 2014 s 46(1).
22 As to regulations made under s 47(1), (2) see the Special Educational Needs and Disability Regulations 2014, SI 2014/1530 (amended by SI 2014/2096; and SI 2015/359).
23 Children and Families Act 2014 s 47(1). See note 22.
24 Children and Families Act 2014 s 47(2)(a). See note 22.
25 Children and Families Act 2014 s 47(2)(b). See note 22.
26 Children and Families Act 2014 s 47(2)(c). See note 22.
27 Ie within the meaning of the Education Act 1996 s 562(1A)(a): see PARA 46 note 8.
28 Children and Families Act 2014 s 48(1)(a).
29 Children and Families Act 2014 s 48(1)(b).
30 Children and Families Act 2014 s 48(1)(c)(i).
31 Ie under the Children and Families Act 2014 s 74: see PARA 974.

32 Children and Families Act 2014 s 48(1)(c)(ii).
33 Children and Families Act 2014 s 48(2)(a).
34 Children and Families Act 2014 s 48(2)(b). Section 48(2)(b) is subject to any contrary provision
    in regulations under s 44(7)(b) (see PARA 964 text to note 24): s 48(3).

966. Personal budgets and direct payments in regard to EHC plans. A local
authority[1] that maintains an EHC plan[2], or is securing the preparation of an
EHC plan, for a child[3] or young person[4] must prepare a personal budget[5] for
him or her if asked to do so by the child's parent[6] or the young person[7].

Regulations[8] may make provision about personal budgets, in particular:

(1)   about requests for personal budgets[9];
(2)   about the amount of a personal budget[10];
(3)   about the sources of the funds making up a personal budget[11];
(4)   for payments ('direct payments') representing all or part of a personal
        budget to be made to a child's parent or a young person, or a person of
        a prescribed description in prescribed circumstances, in order to secure
        provision to which the budget relates[12];
(5)   about the description of provision to which personal budgets and direct
        payments may (and may not) relate[13];
(6)   for a personal budget or direct payment to cover the agreed cost of the
        provision to which the budget or payment relates[14];
(7)   about when, how, to whom and on what conditions direct payments
        may (and may not) be made[15];
(8)   about when direct payments may be required to be repaid and the
        recovery of unpaid sums[16];
(9)   about conditions with which a person or body making direct payments
        must comply before, after or at the time of making a direct payment[17];
(10)   about arrangements for providing information, advice or support in
        connection with personal budgets and direct payments[18].

If the regulations include provision authorising direct payments, they must (a)
require the consent of a child's parent or a young person, or a person of a
prescribed description in prescribed circumstances, to be obtained before direct
payments are made[19]; (b) require the authority to stop making direct payments
where the required consent is withdrawn[20].

Special educational provision[21] acquired by means of a direct payment made
by a local authority is to be treated as having been secured by the authority in
pursuance of its duty under the Children and Families Act 2014[22], subject to any
prescribed conditions or exceptions[23].

If (i) an EHC plan is maintained for a child or young person[24]; and (ii) health
care provision[25] specified in the plan is acquired for him or her by means of a
payment made by a commissioning body[26], the health care provision is to be
treated as having been arranged by the commissioning body in pursuance of its
duty under the 2014 Act[27], subject to any prescribed conditions or exceptions[28].

1   As to the meaning of 'local authority' see PARA 25 (definition applied by the Children and
    Families Act 2014 s 83(7)).
2   As to the meaning of 'EHC plan' see PARA 958.
3   As to the meaning of 'child' see PARA 7 note 6 (definition applied by the Children and Families
    Act 2014 s 83(7)).
4   As to the meaning of 'young person' see PARA 950 note 4.
5   The authority prepares a 'personal budget' for the child or young person if it identifies an
    amount as available to secure particular provision that is specified, or proposed to be specified,
    in the EHC plan, with a view to the child's parent or the young person being involved in
    securing the provision: Children and Families Act 2014 s 49(2).

6   As to the meaning of 'parent' see PARA 7 note 6 (definition applied by the Children and Families Act 2014 s 83(7)).
7   Children and Families Act 2014 s 49(1).
8   As to regulations generally see the Children and Families Act 2014 s 135. As to regulations made under s 49(3), (4) see the Special Educational Needs (Personal Budgets) Regulations 2014, SI 2014/1652 (amended by SI 2014/2096). Note in particular the Special Educational Needs (Personal Budgets) Regulations 2014, SI 2014/1652, reg 4A (added by SI 2014/2096), which provides that a local authority is not required to prepare a personal budget in respect of specified special educational provision where the amount for the specified special educational provision is a notional amount of a larger sum, and the authority is unable to disaggregate the notional amount without causing an adverse impact on other services or where it would not be an efficient use of the authority's resources.
9   Children and Families Act 2014 s 49(3)(a). See note 8.
10 Children and Families Act 2014 s 49(3)(b). See note 8.
11 Children and Families Act 2014 s 49(3)(c). See note 8.
12 Children and Families Act 2014 s 49(3)(d). See note 8.
13 Children and Families Act 2014 s 49(3)(e). See note 8.
14 Children and Families Act 2014 s 49(3)(f). See note 8.
15 Children and Families Act 2014 s 49(3)(g). See note 8.
16 Children and Families Act 2014 s 49(3)(h). See note 8.
17 Children and Families Act 2014 s 49(3)(i). See note 8.
18 Children and Families Act 2014 s 49(3)(j). See note 8.
19 Children and Families Act 2014 s 49(4)(a). See note 8.
20 Children and Families Act 2014 s 49(4)(b). See note 8.
21 As to the meaning of 'special educational provision' see PARA 943.
22 Ie its duty under the Children and Families Act 2014 s 42(2): see PARA 962 note 7.
23 Children and Families Act 2014 s 49(5).
24 Children and Families Act 2014 s 49(6)(a).
25 As to the meaning of 'health care provision' see PARA 946 note 7.
26 Children and Families Act 2014 s 49(6)(b). The reference in the text is to a commissioning body under the National Health Service Act 2006 s 12A(1) (direct payments for health care): see HEALTH SERVICES. 'Commissioning body', in relation to any specified health care provision, means a body that is under a duty to arrange health care provision of that kind in respect of the child or young person: Children and Families Act 2014 s 49(8).
27 Ie its duty under the Children and Families Act 2014 s 42(3): see PARA 962 note 10.
28 Children and Families Act 2014 s 49(7).

(vi)   Special Educational Provision: Functions of Local Authorities, Governing Bodies, etc

967.   Special educational provision: functions of local authorities. A local authority[1] in England[2] may arrange for any special educational provision[3] that it has decided is necessary for a child[4] or young person[5] for whom it is responsible to be made otherwise than in a school[6] or post-16 institution[7] or a place at which relevant early years education is provided[8]. An authority may do so only if satisfied that it would be inappropriate for the provision to be made in a school or post-16 institution or at such a place[9]. Before doing so, the authority must consult the child's parent[10] or the young person[11].

Where a local authority in England makes arrangements for a child or young person for whom it maintains an EHC plan[12] to attend an institution outside England and Wales[13] which specialises in providing for children or young people with special educational needs[14], the arrangements may (in particular) include contributing to or paying (1) fees charged by the institution[15]; (2) the child's or young person's travelling expenses[16]; (3) expenses reasonably incurred in maintaining the child or young person while at the institution or travelling to or from it[17]; (4) expenses reasonably incurred by someone accompanying the child or young person while travelling to or from the institution or staying there[18].

Where (a) a local authority maintains an EHC plan for a child or young person[19]; (b) special educational provision in respect of the child or young person is made at a school, post-16 institution or place at which relevant early years education is provided[20]; and (c) that school, institution or place is named in the EHC plan[21], the local authority must pay any fees payable in respect of education[22] or training[23] provided for the child or young person at that school, institution or place in accordance with the EHC plan[24].

Where (i) a local authority is responsible for a child or young person for whom no EHC plan is maintained[25]; (ii) special educational provision in respect of the child or young person is made at a school, post-16 institution or place at which relevant early years education is provided[26]; and (iii) the local authority is satisfied that the interests of the child or young person require special educational provision to be made[27], and it is appropriate for education or training to be provided to the child or young person at the school, institution or place in question[28], the local authority must pay any fees payable in respect of the special educational provision made at the school, institution or place in question which is required to meet the special educational needs of the child or young person[29]. Where board and lodging are provided for the child or young person at the school, post-16 institution or place mentioned above[30], the authority must also pay any fees in respect of the board and lodging, if satisfied that special educational provision cannot be provided at the school, post-16 institution or place unless the board and lodging are also provided[31].

A local authority in England may supply goods and services[32] to (A) the governing body[33] of a maintained school[34] or maintained nursery school[35] in England[36]; (B) the proprietor[37] of an academy[38]; (C) the governing body of an institution within the further education[39] sector that the authority thinks is or is to be attended by a young person for whom the authority maintains an EHC plan, but only for a specified purpose[40]. A local authority in England may supply goods and services to any authority or other person[41], but only for a specified purpose[42].

Where a local authority in England maintains an EHC plan for a child or young person[43], a person authorised by the authority is entitled to have access at any reasonable time to the premises[44] of a school, post-16 institution or other institution at which education or training is provided in pursuance of the plan, for the purpose of monitoring the education or training[45].

1   As to the meaning of 'local authority' see PARA 25 (definition applied by the Children and Families Act 2014 s 83(7)).
2   As to the meaning of 'England' see PARA 7 note 3.
3   As to the meaning of 'special educational provision' see PARA 943.
4   As to the meaning of 'child' see PARA 7 note 6 (definition applied by the Children and Families Act 2014 s 83(7)).
5   As to the meaning of 'young person' see PARA 950 note 4.
6   As to the meaning of 'school' generally see PARA 91 (definition applied by the Children and Families Act 2014 s 83(7)).
7   As to the meaning of 'post-16 institution' see PARA 943 note 9.
8   Children and Families Act 2014 s 61(1). As to the meaning of 'relevant early years education' see PARA 943 note 17.
9   Children and Families Act 2014 s 61(2).
10   As to the meaning of 'parent' see PARA 7 note 6 (definition applied by the Children and Families Act 2014 s 83(7)).
11   Children and Families Act 2014 s 61(3).
12   As to the meaning of 'EHC plan' see PARA 958.
13   As to the meaning of 'Wales' see PARA 7 note 3.

14 Children and Families Act 2014 s 62(1). As to the meaning of 'special educational needs' see PARA 943. As to the equivalent provision to s 62 in relation to Wales see the Education Act 1996 s 320; and PARA 1018.

15 Children and Families Act 2014 s 62(2)(a).

16 Children and Families Act 2014 s 62(2)(b).

17 Children and Families Act 2014 s 62(2)(c).

18 Children and Families Act 2014 s 62(2)(d).

19 Children and Families Act 2014 s 63(1)(a).

20 Children and Families Act 2014 s 63(1)(b).

21 Children and Families Act 2014 s 63(1)(c).

22 As to references to 'education' see PARA 950 note 11.

23 As to the meaning of 'training' see PARA 943 note 9.

24 Children and Families Act 2014 s 63(2).

25 Children and Families Act 2014 s 63(3)(a).

26 Children and Families Act 2014 s 63(3)(b).

27 Children and Families Act 2014 s 63(3)(b)(i).

28 Children and Families Act 2014 s 63(3)(b)(ii).

29 Children and Families Act 2014 s 63(4).

30 Ie mentioned in the Children and Families Act 2014 s 63(2) or (4).

31 Children and Families Act 2014 s 63(5).

32 The goods and services may be supplied on the terms and conditions that the authority thinks fit, including terms as to payment: Children and Families Act 2014 s 64(3).

33 As to the governing bodies of maintained schools in England see PARA 150 et seq.

34 As to the meaning of 'maintained school' see PARA 943 note 8.

35 As to the meaning of 'maintained nursery school' see PARA 99 note 4 (definition applied by the Children and Families Act 2014 s 83(7)).

36 Children and Families Act 2014 s 64(1)(a).

37 As to the meaning of 'proprietor' see PARA 948 note 21.

38 Children and Families Act 2014 s 64(1)(b). As to the meaning of 'academy' see PARA 346 note 7 (definition applied by s 83(7)).

39 As to the meaning of 'further education' see PARA 23 (definition applied by s 83(7)).

40 See the Children and Families Act 2014 s 64(1), (2). The purpose is that of assisting the governing body or proprietor in the performance of (1) any duty imposed on the body under s 66(2) (duty to use best endeavours to secure special educational provision called for by special educational needs: see PARA 969) (s 64(2)(a)); (2) in the case of a governing body of a community or foundation special school, any duty imposed on the body (s 64(2)(b)). As to references to community or foundations schools see PARA 943 note 8.

41 Ie (other than a governing body or proprietor within the Children and Families Act 2014 s 64(1). As to the meaning of 'person' see PARA 7 note 6.

42 See the Children and Families Act 2014 s 64(4), (5). The purpose is that of assisting the authority or other person in making special educational provision for a child who is receiving relevant early years education, in a case where the authority has decided that the special educational provision is necessary for the child: s 64(5).

43 Children and Families Act 2014 s 65(1).

44 As to the meaning of 'premises' see PARA 62 note 19 (definition applied by the Children and Families Act 2014 s 83(7)).

45 Children and Families Act 2014 s 65(2). Section 65(2) does not apply to the premises of a mainstream post-16 institution in Wales: s 65(3). As to the meaning of 'mainstream post-16 institution' see PARA 943 note 9.

968. Special educational provision at city colleges and academies. Where a child[1] for whom an EHC plan[2] is maintained[3] attends (or proposes to attend) a school[4] which is a city technology college, a city college for the technology of the arts or an academy[5], and the EHC plan is maintained by a local authority[6] in England[7], the Secretary of State[8] may by regulations make provision for securing that arrangements are made[9] for making the special educational provision[10] and any non-educational provision specified in the plan[11]. The regulations may require or authorise a local authority to make payments to the school in respect of the child[12], or to provide any other assistance to the school in respect of the child[13].

Regulations have been made which provide that a local authority may pay to an approved city college[14] all or any part of the cost incurred in respect of securing that the special provision[15] for a relevant child is made[16], and may provide any other assistance to an approved city college for the purpose of securing that the special provision for a relevant child is made[17]. A local authority must keep under review the arrangements so made[18] and in doing so must consult the governing bodies of any city college both in the authority's area[19] and in any neighbouring local authority's area to which the authority makes any payment, supplies any goods and services, or provides any assistance[20].

1　As to the meaning of 'child' see PARA 7 note 6.
2　As to the meaning of 'EHC plan' see PARA 958.
3　Education Act 1996 s 483A(1), (2)(a) (s 483A added by the Learning and Skills Act 2000 s 133; and the Education Act 1996 s 483A(2)(a) amended by the Children and Families Act 2014 Sch 3 Sch 3 paras 1, 44(1), (2)). The statement of special educational needs referred to is one under the Education Act 1996 s 324 (see PARA 1002): see s 483A(2)(a) (as so added and amended).
4　As to the meaning of 'school' see PARA 91.
5　Education Act 1996 s 483A(1), (2)(b) (as added (see note 3); and amended by the Education Act 2002 s 65(3), Sch 7 Pt 2 para 6(1), (4)(a)). As to city technology colleges and city colleges for the technology of the arts see PARA 345. As to the meaning of 'academy' see PARA 346 note 7.
6　As to the meaning of 'local authority' see PARA 25.
7　Education Act 1996 s 483A(1), (3)(a) (s 483A as added (see note 3); s 483A(3)(a) substituted by the Education and Skills Act 2008 s 147(4), (5); and amended by the Children and Families Act 2014 Sch 3 paras 1, 44(1), (3); and by SI 2010/1158). As to the meaning of 'England' see PARA 7 note 3.
8　The legislation refers to 'the appropriate national authority', which means, in relation to a school in England, the Secretary of State: Education Act 1996 s 483A(6A) (s 483A as added (see note 3); s 483A(6A) added by the Education and Skills Act 2008 s 147(4), (7)). As to the Secretary of State see PARA 58.
9　Education Act 1996 s 483A(4) (as added (see note3); and amended by the Education and Skills Act 2008 s 147(4), (6)).
10　As to the meaning of 'special educational provision' see PARAS 943, 989.
11　See the Education Act 1996 s 483A(4)(a), (b) (as added (see note 3); and amended by the Children and Families Act 2014 Sch 3 paras 1, 44(1), (4)). As to the regulations made see the text and notes 14–20.
12　Education Act 1996 s 483A(5)(a) (s 483A as added (see note 3); s 483A(5), (6) amended by SI 2010/1158). No condition or requirement imposed by virtue of the Education Act 1996 s 482(4)(a) (repealed) is to prevent a local authority making payments or providing assistance by virtue of s 483A(5): s 483A(6) (as so added and amended).
13　Education Act 1996 s 483A(5)(b) (as added: see note 3).
14　For these purposes, 'city college' means an academy, a city technology college or a city college for the technology of the arts; and 'approved' means approved by the Secretary of State under the Education Act 1996 s 347(1) (approval of independent schools: see PARA 1045): Education (Special Educational Needs) (City Colleges) (England) Regulations 2002, SI 2002/2071, reg 1(2). A city college will also be regarded as approved if the Secretary of State has consented to the relevant child being educated there: reg 1(3). 'Relevant child' means a child for whom an EHC plan is maintained under the Children and Families Act 2014 s 37 (see PARA 958) and who attends or proposes to attend a city college: Education (Special Educational Needs) (City Colleges) (England) Regulations 2002, SI 2002/2071, reg 1(2) (definition amended by SI 2014/2103).
15　'Special provision' means the special educational provision specified in an EHC plan maintained under the Children and Families Act 2014 s 37(1) (see PARA 958): Education (Special Educational Needs) (City Colleges) (England) Regulations 2002, SI 2002/2071, reg 1(2) (definition substituted by SI 2014/2103).
16　Education (Special Educational Needs) (City Colleges) (England) Regulations 2002, SI 2002/2071, reg 2(1) (amended by SI 2014/2103). Nothing in the Education (Special Educational Needs) (City Colleges) (England) Regulations 2002, SI 2002/2071, affects the duty of a local authority under the Children and Families Act 2014 s 42 (see PARA 962) to secure the

special educational provision which is specified in an EHC plan: Education (Special Educational Needs) (City Colleges) (England) Regulations 2002, SI 2002/2071, reg 4 (substituted by SI 2014/2103).

17 Education (Special Educational Needs) (City Colleges) (England) Regulations 2002, SI 2002/2071, reg 2(2) (amended by SI 2014/2103).
18 Education (Special Educational Needs) (City Colleges) (England) Regulations 2002, SI 2002/2071, reg 3(1).
19 Education (Special Educational Needs) (City Colleges) (England) Regulations 2002, SI 2002/2071, reg 3(2)(a).
20 Education (Special Educational Needs) (City Colleges) (England) Regulations 2002, SI 2002/2071, reg 3(2)(b). This provision applies only to payments made, goods and services supplied, and assistance provided under the Education (Special Educational Needs) (City Colleges) (England) Regulations 2002, SI 2002/2071: see reg 3(2)(b).

969. Special educational provision: functions of governing bodies and others.
Duties are imposed[1] on the appropriate authorities[2] for the following schools and other institutions in England[3]: (1) mainstream schools[4]; (2) maintained nursery schools[5]; (3) 16 to 19 academies[6]; (4) alternative provision academies[7]; (5) institutions within the further education sector[8]; (6) pupil referral units[9]. If a registered pupil[10] or a student[11] at a school or other institution has special educational needs[12], the appropriate authority must, in exercising its functions[13] in relation to the school or other institution, use its best endeavours to secure that the special educational provision[14] called for by the pupil's or student's special educational needs is made[15].

Further duties are imposed[16] on the appropriate authorities[17] of the following schools in England: (a) mainstream schools[18]; (b) maintained nursery schools[19]. The appropriate authority must designate a member of staff at the school (to be known as the 'SEN co-ordinator') as having responsibility for co-ordinating the provision for pupils with special educational needs[20]. Regulations may (i) require appropriate authorities which are subject to the above duty[21] to ensure that SEN co-ordinators have prescribed qualifications or prescribed experience (or both)[22]; (ii) confer other functions relating to SEN co-ordinators on appropriate authorities which are subject to the duty[23].

If (A) special educational provision is made for a child or young person at a maintained school, a maintained nursery school, an academy school, an alternative provision academy or a pupil referral unit[24]; and (B) no EHC plan[25] is maintained for the child[26] or young person[27], the appropriate authority[28] for the school must inform the child's parent[29] or the young person that special educational provision is being made for the child or young person[30].

There is a duty[31] on the governing bodies of maintained schools and maintained nursery schools in England[32]; and the proprietors of academy schools[33], namely that a governing body or proprietor must prepare a report containing SEN information[34].

There is also a statutory right of access to information held by public authorities[35] and parents may request access to their children's personal data[36].

1 Ie by the Children and Families Act 2014 s 66.
2 The 'appropriate authority' for a school or other institution is:
    (1)   in the case of a maintained school, maintained nursery school or institution within the further education sector, the governing body (Children and Families Act 2014 s 66(3)(a));
    (2)   in the case of an academy, the proprietor (s 66(3)(a)(ii));
    (3)   in the case of a pupil referral unit, the management committee (s 66(3)(a)(iii)).
As to the meaning of 'school' generally see PARA 91 (definition applied by s 83(7)). As to the meaning of 'maintained school' see PARA 943 note 8. As to the meaning of 'maintained nursery school' see PARA 99 note 4 (definition applied by s 83(7)). As to the meaning of 'further

education' see PARA 23 (definition applied by s 83(7)). As to the governing bodies of maintained schools in England see PARA 150 et seq. As to the meaning of 'academy' see PARA 346 note 7 (definition applied by s 83(7)). As to the meaning of 'proprietor' see PARA 948 note 21. As to pupil referral units generally see PARA 427 et seq.

3   As to the meaning of 'England' see PARA 7 note 3.
4   Children and Families Act 2014 s 66(1)(a). As to the meaning of 'mainstream school' see PARA 943 note 8.
5   Children and Families Act 2014 s 66(1)(b).
6   Children and Families Act 2014 s 66(1)(c). As to the meaning of '16 to 19 academy' see PARA 346 note 13 (definition applied by s 83(7)).
7   Children and Families Act 2014 s 66(1)(d). As to the meaning of 'alternative provision academy' see PARA 346 note 14 (definition applied by s 83(7)).
8   Children and Families Act 2014 s 66(1)(e).
9   Children and Families Act 2014 s 66(1)(f).
10 As to the meaning of 'registered pupil' see PARA 437 (definition applied by the Children and Families Act 2014 s 83(7)).
11 As to the meaning of 'student' see PARA 67 note 8 (definition applied by the Children and Families Act 2014 s 83(7)).
12 As to the meaning of 'special educational needs' see PARA 943.
13 As to the meaning of 'function' see PARA 18 note 5 (definition applied by the Children and Families Act 2014 s 83(7)).
14 As to the meaning of 'special educational provision' see PARA 943.
15 Children and Families Act 2014 s 66(2).
16 Ie by the Children and Families Act 2014 s 67.
17 The 'appropriate authority' for a school is (1) in the case of a maintained school or maintained nursery school, the governing body (Children and Families Act 2014 s 67(4)(a)); (2) in the case of an academy, the proprietor (s 67(4)(b)).
18 Children and Families Act 2014 s 67(1)(a).
19 Children and Families Act 2014 s 67(1)(b).
20 Children and Families Act 2014 s 67(2).
21 Ie the duty imposed by the Children and Families Act 2014 s 67(2).
22 Children and Families Act 2014 s 67(3)(a). As to regulations under s 69(3) see the Special Educational Needs and Disability Regulations 2014, SI 2014/1530 (amended by SI 2014/2096; and SI 2015/359).
23 Children and Families Act 2014 s 67(3)(b). See note 22.
24 Children and Families Act 2014 s 68(1)(a).
25 As to the meaning of 'EHC plan' see PARA 958.
26 As to the meaning of 'child' see PARA 7 note 6 (definition applied by the Children and Families Act 2014 s 83(7)).
27 As to the meaning of 'young person' see PARA 950 note 4.
28 The 'appropriate authority' for a school is (1) in the case of a maintained school or maintained nursery school, the governing body (Children and Families Act 2014 s 68(3)(a)); (2) in the case of an academy school or an alternative provision academy, the proprietor (s 68(3)(b)); (3) in the case of a pupil referral unit, the management committee (s 68(3)(c)).
29 As to the meaning of 'parent' see PARA 7 note 6 (definition applied by the Children and Families Act 2014 s 83(7)).
30 Children and Families Act 2014 s 68(2).
    If a local authority or other person providing relevant early years education for a child makes special educational provision for him because it is considered that he has special educational needs, and no EHC plan is maintained for the child, and the child's parent has not previously been informed under these provisions of the special educational provision made for the child, the authority or other person concerned must inform the child's parent that special educational provision is being made for him because it is considered that he has special educational needs: School Standards and Framework Act 1998 s 123(3A), (3B) (s 123(3A), (3B) added by the Special Educational Needs and Disability Act 2001 s 7(2); School Standards and Framework Act 1998 s 123(3A) amended by the Children and Families Act 2014 Sch 3 paras 67, 69(1), (6); School Standards and Framework Act 1998 s 123(3B) amended by SI 2010/1158). As to the meaning of 'EHC plan' for these purposes see PARA 958 (definition applied by the School Standards and Framework Act 1998 s 142(8)). As to the duty to have regard to the code of practice see PARA 978. 'Relevant early years education' means, in relation to England, early years provision as defined by the Childcare Act 2006 s 20 (see CHILDREN AND YOUNG PERSONS vol 10 (2012) PARA 1079) which is provided under arrangements made by a local authority in England in pursuance of the duty imposed by s 7 of that Act (see CHILDREN AND YOUNG

PERSONS vol 10 (2012) PARA 1083) (whether or not the local authority provides the early years provision): School Standards and Framework Act 1998 s 123(4) (substituted by the Childcare Act 2006 s 103(1), Sch 2 para 34(b); and amended by SI 2010/1158); Children and Families Act 2014 s 83(2).

31 Ie imposed by the Children and Families Act 2014 s 69.

32 Children and Families Act 2014 s 69(1)(a).

33 Children and Families Act 2014 s 69(1)(b). As to the meaning of 'academy school' see PARA 346 note 12 (definition applied by s 83(7)).

34 Children and Families Act 2014 s 69(2). As to the provision and publication of special needs information see also s 76; and PARA 977.

'SEN information' in s 69 is:

(1) such information as may be prescribed about the implementation of the governing body's or proprietor's policy for pupils at the school with special educational needs (s 69(3)(a));

(2) information as to (a) the arrangements for the admission of disabled persons as pupils at the school (s 69(3)(b)(i)); (b) the steps taken to prevent disabled pupils from being treated less favourably than other pupils (s 69(3)(b)(ii)); (c) the facilities provided to assist access to the school by disabled pupils (s 69(3)(b)(iii)); (d) the plan prepared by the governing body or proprietor under the Equality Act 2010 Sch 10 para 3 (accessibility plan) (see DISCRIMINATION vol 33 (2013) PARA 171) (Children and Families Act 2014 s 69(3)(b)(iv)).

In s 69 'disabled person' means a person who is a disabled person for the purposes of the Equality Act 2010 (see DISCRIMINATION vol 33 (2013) PARA 50); 'disabled pupil' includes a disabled person who may be admitted to a school as a pupil: Children and Families Act 2014 s 69(4).

As to regulations under s 69(3)(a) see the Special Educational Needs and Disability Regulations 2014, SI 2014/1530 (amended by SI 2014/2096; and SI 2015/359).

35 Ie under the Freedom of Information Act 2000: see CONFIDENCE AND INFORMATION PRIVACY vol 19 (2011) PARAS 7, 52; CONSTITUTIONAL AND ADMINISTRATIVE LAW vol 20 (2014) PARA 425 et seq.

36 Ie under the Data Protection 1998: see CONFIDENCE AND INFORMATION PRIVACY vol 19 (2011) PARA 95 et seq. This is where the child cannot do so or gives permission. As to protection of biometric information of children in schools see PARA 69.

(vii) Detained Persons

970. Detained persons generally. Nothing in or made under Part 3 of the Children and Families Act 2014[1] applies to, or in relation to, a child[2] or young person[3] detained[4] in pursuance of (1) an order made by a court[5]; or (2) an order of recall made by the Secretary of State[6].

Regulations[7] may apply any provision of Part 3 of the 2014 Act, with or without modifications, to or in relation to a child or young person detained in pursuance of (a) an order made by a court[8]; or (b) an order of recall made by the Secretary of State[9].

1 Ie the Children and Families Act 2014 Pt 3 (ss 19–83).

2 As to the meaning of 'child' see PARA 7 note 6 (definition applied by the Children and Families Act 2014 s 83(7)).

3 As to the meaning of 'young person' see PARA 950 note 4.

4 For the purpose of the Children and Families Act 2014 Pt 3, 'detained person' means a child or young person who is (1) 18 or under; (2) subject to a detention order (within the meaning of the Education Act 1996 s 562(1A)(a): see PARA 46 note 8); and (3) detained in relevant youth accommodation, and in provisions applying on a person's release, includes a person who, immediately before release, was a detained person: Children and Families Act 2014 ss 70(5), 83(2). As to the meaning of 'relevant youth accommodation' see PARA 949 note 3. As to the time at which a person attains a particular age see PARA 7 note 6. As to the meaning of 'person' see PARA 7 note 6. As to the meaning of 'England' see PARA 7 note 3. Generally as to persons detained in youth accommodation see PARA 547 et seq.

5 Children and Families Act 2014 s 70(1)(a). Section 70(1) is subject to s 70 and also ss 71–75 (see PARA 971 et seq): see s 70(1).

Section 70(1) does not apply to:

(1) s 28 (see PARA 949) (s 70(2)(a));
(2) s 31 (see PARA 952) (s 70(2)(b));
(3) s 77 (see PARA 978) (s 70(2)(c));
(4) s 80 (see PARA 976) (s 70(2)(d));
(5) s 83 (s 70(2)(e));
(6) any amendment made by Pt 3 of a provision which applies to, or in relation to, a child or young person detained in pursuance of (a) an order made by a court (s 70(2)(f)(i)); or (b) an order of recall made by the Secretary of State (s 70(2)(f)(ii)).

6   Children and Families Act 2014 s 70(1)(b). As to the Secretary of State see PARA 58. See note 5.
7   As to regulations generally see the Children and Families Act 2014 s 135. At the date at which this volume states the law no regulations had been made under s 70. As to the Special Educational Needs and Disability (Detained Persons) Regulations 2015, SI 2015/62 see eg PARA 974 note 9. As to relevant guidance affected by these regulations see further PARA 978.
8   Children and Families Act 2014 s 70(3)(a). The Secretary of State must consult the Welsh Ministers before making regulations under s 70(3) which will apply any provision of Pt 3 to, or in relation to, a child or young person who is detained in Wales: s 70(4). As to the Welsh Ministers see PARA 59. As to the meaning of 'Wales' see PARA 7 note 3.
9   Children and Families Act 2014 s 70(3)(b). See note 8.

971.   Assessment of post-detention education, health and care needs of detained persons. In relation to a detained person[1] for whom (1) the home authority[2] is a local authority[3] in England[4]; and (2) no EHC plan[5] is being kept by a local authority[6], a request to the home authority to secure a detained person's EHC needs assessment[7] for the detained person may be made by the appropriate person[8] or the person in charge of the relevant youth accommodation[9] where the detained person is detained[10].

Where (a) such a request is made[11]; (b) the detained person has been brought to the home authority's attention by any person[12] as someone who has or may have special educational needs[13]; or (c) the detained person has otherwise come to the home authority's attention as someone who has or may have special educational needs[14], the home authority must determine whether it may be necessary for special educational provision[15] to be made for the detained person in accordance with an EHC plan[16] on release from detention[17]. In making such a determination[18], the home authority must consult the appropriate person[19]; and the person in charge of the relevant youth accommodation where the detained person is detained[20].

Where the home authority determines that it will not be necessary for special educational provision to be made for the detained person in accordance with an EHC plan on release from detention, it must notify the appropriate person and the person in charge of the relevant youth accommodation where the detained person is detained of the reasons for that determination[21]; and that accordingly it has decided not to secure a detained person's EHC needs assessment for the detained person[22].

Where the detained person has not been assessed[23] during the previous six months[24]; and the home authority determines that it may be necessary for special educational provision to be made for the detained person in accordance with an EHC plan on release from detention[25], the home authority must notify the appropriate person and the person in charge of the relevant youth accommodation where the detained person is detained (i) that it is considering securing a detained person's EHC needs assessment for the detained person[26]; and (ii) that the appropriate person and the person in charge of the relevant youth accommodation where the detained person is detained each have the right to express views to the authority (orally or in writing)[27]; and submit evidence to the authority[28].

The home authority must secure a detained person's EHC needs assessment if, after having regard to any views expressed and evidence submitted as above[29], the authority is of the opinion that the detained person has or may have special educational needs[30]; and it may be necessary for special educational provision to be made for the detained person in accordance with an EHC plan on release from detention[31].

After a detained person's EHC needs assessment has been carried out, the local authority must notify the appropriate person and the person in charge of the relevant youth accommodation where the detained person is detained of (A) the outcome of the assessment[32]; (B) whether it proposes to secure that an EHC plan is prepared for the detained person[33]; and (C) the reasons for that decision[34].

Regulations[35] may make provision about detained persons' EHC needs assessments, in particular:

(aa) about requests to secure a detained person's EHC needs assessment[36];

(bb) imposing time limits in relation to consultation when making a determination[37];

(cc) about giving notice[38];

(dd) about expressing views and submitting evidence[39];

(ee) about how detained persons' EHC needs assessments are to be conducted[40];

(ff) about advice to be obtained in connection with a detained person's EHC needs assessment[41];

(gg) about combining a detained person's EHC needs assessment with other assessments[42];

(hh) about the use for the purposes of a detained person's EHC needs assessment of information obtained as a result of other assessments[43];

(ii) about the use of information obtained as a result of a detained person's EHC needs assessment, including the use of that information for the purposes of other assessments[44];

(jj) about the provision of information, advice and support in connection with a detained person's EHC needs assessment[45].

1   As to the meaning of 'detained person' see PARA 970 note 4.

2   'The home authority' has the same meaning as in the Education Act 1996 Pt X Ch VA (ss 562A–562J) (see PARA 548 note 3), subject to regulations under the Children and Families Act 2014 s 71(7) (see below) (and regulations under the Education Act 1996 s 562J(4) (see PARA 548) made by the Secretary of State may also make provision in relation to the definition of 'the home authority' for the purposes of the Children and Families Act 2014 Pt 3 (ss 19–83)): ss 70(6)(b), 83(2). For the purposes of Pt 3, regulations may provide for the first paragraph of the definition of 'the home authority; in the Education Act 1996 s 562J(1) (the home authority of a looked after child) to apply with modifications in relation to such provisions of the Children and Families Act 2014 Pt 3 as may be specified in the regulations: s 70(7). At the date at which this volume states the law no such regulations had been made.

3   As to the meaning of 'local authority' see PARA 25 (definition applied by the Children and Families Act 2014 s 83(7)).

4   Children and Families Act 2014 s 71(1)(a). As to the meaning of 'England' see PARA 7 note 3.

5   As to the meaning of 'EHC plan' see PARA 958.

6   Children and Families Act 2014 s 71(1)(b).

7   As to the meaning of 'EHC needs assessment' see PARA 957 note 3.

8   Children and Families Act 2014 s 71(2)(a). For the purposes of Pt 3, 'appropriate person', in relation to a detained person, means (1) where the detained person is a child, the detained person's parent; or (2) where the detained person is a young person, the detained person: ss 70(5), 83(2). As to the meaning of 'child' see PARA 7 note 6 (definition applied by s 83(7)). As to the meaning of 'parent' see PARA 7 note 6 (definition applied by s 83(7)). As to the meaning of 'young person' see PARA 950 note 4.

9   As to the meaning of 'relevant youth accommodation' see PARA 949 note 3.
10 Children and Families Act 2014 s 71(2)(b).
11 Children and Families Act 2014 s 71(4)(a). The request referred to is under s 71(2).
12 As to the meaning of 'person' see PARA 7 note 6.
13 Children and Families Act 2014 s 71(4)(b). As to the meaning of 'special educational needs' see PARA 943.
14 Children and Families Act 2014 s 71(4)(c).
15 As to the meaning of 'special educational provision' see PARA 943.
16 As to the meaning of 'EHC plan' see PARA 958.
17 Children and Families Act 2014 s 71(3).
18 Ie under the Children and Families Act 2014 s 71(3).
19 Children and Families Act 2014 s 71(5)(a).
20 Children and Families Act 2014 s 71(5)(b).
21 Children and Families Act 2014 s 71(6)(a).
22 Children and Families Act 2014 s 71(6)(b).
23 Ie under the Children and Families Act 2014 s 71 or under s 36 (see PARA 957).
24 Children and Families Act 2014 s 71(7)(a). As to the meaning of 'month' see PARA 54 note 26.
25 Children and Families Act 2014 s 71(7)(b).
26 Children and Families Act 2014 s 71(8)(a).
27 Children and Families Act 2014 s 71(8)(b)(i). As to the meaning of 'writing' see PARA 76 note 8.
28 Children and Families Act 2014 s 71(8)(b)(ii).
29 Ie under the Children and Families Act 2014 s 71(8).
30 Children and Families Act 2014 s 71(9)(a).
31 Children and Families Act 2014 s 71(9)(b).
32 Children and Families Act 2014 s 71(10)(a).
33 Children and Families Act 2014 s 71(10)(b).
34 Children and Families Act 2014 s 71(10)(c).
35 As to regulations generally see the Children and Families Act 2014 s 135. As to regulations made under the Children and Families Act 2014 s 71(11) see the Special Educational Needs and Disability (Detained Persons) Regulations 2015, SI 2015/62. As to relevant guidance affected by these regulations see further PARA 978.
36 Children and Families Act 2014 s 71(11)(a). The request referred to is a request under s 71(2). See note 35.
37 Children and Families Act 2014 s 71(11)(b). The consultation referred to is under s 71(5). See note 35.
38 Children and Families Act 2014 s 71(11)(c). See note 35.
39 Children and Families Act 2014 s 71(11)(d). The expression of views and submission of evidence referred to is under s 71(8). See note 35.
40 Children and Families Act 2014 s 71(11)(e). See note 35.
41 Children and Families Act 2014 s 71(11)(f). See note 35.
42 Children and Families Act 2014 s 71(11)(g). See note 35.
43 Children and Families Act 2014 s 71(11)(h). See note 35.
44 Children and Families Act 2014 s 71(11)(i). See note 35.
45 Children and Families Act 2014 s 71(11)(j). See note 35.

972.   Securing EHC plans for certain detained persons.   Where, in the light of a detained person's[1] EHC needs assessment[2] it is necessary for special education provision[3] to be made for the detained person in accordance with an EHC plan[4] on release from detention, the home authority[5] must secure that an EHC plan is prepared for him or her[6].

Certain provisions apply in relation to an EHC plan secured as above[7]. Certain other provisions apply where a home authority is securing the preparation of an EHC plan under these provsions[8].

1   As to the meaning of 'detained person' see PARA 970 note 4.
2   As to the meaning of 'EHC needs assessment' see PARA 957 note 3.
3   As to the meaning of 'special educational provision' see PARA 943.
4   As to the meaning of 'EHC plan' see PARA 958.
5   As to the meaning of 'home authority' see PARA 971 note 2.
6   Children and Families Act 2014 s 72(1).
7   See the Children and Families Act 2014 s 72(2).

The provisions of s 37(2)–(5) (see PARA 958) and ss 38–40 (see PARAS 959, 960) apply in relation to an EHC plan secured under s 72(1) as they apply to an EHC plan secured under s 37(1) (see PARA 958), with the following modifications:

   (1)   references to 'the child or young person' are to be read as references to the detained person (s 72(2)(a));

   (2)   references to the local authority are to be read as references to the home authority (s 72(2)(b)); and

   (3)   references to the child's parent or the young person are to be read as references to the appropriate person (s 72(2)(c)).

As to the meaning of 'appropriate person' see PARA 971 note 8.

8   See the Children and Families Act 2014 s 72(3).

The provisions of s 33(2)–(7) (see PARA 958) apply where a home authority is securing the preparation of an EHC plan s 72 as they apply where a local authority is securing a plan under s 37, with the following modifications:

   (1)   references to 'the child or young person' are to be read as references to the detained person (s 72(3)(a));

   (2)   references to the local authority are to be read as references to the home authority (s 72(3)(b));

   (3)   references to the child's parent or the young person are to be read as references to the appropriate person (s 72(3)(c)); and

   (4)   the reference in s 33(2) to s 39(5) and s 40(2) is to be read as a reference to those provisions as applied by s 72(2) (see note 7) (s 72(3)(d)).

973. EHC plans for certain detained persons: appeals and mediation. An appropriate person[1] in relation to a detained person[2] may appeal to the First-tier Tribunal[3] against the matters set out below[4]. The matters are:

   (1)   a decision of the home authority[5] not to secure a detained person's EHC needs assessment[6] for the detained person[7];

   (2)   a decision of the home authority, following a detained person's EHC needs assessment, that it is not necessary for special educational provision[8] to be made for the detained person in accordance with an EHC plan[9] on release from detention[10];

   (3)   where an EHC plan is secured for the detained person (a) the school[11] or other institution named in the plan, or the type of school or other institution named in the plan[12]; (b) if no school or other institution is named in the plan, that fact[13].

Regulations[14] may make provision about appeals to the First-tier Tribunal in respect of detained persons' EHC needs assessments and EHC plans[15], in particular about:

   (i)   making and determining appeals[16];

   (ii)   the powers of the First-tier Tribunal on determining an appeal[17];

   (iii)   unopposed appeals[18].

A person[19] commits an offence if without reasonable excuse that person fails to comply with any requirement (A) in respect of the discovery or inspection of documents[20]; or (B) to attend to give evidence and produce documents[21], where that requirement is imposed by Tribunal Procedure Rules in relation to an appeal under this provision[22]. A person guilty of such an offence[23] is liable on summary conviction to a fine[24].

Certain other provisions about mediation apply with modifications where an appropriate person intends to appeal to the First-tier Tribunal under these provisions[25].

1   As to the meaning of 'appropriate person' see PARA 971 note 8.

2   As to the meaning of 'detained person' see PARA 970 note 4.

3   As to the First-Tier Tribunal see COURTS AND TRIBUNALS vol 24 (2010) PARA 876 et seq. See also PARA 979.

4   See the Children and Families Act 2014 s 73(1). This is subject to s 55 (see PARA 982), as applied by s 73.

5   As to the meaning of 'home authority' see PARA 971 note 2.

6   As to the meaning of 'EHC needs assessment' see PARA 957 note 3.

7   Children and Families Act 2014 s 73(2)(a).

8   As to the meaning of 'special educational provision' see PARA 943.

9   As to the meaning of 'EHC plan' see PARA 958.

10 Children and Families Act 2014 s 73(2)(b).

11 As to the meaning of 'school' generally see PARA 91 (definition applied by the Children and Families Act 2014 s 83(7)).

12 Children and Families Act 2014 s 73(2)(c)(i). The appropriate person may appeal to the First-tier Tribunal under s 73(2)(c) only when an EHC plan is first finalised for the detained person in accordance with s 72 (see PARA 972): s 73(3).

13 Children and Families Act 2014 s 73(2)(c)(ii). See note 12.

14 As to regulations generally see the Children and Families Act 2014 s 135. As to regulations made under the Children and Families Act 2014 s 73(4) see the Special Educational Needs and Disability (Detained Persons) Regulations 2015, SI 2015/62. As to relevant guidance affected by these regulations see further PARA 978.

15 Ie secured under the Children and Families Act 2014 s 72: see PARA 972.

16 Children and Families Act 2014 s 73(4)(a). As to appeals generally see PARA 980.

17 Children and Families Act 2014 s 73(4)(b).

18 Children and Families Act 2014 s 73(4)(c).

19 As to the meaning of 'person' see PARA 7 note 6.

20 Children and Families Act 2014 s 73(5)(a).

21 Children and Families Act 2014 s 73(5)(b).

22 Children and Families Act 2014 s 73(5). The reference in the text is to s 73.

23 Ie an offence under the Children and Families Act 2014 s 73(5).

24 See the Children and Families Act 2014 s 73(6). The fine is a fine not exceeding level 3 on the standard scale: s 73(6). As to the standard scale see SENTENCING AND DISPOSITION OF OFFENDERS vol 92 (2010) PARA 142.

25 See the Children and Families Act 2014 s 73(7), (8), (9) below.

The provisions of s 55(2)–(5) (see PARA 982) apply where an appropriate person intends to appeal to the First-tier Tribunal under s 73 as they apply where a child's parent or young person intends to appeal under s 51 (see PARA 980), with the following modifications:

(1)   references to the child's parent or young person are to be read as references to the appropriate person (s 73(7)(a)); and

(2)   references to mediation under s 53 or s 54 are to be read as references to mediation with the home authority (s 73(7)(b)).

Where, by virtue of s 73(7) (see above), the appropriate person has informed the mediation adviser that he or she wishes to pursue mediation with the home authority:

(a)   the adviser must notify the authority (s 73(8)(a)); and

(b)   the authority must (i) arrange for mediation between it and the appropriate person (s 73(8)(b)(i)); (ii) ensure that the mediation is conducted by an independent person (s 73(8)(b)(ii)); and (iii) participate in the mediation (s 73(8)(b)(iii)).

For this purpose a person is not independent if he or she is employed by a local authority in England (s 73(8)).

Regulations under s 56 (see PARA 982) may make provision for the purposes of s 73(7), (8) (see above), and accordingly s 56 has effect for those purposes with the following modifications:

(A) the references in s 56(1) to commissioning bodies are to be ignored (s 73(9)(a));

(B) the reference in s 56(1)(e) to a child's parent is to be read as a reference to the parent of a detained person who is a child (s 73(9)(b));

(C) the reference in s 56(1)(f) to the child's parent or young person is to be read as a reference to the appropriate person (s 73(9)(c));

(D) in s 56(3), the provisions of s 56(3)(b) and (c) are to be ignored (s 73(9)(d));

(E) s 56(4) is to be ignored (s 73(9)(e)).

974. Duty to keep EHC plans for detained persons. In relation to a detained person[1] (1) for whom a local authority[2] in England[3] was maintaining an EHC plan[4] immediately before the beginning of his or her detention[5]; or (2) for whom the home authority[6] has secured the preparation of an EHC plan[7], the home authority must keep the EHC plan while the person is detained in relevant youth accommodation[8].

Regulations[9] may make provision about the keeping of EHC plans[10], and the disclosure of such plans[11].

The home authority must arrange appropriate special educational provision[12] for the detained person while he or she is detained in relevant youth accommodation[13].

If the EHC plan specifies health care provision[14], the detained person's health services commissioner[15] must arrange appropriate health care provision[16] for the detained person while he or she is detained in relevant youth accommodation[17].

1   As to the meaning of 'detained person' see PARA 970 note 4.
2   As to the meaning of 'local authority' see PARA 25 (definition applied by the Children and Families Act 2014 s 83(7)).
3   As to the meaning of 'England' see PARA 7 note 3.
4   As to the meaning of 'EHC plan' see PARA 958.
5   Children and Families Act 2014 s 74(1)(a). 'Beginning of the detention' has the same meaning as in the Education Act 1996 Pt X Ch VA (ss 562A–562J) (persons detained in youth accommodation) (see PARA 548 note 3): Children and Families Act 2014 ss 70(6)(a), 83(2).
6   As to the meaning of 'home authority' see PARA 971 note 2.
7   Children and Families Act 2014 s 74(1)(a). Such securing of the plan is under s 72: see PARA 972.
8   Children and Families Act 2014 s 74(2). As to the meaning of 'relevant youth accommodation' see PARA 949 note 3.
9   As to regulations generally see the Children and Families Act 2014 s 135. As to regulations made under s 74(3) see the Special Educational Needs and Disability (Detained Persons) Regulations 2015, SI 2015/62. As to relevant guidance affected by these regulations see further PARA 978.
10 Ie under the Children and Families Act 2014 s 74(2).
11 Children and Families Act 2014 s 74(3).
12 For the purposes of the Children and Families Act 2014 s 74(4), 'appropriate special educational provision' is:
    (1)   the special educational provision specified in the EHC plan (s 74(6)(a)); or
    (2)   if it appears to the home authority that it is not practicable for that special educational provision to be provided, educational provision corresponding as closely as possible to that special educational provision (s 74(6)(b)); or
    (3)   if it appears to the home authority that the special educational provision specified in the plan is no longer appropriate for the person, such special educational provision as reasonably appears to the home authority to be appropriate (s 76(6)(c)).
    As to the meaning of 'special educational provision' see PARA 943.
13 Children and Families Act 2014 s 74(4).
14 As to the meaning of 'health care provision' see PARA 946 note 7.
15 In the Children and Families Act 2014 s 74, 'detained person's health services commissioner', in relation to a detained person, means the body that is under a duty under the National Health Service Act 2006 (see HEALTH SERVICES) to arrange for the provision of services or facilities in respect of the detained person during his or her detention: Children and Families Act 2014 s 74(8).
16 For the purposes of the Children and Families Act 2014 s 74(5), 'appropriate health care provision' is:
    (1)   the health care provision specified in the EHC plan (s 74(7)(a)); or
    (2)   if it appears to the detained person's health services commissioner that it is not practicable for that health care provision to be provided, health care provision corresponding as closely as possible to that health care provision (s 74(7)(b)); or
    (3)   if it appears to the detained person's health services commissioner that the health care provision specified in the plan is no longer appropriate for the person, such health care provision as reasonably appears to the detained person's health services commissioner to be appropriate (s 74(7)(c)).
17 Children and Families Act 2014 s 74(5).

975. Supply of goods and services: detained persons. A local authority[1] in England[2] may supply goods and services to any authority or other person[3] making special educational provision[4] for a detained person[5], but only for a certain purpose[6]. The purpose is that of assisting the local authority in the performance of a duty in regard to keeping EHC plans[7].

The goods and services may be supplied on the terms and conditions that the authority thinks fit, including terms as to payment[8].

1 As to the meaning of 'local authority' see PARA 25 (definition applied by the Children and Families Act 2014 s 83(7)).
2 As to the meaning of 'England' see PARA 7 note 3.
3 As to the meaning of 'person' see PARA 7 note 6.
4 As to the meaning of 'special educational provision' see PARA 943.
5 As to the meaning of 'detained person' see PARA 970 note 4.
6 Children and Families Act 2014 s 75(1). That purpose is set out in s 75(2).
7 Children and Families Act 2014 s 75(2). The reference in the text is to a duty under s 74: see PARA 974.
8 Children and Families Act 2014 s 75(3).

(viii) Parents and Young People Lacking Capacity

976. Parents and young people lacking capacity. Regulations[1] may apply any statutory provision[2] with modifications, for the purpose of giving effect to Part 3 of the Children and Families Act 2014[3] in a case where the parent[4] of a child[5], or a young person[6], lacks capacity[7] at the relevant time[8].

Such regulations[9] may in particular include provision for:

(1) references to a child's parent to be read as references to, or as including references to, a representative[10] of the parent[11];

(2) references to a young person to be read as references to, or as including references to, a representative of the young person, the young person's parent, or a representative of the young person's parent[12];

(3) modifications to have effect in spite of a provision of the Mental Capacity Act 2005[13].

1 As to regulations generally see the Children and Families Act 2014 s 135. As to regulations made under s 80(1) see the Special Educational Needs and Disability Regulations 2014, SI 2014/1530 (amended by SI 2014/2096; and SI 2015/359); and the Special Educational Needs and Disability (Detained Persons) Regulations 2015, SI 2015/62.
2 'Statutory provision' means a provision made by or under the Children and Families Act 2014 or any other Act, whenever passed or made: s 80(2).
3 Ie the Children and Families Act 2014 Pt 3 (ss 19–83).
4 As to the meaning of 'parent' see PARA 7 note 6 (definition applied by the Children and Families Act 2014 s 83(7)).
5 As to the meaning of 'child' see PARA 7 note 6 (definition applied by the Children and Families Act 2014 s 83(7)).
6 As to the meaning of 'young person' see PARA 950 note 4.
7 The reference in the Children and Families Act 2014 s 80(1) to lacking capacity is to lacking capacity within the meaning of the Mental Capacity Act 2005 (see MENTAL HEALTH AND CAPACITY vol 75 (2013) PARA 601): Children and Families Act 2014 s 80(5). As to mental capacity see also Special Educational Needs and Disability Code of Practice: 0 to 25 years (Statutory guidance for organisations which work with and support children and young people who have special educational needs or disabilities) (January 2015) Annex 1. As to such guidance generally see PARA 978.
8 Children and Families Act 2014 s 80(1). 'The relevant time' means the time at which, under the statutory provision in question, something is required or permitted to be done by or in relation to the parent or young person: s 80(4).
9 Ie regulations under the Children and Families Act 2014 s 80(1).
10 'Representative', in relation to a parent or young person, means:
   (1) a deputy appointed by the Court of Protection under of the Mental Capacity Act 2005

s 16(2)(b) (see MENTAL HEALTH AND CAPACITY vol 75 (2013) PARA 724) to make decisions on the parent's or young person's behalf in relation to matters within the Children and Families Act 2014 Pt 3 (s 80(6)(a));

(2)   the donee of a lasting power of attorney (within the meaning of the Mental Capacity Act 2005 s 9: see AGENCY vol 1 (2008) PARA 217 et seq) appointed by the parent or young person to make decisions on his or her behalf in relation to matters within the Children and Families Act 2014 Pt 3 (s 80(6)(b));

(3)   an attorney in whom an enduring power of attorney (within the meaning of the Mental Capacity Act 2005 Sch 4: see AGENCY vol 1 (2008) PARA 217 et seq) created by the parent or young person is vested, where the power of attorney is registered in accordance with Sch 4 paras 4, 13 or an application for registration of the power of attorney has been made (Children and Families Act 2014 s 80(6)(c)).

11   Children and Families Act 2014 s 80(2)(a).

12   Children and Families Act 2014 s 80(2)(b).

13   Children and Families Act 2014 s 80(2)(c). The reference is specifically to the Mental Capacity Act 2005 s 27(1)(g) (Act does not permit decisions on discharging parental responsibilities in matters not relating to a child's property to be made on a person's behalf): see MENTAL HEALTH AND CAPACITY vol 75 (2013) PARA 627.

(ix) Provision and Publication of Special Needs Information

977. Provision and publication of special needs information. The Secretary of State[1] must exercise certain powers[2] with a view to securing, in particular, the provision of special needs information[3] which the Secretary of State thinks would be likely to assist the Secretary of State or others in improving the well-being[4] of (1) children in England with special educational needs[5]; and (2) young people aged under 19[6] in England with special educational needs[7].

In each calendar year, the Secretary of State must publish, or arrange to be published, special needs information which has been obtained under the Education Act 1996, where the Secretary of State thinks the publication of the information would be likely to assist the Secretary of State or others in improving the well-being of (a) children in England with special educational needs[8]; and (b) young people aged under 19 in England with special educational needs[9]. Information so published[10] must be published in the form and manner that the Secretary of State thinks fit, except that the names of the children and young people to whom the information relates must not be included[11]. The Secretary of State may make a charge, or arrange for a charge to be made, for documents supplied by virtue of these provisions[12].

1   As to the Secretary of State see PARA 58.

2   Ie the powers listed in the Children and Families Act 2014 s 76(2) (see below). The powers are those of the Secretary of State under the following provisions of the Education Act 1996 (so far as relating to England):

(1)   s 29 (information from local authorities for purposes of Secretary of State's functions: see PARA 48) (Children and Families Act 2014 s 76(2)(a));

(2)   s 408 (information in relation to maintained schools: see PARA 940) (Children and Families Act 2014 s 76(2)(b));

(3)   s 537 (information about schools: see PARA 67) (Children and Families Act 2014 s 76(2)(c));

(4)   s 537A (information about individual pupils: see PARA 68) (Children and Families Act 2014 s 76(2)(d));

(5)   s 537B (information about children receiving funded education outside school: see PARA 70) (Children and Families Act 2014 s 76(2)(e));

(6)   s 538 (information from governing bodies for purposes of Secretary of State's education functions: see PARAS 190, 220) (Children and Families Act 2014 s 76(2)(f)).

3   'Special needs information' means (1) information about children, and young people, in England with special educational needs (Children and Families Act 2014 s 76(7)(a)); and (2) information about special educational provision made for those children and young people (s 76(7)(b)). As to the meaning of 'child' see PARA 7 note 6 (definition applied by s 83(7)). As to the meaning of

'young person' see PARA 950 note 4. As to the meaning of 'England' see PARA 7 note 3. As to the meanings of 'special educational needs' and 'special educational provision' see PARA 943.

4　References in the Children and Families Act 2014 s 76 to the well-being of children and young people with special educational needs are to their well-being so far as relating to:

(1)　physical and mental health and emotional well-being (s 76(8)(a));
(2)　protection from abuse and neglect (s 76(8)(b));
(3)　control by them over their day-to-day lives (s 76(8)(c));
(4)　participation in education, training or recreation (s 76(8)(d));
(5)　social and economic well-being (s 76(8)(e));
(6)　domestic, family and personal relationships (s 76(8)(f));
(7)　the contribution made by them to society (s 76(8)(g)).

5　Children and Families Act 2014 s 76(1)(a).
6　As to the time at which a person attains a particular age see PARA 7 note 6. In regard to the access of young persons aged 19 to 25 with special educational needs to such information see Special Educational Needs and Disability Code of Practice: 0 to 25 years (Statutory guidance for organisations which work with and support children and young people who have special educational needs or disabilities) (January 2015) para 8.50 which states that local authorities must set out in their local offer the support and provision that 19-to 25-year-olds with special educational needs can access regardless of whether they have an EHC plan; and further education colleges must continue to use their best endeavours to secure the special educational provision needed by all young people aged 19 to 25 with special educational needs. As to such guidance generally see PARA 978.
7　Children and Families Act 2014 s 76(1)(b). See note 6. As to duties of governing bodies and others in regard to special educational provision see also PARA 969. There is also a statutory right of access to information held by public authorities and parents may request access to their children's personal data: see PARA 969 note 36.
8　Children and Families Act 2014 s 76(3)(a).
9　Children and Families Act 2014 s 76(3)(b).
10　Ie published under the Children and Families Act 2014 s 76(3).
11　Children and Families Act 2014 s 76(4).
12　Children and Families Act 2014 s 76(5). A charge under s 76(5) must not exceed the cost of supply: s 76(6).

(x)　Code of Practice

978.　Code of practice. The Secretary of State[1] must issue a code of practice giving guidance[2] about the exercise of their functions[3] under Part 3 of the Children and Families Act 2014[4] to:

(1)　local authorities in England[5];
(2)　the governing bodies of schools[6];
(3)　the governing bodies of institutions within the further education[7] sector[8];
(4)　the proprietors[9] of academies[10];
(5)　the management committees of pupil referral units[11];
(6)　the proprietors of certain institutions approved by the Secretary of State[12];
(7)　providers of relevant early years education[13];
(8)　youth offending teams[14];
(9)　persons in charge of relevant youth accommodation[15];
(10)　the National Health Service Commissioning Board[16];
(11)　clinical commissioning groups[17];
(12)　NHS trusts[18];
(13)　NHS foundation trusts[19];
(14)　local health boards[20].

The Secretary of State may revise the code from time to time[21], and must publish the current version of the code[22].

Where the Secretary of State proposes to issue or revise a code of practice[23], he must prepare a draft of the code (or revised code)[24]. The Secretary of State must consult such persons[25] as he thinks fit about the draft and must consider any representations made by them[26]. If the Secretary of State decides to proceed with the draft (in its original form or with modifications), the Secretary of State must lay a copy of the draft before each House of Parliament[27]. The Secretary of State may not take any further steps: (a) in relation to a proposed code, unless the draft is approved by a resolution of each House[28]; or (b) in relation to a proposed revised code, if within the 40-day period[29] either House resolves not to approve the draft[30]. However, this does not prevent a new draft of a proposed code (or proposed revised code) from being laid before Parliament[31]. If, in the case of a proposed code, both Houses resolve to approve[32] the draft[33] or, in the case of a proposed revised code, neither House resolves not to approve[34] the draft[35], the Secretary of State must issue the code or revised code in the form of the draft, and it comes into force on such date as the Secretary of State may by order appoint[36].

The persons listed above[37] must have regard to the code in exercising their functions under Part 3 of the 2014 Act[38], as must those who exercise related functions[39]. The First-tier Tribunal[40] must have regard to any provision of the code that appears to it to be relevant to a question arising on an appeal under Part 3[41].

1   As to the Secretary of State see PARA 58.
2   As to the publication of guidance see the Education Act 1996 s 571; and PARA 60 note 24.
3   As to the meaning of 'function' see PARA 18 note 5 (definition applied by the Children and Families Act 2014 s 83(7)).
4   Ie the Children and Families Act 2014 Pt 3 (ss 19–83).
5   Children and Families Act 2014 s 77(1)(a). As to the meaning of 'local authority' for these purposes see PARA 25 (definition applied by s 83(7)). As to the meaning of 'England' see PARA 7 note 3.
6   Children and Families Act 2014 s 77(1)(b). As to the governing bodies of maintained schools in England see PARA 150 et seq. As to the meaning of 'school' generally see PARA 91 (definition applied by s 83(7)).
7   As to the meaning of 'further education' see PARA 23 (definition applied by the Children and Families Act 2014 s 83(7)).
8   Children and Families Act 2014 s 77(1)(c).
9   As to the meaning of 'proprietor' see PARA 948 note 21.
10 Children and Families Act 2014 s 77(1)(d). As to the meaning of 'academy' see PARA 346 note 7 (definition applied by s 83(7)).
11 Children and Families Act 2014 s 77(1)(e). As to pupil referral units generally see PARA 427 et seq.
12 Children and Families Act 2014 s 77(1)(f). The reference in the text is to institutions approved by the Secretary of State under s 41 (independent special schools and special post-16 institutions: approval: see PARA 961).
13 Children and Families Act 2014 s 77(1)(g). As to the meaning of 'relevant early years education' see PARA 943 note 17.
14 Children and Families Act 2014 s 77(1)(h).
15 Children and Families Act 2014 s 77(1)(i).
16 Children and Families Act 2014 s 77(1)(j). As to the National Health Service Commissioning Board, clinical commissioning groups, NHS trusts, NHS foundation trusts and local health boards see HEALTH SERVICES.
17 Children and Families Act 2014 s 77(1)(k). See note 15.
18 Children and Families Act 2014 s 77(1)(l). See note 15.
19 Children and Families Act 2014 s 77(1)(m). See note 15.
20 Children and Families Act 2014 s 77(1)(n). See note 15.
21 Children and Families Act 2014 s 77(2).
22 Children and Families Act 2014 s 77(3).
23 Ie under the Children and Families Act 2014: see PARA 978.

24 Children and Families Act 2014 s 78(1).
25 As to the meaning of 'person' see PARA 7 note 6.
26 Children and Families Act 2014 s 78(2).
27 Children and Families Act 2014 s 78(3).
28 Children and Families Act 2014 s 78(4)(a).
29 In the Children and Families Act 2014 s 78 '40-day period', in relation to the draft of a proposed revised code, means (1) if the draft is laid before one House on a later day than the day on which it is laid before the other, the period of 40 days beginning with the later of the two days (s 78(8)(a)); and (2) in any other case, the period of 40 days beginning with the day on which the draft is laid before each House (s 78(8)(b)). For the purposes of s 78(8), no account is to be taken of any period during which Parliament is dissolved or prorogued or during which both Houses are adjourned for more than four days: s 78(9).
30 Children and Families Act 2014 s 78(4)(b).
31 Children and Families Act 2014 s 78(7).
32 Ie as mentioned in the Children and Families Act 2014 s 78(4)(a): see head (a) in the text.
33 Children and Families Act 2014 s 78(5)(a).
34 Ie as mentioned in the Children and Families Act 2014 s 78(4)(b): see head (b) in the text.
35 Children and Families Act 2014 s 78(5)(b).
36 Children and Families Act 2014 s 78(6). As to orders made under s 78(6) see the Special Educational Needs (Code of Practice) (Appointed Day) Order 2014, SI 2014/2254; and the Special Educational Needs (Code of Practice) (Appointed Day) Order 2015, SI 2015/893. The second order appoints 1 April 2015 as the day on which the revised 'Special Educational Needs and Disability Code of Practice: 0 to 25 years' (the Code) comes into force. The Code revises and replaces the 'Special Educational Needs and Disability Code of Practice: 0 to 25 years' which came into force on 1 September 2014 (see first order noted above) to reflect the changes made by the Special Educational Needs and Disability (Detained Persons) (England) Regulations 2015, SI 2015/62. To reflect these changes the Code provides guidance on: (1) the procedure for assessing a detained person's education, health and care needs, including the role of local authorities, the person in charge of the relevant youth accommodation, youth offending teams and other bodies; (2) the procedure for developing an education, health and care plan for a detained person; (3) the time-scales within which decisions need to be made; (4) the information and advice to be available to the detained person and, where the detained person is a child, the child's parents; (5) the mediation and appeals procedures available to a detained person, or where the detained person is a child, the child's parents, who disagrees with certain types of decision. As to the publication of guidance see the Education Act 1996 s 571; and PARA 60 note 24.
37 Ie in the Children and Families Act 2014 s 77(1).
38 Children and Families Act 2014 s 77(4).
   The School Standards and Framework Act 1998 also provides that any local authority or other person providing relevant early years education, and any person employed by such an authority or other person or otherwise engaged to provide his services in the provision of such education, is under a duty to have regard to the provisions of the code of practice issued under the Children and Families Act 2014 s 77 (see the School Standards and Framework Act 1998 s 123(1) (amended by the Childcare Act 2006 s 103(1), Sch 2 para 34(a); the Children and Families Act 2014 Sch 3 paras 67, 69(1), (2); and SI 2010/1158)), although the School Standards and Framework Act 1998 s 123(1) does not apply in so far as the person in question is already under a duty to have regard to the provisions of that code of practice (see s 123(1A) (added by the Children and Families Act 2014 Sch 3 paras 67, 69(1), (3))). As to the meaning of 'local authority' for these purposes see PARA 25 (definition applied by the School Standards and Framework Act 1998 s 142(8)). As to the meaning of 'employed' see PARA 298 note 4. In England, 'relevant early years education' means early years provision as defined by the Childcare Act 2006 s 20 (see CHILDREN AND YOUNG PERSONS vol 10 (2012) PARA 1079) which is provided under arrangements made by a local authority in England in pursuance of the duty imposed by s 7 of that Act (see CHILDREN AND YOUNG PERSONS vol 10 (2012) PARA 1083) (whether or not the local authority provides the early years provision): School Standards and Framework Act 1998 s 123(4) (substituted by the Childcare Act 2006 s 103(1), Sch 2 para 34(b); and amended by SI 2010/1158; Children and Families Act 2014 s 83(2). The code of practice may include practical guidance in respect of the provision of relevant early years education for children with special educational needs in circumstances where functions under the Children and Families Act 2014 Pt 3 do not fall to be discharged (School Standards and Framework Act 1998 s 123(2) (amended by the Childcare Act 2006 s 103(1), Sch 2 para 34(a); and the Children and Families Act 2014 Sch 3 paras 67, 69(1), (4))); however, unless the code of practice in question includes such provision, the Secretary of State must publish a document explaining

how the practical guidance contained in the code applies in circumstances where those functions do not fall to be discharged, and the duty imposed by the School Standards and Framework Act 1998 s 123(1) to have regard to the provisions of the relevant code includes a duty to have regard to the provisions of that document (s 123(3) (amended by the Children and Families Act 2014 Sch 3 paras 67, 69(1), (5))). As to the meaning of 'child' see PARA 7 note 6; and as to the meaning of 'special educational needs' see PARA 943 (definitions applied by the School Standards and Framework Act 1998 s 142(8)).

39 See the Children and Families Act 2014 s 77(5).
40 As to the First-Tier Tribunal see COURTS AND TRIBUNALS vol 24 (2010) PARA 876 et seq. See also PARA 979.
41 Children and Families Act 2014 s 77(6).

(xi) Appeals, Mediation and Dispute Resolution

979. First-tier Tribunal. In relation to England[1], appeals under the provisions relating to special educational needs[2] were previously to be made to the Special Educational Needs and Disability Tribunal[3]. The tribunal is now abolished and its functions are transferred to the First-tier Tribunal[4]. All functions relating to an appeal against a decision related to children with special educational needs are assigned to the Health Education and Social Care Chamber of the First-tier Tribunal[5]. Procedure before the chamber is governed by specific rules[6]. Appeals from decisions of the First-tier Tribunal may be made to the Upper Tribunal on a point of law[7].

It should be noted that the First-tier Tribunal can also hear claims of disability discrimination[8].

1 As to the meaning of 'England' see PARA 7 note 3.
2 Ie previously what is now the Education Act 1996 Pt IV (ss 311A–349) (see PARA 989 et seq), and now the Children and Families Act 2014 Pt 3 (ss 19–83) (see PARA 950 et seq), and see generally PARA 941. As to appeals in regard to EHC plans or EHC needs assessments see PARA 980. As to appeals and claims by children see PARA 981. As to appeals in regard to EHC plans for detained persons see PARA 973. As to rights to mediation see PARA 983 et seq.
3 The Special Educational Needs and Disability Tribunal was established under the Education Act 1993 and continued in being under the Education Act 1996 s 333: but see PARA 1034.
4 See the Transfer of Tribunal Functions Order 2008, SI 2008/2833, arts 3(1), 4, Sch 1 Table 1. As to the First-tier Tribunal see COURTS AND TRIBUNALS vol 24 (2010) PARA 874 et seq.
5 First-tier Tribunal and Upper Tribunal (Chambers) Order 2010, SI 2010/2655, art 4(a).
6 See the Tribunal Procedure (First-tier Tribunal) (Health, Education and Social Care Chamber) Rules 2008, SI 2008/2699; and COURTS AND TRIBUNALS vol 24 (2010) PARA 879. As to cases relevant to proceedings relating to appeals concerning special educational needs see those cited in PARA 1036. As to the duty of the Tribunal to have regard to the code of practice issued by the Secretary of State see PARA 1033.
7 See the Tribunals, Courts and Enforcement Act 2007 s 11; and COURTS AND TRIBUNALS vol 24 (2010) PARA 928. As to the Upper Tribunal see COURTS AND TRIBUNALS vol 24 (2010) PARA 883 et seq. As to cases relevant to appeals against tribunal decisions see those cited in PARA 1036.
8 See the Equality Act 2010 Sch 17 paras 1–3; and DISCRIMINATION vol 33 (2013) PARA 343.

980. Appeals in regard to EHC plans or EHC needs assessments. A child's[1] parent[2] or a young person[3] may appeal to the First-tier Tribunal[4] against certain decisions of a local authority[5] and other important issues[6], subject to the provisions on mediation[7]. It is to be stressed that before appealing to the First-Tier Tribunal the possibility of mediation should be considered, and there should be evidence that there has been such consideration[8].

The matters against which an appeal may be made are:

(1) a decision of a local authority not to secure an EHC needs assessment for the child or young person[9];

(2) a decision of a local authority, following an EHC needs assessment, that

it is not necessary for special educational provision to be made for the child or young person in accordance with an EHC plan[10];

(3)   where an EHC plan is maintained for the child or young person[11]:

     (a)   the child's or young person's special educational needs as specified in the plan[12];

     (b)   the special educational provision specified in the plan[13];

     (c)   the school or other institution named in the plan, or the type of school or other institution specified in the plan[14];

     (d)   if no school or other institution is named in the plan, that fact[15];

(4)   a decision of a local authority not to secure a re-assessment of the needs of the child or young person[16] following a request to do so[17];

(5)   a decision of a local authority not to secure the amendment or replacement of an EHC plan it maintains for the child or young person following a review or re-assessment[18];

(6)   a decision of a local authority[19] to cease to maintain an EHC plan for the child or young person[20].

Regulations[21] may make provision about appeals to the First-tier Tribunal in respect of EHC needs assessments and EHC plans, in particular about: (i) other matters relating to EHC plans against which appeals may be brought[22]; (ii) making and determining appeals[23]; (iii) the powers of the First-tier Tribunal on determining an appeal[24]; (iv) unopposed appeals[25].

A person[26] commits an offence if without reasonable excuse that person fails to comply with any requirement in respect of the discovery or inspection of documents, or to attend to give evidence and produce documents[27]. A person guilty of such an offence[28] is liable on summary conviction to a fine[29].

1   As to the meaning of 'child' see PARA 7 note 6 (definition applied by the Children and Families Act 2014 s 83(7)).

2   As to the meaning of 'parent' see PARA 7 note 6 (definition applied by the Children and Families Act 2014 s 83(7)).

3   As to the meaning of 'young person' see PARA 950 note 4. As to the power to make pilot schemes enabling a child to make an appeal see PARA 981.

4   As to the First-Tier Tribunal see COURTS AND TRIBUNALS vol 24 (2010) PARA 876 et seq. See also PARA 979. See also generally the Tribunal Procedure (First-Tier Tribunal) (Health, Education and Social Care Chamber) Rules 2008, SI 2008/2699; and COURTS AND TRIBUNALS vol 24 (2010) PARA 879. As to relevant forms and other information see the Department for Education's website.

5   As to the meaning of 'local authority' see PARA 25 (definition applied by the Children and Families Act 2014 s 83(7)).

6   Ie the matters set out in the Children and Families Act 2014 s 51(2): see heads (1)–(6) in the text.

7   Children and Families Act 2014 s 51(1). See also PARA 983. The provisions on mediation are in s 55: see PARA 982.

8   See further PARA 982.

9   Children and Families Act 2014 s 51(2)(a). As to the meaning of 'EHC needs assessment' see PARA 957 note 3.

10   Children and Families Act 2014 s 51(2)(b). As to the meaning of 'EHC plan' see PARA 958.

11   A child's parent or a young person may appeal to the First-tier Tribunal under the Children and Families Act 2014 s 51(2)(c) (see head (3) in the text) when an EHC plan is first finalised for the child or young person, and following an amendment or replacement of the plan: s 51(3).

12   Children and Families Act 2014 s 51(2)(c)(i). As to the meaning of 'special educational needs' see PARA 943.

13   Children and Families Act 2014 s 51(2)(c)(ii).

14   Children and Families Act 2014 s 51(2)(c)(iii). As to the meaning of 'school' generally see PARA 91 (definition applied by s 83(7)).

15   Children and Families Act 2014 s 51(2)(c)(iv).

16   Ie under the Children and Families Act 2014 s 44: see PARA 964.

17 Children and Families Act 2014 s 51(2)(d).
18 Children and Families Act 2014 s 51(2)(e). The text refers to a review or re-assessment under s 44: see PARA 964.
19 Ie under the Children and Families Act 2014 s 45: see PARA 965.
20 Children and Families Act 2014 s 51(2)(f).
21 As to regulations generally see the Children and Families Act 2014 s 135. As to regulations made under s 51(4) see the Special Educational Needs and Disability Regulations 2014, SI 2014/1530 (amended by SI 2014/2096; and SI 2015/359). Note in particular that the First-Tier Tribunal may, with the agreement of both parties, correct any deficiencies in the EHC plan which relate to the special educational needs or special educational provision for the child or the young person: see the Special Educational Needs and Disability Regulations 2014, SI 2014/1530, reg 43(1). As to the meaning of 'special educational provision' see PARA 943.
22 Children and Families Act 2014 s 51(4)(a). See note 7.
23 Children and Families Act 2014 s 51(4)(b). See note 7.
24 Children and Families Act 2014 s 51(4)(c). Regulations under s 51(4)(c) may include provision conferring power on the First-tier Tribunal, on determining an appeal against a matter, to make recommendations in respect of other matters (including matters against which no appeal may be brought): s 51(5). As to regulations under s 51(4)(c), (5) see the Special Educational Needs and Disability (First-tier Tribunal Recommendation Power) (Pilot) Regulations 2015, SI 2015/358. See also note 7.
25 Children and Families Act 2014 s 51(4)(d). See note 7.
26 As to the meaning of 'person' see PARA 7 note 6.
27 Children and Families Act 2014 s 51(6). The requirements referred to in the text are those imposed by Tribunal Procedure Rules in relation to an appeal under s 51 or regulations under s 51(4)(a) (see the text to note 7).
28 Ie an offence under the Children and Families Act 2014 s 51(6).
29 Children and Families Act 2014 s 51(7). The fine is a fine not exceeding level 3 on the standard scale: see s 51(7). As to the standard scale see SENTENCING AND DISPOSITION OF OFFENDERS vol 92 (2010) PARA 142.

981. Pilot schemes enabling children to make certain appeals and claims. The Secretary of State[1] may by order make pilot schemes enabling children[2] in England[3] to (1) appeal to the First-tier Tribunal[4]; (2) make a claim to the First-tier Tribunal under the Equality Act 2010[5].

Such an order[6] may, in particular, make provision:

(a)   about the age from which children may appeal or make a claim[7];

(b)   in respect of certain appeals[8];

(c)   about the bringing of appeals or making of claims by a child and by his or her parent[9] concurrently[10];

(d)   about determining whether a child is capable of bringing an appeal or making a claim, and the assistance and support a child may require to be able to do so[11];

(e)   enabling a person to exercise a child's rights under an order[12] on behalf of the child[13];

(f)   enabling children to have access to advice and information which is available to a parent or young person in respect of an above appeal or claim[14];

(g)   about the provision of advocacy and other support services to children[15];

(h)   requiring notices to be given to a child (as well as to his or her parent)[16];

(i)   requiring documents to be served on a child (as well as on his or her parent)[17].

The Secretary of State may by order provide that children in England may (i) appeal to the First-tier Tribunal[18]; (ii) make a claim to the First-tier Tribunal under the Equality Act 2010[19].

However the Secretary of State may not make such an order[20] until the end of two years beginning with the day on which the first order is made under the previous provision above[21]. Such an order may, in particular, make provision as set out in heads (a) to (i) above[22].

1   As to the Secretary of State see PARA 58.
2   As to the meaning of 'child' see PARA 7 note 6 (definition applied by the Children and Families Act 2014 s 83(7)).
3   As to the meaning of 'England' see PARA 7 note 3.
4   Children and Families Act 2014 s 58(1)(a). Such appeal is under s 51: see PARA 980. As to the First-Tier Tribunal see COURTS AND TRIBUNALS vol 24 (2010) PARA 876 et seq. See also generally the Tribunal Procedure (First-Tier Tribunal) (Health, Education and Social Care Chamber) Rules 2008, SI 2008/2699; and COURTS AND TRIBUNALS vol 24 (2010) PARA 879.
    An order under the Children and Families Act 2014 s 58(1) may apply a statutory provision, with or without modifications: s 58(3). In s 58(3), 'statutory provision' means a provision made by or under this or any other Act, whenever passed or made: s 58(4).
    At the date at which this volume states the law no order had been made under s 58(1).
    Section 58 is repealed at the end of five years beginning with the day on which the Children and Families Act 2014 was passed: s 58(5). The Act was passed on 13 March 2014.
5   Children and Families Act 2014 s 58(1)(b). The text refers to a claim under the Equality Act 2010 Sch 17 (disabled pupils: enforcement: see PARA 12) that a responsible body in England has contravened Pt 6 Ch 1 (ss 84–89) because of the child's disability: see s 58(1)(b). As to the meaning of 'disability' see PARA 943 note 3.
6   Ie an order under the Children and Families Act 2014 s 58(1).
7   Children and Families Act 2014 s 58(2)(a).
8   Children and Families Act 2014 s 58(2)(b). The reference is to appeals under s 51 (see PARA 980) about mediation and the application of s 55 (see PARA 982).
9   As to the meaning of 'parent' see PARA 7 note 6 (definition applied by the Children and Families Act 2014 s 83(7)).
10 Children and Families Act 2014 s 58(2)(c).
11 Children and Families Act 2014 s 58(2)(d).
12 See note 6.
13 Children and Families Act 2014 s 58(2)(e).
14 Children and Families Act 2014 s 58(2)(f). The reference is to an appeal or claim of a type mentioned in s 58(1).
15 Children and Families Act 2014 s 58(2)(g).
16 Children and Families Act 2014 s 58(2)(h).
17 Children and Families Act 2014 s 58(2)(i).
18 Children and Families Act 2014 s 59(1)(a). Such appeal is under s 51: see PARA 980. An order under s 59(1) may apply a statutory provision, with or without modifications: s 59(4). In s 59(4), 'statutory provision' means a provision made by or under this or any other Act, whenever passed or made: s 59(5).
19 Children and Families Act 2014 s 59(1)(b). Such a claim is under the Equality Act 2010 Sch 17 (disabled pupils: enforcement: see PARA 12) that a responsible body in England has contravened Pt 6 Ch 1 (ss 84–89) because of the child's disability: see s 59(1)(b).
20 Ie an order under the Children and Families Act 2014 s 59(1).
21 Children and Families Act 2014 s 59(2). The reference is to s 58(1): see the text to notes 1–5, and see in particular note 4.
22 See the Children and Families Act 2014 s 59(3)(a)–(i).

982.   Requirement for a certificate from a mediation adviser before making certain appeals.   The provisions below[1] apply where a child's[2] parent[3] or young person[4] intends to appeal[5] to the First-tier Tribunal[6] in respect of a decision of a local authority[7], or in respect of the content of an EHC plan[8] maintained by a local authority[9]. However those provisions do not apply in respect of an appeal concerning only (1) the school[10] or other institution named in an EHC plan[11]; (2) the type of school or other institution specified in an EHC plan[12]; (3) the fact that an EHC plan does not name a school or other institution[13].

The parent or young person may make the appeal only if a mediation adviser has issued[14] a certificate to him or her[15]. A mediation adviser[16] must issue a certificate[17] to the parent or young person if (a) the adviser has provided him or her with information and advice about pursuing mediation[18]; and (b) the parent or young person has informed the adviser that he or she does not wish to pursue mediation[19]. A mediation adviser must issue a certificate[20] to the parent or young person if the adviser has provided him or her with information and advice about pursuing mediation[21], and the parent or young person (i) has informed the adviser that he or she wishes to pursue mediation under the appropriate provision[22]; and (ii) has participated in such mediation[23].

1   Ie the provisions of the Children and Families Act 2014 s 55.
2   As to the meaning of 'child' see PARA 7 note 6 (definition applied by the Children and Families Act 2014 s 83(7)).
3   As to the meaning of 'parent' see PARA 7 note 6 (definition applied by the Children and Families Act 2014 s 83(7)).
4   As to the meaning of 'young person' see PARA 950 note 4.
5   Ie under the Children and Families Act 2014 s 51or regulations made under s 51: see PARA 980.
6   As to the First-Tier Tribunal see COURTS AND TRIBUNALS vol 24 (2010) PARA 876 et seq. See also PARA 979.
7   Children and Families Act 2014 s 55(1)(a). As to the meaning of 'local authority' see PARA 25 (definition applied by s 83(7)).
8   As to the meaning of 'EHC plan' see PARA 958.
9   Children and Families Act 2014 s 55(1)(b).
10 As to the meaning of 'school' generally see PARA 91 (definition applied by the Children and Families Act 2014 s 83(7)).
11 Children and Families Act 2014 s 55(2)(a).
12 Children and Families Act 2014 s 55(2)(b).
13 Children and Families Act 2014 s 55(2)(c).
14 Ie issued under the Children and Families Act 2014 s 55(4) or (5): see the text to notes 16–23.
15 Children and Families Act 2014 s 55(3).
16 In the Children and Families Act 2014 ss 55, 56 'mediation adviser' means an independent person who can provide information and advice about pursuing mediation: s 56(2). For the purposes of s 56(2), a person is not independent if he or she is employed by any of the following: (1) a local authority in England (s 56(3)(a)); (2) a clinical commissioning group (s 56(3)(b)); (3) the National Health Service Commissioning Board (s 56(3)(c)). As to the meaning of 'person' see PARA 7 note 6. As to the meaning of 'England' see PARA 7 note 3. As to clinical commissioning groups and the National Health Service Commissioning Board see HEALTH SERVICES.
17 Ie under the Children and Families Act 2014 s 55(4).
18 Children and Families Act 2014 s 55(4)(a). The reference in the text is to pursuing mediation under s 53 (see PARA 984) or s 54 (see PARA 985).
19 Children and Families Act 2014 s 55(4)(b).
20 Ie under the Children and Families Act 2014 s 55(5).
21 Ie under the Children and Families Act 2014 s 53 (see PARA 984) or s 54 (see PARA 985).
22 Children and Families Act 2014 s 55(5)(a).
23 Children and Families Act 2014 s 55(5)(b).

983.   **Right to mediation.**   Where (1) a decision against which an appeal may be brought[1] is made in respect of a child[2] or young person[3]; or (2) an EHC plan[4] for a child or young person is made, amended or replaced[5], before the end of the prescribed period after the decision is made, or the plan is made, amended or replaced, the local authority[6] must notify the child's parent[7] or the young person of (a) the right to mediation[8]; and (b) the requirement to obtain a relevant certificate[9] before making certain appeals[10].

If the parent or young person wishes to pursue mediation[11], he or she must inform the local authority of (i) that fact[12]; and (ii) the issues in respect of which he or she wishes to pursue mediation ('the mediation issues')[13]. If the mediation issues are, or include, the fact that no health care provision[14], or no health care provision of a particular kind, is specified in the plan, the parent or young person must also inform the local authority of the health care provision which he or she wishes to be specified in the plan[15].

1   Ie brought under the Children and Families Act 2014 s 51: see PARA 980.
2   As to the meaning of 'child' see PARA 7 note 6 (definition applied by the Children and Families Act 2014 s 83(7)).
3   Children and Families Act 2014 s 52(1)(a). As to the meaning of 'young person' see PARA 950 note 4.
4   As to the meaning of 'EHC plan' see PARA 958.
5   Children and Families Act 2014 s 52(1)(b).
6   As to the meaning of 'local authority' see PARA 25 (definition applied by the Children and Families Act 2014 s 83(7)).
7   As to the meaning of 'parent' see PARA 7 note 6 (definition applied by the Children and Families Act 2014 s 83(7)).
8   Children and Families Act 2014 s 52(2)(a). The right to mediation is under s 53 (health care issues: see PARA 984) or 54 (educational and social care issues: see PARA 985).
9   Ie a certificate under the Children and Families Act 2014 s 55: see PARA 982.
10 Children and Families Act 2014 s 52(2)(b).
11 Ie under the Children and Families Act 2014 s 53 (see PARA 984) or s 54 (see PARA 985).
12 Children and Families Act 2014 s 52(3)(a).
13 Children and Families Act 2014 s 52(3)(b).
14 As to the meaning of 'health care provision' see PARA 946 note 7.
15 Children and Families Act 2014 s 52(4).

984.   Mediation: health care issues.   Where (1) the parent[1] or young person[2] informs[3] the local authority[4] that he or she wishes to pursue mediation[5]; and (2) the mediation issues[6] include health care provision[7] specified in the plan or the fact that no health care provision, or no health care provision of a particular kind, is specified in the plan[8], the local authority must notify each relevant commissioning body[9] of (a) the mediation issues[10]; and (b) anything of which it has been informed[11] by the parent or young person[12].

If the mediation issues are limited to the health care provision specified in the plan or the fact that no health care provision, or no health care provision of a particular kind, is specified in the plan, the responsible commissioning body (or, where there is more than one, the responsible commissioning bodies acting jointly) must:

(i)   arrange for mediation between it (or them) and the parent or young person[13];

(ii)   ensure that the mediation is conducted by an independent person[14]; and

(iii)   participate in the mediation[15].

If the mediation issues include anything else (A) the local authority must arrange for mediation between it, each responsible commissioning body and the parent or young person[16]; ensure that the mediation is conducted by an independent person[17]; and participate in the mediation[18]; and (B) each responsible commissioning body must also participate in the mediation[19].

1   As to the meaning of 'parent' see PARA 7 note 6 (definition applied by the Children and Families Act 2014 s 83(7)).
2   As to the meaning of 'young person' see PARA 950 note 4.
3   Ie informs under the Children and Families Act 2014 s 52: see PARA 983.
4   As to the meaning of 'local authority' see PARA 25 (definition applied by the Children and Families Act 2014 s 83(7)).
5   Children and Families Act 2014 s 53(1)(a).
6   As to the meaning of 'mediation issues' see PARA 983.
7   As to the meaning of 'health care provision' see PARA 946 note 7.
8   Children and Families Act 2014 s 53(1)(b). Reference in the text to the plan is a reference to the EHC plan. As to the meaning of 'EHC plan' see PARA 958.

9   In the Children and Families Act 2014 s 53 'responsible commissioning body' (1) if the mediation issues in question are or include the health care provision specified in an EHC plan, means a body that is under a duty to arrange health care provision of that kind in respect of the child or young person (s 53(6)(a)); (2) if the mediation issues in question are or include the fact that no health care provision, or no health care provision of a particular kind, is specified in an EHC plan, means a body that would be under a duty to arrange health care provision of the kind in question if it were specified in the plan (s 53(6)(b)). As to the meaning of 'child' see PARA 7 note 6 (definition applied by s 83(7)).
10 Children and Families Act 2014 s 53(2)(a).
11 Ie informed under the Children and Families Act 2014 s 52(4): see PARA 983.
12 Children and Families Act 2014 s 53(2)(b).
13 Children and Families Act 2014 s 53(3)(a).
14 Children and Families Act 2014 s 53(3)(b). For the purposes of s 53, a person is not independent if he or she is employed by any of the following: (1) a local authority in England (s 53(5)(a)); (2) a clinical commissioning group (s 53(5)(b)); (3) the National Health Service Commissioning Board (s 53(5)(c)). As to the meaning of 'person' see PARA 7 note 6. As to the meaning of 'England' see PARA 7 note 3. As to clinical commissioning groups and the National Health Service Commissioning Board see HEALTH SERVICES.
15 Children and Families Act 2014 s 53(3)(c).
16 Children and Families Act 2014 s 53(4)(a)(i).
17 Children and Families Act 2014 s 53(4)(a)(ii).
18 Children and Families Act 2014 s 53(4)(a)(iii).
19 Children and Families Act 2014 s 53(4)(b).

985.   Mediation: educational and social care issues etc.   Where (1) the parent[1] or young person[2] informs[3] the local authority[4] that he or she wishes to pursue mediation[5]; and (2) the mediation issues[6] do not include health care provision[7] specified in the plan or the fact that no health care provision, or no health care provision of a particular kind, is specified in the plan[8], the local authority must:

(a)   arrange for mediation between it and the parent or young person[9];

(b)   ensure that the mediation is conducted by an independent person[10]; and

(c)   participate in the mediation[11].

1   As to the meaning of 'parent' see PARA 7 note 6 (definition applied by the Children and Families Act 2014 s 83(7)).
2   As to the meaning of 'young person' see PARA 950 note 4.
3   Ie informs under the Children and Families Act 2014 s 52: see PARA 983.
4   As to the meaning of 'local authority' see PARA 25 (definition applied by the Children and Families Act 2014 s 83(7)).
5   Children and Families Act 2014 s 54(1)(a).
6   As to the meaning of 'mediation issues' see PARA 983.
7   As to the meaning of 'health care provision' see PARA 946 note 7.
8   Children and Families Act 2014 s 54(1)(b). Reference in the text to the plan is a reference to the EHC plan. As to the meaning of 'EHC plan' see PARA 958.
9   Children and Families Act 2014 s 54(2)(a).
10 Children and Families Act 2014 s 54(2)(b). For the purposes of s 54, a person is not independent if he or she is employed by a local authority in England: s 54(3). As to the meaning of 'person' see PARA 7 note 6. As to the meaning of 'England' see PARA 7 note 3.
11 Children and Families Act 2014 s 54(2)(c).

986.   Regulations relating to mediation.   Regulations[1] may make provision in relation to mediation[2], in particular:

(1)   about giving notice[3];

(2)   imposing time limits[4];

(3)   enabling a local authority or commissioning body[5] to take prescribed steps following the conclusion of mediation[6];

(4)   about who may attend mediation[7];

(5)   where a child's parent is a party to mediation, requiring the mediator to take reasonable steps to ascertain the views of the child[8];

(6)   about the provision of advocacy and other support services for the parent or young person[9];

(7)   requiring a local authority or commissioning body to pay reasonable travel expenses and other expenses of a prescribed description, up to any prescribed limit[10];

(8)   about exceptions to the requirement that the parent or young person may make the appeal only if a mediation adviser has issued a certificate to him[11];

(9)   about the training[12], qualifications and experience of mediators and mediation advisers[13];

(10)   conferring powers or imposing requirements on local authorities, commissioning bodies, mediators and mediation advisers[14].

1   As to regulations generally see the Children and Families Act 2014 s 135. As to regulations made under s 56(1) see the Special Educational Needs and Disability Regulations 2014, SI 2014/1530 (amended by SI 2014/2096; and SI 2015/359); and the Special Educational Needs and Disability (Detained Persons) Regulations 2015, SI 2015/62.
2   Ie for the purposes of the Children and Families Act 2014 ss 52–55: see also PARAS 982–985.
3   Children and Families Act 2014 s 56(1)(a). See note 1.
4   Children and Families Act 2014 s 56(1)(b). See note 1.
5   In the Children and Families Act 2014 s 56 'commissioning body' means a body that is under a duty to arrange health care provision of any kind: s 56(4). As to the meaning of 'health care provision' see PARA 946 note 7.
6   Children and Families Act 2014 s 56(1)(c). See note 1.
7   Children and Families Act 2014 s 56(1)(d). See note 1.
8   Children and Families Act 2014 s 56(1)(e). See note 1. As to the meanings of 'child' and 'parent' see PARA 7 note 6 (definition applied by the Children and Families Act 2014 s 83(7)).
9   Children and Families Act 2014 s 56(1)(f). See note 1. As to the meaning of 'young person' see PARA 950 note 4.
10 Children and Families Act 2014 s 56(1)(g). See note 1. As to the meaning of 'local authority' see PARA 25 (definition applied by s 83(7)).
11 Children and Families Act 2014 s 56(1)(h). See note 1. The reference in the text is to the requirement in s 55(3): see PARA 982. As to the meaning of 'mediation adviser' see PARA 982 note 16.
12 As to the meaning of 'training' see PARA 943 note 9.
13 Children and Families Act 2014 s 56(1)(i). See note 1.
14 Children and Families Act 2014 s 56(1)(j). See note 1.

987. Resolution of disagreements. A local authority[1] in England[2] must make arrangements with a view to avoiding or resolving disagreements within the provisions of the Children and Families Act 2014 below[3]. One set of disagreements[4] are those about the exercise by the local authority or relevant bodies[5] of their functions[6] under Part 3 of the Children and Families Act 2014[7], where the disagreement is between (1) the local authority or a relevant body[8]; and (2) the parents[9] of children[10], and young people[11], in the authority's area[12]. The other set of disagreements[13] are those about the exercise by the local authority of its functions relating to EHC needs assessments[14], the preparation and review of EHC plans[15], and re-assessment of educational[16], health care and social care needs, where the disagreement is between (a) the local authority and a responsible commissioning body[17]; or (b) a responsible commissioning body and the parents of children, or young people, in the authority's area[18].

A local authority in England must also make arrangements with a view to avoiding or resolving, in each relevant school or post-16 institution[19], the following disagreements[20]. These disagreements[21] are those about the special educational provision[22] made for a child or young person with special educational needs[23] who is a registered pupil[24] or a student[25] at the relevant school or post-16 institution concerned, where the disagreement is between (i) the child's parent, or the young person[26]; and (ii) the appropriate authority[27] for the school or post-16 institution[28]. Arrangements[29] must provide for the appointment of independent persons[30] with the function of facilitating the avoidance or resolution of the disagreements to which the arrangements apply[31].

A local authority in England must take such steps as it thinks appropriate for making the arrangements[32] known to (A) the parents of children in its area with special educational needs[33]; (B) young people in its area with special educational needs[34]; and (C) the head teachers[35], governing bodies, proprietors and principals of schools and post-16 institutions in its area[36]: A local authority in England may take such steps as it thinks appropriate for making the arrangements[37] known to such other persons as it thinks appropriate[38].

1   As to the meaning of 'local authority' see PARA 25 (definition applied by the Children and Families Act 2014 s 83(7)).
2   As to the meaning of 'England' see PARA 7 note 3.
3   Children and Families Act 2014 s 57(1). The reference in the text is to the provisions of s 57(2), (3).
4   Ie disagreements within the Children and Families Act 2014 s 57(2).
5   'Relevant body' means (1) the governing body of a maintained school, maintained nursery school or institution within the further education sector; (2) the proprietor of an academy: Children and Families Act 2014 s 57(10). As to the governing bodies of maintained schools in England see PARA 150 et seq. As to the meaning of 'maintained school' see PARA 943 note 8. As to the meaning of 'maintained nursery school' see PARA 99 note 4 (definition applied by s 83(7)). As to the meaning of 'further education' see PARA 23 (definition applied by s 83(7)). As to the meaning of 'proprietor' see PARA 948 note 21. As to the meaning of 'academy' see PARA 346 note 7 (definition applied by s 83(7)).
6   As to the meaning of 'function' see PARA 18 note 5 (definition applied by the Children and Families Act 2014 s 83(7)).
7   Ie the Children and Families Act 2014 Pt 3 (ss 19–83).
8   Children and Families Act 2014 s 57(2)(a).
9   As to the meaning of 'parent' see PARA 7 note 6 (definition applied by the Children and Families Act 2014 s 83(7)).
10 As to the meaning of 'child' see PARA 7 note 6 (definition applied by the Children and Families Act 2014 s 83(7)).
11 As to the meaning of 'young person' see PARA 950 note 4.
12 Children and Families Act 2014 s 57(2)(b). As to being 'in the area' of a local authority see PARA 944 note 6.
13 Ie disagreements within the Children and Families Act 2014 s 57(3).
14 As to the meaning of 'EHC needs assessment' see PARA 957 note 3.
15 As to the meaning of 'EHC plan' see PARA 958.
16 As to the meaning of 'educational' see PARA 950 note 11.
17 Children and Families Act 2014 s 57(3)(a). 'Responsible commissioning body', in relation to any particular health care provision, means a body that is under a duty to arrange health care provision of that kind in respect of the child or young person concerned: s 57(10). As to the meaning of 'health care provision' see PARA 946 note 7.
18 Children and Families Act 2014 s 57(3)(b).
19 'Relevant school or post-16 institution' means (1) a maintained school; (2) a maintained nursery school; (3) a post-16 institution; (4) an academy; (5) an independent school; (6) a non-maintained special school; (7) a pupil referral unit; (8) a place at which relevant early years education is provided: Children and Families Act 2014 s 57(10). As to the meaning of 'post-16 institution' see PARA 943 note 9. As to the meaning of 'independent school' see PARA 369 (definition applied by s 83(7)). As to the meaning of 'non-maintained special school' see PARA 1042 (definition applied by s 83(7)). As to pupil referral units generally see PARA 427 et seq. As to the meaning of 'relevant early years education' see PARA 943 note 17.
20 Children and Families Act 2014 s 57(4). The reference in the text is to disagreements within s 57(5).
21 Ie the disagreements within the Children and Families Act 2014 s 57(5).
22 As to the meaning of 'special educational provision' see PARA 943.
23 As to the meaning of 'special educational needs' see PARA 943.

24 As to the meaning of 'registered pupil' see PARA 437 (definition applied by the Children and Families Act 2014 s 83(7)).
25 As to the meaning of 'student' see PARA 67 note 8 (definition applied by the Children and Families Act 2014 s 83(7)).
26 Children and Families Act 2014 s 57(5)(a).
27 For the purposes of the Children and Families Act 2014, the 'appropriate authority' for a relevant school or post-16 institution is:
  (1)   in the case of a maintained school, maintained nursery school or non-maintained special school, the governing body (s 57(11)(a));
  (2)   in the case of a post-16 institution, the governing body, proprietor or principal (s 57(11)(b));
  (3)   in the case of an academy or independent school, the proprietor (s 57(11)(c));
  (4)   in the case of a pupil referral unit, the management committee (s 57(11)(d));
  (5)   in the case of a place at which relevant early years education is provided, the provider of the relevant early years education (s 57(11)(e)).
28 Children and Families Act 2014 s 57(5)(b).
29 Ie arrangements within the Children and Families Act 2014 s 57.
30 For the purposes of the Children and Families Act 2014 s 57(6) a person is not independent if he or she is employed by any of the following (1) a local authority in England (s 57(7)(a)); (2) a clinical commissioning group (s 57(7)(b)); (3) the National Health Service Commissioning Board (s 57(7)(c)). As to the meaning of 'person' see PARA 7 note 6. As to clinical commissioning groups and the National Health Service Commissioning Board see HEALTH SERVICES.
31 Children and Families Act 2014 s 57(6).
32 Ie the arrangements under the Children and Families Act 2014 s 57.
33 Children and Families Act 2014 s 57(8)(a).
34 Children and Families Act 2014 s 57(8)(b).
35 As to the meaning of 'head teacher' see PARA 86 note 4 (definition applied by the Children and Families Act 2014 s 83(7)).
36 Children and Families Act 2014 s 57(8)(c).
37 See note 32.
38 Children and Families Act 2014 s 57(9).

988.   Review of resolution of disagreements. The Secretary of State[1] and the Lord Chancellor[2] must carry out a review of how effectively disagreements about the exercise of functions[3] under Part 3 of the Children and Families Act 2014[4] are being resolved[5].

The Secretary of State and the Lord Chancellor must prepare a report on the outcome of the review[6]. The Secretary of State and the Lord Chancellor must lay the report before Parliament before the end of the period of three years beginning with the earliest date on which any provision of this Part comes into force[7].

1 As to the Secretary of State see PARA 58.
2 As to the Lord Chancellor see CONSTITUTIONAL AND ADMINISTRATIVE LAW vol 20 (2014) PARA 256 et seq.
3 As to the meaning of 'function' see PARA 18 note 5 (definition applied by the Children and Families Act 2014 s 83(7)).
4 Ie the Children and Families Act 2014 Pt 3 (ss 19–83).
5 Children and Families Act 2014 s 79(1).
6 Children and Families Act 2014 s 79(2).
7 Children and Families Act 2014 s 79(3).

(3) CHILDREN IN WALES WITH SPECIAL EDUCATIONAL NEEDS AND DISABILITIES

(i) Identification of Children with Special Educational Needs

989.   Meaning in Wales of 'special educational needs', 'special educational provision' and 'learning difficulty'. A child[1] in the area of a local authority in Wales has 'special educational needs' for the purposes of the Education Act 1996 if he has a learning difficulty which calls for special educational provision to be made for him[2]. A child in the area of a local authority in Wales has a 'learning difficulty' for these purposes[3] if:

(1) he has a significantly greater difficulty in learning than the majority of children of his age[4];

(2) he has a disability which either prevents or hinders him from making use of educational facilities of a kind generally provided for children of his age in schools within the area of the local authority[5]; or

(3) he is under compulsory school age[6] and is, or would be if special educational provision were not made for him, likely to fall within head (1) or head (2) above when of that age[7].

However, a child is not to be taken as having a learning difficulty solely because the language (or form of the language) in which he is, or will be, taught is different from a language (or form of a language) which has at any time been spoken in his home[8].

'Special educational provision', in relation to a child in the area of a local authority in Wales, means: (a) in relation to a child who has attained the age of two, educational provision[9] which is additional to, or otherwise different from, the educational provision made generally for children of his age in schools maintained by the local authority (other than special schools)[10]; and (b) in relation to a child under that age, educational provision of any kind[11].

1   For the purposes of the Education Act 1996 Pt IV (ss 311A–349), 'child' also includes any person who has not attained the age of 19 and is a registered pupil at a school: s 312(5). As to the meaning of 'child' generally see PARA 7 note 6. As to the meaning of 'registered pupil' see PARA 437. As to the meaning of 'school' see PARA 91. As to the time at which a person attains a particular age see PARA 7 note 6.
      The definition of 'child' in the Education Act 1996 s 312(5) is not exhaustive; it must extend at least as far as any individual under the age of 19 in respect of whom the local authority does or might owe obligations under the Education Act 1996 Pt IV; and it is not necessary for a person to be 'a registered pupil at a school' to be a 'child' for the purposes of Pt IV: see *Wolverhampton City Council v Special Educational Needs and Disability Tribunal* [2007] EWHC 1117 (Admin), [2007] ELR 418, (2007) Times, 25 May, [2007] All ER (D) 195 (May); *R (on the application of Hill) v Bedfordshire County Council* [2008] EWCA Civ 661, [2008] ELR 660, [2008] All ER (D) 189 (Jun). The definition of 'child' in the Education Act 1996 s 312(5) means a person up to the age of 19 and does not include a person over that age who remains a registered pupil at a school: *R (on the application of B) v Islington London Borough Council* [2010] EWHC 2539 (Admin), [2011] PTSR 716, [2010] NLJR 1190, [2010] All ER (D) 97 (Aug), [2011] PTSR 716. See also *S v Essex County Council* [2000] ELR 718; *Wakefield Metropolitan District Council v E* [2001] EWHC Admin 508, [2002] ELR 203, [2001] All ER (D) 94 (Jul).

2   Education Act 1996 s 312(1) (amended by the Children and Families Act 2014 Sch 3 paras 1, 11(1), (2)), Education Act 1996 s 579(1) (definition added by the Children and Families Act 2014 Sch 3 paras 1, 59(b)). As to the meaning of 'local authority' see PARA 25. As to the meaning of 'Wales' see PARA 7 note 3. As to the effect of the Children and Families Act 2014 see generally PARA 941. See also the Education Act 1996 s 331A; and PARA 941.

3   See the Education Act 1996 s 312(2) (amended by the Apprenticeships, Skills, Children and Learning Act 2009 s 59, Sch 2 paras 1, 6(1), (2); and the Children and Families Act 2014 Sch 3 paras 1, 11(1), (2)). This provision is expressed to be subject to the Education Act 1996 s 312(3) (see the text to note 8) and s 312(3A): see s 312(2) (as so amended). Section 312(2) does not apply: (1) for the purposes of s 15A (local authority functions in respect of full-time education for 16 to 18 year olds: see PARA 34) and s 15B (local authority functions in respect of education for persons over 19: see PARA 36); or (2) a local authority in Wales determining for the purposes of those provisions, whether a child has special educational needs: s 312(3A) (added by the Apprenticeships, Skills, Children and Learning Act 2009 s 59, Sch 2 paras 1, 6(1), (3) ; and amended by the Children and Families Act 2014 paras 1, 11(1), (3))).

4   Education Act 1996 s 312(2)(a). A learning difficulty might, for example, result from a need for speech therapy (*R v Lancashire County Council, ex p M* [1989] 2 FLR 279, 87 LGR 567, CA;

although c f *R v Oxfordshire Education Authority, ex p W* [1987] 2 FLR 193), or from dyslexia (*R v Hampshire Education Authority, ex p J* (1985) 84 LGR 547). See also *R v Secretary of State for Education, ex p C* [1996] ELR 93 (the fact that a child's exceptionally high intelligence enabled him to compensate for dyslexia did not mean that the child did not have special educational needs). However, this is not authority for the proposition that 'giftedness' of itself can constitute a learning difficulty: *R v Portsmouth City Council, ex p Faludy* [1998] 3 FCR 271, [1998] ELR 619; and see [1999] ELR 115, CA (refusing leave to appeal). See also note 5.

5   Education Act 1996 s 312(2)(b) (amended by SI 2010/1158). Exceptional academic ability is not a disability within the meaning of s 312(2)(b): *S v Special Educational Needs Tribunal* [2005] EWHC 196 (Admin), [2005] ELR 443, [2005] All ER (D) 76 (Feb).

6   As to the meaning of 'compulsory school age' see PARA 19.

7   Education Act 1996 s 312(2)(c) (amended by the Education Act 1997 s 57(1), (4), Sch 7 para 23, Sch 8).

8   Education Act 1996 s 312(3). The domestic circumstances in which a child lives would only give the child a learning difficulty for these purposes where there was a direct relationship between the circumstances and the learning difficulty: *R v Wakefield Metropolitan Borough Council, ex p G* [1998] 2 FCR 597, sub nom *G v Wakefield Metropolitan Borough Council* (1998) 96 LGR 69.

9   The following have been held not to amount to educational provision: provision of a lift to ensure a disabled child's access to first floor facilities (*R v Lambeth London Borough Council, ex p MBM* [1995] ELR 374, 94 LGR 122); provision of nursing care to enable a severely disabled child to be safe at school (*Bradford Metropolitan Council v A* [1997] ELR 417); and provision of occupational therapy and physiotherapy (*B v Isle of White Council* [1997] ELR 279). However, a combination of occupational therapy, physiotherapy and speech therapy together has been held to amount to educational provision (*Bromley London Borough Council v Special Educational Needs Tribunal* [1999] 3 All ER 587, [1999] ELR 260, CA); as has speech therapy alone (*R v Lancashire County Council, ex p M* [1989] 2 FLR 279, (1989) 87 LGR 567, CA). See also *A v Hertfordshire County Council* [2006] EWHC 3428 (Admin), [2007] ELR 95, [2006] All ER (D) 302 (Dec) in which the court stated that whether a form of help needed by the child falls within the description 'special educational provision' is a question primarily for the local authority and secondarily for the appeal tribunal's expert judgment; the court will only intervene if the tribunal has gone wrong in law. As to the appeal tribunal see PARA 1034.

10   Education Act 1996 s 312(4)(a) (amended by the School Standards and Framework Act 1998 s 140(1), (3), Sch 30 paras 57, 71(a), Sch 31; SI 2010/1158; and the Education Act 1996 s 312(4) amended by the Children and Families Act 2014 Sch 3 paras 1, 11(1), (4)), Education Act 1996 s 579(1) (definition added by the Children and Families Act 2014 Sch 3 paras 1, 59(b)). In the Education Act 1996 Pt IV (ss 311A–349), 'maintained school' means any community, foundation or voluntary school or any community or foundation special school not established in a hospital: s 312(5) (definition substituted by the School Standards and Framework Act 1998 s 140(1), Sch 30 paras 57, 71(b)). As to the meaning of references to a community, foundation or voluntary school or a community or foundation special school see PARA 106.

11   Education Act 1996 s 312(4)(b), Education Act 1996 s 579(1) (definition as added: see note 10).

990. Children for whom local authority is responsible. A local authority[1] is responsible[2] for a child[3] if he is in its area[4] and:

    (1)   he is a registered pupil[5] at a maintained school[6] or maintained nursery school[7];

    (2)   education is provided for him at a school[8] which is not a maintained school or maintained nursery school but is so provided at the expense of the authority[9];

    (3)   he does not come within head (1) or head (2) above but is a registered pupil at a school and has been brought to the authority's attention as having (or probably having) special educational needs[10]; or

    (4)   he is not a registered pupil at a school but is not under the age of two or over compulsory school age[11] and has been brought to its attention as having (or probably having) special educational needs[12].

1   As to the meaning of 'local authority' see PARA 25.

2 Ie for the purposes of the Education Act 1996 Pt IV (ss 311A–349). See *Wolverhampton City Council v Special Educational Needs and Disability Tribunal* [2007] EWHC 1117 (Admin), [2007] ELR 418, (2007) Times, 25 May, [2007] All ER (D) 195 (May).
3 As to the meaning of 'child' see PARA 989 note 1.
4 Education Act 1996 s 321(3) (amended by SI 2010/1158). As to the effect of the Children and Families Act 2014 see generally PARA 941. See also the Education Act 1996 s 331A; and PARA 941.
5 As to the meaning of 'registered pupil' see PARA 437.
6 As to the meaning of 'maintained school' see PARA 989 note 10.
7 Education Act 1996 s 321(3)(a) (amended by the School Standards and Framework Act 1998 s 140(1), Sch 30 paras 57, 76(a); and the Education Act 2002 s 215(1), Sch 21 para 42). As to the meaning of 'maintained nursery school' see PARA 99 note 4.
8 As to the meaning of 'school' see PARA 91.
9 Education Act 1996 s 321(3)(b) (substituted by the School Standards and Framework Act 1998 s 140(1), Sch 30 paras 57, 76(b); and amended by Education Act 2002 Sch 21 para 42).
10 Education Act 1996 s 321(3)(c). As to the meaning of 'special educational needs' see PARA 989.
11 As to the meaning of 'compulsory school age' see PARA 19. As to the time at which a person attains a particular age see PARA 7 note 6.
12 Education Act 1996 s 321(3)(d).

991. General duty of local authority towards children for whom it is responsible. A local authority[1] must exercise its powers[2] with a view to securing that, of the children[3] for whom it is responsible[4], it identifies those children who have special educational needs[5] and in relation to whom it is necessary for the authority to determine the special educational provision[6] for which any learning difficulty[7] each child may have calls[8].

1 As to the meaning of 'local authority' see PARA 25.
2 As to the general duties and functions of local authorities in relation to education see PARA 25 et seq.
3 As to the meaning of 'child' see PARA 989 note 1.
4 As to the children for whom the local authority is responsible see PARA 990.
5 See the Education Act 1996 s 321(1), (2)(a) (s 321(1) amended by SI 2010/1158). As to the meaning of 'special educational needs' see PARA 989. As to the effect of the Children and Families Act 2014 see generally PARA 941. See also the Education Act 1996 s 331A; and PARA 941. See also the Education Act 1996 s 331A; and PARA 941.
6 As to the meaning of 'special educational provision' see PARA 989.
7 As to the meaning of 'learning difficulty' see PARA 989.
8 See the Education Act 1996 s 321(1), (2)(b) (s 321(1) amended by SI 2010/1158). As to the liability of local authorities in failing to diagnose learning difficulties see PARA 1039.

992. Duties of health service bodies to notify parent of special educational needs. Where a clinical commissioning group[1], a local health board[2], a National Health Service trust[3] or an NHS foundation trust[4], in the course of exercising any of its functions[5] in relation to a child[6] who is under compulsory school age[7], forms the opinion that he has (or probably has) special educational needs[8], the board or other body must:

(1) inform the child's parent[9] of its opinion and of its duty under head (2) below[10]; and

(2) after giving the parent an opportunity to discuss that opinion with an officer of the board or other body, bring it to the attention of the appropriate local authority[11].

If the board or other body is of the opinion that a particular voluntary organisation is likely to be able to give the parent advice or assistance in connection with any special educational needs that the child may have, it must inform the parent accordingly[12].

1 As to clinical commissioning groups see HEALTH SERVICES.

2   As to local health boards see HEALTH SERVICES vol 54 (2008) PARA 74.
3   As to NHS trusts see HEALTH SERVICES vol 54 (2008) PARA 155 et seq.
4   As to NHS Foundation trusts see HEALTH SERVICES vol 54 (2008) PARA 174 et seq.
5   As to the meaning of 'functions' see PARA 18 note 5.
6   As to the meaning of 'child' see PARA 989 note 1.
7   As to the meaning of 'compulsory school age' see PARA 19.
8   Education Act 1996 s 332(1) (amended by the Education Act 1997 s 57(1), Sch 7 para 24; SI 2000/90; the Health and Social Care (Community Health and Standards) Act 2003 s 34, Sch 4 paras 104, 105; SI 2007/961; and the Health and Social Care Act 2012 Sch 5 paras 77, 79(1), (2)). As to the meaning of 'special educational needs' see PARA 989. As to the effect of the Children and Families Act 2014 see generally PARA 941. See also the Education Act 1996 s 331A; and PARA 941.
9   As to the meaning of 'parent' see PARA 7 note 6.
10 Education Act 1996 s 332(2)(a) (s 332(2) amended by the Health and Social Care Act 2012 Sch 7 paras 77, 79(1), (3)).
11 Education Act 1996 s 332(2)(b) (amended by SI 2007/961; SI 2010/1158; and the Health and Social Care Act 2012 Sch 5 paras 77, 79(1), (3)). As to the meaning of 'local authority' see PARA 25.
12 Education Act 1996 s 332(3) (amended by SI 2007/961).

993.   Children subject to detention. No provision of, or made under, the Part of the Education Act 1996 relating to special educational needs[1] applies in relation to a child[2] who is subject to a detention order[3] and detained in relevant youth accommodation[4].

Where a child who has been subject to a detention order is released having, immediately before release, been detained in relevant youth accommodation[5], a statement which was maintained for the child by a local authority[6] immediately before the beginning of the detention[7] is, from the child's release, to be treated as being maintained[8] by that authority[9]. However, where, on the child's release, a local authority ('the new authority') other than the authority mentioned above ('the old authority') becomes responsible[10] for the child[11], the old authority must transfer the statement to the new authority[12], and from the child's release, the statement is to be treated as being maintained[13] by the new authority[14].

1   Ie the Education Act 1996 Pt IV (ss 311A–349). As to the meaning of 'special educational needs' see PARA 989.
2   As to the meaning of 'child' see PARA 989 note 1.
3   As to when a person is subject to a detention order see PARA 46 note 8.
4   Education Act 1996 s 312A(1) (s 312A added by the Apprenticeships, Skills, Children and Learning Act 2009 s 52(1), (2)). As to the meaning of 'relevant youth accommodation' see PARA 46 note 9. As to the effect of the Children and Families Act 2014 see generally PARA 941. See also the Education Act 1996 s 331A; and PARA 941.
5   Education Act 1996 s 312A(2) (as added: see note 4).
6   Ie under the Education Act 1996 s 324: see PARA 1002. As to the meaning of 'local authority' see PARA 25.
7   'The beginning of the detention' means: (1) the beginning of the period of detention in relevant youth accommodation (Education Act 1996 s 312A(4)(a) (as added: see note 4)); or (2) where that period is part of a continuous period, comprising periods of detention in relevant youth accommodation and in other accommodation, the beginning of that continuous period (s 312A(4)(b) (as so added)). For these purposes, it is immaterial whether or not a period of detention is pursuant to a single order: s 312A(5) (as so added).
8   Ie under the Education Act 1996 s 324: see PARA 1002.
9   Education Act 1996 s 312A(3) (as added (see note 4); and amended by SI 2010/1158). This provision is expressed to be subject to s 312A(6) (see the text to notes 10–14): see s 312A(3) (as so added).
10 Ie for the purposes of the Education Act 1996 Pt IV (ss 311A–349).
11 Education Act 1996 s 312A(6) (as added (see note 4); and amended by SI 2010/1158).
12 Education Act 1996 s 312A(6)(a) (as added: see note 4).
13 Ie under the Education Act 1996 s 324: see PARA 1002.
14 Education Act 1996 s 312A(6)(b) (as added: see note 4).

(ii) Assessment of Special Educational Needs

994. Assessment of educational needs. Where a local authority[1] is of the opinion that a child[2] for whom it is responsible[3] is, or probably is: (1) a child who has special educational needs[4]; and (2) a child in relation to whom it is necessary for the authority to determine the special educational provision[5] for which any learning difficulty[6] he may have calls[7], the authority must serve a notice[8] on the child's parent[9] informing him[10]:

(a) that it is considering whether to make an assessment of the child's educational needs[11];

(b) of the procedure to be followed in making the assessment[12];

(c) of the name of the officer of the authority from whom further information may be obtained[13]; and

(d) of the parent's right to make representations, and submit written[14] evidence, to the authority within such period as may be specified in the notice[15].

Where a local authority has served such a notice and the period specified in the notice has expired[16], and the authority remains of the opinion, after taking into account any representations made and any evidence submitted to it in response to the notice, that the child falls, or probably falls, within heads (1) and (2) above[17], it must make an assessment of his educational needs[18]. Where an authority decides to make such an assessment, it must give notice in writing to the child's parent of that decision and of its reasons for making it[19].

Where, at any time after serving such a notice, an authority decides not to assess the educational needs of the child concerned it must give notice in writing to the child's parent of its decision[20].

Regulations[21] make provision as to the manner in which assessments are to be conducted[22] and in connection with such other matters relating to the making of assessments as the Welsh Ministers[23] consider appropriate[24].

1 As to the meaning of 'local authority' see PARA 25.

2 As to the meaning of 'child' see PARA 989 note 1.

3 As to the children for whom the local authority is responsible see PARA 990.

4 See the Education Act 1996 s 323(2)(a). As to the meaning of 'special educational needs' see PARA 989. As to the effect of the Children and Families Act 2014 see generally PARA 941. See also the Education Act 1996 s 331A; and PARA 941.

5 As to the meaning of 'special educational provision' see PARA 989.

6 As to the meaning of 'learning difficulty' see PARA 989.

7 See the Education Act 1996 s 323(2)(b).

8 Regulations may provide that where a local authority is under a duty under the Education Act 1996 s 323 to serve any notice, the duty must be performed within the prescribed period (see Sch 26 para 3(3)(a) (Sch 26 para 3(3), (4) substituted by the Special Educational Needs and Disability Act 2001 s 42(1), Sch 8 Pt I para 14(1), (3); and amended by SI 2010/1158)), and that, where an authority has served a notice under the Education Act 1996 s 323(1) on a child's parent, it must decide within the prescribed period whether or not to make an assessment of the child's educational needs (Sch 26 para 3(3)(b) (as so substituted and amended)). Provision made under Sch 26 para 3(3) may be subject to prescribed exceptions, and does not relieve the authority of the duty to serve a notice, or make a decision or assessment, which has not been served or made within the prescribed period: Sch 26 para 3(4) (as so substituted and amended). 'Prescribed' means prescribed by regulations; and 'regulations' means regulations made by the Secretary of State or, in relation to Wales, the Welsh Ministers: see s 579(1) but see also PARA 941. As to the Secretary of State see PARA 58. As to the Welsh Ministers see PARA 59. As to the meaning of 'Wales' see PARA 7 note 3. The functions of the Secretary of State under Sch 26, so far as exercisable in relation to Wales, were originally transferred to the National Assembly for Wales (see the National Assembly for Wales (Transfer of Functions) Order 1999, SI 1999/672, art 2, Sch 1) and are now vested in the Welsh Ministers (see the Government of Wales Act 2006

s 162(1), Sch 11 para 30); but see also PARA 941. Provision for the service of notices in relation to Wales is made by the Education (Special Educational Needs) (Wales) Regulations 2002, SI 2002/152, regs 4–5.

9 As to the meaning of 'parent' see PARA 7 note 6.

10 Education Act 1996 s 323(1) (amended by SI 2010/1158). Where an authority serves notice on a child's parent that it is considering whether to make an assessment, provision for the content and service of that notice, and for the service of further notifications concerning the assessment, is made in relation to Wales by the Education (Special Educational Needs) (Wales) Regulations 2002, SI 2002/152, regs 6(1)–(3), 12(1)–(5) (reg 6(2) amended by SI 2010/1142).

11 Education Act 1996 s 323(1)(a) (amended by the Special Educational Needs and Disability Act 2001 s 42(1), Sch 8 para 11(1)).

12 Education Act 1996 s 323(1)(b).

13 Education Act 1996 s 323(1)(c).

14 As to the meaning of 'written' see PARA 76 note 8.

15 Education Act 1996 s 323(1)(d). The period must not be less than 29 days beginning with the date on which the notice is served: s 323(1)(d). When making an assessment of special educational needs an authority is required to take into consideration any representations made by, and any evidence submitted by or at the request of, the child's parent under s 323(1)(d): see in relation to Wales the Education (Special Educational Needs) (Wales) Regulations 2002, SI 2002/152, reg 11(a), (b).

16 Education Act 1996 s 323(3)(a) (amended by SI 2010/1158).

17 Education Act 1996 s 323(3)(b).

18 Education Act 1996 s 323(3). Regulations may provide that where a local authority is under a duty to make an assessment, the duty must be performed within the prescribed period: Sch 26 para 3(3)(d) (as substituted and amended: see note 8). Provision made under Sch 26 para 3(3) may be subject to prescribed exceptions, and does not relieve the authority of the duty to serve a notice, or make a decision or assessment, which has not been served or made within the prescribed period: Sch 26 para 3(4) (as so substituted). When making an assessment, an authority must take into consideration any representations made by the child's parent under s 323(1)(d) (see head (d) in the text) or s 329A(3)(d) (see PARA 1001), any evidence submitted by or at the request of the child's parent under either of those provisions, and the advice obtained, in relation to Wales, under the Education (Special Educational Needs) (Wales) Regulations 2002, SI 2002/152, reg 7 (see PARA 995): see the Education (Special Educational Needs) (Wales) Regulations 2002, SI 2002/152, reg 11(a)–(c). As to the documents which must be served in relation to Wales where an authority has made an assessment of the educational needs of a child see the Education (Special Educational Needs) (Wales) Regulations 2002, SI 2002/152, reg 17(1).

    If a local authority forms the opinion that at the time in question it is not necessary to determine the child's special educational needs because progress appears to be made by remedial measures privately paid for, that is not a failure on the authority's part to perform its statutory duties; rather, it is the performance of those duties in a particular way; the initiation of an assessment is only required where and when the authority is of the opinion that the child falls within the Education Act 1996 s 323(3), including being of the opinion that it is necessary for it to determine special educational provision required in the child's case. The fact that the authority is not of that opinion is not a failure to perform its duty: *C v Lambeth London Borough Council and the Special Educational Needs Tribunal* [1999] ELR 350 at 355 per Keene J. See also *H v Kent County Council and the Special Educational Needs Tribunal* [2000] ELR 660 at 672 (a failure to carry out an assessment does not amount to a breach of the right to education under the Convention for the Protection of Human Rights and Fundamental Freedoms (Rome, 4 November 1950; TS 71 (1953) Cmd 8969), First Protocol (Paris, 20 March 1952; TS 46 (1954); Cmd 9221) art 2 (see PARA 3)); Application 57325/00 *DH v Czech Republic* (2007) 47 EHRR 59, [2008] ELR 17, 23 BHRC 526, ECtHR (claim in respect of discrimination on grounds of racial origin in applying national rules as to assessment of special educational needs).

19 Education Act 1996 s 323(4) (amended by SI 2010/1158). Provision for the content and service of notices under the Education Act 1996 s 323(4), and for the time limit within which the assessment must be completed, is made in relation to Wales by the Education (Special Educational Needs) (Wales) Regulations 2002, SI 2002/152, regs 4, 6(1)–(3), 12(6)–(10) (amended by SI 2010/1142).

20 Education Act 1996 s 323(6) (amended by SI 2010/1158). The time limits within which such a decision must be notified to the child's parents are prescribed in relation to Wales by the Education (Special Educational Needs) (Wales) Regulations 2002, SI 2002/152, reg 12(1), (5)–(7) (amended by SI 2010/1142).

21 In relation to Wales see the Education (Special Educational Needs) (Wales) Regulations 2002, SI 2002/152, Pt II (regs 6–13).
22 Education Act 1996 Sch 26 para 3(1)(a).
23 See note 8.
24 Education Act 1996 Sch 26 para 3(1)(c).

995. Advice in connection with the making of assessments. Regulations[1] must make provision as to the advice which a local authority[2] is to seek in making assessments[3] and must require the authority, except in such circumstances as may be prescribed[4], to seek medical, psychological and educational advice and such other advice as may be prescribed[5].

1 'Regulations' means regulations made by the Secretary of State or, in relation to Wales, the Welsh Ministers: see the Education Act 1996 s 579(1) but see also PARA 941. As to the Secretary of State see PARA 58. As to the Welsh Ministers see PARA 59. As to the meaning of 'Wales' see PARA 7 note 3. The functions of the Secretary of State under the Education Act 1996 Sch 26, so far as exercisable in relation to Wales, were originally transferred to the National Assembly for Wales (see the National Assembly for Wales (Transfer of Functions) Order 1999, SI 1999/672, art 2, Sch 1) and are now vested in the Welsh Ministers (see the Government of Wales Act 2006 s 162(1), Sch 11 para 30).
2 As to the meaning of 'local authority' see PARA 25.
3 Education Act 1996 Sch 26 para 2(1) (amended by SI 2010/1158). 'Assessment' means an assessment of a child's educational needs under s 323 (see PARA 994): Sch 26 para 1. As to the meaning of 'child' see PARA 989 note 1. As to the effect of the Children and Families Act 2014 see generally PARA 941. See also the Education Act 1996 s 331A; and PARA 941.
4 'Prescribed' means prescribed by regulations: Education Act 1996 s 579(1).
5 Education Act 1996 Sch 26 para 2(2). As to advice from the child's parent in relation to Wales see the Education (Special Educational Needs) (Wales) Regulations 2002, SI 2002/152, reg 7(1)(a). As to educational advice from the child's head teacher or other person responsible for his educational provision in Wales see regs 7(1)(b), 8. As to medical advice from the health authority, which must obtain the advice from a fully registered medical practitioner, in relation to Wales see regs 7(1)(c), 9 (reg 9 amended by SI 2002/3135). As to psychological advice from an educational psychologist in Wales see the Education (Special Educational Needs) (Wales) Regulations 2002, SI 2002/152, regs 7(1)(d), 10. As to advice from a social worker in Wales see reg 7(1)(e) (substituted by SI 2010/1142). As to any other advice which the local authority considers appropriate for the purpose of arriving at a satisfactory assessment in relation to Wales see the Education (Special Educational Needs) (Wales) Regulations 2002, SI 2002/152, reg 7(1)(f). 'Any other advice' under reg 7(1)(f) may include further medical advice which allows an authority to plug gaps in advice already given under regs 7(1)(c), 9: *R v Comr for Local Administration, ex p S* [1999] ELR 102.
    Provision is also made as to the nature and source of the advice required to be sought and the circumstances in which it is required to be sought: in relation to Wales see the Education (Special Educational Needs) (Wales) Regulations 2002, SI 2002/152, reg 7(2)–(5).

996. Attendance for examination. Where a local authority[1] is considering whether to make an assessment[2], it may serve a notice[3] on the parent[4] of the child[5] concerned requiring the child's attendance for examination in accordance with the provisions of the notice[6]. Such a notice must:

(1)   state the purpose of the examination[7];
(2)   state the time and place at which the examination will be held[8];
(3)   name an officer of the authority from whom further information may be obtained[9];
(4)   inform the parent that he may submit such information to the authority as he may wish[10]; and
(5)   inform the parent of his right[11] to be present at the examination[12].

1 As to the meaning of 'local authority' see PARA 25.
2 As to the meaning of 'assessment' see PARA 995 note 3.
3 Provision for the service of notices is made in relation to Wales by the Education (Special Educational Needs) (Wales) Regulations 2002, SI 2002/152, regs 4–5.

4   As to the meaning of 'parent' see PARA 7 note 6.
5   As to the meaning of 'child' see PARA 989 note 1.
6   Education Act 1996 Sch 26 para 4(1) (amended by the Special Educational Needs and Disability Act 2001 s 42(1), Sch 8 Pt I para 11(2); and SI 2010/1158). Any parent who fails without reasonable excuse to comply with any requirements of a notice served on him under the Education Act 1996 Sch 26 para 4 commits an offence if the notice relates to a child who is not over compulsory school age at the time stated in it as the time for holding the examination: Sch 26 para 5(1). As to the meaning of 'compulsory school age' see PARA 19. A person guilty of such an offence is liable on summary conviction to a fine not exceeding level 2 on the standard scale: Sch 26 para 5(2). As to the standard scale see SENTENCING AND DISPOSITION OF OFFENDERS vol 92 (2010) PARA 142. As to the effect of the Children and Families Act 2014 see generally PARA 941. See also the Education Act 1996 s 331A; and PARA 941.
7   Education Act 1996 Sch 26 para 4(3)(a).
8   Education Act 1996 Sch 26 para 4(3)(b).
9   Education Act 1996 Sch 26 para 4(3)(c).
10 Education Act 1996 Sch 26 para 4(3)(d).
11 The parent of a child examined under the Education Act 1996 Sch 26 para 4 has the right to be present at the examination if he so desires: Sch 26 para 4(2).
12 Education Act 1996 Sch 26 para 4(3)(e).

997.   Assessment of educational needs of children under two.   Where a local authority[1] is of the opinion that a child[2] in its area who is under the age of two[3] is, or probably is:

(1)   a child who has special educational needs[4]; and

(2)   a child in relation to whom it is necessary for the authority to determine the special educational provision[5] for which any learning difficulty[6] he may have calls[7],

the authority may, with the consent of the child's parent[8], make an assessment of the child's educational needs[9], and must make such an assessment if requested to do so by the parent[10].

After making such an assessment, the authority may, in such manner as it considers appropriate, make a statement of the child's special educational needs[11], and may maintain that statement[12].

1   As to the meaning of 'local authority' see PARA 25.
2   As to the meaning of 'child' see PARA 989 note 1.
3   As to the time at which a person attains a particular age see PARA 7 note 6.
4   Education Act 1996 s 331(1), (2)(a) (s 331(1) amended by SI 2010/1158). As to the meaning of 'special educational needs' see PARA 989. As to the effect of the Children and Families Act 2014 see generally PARA 941. See also the Education Act 1996 s 331A; and PARA 941.
5   As to the meaning of 'special educational provision' see PARA 989.
6   As to the meaning of 'learning difficulty' see PARA 989.
7   Education Act 1996 s 331(1), (2)(b) (s 331(1) as amended: see note 4).
8   As to the meaning of 'parent' see PARA 7 note 6.
9   Education Act 1996 s 331(1)(a). An assessment must be made in such manner as the authority considers appropriate: s 331(3). However, when making an assessment, an authority must take into consideration any representations made by the child's parent under s 323(1)(d) (see PARA 994) or s 329A(3)(d) (see PARA 1001), any evidence submitted by or at the request of the child's parent under either of those provisions, and the advice obtained, in relation to Wales, under the Education (Special Educational Needs) (Wales) Regulations 2002, SI 2002/152, reg 7 (see PARA 995): see the reg 11(a)–(c).
10 Education Act 1996 s 331(4)(b).
11 Education Act 1996 s 331(4)(a). As to statements of special educational needs see PARA 1002 et seq.
12 Education Act 1996 s 331(4)(b).

998.   Assessment of persons above compulsory school age.   The Welsh Ministers[1] may at any time arrange for an assessment[2] to be conducted of a person[3]: (1) who is in his last year of compulsory schooling or who is over compulsory school age[4] but has not attained the age of 25[5]; (2) who appears to the Welsh Ministers to have a learning difficulty[6]; and (3) who is receiving, or in the opinion of the Welsh Ministers is likely to receive, post-16 education or training[7] or higher education[8].

If a local authority in Wales[9] maintains a statement of special educational needs[10] for a person[11], and the Welsh Ministers believe that the person will leave school at the end of his last year of compulsory schooling to receive post-16 education or training or higher education[12], the Welsh Ministers must arrange for an assessment of the person to be conducted at some time during the person's last year of compulsory schooling[13].

A local authority in Wales must send a copy of a statement of a person's special educational needs[14] to the Welsh Ministers on their request[15].

1   As to the Welsh Ministers see PARA 59.
2   An assessment of a person is an assessment resulting in a written report of:
     (1)   his educational and training needs (Learning and Skills Act 2000 s 140(4)(a)); and
     (2)   the provision required to meet them (s 140(4)(b)).
     As to the meaning of 'written' see PARA 76 note 8. Section 140(4) requires the following: (a) an assessment of (i) the subject's educational and training needs; and (ii) of the provision required to meet them; (b) a written report of that assessment. The assessment should not be merely a set of recommendations as to what would in theory, or ideally, be required, but should identify what can actually (and realistically) be provided. The report is the result of the assessment and must reasonably reflect in sufficiently clear and intelligible form the conclusions of the assessment: *R (on the application of A) v Bromley Borough Council* [2008] EWHC 2449 (Admin), [2008] All ER (D) 86 (Sep). See also *R (on the application of P (a child) by his mother and litigation friend KP) v Royal Borough of Windsor and Maidenhead* [2010] EWHC 1408 (Admin), [2010] ELR 837, [2010] All ER (D) 179 (Jun).
     For the purposes of the Education Act 1996 a person is subject to learning difficulty assessment if (A) an assessment under the Learning and Skills Act 2000 s 140 (learning difficulty assessments: Wales) has been conducted in respect of the person; or (B) arrangements for such an assessment to be conducted in respect of the person have been made or are required to be made: Education Act 1996 s 579(1A) (added by the Children and Families Act 2014 Sch 3 paras 1, 59(c)).
3   Learning and Skills Act 2000 s 140(3) (amended by the Education and Skills Act 2008 s 169, Sch 1 Pt 2 paras 75, 77(c)).
4   As to the meaning of 'compulsory school age' see PARA 19.
5   Learning and Skills Act 2000 s 140(3)(a). As to the time at which a person attains a particular age see PARA 7 note 6.
6   Learning and Skills Act 2000 s 140(3)(b) (amended by the Education and Skills Act 2008 s 169, Sch 1 Pt 2 paras 75, 77(d)). As to the meaning of 'learning difficulty' see PARA 791 note 6 (definition applied by the Learning and Skills Act 2000 s 140(3)(b) (as so amended)).
7   Ie post-16 education or training within the meaning of the Learning and Skills Act 2000 Pt II (ss 31–41): see s 32(6)–(7); and PARA 790 note 2.
8   Learning and Skills Act 2000 s 140(3)(c) (amended by the Education and Skills Act 2008 s 169, Sch 1 Pt 2 paras 75, 77(e)). As to the meaning of 'higher education' see PARA 24 (definition applied by the Learning and Skills Act 2000 s 140(3)(c) (as so amended)).
9   'Local authority in Wales' has the same meaning as in the Education Act 1996 (see PARA 25): Learning and Skills Act 2000 s 140(5A) (added by SI 2010/1158). As to the meaning of 'Wales' see PARA 7 note 3.
10   Ie a statement maintained under the Education Act 1996 s 324: see PARA 1002.
11   Learning and Skills Act 2000 s 140(1)(a) (amended by the Education and Skills Act 2008 s 169, Sch 1 Pt 2 paras 75, 77(a); and SI 2010/1158).
12   Learning and Skills Act 2000 s 140(1)(b) (amended by the Education and Skills Act 2008 s 169, Sch 1 Pt 2 paras 75, 77(b)).
13   Learning and Skills Act 2000 s 140(2) (amended by the Education and Skills Act 2008 s 169, Sch 1 Pt 2 paras 75, 77(c)).
14   Ie a statement maintained under the Education Act 1996 s 324: see PARA 1002.
15   Learning and Skills Act 2000 s 140(5) (amended by the Education and Skills Act 2008 s 169, Sch 1 Pt 2 paras 75, 77(f); and SI 2010/1158).

999. Assessment of educational needs at request of child's parent. Where:

(1) the parent[1] of a child[2] for whom a local authority[3] is responsible[4] but for whom no statement of special educational needs[5] is maintained[6] asks the authority to arrange for an assessment of special educational needs to be made[7] in respect of the child[8];

(2) no such assessment has been made within the period of six months[9] ending with the date on which the request is made[10]; and

(3) it is necessary for the authority to make such an assessment[11], the authority must comply with the request[12].

If in any case where heads (1) and (2) above apply the authority determines not to comply with the request, it must give notice in writing[13] of that fact to the child's parent[14] and the parent may appeal against the determination to the Tribunal[15]. The Tribunal may either dismiss the appeal[16] or order the authority to arrange for an assessment to be made in respect of the child[17]. If the Tribunal makes an order, the local authority concerned must comply with the order before the end of the prescribed period beginning with the date on which it is made[18]. If the parent of a child, or a child, has appealed to the Tribunal against a decision of the authority[19], and the authority notifies the Tribunal that it has determined that it will not, or will no longer, oppose the appeal[20], the appeal is to be treated as having been determined in favour of the appellant[21]. In such a case the Tribunal is not required to make any order[22] and the authority must make an assessment of the child's educational needs before the end of the prescribed period[23].

1 As to the meaning of 'parent' see PARA 7 note 6.
2 As to the meaning of 'child' see PARA 989 note 1.
3 As to the meaning of 'local authority' see PARA 25.
4 As to the children for whom a local authority is responsible see PARA 990.
5 As to the meaning of 'special educational needs' see PARA 989.
6 Ie under the Education Act 1996 s 324: see PARA 1002.
7 Ie under the Education Act 1996 s 323: see PARA 994.
8 Education Act 1996 s 329(1)(a) (amended by SI 2010/1158). As to the effect of the Children and Families Act 2014 see generally PARA 941. See also the Education Act 1996 s 331A; and PARA 941.
9 As to the meaning of 'month' see PARA 54 note 26.
10 Education Act 1996 s 329(1)(b).
11 Education Act 1996 s 329(1)(c).
12 Education Act 1996 s 329(1). Regulations may provide that where a request has been made to a local authority under s 329(1), it must decide within the prescribed period whether or not to comply with the request: Sch 26 para 3(3)(c) (Sch 26 para 3(3), (4) substituted by the Special Educational Needs and Disability Act 2001 s 42(1), Sch 8 Pt I para 14(1), (3); and the Education Act 1996 Sch 26 para 3(3)(c) amended by SI 2010/1158). Provision made under the Education Act 1996 Sch 26 para 3(3) may be subject to prescribed exceptions, and does not relieve the authority of the duty to serve a notice, or make a decision or assessment, which has not been served or made within the prescribed period: Sch 26 para 3(4) (as so substituted). 'Prescribed' means prescribed by regulations; and 'regulations' means regulations made by the Secretary of State or, in relation to Wales, the Welsh Ministers: see s 579(1) but see PARA 941. As to the Secretary of State see PARA 58. As to the Welsh Ministers see PARA 59. As to the meaning of 'Wales' see PARA 7 note 3. The functions of the Secretary of State under the Education Act 1996 Sch 26, so far as exercisable in relation to Wales, were originally transferred to the National Assembly for Wales (see the National Assembly for Wales (Transfer of Functions) Order 1999, SI 1999/672, art 2, Sch 1) and are now vested in the Welsh Ministers (see the Government of Wales Act 2006 s 162(1), Sch 11 para 30).

    As to the provision made in relation to Wales see the Education (Special Educational Needs) (Wales) Regulations 2002, SI 2002/152, regs 4, 6(4), 12(2), (5) (reg 6(4) amended by SI 2010/1142). See also *H v Kent County Council and the Special Educational Needs Tribunal* [2000] ELR 660 at 672 per Grigson J (a failure to carry out an assessment requested under the Education Act 1996 s 329 does not amount to a breach of the right to education under the

Convention for the Protection of Human Rights and Fundamental Freedoms (Rome, 4 November 1950; TS 71 (1953); Cmd 8969), First Protocol (Paris, 20 March 1952; TS 46 (1954); Cmd 9221) art 2 (see PARA 3)).

13 As to the meaning of 'writing' see PARA 76 note 8.

14 Education Act 1996 s 329(2)(a) (amended by the Special Educational Needs and Disability Act 2001 s 42(1), Sch 8 paras 1, 8(1)). A notice under the Education Act 1996 s 329(2)(a) must inform the parent of the right of appeal under s 329(2)(b) (see the text to note 15) and must contain such other information as may be prescribed: s 329(2A) (added by the Special Educational Needs and Disability Act 2001 Sch 8 paras 1, 8(2)). Regulations may provide that where a local authority is under a duty under the Education Act 1996 s 329 to serve a notice, the duty must be performed within the prescribed period: Sch 26 para 3(3)(a) (as substituted: see note 12). Provision made under Sch 26 para 3(3) may be subject to prescribed exceptions, and does not relieve the authority of the duty to serve a notice, or make a decision or assessment, which has not been served or made within the prescribed period: Sch 26 para 3(4) (as so substituted). As to the service of notices under s 329(2) see in relation to Wales the Education (Special Educational Needs) (Wales) Regulations 2002, SI 2002/152, regs 4, 12(2), (5), 17(2), (9).

If a local authority is required to give notice to or serve a document on a parent of a child under the Education Act 1996 s 329 or Sch 26 para 3 the local authority must give notice to, or serve the document on, the child as well as on the parent: s 332ZB(1)(c), (e), (2) (s 332ZB added by the Education (Wales) Measure 2009 s 2 (amended by SI 2010/1148); and the Education Act 1996 s 332ZB(1) amended by the Children and Families Act 2014 Sch 3 paras 1, 22). Any provision applicable to notices given to or documents served on a parent applies equally to notices given to or documents served on a child: Education Act 1996 s 332ZB(3) (as so added).

15 Education Act 1996 s 329(2)(b). As to the role of parallel judicial review proceedings in such cases see *R v Worcestershire County Council, ex p S* [1999] ELR 46. 'The Tribunal', in relation to an appeal, means the Special Educational Needs Tribunal for Wales: see s 313(5) (substituted by the Education Act 2002 s 195, Sch 18 paras 1, 2; and amended by SI 2008/2833; and the Children and Families Act 2014 Sch 3 paras 1, 12(1), (3)). As to the Special Educational Needs Tribunal for Wales see PARA 1034.

The rights of a parent of a child to appeal to the Tribunal under the Education Act 1996 s 329(2)(b) may be exercised by the child: see s 332ZA(1)(d), (2) (s 332ZA added by the Education (Wales) Measure 2009 s 1; and the Education Act 1996 s 332ZA(1) amended by the Children and Families Act 2014 Sch 3 paras 1, 21). The child's rights are exercisable concurrently with the parent's rights: Education Act 1996 s 332ZA(3) (as so added). The exercise of such rights is subject to provision made by regulations under s 332ZC (see PARA 1030) and s 336(1) (see PARA 1035): s 332ZA(4) (as so added).

16 Education Act 1996 s 329(3)(a). As to appeals from Tribunal decisions see PARA 1036.

17 Education Act 1996 s 329(3)(b).

18 Education Act 1996 s 336A(1) (s 336A added by the Special Educational Needs and Disability Act 2001 s 4; and the Education Act 1996 s 336A(1) amended by SI 2010/1158)). For these purposes, 'prescribed' means prescribed by regulations made by the Welsh Ministers with the agreement of the Secretary of State: Education Act 1996 s 336A(2) (s 336A as so added; s 336A(2) substituted by the Education Act 2002 s 195, Sch 18 paras 1, 6; and amended by the Children and Families Act 2014 Sch 3 paras 1, 35). Provision governing compliance with orders of the Tribunal is made in relation to Wales by the Special Educational Needs Tribunal for Wales Regulations 2012, SI 2012/322. For an attempt to compel compliance with an order via mandatory order see *R v Brent London Borough Council and Vassie (Chairman of the Special Educational Needs Tribunal), ex p AF* [2000] ELR 550.

19 See the Education Act 1996 s 326A(1)(a) (s 326A added by the Special Educational Needs and Disability Act 2001 s 5; and the Education Act 1996 s 326A(1)(a) substituted by the Children and Families Act 2014 Sch 3 paras 1, 18(1), (2)). Such appeal is under the Education Act 1996 s 325 (see PARA 1009), s 328 or s 329A (see PARA 1009) or Sch 27 para 8(3) (see PARA 1013): see s 326A(1)(a) (as added and amended).

20 Education Act 1996 s 326A(1)(b) (as added: see note 19).

21 Education Act 1996 s 326A(2) (as added: see note 19).

22 See the Education Act 1996 s 326A(3) (as added: see note 19).

23 See the Education Act 1996 s 326A(4)(b) (as added: see note 19). For these purposes 'prescribed' means prescribed by regulations made by the Welsh Ministers: s 326A(6) (as so added; substituted by the Education Act 2002 s 195, Sch 18 paras 1, 3; and amended by the Children and Families Act 2014 Sch 3 paras 1, 18(1), (3)). As to the provision made see in relation to Wales the Special Educational Needs Tribunal for Wales Regulations 2012, SI 2012/322.

1000. Reviews of educational needs. Regulations[1] may prescribe the frequency with which assessments of educational needs[2] are to be repeated in respect of children[3] for whom statements of special educational needs[4] are maintained[5].

Where:

(1) the parent[6] of a child for whom a statement is maintained asks the local authority[7] to arrange for an assessment to be made in respect of the child[8];

(2) no assessment has been made within the period of six months[9] ending with the date on which the request is made[10]; and

(3) it is necessary for the authority to make a further assessment[11],

the authority must comply with the request[12]. If in any case where heads (1) and (2) above apply, the authority determines not to comply with the request it must give notice in writing[13] of that fact to the child's parent[14] and the parent may appeal against the determination to the Tribunal[15]. The Tribunal may either dismiss the appeal[16] or order the authority to arrange for an assessment to be made in respect of the child[17]. If the Tribunal makes an order, the local authority concerned must comply with the order before the end of the prescribed period beginning with the date on which it is made[18]. If the parent of a child, or a child, has appealed to the Tribunal against a decision of the authority[19], and the authority notifies the Tribunal that it has determined that it will not, or will no longer, oppose the appeal[20], the appeal is to be treated as having been determined in favour of the appellant[21]. In such a case the Tribunal is not required to make any order[22] and the authority must make an assessment of the child's educational needs before the end of the prescribed period[23].

A statement of special educational needs must be reviewed by the local authority[24]:

(a) on the making of an assessment in respect of the child concerned[25];

(b) where the child concerned has been subject to a detention order[26], and immediately before release was detained in relevant youth accommodation[27], on the child's release from detention[28]; and

(c) in any event, within the period of 12 months beginning with the making of the statement or, as the case may be, with the previous review[29].

Regulations may make provision as to the manner in which reviews of such statements are to be conducted[30], as to the participation in such reviews of such persons as may be prescribed[31], and in connection with such other matters relating to such reviews as the Secretary of State or, in relation to Wales, the Welsh Ministers considers appropriate[32].

1   'Regulations' means regulations made by the Secretary of State or, in relation to Wales, the Welsh Ministers: see the Education Act 1996 s 579(1) and see PARA 941. As to the Secretary of State see PARA 58. As to the Welsh Ministers see PARA 59. As to the meaning of 'Wales' see PARA 7 note 3. The functions of the Secretary of State under ss 326A, 328, 336A, so far as exercisable in relation to Wales, were originally transferred to the National Assembly for Wales (see the National Assembly for Wales (Transfer of Functions) Order 1999, SI 1999/672, art 2, Sch 1) and are now vested in the Welsh Ministers (see the Government of Wales Act 2006 s 162(1), Sch 11 para 30).

2   Ie under the Education Act 1996 s 323: see PARA 994.

3   As to the meaning of 'child' see PARA 989 note 1.

4   As to the meaning of 'special educational needs' see PARA 989. As to statements of special educational needs see PARA 1002 et seq.

5   Education Act 1996 s 328(1). As to the effect of the Children and Families Act 2014 see generally PARA 941. See also the Education Act 1996 s 331A; and PARA 941.

     Statements of special educational needs are maintained under s 324: see PARA 1002. Provision as to the frequency with which the educational needs of a child in respect of whom a statement is maintained are reviewed, and as to the procedure for such reviews, is made in relation to Wales by the Education (Special Educational Needs) (Wales) Regulations 2002, SI 2002/152, regs 18, 20–22 (reg 18 amended by SI 2003/1717; and SI 2010/1142; and the Education (Special Educational Needs) (Wales) Regulations 2002, SI 2002/152, regs 21, 22 amended by SI 2010/1142).

6 As to the meaning of 'parent' see PARA 7 note 6.
7 As to the meaning of 'local authority' see PARA 25.
8 Education Act 1996 s 328(2)(a) (amended by SI 2010/1158).
9 As to the meaning of 'month' see PARA 54 note 26.
10 Education Act 1996 s 328(2)(b).
11 Education Act 1996 s 328(2)(c).
12 Education Act 1996 s 328(2). Regulations may make provision requiring the local authority, where, after conducting an assessment under s 323 (see PARA 994) of the educational needs of a child for whom a statement is maintained under s 324 (see PARA 1002), it determines not to amend the statement, to serve on the parent of the child a notice giving the prescribed information: Sch 26 para 3(1)(b) (amended by SI 2010/1158). Regulations may provide that where a local authority is under a duty under regulations under the Education Act 1996 Sch 26 para 3(1)(b), to serve any notice, the duty must be performed within the prescribed period, and that where a local authority is under a duty to make an assessment, the duty must be performed within the prescribed period: Sch 26 para 3(3)(a), (d) (Sch 26 para 3(3) substituted by the Special Educational Needs and Disability Act 2001 s 42(1), Sch 8 Pt 1 paras 1, 14(1), (3); the Education Act 1996 Sch 26 para 3(3)(a) amended by the Education and Inspections Act 2006 s 174(1), (2); and the Education Act 1996 Sch 26 para 3(3)(a), (d) amended by SI 2010/1158). Where a child's parent asks an authority to arrange for an assessment and no assessment has been made for that child within the period of six months ending with the date on which the request is made, provision for the giving of notices by the authority is made in relation to Wales by the Education (Special Educational Needs) (Wales) Regulations 2002, SI 2002/152, regs 4, 6(2), (4), 12(2) (reg 6(2), (4) amended by SI 2010/1142).
13 As to the meaning of 'writing' see PARA 76 note 8. Provision for the service of notices generally is made in relation to Wales by the Education (Special Educational Needs) (Wales) Regulations 2002, SI 2002/152, regs 4–5.
14 Education Act 1996 s 328(3)(a) (amended by the Special Educational Needs and Disability Act 2001 s 42(1), Sch 8 paras 1, 7(1)). A notice under the Education Act 1996 s 328(3)(a) must inform the parent of the right of appeal under s 328(3)(b) (see the text to note 15) and contain such other information as may be prescribed: s 328(3A) (s 328(3A), (3B) added by the Special Educational Needs and Disability Act 2001 Sch 8 paras 1, 7(2)). Regulations may also provide that where a local authority is under a duty under the Education Act 1996 s 328 to serve any notice, the duty must be performed within the prescribed period: s 328(3B) (as so added; and amended by SI 2010/1158).
    If a local authority is required to give notice to or serve a document on a parent of a child under s 328 or Sch 27 para 2A or 2B(2) (see notes 25, 29) the local authority must give notice to, or serve the document on, the child as well as on the parent: s 332ZB(1)(b), (f), (g), (2) (s 332ZB added by the Education (Wales) Measure 2009 s 2 (amended by SI 2010/1148); and the Education Act 1996 s 332ZB(1) amended by the Children and Families Act 2014 Sch 3 paras 1, 22). Any provision applicable to notices given to or documents served on a parent applies equally to notices given to or documents served on a child: Education Act 1996 s 332ZB(3) (as so added).
15 Education Act 1996 s 328(3)(b). As to the meaning of 'the Tribunal' see PARA 999 note 15. The rights of a parent of a child to appeal to the Tribunal under s 328(3)(b) may be exercised by the child: see s 332ZA(1)(c), (2) (s 332ZA added by the Education (Wales) Measure 2009 s 1; and the Education Act 1996 s 332ZA(1) amended by the Children and Families Act 2014 Sch 3 paras 1, 21). The child's rights are exercisable concurrently with the parent's rights: Education Act 1996 s 332ZA(3) (as so added). The exercise of such rights is subject to provision made by regulations under s 332ZC (see PARA 1030) and s 336(1) (see PARA 1035): s 332ZA(4) (as so added).
16 Education Act 1996 s 328(4)(a). As to appeals from Tribunal decisions see PARA 1036.
17 Education Act 1996 s 328(4)(b).
18 Education Act 1996 s 336A(1) (s 336A added by the Special Educational Needs and Disability Act 2001 s 4; and the Education Act 1996 s 336A(1) amended by SI 2010/1158). For these purposes, 'prescribed' means prescribed by regulations made by the Welsh Ministers with the agreement of the Secretary of State: Education Act 1996 s 336A(2) (s 336A as so added; s 336A(2) substituted by the Education Act 2002 s 195, Sch 18 paras 1, 6; and amended by the Children and Families Act 2014 Sch 3 paras 1, 35). Provision governing compliance with orders

of the Tribunal is made in relation to Wales by the Special Educational Needs Tribunal for Wales Regulations 2012, SI 2012/322. For an attempt to compel compliance with an order via mandatory order see *R v Brent London Borough Council and Vassie (Chairman of the Special Educational Needs Tribunal), ex p AF* [2000] ELR 550.

19 See the Education Act 1996 s 326A(1)(a) (s 326A added by the Special Educational Needs and Disability Act 2001 s 5; and the Education Act 1996 s 326A(1)(a) substituted by the Children and Families Act 2014 Sch 3 paras 1, 18(1), (2)).

20 Education Act 1996 s 326A(1)(b) (as added: see note 19).

21 Education Act 1996 s 326A(2) (as added: see note 19).

22 See the Education Act 1996 s 326A(3) (as added: see note 19).

23 See the Education Act 1996 s 326A(4)(b) (as added: see note 19). For these purposes 'prescribed' means prescribed by regulations made by the Welsh Ministers: s 326A(6) (as so added; substituted by the Education Act 2002 s 195, Sch 18 paras 1, 3; and amended by the Children and Families Act 2014 Sch 3 paras 1, 18(1), (3))). As to the provision made in relation to Wales see the Special Educational Needs Tribunal for Wales Regulations 2012, SI 2012/322.

24 Education Act 1996 s 328(5) (amended by SI 2010/1158).

25 Education Act 1996 s 328(5)(a). Such a review is called a 're-assessment review': Sch 27 para 1 (substituted by the Special Educational Needs and Disability Act 2001 s 10, Sch 1 paras 1, 2). If, following such a review, a local authority proposes to amend a statement, it must serve on the parent of the child concerned a copy of the proposed amended statement: Education Act 1996 Sch 27 para 2A(2) (Sch 27 para 2A added by the Special Educational Needs and Disability Act 2001 s 10, Sch 1 paras 1, 3; and the Education Act 1996 Sch 27 para 2A(2) amended by SI 2010/1158). The copy of the proposed amended statement must not specify any prescribed matter nor any matter in pursuance of the Education Act 1996 s 324(4) (see PARA 1002): see Sch 27 paras 2(3), (4), 2A(3) (Sch 27 para 2(3), (4) substituted by the Special Educational Needs and Disability Act 2001 Sch 1 paras 1, 3; and the Education Act 1996 Sch 27 para 2A(3) as so added).

When serving a copy of a proposed amended statement under the Education Act 1996 Sch 27 para 2A, the local authority must also serve on the parent a written notice explaining (to the extent that they are applicable) the arrangements under Sch 27 para 3 for enabling the parent to express a preference as to his choice of school (see PARA 1012), the parent's right to make representations to the authority as to the content of the proposed statement (ie the effect of Sch 27 para 4: see PARA 1011), and the provisions for appealing against the contents of a statement (ie under s 326: see PARA 1010), and containing such other information as may be prescribed: see Sch 27 para 2B(1)(b), (2), (3) (Sch 27 para 2B added by the Special Educational Needs and Disability Act 2001 Sch 1 paras 1, 3; and the Education Act 1996 Sch 27 para 2B(2) amended by SI 2010/1158). The notice which must be served by an authority on a parent pursuant to the Education Act 1996 Sch 27 para 2B(2) to accompany a copy of a proposed statement must contain the prescribed information: see in relation to Wales the Education (Special Educational Needs) (Wales) Regulations 2002, SI 2002/152, reg 14(a), Sch 1 Pt A (amended by SI 2010/1142). The time limits within which notice must be served under the Education Act 1996 Sch 27 paras 2A, 2B(2) are prescribed in relation to Wales by the Education (Special Educational Needs) (Wales) Regulations 2002, SI 2002/152, reg 17(1)–(4), (9). See also note 14.

26 Education Act 1996 s 328(5)(aa)(i) (s 328(5)(aa) (added by the Apprenticeships, Skills, Children and Learning Act 2009 s 52(1), (3)). As to when a person is subject to a detention order see PARA 46 note 8.

27 Education Act 1996 s 328(5)(aa)(ii) (as added: see note 26). As to the meaning of 'relevant youth accommodation' see PARA 46 note 9.

28 Education Act 1996 s 328(5)(aa) (as added: see note 26).

29 Education Act 1996 s 328(5)(b). Such a review is called a 'periodic review': see Sch 27 para 1 (as substituted: see note 25). If, following such a review, a local authority proposes to amend a statement, it must serve on the parent of the child concerned a copy of the existing statement, and an amendment notice: Sch 27 para 2A(4) (as added (see note 25); and amended by SI 2010/1158). An 'amendment notice' is a notice in writing giving details of the amendments to the statement proposed by the authority: Education Act 1996 Sch 27 para 2A(6) (as so added). When serving an amendment notice under Sch 27 para 2A, the authority must also serve on the parent a written notice explaining (to the extent that they are applicable) the arrangements under Sch 27 para 3 for enabling the parent to express a preference as to his choice of school (see PARA 1012), the parent's right to make representations to the authority as to the content of the proposed statement (ie the effect of Sch 27 para 4: see PARA 1011), and the provisions for appealing against the contents of a statement (ie under s 326: see PARA 1010), and containing such other information as may be prescribed: Sch 27 para 2B(1)(c), (2), (3) (as added: see

note 25). As to the time limits within which a statement must be amended following the service of a notice under Sch 27 para 2A(4) see in relation to Wales the Special Educational Needs Tribunal for Wales Regulations 2012, SI 2012/322. See also note 14.

30 Education Act 1996 s 328(6)(a).

31 Education Act 1996 s 328(6)(b). At the request of the local authority, the governing body, head teacher and staff of non-maintained special schools must participate in any review conducted by the authority pursuant to s 328 of a statement under s 324, which relates to any registered pupil at the school, making no charge to the authority for such participation: see in relation to Wales the Education (Special Schools) Regulations 1994, SI 1994/652, reg 5, Schedule para 19(2) (revoked, in relation to England, by SI 1999/2257; and applied in relation to Wales by virtue of the Education Act 1996 s 582(3), Sch 39 para 1; Interpretation Act 1978 s 17(2)(b)). As to the meaning of 'special school' see PARA 1041. Similar provision is made (in relation to England and Wales) in connection with the proprietor, head teacher and professional staff of independent schools: see the Education (Special Educational Needs) (Approval of Independent Schools) Regulations 1994, SI 1994/651, reg 4, Sch 2 para 8(5), (6) (Sch 2 para 8(5) amended by SI 2010/1142; regulations applied by virtue of the Education Act 1996 s 582(3), Sch 39 para 1; Interpretation Act 1978 s 17(2)(b)). As to independent schools see PARA 369 et seq.

32 Education Act 1996 s 328(6)(c).

1001. Review or assessment of educational needs at request of responsible body. If:

(1) a child[1] is a registered pupil[2] at a relevant school[3] (whether or not he is a child in respect of whom a statement of special educational needs[4] is maintained)[5];

(2) the responsible body[6] asks the local authority[7] to arrange for an assessment of educational needs[8] to be made in respect of the child[9]; and

(3) no such assessment has been made within the period of six months[10] ending with the date on which the request is made[11],

then, if it is necessary for the authority to make an assessment or further assessment of educational needs, it must comply with the request[12]. Before deciding whether to comply with the request, the authority must serve on the child's parent a notice[13] informing him:

(a) that it is considering whether to make an assessment of the child's educational needs[14];

(b) of the procedure to be followed in making the assessment[15];

(c) of the name of its officer from whom further information may be obtained[16]; and

(d) of the parent's right to make representations[17], and submit written evidence[18], to the authority before the end of the period specified in the notice[19].

If a local authority decides[20] to make an assessment of educational needs, it must give written notice to the child's parent and to the responsible body which made the request, of the decision and of its reasons for making it[21]. If, however, after serving a notice[22], the authority decides not to assess the educational needs of the child, it must give written notice of the decision and of its reasons for making it to the child's parent and to the responsible body which made the request[23], and the parent may appeal against the decision to the Tribunal[24]. The Tribunal may either dismiss the appeal[25] or order the authority to arrange for an assessment to be made in respect of the child[26]. If the Tribunal makes an order, the local authority concerned must comply with the order before the end of the prescribed period beginning with the date on which it is made[27]. If the parent of a child, or a child, has appealed to the Tribunal against a decision of the authority[28], and the authority notifies the Tribunal that it has determined that it will not, or will no longer, oppose the appeal[29], the appeal is to be treated as having been determined in favour of the appellant[30]. In such a case the Tribunal is not required to make any order[31] and the authority must make an assessment of the child's educational needs before the end of the prescribed period[32].

1 As to the meaning of 'child' see PARA 989 note 1.
2 As to the meaning of 'registered pupil' see PARA 437. The Education Act 1996 s 329A applies to a child for whom relevant early years education (or, in relation to Wales, until a day to be appointed, nursery education) is provided as it applies to a child who is a registered pupil at a relevant school (see note 3): s 329A(11) (s 329A added by the Special Educational Needs and Disability Act 2001 s 8; and the Education Act 1996 s 329A(11) amended by the Childcare Act 2006 s 103(1), Sch 2 para 22(1), (2)). 'Relevant early years education' has the same meaning as it has (in relation to Wales) in s 123 except that it does not include early years education provided by a local authority at a maintained nursery school: Education Act 1996 s 329A(14)(a), (b) (s 329A as so added; s 329A(14) substituted by the Childcare Act 2006 s 103(1), Sch 2 para 22(1), (4), and amended by SI 2010/1158; and the Children and Families Act 2014 Sch 3 paras 1, 20). As to the meaning of 'Wales' see PARA 7 note 3. As to the meaning of 'maintained nursery school' see PARA 99 note 4. As to the meaning of 'pupil' see PARA 20 note 4.
    'Relevant nursery education' has the same meaning as in the School Standards and Framework Act 1998 s 123 (see PARA 1033 note 17), except that it does not include nursery education provided by a local authority at a maintained nursery school: Education Act 1996 s 329A(14) (as so added; and amended by SI 2010/1158).
3 'Relevant school' means a maintained school; a maintained nursery school; a pupil referral unit; an independent school; an alternative provision academy that is not an independent school; and a school approved under the Education Act 1996 s 342 (see PARA 1042): s 329A(12) (as added (see note 2); and amended by the Education Act 2011 Sch 13 paras 9(1), (4)). As to the meaning of 'maintained school' see PARA 989 note 10. As to pupil referral units see PARA 427 et seq. As to the meaning of 'independent school' see PARA 369. As to the meaning of 'alternative provision academy' see PARA 346 note 14.
4 As to the meaning of 'special educational needs' see PARA 989.
5 Education Act 1996 s 329A(1)(a) (as added: see note 2). Statements of special educational needs are maintained under s 324: see PARA 1002. As to the effect of the Children and Families Act 2014 see generally PARA 941. See also the Education Act 1996 s 331A; and PARA 941.
6 'The responsible body' means: (1) in relation to a maintained nursery school or a pupil referral unit, the head teacher; (2) in relation to any other relevant school, the proprietor or head teacher; and (3) in relation to a provider of relevant early years education (or, in relation to Wales, until a day to be appointed, nursery education), the person or body of persons responsible for the management of the provision of that early years or nursery education: Education Act 1996 s 329A(13) (as added (see note 2); and amended by the Education Act 2002 s 215(1), Sch 21 para 44; and the Childcare Act 2006 s 103(1), Sch 2 para 22(1), (3)). As to the meaning of 'head teacher' see PARA 86 note 4. As to the meaning of 'proprietor' see PARA 51 note 4. As to the meaning of 'person' see PARA 7 note 6. At the date at which this volume states the law the amendments made to head (3) above by the Childcare Act 2006 s 103(1), Sch 2 para 22(1), (3) do not apply fully in relation to Wales.
7 As to the meaning of 'local authority' see PARA 25.
8 Ie under the Education Act 1996 s 323: see PARA 994.
9 Education Act 1996 s 329A(1)(b) (as added (see note 2); and amended by SI 2010/1158).
10 As to the meaning of 'month' see PARA 54 note 26.
11 Education Act 1996 s 329A(1)(c) (as added: see note 2).
12 Education Act 1996 s 329A(2) (as added: see note 2). Where a responsible body asks an authority to arrange for an assessment and no assessment has been made for that child within the period of six months ending with the date on which the request is made, provision for the giving of notices by the authority is made in relation to Wales by the Education (Special Educational Needs) (Wales) Regulations 2002, SI 2002/152, regs 4, 6(2), (5)–(6) (reg 6 amended by SI 2010/1142). When making an assessment an authority must take into consideration any representations made by the child's parent under the Education Act 1996 s 323(1)(d) (see PARA 994) or s 329A(3)(d) (see the text to notes 17–19), together with any evidence submitted by or at the request of the child's parent under either of those provisions, and the advice obtained, in relation to Wales, under the Education (Special Educational Needs) (Wales) Regulations 2002, SI 2002/152, reg 7 (see PARA 995): see reg 11(a)–(c).
13 Regulations may provide that where a local authority is under a duty under the Education Act 1996 s 329A to serve any notice, the duty must be performed within the prescribed period (see Sch 26 para 3(3)(a) (Sch 26 para 3(3), (4) substituted by the Special Educational Needs and Disability Act 2001 s 42(1), Sch 8 Pt I para 14(1), (3); and the Education Act 1996 Sch 26

para 3(3)(a), (b) amended by SI 2010/1158)), and that where a local authority has served a notice under the Education Act 1996 329A(3) on a child's parent, it must decide within the prescribed period whether or not to make an assessment of the child's educational needs (Sch 26 para 3(3)(b) (as so substituted and amended)). Provision made under Sch 26 para 3(3) may be subject to prescribed exceptions, and does not relieve the authority of the duty to serve a notice, or make a decision or assessment, which has not been served or made within the prescribed period: Sch 26 para 3(4) (as so substituted). 'Prescribed' means prescribed by regulations made by the Welsh Ministers: see ss 329A(15) (as added (see note 2); and amended by the Children and Families Act 2014 Sch 3 paras 1, 20(1), (3)), and the Education Act 1996 579(1). As to provision for the service of notices in relation to Wales see the Education (Special Educational Needs) (Wales) Regulations 2002, SI 2002/152, regs 4–5. See also note 23.

The functions under the Education Act 1996 ss 326A, 329A, 336A so far as exercisable in relation to Wales, were originally transferred to the National Assembly for Wales (see the National Assembly for Wales (Transfer of Functions) Order 1999, SI 1999/672, art 2, Sch 1) and are now vested in the Welsh Ministers (see the Government of Wales Act 2006 s 162(1), Sch 11 para 30). As to the Welsh Ministers see PARA 59.

14 Education Act 1996 s 329A(3)(a) (as added: see note 2). Where an authority serves on a child's parent notice that it is considering whether to make an assessment, provision for the content and service of that notice is made in relation to Wales by the Education (Special Educational Needs) (Wales) Regulations 2002, SI 2002/152, regs 4, 6(1)–(3), 12(3)–(5) (reg 6 amended by SI 2010/1142).

15 Education Act 1996 s 329A(3)(b) (as added: see note 2).

16 Education Act 1996 s 329A(3)(c) (as added: see note 2).

17 The authority must take into account any representations made, and any evidence submitted, to it in response to the notice: see the Education Act 1996 s 329A(6) (as added: see note 2); and the Education (Special Educational Needs) (Wales) Regulations 2002, SI 2002/152, reg 11(a), (b).

18 As to the meaning of 'written' see PARA 76 note 8. See also note 17.

19 Education Act 1996 s 329A(3)(d) (as added: see note 2). The period specified in the notice must not be less than 29 days beginning with the date on which the notice is served (s 329A(4) (as so added)), and the authority may not decide whether to comply with the request until the specified period has expired (s 329A(5) (as so added)).

20 Ie as a result of the Education Act 1996 s 329A.

21 Education Act 1996 s 329A(7) (as added (see note 2); and amended by SI 2010/1158). Where no notice has been given in relation to a particular assessment and an authority serves notice on a child's parent that it is considering whether to make an assessment, provision for the content and service of that notice, and for the time limit within which the assessment must be completed, is made in relation to Wales by the Education (Special Educational Needs) (Wales) Regulations 2002, SI 2002/152, regs 4, 6(1)–(3), 12(6)–(10) (regs 6, 12 amended by SI 2010/1142).

22 Ie under the Education Act 1996 s 329A(3): see the text to notes 13–19.

23 Education Act 1996 s 329A(8)(a) (as added: see note 2). A notice given under s 329A(8)(a) to the child's parent must inform the parent of his right to appeal, and must contain such other information (if any) as may be prescribed: s 329A(9) (as so added). Provision in this regard is made in relation to Wales by the Education (Special Educational Needs) (Wales) Regulations 2002, SI 2002/152, reg 12(3)–(5).

If a local authority is required to give notice to or serve a document on a parent of a child under the Education Act 1996 s 329A(8) or Sch 26 para 3 (see note 13) the local authority must give notice to, or serve the document on, the child as well as on the parent: s 332ZB(1)(d), (e), (2) (s 332ZB added by the Education (Wales) Measure 2009 s 2 (amended by SI 2010/1148); and the Education Act 1996 s 332ZB(1) amended by the Children and Families Act 2014 Sch 3 paras 1, 22). Any provision applicable to notices given to or documents served on a parent applies equally to notices given to or documents served on a child: Education Act 1996 s 332ZB(3) (as so added).

24 Education Act 1996 s 329A(8)(b) (as added: see note 2). As to the meaning of 'the Tribunal' see PARA 999 note 15. The rights of a parent of a child to appeal to the Tribunal under s 329A(8)(b) may be exercised by the child: see s 332ZA(1)(e), (2) (s 332ZA added by the Education (Wales) Measure 2009 s 1; and the Education Act 1996 s 332ZA(1) amended by the Children and Families Act 2014 Sch 3 paras 1, 21). The child's rights are exercisable concurrently with the parent's rights: Education Act 1996 s 332ZA(3) (as so added). The exercise of such rights is subject to provision made by regulations under s 332ZC (see PARA 1030) and s 336(1) (see PARA 1035): s 332ZA(4) (as so added).

25 Education Act 1996 s 329A(10)(a) (as added: see note 2). As to appeals from Tribunal decisions see PARA 1036.

26 Education Act 1996 s 329A(10)(b) (as added: see note 2).
27 Education Act 1996 s 336A(1) (s 336A added by the Special Educational Needs and Disability
    Act 2001 s 4; and the Education Act 1996 s 336A(1) amended by SI 2010/1158). For these
    purposes, 'prescribed' means prescribed by regulations made by the Welsh Ministers with the
    agreement of the Secretary of State: Education Act 1996 s 336A(2) (s 336A as so added;
    s 336A(2) substituted by the Education Act 2002 s 195, Sch 18 paras 1, 6; and amended by the
    Children and Families Act 2014 Sch 3 paras 1, 35). Provision governing compliance with orders
    of the Tribunal is made in relation to Wales by the Special Educational Needs Tribunal for Wales
    Regulations 2012, SI 2012/322. For an attempt to compel compliance with an order via
    mandatory order see *R v Brent London Borough Council and Vassie (Chairman of the Special
    Educational Needs Tribunal), ex p AF* [2000] ELR 550.
28 See the Education Act 1996 s 326A(1)(a) (s 326A added by the Special Educational Needs and
    Disability Act 2001 s 5; and the Education Act 1996 s 326A(1)(a) substituted by the Children
    and Families Act 2014 Sch 3 paras 1, 18(1), (2)).
29 Education Act 1996 s 326A(1)(b) (as added: see note 28).
30 Education Act 1996 s 326A(2) (as added: see note 28).
31 See the Education Act 1996 s 326A(3) (as added: see note 28).
32 See the Education Act 1996 s 326A(4)(b) (as added: see note 28). For these purposes 'prescribed'
    means prescribed by regulations made by the Welsh Ministers: s 326A(6) (s 326A as so added;
    s 326A(6) substituted by the Education Act 2002 s 195, Sch 18 paras 1, 3; and amended by the
    Children and Families Act 2014 Sch 3 paras 1, 18(1), (3). As to the provision made in relation
    to Wales see the Special Educational Needs Tribunal for Wales Regulations 2012, SI 2012/322.

(iii) Statements of Special Educational Needs

1002. Statement of special educational needs. If, in the light of an assessment[1]
of any child's[2] educational needs and of any representations made by the child's
parent[3], it is necessary for the local authority[4] to determine the special
educational provision[5] for which any learning difficulty[6] he may have calls, the
authority must make and maintain a statement of his special educational needs[7].
The statement must be in such form and contain such information as may be
prescribed[8] and, in particular, must give details of the authority's assessment of
the child's special educational needs[9] and specify the special educational
provision to be made for the purpose of meeting those needs[10]. The statement
must:
(1)   specify the type of school[11] or other institution which the local authority
       considers would be appropriate for the child[12];
(2)   if it is not required[13] to specify the name of any school in the statement,
       specify the name of any school[14] or institution (whether in the United
       Kingdom[15] or elsewhere) which it considers would be appropriate for
       the child and should be specified in the statement[16]; and
(3)   specify any special educational provision otherwise than in schools for
       the child for which it makes arrangements[17] and which it considers
       should be specified in the statement[18].
Where a local authority maintains a statement of a child's special educational
needs, then:
(a)   unless the child's parent has made suitable arrangements[19], the authority
       must arrange that the special educational provision specified in the
       statement is made for the child[20], and may arrange that any
       non-educational provision specified in the statement is made for him in
       such manner as it considers appropriate[21]; and
(b)   if the name of a maintained school or maintained nursery school is
       specified in the statement, the governing body of the school must admit
       the child to the school[22].

1   Ie under the Education Act 1996 s 323: see PARA 994.

2   As to the meaning of 'child' see PARA 989 note 1.
3   Ie in pursuance of the Education Act 1996 Sch 27: see PARA 1011. As to the meaning of 'parent' see PARA 7 note 6.
4   As to the meaning of 'local authority' see PARA 25.
5   As to the meaning of 'special educational provision' see PARA 989.
6   As to the meaning of 'learning difficulty' see PARA 989.
7   Education Act 1996 s 324(1) (amended by SI 2010/1158). As to the meaning of 'special educational needs' see PARA 989. As to the effect of the Children and Families Act 2014 see generally PARA 941. See also the Education Act 1996 s 331A; and PARA 941. A local authority is only required to make and maintain a statement of special educational needs until a person's 19th birthday: *R (on the application of B) v Islington London Borough Council* [2010] EWHC 2539 (Admin), [2010] NLJR 1190, [2011] PTSR 716, [2010] All ER (D) 97 (Aug). The local authority has a wide discretion as to whether a statement is needed (see eg *R v Secretary of State for Education and Science, ex p Lashford* [1988] 1 FLR 72, (1987) 86 LGR 13, CA; *R v Isle of Wight County Council, ex p S* (1992) Times, 2 November, CA) although it must have regard to the code of practice made under the Education Act 1996 s 313 (see PARA 1033). As to the parental right of appeal against the content of a statement see PARA 1010. As to the application of the Education Act 1996 s 324 to new schools, see in relation to Wales the New School (Admissions) (Wales) Regulations 2006, SI 2006/175, regs 3, 9, Schedule paras 1(a), 2, 3.
8   Education Act 1996 s 324(2). 'Prescribed' means prescribed by regulations; and 'regulations' means regulations made by the Secretary of State or, in relation to Wales, the Welsh Ministers: see s 579(1) but see PARA 941. As to the Secretary of State see PARA 58. As to the Welsh Ministers see PARA 59. As to the meaning of 'Wales' see PARA 7 note 3. The functions of the Secretary of State under s 324, Sch 27, so far as exercisable in relation to Wales, were originally transferred to the National Assembly for Wales (see the National Assembly for Wales (Transfer of Functions) Order 1999, SI 1999/672, art 2, Sch 1) and are now vested in the Welsh Ministers (see the Government of Wales Act 2006 s 162(1), Sch 11 para 30).
    A statement of special educational needs must be in a form substantially corresponding to that set out, in relation to Wales, in the Education (Special Educational Needs) (Wales) Regulations 2002, SI 2002/152, Sch 2: see the reg 16(a), Sch 2 (amended by SI 2010/1142). A statement must contain the specified information (see the Education (Special Educational Needs) (Wales) Regulations 2002, SI 2002/152, reg 16(b)), arranged into six parts:
    (1)   Introduction: the name of the local authority making the statement, particulars of the child and the child's parent or person responsible, and details of the advice taken into consideration by the authority in assessing the child's needs (see PARA 995) (Sch 2 Pt 1, Appendices A–G);
    (2)   Special Educational Needs: the special educational needs of the child calling for special educational provision, as assessed by the authority (Sch 2 Pt 2);
    (3)   Special Educational Provision: the objectives which the special educational provision for the child should aim to meet, the educational provision considered appropriate to meet those needs and objectives, and the arrangements to be made for monitoring the proposed educational provision (Sch 2 Pt 3);
    (4)   Placement: the type of school (or the name of the school) considered appropriate for the child's needs (Sch 2 Pt 4);
    (5)   Non-educational Needs: the non-educational needs of the child for which the authority considers provision is appropriate if the child is to properly benefit from the special educational provision specified in head (3) above (Sch 2 Pt 5); and
    (6)   Non-educational Provision: any non-educational provision proposed to be made available to the child, including the arrangements for its provision, the objectives of the provision, and the arrangements for monitoring progress in meeting those objectives (Sch 2 Pt 6).
Additionally, the statement must be dated and authenticated by the signature of a duly authorised officer of the authority concerned (reg 16(c)), and it must set out whether it is the first statement made by the authority for the child or a subsequent statement (reg 16(d)). It must indicate on the front page if it is: (a) amended pursuant to an annual review, and the date of any such annual review; or (b) whether it is amended pursuant to a review other than an annual review, and the date of any such review; or (c) whether it is amended pursuant to an order of the Tribunal (see PARA 999 note 15), and the date of any such order; or (d) whether it is amended pursuant to a direction of the Secretary of State or the Welsh Ministers, as the case may be, and the date of any such direction: reg 16(e).
    In relation to heads (2) and (3) above, it was held in *G v Barnet London Borough Council and the Special Educational Needs Tribunal* [1998] ELR 480 at 483 per Ognall J that a child's religious and cultural background does not constitute a special educational need in its own right.

However, in *A v Special Educational Needs and Disability Tribunal* [2003] EWHC 3368 (Admin), [2004] ELR 293, [2003] All ER (D) 363 (Nov), a decision maker was required to take account of a child's religious and cultural background (in this case, Jewishness) in assessing how special educational needs should be met.

In relation to head (3) above, provision is not required to be made for matters of background and comment, nor even for needs which do not amount to educational needs: *W v Leeds City Council* [2005] EWCA Civ 988, [2005] ELR 617, [2005] All ER (D) 487 (Jul). The regulations require the statement to specify, in particular, any appropriate facilities and equipment, staffing arrangements and curriculum: see in relation to Wales the Education (Special Educational Needs) (Wales) Regulations 2002, SI 2002/152, Sch 2 Pt 3. The courts have approached this by acknowledging the importance of flexibility: see eg *R v Cumbria County Council, ex p P* [1995] ELR 337 at 348, where Schiemann J concluded that it would not be appropriate to issue a declaration that where speech therapy was required the number and length of weekly sessions should be specified in the statement, because there was 'a whole spectrum of help which any individual child can receive from variously qualified and unqualified persons so as to help him achieve the maximum of what he is capable of achieving'. See also *L v Clarke and Somerset County Council* [1998] ELR 129 at 136, where Laws J observed: 'A requirement that the help to be given should be specified in a statement in terms of hours per week is not an absolute and universal precondition of the legality of the statement … There will be some cases where flexibility should be retained', although he concluded (at 137): 'The real question … in relation to any particular statement is whether it is so specific and so clear as to leave no room for doubt as to what has been decided is necessary in the individual case. Very often a specification of hours per week will no doubt be necessary and there will be a need for that to be done'. This guidance was considered in *C v Special Educational Needs Tribunal* [1999] ELR 5 at 11 per Richards J; *C v Buckinghamshire County Council and the Special Educational Needs Tribunal* [1999] ELR 179 at 189, CA, per Thorpe LJ; *Bromley London Borough Council v Special Educational Needs Tribunal* [1999] 3 All ER 587 at 597, [1999] ELR 260 at 297, CA, per Sedley LJ; *H v Leicestershire County Council* [2000] ELR 471 at 484–485 per Dyson J; *S v City and Council of Swansea and Confrey* [2000] ELR 315 at 327–328 per Sullivan J; *E v Rotherham Metropolitan Borough Council* [2001] EWHC Admin 432 at [25], [2002] ELR 266, [2001] All ER (D) 1 (Jun) per Bell J; *E v Flintshire County Council* [2002] EWHC 388 (Admin) at [19], [2002] ELR 378, [2002] All ER (D) 309 (Feb) per Newman J; *E v Newham London Borough Council* [2002] EWHC 915 (Admin) at [24], [2002] ELR 453, [2002] All ER (D) 191 (May) per Stanley Burnton J (affd [2003] EWCA Civ 09, [2003] LGR 547, [2003] ELR 286); *R (on the application of IPSEA Ltd) v Secretary of State for Education and Skills* [2003] EWCA Civ 07 at [14], [2003] ELR 393, [2003] All ER (D) 121 (Jan) per Hale LJ (any flexibility built into a statement must meet needs of the child not the system). As to the requirement that a statement be sufficiently specific so as to enable a child's particular needs to be met see also *R (on the application of W) v Bedfordshire County Council and B* [2001] EWHC Admin 47, [2001] ELR 645, sub nom *R (on the application of Weedon) v Bedfordshire County Council* [2001] All ER (D) 265 (Jan); *E v Newham London Borough Council* at [36] per Stanley Burnton J. As to doubts expressed regarding the lawfulness of delegating the decision as to the final content of the provision under head (3) above see *C v Special Educational Needs Tribunal* (above) at 13 per Richards J; cf *Bromley London Borough Council v Special Educational Needs Tribunal*; *S v Hackney London Borough Council* [2001] EWHC Admin 572, [2002] ELR 45, [2001] All ER (D) 182 (Jul).

Where educational provision is appropriate, it should be included within part 3 of the statement (see head (3) above); but there is no reason why, if it was considered necessary, part 4 of the statement (see head (4) above) should not contain a reference to the provision as the measure that is appropriate for the time being, and a reference to the type of school to which a placement would be appropriate in the event that a vacancy should arise: *Wandsworth London Borough Council v K* [2003] EWHC 1424 (Admin), [2003] ELR 554, [2003] All ER (D) 248 (Jun).

9   Education Act 1996 s 324(3)(a).
10 Education Act 1996 s 324(3)(b). The educational provision to be specified includes the particulars required by s 324(4) (see heads (1)–(3) in the text): see s 324(3)(b). The precise nature of the requirement in s 324(3)(b) to specify the special educational provision to be made for the purpose of meeting the child's needs was considered in *R v Secretary of State for Education and Science, ex p E* [1993] 2 FCR 753, [1992] 1 FLR 377, CA (specified provision must address each of the needs specified in the statement). See also *R v Mid-Glamorgan County Council, ex p B* [1995] ELR 168; *R v Kingston upon Thames London Borough Council and Hunter* [1997] ELR 223. However, a cautious approach is needed. It has been held that *R v Secretary of State for Education, ex p E* (above) does not justify a detailed comparison between

the parts of a statement in support of a challenge to its sufficiency: see *Re L* [1994] ELR 16 at 22 per Leggatt LJ, CA. The Tribunal is entitled to take account of evidence from the local authority as to how it intends to implement a commitment in the statement which leaves some room for doubt (*Joyce v Dorset County Council* [1997] ELR 26) or as to how the authority has classified provision to be made (for example, as educational or non-educational) (*C v Special Educational Needs Tribunal* [1997] ELR 390, applying *Re L*). See also *B v Isle of Wight Council* [1997] ELR 279; *R v Northamptonshire County Council, ex p Marshall* [1998] Ed CR 262; *C v Special Educational Needs Tribunal and Greenwich London Borough Council* [1999] ELR 5; *R v Hackney London Borough Council, ex p GC* [1996] ELR 142, CA. See also note 17.

The local authority's duty is to make suitable provision, not necessarily the best possible provision: *R v Surrey County Council Education Committee, ex p H* (1984) 83 LGR 219, CA. In relation to that case it has been said: 'it is ... fair to read that case ... as endorsing the limitation of the authority's duty under [the Education Act 1996 s 324] to the selection of an appropriate school. Although the statutory regard to cost is relevant only as a constraint on parental choice ... there is nothing in the statutory scheme which calls upon the local authority to specify the optimum available provision and much in its general duty of financial husbandry to entitle it to choose the least expensive of the appropriate options': *R v Cheshire County Council, ex p C* [1998] ELR 66 at 78 per Sedley J.

In order to comply with the Education Act 1996 s 324(3), an authority may not specify either directly or indirectly that parents are to supply some or all of the needs: *R(A) v Cambridgeshire County Council* [2002] EWHC 2391 (Admin), [2003] ELR 464, sub nom *R(on the application of FJ) v Cambridgeshire County Council* [2002] All ER(D) 183 (Nov); *DM & KC v Essex County Council* [2003] EWHC 135 (Admin), [2003] ELR 419 (parents did not consent to the regime being proposed). However, there is no offence against this principle if the parent is required to co-operate and liaise with those providing the child's educational programme when the child is at home during times of non-educational care: *R (on the application of KW) v Special Educational Needs Tribunal and Rochdale Metropolitan Borough Council* [2003] EWHC 1770 (Admin), [2003] ELR 566, [2003] All ER (D) 341 (Jul).

11 As to the meaning of 'school' see PARA 91. Naming a boarding school is not likely to contravene the Convention for the Protection of Human Rights and Fundamental Freedoms (Rome, 4 November 1950; TS 71 (1953); Cmd 8969) art 8 (right to respect for a person's private and family life: see PARA 3; and RIGHTS AND FREEDOMS vol 88A (2013) PARA 317 et seq): *CB v Merton London Borough Council* [2002] EWHC 877 (Admin) at [19], [2002] ELR 441, [2002] All ER (D) 271 (Apr) per Sullivan J.

12 Education Act 1996 s 324(4)(a) (amended by SI 2010/1158). See also in relation to Wales the Education (Special Educational Needs) (Wales) Regulations 2002, SI 2002/152, reg 16(b), Sch 2 Pt 4; and note 8 head (4). See *R (on the application of M) v Sutton London Borough Council* [2007] EWCA Civ 1205, [2008] ELR 123, [2007] All ER (D) 322 (Nov) (the nomination of particular school conditional upon the child's parents taking responsibility for getting him to and from school, failing which the authority confined itself to specifying the type of school, did not breach its duty under the Education Act 1996 s 324(4)(a)).

13 Ie under the Education Act 1996 Sch 27.

14 If a local authority is considering specifying the name of a maintained school or maintained nursery school in a statement, it must serve a copy of the proposed statement on, and consult, each affected body: see the Education Act 1996 Sch 27 para 3A(1)(a), (2) (Sch 27 para 3A added by the Special Educational Needs and Disability Act 2001 s 10, Sch 1 paras 1, 7; and the Education Act 1996 Sch 27A para 3A(1)(a) amended by the Education Act 2002 s 215(1), Sch 21 para 58(a), SI 2010/1158). For these purposes, 'affected body' means the governing body of any school which the local authority is considering specifying and, if a school which the authority is considering specifying is maintained by another local authority, that authority: Education Act 1996 Sch 27 para 3A(3) (as so added; and amended by SI 2010/1158). As to the meaning of 'maintained school' see PARA 989 note 10. As to the meaning of 'maintained nursery school' see PARA 99 note 4. As to the governing bodies of maintained schools in Wales see PARA 195 et seq.

Provision for the service of documents is made in relation to Wales by the Education (Special Educational Needs) (Wales) Regulations 2002, SI 2002/152, reg 5.

15 As to the meaning of 'United Kingdom' see PARA 73 note 3.

16 Education Act 1996 s 324(4)(b). See also in relation to Wales the Education (Special Educational Needs) (Wales) Regulations 2002, SI 2002/152, reg 16(b), Sch 2 Pt 4; and note 8 head (4). This does not, however, require the name of a school or institution to be specified if the child's parent has made suitable arrangements for the special educational provision specified in the statement to be made for the child: Education Act 1996 s 324(4A) (added by the Special Educational Needs and Disability Act 2001 s 9). As to what comprises 'suitable arrangements' see note 19. A

local authority is only required to specify the name of a school in a statement if it considers the school appropriate and that it should be specified; in other words, the authority has a discretion as to whether or not to name a school in a statement: *Richardson v Solihull Metropolitan Borough Council, White v Ealing London Borough Council, Hereford and Worcester County Council v Lane* [1999] 1 FCR 356, [1998] ELR 319, CA. See also *R v Kent County Council, ex p AMS* [2000] ELR 209; *R (on the application of M) v Sutton London Borough Council* [2007] EWCA Civ 1205, [2008] ELR 123, [2007] All ER (D) 322 (Nov).

17 Ie under the Education Act 1996 s 319: see PARA 1017. See also *Tottman v Hertfordshire County Council* [2004] EWCA Civ 927, [2005] LGR 262, [2004] All ER (D) 370 (Jun) (once the Tribunal had found that the child's special educational needs could be met at a local authority school, it had no obligation to specify what should occur outside the school working day); *J v Special Educational Needs and Disability Tribunal* [2005] EWHC 3315 (Admin), [2005] All ER (D) 125 (Dec) (Tribunal entitled to conclude that a claimant's statement of special educational needs could be met appropriately by a school without prescribing a continuation of 'applied behaviour analysis' (ABA), which had been undertaken largely at home).

18 Education Act 1996 s 324(4)(c). See also in relation to Wales the Education (Special Educational Needs) (Wales) Regulations 2002, SI 2002/152, reg 16(b), Sch 2 Pt 4; and note 8 head (4). Local authorities must not fetter their discretion in determining the provision to be made: *R v Newham London Borough Council, ex p R* [1995] ELR 156. It is not, however, unlawful to have a policy to guide the authority in the exercise of its discretion as to whether or not to make a statement: *R v Cumbria County Council, ex p P* [1995] ELR 337; *R v Cumbria County Council, ex p B* [1995] 3 FCR 252, sub nom *R v Cumbria County Council, ex p NB* [1996] ELR 65.

19 'If the parents make suitable arrangements they effectively relieve the local authority of its duty': *R v Governors of Hasmonean High School, ex p N and E* [1994] ELR 343 at 355, CA, per Glidewell LJ. 'The question of 'suitable arrangements' is a question of funding the necessary schooling': *G v Barnet London Borough Council* [1998] ELR 480 at 486 per Ognall J. In *White v Ealing London Borough Council, Richardson v Solihull Metropolitan Borough Council, Solihull Metropolitan Borough Council v Finn* [1998] 1 FCR 344, [1998] ELR 203, the parents of an autistic child had raised funds in order to send the child to an independent residential school of their choice, which was meeting his needs; however, it was held that this did not mean that the parents had made 'suitable arrangements' since such arrangements had to include arrangements for funding for a reasonable period of time: 'It would have been unreasonable to decide that suitable arrangements had been made because the parents would be able to finance [the child's] schooling by future fund raising. Quite apart from the worrying uncertainty of relying on the kinds of activities in which the parents had engaged in order to get [the child] started at the school as a source of finance, it is unreasonable for an authority to seek to relieve itself of its statutory duties by relying on parents to raise finance in this way' (at 225 per Dyson J). See also *R v Hackney London Borough Council, ex p GC* [1996] ELR 142, CA. The Education Act 1996 s 324(5) has been used as the basis for a decision allowing the Family Court to make other suitable arrangements for a child's education, even if the Tribunal takes a different view: *X County Council v DW, PW and SW* [2005] EWHC 162 (Fam), [2005] 2 FLR 508 (Family Court was in no worse a position than a parent under the Education Act 1996 s 324(5)).

20 Education Act 1996 s 324(5)(a)(i) (s 324(5) amended by SI 2010/1158). See *R v Brent London Borough Council and Vassie (Chairman of the Special Educational Needs Tribunal), ex p AF* [2000] ELR 550. As to the making of special educational provision for a child attending (or proposing to attend) a city technology college, a city college for the technology of the arts or an academy, see the Education Act 1996 s 483A; and PARA 1015.

21 Education Act 1996 s 324(5)(a)(ii). '[Section 324(5)(a)] differentiates explicitly between special educational provision and 'non-educational provision'. It thus anticipates that both will appear in the statement, and it prescribes a duty on the [local authority] to arrange for the former and a discretion in the [local authority] to arrange for the latter': *Bromley London Borough Council v Special Educational Needs Tribunal* [1999] ELR 260 at 291, CA, per Sedley LJ. The distinction between 'educational' and 'non-educational provision' for this purpose was explained thus: 'there is between the unequivocally educational and the unequivocally non-educational a shared territory of provision which can be intelligibly allocated to either ... The potentially large intermediate area of provision which is capable of ranking as educational or non-educational is not made the subject of any statutory prescription precisely because it is for the [local authority], and if necessary the [Tribunal], to exercise a case-by-case judgment which no prescriptive legislation could ever hope to anticipate': *Bromley London Borough Council v Special Educational Needs Tribunal* at 295–296 per Sedley LJ. The duty to provide the special educational provision specified in the statement is mandatory: *R (N) v North*

Tyneside Borough Council (IPSEA Intervening) [2010] EWCA Civ 135, [2010] ELR 312, [2010] All ER (D) 115 (Jun). See also *Bradford Metropolitan Council v A* [1997] ELR 417 (a local authority was justified in regarding the provision in a statement for a nurse for a pupil with special educational needs as non-educational provision).

22 Education Act 1996 s 324(5)(b) (amended by the School Standards and Framework Act 1998 s 140(1), Sch 30 paras 57, 77(a); and the Education Act 2002 s 215(1), Sch 21 para 43). The Education Act 1996 s 324(5)(b) has effect regardless of any duty imposed on the governing body of a school by the School Standards and Framework Act 1998 s 1(6) (limits on class sizes: see PARA 234) (Education Act 1996 s 324(5A) (added by the School Standards and Framework Act 1998 s 140(1), Sch 30 paras 57, 77(b))), and does not affect any power to exclude from a school a pupil who is already a registered pupil there (Education Act 1996 s 324(6)). As to the meaning of 'pupil' see PARA 20 note 4. As to the meaning of 'registered pupil' see PARA 437. As to the exclusion of pupils see PARA 517 et seq. The duty under s 324(5)(b) to admit the child to the school specified in the child's statement is mandatory: *R v Chair of Governors and Headteacher of A and S School, ex p T* [2000] ELR 274.

1003. Copy of proposed statement of child's special educational needs.

Before making a statement of special educational needs[1], a local authority[2] must serve on the parent[3] of the child[4] concerned a copy of the proposed statement[5]. When serving the copy, the authority must also serve on the parent a written[6] notice explaining (to the extent that they are applicable) the arrangements for enabling the parent to express a preference as to his choice of school[7], the parent's right to make representations to the authority as to the content of the proposed statement[8], and the provisions for appealing against a statement[9]. The notice must also contain such other information as may be prescribed[10].

1 Ie a statement under the Education Act 1996 s 324 (see PARA 1002): see Sch 27 para 1 (substituted by the Special Educational Needs and Disability Act 2001 s 10, Sch 1 paras 1, 2). As to the meaning of 'special educational needs' see PARA 989.

2 As to the meaning of 'local authority' see PARA 25.

3 As to the meaning of 'parent' see PARA 7 note 6. Provision for the service of documents is made in relation to Wales by the Education (Special Educational Needs) (Wales) Regulations 2002, SI 2002/152, reg 5. The time limits within which notice must be served under the Education Act 1996 Sch 27 para 2(1) are prescribed in relation to Wales by the Education (Special Educational Needs) (Wales) Regulations 2002, SI 2002/152, reg 17(1), (3), (4), (9).

   If a local authority is required to give notice to or serve a document on a parent of a child under the Education Act 1996 Sch 27 para 2B(2) the local authority must give notice to, or serve the document on, the child as well as on the parent: s 332ZB(1)(g), (2) (s 332ZB added by the Education (Wales) Measure 2009 s 2 (amended by SI 2010/1148); and the Education Act 1996 s 332ZB(1) amended by the Children and Families Act 2014 Sch 3 paras 1, 22). Any provision applicable to notices given to or documents served on a parent applies equally to notices given to or documents served on a child: Education Act 1996 s 332ZB(3) (as so added).

4 As to the meaning of 'child' see PARA 989 note 1.

5 Education Act 1996 Sch 27 para 2(1) (Sch 27 para 2 substituted by the Special Educational Needs and Disability Act 2001 Sch 1 paras 1, 3). As to the effect of the Children and Families Act 2014 see generally PARA 941. See also the Education Act 1996 s 331A; and PARA 941. The copy of the proposed statement must not specify any prescribed matter or any matter in pursuance of the Education Act 1996 s 324(4) (see PARA 1002): see Sch 27 para 2(2)–(4) (as so substituted). 'Prescribed' means prescribed by regulations; and 'regulations' means regulations made by the Secretary of State or, in relation to Wales, the Welsh Ministers: see s 579(1) and see PARA 941. As to the Secretary of State see PARA 58. As to the Welsh Ministers see PARA 59. As to the meaning of 'Wales' see PARA 7 note 3. The functions of the Secretary of State under the Education Act 1996 Sch 27, so far as exercisable in relation to Wales, were originally transferred to the National Assembly for Wales (see the National Assembly for Wales (Transfer of Functions) Order 1999, SI 1999/672, art 2, Sch 1) and are now vested in the Welsh Ministers (see the Government of Wales Act 2006 s 162(1), Sch 11 para 30).

6 As to the meaning of 'written' see PARA 76 note 8.

7 Ie arrangements under the Education Act 1996 Sch 27 para 3 (see PARA 1012): see Sch 27 para 2B(1)(a), (2)(a) (Sch 27 para 2B added by the Special Educational Needs and Disability Act 2001 Sch 1 paras 1, 3).

8   Ie the effect of the Education Act 1996 Sch 27 para 4 (see PARA 1011): see Sch 27 para 2B(1)(a), (2)(b) (as added: see note 7).
9   Ie the right of appeal under the Education Act 1996 s 326 (see PARA 1010): see Sch 27 para 2B(1)(a), (2)(c) (as added: see note 7).
10   Education Act 1996 Sch 27 para 2B(3) (as added: see note 7). The notice must contain the information specified in the required Notice to Parent, including the procedure by which the parents may discuss the statement with the authority, lists of the maintained primary or secondary schools in the area and lists of approved non-maintained and independent schools, the procedure to be followed if the parents nominate a school, and the consultation process generally: see in relation to Wales the Education (Special Educational Needs) (Wales) Regulations 2002, SI 2002/152, reg 14(a), Schedule 1 Pt A (amended by SI 2010/1142). Copies of all the advice given to the authority during the child's assessment for the statement must also be attached to the Notice to Parent: see in relation to Wales the Education (Special Educational Needs) (Wales) Regulations 2002, SI 2002/152, Schedule 1 Pt A (as so amended). The time limits within which notice must be served under the Education Act 1996 Sch 27 para 2B(2) are prescribed in relation to Wales by the Education (Special Educational Needs) (Wales) Regulations 2002, SI 2002/152, reg 17(1)–(2), (9).

1004.   Time limit for making the statement of child's special educational needs. Regulations[1] may provide that, where a local authority[2] is under a duty[3] to make a statement of special educational needs[4], the duty to make the statement, or any step required to be taken for or in connection with the performance of the duty or the maintenance of the statement (including any step in relation to the amendment of the statement) must, subject to prescribed[5] exceptions, be performed within the prescribed period[6]. Such provision does not relieve the authority of the duty to make a statement, or take any step, which has not been performed or taken within that period[7].

1   'Regulations' means regulations made by the Secretary of State or, in relation to Wales, the Welsh Ministers: see the Education Act 1996 s 579(1) and see PARA 941. As to the Secretary of State see PARA 58. As to the Welsh Ministers see PARA 59. As to the meaning of 'Wales' see PARA 7 note 3. The functions of the Secretary of State under the Education Act 1996 Sch 27, so far as exercisable in relation to Wales, were originally transferred to the National Assembly for Wales (see the National Assembly for Wales (Transfer of Functions) Order 1999, SI 1999/672, art 2, Sch 1) and are now vested in the Welsh Ministers (see the Government of Wales Act 2006 s 162(1), Sch 11 para 30).
2   As to the meaning of 'local authority' see PARA 25.
3   Ie subject to compliance with the Education Act 1996 Sch 27 paras 1–4.
4   Ie a statement under the Education Act 1996 s 324 (see PARA 1002): see Sch 27 para 1 (substituted by the Special Educational Needs and Disability Act 2001 s 10, Sch 1 paras 1, 2). As to the meaning of 'special educational needs' see PARA 989.
5   'Prescribed' means prescribed by regulations: Education Act 1996 s 579(1).
6   Education Act 1996 Sch 27 para 5(3) (substituted by the Education and Inspections Act 2006 s 174(1), (3)(a)). As to the effect of the Children and Families Act 2014 see generally PARA 941. See also the Education Act 1996 s 331A; and PARA 941. The time limits for the performance of local authority duties in this regard are prescribed in relation to Wales by the Education (Special Educational Needs) (Wales) Regulations 2002, SI 2002/152, reg 17.
7   Education Act 1996 Sch 27 para 5(4).

1005.   Service of statement of child's special educational needs. Where a local authority[1] makes or amends a statement of special educational needs[2] it must serve a copy[3] of the statement, or the amended statement, on the parent[4] of the child[5] concerned[6]. At the same time, the authority must give the parent written notice[7] of the right to appeal[8] against (1) the description in the statement of the authority's assessment of the child's special educational needs[9]; (2) the special educational provision[10] specified in the statement (including the name of the school[11] specified in the statement)[12]; or (3) if no school is named in the statement, that fact[13]. The notice must also contain such other information as may be prescribed[14].

1   As to the meaning of 'local authority' see PARA 25.
2   Ie a statement under the Education Act 1996 s 324 (see PARA 1002): see Sch 27 para 1 (substituted by the Special Educational Needs and Disability Act 2001 s 10, Sch 1 paras 1, 2). As to the meaning of 'special educational needs' see PARA 989. As to amending statements see PARA 1006.
3   Provision for the service of documents is made in relation to Wales by the Education (Special Educational Needs) (Wales) Regulations 2002, SI 2002/152, reg 5.
4   As to the meaning of 'parent' see PARA 7 note 6.
5   As to the meaning of 'child' see PARA 989 note 1. If a local authority is required to give notice to or serve a document on a parent of a child under the Education Act 1996 Sch 27 para 6 the local authority must give notice to, or serve the document on, the child as well as on the parent: s 332ZB(1)(h), (2) (s 332ZB added by the Education (Wales) Measure 2009 s 2 (amended by SI 2010/1148); and the Education Act 1996 s 332ZB(1) amended by the Children and Families Act 2014 Sch 3 paras 1, 22). Any provision applicable to notices given to or documents served on a parent applies equally to notices given to or documents served on a child: Education Act 1996 s 332ZB(3) (as so added).
6   Education Act 1996 Sch 27 para 6(1) (Sch 27 para 6 substituted by the Special Educational Needs and Disability Act 2001 s 10, Sch 1 paras 1, 14; and the Education Act 1996 Sch 27 para 6(1) amended by SI 2010/1158). As to the effect of the Children and Families Act 2014 see generally PARA 941. See also the Education Act 1996 s 331A; and PARA 941. The time limits for the performance of local authority duties in connection with the service of notices under Sch 27 para 6 are prescribed in relation to Wales by the Education (Special Educational Needs) (Wales) Regulations 2002, SI 2002/152, reg 17(3)–(4), (9).
7   As to the meaning of 'written' see PARA 76 note 8. As to the time limits for the service of notices see note 6.
8   Ie under the Education Act 1996 s 326(1): see PARA 1010.
9   Education Act 1996 Sch 27 para 6(2)(a) (as substituted: see note 6).
10   As to the meaning of 'special educational provision' see PARA 989.
11   As to the meaning of 'school' see PARA 91.
12   Education Act 1996 Sch 27 para 6(2)(b) (as substituted: see note 6).
13   Education Act 1996 Sch 27 para 6(2)(c) (as substituted: see note 6).
14   Education Act 1996 Sch 27 para 6(3) (as substituted: see note 6). 'Prescribed' means prescribed by regulations; and 'regulations' means regulations made by the Secretary of State or, in relation to Wales, the Welsh Ministers: see s 579(1) and see PARA 941. As to the regulations made see in relation to Wales the Education (Special Educational Needs) (Wales) Regulations 2002, SI 2002/152, reg 14. As to the Secretary of State see PARA 58. As to the Welsh Ministers see PARA 59. The functions of the Secretary of State under Sch 27, so far as exercisable in relation to Wales, were originally transferred to the National Assembly for Wales (see the National Assembly for Wales (Transfer of Functions) Order 1999, SI 1999/672, art 2, Sch 1) and are now vested in the Welsh Ministers (see the Government of Wales Act 2006 s 162(1), Sch 11 para 30).

1006. Amendments to a statement. A local authority[1] must not amend a statement of special educational needs[2] except in compliance with an order of the Tribunal[3], as directed by the Welsh Ministers[4], or in accordance with the appropriate procedure[5]. Subject to specific provisions relating to proposed amendments to statements following periodic reviews[6], if an authority proposes to amend a statement, it must serve[7] on the parent[8] of the child[9] concerned a copy of the existing statement and an amendment notice[10]. When serving an amendment notice, the authority must also serve on the parent a written notice explaining (to the extent that they are applicable) the arrangements for enabling the parent to express a preference as to his choice of school[11], the parent's right to make representations to the authority as to the content of the proposed statement[12], and the provisions for appealing against a statement[13]. The notice must also contain such other information as may be prescribed[14].

1   As to the meaning of 'local authority' see PARA 25.
2   Ie a statement under the Education Act 1996 s 324 (see PARA 1002): see Sch 27 para 1 (substituted by the Special Educational Needs and Disability Act 2001 s 10, Sch 1 paras 1, 2). As to the meaning of 'special educational needs' see PARA 989. An authority is required to amend a statement before 15 February in the calendar year of the child's transfer between phases of his

schooling: see in relation to Wales the Education (Special Educational Needs) (Wales) Regulations 2002, SI 2002/152, reg 19. Where a local authority amends a statement it must serve a copy of the amended statement on the parent of the child concerned: see the Education Act 1996 Sch 27 para 6(1); and PARA 1005.

3   Education Act 1996 Sch 27 para 2A(1)(a) (Sch 27 para 2A added by the Special Educational Needs and Disability Act 2001 s 10, Sch 1 paras 1, 3). As to the effect of the Children and Families Act 2014 see generally PARA 941. See also the Education Act 1996 s 331A; and PARA 941. As to the meaning of 'the Tribunal' see PARA 999 note 15. As to the powers of the Tribunal to order that amendments be made to statements, and for the requirements as to compliance, see PARAS 1007, 1010, 1035.

4   Ie under the Education Act 1996 s 442(4) (see PARA 445): Sch 27 para 2A(1)(b) (as added: see note 3). As to the Welsh Ministers see PARA 59. The functions of the Secretary of State under Sch 27, so far as exercisable in relation to Wales, were originally transferred to the National Assembly for Wales (see the National Assembly for Wales (Transfer of Functions) Order 1999, SI 1999/672, art 2, Sch 1) and are now vested in the Welsh Ministers (see the Government of Wales Act 2006 s 162(1), Sch 11 para 30). As to the Secretary of State see PARA 58.

5   Education Act 1996 Sch 27 para 2A(1)(c) (as added: see note 3). The appropriate procedure is that laid down in Sch 27: see Sch 27 para 2A(1)(c) (as so added).

6   Ie the Education Act 1996 Sch 2A(4): see PARA 1000 note 29.

7   Provision for the service of documents is made in relation to Wales by the Education (Special Educational Needs) (Wales) Regulations 2002, SI 2002/152, reg 5. The time limits within which notice must be served under the Education Act 1996 Sch 27 para 2A are prescribed in relation to Wales by the Education (Special Educational Needs) (Wales) Regulations 2002, SI 2002/152, reg 17(1)–(4), (9).

8   As to the meaning of 'parent' see PARA 7 note 6.

9   As to the meaning of 'child' see PARA 7 note 6. If a local authority is required to give notice to or serve a document on a parent of a child under the Education Act 1996 Sch 27 para 2A the local authority must give notice to, or serve the document on, the child as well as on the parent: s 332ZB(1)(f), (2) (s 332ZB added by the Education (Wales) Measure 2009 s 2 (amended by SI 2010/1148); and the Education Act 1996 s 332ZB(1) amended by the Children and Families Act 2014 Sch 3 paras 1, 22). Any provision applicable to notices given to or documents served on a parent applies equally to notices given to or documents served on a child: Education Act 1996 s 332ZB(3) (as so added).

10   See the Education Act 1996 Sch 27 para 2A(4), (5) (as added: see note 3). An 'amendment notice' is a notice in writing giving details of the amendments to the statement proposed by the authority: Sch 27 paras 1, 2A(6) (Sch 27 para 1 (as substituted (see note 1); and Sch 27 para 2(6) as so added). As to the meaning of 'writing' see PARA 76 note 8. If a local authority is considering amending a statement: (1) if no school was specified in the statement before the amendment, so that a maintained school or maintained nursery school will be specified in it; or (2) if a school was specified in the statement before the amendment, so that a different school, which is a maintained school or maintained nursery school, will be specified in it, the authority must serve a copy of the proposed amended statement, or of the existing statement and of the amendment notice, on each affected body, and must consult each affected body: see Sch 27 para 3A(1)(b), (2) (Sch 27 para 3A added by the Special Educational Needs and Disability Act 2001 s 10, Sch 1 paras 1, 7; and amended by SI 2010/1158; and the Education Act 1996 Sch 27 para 3A(1)(b) further amended by the Education Act 2002 s 215(1), Sch 21 para 58). For these purposes, 'affected body' means the governing body of any school which the local authority is considering specifying and, if a school which the authority is considering specifying is maintained by another local authority, that authority: Education Act 1996 Sch 27 para 3A(3) (as so added and amended). As to the meaning of 'maintained school' see PARA 989 note 10. As to the meaning of 'maintained nursery school' see PARA 99 note 4. As to the governing bodies of maintained schools in Wales see PARA 195 et seq.

11   Ie the arrangements under the Education Act 1996 Sch 27 para 3 (see PARA 1012): see Sch 27 para 2B(1)(c), (2)(a) (Sch 27 para 2B added by the Special Educational Needs and Disability Act 2001 Sch 1 paras 1, 3; and amended by SI 2010/1158).

12   Ie the effect of the Education Act 1996 Sch 27 para 4 (see PARA 1011): see Sch 27 para 2B(1)(c), (2)(b) (as added and amended: see note 11).

13   Ie the right of appeal under the Education Act 1996 s 326 (see PARA 1010): see Sch 27 para 2B(1)(c), (2)(c) (as added and amended: see note 11).

14   Education Act 1996 Sch 27 para 2B(3) (as added: see note 11). 'Prescribed' means prescribed by regulations; and 'regulations' means regulations made by the Secretary of State or the Welsh Ministers: see s 579(1), and see PARA 941. The notice must contain the information specified in the required Notice to Parent, including information relating to the existing statement of special

educational needs, the proposed amendment, the procedure by which the parents may discuss the statement with the authority, lists of the maintained primary or secondary schools in the area and lists of approved non-maintained and independent schools, the procedure to be followed if the parents nominate a school, the consultation process generally, and the provision for appealing against the final amended statement: see in relation to Wales the Education (Special Educational Needs) (Wales) Regulations 2002, SI 2002/152, reg 14(a), Schedule 1 Pt A (amended by SI 2010/1142). The time limits within which notice must be served under the Education Act 1996 Sch 27 para 2B(2) are prescribed in relation to Wales by the Education (Special Educational Needs) (Wales) Regulations 2002, SI 2002/152, reg 17(1)–(4), (9).

1007. Procedure for ceasing to maintain a statement of child's special educational needs. A local authority[1] may not cease to maintain a statement of special educational needs[2] unless it is no longer necessary to maintain it[3]. Where an authority determines to cease to maintain a statement[4] it must give notice in writing[5] of that fact to the child's[6] parent[7], and the parent may appeal against the determination to the Tribunal[8]. The Tribunal may dismiss the appeal[9], or order the local authority to continue to maintain the statement in its existing form or with such amendments of the description in the statement of the authority's assessment of the child's special educational needs, or the special educational provision[10] specified in the statement, and such other consequential amendments, as the Tribunal may determine[11]. If the Tribunal makes an order, the local authority concerned must comply with the order before the end of the prescribed period beginning with the date on which it is made[12].

1 As to the meaning of 'local authority' see PARA 25.
2 Ie a statement under the Education Act 1996 s 324 (see PARA 1002): see Sch 27 para 1 (substituted by the Special Educational Needs and Disability Act 2001 s 10, Sch 1 paras 1, 2). As to the meaning of 'special educational needs' see PARA 989.
3 Education Act 1996 Sch 27 paras 9(1), 11(1) (both amended by SI 2010/1158; and Sch 27 para 9(1) further amended by the Special Educational Needs and Disability Act 2001 ss 10, 42(6), Sch 1 paras 1, 16(g), Sch 9). As to the effect of the Children and Families Act 2014 see generally PARA 941. See also the Education Act 1996 s 331A; and PARA 941. The general prohibition on ceasing to maintain a statement under Sch 27 para 9(1) does not apply where the local authority: (1) ceases to maintain a statement for a child who has ceased to be a child for whom it is responsible (Sch 27 para 9(2)(a) (amended by the Special Educational Needs and Disability Act 2001 Sch 1 paras 1, 16(h))); or (2) is ordered to cease to maintain a statement under the Education Act 1996 s 326(3)(c) (see PARA 1010) (Sch 27 para 9(2)(c)). The necessity to maintain a statement by way of exception to Sch 27 para 9(1) may arise only in accordance with Sch 27 para 11 (see the text to notes 4–11): see Sch 27 para 9(1) (as so amended). As to the meaning of 'child' see PARA 989 note 1. See also note 6. As to the children for whom the local authority is responsible see PARA 990. As to the relationship between Sch 27 paras 9 and 11 see *Wolverhampton City Council v Special Educational Needs and Disability Tribunal* [2007] EWHC 1117 (Admin), [2007] ELR 418, (2007) Times, 25 May, [2007] All ER (D) 195 (May); *R (on the application of Hill) v Bedfordshire County Council* [2008] EWCA Civ 661, [2008] ELR 660, [2008] All ER (D) 189 (Jun). See also *Wakefield Metropolitan District Council v E* [2001] EWHC Admin 508, [2002] ELR 203 (per curiam). As to circumstances in which an authority may not cease to maintain a statement see *R (on the application of Wilson) v Blaenau Gwent County Borough Council* [2003] EWHC 2880 (Admin), [2004] ELR 152, [2003] All ER (D) 214 (Nov).
4 Education Act 1996 Sch 27 para 11(2) (amended by SI 2010/1158). Except where there is an appeal to the Tribunal under the Education Act 1996 Sch 27 para 11, a local authority may only cease to maintain a statement under Sch 27 para 11 within the prescribed period beginning with the service of the notice under Sch 27 para 11(2) (see the text to notes 5–7): Sch 27 para 11(4) (amended by SI 2010/1158; and the Education (Wales) Measure 2009 s 23, Schedule paras 1, 5(b)). As to the meaning of 'the Tribunal' see PARA 999 note 15.
   'Prescribed' means prescribed by regulations; and 'regulations' means regulations made by the Secretary of State or, in relation to Wales, the Welsh Ministers: see the Education Act 1996 s 579(1), and see PARA 941. As to the Secretary of State see PARA 58. As to the Welsh Ministers see PARA 59. As to the meaning of 'Wales' see PARA 7 note 3. The functions of the Secretary of State under Sch 27, so far as exercisable in relation to Wales, were originally transferred to the

National Assembly for Wales (see the National Assembly for Wales (Transfer of Functions) Order 1999, SI 1999/672, art 2, Sch 1) and are now vested in the Welsh Ministers (see the Government of Wales Act 2006 s 162(1), Sch 11 para 30). The time limits within which the local authority may cease to maintain a statement following service of a notice under the Education Act 1996 Sch 27 para 11(1) are prescribed in relation to Wales by the Education (Special Educational Needs) (Wales) Regulations 2002, SI 2002/152, reg 17(8)–(9).

The rationale and effect of the Education Act 1996 Sch 27 para 11(4) were explained in *R v Oxfordshire County Council, ex p Roast* [1996] ELR 381; but see the Education Act 1996 Sch 27 para 11(5) (see note 8), which was enacted after that case.

5   As to the meaning of 'writing' see PARA 76 note 8.

6   For the purposes of the Education Act 1996 Sch 27 para 11, 'child' means a child who was the subject of a statement of special educational needs at the time when the local authority decided to give notice to determine to cease maintaining that statement: *S v Essex County Council* [2000] ELR 718 at 729 per Turner J; cf *Wakefield Metropolitan District Council v E* [2001] EWHC Admin 508, [2002] ELR 203, [2003] All ER (D) 214 (Nov).

7   Education Act 1996 Sch 27 para 11(2)(a) (amended by the Special Educational Needs and Disability Act 2001 s 42(1), Sch 8 paras 1, 10(1)). A notice under the Education Act 1996 Sch 27 para 11(2)(a) must inform the parent of the right of appeal under Sch 27 para 11(2)(b) (see the text to note 8) and contain such other information as may be prescribed: Sch 27 para 11(2A) (added by the Special Educational Needs and Disability Act 2001 Sch 8 paras 1, 10(2)). Where the local authority determines to cease to maintain a statement following a periodic review or a re-assessment review, regulations may provide that a notice under the Education Act 1996 Sch 27 para 11(2)(a) must be given within the prescribed period beginning with the date of the review: Sch 27 para 11(2B) (added by the Education and Inspections Act 2006 s 174(1), (3)(b); and amended by SI 2010/1158). As to the provision made see in relation to Wales the Education (Special Educational Needs) (Wales) Regulations 2002, SI 2002/152, reg 17.

If a local authority is required to give notice to or serve a document on a parent of a child under the Education Act 1996 Sch 27 para 11 the local authority must give notice to, or serve the document on, the child as well as on the parent: s 332ZB(1)(j), (2) (s 332ZB added by the Education (Wales) Measure 2009 s 2 (amended by SI 2010/1148); and the Education Act 1996 s 332ZB(1) amended by the Children and Families Act 2014 Sch 3 paras 1, 22). Any provision applicable to notices given to or documents served on a parent applies equally to notices given to or documents served on a child: Education Act 1996 s 332ZB(3) (as so added).

8   Education Act 1996 Sch 27 para 11(2)(b). A local authority may not under Sch 27 para 11 cease to maintain a statement if (1) there has been an appeal under Sch 27 para 11 against the authority's determination to cease to maintain the statement; and (2) the appeal has not been determined by the Tribunal or withdrawn: Sch 27 para 11(5) (added by the Special Educational Needs and Disability Act 2001 s 6; and amended by SI 2010/1158; and the Education (Wales) Measure 2009 s 23, Schedule paras 1, 5(c)).

The rights of a parent of a child to appeal to the Tribunal under the Education Act 1996 s 329(2)(b) may be exercised by the child: see s 332ZA(1)(g), (2) (s 332ZA added by the Education (Wales) Measure 2009 s 1; and the Education Act 1996 s 332ZA(1) amended by the Children and Families Act 2014 Sch 3 paras 1, 21). The child's rights are exercisable concurrently with the parent's rights: Education Act 1996 s 332ZA(3) (as so added). The exercise of such rights is subject to provision made by regulations under s 332ZC (see PARA 1222) and s 336(1) (see PARA 1235): s 332ZA(4) (as so added). As to the meaning of 'parent' see PARA 7 note 6.

9   Education Act 1996 Sch 27 para 11(3)(a). As to appeals from Tribunal decisions see PARA 1036.

10   As to the meaning of 'special educational provision' see PARA 989.

11   Education Act 1996 Sch 27 para 11(3)(b) (amended by SI 2010/1158).

12   Education Act 1996 s 336A(1) (s 336A added by the Special Educational Needs and Disability Act 2001 s 4; and the Education Act 1996 s 336A(1) amended by SI 2010/1158). For these purposes, 'prescribed' means prescribed by regulations made by the Welsh Ministers with the agreement of the Secretary of State: Education Act 1996 s 336A(2) (s 336A as so added; and s 336A(2) substituted by the Education Act 2002 s 195, Sch 18 paras 1, 6; and amended by the Children and Families Act 2014 Sch 3 paras 1, 35). Provision governing compliance with orders of the Tribunal is made in relation to Wales by the Special Educational Needs Tribunal for Wales Regulations 2012, SI 2012/322. For an attempt to compel compliance with an order via mandatory order see *R v Brent London Borough Council and Vassie (Chairman of the Special Educational Needs Tribunal), ex p AF* [2000] ELR 550.

1008. Keeping, disclosure and transfer of statements of child's special educational needs. Regulations[1] may make provision:

(1) as to the keeping and disclosure of statements of special educational needs[2]; and

(2) where a local authority[3] becomes responsible for a child[4] for whom a statement is maintained by another authority, for the transfer of the statement to it and for the statutory provisions relating to special educational needs[5] to have effect as if the duty to maintain the transferred statement were its duty[6].

1 'Regulations' means regulations made by the Secretary of State or, in relation to Wales, the Welsh Ministers: see the Education Act 1996 s 579(1), and see PARA 941. As to the Secretary of State see PARA 58. As to the Welsh Ministers see PARA 59. As to the meaning of 'Wales' see PARA 7 note 3. The functions of the Secretary of State under the Education Act 1996 Sch 27, so far as exercisable in relation to Wales, were originally transferred to the National Assembly for Wales (see the National Assembly for Wales (Transfer of Functions) Order 1999, SI 1999/672, art 2, Sch 1) and are now vested in the Welsh Ministers (see the Government of Wales Act 2006 s 162(1), Sch 11 para 30).

2 Education Act 1996 Sch 27 para 7(1). As to the effect of the Children and Families Act 2014 see generally PARA 941. See also the Education Act 1996 s 331A; and PARA 941. A statement of special educational needs is one under s 324 (see PARA 1002): see Sch 27 para 1 (substituted by the Special Educational Needs and Disability Act 2001 s 10, Sch 1 paras 1, 2). As to the meaning of 'special educational needs' see PARA 989. Provision restricting the disclosure of statements of special educational needs without the consent of the child concerned is made in relation to Wales by the Education (Special Educational Needs) (Wales) Regulations 2002, SI 2002/152, reg 24 (amended by SI 2010/1142).

3 As to the meaning of 'local authority' see PARA 25.

4 As to the meaning of 'child' see PARA 989 note 1. As to the children for whom a local authority is responsible see PARA 990.

5 Ie the Education Act 1996 Pt IV (ss 311A–349).

6 Education Act 1996 Sch 27 para 7(2). Provision for the transfer of a statement where a child in respect of whom a statement is maintained moves from the area of the authority which maintains the statement into that of another is made in relation to Wales by the Education (Special Educational Needs) (Wales) Regulations 2002, SI 2002/152, reg 23 (amended by SI 2010/1142).

1009. Appeal against decision not to make statement. If, after making an assessment of the educational needs[1] of any child[2] for whom no statement of special educational needs[3] is maintained[4], the local authority[5] does not propose to make such a statement, it must give notice in writing[6] of its decision to the child's parent[7]. In such a case, the child's parent[8] may appeal against the decision to the Tribunal[9].

The Tribunal may: (1) dismiss the appeal[10]; (2) order the local authority to make and maintain a statement[11]; or (3) remit the case to the authority for it to reconsider whether, having regard to any observations made by the Tribunal, it is necessary for the authority to determine the special educational provision[12] for which any learning difficulty[13] the child may have calls[14]. If the Tribunal makes an order, the local authority concerned must comply with the order before the end of the prescribed period beginning with the date on which it is made[15]. If the parent of a child, or a child, has appealed to the Tribunal against a decision of the authority[16] and the authority notifies the Tribunal that it has determined that it will not, or will no longer, oppose the appeal[17], the appeal is to be treated as having been determined in favour of the appellant[18]. In such a case the Tribunal is not required to make any order[19] and the authority must make a statement[20] of the child's educational needs before the end of the prescribed period[21].

1 Ie under the Education Act 1996 s 323: see PARA 994.

2   As to the meaning of 'child' see PARA 989 note 1.

3   As to the meaning of 'special educational needs' see PARA 989.

4   Ie under the Education Act 1996 s 324: see PARA 1002.

5   As to the meaning of 'local authority' see PARA 25.

6   As to the meaning of 'writing' see PARA 76 note 8.

7   Education Act 1996 s 325(1) (amended by the Special Educational Needs and Disability Act 2001 s 42(1), (6), Sch 8 paras 1, 6(1), Sch 9; and SI 2010/1158). As to the meaning of 'parent' see PARA 7 note 6. As to the effect of the Children and Families Act 2014 see generally PARA 941. See also the Education Act 1996 s 331A; and PARA 941. A notice under s 325(1) must inform the parent of the right of appeal under s 325(2) (see the text to notes 8–9) and contain such other information as may be prescribed: s 325(2A) (s 325(2A), (2B) added by the Special Educational Needs and Disability Act 2001 Sch 8 paras 1, 6(2)). Regulations may provide that where a local authority is under a duty under the Education Act 1996 s 325 to serve any notice, the duty must be performed within the prescribed period: s 325(2B) (as so added; and amended by SI 2010/1158). 'Prescribed' means prescribed by regulations; and 'regulations' means regulations made by the Secretary of State or, in relation to Wales, the Welsh Ministers: see s 579(1), and see PARA 941. As to the Secretary of State see PARA 58. As to the Welsh Ministers see PARA 59. As to the meaning of 'Wales' see PARA 7 note 3. The functions of the Secretary of State under the Education Act 1996 s 325, so far as exercisable in relation to Wales, were originally transferred to the National Assembly for Wales (see the National Assembly for Wales (Transfer of Functions) Order 1999, SI 1999/672, art 2, Sch 1) and are now vested in the Welsh Ministers (see the Government of Wales Act 2006 s 162(1), Sch 11 para 30). Provision for the service of notices is made in relation to Wales by the Education (Special Educational Needs) (Wales) Regulations 2002, SI 2002/152, regs 4–5. The time limits within which notice must be served under the Education Act 1996 s 325(1) are prescribed in relation to Wales by the Education (Special Educational Needs) (Wales) Regulations 2002, SI 2002/152, reg 17(1), (9).

If a local authority is required to give notice to or serve a document on a parent of a child under the Education Act 1996 s 325 the local authority must give notice to, or serve the document on, the child as well as on the parent: s 332ZB(1)(a), (2) (s 332ZB added by the Education (Wales) Measure 2009 s 2 (amended by SI 2010/1148); and the Education Act 1996 s 332ZB(1) amended by the Children and Families Act 2014 Sch 3 paras 1, 22). Any provision applicable to notices given to or documents served on a parent applies equally to notices given to or documents served on a child: Education Act 1996 s 332ZB(3) (as so added).

8   A foster-parent can be a parent for this purpose: *Fairpo v Humberside County Council* [1997] 1 All ER 183, [1997] ELR 12. The child may attend the hearing and the Tribunal may permit the child to give evidence and to address the Tribunal on the subject matter of the appeal: see in relation to Wales the Special Educational Needs Tribunal for Wales Regulations 2012, SI 2012/322.

The rights of a parent of a child to appeal to the Tribunal under the Education Act 1996 s 325(2) may be exercised by the child: see s 332ZA(1)(a), (2) (s 332ZA added by the Education (Wales) Measure 2009 s 1; and the Education Act 1996 s 332ZA(1) amended by the Children and Families Act 2014 Sch 3 paras 1, 21). The child's rights are exercisable concurrently with the parent's rights: Education Act 1996 s 332ZA(3) (as so added). The exercise of such rights is subject to provision made by regulations under s 332ZC (see PARA 1030) and s 336(1) (see PARA 1035): s 332ZA(4) (as so added).

9   Education Act 1996 s 325(2). As to the meaning of 'the Tribunal' see PARA 999 note 15. There is nothing in the language or the structure of s 325 to shut out the apparent right of appeal merely because an intervening appeal resulted in remission requiring a fresh decision; the Tribunal's safeguard lies in its power under the appropriate procedural rules to strike out appeals which are scandalous, frivolous or vexatious: *O v Harrow London Borough Council* [2001] EWCA Civ 2046, [2002] 1 WLR 928, [2002] ELR 195 (a single assessment of a child's educational needs may found successive appeals where an authority has failed to make a statement following an earlier appeal). As to the procedure on appeals see PARA 1034 et seq.

10   Education Act 1996 s 325(3)(a). As to appeals from Tribunal decisions see PARA 1036.

11   Education Act 1996 s 325(3)(b) (amended by SI 2010/1158).

12   As to the meaning of 'special educational provision' see PARA 989.

13   As to the meaning of 'learning difficulty' see PARA 989.

14   Education Act 1996 s 325(3)(c).

15   Education Act 1996 s 336A(1) (s 336A added by the Special Educational Needs and Disability Act 2001 s 4; and the Education Act 1996 s 336A(1) amended by SI 2010/1158). For these purposes, 'prescribed' means prescribed by regulations made by the Welsh Ministers with the agreement of the Secretary of State: Education Act 1996 s 336A(2) (s 336A as so added; and s 336A(2) substituted by the Education Act 2002 s 195, Sch 18 paras 1, 6; and amended by the

Children and Families Act 2014 Sch 3 paras 1, 35). Provision governing compliance with orders of the Tribunal is made in relation to Wales by the Special Educational Needs Tribunal for Wales Regulations 2012, SI 2012/322. For an attempt to compel compliance with an order via mandatory order see *R v Brent London Borough Council and Vassie (Chairman of the Special Educational Needs Tribunal), ex p AF* [2000] ELR 550.

16 See the Education Act 1996 s 326A(1)(a) (s 326A added by the Special Educational Needs and Disability Act 2001 s 5; and the Education Act 1996 s 326A(1)(a) substituted by the Children and Families Act 2014 Sch 3 paras 1, 18(1), (2)).

17 Education Act 1996 s 326A(1)(b) (as added: see note 16).

18 Education Act 1996 s 326A(2) (as added: see note 16).

19 See the Education Act 1996 s 326A(3) (as added: see note 16).

20 Ie under the Education Act 1996 s 324: see PARA 1002. An authority required by the Education Act 1996 s 326A(4)(a) to make a statement under s 324 must maintain the statement under that section: s 326A(5) (as added: see note 16).

21 See the Education Act 1996 s 326A(4)(a) (as added: see note 16). For these purposes 'prescribed' means prescribed by regulations made by the Welsh Ministers: s 326A(6) (as so added; substituted by the Education Act 2002 s 195, Sch 18 paras 1, 3; and amended the Children and Families Act 2014 Sch 3 paras 1, 18(1), (3)). As to the provision made see in relation to Wales the Special Educational Needs Tribunal for Wales Regulations 2012, SI 2012/322.

1010. Appeal against contents of statement. The parent[1] of a child[2] for whom a local authority[3] maintains a statement of special educational needs[4] may:

(1)   when the statement is first made[5];

(2)   if an amendment is made to the statement[6]; or

(3)   if, after conducting an assessment of the educational needs of the child[7], the authority determines not to amend the statement[8],

appeal to the Tribunal[9] against any of the following:

(a)   the description in the statement of the authority's assessment of the child's special educational needs[10];

(b)   the special educational provision[11] specified in the statement (including the name of a school[12] so specified)[13]; or

(c)   if no school is so specified, that fact[14].

The Tribunal may: (i) dismiss the appeal[15]; (ii) order the authority to amend the statement, so far as it describes the authority's assessment of the child's special educational needs or specifies the special educational provision, and make such other consequential amendments to the statement as the Tribunal thinks fit[16]; or (iii) order the authority to cease to maintain the statement[17]. If the Tribunal makes an order, the local authority concerned must comply with the order before the end of the prescribed period beginning with the date on which it is made[18].

1   As to the meaning of 'parent' see PARA 7 note 6.

2   As to the meaning of 'child' see PARA 989 note 1. The rights of a parent of a child to appeal to the Tribunal under the Education Act 1996 s 326(1) may be exercised by the child: see s 332ZA(1)(b), (2) (s 332ZA added by the Education (Wales) Measure 2009 s 1; and the Education Act 1996 s 332ZA(1) amended by the Children and Families Act 2014 Sch 3 paras 1, 21). The child's rights are exercisable concurrently with the parent's rights: Education Act 1996 s 332ZA(3) (as so added). The exercise of such rights is subject to provision made by regulations under s 332ZC (see PARA 1030) and s 336(1) (see PARA 1035): s 332ZA(4) (as so added). As to the meaning of 'Tribunal' see PARA 999 note 15.

3   As to the meaning of 'local authority' see PARA 25.

4   Ie under the Education Act 1996 s 324: see PARA 1002. As to the meaning of 'special educational needs' see PARA 989.

5   Education Act 1996 s 326(1)(a) (s 326(1) substituted by the Special Educational Needs and Disability Act 2001 s 10, Sch 1 paras 18, 19). As to the effect of the Children and Families Act 2014 see generally PARA 941. See also the Education Act 1996 s 331A; and PARA 941.

6   Education Act 1996 s 326(1)(b) (as substituted: see note 5). As to the amendment of statements see PARA 1006. Section 326(1)(b) does not apply where the amendment is made in pursuance of

Sch 27 para 8 (change of named school: see PARA 1013), or Sch 27 para 11(3)(b) (amendment ordered by Tribunal: see PARA 1007), or directions under s 442 (revocation of school attendance order: see PARA 445): s 326(2)(a), (b).

7 Ie under the Education Act 1996 s 323: see PARA 994.

8 Education Act 1996 s 326(1)(c) (as substituted: see note 5). Section 326(1)(c) does not apply to a determination made following the service of notice under Sch 27 para 2A (amendment by local authority: see PARA 1000) of a proposal to amend the statement: s 326(2) (amended by the Special Educational Needs and Disability Act 2001 Sch 1 paras 18, 20).

9 Education Act 1996 s 326(1) (as substituted (see note 5); and amended by SI 2010/1158). Before determining any such appeal the Tribunal may, with the agreement of the parties, correct any deficiency in the statement: s 326(5).

10 Education Act 1996 s 326(1A)(a) (s 326(1A) added by the Special Educational Needs and Disability Act 2001 Sch 1 paras 18, 19).

11 As to the meaning of 'special educational provision' see PARA 989.

12 As to the meaning of 'school' see PARA 91.

13 Education Act 1996 s 326(1A)(b) (as added: see note 10). In R (on the application of S) v Norfolk County Council [2004] EWHC 404 (Admin), [2004] ELR 259, the local authority had proposed to discontinue funding a child's college placement after allegations that staff had committed offences against children at the college; notwithstanding the prospective criminal proceedings, an interim injunction was granted compelling the authority to continue the funding for a limited period, pending an appeal lodged by the child's mother against amendments made to the school specified in the child's statement. As to an appeal involving disagreement between the parents and the authority in regard to the meaning in the statement of teaching in small groups see K & K v The Authority (SEN) [2013] UKUT 624 (AAC). As to the naming of schools in a statement subject to appeal see further note 16.

14 Education Act 1996 s 326(1A)(c) (as added: see note 10). As to the naming of schools in a statement subject to appeal see further note 16.

15 Education Act 1996 s 326(3)(a). As to appeals from Tribunal decisions see PARA 1036.

16 Education Act 1996 s 326(3)(b). The Tribunal must not order the local authority to specify the name of any school in the statement (either in substitution for an existing name or in a case where no school is named) unless: (1) the parent has expressed a preference for the school in pursuance of arrangements under Sch 27 para 3 (see PARA 1012) (s 326(4)(a)); or (2) in the proceedings the parent, the authority, or both, have proposed the school (s 326(4)(b)); or, as from a day to be appointed, (3) in the proceedings the child has proposed the school (whether or not the parent, the local authority or both have also proposed the school) (s 326(4)(c) (added by the Education (Wales) Measure 2009 s 23, Schedule paras 1, 2(b); and amended by the Children and Families Act 2014 Sch 3 paras 1, 17). As to the meaning of 'Wales' see PARA 7 note 3.

'Proposed' should be construed as including an acceptance of a suggested school rather than as a reference to a proposal made unprompted: see Manchester City Council v Special Educational Needs Tribunal and P [2000] ELR 144. As to the date from which funding consequent on an amendment ordered by the Tribunal should be provided see R v Barnet London Borough Council, ex p G [1998] ELR 281, CA; cf R v Kent County Council, ex p W [1995] 2 FCR 342, [1995] ELR 362, 94 LGR 271. The Tribunal could conceivably order provision that is less than that proposed by the local authority or sought by the parent: see Re A [2000] ELR 639.

In Camden London Borough Council v Hodin and White [1996] ELR 430, the court refused to impose a stay to prevent implementation of the Tribunal's decision that a statement should be amended pending an appeal against that decision. See also R v Mid-Glamorgan County Council, ex p B [1995] ELR 168. There is no right of appeal to the Tribunal against a statement which has already been amended in accordance with an order of the Tribunal, as to give such a right would defeat the legislative purpose of the scheme: D v East Sussex County Council [2005] EWCA Civ 323, [2005] ELR 388, [2005] All ER (D) 354 (Mar). In ordering that a statement is to be amended, it is not open for the Tribunal to range freely over the statement; its power is limited in its application to cases where an amendment is necessary for the resolution of an issue that is before the Tribunal: see M v Essex County Council [2001] EWHC Admin 956, [2001] All ER (D) 45 (Nov). In W v Leeds City Council [2005] EWCA Civ 988, [2005] ELR 617, [2005] All ER (D) 487 (Jul), the Court of Appeal agreed that it had been within the proper ambit of the Tribunal's control over its own process to agree a late proposal for an amendment to the statement and that it had not curtailed proper analysis of the child's needs.

17 Education Act 1996 s 326(3)(c). See Wilkin v Goldthorpe [1998] ELR 345.

18 Education Act 1996 s 336A(1) (s 336A added by the Special Educational Needs and Disability Act 2001 s 4; Education Act 1996 s 336A(1) amended by SI 2010/1158). For these purposes, 'prescribed' means prescribed by regulations made by the Welsh Ministers with the agreement of

the Secretary of State: Education Act 1996 s 336A(2) (s 336A as so added; s 336A(2) substituted by the Education Act 2002 s 195, Sch 18 paras 1, 6; and amended by the Children and Families Act 2014 Sch 3 paras 1, 35). As to the Secretary of State see PARA 58. As to the Welsh Ministers see PARA 59. Provision governing compliance with orders of the Tribunal is made in relation to Wales by the Special Educational Needs Tribunal for Wales Regulations 2012, SI 2012/232. In *R v Brent London Borough Council and Vassie (Chairman of the Special Educational Needs Tribunal), ex p AF* [2000] ELR 550, an attempt was made via mandatory order to compel a local authority to implement the special educational provisions set out in the statement but it failed as a local authority normally has no power to direct the school as to implementation.

1011. Right of parent to make representations as to statements and proposed amendments. A parent[1] on whom there has been served a copy of a proposed statement of special educational needs[2], a proposed amended statement[3], or an amendment notice[4], may[5] make representations (or further representations) to the local authority[6] about the content of the proposed statement or the statement as it will have effect if amended in the way proposed by the authority[7], and may require the authority to arrange a meeting[8] between him and an officer of the authority at which the proposed statement or the statement as it will have effect if amended in the way proposed by the authority can be discussed[9].

1   As to the meaning of 'parent' see PARA 7 note 6. As to the requirement that where a local authority in Wales is required to give notice to or serve a document on a parent of a child under Sch 27 para 2A (see the text to notes 3, 4) the local authority must also give notice to, or serve the document on, the child: see s 332ZB(1)(f), (2); and PARA 1000.

2   Ie served under the Education Act 1996 Sch 27 para 2: see PARA 1003. As to statements of special educational needs see s 324; and PARA 1002. As to the meaning of 'special educational needs' see PARA 989.

3   Ie served under the Education Act 1996 Sch 27 para 2A: see PARA 1000. If a local authority amends a statement following service of a proposed amended statement under Sch 27 para 2A, the amended statement made may be in the form proposed or in a form modified in the light of the representations made by the parent: Sch 27 para 5(2A) (added by the Special Educational Needs and Disability Act 2001 Sch 1 paras 1, 13; and amended by SI 2010/1158). See note 6.

4   Ie served under the Education Act 1996 Sch 27 para 2A: see PARA 1000. As to the meaning of 'amendment notice' see PARA 1006 note 10. If a local authority amends a statement following service of an amendment notice, the amendments may be those proposed in the notice or amendments modified in the light of the representations made by the parent: Sch 27 para 5(2B) (added by the Special Educational Needs and Disability Act 2001 Sch 1 paras 1, 13; and amended by SI 2010/1158).

     When amending a statement in a case where there is a real prospect of appeal, a local authority is not bound to consider whether it would be better not to name a school rather than name a school so as to avoid any delay which might arise whilst it was seeking to find whether a particular school was appropriate or available: *R v Kent County Council, ex p AMS* [2000] ELR 209.

5   Education Act 1996 Sch 27 para 4(1) (amended by the Special Educational Needs and Disability Act 2001 Sch 1 paras 1, 8(a)). As to the effect of the Children and Families Act 2014 see generally PARA 941. See also the Education Act 1996 s 331A; and PARA 941.

6   As to the meaning of 'local authority' see PARA 25.

7   Education Act 1996 Sch 27 para 4(1)(a) (amended by the Special Educational Needs and Disability Act 2001 Sch 1 paras 1, 8(b); SI 2010/1158). Any such representations must be made within the period of 15 days beginning with the date on which the written notice mentioned in the Education Act 1996 Sch 27 para 2B (see PARAS 1000, 1003, 1006) was served on the parent, or, if a meeting has (or meetings have) been arranged under Sch 27 para 4(1)(b) or para 4(2) (see the text to notes 8–9), with the date fixed for that meeting (or the last of those meetings): Sch 27 para 4(4) (amended by the Special Educational Needs and Disability Act 2001 Sch 1 paras 1, 10).

     Where representations are made to a local authority under the Education Act 1996 Sch 27 para 4(1)(a), the authority may not make or amend the statement until it has considered the representations and the period or the last of the periods allowed by Sch 27 para 4 for making requirements or further representations (see notes 8–9) has expired: Sch 27 para 5(1) (amended by the Special Educational Needs and Disability Act 2001 Sch 1 paras 1, 11; and amended by SI 2010/1158). If an authority makes a statement, it may be in the form originally proposed (except as to the matters required to be excluded from the copy of the proposed statement) or in a form modified in the light of the representations: Education Act 1996 Sch 27 para 5(2) (amended by the Special Educational Needs and Disability Act 2001 Sch 1 paras 1, 12; SI 2010/1158). As to time limits in relation to the making or amendment of statements see PARA 1004. If the authority changes its view about making a statement after issuing a draft it does not necessarily act unlawfully: *R v Isle of Wight County Council, ex p RS and AS* [1994] 1 FCR 641, sub nom *R v Isle of Wight County Council, ex p RS, R v Isle of Wight County Council, ex p AS* [1993] 1 FLR 634, CA.

8   Such a requirement must be made within the period of 15 days beginning with the date on which the written notice mentioned in the Education Act 1996 Sch 27 para 2B (see PARAS 1000, 1003, 1006) was served on the parent: Sch 27 para 4(5) (amended by the Special Educational Needs and Disability Act 2001 Sch 1 paras 1, 10).

9   Education Act 1996 Sch 27 para 4(1)(b) (amended by the Special Educational Needs and Disability Act 2001 Sch 1 paras 1, 8(b)). Where a parent, having attended a meeting arranged by a local authority under the Education Act 1996 Sch 27 para 4(1)(b) in relation to a proposed statement or an amendment proposed following a re-assessment review, disagrees with any part of the assessment in question, he may require the authority to arrange such meeting or meetings as it considers will enable him to discuss the relevant advice with the appropriate person or persons: Sch 27 para 4(2) (amended by the Special Educational Needs and Disability Act 2001 Sch 1 Pt 1 paras 1, 9; SI 2010/1158). Such a requirement must be made within the period of 15 days beginning with the date fixed for the meeting arranged under the Education Act 1996 Sch 27 para 4(1)(b): Sch 27 para 4(6). 'Relevant advice' means such of the advice given to the authority in connection with the assessment as it considers to be relevant to that part of the assessment with which the parent disagrees; and 'appropriate person' means the person who gave the relevant advice or any other person who, in the opinion of the authority, is the appropriate person to discuss it with the parent: Sch 27 para 4(3). As to the meaning of 're-assessment review' see PARA 1000 note 25.

1012.   Choice of school. Every local authority[1] must make arrangements for enabling a parent[2] upon whom has been served a copy of a proposed statement of special educational needs[3], a copy of a proposed amended statement[4], or an amendment notice[5] containing a proposed amendment[6] to be specified in a statement[7], to express a preference as to the maintained school[8] at which he wishes education to be provided for his child and to give reasons for his preference[9].

Where a local authority makes a statement in a case where the parent of the child concerned has expressed a preference in pursuance of such arrangements as to the school at which he wishes education to be provided for his child, it must, unless the school is unsuitable to the child's age, ability or aptitude or to his special educational needs[10], or the attendance of the child at the school would be incompatible with the provision of efficient education for the children with whom he would be educated or the efficient use of resources[11], specify the name of that school in the statement[12].

1   As to the meaning of 'local authority' see PARA 25.
2   Education Act 1996 Sch 27 para 3(1) (amended by the Special Educational Needs and Disability Act 2001 s 10, Sch 1 paras 1, 4; SI 2010/1158). As to the meaning of 'parent' see PARA 7 note 6. As to the effect of the Children and Families Act 2014 see generally PARA 941. See also the Education Act 1996 s 331A; and PARA 941.
3   Education Act 1996 Sch 27 para 3(1)(a) (amended by the Special Educational Needs and Disability Act 2001 Sch 1 paras 1, 4). As to statements of special educational needs see the Education Act 1996 s 324; and PARA 1002. Copies of proposed statements are required to be served under the Education Act 1996 Sch 27 para 2: see PARA 1003. As to the meaning of 'special educational needs' see PARA 989.
4   Education Act 1996 Sch 27 para 3(1)(b) (amended by the Special Educational Needs and Disability Act 2001 Sch 1 paras 1, 4). Copies of proposed amended statements are required to be served under the Education Act 1996 Sch 27 para 2A: see PARA 1000.
5   As to the meaning of 'amendment notice' see PARA 1006 note 10.
6   The proposed amendment must, for this purpose, be about the type or name of a school or institution, or the provision made for the child concerned under arrangements made under the

Education Act 1996 s 319 (special educational provision otherwise than in schools: see PARA 1017): Sch 27 para 3(1)(c) (amended by the Special Educational Needs and Disability Act 2001 Sch 1 paras 1, 4). As to the meaning of 'school' see PARA 91. As to the meaning of 'child' see PARA 989 note 1.

7 Education Act 1996 Sch 27 para 3(1)(c) (as amended: see note 6). The amendment notices referred to are those required to be served under Sch 27 para 2A: see PARA 1000.

8 As to the meaning of 'maintained school' see PARA 989 note 10.

9 Education Act 1996 Sch 27 para 3(1) (amended by the School Standards and Framework Act 1998 s 140(1), Sch 30 paras 57, 186(1), (2)(a)). Any such preference must be expressed or made within the period of 15 days beginning with the date on which the written notice mentioned in the Education Act 1996 Sch 27 para 2B (see PARAS 1000, 1003, 1006) was served on the parent, or if a meeting has (or meetings have) been arranged under Sch 27 para 4(1)(b) or para 4(2) (see PARA 1011), with the date fixed for that meeting (or the last of those meetings): Sch 27 para 3(2) (amended by the Special Educational Needs and Disability Act 2001 Sch 1 paras 1, 5). As to the general principle that children be educated in accordance with parental wishes: see PARA 7.

10 Education Act 1996 Sch 27 para 3(3)(a).

11 Education Act 1996 Sch 27 para 3(3)(b).

12 Education Act 1996 Sch 27 para 3(3) (amended by SI 2010/1158). Where the parents and the local authority cannot agree on the school to be named, but one alternative would result in significant additional expenditure, then provided both schools are appropriate for the child's special educational needs, the authority is entitled to justify sending the child to a school other than that of the parents' choice: *Surrey County Council v P* [1997] ELR 516 at 523 per Kay J. When deciding whether the parent's choice or its choice should prevail, the local authority may have regard to its own resources but should balance the disadvantages to its resources with the advantages to the child of attending the school chosen by the parents: *F v Harrow London Borough Council* (1997) Times, 29 December. Under the Education Act 1996, the scheme for special educational provision is for children for whom an authority was 'responsible' (ie the children in its area: see s 321(3); and PARA 990); this indicates that the resources concerned for the purposes of Sch 27 para 3(3) are those of the responsible local authority: *B v Harrow London Borough Council* [2000] 1 All ER 876 at 881–882, [2000] 1 WLR 223 at 228–229, [2000] ELR 109 at 115, HL, per Lord Slynn of Hadley (the fact that the admission of a child to the school of the parents' choice would mean that the school was above its approved admission limit was held to be a legitimate ground for not naming that school contrary to the parents' wishes).

The House of Lords in *B v Harrow London Borough Council* (above) also considered the relevance of the Education Act 1996 s 9 (general principle of adherence to parental wishes: see PARA 7), and held that s 9 did not mean that parental preference was to prevail unless it involved unreasonable public expenditure. 'In dealing with special schools, the authority must also observe the specific provisions of para 3(3) of Sch 27. This does not mean that the parent loses the right to express a preference. A preference may be expressed but is subject to the qualifications set out in para 3(3), one of which is the efficient use of resources': *B v Harrow London Borough Council* at 882–883, at 229, and at 116 per Lord Slynn of Hadley. See also *R (on the application of MH) v Special Educational Needs and Disability Tribunal* [2004] EWCA Civ 770, [2004] LGR 844, [2004] ELR 424 (parents had the right to insist on a particular school, except where either the 'unsuitability' or 'incompatibility' condition in the Education Act 1996 Sch 27 para 3(3) applied). As to the principle of adherence to parental wishes in the making of special educational provision see further *R (on the application of Oxfordshire County Council) v GB* [2001] EWCA Civ 1358, [2002] LGR 279, [2002] ELR 8; *Hampshire County Council v R* [2009] EWHC 626 (Admin), [2009] ELR 371, [2009] All ER (D) 87 (Feb). As to the interaction between the Education Act 1996 Sch 27 para 3 and s 316 (duty to educate children with special educational needs in mainstream schools: see PARA 1014) see *R (on the application of MH) v Special Educational Needs and Disability Tribunal.*

The Education Act 1996 Sch 27 para 3 applies only to maintained schools but local authorities (and, on appeal, the Tribunal: see PARA 979 et seq) must take into account the general principle of adherence to parental preference under s 9 in relation to all preferred schools, including independent schools: *B v Gloucestershire County Council* [1998] ELR 539. See also *R v West Sussex County Council, ex p S* [1999] ELR 40; *S and S v Bracknell Forest Borough Council and the Special Educational Needs Tribunal* [1999] ELR 51; *Catchpole v Buckingham County Council and Special Needs Tribunal* [1999] LGR 321, sub nom *C v Buckinghamshire County Council and the Special Educational Needs Tribunal* [1999] ELR 179, CA; *W-R v Solihull Metropolitan Borough Council* [1999] ELR 528; *S v Metropolitan Borough of Dudley* [2000] ELR 330.

As to the extent to which the right to education in accordance with the parents' religious and philosophical convictions under the Convention for the Protection of Human Rights and Fundamental Freedoms (Rome, 4 November 1950; TS 71 (1953) Cmd 8969) extends to choice of school or provision in relation to children with special educational needs see PARA 3.

1013. Request for change of named school. Where:

(1)   the parent[1] of a child[2] for whom a statement of special educational needs[3] is maintained which specifies the name of a school[4] or institution asks the local authority[5] to substitute for that name the name of a maintained school[6] or maintained nursery school[7] specified by the parent[8]; and

(2)   the request is not made less than 12 months[9] after whichever is the later of: (a) an earlier request[10] for the substitution of a name[11]; (b) the service[12] of a copy of a statement or amended statement[13]; or (c) if there is an appeal to the Tribunal[14], the date when the appeal is concluded[15],

the local authority must comply with the request unless[16] the school is unsuitable to the child's age, ability or aptitude or to his special educational needs[17], or the attendance of the child at the school would be incompatible with the provision of efficient education for the children with whom he would be educated or the efficient use of resources[18].

Where the local authority determines not to comply with the request[19], it must give notice in writing[20] of that fact to the child's parent[21], and the parent may appeal against the determination to the Tribunal[22]. The Tribunal may dismiss the appeal[23], or order the local authority to substitute for the name of the school or other institution specified in the statement the name of the school specified by the parent[24]. If the Tribunal makes an order, the local authority concerned must comply with the order before the end of the prescribed period beginning with the date on which it is made[25]. If the parent of a child, or a child, has appealed to the Tribunal against a decision of the authority[26], and the authority notifies the Tribunal that it has determined that it will not, or will no longer, oppose the appeal[27], the appeal is to be treated as having been determined in favour of the appellant[28]. In such a case the Tribunal is not required to make any order[29] and the authority must make an assessment of the child's educational needs before the end of the prescribed period[30].

1   As to the meaning of 'parent' see PARA 7 note 6.
2   As to the meaning of 'child' see PARA 989 note 1.
3   Ie a statement under the Education Act 1996 s 324 (see PARA 1002): see Sch 27 para 1 (substituted by the Special Educational Needs and Disability Act 2001 s 10, Sch 1 Pt 1 paras 1, 2). As to the meaning of 'special educational needs' see PARA 989.
4   As to the meaning of 'school' see PARA 91.
5   As to the meaning of 'local authority' see PARA 25.
6   As to the meaning of 'maintained school' see PARA 989 note 10.
7   As to the meaning of 'maintained nursery school' see PARA 99 note 4.
8   Education Act 1996 Sch 27 para 8(1)(a) (amended by the School Standards and Framework Act 1998 s 140(1), Sch 30 paras 57, 186(3); and the Education Act 2002 s 215(1), Sch 21 para 58(b); SI 2010/1158). As to the effect of the Children and Families Act 2014 see generally PARA 941. See also the Education Act 1996 s 331A; and PARA 941. As to the general principle of that children be educated in accordance with parental wishes: see PARA 7.
9   As to the meaning of 'month' see PARA 54 note 26.
10   Ie under the Education Act 1996 Sch 27 para 8.
11   Education Act 1996 Sch 27 para 8(1)(b)(i).
12   Ie under the Education Act 1996 Sch 27 para 6: see PARA 1005.
13   Education Act 1996 Sch 27 para 8(1)(b)(ii) (amended by the Special Educational Needs and Disability Act 2001 s 10, Sch 1 paras 1, 15(e)).

14 Ie under the Education Act 1996 s 326 (see PARA 1010) or Sch 27 para 8 (see the text to notes 19–30). As to the meaning of 'the Tribunal' see PARA 999 note 15.

15 Education Act 1996 Sch 27 para 8(1)(b)(iv) (amended by the Education (Wales) Measure 2009 s 23, Schedule paras 1, 5(a)).

16 Education Act 1996 Sch 27 para 8(2) (amended by SI 2010/1158). Regulations may provide that, where a local authority is under a duty to comply with a request under the Education Act 1996 Sch 27 para 8, the duty must, subject to prescribed exceptions, be performed within the prescribed period: Sch 27 para 8(5) (amended by SI 2010/1158). Such provision does not relieve the authority of the duty to comply with such a request which has not been complied with within that period: Education Act 1996 Sch 27 para 8(6). 'Regulations' means regulations made by the Secretary of State or, in relation to Wales, the Welsh Ministers; and 'prescribed' means prescribed by regulations: see s 579(1), and see PARA 941. As to the Secretary of State see PARA 58. As to the Welsh Ministers see PARA 59. The time limits within which a request under Sch 27 para 8(1) must be responded to are prescribed in relation to Wales by the Education (Special Educational Needs) (Wales) Regulations 2002, SI 2002/152, reg 17(5), (9).

The Education Act 1996 Sch 27 para 8 has a very limited scope, being concerned only with a change in the name of the school specified in part 4 of an existing statement (see PARA 1192); the power to change the name of the school does not carry with it a power to change the type of school: *Slough Borough Council v C* [2004] EWHC 1759 (Admin), [2005] LGR 368, [2004] ELR 546. As to the interaction between the Education Act 1996 Sch 27 para 8 and the process set out in s 316(3) (duty to educate children with special educational needs in mainstream schools: see PARA 1014) see *Slough Borough Council v C*; *R (on the application of MH) v Special Educational Needs and Disability Tribunal* [2004] EWCA Civ 770, [2004] LGR 844, [2004] ELR 424.

17 Education Act 1996 Sch 27 para 8(2)(a).

18 Education Act 1996 Sch 27 para 8(2)(b). As to such incompatibility see the cases cited at PARA 1012 note 12.

19 Education Act 1996 Sch 8 para 8(3) (amended by SI 2010/1158).

20 As to the meaning of 'writing' see PARA 76 note 8.

21 Education Act 1996 Sch 27 para 8(3)(a) (amended by the Special Educational Needs and Disability Act 2001 Sch 8 paras 1, 9(1)). A notice under the Education Act 1996 Sch 27 para 8(3)(a) must inform the parent of the right of appeal under Sch 27 para 8(3)(b) (see the text and note 22) and must contain such other information as may be prescribed: Sch 27 para 8(3A) (added by the Special Educational Needs and Disability Act 2001 Sch 8 paras 1, 9(2)). Provision for the service of notices is made in relation to Wales by the Education (Special Educational Needs) (Wales) Regulations 2002, SI 2002/152, regs 4–5. The time limits within which notice must be given under the Education Act 1996 Sch 27 para 8(3) are prescribed in relation to Wales by Education (Special Educational Needs) (Wales) Regulations 2002, SI 2002/152, reg 17(5), (9).

If a local authority is required to give notice to or serve a document on a parent of a child under the Education Act 1996 Sch 27 para 8 the local authority must give notice to, or serve the document on, the child as well as on the parent: s 332ZB(1)(i), (2) (s 332ZB added by the Education (Wales) Measure 2009 s 2 (amended by SI 2010/1148); and the Education Act 1996 s 332ZB(1) amended by the Children and Families Act 2014 Sch 3 paras 1, 21). Any provision applicable to notices given to or documents served on a parent applies equally to notices given to or documents served on a child: Education Act 1996 s 332ZB(3) (as so added).

22 Education Act 1996 Sch 27 para 8(3)(b). The rights of a parent of a child to appeal to the Tribunal under Sch 27 para 8(3)(b) may be exercised by the child: see s 332ZA(1)(f), (2) (s 332ZA added by the Education (Wales) Measure 2009 s 1; and the Education Act 1996 s 332ZA(1) amended by the Children and Families Act 2014 Sch 3 paras 1, 21). The child's rights are exercisable concurrently with the parent's rights: Education Act 1996 s 332ZA(3) (as so added). The exercise of such rights is subject to provision made by regulations under s 332ZC (see PARA 1030) and s 336(1) (see PARA 1035): s 332ZA(4) (as so added).

23 Education Act 1996 Sch 27 para 8(4)(a). As to appeals from Tribunal decisions see PARA 1036.

24 Education Act 1996 Sch 27 para 8(4)(b) (amended by SI 2010/1158). As to the influence of the costs to be taken into account by the Tribunal when determining compliance with a parental preference see *Wardle-Heron v Newham London Borough Council* [2002] EWHC 2806 (Admin), [2004] ELR 68, [2002] All ER (D) 114 (Dec); *S v Somerset County Council* [2002] EWHC 1808 (Admin), [2003] ELR 78, [2002] All ER (D) 387 (Jul); and see PARA 7 note 7.

25 Education Act 1996 s 336A(1) (s 336A added by the Special Educational Needs and Disability Act 2001 s 4; Education Act 1996 s 336A(1) amended by SI 2010/1158). For these purposes, 'prescribed' means prescribed by regulations made by the Welsh Ministers with the agreement of the Secretary of State: Education Act 1996 s 336A(2) (s 336A as so added; s 336A(2) substituted

by the Education Act 2002 s 195, Sch 18 paras 1, 6; and amended by the Children and Families Act 2014 Sch 3 paras 1, 35). Provision governing compliance with orders of the Tribunal is made in relation to Wales by the Special Educational Needs Tribunal for Wales Regulations 2012, SI 2012/322. For an attempt to compel compliance with an order via mandatory order see *R v Brent London Borough Council and Vassie (Chairman of the Special Educational Needs Tribunal), ex p AF* [2000] ELR 550.

26 See the Education Act 1996 s 326A(1)(a) (s 326A added by the Special Educational Needs and Disability Act 2001 s 5; and the Education Act 1996 s 326A(1)(a) amended by the Children and Families Act 2014 Sch 3 paras 1, 18(1), (2).

27 Education Act 1996 s 326A(1)(b) (as added: see note 26).

28 Education Act 1996 s 326A(2) (as added: see note 26).

29 See the Education Act 1996 s 326A(3) (as added: see note 26).

30 See the Education Act 1996 s 326A(4)(b) (as added: see note 26). For these purposes 'prescribed' means prescribed by regulations made by the Welsh Ministers: s 326A(6) (as so added; substituted by the Education Act 2002 s 195, Sch 18 paras 1, 3; and amended by the Children and Families Act 2014 Sch 3 paras 1, 18(1), (3)). As to the provision made in relation to Wales see the Special Educational Needs Tribunal for Wales Regulations 2012, SI 2012/322.

(iv) Special Educational Provision: Functions of Local Authorities, Governing Bodies, etc

1014. Children with special educational needs generally to be educated in mainstream schools. A child[1] with special educational needs[2] who should be educated in a school[3] must be educated in a mainstream school[4] if no statement of the child's special educational needs is maintained[5] for the child[6]. If such a statement is maintained[7], the child must be educated in a mainstream school unless that is incompatible with either the wishes of his parent[8] or the provision of efficient education for other children[9]. These requirements do not, however, prevent a child from being educated in an independent school which is not a mainstream school[10], or an approved special school[11], if the cost is met otherwise than by a local authority[12]; nor do they affect the operation of certain provisions relating to the making of special educational provision at non-maintained schools[13] or enabling parents to express a preference as to the maintained school at which they wish education to be provided for their child[14]. An authority[15] must have regard to guidance about these requirements[16] issued by the Welsh Ministers[17].

1 As to the meaning of 'child' see PARA 989 note 1.

2 As to the meaning of 'special educational needs' see PARA 989.

3 Education Act 1996 s 316(1) (s 316 substituted by the Special Educational Needs and Disability Act 2001 s 1). As to the meaning of 'school' see PARA 91. As to the effect of the Children and Families Act 2014 see generally PARA 941. See also the Education Act 1996 s 331A; and PARA 941.

4 'Mainstream school' means any school other than: (1) a special school; or (2) an independent school which is not a city technology college, a city college for the technology of the arts, or an academy: Education Act 1996 s 316(4) (as substituted (see note 3); and amended by the Education Act 2002 s 65(3), Sch 7 Pt 2 para 6(1), (3)). As to the meaning of 'special school' see PARA 1041. As to the meaning of 'independent school' see PARA 369. As to city technology colleges and city colleges for the technology of the arts see PARA 345. As to the meaning of 'academy' see PARA 346 note 7.

5 Ie under the Education Act 1996 s 324: see PARA 1002.

6 Education Act 1996 s 316(2) (as substituted: see note 3). This does not, however, require a child to be educated in a mainstream school during any period in which: (1) he is admitted to a special school for the purposes of an assessment under s 323 (see PARA 994) of his educational needs and his admission to that school is with the agreement of the local authority, the governing body of the school or, if the school is in England, its head teacher, the child's parent, and any person whose advice is to be sought in accordance with regulations made under Sch 26 para 2 (see PARA 995) (s 316(2)(a) (s 316A added by the Special Educational Needs and Disability Act 2001 s 1; and amended by SI 2010/1158; and the Children and Families Act 2014 Sch 3 paras 1,

14(1), (2)(a)); (2) he remains admitted to a special school, in prescribed circumstances, following an assessment under the Education Act 1996 s 323 at that school (s 316A(2)(b) (as so added)); (3) he is admitted to a special school, following a change in his circumstances, with the agreement of the local authority, the governing body of the school or, if the school is in England, its head teacher, and his parent (s 316A(2)(c) (as so added and amended; and further amended by the Children and Families Act 2014 Sch 3 paras 1, 14(1), (2)(b)); or (4) he is admitted to a community or foundation special school which is established in a hospital (Education Act 1996 s 316A(2)(d) (as so added)). As to the meaning of 'local authority' see PARA 25. As to the meaning of 'head teacher' see PARA 86 note 4. As to the governing bodies of maintained schools in Wales see PARA 195 et seq. As to the meanings of 'England' and 'Wales' see PARA 7 note 3. As to the meaning of 'parent' see PARA 7 note 6. As to the meaning of references to a community or foundation special school see PARA 106.

'Prescribed' means prescribed in regulations made by the Welsh Ministers: see s 316A(10) (as so added; and amended by the Children and Families Act 2014 Sch 3 paras 1, 14(1), (4)), Education Act 1996 s 579(1). As to the Welsh Ministers see PARA 59. The functions under the Education Act 1996 s 316A in relation to Wales were originally vested in the National Assembly for Wales and are now exercisable by the Welsh Ministers by virtue of the Government of Wales Act 2006 s 162(1), Sch 11 paras 30, 32.

If a child without a statement has been admitted to a special school for the purposes of an assessment, as provided for in the Education Act 1996 s 316A(2), he may remain at that school either until the expiry of ten school days after the authority serves a notice under s 325 (see PARA 1009) informing the child's parent that it does not propose to make a statement, or until a statement is made: see in relation to Wales the Education (Special Educational Needs) (Wales) Regulations 2002, SI 2002/152, reg 13. As to the meaning of 'school day' see PARA 229 note 6.

See *MA v Borough of Kensington and Chelsea (SEN)* [2015] UKUT 186 (AAC) in which it was held that there had been no infringement of the Education Act 1996 s 316 where a specialist unit for children autistic spectrum disorder (ASD) was part of a mainstream school rather than a separate special school.

As to the relationship between the Education Act 1996 ss 9 and 316 (as to s 9 see PARA 7) see *KC v London Borough of Hammersmith and Fulham (SEN)* [2015] UKUT 177 (AAC).

7   Ie under the Education Act 1996 s 324: see PARA 1002.

8   Education Act 1996 s 316(3)(a) (as substituted: see note 3). If a local authority decides to make a statement of a child's special educational needs under s 324 (see PARA 1002) but decides not to name in the statement the school for which a parent has expressed a preference under Sch 27 para 3 (parents' right to express a preference for a particular school: see PARA 1202), then the authority, in making the statement, nonetheless complies with s 316(3): s 316A(4) (as added and amended: see note 6). The parents' right to express a preference under Sch 27 para 3 (if lawfully invoked by the parent) constitutes no more than the nomination of a candidate for the authority to consider, and the process set out in s 316 comes into operation where that nomination process has been exhausted; in carrying out the process set out in s 316, the authority, and hence the Tribunal, has a discretion to consider particular schools as candidates for naming in part 4 of the statement (see PARA 1002): *R (on the application of MH) v Special Educational Needs and Disability Tribunal* [2004] EWCA Civ 770, [2004] LGR 844, [2004] ELR 424. The process set out in the Education Act 1996 s 316(3) does not apply to a determination under Sch 27 para 8 where none of the conditions in Sch 27 para 8(2) has been met (see PARA 1013): *Slough Borough Council v C* [2004] EWHC 1759 (Admin), [2005] LGR 368, [2004] ELR 546 (distinguishing *R (on the application of MH) v Special Educational Needs and Disability Tribunal* (above)).

The question of compatibility with parental wishes under the Education Act 1996 s 316 (as originally enacted) (which provided that the duty (subject to conditions) to educate in a non-special school unless that would be incompatible with the wishes of the child's parent applied in respect of any child with special educational needs) was considered in *L v Hereford and Worcester County Council* [2000] ELR 375; *R v Brent London Borough Council and Vassie (Chairman of the Special Educational Needs Tribunal), ex p AF* [2000] ELR 550; *L v Worcestershire County Council and Hughes* [2000] ELR 674, sub nom *Lane v Worcestershire County Council* [2000] All ER (D) 333, CA.

9   Education Act 1996 s 316(3)(b) (as substituted: see note 3). See further note 8. A local authority may, in relation to its mainstream schools taken as a whole, rely on the exception in s 316(3)(b) only if it shows that there are no reasonable steps that it could take to prevent the incompatibility: s 316A(5) (as added and amended: see note 6). An authority in relation to a particular mainstream school (ie in relation to a maintained school or maintained nursery school, the local authority or the school's governing body; and in relation to a pupil referral unit, the local authority (s 316A(11) (as so added and amended; and further amended by the Education Act 2002 s 215, Sch 21 para 38, Sch 22 Pt 3)) may rely on the exception in the

Education Act 1996 s 316(3)(b) only if it shows that there are no reasonable steps that it or another authority in relation to the school could take to prevent the incompatibility: s 316A(6) (as so added). The exception in s 316(3)(b) does not permit a governing body to fail to comply with the duty imposed by s 324(5)(b) (see PARA 1002): s 316A(7) (as so added). As to the meaning of 'maintained school' see PARA 989 note 10. As to the meaning of 'maintained nursery school' see PARA 99 note 4. As to pupil referral units see PARA 427 et seq.

10 Education Act 1996 s 316A(1)(a) (as added: see note 6).
11 Ie a special school approved under the Education Act 1996 s 342 (approval of non-maintained special schools: see PARA 1042): s 316A(1)(b) (as added: see note 6).
12 Education Act 1996 s 316A(1) (as added and amended: see note 6).
13 Ie the Education Act 1996 s 348 (see PARA 1016): s 316A(3)(a) (as added: see note 6).
14 Ie the Education Act 1996 Sch 27 para 3 (see PARA 1012): s 316A(3)(b) (as added: see note 6). See also note 8.
15 Ie in relation to a maintained school or maintained nursery school, the local authority or the school's governing body; and in relation to a pupil referral unit, the local authority: Education Act 1996 s 316A(11) (as added and amended: see note 9).
16 Ie the requirements of the Education Act 1996 ss 316, 316A.
17 Education Act 1996 s 316A(8) (as added (see note 6); and amended by the Children and Families Act 2014 Sch 3 paras 14(1), (3)). Such guidance must, in particular, relate to steps which may, or may not, be regarded as reasonable for the purposes of the Education Act 1996 s 316A(5), (6) (see note 9): s 316A(9) (as so added).

1015. Special educational provision at city colleges and academies. Where:

(1) a child[1] for whom a statement of special educational needs[2] is maintained[3] attends (or proposes to attend) a school[4] which is a city technology college, a city college for the technology of the arts or an academy[5]; and

(2) the statement of special educational needs is maintained by a local authority[6] in Wales[7] and the Welsh Ministers[8] consent to the child being educated at the school[9],

the Welsh Ministers[10] may by regulations make provision for securing that arrangements are made[11] for making the special educational provision[12] and any non-educational provision specified in the statement[13]. The regulations may require or authorise a local authority to make payments to the school in respect of the child[14], or to provide any other assistance to the school in respect of the child[15].

1 As to the meaning of 'child' see PARA 7 note 6.
2 As to the meaning of 'special educational needs' see PARAS 943, 989.
3 Education Act 1996 s 483A(1), (2)(a) (s 483A added by the Learning and Skills Act 2000 s 133; and the Education Act 1996 s 483A(2)(a) amended by the Children and Families Act 2014 Sch 3 Sch 3 paras 1, 44(1), (2)). The statement of special educational needs referred to is one under the Education Act 1996 s 324 (see PARA 1002): see s 483A(2)(a) (as so added and amended).
4 As to the meaning of 'school' see PARA 91.
5 Education Act 1996 s 483A(1), (2)(b) (as added (see note 3); and amended by the Education Act 2002 s 65(3), Sch 7 Pt 2 para 6(1), (4)(a)). As to city technology colleges and city colleges for the technology of the arts see PARA 345. As to the meaning of 'academy' see PARA 346 note 7.
6 As to the meaning of 'local authority' see PARA 25.
7 As to the meaning of 'Wales' see PARA 7 note 3.
8 As to the Welsh Ministers see PARA 59.
9 Education Act 1996 s 483A(1), (3)(b) (s 483A as added (see note 3); s 483A(3)(a), (b) substituted by the Education and Skills Act 2008 s 147(4), (5); and amended by SI 2010/1158).
10 The legislation refers to 'the appropriate national authority', which means, in relation to a school in Wales, the Welsh Ministers: Education Act 1996 s 483A(6A) (s 483A as added (see note 3); s 483A(6A) added by the Education and Skills Act 2008 s 147(4), (7)).
11 Education Act 1996 s 483A(4) (as added (see note 3); and amended by the Education and Skills Act 2008 s 147(4), (6)).
12 As to the meaning of 'special educational provision' see PARAS 943, 989.

13 See the Education Act 1996 s 483A(4)(a), (b) (as added (see note 3); and amended by the Children and Families Act 2014 Sch 3 paras 1, 44(1), (4)). As to the regulations made in relation to England, see notes 18–24. At the date at which this volume states the law no regulations had been made in relation to Wales.

14 Education Act 1996 s 483A(5)(a) (s 483A as added (see note 3); s 483A(5), (6) amended by SI 2010/1158). No condition or requirement imposed by virtue of the Education Act 1996 s 482(4)(a) (repealed) is to prevent a local authority making payments or providing assistance by virtue of s 483A(5): s 483A(6) (as so added and amended).

15 Education Act 1996 s 483A(5)(b) (as added: see note 3).

1016. Payment of fees for special education at non-maintained schools.
Where:

(1) special educational provision[1] in respect of a child[2] with special educational needs[3] is made at a school[4] which is not a maintained school[5]; and

(2) the child is in the area of a local authority in Wales[6];

(3) either the name of the school is specified in a statement in respect of the child[7] or the local authority is satisfied[8] both that his interests require the necessary special educational provision to be made for him at a school which is not a maintained school[9], and that it is appropriate for the child to be provided with education at the particular school[10],

the local authority must pay the whole of the fees payable in respect of the education provided for the child at the school[11]; and if board and lodging are provided for him at the school[12], and the authority is satisfied that the necessary special educational provision cannot be provided for him at the school unless the board and lodging are also provided[13], the authority must pay the whole of the fees payable in respect of the board and lodging[14].

1   As to the meaning of 'special educational provision' see PARA 989.
2   As to the meaning of 'child' see PARA 989 note 1.
3   As to the meaning of 'special educational needs' see PARA 989.
4   As to the meaning of 'school' see PARA 91.
5   Education Act 1996 s 348(1)(a). 'Maintained school' means a school maintained by a local authority: s 348(3) (substituted by the School Standards and Framework Act 1998 s 140(1), Sch 30 paras 57, 84; and amended by SI 2010/1158). As to schools maintained by local authorities see PARA 99 et seq. As to the meaning of 'local authority' see PARA 25.
6   Education Act 1996 s 348(1)(aa) (added by the Children and Families Act 2014 Sch 3 paras 1, 38). As to the meaning of 'Wales' see PARA 7 note 3.
7   Ie a statement under the Education Act 1996 s 324: see PARA 1002.
8   Education Act 1996 s 348(1)(b) (amended by SI 2010/1158).
9   Education Act 1996 s 348(1)(b)(i).
10 Education Act 1996 s 348(1)(b)(ii). See further *White v Ealing London Borough Council, Richardson v Solihull Metropolitan Borough Council, Solihull Metropolitan Borough Council v Finn* [1998] ELR 203 at 223 per Dyson J; *Richardson v Solihull Metropolitan Borough Council, White v Ealing London Borough Council, Hereford and Worcester County Council v Lane* [1998] ELR 319 at 339–340, CA, per Schiemann LJ (who also held (at 339–340) that the Education Act 1996 s 348 does not impose any duty to specify the name of the school in the statement).
11 Education Act 1996 s 348(2) (amended by SI 2010/1158). The operation of the Education Act 1996 s 348 is not affected by s 316 (duty to educate children with special educational needs in mainstream schools): see s 316A(3); and PARA 1014.
12 Education Act 1996 s 348(2)(a).
13 Education Act 1996 s 348(2)(b).
14 Education Act 1996 s 348(2). As to the payment of fees where arrangements have been made under Pt IV (ss 311A–349) or the Children and Families Act 2014 Pt 3 (ss 19–83) (see PARA 950 et seq) for the provision of primary or secondary education for a pupil at a school not maintained by a local authority see also (until a day to be appointed) the Education Act 1996 s 517 (amended by SI 1999/2260; SI 2010/1158; and the Children and Families Act 2014 Sch 3

paras 1, 51; prospectively repealed by the School Standards and Framework Act 1998
s 140(1), (3), Sch 30 paras 57, 138, Sch 31). At the date at which this volume states the law, no
such day had been appointed.

1017.   Special educational provision otherwise than in schools.   Where a local
authority[1] is satisfied that it would be inappropriate for the special educational
provision[2] for which a learning difficulty[3] of a child[4] in its area calls[5], or for any
part of any such provision[6], to be made in a school[7], it may arrange for the
provision (or, as the case may be, for that part of it) to be made otherwise than in
a school[8]. Before making such an arrangement, a local authority must consult the
child's parent[9].

1   As to the meaning of 'local authority' see PARA 25.
2   As to the meaning of 'special educational provision' see PARA 989.
3   As to the meaning of 'learning difficulty' see PARA 989.
4   As to the meaning of 'child' see PARA 989 note 1.
5   Education Act 1996 s 319(1)(a). As to the effect generally of the Children and Families Act 2014
    see PARA 941. See also the Education Act 1996 s 311A; and PARA 941.
6   Education Act 1996 s 319(1)(b).
7   As to the meaning of 'school' see PARA 91.
8   Education Act 1996 s 319(1) (amended by SI 2010/1158). The statutory provisions relating to
    special educational needs (ie the Education Act 1996 ss 311A–324 and now only applying to
    Wales: see PARA 941) contemplate a number of stages that a local authority must go through
    when deciding on whether and how to provide special educational provision for a child with
    learning difficulties. If, as a result of that process, the local authority decides that special
    educational provision is called for, it is at that stage that s 319 applies. In answering the question
    whether it is satisfied that it would be 'inappropriate' for the special educational provision to be
    made in a school or not, it is not enough for the local authority to ask simply 'can' the school
    meet the statement of needs set out in the statement under s 324 (see PARA 1002); the authority
    has to see if a school would 'not be suitable' or 'would not be proper', and to do that it has to
    take into account all the circumstances of the case in hand which might include consideration of
    the following matters (depending on the facts of the particular case): the child's background and
    medical history; the particular educational needs of the child; the facilities that can be provided
    by a school; the facilities that could be provided other than in a school; the comparative cost of
    the possible alternatives to the child's educational provisions; the child's reaction to education
    provisions, either at a school or elsewhere; the parents' wishes; and any other particular
    circumstances that apply to a particular child: *R (on the application of M) v Hounslow London
    Borough Council* [2009] EWCA Civ 859, [2010] 2 All ER 467, [2010] LGR 468, [2009] All ER
    (D) 17 (Sep). If the local authority is not satisfied that it would be inappropriate for the special
    educational provision to be made in a school, then it must decide whether the education is to be
    in a maintained school under the Education Act 1996 s 316(3), or if not, under s 316A (see PARA
    1204): *R (on the application of M) v Hounslow London Borough Council* (above). Where the
    school provision by the local authority is regarded as appropriate, there is no power under the
    Education Act 1996 s 319(1) to make arrangements for non-school provision: *T v Special
    Educational Needs Tribunal and Wiltshire County Council* [2002] EWHC 1474 (Admin),
    [2002] ELR 704.
9   Education Act 1996 s 319(2) (amended by SI 2010/1158). As to the meaning of 'parent' see
    PARA 7 note 6. As to the exercise of the duty to consult see JUDICIAL REVIEW vol 61 (2010) PARA
    627.

1018.   Provision outside England and Wales for certain children.   A local
authority[1] may make such arrangements as it thinks fit to enable a child[2] for
whom it maintains a statement of special educational needs[3] to attend an
institution outside England and Wales[4] which specialises in providing for
children with special needs[5]. Where a local authority makes such arrangements
in respect of a child, those arrangements may in particular include contributing
to or paying[6]:

   (1)   fees charged by the institution[7];

(2) expenses reasonably incurred in maintaining the child while he is at the institution or travelling to or from it[8];

(3) the child's travelling expenses[9]; and

(4) expenses reasonably incurred by any person accompanying the child while he is travelling or staying at the institution[10].

This power is without prejudice to any other powers of a local authority[11].

1 As to the meaning of 'local authority' see PARA 25.
2 As to the meaning of 'child' see PARA 7 note 6.
3 Ie a statement maintained under the Education Act 1996 s 324: see PARA 1002. As to the meaning of 'special educational needs' see PARA 989. As to England see also the Children and Families Act 2014 s 62; and PARA 967; see also PARA 943.
4 As to the meaning of 'Wales' see PARA 7 note 3.
5 Education Act 1996 s 320(1) (amended by SI 2010/1158). 'Children with special needs' means children who have particular needs which would be special educational needs if those children were in England and Wales: Education Act 1996 s 320(2). As to the effect generally of the Children and Families Act 2014 see PARA 941. See also the Education Act 1996 s 311A; and PARA 941.
6 Education Act 1996 s 320(3) (amended by SI 2010/1158).
7 Education Act 1996 s 320(3)(a).
8 Education Act 1996 s 320(3)(b).
9 Education Act 1996 s 320(3)(c).
10 Education Act 1996 s 320(3)(d).
11 Education Act 1996 s 320(4) (amended by SI 2010/1158).

1019. Duty to inform parents where special educational provision is made. If a child[1] for whom no statement of special educational needs[2] is maintained[3] is a registered pupil[4] at a community, foundation or voluntary school[5] or a maintained nursery school[6] or a pupil referral unit in Wales[7], and special educational provision[8] is made for him at the school because it is considered that he has special educational needs[9], and the child's parent[10] has not previously been informed[11] of special educational provision made for him at the school[12], then: (1) if the school is a pupil referral unit, the local authority[13] must secure that the head teacher[14] informs the child's parent that special educational provision is being made for him at the school because it is considered that he has special educational needs[15]; and (2) in any other case, the governing body[16] must inform the child's parent that special educational provision is being made for him there because it is considered that he has special educational needs[17].

If a local authority or other person providing relevant nursery education[18] for a child makes special educational provision for him because it is considered that he has special educational needs[19], and no statement of special educational needs[20] is maintained for the child[21], and the child's parent has not previously been informed[22] of the special educational provision made for the child[23], the authority or other person concerned must inform the child's parent that special educational provision is being made for him because it is considered that he has special educational needs[24].

1 As to the meaning of 'child' see PARA 989 note 1.
2 As to the meaning of 'special educational needs' see PARA 989.
3 Ie under the Education Act 1996 s 324: see PARA 1002.
4 As to the meaning of 'registered pupil' see PARA 437.
5 As to the meaning of references to a community, foundation or voluntary school see PARA 106.
6 Education Act 1996 s 317A(1)(a)(i) (s 317A added by the Special Educational Needs and Disability Act 2001 s 7(1); and the Education Act 1996 s 317A(1)(a)(i) amended by the Education Act 2002 s 215(1), Sch 21 para 40). As to the meaning of 'maintained nursery school' see PARA 99 note 4. As to the effect generally of the Children and Families Act 2014 see PARA 941. See also the Education Act 1996 s 311A; and PARA 941.

7   Education Act 1996 s 317A(1)(a)(ii) (as added: see note 6). As to pupil referral units see PARA
     427 et seq. As to the meaning of 'Wales' see PARA 7 note 3. As to the effect generally of the
     Children and Families Act 2014 see PARA 941. See also the Education Act 1996 s 311A; and
     PARA 941.
8   As to the meaning of 'special educational provision' see PARA 989.
9   Education Act 1996 s 317A(1)(b) (as added: see note 6).
10   As to the meaning of 'parent' see PARA 7 note 6.
11   Ie under the Education Act 1996 s 317A.
12   Education Act 1996 s 317A(1)(c) (as added: see note 6).
13   As to the meaning of 'local authority' see PARA 25.
14   As to the meaning of 'head teacher' see PARA 86 note 4.
15   Education Act 1996 s 317A(2) (as added: see note 6).
16   As to the governing bodies of maintained schools in Wales see PARA 195 et seq.
17   Education Act 1996 s 317A(3) (as added: see note 6).
18   'Relevant nursery education' means nursery education which is provided: (1) by a local
     authority; or (2) by any other person who is in receipt of financial assistance given by such an
     authority and whose provision of nursery education is taken into account by the authority in
     formulating proposals for the purposes of the School Standards and Framework Act 1998
     s 120(2)(a) (repealed): s 123(4) (amended by SI 2010/1158). As to the meaning of 'nursery
     education' see PARA 95.
        As from a day to be appointed, the School Standards and Framework Act 1998 s 123(3A)(a)
     is amended so as to refer to relevant early years education, instead of relevant nursery education
     (see s 123(3A)(a) (as added (see note 19); and prospectively amended by the Childcare Act 2006
     s 103(1), Sch 2 para 34(a))); in Wales, 'relevant early years education' means nursery education
     which is provided by a local authority in Wales, or by any other person who is in receipt of
     financial assistance given by such an authority under arrangements made by it in pursuance of
     the duty imposed by the School Standards and Framework Act 1998 s 118 (see PARA 96) (see
     s 123(4) (prospectively substituted by the Childcare Act 2006 s 103(1), Sch 2 para 34(b); and
     amended by SI 2010/1158)). At the date at which this volume states the law no such day had
     been appointed in relation to Wales.
19   School Standards and Framework Act 1998 s 123(3A)(a) (s 123(3A), (3B) added by the Special
     Educational Needs and Disability Act 2001 s 7(2)). As to the prospective amendment of this
     provision see note 18.
20   Ie under the Education Act 1996 s 324: see PARA 1002.
21   School Standards and Framework Act 1998 s 123(3A)(b) (as added: see note 19).
22   Ie under the School Standards and Framework Act 1998 s 123(3B): see the text to note 24.
23   School Standards and Framework Act 1998 s 123(3A)(c) (as added: see note 19).
24   School Standards and Framework Act 1998 s 123(3B) (as added (see note 19); and amended by
     SI 2010/1158). As to the duty to have regard to the code of practice see PARA 978.

1020. Duties of governing body in relation to pupils with special educational needs.

The governing body[1] of a community, foundation or voluntary school[2] or a maintained nursery school[3] must[4]:

(1)   use its best endeavours, in exercising its functions[5] in relation to the
       school, to secure that, if any registered pupil[6] has special educational
       needs[7], the special educational provision[8] for which his learning
       difficulty[9] calls is made[10];

(2)   secure that, where the responsible person[11] has been informed by the
       local authority[12] that a registered pupil has special educational needs,
       those needs are made known to all who are likely to teach him[13]; and

(3)   secure that the teachers in the school are aware of the importance of
       identifying, and providing for, those registered pupils who have special
       educational needs[14];

(4)   to the extent that it appears necessary or desirable for the purpose of
       co-ordinating provision for children[15] with special educational needs, in
       exercising functions relating to the provision for such children, consult
       the local authority and the governing bodies of other such schools[16];

(5)   designate a member of the staff at the school (to be known as the

'special educational needs co-ordinator') as having responsibility for
co-ordinating the provision for pupils with special educational needs[17].
Where a child who has special educational needs is being educated in a
community, foundation or voluntary school or a maintained nursery school,
those concerned with making special educational provision for the child must
secure, so far as is reasonably practicable and is compatible with[18]:

(a)   the child receiving the special educational provision for which his
      learning difficulty calls[19];

(b)   the provision of efficient education for the children with whom he will
      be educated[20]; and

(c)   the efficient use of resources[21],

that the child engages in the activities of the school together with children who
do not have special educational needs[22].

1   As to the governing bodies of maintained schools in Wales see PARA 195 et seq.
2   As to the meaning of references to a community, foundation or voluntary school see PARA 106.
3   As to the meaning of 'maintained nursery school' see PARA 99 note 4.
4   Education Act 1996 s 317(1) (amended by the Education Act 2002 s 215(1), Sch 21
    para 39(1), (2)). As to the effect generally of the Children and Families Act 2014 see PARA 941.
    See also the Education Act 1996 s 311A; and PARA 941.
5   As to the meaning of 'functions' see PARA 18 note 5.
6   As to the meaning of 'registered pupil' see PARA 437.
7   As to the meaning of 'special educational needs' see PARA 989.
8   As to the meaning of 'special educational provision' see PARA 989.
9   As to the meaning of 'learning difficulty' see PARA 989.
10 Education Act 1996 s 317(1)(a). As to the effect generally of the Children and Families Act 2014
    see PARA 941. See also the Education Act 1996 s 311A; and PARA 941.
11 'The responsible person' means the head teacher or the appropriate governor (that is, the
    chairman of the governing body or, where the governing body has designated another governor
    for these purposes, that other governor): Education Act 1996 s 317(2) (substituted by the
    Education Act 2002 Sch 21 para 39(1), (3)). As to the meaning of 'head teacher' see PARA 86
    note 4.
12 As to the meaning of 'local authority' see PARA 25.
13 Education Act 1996 s 317(1)(b) (amended by SI 2010/1158).
14 Education Act 1996 s 317(1)(c).
15 As to the meaning of 'child' see PARA 989 note 1.
16 See the Education Act 1996 s 317(3)(a) (amended by the School Standards and Framework
    Act 1998 s 140(1), (3), Sch 30 paras 57, 74(1), (4)(a), Sch 31; the Education Act 2002 Sch 21
    para 39(1), (4); and SI 2010/1158).
17 Education Act 1996 s 317(3A) (s 317(3A), (3B) added by the Education and Inspections
    Act 2006 s 173). Regulations may: (1) require the governing bodies of schools falling within the
    Education Act 1996 s 317(3A) to ensure that special educational needs co-ordinators have
    prescribed qualifications or prescribed experience (or both) (s 317(3B)(a) (as so added)); and (2)
    confer on the governing bodies of those schools other functions relating to special educational
    needs co-ordinators (s 317(3B)(b) (as so added)). 'Regulations' means regulations made by the
    Secretary of State or, in relation to Wales, the Welsh Ministers: see s 579(1), and see PARA 941.
    As to the Secretary of State see PARA 58. As to the Welsh Ministers see PARA 59. As to the
    meaning of 'Wales' see PARA 7 note 3. The functions of the Secretary of State under s 317, so far
    as exercisable in relation to Wales, were originally transferred to the National Assembly for
    Wales (see the National Assembly for Wales (Transfer of Functions) Order 1999, SI 1999/672,
    art 2, Sch 1) and are now vested in the Welsh Ministers (see the Government of Wales Act 2006
    s 162(1), Sch 11 para 30). As to the regulations made see the Education (Special Educational
    Needs Co-ordinators) (England) Regulations 2008, SI 2008/2945 (amended by SI 2009/1387).
    At the date at which this volume states the law no such regulations had been made in relation to
    Wales.
18 Education Act 1996 s 317(4) (amended by the School Standards and Framework Act 1998
    Sch 30 paras 57, 74(1), (5)).
19 Education Act 1996 s 317(4)(a).
20 Education Act 1996 s 317(4)(b).

21 Education Act 1996 s 317(4)(c).
22 Education Act 1996 s 317(4).

1021. Access for local authority to certain schools. Where a local authority[1] maintains a statement of special educational needs[2] for a child[3], and in pursuance of the statement education is provided for the child at a school maintained[4] by another local authority or at an independent school[5], any person[6] authorised by the local authority is entitled to have access at any reasonable time to the premises[7] of any such school for the purpose of monitoring the special educational provision[8] made in pursuance of the statement for the child at the school[9].

1 As to the meaning of 'local authority' see PARA 25.
2 Ie under the Education Act 1996 s 324: see PARA 1002. As to the meaning of 'special educational needs' see PARA 989.
3 Education Act 1996 s 327(1)(a) (amended by SI 2010/1158). As to the meaning of 'child' see PARA 989 note 1. As to the effect generally of the Children and Families Act 2014 see PARA 941. See also the Education Act 1996 s 311A; and PARA 941.
4 As to the meaning of 'maintained school' see PARA 989 note 10.
5 Education Act 1996 s 327(1)(b) (substituted by the School Standards and Framework Act 1998 s 140(1), Sch 30 paras 57, 78; and amended by the Education Act 2002 s 173; and SI 2010/1158). As to the meaning of 'independent school' see PARA 369.
6 As to the meaning of 'person' see PARA 7 note 6.
7 As to the meaning of 'premises' see PARA 62 note 19.
8 As to the meaning of 'special educational provision' see PARA 989.
9 Education Act 1996 s 327(2) (amended by SI 2010/1158).

1022. Provision of goods and services in connection with special educational needs. A local authority[1] may, for the purpose only of assisting the governing bodies[2] of community, foundation or voluntary schools[3] or maintained nursery schools[4] (in its or any other area) in the performance of their duties in relation to pupils with special educational needs[5], or the governing bodies of community or foundation special schools[6] (in its or any other area) in the performance of their duties[7], supply goods or services to those bodies[8].

A local authority may supply goods and services to any authority in Wales or other person[9] for the purpose of assisting them in making for a child[10] any special educational provision[11] for which any learning difficulty[12] of the child calls[13].

These provisions[14] are without prejudice to the generality of any other power of local authorities to supply goods or services[15].

1 As to the meaning of 'local authority' see PARA 25.
2 As to the governing bodies of maintained schools in Wales see PARA 195 et seq.
3 As to the meaning of references to a community, foundation or voluntary school see PARA 106.
4 As to the meaning of 'maintained nursery school' see PARA 99 note 4.
5 Education Act 1996 s 318(1)(a). The duties referred to are those duties under the Education Act 1996 s 317(1)(a) (see PARA 1020): see s 318(1)(a). As to the effect generally of the Children and Families Act 2014 see PARA 941. See also the Education Act 1996 s 311A; and PARA 941.
6 As to the meaning of references to a community or foundation special school see PARA 106.
7 Education Act 1996 s 318(1)(b).
8 Education Act 1996 s 318(1) (amended by the School Standards and Framework Act 1998 Sch 30 paras 57, 75(1), (2); the Education Act 2002 Sch 21 para 41(1), (2); and SI 2010/1158). The terms on which goods or services are supplied by local authorities under the Education Act 1996 s 318 to the governing bodies of community, foundation or voluntary schools, maintained nursery schools or community or foundation special schools in any other area may, in such circumstances as may be prescribed, include such terms as to payment as may be prescribed: s 318(2) (amended by the School Standards and Framework Act 1998 s 140(1), Sch 30 paras 57, 75(1), (3); the Education Act 2002 s 215(1), Sch 21 para 41(1), (3); and

SI 2010/1158). 'Prescribed' means prescribed by regulations; and 'regulations' means regulations made by the Secretary of State or, in relation to Wales, the Welsh Ministers: see the Education Act 1996 s 579(1), and see PARA 941. As to the Secretary of State see PARA 58. As to the Welsh Ministers see PARA 59. As to the meaning of 'Wales' see PARA 7 note 3. The functions of the Secretary of State under s 318, so far as exercisable in relation to Wales, were originally transferred to the National Assembly for Wales (see the National Assembly for Wales (Transfer of Functions) Order 1999, SI 1999/672, art 2, Sch 1) and are now vested in the Welsh Ministers (see the Government of Wales Act 2006 s 162(1), Sch 11 para 30).

Where a local authority supplies, under the Education Act 1996 s 318(1), goods or services to the governing body of a school which it does not maintain, and which is in the area of another local authority, the terms on which the authority supplies those goods or services may include such terms as to payment as can reasonably be expected to secure that the full cost (but not more than the full cost) of the provision is recovered by the authority: Education (Payment for Special Educational Needs Supplies) Regulations 1999, SI 1999/710, reg 2 (amended by SI 2010/1142).

9   Ie other than a governing body within the Education Act 1996 s 318(1): see the text to notes 1–8.
10 As to the meaning of 'child' see PARA 989 note 1.
11 As to the meaning of 'special educational provision' see PARA 989.
12 As to the meaning of 'learning difficulty' see PARA 989.
13 Education Act 1996 s 318(3B) (added by the Education Act 2002 s 194(2)(b); and amended by the Children and Families Act 2014 Sch 3 paras 1, 16(1), (3)). As to the power of the Welsh Ministers to make regional provision for special educational needs see PARA 1024.
14 Ie the provisions of the Education Act 1996 s 318.
15 Education Act 1996 s 318(4) (amended by SI 2010/1158). As to the supply of goods and services by local authorities generally see LOCAL GOVERNMENT vol 69 (2009) PARA 495.

1023.   Review of arrangements for special educational provision.   A local authority[1] must keep under review the arrangements made by it for special educational provision[2]. In doing so the authority must, to the extent that it appears necessary or desirable for the purpose of co-ordinating provision for children[3] with special educational needs[4], consult the governing bodies[5] of community, foundation and voluntary schools, community and foundation special schools[6] and maintained nursery schools[7] in its area[8].

1   As to the meaning of 'local authority' see PARA 25.
2   Education Act 1996 s 315(1) (amended by SI 2010/1158). As to the meaning of 'special educational provision' see PARA 989. As to the effect generally of the Children and Families Act 2014 see PARA 941. See also the Education Act 1996 s 311A; and PARA 941.
    This duty is effectively limited to the assessment and provision of appropriate places and does not extend to monitoring every pupil: *P v Harrow London Borough Council* [1993] 2 FCR 341, [1993] 1 FLR 723 (decided under previous legislation; pupil placed in an independent school); applied in *R (on the application of Campbell) v Special Educational Needs and Disability Tribunal* [2003] EWHC 1590 (Admin), [2004] ELR 111, [2003] All ER (D) 309 (Jun).
3   As to the meaning of 'child' see PARA 989 note 1.
4   As to the meaning of 'special educational needs' see PARA 989.
5   As to the governing bodies of maintained schools in Wales see PARA 195 et seq.
6   As to the meaning of references to a community, foundation or voluntary school or a community or foundation special school see PARA 106.
7   As to the meaning of 'maintained nursery school' see PARA 99 note 4.
8   Education Act 1996 s 315(2) (amended by the School Standards and Framework Act 1998 s 140(1), Sch 30 paras 57, 73; and the Education Act 2002 s 215(1), Sch 21 para 37). As to the exercise of the duty to consult see JUDICIAL REVIEW vol 61 (2010) PARA 627.

1024.   Regional provision for special educational needs.   The Welsh Ministers[1] may direct local authorities[2] to consider whether they (or any of them) would be able to carry out their special education functions[3], in respect of children[4] with the special educational needs specified in the direction, more efficiently or effectively if regional provision[5] were made[6]. The authorities to whom a direction is given must report their conclusions to the Welsh Ministers no later than the time specified in the direction[7]. Such a direction may be given to local authorities generally or to one or more authorities specified in the direction[8].

Where the Welsh Ministers are of the opinion that two or more local authorities would be able to carry out their special education functions, in respect of children falling within a particular description, more effectively or efficiently if regional provision were made in relation to the areas of those authorities, the Welsh Ministers may give one or more of the directions specified[9] for the purpose of securing that regional provision is made in relation to the description of children from the areas specified in the direction[10].

Where (1) the Welsh Ministers have given a direction[11]; and (2) either proposals have been published in accordance with the direction, or the time allowed under the direction for the publication of the proposals has expired, the Welsh Ministers may make any proposals that could have been made in accordance with the direction[12].

Any person may object to proposals published[13]. Objections must be sent in writing to the Welsh Ministers before the end of 28 days beginning with the day on which the proposals were published[14].

The Welsh Ministers may, after considering any objections made[15] (and not withdrawn) adopt the proposals with or without modifications, or determine not to adopt the proposals[16].

1 As to the Welsh Ministers see PARA 59.
2 As to the meaning of 'local authority' see the School Standards and Organisation (Wales) Act 2013 s 98(3).
3 'Special education functions' means functions under the Education Act 1996 Pt IV (ss 311A–349) (special educational needs) (see PARA 989 et seq): see the School Standards and Organisation (Wales) Act 2013 s 64.
4 As to the meaning of 'child' see PARA 989 note 1 (definition applied by the School Standards and Organisation (Wales) Act 2013 s 98(1)).
5 'Regional provision' means (1) provision of education for children belonging to the areas of different local authorities, at a school maintained by one of those authorities, or (2) provision made by two or more local authorities for goods or services to be supplied by one of the authorities (a) to the other or others, or (b) to one or more governing bodies of schools maintained by the other authority or authorities: see the School Standards and Organisation (Wales) Act 2013 s 64.
6 See the School Standards and Organisation (Wales) Act 2013 s 65(1).
7 See the School Standards and Organisation (Wales) Act 2013 s 65(2).
8 See the School Standards and Organisation (Wales) Act 2013 s 65(3).
9 Ie specified in the School Standards and Organisation (Wales) Act 2013 s 66(3).
    The directions are (1) that a local authority exercise its powers to make proposals to establish, alter or discontinue schools; (2) that the governing body of a foundation or voluntary school exercise its powers to make proposals to alter its school; (3) that two or more local authorities make arrangements under which provision for education is made by one of the authorities in respect of persons from the area (or areas) of the other authority (or authorities), and provision is made for determining the payments to be made under the arrangements in respect of the provision of that education; (4) that two or more local authorities make arrangements that provide for one of those authorities to supply to the other (or others) goods or services to be specified in the arrangements on terms (including terms as to payment) to be so specified; (5) that a local authority and the governing bodies of one or more foundation or voluntary schools make arrangements that provide for the authority to supply to the governing bodies goods or services to be specified in the arrangements, on terms (including terms as to payment) to be so specified: see the School Standards and Organisation (Wales) Act 2013 s 66(3). In regard to s 66(3) see further s 66(4), (5). As to the meaning of 'powers to make proposals to establish, alter or discontinue schools' and 'powers to make proposals to alter its school' see s 83(1). Further provision about proposals made after a direction under s 66 is made: see s 67.
10 See the School Standards and Organisation (Wales) Act 2013 s 66(1), (2).

11 Ie a direction under the School Standards and Organisation (Wales) Act 2013 s 66.
12 See the School Standards and Organisation (Wales) Act 2013 s 68.
13 See the School Standards and Organisation (Wales) Act 2013 s 69(1). The reference is to proposals published under s 69.
14 See the School Standards and Organisation (Wales) Act 2013 s 69(2).
15 Ie objections made in accordance with the School Standards and Organisation (Wales) Act 2013 s 69.
16 See the School Standards and Organisation (Wales) Act 2013 s 70.

1025. Duty of certain bodies to help local authority. Where it appears to a local authority[1] that another local authority, the National Health Service Commissioning Board, a clinical commissioning group[2] or a local health board[3] could, by taking any specified action, help in the exercise of any of their functions relating to special educational needs[4], it may request the help of that body, specifying the action in question[5]. A body whose help is so requested must comply with the request unless[6]:

(1)   it considers that the help requested is not necessary for the purpose of the exercise of those functions by the local authority that made the request[7]; or

(2)   in a case where the request is made of the National Health Service Commissioning Board, a clinical commissioning group or a local health board, if that body considers that, having regard to the resources available to it for the purpose of the exercise of its functions under the National Health Service Act 2006 or the National Health Service (Wales) Act 2006, it is not reasonable for it to comply with the request[8]; or

(3)   in a case where the request is made of a local authority, if that authority considers that the request is not compatible with its own statutory or other duties and obligations or unduly prejudices the discharge of any of its functions[9].

Regulations[10] may provide that, where a local authority, the National Health Service Commissioning Board, a clinical commissioning group or local health board are under a duty by virtue of head (1), (2) or (3) above to comply with a request to help a local authority in the making of an assessment[11] or a statement[12] of special educational needs, it must, subject to prescribed[13] exceptions, comply with the request within the prescribed period[14].

1   As to the meaning of 'local authority' see PARA 25.
2   As to the National Health Service Commissioning Board and clinical commissioning groups see HEALTH SERVICES.
3   As to local health boards see HEALTH SERVICES vol 54 (2008) PARA 74.
4   Ie its functions under the Education Act 1996 Pt IV (ss 311A–349). As to the meaning of 'special educational needs' see PARA 989. As to the meaning of 'functions' see PARA 18 note 5.
5   Education Act 1996 s 322(1) (amended by SI 2010/1158; and the Health and Social Care Act 2012 Sch 5 paras 77, 78(1), (2)). As to the effect generally of the Children and Families Act 2014 see PARA 941. See also the Education Act 1996 s 311A; and PARA 941.
       It has been judicially observed that the Education Act 1996 s 322, by imposing a separate duty on health bodies to help local authorities, would not have been required were the definition of public expenditure used for the purposes of s 9 (see PARA 7) wide and comprehensive enough to include costs incurred by health bodies and social services: *S v Somerset County Council* [2002] EWHC 1808 (Admin) at [30]–[31], [2003] ELR 78 per Sir Richard Tucker.
6   Education Act 1996 s 322(2) (amended by the Health and Social Care Act 2012 Sch 5 paras 77, 78(1), (3)).
7   Education Act 1996 s 322(2)(a) (amended by SI 2010/1158).
8   See the Education Act 1996 s 322(2)(b), (3)(a) (amended by the National Health Service (Consequential Provisions) Act 2006 s 2, Sch 1 paras 181, 182; SI 2000/90; SI 2007/961; SI 2010/1158; and the Health and Social Care Act 2012 Sch 5 paras 77, 78(1), (4)). This does

not absolve the local authority of its duty under the Education Act 1996 s 324(5)(a) (see PARA 1002) to ensure that the specified provision is made, for that is a duty that is not delegable: *R v Harrow London Borough Council, ex p M* [1997] 3 FCR 761, [1997] ELR 62. See also *R v Brent and Harrow Health Authority, ex p Harrow London Borough Council* [1997] 3 FCR 765, [1997] ELR 187 (a health body was entitled to ration its resources and refuse to meet a request by a local authority for provision of speech therapy, occupational therapy and physiotherapy).

9 See the Education Act 1996 s 322(2)(b), (3)(b) (amended by SI 2010/1158).

10 'Regulations' means regulations made by the Secretary of State or, in relation to Wales, the Welsh Ministers: see the Education Act 1996 s 579(1), and see PARA 941. As to the Secretary of State see PARA 58. As to the Welsh Ministers see PARA 59. As to the meaning of 'Wales' see PARA 7 note 3. The functions of the Secretary of State under s 322, so far as exercisable in relation to Wales, were originally transferred to the National Assembly for Wales (see the National Assembly for Wales (Transfer of Functions) Order 1999, SI 1999/672, art 2, Sch 1) and are now vested in the Welsh Ministers (see the Government of Wales Act 2006 s 162(1), Sch 11 para 30).

11 Ie under the Education Act 1996 s 323: see PARA 994.

12 Ie under the Education Act 1996 s 324: see PARA 1002.

13 'Prescribed' means prescribed by regulations: Education Act 1996 s 579(1).

14 Education Act 1996 s 322(4) (amended by SI 2000/90; SI 2007/961; SI 2010/1158; and the Health and Social Care Act 2012 Sch 5 paras 77, 78(1), (5)). As to the regulations made in relation to Wales see the Education (Special Educational Needs) (Wales) Regulations 2002, SI 2002/152, reg 12(8)–(10) (amended by SI 2010/1172).

1026. Duty of local authority to provide advice and information to parents of children with special educational needs. A local authority[1] must arrange for any child[2] in its area with special educational needs[3], for a parent[4] of any such child and for a case friend for any such child[5], to be provided with advice and information about matters relating to those needs[6]; and must take such steps as it considers appropriate for making the services so provided known to children in its area[7], parents of children in its area[8], head teachers[9] and proprietors[10] of schools[11] in its area[12], and such other persons[13] as it considers appropriate[14]. In making the arrangements, the authority must have regard to any guidance given by the Welsh Ministers[15]; and the arrangements must comply with any provisions made in regulations by the Welsh Ministers that relate to the arrangements[16].

1 As to the meaning of 'local authority' see PARA 25.

2 As to the meaning of 'parent' see PARA 7 note 6.

3 As to the meaning of 'special educational needs' see PARA 989.

4 As to the meaning of 'child' see PARA 989 note 1.

5 As to case friends see PARA 1030.

6 Education Act 1996 s 332AA(1) (s 332AA added by the Education (Wales) Measure 2009 s 4(1), (3) (amended by SI 2010/1148); and the Education Act 1996 s 332AA(1) amended by the Children and Families Act 2014 Sch 3 paras 1, 25(1), (2))). As to the effect generally of the Children and Families Act 2014 see PARA 941. See also the Education Act 1996 s 311A; and PARA 941.

7 Education Act 1996 s 332AA(4)(a) (as added: see note 16).

8 Education Act 1996 s 332AA(4)(b) (as added: see note 16).

9 As to the meaning of 'head teacher' see PARA 86 note 4.

10 As to the meaning of 'proprietor' see PARA 51 note 4.

11 As to the meaning of 'school' see PARA 91.

12 Education Act 1996 s 332AA(4)(c) (as added: see note 16).

13 As to the meaning of 'person' see PARA 7 note 6.

14 Education Act 1996 s 332AA(4)(d) (as added: see note 16).

15 Education Act 1996 s 332AA(2) (as added: see note 16). As to the publication of guidance see s 571; and PARA 60 note 24. As to the Welsh Ministers see PARA 59.

16 Education Act 1996 s 332AA(3) (as added: see note 16). At the date at which this volume states the law no such regulations had been made.

1027. Provision of information by governing bodies. The governing body[1] of a community, foundation or voluntary school[2], a maintained nursery school[3], or a community or foundation special school[4] must include special needs information[5] in the governors' report[6].

1   As to the governing bodies of maintained schools in Wales see PARA 195 et seq.
2   As to the meaning of references to a community, foundation or voluntary school see PARA 106.
3   As to the meaning of 'maintained nursery school' see PARA 99 note 4.
4   As to the meaning of references to a community or foundation special school see PARA 106.
5   'Special needs information' means: (1) such information as may be prescribed about the implementation of the governing body's policy for pupils with special educational needs; and (2) information as to the arrangements for the admission of disabled persons as pupils at the school, the steps taken to prevent disabled pupils from being treated less favourably than other pupils, the facilities provided to assist access to the school by disabled pupils, and the plan prepared by the governing body under the Equality Act 2010 Sch 10 para 3 (see PARA 11): Education Act 1996 s 317(6) (s 317(5), (6) substituted by the Education Act 2005 s 117, Sch 18 para 2; and the Education Act 1996 s 317(6) amended by the Equality Act 2010 s 211(1), Sch 26 Pt 1 paras 35, 36(1), (2)). For the purposes of head (2) above, 'disabled person' means a person who is a disabled person for the purposes of the Equality Act 2010 (see DISCRIMINATION vol 33 (2013) PARA 50 et seq); and s 89 (see PARA 9) and Sch 10 para 6 (see PARA 11) of that Act apply for these purposes as they apply for the purposes of Pt 6 and Sch 10 to that Act: Education Act 1996 s 317(6A) (added by the Special Educational Needs and Disability Act 2001 s 14(2); and substituted by the Equality Act 2010 s 211(1), Sch 26 Pt 1 paras 35, 36(1), (3)). As to the meaning of 'pupil' see PARA 20 note 4. As to the meaning of 'special educational needs' see PARA 989. 'Prescribed' means prescribed by regulations; and 'regulations' means regulations made by the Secretary of State or, in relation to Wales, the Welsh Ministers: see the Education Act 1996 s 579(1), and see PARA 941. As to the Secretary of State see PARA 58. As to the Welsh Ministers see PARA 59. As to the meaning of 'Wales' see PARA 7 note 3. The functions of the Secretary of State under s 317, so far as exercisable in relation to Wales, were originally transferred to the National Assembly for Wales (see the National Assembly for Wales (Transfer of Functions) Order 1999, SI 1999/672, art 2, Sch 1) and are now vested in the Welsh Ministers (see the Government of Wales Act 2006 s 162(1), Sch 11 para 30).
      As to the regulations made under the Education Act 1996 s 317(5) in relation to Wales see the Education (Special Educational Needs) (Information) (Wales) Regulations 1999, SI 1999/1442.
6   Education Act 1996 s 317(5) (as substituted (see note 5); and amended by the Children and Families Act 2014 Sch 3 paras 1, 15). The governors' report referred to is that prepared under the Education Act 2002 s 30(1) (see PARA 218): see the Education Act 1996 s 317(5) (as so substituted and amended). As to the effect generally of the Children and Families Act 2014 see PARA 941. See also the Education Act 1996 s 311A; and PARA 941.

1028. Duty of local authority in relation to disagreements between local authorities, governing bodies and parents. A local authority[1] must make arrangements with a view to avoiding or resolving disagreements between governing bodies of maintained schools[2] and the local authority (on the one hand) and children[3] in its area or parents[4] of children in its area (on the other) about the exercise of the statutory functions[5] relating to special educational needs[6]. The arrangements must provide for the appointment of independent persons with the functions of facilitating the avoidance or resolution of such disagreements[7]. In making the arrangements, the authority must have regard to any guidance given by the Welsh Ministers[8]; and the arrangements must comply with any provisions made in regulations by the Welsh Ministers that relate to the arrangements[9]. The arrangements cannot affect the entitlement of a child or a parent of a child to appeal to the Tribunal[10], and the authority must take such steps as it considers appropriate to make that fact known to children, to parents of children and to case friends[11] for children in its area[12].

1   As to the meaning of 'local authority' see PARA 25.

2 As to the meaning of 'maintained school' see PARA 989 note 10. As to the governing bodies of maintained schools in Wales see PARA 195 et seq.
3 As to the meaning of 'child' see PARA 989 note 1.
4 As to the meaning of 'parent' see PARA 7 note 6.
5 Ie functions under the Education Act 1996 Pt IV (ss 311A–349).
6 See the Education Act 1996 s 332BA(1)(a), (b), (8) (s 332BA added by the Education (Wales) Measure 2009 s 5(1), (3) (amended by SI 2010/1148); and the Education Act 2014 s 332BA(1) amended by the Children and Families Act 2014 Sch 3 paras 1, 27(1), (2)). As to the meaning of 'special educational needs' see PARA 989. As to the effect generally of the Children and Families Act 2014 see PARA 941. See also the Education Act 1996 s 311A; and PARA 941.
   The authority must take such steps as it considers appropriate for making the arrangements under the Education Act 1996 s 332BA(1) known to children in its area, parents of children in its area, head teachers and proprietors of schools in its area, and such other persons as it considers appropriate: s 332BA(6) (as so added). As to the meaning of 'head teacher' see PARA 86 note 4. As to the meaning of 'proprietor' see PARA 51 note 4.
7 Education Act 1996 s 332BA(3) (as added: see note 6).
8 Education Act 1996 s 332BA(4) (as added: see note 6). As to the publication of guidance see s 571; and PARA 60 note 24. As to the Welsh Ministers see PARA 59.
9 Education Act 1996 s 332BA(5) (as added: see note 6). At the date at which this volume states the law no such regulations had been made.
10 As to the meaning of 'the Tribunal' see PARA 999 note 15.
11 As to case friends see PARA 1030.
12 Education Act 1996 s 332BA(7) (as added: see note 6).

1029. Duty of local authority in relation to disagreements between parents and proprietors. A local authority[1] must make arrangements with a view to avoiding or resolving, in each relevant school[2], disagreements between[3]: (1) a relevant child[4] and the proprietor of the school about the special educational provision made for that child[5]; and (2) the parents of a relevant child and the proprietor of the school about the special educational provision made for that child[6]. The arrangements must provide for the appointment of independent persons with the functions of facilitating the avoidance or resolution of such disagreements[7]. In making the arrangements, the authority must have regard to any guidance given by the Welsh Ministers[8]; and the arrangements must comply with any provisions made in regulations by the Welsh Ministers that relate to the arrangements[9]. The arrangements cannot affect the entitlement of a child or a parent of a child to appeal to the Tribunal[10], and the authority must take such steps as it considers appropriate to make that fact known to children, to parents of children and to case friends[11] for children in its area[12].

1 As to the meaning of 'local authority' see PARA 25.
2 For these purposes a school is a relevant school in relation to a child if it is: (1) a maintained school or a maintained nursery school; (2) a pupil referral unit; (3) an independent school named in the statement maintained for the child under the Education Act 1996 s 324 (see PARA 1002), or (4) a school approved under s 342 (see PARA 1042): s 332BA(9) (s 332BA added by the Education (Wales) Measure 2009 s 5(1), (3) (amended by SI 2010/1148)). As to the meaning of 'school' see PARA 91. As to the meaning of 'child' see PARA 989 note 1. As to the meaning of 'maintained school' see PARA 989 note 10. As to the meaning of 'maintained nursery school' see PARA 99 note 4. As to pupil referral units see PARA 427 et seq. As to the meaning of 'independent school' see PARA 369.
3 Education Act 1996 s 332BA(2) (as added (see note 2); and amended by the Children and Families Act 2014 Sch 3 paras 1, 27(1), (2)). As to the meaning of 'special educational needs' see PARA 989. As to the effect generally of the Children and Families Act 2014 see PARA 941. See also the Education Act 1996 s 311A; and PARA 941.
   The authority must take such steps as it considers appropriate for making the arrangements under the Education Act 1996 s 332BA(2) known to children in its area, parents of children in its area, head teachers and proprietors of schools in its area, and such other persons as it considers appropriate: s 332BA(6) (as so added). As to the meaning of 'parent' see PARA 7 note 6. As to the meaning of 'head teacher' see PARA 86 note 4. As to the meaning of 'proprietor' see PARA 51 note 4.

4 'Relevant child' means a child who has special educational needs and is a registered pupil at a relevant school: Education Act 1996 s 332BA(8) (as added: see note 2). As to the meaning of 'special educational needs' see PARA 989. As to the meaning of 'registered pupil' see PARA 437.
5 Education Act 1996 s 332BA(2)(a) (as added: see note 2).
6 Education Act 1996 s 332BA(2)(b) (as added: see note 2).
7 Education Act 1996 s 332BA(3) (as added: see note 2).
8 Education Act 1996 s 332BA(4) (as added: see note 2). As to the publication of guidance see s 571; and PARA 60 note 24. As to the Welsh Ministers see PARA 59.
9 Education Act 1996 s 332BA(5) (as added: see note 2). At the date at which this volume states the law no such regulations had been made.
10 As to the meaning of 'the Tribunal' see PARA 999 note 15.
11 As to case friends see PARA 1030.
12 Education Act 1996 s 332BA(7) (as added: see note 2).

1030. Case friends. The Welsh Ministers[1] may provide by regulations[2] for a child[3] to have a person (known as a 'case friend'): (1) to make representations on behalf of a child with a view to avoiding or resolving disagreements about the exercise by local authorities[4] of the statutory functions relating to special educational needs[5]; and (2) to exercise the rights of a child to appeal to the Welsh Tribunal[6] on the child's behalf[7]. A child's case friend must: (a) make representations and exercise rights fairly and competently[8]; (b) have no interest adverse to that of the child[9]; (c) ensure that all steps and decisions taken by the case friend are for the benefit of the child and take account of the child's views[10].

1 As to the Welsh Ministers see PARA 59.
2 The regulations may (among other things): (1) confer functions on the Tribunal; (2) make provision about procedures in relation to case friends; (3) make provision about the appointment and removal of case friends; (4) specify the circumstances in which a person may or may not act as a case friend; (5) specify the circumstances in which a child must have a case friend; (6) specify further requirements in respect of the conduct of case friends: Education Act 1996 s 332ZC(3)(a)–(f) (s 332ZC added by the Education (Wales) Measure 2009 s 3 (amended by SI 2010/1148); and the Education Act 1996 s 332ZC(3)(a) amended by the Children and Families Act 2014 Sch 3 paras 1, 23(1), (3)). As to the meaning of 'functions' see PARA 18 note 5. As to the meaning of 'Tribunal' see PARA 999 note 15. As to regulations made under the Education Act 1996 s 332ZC(1), (3) see the Special Educational Needs Tribunal for Wales Regulations 2012, SI 2012/322.
3 As to the meaning of 'child' see PARA 989 note 1.
4 As to the meaning of 'local authority' see PARA 25.
5 Education Act 1996 s 332ZC(1)(a) (as added (see note 2); and amended by the Children and Families Act 2014 Sch 3 paras 1, 23(1), (2)). The functions referred to are those under the Education Act 1996 Pt IV (ss 311A–349): see s 332ZC(1)(a) (as so added). As to the meaning of 'special educational needs' see PARA 989. As to independent advocacy services see PARA 1031. As to the effect generally of the Children and Families Act 2014 see PARA 941. See also the Education Act 1996 s 311A; and PARA 941.
6 Ie the rights under the Education Act 1996 s 332ZA: see PARAS 999–1001, 1007, 1009, 1010, 1013.
7 Education Act 1996 s 332ZC(1)(b) (as added: see note 2).
8 Education Act 1996 s 332ZC(2)(a) (as added: see note 2).
9 Education Act 1996 s 332ZC(2)(b) (as added: see note 2).
10 Education Act 1996 s 332ZC(2)(c) (as added: see note 2).

1031. Independent advocacy services. Every local authority[1] in must[2]: (1) make arrangements for the provision of independent advocacy services in its area[3]; (2) refer any child[4] in its area who requests independent advocacy services to a service provider[5]; (3) refer any person[6] who is a case friend[7] for a child in its area and who requests independent advocacy services to a service provider[8]. 'Independent advocacy services' are services providing advice and assistance (by way of representation or otherwise) to a child (a) making, or intending to make an appeal[9] to the Tribunal[10]; or (b) considering whether to appeal[11] to the Tribunal[12]; or (c) taking part in or intending to take part in dispute resolution arrangements[13].

In making the arrangements, every local authority must have regard to the principle that any services provided under the arrangements must be independent of any person who is the subject of an appeal to the Tribunal[14], or involved in investigating or adjudicating on such an appeal[15]. The arrangements must comply with any provisions made in regulations by the Welsh Ministers that relate to the arrangements[16]. The arrangements may include provision for payments to be made to, or in relation to, any person carrying out functions[17] in accordance with the arrangements[18].

Every local authority must take such steps as it considers appropriate for making the arrangements known to[19] children in its area[20], parents[21] of children in its area[22], head teachers[23] and proprietors[24] of schools[25] in its area[26], and such other persons as it considers appropriate[27].

A local authority must have regard to any guidance given from time to time by the Welsh Ministers[28].

1 As to the meaning of 'local authority' see PARA 25.
2 Education Act 1996 s 332BB(1) (s 332BB added by the Education (Wales) Measure 2009 s 6 (amended by SI 2010/1148); and the Education Act 1996 s 332BB(1) amended by the Children and Families Act 2014 Sch 3 paras 1, 28(1), (2)). As to the effect generally of the Children and Families Act 2014 see PARA 941. See also the Education Act 1996 s 311A; and PARA 941.
3 Education Act 1996 s 332BB(1)(a) (as added: see note 2).
4 As to the meaning of 'child' see PARA 989 note 1.
5 Education Act 1996 s 332BB(1)(b) (as added: see note 2).
6 As to the meaning of 'person' see PARA 7 note 6.
7 As to case friends see PARA 1030.
8 Education Act 1996 s 332BB(1)(c) (as added: see note 2).
9 Ie under the Education Act 1996 s 332ZA: see PARAS 999–1001, 1007, 1009, 1010, 1013.
10 Education Act 1996 s 332BB(2)(a) (as added: see note 2). As to the meaning of 'the Tribunal' see PARA 999 note 15.
11 Ie under the Education Act 1996 s 332ZA: see PARAS 999–1001, 1007, 1009, 1010, 1013.
12 Education Act 1996 s 332BB(2)(b) (as added: see note 2).
13 Education Act 1996 s 332BB(2)(c) (as added: see note 2). Dispute resolution arrangements are arrangements made under s 332BA (see PARAS 1028, 1029): see s 332BB(2)(c) (as so added).
14 Education Act 1996 s 332BB(3)(a) (as added: see note 2).
15 Education Act 1996 s 332BB(3)(b) (as added: see note 2).
16 Education Act 1996 s 332BB(4) (as added: see note 2). At the date at which this volume states the law no such regulations had been made.
17 As to the meaning of 'functions' see PARA 18 note 5.
18 Education Act 1996 s 332BB(6) (as added: see note 2).
19 Education Act 1996 s 332BB(5) (as added (see note 2); and amended by the Children and Families Act 2014 Sch 3 paras 1, 28(1), (2)).
20 Education Act 1996 s 332BB(5)(a) (as added: see note 2).
21 As to the meaning of 'parent' see PARA 7 note 6.
22 Education Act 1996 s 332BB(5)(b) (as added: see note 2).
23 As to the meaning of 'head teacher' see PARA 86 note 4.
24 As to the meaning of 'proprietor' see PARA 51 note 4.
25 As to the meaning of 'school' see PARA 91.
26 Education Act 1996 s 332BB(5)(c) (as added: see note 2).
27 Education Act 1996 s 332BB(5)(d) (as added: see note 2).
28 Education Act 1996 s 332BB(7) (as added: see note 2). As to the publication of guidance see s 571; and PARA 60 note 24.

(v) Detained Persons

1032. Detained persons with special educational needs. Where, immediately before the beginning of the detention, a local authority in Wales was maintaining a statement of special educational needs for a detained person, the authority must keep the statement while the person is detained in relevant youth accommodation[1]. Best endeavours must be used to secure that appropriate special educational provision is made for the detained person while the person is detained[2]. A local authority in Wales may supply goods and services to the host authority or any other person making the special educational provision in question[3].

1 See the Education Act 1996 s 562C(1), (2); and PARA 549.
2 See the Education Act 1996 s 562C(3); and PARA 549.
3 See the Education Act 1996 s 562D; and PARA 549.

(vi) Code of Practice

1033. Code of practice. The Welsh Ministers[1] must issue, and may from time to time revise, a code of practice giving practical guidance in respect of the discharge by local authorities[2] and the governing bodies of maintained schools[3] and maintained nursery schools[4] of their functions[5] under the statutory provisions relating to special educational needs[6]. The Welsh Ministers must publish the code as for the time being in force[7].

Where the Welsh Ministers propose to issue or revise a code of practice, they must prepare a draft of the code (or revised code)[8]. The Welsh Ministers must consult such persons[9] about the draft as they think fit and must consider any representations made by those persons[10]. If the Welsh Ministers determine to proceed with the draft (either in its original form or with such modifications[11] as they think fit) they must follow the appropriate statutory procedure[12], and if the draft is approved following such procedure[13], the Welsh Ministers must issue the code in the form of the draft, and the code comes into effect on such day as the Welsh Ministers may by order appoint[14].

It is the duty of:

(1)　local authorities, and governing bodies of maintained schools and maintained nursery schools, exercising their functions under the statutory provisions relating to special educational needs[15]; and

(2)　any other person exercising any function for the purpose of the discharge by local authorities, and such governing bodies, of those functions[16],

to have regard to the provisions of the code[17]; and on any appeal under those provisions to the Tribunal[18], the Tribunal must have regard to any provision of the code which appears to it to be relevant to any question arising on the appeal[19].

1 As to the Welsh Ministers see PARA 59. The functions of the Secretary of State under the Education Act 1996 s 313 and the School Standards and Framework Act 1998 s 123, so far as exercisable in relation to Wales, were originally transferred to the National Assembly for Wales (see the National Assembly for Wales (Transfer of Functions) Order 1999, SI 1999/672, art 2, Sch 1) and are now vested in the Welsh Ministers (see the Government of Wales Act 2006 s 162(1), Sch 11 para 30). As to the Secretary of State see PARA 58.
2 As to the meaning of 'local authority' see PARA 25.
3 As to the meaning of 'maintained school' see PARA 989 note 10. As to the governing bodies of maintained schools in Wales see PARA 195 et seq.
4 As to the meaning of 'maintained nursery school' see PARA 99 note 4.
5 As to the meaning of 'functions' see PARA 18 note 5.
6 See the Education Act 1996 s 313(1) (amended by the School Standards and Framework Act 1998 s 140(1), Sch 30 paras 57, 72; the Education Act 2002 s 215(1), Sch 21 para 36; SI 2010/1158; and the Children and Families Act 2014 Sch 3 paras 1, 12(1), (2)). The functions

referred to are those under the Education Act 1996 Pt IV (ss 311A–349): see s 313(1) (as so amended). As to the effect of the Children and Families Act 2014 see generally PARA 941. See also the Education Act 1996 s 331A; and PARA 941.

7   Education Act 1996 s 313(4) (amended by the Children and Families Act 2014 Sch 3 paras 1, 12(1), (2)).

8   Education Act 1996 s 314(1) (amended by the Children and Families Act 2014 Sch 3 paras 1, 13(1), (2)).

9   As to the meaning of 'person' see PARA 7 note 6.

10 Education Act 1996 s 314(2) (amended by the Children and Families Act 2014 Sch 3 paras 1, 13(1), (3)).

11 As to the meaning of 'modifications' see PARA 21 note 15.

12 See the Education Act 1996 s 314(3) (amended by the Children and Families Act 2014 Sch 3 paras 1, 13(1), (4)). The Welsh Ministers, they must lay the draft code before the National Assembly for Wales: see the Education Act 1996 s 314(3) (as so amended); Government of Wales Act 2006 s 86. As to the laying of documents before Parliament see STATUTES AND LEGISLATIVE PROCESS vol 96 (2012) PARA 1052. As to the National Assembly for Wales see CONSTITUTIONAL AND ADMINISTRATIVE LAW vol 20 (2014) PARA 351 et seq.

13 Ie if it is approved by a resolution of the National Assembly for Wales: see the Education Act 1996 s 314(4) (amended by the Children and Families Act 2014 Sch 3 paras 1, 13(1), (5)); Government of Wales Act 2006 s 86.

14 See the Education Act 1996 s 314(4) (as amended: see note 13). As to the order made see the Special Educational Needs Code of Practice (Appointed Day) (Wales) Order 2002, SI 2002/156.

15 See the Education Act 1996 s 313(2)(a) (amended by SI 2010/1158).

16 See the Education Act 1996 s 313(2)(b) (amended by SI 2010/1158).

17 Education Act 1996 s 313(2). As to the duty to have regard to the code see *R (on the application of S) v Brent London Borough Council, R (on the application of T) v Head Teacher of Wembley High School, R (on the application of P) v Oxfordshire County Council Exclusion Appeals Panel* [2002] EWCA Civ 693 at [15], [2002] ELR 556, [2002] All ER (D) 277 (May) per Schiemann LJ (the guidance is not direction and certainly not rules but cannot be neglected).
    The School Standards and Framework Act 1998 also provides that any local authority or other person providing relevant nursery education, and any person employed by such an authority or other person or otherwise engaged to provide his services in the provision of such education, is under a duty to have regard to the provisions of the code of practice issued under the Education Act 1996 s 313(2) (see the School Standards and Framework Act 1998 s 123(1) (amended by the Children and Families Act 2014 Sch 3 paras 67, 69(1), (2); and SI 2010/1158)), although the School Standards and Framework Act 1998 s 123(1) does not apply in so far as the person in question is already under a duty to have regard to the provisions of that code of practice (see s 123(1A) (added by the Children and Families Act 2014 Sch 3 paras 67, 69(1), (3))). As to the meaning of 'local authority' see PARA 25 (definition applied by the School Standards and Framework Act 1998 s 142(8)). As to the meaning of 'employed' see PARA 298 note 4. 'Relevant nursery education' means nursery education which is provided by a local authority, or by any other person who is in receipt of financial assistance given by such an authority and whose provision of nursery education is taken into account by the authority in formulating proposals for the purposes of the School Standards and Framework Act 1998 s 120(2)(a) (repealed): s 123(4) (amended by SI 2010/1158). As to the meaning of 'nursery education' see PARA 95. The code of practice may include practical guidance in respect of the provision of relevant nursery education for children with special educational needs in circumstances where functions under the Education Act 1996 Pt IV do not fall to be discharged (School Standards and Framework Act 1998 s 123(2) (amended by the Children and Families Act 2014 Sch 3 paras 67, 69(1), (4))); however, unless the code of practice in question includes such provision, the Welsh Ministers must publish a document explaining how the practical guidance contained in the code applies in circumstances where functions under the Education Act 1996 Pt IV do not fall to be discharged, and the duty imposed by the School Standards and Framework Act 1998 s 123(1) to have regard to the provisions of the code includes a duty to have regard to the provisions of that document (s 123(3) (amended by the Children and Families Act 2014 Sch 3 paras 67, 69(1), (5))). As to the meaning of 'child' see PARAS 7 note 6, 989 note 1; and as to the meaning of 'special educational needs' see PARAS 943, 989 (definitions applied by the School Standards and Framework Act 1998 s 142(8)). As from a day to be appointed, these provisions are amended so as to refer to relevant early years education, instead of relevant nursery education (see the School Standards and Framework Act 1998 s 123(1), (2) (as so amended; and prospectively amended by the Childcare Act 2006 s 103(1), Sch 2 para 34(a))); in Wales 'relevant early years education' means nursery education which is provided by a local authority in Wales, or by any other person who is in receipt of financial assistance given by such

an authority under arrangements made by it in pursuance of the duty imposed by the School Standards and Framework Act 1998 s 118 (see PARA 96) (see s 123(4) (prospectively substituted by the Childcare Act 2006 s 103(1), Sch 2 para 34(b); and amended by SI 2010/1158)). At the date at which this volume states the law no such day had been appointed in relation to Wales.
18 As to the meaning of 'the Tribunal' see PARA 999 note 15. As to such appeals see PARA 1037.
19 Education Act 1996 s 313(3).

(vii) Appeals

1034. Special Educational Needs Tribunal for Wales. There continues to be a tribunal known as the Special Educational Needs Tribunal for Wales[1], which must exercise the jurisdiction conferred[2] on it[3].

There is a President of the Tribunal[4] and a panel of persons ('the chairmen's panel') who may serve as chairman of the Tribunal[5], and the Welsh Ministers[6], with the agreement of the Secretary of State[7], must appoint a panel of persons ('the lay panel') who may serve as the other two members of the Tribunal apart from the chairman[8]. The Welsh Ministers may pay to the President, and to any other person in respect of his service as a member of the Tribunal, such remuneration and allowances as the Welsh Ministers may determine[9]. The Welsh Ministers may provide such staff and accommodation as the Tribunal may require[10]; and may defray the expenses of the Tribunal to such amount as they may determine[11].

Regulations[12] made by the Welsh Ministers with the agreement of the Secretary of State may: (1) provide for the jurisdiction of the Tribunal to be exercised by such number of tribunals as may be determined from time to time by the President[13]; and (2) make such other provision in connection with the establishment and continuation of the Tribunal as the Welsh Ministers, with the agreement of the Secretary of State, consider necessary or desirable[14].

1 Education Act 1996 s 333(1ZA) (s 333(1ZA), (1ZB) added by SI 2008/2833; and the Education Act 1996 s 333(1ZB) repealed by the Children and Families Act 2014 Sch 3 paras 1, 31(1), (2)).
2 Ie by the Education Act 1996 Pt IV (ss 311A–349).
3 Education Act 1996 s 333(1) (substituted by the Special Educational Needs and Disability Act 2001 s 42(1), Sch 8 Pt 1 paras 1, 3; and amended by SI 2008/2833; and the Children and Families Act 2014 Sch 3 paras 1, 31(1), (3)(a)). As to the jurisdiction of the Tribunal see PARA 1037. Like the First-tier Tribunal (see PARA 979), the Special Educational Needs Tribunal for Wales can also hear disability discrimination claims: see the Equality Act 2010 Sch 17 paras 1–3; and DISCRIMINATION vol 33 (2013) PARA 343.
4 See the Education Act 1996 s 333(2)(a), (3) (s 333(2)(a) amended by SI 2008/2833; and the Children and Families Act 2014 Sch 3 paras 1, 31(1), (3)(b)). No person may be appointed President unless he satisfies the judicial-appointment eligibility condition on a five-year basis: see s 334(1) (amended by the Tribunals, Courts and Enforcement Act 2007 s 50, Sch 10 Pt 1 para 28). As to the judicial-appointment eligibility condition on a five-year basis see COURTS AND TRIBUNALS vol 24 (2010) PARA 645. If, in the opinion of the Lord Chancellor and of the Lord Chief Justice, the President is unfit to continue in office or is incapable of performing his duties, the Lord Chancellor may, with the concurrence of the Lord Chief Justice, revoke his appointment: Education Act 1996 s 334(3) (amended by the Constitutional Reform Act 2005 s 15(1), Sch 4 Pt 1 para 259). As to the Lord Chancellor see CONSTITUTIONAL AND ADMINISTRATIVE LAW vol 20 (2014) PARA 255 et seq. As to the Lord Chief Justice see COURTS AND TRIBUNALS vol 24 (2010) PARA 604. The President may resign office by notice in writing to the Lord Chancellor, and is eligible for re-appointment if he ceases to hold office: see the Education Act 1996 s 334(5). As to the meaning of 'writing' see PARA 76 note 8. As to the service of notices see PARA 76.
5 See the Education Act 1996 s 333(2)(b), (3) (s 333(2)(b) amended by SI 2008/2833; and the Children and Families Act 2014 Sch 3 paras 1, 31(1), (3)(b))). No person may be appointed member of the chairmen's panel unless he satisfies the judicial-appointment eligibility condition on a five-year basis: see the Education Act 1996 s 334(1) (amended by the Tribunals, Courts and Enforcement Act 2007 s 50, Sch 10 Pt 1 para 28). Each member of the chairmen's panel holds

and vacates office under the terms of the instrument under which he is appointed: see the Education Act 1996 s 334(4). A member of the chairmen's panel may resign office by notice in writing to the Lord Chancellor, and is eligible for re-appointment if he ceases to hold office: see s 334(5).

6   As to the Welsh Ministers see PARA 59.
7   As to the Secretary of State see PARA 58.
8   See the Education Act 1996 s 333(2)(c), (4) (both amended by SI 2008/2833; and the Education Act 1996 s 333(2)(c) amended by the Children and Families Act 2014 Sch 3 paras 1, 31(1), (3)(b))). No person may be appointed member of the lay panel unless he satisfies such requirements as may be prescribed in regulations made by the Welsh Ministers with the agreement of the Secretary of State: Education Act 1996 s 334(2) (amended by SI 2008/2833). As to the regulations made see the see the Special Educational Needs Tribunal for Wales Regulations 2012, SI 2012/322 (amended by SI 2012/1418; and SI 2012/3006). Each member of the lay panel holds and vacates office under the terms of the instrument under which he is appointed: Education Act 1996 s 334(4). A member of the lay panel may resign office by notice in writing to the Welsh Ministers, and is eligible for re-appointment if he ceases to hold office: see s 334(5) (amended by SI 2008/2833).
9   Education Act 1996 s 335(1) (substituted by SI 2008/2833).
10   Education Act 1996 s 333(6) (substituted by SI 2008/2833; and amended by the Children and Families Act 2014 Sch 3 paras 1, 31(1), (3)(d)).
11   Education Act 1996 s 335(2) (substituted by SI 2008/2833).
12   As to the regulations made see note 8.
13   Education Act 1996 s 333(5)(a) (s 333(5) amended by SI 2008/2833; and the Children and Families Act 2014 Sch 3 paras 1, 31(1), (3)(c)).
14   Education Act 1996 s 333(5)(b) (as amended: see note 13).

1035.   Proceedings. Regulations[1] made by the Welsh Ministers[2] may make provision about the proceedings of the Tribunal[3] on an appeal under the Education Act 1996[4] and the initiation of such an appeal[5]. The regulations may, in particular, include provision:

(1)   as to the period within which, and the manner in which, appeals are to be instituted[6];

(2)   where the jurisdiction of the Tribunal is being exercised by more than one tribunal, for determining by which tribunal any appeal is to be heard, and for the transfer of proceedings from one tribunal to another[7];

(3)   for enabling any functions[8] which relate to matters preliminary or incidental to an appeal to be performed by the President, or by the chairman[9];

(4)   for hearings to be conducted in the absence of any member other than the chairman[10];

(5)   as to the persons[11] who may appear on behalf of the parties[12];

(6)   for granting any person such disclosure or inspection of documents or right to further particulars as might be granted by the county court[13];

(7)   requiring persons to attend to give evidence and produce documents[14];

(8)   for authorising the administration of oaths[15] to witnesses[16];

(9)   for the determination of appeals without a hearing in circumstances prescribed in the regulations[17];

(10)   as to the withdrawal of appeals[18];

(11)   for the award of costs or expenses[19];

(12)   for taxing or otherwise settling any such costs or expenses (and, in particular, for enabling such costs to be taxed in the county court)[20];

(13)   for the registration and proof of decisions and orders[21];

(14)   for enabling the Tribunal to review its decisions, or revoke or vary its orders, in such circumstances as may be determined in accordance with the regulations[22];

(15)   enabling the Tribunal to stay proceedings on an appeal[23]; and

(16)   for adding and substituting parties[24].

Proceeding before the Tribunal must be held in private, except in circumstances prescribed in the regulations[25].

The Tribunal must conduct the hearing in such manner as it considers the most suitable to the clarification of the issues and generally to the just handling of the proceedings, and must seek, as far as appears to it appropriate, to avoid formality in its proceedings[26]. The Tribunal has a wide discretion to permit a party before it to raise new issues[27] and to admit late written evidence in wholly exceptional cases[28].

Part I of the Arbitration Act 1996[29] (which makes provision for the fair resolution of disputes by an impartial tribunal and for the means of resolution to be determined, so far as practicable, in accordance with the wishes of the parties) does not apply to proceedings before the Tribunal but regulations made by the Welsh Ministers may make provision corresponding to any provision of that Part[30].

1   As to the regulations made see the Special Educational Needs Tribunal for Wales Regulations 2012, SI 2012/322 (amended by SI 2012/1418; and SI 2012/3006).

2   As to the Welsh Ministers see PARA 59.

3   As to the Special Educational Needs Tribunal for Wales see PARA 1034. As to the jurisdiction of the Tribunal see PARA 1037. As to the equivalent tribunal in relation to England see PARA 979.

4   Ie under the Education Act 1996 Pt IV (ss 311A–349).

5   Education Act 1996 s 336(1) (amended by SI 2008/2833; and the Children and Families Act 2014 Sch 3 paras 1, 33(1), (2)(a)). The regulations may make provision for such an appeal to be heard, in circumstances prescribed in the regulations, with a claim in relation to a contravention of the Equality Act 2010 Pt 6 Ch 1 (ss 84–89) (see PARA 12): Education Act 1996 s 336(4A) (added by the Special Educational Needs and Disability Act 2001 s 42(1), Sch 8 Pt 1 paras 1, 13(1), (5); and amended by SI 2008/2833; and the Equality Act 2010 s 211(1), Sch 26 Pt 1 paras 35, 37). As to the effect generally of the Children and Families Act 2014 see PARA 941. See also the Education Act 1996 s 311A; and PARA 941.

6   Education Act 1996 s 336(2)(a). See *R v Special Educational Needs Tribunal, ex p KL* [1997] ELR 504. On the question of when it is appropriate for the Tribunal to adjourn its proceedings see *L v Royal Borough of Kensington and Chelsea* [1997] ELR 155; *Ligouri v City of Salford and Special Educational Needs Tribunal* [1997] ELR 455; *R v Cheshire County Council, ex p C* [1998] ELR 66 at 73 per Sedley J; *West Glamorgan County Council v Confrey* [1998] ELR 121 at 123. See also *S v Hounslow London Borough Council and Vassie* [2001] ELR 88 at [66] per Tomlinson J, who declined to rule on the conflict of authority, both tests being satisfied in the instant case.

The power of the Tribunal to strike out an appeal for want of prosecution was considered in *White v Aldridge QC and Ealing London Borough Council* [1999] ELR 58; on appeal [1999] ELR 150, [1998] All ER (D) 672, CA. See also *G v Barnet London Borough and Aldridge QC (President of Special Educational Needs Tribunal)* [1999] ELR 161 (new material may have allowed different outcome); *Glasner v South Gloucestershire Council* [2000] ELR 136; *O v Harrow London Borough Council* [2001] EWCA Civ 2046 at [22], [2002] 1 WLR 928, [2002] ELR 195 per Simon Brown LJ; *R (on the application of A) v Lambeth London Borough Council* [2002] ELR 231 at [24] per Ouseley J (issue estoppel not to be applied in all cases).

As to natural justice in the Tribunal proceedings see *Richardson v Solihull Metropolitan Borough Council, White v Ealing London Borough Council, Hereford and Worcester County Council v Lane* [1999] 1 FCR 356, [1998] ELR 319, CA (suggested school not in contemplation of either party; expert member of Tribunal may apply expert knowledge); cf *S v Hackney London Borough Council* [2001] EWHC Admin 572, [2002] ELR 45, [2001] All ER (D) 182 (Jul) (no duty to assume parental preferences other than those advanced). See also *Rhondda Cynon Taff Borough Council v Special Educational Needs Tribunal* [2001] EWHC (Admin) 823 at [14], [2002] ELR 290 per Newman J (no need for Tribunal to allow local authority to suggest cheaper alternatives). Where an omission of factual evidence is relevant, ignorance of that fact may be a source of unfairness, and only exceptionally would relief not be given: *Ali v Kirklees Metropolitan Council* [2001] EWCA Civ 582 at [20], [2001] LGR 448, [2001] ELR 657 per Sedley LJ.

7   Education Act 1996 s 336(2)(b) (amended by SI 2008/2833; and the Children and Families Act 2014 Sch 3 paras 1, 33(1), (2)(b)). A Tribunal cannot remit papers relating to a quashed decision to a freshly-constituted Tribunal: *R v Special Educational Needs Tribunal, ex p Fisher* [1999] ELR 417.

8   As to the meaning of 'functions' see PARA 18 note 5.

9   Education Act 1996 s 336(2)(c). As to the President and chairmen of the Tribunal see PARA 1034.

10   Education Act 1996 s 336(2)(e).

11   As to the meaning of 'person' see PARA 7 note 6.

12   Education Act 1996 s 336(2)(f).

13   Education Act 1996 s 336(2)(g) (amended by the Special Educational Needs and Disability Act 2001 s 42(1), Sch 8 paras 1, 13(1), (2)(b); and the Crime and Courts Act 2013 Sch 9 para 52(1)(b), (2)). Any person who without reasonable excuse fails to comply with any requirement in respect of the disclosure or inspection of documents imposed by regulations by virtue of the Education Act 1996 s 336(2)(g) is guilty of an offence: see s 336(5)(a). The penalty for such an offence is, on summary conviction, a fine not exceeding level 3 on the standard scale: see s 336(6). As to the standard scale see SENTENCING AND DISPOSITION OF OFFENDERS vol 92 (2010) PARA 142.

14   Education Act 1996 s 336(2)(h). Any person who without reasonable excuse fails to comply with any requirement imposed by regulations by virtue of s 336(2)(h) is guilty of an offence: see s 336(5)(b). The penalty for such an offence is, on summary conviction, a fine not exceeding level 3 on the standard scale: see s 336(6). As to the right of the parties to give evidence and call witnesses see *H v Gloucestershire County Council* [2000] ELR 357 (representative of the local authority does not count as a witness). The Welsh Ministers may pay such allowances for the purpose of or in connection with the attendance of persons at the Tribunal as the Welsh Ministers may determine: Education Act 1996 s 336(3) (substituted by SI 2008/2833; and amended by the Children and Families Act 2014 Sch 3 paras 1, 33(1), (2)(e)).

15   'Oath' includes affirmation and declaration: Interpretation Act 1978 s 5, Sch 1. As to oaths, affirmations and declarations see CIVIL PROCEDURE vol 11 (2009) PARA 1021 et seq.

16   Education Act 1996 s 336(2)(i).

17   Education Act 1996 s 336(2)(j) (amended by SI 2008/2833). As to an agreement by the parties to amend part 2 of a statement of special educational needs see *Crean v Somerset County Council* [2002] ELR 152. As to statements of special educational needs see PARA 1002 et seq.

18   Education Act 1996 s 336(2)(k).

19   Education Act 1996 s 336(2)(l). In connection with the matter of costs see *C v Lambeth London Borough Council* [1999] ELR 350, (1999) Times, 27 May.

20   Education Act 1996 s 336(2)(m).

21   Education Act 1996 s 336(2)(n). As to the form of decisions see *DC v London Borough of Ealing* [2010] UKUT 10 (AAC). As to guidance on the giving of reasons by Tribunals see *DC v London Borough of Ealing* (above); *S v Special Educational Needs Tribunal* [1995] 1 WLR 1627 at 1636, [1996] ELR 102 at 112 per Latham J. See also *Re L* [1994] ELR 16, CA; *Staffordshire County Council v J and J* [1996] ELR 418 at 424 per Collins J; *Joyce v Dorset County Council* [1997] ELR 26 at 34 per Latham J; *B v Isle of Wight Council* [1997] ELR 279 at 286–289 per McCullough J; *C v Special Educational Needs Tribunal* [1997] ELR 390 at 402–403 per Dyson J (no need to give reasons for refusing a review); *L v Kent County Council and Special Educational Needs Tribunal* [1998] ELR 140 at 147 per Collins J (inadequacy of reasons may indicate an error of law); *H v Kent County Council* [2000] ELR 660 at 669 per Grigson J (reasons should deal with the substantial issues and indicate which evidence had been accepted or rejected so that an aggrieved party may identify the basis of the decision); *H v Leicestershire County Council* [2000] ELR 471 at 488 per Dyson J; *L v Devon County Council* [2001] EWHC Admin 958, [2001] All ER (D) 155 (Nov) (tribunal failed to provide adequate reasons as to rejection of expert evidence); *Crean v Somerset County Council* [2002] ELR 152; *M v Worcestershire County Council* [2002] EWHC 1292 (Admin) at [10]–[11], [2003] ELR 31 per Collins J; *S v Special Educational Needs Tribunal* [2002] EWHC 1047 (Admin) at [52], [2003] ELR 85 per Goldring J; *M v Brighton and Hove City Council* [2003] EWHC 1722 (Admin) at [23], [2003] ELR 752 per Leveson J; *R (on the application of L) v Waltham Forest London Borough Council* [2003] EWHC 2907 (Admin) at [13]–[14], [2004] ELR 161 per Beatson J (expert evidence of child's progress at school rejected; incumbent on the Tribunal to give a brief reason for so doing).

22   Education Act 1996 s 336(2)(o) (amended by SI 2008/2833; and the Children and Families Act 2014 Sch 3 paras 1, 33(1), (2)(b)). Challenges to the adequacy of reasons may be sought via a review of a Tribunal's decision under the regulations as an alternative to an appeal to the High Court (see PARA 1036): *South Glamorgan County Council v L and M* [1996] ELR 400. For

guidance as to when the interests of justice may require a review see *Dean v East Sussex County Council* [2005] EWCA Civ 323, [2005] ELR 388, [2005] All ER (D) 354 (Mar).

23 Education Act 1996 s 336(2)(p) (s 336(2)(p), (q) added by the Education (Wales) Measure 2009 s 7(1), (3); and the Education Act 1996 s 336(2)(p) amended by the Children and Families Act 2014 Sch 3 paras 1, 33(1), (2)(b))).

24 Education Act 1996 s 336(2)(q) (as added: see note 23).

25 Education Act 1996 s 336(2A) (added by the Special Educational Needs and Disability Act 2001 s 42(1), Sch 8 paras 1, 13(1), (3); and amended by SI 2008/2833; and the Children and Families Act 2014 Sch 3 paras 1, 33(1), (2)(c)). As to the duty of the Tribunal to have regard to the code of practice issued by the Welsh Ministers see PARA 1033.

26 See the Special Educational Needs Tribunal for Wales Regulations 2012, SI 2012/322, reg 45(2); *R v Special Educational Needs Tribunal, ex p KL* [1997] ELR 504 at 505 per Popplewell J. Tribunal members should, however, avoid any discussion or informal contact with one party or its witnesses during the course of the hearing: *Joyce v Dorset County Council* [1997] ELR 26.

27 See the Special Educational Needs Tribunal for Wales Regulations 2012, SI 2012/322, reg 45(4) (the parent and/or the authority may rely on grounds not stated in the notice of appeal or the statement of case); and *L v Salford City Council* [1998] ELR 28.

28 See the Special Educational Needs Tribunal for Wales Regulations 2012, SI 2012/322, reg 50; and *Duncan v Bedfordshire County Council* [1997] ELR 299. The words 'wholly exceptional' in the Special Educational Needs Tribunal Regulations 2001, SI 2001/600, reg 33 (ie the predecessor of the Special Educational Needs Tribunal for Wales Regulations 2012, SI 2012/322, reg 50) do not refer to the case as a whole but to the circumstances surrounding the application to adduce the relevant material: *I v Redbridge London Borough Council* [2005] EWHC 3010 (Admin), [2005] All ER (D) 378 (Nov).

29 Ie the Arbitration Act 1996 Pt I (ss 1–84): see ARBITRATION vol 2 (2008) PARA 1209 et seq.

30 Education Act 1996 s 336(4) (amended by the Special Educational Needs and Disability Act 2001 s 42(1), Sch 8 paras 1, 13(1), (4); SI 2008/2833; and the Children and Families Act 2014 Sch 3 paras 1, 33(1), (2)(e)).

1036. Appeals to the Upper Tribunal. A party to any proceedings under the statutory provisions relating to special educational needs[1] before the Tribunal[2] may appeal to the Upper Tribunal[3] on any point of law arising from a decision made by the Tribunal in those proceedings[4]. An appeal may be brought only if, on an application made by the party concerned, the Tribunal or the Upper Tribunal has given its permission for the appeal to be brought[5].

1 Ie under the Education Act 1996 Pt IV (ss 311A–349): see PARA 989 et seq.

2 As to the Special Educational Needs Tribunal for Wales see PARA 1034.

3 As to the Upper Tribunal see COURTS AND TRIBUNALS vol 24 (2010) PARA 883 et seq.

4 Education Act 1996 s 336ZB(1) (s 336ZB added by SI 2008/2833; and the Education Act 1996 s 336ZB(1) amended by the Children and Families Act 2014 Sch 3 paras 1, 34(1), (2)(a)). As to the effect generally of the Children and Families Act 2014 see PARA 941. See also the Education Act 1996 s 311A; and PARA 941. See *CP v M Technology School* [2010] UKUT 314 (AAC), [2010] ELR 757. See also note 5.

5 Education Act 1996 s 336ZB(2) (as added: see note 4); and amended by the Children and Families Act 2014 Sch 3 paras 1, 34(1), (2)(b)). The Tribunals, Courts and Enforcement Act 2007 s 12 (proceedings on appeal to Upper Tribunal: see COURTS AND TRIBUNALS vol 24 (2010) PARA 928) applies in relation to appeals to the Upper Tribunal under the Education Act 1996 s 336ZB as it applies in relation to appeals to it under the Tribunals, Courts and Enforcement Act 2007 s 11, but as if references to the First-tier Tribunal were references to the Tribunal: Education Act 1996 s 336ZB(3) (as so added; and amended by the Children and Families Act 2014 Sch 3 paras 1, 34(1), (2)(c)). As to the giving by the Tribunal of reasons for its decision see *DC v London Borough of Ealing* [2010] UKUT 10 (AAC); *NA v London Borough of Barnet* [2010] UKUT 180 (AAC), [2010] ELR 617.

   Prior to the enactment of s 336ZB, appeals from the Special Educational Needs Tribunal for Wales were to the High Court: see the Tribunals and Inquiries Act 1992 s 11 (repealed). The following cases decided in relation to appeals so made continue to have relevance. As to the giving by the Tribunal of reasons for its decision see *H v East Sussex County Council* [2009] EWCA Civ 249, [2009] ELR 161, [2009] All ER (D) 304 (Mar). As to questions of law and questions of educational judgment see *C v Special Educational Needs Tribunal* [1997] ELR 390. See also *G v London Borough of Barnet and Special Educational Needs Tribunal* [1998] ELR

480 at 485 per Ognall J; *S v Special Educational Needs Tribunal* [2002] EWHC 1047 (Admin) at [51], [2003] ELR 85 per Goldring J (citing *Russell v Royal Borough of Kingston upon Thames* (6 November 1996, unreported) per McCullough J). As to whether points which had not been raised before the tribunal may be raised before the court on appeal see *B v Harrow London Borough Council* [2000] 1 All ER 876, [2000] 1 WLR 223, HL; and see *B v Special Educational Needs Tribunal* [1999] LGR 144 at 148, [1998] 3 FCR 231 at 236, CA, per Sir Christopher Staughton (it would be wrong to penalise claimant for not having raised point of statutory construction before tribunal when it was in the public interest for the point to be decided); *T v Special Educational Needs Tribunal and Wiltshire County Council* [2002] EWHC 1474 (Admin), [2002] ELR 704 (claimant represented by competent solicitor; point raised not of sufficient general importance). See also *Way v Poole Borough Council* [2007] EWCA Civ 1145, [2008] ELR 232, [2008] All ER (D) 263 (Jan) (matters not raised on appeal to the court will not be considered by the Court of Appeal on appeal from the court).

In relation to appeals, the chairman of the panel (but not the Tribunal itself) should be named as one of the respondents to the appeal; the chairman has no right to appear and be heard but may ask the court for permission to do so: see *S and C v Special Educational Needs Tribunal* [1997] ELR 242; *S (A Minor) v Special Educational Needs Tribunal* [1996] 2 All ER 286, [1996] 1 WLR 382, [1996] ELR 228, CA. In *Sunderland City Council v P and C* [1996] ELR 283, it was held that the court's power to order that a person be added as a party to proceedings could not be used in respect of an appeal against the decision of the Special Educational Needs Tribunal. See also *Fairpo v Humberside County Council* [1997] 1 All ER 183, [1997] ELR 12; *Phillips v Derbyshire County Council* [1997] ELR 461; *Re F* [1999] ELR 251; *Bromley London Borough Council v Special Educational Needs Tribunal* [1999] 3 All ER 587, [1999] ELR 260, CA (extension of time for appealing); *Camden London Borough Council v Hodin and White* [1996] ELR 430 (inappropriate to exercise court's power to impose a stay of the implementation of a Tribunal decision pending an appeal to the High Court).

The right of appeal has largely superseded judicial review as a mechanism for challenging decisions of the Tribunal: see *R v Special Educational Needs Tribunal, ex p F* [1996] ELR 213; *R v Special Educational Needs Tribunal, ex p South Glamorgan County Council* [1996] ELR 326; but see also *R v Special Educational Needs Tribunal, ex p KL* [1997] ELR 504. As to judicial review see JUDICIAL REVIEW.

1037. Jurisdiction. The Special Educational Needs Tribunal for Wales, in relation to Wales[1], exercises the jurisdiction conferred by statutory provisions relating to special educational needs[2] to hear appeals against:

(1) local authority determinations not to comply with a parental request for an assessment of the educational needs of a child in respect of whom a statement of special educational needs is maintained[3];

(2) local authority determinations not to comply with a parental request for an assessment of the educational needs of a child in respect of whom no statement is maintained[4];

(3) local authority determinations not to comply with a request for an assessment of the educational needs of a child made by a responsible body[5];

(4) local authority determinations not to comply with a request to change the name of a school or institution specified in a statement of special educational needs[6];

(5) local authority decisions not to make a statement of special educational needs[7];

(6) the content of a statement of special educational needs[8]; and

(7) local authority determinations to cease to maintain a statement of special educational needs[9].

1 As to the Special Educational Needs Tribunal for Wales see PARA 1034. As to the meaning of 'Wales' see PARA 7 note 3. As to appeals to the First-tier Tribunal in relation to England see PARA 979. As to the meaning of 'England' see PARA 7 note 3. Like the First-tier Tribunal, the Special Educational Needs Tribunal for Wales can also hear disability discrimination claims: see the Equality Act 2010 Sch 17 paras 1–3; and DISCRIMINATION vol 33 (2013) PARA 343.

2 Ie the jurisdiction conferred by the Education Act 1996 Pt IV (ss 311A–349).
3 See the Education Act 1996 s 328(3)(b); and PARA 1000.
4 See the Education Act 1996 s 329(2)(b); and PARA 999.
5 See the Education Act 1996 s 329A(8)(b), (10); and PARA 1001.
6 See the Education Act 1996 Sch 27 para 8(3)(b); and PARA 1013.
7 See the Education Act 1996 s 325(2); and PARA 1009.
8 See the Education Act 1996 s 326(1); and PARA 1010.
9 See the Education Act 1996 Sch 27 para 11(2)(b); and PARA 1007.

1038. Pilot schemes for children to make certain appeals and claims.
Provision was made for the piloting of the provisions[1] relating to special educational needs appeals by children[2]. The pilot ran in Carmarthenshire and Wrexham from 6 March 2012 and, although originally due to end on 30 June 2015, was in fact closed in January 2015[3]. The provisions thus took effect across the whole of Wales in January 2015[4].

1 Ie the provisions of the Education Act 1996 Pt IV (ss 311A–349), as amended by the Education (Wales) Measure 2009 Pt 1 (ss 1–20): see s 17(1). As to such amendments see in particular the Education Act 1996 s 332ZA; and PARAS 999–1001, 1007, 1009, 1010, 1013.
2 See the Education (Wales) Measure 2009 s 17 (amended by SI 2011/1651); the Education (Wales) Measure 2009 s 18 (amended by SI 2010/1148; SI 2011/1651); and the Education (Wales) Measure 2009 s 25. For these purposes, 'child' includes any person who has not attained the age of 19 and is a registered pupil at a school: Education (Wales) Measure 2009 s 19(1). As to the time at which a person attains a particular age see PARA 7 note 6.
3 A period beginning on 6 March 2012 and ending on 30 June 2015 was specified in relation to the specified local authorities and areas: see the Education (Wales) Measure 2009 (Pilot) Regulations 2012, SI 2012/321, regs 2, 3. However, the 2012 regulations were revoked with effect from 5 January 2015 by the Education (Wales) Measure 2009 (Pilot) (Revocation) Regulations 2014, SI 2014/3267.
4 See eg the ministerial statement *Written Statement – Children's Right to Make Special Educational Needs Appeals and Claims of Disability Discrimination to the Special Educational Needs Tribunal for Wales* (26 June 2014), available at the date at which this volume states the law on the on the Welsh government website. As to the meaning of 'Wales' see PARA 7 note 3.

(4) LIABILITY FOR FAILURE TO PROVIDE ADEQUATELY FOR SPECIAL EDUCATIONAL NEEDS

1039. Liability of local authorities for failure to provide adequately for children with special educational needs. The failure of local authorities to diagnose learning difficulties or to make suitable education provision for children with special educational needs has been the subject of claims[1] for breach of statutory duty and negligence[2].

Whilst the statutory duties imposed on local authorities are of the greatest importance and the failure to fulfil them could have a serious effect on a child's education, it does not appear that Parliament intended that there should be a remedy of damages for breach of statutory duty in respect of such matters[3]. Rather, the general nature of the duties imposed by the education legislation on local authorities in the context of a national education system, and the remedies available by way of appeal and judicial review, indicate that Parliament did not intend to create a statutory remedy by way of damages[4].

However, it does not follow that a local authority can never be liable in common law negligence for damage resulting from acts done in the course of the performance of a statutory duty by it or its servants or agents[5]. Advice given by educational psychologists has been the subject of such claims[6]. Where a person is employed by a local authority to carry out professional services as part of the fulfilment of the authority's statutory duty, there is no overriding reason in principle why that person should not owe a duty of care to the child[7], nor is there any overriding reason in principle why, if that duty of care is broken, the authority as employer or principal should not be vicariously liable[8]. This is subject to the qualification that, for there to be liability arising from the performance of professional duties by, for example, an educational psychologist in relation to a particular child, it must be a situation where the law recognises a duty of care[9]. If an educational psychologist is specifically called in to advise in relation to the assessment and future provision for a specific child, and it is clear that the parents acting for the child and the teachers would follow that advice, then prima facie a duty of care arises; the question is whether in the particular circumstances the necessary nexus has been shown[10]. The result of a failure by an educational psychologist to take care may be that the child suffers emotional or psychological or even physical harm, which may constitute damage for the purpose of the common law if foreseeability and causation are established[11]. A failure to ameliorate the effects of a congenital condition may also constitute damage for this purpose[12]. A claim made on either of these bases is a claim for personal injury which falls under the head of general damages[13].

Whilst there are no reasons of public policy why the courts should never recognise the vicarious liability of local authorities in situations such as these[14], there may, however, be cases where it may be wrong to recognise such a vicarious liability as it may interfere with the performance of the local authority's duties[15].

Whether local authorities generally owe a common law duty of care to pupils to take reasonable care in discharging their statutory functions is less clear[16]. It has been said that the courts should hesitate before imposing a common law duty of care in the exercise of discretionary powers or duties conferred by Parliament for social welfare purposes[17], and that a common law duty of care in the exercise of statutory discretions can only arise in relation to an authority which has decided an issue so carelessly that no reasonable authority could have reached that decision[18]. However, there is no universally recognised principle that a claim at common law in negligence should never be possible[19]. In practice, since the authority can only act through its employees or agents, and if they are negligent vicarious liability will arise, it may rarely be necessary to invoke a claim for direct liability[20].

While concerned with special educational needs, the potential scope of these rulings may extend to other areas of education as well[21].

1   As to the nature of statutory duty see STATUTES AND LEGISLATIVE PROCESS vol 96 (2012) PARA 721 et seq. As to breach of statutory duty see further STATUTES AND LEGISLATIVE PROCESS vol 96 (2012) PARA 752 et seq; TORT vol 97 (2015) PARA 500 et seq. As to negligence in relation to statutory powers see CONSTITUTIONAL AND ADMINISTRATIVE LAW vol 20 (2014) PARA 653; NEGLIGENCE vol 78 (2010) PARAS 17–19; TORT vol 97 (2015) PARA 502.

2   See e g *Phelps v Hillingdon London Borough Council, Anderton v Clwyd County Council, Jarvis v Hampshire County Council, G v Bromley London Borough Council* [2001] 2 AC 619, [2000] 4 All ER 504, [2000] ELR 499, HL, where the House of Lords decided four appeals raising related issues together. In *Phelps v Hillingdon London Borough Council* [1998] ELR 38, [1997] 3 FCR 621 (on appeal [1999] 1 All ER 421, [1999] 1 WLR 500, CA), the claimant brought proceedings against the defendant local authority claiming damages for breach of statutory duty (and negligence in the alternative), alleging that despite the claimant being assessed by an educational psychologist, her dyslexia remained undiagnosed and that the local authority had failed to appreciate her learning difficulties and to make appropriate arrangements. In *Anderton v Clwyd County Council* [1998] ELR 533 (on appeal [1999] ELR 1, CA), the claimant, who also had dyslexia, claimed that she had suffered psychological problems due to the failure of the local authority to make suitable educational provision for her. In *Jarvis v Hampshire County Council* [1999] Ed CR 785 (on appeal [2000] ELR 36, CA), the claimant brought proceedings against an educational psychologist and the local authority on the

grounds of negligence and breach of statutory duty in not providing competent advice through the authority's psychology service. In *G v Bromley London Borough Council* (4 March 1999, unreported), the claimant suffered from muscular dystrophy and claimed that the local authority had negligently, and in breach of its statutory duty, failed to provide him with a proper education.

See also *X (Minors) v Bedfordshire County Council, M (A Minor) v Newham London Borough Council, E (A Minor) v Dorset County Council, Christmas v Hampshire County Council, Keating v Mayor and Burgesses of Bromley London Borough Council* [1995] 2 AC 633, [1995] 3 All ER 353, HL, where the House of Lords heard five appeals together, three of which involved claims either in negligence or for breach of statutory duty under the education legislation against local authorities in failing to provide appropriate special education.

3   *Phelps v Hillingdon London Borough Council, Anderton v Clwyd County Council, Jarvis v Hampshire County Council, G v Bromley London Borough Council* [2001] 2 AC 619 at 652, [2000] 4 All ER 504 at 516–517, [2000] ELR 499 at 515, HL, per Lord Slynn of Hadley.

4   *Phelps v Hillingdon London Borough Council, Anderton v Clwyd County Council, Jarvis v Hampshire County Council, G v Bromley London Borough Council* [2001] 2 AC 619 at 652, [2000] 4 All ER 504 at 517, [2000] ELR 499 at 515, HL, per Lord Slynn of Hadley. See also *X (Minors) v Bedfordshire County Council, M (A Minor) v Newham London Borough Council, E (A Minor) v Dorset County Council, Christmas v Hampshire County Council, Keating v Mayor and Burgesses of Bromley London Borough Council* [1995] 2 AC 633 at 762, [1995] 3 All ER 353 at 392, [1995] ELR 404 at 447, HL, per Lord Browne-Wilkinson ('If, despite the complex machinery for consultation and appeals contained in the [Education Act 1981], the scheme fails to provide the benefit intended that is a matter more appropriately remedied by way of the ombudsman ... than by way of litigation').

5   *Phelps v Hillingdon London Borough Council, Anderton v Clwyd County Council, Jarvis v Hampshire County Council, G v Bromley London Borough Council* [2001] 2 AC 619 at 652–653, [2000] 4 All ER 504 at 517, [2000] ELR 499 at 515, HL, per Lord Slynn of Hadley (applying *Barrett v Enfield London Borough Council* [2001] 2 AC 550, [1999] 3 All ER 193, HL). As to the liability of an employer for the torts of his employee or of an independent contractor see TORT vol 97 (2015) PARA 767 et seq.

6   As regards the role of the educational psychology service in *E (A Minor) v Dorset County Council* (reported in *X (Minors) v Bedfordshire County Council, M (A Minor) v Newham London Borough Council, E (A Minor) v Dorset County Council, Christmas v Hampshire County Council, Keating v Mayor and Burgesses of Bromley London Borough Council* [1995] 2 AC 633, [1995] 3 All ER 353, [1995] ELR 404, HL), the House of Lords was clear that the local authority was providing a service (ie psychological advice) to the public. Although the service could not be provided without statutory authority, once the decision was taken to offer such a service, a statutory body was in general in the same position as any private individual or organisation holding itself out as offering such a service, and it owed a duty of care to persons using the service; it was nevertheless important to establish the factual background to the operation of educational psychology services: see *X (Minors) v Bedfordshire County Council, M (A Minor) v Newham London Borough Council, E (A Minor) v Dorset County Council, Christmas v Hampshire County Council, Keating v Mayor and Burgesses of Bromley London Borough Council* at 762–763, at 392, and at 447–448 per Lord Browne-Wilkinson. As regards individual psychologists and the question whether they owed a duty of care and whether the authority might be liable if a psychologist was found to be negligent, Lord Browne-Wilkinson went on to say (at 763–764, at 393, and at 448–449) that 'psychologists hold themselves out as having special skills and they are ... like any other professional bound to possess such skills and exercise them carefully'. If a conflict of duty could be shown between the professional's duties to the claimant and his duty to his employer, or if there was a conflict between the professional being under a duty of care to the claimant and the discharge by the authority of its statutory duties, the trial judge might have to limit or exclude the duty of care owed to the claimant, but in this case Lord Browne-Wilkinson could not see any such conflict and also considered that there could be liability for advice given by education officers. As to education officers see further *Carty v Croydon London Borough Council* [2005] EWCA Civ 19, [2005] 2 All ER 517, [2005] 1 FCR 554 (education officers can owe a common law duty of care to children with special educational needs, and authorities can be vicariously liable for the negligence of such officers; liability is not limited to persons who have been trained and qualify as members of a recognised profession or who are subject to professional disciplinary procedures).

7   *Phelps v Hillingdon London Borough Council, Anderton v Clwyd County Council, Jarvis v Hampshire County Council, G v Bromley London Borough Council* [2001] 2 AC 619 at 653–654, [2000] 4 All ER 504 at 517–518, [2000] ELR 499 at 516–517, HL, per Lord Slynn of Hadley. As to duty of care generally see NEGLIGENCE vol 78 (2010) PARA 1 et seq.

8   *Phelps v Hillingdon London Borough Council, Anderton v Clwyd County Council, Jarvis v Hampshire County Council, G v Bromley London Borough Council* [2001] 2 AC 619 at 653–655, [2000] 4 All ER 504 at 517, 519, [2000] ELR 499 at 516, 518, HL, per Lord Slynn of Hadley.

9   See *Phelps v Hillingdon London Borough Council, Anderton v Clwyd County Council, Jarvis v Hampshire County Council, G v Bromley London Borough Council* [2001] 2 AC 619 at 654, [2000] 4 All ER 504 at 518, [2000] ELR 499 at 516–517, HL, per Lord Slynn of Hadley. 'A school which accepts a pupil assumes responsibility not only for his physical well-being but also for his educational needs ... The head teacher, being responsible for the school, himself comes under a duty of care to exercise the reasonable skills of a headmaster in relation to such educational needs. If it comes to the attention of the headmaster that a pupil is under-performing, he does owe a duty to take such steps as a reasonable teacher would consider appropriate to try to deal with such under-performance ... If such a head teacher gives advice to parents, then ... he must exercise the skills and care of a reasonable teacher in giving such advice. Similarly, in the case of the advisory teacher brought in to advise on the educational needs of a specific pupil, if he knows that his advice will be communicated to the pupil's parents he must foresee that they will rely on such advice. Therefore, in giving that advice he owes a duty to the child to exercise the skill and care of a reasonable advisory teacher ... The headmaster and advisory teachers were not under any duty to exercise a higher degree of skill such as that of an educational psychologist': *X (Minors) v Bedfordshire County Council, M (A Minor) v Newham London Borough Council, E (A Minor) v Dorset County Council, Christmas v Hampshire County Council, Keating v Mayor and Burgesses of Bromley London Borough Council* [1995] 2 AC 633 at 766, [1995] 3 All ER 353 at 395–396, 1995] ELR 404 at 451, HL, per Lord Browne-Wilkinson.

10 See *Phelps v Hillingdon London Borough Council, Anderton v Clwyd County Council, Jarvis v Hampshire County Council, G v Bromley London Borough Council* [2001] 2 AC 619 at 654, [2000] 4 All ER 504 at 518, [2000] ELR 499 at 517, HL, per Lord Slynn of Hadley. See also *X (Minors) v Bedfordshire County Council, M (A Minor) v Newham London Borough Council, E (A Minor) v Dorset County Council, Christmas v Hampshire County Council, Keating v Mayor and Burgesses of Bromley London Borough Council* [1995] 2 AC 633 at 766, [1995] 3 All ER 353 at 395–396, [1995] ELR 404 at 451, HL, per Lord Browne-Wilkinson.

11 *Phelps v Hillingdon London Borough Council, Anderton v Clwyd County Council, Jarvis v Hampshire County Council, G v Bromley London Borough Council* [2001] 2 AC 619 at 654, [2000] 4 All ER 504 at 518, [2000] ELR 499 at 516–517, HL, per Lord Slynn of Hadley.

12 See *Phelps v Hillingdon London Borough Council, Anderton v Clwyd County Council, Jarvis v Hampshire County Council, G v Bromley London Borough Council* [2001] 2 AC 619 at 654, [2000] 4 All ER 504 at 518, [2000] ELR 499 at 517, HL, where Lord Slynn of Hadley expressed the view that there is no reason in principle to rule out claims for injury deriving from a failure by an educational psychologist to diagnose a congenital condition and to take appropriate action as a result of which a child's level of achievement is reduced, leading to loss of employment and wages. See also his remarks at 664, at 528, and at 529, quoting *Phelps v Hillingdon London Borough Council* [1997] 3 FCR 621 at 648, [1998] ELR 38 at 64 per Garland J. As to the possibility of claiming for consequential economic loss, falling under the head of special damages, see further *Phelps v Hillingdon London Borough Council, Anderton v Clwyd County Council, Jarvis v Hampshire County Council, G v Bromley London Borough Council* (above) at 670, at 533, and at 534 per Lord Clyde; *Adams v Bracknell Forest Borough Council* [2004] UKHL 29, [2005] 1 AC 76, [2004] 3 All ER 897. See also *Devon County Council v Clarke* [2005] EWCA Civ 266, [2005] 1 FCR 752, sub nom *Clarke v Devon County Council* [2005] ELR 375 (award of compensation made for loss of employment and earnings where the evidence was sufficient to find that, but for the breach of duty, the claimant would have been taught differently, and that he would have derived benefit which would have helped him to overcome his problems); *Skipper v Calderdale Metropolitan Borough Council* [2006] EWCA Civ 238, [2006] ELR 322, [2006] All ER (D) 203 (Mar) (claim for humiliation, lost confidence and lost self-esteem, and for lost earning capacity).

13 *Adams v Bracknell Forest Borough Council* [2004] UKHL 29, [2005] 1 AC 76, [2004] 3 All ER 897, approving *Robinson v St Helens Metropolitan Borough Council* [2002] EWCA Civ 1099 at [21], [2002] ELR 681, [2003] PIQR P128 per Stuart-Smith LJ (negligent failure to ameliorate the consequences of dyslexia by appropriate teaching may be said to continue the injury, in the same way that the negligent failure to cure or ameliorate a congenital physical condition so that it continues could give rise to an action for personal injuries).

A personal injury claim is subject to the provisions of the Limitation Act 1980 ss 11, 14 (ie three years from accrual or from the claimant's date of knowledge): see LIMITATION PERIODS vol 68 (2008) PARAS 998–999. The exercise of discretion to extend the time limit under s 33 (see

LIMITATION PERIODS vol 68 (2008) PARA 1001) is subject to the question of proportionality: *Adams v Bracknell Forest Borough Council* (above) (the potential injustice to the defendant in having to defend the claim was such as to preclude any exercise of discretion), approving *Robinson v St Helens Metropolitan Borough Council* at [32]–[33] per Stuart-Smith LJ. The standard to be applied in fixing knowledge is that of a person assumed to be suffering from untreated dyslexia; personal characteristics are otherwise irrelevant: *Adams v Bracknell Forest Borough Council* (above). See also *Rowe v Kingston upon Hull County Council* [2003] EWCA Civ 1281, [2003] ELR 771, [2003] All ER (D) 426 (Jul); and *Skipper v Calderdale Metropolitan Borough Council* [2006] EWCA Civ 238, [2006] ELR 322, [2006] All ER (D) 203 (Mar).

14   See *Phelps v Hillingdon London Borough Council, Anderton v Clwyd County Council, Jarvis v Hampshire County Council, G v Bromley London Borough Council* [2001] 2 AC 619 at 672, [2000] 4 All ER 504 at 534–535, [2000] ELR 499 at 536, HL, per Lord Clyde.

15   See *Phelps v Hillingdon London Borough Council, Anderton v Clwyd County Council, Jarvis v Hampshire County Council, G v Bromley London Borough Council* [2001] 2 AC 619 at 652–655, [2000] 4 All ER 504 at 517–519, [2000] ELR 499 at 516–518, HL, per Lord Slynn of Hadley; *X (Minors) v Bedfordshire County Council, M (A Minor) v Newham London Borough Council, E (A Minor) v Dorset County Council, Christmas v Hampshire County Council, Keating v Mayor and Burgesses of Bromley London Borough Council* [1995] 2 AC 633, [1995] 3 All ER 353, [1995] ELR 404, HL. 'It is important that those engaged in the provision of educational services under the statutes should not be hampered by the imposition of such vicarious liability. I do not, however, see that to recognise the existence of the duties necessarily leads or is likely to lead to that result. The recognition of a duty of care does not of itself impose unreasonably high standards': *Phelps v Hillingdon London Borough Council, Anderton v Clwyd County Council, Jarvis v Hampshire County Council, G v Bromley London Borough Council* (above) at 655, at 519, and at 518 per Lord Slynn of Hadley. Lord Nicholls of Birkenhead distinguished cases where there is 'manifest incompetence or negligence comprising specific, identifiable mistakes', such as where a teacher 'carelessly teaches the wrong syllabus for an external examination', from a more general claim that a child did not receive an adequate education at the school or that a particular teacher failed to teach properly (*Phelps v Hillingdon London Borough Council, Anderton v Clwyd County Council, Jarvis v Hampshire County Council, G v Bromley London Borough Council* (above) at 667, at 530–531, and at 531–532), and he emphasised that 'proof of under-performance by a child is not by itself evidence of negligent teaching', given the range of external factors that can affect it (*Phelps v Hillingdon London Borough Council, Anderton v Clwyd County Council, Jarvis v Hampshire County Council, G v Bromley London Borough Council* (above) at 668, at 531, and at 532).

16   The question of whether local authorities can be directly liable (rather than vicariously liable for the act of, for example, a teacher or psychologist) was left open in *Phelps v Hillingdon London Borough Council, Anderton v Clwyd County Council, Jarvis v Hampshire County Council, G v Bromley London Borough Council* [2001] 2 AC 619 at 668, [2000] 4 All ER 504 at 531, [2000] ELR 499 at 533, HL, per Lord Nicholls of Birkenhead. Lord Slynn of Hadley (at 658, at 522, and at 521) was of the opinion that an authority would not be directly liable for the way it had established arrangements to meet its statutory duties towards children with special educational needs, but might be directly liable if it employed teachers and others who were not qualified or competent to undertake their duties. See also *Carty v Croydon London Borough Council* [2005] EWCA Civ 19, [2005] 2 All ER 517, [2005] 1 WLR 2312; *Connor v Surrey County Council* [2010] EWCA Civ 286, [2011] QB 429, [2010] 3 All ER 905.

17   *X (Minors) v Bedfordshire County Council, M (A Minor) v Newham London Borough Council, E (A Minor) v Dorset County Council, Christmas v Hampshire County Council, Keating v Mayor and Burgesses of Bromley London Borough Council* [1995] 2 AC 633 at 762, [1995] 3 All ER 353 at 392, [1995] ELR 404 at 447, HL, per Lord Browne-Wilkinson.

18   *X (Minors) v Bedfordshire County Council, M (A Minor) v Newham London Borough Council, E (A Minor) v Dorset County Council, Christmas v Hampshire County Council, Keating v Mayor and Burgesses of Bromley London Borough Council* [1995] 2 AC 633 at 761, [1995] 3 All ER 353 at 391, [1995] ELR 404 at 446, HL, per Lord Browne-Wilkinson. However, the analysis of the Court of Appeal in *Connor v Surrey County Council* [2010] EWCA Civ 286, [2011] QB 429, [2010] 3 All ER 905, especially at [64]–[67] per Laws LJ, shows that, at least in some situations, a duty of care may nevertheless arise.

19   *Phelps v Hillingdon London Borough Council, Anderton v Clwyd County Council, Jarvis v Hampshire County Council, G v Bromley London Borough Council* [2001] 2 AC 619 at 658, [2000] 4 All ER 504 at 522, [2000] ELR 499 at 521, HL, per Lord Slynn of Hadley (where he did not accept the dictum of Lord Browne-Wilkinson in *X (Minors) v Bedfordshire County Council, M (A Minor) v Newham London Borough Council, E (A Minor) v Dorset County Council, Christmas v Hampshire County Council, Keating v Mayor and Burgesses of Bromley*

London Borough Council [1995] 2 AC 633 at 762, [1995] 3 All ER 353 at 392, [1995] ELR 404 at 447, HL, that a local authority owed no common law duty of care in the exercise of the powers and discretions relating to children with special educational needs specifically conferred on it by the Education Act 1981).

20   *Phelps v Hillingdon London Borough Council, Anderton v Clwyd County Council, Jarvis v Hampshire County Council, G v Bromley London Borough Council* [2001] 2 AC 619 at 658, [2000] 4 All ER 504 at 522, [2000] ELR 499 at 521, HL, per Lord Slynn of Hadley.

21   See eg *R (on the application of B) v Head Teacher of Alperton Community School, R (on the application of T) v Head Teacher of Wembley High School, R (on the application of C) v Governing Body of the Cardinal Newman Roman Catholic School* [2001] EWHC 229 (Admin), [2002] LGR 132, [2001] ELR 359 (where Newman J held that *Phelps v Hillingdon London Borough Council, Anderton v Clwyd County Council, Jarvis v Hampshire County Council, G v Bromley London Borough Council* [2001] 2 AC 619, [2000] 4 All ER 504, [2000] ELR 499, HL, is 'authority against the submission that a private law right to education exists in English law'). See also *Bradford-Smart v West Sussex County Council* [2001] ELR 138; affd on different grounds [2002] EWCA Civ 07, [2002] 1 FCR 425, [2002] ELR 139 (a duty may be imposed on a person who had control of a potential assailant; but there is no liability if bullying occurred outside school with no apparent impact on educational progress).

(5) INSTITUTIONS MAKING SPECIAL EDUCATIONAL PROVISION

1040.   Mainstream schools. A child with special educational needs who should be educated in a school should in general be educated in a mainstream school[1]. A child with special educational needs may, however, in appropriate circumstances be educated in a special school[2], an independent school[3], a non-maintained school in Wales[4], a city college or an academy[5], an institution outside England and Wales[6], or in an institution which is not a school[7].

1   As to England see the Children and Families Act 2014 ss 33–35; and PARAS 954–956. As to Wales see the Education Act 1996 s 316; and PARA 1014.
2   See PARAS 1041–1044. See also the Children and Families Act 2014 s 34(4); and PARA 955.
3   See PARAS 1045–1046.
4   See PARA 1016. As to England see also the Children and Families Act 2014 s 63; and PARA 967.
5   See PARA 1015.
6   As to England see the Children and Families Act 2014 s 62; and PARA 967. As to Wales see the Education Act 1996 s 320; and PARA 1018.
7   As to England see the Children and Families Act 2014 s 61; and PARA 967. As to Wales see the Education Act 1996 s 319; and PARA 1017.

1041.   Special schools. A school[1] is a 'special school' if it is specially organised to make special educational provision[2] for pupils[3] with special educational needs[4], and it is (1) maintained by a local authority[5]; (2) an academy school[6]; or (3) a non-maintained special school[7].

1   As to the meaning of 'school' see PARA 91.
2   As to the meaning of 'special educational provision' see PARAS 943, 989.
3   As to the meaning of 'pupil' see PARA 20 note 4.
4   As to the meaning of 'special educational needs' see PARAS 943, 989.
5   Education Act 1996 s 337(a) (s 337 substituted by the Children and Families Act 2014 Sch 3 paras 1, 36). As to the meaning of 'local authority' see PARA 25. As to maintained schools see PARA 99 et seq.
6   Education Act 1996 s 337(b) (as added: see note 5). As to the meaning of 'academy school' see PARA 346 note 12.
7   Education Act 1996 s 337(c) (as added: see note 5). As to the meaning of 'non-maintained special school' see PARA 1042.

1042.   Approval of non-maintained special schools. The appropriate national authority[1] may approve[2] any school which is specially organised to make special

educational provision[3] for pupils[4] with special educational needs[5], and is not a
community or foundation special school[6] or an academy school[7], and may give
approval before or after the school is established[8]. A school that is so approved[9]
is known as a 'non-maintained special school'[10].

Regulations[11] may make provision as to the requirements which are to be
complied with as a condition of approval[12], and as to the requirements which are
to be complied with by a school while approved[13]. The requirements which may
be imposed by the regulations include requirements: (1) which call for
arrangements to be approved by the appropriate national authority[14]; or (2) as to
the organisation of any special school as a primary school[15] or as a secondary
school[16]. Regulations[17] may make provision for an appeal against a decision of
the Secretary of State not to approve, not to approve a change to, or to withdraw
approval from, relevant arrangements[18] in relation to such a non-maintained
special school in England[19].

1 'The appropriate national authority' means, in relation to a school in England, the Secretary of
   State; and, in relation to a school in Wales, the Welsh Ministers: Education Act 1996 s 337A
   (added by the Education and Skills Act 2008 s 142(1)). As to the meaning of 'school' see PARA
   91. As to the meanings of 'England' and 'Wales' see PARA 7 note 3. As to the Secretary of State
   see PARA 58. As to the Welsh Ministers see PARA 59.
2 Ie under the Education Act 1996 s 342. As to the approval of independent schools in Wales see
   PARA 1045.
3 As to the meaning of 'special educational provision' see PARAS 943, 989.
4 As to the meaning of 'pupil' see PARA 20 note 4.
5 Education Act 1996 s 342(1)(a) (s 342 substituted by the School Standards and Framework
   Act 1998 s 140(1), Sch 30 para 82). As to the meaning of 'special educational needs' see PARAS
   943, 989.
6 As to the meaning of references to a community or foundation special school see PARA 106.
7 Education Act 1996 s 342(1)(b) (as substituted (see note 5); and amended by the Children and
   Families Act 2014 Sch 3 paras 1, 37). As to the meaning of 'academy school' see PARA 346 note
   12.
8 Education Act 1996 s 342(1) (as substituted (see note 5); and amended by the Education and
   Skills Act 2008 ss 142(2), (3), 169(2), Sch 2). As to the meaning of 'establish' see PARA 110
   note 2. Any school which was a special school immediately before 1 April 1994 must be treated,
   subject to the Education Act 1996 s 342(4) (see the text to note 13), as approved under s 342:
   s 342(3) (as so substituted). As to the meaning of 'special school' see PARA 1041. 1 April 1994
   was the date on which the Education Act 1993 s 184, which made provision in connection with
   proposals for the establishment or alteration of maintained or grant-maintained special schools,
   was brought into force by the Education Act 1993 (Commencement No 3 and Transitional
   Provisions) Order 1994, SI 1994/507. The Education Act 1993 s 184 was repealed by the
   Education Act 1996 and replaced by s 340 (itself now repealed).
9 Ie under the Education Act 1996 s 342.
10 See the Education Act 1996 s 337A (as added: see note 1). A school approved under s 342(1) is
   not susceptible to judicial review: *R v Muntham House School, ex p R* [2000] LGR 255, [2000]
   ELR 287. As to judicial review see JUDICIAL REVIEW.
11 'Regulations' means regulations made by the Secretary of State or, in relation to Wales, the
   Welsh Ministers: see the Education Act 1996 s 579(1). The appropriate national authority may
   by order make such modifications of any trust deed or other instrument relating to a school as,
   after consultation with the governing body or other proprietor of the school, appear to it to be
   necessary to enable the governing body or proprietor to meet any requirement imposed by
   regulations under s 342: s 349(1)(a) (amended by the Education and Skills Act 2008
   ss 147(1), (2), 169(2), Sch 2; and the Academies Act 2010 s 14, Sch 2 paras 1, 3). Any
   modification made by such an order may be made to have permanent effect or to have effect for
   such period as may be specified in the order: Education Act 1996 s 349(2). As to the meaning of
   'modifications' see PARA 21 note 15. As to the meaning of 'trust deed' see PARA 108 note 6. As
   to the governing bodies of maintained schools in England see PARA 150 et seq; and in Wales see
   PARA 195 et seq. As to the meaning of 'proprietor' see PARA 51 note 4. Such orders, being of
   local effect, are not recorded in this work.
12 Education Act 1996 s 342(2) (as substituted: see note 5). As to the regulations made see, in
   relation to England, the Non-Maintained Special Schools (England) Regulations 2015,

SI 2015/728; and, in relation to Wales, the Education (Special Schools) Regulations 1994, SI 1994/652 (the latter regulations having effect as if made under the Education Act 1996 s 342 by virtue of s 582(3), Sch 39 para 1 and the Interpretation Act 1978 s 17(2)(b)).

13　Education Act 1996 s 342(4)(a) (as substituted: see note 5). As to the provision made see note 12. As to the withdrawal of approval see PARAS 1043, 1044.

14　Education Act 1996 s 342(5)(a) (as substituted (see note 5); and amended by the Education and Skills Act 2008 s 142(2), (4)).

15　As to the meaning of 'primary school' see PARA 91.

16　Education Act 1996 s 342(5)(b) (as substituted: see note 5). As to the meaning of 'secondary school' see PARA 91.

17　See the Non-Maintained Special Schools (England) Regulations 2015, SI 2015/728.

18　'Relevant arrangements' means arrangements that require the approval of the Secretary of State by virtue of the Education Act 1996 s 342(5)(a) (see the text to note 14): s 342B(2) (s 342B added by the Education and Skills Act 2008 s 145).

19　See the Education Act 1996 s 342B(1)(b) (as added: see note 18). The regulations must provide that such an appeal lies to the First-tier Tribunal (s 342B(3)(a) (as so added)), and must be brought by the proprietor of the school in question (s 342B(3)(b) (as so added)). As to the First-tier Tribunal see COURTS AND TRIBUNALS vol 24 (2010) PARA 874 et seq.

1043. Withdrawal of approval of non-maintained special schools in England.

Regulations[1] may make provision as to the withdrawal of approval[2] from a non-maintained special school[3] at the request of the proprietor[4] or on the ground that there has been a failure to comply with any prescribed[5] requirement[6].

Regulations[7] may make provision for an appeal against a decision of the Secretary of State to withdraw approval from a non-maintained special school in England[8] otherwise than at the request of the proprietor[9]. The regulations must provide that such an appeal lies to the First-tier Tribunal[10], and must be brought by the proprietor of the school in question[11]; and the regulations may in particular make provision prohibiting the Secretary of State from acting on a decision to withdraw approval during the period in which an appeal against the decision could be brought[12], or where an appeal has been brought, the appeal has not been determined, withdrawn or otherwise disposed of[13].

1　'Regulations' means regulations made by the Secretary of State or, in relation to Wales, the Welsh Ministers: see the Education Act 1996 s 579(1). As to the Secretary of State see PARA 58. As to the Welsh Ministers see PARA 59. The functions of the Secretary of State under s 342, so far as exercisable in relation to Wales, were originally transferred to the National Assembly for Wales (see the National Assembly for Wales (Transfer of Functions) Order 1999, SI 1999/672, art 2, Sch 1) and are now vested in the Welsh Ministers (see the Government of Wales Act 2006 s 162(1), Sch 11 para 30).

　　As to the regulations made in relation to England see the Non-Maintained Special Schools (England) Regulations 2015, SI 2015/728; and in relation to Wales see the Education (Special Schools) Regulations 1994, SI 1994/652 (amended by SI 2009/2544) (having effect as if made under the Education Act 1996 s 342(4)(b) by virtue of s 582(3), Sch 39 para 1 and the Interpretation Act 1978 s 17(2)(b). As to the meanings of 'England' and 'Wales' see PARA 7 note 3.

2　Ie approval under the Education Act 1996 s 342, including approval treated as given under s 342(3): see PARA 1042.

3　As to the meaning of 'non-maintained special school' see PARA 1042.

4　As to the meaning of 'proprietor' see PARA 51 note 4.

5　'Prescribed' means prescribed by regulations: Education Act 1996 s 579(1).

6　See the Education Act 1996 s 342(4)(b) (s 342 substituted by the School Standards and Framework Act 1998 s 140(1), Sch 30 paras 57, 82). As to the prescribed requirements see PARA 1042. As to the withdrawal of approval in urgent cases see PARA 1044. As to the withdrawal of approval of independent schools in Wales see PARA 1046.

　　The appropriate national authority may by order make such modifications of any trust deed or other instrument relating to a school as, after consultation with the governing body or other proprietor of the school, appear to it to be necessary to enable the governing body or proprietor to meet any requirement imposed by regulations under the Education Act 1996 s 342: s 349(1)(a) (amended by the Education and Skills Act 2008 ss 147(1), (2), 169(2), Sch 2; and the

Academies Act 2010 s 14, Sch 2 paras 1, 3). Any modification made by such an order may be made to have permanent effect or to have effect for such period as may be specified in the order: Education Act 1996 s 349(2). 'The appropriate national authority' means, in relation to a school in England, the Secretary of State; and, in relation to a school in Wales, the Welsh Ministers: s 337A (added by the Education and Skills Act 2008 s 142(1)). As to the meaning of 'modifications' see PARA 21 note 15. As to the meaning of 'trust deed' see PARA 108 note 6. As to the meaning of 'school' see PARA 91. As to the governing bodies of maintained schools in England see PARA 150 et seq; and in Wales see PARA 195 et seq. Such orders, being of local effect, are not recorded in this work.

7   See the Non-Maintained Special Schools (England) Regulations 2015, SI 2015/728.
8   Ie by virtue of the Education Act 1996 s 342(4)(b): see the text to notes 1–6.
9   Education Act 1996 s 342B(1)(a) (s 342B added by the Education and Skills Act 2008 s 145).
10 Education Act 1996 s 342B(3)(a) (as added: see note 9). As to the First-tier Tribunal see COURTS AND TRIBUNALS vol 24 (2010) PARA 874 et seq.
11 Education Act 1996 s 342B(3)(b) (as added: see note 9).
12 Education Act 1996 s 342B(4)(a) (as added: see note 9).
13 Education Act 1996 s 342B(4)(b) (as added: see note 9).

1044. Withdrawal of approval of non-maintained special schools in England in urgent cases.

Regulations[1] may make provision conferring power on a justice of the peace[2], on the application of the Secretary of State, to make an order in an urgent case that a non-maintained special school[3] in England[4] should cease to be approved[5].

Regulations[6] may make provision for an appeal against the making of such an order by a justice of peace[7]. The regulations must provide that such an appeal lies to the First-tier Tribunal[8], and must be brought by the proprietor[9] of the school in question[10].

1   'Regulations' means regulations made by the Secretary of State: Education Act 1996 s 579(1). As to the Secretary of State see PARA 58. As to regulations see note 6.
2   As to justices of the peace see MAGISTRATES vol 71 (2013) PARA 401 et seq.
3   As to the meaning of 'non-maintained special school' see PARA 1042.
4   As to the meaning of 'England' see PARA 7 note 3.
5   Education Act 1996 s 342A(1) (s 342A added by the Education and Skills Act 2008 s 144). The approval referred to is that under the Education Act 1996 s 342 (see PARA 1042): see s 342A(1) (as so added). The regulations may in particular make provision corresponding, with or without modifications, to that made in the Education and Skills Act 2008 s 120(2)–(7) (emergency orders in relation to registered independent educational institutions), or s 122 of that Act (notification) (see PARA 404): Education Act 1996 s 342A(2) (as so added). As to the meaning of 'modifications' see PARA 21 note 15.
6   See the Non-Maintained Special Schools (England) Regulations 2015, SI 2015/728.
7   See the Education Act 1996 s 342C(1) (s 342C added by the Education and Skills Act 2008 s 145).
8   Education Act 1996 s 342C(2)(a) (as added: see note 7). As to the First-tier Tribunal see COURTS AND TRIBUNALS vol 24 (2010) PARA 874 et seq.
9   As to the meaning of 'proprietor' see PARA 51 note 4.
10 Education Act 1996 s 342C(2)(b) (as added: see note 7).

1045. Approval of independent schools in Wales.

The Welsh Ministers[1] may approve[2] an independent school[3] in Wales as suitable for the admission of children[4] for whom statements of special educational needs[5] are maintained[6]. An approval may be given subject to such conditions[7] as the Welsh Ministers see fit to impose[8].

No person[9] may so exercise his functions[10] that a relevant child[11] is educated in an independent school unless[12]: (1) the school is for the time being approved by the Welsh Ministers as suitable for the admission of children for whom statements of special educational needs are[13] maintained[14]; or (2) the Welsh Ministers are satisfied that there is a place available for the child at the school and consent to the child being educated there[15].

1   As to the Welsh Ministers see PARA 59.

2   Regulations may make provision as to the requirements which are to be complied with by a school as a condition of its approval under the Education Act 1996 s 347 (s 347(2)(a)), and the requirements which are to be complied with by a school while an approval under s 347 is in force in respect of it (s 347(2)(b)). 'Regulations' means regulations made by the Welsh Ministers: see the Education Act 1996 s 579(1). By virtue of s 582(3), Sch 39 Pt I para 1, the Education (Special Educational Needs) (Approval of Independent Schools) Regulations 1994, SI 1994/651, have effect as if made under the Education Act 1996 s 347. As to the requirements with which an independent school must comply as a condition of its approval see the Education (Special Educational Needs) (Approval of Independent Schools) Regulations 1994, SI 1994/651, reg 3, Sch 1 (amended by SI 1998/417; and SI 2010/1142). As to the requirements which are to be complied with by a school while an approval under the Education Act 1996 s 347 is in force see the Education (Special Educational Needs) (Approval of Independent Schools) Regulations 1994, SI 1994/651, reg 4, Schs 1, 2 (Sch 1 as so amended; Sch 2 amended by SI 1998/417; SI 2001/3710; SI 2005/2929; SI 2010/1142; and SI 2010/2431).

      The Welsh Ministers may by order make such modifications of any trust deed or other instrument relating to a school in Wales as, after consultation with the governing body or other proprietor of the school, appear to them to be necessary to enable the governing body or proprietor to meet any requirement imposed by regulations under the Education Act 1996 s 347: s 349(1A) (added by the Education and Skills Act 2008 s 147(1), (3)). As to the meaning of 'modifications' see PARA 21 note 15. As to the meaning of 'trust deed' see PARA 108 note 6. As to the meaning of 'school' see PARA 91. As to the meaning of 'Wales' see PARA 7 note 3. As to the meaning of 'proprietor' see PARA 51 note 4. Such orders, being of local effect, are not recorded in this work.

3   As to the meaning of 'independent school' see PARA 369.

4   As to the meaning of 'child' see PARA 989 note 1.

5   Ie statements maintained under the Education Act 1996 s 324: see PARA 1002. As to the meaning of 'special educational needs' see PARA 989.

6   Education Act 1996 s 347(1) (amended by the Education and Skills Act 2008 s 146(1), (2)(a)). Where, immediately before 1 September 2009 (ie the date of the coming into force of the Education and Skills Act 2008 s 146), a relevant child was being educated in an independent school in England and the school was for the time being approved by the Secretary of State under the Education Act 1996 s 347, or the Secretary of State had consented to the child being educated there under s 347(5)(b) (see the text to note 15), on that date the Welsh Ministers were deemed to have consented, under s 347(5)(b), to the child being educated at the school: see the Education and Skills Act 2008 s 148(1), (3). The Welsh Ministers may withdraw consent so deemed to have been given as if it had in fact been given: s 148(4). 'A relevant child' means a child with special educational needs (1) for whom a local authority in Wales maintains a statement under the Education Act 1996 s 324 (see PARA 1002); or (2) for whom no local authority maintains such a statement and who is in the area of a local authority in Wales: Education and Skills Act 2008 s 148(2) (amended by SI 2010/1158). 'Child' has the same meaning as in the Education Act 1996 Pt IV (ss 311A–349) (see note 4): Education and Skills Act 2008 s 148(5). As to the meaning of 'local authority' see PARA 25. As to the meaning of 'England' see PARA 7 note 3. As to the Secretary of State see PARA 58. As to the withdrawal of consent generally see PARA 1046.

7   Ie in addition to those prescribed: see the Education Act 1996 s 347(3). 'Prescribed' means prescribed by regulations: s 579(1). As to the regulations made see note 2.

8   Education Act 1996 s 347(3) (amended by the Education and Skills Act 2008 s 146(1), (3)).

9   As to the meaning of 'person' see PARA 7 note 6.

10   Ie his functions under the Education Act 1996 Pt IV (ss 311A–349). Section 347(5) does not apply to a local authority in Wales deciding, for the purposes of s 324(5) (see PARA 1002), whether a parent has made suitable arrangements: s 347(5A) (added by the Special Educational Needs and Disability Act 2001 s 42(1), Sch 8 Pt 1 paras 1, 12; and amended by the Education and Skills Act 2008 s 146(1), (7)(a); and SI 2010/1158). As to the meaning of 'functions' see PARA 18 note 5. As to the meaning of 'parent' see PARA 7 note 6.

11   'A relevant child' means a child with special educational needs: (1) for whom a local authority in Wales maintain a statement under the Education Act 1996 s 324 (see PARA 1192) (s 347(5ZA)(a) (s 347(5ZA) added by the Education and Skills Act 2008 s 146(1), (6); and amended by SI 2010/1158)); or (2) for whom no local authority maintain such a statement and who is in the area of a local authority in Wales (Education Act 1996 s 347(5ZA)(b) (as so added and amended)).

12   Education Act 1996 s 347(5) (amended by the Education and Skills Act 2008 s 146(1), (5)(a)).

13   Ie under the Education Act 1996 s 324: see PARA 1002.

14 Education Act 1996 s 347(5)(a) (amended by the Education and Skills Act 2008 s 146(1), (5)(b)). In relation to approval or consent for the purposes of the Education Act 1996 s 347(5), it has been held that while the [Welsh Ministers] are entitled to have a policy in relation to the approval of schools under s 347(5)(a) and the giving or withholding of consent under s 347(5)(b) (see the text to note 15), a policy cannot lawfully be applied inflexibly, and the possibility of exceptions must always be applied: see *R v Secretary of State for Education and Employment, ex p P* [2000] ELR 300 at 304–305 per Dyson J (citing *British Oxygen Co Ltd v Minister of Technology* [1971] AC 610, [1970] 3 All ER 165, HL).

15 Education Act 1996 s 347(5)(b) (amended by the Education Act 2002 s 174; Education and Skills Act 2008 s 146(1), (5)(c)). This provision, making special provision for ad hoc consent for a non-approved independent school, cannot properly be interpreted to mean that in the maintained sector a child could lawfully be sent to a school which was not for the time being approved by the [Welsh Ministers] and at which they did not consent to the child being educated: see *Sunderland City Council v P and C* [1996] ELR 283 at 293–294 per Brooke J. See also note 14.

1046. Withdrawal of approval of independent schools in Wales.

In any case where there is a failure to comply with a condition of an approval of an independent school[1], the Welsh Ministers may withdraw their approval[2]. Regulations[3] may make provision as to the withdrawal of approval from a school at the request of the proprietor[4] or on the ground that there has been a failure to comply with any prescribed[5] requirement[6].

1 Ie a condition imposed by the Welsh Ministers under the Education Act 1996 s 347(3): see PARA 1045. As to the Welsh Ministers see PARA 59. As to the meaning of 'independent school' see PARA 369.

2 Education Act 1996 s 347(4) (amended by the Education and Skills Act 2008 s 146(1), (4)). As to withdrawal of approval see *R v Secretary of State for Education and Employment, ex p McCarthy* (1996) Times, 24 July.

3 'Regulations' means regulations made by the Welsh Ministers: see the Education Act 1996 s 579(1).

4 As to the meaning of 'proprietor' see PARA 51 note 4.

5 'Prescribed' means prescribed by regulations: Education Act 1996 s 579(1). As to the prescribed requirements see PARA 1045 note 7.

6 Education Act 1996 s 347(2)(c). The Welsh Ministers may withdraw their approval of a school on the ground that, in the case of that school, there has been a failure to comply with any of the requirements which are to be complied with by a school while an approval under s 347 is in force in respect of it: see the Education (Special Educational Needs) (Approval of Independent Schools) Regulations 1994, SI 1994/651, reg 5(1). The Welsh Ministers must not, however, unless they are of the opinion that it is necessary or expedient to do so in the interests of the health, safety or welfare of children at the school, so withdraw their approval without consulting the proprietor of the school and, if the proprietor so requests, affording the school a specified period within which to comply with the requirement with which the school has not complied: see reg 5(2). The Welsh Ministers must also withdraw their approval of a school if the proprietor in writing requests them to do so: see reg 5(3). As to the meaning of 'child' see PARA 989 note 1. As to the meaning of 'writing' see PARA 76 note 8. The Education (Special Educational Needs) (Approval of Independent Schools) Regulations 1994, SI 1994/651, have effect as if made under the Education Act 1996 s 347(2) by virtue of s 582(3), Sch 39 para 1.

8. TEACHERS AND RELATED STAFF

(1) QUALIFICATION, REGISTRATION AND OTHER REQUIREMENTS FOR TEACHING STAFF

(i) Requirements for Teaching Staff

1047. Meaning of 'qualified teacher'. A reference in the Education Acts[1] to a 'qualified teacher' is a reference to a person who satisfies requirements specified in regulations[2]. A requirement of such regulations may relate to:

(1)   the possession of a specified qualification[3] or experience of a specified kind[4];

(2)   participation in or completion of a specified programme or course of training[5];

(3)   compliance with a specified condition[6];

(4)   an exercise of discretion by the Secretary of State, the Welsh Ministers or another specified person[7].

The Welsh Ministers must consult[8] the Education Workforce Council, before making any such regulations which make provision by reference to the content of a course or programme[9] or to the standard of education or training provided through a course or programme[10].

1   As to the meaning of 'the Education Acts' see PARA 1 note 13 (definition applied by the Education Act 2002 s 212(2), (3)).
2   Education Act 2002 s 132(1). 'Regulations' means regulations made under the Education Act 2002 by the Secretary of State (in relation to England) or by the Welsh Ministers (in relation to Wales): s 212(1). As to the Secretary of State see PARA 58. As to the Welsh Ministers see PARA 59. As to the meanings of 'England' and 'Wales' see PARA 7 note 3. The functions under the Education Act 2002 s 132 in relation to Wales were originally vested in the National Assembly for Wales and are now exercisable by the Welsh Ministers by virtue of the Government of Wales Act 2006 s 162(1), Sch 11 paras 30, 32. As to the regulations made under the Education Act 2002 s 132 see the Education (School Teachers' Qualifications) (England) Regulations 2003, SI 2003/1662 (amended by SI 2007/2782; SI 2012/431; SI 2012/1736; and SI 2014/2697); and the School Teachers' Qualifications (Wales) Regulations 2012, SI 2012/724.
3   A power under the Education Act 2002 ss 132–140 to make provision by reference to a specified qualification, a specified course of education or training or a specified programme includes power to make provision: (1) by reference to a class or description of qualification, course or programme (s 145(1)(a)); (2) by reference to the institution, or class or description of institution, which awards the qualification or provides the course or programme (s 145(1)(b)); (3) which confers discretion on the Secretary of State, the Welsh Ministers, the Higher Education Funding Council for Wales, the General Teaching Council for Wales (now the Education Workforce Council) or another specified person (s 145(1)(c) (amended by the Education Act 2011 Sch 2 par 19(1), (4), Sch 5 para 17(a)). A discretion under the Education Act 2002 s 145(1)(c) (see head (3) above) may, in particular, refer to approval or accreditation of a qualification, course or programme or institution: s 145(2). Regulations made by virtue of s 145(1) may impose a duty on the Higher Education Funding Council for Wales: s 145(3) (amended by the Education Act 2011 Sch 5 para 17(b)). As to the regulations made under the Education Act 2002 s 145 see the Education (School Teachers' Qualifications) (England) Regulations 2003, SI 2003/1662 (amended by SI 2007/2782; SI 2012/431; SI 2012/1736; and SI 2014/2697); the Head Teachers' Qualifications and Registration (Wales) Regulations 2005, SI 2005/1227; the Education (Specified Work and Registration) (Wales) Regulations 2010, SI 2010/2710; the School Teachers' Qualifications (Wales) Regulations 2012, SI 2012/724; and the Education (Specified Work) (England) Regulations 2012, SI 2012/762. As to the Education Workforce Council (formerly the General Teaching Council for Wales) see PARA 1075. As to the Higher Education Funding Council for Wales see PARA 691 et seq. As to the meaning of 'person' see PARA 7 note 6.
4   Education Act 2002 s 132(2)(a).
5   Education Act 2002 s 132(2)(b). As to the specification of courses see note 3.
6   Education Act 2002 s 132(2)(c).

7 Education Act 2002 s 132(2)(d).
8 As to the exercise of the duty to consult see JUDICIAL REVIEW vol 61 (2010) PARA 627.
9 Education Act 2002 s 132(4)(a) (s 132(4) amended by the Education (Wales) Act 2014 Sch 3 para 1(1), (4)).
10 Education Act 2002 s 132(4)(b).

1048. Requirement for teachers at schools and head teachers of schools to be qualified. Regulations[1] may provide that specified work may not be carried out by a person in a school[2] in England unless he: (1) is a qualified teacher[3]; or (2) satisfies specified requirements[4]. Regulations specifying work for these purposes may make provision by reference to one or more specified activities[5] or to the circumstances in which activities are carried out[6]. A requirement of such regulations may, in particular, relate to:

(a) the possession of a specified qualification[7] or experience of a specified kind[8];

(b) participation in or completion of a specified programme or course of training[9];

(c) compliance with a specified condition[10];

(d) an exercise of discretion by the Secretary of State, the Welsh Ministers, another specified person[11] or another person of a specified description[12].

Regulations[13] may provide that a person may serve as the head teacher[14] of a school[15] only if he is a qualified teacher[16], and only if he has, in addition to any qualification so required, a specified qualification[17].

1 'Regulations' means regulations made under the Education Act 2002 by the Secretary of State (in relation to England) or by the Welsh Ministers (in relation to Wales): s 212(1). As to the Secretary of State see PARA 58. As to the Welsh Ministers see PARA 59. As to the meanings of 'England' and 'Wales' see PARA 7 note 3. The functions under the Education Act 2002 ss 133–135 in relation to Wales were originally vested in the National Assembly for Wales and are now exercisable by the Welsh Ministers by virtue of the Government of Wales Act 2006 s 162(1), Sch 11 paras 30, 32. As to the regulations made under the Education Act 2002 s 133 see the Education (Specified Work and Registration) (Wales) Regulations 2010, SI 2010/2710; and the Education (Specified Work) (England) Regulations 2012, SI 2012/762 (amended by SI 2012/1736).
2 For these purposes, 'school' means a school maintained by a local authority or a special school not so maintained: Education Act 2002 s 133(6) (amended by SI 2010/1158). As to the meaning of 'school' see PARA 91; as to the meaning of 'local authority' see PARA 25; and as to the meaning of 'special school' see PARA 1041 (definitions applied by the Education Act 2002 s 212(2), (3)). 'Schools' can include certain types of academy (see further PARA 91) and as academies see PARA 345 et seq.
3 Education Act 2002 s 133(1)(a) (s 133(1) amended by the Education (Wales) Act 2014 Sch 3 para 1(1), (5)). As to the meaning of 'qualified teacher' see PARA 1047.
4 Education Act 2002 s 133(1)(b). Regulations may limit the period of time during which work may be carried out by a person in reliance on s 133(1)(b): s 133(5). As to the requirement to be registered in Wales see the Education (Wales) Act 2014 s 9, 10; and PARA 1075 note 10.
5 Education Act 2002 s 133(2)(a). Provision by virtue of s 133(2) may, in particular, be made by reference to an activity specified in a document of the kind mentioned in s 124(3) (pay and conditions orders: see PARA 1078): s 133(3).
6 Education Act 2002 s 133(2)(b).
7 As to the specification of qualifications see PARA 1047 note 3.
8 Education Act 2002 s 133(4)(a).
9 Education Act 2002 s 133(4)(b). As to the specification of courses see PARA 1047 note 3.
10 Education Act 2002 s 133(4)(c).
11 As to the meaning of 'person' see PARA 7 note 6.
12 Education Act 2002 s 133(4)(d).
13 As to the regulations made under the Education Act 2002 s 135 see the Head Teachers' Qualifications and Registration (Wales) Regulations 2005, SI 2005/1227 (amended by SI 2007/2811; and SI 2011/1769).

14 As to the meaning of 'head teacher' see PARA 538 note 6 (definition applied by the Education Act 2002 s 212(2), (3)).
15 For the purposes, 'school' means: (1) a school maintained by a local authority; or (2) a special school not so maintained: s 135(5) (amended by SI 2010/1158). See note 2.
16 Education Act 2002 s 135(1).
17 See the Education Act 2002 s 135(2). Regulations under s 135(2) do not prevent a person from carrying out the functions of the head teacher of a school: (1) pending the appointment of a head teacher (s 135(4)(a)); or (2) in the absence of the head teacher (s 135(4)(b)). A provision of regulations under s 135(2) does not apply to a person who has been appointed as the head teacher of a school before the commencement of the provision: s 135(3).

1049. Requirements to be met by teachers at, and principals of, further education institutions in Wales. Regulations[1] may: (1) prohibit the provision of education[2] at a further education institution in Wales by a person who does not have a specified qualification[3]; (2) prohibit the provision of education at a further education institution in Wales by a person unless he is serving or has served a probationary period[4]; (3) specify conditions to be complied with by or in respect of persons providing education at a further education institution[5]; and (4) provide that a person may serve as the principal of a further education institution in Wales only if he has a specified qualification[6].

The Welsh Ministers may by regulations[7]: (i) prohibit the provision by a further or higher education institution in Wales of a course, which is designed to lead to the award of a qualification specified under heads (1) and (4) above, without their approval[8]; (ii) enable the Welsh Ministers to determine the number of persons who may undertake a course, which is designed to lead to the award of a qualification specified under heads (1) and (4) above, at a further or higher education institution in Wales[9]; (iii) enable the Welsh Ministers to determine the number of persons in different categories who may undertake a course, which is designed to lead to the award of a qualification specified under heads (1) and (4) above, at a further or higher education institution in Wales[10].

1 'Regulations' means regulations made under the Education Act 2002 by the Secretary of State (in relation to England) or by the Welsh Ministers (in relation to Wales): s 212(1). As to the Secretary of State see PARA 58. As to the Welsh Ministers see PARA 59. As to the meanings of 'England' and 'Wales' see PARA 7 note 3. The functions under the Education Act 2002 ss 136–138, 140 in relation to Wales were originally vested in the National Assembly for Wales and are now exercisable by the Welsh Ministers by virtue of the Government of Wales Act 2006 s 162(1), Sch 11 paras 30, 32. As to the regulations made under the Education Act 2002 s 136 see the Further Education (Providers of Education) (England) Regulations 2006, SI 2006/3199 (amended by SI 2009/1924; and SI 2012/979); and the Persons Providing Education at Further Education Institutions in Wales (Conditions) Regulations 2007, SI 2007/2220. In addition, by virtue of the Interpretation Act 1978 s 17(2)(b), the Education (Teachers' Qualifications and Health Standards) (Wales) Regulations 1999, SI 1999/2817 (amended by SI 2002/1663; SI 2002/2938; SI 2003/140; SI 2003/2458; SI 2004/1744; SI 2004/1729; SI 2004/2733; and SI 2012/724), made under the Education Reform Act 1988 s 218(1) (repealed) have effect as if made under the Education Act 2002 s 136. Note that the Education Act 2002 ss 136(a), (b), 137, 138 have ceased to have effect in relation to England: see notes 3, 4, 6, 8.
   Regulations under any of ss 136–138 may provide that a specified provision of the regulations is not to apply where a specified condition, which may refer to the opinion of a specified person, is satisfied (s 140(1)); and such regulations may impose a function on a local authority, or the governing body of a further or higher education institution (s 140(2) (amended by SI 2010/1158)). As to the meaning of 'person' see PARA 7 note 6. As to the meaning of 'functions' see PARA 18 note 5; and as to the meaning of 'local authority' see PARA 25 (definitions applied by the Education Act 2002 s 212(2), (3)). As to the meaning of 'governing body' under the Further and Higher Education Act 1992 in relation to a further education institution see PARA 560 note 6. As to the meaning of 'governing body' under the Education Reform Act 1988 in relation to a higher education institution see PARA 628 note 2. 'Further education institution' means an institution which: (1) provides further education and is maintained by a local authority; or (2) is within the further education sector: Education

Act 2002 s 140(3) (amended by SI 2010/1158). As to the meaning of 'further education' see PARA 23 (definition applied by the Education Act 2002 s 212(2), (3)). As to the meaning of 'institution within the further education sector' see PARA 555. 'Higher education institution' means an institution which: (a) is within the higher education sector; and (b) receives financial support under the Further and Higher Education Act 1992 s 65 (administration of funds by higher education funding councils: see PARA 701): Education Act 2002 s 140(3). As to the meaning of 'institution within the higher education sector' see PARA 619.

2   'Education' includes vocational, social, physical and recreational training: Education Act 2002 s 140(3).

3   Education Act 2002 s 136(a) (amended by the Deregulation Act 2015 Sch 15 para 8(2)(a)). As to the specification of qualifications see PARA 1047 note 3. The Education Act 2002 s 136(a) ceased to have effect in relation to England under the Deregulation Act 2014 Sch 15 para 8(1)(a).

4   Education Act 2002 s 136(b) (amended by the Deregulation Act 2015 Sch 15 para 8(2)(b)). The Education Act 2002 s 136(b) ceased to have effect in relation to England under the Deregulation Act 2014 Sch 15 para 8(1)(b)).

5   Education Act 2002 s 136(c).

6   Education Act 2002 s 137(1) (amended by the Deregulation Act 2015 Sch 15 para 8(2)(c)). The Education Act 2002 s 137 ceased to have effect in relation to England under the Deregulation Act 2014 Sch 15 para 8(1)(c). Regulations under the Education Act 2002 s 137(1) do not prevent a person from serving as the principal of an institution while he is following a course or programme which is of a kind specified in the regulations, and is designed to lead to the award of a qualification specified under s 137(1): s 137(2). As from a day to be appointed under the Further Education and Training Act 2007 s 32(4), regulations under the Education Act 2002 s 137(1) may limit the period of time during which a person may serve as the principal of an institution in reliance on s 137(2): s 137(2A) (prospectively added (so far as relating to Wales) by the Further Education and Training Act 2007 s 23(1), (2)). At the date at which this volume states the law no such day had been appointed. A provision of regulations made under the Education Act 2002 s 137(1) by the Welsh Ministers in relation to Wales does not apply to a person who has been appointed as the principal of an institution in England or Wales before the commencement of the provision: s 137(3) (amended by the Further Education and Training Act 2007 s 23(1), (3)(b)). Nor do such regulations prevent a person from carrying out the functions of the principal of an institution pending the appointment of a principal (Education Act 2002 s 137(4)(a)), or in the absence of the principal (s 137(4)(b)). As to the regulations made see the Further Education (Principals' Qualifications) (England) (Revocation) Regulations 2010, SI 2010/2269. See also note 1.

7   At the date at which this volume states the law no such regulations had been made. However, by virtue of the Interpretation Act 1978 s 17(2)(b), the Education (Schools and Further and Higher Education) Regulations 1989, SI 1989/351 (revoked, in relation to England, by SI 2008/1701), made under the Education Reform Act 1988 s 218 (repealed) have effect as if made under the Education Act 2002 s 138(1), (3).

8   Education Act 2002 s 138(1), (3)(a). The Education Act 2002 s 138 ceased to have effect in relation to England under the Deregulation Act 2014 Sch 15 para 8(1)(d)). See also note 1.

    As from a day to be appointed, the following provisions are added: For the purposes of the Education Act 2002 s 138(3), a university to which an approved plan relates is to be treated (in any case where it would not be so treated but for this provision) as being a higher education institution; and 'approved plan', in the above provision, has the meaning given in the Higher Education (Wales) Act 2015 s 7: Education Act 2002 s 140(4), (5) (prospectively added by the Higher Education (Wales) Act 2015 Schedule para 6). At the date at which this volume states the law no such day had been appointed. See generally PARA 719.

9   Education Act 2002 s 138(1), (3)(b). See also notes 1, 8.

10 Education Act 2002 s 138(1), (3)(c). See also notes 1, 8.

1050.   Requirements for teachers as to health and physical capacity.

Regulations[1] may provide that certain activities may be carried out only by a person who satisfies specified conditions as to health or physical capacity[2]. The activities to which this requirement relates are:

(1)   an activity of a prescribed[3] kind performed in the course of the provision of education[4] at a school[5], or a further education institution[6];

(2)   an activity of a prescribed kind performed in the course of the provision of education by a person otherwise than in a school or a further

education institution[7] and under a contract of employment[8] or for services where the other party is a local authority or a person[9] exercising a function[10] relating to the provision of education on behalf of a local authority[11];

(3)   an activity of a prescribed kind, other than the provision of education, where: (a) the activity is carried out by a person under a contract of employment or for services[12]; (b) the other party to the contract is a local authority which entered into the contract for purposes connected with any of its education functions[13], the governing body of a school[14], or a further education institution[15]; and (c) the activity regularly brings the person into contact with children[16].

1   'Regulations' means regulations made under the Education Act 2002 by the Secretary of State (in relation to England) or by the Welsh Ministers (in relation to Wales): s 212(1). As to the Secretary of State see PARA 58. As to the Welsh Ministers see PARA 59. As to the meanings of 'England' and 'Wales' see PARA 7 note 3. The functions under the Education Act 2002 s 141 in relation to Wales were originally vested in the National Assembly for Wales and are now exercisable by the Welsh Ministers by virtue of the Government of Wales Act 2006 s 162(1), Sch 11 paras 30, 32. As to the regulations made under the Education Act 2002 s 141 see the Education (Health Standards) (England) Regulations 2003, SI 2003/3139; and the Education (Health Standards) (Wales) Regulations 2004, SI 2004/2733. In addition, by virtue of the Interpretation Act 1978 s 17(2)(b), the Education (Teachers' Qualifications and Health Standards) (Wales) Regulations 1999, SI 1999/2817 (amended by SI 2002/1663; SI 2002/2938; SI 2003/140; SI 2003/2458; SI 2004/1744; SI 2004/1729; SI 2004/2733; and SI 2012/724), made under the Education Reform Act 1988 s 218(1) (repealed) have effect as if made under the Education Act 2002 s 141.
2   Education Act 2002 s 141(1). As to whether such regulations can impose a public law duty on the employer to dismiss see the following cases (decided under previous legislation, ie the Education (Teachers' Qualifications and Health Standards) (England) Regulations 1999, SI 1999/2166 (revoked)): *R (on the application of Verner) v Derby City Council, R (on the application of Sheppard) v Norfolk County Council, R (on the application of Ridley) v St Thomas More Roman Catholic High School* [2003] EWHC 2708 (Admin), [2004] ICR 535, [2004] LGR 786 (where a teacher successfully applied for ill-health retirement benefit the onus was on him to arrange for termination of the employment); c f *R (on the application of Dorling) v Sheffield City Council* [2002] EWHC 2505 (Admin), [2003] ICR 424, [2003] ELR 486 (illness resulting in incapacity to fulfil employment obligations does not give rise to an automatic termination of a contract of employment). See also *Healey v Bridgend County Borough Council* [2002] EWCA Civ 1996, [2004] ICR 561n, [2002] All ER (D) 204 (Nov) (employee who applied voluntarily for ill-health retirement benefits and passed paperwork to employer had made a decision to retire).
3   'Prescribed' means prescribed by regulations: Education Act 2002 s 212(1).
4   'Education' includes vocational, social, physical and recreational training: Education Act 2002 s 141(5).
5   Education Act 2002 s 141(2)(a). 'School' means a school maintained by a local authority or a special school not so maintained: s 141(5) (amended by SI 2010/1158). As to the meaning of 'school' see PARA 91; as to the meaning of 'local authority' see PARA 25; and as to the meaning of 'special school' see PARA 1041 (definitions applied by the Education Act 2002 s 212(2), (3)). 'Schools' can include certain types of academy (see further PARA 91) and as to academies generally see PARA 345 et seq.
6   Education Act 2002 s 141(2)(b). 'Further education institution' has the meaning given by s 140 (see PARA 1049 note 1): s 141(5).
7   Education Act 2002 s 141(3)(a).
8   As to the meaning of 'contract of employment' see PARA 268 note 3.
9   As to the meaning of 'person' see PARA 7 note 6.
10 As to the meaning of 'functions' see PARA 18 note 5 (definition applied by the Education Act 2002 s 212(2), (3)).
11 Education Act 2002 s 141(3)(b) (amended by SI 2010/1158).
12 Education Act 2002 s 141(4)(a).
13 Education Act 2002 s 141(4)(b)(i) (s 141(4)(b) substituted by SI 2010/1158). As to the meaning of 'education functions' see PARA 25 (definition applied by the Education Act 2002 s 212(2), (3)).

14 Education Act 2002 s 141(4)(b)(ii) (as substituted: see note 13). As to the governing bodies of maintained schools in England see PARA 150 et seq; and in Wales see PARA 195 et seq.

15 Education Act 2002 s 141(4)(b)(iii) (as substituted: see note 13). As to the meaning of 'governing body' under the Further and Higher Education Act 1992 in relation to a further education institution see PARA 560 note 6.

16 Education Act 2002 s 141(4)(c). 'Child' means a person who has not attained the age of 18 years: s 141(5). As to the time at which a person attains a particular age see PARA 7 note 6.

1051. Service of induction period for teachers in England. Regulations[1] may make provision for, and in connection with, requiring persons employed[2] as teachers at relevant schools[3] in England, subject to such exceptions as may be provided by or under the regulations, to have satisfactorily completed an 'induction period'[4] of not less than three school terms[5]:

(1) in a relevant school[6];
(2) in such circumstances as may be prescribed[7], a nursery school[8] that is not maintained by a local authority, and is not a special school[9];
(3) in such circumstances as may be prescribed, an independent school[10] or an alternative provision academy[11] that is not an independent school[12]; or
(4) in such circumstances as may be prescribed, an institution within the further education[13] sector (or an institution within the further education sector of a prescribed description) or a 16 to 19 academy[14].

Such regulations may, in particular, make provision:

(a) as to the length of the induction period in any prescribed circumstances[15];
(b) as to periods of employment which are to count towards the induction period[16];
(c) as to the number of induction periods that a person may serve, and the circumstances in which a person may serve more than one induction period[17];
(d) precluding a relevant school, in such circumstances as may be prescribed, from being one at which an induction period may be served[18];
(e) as to supervision and training during a person's induction period[19];
(f) authorising the Secretary of State to determine the standards against which a person is to be assessed for the purpose of deciding whether the person has satisfactorily completed an induction period[20];
(g) requiring the appropriate body to decide whether a person (i) has achieved those standards and has accordingly satisfactorily completed his or her induction period[21]; or (ii) should have his or her induction period extended by such period as may be determined by the appropriate body[22]; or (iii) has failed satisfactorily to complete his or her induction period[23];
(h) requiring the head teacher of a school to make a recommendation to the appropriate body as to whether a person has achieved the standards mentioned in head (f) above[24];
(i) requiring the appropriate body to inform the Secretary of State of any decision under head (g) above[25];
(j) requiring the employer of a person employed as a teacher at a relevant school to secure (i) the termination of that person's employment as a teacher[26]; or (ii) that the person only undertakes such teaching duties as may be determined in accordance with the regulations, in such

circumstances following a decision that the person has failed satisfactorily to complete his or her induction period as may be prescribed[27];

(k) authorising or requiring the appropriate body to exercise such other functions[28] as may be prescribed (which may include functions with respect to the provision of assistance to schools, institutions within the further education sector or 16 to 19 academies or of training for teachers[29];

(l) authorising the appropriate body in such circumstances as may be prescribed to make such reasonable charges in connection with the exercise of its functions under the regulations as it may determine[30];

(m) requiring any person or body exercising any prescribed function under the regulations to have regard to any guidance given from time to time by the Secretary of State as to the exercise of that function[31].

Such regulations must include provision conferring on a person aggrieved by a decision under head (g) above a right to appeal against the decision to the Secretary of State[32], and a decision on such an appeal is to be final[33]. The regulations may make provision for, or for the determination in accordance with the regulations of, such matters relating to appeals as the Secretary of State considers necessary or expedient[34].

1 'Regulations' means regulations made by the Secretary of State in relation to England: Education Act 2002 s 212(1). As to the Secretary of State see PARA 58. As to the meaning of 'England' see PARA 7 note 3. As to the regulations made see the Education (Induction Arrangements for School Teachers) (England) Regulations 2012, SI 2012/1115. As to a 2014 decision involving the 2012 Regulations see *Mosekari v London Borough of Lewisham* [2014] EWHC 3617 (Admin), [2015] ELR 31.

2 As to the meaning of 'person' see PARA 7 note 6.

3 'Relevant school' means a school maintained by a local authority or a special school not so maintained: Education Act 2002 s 135A(4) (ss 135A–135C added by the Education Act 2011 s 9). As to the meaning of 'local authority' see PARA 25 (definition applied by the Education Act 2002 s 212(1) (amended by SI 2010/1158)). As to the meaning of 'special school' see PARA 1041 (definition applied by the Education Act 2002 s 212(2), (3)). As to schools maintained by local authorities see PARA 99. As to the meaning of 'school' generally see PARA 91 (definition applied by the Education Act 2002 s 212(2), (3)). As to the governing bodies of maintained schools in England see PARA 150 et seq. 'Schools' can include certain types of academy (see further PARA 91) and as to academies generally see PARA 345 et seq.

The Education Act 1996 ss 496, 497 (default powers of Secretary of State: see PARAS 64, 65) have effect in relation to the duties imposed and powers conferred by virtue of the Education Act 2002 s 135A as if the bodies to which those provisions apply included (1) the governing body of a special school that is not maintained by a local authority; (2) the governing body (within the meaning given by the Further and Higher Education Act 1992 s 90(1) (see PARA 560 note 6)) of an institution within the further education sector; (3) the appropriate body (within the meaning of the Education Act 2002 s 135A: see note 15): s 135C(4) (as so added).

4 During the induction period which a person is required to serve by virtue of regulations under the Education Act 2002 s 135A, the provisions of s 131 (appraisal of teachers' performance: see PARA 1052) and regulations under that provision do not apply to the person: s 135C(1) (as added: see note 3).

5 Education Act 2002 s 135A(1) (as added: see note 3). In the application of s 135A to an institution within the further education sector or a 16 to 19 academy a reference to a school term is to be read as a reference to a term of the institution, and a reference to the head teacher of a school is to be read as a reference to the principal of the institution: s 135A(5) (as so added; and amended by the Education Act 2011 Sch 13 para 13(2)(c)). As to the meaning of '16 to 19 academy' see PARA 346 note 13 (definition applied by the Education Act 2002 s 212(2), (3)).

6 Education Act 2002 s 135A(1)(a) (as added: see note 3). As to service of an induction period for teachers in Wales see the Education (Wales) Act 2014 s 17; and PARA 1075 note 16.

7 'Prescribed' means prescribed by regulations: Education Act 2002 s 212(1).

8 As to the meaning of 'nursery school' see PARA 91 (definition applied by the Education Act 2002 s 212(2), (3)).

9   Education Act 2002 s 135A(1)(b) (as added: see note 3).
10 As to the meaning of 'independent school' see PARA 369 (definition applied by the Education Act 2002 s 212(2), (3)).
11 As to the meaning of 'alternative provision academy' see PARA 346 note 14 (definition applied by the Education Act 2002 s 212(2), (3)).
12 Education Act 2002 s 135A(1)(c) (as added (see note 3); and amended by SI 2012/976).
13 As to the meaning of 'further education' see PARA 23 (definition applied by the Education Act 2002 s 212(2), (3)).
14 Education Act 2002 s 135A(1)(d) (as added (see note 3); and amended by the Education Act 2011 Sch 13 para 13(1)(2)(a)). Regulations under the Education Act 2002 s 135A(1)(d) may, in particular (1) provide that an induction period may not be begun without approval of the appropriate body for the serving of that induction period (s 135A(3)(a) (as so added)); (2) provide for approval to be general or specific (s 135A(3)(b) (as so added)); (3) make provision (including transitional provision) about the withdrawal of approval (s 135A(3)(c) (as so added)); (4) impose conditions or limitations on the appropriate body's power to give or withhold approval (s 135A(3)(d) (as so added)). For these purposes 'the appropriate body' means such person or body (including a local authority) as may be prescribed by, or determined by the Secretary of State in accordance with, regulations under the s 135A (and such regulations may provide for an appropriate body which is not a local authority to include a representative of such an authority): s 135A(4) (as so added).
15 Education Act 2002 s 135A(2)(a) (as added: see note 3).
16 Education Act 2002 s 135A(2)(b) (as added: see note 3).
17 Education Act 2002 s 135A(2)(c) (as added: see note 3).
18 Education Act 2002 s 135A(2)(d) (as added: see note 3).
19 Education Act 2002 s 135A(2)(e) (as added: see note 3).
20 Education Act 2002 s 135A(2)(f) (as added: see note 3).
21 Education Act 2002 s 135A(2)(g)(i) (as added: see note 3).
22 Education Act 2002 s 135A(2)(g)(ii) (as added: see note 3).
23 Education Act 2002 s 135A(2)(g)(iii) (as added: see note 3).
24 Education Act 2002 s 135A(2)(h) (as added: see note 3).
25 Education Act 2002 s 135A(2)(i) (as added: see note 3).
26 Education Act 2002 s 135A(2)(j)(i) (as added: see note 3).
27 Education Act 2002 s 135A(2)(j)(ii) (as added: see note 3). Where, in accordance with a requirement imposed by virtue of s 135A(2)(j)(ii), a teacher employed at a school maintained by a local authority continues to be employed at the school, but is not undertaking his or her normal teaching duties there, any costs incurred by the local authority in respect of the teacher's emoluments are not to be met from the school's budget share for any funding period except in so far as the authority have good reason for deducting those costs, or any part of those costs, from that share: s 135C(2) (as so added). Nothing in s 135C(2) applies to a maintained school at any time when the school does not have a delegated budget: s 135C(2) (as so added). In s 135C(2) the references to a school's budget share and to a school not having a delegated budget have the same meaning as in the School Standards and Framework Act 1998 Pt II (ss 20–83); and 'funding period', in relation to a school's budget share, has the same meaning as in that Part (see PARA 315 note 3): Education Act 2002 s 135C(3) (as so added). As to delegated budgets see PARA 323.
28 As to the meaning of 'functions' see PARA 18 note 5 (definition applied by the Education Act 2002 s 212(2), (3)).
29 Education Act 2002 s 135A(2)(k) (as added (see note 3); and amended by the Education Act 2011 Sch 13 para 13(1), (2)(b)).
30 Education Act 2002 s 135A(2)(l) (as added: see note 3).
31 Education Act 2002 s 135A(2)(m) (as added: see note 3).
32 Education Act 2002 s 135B(1) (as added: see note 3).
33 Education Act 2002 s 135B(2) (as added: see note 3).
34 Education Act 2002 s 135B(3) (as added: see note 3).

1052. Appraisal of performance of teachers in England. Regulations[1] may require the appraisal of the performance of teachers in England in a manner specified by the regulations[2], and at times specified by or determined in accordance with the regulations[3]. The regulations may impose a duty on: (1) a local authority[4]; (2) the governing body of a school[5] or institution[6]; (3) the head teacher[7] of a school or the principal of an institution[8]. The regulations may require or permit an appraisal to be carried out in a manner which confers a discretion on a person[9] specified by or chosen or determined in accordance with the regulations[10], and permit a person listed in heads (1) to (3) above on whom a duty is imposed to delegate that duty in whole or in part[11]. The regulations may require or permit a person listed in heads (1) to (3) above to have regard to the results of an appraisal in the performance of a function[12] specified by the regulations[13]. The results of an appraisal may be used in determining a teacher's remuneration[14].

Before making such regulations, the Secretary of State must consult[15] such of the following as appear to him to be appropriate: (a) associations of local authorities in England[16]; (b) local authorities in England[17]; (c) bodies representing the interests of governing bodies in England[18]; (d) bodies representing the interests of teachers in England[19].

1 'Regulations' means regulations made under the Education Act 2002 by the Secretary of State (in relation to England) or by the Welsh Ministers (in relation to Wales): see s 212(1). As to the Secretary of State see PARA 58. As to the Welsh Ministers see PARA 59. As to the meanings of 'England' and 'Wales' see PARA 7 note 3. The functions under the Education Act 2002 s 131 in relation to Wales were originally vested in the National Assembly for Wales and are now exercisable by the Welsh Ministers by virtue of the Government of Wales Act 2006 s 162(1), Sch 11 paras 30, 32.
     As to the regulations made under the Education Act 2002 s 131 see the School Teacher Appraisal (Wales) Regulations 2011, SI 2011/2940; the Education (School Teachers' Appraisal) (England) Regulations 2012, SI 2012/115 (amended by SI 2012/431; and SI 2012/2055); and the Education (School Developments Plans) (Wales) Regulations 2014, SI 2014/2677.
2 Education Act 2002 s 131(1)(a) (s 131(1) amended by the Education (Wales) Act 2014 Sch 3 para 1(1), (3)). As to the meaning of 'England' see PARA 7 note 3. As to appraisal of registered persons in Wales see the Education (Wales) Act 2014 s 23; and PARA 1075 note 21.
3 Education Act 2002 s 131(1)(b).
4 Education Act 2002 s 131(2)(a) (amended by SI 2010/1158). As to the meaning of 'local authority' see PARA 25 (definition applied by the Education Act 2002 s 212(1)).
5 As to the meaning of 'school' see PARA 91 (definition applied by the Education Act 2002 s 212(2), (3)). As to the governing bodies of maintained schools in England see PARA 150 et seq; and in Wales see PARA 195 et seq. 'Schools' can include certain types of academy (see further PARA 91) and as to academies generally see PARA 345 et seq.
6 Education Act 2002 s 131(2)(b). As to the meaning of 'governing body' under the Further and Higher Education Act 1992 in relation to a further education institution see PARA 560 note 6.
7 As to the meaning of 'head teacher' see PARA 538 note 6 (definition applied by the Education Act 2002 s 212(2), (3)).
8 Education Act 2002 s 131(2)(c).
9 As to the meaning of 'person' see PARA 7 note 6.
10 Education Act 2002 s 131(3)(a).
11 Education Act 2002 s 131(3)(b).
12 As to the meaning of 'function' see PARA 18 note 5 (definition applied by the Education Act 2002 s 212(2), (3)).
13 Education Act 2002 s 131(4).
14 Education Act 2002 s 131(5). As to the determination of teachers' remuneration see PARA 1076 et seq.
15 As to the exercise of the duty to consult see JUDICIAL REVIEW vol 61 (2010) PARA 627.
16 Education Act 2002 s 131(6)(a) (amended by SI 2010/1158).
17 Education Act 2002 s 131(6)(b) (amended by SI 2010/1158).
18 Education Act 2002 s 131(6)(c).
19 Education Act 2002 s 131(6)(d) (amended by SI 2010/1080).

(ii) Prohibitions and Restrictions on Employment of Teaching Staff

1053. Regulation under the Safeguarding Vulnerable Groups Act 2006. The Safeguarding Vulnerable Groups Act 2006 makes provision for the establishment of the Disclosure and Barring Service (initially the Independent Safeguarding

Authority) with responsibility for the maintenance of lists of persons barred from carrying out regulated activities in respect of children and vulnerable adults[1]. Regulated activities include any form of teaching, training or instruction of children (unless the teaching, training or instruction is merely incidental to teaching, training or instruction of persons who are not children), and any form of training, teaching or instruction provided wholly or mainly for vulnerable adults[2].

1 As to the Disclosure and Barring Service and its functions see CHILDREN AND YOUNG PERSONS vol 9 (2012) PARA 672 et seq.
2 See the Safeguarding Vulnerable Groups Act 2006 s 5, Sch 4; and CHILDREN AND YOUNG PERSONS vol 9 (2012) PARA 684.

(2) TEACHER TRAINING

1054. Responsibility for teacher training. The body corporate[1], originally established under the Education Act 1994[2] as the Teacher Training Agency, and later known as the Training and Development Agency for Schools[3], was abolished as from 1 April 2012[4]. The functions previously exercised by the Agency are now to be exercised by the Secretary of State[5] (in relation to England)[6] and the Welsh Ministers[7] (in relation to Wales)[8]. The National College for Teaching and Leadership and the Education Workforce Council are now the bodies responsible for teacher training.

1 As to bodies corporate see COMPANIES vol 14 (2009) PARA 2; CORPORATIONS vol 24 (2010) PARA 301 et seq.
2 Ie under the Education Act 1994 s 1(1) (repealed).
3 See the Education Act 2005 s 74 (repealed). Sections 74–84, Sch 13 are repealed by the Education Act 2011 s 14.
4 The Education Act 2005 ss 74–84, Sch 13 are repealed by the Education Act 2011 s 14 as from 1 April 2012.
5 As to the Secretary of State see PARA 58. As to the Education Act 2005 s 94 in regard to provision of information to the Secretary of State by the Higher Education Funding Council for Wales see PARA 1065.
6 As to the meaning of 'England' see PARA 7 note 3.
7 As to the Welsh Ministers see PARA 59.
8 See the Education Act 2002 s 14, the Education Act 2005 ss 84A, 84B; and PARAS 78, 1055. As to the transfer of staff, property, rights and liabilities from the Agency to the Secretary of State see the Education Act 2011 s 17, Sch 6. As to the meaning of 'Wales' see PARA 7 note 3.

1055. Duty of Welsh Ministers with respect to teacher training and power to promote careers in school workforce in Wales. In carrying out their general duties[1], the Welsh Ministers[2] must in particular make such arrangements as they consider expedient for securing that sufficient facilities are available for the training of teachers[3] to serve in (1) schools maintained by local authorities in Wales[4]; (2) institutions in Wales within the further education[5] sector[6]; and (3) institutions in Wales which are maintained by local authorities in Wales and provide higher education[7] or further education (or both)[8].

The Welsh Ministers may promote careers in the school workforce[9] in Wales[10]. The Welsh Ministers may exercise this power[11] jointly with the Secretary of State[12] or any other person[13] with functions[14] relating to careers in the school workforce[15].

The Welsh Ministers may make arrangements for the above power to be exercised on their behalf by any other person[16]. Such arrangements[17] may, in particular, make provision for that power to be exercised (1) to the extent, and on the terms, specified in the arrangements[18]; (2) generally or in such circumstances as are specified in the arrangements[19]; (3) jointly with any person with whom it can be exercised[20] jointly by the Welsh Ministers[21].

1 Ie their duties under the Education Act 1996 ss 10, 11: see PARA 60.
2 As to the Welsh Ministers see PARA 59.
3 As to the meaning of references to the training of teachers see PARA 24 note 2. See also PARA 1059 note 3.
4 Education Act 2005 s 84A(1) (s 84A added by the Education Act 2011 s 15(4), (5)). As to the meaning of 'local authority' see PARA 25 (definition applied by the Education Act 2005 s 100(3)). As to the meaning of 'maintained school' see PARA 1059 note 3. As to the meaning of 'Wales' see PARA 7 note 3.
5 As to the meaning of 'further education' see PARA 23 (definition applied by the Education Act 2005 s 100(3)).
6 Education Act 2005 s 84A(2) (as added: see note 3).
7 As to the meaning of 'higher education' see PARA 24 (definition applied by the Education Act 2005 s 100(3)).
8 Education Act 2005 s 84A(3) (as added: see note 3).
9 As to the meaning of 'school workforce' see PARA 1059 note 3.
10 Education Act 2005 s 84B(1) (s 84A added by the Education Act 2011 s 15(4), (5)). As to the meaning of 'Wales' see PARA 7 note 3.
11 Ie the power conferred by the Education Act 2005 s 84B(1).
12 As to the Secretary of State see PARA 58.
13 As to the meaning of 'person' see PARA 7 note 6.
14 As to the meaning of 'functions' see PARA 18 note 5 (definition applied by the Education Act 2005 s 100(3)).
15 Education Act 2005 s 84B(2) (as added: see note 3).
16 Education Act 2005 s 84B(3) (as added: see note 3). Arrangements under s 84B(3) do not prevent the power conferred by s 84B(1) from being exercised by the Welsh Ministers: s 84B(5) (as so added).
17 Ie arrangements under the Education Act 2005 s 84B(3).
18 Education Act 2005 s 84B(4)(a) (as added: see note 3).
19 Education Act 2005 s 84B(4)(b) (as added: see note 3).
20 Ie by virtue of the Education Act 2005 s 84B(2): see the text to notes 4–8.
21 Education Act 2005 s 84B(4)(c) (as added: see note 3).

1056. Powers of bodies to provide financial support. With its abolition in 2012[1], the Training and Development Agency for Schools obviously no longer has a role in the funding of training and development, although other bodies do. The Secretary of State[2], the Higher Education Funding Council for Wales[3] and any other relevant funding body may exercise any of their functions jointly[4]. 'Other relevant funding body' means the Higher Education Funding Council for England or the Welsh Ministers[5] to the extent that they are discharging their further education functions[6].

1 See PARA 1054.
2 As to the Secretary of State see PARA 58.
3 As to the Higher Education Funding Councils for England and Wales see PARA 691 et seq. As to the exchange of information between the Secretary of State and the Higher Education Funding Council for Wales see the Education Act 2005 s 94; and PARA 1065. Section 92 does not apply in relation to the functions of the Higher Education Funding Council for England in its capacity as principal regulator (within the meaning of the Charities Act 2011 s 25: see CHARITIES vol 8 (2015) PARA 320): Education Act 2005 s 92(5) (added by SI 2010/501; and amended by the Charities Act 2011 Sch 7 para 104)).
4 Education Act 2005 s 92(1) (amended by the Education Act 2011 s 15(4), (6)(a)). The reference in the Education Act 2005 s 92(1) to the functions of the Secretary of State is to the functions of the Secretary of State relating to training for members of the school workforce: s 92(2A) (added by the Education Act 2011 s 15(4), (6)(c)).
5 As to the Welsh Ministers see PARA 59. The functions under the Education Act 2005 s 92 were originally vested in the National Assembly for Wales and are now exercisable by the Welsh Ministers by virtue of the Government of Wales Act 2006 s 162(1), Sch 11 paras 30, 32. As to the meaning of 'Wales' see PARA 7 note 3.

6 Education Act 2005 s 92(2) (amended by SI 2005/3238; SI 2010/1080; the Education Act 2011 Sch 16 paras 24, 27; and the Deregulation Act 2015 Sch 14 Pt 2 pars 47, 48). The reference in the text to the Welsh Ministers' further education functions is a reference to functions under the Learning and Skills Act 2000 Pt 2 (ss 31–41) (see PARA 789 et seq).

1057. Further conditions imposed in relation to grants paid to the Higher Education Funding Council for England by the Secretary of State. In relation to England[1], the Secretary of State[2] must, when making any grant to the Higher Education Funding Council for England[3], impose a condition requiring the Council to impose a condition regarding student fees and fair access to higher education in relation to any grants, loans or other payments made by that body to the governing body[4] of a relevant institution[5]. If a governing body in England fails to comply with that requirement, the Director of Fair Access to Higher Education[6] may direct the Higher Education Funding Council for England or the Secretary of State (or both) to impose specified financial requirements on the governing body[7].

1 As to the meaning of 'England' see PARA 7 note 3. As to the corresponding powers in relation to Wales see PARA 1058.
2 As to the Secretary of State see PARA 58.
3 Ie under the Further and Higher Education Act 1992 s 68: see PARA 712. As to the Higher Education Funding Council for England see PARA 691.
4 As to the meaning of 'governing body' see PARA 717 note 5.
5 See the Higher Education Act 2004 s 23; and PARA 717. As to the meaning of 'relevant institution' see PARA 717 note 6.
6 As to the Director of Fair Access to Higher Education see PARA 911.
7 See the Higher Education Act 2004 s 37; and PARA 720.

1058. Further conditions imposed in relation to grants paid to the Higher Education Funding Council for Wales by the Welsh Ministers. Under the Higher Education Act 2004, when making any grant to the Higher Education Funding Council for Wales[1], the Welsh Ministers[2] had to impose a condition requiring the Council to impose a condition regarding student fees and fair access to higher education in relation to any grants, loans or other payments made by the Council to the governing body[3] of a relevant institution[4]. If a governing body in Wales[5] failed to comply with such a requirement, the Council could enforce the relevant condition by imposing financial requirements on the governing body in pursuance of any condition[6].

1 Ie under the Further and Higher Education Act 1992 s 68(1) (see PARA 712) or the Education Act 2005 s 88(1) (see PARA 1063). As to the Higher Education Funding Council for Wales see PARA 691 et seq.
2 As to the Welsh Ministers see PARA 59.
3 As to the meaning of 'governing body' see PARA 717 note 5.
4 See the Higher Education Act 2004 s 27. This provision is repealed as from 1 September 2015: see the Higher Education (Wales) Act 2015 s 58, Sch 1; and the Higher Education (Wales) Act 2015 (Commencement No 1 Order and Saving Provision) Order 2015, SI 2015/1327. As to the meaning of 'relevant institution' see PARA 717 note 6.
5 As to the meaning of 'Wales' see PARA 7 note 3.
6 See the Higher Education Act 2004 s 38. This provision is repealed as from 1 September 2015: see the Higher Education (Wales) Act 2015 Sch 1; and the Higher Education (Wales) Act 2015 (Commencement No 1 Order and Saving Provision) Order 2015, SI 2015/1327.

1059. Efficiency studies and research in England. The Secretary of State[1] may arrange for the promotion or carrying out by any person[2] of studies designed to improve economy, efficiency and effectiveness in the management or operations of a qualifying person[3]. A person promoting or carrying out such studies at the request of the Secretary of State may require the qualifying person concerned to provide him, or a person authorised by him, with such information, and to make its accounts and such other documents available to him, or a person authorised by him, for inspection, as he may reasonably require for that purpose[4].

1   As to the Secretary of State see PARA 58.
2   As to the meaning of 'person' see PARA 7 note 6.
3   See the Education Act 2005 ss 93(1), 100(1) (s 93(1) amended by the Education Act 2011 s 15(4), (7)(a)). 'Qualifying person' means a training provider receiving financial assistance under the Education Act 2002 s 14 from the Secretary of State (see PARAS 78, 615): Education Act 2005 s 93(3) (amended by the Education Act 2011 s 15(4), (7)(c)). 'Training provider' means a person who provides training for members of the school workforce: Education Act 2005 s 100(1) (definition amended by the Education Act 2011 s 15(4), (9)(c)).

     'The school workforce' and 'member of the school workforce' are to be read in accordance with the Education Act 2005 s 100(1A): s 100(1) (definition amended by the Education Act 2011 s 15(4), (9)(b)). For the purposes of the Education Act 2005 Pt 3 (ss 84A–100) the school workforce consists of the following members: (1) persons who work in schools; and (2) other persons who are teachers or who carry out work that consists of or includes teaching: s 100(1A) (added by the Education Act 2011 s 15(4), (9)(b)).

     References in the Education Act 2005 Pt 3 to 'training', in relation to teachers or other members of the school workforce (including references to the provision of training 'for' teachers or other members of the school workforce), include: (a) any training or education with the object of fitting persons to be teachers or other members of the school workforce, or to be better teachers or other members of the school workforce (ss 96(1)(a), 100(1)); and (b) any assessment related to the award of any qualification or status as a teacher or other member of the school workforce (ss 96(1)(b), 100(1)). As to the meaning of references to training in relation to teachers or other members of the school workforce in general see PARA 24 note 2.

     The governing body of a maintained school may: (i) provide courses of initial or further training for school teachers (Education Act 2005 s 95(1)(a)); (ii) provide courses of training for other members of the school workforce (s 95(1)(b)); or (c) join in partnership with other training providers, or (alone or jointly with other training providers) establish a body, for the purpose of providing training falling within head (i) or (ii) above (s 95(1)(c)). It is immaterial for these purposes whether or not the training constitutes higher education: s 95(2). In relation to an exercise of the powers so conferred, the governing body has all the same supplementary and incidental powers as it has in relation to the conduct of the school (s 95(3)); and any exercise by the governing body of a maintained school of the powers so conferred is not to be treated, for the purposes of the School Standards and Framework Act 1998 Pt II Ch IV (ss 45–53A) (financing of maintained schools: see PARA 315 et seq) as being undertaken for the purposes of the school (Education Act 2005 s 95(4)). The School Standards and Framework Act 1998 s 80 (exercise of power by a maintained school to provide further education: see PARA 588) does not apply in relation to any course of training that is provided under the Education Act 2005 s 95: s 95(5). Nothing in s 95 is to be read as affecting the power of the governing body of a school, as an ordinary incident of the conduct of the school to provide training for members of the school workforce who work at the school (s 95(6)(a)), or to participate in the provision of training for members of the school workforce as part of a course provided by another training provider (s 95(6)(b)). As to the governing bodies of maintained schools in England see PARA 150 et seq; and in Wales see PARA 195 et seq. 'Maintained school' means a community, foundation or voluntary school; a community or foundation special school; or a maintained nursery school: s 100(1). As to the meaning of references to a community, foundation or voluntary school or a community or foundation special school see PARA 106. As to the meaning of 'maintained nursery school' see PARA 99 note 4; and as to the meaning of 'higher education' see PARA 24 (definitions applied by s 100(3)). Maintained schools potentially include academies; as to academies generally see PARA 345 et seq.
4   Education Act 2005 s 93(2) (amended by the Education Act 2011 s 15(4), (7)(b)).

1060. Efficiency studies and research in Wales. The Higher Education Funding Council for Wales[1] may arrange for the promotion or carrying out by any person[2] of studies designed to improve economy, efficiency and effectiveness in the management or operations of a qualifying person[3]. A person promoting or carrying out such studies at the request of the Council may require the qualifying person concerned to provide him, or a person authorised by him, with such information[4], and to make its accounts and such other documents available to him, or a person authorised by him, for inspection[5], as he may reasonably require for that purpose[6].

The Higher Education Funding Council for Wales may carry out or commission such research as it considers appropriate with a view to improving the training of teachers[7] or the standards of teaching[8].

1 As to the Higher Education Funding Council for Wales see PARA 691 et seq.
2 As to the meaning of 'person' see PARA 7 note 6.
3 Education Act 2005 s 93(1). 'Qualifying person' means the governing body of an eligible institution, as defined by s 85(3) (see PARA 1062), receiving financial support under Pt 3 (ss 84A–100) from the Higher Education Funding Council for Wales: s 93(3)(b).
4 Education Act 2005 s 93(2)(a) (s 93(2) amended by the Education Act 2011 s 15(4), (7)(b)).
5 Education Act 2005 s 93(2)(b).
6 Education Act 2005 s 93(2).
7 Education Act 2005 s 89(a). As to the meaning of references to the training of teachers see PARA 24 note 2. As to the power of maintained schools to provide training for the school workforce see ss 95, 96; and PARA 1059 note 3.
8 Education Act 2005 s 89(b).

1061. Financial assistance for the training of teachers. The Secretary of State[1] (in relation to England[2]) or the Welsh Ministers[3] (in relation to Wales[4]) may give, or make arrangements for the giving of, financial assistance to any person[5] for or in connection with enabling any persons to receive any training for teachers or for non-teaching staff, or the provision of any form of training for teachers or for non-teaching staff[6].

1 As to the Secretary of State see PARA 58.
2 As to the meaning of 'England' see PARA 7 note 3.
3 As to the Welsh Ministers see PARA 59. The functions under the Education Act 2002 s 14 in relation to Wales were originally vested in the National Assembly for Wales and are now exercisable by the Welsh Ministers by virtue of the Government of Wales Act 2006 s 162(1), Sch 11 paras 30, 32.
4 As to the meaning of 'Wales' see PARA 7 note 3.
5 As to the meaning of 'person' see PARA 7 note 6.
6 See the Education Act 2002 s 14(1), (2)(ca), (g); and PARA 78.

1062. The Higher Education Funding Council for Wales as a funding agency for teacher training. The Higher Education Funding Council for Wales[1] is responsible for administering funds made available to it by the Welsh Ministers and others for the purpose of providing financial support for the carrying on by eligible institutions of qualifying activities[2], namely: (1) the provision of teacher training[3]; (2) the provision of facilities, and the carrying on of other activities, by eligible institutions which the governing bodies of those institutions[4] consider it necessary or desirable to provide or carry on for the purpose of or in connection with activities within head (1) above[5]; (3) the provision by any person[6] of services for the purposes of, or in connection with, such activities[7].

The institutions eligible for funding by the Council under the Education Act 2005[8] ('eligible institutions') are: (a) any institution in Wales[9] within the higher or further education sector[10]; (b) the Open University[11]; (c) any school in Wales[12]; (d) any other institution or body in Wales designated by order of the Welsh Ministers[13]; and (e) any partnership or association of eligible institutions, or body established by one or more such institutions, for the purpose of carrying on qualifying activities[14].

The Higher Education Funding Council for Wales may, subject to such terms and conditions[15] as the Council thinks fit[16]: (i) make grants, loans or other payments in respect of expenditure incurred or to be incurred by the governing body of an eligible institution for the purposes of activities qualifying for funding by the Council by virtue of head (1) or head (2) above[17]; and (ii) make grants, loans or other payments in respect of expenditure incurred or to be incurred for the purposes of the provision of services as mentioned in head (3) above[18]. Before exercising its discretion under head (i) or head (ii) above with respect to the terms and conditions to be imposed in relation to any grants, loans or other payments, the Council must consult the specified bodies[19].

In exercising its functions in relation to grants, loans and other payments, the Council must have regard to any forecast of demand for newly-qualified teachers notified to it by the Welsh Ministers and, in relation to any particular institution, to any assessment of the quality of the teacher training provided by that institution made by Her Majesty's Chief Inspector of Education and Training in Wales[20] or to which the Council thinks it is appropriate to have regard or to which the Welsh Ministers direct it to have regard[21].

In exercising its functions in relation to the provision of financial support for qualifying activities, the Council must have regard to the desirability of not discouraging any institution for whose activities financial support is provided under the Education Act 2005[22] from maintaining or developing its funding from other sources[23]. The Council also must have regard (so far as it thinks it appropriate to do so in the light of any other relevant considerations) to the desirability of maintaining: (A) what appears to it to be an appropriate balance in the support given by it as between institutions which are of a denominational character[24] and other institutions[25]; and (B) any distinctive characteristics of any eligible institution for whose activities financial support is provided[26]. The Council must also take such steps as appear to it appropriate to secure that the governing body of any institution which provides a course of initial teacher training funded by the Council makes available such information relating to the course, in such manner and to such persons, as the Council may require[27].

In exercising its functions[28], the Council must comply with any general directions given to it by the Welsh Ministers about the exercise of those functions[29].

1   As to the Higher Education Funding Council for Wales see PARA 691 et seq. The Welsh Ministers may by order confer or impose on the Council such functions supplementary to its functions under the Education Act 2005 Pt 3 (ss 84A–100) as the Welsh Ministers think fit: s 90(1). For these purposes, a function is a supplementary function in relation to the Council if: (1) it is exercisable for the purposes of the exercise by the Welsh Ministers of their functions under any enactment (s 90(2)(a)); and (2) it relates to, or to the activities of, an eligible institution (s 90(2)(b)). Before making such an order, the Welsh Ministers must carry out such consultation as appears to them to be appropriate: s 90(3). The Council may carry out such activities ancillary to its functions under Pt 3 as the Welsh Ministers may direct: s 90(4). In ss 86–91, 'eligible institution' is to be read in accordance with s 85(3) (see heads (a)–(e) in the text): s 85(5). At the date at which this volume states the law no order had been made under s 90. As to the Welsh Ministers see PARA 59. The functions under the Education Act 2005 Pt 3 in relation to Wales were originally vested in the National Assembly for Wales and are now exercisable by the Welsh Ministers by virtue of the Government of Wales Act 2006 s 162(1), Sch 11 paras 30, 32. As to the meaning of 'Wales' see PARA 7 note 3. As to the meaning of 'functions' see PARA 18 note 5 (definition applied by the Education Act 2005 s 100(3)). As to the exercise of the duty to consult see JUDICIAL REVIEW vol 61 (2010) PARA 627. As to directions generally see PARA 75. As to the giving of directions by the Welsh Ministers under Pt 3 see also the text to notes 28–29. As to the functions of the Welsh Ministers with respect to teacher training and the power to promote careers in the school workforce see the Education Act 2005 ss 84A, 84B; and PARA 1055.

2   See the Education Act 2005 s 85(1). The Higher Education Funding Council for Wales and any other relevant funding body may exercise any of their functions jointly: see s 92(1). As to the

meaning of 'other relevant funding body' see PARA 1056 note 2. The Welsh Ministers may by order authorise the Council to exercise its functions under Pt 3 (ss 84A–100) jointly with a body specified in the order, and the specified body to exercise its functions jointly with the Council: s 92(4). At the date at which this volume states the law no such order had been made.

3   Education Act 2005 s 85(2)(a). As to the meaning of references to teacher training see PARA 24 note 2. See also PARA 1059 note 3.

4   'Governing body', in relation to an institution conducted by a company, is to be read in accordance with an order under the Education Act 2005 s 100(2): s 100(1). The Welsh Ministers may by order provide for references in ss 85–91 to the governing body of an institution, in relation to an institution which is conducted by a company, to be read as references to the governing body provided for in the instrument of government, or to the company, or to both: s 100(2). At the date at which this volume states the law no such order had been made.

5   Education Act 2005 s 85(2)(b).

6   As to the meaning of 'person' see PARA 7 note 6.

7   Education Act 2005 s 85(2)(c).

8   Ie under the Education Act 2005 Pt 3 (ss 84A–100).

9   For the purposes of the Education Act 2005 s 85(3), an institution or body is in Wales if its activities are carried on, or principally carried on, in Wales: s 85(4).

10 Education Act 2005 s 85(3)(a). As to the meaning of 'institution within the higher education sector' see PARA 619. As to the meaning of 'institution within the further education sector' see PARA 555.

11 Education Act 2005 s 85(3)(b).

12 Education Act 2005 s 85(3)(c). As to the meaning of 'school' see PARA 91 (definition applied by s 100(3)).

13 Education Act 2005 s 85(3)(d). Such orders, being of local effect, are not recorded in this work.

14 Education Act 2005 s 85(3).

15 The terms and conditions on which the Council may make any such grants, loans or other payments may in particular: (1) enable the Council to require the repayment, in whole or in part, of sums paid by the Council if any of the terms and conditions subject to which the sums were paid is not complied with (Education Act 2005 s 86(2)(a)); and (2) require the payment of interest in respect of any period during which a sum due to the Council in accordance with any of the terms and conditions remains unpaid (s 86(2)(b)). The power of the Council to impose conditions on the making of any such grants, loans or other payments to an eligible institution includes in particular power to impose conditions prohibiting, restricting or requiring the charging of fees in connection with the carrying out by that institution of qualifying activities: s 86(3). Where a condition is imposed under s 86(3) in connection with any grant, loan or other payment made to an eligible institution (s 86(4)(a)), and the grant, loan or other payment is to any extent made in respect of persons undertaking training which is provided in whole or in part by another training provider (s 86(4)(b)), then, for the purposes of the condition, fees payable by such persons to the other training provider are to be regarded as fees charged by the eligible institution (s 86(4)). The terms and conditions must not relate to the application of any sums derived otherwise than from the Council; but this provision does not affect the power to impose conditions by virtue of s 86(3): s 86(5). As to the meaning of 'training provider' see PARA 1059 note 3.

16 See the Education Act 2005 s 86(1).

17 Education Act 2005 s 86(1)(a).

18 Education Act 2005 s 86(1)(b).

19 See the Education Act 2005 s 87(2). The Council must consult such of the following bodies as appear to it to be appropriate to consult in the circumstances: (1) such bodies representing the interests of eligible institutions as appear to the Council to be concerned (s 87(2)(a)); and (2) the governing body of any particular eligible institution which appears to the Council to be concerned (s 87(2)(b)).

20 As to Her Majesty's Chief Inspector of Education and Training in Wales see PARA 1148.

21 Education Act 2005 s 86(6). As to the giving of directions see also the text to notes 28–29.

22 Ie under the Education Act 2005 Pt 3 (ss 84A–100).

23 Education Act 2005 s 87(1). This provision does not affect the power by virtue of s 86(3) (see note 15) to impose conditions prohibiting or restricting the charging of fees: s 87(5).

24 For the purposes of the Education Act 2005 Pt 3 (ss 84A–100), an institution is 'of a denominational character' if: (1) at least one-quarter of the members of the governing body of the institution, or in the case of a school at least one-fifth, are persons appointed to represent the interests of a religion or religious denomination (s 97(a)); or (2) any of the property held for the purposes of the institution is held upon trusts which provide that, in the event of the discontinuance of the institution, the property concerned is to be held for, or sold and the

proceeds of sale applied for, the benefit of a religion or religious denomination (s 97(b)); or (3) any of the property held for the purposes of the institution is held on trust for or in connection with the provision of education, or the conduct of an educational institution, in accordance with the tenets of a religion or religious denomination (s 97(c)).

25 Education Act 2005 s 87(3)(a).
26 Education Act 2005 s 87(3)(b).
27 Education Act 2005 s 87(4).
28 Ie under the Education Act 2005 Pt 3 (ss 84A–100).
29 See the Education Act 2005 s 91(1), (2). If it appears to the Welsh Ministers that the financial affairs of an eligible institution have been or are being mismanaged, the Welsh Ministers may, after consulting the Council and the institution, give such directions to the Council about the provision of financial support in respect of the activities carried on by the institution as the Welsh Ministers consider necessary or expedient by reason of the mismanagement: s 91(3). Directions under s 91 must be contained in an order made by the Welsh Ministers: s 91(4). At the date at which this volume states the law no such order had been made.

1063. Grants to the Higher Education Funding Council for Wales made by the Welsh Ministers; terms and conditions. The Welsh Ministers[1] may make grants to the Higher Education Funding Council for Wales[2] of such amounts and subject to such terms and conditions as the Welsh Ministers may determine[3]. The terms and conditions subject to which such grants are made by the Welsh Ministers to the Council:

(1)   may in particular impose requirements to be complied with in respect of every institution, or every institution falling within a class or description specified in the terms and conditions, being requirements to be complied with in the case of any institution to which the requirements apply before financial support of any amount or description so specified is provided by the Council in respect of activities carried on by the institution[4]; but

(2)   may not otherwise relate to the provision of financial support by the Council in respect of activities carried on by any particular institution or institutions[5].

The terms and conditions may not be framed by reference to criteria for the selection and appointment of academic staff and for the admission of students[6]. The terms and conditions may in particular enable the Welsh Ministers to require the repayment, in whole or in part, of sums paid by it if any of the terms and conditions subject to which the sums were paid is not complied with[7], and require the payment of interest in respect of any period during which a sum due to the Welsh Ministers in accordance with any of the terms and conditions remains unpaid[8].

1   As to the Welsh Ministers see PARA 59. The functions under the Education Act 2005 Pt 3 (ss 84A–100) in relation to Wales were originally vested in the National Assembly for Wales and are now exercisable by the Welsh Ministers by virtue of the Government of Wales Act 2006 s 162(1), Sch 11 paras 30, 32. As to the meaning of 'Wales' see PARA 7 note 3. As to the functions of the Welsh Ministers with respect to teacher training and the power to promote careers in the school workforce see the Education Act 2005 ss 84A, 84B; and PARA 1055.
2   As to the Higher Education Funding Council for Wales see PARA 691 et seq. As to the Higher Education Funding Council for Wales as a funding agency for teacher training, and as to general directions as to the performance by the Council of its functions, see PARA 1062.
3   Education Act 2005 s 88(1). As to further conditions imposed in relation to grants paid to the Higher Education Funding Council for Wales see PARA 1064.
4   Education Act 2005 s 88(2)(a).
5   Education Act 2005 s 88(2)(b).
6   Education Act 2005 s 88(3).
7   Education Act 2005 s 88(4)(a).
8   Education Act 2005 s 88(4)(b).

1064. Further conditions imposed in relation to grants paid to the Higher Education Funding Council for Wales. Under the Higher Education Act 2004, when making any grant to the Higher Education Funding Council for Wales[1], the Welsh Ministers[2] had to impose a condition requiring the Council to impose a condition regarding student fees and fair access to higher education in relation to any grants, loans or other payments made by the Council, to the governing body[3] of a relevant institution[4]. If a governing body in Wales failed to comply with such a requirement, the Council could enforce the relevant condition by imposing financial requirements on the governing body in pursuance of any condition[5].

1 Ie under the Education Act 2005 s 88(1): see PARA 1063. As to the Higher Education Funding Council for Wales see PARA 691 et seq.
2 As to the Welsh Ministers see PARA 59. As to the functions of the Welsh Ministers with respect to teacher training and the power to promote careers in the school workforce see the Education Act 2005 ss 84A, 84B; and PARA 1055.
3 As to the meaning of 'governing body' see PARA 717 note 5.
4 See the Higher Education Act 2004 s 27. This provision is repealed as from 1 September 2015: see the Higher Education (Wales) Act 2015 s 58, Sch 1; and the Higher Education (Wales) Act 2015 (Commencement No 1 Order and Saving Provision) Order 2015, SI 2015/1327. As to the meaning of 'relevant institution' see PARA 717 note 6.
5 See the Higher Education Act 2004 s 38. This provision is repealed as from 1 September 2015: see the Higher Education (Wales) Act 2015 Sch 1; and the Higher Education (Wales) Act 2015 (Commencement No 1 Order and Saving Provision) Order 2015, SI 2015/1327.

1065. Provision of information. The Higher Education Funding Council for Wales[1] may give the Secretary of State[2] information for the purposes of the exercise of the Secretary of State's functions[3] relating to training[4] for members of the school workforce[5].

The Secretary of State may give the Council information for the purposes of the exercise of its functions under any enactment[6].

Certain persons and bodies[7] must (1) give the Secretary of State such information as the Secretary of State may require for the purpose of the exercise of the Secretary of State's functions relating to training for members of the school workforce[8]; (2) give the Council such information as it may require for the purpose of the exercise of their functions under any enactment[9].

1 As to the Higher Education Funding Council for Wales see PARA 691 et seq.
2 As to the Secretary of State see PARA 58.
3 As to the meaning of 'functions' see PARA 18 note 5 (definition applied by the Education Act 2005 s 100(3)).
4 As to the meaning of 'training' see PARA 1059 note 3.
5 Education Act 2005 s 94(1) (s 94 substituted by the Education Act 2011 s 15(4), (8)). As to the meanings of 'member of the school workforce' and 'school workforce' see PARA 1059 note 3. As to the Secretary of State's functions relating to such training generally see PARAS 1054, 1061.
6 Education Act 2005 s 94(2) (as substituted: see note 5).
7 Ie the persons and bodies mentioned in the Education Act 2005 s 94(4): (1) a person receiving, or who has received or applied for, a grant, loan or other payment under s 86 (see PARA 1062), or financial assistance from the Secretary of State under the Education Act 2002 s 14 (see PARAS 78, 615) (Education Act 2005 s 94(4)(a) (as substituted: see note 5); (2) a local authority (s 94(4)(b) (as so substituted). As to the meaning of 'local authority' see PARA 25 (definition applied by the Education Act 2005 s 100(3)).
8 Education Act 2005 s 94(3)(a) (as substituted: see note 5).
9 Education Act 2005 s 94(3)(b) (as substituted: see note 5).

(3) REGULATION OF TEACHING

(i) Regulation of Teacher Conduct in England

1066.   Regulation by Secretary by State and National College for Teaching and Leadership.   The General Teaching Council for England was established as a body corporate[1] under the Teaching and Higher Education Act 1998[2] and there were provisions under that Act both about the Council and its functions[3]. However the Council was abolished as from 1 April 2012[4] and its staff, property, rights and liabilities transferred to the Secretary of State[5]. The Secretary of State thus became responsible for the regulation of teacher conduct in England[6]. The National College for Teaching and Leadership operates as the regulator of the teaching profession on behalf of the Secretary of State[7].

1   As to bodies corporate see COMPANIES vol 14 (2009) PARA 2; CORPORATIONS vol 24 (2010) PARA 301 et seq.
2   See the Teaching and Higher Education Act 1998 s 1(1) (as substituted (see note 4); now repealed). See note 3.
3   See the Teaching and Higher Education Act 1998 Pt 1 Ch 1 (ss 1–15A) which are amended by the Education Act 2011 with the effect that the provisions generally applied only to the General Teaching Council for Wales (renamed as the Education Workforce Council) but most of the provisions are now repealed. As to regulation of teacher conduct in Wales see PARA 1075.
4   See the Teaching and Higher Education Act 1998 s 1 (amended by the Education Act 2011 s 7; now repealed). See note 3.
5   See the Education Act 2011 s 12, Sch 3 (now repealed). See note 3.
6   See PARA 1067 et seq.
7   See the guidance document *'Teacher Misconduct: Regulating The Teaching Profession'* available at the date at which this volume states the law on the Government website.

1067.   Application of provisions on teacher misconduct generally.   The relevant provisions of the Education Act 2002 on teacher misconduct[1] apply to a person[2] who is employed or engaged to carry out teaching work[3] at (1) a school[4] in England[5]; (2) a sixth form college in England[6]; (3) a 16 to 19 academy[7]; (4) relevant youth accommodation in England[8]; or (5) a children's home[9] in England[10].

1   Ie the Education Act 2002 ss 141B–141E: see PARA 1068 et seq.
2   As to the meaning of 'person' see PARA 7 note 6.
3   'Teaching work' means work of a kind specified in regulations under the Education Act 2002 s 141A (and such regulations may make provision by reference to specified activities or by reference to the circumstances in which activities are carried out): Education Act 2002 s 141A(2) (s 141A added by the Education Act 2011 s 8(1)). As to the regulations made see the Teachers' Disciplinary (England) Regulations 2012, SI 2012/560 (amended by SI 2014/1685).
4   As to the meaning of 'school' see PARA 91 (definition applied by the Education Act 2002 s 212(2), (3)).
5   Education Act 2002 s 141A(1)(a) (s 141A added by the Education Act 2011 s 8(1)). As to the meaning of 'England' see PARA 7 note 3.
6   Education Act 2002 s 141A(1)(b) (as added: see note 5).
7   Education Act 2002 s 141A(1)(ba) (as added (see note 5); and amended by the Education Act 2011 Sch 13 para 13(1), (3)). As to the meaning of '16 to 19 academy' see PARA 346 note 13 (definition applied by the Education Act 2002 s 212(2), (3)).
8   Education Act 2002 s 141A(1)(c) (as added: see note 5).
9   'Children's home' has the same meaning as in the Care Standards Act 2000 (see CHILDREN AND YOUNG PERSONS vol 10 (2012) PARA 992): Education Act 2002 s 141A(2) (as added: see note 3).
10 Education Act 2002 s 141A(1)(d) (as added: see note 5).

1068.   Investigation of disciplinary cases by the Secretary of State.   The Secretary of State[1] may investigate a case where an allegation is referred to the

Secretary of State that a person[2] may be guilty of unacceptable professional conduct or conduct that may bring the teaching profession into disrepute, or has been convicted (at any time) of a relevant offence[3]. Where the Secretary of State finds on an investigation of a case[4] that there is a case to answer, the Secretary of State must decide whether to make a prohibition order[5] in respect of the person[6].

There is provision about the regulations to be made[7] by the Secretary of State, including provision about the procedures to be followed[8], prohibition and interim prohibition orders[9], appeals against prohibition orders[10], and supplementary provisions[11].

1   As to the Secretary of State see PARA 58.
2   Ie a person to whom the Education Act 2002 s 141B applies: see s 141A; and PARA 1067.
3   Education Act 2002 s 141B(1) (s 141B added by the Education Act 2011 s 8(1)). As to the meaning of 'person' see PARA 7 note 6. 'Relevant offence', in relation to a person, means (1) in the case of a conviction in England and Wales, a criminal offence other than one having no material relevance to the person's fitness to be a teacher; and (2) in the case of a conviction elsewhere, an offence which, if committed in England and Wales, would be within head (1) above: Education Act 2002 s 141B(4) (as so added). As to the meanings of 'England' and 'Wales' see PARA 7 note 3.
4   Ie under the Education Act 2002 s 141B(1).
5   A 'prohibition order' means an order prohibiting the person to whom it relates from carrying out teaching work: s 141B(4) (as added: see note 3). As to the meaning of 'teaching work' see PARA 1067 note 3 (definition applied by s 141B(4) (as so added)).
6   Education Act 2002 s 141B(2) (as added: see note 3).
7   Ie under the Education Act 2002 s 141B.
8   See the Education Act 2002 s 141B(3) (as added: see note 3), Sch 11A para 2 (Sch 11A added by the Education Act 2002 s 8(2); and the Education Act 2002 Sch 11A para 2 amended by SI 2012/3006). As to the regulations made see the Teachers' Disciplinary (England) Regulations 2012, SI 2012/560 (amended by SI 2014/1685).
9   See the Education Act 2002 Sch 11A paras 3, 4 (as added: see note 8).
10 See the Education Act 2002 Sch 11A para 5 (as added: see note 8).
11 See the Education Act 2002 Sch 11A para 6 (as added: see note 8).

1069.   List of persons prohibited from teaching etc.   The Secretary of State[1] must keep a list containing (1) the names of persons[2] in relation to whom a prohibition order[3] has effect[4]; and (2) the names of persons who have begun, but have failed satisfactorily to complete, an induction period[5] in such circumstances as may be prescribed[6].

The Secretary of State may include on the list the name of any person who has been prohibited from teaching in Wales[7], Scotland or Northern Ireland that the Secretary of State thinks appropriate to include on the list[8].

The Secretary of State must secure that, where the name of a person is included on the list because an interim prohibition order[9] has effect in respect of the person, there is an indication on the list to that effect[10]. The Secretary of State must secure that, where the name of a person is included on the list because the person has failed satisfactorily to complete an induction period[11], there is an indication on the list to that effect[12].

The list may contain such other information in relation to the persons whose names are included on it as the Secretary of State considers appropriate[13]. The list must also be available for inspection by members of the public[14].

1   As to the Secretary of State see PARA 58.
2   As to the meaning of 'person' see PARA 7 note 6.
3   As to the meaning of 'prohibition order' see PARA 1068 note 5 (definition applied by the Education Act 2002 s 141C(7) (s 141C added by the Education Act 2011 s 8(1))).
4   Education Act 2002 s 141C(1)(a) (as added: see note 3).
5   Ie an induction period under the Education Act 2002 s 135A: see PARA 1051.

6   Education Act 2002 s 141C(1)(b) (as added: see note 3). 'Prescribed' means prescribed by regulations; and 'regulations' means regulations made by the Secretary of State: see s 212(1). As to the regulations made see the Education (Induction Arrangements for School Teachers) (England) Regulations 2012, SI 2012/1115.

7   As to the meaning of 'Wales' see PARA 7 note 3.

8   Education Act 2002 s 141C(2) (as added: see note 3).

9   'Interim prohibition order' means an order made by virtue of the Education Act 2002 Sch 11A para 3 (see the note to PARA 1068 note 9): s 141C(7) (as added: see note 3).

10   Education Act 2002 s 141C(3) (as added: see note 3).

11   See note 5.

12   Education Act 2002 s 141C(4) (as added: see note 3).

13   Education Act 2002 s 141C(5) (as added: see note 3).

14   Education Act 2002 s 141C(6) (as added: see note 3).

1070. Supply of information following dismissal, resignation, etc. The following provisions[1] apply where a relevant employer[2] has ceased to use the services of a teacher because the teacher has been guilty of serious misconduct[3]. The provisions also apply where a relevant employer might have ceased to use the services of a teacher as mentioned above[4] had the teacher not ceased to provide those services[5].

The employer must consider whether it would be appropriate to provide prescribed[6] information about the teacher to the Secretary of State[7].

1   Ie the provisions of the Education Act 2002 s 141D.

2   'Relevant employer' means (1) a local authority; (2) a person exercising a function relating to the provision of education on behalf of a local authority; (3) the proprietor of a school or 16 to 19 academy; (4) a sixth form college corporation; (5) a person who employs a person to teach in a children's home or in relevant youth accommodation; 'education' includes vocational, social, physical and recreational training; 'children's home' has the same meaning as in the Care Standards Act 2000 (see CHILDREN AND YOUNG PERSONS vol 10 (2012) PARA 992); 'services' includes professional and voluntary services; and 'teacher' means a person within the Education Act 2002 s 141A(1) (see PARA 1067): s 141D(4) (s 141D added by the Education Act 2011 s 8(1); and the Education Act 2002 s 141D(4) amended by the Education Act 2011 Sch 13 para 13(1), (4)). As to the meaning of 'local authority' see PARA 25; as to the meaning of 'school' see PARA 91; and as to the meaning of '16 to 19 academy' see PARA 346 note 13 (definitions applied by the Education Act 2002 s 212(2), (3)).

3   Education Act 2002 s 141D(1) (as added: see note 2). As to the supply of information generally in Wales see the Education (Wales) Act 2014 ss 33–37; and PARA 1075 notes 27, 28.

4   Ie in the Education Act 2002 s 141D(1).

5   Education Act 2002 s 141D(2) (as added: see note 2).

6   'Prescribed' means prescribed by regulations; and 'regulations' means regulations made by the Secretary of State: see the Education Act 2002 s 212(1). See note 7.

7   Education Act 2002 s 141D(3) (as added: see note 2). As to the information prescribed for the purposes of the Education Act 2002 s 141D(3) see the Teachers' Disciplinary (England) Regulations 2012, SI 2012/560, reg 20.

1071. Supply of information by contractor, agency, etc. The following provisions[1] apply where arrangements have been made by a person[2] (the 'agent') for a teacher to carry out work at the request of or with the consent of a relevant employer[3] (whether or not under a contract) and the agent has terminated the arrangements because the teacher[4] has been guilty of serious misconduct[5]. The provisions also apply where the agent (1) might have terminated the arrangements[6] had the teacher not terminated them[7]; or (2) might have refrained from making new arrangements because of the teacher's serious misconduct had the teacher not ceased to be available for work[8].

The agent must consider whether it would be appropriate to provide prescribed[9] information about the teacher to the Secretary of State[10].

1   Ie the provisions of the Education Act 2002 s 141E.

2 As to the meaning of 'person' see PARA 7 note 6.
3 As to the meaning of 'relevant employer' see PARA 1070 note 2 (definition applied by the Education Act 2002 s 141E(4) (s 141E added by the Education Act 2011 s 8(1))). As to the supply of information by a contractor, agency, etc in Wales see the Teacher and Higher Education Act 1988 s 15A; and PARA 1075 note 28.
4 As to the meaning of 'teacher' see PARA 1070 note 2 (definition applied by the Education Act 2002 s 141E(4) (as added: see note 3)).
5 Education Act 2002 s 141E(1) (as added: see note 3).
6 Ie the arrangements as mentioned in the Education Act 2002 s 141E(1).
7 Education Act 2002 s 141E(2)(a) (as added: see note 3).
8 Education Act 2002 s 141E(2)(b) (as added: see note 3).
9 'Prescribed' means prescribed by regulations; and 'regulations' means regulations made by the Secretary of State: see the Education Act 2002 s 212(1). See note 10.
10 Education Act 2002 s 141E(3) (as added: see note 3). As to the Secretary of State see PARA 58. As to the information prescribed for the purposes of s 141E(3) see the Teachers' Disciplinary (England) Regulations 2012, SI 2012/560, reg 20.

1072.   Restrictions on reporting alleged offences by teachers.   The following provisions[1] apply where a person[2] who is employed or engaged as a teacher at a school[3] is the subject of an allegation which (1) is an allegation that the person is or may be guilty of a relevant criminal offence[4]; and (2) is made by or on behalf of a registered pupil at the school[5].

No matter relating to the person is to be included in any publication[6] if it is likely to lead members of the public to identify the person as the teacher who is the subject of the allegation[7].

Any person may make an application to a magistrates' court for an order dispensing with the above restrictions[8]. The court may make an order dispensing with the restrictions, to the extent specified in the order, if it is satisfied that it is in the interests of justice to do so, having regard to the welfare of the person who is the subject of the allegation, and the victim of the offence to which the allegation relates[9].

In the case of a decision to make or refuse to make such an order[10], certain persons[11] may, in accordance with Criminal Procedure Rules[12] appeal to the Crown Court against the decision, or appear or be represented at the hearing of such an appeal[13]. On such an appeal[14], the Crown Court may make such order as is necessary to give effect to its determination of the appeal, and may make such incidental or consequential orders as appear to it to be just[15].

The above restrictions[16] cease to apply once proceedings for the offence have been instituted[17]. The restrictions[18] also cease to apply if (a) the Secretary of State[19] publishes information about the person who is the subject of the allegation in connection with an investigation or decision[20] relating to the same allegation[21]; or (b) the Education Workforce Council[22] publishes information about the person who is the subject of the allegation in connection with an investigation, hearing or determination[23] relating to the same allegation[24].

The above restrictions[25] also cease to apply if (i) the person who is the subject of the allegation includes a matter in a publication[26]; or (ii) another person includes a matter in a publication with the written consent of the person who is the subject of the allegation, and, in either case, the inclusion of the matter in the publication would otherwise be in breach of the relevant provision[27].

1 Ie the provisions of the Education Act 2002 s 141F.
2 As to the meaning of 'person' see PARA 7 note 6.
3 As to the meaning of 'school' see PARA 91 (definition applied by the Education Act 2002 s 212(2), (3)).
4 Education Act 2002 s 141F(1), (2)(a) (s 141F added by the Education Act 2011 s 13(1)). 'Relevant criminal offence', in relation to a person employed or engaged as a teacher at a school,

means an offence against the law of England and Wales where the victim of the offence is a registered pupil at the school: Education Act 2002 s 141F(14) (as so added). As to the meanings of 'England' and 'Wales' see PARA 7 note 3. As to the meaning of 'registered pupil' see PARA 437 (definition applied by s 212(2), (3)).

5 Education Act 2002 s 141F(1), (2)(b) (as added: see note 4).

6 'Publication' includes any speech, writing, relevant programme or other communication in whatever form, which is addressed to the public at large or any section of the public (and for this purpose, every relevant programme is to be taken to be so addressed), but does not include an indictment or other document prepared for use in particular legal proceedings, or a document published by the regulator of a profession of which the person who is the subject of the allegation is a member in connection with disciplinary proceedings in relation to the person; and 'relevant programme' means a programme included in a programme service, within the meaning of the Broadcasting Act 1990 (see BROADCASTING vol 4 (2011) PARA 507 note 11): Education Act 2002 s 141F(14) (as added: see note 4).

7 Education Act 2002 s 141F(3) (as added: see note 4).

8 Education Act 2002 s 141F(4) (as added: see note 4). The reference to the above restrictions is a reference to the restrictions imposed by s 141F(3): see the text to notes 6, 7. As to magistrates' courts see MAGISTRATES.

9 Education Act 2002 s 141F(5) (as added: see note 4). The power under s 141F(5) may be exercised by a single justice: s 141F(6) (as so added).

10 Ie an order under the Education Act 2002 s 141F(5): see the text to note 9.

11 Ie a person mentioned in the Education Act 2002 s 141F(8). The persons referred to in s 141F(7) are a person who was a party to the proceedings on the application for the order and any other person with the leave of the Crown Court: s 141F(8) (as so added). As to the Crown Court generally see COURTS AND TRIBUNALS vol 24 (2010) PARA 716 et seq.

12 Ie the Criminal Procedure Rules 2014, SI 2014/1610: see CRIMINAL PROCEDURE vol 27 (2010) PARA 110 et seq.

13 Education Act 2002 s 141F(7) (as added: see note 4).

14 Ie under the Education Act 2002 s 141F(7): see the text to notes 10–13.

15 Education Act 2002 s 141F(9) (as added: see note 4).

16 Ie the restrictions in the Education Act 2002 s 141F(3): see the text to notes 6, 7.

17 Education Act 2002 s 141F(10) (as added: see note 4). For these purposes, proceedings for an offence are instituted at the earliest of the following times: (1) when a justice of the peace issues a summons or warrant under the Magistrates' Courts Act 1980 s 1 (see MAGISTRATES vol 71 (2013) PARA 429) in respect of the offence; (2) when a relevant prosecutor issues a written charge and requisition or single justice procedure notice in respect of the offence; (3) when a person is charged with the offence after being taken into custody without a warrant; (4) when a bill of indictment is preferred by virtue of the Administration of Justice (Miscellaneous Provisions) Act 1933 s 2(2)(b) (see CRIMINAL PROCEDURE vol 27 (2010) PARA 325): Education Act 2002 s 141F(15) (as so added; and amended by the Criminal Justice and Courts Act 2015 Sch 11 para 19(1), (2)). For the above purposes, 'relevant prosecutor', 'requisition', 'single justice procedure notice' and 'written charge' have the same meaning as in the Criminal Justice Act 2003 s 29 (see CRIMINAL PROCEDURE vol 27 (2010) PARA 124): Education Act 2002 s 141F(16) (added by the Criminal Justice and Courts Act 2015 Sch 11 para 19(1), (3)).

18 See note 16.

19 As to the Secretary of State see PARA 58.

20 Ie an investigation or decision under the Education Act 2002 s 141B (investigation of disciplinary cases by Secretary of State): see PARA 1068.

21 Education Act 2002 s 141F(11)(a) (as added: see note 4).

22 Ie renamed as such, formerly the General Teaching Council for Wales: see PARA 1075.

23 Ie under the Teaching and Higher Education Act 1998 Sch 2 (investigation of disciplinary cases by the General Teaching Council for Wales) (repealed): see PARA 1075.

24 Education Act 2002 s 141F(11)(b) (as added: see note 4).

25 See note 16.

26 Education Act 2002 s 141F(12)(a) (as added: see note 4).

27 Education Act 2002 s 141F(12)(b) (as added: see note 4). The reference to the relevant provision is a reference to s 141F(3): see the text to notes 6, 7. Written consent is to be ignored for the purposes of s 141F(12)(b) if it is proved that any person interfered unreasonably with the peace or comfort of the person giving the consent, with intent to obtain it: s 141F(13) (as so added).

1073. Offence of breach of reporting restrictions. The following provisions[1] apply if a publication includes any matter in breach of the relevant restrictions[2].

Where the publication is a newspaper or periodical, any proprietor, any editor and any publisher of the newspaper or periodical is guilty of an offence[3]. Where the publication is a programme included in a programme service[4], the following are guilty of an offence: any body corporate[5] engaged in providing the programme service in which the programme is included, and any person[6] having functions in relation to the programme corresponding to those of an editor of a newspaper[7]. In the case of any other publication, any person publishing it is guilty of an offence[8].

A person guilty of such an offence is liable on summary conviction to a fine[9]. If an offence committed by a body corporate is proved to have been committed with the consent or connivance of, or to be attributable to any neglect on the part of, an officer[10], the officer as well as the body corporate is guilty of the offence and liable to be proceeded against and punished accordingly[11].

There are also supplementary provisions about the above offence[12] to ensure compliance with European Union legislation[13].

1 Ie the provisions of the Education Act 2002 s 141G.
2 Education Act 2002 s 141G(1) (s 141G added by the Education Act 2011 s 13(1).
3 Education Act 2002 s 141G(2) (as added: see note 2).
4 Ie within the meaning of the Broadcasting Act 1990: see BROADCASTING vol 4 (2011) PARA 507 note 11.
5 As to bodies corporate see COMPANIES vol 14 (2009) PARA 2; CORPORATIONS vol 24 (2010) PARA 301 et seq.
6 As to the meaning of 'person' see PARA 7 note 6.
7 Education Act 2002 s 141G(3) (as added: see note 2).
8 Education Act 2002 s 141G(4) (as added: see note 2).
9 Education Act 2002 s 141G(5) (as added: see note 2). Such a person is liable to a fine not exceeding level 5 on the standard scale: see s 141G(5) (as so added). As to the standard scale see SENTENCING AND DISPOSITION OF OFFENDERS vol 92 (2010) PARA 142.
10 'Officer' means a director, manager, secretary or other similar officer of the body, or a person purporting to act in any such capacity: Education Act 2002 s 141G(7) (as added: see note 2). If the affairs of a body corporate are managed by its members, 'director' in s 141G(7) means a member of that body: s 141G(8) (as so added).
11 Education Act 2002 s 141G(6) (as added: see note 2).
12 Ie the under the Education Act 2002 s 141G.
13 See the Education Act 2002 Sch 11B (added by the Education Act 2011 s 13, Sch 4; and amended by SI 2012/1809).

1074. Defence to a charge of breach of reporting restrictions. Where a person[1] is charged with an offence of breach of reporting restrictions[2], it is a defence for the person to prove either of the matters mentioned[3] below[4].

The matters are (1) that, at the time of the alleged offence, the person was not aware, and neither suspected nor had reason to suspect, that the publication included the matter in question[5]; and (2) that, at the time of the alleged offence, the person was not aware, and neither suspected nor had reason to suspect, that the allegation in question had been made[6].

1 As to the meaning of 'person' see PARA 7 note 6.
2 Ie an offence under the Education Act 2002 s 141G: see PARA 1073.
3 Ie in the Education Act 2002 s 141H(2).
4 Education Act 2002 s 141H(1) (s 141H added by the Education Act 2011 s 13(1)).
5 Education Act 2002 s 141H(2)(a) (as added: see note 4).
6 Education Act 2002 s 141H(2)(b) (as added: see note 4).

(ii) Regulation of Teacher Conduct in Wales

1075. Regulation by the Education Workforce Council. With the abolition of the General Teaching Council for England[1], the relevant amended provisions of the Teaching and Higher Education Act 1998[2] applied only to the General Teaching Council for Wales. However from April 2015 the General Teaching Council for Wales was reformed, renamed and replaced by a new body, the Education Workforce Council, by the Education (Wales) Act 2014[3].

The Education (Wales) Act 2014 introduced a new registration system for the whole education workforce in Wales. Amongst other things, it also harmonises school term dates and removes the appointment of the Her Majesty's Chief Inspector of Education and Training in Wales and Her Majesty's inspectors of education and training in Wales[4].

Of most significance to teachers and related staff and their regulation is Part 2 of the 2014 Act[5] which makes provision about (1) the reform of the General Teaching Council for Wales[6] and its renaming as the Education Workforce Council; (2) the registration of certain persons who educate children and young people; (3) the regulation of registered persons, including the obligation of registered persons to comply with a code specifying the standards of professional conduct and practice, and the action that can be taken against a registered person; and (4) the sharing of information about registered persons[7].

In brief the provisions of Part 2 include those covering the Education Workforce Council generally, its aims and functions and directions by it[8], the provision of advice and promotion of careers by the Council[9], registration of the Council including the register and registration[10], appeals against refusal of registration[11] and registration fees and further provision[12], requirements to be satisfied in order to provide services including for school teachers and school learning support workers[13], further education teachers[14] and further education learning support workers[15], induction and appraisal of registered persons including the requirement to undertake a period of induction[16], induction assessment standards[17], appeals against induction decisions[18], induction intervention powers and definitions[19], special provision for maintained schools with delegated budgets[20], appraisal of registered persons[21], code of conduct and practice for registered persons[22], disciplinary functions of the Council[23], conditional registration orders[24], suspension orders and prohibition orders[25], appeals against disciplinary orders[26], information duties including the Council's duty to maintain records[27], the supply of information by the Welsh Ministers, the Council, employers, agents and contractors[28], and directions to secure compliance with information duties[29], and transfer of registrations of persons already registered and transitory matters on registration eligibility[30].

1   See PARA 1066.
2   Ie the Teaching and Higher Education Act 1998 Pt 1 Ch 1 (ss 1–15A), Schs 1, 2: see PARA 1066 note 3. The provisions of Part 1 Ch 1 (except for s 15A: see note 28) are repealed by the Education (Wales) Act 2014 Sch 3 Pt 2 para 3 Table 2.
3   Ie in particular the Education (Wales) Act 2014 Pt 2 (ss 2–41), Schs 1, 2.
4   Ie under the Education Act 2005 s 19: see PARA 1148. As to the meaning of 'Wales' see PARA 7 note 3.
5   Ie the Education (Wales) Act 2014 Pt 2 (ss 2–41), Schs 1, 2 (Education Workforce).
6   As to the General Teaching Council for Wales see the text to notes 1–3.
7   See the Education (Wales) Act 2014 s 1(2).
8   See the Education (Wales) Act 2014 ss 2–6, Sch 1; and Education Workforce Council (Main Functions) (Wales) Regulations 2015, SI 2015/140; and the Education Workforce Council (Additional Functions and Revocation) (Wales) Order 2015, SI 2015/194.
9   See the Education (Wales) Act 2014 ss 7, 8. See also the Education Act 2005 s 84B; and PARA 1055.
10 See the Education (Wales) Act 2014 ss 9, 10, Sch 2; and the Education Workforce Council (Main Functions) (Wales) Regulations 2015, SI 2015/140.
11 See the Education (Wales) Act 2014 s 11.

12 See the Education (Wales) Act 2014 ss 12, 13; the Education Workforce Council (Main Functions) (Wales) Regulations 2015, SI 2015/140; and the '.
13 See the Education (Wales) Act 2014 s 14; and the Education Workforce Council (Main Functions) (Wales) Regulations 2015, SI 2015/140.
14 See the Education (Wales) Act 2014 s 15; and the Education Workforce Council (Main Functions) (Wales) Regulations 2015, SI 2015/140.
15 See the Education (Wales) Act 2014 s 16.
16 See the Education (Wales) Act 2014 s 17; and the Education (Induction Arrangements for School Teachers) (Wales) Regulations 2015, SI 2015/484.
17 See the Education (Wales) Act 2014 s 18.
18 See the Education (Wales) Act 2014 s 19; and the Education (Induction Arrangements for School Teachers) (Wales) Regulations 2015, SI 2015/484.
19 See the Education (Wales) Act 2014 ss 20, 21.
20 See the Education (Wales) Act 2014 s 22.
21 See the Education (Wales) Act 2014 s 23.
22 See the Education (Wales) Act 2014 ss 24, 25; and the Education Workforce Council (Main Functions) (Wales) Regulations 2015, SI 2015/140.
23 See the Education (Wales) Act 2014 ss 26–28; and the Education Workforce Council (Main Functions) (Wales) Regulations 2015, SI 2015/140.
24 See the Education (Wales) Act 2014 s 29.
25 See the Education (Wales) Act 2014 ss 30, 31.
26 See the Education (Wales) Act 2014 s 32.
27 See the Education (Wales) Act 2014 s 33; and the Education Workforce Council (Main Functions) (Wales) Regulations 2015, SI 2015/140.
28 See the Education (Wales) Act 2014 ss 34–37; the Education Workforce Council (Main Functions) (Wales) Regulations 2015, SI 2015/140; and the Education Workforce Council (Registration Fees) (Wales) Regulations 2015, SI 2015/195. As to the Welsh Ministers see PARA 59. As to the supply of information by a contractor, agency, etc in Wales see the Teaching and Higher Education Act 1988 s 15A (added by the Education Act 2002 Sch 21 para 83; and amended by the Safeguarding Vulnerable Groups Act 2006 Sch 9 paras 2, 6; and the Education Act 2011 Sch 2 paras 1, 12).
29 See the Education (Wales) Act 2014 s 38.
30 See the Education (Wales) Act 2014 ss 39, 40.

(4) PAY AND CONDITIONS OF TEACHING STAFF

(i) Statutory Conditions of Employment of Teachers

1076. Establishment and functions of the School Teachers' Review Body. The review body, established under the School Teachers' Pay and Conditions Act 1991[1], is preserved under the Education Act 2002 and is known as the School Teachers' Review Body[2].

The School Teachers' Review Body must consider any matter which is referred to it by the Secretary of State[3] and which relates to: (1) the remuneration of school teachers[4]; or (2) other conditions of employment of school teachers which relate to their professional duties or working time[5]. Before reporting on a matter so referred to it, the Review Body must: (a) notify each relevant body[6]; (b) give each relevant body an opportunity to submit evidence and make representations[7]; and (c) give the Secretary of State an opportunity to submit evidence and make representations[8].

Following consideration of any such matter, the Review Body must report to the Prime Minister[9] and the Secretary of State in accordance with any direction[10] of the Secretary of State about: (i) a consideration to which it is to have particular regard[11]; (ii) a matter on which it is to make a recommendation[12]; or (iii) the time within which it is to report[13]. Where the Prime Minister and the Secretary of State receive such a report, they must arrange for it to be published[14].

1   Ie the body established under the School Teachers' Pay and Conditions Act 1991 s 1 (repealed) to examine and report on such matters relating to the statutory conditions of employment of school teachers in England and Wales as may from time to time be referred to it by the Secretary of State.
2   See the Education Act 2002 s 119(1). As to the constitution of the Review Body see PARA 1077.
3   As to the Secretary of State see PARA 58.
4   Education Act 2002 s 120(1)(a). 'School teacher' means a person who is a school teacher for the purposes of the Secretary of State's power under the Education Act 2002 s 122 (see PARA 1078) to make orders about remuneration and other conditions of employment: s 120(2).
5   Education Act 2002 s 120(1)(b). See *Wandsworth London Borough Council v National Association of Schoolmasters/Union of Women Teachers* [1994] ELR 170, (1993) 92 LGR 91, CA (a dispute between members of a teaching union and their employers over the carrying out of National Curriculum assessments was held to be a trade dispute within the terms of the Trade Union and Labour Relations (Consolidation) Act 1992 s 244 (see EMPLOYMENT vol 41A (2014) PARAS 1360–1362) because it related to the statutory conditions of employment of teachers defined in the School Teachers' Pay and Conditions Act 1991 (repealed)). See also *P (A Minor) v National Association of Schoolmasters/Union of Women Teachers* [2003] UKHL 8, [2003] 2 AC 663, [2003] 1 All ER 993 (dispute between members of a teaching union and their head teacher and governors over the return of an excluded pupil to their classes was a dispute as to the teachers' terms and conditions of employment).
6   Education Act 2002 s 121(1)(a). In relation to a matter referred to the Review Body, 'relevant body' means such of the following as appear to the Review Body to be appropriate to consult about the matter: (1) associations of local authorities; (2) local authorities; (3) bodies representing the interests of governing bodies of schools; and (4) bodies representing the interests of teachers: s 121(2) (amended by SI 2010/1158). As to the meaning of 'local authority' see PARA 25; and as to the meaning of 'school' see PARA 91 (definitions applied by the Education Act 2002 s 212(2), (3)). As to the governing bodies of maintained schools in England see PARA 150 et seq; and in Wales see PARA 195 et seq. As to the exercise of the duty to consult see JUDICIAL REVIEW vol 61 (2010) PARA 627.
7   Education Act 2002 s 121(1)(b). The Review Body may: (1) determine the manner in which each relevant body is permitted to submit evidence or make representations (s 121(3)(a)); and (2) make different determinations in respect of different relevant bodies (s 121(3)(b)).
8   Education Act 2002 s 121(1)(c).
9   As to the Prime Minister see CONSTITUTIONAL AND ADMINISTRATIVE LAW vol 20 (2014) PARA 203 et seq.
10 A direction under the Education Act 2002 s 120(3) may be varied or revoked: s 120(5).
11 Education Act 2002 s 120(3)(a).
12 Education Act 2002 s 120(3)(b).
13 Education Act 2002 s 120(3)(c).
14 Education Act 2002 s 120(4).

1077. Constitution and proceedings. The School Teachers' Review Body[1] is to consist of not less than five and not more than nine members (including the chairman)[2]. The chairman of the Review Body is appointed by the Prime Minister[3], and the other members are appointed by the Secretary of State[4]. The Secretary of State may appoint a member of the Body to act as deputy chairman[5]. Members hold and vacate office in accordance with their terms of appointment[6]. The Secretary of State may pay remuneration and allowances and make other payments to a member of the Body, the chairman and the deputy chairman[7].

The Review Body must determine its own proceedings, including any provision for a quorum[8]. The validity of proceedings of the Review Body is not affected by a vacancy in the membership[9], a vacancy in the position of chairman[10], or a defect in the appointment of a member[11].

1   As to the establishment of the School Teachers' Review Body see PARA 1076.
2   Education Act 2002 Sch 11 para 1.
3   See the Education Act 2002 s 119(2). The chairman may by notice in writing to the Prime Minister resign as chairman (Sch 11 para 6(a)), or resign as chairman and as a member of the Body (Sch 11 para 6(b)). The Prime Minister may dismiss the chairman on the grounds set out in

Sch 11 para 4 (see note 4) either so as to dismiss the chairman only from that office or also from membership of the Body: see Sch 11 para 7. If the chairman ceases to be a member of the Body he also ceases to be chairman: Sch 11 para 8. As to the Prime Minister see CONSTITUTIONAL AND ADMINISTRATIVE LAW vol 20 (2014) PARA 203 et seq. As to the meaning of 'writing' see PARA 76 note 8.

4   See the Education Act 2002 s 119(3). A member may resign by notice in writing to the Secretary of State: Sch 11 para 3. The Secretary of State may by notice in writing dismiss a member if the member (1) is adjudged bankrupt or has a debt relief order made in respect of him (under the Insolvency Act 1986 Pt VIIA (ss 251A–251X) (see BANKRUPTCY AND INDIVIDUAL INSOLVENCY vol 5 (2013) PARA 101 et seq); (2) enters into an arrangement with his creditors; or (3) is, in the opinion of the Secretary of State, unable, unfit or unwilling to perform his duties whether by reason of physical or mental illness or otherwise: Education Act 2002 Sch 11 para 4 (amended by SI 2012/2404). As to the Secretary of State see PARA 58. As to the making of bankruptcy orders see BANKRUPTCY AND INDIVIDUAL INSOLVENCY vol 5 (2013) PARA 198 et seq. As to arrangements with creditors see BANKRUPTCY AND INDIVIDUAL INSOLVENCY vol 5 (2013) PARA 852 et seq.
5   Education Act 2002 Sch 11 para 9. The deputy chairman may by notice in writing to the Secretary of State resign as deputy chairman, or resign as deputy chairman and as a member of the Body: Sch 11 para 10. If the deputy chairman ceases to be a member of the Body he also ceases to be deputy chairman: Sch 11 para 11.
6   Education Act 2002 Sch 11 para 2. This provision is expressed to be subject to Sch 11 paras 3–15: see notes 3–5 and the text to notes 7–11.
7   See the Education Act 2002 Sch 11 para 12. A member of the School Teachers' Review Body in receipt of remuneration is disqualified for membership of the House of Commons: see the House of Commons Disqualification Act 1975 s 1(1)(f), Sch 1 Pt III (amended by the Education Act 2002 Sch 11 para 5); and PARLIAMENT vol 78 (2010) PARA 908.
8   Education Act 2002 Sch 11 para 13.
9   Education Act 2002 Sch 11 para 14(a).
10 Education Act 2002 Sch 11 para 14(b).
11 Education Act 2002 Sch 11 para 14(c).

1078. Pay and conditions orders. The Secretary of State[1] may by order[2] ('a pay and conditions order') make provision for the determination of the remuneration of school teachers[3] and other conditions of employment of school teachers which relate to their professional duties or working time[4]. However, such an order may make provision about a matter only if the Secretary of State has referred the matter to the School Teachers' Review Body[5], and considered its report[6]; and the Secretary of State may not make an order[7] unless he has consulted such of the following as appear to him to be appropriate to consult having regard to the content of the order: (1) associations of local authorities[8]; (2) local authorities[9]; (3) bodies representing the interests of governing bodies of schools[10]; and (4) bodies representing the interests of teachers[11].

A pay and conditions order is made by statutory instrument[12], and may make provision by reference to a document[13]. A pay and conditions order may, in particular[14]:

(a)   confer discretion on a local authority or a governing body[15];
(b)   confer a function (which may include the administration of a test or assessment, the exercise of a discretion or the exercise of a supervisory or appellate jurisdiction) on the Secretary of State or on a specified person who has agreed with the Secretary of State to perform that function[16];
(c)   require a discretion or function conferred under head (a) or head (b) above to be exercised having regard to guidance given by the Secretary of State or another specified person[17];
(d)   make provision for the determination of a teacher's remuneration by reference to any matter including, in particular, his qualifications, experience, duties, aptitude or previous salary[18];

(e)   make provision for a right of appeal specified by or determined in accordance with the order[19];

(f)   limit the aggregate amount of an allowance, or of a number of allowances, payable to teachers in a school[20];

(g)   set a lower or upper limit on the number or proportion of teachers in a school who are paid on a specified scale[21];

(h)   set a lower or upper limit on the number or proportion of teachers in a school who are paid a specified allowance[22];

(i)   provide for special provisions to apply in relation to a description of school specified by or determined in accordance with the order[23];

(j)   provide for the determination of a question of the interpretation or application of a provision of the order[24].

Provision under head (e) or head (j) above may confer jurisdiction on a court, tribunal, person or body[25] and provide for a matter to be settled by agreement between, or in a manner agreed between, teachers and local authorities or teachers and governing bodies[26].

Where a pay and conditions order applies to a school teacher: (i) his remuneration must be determined and paid in accordance with any provision of the order which applies to him[27]; (ii) a provision of the order which relates to a condition of employment other than remuneration and which applies to him has effect as a term of his contract of employment[28]; and (iii) a term of that contract has no effect in so far as it makes provision which is prohibited by the order or which is otherwise inconsistent with a provision of the order[29].

A local authority and the governing body of a school must have regard to any guidance issued by the Secretary of State about the procedure to be followed in applying provisions of a pay and conditions order[30]. Where an employer fails to follow such guidance, the failure will not give rise to civil liability[31], but a court or tribunal may take the failure into account in any proceedings[32].

1   As to the Secretary of State see PARA 58.
2   Such an order may: (1) make provision which applies generally or only in a specified case or in specified circumstances (Education Act 2002 s 124(1)(a)); (2) make different provision for different cases or circumstances (s 124(1)(b)); (3) make transitional provision (s 124(1)(c)); (4) make provision by reference to the exercise of another power under the Education Act 2002 (s 124(2)). As to the order made see the School Teachers' Pay and Conditions Order 2015, SI 2015/1582; and note 13.
3   Education Act 2002 s 122(1)(a). A person is a school teacher for these purposes if: (1) he is a qualified teacher (s 122(3)(a)); (2) he provides primary or secondary education under a contract of employment or for services (s 122(3)(b)); (3) the other party to the contract is a local authority or the governing body of a foundation, voluntary aided or foundation special school (s 122(3)(c) (amended by SI 2010/1158)); and (4) the contract requires him to carry out work of a kind which is specified by regulations under the Education Act 2002 s 133(1) (see PARA 1048) (s 122(3)(d)). As to the meaning of 'qualified teacher' see PARA 1047. As to the meaning of 'primary education' see PARA 20; and as to the meaning of 'secondary education' see PARA 21 (definitions applied by s 212(2), (3)). As to the meaning of 'contract of employment' see PARA 268 note 3. As to contracts for services see EMPLOYMENT vol 39 (2014) PARAS 1, 2. As to the meaning of 'local authority' see PARA 25 (definition applied by s 212(1)). As to the meaning of references to a foundation, voluntary or foundation special school see PARA 106. A person is also a school teacher for these purposes if he serves as the head teacher of a school maintained by a local authority: s 122(4) (amended by SI 2010/1158). As to the meaning of 'head teacher' see PARA 538 note 6 (definition applied by the Education Act 2002 s 212(2), (3)). A person is also a school teacher for these purposes if his case satisfies heads (2), (3) and (4) above and: (a) he possesses a prescribed qualification (s 122(5)(a)); (b) he provides education of a prescribed kind or in prescribed circumstances, or both (s 122(5)(b)); (c) he is undertaking training of a prescribed kind, or obtaining experience of a prescribed kind, with a view to becoming a qualified teacher (s 122(5)(c)); (d) he is within a prescribed class of persons awaiting assessment for the purpose of becoming a qualified teacher (s 122(5)(d)); or (e) he is within a prescribed

class of persons awaiting the award of a qualification (s 122(5)(e)). In s 122, 'prescribed' means prescribed by an order under s 122 (see note 2): s 122(8). A person providing education in an establishment maintained by a local authority in the exercise of a social services function is not a school teacher for these purposes: s 122(6).

4 Education Act 2002 s 122(1)(b).

5 Ie under the Education Act 2002 s 120 (see PARA 1076): see s 125(1)(a). As to the School Teachers' Review Body see PARA 1076.

6 Education Act 2002 s 125(1)(b). Section 125(1) does not apply: (1) to subsidiary provision (s 125(2)(a)); or (2) in a case where the Secretary of State has consulted the chairman of the Review Body about disapplying s 125(1) (s 125(2)(b)). Provision is subsidiary for the purpose of head (1) above if the Secretary of State thinks that it: (a) concerns only the criteria for entry into or exit from a particular class of teachers for purposes of remuneration (s 125(3)(a)); (b) concerns only the criteria for moving from one scale of remuneration to another (s 125(3)(b)); (c) concerns only the implementation or application of a system or principle on which the Review Body has reported (s 125(3)(c)); (d) prescribes a matter for the purpose of s 122(5) (see note 3) (s 125(3)(d)); (e) is made under s 123(4) (see note 18) (s 125(3)(e)); or (f) is minor, consequential, temporary, transitional or designed to resolve an anomaly (s 125(3)(f)). The Secretary of State may by order provide that provision of a specified kind (which may be described wholly or partly by reference to an opinion of the Secretary of State or another person): (i) is subsidiary for the purpose of s 125(2)(a) (see head (1) above) (s 125(4)(a)); or (ii) is to cease to be subsidiary for that purpose (s 125(4)(b)). An order under s 125(4) may amend s 125(3): s 125(5). As to the meaning of 'person' see PARA 7 note 6. At the date at which this volume states the law no such order had been made.

7 Ie an order under either the Education Act 2002 s 122 (see the text to notes 1–4) or 125(4)(a) (see note 6).

8 Education Act 2002 s 126(a) (amended by SI 2010/1158). As to the exercise of the duty to consult see JUDICIAL REVIEW vol 61 (2010) PARA 627.

9 Education Act 2002 s 126(b) (amended by SI 2010/1158).

10 Education Act 2002 s 126(c). As to the meaning of 'school' see PARA 91 (definition applied by s 212(2), (3)). As to the governing bodies of maintained schools in England see PARA 150 et seq; and in Wales see PARA 195 et seq. 'Schools' can include certain types of academy (see further PARA 91) and as to academies generally see PARA 345 et seq.

11 Education Act 2002 s 126(d).

12 See the Education Act 2002 s 210 (amended by the Childcare Act 2006 ss 48, 103(2), Sch 1, para 16, Sch 3, Pt 1; the Learner Travel (Wales) Measure 2008 ss 20, 21(1), (3); the Learning and Skills (Wales) Measure 2009 s 20(1), (2)(a); the Apprenticeships, Skills, Children and Learning Act 2009 s 123(2), Sch 6, paras 54, 56; the Education Act 2011 s 67(1), Sch 16, paras 18, 21; and the Education (Wales) Act 2014 Sch 3, Pt 1, para 1(1), (6)).

13 Education Act 2002 s 124(3). An order which makes provision by reference to a document must include provision about publication of the document (s 124(3)(a)); and a reference in s 124 to an order includes a reference to a document referred to by an order (s 124(3)(b)). The School Teachers' Pay and Conditions Order 2015, SI 2015/1582, provides that the Document (ie the document entitled 'School Teachers' Pay and Conditions Document 2015 and Guidance on School Teachers' Pay and Conditions' published on the website of the Department for Education) has effect on and after 1 September 2015 for the purposes of determining (1) the remuneration of school teachers; and (2) other conditions of employment of school teachers which relate to their professional duties and working time: see the School Teachers' Pay and Conditions Order 2015, SI 2015/1582, arts 1, 2.

14 Education Act 2002 s 123(1). An order may make retrospective provision, but not so as to reduce remuneration in respect of a period wholly or partly before the making of the order, or alter a condition of employment to the detriment of a teacher in respect of a period wholly or partly before the making of the order: s 123(3). For special provisions as to schools in education action zones see PARA 1079; and for special provisions for teachers on transfer of employment see PARA 1080.

15 Education Act 2002 s 123(1)(a) (amended by SI 2010/1158).

16 Education Act 2002 s 123(1)(b). As to the meaning of 'function' see PARA 18 note 5 (definition applied by s 212(2), (3)).

17 Education Act 2002 s 123(1)(c). As to the publication of guidance see the Education Act 1996 s 571 (applied by the Education Act 2002 s 212(2), (3)); and PARA 60.

18 Education Act 2002 s 123(1)(d). The Secretary of State may by order provide: (1) that a payment or entitlement of a specified kind is or is not to be treated as remuneration (s 123(4)(a)); (2) that a specified matter is or is not to be treated for that purpose as relating to the professional duties of school teachers (s 123(4)(b)); (3) that a specified matter is or is not to

be treated for that purpose as relating to the working time of school teachers (s 123(4)(c)). As to the regulations made see the School Teachers' Incentive Payments (England) Order 2010, SI 2010/738; and the School Teachers' Incentive Payments (England) Order 2012, SI 2012/878. By virtue of the Interpretation Act 1978 s 17(2)(b), the School Teachers' Remuneration, Professional Duties and Working Time Order 1992, SI 1992/3069, the School Teachers' Remuneration Order 2000, SI 2000/2324 (regarding lump sum incentive payments), and the School Teachers' Remuneration Order 2002, SI 2002/2103 (regarding personal bonus payments to school teachers taking part in the Excellence Fellowship scheme with a higher education institution), also have effect as if made under the Education Act 2002 s 123(4).

19 Education Act 2002 s 123(1)(e).
20 Education Act 2002 s 123(1)(f).
21 Education Act 2002 s 123(1)(g).
22 Education Act 2002 s 123(1)(h).
23 Education Act 2002 s 123(1)(i).
24 Education Act 2002 s 123(1)(j).
25 Education Act 2002 s 123(2)(a).
26 Education Act 2002 s 123(2)(b) (amended by SI 2010/1158).
27 Education Act 2002 s 122(2)(a). In the application of s 122(2): (1) it is immaterial whether someone other than the party mentioned in s 122(3)(c) (see note 3) provides or is responsible for providing all or part of a teacher's remuneration (s 122(7)(a)); (2) it is immaterial whether someone other than the party mentioned in s 122(3)(c) is treated wholly or partly as a teacher's employer for some or all purposes by virtue of an enactment (s 122(7)(b)); and (3) in relation to a person who provides education under a contract for services, a reference to his contract of employment is a reference to the contract for services (s 122(7)(c)).
28 Education Act 2002 s 122(2)(b). See also note 27.
29 Education Act 2002 s 122(2)(c). See also note 27.
30 See the Education Act 2002 s 127(1), (2) (amended by SI 2010/1158). The Secretary of State may not issue guidance under s 127(1) unless he has consulted such of the following as appear to him to be appropriate to consult having regard to the nature of the guidance: (1) associations of local authorities (s 127(4)(a) (s 127(4)(a), (b) amended by SI 2010/1158)); (2) local authorities (Education Act 2002 s 127(4)(b) (as so amended)); (3) bodies representing the interests of governing bodies of schools (s 127(4)(c)); and (4) bodies representing the interests of teachers (s 127(4)(d)).
31 Education Act 2002 s 127(3)(a).
32 Education Act 2002 s 127(3)(b).

1079. Special provisions as to schools in education action zones. On the application of the governing body[1] of a school[2] which forms part of an education action zone[3], the Secretary of State[4] may by order[5] provide that a pay and conditions order[6] will not apply to any school teacher[7] at the school[8]. A governing body may not make such an application unless it has consulted each school teacher at the school[9]. An application must specify a date for commencement of the order sought[10].

Where such an order is in force in respect of a school: (1) the governing body must determine the remuneration and other conditions of employment of each school teacher at the school[11]; (2) the local authority[12] must do anything necessary to give effect to the governing body's determination[13]; and (3) pending a determination under head (1) above, the terms on which a school teacher works at the school must remain unchanged[14].

The Secretary of State may make regulations[15] about the application of a pay and conditions order[16] where an order disapplying those provisions[17] is revoked[18], or lapses in whole or in part because one or more schools to which the order relates cease to form part of an education action zone[19].

1 As to the governing bodies of maintained schools in England see PARA 150 et seq; and in Wales see PARA 195 et seq.
2 As to the meaning of 'school' see PARA 91 (definition applied by the Education Act 2002 s 212(2), (3)). 'Schools' can include certain types of academy (see further PARA 91); as to academies generally see PARA 345 et seq.

3 Ie for the purposes of the School Standards and Framework Act 1998 Pt I Ch III (ss 10–12): see PARA 344.
4 As to the Secretary of State see PARA 58.
5 At the date at which this volume states the law no such order had been made.
6 Ie under the Education Act 2002 s 122(2): see PARA 1078.
7 As to the meaning of 'school teacher' see PARA 1078 note 3 (definition applied by the Education Act 2002 s 128(7)).
8 See the Education Act 2002 s 128(1), (2).
9 Education Act 2002 s 128(4). As to the exercise of the duty to consult see JUDICIAL REVIEW vol 61 (2010) PARA 627.
10 Education Act 2002 s 128(5). The date specified must not precede the expiry of the period of three months beginning with the date on which the application is made (s 128(5)(a)); and an order made on the application must provide that it comes into force on the date specified in the application or on a later date which is agreed between the Secretary of State and the governing body and which is specified in the order (s 128(5)(b)). As to the meaning of 'month' see PARA 54 note 26.
11 Education Act 2002 s 128(3)(a).
12 As to the meaning of 'local authority' see PARA 25 (definition applied by the Education Act 2002 s 212(1)).
13 Education Act 2002 s 128(3)(b) (amended by SI 2010/1158).
14 Education Act 2002 s 128(3)(c). Section 128(3)(c) applies irrespective of any new order made under s 122 (see PARA 1078): see s 128(3)(c).
15 At the date at which this volume states the law no such regulations had been made.
16 Ie under the Education Act 2002 s 122(2): see PARA 1078.
17 Ie an order under the Education Act 2002 s 128(2): see the text to notes 1–8.
18 Education Act 2002 s 128(6)(a).
19 Education Act 2002 s 128(6)(b).

1080. Special provisions for teachers on transfer of employment. A pay and conditions order[1] does not apply to a person if: (1) a maintained school[2] is established in place of an independent school[3] in pursuance of proposals published under the relevant school organisation provisions[4]; and (2) the person becomes a school teacher[5] in the maintained school in accordance with the Transfer of Undertakings (Protection of Employment) Regulations 2006[6]. However, if the school teacher gives notice in writing[7] to his new employer, then the order does apply to him in respect of the period beginning with: (a) a date specified in the notice[8]; (b) if no such date is specified, a date agreed between the teacher and the new employer[9]; or (c) if no date is so specified or agreed, the date on which the employer receives the notice[10]. Where the governing body of a foundation, voluntary aided or foundation special school receives such a notice, it must inform the local authority[11].

1 Ie the Education Act 2002 s 122(2): see PARA 1078.
2 'Maintained school' means a community school, a foundation school, a voluntary school, a community special school, a foundation special school, or a maintained nursery school: Education Act 2002 s 129(5). As to the meaning of references to a community, foundation or voluntary school or a community or foundation special school see PARA 106. As to the meaning of 'maintained nursery school' see PARA 99 note 4 (definition applied by s 212(2), (3)).
3 As to the meaning of 'independent school' see PARA 369 (definition applied by the Education Act 2002 s 212(2), (3)).
4 Education Act 2002 s 129(1)(a) (amended by the Education and Inspections Act 2006 s 30, Sch 3 para 47(1), (2)). 'The relevant school organisation provisions' means: (1) in relation to England, the School Standards and Framework Act 1998 s 28 (repealed), s 28A (repealed) or s 31 (repealed), the Education Act 2005 s 66 (repealed) or the Education and Inspections Act 2006 s 7 (see PARA 111) or s 11 (see PARA 113); and (2) in relation to Wales, the School Standards and Framework Act 1998 s 28 (repealed) or s 31 (repealed) or the School Standards and Organisation (Wales) Act 2013 Pt 3 (ss 38–56) (see PARA 139 et seq): Education Act 2002 s 129(6) (added by the Education and Inspections Act 2006 s 30, Sch 3 para 47(1), (3); and amended by the School Standards and Organisation (Wales) Act 2013 Sch 5 para 21(1), (7)). As to the meanings of 'England' and 'Wales' see PARA 7 note 3.

5   As to the meaning of 'school teacher' see PARA 1078 note 3 (definition applied by the Education Act 2002 s 129(4)).

6   Education Act 2002 s 129(1)(b) (amended by SI 2006/246). As to the Transfer of Undertakings (Protection of Employment) Regulations 2006, SI 2006/246, see EMPLOYMENT vol 39 (2014) PARA 136 et seq.

7   As to the meaning of 'writing' see PARA 76 note 8. As to the service of notices and documents see the Education Act 1996 s 572 (applied by the Education Act 2002 s 212(2), (3)); and PARA 76.

8   Education Act 2002 s 129(2)(a).

9   Education Act 2002 s 129(2)(b).

10 Education Act 2002 s 129(2)(c).

11 Education Act 2002 s 129(3) (amended by SI 2010/1158). As to the meaning of 'local authority' see PARA 25 (definition applied by the Education Act 2002 s 212(2), (3)).

(ii) Pensions and Benefits for Teachers etc

1081. Superannuation of teachers. Teachers' superannuation and pensions were, until 1965, governed mainly by the Teachers (Superannuation) Acts 1918 to 1956[1]. The Teachers' Superannuation Act 1965 provided for the making of superannuation regulations, and introduced pensions for the widows and other dependants of teachers[2]. Teachers' superannuation was then governed by regulations made under the Superannuation Act 1972[3], and now there is also the effect of the provisions of the Public Service Pensions Act 2013 to be considered[4].

Under the Superannuation Act 1972, the Secretary of State[5] may, by regulations[6] made with the consent of the Minister for the Civil Service[7], make provision with respect to the pensions, allowances or gratuities[8] which, subject to the fulfilment of such requirements and conditions as may be prescribed by the regulations, are to be, or may be, paid to or in respect of teachers[9] by the Secretary of State or, in the case of injury benefit[10], by the Secretary of State, an employer of teachers or such other person as the Secretary of State may consider appropriate and may specify in the regulations[11].

Where such regulations make provision with respect to money purchase benefits[12], they may also: (1) include provision enabling a person to elect for such money purchase benefits as are to be provided to or in respect of him under the regulations to be purchased from any authorised provider[13] whom he may specify[14]; and (2) provide[15] that the making of such an election has the effect, in such cases as may be specified in the regulations, of discharging any liability of the Secretary of State to pay those benefits to or in respect of that person[16]. However, no regulations may be so framed as to have the effect that any money purchase benefits to be provided under them may only be provided in a manner which discharges that liability of the Secretary of State[17].

Before making any regulations under the provisions described above, the Secretary of State must consult with representatives of local authorities and teachers and with such representatives of other persons likely to be affected by the proposed regulations as appear to him to be appropriate[18].

Under the Public Service Pensions Act 2013, the Secretary of State, with the consent of the Treasury[19], may by regulations[20] establish schemes ('scheme regulations') for the payment of pensions and other benefits to or in respect of teachers[21]. Scheme regulations for such a scheme may secure that no injury benefits are to be provided for teachers under regulations under the Superannuation Act 1972[22] that are connected with it[23].

The 2013 Act includes generally provision that may be made by such regulations[24], provisions as to the governance of schemes made by such regulations[25], provisions as to the procedure for making scheme regulations[26], provisions as to cost control[27], provisions as to the administration of schemes[28] and supplementary provisions[29].

Scheme regulations may establish such a scheme as a defined benefits scheme, a defined contributions scheme, or a scheme of any other description[30].

Both the normal pension age[31] and the deferred pension age[32] of teachers under such a scheme must be the same as that person's state pension age[33], or 65, if that is higher[34].

Subject to specified exceptions, no benefits are to be provided under specified schemes for teachers to or in respect of a person in relation to the person's service after 31 March 2015 except under a defined contributions scheme[35].

1   The Teachers (Superannuation) Acts 1918 to 1956 have been repealed: see e g the Teachers' Superannuation Act 1965.
2   The Teachers' Superannuation Act 1965 was repealed by, and consolidated in, the Teachers' Superannuation Act 1967, which itself was repealed with savings by the Superannuation Act 1972.
3   See the Superannuation Act 1972 s 9; and the text to notes 4–18.
4   As to the Public Service Pensions Act 2013 see the text to notes 19–35. See also CONSTITUTIONAL AND ADMINISTRATIVE LAW vol 20 (2014) PARA 298; PERSONAL AND OCCUPATIONAL PENSIONS.
5   As to the Secretary of State see PARA 58.
6   As to the regulations made under the Superannuation Act 1972 s 9 see the Teachers' Superannuation (Additional Voluntary Contributions) Regulations 1994, SI 1994/2924 (see PARA 1083); and the Teachers' Pensions Regulations 2010, SI 2010/990 (see PARA 1082).
7   As to the Minister for the Civil Service see CONSTITUTIONAL AND ADMINISTRATIVE LAW vol 20 (2014) PARA 235. The responsibility for pensions was transferred from the Minister for the Civil Service to the Treasury (see the Transfer of Functions (Minister for the Civil Service and Treasury) Order 1981, SI 1981/1670, art 2(b)) and then reverted from the Treasury to the Minister for the Civil Service (see the Transfer of Functions (Treasury and Minister for the Civil Service) Order 1995, SI 1995/269, art 3, Schedule).
8   Regulations under the Superannuation Act 1972 s 9 may provide, notwithstanding anything in the Pensions (Increase) Act 1971, that the cost of increases under the Pensions (Increase) Act 1971 of such of the pensions, allowances or gratuities payable under the regulations as may be prescribed by the regulations, or such part of those increases as may be so prescribed, are to be defrayed by contributions from employers of teachers or from such other persons or classes of person (apart from teachers) as the Secretary of State may consider appropriate and may specify in the regulations, or by contributions from such of those employers or other persons as may be so specified: Superannuation Act 1972 s 9(3A) (s 9(3A) added by the Pensions (Miscellaneous Provisions) Act 1990 ss 4(1), 8(3), 11(2)). Any provisions of the Pensions (Increase) Act 1971, or of regulations made under s 5, relating to liability for the cost of increases of pensions, allowances or gratuities payable under the regulations have effect subject to the provisions of any regulations made by virtue of the Superannuation Act 1972 s 9(3A) and for the time being in force: s 9(3A) (as so added). As to the Pensions (Increase) Act 1971 and the regulations so made see PERSONAL AND OCCUPATIONAL PENSIONS vol 80 (2013) PARA 309.
9   'Teachers' includes such persons as may be prescribed by regulations made under the Superannuation Act 1972 s 9, being persons employed otherwise than as teachers: (1) in a capacity connected with education which to a substantial extent involves the control or supervision of teachers; or (2) in employment which involves the performance of duties in connection with the provision of education or services ancillary to education: s 9(6). An educational counsellor is capable of being a teacher for the purposes of the Superannuation Act 1972 s 9: see *Owens v Dudley Metropolitan Borough Council* [2011] EWCA Civ 359, [2012] ICR 453.
10 'Injury benefit' means a pension, allowance or gratuity payable under the regulations to or in respect of a teacher in consequence of any injury sustained, or disease contracted, by him in the course of his employment in that capacity: Superannuation Act 1972 s 9(6) (definition added by the Pensions (Miscellaneous Provisions) Act 1990 ss 8(6), 11(3)). The subsidiary powers of local authorities exercisable by virtue of the Local Government Act 1972 s 111 (see LOCAL GOVERNMENT vol 69 (2009) PARA 462) are taken to include, and to have at all times included, power to pay, or arrange for the payment of, injury benefit to or in respect of teachers: Superannuation Act 1972 s 9(5A) (added by the Pensions (Miscellaneous Provisions) Act 1990

ss 4(1), 8(3), 11(2)). However, the Local Government Act 1972 s 111 ceases to confer any such power on an authority as from the coming into force of the first regulations under the Superannuation Act 1972 s 9 which make provision for the payment of injury benefit by a local education authority to or in respect of teachers: s 9(5A) (as so added). As to local authorities and their education functions see PARA 25.

11 Superannuation Act 1972 s 9(1) (amended by the Pensions (Miscellaneous Provisions) Act 1990 s 11(1)); and see the Superannuation Act 1972 s 1(1). The Superannuation Act 1972 s 9(1) is subject to the Public Service Pensions Act 2013 ss 18, 19 (restrictions on benefits provided under existing schemes) (see PERSONAL AND OCCUPATIONAL PENSIONS): Superannuation Act 1972 s 9(1A) (added by the Public Service Pensions Act 2013 Sch 8 paras 6, 9). Without prejudice to the generality of the Superannuation Act 1972 s 9(1), regulations under s 9 may include all or any of the provisions referred to in Sch 3 (see PERSONAL AND OCCUPATIONAL PENSIONS vol 80 (2013) PARA 321), and may make different provision as respects different classes of persons and different circumstances: s 9(2). Where the regulations provide for the making of any such payment as is referred to in Sch 3 para 3, 5 or 6, they may also provide for the payment to be made by the Secretary of State: s 9(3). Where regulations under s 9 provide for the establishment of a superannuation fund, the regulations may also provide for the payment by the Secretary of State of the administrative expenses of the persons by whom, in accordance with the regulations, the fund is to be administered, and of such travelling, subsistence and other allowances to those persons as the Secretary of State may, with the consent of the Minister for the Civil Service, determine: s 9(4). As to the meaning of 'person' see PARA 7 note 6.

12 'Money purchase benefits', in relation to a member of a personal or occupational pension scheme or the widow or widower of a member of such a scheme, means benefits the rate or amount of which is calculated by reference to a payment or payments made by the member or by any other person in respect of the member and which are not average salary benefits: Superannuation Act 1972 s 9(6) (definition added by the Pensions (Miscellaneous Provisions) Act 1990 s 8(6); and amended by the Pension Schemes Act 1993 s 190, Sch 8 para 7); Pension Schemes Act 1993 s 181(1) (definition amended by SI 2005/2053; and the Pensions Act 2011 s 29(1)).

13 'Authorised provider', in relation to the investment of any sums paid by way of voluntary contributions or the provision of any benefit, means: (1) a person who has permission under the Financial Services and Markets Act 2000 Pt IVA (ss 55A–55Z4) (see FINANCIAL SERVICES AND INSTITUTIONS) to invest such sums or, as the case may be, to provide that benefit; (2) an EEA firm of a kind mentioned in s 31(1)(b), s 425(1)(a), Sch 3 para 5(a), (b) or (c), which has permission under Sch 3 para 15, as a result of qualifying for authorisation under Sch 3 para 12 (see FINANCIAL SERVICES AND INSTITUTIONS vol 48 (2008) PARA 315), to invest such sums or, as the case may be, to provide that benefit and which satisfies the conditions applicable to it which are specified in the Superannuation Act 1972 s 1(9B)–(9D); or (3) an EEA firm of a kind mentioned in the Financial Services and Markets Act 2000 Sch 3 para 5(d), which has permission under Sch 3 para 15, as a result of qualifying for authorisation under Sch 3 para 12 (see FINANCIAL SERVICES AND INSTITUTIONS vol 48 (2008) PARA 315), to invest such sums or, as the case may be, to provide that benefit: Superannuation Act 1972 s 1(9) (definition substituted by SI 2001/3649; and amended by the Financial Services Act 2012 Sch 18 para 35); definition applied by the Superannuation Act 1972 s 9(6) (amended by SI 2001/3649).

14 Superannuation Act 1972 s 9(2A)(a) (s 9(2A) added by the Pensions (Miscellaneous Provisions) Act 1990 ss 4(1), 8(3), 11(2)).

15 Ie notwithstanding the Superannuation Act 1972 s 9(1): see the text to notes 5–11.

16 Superannuation Act 1972 s 9(2A)(b) (as added: see note 14).

17 Superannuation Act 1972 s 9(2A) (as added: see note 14).

18 Superannuation Act 1972 s 9(5) (amended by SI 2010/1158). As to the exercise of the duty to consult see JUDICIAL REVIEW vol 61 (2010) PARA 627.

19 As to the Treasury see CONSTITUTIONAL AND ADMINISTRATIVE LAW vol 20 (2014) PARA 263 et seq.

20 As to the regulations made see the Teachers' Pension Scheme Regulations 2014, SI 2014/512 (fully in force on 1 April 2015, and amended with effect from 1 April 2015 by SI 2014/2652), which establish a career average re-valued earnings scheme for the payment of pensions and other benefits to and in respect of teachers. See further PARA 1082.

21 Public Service Pensions Act 2013 ss 1(1), (2)(d), (3), (4), 2, Sch 2 para 8. 'Teachers' includes persons employed otherwise than as teachers (1) in a capacity connected with education which to a substantial extent involves the control or supervision of teachers, or (2) in employment which involves the performance of duties in connection with the provision of education or services ancillary to education, and who are specified in scheme regulations: Sch 1 para 4. As to certain modifications of the 2013 Act provisions in certain circumstances see the Teachers'

Pension Scheme (Consequential Provisions) Regulations 2015, SI 2015/436, made under the Public Service Pensions Act 2013 ss 1(1), (2)(d), 2(1). See also the Teachers (Compensation for Redundancy and Premature Retirement) Regulations 2015, SI 2015/601, made under the Public Service Pensions Act 2013 s 1.

22 Ie the Superannuation Act 1972 s 9: see the text to notes 4–18.

23 See the Public Service Pensions Act 2013 s 19, Sch 6 para 5.

24 See the Public Service Pensions Act 2013 s 3, Sch 3. As to certain modifications of the 2013 Act provisions in certain circumstances see the Teachers' Pension Scheme (Consequential Provisions) Regulations 2015, SI 2015/436, made under the Public Service Pensions Act 2013 s 3(1), (2), (3)(a), (4). See also the Teachers (Compensation for Redundancy and Premature Retirement) Regulations 2015, SI 2015/601, made under the Public Service Pensions Act 2013 s 3, Sch 3.

25 See the Public Service Pensions Act 2013 ss 4–7.

26 See the Public Service Pensions Act 2013 ss 21–24.

27 See the Public Service Pensions Act 2013 ss 11–13 (s 12 not fully in force at the date at which this volume states the law: see SI 2015/4); and the Public Service Pensions (Employer Cost Cap) Regulations 2014, SI 2014/575.

28 See the Public Service Pensions Act 2013 ss 14–17.

29 See the Public Service Pensions Act 2013 ss 25, 26.

30 See the Public Service Pensions Act 2013 s 8(1). A scheme under s 1 which is a defined benefits scheme must be (1) a career average revalued earnings scheme; or (2) a defined benefits scheme of such other description (not being a final salary scheme) as Treasury regulations may specify: s 8(2), (3). A scheme under s 1 is a 'career average revalued earnings scheme' if (a) the pension payable to or in respect of a person, so far as it is based on the person's pensionable service, is determined by reference to the person's pensionable earnings in each year of pensionable service; and (b) those earnings, or a proportion of those earnings accrued as a pension, are under the scheme revalued each year until the person leaves pensionable service: s 8(4). Provision is also made for revaluation: see s 9 (not fully in force at the date at which this volume states the law: see SI 2015/4).

31 'Normal pension age', in relation to a person and a scheme, means the earliest age at which the person is entitled to receive benefits under the scheme (without actuarial adjustment) on leaving the service to which the scheme relates (and disregarding any special provision as to early payment of benefits on the grounds of ill-health or otherwise: Public Service Pensions Act 2013 s 10(5)(a).

32 'Deferred pension age', in relation to a person and a scheme, means the earliest age at which the person is entitled to receive benefits under the scheme (without actuarial adjustment) after leaving the service to which the scheme relates at a time before normal pension age (and disregarding any special provision as to early payment of benefits on the grounds of ill-health or otherwise): Public Service Pensions Act 2013 s 10(5)(b).

33 'State pension age', in relation to a person, means the pensionable age of the person as specified from time to time in the Pensions Act 1995 Sch 4 Pt I: see the Public Service Pensions Act 2013 s 10(5)(c).

34 See the Public Service Pensions Act 2013 s 10(1), (3).

35 See the Public Service Pensions Act 2013 s 18(1)–(3), (4)(b). As to the specified schemes and specified exceptions, see Sch 5 para 18. Benefits in relation to a person's service include benefits relating to the person's death in service: s 18(9). See further s 18(5), (5A), (6)–(8) (s 18(5A) added by the Pensions Act 2014 s 52(1), (2)) (the Public Service Pensions Act 2013 s 18 not fully in force at the date at which this volume states the law: see SI 2014/839). As to preservation of a final salary link, however, see the Public Service Pensions Act 2013 s 20, Sch 7.

1082. The teachers' pension scheme. The Teachers' Pensions Regulations 2010[1] came into force on 1 September 2010[2]. The regulations define pensionable employment[3] and make provision as to contributions by employees and employers[4]. Provision is made for the calculation of benefits[5] which include retirement benefits[6], incapacity and ill health benefits[7], additional pensions[8], and other benefits[9]. Death grants are payable in specified circumstances[10], as are family benefits for surviving partners and children[11], and benefits for pension credit members[12]. General provision is made as to the payment of benefits[13] and financial matters relating to the scheme[14].

The Teachers' Pension Scheme Regulations 2014[15], which establish a career average re-valued earnings scheme for the payment of pensions and other benefits to and in respect of teachers, came into force on 1 April 2015[16]. They contain governance provisions including delegation of the scheme manager's functions and establishment of the Teachers' Pension Scheme Pension Board and the Teachers' Pension Scheme Advisory Board[17], provide for scheme membership[18], provide for the establishment of a member's pension accounts in relation to a continuous period of pensionable service under this scheme[19], provide for a member's entitlement to payment of retirement benefits[20], provide for death grants and survivors' benefits[21], provide for benefits for pension credit members[22], provide for the payment and calculation of pension benefits[23], provide for the payment of contributions by members and employers and also the repayment of a member's contributions after short-service[24], provide for the payment and receipt of transfer values including club transfers[25], and contain supplementary provisions on matters including employment records and the provision of information between the scheme and members[26].

1   Ie the Teachers' Pensions Regulations 2010, SI 2010/990. The Marriage (Same Sex Couples) Act 2013 s 11(1), (2), Sch 3 paras 1–3 (see MATRIMONIAL AND CIVIL PARTNERSHIP LAW vol 72 (2015) PARA 2) do not apply to the Teachers' Pensions Regulations 2010, SI 2010/990: see the Marriage (Same Sex Couples) Act 2013 (Consequential and Contrary Provisions and Scotland) Order 2014, SI 2014/560, Sch 2 para 5(kkk).

2   See the Teachers' Pensions Regulations 2010, SI 2010/990, reg 1. The regulations revoked the Teachers' Pensions Regulations 1997, SI 1997/3001. As to the savings and transitional provision made see the Teachers' Pensions Regulations 2010, SI 2010/990, reg 138(3), Sch 13 (amended by SI 2011/614; and SI 2013/275). In regard to the marriage of, and living together as, a same sex couple see the Teachers' Pensions Regulations 2010, SI 2010/990, regs 2A, 2B (regs 2A, 2B added by SI 2014/560; and the Teachers' Pensions Regulations 2010, SI 2010/990, reg 2A amended by SI 2014/3061).

3   See the Teachers' Pensions Regulations 2010, SI 2010/990, regs 5–14H (regs 6–11 amended by SI 2012/2770; the Teachers' Pensions Regulations 2010, SI 2010/990, reg 7 amended by SI 2011/614; SI 2014/3255; SI 2014/424; the Teachers' Pensions Regulations 2010, SI 2010/990, reg 9 amended by SI 2014/424; the Teachers' Pensions Regulations 2010, SI 2010/990, reg 13 amended by SI 2014/2651; the Teachers' Pensions Regulations 2010, SI 2010/990, regs 14A–14H added by SI 2014/424; and the Teachers' Pensions Regulations 2010, SI 2010/990, regs 14A, 14F also amended by SI 2014/2651).

4   See the Teachers' Pensions Regulations 2010, SI 2010/990, regs 15–36A (reg 15 amended by SI 2014/3255; the Teachers' Pensions Regulations 2010, SI 2010/990, reg 16 amended by SI 2012/673; and SI 2014/2651; the Teachers' Pensions Regulations 2010, SI 2010/990, reg 17 amended by SI 2014/2651; the Teachers' Pensions Regulations 2010, SI 2010/990, reg 18 amended by SI 2013/275; the Teachers' Pensions Regulations 2010, SI 2010/990, reg 19 amended by SI 2011/614; the Teachers' Pensions Regulations 2010, SI 2010/990, reg 22 amended by SI 2011/614; and SI 2014/3255; the Teachers' Pensions Regulations 2010, SI 2010/990, reg 30 amended by SI 2014/2651; the Teachers' Pensions Regulations 2010, SI 2010/990, reg 31 amended by SI 2011/614; and SI 2014/2651; and the Teachers' Pensions Regulations 2010, SI 2010/990, regs 31A, 32A, 33–33E, 34–34D, 35–35G substituted and added by SI 2014/2651). As to additional voluntary contributions see PARA 1083. As to compensation for redundancy and premature retirement see PARA 1085.

5   See the Teachers' Pensions Regulations 2010, SI 2010/990, regs 37–56 (regs 39, 40, 43 amended by SI 2011/614; the Teachers' Pensions Regulations 2010, SI 2010/990, reg 40 amended by SI 2014/3255; and the Teachers' Pensions Regulations 2010, SI 2010/990, regs 44, 51 and 55 amended by SI 2014/2651).

6   See the Teachers' Pensions Regulations 2010, SI 2010/990, regs 57–64D (reg 59 amended by SI 2014/2651; and the Teachers' Pensions Regulations 2010, SI 2010/990, regs 64–64D substituted and added by SI 2014/2651).

7   See the Teachers' Pensions Regulations 2010, SI 2010/990, regs 65–72 (reg 71 amended by SI 2014/2651). See *Department for Education v Molyneux* [2012] EWCA Civ 193, [2012] ELR 357, [2012] ICR D30, [2012] All ER (D) 183 (Feb) (decision under the Teachers' Regulations 1997, SI 1997/3001).

8   See the Teachers' Pensions Regulations 2010, SI 2010/990, regs 73–76 (regs 73, 75 amended by SI 2011/614).

9   See the Teachers' Pensions Regulations 2010, SI 2010/990, regs 77–81.

10 See the Teachers' Pensions Regulations 2010, SI 2010/990, regs 82–87.

11 See the Teachers' Pensions Regulations 2010, SI 2010/990, regs 88–101 (reg 94 amended by SI 2014/2651; the Teachers' Pensions Regulations 2010, SI 2010/990, regs 95, 98 101 amended by SI 2011/614; and the Teachers' Pensions Regulations 2010, SI 2010/990, regs 95 and 98 also amended by SI 2014/3255)).

12 See the Teachers' Pensions Regulations 2010, SI 2010/990, regs 102–106 (reg 105 amended by SI 2012/673).

13 See the Teachers' Pensions Regulations 2010, SI 2010/990, regs 107–124 (reg 112 amended by SI 2011/614; the Teachers' Pensions Regulations 2010, SI 2010/990, regs 116, 118 and 119 amended by SI 2012/673; and the Teachers' Pensions Regulations 2010, SI 2010/990, regs 117 and 119 amended and reg 123 substituted by SI 2014/2651).

14 See the Teachers' Pensions Regulations 2010, SI 2010/990, regs 125–129 (reg 128 revoked by SI 2013/275; and the Teachers' Pensions Regulations 2010, SI 2010/990, reg 129 amended by SI 2011/614).

15 Ie the Teachers' Pension Scheme Regulations 2014, SI 2014/512, made under the Public Service Pensions Act 2013 ss 1, 4, 5, 7, 8, 14, 18, Sch 1, 2, 3, 6, 7. See further PARA 1081 text to notes 19–35.

16 Ie fully in force on 1 April 2015, and amended with effect from the same date by SI 2014/2652, and SI 2015/592.

17 See the Teachers' Pension Scheme Regulations 2014, SI 2014/512, Pt 2 (regs 7–13) (regs 7, 9 amended by SI 2014/2652).

18 See the Teachers' Pension Scheme Regulations 2014, SI 2014/512, Pt 3 (regs 14–41) (regs 19, 31, 41 amended by SI 2014/2652). The Teachers' Pension Scheme Regulations 2014, SI 2014/512, Pt 3 sets out the key concepts of eligible employment and pensionable earnings, and contains eligibility and auto-enrolment provisions. Regulations 3, 14, Sch 1 (reg 3, Sch 1 amended by SI 2014/2652) describe eligible employment.

19 See the Teachers' Pension Scheme Regulations 2014, SI 2014/512, Pt 4 (regs 42–81) (reg 65 amended by SI 2015/592). The Teachers' Pension Scheme Regulations 2014, SI 2014/512, Pt 4 explains how the amount of accrued pension is calculated, provides for the establishment of pension accounts, provides for the establishment of the active member's account (and provides for the proportion of pensionable earnings accrued as pension to be re-valued each year until the member leaves pensionable service), provides for the establishment of additional pension accounts, provides for deferred members' accounts and explains how the provisional amount of deferred pension is calculated, provides for the establishment of pensioner members' accounts and provides for the establishment of pension credit members' accounts. Regulations 3, 46, 186, Sch 2 (amended by SI 2014/2652) make provision for pension flexibilities.

20 See the Teachers' Pension Scheme Regulations 2014, SI 2014/512, Pt 5 (regs 82–125) (reg 117 amended by SI 2014/2652). The Teachers' Pension Scheme Regulations 2014, SI 2014/512, Pt 5 sets out the key concept of qualifying service.

21 See the Teachers' Pension Scheme Regulations 2014, SI 2014/512, Pt 6 (regs 126–152) (regs 117, 147, 150 amended by SI 2014/2652).

22 See the Teachers' Pension Scheme Regulations 2014, SI 2014/512, Pt 7 (regs 153–160).

23 See the Teachers' Pension Scheme Regulations 2014, SI 2014/512, Pt 8 (regs 161–183) (regs 174, 182 amended by SI 2014/2652). The Teachers' Pension Scheme Regulations 2014, SI 2014/512, Pt 8 also provides for the recovery and suspension of benefits in certain cases.

24 See the Teachers' Pension Scheme Regulations 2014, SI 2014/512, Pt 9 (regs 184–196) (regs 185, 192, 196 amended by SI 2014/2652). See also note 19.

25 See the Teachers' Pension Scheme Regulations 2014, SI 2014/512, Pt 10 (regs 197–218) (regs 200, 201, 203, 205, 209, 211 amended by SI 2014/2652).

26 See the Teachers' Pension Scheme Regulations 2014, SI 2014/512, Pt 11 (regs 219–225) (regs 219, 220, 223, 225 amended by SI 2014/2652). The Teachers' Pension Scheme Regulations 2014, SI 2014/512, reg 224, Sch 3 (Sch 3 amended by SI 2014/2652; and SI 2015/592) make transitional provision, and the Teachers' Pension Scheme Regulations 2014, SI 2014/512, reg 225, Sch 4 (added by SI 2014/2652) relate to scheme valuation and employer cost cap.

1083. Additional voluntary contributions. Teachers may pay additional voluntary contributions to improve their pension provision[1]. The Teachers' Superannuation (Additional Voluntary Contributions) Regulations 1994[2] make provision in relation to eligibility to make additional voluntary contributions[3], the making and acceptance of elections[4] to pay regular and lump sum contributions[5], and the variation and cancellation of such elections[6]. Provision is made for the investment of contributions[7], inward[8] and outward transfers[9], retirement[10] and the repayment of investments in certain cases[11]. Benefits may include lump sum death benefits[12] and pension sharing on divorce[13]. The regulations also contain provisions in relation to payments to be made by the Secretary of State[14], information to be given to him[15] and the determination of questions by him[16].

Account should also be taken generally of the Public Service Pensions Act 2013, and regulations made under it[17].

1 As to teachers' pension schemes see PARA 1082; and as to the power to make pension schemes for teachers see PARA 1081.
2 Ie the Teachers' Superannuation (Additional Voluntary Contributions) Regulations 1994, SI 1994/2924.
3 See the Teachers' Superannuation (Additional Voluntary Contributions) Regulations 1994, SI 1994/2924, reg 7 (amended by SI 1997/3001; and SI 2010/990).
4 See the Teachers' Superannuation (Additional Voluntary Contributions) Regulations 1994, SI 1994/2924, reg 3 (amended by SI 2006/736; and SI 2015/594).
5 See the Teachers' Superannuation (Additional Voluntary Contributions) Regulations 1994, SI 1994/2924, regs 4–5 (reg 4 amended by SI 2015/594; and the Teachers' Superannuation (Additional Voluntary Contributions) Regulations 1994, SI 1994/2924, reg 5 amended by SI 2000/666; SI 2006/3122; SI 2011/614; and SI 2015/594). As to the payment of contributions and the amount of regular contributions see the Teachers' Superannuation (Additional Voluntary Contributions) Regulations 1994, SI 1994/2924, reg 8 (amended by SI 2006/736).
6 See the Teachers' Superannuation (Additional Voluntary Contributions) Regulations 1994, SI 1994/2924, reg 6 (amended by SI 2006/3122; and SI 2015/594).
7 See the Teachers' Superannuation (Additional Voluntary Contributions) Regulations 1994, SI 1994/2924, reg 9.
8 See the Teachers' Superannuation (Additional Voluntary Contributions) Regulations 1994, SI 1994/2924, reg 10 (amended by SI 2006/736; and SI 2015/594).
9 See the Teachers' Superannuation (Additional Voluntary Contributions) Regulations 1994, SI 1994/2924, reg 11 (amended by SI 2000/3028; SI 2006/2214; SI 2010/990; SI 2011/614; and SI 2015/594).
10 See the Teachers' Superannuation (Additional Voluntary Contributions) Regulations 1994, SI 1994/2924, reg 12 (amended by SI 2000/666; SI 2006/736; SI 2006/3122; SI 2008/541; SI 2010/990; and SI 2011/614).
11 See the Teachers' Superannuation (Additional Voluntary Contributions) Regulations 1994, SI 1994/2924, reg 15 (amended by SI 1997/3001; SI 2006/736; and SI 2010/990).
12 See the Teachers' Superannuation (Additional Voluntary Contributions) Regulations 1994, SI 1994/2924, reg 13. As to payments in respect of deceased persons see reg 18.
13 See the Teachers' Superannuation (Additional Voluntary Contributions) Regulations 1994, SI 1994/2924, reg 13A (added by SI 2000/3028; and amended by SI 2006/736; SI 2006/3122; SI 2010/990; and SI 2015/594).
14 See the Teachers' Superannuation (Additional Voluntary Contributions) Regulations 1994, SI 1994/2924, reg 16 (amended by SI 1997/3001; SI 2006/736; SI 2006/3122; SI 2008/541; SI 2010/990; and SI 2015/594). As to the Secretary of State see PARA 58.
15 See the Teachers' Superannuation (Additional Voluntary Contributions) Regulations 1994, SI 1994/2924, reg 17.
16 See the Teachers' Superannuation (Additional Voluntary Contributions) Regulations 1994, SI 1994/2924, reg 19.
17 See the Public Service Pensions Act 2013 (not fully in force at the date at which this volume states the law), the Teachers' Pension Scheme Regulations 2014, SI 2014/512; and PARAS 1081, 1082.

1084. Elementary school teachers' superannuation. The Elementary School Teachers (Superannuation) Act 1898[1] created a pension scheme for certificated teachers[2]. It provided a deferred annuity[3], a superannuation allowance[4] and a disablement allowance[5]. Provision was also made in relation to the making of decisions[6], forfeiture for misconduct[7] and the payment and assignment of annuities and allowances[8].

Account should also be taken generally of the Public Service Pensions Act 2013, and regulations made under it[9].

1   The Elementary School Teachers (Superannuation) Act 1898 was amended by the Elementary School Teachers (Superannuation) Act 1912 and applied to Jersey by the Elementary School Teachers Superannuation (Jersey) Act 1900. As to the rules made under the Elementary School Teachers (Superannuation) Act 1898 s 6 (amended by virtue of SI 1984/539) see the Elementary School Teachers Superannuation Rules 1919, SR & O 1920/2298 (amended by the Administration of Estates (Small Payments) Act 1965 ss 1(1)(c), 6, Sch 1 Pt III; and SI 1950/60).

2   Prior to 1 April 1945, 'certificated teachers' meant a teacher who was recognised under the Education Code as a certificated teacher for public elementary schools: Elementary School Teachers (Superannuation) Act 1898 s 11; Teachers (Superannuation) Act 1945 s 11(2) (repealed). In relation to any subsequent period, 'certificated teacher' meant any person who would for the time being have been recognised as a certificated teacher under the regulations which were in force with respect to such recognition immediately before 1 April 1945 if those regulations had remained in force thereafter: s 11(2) (repealed). For these purposes, 'Education Code' meant such minutes of the Education Department as were for the time being in force for the purpose of the Elementary Education Act 1870: Elementary School Teachers (Superannuation) Act 1898 s 11.

3   See the Elementary School Teachers (Superannuation) Act 1898 s 1 (amended by the Teachers (Superannuation) Act 1925 s 23(3); the Elementary School Teachers (Superannuation) Act 1912 s 1(1), (2); the Teachers (Superannuation) Act 1945 s 11(1); SI 1995/2986; and by virtue of Decimal Currency Act 1969 s 10(1)). As to the collection of contributions and the deferred annuity fund see the Elementary School Teachers (Superannuation) Act 1898 s 3 (amended by the School Teachers (Superannuation) Act 1918 s 12(4)).

4   See the Elementary School Teachers (Superannuation) Act 1898 s 1 (as amended: see note 3).

5   See the Elementary School Teachers (Superannuation) Act 1898 s 2 (amended by the Elementary School Teachers (Superannuation) Act 1912 s 1(3); the School Teachers (Superannuation) Act 1918 ss 12(4), 13(3); and by virtue of Decimal Currency Act 1969 s 10(1)).

6   See the Elementary School Teachers (Superannuation) Act 1898 s 7.

7   See the Elementary School Teachers (Superannuation) Act 1898 s 8.

8   See the Elementary School Teachers (Superannuation) Act 1898 s 9 (amended by the Teachers (Superannuation) Act 1956 s 21).

9   See the Public Service Pensions Act 2013 (not fully in force at the date at which this volume states the law), the Teachers' Pension Scheme Regulations 2014, SI 2014/512; and PARAS 1081, 1082.

1085.   Compensation for redundancy and premature retirement. Regulations provide for compensation to teachers on redundancy and premature retirement[1]. A teacher who is entitled to a statutory redundancy payment[2] may claim compensation from his employer[3].

A teacher who immediately before his employment ceased was employed in relevant employment[4], who had attained the age of 55 but had not attained the age of 65[5], and who satisfied certain conditions[6] is entitled to be credited with an additional service credit[7]. A teacher thus credited is entitled to a lump sum compensation and to annual compensation calculated in accordance with the regulations[8]. The regulations also provide for compensation to be paid after the teacher's death[9].

Separate provision is made as to compensation payable for loss of employment or loss or diminution of emoluments consequent upon the reorganisation of education authorities in inner London[10]; and provision is also made for payment of compensation to teachers employed by a local authority, other than those employed in schools or further or higher education institutions, and to certain administrative and support staff for redundancy or loss of remuneration caused by local government reorganisation[11].

Account should also be taken generally of the Public Service Pensions Act 2013, and regulations made under it[12].

1   Ie the Teachers (Compensation for Redundancy and Premature Retirement) Regulations 1997, SI 1997/311. Part IV (regs 7–10) introduces provisions for mandatory compensation for premature retirement. As to dismissal by reason of redundancy generally see EMPLOYMENT vol 41 (2014) PARA 835 et seq. See also *Healey v Bridgend County Council* [2002] EWCA Civ 1996, [2004] ICR 561n, [2002] All ER (D) 204 (Nov).

2   Ie under the Employment Rights Act 1996 Pt XI (ss 135–181) (see EMPLOYMENT vol 41 (2014) PARA 835 et seq): see the Teachers (Compensation for Redundancy and Premature Retirement) Regulations 1997, SI 1997/311, reg 4(1).

3   See the Teachers (Compensation for Redundancy and Premature Retirement) Regulations 1997, SI 1997/311, reg 5 (amended by SI 1999/608; and SI 2010/1172). Such compensation must not exceed the difference between the statutory redundancy payment and the payment he would have been entitled to if the Employment Rights Act 1996 s 227(1)(c) (see EMPLOYMENT vol 39 (2014) PARA 147) had been repealed: see the Teachers (Compensation for Redundancy and Premature Retirement) Regulations 1997, SI 1997/311, reg 5. In the case of a person employed at an aided school, compensation is payable by the 'appropriate person', namely the local authority, and in any other case is payable by the person by whom he was employed: reg 2(2) (definition substituted by SI 1999/608; and amended by SI 2010/1172). The Teachers (Compensation for Redundancy and Premature Retirement) Regulations 1997, SI 1997/311, also provide for discretionary compensation for termination of employment: see reg 6 (substituted by SI 2006/2216; and amended by SI 2010/1172).

4   See the Teachers (Compensation for Redundancy and Premature Retirement) Regulations 1997, SI 1997/311, reg 4(6)(a). As to relevant employment see reg 3 (amended by SI 1998/2256; SI 1999/608; SI 2000/664; SI 2006/3122; and SI 2010/990).

5   See the Teachers (Compensation for Redundancy and Premature Retirement) Regulations 1997, SI 1997/311, reg 4(7)(a) (amended by SI 2010/990).

6   As to these conditions see the Teachers (Compensation for Redundancy and Premature Retirement) Regulations 1997, SI 1997/311, reg 4(6)(c), (7)(b)–(e) (amended by SI 1998/2256; SI 2006/3122; and SI 2010/990). Only teachers who have not received discretionary compensation for termination under the Teachers (Compensation for Redundancy and Premature Retirement) Regulations 1997, SI 1997/311, reg 6 may be credited with an additional period of service: see reg 4(6)(b).

7   See the Teachers (Compensation for Redundancy and Premature Retirement) Regulations 1997, SI 1997/311, reg 11.

8   See the Teachers (Compensation for Redundancy and Premature Retirement) Regulations 1997, SI 1997/311, reg 12 (amended by SI 1998/2256; SI 2010/990).

9   See the Teachers (Compensation for Redundancy and Premature Retirement) Regulations 1997, SI 1997/311, reg 14 (amended by SI 2010/990).

10 See the Education (Reorganisation in Inner London) (Compensation) Regulations 1989, SI 1989/1139 (amended by the Employment Rights (Dispute Resolution) Act 1998 s 1(2)(a); SI 1990/1433; and SI 1996/1935).

11 See the Local Government Reorganisation (Compensation for Redundancy or Loss of Remuneration) (Education) Regulations 1996, SI 1996/1240.

12 See the Public Service Pensions Act 2013 (not fully in force at the date at which this volume states the law), the Teachers' Pension Scheme Regulations 2014, SI 2014/512; and PARAS 1081, 1082.

(iii)   Pay, Conditions and Pensions at Academies

1086.   Pay, conditions and pensions at academies.   Staff at maintained schools are employed by the local authority or the governing body[1], and there are statutory provisions relating to teachers' pay and conditions, and pensions[2] which are set out elsewhere in this title. However, in an academy, it is the academy trust that employs the staff[3], and it follows the requirements set out in its funding agreement[4] rather than national legislation. The model funding agreement, for example, contains clauses specifying teachers' pay, and conditions of service are the responsibility of the academy trust[5]. The academy trust is also responsible for the pension arrangements of academy's staff, and must arrange for the transfer if a school is converting from maintained to academy status[6].

1   As to staffing of schools see PARA 268 et seq.

2 See PARA 1076 et seq.
3 As to the meaning of 'academy' see PARA 346 note 7. As to academy arrangements and academies generally see PARA 345 et seq. As to staffing of academies see PARA 358.
4 As to funding agreements see PARA 346.
5 Model funding agreements for the various types of academies can be found on the Department for Education website.
6 See the Department for Education document '*Convert to an academy: guide for schools*'. As to the conversion of schools into academies see PARAS 350–351.

(5) TEACHERS' DUTY OF CARE TOWARDS PUPILS

1087. The teacher's duties towards the pupil: common law and statutory. The teacher's duty at common law is to take such care of the children in his charge as a careful parent would take of his own children[1]. The standard of care generally expected of a teacher is that of a reasonably prudent parent judged not in the context of his own home but in that of a school[2], or the standard of a reasonable parent of a rather large family[3]. The general position that the duty of care is that of the reasonably careful and prudent father towards his own children is helpful when considering, for example, individual instructions to individual children in a school, but that rule may sometimes be unrealistic in the context of a large group[4].

It is the statutory duty of every employee (including a teacher) while at work to take reasonable care for the health and safety of himself and of other persons who may be affected by his acts or omissions at work[5]. In addition, there is a statutory duty imposed on teachers as part of their conditions of employment to promote the safety and well-being of pupils and to maintain good order and discipline among pupils[6].

While the prevention of bullying among pupils is within a teacher's ordinary duty of care[7], the occasions when a school would be in breach of duty for a failure to take steps within its power to combat the harmful behaviour of one pupil towards another even when they were outside school would be few and far between[8].

Teachers may owe a duty of care in respect of the under-performance of pupils in some circumstances[9].

1 *Williams v Eady* (1893) 10 TLR 41, CA.
2 *Lyes v Middlesex County Council* (1962) 61 LGR 443. 'A lot of pupils are apt to make much more noise even than a few children in a small home and there is ... more skylarking and a bit of rough play': *Lyes v Middlesex County Council* at 446 per Edmund Davies J.
3 *Jacques v Oxfordshire County Council* (1967) 66 LGR 440 at 444 per Waller J. Compare and contrast the court's decisions in *Butt v Cambridgeshire and Isle of Ely County Council* (1969) 68 LGR 81, CA, and *Black v Kent County Council* (1983) 82 LGR 39, CA. Both *Butt v Cambridgeshire and Isle of Ely County Council* and *Black v Kent County Council* were cases of eye injuries caused by young children using sharp-pointed scissors. In *Butt v Cambridgeshire and Isle of Ely County Council* (class of 37 nine and ten-year-old girls) the local education authority was held not liable for the injury. In *Black v Kent County Council* (class of 25 seven-year-olds) the authority was held liable.
    The gradual raising of the standard of care expected in schools is evident from the cases. See eg *Rich v LCC* [1953] 2 All ER 376, [1953] 1 WLR 895, CA (heap of coke lying unfenced on part of senior school playground; plaintiff lost an eye when another young boy threw a piece of coke at him; it was held that the authority was not obliged to prevent the boys having access to the coke; the supervision of the boys was held to be adequate and therefore the authority was not liable); *Clark v Monmouthshire County Council* (1954) 52 LGR 246, CA (boy stabbed in leg by another boy in playground during break; staff did not know that the other boy was carrying a knife; at time of accident no prefect on duty in playground; master in charge passed through the playground twice during break; the authority was held not negligent ('The duty of a school does not extend to constant supervision of all the boys all the time': at 247–248 per

Denning LJ)). See also *Suckling v Essex County Council* (1955) Times, 27 January (plaintiff injured during horseplay involving a scorer knife which another boy had taken from a cupboard while the teacher was out of the room), where Vaisey J stated that it seemed to him that if he were to hold that every school with small children was committing an actionable wrong in leaving unlocked such implements as these scorer knives he would be putting an altogether excessive burden on educational establishments. Not only would it be difficult for them to be conducted in a successful and reasonable manner, but it would run the serious risk of turning these children into the votaries of the principle of safety first. He said that it was better that a boy should break his neck than allow other people to break his spirit. This decision and the tenor of the judge's language do not accord with the line of authority beginning with *Williams v Eady* (1893) 10 TLR 41, CA (see the text to note 1), in which a boy played with a bottle containing phosphorus which was in a conservatory to which the pupils had access; the bottle burst, and the phosphorus exploded and injured the plaintiff; and it was held that a schoolmaster is bound to take such care of his boys as a careful father would take of his boys, and is bound to take notice of the ordinary nature of young boys, their tendency to do mischievous acts, and their propensity to meddle with anything that came in their way, and that, having phosphorus in his house, he was bound not to leave it in any place in which they might get at it (at 42 per Lord Esher MR)). See also *Martin v Middlesbrough Corpn* (1965) 63 LGR 385, CA (girl slipped on icy playground and cut her hand on a piece of broken milk-bottle glass lying on a grating; broken milk bottles were often found on the playground; it was held there was a very serious risk of serious injury and the authority was liable); *Beaumont v Surrey County Council* (1968) 66 LGR 580 (discarded piece of elastic from mini-trampoline deposited, uncovered, in litter bin in loggia of school and found by pupils during next day's morning break; despite supervision of break by two masters, four prefects, four sub-prefects and four monitors, no member of staff was at loggia or on the playground when the plaintiff was injured in horseplay with the elastic; it was held: (1) the possibility of physical injury from use of, or horseplay with, the elastic was foreseeable; (2) if the school system of supervision had been working properly the horseplay would have been stopped; (3) the authority fell short of the high standards the law demanded of it); *Norman v Inner London Education Authority* (1974) Times, 14 December (unlabelled beaker of sulphuric acid left on bench in chemistry laboratory in master's absence; boy filled syringe from beaker and squirted it in another boy's eye; it was held that the master's failure to give a specific warning of the danger involved a departure from the very high standards demanded); *Moore v Hampshire County Council* (1981) 80 LGR 481, CA (girl born with dislocated hips, forbidden by parent to take part in physical education (PE); the headmistress noted fact, but the girl told PE teacher untruthfully that she was allowed by the doctor to do PE and, in attempting a handstand in PE class, fell and broke an ankle; it was held that the teacher had failed to conform to the standard of care required in that she failed to supervise the girl's ability to do a handstand, as her special condition required, and in allowing her to take part in the PE class without first checking that she was allowed to do so); *Gough v Upshire Primary School* [2002] ELR 169, QBD (no liability in respect of a pupil who fell when sliding down banister at school); *Pierce v West Sussex County Council* [2013] EWCA Civ 1230, [2013] All ER (D) 166 (Oct) (in regard to an accident in the context of skylarking at a water fountain, it was found that the local authority was not liable; the school and therefore the authority were not under a duty to safeguard children in all circumstances). There are a number of cases involving negligence in the context of swimming lessons e g see *Woodland v Essex County Council* [2013] UKSC 66, [2014] AC 537, [2014] 1 All ER 482 (and the related case *Woodland v Maxwell* [2015] EWHC 273 (QB), [2015] All ER (D) 162 (Feb), also considered at PARA 1088 note 2). As to the supervision of pupils see further PARA 1088.

4   Eg when applied to an incident of horseplay in a school of 900 pupils: *Beaumont v Surrey County Council* (1968) 66 LGR 580 at 585 per Geoffrey Lane J.

5   See the Health and Safety at Work etc Act 1974 s 7; and HEALTH AND SAFETY AT WORK vol 52 (2014) PARA 410.

6   See the document entitled 'School Teachers' Pay and Conditions Document 2015 and Guidance on School Teachers' Pay and Conditions' (published on the website of the Department for Education) paras 52.8, 52.9, which document is given effect by the School Teachers' Pay and Conditions Order 2015, SI 2015/1582, as from 1 September 2015. See further PARA 1078. As to the promotion of good behaviour and the prevention of the breakdown of discipline see PARA 509 et seq; and as to the restraint and search of pupils see PARA 541 et seq.

7   See eg *Scott v Lothian Regional Council* (29 September 1998, unreported). See also PARA 596.

8   *Bradford-Smart v West Sussex County Council* [2002] EWCA Civ 07, [2002] LGR 489, [2002] ELR 139; revsg on this point [2001] ELR 138, [2001] All ER (D) 1731.

9   See *X (Minors) v Bedfordshire County Council* [1995] 2 AC 633, [1995] 3 All ER 353, [1995] ELR 404, HL; *Phelps v Hillingdon London Borough Council, Anderton v Clwyd County*

Council, Jarvis v Hampshire County Council, G v Bromley London Borough Council [2001] 2 AC 619, [2000] 4 All ER 504, [2000] ELR 499, HL; *DN v Greenwich London Borough Council* [2004] EWCA Civ 1659, [2005] LGR 597, [2005] 1 FCR 112; *Carty v Croydon London Borough Council* [2005] EWCA Civ 19, [2005] 2 All ER 517, [2005] 1 WLR 2312; *Skipper v Calderdale Metropolitan Borough Council* [2006] EWCA Civ 238, [2006] ELR 322, [2006] All ER (D) 203 (Mar); *Connor v Surrey County Council* [2010] EWCA Civ 286, [2011] QB 429, [2010] 3 All ER 905 (in which the court considered the divide between duties arising in private and public law). See further PARA 1039.

1088. Liability for negligent supervision of pupils. Negligence in the supervision of pupils may render those charged with their care liable to compensate the pupils or any other person suffering injury or damage as a result[1]. The duty is to take at least such care of the pupils as a careful parent would take of his children[2], and the ordinary principles of vicarious liability[3] apply where the negligence is that of a teacher[4]. The age of the pupil[5] and the nature of the activity[6] in which he is taking part are material factors in determining the degree of supervision demanded. For example, the release of a very young child from school before the scheduled time in certain circumstances has been held to be negligent[7]. School trips present particular risks requiring careful supervision[8].

1 Supervision is an incident of the giving of secular instruction, which includes proper recreation periods, and the duty to provide supervision lies on the education authority or body of governors as the case may be: see *Greenwood v Atherton* [1938] 2 All ER 475 at 478 per Lewis J; affd [1939] 1 KB 388, [1938] 4 All ER 686, CA (the duty of supervision was held to be a public duty and protected by the Public Authorities Protection Act 1893 (repealed)). As to a teacher's general duty towards pupils see PARA 1087.

2 *Williams v Eady* (1893) 10 TLR 41 at 42, CA, per Lord Esher MR. 'That test has been the one adopted ever since': *Rich v LCC* [1953] 2 All ER 376 at 379, [1953] 1 WLR 895 at 900, CA, per Singleton LJ. However 'one has to visualise a parent with a very large family': *Ricketts v Erith Borough Council* [1943] 2 All ER 629 at 631 per Tucker J. 'School authorities ... must strike some balance between the meticulous supervision of children every moment of the time when they are under their care, and the very desirable object of encouraging the sturdy independence of children as they grow up; ... encouragement ... must start at quite an early age': *Jeffery v LCC* (1954) 52 LGR 521 at 523 per McNair J (a five-year-old child climbed on to a glass roof, fell and sustained fatal injuries).

In later cases a higher standard of care has been required than that in *Williams v Eady*: see eg *Lyes v Middlesex County Council* (1962) 61 LGR 443 (plaintiff's hand caused to break glass in door by fellow pupil's prank; glass too thin for the rough-and-tumble of school life); *Reffell v Surrey County Council* [1964] 1 All ER 743, [1964] 1 WLR 358 (dangerous door); *Beaumont v Surrey County Council* (1968) 66 LGR 580 (it is a schoolmaster's duty, bearing in mind the known propensities of children between the ages of 11 and 18, to take all reasonable and proper steps to prevent any of the pupils under his care from suffering injury from inanimate objects, from the actions of their fellow pupils, or from a combination of the two). As to supervision in school playgrounds see *Langham v Governors of Wellingborough School and Fryer* (1932) 101 LJKB 513, CA (golf ball, hit with stick in playground, flew through open door to strike plaintiff, inside school building, in the eye; no express evidence as to supervision in the playground; claim failed); *Rawsthorne v Ottley* [1937] 3 All ER 902 (tip-up lorry with single driver delivered coke to school playground; a pupil jumped on to lorry behind driver's cab; when tipping part of lorry was released it fell and crushed claimant pupil's leg; headmaster not negligent in leaving boys in playground without supervision); *Clark v Monmouthshire County Council* (1954) 52 LGR 246, CA (the duty of a schoolmaster does not extend to constant supervision of all the boys in his care all the time); *Mays v Essex County Council* (1975) Times, 11 October (school under no legal duty to supervise the early arrivals in the playground before school began nor to prevent children sliding on ice); *Webster v Ridgeway Foundation School* [2010] EWHC 157 (QB), [2010] ELR 694, [2010] All ER (D) 52 (Feb) (school not in breach of duty of care where pupil attacked on school premises after end of school day. In this case arguments were also raised on the claimant's part in respect of the Human Rights Act 1998: see PARA 3); cf *Kearn-Price v Kent County Council* [2002] EWCA Civ 1539, [2003] ELR 17, [2003] PIQR P167, [2002] All ER (D) 440 (Oct) (full-size leather football caused injury during pre-school period to pupil who had been behaving reasonably as a mere bystander in a playground; enforcement of ban on such footballs would have prevented injury; duty not unduly onerous, even shortly before registration started). See also *Jeffery v LCC*; *Price v Caernarvonshire County Council* (1960) Times, 11 February, CA; *Newton v East Ham Corpn* [1963] CLY 2426; *Martin v Middlesbrough Corpn* (1965) 63 LGR 385, CA; *Beaumont v Surrey County Council*; *Ward v Hertfordshire County Council* [1970] 1 All ER 535, [1970] 1 WLR 356, CA (unsupervised race in playground and pupil tripped and struck head against flint wall; it was held that the local education authority was not liable: (1) because the wall was not dangerous, bearing in mind its nature, typicality and long-standing and the fact that complaints had never been made against it; (2) since the accident occurred in the ordinary course of play the lack of supervision was irrelevant: it is impossible so to supervise children that they never fall down and hurt themselves); *Simonds v Isle of Wight Council* [2003] EWHC 2303 (QB), [2004] ELR 59, [2003] 39 LS Gaz R 40, (2003) Times, 9 October, [2003] All ER (D) 156 (Sep) (child broke arm on sports day while playing on swings unsupervised, having spent some time with his mother; school not liable; playing fields could not be made free of all hazards; fact that potential hazard had been diagnosed by school did not impose duty to make access or use impossible); *Palmer v Cornwall County Council* [2009] EWCA Civ 456, [2009] ELR 314, [2009] All ER (D) 191 (May) (inadequate supervision of playground resulting in stones being thrown and causing injury); *Pierce v West Sussex County Council* [2013] EWCA Civ 1230, [2013] All ER (D) 166 (Oct) (in regard to an accident in the context of skylarking at a water fountain, it was found that the local authority was not liable; the school and therefore the authority were not under a duty to safeguard children in all circumstances); *Woodland v Maxwell* [2015] EWHC 273 (QB), [2015] All ER (D) 162 (Feb) (swim teacher, lifeguard and consequently local authority liable in negligence to claimant, a ten-year-old girl who had been taking part in a group swimming lesson when she got into difficulties and suffered serious brain injury as a result of loss of oxygen to the brain) (see also the related case: *Woodland v Essex County Council* [2013] UKSC 66, [2014] AC 537, [2014] 1 All ER 482). As to arrangements by councils for patrolling school crossings see ROAD TRAFFIC vol 89 (2011) PARAS 572–573.

3   See TORT vol 97 (2015) PARA 767 et seq.

4   *Smith v Martin and Kingston-upon-Hull Corpn* [1911] 2 KB 775, CA. The education authority may, of course, also be responsible for the torts of other employees: see *Shrimpton v Hertfordshire County Council* (1911) 104 LT 145, HL (attendance officer); *Knott v LCC* [1934] 1 KB 126 at 138, CA, per Lord Wright, and at 142–143 per Slesser LJ (school-keeper). Cf *Smith v Glasgow Corpn* 1952 SLT 62, Sh Ct. See also *Alexis v Newham London Borough Council* [2009] EWHC 1323 (QB), [2009] ICR 1517, [2009] ELR 453 (no breach of duty by education authority where pupil contaminated a teacher's drink). See also *Woodland v Maxwell* [2015] EWHC 273 (QB), [2015] All ER (D) 162 (Feb); and note 2.

5   The duty to safeguard pupils' health and safety (see PARA 1087) has particular application in the case of young children: see eg *Jefferey v LCC* (1954) 52 LGR 521; *Carmarthenshire County Council v Lewis* [1955] AC 549, [1955] 1 All ER 565, HL (boy aged four, left unattended for 10 minutes, walked out of school to busy road where he caused a lorry to swerve so that it struck a telegraph pole and the driver was killed; it was held that there was a lack of reasonable precautions by the authority; the accident was foreseeable, and the authority was negligent and liable in damages); *Barnes (An Infant) v Hampshire County Council* [1969] 3 All ER 746, [1969] 1 WLR 1563, HL (small children released from school by their teachers five minutes before scheduled time; a girl was injured on a nearby main road, before the mother arrived to meet her; the school authority was held to be negligent; a school is not required to detain small children until their parents collect them, but must adhere to the timetable of which the parents had been informed). See also *Jenney (a minor) v North Lincolnshire County Council* [2000] LGR 269, sub nom *J v North Lincolnshire County Council* [2000] ELR 245, [2000] PIQR P84, CA (school liable for injuries suffered by a child who wandered out of school premises into the path of a car).
     See also *Orchard v Lee* [2009] EWCA Civ 295, [2009] ELR 178, [2009] PIQR P285 (injury caused to a member of staff by a 13 year old pupil while engaged in horseplay).

6   The duty of care appropriate in sport and physical education may call for more than usual forethought and supervision: see *Gibbs v Barking Corpn* [1936] 1 All ER 115 (extent of instructor's duty in supervising vaulting over a horse); *Gillmore v LCC* [1938] 4 All ER 331 (accident during exercises on slippery floor); *Ralph v LCC* (1947) 111 JP 548, CA (accident during game of touch; plaintiff's hand went through glass partition); *Wright v Cheshire County Council* [1952] 2 All ER 789, CA (gymnastic exercises; degree of supervision required); cf *Barnes (An Infant) v Hampshire County Council* [1969] 3 All ER 746, [1969] 1 WLR 1563, HL; *Conrad v Inner London Education Authority* (1967) 111 Sol Jo 684, 65 LGR 543, CA (accident in judo class); *Affutu-Nartoy v Clarke* (1984) Times, 9 February (whether a teacher should tackle pupils when playing rugby football with them); *Van Oppen v Clerk to the*

Trustees of the Bedford Charity [1989] 3 All ER 389, [1990] 1 WLR 235, CA (school under no duty to insure a pupil against accidental rugby injury or to inform or advise a parent of the need for personal accident insurance); *Fowles v Bedfordshire County Council* [1996] ELR 51, [1995] PIQR P389, CA (no warnings or prohibitions posted in respect of gymnastics at youth centre involving danger to participant; contributory negligence); *Smoldon v Whitworth* [1997] ELR 249, [1997] PIQR P133, CA (referee in breach of duty of care through negligent refereeing of rugby match; the Court of Appeal recommended (per curiam) a general practice of insuring against rugby injuries). See also *Pierce v West Sussex County Council* [2013] EWCA Civ 1230, [2013] All ER (D) 166 (Oct); and *Woodland v Essex County Council* [2013] UKSC 66, [2014] AC 537, [2014] 1 All ER 482 (and the related case *Woodland v Maxwell* [2015] EWHC 273 (QB), [2015] All ER (D) 162 (Feb)); and PARA 1087 note 3.

As to school trips see note 8. For cases involving danger from machines see *Smerkinich v Newport Corpn* (1912) 10 LGR 959, 76 JP 454; *Butt v Inner London Education Authority* (1968) 66 LGR 379, CA. As to an accident with an unguarded cooker see *Fryer v Salford Corpn* [1937] 1 All ER 617, CA.

The standard of care is especially high in relation to children with disability: *Ellis v Sayers Confectioners Ltd* (1963) 61 LGR 299, 107 Sol Jo 252, CA; *Moore v Hampshire County Council* (1981) 80 LGR 481, CA.

7   Cf *Carmarthenshire County Council v Lewis* [1955] AC 549, [1955] 1 All ER 565, HL (cited in note 5); *Nwabudike v Southwark London Borough Council* [1997] ELR 35, (1996) 140 Sol Jo LB 128; *Wilson v Governors of Sacred Heart Roman Catholic School* [1998] ELR 637, [1998] 1 FLR 663, CA; *Jenney (A Minor) v North Lincolnshire County Council* [2000] LGR 269, sub nom *J v North Lincolnshire County Council* [2000] ELR 245, CA.

8   See *Porter v City of Bradford Metropolitan Council* (14 January 1985, unreported), CA. As to the nature of the duty of care, and the standard of care, required when pupils are taken on a school trip see *Chittock v Woodbridge School* [2002] EWCA Civ 915, [2002] ELR 735, [2003] PIQR P81 (pupil injured in skiing trip accident).

9. STUDENTS

(1) STATUS OF STUDENTS; COMPLAINTS AND RIGHTS OF REDRESS

1089. Students' legal relationship with higher education institutions. It is now accepted that a student stands in a contractual relationship with a university whatever the nature of the institution he attends[1]. Nevertheless, this does not necessarily mean that decisions of universities about such matters as awards of degrees, progression to the next stage of a course or disciplinary matters are not amenable to judicial review[2].

In relation to issues which do not touch upon matters of academic judgment, the Higher Education Act 2004 introduced a statutory scheme for the review of complaints made by students or former students at qualifying institutions or by students working towards the grant of one of the qualifying institution's awards[3].

1 *Clark v University of Lincolnshire and Humberside* [2000] 3 All ER 752, [2000] 1 WLR 1988, [2000] ELR 345, CA. See also *Cadells v Balfour* (1898) S Ct 1138 (1890) 17 R 1138, Ct of Sess; *Herring v Templeman* [1973] 3 All ER 569 at 584–585, CA, per Russell LJ; *Moran v University College Salford (No 2)* [1994] ELR 187, CA; cf *Thomson v University of London* (1864) 33 LJ Ch 625 per Kindersley VC; *Green v Master and Fellows of St Peter's College Oxford* (1896) Times, 10 February per Wills J; *R v Aston University Senate, ex p Roffey* [1969] 2 QB 538, sub nom *R v Senate of University of Aston, ex p Roffey* [1969] 2 All ER 964. Such contractual status notwithstanding, however, a student's 'civil right' for the purposes of the Convention for the Protection of Human Rights and Fundamental Freedoms (Rome, 4 November 1950; TS 71 (1953) Cmd 8969) art 6(1) was not being determined by an academic appeals committee of the university when considering matters relating to the failure to award him an MA: see *Hanuman v United Kingdom* [2000] ELR 685, ECtHR; and PARA 3.

2 See *R v Manchester Metropolitan University, ex p Nolan* [1994] ELR 380; *R v University of Humberside, ex p Cousens* [1995] CLY 1947, CA; *R v Board of Governors of Sheffield Hallam University, ex p R* [1995] ELR 267; *R v University College London, ex p Christofi* (18 June 1997, unreported); *R v Liverpool John Moores University, ex p Hayes* [1998] ELR 261; *R v University of Portsmouth, ex p Lakareber* [1999] ELR 135, CA; *R v Cambridge University, ex p Beg* [1999] ELR 404; *Iqbal Sandhu v University of Central England* [1999] ELR 419, CA; *R v Cranfield University Senate, ex p Bashir* [1999] ELR 317, CA; *R v South Bank University, ex p Coggeran* [2001] ELR 42, [2000] ICR 1342, CA; *R v Chelsea College of Art and Design, ex p Nash* [2000] ELR 686; *R (on the application of Persaud) v University of Cambridge* [2001] EWCA Civ 534, [2001] ELR 480; *R (on the application of M) v University of the West of England* [2001] ELR 458, CA; *R (on the application of Isolyn Burgess) v South Bank University* [2001] ELR 300; *Abramova v Oxford Institute of Legal Practice* [2011] EWHC 613 (QB), [2011] All ER (D) 229 (Mar). As to judicial review generally see JUDICIAL REVIEW.

   Where a decision concerning a student is amenable to judicial review, there is sufficient procedural flexibility within the Civil Procedure Rules 1998, SI 1998/3132, to enable a student to pursue a claim against a university in contract even though it might more appropriately be brought via judicial review, and the claim would not be struck out by the court for that reason unless the court was satisfied that there had been an abuse of the process of the court in the circumstances, including a delay in instituting proceedings: *Clark v University of Lincolnshire and Humberside* [2000] 3 All ER 752 at 761, [2000] 1 WLR 1988 at 1997–1998, [2000] ELR 345 at 355 per Lord Woolf MR, CA. See also *R (on the application of Maxwell) v Office of the Independent Adjudicator for Higher Education* [2011] EWCA Civ 1236, [2012] PTSR 884, [2011] All ER (D) 232 (Oct) (adjudicator not bound to make positive statement of finding of disability discrimination by University; application for judicial review refused).

3 See the Higher Education Act 2004 Pt 2 (ss 11–21); and PARA 1090 et seq. 'Academic judgment' is not defined in the Higher Education Act 2004. The jurisdiction of a visitor to the institution is ousted in respect of the matters covered by s 20 (qualifying student complaints: see PARA 1090) and s 46 (disputes between a member of staff and the qualifying institution: see PARA 630). As to the jurisdiction of visitors see PARA 629.

1090. Review of student complaints under statutory scheme. The governing body[1] of every qualifying institution[2] in England and Wales must comply with any obligation imposed upon it by a scheme for the review of qualifying complaints that is provided by the designated operator[3] of the statutory student complaints scheme[4].

A 'qualifying complaint' means a complaint about an act or omission of a qualifying institution which is made by a person: (1) as a student or former student at that institution[5]; or (2) as a student or former student at another institution (whether or not a qualifying institution) undertaking a course of study, or programme of research, leading to the grant of one of the qualifying institution's awards[6]. However, this is subject to the provisos[7] that a complaint which falls within these criteria is not a qualifying complaint to the extent that it relates to matters of academic judgment[8], and that the designated operator may determine that a complaint about an act or omission of specified qualifying institutions[9] is a qualifying complaint only if it is made by a person who is undertaking or has undertaken a particular course or a course of a particular description[10].

For the purposes of the law of defamation, any proceedings relating to the review, under the scheme for the review of qualifying complaints provided by the designated operator, of a qualifying complaint are to be treated as if they were proceedings before a court[11].

The visitor of a qualifying institution has no jurisdiction in respect of any complaint[12]: (a) if it is made in respect of an application for admission to the qualifying institution as a student[13]; or (b) if it is made by a person as a student or former student at the qualifying institution[14], or as a student or former student at another institution (whether or not a qualifying institution) undertaking a course of study, or programme of research, leading to the grant of one of the qualifying institution's awards[15].

1　In the Higher Education Act 2004 Pt 2 (ss 11–21), 'governing body' has the meaning given by the Further and Higher Education Act 1992 s 90(1), but subject to any provision made by virtue of s 90(2) (see PARA 560 note 6): Higher Education Act 2004 s 21.

2　For the purposes of the Higher Education Act 2004 Pt 2 (ss 11–21), 'qualifying institution' means any of the following institutions in England or Wales: (1) a university, whether or not receiving financial support under the Further and Higher Education Act 1992 s 65 (see PARA 701), whose entitlement to grant awards is conferred or confirmed by an Act of Parliament, a Royal Charter, or an order under the Further and Higher Education Act 1992 s 76 (see PARA 685) (Higher Education Act 2004 ss 11(a), 21); (2) a constituent college, school or hall or other institution of a university falling within head (1) above (s 11(b)); (3) an institution conducted by a higher education corporation (s 11(c)); (4) a designated institution, as defined by the Further and Higher Education Act 1992 s 72(3) (see PARA 701 note 5) (Higher Education Act 2004 s 11(d)); (5) an institution (other than one within s 11(a)–(d), (f)) which provides higher education courses which are designated for the purposes of the Teaching and Higher Education Act 1998 s 22 (see PARAS 1096, 1097) by or under regulations thereunder (Higher Education Act 2004 s 11(e) (s 11(e), (f) added (prospectively, so far as relating to Wales) by the Consumer Rights Act 2015 s 89(1), (2))); and (6) an institution (other than one within s 11(a)–(e)) whose entitlement to grant awards is conferred by an order under the Further and Higher Education Act 1992 s 76(1) (see PARA 685) (Higher Education Act 2004 s 11(f) (as so added)). For the purposes of Pt 2, 'award' means any degree, diploma, certificate or other academic award or distinction: s 21. As to the meaning of 'higher education corporation' see PARA 645 (definition applied by s 21). As to the meanings of 'England' and 'Wales' see PARA 7 note 3. As to the meaning of 'university' see PARA 621.

3　As to the meaning of 'designated operator' see PARA 1091 note 4.

4　See the Higher Education Act 2004 s 15(1). The duty imposed by s 15(1) applies from the effective date of the designation and ceases to apply only if the designation is terminated:

s 15(2). As to the meaning of 'the effective date' see PARA 1091 note 12. The obligations referred to in s 15(1) include any obligation to pay fees to the designated operator of the statutory student complaints scheme: s 15(3).

5   Higher Education Act 2004 s 12(1)(a).

6   Higher Education Act 2004 ss 12(1)(b), 21. See note 5.

7   Higher Education Act 2004 s 12(1) (s 12(1) amended, s 12(3) added, by the Consumer Rights Act 2015 s 89(1), (3)). Note that at the date at which this volume states the law these amendments had not been brought into force in relation to Wales. See note 2.

8   Higher Education Act 2004 s 12(2). 'Academic judgment' is not defined by the Higher Education Act 2004. As to the scope of the operation of s 12(2) see *R (on the application of Gopikrishna) v Office of the Independent Adjudicator for Higher Education* [2015] EWHC 207 (Admin), [2015] ELR 190, [2015] All ER (D) 160 (Feb) (The statutory academic decision immunity applied where the central subject of the complaint was a dispute about academic judgment ... An academic institution could not expect that any claim for academic judgment immunity would be accepted uncritically. On the assumption that a complaint was one made, not to a court, but to the Office of the Independent Adjudicator (OIA), if there was objective evidence of matters which suggested procedural unfairness, bias, impropriety, or the kind of administrative irrationality or perversity which the court could consider, then the OIA might properly regard a complaint to it against a university's decision as one which it was competent to determine, notwithstanding the academic context within which it arose). As to the OIA see PARA 1091 note 5. As to a student's legal relationship with a higher education institution see PARA 1089.

9   Ie qualifying institutions within the Higher Education Act 2004 s 11(e) or (f) (see note 2).

10 Higher Education Act 2004 s 12(3) (as added: see note 7).

11 Higher Education Act 2004 s 17(1), (3). For the purposes of the law of defamation, absolute privilege attaches to the publication of: (1) any decision or recommendation made under the scheme by a person responsible for reviewing a qualifying complaint (s 17(2)(a)); and (2) any report under Sch 3 para 6 or Sch 3 para 7 (see PARA 1093) (s 17(2)(b)). As to privilege in the law of defamation see DEFAMATION vol 32 (2012) PARA 594 et seq.

12 Higher Education Act 2004 s 20(1). As to the jurisdiction of visitors see PARA 629. As to the exclusion of the visitor's jurisdiction in relation to certain disputes involving a member of staff or the qualifying institution (or both) see PARA 630.

13 Higher Education Act 2004 s 20(2).

14 Higher Education Act 2004 s 20(3)(a).

15 Higher Education Act 2004 s 20(3)(b).

1091. Designation of operator of statutory student complaints scheme. The Secretary of State[1] may, for the purposes of the provisions relating to the review of student complaints[2], designate a body corporate[3] as the designated operator[4] for England as from a date specified in the designation[5]. The Welsh Ministers[6] may, for the purposes of the provisions relating to the review of student complaints, designate a body corporate as the designated operator for Wales as from a date specified in the designation[7].

The Secretary of State or the Welsh Ministers may not designate a body in this way unless satisfied that the body:

(1)   meets all of the conditions[8] to be met by an operator of the student complaints scheme[9];

(2)   is providing a scheme for the review of qualifying complaints[10] that meets all of the conditions to be met by a student complaints scheme[11], or is proposing to provide such a scheme from a date not later than the effective date[12];

(3)   has consulted interested parties[13] about the provisions of that scheme[14]; and

(4)   consents to the designation[15].

If a body is so designated, the Secretary of State or the Welsh Ministers must, before the effective date, give the body notice of the designation[16] and publish notice of the designation in such manner as he or they think fit[17].

1   As to the Secretary of State see PARA 58.
2   Ie for the purposes of the Higher Education Act 2004 Pt 2 (ss 11–21).
3   As to bodies corporate see COMPANIES vol 14 (2009) PARA 2; CORPORATIONS vol 24 (2010) PARA 301 et seq.
4   In the Higher Education Act 2004 Pt 2 (ss 11–21), any reference to the 'designated operator' is, in relation to an institution in England, a reference to the body designated under s 13(1), and, in relation to an institution in Wales, a reference to the body designated under s 13(2) (see the text to notes 6–7): ss 13(5)(b), 21. As to the meanings of 'England' and 'Wales' see PARA 7 note 3.
5   Higher Education Act 2004 s 13(1). The Office of the Independent Adjudicator (OIA) was chosen to operate this scheme, to which all universities in England and Wales must subscribe. Its role is to review individual complaints by students against universities, although it has no regulatory powers over universities and cannot punish or fine them. The OIA is a company limited by guarantee and is governed by its memorandum and articles of association, as amended. The OIA is a registered charity, registered in England and Wales. At the date at which this volume states the law, additional providers offering higher education courses are being required to join the OIA Scheme; this will thus broaden the range of students able to use the scheme, and membership, rules and procedures will be updated accordingly. See further the OIA website.
6   As to the Welsh Ministers see PARA 59. The functions under the Higher Education Act 2004 Pt 2 (ss 11–21) were originally vested in the National Assembly for Wales and are now exercisable by the Welsh Ministers by virtue of the Government of Wales Act 2006 s 162(1), Sch 11 paras 30, 32.
7   Higher Education Act 2004 s 13(2). See note 5.
8   Ie all of the conditions set out in the Higher Education Act 2004 Sch 1 (see PARA 1092).
9   Higher Education Act 2004 s 13(3)(a).
10 As to the meaning of 'qualifying complaint' see PARA 1090.
11 Ie all of the conditions set out in the Higher Education Act 2004 Sch 2 (see PARA 1092).
12 Higher Education Act 2004 s 13(3)(b). In Pt 2 (ss 11–21), 'the effective date', in relation to the designation of a body corporate under s 13, means the date specified in the designation as the date from which the body is designated as designated operator: ss 13(5)(a), 21.
13 In the Higher Education Act 2004 Pt 2 (ss 11–21), 'interested parties', in relation to a scheme for the review of qualifying complaints provided or to be provided by a body corporate, means: (1) qualifying institutions in England or Wales (as the case may be); and (2) persons selected by the body corporate from amongst those it considers to represent the interests of students at qualifying institutions in England or Wales (as the case may be): s 21. As to the meaning of 'qualifying institution' see PARA 1090 note 2. As to the meaning of 'person' see PARA 7 note 6.
14 Higher Education Act 2004 s 13(3)(c). As to the exercise of the duty to consult see JUDICIAL REVIEW vol 61 (2010) PARA 627.
15 Higher Education Act 2004 s 13(3)(d).
16 Higher Education Act 2004 s 13(4)(a).
17 Higher Education Act 2004 s 13(4)(b).

1092.   Conditions to be met by a student complaints scheme and by the operator of a student complaints scheme.   The conditions to be met by an operator of the student complaints scheme[1] are: (1) that the body corporate[2] is a suitable person[3] to be the designated operator[4] (condition 'A')[5]; and (2) the body corporate is capable of providing in an effective manner, on and after the effective date[6], a scheme for the review of qualifying complaints[7] which meets all of the conditions set out in heads (a) to (h) below (condition 'B')[8].

The conditions to be met by a student complaints scheme[9] are:

(a)   that at any given time the scheme relates (as the case may be) to every institution in England, to every institution in Wales, or to every institution in England and Wales, that is a qualifying institution at that time[10];

(b)   that the scheme provides that every qualifying complaint made about the qualifying institutions to which it relates is capable of being referred under the scheme[11];

(c)   that the scheme requires every qualifying complaint referred under the scheme to be reviewed by an individual who is independent of the parties[12], and is suitable to review that complaint[13];

(d)   that the scheme requires a reviewer[14] to make a decision as to the extent to which a qualifying complaint is justified, and to make that decision as soon as reasonably practicable[15];

(e)   that the scheme provides that, in a case where a reviewer decides that a qualifying complaint is to any extent justified, the reviewer[16]: (i) may recommend the governing body of the institution to which the complaint relates to do anything specified in the recommendation (which may include the payment of sums so specified), and to refrain from doing anything so specified[17]; but (ii) may not require any person to do, or refrain from doing, anything[18];

(f)   that the scheme requires a reviewer to notify the parties to a qualifying complaint in writing[19] of the decision the reviewer has made[20], the reviewer's reasons for making that decision[21], and, if the reviewer makes a recommendation, that recommendation, and the reviewer's reasons for making that recommendation[22];

(g)   that the scheme does not require complainants to pay any fees in connection with the operation of the scheme[23];

(h)   that any fees payable under the scheme by the qualifying institutions to which it relates do not exceed the amount incurred by the operator, taking one year with another, in providing the scheme in relation to those institutions[24].

A scheme does not fail to meet the conditions set out in heads (a) to (h) above only because it also relates to bodies that are not qualifying institutions[25]; and a scheme which relates to such bodies does not fail to meet the conditions only because the provisions of the scheme that apply to such bodies do not meet those conditions[26].

1   Ie the conditions referred to in the Higher Education Act 2004 s 13(3)(a) (see PARA 1091) and other provisions of Pt 2 (ss 11–21): Sch 1 para 1. As to the designation of an operator of the statutory student complaints scheme see PARA 1091.
2   Ie the body corporate designated under the Higher Education Act 2004 s 13 (see PARA 1091).
3   As to the meaning of 'person' see PARA 7 note 6.
4   As to the meaning of 'designated operator' see PARA 1091 note 4.
5   Higher Education Act 2004 Sch 1 para 2.
6   As to the meaning of 'the effective date' see PARA 1091 note 12.
7   As to the meaning of 'qualifying complaint' see PARA 1090.
8   Higher Education Act 2004 Sch 1 para 3.
9   Ie the conditions referred to in the Higher Education Act 2004 s 13(3)(b) (see PARA 1091) and other provisions of Pt 2: Sch 2 para 1. Regulations made, in relation to schemes relating to qualifying institutions in England, by the Secretary of State or, in relation to schemes relating to qualifying institutions in Wales, by the Welsh Ministers may amend Sch 2 paras 1–11 (see the text to notes 10–26): Sch 2 para 12(1), (2). At the date at which this volume states the law, no regulations had been made under Sch 2 para 12. As to the meaning of 'qualifying institution' see PARA 1090 note 2. As to the meanings of 'England' and 'Wales' see PARA 7 note 3. As to the Secretary of State see PARA 58. As to the Welsh Ministers see PARA 59. The functions under Sch 2 were originally vested in the National Assembly for Wales and are now exercisable by the Welsh Ministers by virtue of the Government of Wales Act 2006 s 162(1), Sch 11 paras 30, 32.
10   Higher Education Act 2004 Sch 2 para 2.
11   Higher Education Act 2004 Sch 2 para 3(1). A scheme does not fail to meet this condition only because it contains some or all of the following: (1) provision that qualifying complaints are to be referred under the scheme within a time limit specified in, or determined in accordance with, the scheme (Sch 2 para 3(2)(a)); (2) provision that, where a qualifying complaint is made about a qualifying institution which provides an internal procedure for the review of complaints, the complaint is not to be referred under the scheme until the complainant has exhausted the internal procedure (Sch 2 para 3(2)(b)); (3) provision that a qualifying complaint is not to be

referred under the scheme if relevant proceedings have been concluded, or if relevant proceedings that have not been concluded have not been stayed (Sch 2 para 3(2)(c)). 'Relevant proceedings' means proceedings relating to the subject matter of the qualifying complaint that have been brought at first instance before a court or tribunal: Sch 2 para 3(3).

12 'Parties', in relation to a qualifying complaint, means: (1) the person making a qualifying complaint ('the complainant'); and (2) the governing body of the institution about which the complaint is made: Higher Education Act 2004 Sch 2 para 11. As to the meaning of 'governing body' see PARA 1090 note 1.

13 Higher Education Act 2004 Sch 2 para 4.

14 'Reviewer', in relation to the review of a qualifying complaint under a scheme, means the individual who is reviewing the complaint: Higher Education Act 2004 Sch 2 para 11.

15 Higher Education Act 2004 Sch 2 para 5(1). A scheme does not fail to meet this condition only because it contains provision that a reviewer may dismiss a qualifying complaint without consideration of the merits if the reviewer considers the complaint to be frivolous or vexatious: Sch 2 para 5(2).

16 Higher Education Act 2004 Sch 2 para 6.

17 Higher Education Act 2004 Sch 2 para 6(a).

18 Higher Education Act 2004 Sch 2 para 6(b).

19 As to the meaning of 'writing' see PARA 76 note 8.

20 Higher Education Act 2004 Sch 2 para 7(a).

21 Higher Education Act 2004 Sch 2 para 7(b).

22 Higher Education Act 2004 Sch 2 para 7(c).

23 Higher Education Act 2004 Sch 2 para 8.

24 Higher Education Act 2004 Sch 2 para 9.

25 Higher Education Act 2004 Sch 2 para 10(1).

26 Higher Education Act 2004 Sch 2 para 10(2).

1093. Duties of the designated operator of a student complaints scheme. The designated operator[1] of a student complaints scheme must comply with the duties set out in heads (1) to (7) below[2], which apply from the relevant date[3] and cease to apply only if the designation is terminated[4]. The duties are:

(1)   that the designated operator must provide a scheme for the review of qualifying complaints[5] which meets all of the conditions[6] to be met by a student complaints scheme[7];

(2)   that the designated operator must publish the latest version of the scheme in such manner as it thinks fit[8];

(3)   that the designated operator must not make any change to a provision of the scheme to which a condition to be met by a student complaints scheme[9] relates unless the operator has first consulted interested parties about the proposed change, and notified the Secretary of State[10] or the Welsh Ministers[11] (as the case requires) of the proposed change[12];

(4)   that the designated operator must comply with any requirements that the scheme imposes on it[13];

(5)   that the designated operator must produce an annual report on the scheme and its operation[14], and publish the report in such manner as it thinks fit[15];

(6)   that the designated body must comply with any request from the Secretary of State or the Welsh Ministers to conduct a review of the scheme or its operation (or any aspect of either of those matters)[16], and report the results of the review to the Secretary of State or the Welsh Ministers[17], within such time as he or they may specify[18];

(7)   that the designated operator must provide the Secretary of State or the Welsh Ministers with such information about itself, and the scheme and its operation, as the Secretary of State or the Welsh Ministers may reasonably require for the purposes of his or their functions under the provisions[19] relating to the review of student complaints[20].

1   As to the meaning of 'designated operator' see PARA 1091 note 4.
2   See the Higher Education Act 2004 s 14.
3   The 'relevant date' means: (1) in relation to the duties set out in the Higher Education Act 2004
    Sch 3 paras 3–5, 8 (see heads (2)–(4), (7) in the text), the date on which notice of designation is
    received in accordance with s 13(4)(a) (see PARA 1091); and (2) in relation to the duties set out
    in Sch 3 paras 2, 6–7 (see heads (1), (5), (6) in the text), the effective date of the designation:
    Sch 3 para 9(2). As to the meaning of 'the effective date' see PARA 1091 note 12.
4   See the Higher Education Act 2004 Sch 3 paras 1, 9(1). As to the termination of a designation
    see PARA 1094.
5   As to the meaning of 'qualifying complaint' see PARA 1090.
6   Ie the conditions set out in the Higher Education Act 2004 Sch 2 (see PARA 1092).
7   Higher Education Act 2004 Sch 3 para 2.
8   Higher Education Act 2004 Sch 3 para 3. Where by virtue of Sch 3 the designated operator is
    under a duty to publish information, it must, in choosing the manner in which the information
    is to be published, have regard to the object of making that information available to interested
    parties: Sch 3 para 10. As to the meaning of 'interested parties' see PARA 1091 note 13.
9   Ie a condition set out in the Higher Education Act 2004 Sch 2 (see PARA 1092).
10 As to the Secretary of State see PARA 58.
11 As to the Welsh Ministers see PARA 59. The functions under the Higher Education Act 2004
    Sch 3 were originally vested in the National Assembly for Wales and are now exercisable by the
    Welsh Ministers by virtue of the Government of Wales Act 2006 s 162(1), Sch 11 paras 30, 32.
12 Higher Education Act 2004 Sch 3 para 4.
13 Higher Education Act 2004 Sch 3 para 5.
14 Higher Education Act 2004 Sch 3 para 6(1)(a). The report must include information about: (1)
    complaints referred under the scheme (Sch 3 para 6(2)(a)); (2) the decisions and
    recommendations made by reviewers (Sch 3 para 6(2)(b)); (3) the extent to which
    recommendations made by reviewers have been followed (Sch 3 para 6(2)(c)); and (4) the way in
    which the operator has used the fees (if any) paid in connection with the scheme (Sch 3
    para 6(2)(d)).
15 Higher Education Act 2004 Sch 3 para 6(1)(b). As to publication of the report see note 8. As to
    privilege in relation to defamation attaching to the report see PARA 1090 note 8.
16 See the Higher Education Act 2004 Sch 3 para 7(1)(a), (2). In conducting the review, the
    designated body must comply with any particular requirements imposed by the Secretary of
    State or the Welsh Ministers: Sch 3 para 7(3).
17 See the Higher Education Act 2004 Sch 3 para 7(1)(b), (2). As to privilege in relation to
    defamation attaching to the report see PARA 1090 note 8.
18 See the Higher Education Act 2004 Sch 3 para 7(2).
19 Ie under the Higher Education Act 2004 Pt 2 (ss 11–21).
20 Higher Education Act 2004 Sch 3 para 8.

1094.   Duration of designation of the operator of a student complaints scheme.   The designation of a body as operator of a student complaints scheme[1] continues until it is terminated in accordance with the following provisions[2]. The designation is terminated:

(1)   if the designated operator[3] and the appropriate national authority[4] make an agreement which specifies a date when the designation is to terminate[5]; and in such a case, the designation is terminated on the date specified in the agreement[6];

(2)   if the designated operator gives the appropriate national authority notice which specifies a date when the designation is to terminate[7]; and in such a case, the designation is terminated on the date specified in the notice[8];

(3)   if the appropriate national authority gives the designated operator notice which specifies a date when the designation is to terminate[9]; and in such a case, the designation is terminated on the date specified in the notice[10];

(4)   if the designated operator ceases to exist[11]; and in such a case, the designation is terminated on the date when the operator ceases to exist[12].

Where the designated operator and the appropriate national authority have made an agreement under head (1) above[13], the designated operator has given notice under head (2) above[14], or where the appropriate national authority has given notice under head (3) above[15]: (a) the designated operator and the appropriate national authority may not make an agreement or a new agreement under head (1)[16]; (b) the designated operator may not give a notice or a new notice under head (2)[17]; and (c) the appropriate national authority may not give a notice (except in accordance with specified conditions[18]), nor give a new notice, under head (3)[19]. The original instrument of termination is superseded only if notice is given under head (3) above in accordance with the conditions mentioned in head (c)[20], or if the designation in question is terminated under head (4) above where the operator ceases to exist[21].

If the designation of a body is terminated, the appropriate national authority must publish notice of the termination in such manner as it thinks fit[22].

Where an agreement to terminate a designation has been made under head (1) above[23], notice to terminate a designation has been given under head (2) or (3) above[24], or the designated operator has ceased to exist[25], the appropriate national authority may by order[26] make such provision as it thinks fit for, or in connection with, the review of qualifying complaints[27]. Such provision may include any one or more of the following:

(i)   provision requiring the designated operator to provide the scheme[28] in accordance with specified[29] requirements[30];

(ii)   provision modifying, or requiring the designated operator to modify, the provisions of the scheme[31];

(iii) provision about the fees payable under the scheme, including provision requiring the repayment of fees already paid[32];

(iv)   provision for a specified person[33] to take over provision of the scheme[34];

(v)   provision for any provision relating to the review of student complaints[35] that applies in relation to a scheme provided by the designated operator to apply, with or without modifications, in relation to a scheme provided by a person specified by virtue of head (iv) above[36];

(vi)   provision for a specified person[37] to review qualifying complaints, or specified descriptions of qualifying complaints, otherwise than under the scheme[38];

(vii) provision requiring the payment of fees by the governing bodies[39] of qualifying institutions[40] to a person specified by virtue of head (vi) above[41];

(viii) provision requiring the designated operator to provide such information and assistance as the appropriate national authority considers necessary for the appropriate national authority to make appropriate provision[42], or for any person to comply with, or act under or in accordance with, such provision[43].

1 Ie the designation of a body under the Higher Education Act 2004 s 13 (see PARA 1091).
2 See the Higher Education Act 2004 s 16(1), Sch 4 para 1.
3 As to the meaning of 'designated operator' see PARA 1091 note 4.
4 Ie the Secretary of State or the Welsh Ministers, as the case may be. As to the Secretary of State see PARA 58. As to the Welsh Ministers see PARA 59. The functions under the Higher Education

Act 2004 Sch 4 in relation to Wales were originally vested in the National Assembly for Wales and are now exercisable by the Welsh Ministers by virtue of the Government of Wales Act 2006 s 162(1), Sch 11 paras 30, 32. As to the meaning of 'Wales' see PARA 7 note 3.

5   Higher Education Act 2004 Sch 4 para 2. Such an agreement may not be varied or cancelled: Sch 4 para 13(1). Accordingly, such an agreement continues in force until the designation is terminated in accordance with the agreement, or until the agreement is superseded in accordance with Sch 4 para 12 (see the text to notes 20–21): Sch 4 para 13(2).

6   Higher Education Act 2004 Sch 4 para 3.

7   Higher Education Act 2004 Sch 4 para 4(1). Such notice is valid only if the period between the date when the notice is given, and the date specified in the notice, is one year or longer: Sch 4 para 4(2). Such notice may not be varied or revoked: Sch 4 para 14(1). Accordingly, such notice continues in force until the designation is terminated in accordance with the notice, or until the notice is superseded in accordance with Sch 4 para 12 (see the text to notes 20–21): Sch 4 para 14(2).

8   Higher Education Act 2004 Sch 4 para 5.

9   Higher Education Act 2004 Sch 4 para 6(1). Such notice may not be given unless the appropriate national authority is no longer satisfied that the designated operator meets all of the conditions in Sch 1 (see PARA 1092) (Sch 4 para 6(2)(a)), or is satisfied that the designated operator has failed to comply with s 14 (see PARA 1093) (Sch 4 para 6(2)(b)). Notice under Sch 4 para 6 is valid only if the period between the date when the notice is given, and the date specified in the notice, is such as the appropriate national authority considers reasonable: Sch 4 para 6(3). The notice may not be varied or revoked: Sch 4 para 14(1). Accordingly, such notice continues in force until the designation is terminated in accordance with the notice, or until the notice is superseded in accordance with Sch 4 para 12 (see the text to notes 20–21): Sch 4 para 14(2).

10   Higher Education Act 2004 Sch 4 para 7.

11   Higher Education Act 2004 Sch 4 para 8.

12   Higher Education Act 2004 Sch 4 para 9.

13   Higher Education Act 2004 Sch 4 para 10(1)(a).

14   Higher Education Act 2004 Sch 4 para 10(1)(b).

15   Higher Education Act 2004 Sch 4 para 10(1)(c).

16   Higher Education Act 2004 Sch 4 para 11(1)(a).

17   Higher Education Act 2004 Sch 4 para 11(1)(b).

18   The appropriate national authority may give a notice under the Higher Education Act 2004 Sch 4 para 6 (see head (3) in the text) if: (1) the original instrument of termination is an agreement under Sch 4 para 2 (see head (1) in the text) or a notice under Sch 4 para 4 (see head (2) in the text) (Sch 4 para 11(2)(a)); and (2) the termination date specified in the notice under Sch 4 para 6 falls before the termination date specified in the original instrument of termination (Sch 4 para 11(2)(b)). For the purposes of Sch 4 Pt 2 paras 10–14, 'original instrument of termination' means the agreement or notice referred to in Sch 4 para 10(1) (see the text to notes 13–15); and 'termination date' means the date specified in an agreement under Sch 4 para 2, or notice under Sch 4 para 4 or Sch 4 para 6, as the date when the designation in question is to terminate: Sch 4 para 10(2).

19   Higher Education Act 2004 Sch 4 para 11(1)(c).

20   See the Higher Education Act 2004 Sch 4 para 12(a).

21   See the Higher Education Act 2004 Sch 4 para 12(b).

22   Higher Education Act 2004 s 16(2).

23   Higher Education Act 2004 s 18(1)(a).

24   Higher Education Act 2004 s 18(1)(b).

25   Higher Education Act 2004 s 18(1)(c).

26   At the date at which this volume states the law no such order had been made.

27   Higher Education Act 2004 s 18(1). As to the meaning of 'qualifying complaint' see PARA 1090.

28   For the purposes of the Higher Education Act 2004 s 18, 'the scheme' means the scheme for the review of qualifying complaints that the designated operator provides or has been providing: s 18(4).

29   'Specified' means specified in an order under the Higher Education Act 2004 s 18: s 18(4).

30   Higher Education Act 2004 s 18(2)(a).

31   Higher Education Act 2004 s 18(2)(b).

32   Higher Education Act 2004 s 18(2)(c).

33   The Secretary of State or the Welsh Ministers may be specified by virtue of the Higher Education Act 2004 s 18(2)(d): s 18(3). As to the meaning of 'person' see PARA 7 note 6.

34   Higher Education Act 2004 s 18(2)(d).

35   Ie any provision of the Higher Education Act 2004 Pt 2 (ss 11–21).

36 Higher Education Act 2004 s 18(2)(e).
37 The Secretary of State or the Welsh Ministers may not be specified by virtue of the Higher Education Act 2004 s 18(2)(f): s 18(3).
38 Higher Education Act 2004 s 18(2)(f).
39 As to the meaning of 'governing body' see PARA 1090 note 1.
40 As to the meaning of 'qualifying institution' see PARA 1090 note 2.
41 Higher Education Act 2004 s 18(2)(g).
42 Ie provision under the Higher Education Act 2004 s 18 (see the text to notes 23–41).
43 Higher Education Act 2004 s 18(2)(h)(ii).

(2) STUDENT SUPPORT

(i) The Statutory System for providing Financial Support for Students

A. INTRODUCTION

1095. The statutory framework. The current system governing the provision of financial support for students, under which the Secretary of State[1] or, as appropriate, the Welsh Ministers[2] may make grants or loans for the purpose, was introduced as from 16 July 1998 by the Teaching and Higher Education Act 1998[3]. This system replaced the system formerly operated under the Education Act 1962 (and related provisions), which regulated the making of awards and grants by local authorities[4], and the system under the Education (Student Loans) Act 1990, which made provision in connection with the making of loans to students in higher education[5].

The former legislation continues, however, to have effect in certain circumstances. The Education Act 1962 and its associated provisions, and any subordinate legislation made or to be made thereunder, continue to have effect with respect to or otherwise in connection with awards bestowed before 1 January 1999 or to the bestowing of awards, or awards bestowed, on any student attending prescribed courses[6]. The Education (Student Loans) Act 1990 and subordinate legislation made or to be made thereunder continue to have effect in relation to loans made before 13 August 1998 or to the making of loans to students attending prescribed courses[7]. The provisions of the Education (Student Loans) Act 1990 relating to the assignment of public sector loans and the making of arrangements in connection with such assignments[8] continue in operation[9].

Provision is made for the Secretary of State to repay amounts payable in respect of loans received under the Education (Student Loans) Act 1990[10] or under the Teaching and Higher Education Act 1998[11] by eligible persons who fulfil prescribed conditions[12]. Provision is made also for reducing or extinguishing the amounts payable in respect of such loans by such persons[13].

1 As to the Secretary of State see PARA 58.
2 As to the Welsh Ministers see PARA 59.
3 Ie the Teaching and Higher Education Act 1998 Pt II Ch I (ss 22–28) (see PARA 1096 et seq). As to grants made to Higher Education Funding Councils see PARA 712.
4 The legislation regulating the making of grants and awards by local authorities (ie the Education Act 1962 ss 1–4, Sch 1, and provisions of the Education Act 1973, the Education (Fees and Awards) Act 1983, and the Education Reform Act 1988) was repealed by the Teaching and Higher Education Act 1998 Sch 4, with effect from 1 January 1999: see the Teaching and Higher Education Act 1998 (Commencement No 4 and Transitional Provisions) Order 1998, SI 1998/3237, art 2.
5 The Education (Student Loans) Act 1990 was repealed by the Teaching and Higher Education Act 1998 Sch 4, with effect from 13 August 1998: see the Teaching and Higher Education

Act 1998 (Commencement No 2 and Transitional Provisions) Order 1998, SI 1998/2004, art 2. The Education (Student Loans) Acts 1996 and 1998, which amended the Education (Student Loans) Act 1990, were also repealed as from that date.

6 See the Teaching and Higher Education Act 1998 (Commencement No 4 and Transitional Provisions) Order 1998, SI 1998/3237, arts 3, 4.

7 See the Teaching and Higher Education Act 1998 (Commencement No 2 and Transitional Provisions) Order 1998, SI 1998/2004, arts 3(1), (2)(a), 4.

8 Ie the Education (Student Loans) Act 1990 s 1A (repealed).

9 See the Teaching and Higher Education Act 1998 (Commencement No 2 and Transitional Provisions) Order 1998, SI 1998/2004, art 3(2)(b), (c).

10 Ie under the Education (Student Loans) Act 1990 s 1 (repealed).

11 Ie under the Teaching and Higher Education Act 1998 s 22 (see PARAS 1096–1097).

12 See the Education Act 2002 s 186(1); and PARA 1104.

13 See the Education Act 2002 s 186(1); and PARA 1104.

B. FINANCIAL SUPPORT

1096. Provision of financial support for students. Regulations[1] must make provision authorising or requiring the Secretary of State or the Welsh Ministers[2] to make grants or loans, for any prescribed[3] purposes, to eligible students in connection with their undertaking higher education courses[4], or further education courses[5], which are designated[6] by or under the regulations[7]. Such regulations may, in particular, make provision:

(1) for determining whether a person is an eligible student in relation to any available[8] grant or loan[9];

(2) prescribing, in relation to any such grant or loan and an academic year, the maximum amount available to any person for any prescribed purpose for that year[10];

(3) where the amount of any such grant or loan may vary to any extent according to a person's circumstances, for determining, or enabling the determination of the amount required or authorised to be paid to him[11];

(4) prescribing categories of attendance on higher education courses or further education courses which are to qualify for any purposes of the regulations[12];

(5) for any grant[13] to be made available on such terms and conditions as may be prescribed by, or determined by the Secretary of State or Welsh Ministers under, the regulations, including terms and conditions requiring repayments to be made in circumstances so prescribed or determined[14];

(6) requiring the making of payments in respect of any such grant to be suspended or terminated in any such circumstances[15];

(7) prescribing requirements or other provisions, whether as to repayment or otherwise, which are for the time being to apply in relation to loans[16] (including requirements or other provisions taking effect during the currency of such loans so as to add to, or otherwise modify[17], those for the time being applying in relation to the loans)[18];

(8) authorising grants in respect of fees payable in connection with courses to be paid directly to institutions charging the fees[19];

(9) requiring prescribed amounts payable to eligible students under loans[20] to be paid directly to institutions to whom those persons are liable to make payments[21];

(10) modifying any enactment or instrument (whenever passed or made) so as to provide for the treatment, in connection with any calculation with

respect to the income (however defined) of persons to whom grants or loans are made[22], of amounts due from or payable to such persons under such grants or loans[23];

(11) for appeals with respect to matters arising under the regulations (including provision for determining, or enabling the determination of the procedure to be followed in connection with appeals)[24].

1 'Regulations' means regulations made by the Secretary of State or, in relation to Wales, the Welsh Ministers (see note 2) under the Teaching and Higher Education Act 1998: see s 43(1); Higher Education Act 2004 s 44(1). As to the Secretary of State see PARA 58. As to the meaning of 'Wales' see PARA 7 note 3. As to the Welsh Ministers see PARA 59.

2 In relation to Wales, the functions of the Secretary of State under the Teaching and Higher Education Act 1998 s 22 are transferred to the Welsh Ministers, except so far as they relate to the making of any provision authorised by s 22(2)(a), (2)(c), (2)(j) or s 22(2)(k) (see heads (1), (3), (10) and (11) in the text), s 22(3)(e) or s 22(3)(f) (see note 18): Higher Education Act 2004 s 44(1). The functions of the Secretary of State under the Teaching and Higher Education Act 1998 s 22 are exercisable concurrently with the Welsh Ministers so far as they relate to the making in relation to Wales of any provision authorised by s 22(2)(a), (2)(c) or s 22(2)(k): Higher Education Act 2004 s 44(2). The functions under the Teaching and Higher Education Act 1998 s 22 (as so transferred by the Higher Education Act 2004 s 44) were originally vested in the National Assembly for Wales and are now exercisable by the Welsh Ministers by virtue of the Government of Wales Act 2006 s 162(1), Sch 11 paras 30, 32.

3 'Prescribed' means prescribed by regulations: Teaching and Higher Education Act 1998 s 43(1).

4 Teaching and Higher Education Act 1998 s 22(1)(a). For the purposes of Pt II Ch I (ss 22–28), 'higher education course' has the meaning given by regulations under s 22: s 28(1). Regulations under s 22 may provide for courses provided wholly or partly outside the United Kingdom to be higher education courses for the purposes of Pt II Ch 1: s 28(2). As to the meaning of 'United Kingdom' see PARA 73 note 3. As to the regulations made see note 7.

5 Teaching and Higher Education Act 1998 s 22(1)(b). For the purposes of Pt II Ch I (ss 22–28), 'further education course' has the meaning given by regulations under s 22: s 28(1). Regulations under s 22 may provide for courses provided wholly or partly outside the United Kingdom to be further education courses for the purposes of Pt II Ch 1: s 28(2). As to the regulations made see note 7.

6 Ie designated for the purposes of the Teaching and Higher Education Act 1998 s 22.

7 Teaching and Higher Education Act 1998 s 22(1) (amended by the Learning and Skills Act 2000 s 146(1), (2)(a)). As to the transfer of the functions in relation to the making or granting of loans to eligible students see PARA 1098. As to the delegation of such functions see PARA 1099. As to the sale of student loans see PARA 1105 et seq.

As to the regulations currently having effect under the Teaching and Higher Education Act 1998 s 22 see the Assembly Learning Grant (Further Education) Regulations 2007, SI 2007/2314; the Education (Student Loans) (Repayment) Regulations 2009, SI 2009/470 (amended by SI 2010/661; SI 2011/784; SI 2012/836; SI 2012/1309; SI 2013/388; SI 2013/591; SI 2013/607; SI 2013/1881; and SI 2014/651); the Assembly Learning Grant (Further Education) Regulations 2009, SI 2009/2158; the Assembly Learning Grants and Loans (Higher Education) (Wales) Regulations 2009, SI 2009/2737 (amended by SI 2011/1043); the Cancellation of Student Loans for Living Costs Liability (Wales) Regulations 2010, SI 2010/1704; the Education (Student Support) Regulations 2011, SI 2011/1986 (amended by SI 2012/1653; SI 2013/235; SI 2013/630; SI 2013/1728; SI 2013/3106; SI 2014/1766, SI 2014/2103, and SI 2014/2765); the Cancellation of Student Loans for Living Costs Liability (Wales) Regulations 2011, SI 2011/1654; the Cancellation of Student Loans for Living Costs Liability (Wales) Regulations 2012, SI 2012/1518; the Cancellation of Student Loans for Living Costs Liability (Wales) Regulations 2013, SI 2013/1396; the Cancellation of Student Loans for Living Costs Liability (Wales) Regulations 2014, SI 2014/1314; the Education (Student Support) (Wales) Regulations 2015, SI 2015/54 (amended by SI 2015/1505); the Cancellation of Student Loans for Living Costs Liability (Wales) Regulations 2015, SI 2015/1418; and the Education (Student Support) (Wales) (Amendment) Regulations 2015, SI 2015/1505. As to the test for eligibility in relation to students from outside the United Kingdom see *R (on the application of Haracoglou) v Department for Education and Skills* [2001] EWHC 678 (Admin), [2002] ELR 177, [2001] All ER (D) 92 (Aug) (test for determining residency was whether student would have been resident in the United Kingdom in any event, even if she had not been completing her degree course); Case C-209/03 *R (on the application of Bidar) v Ealing London Borough Council* [2005] QB 812, [2005] All ER (EC) 687 (Mar), ECJ (national legislation could not make settlement a condition of eligibility while precluding a national of another member state from obtaining the status of settled person as a student) (both cases decided under previous legislation); *R (on the application of Arogundade) v Secretary of State for Business, Innovation and Skills* [2013] EWCA Civ 823, [2013] All ER (D) 177 (Jul) (eligibility on ground of being ordinarily resident could not include period of unlawful residence); *R (on the application of Tigere) v Secretary of State for Business, Innovation and Skills* [2014] EWCA Civ 1216, [2015] ELR 47, [2014] All ER (D) 85 (Sep) (Secretary of State justified in promulgating bright line rule on basic category of eligible students).

The following regulations made under the Teaching and Higher Education Act 1998 s 22 provide for limited numbers of eligible applicants to receive financial support by reason of their attendance at certain designated courses: the Education (Student Support) (European University Institute) Regulations 2010, SI 2010/447 (amended by SI 2011/83; SI 2011/2430; SI 2012/3059; SI 2013/630; and SI 2013/1728); the Education (Student Support) (College of Europe) Regulations 2010, SI 2010/960; the Education (Student Support) Regulations 2011, SI 2011/1986 (as so amended); the Further Education Loans Regulations 2012, SI 2012/1818 (amended by SI 2014/290; SI 2014/1766; and SI 2015/181); and the Education (European University Institute) (Wales) Regulations 2014, SI 2014/3037.

8   Ie available under the Teaching and Higher Education Act 1998 s 22.
9   Teaching and Higher Education Act 1998 s 22(2)(a). As to such loans see also note 18.
10   Teaching and Higher Education Act 1998 s 22(2)(b).
11   Teaching and Higher Education Act 1998 s 22(2)(c).
12   Teaching and Higher Education Act 1998 s 22(2)(d).
13   Ie under the Teaching and Higher Education Act 1998 s 22.
14   Teaching and Higher Education Act 1998 s 22(2)(e).
15   Teaching and Higher Education Act 1998 s 22(2)(f).
16   Ie under the Teaching and Higher Education Act 1998 s 22.
17   As to the meaning of 'modify' see PARA 21 note 15.
18   Teaching and Higher Education Act 1998 s 22(2)(g). The provision which may be made by virtue of s 22(2)(g) in relation to loans under s 22 includes provision: (1) for such loans to bear compound interest at such rates, and calculated in such manner, as may be prescribed from time to time (s 22(3)(a)); (2) for such loans to be repaid in such manner, at such times, and to such person or body as may be prescribed from time to time (s 22(3)(b)); (3) for the payment, in respect of amounts overpaid by borrowers, of interest at such rate, and calculated in such manner, as may be determined by the Secretary of State or Welsh Ministers from time to time (s 22(3)(c)); (4) for a borrower not to be liable to make any repayment in respect of such a loan during such period as may be prescribed from time to time, or in such circumstances as may be so prescribed, including provision for the cancellation of any further such liability of the borrower in any such circumstances (s 22(3)(d)); (5) with respect to sums which a borrower receives, or is entitled to receive, under such a loan after the commencement of his bankruptcy or the date of the sequestration of his estate (s 22(3)(e)); (6) with respect to the effect of bankruptcy upon a borrower's liability to make repayments in respect of such a loan (whether the repayments relate to sums which the borrower receives, or is entitled to receive, before or after the commencement of the bankruptcy) (s 22(3)(f) (added by the Higher Education Act 2004 s 42(1))); (7) with respect to sums which a borrower receives, or is entitled to receive, under such a loan before or after a voluntary arrangement under the Insolvency Act 1986 Pt 8 (ss 252–263G) or the Insolvency (Northern Ireland) Order 1989, SI 1989/2405, Pt 8 (individual voluntary arrangements: see BANKRUPTCY AND INDIVIDUAL INSOLVENCY vol 5 (2013) PARA 43 et seq) takes effect in respect of the borrower (Teaching and Higher Education Act 1998 s 22(3)(g) (s 22(3)(g), (h) added by the Apprenticeships, Skills, Children and Learning Act 2009 s 257(1), (2))); (8) excluding or modifying the application of the Insolvency Act 1986 Pt 8 or the Insolvency (Northern Ireland) Order 1989, SI 1989/2405, Pt 8, in relation to liability to make repayments in respect of such a loan (whether the repayments relate to sums which the borrower receives, or is entitled to receive, before or after a voluntary arrangement takes effect in respect of the borrower) (Teaching and Higher Education Act 1998 s 22(3)(h) (as so added)). As to the meaning of 'person' see PARA 7 note 6.

In relation to loans under the Teaching and Higher Education Act 1998 s 22:
(a)   the rates prescribed by regulations made in pursuance of s 22(3)(a) must be lower than those prevailing on the market (s 22(4)(a)(i) (s 22(4)(a) substituted (in relation to a student who begins a course on or after 1 September 2012) by the Education Act 2011 s 76(1))); or must be no higher than those prevailing on the market, where the other terms on which such loans are provided are more favourable to borrowers than those prevailing on the market (Teaching and Higher Education Act 1998 s 22(4)(a)(ii) (as so substituted)); and

(b)   such regulations may make provision, for the purpose of calculating the interest to be borne by such loans, for repayments by borrowers to be treated as having been made or received on such date or dates as may be prescribed by the regulations (s 22(4)(b)).

For prescribed exceptions to the rate limits imposed by s 22(4)(a) see the Education (Student Loans) (Repayment) (Amendment) (No 2) Regulations 2012, SI 2012/1309, reg 15.The Consumer Credit Act 1974 (see CONSUMER CREDIT vol 21 (2011) PARA 1 et seq) does not regulate loans made in accordance with regulations under the Teaching and Higher Education Act 1998 s 22: Sale of Student Loans Act 2008 s 8(1). This provision must be treated as always having had effect: s 8(2) (amended by SI 2013/1881). As to the Sale of Student Loans Act 2008 s 8 see further PARA 1097 note 2.

19 Teaching and Higher Education Act 1998 s 22(2)(h) (amended by the Learning and Skills Act 2000 ss 146(1), (2)(b), 153, Sch 11).
20 Ie under the Teaching and Higher Education Act 1998 s 22.
21 Teaching and Higher Education Act 1998 s 22(2)(i) (amended by the Higher Education Act 2004 s 43).
22 Ie under the Teaching and Higher Education Act 1998 s 22.
23 Teaching and Higher Education Act 1998 s 22(2)(j).
24 Teaching and Higher Education Act 1998 s 22(2)(k).

1097.   Arrangements for the recovery of loans. Regulations[1] may make such provision as the Secretary of State considers necessary or expedient in connection with the recovery of amounts due from borrowers under loans[2]. The regulations may include provision for:

(1)   imposing on employers[3], or (as the case may be) such other persons or bodies as may be prescribed[4], requirements with respect to: (a) the making of deductions in respect of amounts so due (or, in any prescribed circumstances, amounts assessed in accordance with the regulations to be so due) from emoluments payable to borrowers[5]; (b) the collection by other means of such amounts[6]; and (c) the transmission of amounts so deducted or collected to the Secretary of State in accordance with directions given by him[7];

(2)   imposing on employers, or such other persons or bodies as may be prescribed, requirements with respect to the keeping and production of records for such purposes as may be prescribed[8];

(3)   imposing on borrowers requirements with respect to the provision of such information[9] and the keeping and production of such documents and records[10] relating to their income as may be prescribed[11];

(4)   requiring the payment, by persons or bodies to whom requirements imposed in pursuance of any of heads (1) to (3) above apply, of penalties in cases of non-compliance with such requirements (or penalties otherwise framed by reference to such requirements)[12], and interest in respect of periods when such penalties are due but unpaid[13];

(5)   requiring the payment by borrowers, in respect of periods when amounts due under their loans are unpaid, of interest[14] or both such interest and one or more surcharges (together with further interest in respect of periods when such surcharges are due but unpaid)[15];

(6)   enabling the Secretary of State to require the reimbursement by borrowers of costs or expenses of any prescribed description incurred by him in connection with the recovery of unpaid amounts[16];

(7)   applying or extending with or without modification[17], for purposes connected with the recovery of amounts under regulations[18], any of the provisions of the Taxes Acts[19] or of PAYE regulations[20];

(8)   determining the priority as between certain deductions falling to be made by employers[21] and other deductions falling to be made[22] from emoluments payable to borrowers[23].

1 'Regulations' means regulations made by the Secretary of State under the Teaching and Higher
   Education Act 1998: s 43(1). Regulations made under s 22 by the Secretary of State must
   provide that no provision made by virtue of s 22(5) is to apply in relation to any loan made
   under s 22 by the Welsh Ministers unless the Welsh Ministers: (1) have determined, in relation to
   any loan or description of loan, that repayments are to be collected by the Commissioners for
   Her Majesty's Revenue and Customs; and (2) have given notice of that determination to the
   Secretary of State and to the person liable to make the repayments: Higher Education Act 2004
   s 44(3) (amended by virtue of the Commissioners for Her Majesty's Revenue and Customs
   Act 2005 s 50). As to the Secretary of State see PARA 58. As to the Welsh Ministers see PARA 59.
   As to the making of loans see PARA 1096. As to the regulations made under the Teaching and
   Higher Education Act 1998 s 22(5) see the Education (Student Loans) (Repayment)
   Regulations 2009, SI 2009/470 (amended by SI 2010/661; SI 2011/784; SI 2012/836;
   SI 2012/1309; SI 2013/388; SI 2013/591; SI 2013/607; SI 2013/1881; and SI 2014/651).
2 Teaching and Higher Education Act 1998 s 22(5). The Consumer Credit Act 1974 (see
   CONSUMER CREDIT vol 21 (2011) PARA 1 et seq) does not regulate loans made in accordance
   with regulations under the Teaching and Higher Education Act 1998 s 22: Sale of Student Loans
   Act 2008 s 8(1). This provision must be treated as always having had effect: s 8(2) (amended by
   SI 2013/1881). As to the transfer of the Secretary of State's functions in relation to the recovery
   of amounts due in respect of loans made to eligible students see PARA 1098. As to the delegation
   of such functions see PARA 1099. As to the sale of student loans see PARA 1105 et seq.
3 'Employers' means persons who make payments of, or on account of, PAYE income: Teaching
   and Higher Education Act 1998 s 22(6)(a) (amended by the Income Tax (Earnings and Pensions)
   Act 2003 s 722, Sch 6 Pt 2 para 236(b)). 'PAYE income' has the meaning given by the Income
   Tax (Earnings and Pensions) Act 2003 s 683 (see INCOME TAXATION vol 58 (2014) PARA 927):
   Interpretation Act 1978 s 5, Sch 1 (definition added by the Income Tax (Earnings and Pensions)
   Act 2003 s 722, Sch 6 Pt 2 para 148). As to the meaning of 'person' see PARA 7 note 6.
4 'Prescribed' means prescribed by regulations: Teaching and Higher Education Act 1998 s 43(1).
5 Teaching and Higher Education Act 1998 s 22(5)(a)(i).
6 Teaching and Higher Education Act 1998 s 22(5)(a)(ii).
7 Teaching and Higher Education Act 1998 s 22(5)(a)(iii).
8 Teaching and Higher Education Act 1998 s 22(5)(b).
9 Teaching and Higher Education Act 1998 s 22(5)(c)(i).
10 Teaching and Higher Education Act 1998 s 22(5)(c)(ii).
11 Teaching and Higher Education Act 1998 s 22(5)(c).
12 See the Teaching and Higher Education Act 1998 s 22(5)(d)(i).
13 Teaching and Higher Education Act 1998 s 22(5)(d)(ii). Interest required to be paid, by virtue of
   s 22(5)(d), by regulations under s 22 must be paid without any deduction of income tax and
   must not be taken into account in computing any income, profits or losses for any tax purposes:
   s 22(10) (added by the Finance Act 2003 s 147(3)).
14 Teaching and Higher Education Act 1998 s 22(5)(e)(i). The interest in question is applied to
   such amounts at a rate calculated otherwise than in accordance with s 22(4)(a) (see PARA 1096
   note 18): see s 22(5)(e)(i).
15 Teaching and Higher Education Act 1998 s 22(5)(e)(ii).
16 Teaching and Higher Education Act 1998 s 22(5)(f).
17 As to the meaning of 'modification' see PARA 21 note 15.
18 Ie made by virtue of the Teaching and Higher Education Act 1998 s 22(5).
19 As to the meaning of 'the Taxes Acts' see the Taxes Management Act 1970 s 118(1); and
   INCOME TAXATION vol 58 (2014) PARA 24 (definition applied by the Teaching and Higher
   Education Act 1998 s 22(6)(b)).
20 Teaching and Higher Education Act 1998 s 22(5)(g) (amended by the Income Tax (Earnings and
   Pensions) Act 2003 Sch 6 Pt 2 para 236(a)). 'PAYE regulations' means regulations under the
   Income Tax (Earnings and Pensions) Act 2003 s 684 (see INCOME TAXATION vol 58 (2014) PARA
   932): Interpretation Act 1978 s 5, Sch 1 (definition added by the Income Tax (Earnings and
   Pensions) Act 2003 s 722, Sch 6 Pt 2 para 148).
21 Ie deductions falling to be made by virtue of the Teaching and Higher Education Act 1998
   s 22(5)(a)(i) (see head (1)(a) in the text).
22 Ie falling to be made by virtue of other enactments (whenever passed).
23 Teaching and Higher Education Act 1998 s 22(5)(h).

1098.   Transfer of functions relating to student support. If the appropriate
national authority[1] so determines, any function[2] exercisable by it by virtue of
provisions relating to the making of grants or loans to students or the recovery of

amounts due in respect of such loans[3] is, to such extent as is specified in the determination, exercisable instead by such body as is so specified which is either[4]:

(1) a local authority[5]; or

(2) the governing body of an institution with which eligible students[6] are undertaking courses[7].

A body by whom any function is for the time being so exercisable must comply with any directions given by the appropriate national authority as to the exercise of that function[8]. The appropriate national authority may pay, to any body or person[9] by whom any transferred function is so exercisable, such amounts as the appropriate national authority considers appropriate for the purpose of meeting expenditure incurred or to be incurred by that body or person in making[10] grants or loans[11], or by way of administrative expenses[12], in, or in connection with, the exercise of that function[13].

1 Ie the Secretary of State or, in relation to Wales, the Welsh Ministers. The functions of the Secretary of State under the Teaching and Higher Education Act 1998 s 23 are transferred to the Welsh Ministers so far as they relate to functions which are exercisable by the Welsh Ministers under regulations under s 22 (see PARA 1096): Higher Education Act 2004 s 44(4). As to the Secretary of State see PARA 58. As to the meaning of 'Wales' see PARA 7 note 3. As to the Welsh Ministers see PARA 59. The functions under the Teaching and Higher Education Act 1998 s 23 (as so transferred) were originally vested in the National Assembly for Wales and are now exercisable by the Welsh Ministers by virtue of the Government of Wales Act 2006 s 162(1), Sch 11 paras 30, 32.

2 As to the meaning of 'function' see PARA 18 note 5. In relation to any function which, by virtue of the Teaching and Higher Education Act 1998 s 23(1) is exercisable to a specified extent, references in any other provision of s 23 to the exercise of that function are accordingly to its exercise to that extent: s 23(10). As to the delegation of functions see PARA 1099.

3 Ie any function exercisable by virtue of regulations under the Teaching and Higher Education Act 1998 s 22 (see PARAS 1096–1097).

4 Teaching and Higher Education Act 1998 s 23(1). As to the bringing of appeals arising out of the exercise of transferred functions see PARA 1100.

5 Teaching and Higher Education Act 1998 s 23(1)(a) (amended by SI 2010/1158). As to the meaning of 'local authority' see PARA 25 (definition applied by the Teaching and Higher Education Act 1998 s 43(1) (amended by SI 2010/1158)).

6 Ie within the meaning of the regulations under the Teaching and Higher Education Act 1998 s 22 (see PARAS 1096–1097).

7 Teaching and Higher Education Act 1998 s 23(1)(b) (amended by the Learning and Skills Act 2000 s 146(1), (3)).

8 Teaching and Higher Education Act 1998 s 23(2). Where any function is so exercisable by a local authority, the functions are taken to be a function of that authority for the purposes of:

(1) in the case of an authority which is not operating executive arrangements, the Local Government Act 1972 s 101 (see LOCAL GOVERNMENT vol 69 (2009) PARA 370) (Teaching and Higher Education Act 1998 s 23(3)(a) (s 23(3) substituted, in relation to England, by SI 2001/2237; and, in relation to Wales, by SI 2002/808; and amended by SI 2010/1158));

(2) the Deregulation and Contracting Out Act 1994 s 70 (see LOCAL GOVERNMENT vol 69 (2009) PARA 407) (Teaching and Higher Education Act 1998 s 23(3)(b) (as so substituted and amended)); and

(3) in the case of an authority which is operating executive arrangements, the Local Government Act 2000 s 13 (see LOCAL GOVERNMENT vol 69 (2009) PARA 324) (Teaching and Higher Education Act 1998 s 23(3)(c) (as so substituted and amended)); and accordingly: (a) if, or to the extent that, that function is the responsibility of the executive of that authority the Local Government Act 2000 ss 14–16 (see LOCAL GOVERNMENT vol 69 (2009) PARAS 357–359), and any regulations made under ss 17–20 (see LOCAL GOVERNMENT vol 69 (2009) PARAS 360–363), apply (Teaching and Higher Education Act 1998 s 23(3)(c)(i) (as so substituted and amended)); or (b) if, or to the extent that, that function is not the responsibility of that executive, the Local

Government Act 1972 s 101 (see LOCAL GOVERNMENT vol 69 (2009) PARA 370) applies (Teaching and Higher Education Act 1998 s 23(3)(c)(ii) (as so substituted and amended)).

As to the meanings of 'executive arrangements' and 'executive' see the Local Government Act 2000 ss 10–11 (see LOCAL GOVERNMENT vol 69 (2009) PARAS 303, 327) (definitions applied by the Teaching and Higher Education Act 1998 s 23(11) (added, in relation to England, by SI 2001/2237; and, in relation to Wales, by SI 2002/808)).

9   As to the meaning of 'person' see PARA 7 note 6.
10 Ie under the Teaching and Higher Education Act 1998 s 22 (see PARA 1096).
11 Teaching and Higher Education Act 1998 s 23(7)(a)(i).
12 Teaching and Higher Education Act 1998 s 23(7)(a)(ii).
13 Teaching and Higher Education Act 1998 s 23(7)(a). Any payment under s 23(7)(a) may be made subject to such terms and conditions as the appropriate national authority may determine; and any such conditions may in particular: (1) require the provision of returns or other information before any such payment is made (s 23(8)(a)); and (2) relate to the use of the amount paid or require the repayment in specified circumstances of all or part of the amount paid (s 23(8)(b)).

1099.   Delegation of functions relating to student support.   The appropriate national authority[1] may make arrangements for any person[2] or body specified in the arrangements to exercise on its behalf, to such extent as is so specified, any function[3] exercisable by the appropriate national authority by virtue of the provisions relating to the making of grants or loans to students or the recovery of amounts due in respect of such loans[4], including any such function in relation to appeals[5]. Any such arrangements do not prevent the appropriate national authority from exercising the function in question itself[6].

The appropriate national authority may pay to any body or person by whom any function is so exercisable: (1) such amounts as the appropriate national authority considers appropriate for the purpose of meeting expenditure incurred or to be incurred by that body or person in making[7] grants or loans[8], or by way of administrative expenses[9], in, or in connection with, the exercise of that function[10]; and (2) such remuneration as the appropriate national authority may determine[11].

1   Ie the Secretary of State or, in relation to Wales, the Welsh Ministers. The functions of the Secretary of State under the Teaching and Higher Education Act 1998 s 23 are transferred to the Welsh Ministers so far as they relate to functions which are exercisable by the Welsh Ministers under regulations under s 22 (see PARA 1096): Higher Education Act 2004 s 44(4). As to the Secretary of State see PARA 58. As to the meaning of 'Wales' see PARA 7 note 3. As to the Welsh Ministers see PARA 59. The functions under the Teaching and Higher Education Act 1998 s 23 (as so transferred) were originally vested in the National Assembly for Wales and are now exercisable by the Welsh Ministers by virtue of the Government of Wales Act 2006 s 162(1), Sch 11 paras 30, 32.
2   As to the meaning of 'person' see PARA 7 note 6.
3   As to the meaning of 'function' see PARA 18 note 5. In relation to any function which, by virtue of the Teaching and Higher Education Act 1998 s 23(4) is exercisable to a specified extent, references in any other provision of s 23 to the exercise of that function are accordingly to its exercise to that extent: s 23(10).
4   Ie any function exercisable by virtue of regulations under the Teaching and Higher Education Act 1998 s 22 (see PARAS 1096–1097).
5   Teaching and Higher Education Act 1998 s 23(4). As to the bringing of appeals arising out of the exercise of delegated functions see PARA 1100.
6   Teaching and Higher Education Act 1998 s 23(5).
7   Ie under the Teaching and Higher Education Act 1998 s 22 (see PARA 1096).
8   Teaching and Higher Education Act 1998 s 23(7)(a)(i).
9   Teaching and Higher Education Act 1998 s 23(7)(a)(ii).
10 Teaching and Higher Education Act 1998 s 23(7)(a). Any payment under s 23(7)(a) may be made subject to such terms and conditions as the appropriate national authority may determine; and any such conditions may in particular: (1) require the provision of returns or other

information before any such payment is made (s 23(8)(a)); and (2) relate to the use of the amount paid or require the repayment in specified circumstances of all or part of the amount paid (s 23(8)(b)).

11 Teaching and Higher Education Act 1998 s 23(7)(b).

1100. Appeals relating to the exercise of transferred or delegated functions. The appropriate national authority[1] may make provision for enabling appeals to be made, to a person[2] or body appointed by it for the purpose[3], with respect to such matters arising out of the exercise by any person or body of any function[4] relating to the making of grants or loans to students or the recovery of amounts due in respect of such loans, transferred[5] or delegated[6] to him, as the appropriate national authority may determine[7].

1 Ie the Secretary of State or, in relation to Wales, the Welsh Ministers. The functions of the Secretary of State under the Teaching and Higher Education Act 1998 s 23 are transferred to the Welsh Ministers so far as they relate to functions which are exercisable by the Welsh Ministers under regulations under s 22 (see PARA 1096): Higher Education Act 2004 s 44(4). As to the Secretary of State see PARA 58. As to the meaning of 'Wales' see PARA 7 note 3. As to the Welsh Ministers see PARA 59. The functions under the Teaching and Higher Education Act 1998 s 23 (as so transferred) were originally vested in the National Assembly for Wales and are now exercisable by the Welsh Ministers by virtue of the Government of Wales Act 2006 s 162(1), Sch 11 paras 30, 32.
2 As to the meaning of 'person' see PARA 7 note 6.
3 Teaching and Higher Education Act 1998 s 23(6)(b). The appropriate national authority may pay to any person or body appointed by it under s 23(6) such remuneration or administrative expenses (or both) as the appropriate national authority may determine: s 23(9).
4 As to the meaning of 'function' see PARA 18 note 5. In relation to any function which, by virtue of the Teaching and Higher Education Act 1998 s 23(1) (see PARA 1250) or s 23(4) (see PARA 1099) is exercisable to a specified extent, references in any other provision of s 23 to the exercise of that function are accordingly to its exercise to that extent: s 23(10).
5 Ie in accordance with the Teaching and Higher Education Act 1998 s 23(1) (see PARA 1098).
6 Ie in accordance with the Teaching and Higher Education Act 1998 s 23(4) (see PARA 1099).
7 See the Teaching and Higher Education Act 1998 s 23(6)(a).

1101. Information in connection with student loans. Any information which is held by the Commissioners for Her Majesty's Revenue and Customs[1], or by a person[2] providing services to those Commissioners and in connection with the provision of those services[3], may, for the purpose of enabling or assisting the recipient to exercise any function[4] in connection with the operation of the student loans scheme[5], be supplied to[6]:

(1)   the Secretary of State or the Welsh Ministers[7];

(2)   any person or body acting on behalf of the Secretary of State or the Welsh Ministers under the delegation of functions provisions[8]; or

(3)   any authority or governing body by whom any function of the Secretary of State or the Welsh Ministers is for the time being exercisable to any extent by virtue of the transfer of functions provisions[9].

Information supplied under these provisions must not be supplied by the recipient to any other person or body unless it is supplied to a person or body to whom it could be so supplied[10], or for the purposes of any civil or criminal proceedings arising out of the student loans scheme or provisions relating to the making of grants or loans to students or the recovery of amounts due in respect of such loans[11] so far as having effect in relation to grants made in pursuance of the Welsh Ministers' functions[12]. These provisions[13] extend only to the supply of information by or under the authority of the Commissioners for Her Majesty's Revenue and Customs[14].

1   Teaching and Higher Education Act 1998 s 24(1)(a) (amended by virtue of the Commissioners for Revenue and Customs Act 2005 s 50). As to the Commissioners for Her Majesty's Revenue and Customs see INCOME TAXATION vol 58 (2014) PARA 33.

2   As to the meaning of 'person' see PARA 7 note 6.

3   Teaching and Higher Education Act 1998 s 24(1)(b).

4   As to the meaning of 'function' see PARA 18 note 5.

5   'The student loans scheme' means the provisions of regulations under the Teaching and Higher Education Act 1998 s 22 (see PARAS 1096–1097) (or any corresponding Northern Ireland legislation), so far as having effect in relation to loans under s 22, or regulations under the Education (Scotland) Act 1980 s 73(f) made with respect to loans: Teaching and Higher Education Act 1998 s 24(6)(c).

6   The Teaching and Higher Education Act 1998 s 24 does not limit the circumstances in which information may be supplied apart therefrom: s 24(5).

7   See the Teaching and Higher Education Act 1998 s 24(2)(a) (s 24(2) amended by the Further and Higher Education (Governance and Information) (Wales) Act 2014 s 9(a)(i)). As to the Secretary of State see PARA 58; and as to the Welsh Ministers see PARA 59. The Teaching and Higher Education Act 1998 s 24(2) also makes provision for the supply of information to a corresponding Northern Ireland body. Information to which s 24(2) applies may also be supplied to: (1) the Welsh Ministers; (2) any person or body acting on behalf of the Welsh Ministers under s 23(4) (see PARA 1099); or (3) any authority or governing body by whom any function of the Welsh Ministers is for the time being exercisable to any extent by virtue of section 23(1) (see PARA 1098), for the purpose of enabling or assisting the recipient to exercise any function in connection with regulations under s 22 (see PARAS 1096–1097) so far as having effect in relation to grants under s 22: s 24(2A) (added by the Further and Higher Education (Governance and Information) (Wales) Act 2014 s 9(b)). As to the meaning of 'local authority' see PARA 25 (definition applied by the Teaching and Higher Education Act 1998 s 43(1) (amended by SI 2010/1158)).

8   Teaching and Higher Education Act 1998 s 24(2)(b) (as amended: see note 7). 'The delegation of functions provisions' means s 23(4) (see PARA 1099), or any corresponding Northern Ireland legislation, or the Education (Scotland) Act 1980 s 73A(3): Teaching and Higher Education Act 1998 s 24(6)(a). See also note 7.

9   Teaching and Higher Education Act 1998 s 24(2)(c) (as amended: see note 7). 'The transfer of functions provisions' means s 23(1) (see PARA 1098), or any corresponding Northern Ireland legislation, or the Education (Scotland) Act 1980 s 73A(1): Teaching and Higher Education Act 1998 s 24(6)(b). See also note 7.

10 Teaching and Higher Education Act 1998 s 24(3)(a) (s 24(3) amended by the Further and Higher Education (Governance and Information) (Wales) Act 2014 s 9(c)(i), (c)(ii)). The reference in the text to provisions is to those under s 24(2) (see the text and notes 4–9) and s 24(2A) (see note 7).

11 Ie regulations under the Teaching and Higher Education Act 1998 s 22 (see PARAS 1096–1097).

12 Teaching and Higher Education Act 1998 s 24(3)(b) (as amended: see note 10). The reference in the text to the Welsh Ministers' functions is to those under s 22 (see PARAS 1096–1097).

13 Ie the Teaching and Higher Education Act 1998 s 24(2), (2A), (3) (see the text and notes 4–12).

14 Teaching and Higher Education Act 1998 s 24(4) (amended by virtue of the Commissioners for Revenue and Customs Act 2005 s 50; and by the Further and Higher Education (Governance and Information) (Wales) Act 2014 s 9(d)). Where the Commissioners for Her Majesty's Revenue and Customs provide information to a person under the Teaching and Higher Education Act 1998, the Commissioners for Revenue and Customs Act 2005 s 19 (wrongful disclosure: see INCOME TAXATION vol 59 (2014) PARA 2325) applies to the disclosure of the information by the person as it applies to the disclosure of information in contravention of a provision of that Act: Teaching and Higher Education Act 1998 s 24(7) (s 24(7)–(11) added by the Sale of Student Loans Act 2008 s 7(1), (6)). But the Commissioners for Revenue and Customs Act 2005 s 19 does not apply to disclosure: (1) in accordance with the Teaching and Higher Education Act 1998 s 24 (s 24(8)(a) (as so added)); (2) in accordance with another enactment (s 24(8)(b) (as so added)); or (3) in circumstances specified in the Commissioners for Revenue and Customs Act 2005 s 18(2)(c), (d), (e) or (h) (see INCOME TAXATION vol 59 (2014) PARA 2325) (Teaching and Higher Education Act 1998 s 24(8)(c) (as so added)). In s 24(7): (a) information provided to a person (P) must be treated as being provided both to P and to any person on whose behalf P acts or by whom P is employed (s 24(9)(a) (as so added)); (b) information provided to a person (P) and disclosed by P to another person (P2) in accordance with s 24 must be treated as being provided also to P2 (and to any person on whose behalf P2 acts or by whom P2 is employed) (s 24(9)(b) (as so added)); and (c) the reference to disclosure by the person to whom information was provided (P) includes a reference to disclosure by any

person acting on behalf of, or employed by, P (or a person to whom it is treated as being provided by virtue of head (a) or head (b) above) (s 24(9)(c) (as so added)). In the application of the Commissioners for Revenue and Customs Act 2005 s 18(2)(c), (d) by virtue of the Teaching and Higher Education Act 1998 s 24(8)(c) (see head (3) above) a reference to functions of the Revenue and Customs must be taken as a reference to functions of the person making the disclosure in connection with student grants or loans: s 24(10) (as so added; and amended by the Further and Higher Education (Governance and Information) (Wales) Act 2014 s 9(e)). In the application of the Commissioners for Revenue and Customs Act 2005 s 19 by virtue of the Teaching and Higher Education Act 1998 s 24(7), 'revenue and customs information' means information provided by the Commissioners (but subject to the express exclusion in the Commissioners for Revenue and Customs Act 2005 s 19(2)): Teaching and Higher Education Act 1998 s 24(11) (as so added).

1102. Information in connection with student support. Regulations[1] may provide that a student support authority may supply student support information[2] of a prescribed[3] description to a prescribed person for a prescribed purpose[4]. Such regulations may also provide that information may be supplied under the regulations only if prescribed conditions are met[5]. Such regulations may not allow information to be supplied except with the consent of every individual to whom the information relates, given in such manner as may be prescribed[6], unless the supply of information is for the purposes of any civil or criminal proceedings arising out of the student support scheme[7].

These provisions do not limit the circumstances in which information may otherwise[8] be supplied[9].

1 'Regulations' means: (1) in relation to a student support authority falling within any of s 45(7)(a)–(c) (see heads (a)–(c) below), regulations made by the Secretary of State; and (2) in relation to a student support authority falling within any of s 45(7)(d)–(f) (see heads (d)–(f) below), regulations made by the Welsh Ministers: s 45(8). 'Student support authority' means:
    (a)   the Secretary of State (s 45(7)(a));
    (b)   any authority or governing body by whom any function of the Secretary of State is for the time being exercisable to any extent by virtue of the Teaching and Higher Education Act 1998 s 23(1) (see PARA 1098) (Higher Education Act 2004 s 45(7)(b));
    (c)   any person acting on behalf of the Secretary of State to any extent by virtue of the Teaching and Higher Education Act 1998 s 23(4) (see PARA 1099) (Higher Education Act 2004 s 45(7)(c));
    (d)   the Welsh Ministers (s 45(7)(d));
    (e)   any authority or governing body by whom any function of the Welsh Ministers is for the time being exercisable to any extent by virtue of the Teaching and Higher Education Act 1998 s 23(1) (Higher Education Act 2004 s 45(7)(e)); and
    (f)   any person acting on behalf of the Welsh Ministers to any extent by virtue of the Teaching and Higher Education Act 1998 s 23(4) (Higher Education Act 2004 s 45(7)(f)).
As to the Secretary of State see PARA 58. As to the Welsh Ministers see PARA 59. The functions under s 45 were originally vested in the National Assembly for Wales and are now exercisable by the Welsh Ministers by virtue of the Government of Wales Act 2006 s 162(1), Sch 11 paras 30, 32. As to the meaning of 'person' see PARA 7 note 6.
As to the regulations made see the Education (Supply of Student Support Information to Governing Bodies) Regulations 2006, SI 2006/141; Supply Of Student Support Information To Governing Bodies (Wales) Regulations 2006, SI 2006/2828.
2 'Student support information', in relation to a student support authority, means any information which the student support authority holds in connection with, or in consequence of, the exercise of any function relating to the operation of the student support scheme; and 'student support scheme' means the provisions of regulations under the Teaching and Higher Education Act 1998 s 22 (see PARAS 1096–1097): Higher Education Act 2004 s 45(8).
3 'Prescribed' means prescribed by regulations: Higher Education Act 2004 s 45(8).
4 Higher Education Act 2004 s 45(1). A person may not be prescribed under s 45(1) unless the person: (1) is the governing body of an institution with which eligible students (as defined for the purposes of the student support scheme) are undertaking courses (s 45(2)(a)); or (2) is a person who appears to the Secretary of State or, as the case may be, the Welsh Ministers to be exercising functions of a public nature (s 45(2)(b)).

5 Higher Education Act 2004 s 45(5).
6 Higher Education Act 2004 s 45(3).
7 Higher Education Act 2004 s 45(4).
8 Ie apart from the Higher Education Act 2004 s 45.
9 Higher Education Act 2004 s 45(6).

1103. Power to ensure parity of provision as respects attendance at Scottish institutions. The Secretary of State[1] was required, not later than 16 January 1999[2], to appoint an independent body to review the arrangements for England and Wales[3] relating to the payment of grants in respect of fees payable in connection with attendance on the final honours year of first degree courses at higher education institutions in Scotland[4]. The Secretary of State was required to invite the Scottish higher education principals, the Committee of Vice-Chancellors and Principals, and such other bodies as he considered appropriate, to make representations to such body, and the report of the body was required to be laid before each House of Parliament not later than 1 April 2000[5].

In the event that that body recommended that such arrangements[6] should be modified[7], the Secretary of State was empowered to modify those arrangements so as to secure that they were no less favourable than the arrangements made under corresponding Scottish legislation[8].

1 As to the Secretary of State see PARA 58.
2 Ie six months after the Teaching and Higher Education Act 1998 was passed (ie received Royal Assent). The Act was passed on 16 July 1998.
3 For the purposes of the Teaching and Higher Education Act 1998 s 25(4), (6), any reference to the arrangements for England and Wales is a reference to arrangements made either under the Education Act 1962 (repealed) (see PARA 1247) or under the Teaching and Higher Education Act 1998 s 22 (see PARAS 1096–1097). As to the meanings of 'England' and 'Wales' see PARA 7 note 3.
4 Teaching and Higher Education Act 1998 s 25(4). As to the power of the Secretary of State to make arrangements relating to the payment of grants in respect of fees payable in connection with courses see PARA 1096.
5 Teaching and Higher Education Act 1998 s 25(5). As to the report see the *Report of the Scottish Fee Support Review* (March 2000).
6 Ie the arrangements referred to in the Teaching and Higher Education Act 1998 s 25(4) (see the text to notes 1–4).
7 Ie in accordance with the Teaching and Higher Education Act 1998 s 25(6). As to the meaning of 'modified' see PARA 25 note 15.
8 Teaching and Higher Education Act 1998 s 25(6). The corresponding Scottish legislation is comprised of regulations under the Education (Scotland) Act 1980 s 73(f) for the payment of allowances in respect of fees payable as mentioned in the Teaching and Higher Education Act 1998 s 25(4) (see the text to notes 1–4): s 25(6).

C. ADJUSTMENT OF ARRANGEMENTS FOR THE RECOVERY OF STUDENT LOANS

1104. Student loans. Regulations[1] may make provision for:
(1) the repayment by the Secretary of State of amounts payable in respect of certain loans[2];
(2) reducing or extinguishing the amounts payable in respect of certain loans[3].
The regulations may, in particular, make provision:
(a) for determining whether a person is eligible for the purposes of the regulations[4];
(b) prescribing the circumstances and manner in which, and the times at which, payments are to be made, or amounts are to be reduced or extinguished[5];

(c) allowing retrospective adjustments for the purposes of the regulations, including provision allowing the Secretary of State to require reimbursement of repayments, or to alter the amounts reduced or extinguished[6];

(d) for imposing on employers, or such other persons[7] or bodies as may be prescribed, requirements with respect to information to be given to the Secretary of State[8];

(e) for the reimbursement by the Secretary of State of costs incurred by persons or bodies in complying with any such requirements[9];

(f) for appeals with respect to matters arising under the regulations (including provision for determining, or enabling the determination of the procedure to be followed in connection with the appeals)[10].

The Secretary of State may make arrangements for any person or body specified in the arrangements to exercise on his behalf, to such extent as is so specified, any function exercisable by him by virtue of the regulations (including any such function in relation to appeals)[11].

1 'Regulations' means regulations made under the Education Act 2002 s 186 by the Secretary of State: s 186(9). As to the Secretary of State see PARA 58. As to the regulations made see the Education (Teacher Student Loans) (Repayment etc) Regulations 2003, SI 2003/1917 (amended by SI 2005/3309; SI 2012/555; SI 2012/956; and SI 2012/979 (England)). As to the sale of student loans see PARA 1105 et seq.

2 Education Act 2002 s 186(1)(a). The loans referred to in the text are: (1) loans received under arrangements made under the Education (Student Loans) Act 1990 s 1 (repealed) (see PARA 1095) by eligible persons who fulfil prescribed conditions (Education Act 2002 s 186(2)(a)); (2) loans received under arrangements made under the Teaching and Higher Education Act 1998 s 22 (see PARAS 1096–1097) by eligible persons who fulfil prescribed conditions (Education Act 2002 s 186(2)(b)); (3) loans received for educational purposes under such other arrangements as may be prescribed by the regulations, including arrangements made outside England and Wales, by eligible persons who fulfil prescribed conditions (s 186(2)(c)). 'Prescribed' means prescribed by regulations: s 186(9). As to the meanings of 'England' and 'Wales' see PARA 7 note 3.

3 Education Act 2002 s 186(1)(b). The loans referred to in the text are those mentioned in s 186(2)(a), (b) (see note 2 heads (1), (2)): see s 186(1)(b).

4 Education Act 2002 s 186(3)(a).

5 Education Act 2002 s 186(3)(b).

6 Education Act 2002 s 186(3)(c).

7 As to the meaning of 'person' see PARA 7 note 6.

8 Education Act 2002 s 186(3)(d).

9 Education Act 2002 s 186(3)(e).

10 Education Act 2002 s 186(3)(f).

11 Education Act 2002 s 186(4). Any arrangements made under s 186(4) do not prevent the Secretary of State from exercising the function in question himself: s 186(5). The Secretary of State may pay to any person or body by whom any function is exercisable by virtue of s 186(4) such amounts as he considers appropriate for the purpose of meeting expenditure incurred or to be incurred by that person or body in, or in connection with, the exercise of that function: s 186(6). Any payment under s 186(6) may be made subject to such terms and conditions as the Secretary of State may determine: s 186(7). Such conditions may in particular: (1) require the provision of returns or other information before any such payment is made (s 186(8)(a)); (2) relate to the use of the amount paid or require the repayment in specified circumstances of all or part of the amount paid (s 186(8)(b)).

D. SALE OF STUDENT LOANS

1105. Power of the Secretary of State to make transfer arrangements regarding student loans. The Secretary of State[1] may enter into arrangements ('transfer arrangements') under which rights of the Secretary of State in respect of student loans[2] are transferred to another person[3] ('the loan purchaser')[4]. Transfer arrangements may relate to specified loans or a specified class of loan[5], and some or all of the Secretary of State's rights[6]. Transfer arrangements may include provision:

(1)   transferring to the loan purchaser an obligation of the Secretary of State in connection with a loan[7];

(2)   transferring to the loan purchaser the benefit of an obligation or undertaking of the borrower in respect of a loan (whether deriving from loan regulations or from arrangements agreed between the borrower and the Secretary of State in respect of the loan ('loan arrangements'))[8];

(3)   for warranties or indemnities or other obligations of the Secretary of State[9];

(4)   enabling the Secretary of State to require a loan purchaser to make specified arrangements in connection with the administration of loans (whether by appointing a specified agent for specified purposes, or otherwise)[10];

(5)   prohibiting the loan purchaser from making specified arrangements without the Secretary of State's consent[11];

(6)   specifying consequences of the breach of a provision of the transfer arrangements[12].

Transfer arrangements may also include provision:

(a)   for repayments and other sums to be paid by the Secretary of State to the loan purchaser (having been collected by or on behalf of the Secretary of State)[13], for those payments to be made by reference to estimates[14], and for repayments to or deductions by the Secretary of State in case of overpayment[15];

(b)   as to who is entitled to interest, penalties or charges imposed or incurred after the transfer[16];

(c)   for the Secretary of State to pay compensation to the loan purchaser in connection with certain matters[17];

(d)   for undertakings by the Secretary of State about the power to make loan regulations[18];

(e)   for repurchase in specified circumstances[19];

(f)   for the appointment of a person to consider disputes between the loan purchaser and the borrower in respect of a transferred loan[20];

(g)   for making consequential amendment of a document forming part of, or issued in connection with, loan arrangements[21].

Transfer arrangements may also include any provision that the Secretary of State thinks appropriate (in addition to those specifically permitted by heads (1) to (6) and (a) to (g) above)[22].

Transfer arrangements must have effect (and, in particular, a provision transferring rights or obligations is sufficient to effect the transfer)[23]. Transfer arrangements may be made without the borrower's consent[24] and without notice to the borrower[25]. However, the Secretary of State must take reasonable steps to notify the borrower within three months[26] of transfer arrangements taking effect[27]. The Secretary of State may incur expenditure in connection with transfer arrangements[28].

The statutory provisions in respect of the supply of information have effect in relation to the sale of student loans[29].

1   As to the Secretary of State see PARA 58. As to the power of the Welsh Ministers to enter into transfer arrangements see PARA 1109.

2 'Student loans' means loans made by the Secretary of State in accordance with regulations under
the Teaching and Higher Education Act 1998 s 22 ('loan regulations') (see PARAS 1096–1097):
Sale of Student Loans Act 2008 s 1(2). A reference in loan regulations to the Secretary of State
as lender includes a reference to a loan purchaser: s 5(1). Regulations by virtue of the Teaching
and Higher Education Act 1998 s 22(5)(a)(iii) (loan regulations: repayment) (see PARA 1097)
may make provision for the transmission of amounts by a specified person (or body) other than
a borrower's employer, to a loan purchaser, and in accordance with directions given by the
Secretary of State: Sale of Student Loans Act 2008 s 5(2). Regulations by virtue of the Teaching
and Higher Education Act 1998 s 22(5)(f) (loan regulations: repayment) (see PARA 1097) may
enable the Secretary of State to require the reimbursement of costs or expenses incurred by a
loan purchaser: Sale of Student Loans Act 2008 s 5(3). Amendments of loan regulations may
have effect in respect of transferred loans (s 5(4)) and this includes amendments which have
effect in respect of loans made before the amendments are made (s 5(5)). But in amending loan
regulations the Secretary of State must aim to ensure that no borrower whose loan is transferred
is in a worse position, as the result of the amendment, than would have been the case had the
loan not been transferred: s 5(6). Section 5(6) also applies to making or amending regulations
under the Education Act 2002 s 186 (see PARA 1104): Sale of Student Loans Act 2008 s 5(7).
3 As to the meaning of 'person' see PARA 7 note 6.
4 Sale of Student Loans Act 2008 s 1(1). A loan in respect of which transfer arrangements are
made may be referred to as a 'transferred loan': s 1(8).
5 Sale of Student Loans Act 2008 s 1(3)(a).
6 Sale of Student Loans Act 2008 s 1(3)(b).
7 Sale of Student Loans Act 2008 s 1(4)(a).
8 Sale of Student Loans Act 2008 s 1(4)(b).
9 Sale of Student Loans Act 2008 s 1(4)(c).
10 Sale of Student Loans Act 2008 s 1(4)(d).
11 Sale of Student Loans Act 2008 s 1(4)(e).
12 Sale of Student Loans Act 2008 s 1(4)(f).
13 Sale of Student Loans Act 2008 s 2(2)(a).
14 Sale of Student Loans Act 2008 s 2(2)(b).
15 Sale of Student Loans Act 2008 s 2(2)(c).
16 Sale of Student Loans Act 2008 s 2(3).
17 See the Sale of Student Loans Act 2008 s 2(4). The compensation may be: (1) to reflect
regulations under the Education Act 2002 s 186 (see PARA 1104) (Sale of Student Loans
Act 2008 s 2(4)(a)); (2) in connection with amendments of loan regulations (s 2(4)(b)); or (3) in
other specified circumstances (s 2(4)(c)).
18 See the Sale of Student Loans Act 2008 s 2(5). In particular: (1) the Secretary of State may
undertake to exercise the power so as to achieve a specified result (s 2(5)(a)); (2) the Secretary of
State may undertake not to exercise the power so as to achieve a specified result (s 2(5)(b)); (3)
the Secretary of State may undertake to follow, or not to follow, a specified procedure in
connection with the power (s 2(5)(c)); and (4) a loan purchaser may enforce an undertaking by
way of legal proceedings in public law, private law or both (s 2(5)(e)). In s 2(5) the reference to
loan regulations includes a reference to regulations under the Education Act 2002 s 186 (see
PARA 1104): Sale of Student Loans Act 2008 s 2(6).
19 Sale of Student Loans Act 2008 s 2(7).
20 Sale of Student Loans Act 2008 s 2(8).
21 Sale of Student Loans Act 2008 s 2(9).
22 Sale of Student Loans Act 2008 s 2(1).
23 Sale of Student Loans Act 2008 s 1(5).
24 Sale of Student Loans Act 2008 s 1(6)(a).
25 Sale of Student Loans Act 2008 s 1(6)(b).
26 As to the meaning of 'month' see PARA 54 note 26.
27 Sale of Student Loans Act 2008 s 1(7).
28 Sale of Student Loans Act 2008 s 2(10).
29 Ie the Teaching and Higher Education Act 1998 s 24 (see PARA 1101) has effect with the
following three modifications: Sale of Student Loans Act 2008 s 7(1). Modification 1 is that the
permitted purposes for disclosure (under the Teaching and Higher Education Act 1998 s 24(2))
include purposes in connection with loans that have been or may be transferred (including
onward disclosure by virtue of the Sale of Student Loans Act 2008 s 7(4)): s 7(2). Modification 2
is that the Teaching and Higher Education Act 1998 s 24(2)(b) permits disclosure to a person or
body who acts on behalf of the Secretary of State under the delegation of functions provisions,
whether the person or body requires the information in that capacity or in the capacity of agent
of a loan purchaser: Sale of Student Loans Act 2008 s 7(3). Modification 3 is that the class of

permitted onwards disclosure (under the Teaching and Higher Education Act 1998 s 24(3)) includes (a) in the case of information which does not relate to a person whose identity is specified in the disclosure or can be deduced from it, disclosure for purposes in connection with loans that have been or may be transferred (Sale of Student Loans Act 2008 s 7(4)(a)); and (b) in any case, disclosure to an actual loan purchaser (or its agent) for purposes in connection with a transferred loan (s 7(4)(b)). The reference in s 7(4)(b) to an agent includes an auditor: s 7(5).

1106. Onward sales of student loans. Rights transferred by transfer arrangements[1] may be further transferred by arrangements between the loan purchaser[2] and another person[3]. However, this is subject to any provision of transfer arrangements prohibiting, restricting or controlling further transfer[4].

Further transfer arrangements may include provision:

(1) transferring to the further transferee an obligation of the loan purchaser in connection with a loan[5];

(2) transferring to the further transferee the benefit of an obligation or undertaking of the borrower in respect of a loan (however deriving)[6];

(3) transferring to the further transferee the benefit of warranties or indemnities or other obligations of the Secretary of State[7] under transfer arrangements[8].

Transfer arrangements may: (a) prohibit the making of further transfer arrangements without the Secretary of State's consent[9]; (b) require further transfer arrangements to be effected by way of novation[10] or other arrangements to which the Secretary of State is a party[11]; (c) include provision by virtue of which the Secretary of State is automatically a party to further transfer arrangements (and may enforce any of their terms)[12]. In entering into transfer arrangements the Secretary of State must ensure (whether by reliance on head (b) or (c) above or otherwise) that he will be party to any further transfer arrangements[13].

The Secretary of State may enter into arrangements, under or in accordance with transfer arrangements, in connection with further transfer[14].

1 As to the meaning of 'transfer arrangements' see PARA 1105.
2 As to the meaning of 'loan purchaser' see PARA 1105.
3 Sale of Student Loans Act 2008 s 3(1). Such arrangements are known as 'further transfer arrangements': see s 3(1). As to the meaning of 'person' see PARA 7 note 6. In the Sale of Student Loans Act 2008 (including s 3) a reference to transfer arrangements includes a reference to further transfer arrangements: s 3(2). In the application of the Sale of Student Loans Act 2008 to further transfer arrangements: (1) a reference to a loan purchaser is a reference to the transferee under the further transfer arrangements ('the further transferee') (s 3(3)(a)); and (2) in s 1(3)(b), (4)(a), (c), (7) (see PARA 1105) a reference to the Secretary of State is a reference to the transferor under the further transfer arrangements (s 3(3)(b)). References in s 3 to the further transfer of transferred rights do not include references to arrangements under which: (a) transferred rights become held on trust (s 3(9)(a)); (b) other equitable interests are created or transferred in relation to transferred rights (s 3(9)(b)); or (c) securities are granted in respect of transferred rights (s 3(9)(c)).
4 Sale of Student Loans Act 2008 s 3(4).
5 Sale of Student Loans Act 2008 s 3(5)(a).
6 Sale of Student Loans Act 2008 s 3(5)(b).
7 As to the Secretary of State see PARA 58. As to the power of the Welsh Ministers to enter into transfer arrangements see PARA 1109.
8 Sale of Student Loans Act 2008 s 3(5)(c).
9 Sale of Student Loans Act 2008 s 3(6)(a).
10 As to novation see CONTRACT vol 22 (2012) PARA 598 et seq.
11 Sale of Student Loans Act 2008 s 3(6)(b).
12 Sale of Student Loans Act 2008 s 3(6)(c).
13 Sale of Student Loans Act 2008 s 3(7).
14 Sale of Student Loans Act 2008 s 3(8).

1107. Report about transfer arrangements for student loans. After entering into transfer arrangements[1] the Secretary of State[2] must lay before Parliament[3] a report about the arrangements[4]. The report must include information about the extent to which the arrangements give good value; and for that purpose the report must reflect any guidance given by the Treasury[5] about assessing value for money (including guidance to the accounting officer of the Secretary of State's department)[6]. The report must be laid during the period of three months[7] beginning with the date on which the Secretary of State enters into the transfer arrangements[8].

1　As to the meaning of 'transfer arrangements' see PARA 1105. The Sale of Student Loans Act 2008 s 4 does not apply to further transfer arrangements (despite s 3(2): see PARA 1106 note 3): s 4(4).

2　As to the Secretary of State see PARA 58. As to the power of the Welsh Ministers to enter into transfer arrangements see PARA 1109.

3　As to the laying of documents before Parliament see STATUTES AND LEGISLATIVE PROCESS vol 96 (2012) PARA 1052.

4　Sale of Student Loans Act 2008 s 4(1).

5　As to the meaning of 'Treasury' see PARA 54 note 20.

6　Sale of Student Loans Act 2008 s 4(2).

7　As to the meaning of 'month' see PARA 54 note 26.

8　Sale of Student Loans Act 2008 s 4(3).

1108. Repayment of student loans. Loan regulations[1], loan arrangements[2] or transfer arrangements[3] may include provision about repayment of loans to a loan purchaser[4]. In particular, regulations or arrangements may provide for: (1) collection by a person[5] acting on behalf of a loan purchaser[6]; (2) collection by Her Majesty's Commissioners for Revenue and Customs[7]. A provision of loan regulations or loan arrangements which requires money to be paid to the Secretary of State[8] or into the Consolidated Fund[9] (whether as repayment, interest, charge or penalty) must be treated in relation to a transferred loan[10] as requiring payment to the loan purchaser (whether directly, through the Secretary of State or through another agent)[11].

1　As to the meaning of 'loan regulations' see PARA 1105 note 2.

2　As to the meaning of 'loan arrangements' see PARA 1105.

3　As to the meaning of 'transfer arrangements' see PARA 1105. See also PARA 1106 note 3.

4　Sale of Student Loans Act 2008 s 6(1). As to the meaning of 'loan purchaser' see PARA 1105.

5　As to the meaning of 'person' see PARA 7 note 6.

6　Sale of Student Loans Act 2008 s 6(2)(a).

7　Sale of Student Loans Act 2008 s 6(2)(b). As to the Commissioners for Her Majesty's Revenue and Customs see INCOME TAXATION vol 58 (2014) PARA 33.

8　As to the Secretary of State see PARA 58. As to the power of the Welsh Ministers to enter into transfer arrangements see PARA 1109.

9　As to the Consolidated Fund see CONSTITUTIONAL AND ADMINISTRATIVE LAW vol 20 (2014) PARA 480 et seq.

10　As to the meaning of 'transferred loan' see PARA 1105 note 4.

11　Sale of Student Loans Act 2008 s 6(3). Section 6(3) is subject to any provision included in transfer arrangements by virtue of s 2 (see PARA 1105): s 6(4).

1109. Power of the Welsh Ministers to enter into transfer arrangements. The Welsh Ministers[1] may enter into arrangements ('Welsh transfer arrangements') under which rights of theirs in respect of student loans[2] are transferred to another person[3].

1　As to the Welsh Ministers see PARA 59.

2   'Student loans' means loans made by the Welsh Ministers in accordance with regulations under the Teaching and Higher Education Act 1998 s 22 (see PARAS 1096–1097): Sale of Student Loans Act 2008 s 9(2).

3   See the Sale of Student Loans Act 2008 s 9(1), (3). As to the meaning of 'person' see PARA 7 note 6. The provisions of the Sale of Student Loans Act 2008 apply in relation to Welsh transfer arrangements as to arrangements made under s 1(1) (see PARA 1105): s 9(3). In connection with Welsh transfer arrangements references to the Secretary of State are to be read as references to the Welsh Ministers, except in s 2(4)(a), s 2(5) in so far as it has effect by virtue of s 2(6), and s 5(2), (3) (see PARA 1105): s 9(4). Nothing in the Sale of Student Loans Act 2008 confers a power on the Welsh Ministers to make regulations under a provision which does not otherwise confer power on them; in particular, the provision permitted to be made by virtue of s 5(2), (3) (see PARA 1105) and s 6(2)(b) (see PARA 1108) is to be made by the Secretary of State in connection with Welsh transfer arrangements: s 9(5). Section 4 (see PARA 1107) does not apply to Welsh transfer arrangements: s 9(6). As to the Secretary of State see PARA 58.

(ii) Eligibility of Students for Financial Awards

1110.   Making of discretionary awards.   The appropriate national authority[1] may, as respects any awards (however described) as may be specified by regulations, being awards in connection with courses of education or training or the undertaking of research, make regulations authorising the adoption of rules of eligibility which confine the awards to persons having such connection with the United Kingdom[2] or any part of it as may be specified in the regulations[3].

1   Ie the Secretary of State or, in relation to Wales, the Welsh Ministers. As to the Secretary of State see PARA 58. As to the Welsh Ministers see PARA 59. As to the meaning of 'Wales' see PARA 7 note 3. The functions of the Secretary of State under the Education (Fees and Awards) Act 1983 s 2, so far as exercisable in relation to Wales, were transferred to the National Assembly for Wales (see the National Assembly for Wales (Transfer of Functions) Order 1999, SI 1999/672, art 2, Sch 1) and are now vested in the Welsh Ministers (see the Government of Wales Act 2006 s 162(1), Sch 11 para 30).

2   For these purposes, references to the United Kingdom include references to the Channel Islands and the Isle of Man, but the Education (Fees and Awards) Act 1983 does not extend to Northern Ireland: see s 3. As to the meaning of 'United Kingdom' generally see PARA 73 note 3.

3   Education (Fees and Awards) Act 1983 s 2(1), (3)(b) (s 2(3)(b) amended by the Teaching and Higher Education Act 1998 s 44(2), Sch 4). The regulations may provide for exceptions and make different provision for different cases or purposes: Education (Fees and Awards) Act 1983 s 2(2).

As to the regulations made under the Education (Fees and Awards) Act 1983 s 2 see the Local Education Authority (Post-Compulsory Education Awards) Regulations 1999, SI 1999/229 (amended by SI 2000/2057; revoked, in relation to Wales, by SI 2002/1856); the Education (Fees and Awards) (England) Regulations 2007, SI 2007/779 (amended by SI 2011/87; SI 2011/1987; SI 2012/765; SI 2012/956; and SI 2012/1653); the Education (Fees and Awards) (Wales) Regulations 2007, SI 2007/2310 (amended by SI 2011/1978; and SI 2013/1792); the Education (Fees and Awards) (Wales) Regulations 2008, SI 2008/1259; and the Education (Student Fees, Awards and Support) (Wales) Regulations 2011, SI 2011/1978.

1111.   Power to charge higher fees for students not connected with the United Kingdom.   In respect of certain institutions[1], the appropriate national authority[2] may make regulations requiring or authorising the charging of fees[3] which are higher in the case of students not having such connection with the United Kingdom[4] or any part of it as may be specified in the regulations than in the case of students having such a connection[5]. The regulations may provide for exceptions and make different provision for different cases or purposes[6].

1   The Education (Fees and Awards) Act 1983 s 1 applies to the following higher education institutions:
    (1)   any university, university college or college, school, hall or other institution of a university (s 1(3)(a));

(2) any institution within the higher education sector (s 1(3)(b) (substituted by the Further and Higher Education Act 1992 s 93(1), Sch 8 Pt I para 19));

(3) any institution which provides higher education or further education (or both) and is either: (a) maintained by a local authority; or (b) substantially dependent for its maintenance on public funds and either is specified in the regulations made under the Education (Fees and Awards) Act 1983 s 1 or is of a class or description so specified (s 1(3)(c), (3A) (s 1(3)(c) substituted, and s 1(3A) added, by the Education Reform Act 1988 s 237(1), Sch 12 para 91; Education (Fees and Awards) Act 1983 s 1(3)(c) amended by SI 2010/1158));

(4) any training provider, within the meaning of the Education Act 2005 Pt 3 (ss 74–100) (see PARA 1059 note 3), who is receiving financial assistance from the Secretary of State or the Welsh Ministers under the Education Act 2002 s 14 (see PARA 78), or from a person who is receiving financial assistance under s 14 (Education (Fees and Awards) Act 1983 s 1(3)(e) (added by the Education Act 1994 s 24, Sch 2 para 7; and substituted by the Education Act 2005 s 98, Sch 14 para 9); and amended by the Education Act 2011 Sch 5 para 5); and

(5) any institution eligible for funding by the Higher Education Funding Council for Wales under the Education Act 2005 Pt 3 (Education (Fees and Awards) Act 1983 s 1(3)(ee) (added by the Education Act 2005 Sch 14 para 9)).

The Education (Fees and Awards) Act 1983 s 1 also applies to certain further education institutions: see PARA 614. As to the meaning of 'university' see PARA 621. As to the meaning of 'institution within the higher education sector' see PARA 619; as to the meaning of 'higher education' see PARA 24; as to the meaning of 'further education' see PARA 23; and as to the meaning of 'local authority' see PARA 25 (definitions applied by s 1(4) (amended by the Education Act 1996 s 582(1), Sch 37 para 57; Education Reform Act 1988 s 237, Sch 12 Part III para 91; and SI 2010/1158)). As to the Training and Development Agency for Schools see PARA 1054. 'Public funds' means assistance from a local authority or grants under the Education Act 1996 s 485 (see PARA 82): Education (Fees and Awards) Act 1983 s 1(4) (as so amended). As to the Higher Education Funding Council for Wales see PARA 691 et seq.

2   Ie the Secretary of State or, in relation to Wales, the Welsh Ministers. As to the Secretary of State see PARA 58. As to the Welsh Ministers see PARA 59. As to the meaning of 'Wales' see PARA 7 note 3. The functions of the Secretary of State under the Education (Fees and Awards) Act 1983 s 1, so far as exercisable in relation to Wales, were transferred to the National Assembly for Wales (see the National Assembly for Wales (Transfer of Functions) Order 2006, SI 2006/1458, arts 2(a), 3) and are now vested in the Welsh Ministers (see the Government of Wales Act 2006 s 162(1), Sch 11 para 30).

3   'Fees' includes charges however described (including charges for board and lodging): Education (Fees and Awards) Act 1983 s 1(4).

4   References to the United Kingdom include references to the Channel Islands and the Isle of Man, but the Education (Fees and Awards) Act 1983 does not extend to Northern Ireland: see s 3. As to the meaning of 'United Kingdom' generally see PARA 73 note 3.

5   Education (Fees and Awards) Act 1983 s 1(1).

As to the regulations made under the Education (Fees and Awards) Act 1983 s 1 see the Education (Fees and Awards) (England) Regulations 2007, SI 2007/779 (amended by SI 2011/87; SI 2011/1987; SI 2012/765; SI 2012/956; and SI 2012/1653); the Education (Fees and Awards) (Wales) Regulations 2007, SI 2007/2310 (amended by SI 2011/1978; and SI 2013/1792); the Education (Fees and Awards) (Wales) Regulations 2008, SI 2008/1259. See *R (on the application of Mitchell) v Coventry University and the Secretary of State for Education and Employment* [2001] ELR 594, [2001] All ER (D) 34 (Mar), where it was held that the purpose behind the regulations was a reasonable and objective justification for the discrimination which resulted, so there was no conflict with the Convention for the Protection of Human Rights and Fundamental Freedoms (Rome, 4 November 1950; TS 71 (1953); Cmd 8969) art 14 or with the First Protocol (Paris, 20 March 1952; TS 46 (1954); Cmd 9221) art 2 (see PARA 3).

6   Education (Fees and Awards) Act 1983 s 1(2).

(iii) Particular Scholarships

1112.   Industrial scholarships. The appropriate national authority[1] may award industrial scholarships or make payments to any other person[2] in respect of the award of such scholarships by that person[3].

'Industrial scholarships' are scholarships (however described) tenable by persons undertaking full-time courses[4] of higher education[5] provided by a university, college or other institution in the United Kingdom[6], being courses which appear to the appropriate national authority or, as the case may be, the person awarding the scholarships to be relevant to a career in industry[7].

1　Ie the Secretary of State or, in relation to Wales, the Welsh Ministers. As to the Secretary of State see PARA 58. As to the Welsh Ministers see PARA 59. As to the meaning of 'Wales' see PARA 7 note 3. The functions of the Secretary of State under the Education Act 1980 s 20, so far as exercisable in relation to Wales, were transferred to the National Assembly for Wales (see the National Assembly for Wales (Transfer of Functions) Order 1999, SI 1999/672, art 2, Sch 1) and are now vested in the Welsh Ministers (see the Government of Wales Act 2006 s 162(1), Sch 11 para 30).
2　As to the meaning of 'person' see PARA 7 note 6.
3　Education Act 1980 s 20(1).
4　The reference to a full-time course includes a reference to a course consisting of alternate periods of full-time study in the university, college or institution in question and associated industrial, professional or commercial experience: Education Act 1980 s 20(3)(a), (b).
5　As to the meaning of 'higher education' see PARA 24 (definition applied by Education Act 1980 s 38(3) (substituted by the Education Act 1996 s 582(1), Sch 37 para 47(1), (3))).
6　The reference to a course provided by a university, college or institution in the United Kingdom includes a reference to a course provided by such a university, college or institution in conjunction with a university, college or other institution in another country: Education Act 1980 s 20(3). As to the meaning of 'United Kingdom' see PARA 73 note 3.
7　Education Act 1980 s 20(2).

1113. Commonwealth Scholarship Commission. The Commonwealth Scholarship Commission[1] is charged with the duty of: (1) selecting the recipients[2] of awards arising out of the Commonwealth Scholarship and Fellowship Plan[3] to persons coming to the United Kingdom[4]; (2) making arrangements for placing the recipients at institutions within the further education sector[5] or higher education sector[6], at 16 to 19 academies[7] or at other appropriate establishments in the United Kingdom, and for the supervision of their work during the currency of their awards[8]; (3) selecting persons to put forward as candidates from the United Kingdom for awards arising out of the Plan and to be granted in countries outside the United Kingdom[9]; and (4) discharging any other functions under the Plan which the Secretary of State may assign to the Commission[10].

The Commission consists of a chairman and not less than nine nor more than 14 other members appointed by the Secretary of State[11]. The Commission may appoint committees to assist it in the discharge of its functions, and may delegate the discharge of its functions to such a committee, with or without restrictions or conditions[12]. In the discharge of its functions the Commission must comply with any directions given to it by the Secretary of State[13]. The expenses of the Commission, up to such amount as may be approved by the Secretary of State with the consent of the Treasury[14], may be defrayed by the Secretary of State[15].

The Commission must make an annual report to the Secretary of State on the discharge of its functions[16], and the Secretary of State must lay a copy of every such report before Parliament[17].

1　The existence of the Commission known as the Commonwealth Scholarship Commission in the United Kingdom continues by virtue of the International Development Act 2002 s 13(1). As to financial assistance under the International Development Act 2002 see also PARA 80.
2　Persons selected must be Commonwealth citizens or British protected persons (within the meaning of the British Nationality Act 1981) except where the Commission for special reasons, approved by the Secretary of State, otherwise determines: International Development Act 2002 s 14(4). As to Commonwealth citizens see BRITISH NATIONALITY vol 4 (2011) PARA 409. As to British protected persons see BRITISH NATIONALITY vol 4 (2011) PARAS 408, 476–480. As to the Secretary of State see PARA 58.

3 The 'Commonwealth Scholarship and Fellowship Plan' means the plan so named which was put forward by the Commonwealth Development Conference held at Oxford in July 1959: International Development Act 2002 s 14(6). The origin of the Commonwealth Scholarship and Fellowship Plan was a speech by Sydney Smith, former president of the University of Toronto and then Canadian Minister for External Affairs, delivered at the Eighth Quinquennial Congress of Commonwealth Universities at Montreal in September 1958. From that conference there emerged the proposal to establish a new scheme of Commonwealth scholarships and fellowships. The purpose and operation of the scheme were elaborated at the first Commonwealth Development Conference held at Oxford in July 1959. The first Commonwealth Scholars took up their awards in 1960.

4 International Development Act 2002 s 14(1)(a). The Secretary of State may make such awards as are mentioned in s 14(1)(a): s 14(5)(a). For these purposes, 'United Kingdom' includes the Channel Islands and the Isle of Man: s 14(6). As to the meaning of 'United Kingdom' generally see PARA 73 note 3.

5 As to the meaning of 'institution within the further education sector' see PARA 555 (definition applied by the International Development Act 2002 s 14(6)).

6 As to the meaning of 'institution within the higher education sector' see PARA 619 (definition applied by the International Development Act 2002 s 14(6)).

7 As 16 to 19 academies see PARA 346 note 13. As to academies see PARA 345 et seq.

8 International Development Act 2002 s 14(1)(b) (amended by the Education Act 2011 Sch 13 para 12).

9 International Development Act 2002 s 14(1)(c). The Secretary of State may make such awards as are mentioned in s 14(1)(c): s 14(5)(b).

10 International Development Act 2002 s 14(1)(d).

11 International Development Act 2002 s 13(2). Not less than four of the members must be persons appointed as the holders of high academic office: s 13(3). A member of the Commission holds and vacates office in accordance with the terms of his appointment and is eligible for re-appointment, but may at any time resign his office by notice in writing to the Secretary of State: Sch 2 para 1. As to the meaning of 'writing' see PARA 76 note 8. The quorum at any meeting of the Commission is six and the validity of any proceedings of the Commission is not affected by any vacancy in its number or any defect in the appointment of a member: Sch 2 para 2.

12 International Development Act 2002 Sch 2 para 3(1), (3). Any such committee may include persons who are not members of the Commission: Sch 2 para 3(2).

13 International Development Act 2002 s 14(2). No direction is to be given for the selection or rejection of any particular person for an award or as a candidate for an award: s 14(3).

14 As to the meaning of 'Treasury' see PARA 54 note 20.

15 International Development Act 2002 Sch 2 para 4(1). Such expenses include the payment of travelling and other allowances to members of the Commission or of any committee of the Commission and to persons chosen by the Commission to act as advisers: Sch 2 para 4(2).

16 See the International Development Act 2002 Sch 2 para 5(1).

17 International Development Act 2002 Sch 2 para 5(2). As to the laying of documents before Parliament see STATUTES AND LEGISLATIVE PROCESS vol 96 (2012) PARA 1052.

1114. Marshall Aid Commemoration Commission. The Marshall Aid Commemoration Commission was established by the Marshall Aid Commemoration Act 1953[1]. The Commission consists of not less than seven nor more than ten members appointed by the Secretary of State[2].

The Commission's functions are to give effect to arrangements made by or with the approval of the Secretary of State: (1) for administering the grants provided by Parliament for Marshall scholarships[3]; (2) for the selection of the persons to receive Marshall scholarships[4]; and (3) for the placing of the holders of Marshall scholarships in universities or university colleges in the United Kingdom[5]. The Commission also discharges such other functions in connection with Marshall scholarships as may be conferred on it by such arrangements[6].

The Commission is obliged to make an annual report to the Secretary of State on the discharge by it of its functions, and the Secretary of State must lay a copy of every such report before each House of Parliament[7].

The Commission must prepare accounts of its expenditure in such form as the Secretary of State may with the approval of the Treasury[8] direct, and must submit the accounts to the Secretary of State at such time as he may direct[9].

1   The Marshall Aid Commemoration Act 1953 and the Marshall Scholarships Act 1959, which may together be cited as the Marshall Aid Commemoration Acts 1953 and 1959 (see the Marshall Scholarships Act 1959 s 2), provide for the granting of Marshall scholarships tenable at universities or university colleges in the United Kingdom by citizens of the United States of America who are graduates of recognised institutions of higher learning in the United States of America: Marshall Aid Commemoration Act 1953 s 1. The Secretary of State may make, out of moneys provided by Parliament, grants to the Commission to defray the expenditure of the Commission incurred for the said purpose, including administrative expenses: s 1. As to the meaning of 'United Kingdom' see PARA 73 note 3. As to the Secretary of State see PARA 58.
    Marshall scholarships were established in commemoration of the assistance received by the United Kingdom after the 1939–45 war under the European Recovery Programme known as Marshall Aid. The Marshall Aid Commemoration Act 1953 provided for up to 12 scholarships to be granted in each year; the Marshall Scholarships Act 1959 substituted for the reference to 12 scholarships a reference to 24 or such greater number as Her Majesty might by Order in Council from time to time determine: see the Marshall Scholarships Act 1959 s 1(1). The Marshall Scholarships Order 1972, SI 1972/961 (revoked) increased the maximum number to 30 each year. The Marshall Scholarships Order 1990, SI 1990/990, further increased the maximum number of annual scholarships to 40.
2   Marshall Aid Commemoration Act 1953 s 2(2). Not less than two of the Commission's members must be chosen as persons of eminence in academic matters, and the Secretary of State may designate one of the members to be chairman of the Commission: s 2(2). The Commission's quorum is four (s 2(3)) but so long as it is quorate the Commission has power to act notwithstanding any vacancy in its number (s 2(4)). Terms of office of members of the Commission are determined by the Secretary of State: s 2(5). A member of the Commission is eligible for re-appointment on vacating office: s 2(5).
3   Marshall Aid Commemoration Act 1953 s 2(1)(a).
4   Marshall Aid Commemoration Act 1953 s 2(1)(b).
5   Marshall Aid Commemoration Act 1953 s 2(1)(c).
6   Marshall Aid Commemoration Act 1953 s 2(1).
7   See the Marshall Aid Commemoration Act 1953 s 2(6). As to the laying of documents before Parliament see STATUTES AND LEGISLATIVE PROCESS vol 96 (2012) PARA 1052.
8   As to the meaning of 'Treasury' see PARA 54 note 20.
9   Marshall Aid Commemoration Act 1953 s 2(7). On or before 30 November in any year the Secretary of State must transmit the Commission's accounts for the financial year last ended to the Comptroller and Auditor General, who must examine and certify the accounts and lay before Parliament copies of the accounts together with his report on them: s 2(7). As to the Comptroller and Auditor General see CONSTITUTIONAL AND ADMINISTRATIVE LAW vol 20 (2014) PARAS 494–496.

(3) STUDENTS' UNIONS

(i) Meaning of 'Students' Union' and Applicable Establishments

1115.   Meaning of 'students' union'. The Education Act 1994 contains provisions relating to students' unions[1]. For those purposes, a 'students' union' means:

(1)   an association of the generality of students[2] at an establishment[3] to which the Education Act 1994 applies[4] whose principal purposes include promoting the general interests of its members as students[5]; or

(2)   a representative body (whether an association or not) whose principal purposes include representing the generality of students at such an establishment in academic, disciplinary or other matters relating to the government of the establishment[6].

References to a students' union include an association or body which consists wholly or mainly of:

(a) constituent or affiliated associations or bodies which are themselves students' unions[7]; or

(b) representatives of such constituent or affiliated associations[8],

and which fulfils the functions of a students' union[9] in relation to students at an establishment to which the Education Act 1994 applies[10].

An association or body may be a students' union in relation to more than one establishment but not in relation to establishments generally in the United Kingdom or a part of the United Kingdom[11].

1 See the Education Act 1994 Pt II (ss 20–22). A students' union may be a charity: see CHARITIES vol 8 (2015) PARAS 20, 307.

2 References in the Education Act 1994 s 20 to an association of the generality of students, or of any description of students, include:

  (1) any association which the generality of students, or of students of that description, may join, whether or not it has in membership a majority of them (s 20(5)(a)); and

  (2) any association which would fall within head (1) if the references there to students were confined to full-time students (s 20(5)(b)),

  and references to a representative body whose principal purposes include representing the generality of students, or of any description of students, must be similarly construed (s 20(5)).

3 References to a students' union include an association or body which would fall within the Education Act 1994 s 20(1) if for the references to the generality of students at the establishment there were substituted a reference to:

  (1) the generality of undergraduate students, or graduate students, at the establishment (s 20(2)(a)); or

  (2) the generality of students at a particular hall of residence of the establishment (s 20(2)(b)).

4 As to the establishments to which the Education Act 1994 Pt II (ss 20–22) applies see PARA 1116.

5 Education Act 1994 s 20(1)(a).

6 Education Act 1994 s 20(1)(b). A students' union has purposes and functions which are distinct from those of the establishment to which it relates and is an entity separate from that establishment which nevertheless has a supervisory role: *Customs and Excise Comrs v University of Leicester Students' Union* [2001] EWCA Civ 1972, [2002] STC 147, [2002] ELR 347. However, a students' union does not have a public law or statutory character such as to make its decisions amenable to judicial review: *R v Thames Valley University Students Union, ex p Ogilvy* [1997] CLY 2149.

7 Education Act 1994 s 20(3)(a). The reference to bodies which are themselves students' unions is a reference to bodies which are student unions within s 20(1) or s 20(2) (see the text to notes 1–6): see s 20(3)(a).

8 Education Act 1994 s 20(3)(b).

9 Ie within the Education Act 1994 s 20(1) or s 20(2) (see the text to notes 1–6).

10 Education Act 1994 s 20(3).

11 Education Act 1994 s 20(4). As to the meaning of 'United Kingdom' see PARA 73 note 3.

1116. Applicable establishments. The establishments in England and Wales[1] to which the provisions of the Education Act 1994[2] relating to students' unions[3] apply are:

  (1) any university[4] receiving financial support under the Further and Higher Education Act 1992[5];

  (2) any institution conducted by a higher education corporation[6] or further education corporation[7];

  (3) any sixth form college[8];

  (4) any institution designated[9] as eligible to receive support from funds administered by a Higher Education Funding Council[10];

  (5) any institution designated[11] as eligible to receive support from funds administered by a further education funding council[12];

  (6) any institution substantially dependent on financial support under the

provision[13] relating to applications for support for the provision of facilities for part-time, or adult, further education[14];

(7)   any institution designated, or of a description designated, by order of the Secretary of State[15];

(8)   any college[16], school or hall in an establishment within any of heads (1) to (7) above[17].

1   As to the meanings of 'England' and 'Wales' see PARA 7 note 3.
2   Ie the Education Act 1994 Pt II (ss 20–22).
3   As to the meaning of 'students' union' see PARA 1115.
4   As to the meaning of 'university' for the purposes of the Further and Higher Education Act 1992 see PARA 621 note 3. As to universities generally see PARA 621 et seq.
5   Education Act 1994 s 21(1)(a). The relevant provision of the Further and Higher Education Act 1992 is s 65 (see PARA 701).
6   Ie within the meaning of the Further and Higher Education Act 1992 (see PARA 645).
7   Education Act 1994 s 21(1)(b). A further education corporation is a further education corporation within the meaning of the Further and Higher Education Act 1992 (see PARA 555 note 3).
8   Education Act 1994 s 21(1)(ba) (added by SI 2010/1080).
9   Ie under the Education Reform Act 1988 s 129 (see PARA 671).
10 Education Act 1994 s 21(1)(c). As to the Higher Education Funding Councils see PARA 691 et seq.
11 Ie under the Further and Higher Education Act 1992 s 28 (see PARA 572).
12 Education Act 1994 s 21(1)(d).
13 Ie under the Further and Higher Education Act 1992 s 6(5) (repealed).
14 Education Act 1994 s 21(1)(e). For the purposes of s 21(1)(e), an institution is substantially dependent on financial support under the Further and Higher Education Act 1992 s 6(5) (repealed) in any year in which such support amounts to 25% or more of its income: Education Act 1994 s 21(3). For this purpose, 'year' means an accounting year of the institution; and 'income' means receipts of any description, including capital receipts: s 21(3).
15 Education Act 1994 s 21(1)(f). As to the Secretary of State see PARA 58. At the date at which this volume states the law no such order had been made.
16 'College' includes any institution in the nature of a college: Education Act 1994 s 21(4).
17 Education Act 1994 s 21(1)(g).

(ii) Duties of Governing Bodies in relation to Students' Unions

1117.   General duty of governing body in relation to students' unions. The governing body[1] of every establishment to which the provisions of the Education Act 1994[2] relating to students' unions[3] apply must take such steps as are reasonably practicable to secure that any students' union for students at the establishment operates in a fair and democratic manner and is accountable for its finances[4].

1   References in the Education Act 1994 Pt II (ss 20–22) to the governing body of an establishment are references to the executive governing body which has responsibility for the conduct of affairs of the establishment and the management and administration of its revenue and property: s 21(5). As to the establishments in England and Wales to which Pt II applies see PARA 1116.
2   Ie the Education Act 1994 Pt II (ss 20–22).
3   As to the meaning of 'students' union' see PARA 1115.
4   Education Act 1994 s 22(1).

1118.   Duties regarding constitution of students' unions. The governing body[1] of every establishment to which the provisions of the Education Act 1994[2] relating to students' unions[3] apply[4] must take such steps as are reasonably practicable to secure that the following requirements are observed by or in relation to any students' union for students at the establishment[5]. The requirements are that the union must have a written constitution[6] and that the provisions of the constitution must be subject to the approval of the governing body and must be subject to review by that body at intervals of not more than five years[7].

1   As to the meaning of 'governing body' see PARA 1117 note 1.
2   Ie the Education Act 1994 Pt II (ss 20–22).
3   As to the meaning of 'students' union' see PARA 1115.
4   As to the establishments in England and Wales to which the provisions relating to students' unions apply see PARA 1116.
5   Education Act 1994 s 22(2).
6   Education Act 1994 s 22(2)(a). As to the meaning of 'written' see PARA 76 note 8.
7   Education Act 1994 s 22(2)(b).

1119.   Duties regarding students' right not to join students' unions.   A student must have the right not to be a member[1] of the students' union[2], or, in the case of a representative body which is not an association[3], to signify that he does not wish to be represented by it[4], and students who exercise that right must not be unfairly disadvantaged, with regard to the provision of services or otherwise, by reason of their having done so[5]. The governing body of every establishment to which the provisions of the Education Act 1994[6] relating to students' unions apply[7] must take such steps as are reasonably practicable to secure that this requirement is observed by or in relation to any students' union for students at the establishment[8].

1   In the Education Act 1994 s 22, the expression 'members', in relation to a representative body which is not an association, means those whom it is the purpose of the union to represent, excluding any student who has exercised the right referred to in s 22(2)(c)(ii) (see the text to notes 3–4): s 22(7).
2   Education Act 1994 s 22(2)(c)(i). As to the meaning of 'students' union' see PARA 1115. The governing body must bring to the attention of all students, at least once a year, and must include in any information which is generally made available to persons considering whether to become students at the establishment, information as to the right referred to in s 22(2)(c)(i) or in s 22(2)(c)(ii) (see the text to notes 3–4) (s 22(5)(a)), and details of any arrangements it has made for services of a kind which a students' union at the establishment provides for its members to be provided for students who are not members of the union (s 22(5)(b)). As to the meaning of 'governing body' see PARA 1117 note 1.
      For the purposes of s 22(2), (4) and (5), the expression 'all students' is to be construed as follows:
      (1)   in relation to an association or body which is a students' union by virtue of s 20(1) (see PARA 1115), the reference is to all students at the establishment (s 22(6)(a));
      (2)   in relation to an association or body which is a students' union by virtue of s 20(2) (see PARA 1115), the reference is to all undergraduate, or all graduate, students at the establishment or to all students at the hall of residence in question, as the case may be (s 22(6)(b));
      (3)   in relation to an association or body which is a students' union by virtue of s 20(3) (see PARA 1115), the reference is to all the students who by virtue of s 20(1) or s 20(2) are comprehended by that expression in relation to its constituent or affiliated associations or bodies (s 22(6)(c)).
3   As to the meaning of 'association' see PARA 1115 note 2.
4   Education Act 1994 s 22(2)(c)(ii).
5   Education Act 1994 s 22(2)(c). Students who claim to have been unfairly disadvantaged by reason of their having exercised the right not to be a member of the union or not to be represented by a representative body have the right to make a complaint (see PARA 1123).
6   Ie the Education Act 1994 Pt II (ss 20–22).
7   As to the establishments in England and Wales to which the provisions relating to students' unions apply see PARA 1116.
8   Education Act 1994 s 22(2).

1120. Duties regarding appointment, election and tenure of union officers.
The governing body[1] of every establishment to which the provisions of the
Education Act 1994[2] relating to students' unions[3] apply[4] must take such steps as
are reasonably practicable to secure that the following requirements are observed
by or in relation to any students' union for students at the establishment[5]. The
requirements are that:

(1)   appointment to major union offices must be by election in a secret ballot
        in which all members[6] are entitled to vote[7];

(2)   the governing body must satisfy itself that the elections are fairly and
        properly conducted[8]; and

(3)   a person must not hold sabbatical union office, or paid elected union
        office, for more than two years in total at the establishment[9].

1   As to the meaning of 'governing body' see PARA 1117 note 1.
2   Ie the Education Act 1994 Pt II (ss 20–22).
3   As to the meaning of 'students' union' see PARA 1115.
4   As to the establishments in England and Wales to which the provisions relating to students'
    unions apply see PARA 1116.
5   Education Act 1994 s 22(2).
6   As to the meaning of 'members' see PARA 1119 note 1.
7   Education Act 1994 s 22(2)(d). Section 22(2)(d) does not apply in the case of an establishment
    where the students, or the great majority of them, are provided with materials for private study
    and are not required to attend the establishment to any significant extent or at all (ie an 'open or
    distance learning establishment'): s 22(9).
8   Education Act 1994 s 22(2)(e).
9   Education Act 1994 s 22(2)(f).

1121. Duties regarding financial affairs of students' unions. The governing
body[1] of every establishment to which the provisions of the Education Act 1994[2]
relating to students' unions[3] apply[4] must take such steps as are reasonably
practicable to secure that the following requirements are observed by or in
relation to any students' union for students at the establishment[5]. The
requirements are that:

(1)   the financial affairs of the union must be properly conducted and
        appropriate arrangements must exist for the approval of the union's
        budget, and the monitoring of its expenditure, by the governing body[6];

(2)   financial reports of the union must be published annually or more
        frequently, and must be made available to the governing body and to all
        students[7], and each such report must contain, in particular, a list of the
        external organisations to which the union has made donations in the
        period to which the report relates[8], and details of those donations[9]; and

(3)   the procedure for allocating resources to groups or clubs must be fair
        and must be set down in writing[10] and freely accessible to all students[11].

1   As to the meaning of 'governing body' see PARA 1117 note 1.
2   Ie the Education Act 1994 Pt II (ss 20–22).
3   As to the meaning of 'students' union' see PARA 1115.
4   As to the establishments in England and Wales to which the provisions relating to students'
    unions apply see PARA 1116.
5   Education Act 1994 s 22(2).
6   Education Act 1994 s 22(2)(g).
7   As to the meaning of 'all students' see PARA 1119 note 2.
8   Education Act 1994 s 22(2)(h)(i).
9   Education Act 1994 s 22(2)(h)(ii).
10 As to the meaning of 'writing' see PARA 76 note 8.
11 Education Act 1994 s 22(2)(i).

1122. Duties regarding affiliations of students' unions. The governing body[1] of every establishment to which the provisions of the Education Act 1994[2] relating to students' unions[3] apply[4] must take such steps as are reasonably practicable to secure that the following requirements are observed by or in relation to any students' union for students at the establishment[5]. The requirements are that:

(1) if the union decides to affiliate to an external organisation[6], it must publish notice of its decision stating the name of the organisation[7], and details of any subscription or similar fee paid or proposed to be paid, and of any donation made or proposed to be made, to the organisation[8], and any such notice must be made available to the governing body and to all students[9];

(2) where the union is affiliated to any external organisations, a report must be published annually or more frequently containing a list of the external organisations to which the union is currently affiliated[10], and details of subscriptions or similar fees paid, or donations made, to such organisations in the past year (or since the last report)[11], and such reports must be made available to the governing body and to all students[12]; and

(3) there must be procedures for the review of affiliations to external organisations under which the current list of affiliations is submitted for approval by members[13] annually or more frequently[14], and at such intervals of not more than a year as the governing body may determine, a requisition may be made by such proportion of members (not exceeding 5 per cent) as the governing body may determine, that the question of continued affiliation to any particular organisation be decided upon by a secret ballot in which all members are entitled to vote[15].

1 As to the meaning of 'governing body' see PARA 1117 note 1.
2 Ie the Education Act 1994 Pt II (ss 20–22).
3 As to the meaning of 'students' union' see PARA 1115.
4 As to the establishments in England and Wales to which the provisions relating to students' unions apply see PARA 1116.
5 Education Act 1994 s 22(2).
6 For the purposes of the Education Act 1994 s 22(2)(j)–(l), the references to affiliation to an external organisation, in relation to a students' union for students at an establishment, include any form of membership of, or formal association with, an organisation whose purposes are not confined to purposes connected with that establishment: s 22(8).
7 Education Act 1994 s 22(2)(j)(i).
8 Education Act 1994 s 22(2)(j)(ii).
9 Education Act 1994 s 22(2)(j). As to the meaning of 'all students' see PARA 1119 note 2.
10 Education Act 1994 s 22(2)(k)(i).
11 Education Act 1994 s 22(2)(k)(ii).
12 Education Act 1994 s 22(2)(k).
13 As to the meaning of 'members' see PARA 1119 note 1.
14 Education Act 1994 s 22(2)(l)(i).
15 Education Act 1994 s 22(2)(l)(ii). Section 22(l)(ii) does not apply in the case of an establishment where the students, or the great majority of them, are provided with materials for private study and are not required to attend the establishment to any significant extent or at all (ie an 'open or distance learning establishment'): s 22(9).

1123. Duties regarding complaints in relation to students' unions. The governing body[1] of every establishment to which the provisions of the Education Act 1994[2] relating to students' unions[3] apply[4] must take such steps as are reasonably practicable to secure that the following requirements are observed by or in relation to any students' union for students at the establishment[5]. The requirements are that:

(1) there must be a complaints procedure available to all students[6] or groups of students who are dissatisfied in their dealings with the union[7], or claim to be unfairly disadvantaged by reason of their having exercised the right not to be a member[8] of the union[9] or not to be represented by a representative body[10], which must include provision for an independent person appointed by the governing body to investigate and report on complaints[11]; and

(2) complaints must be dealt with promptly and fairly and where a complaint is upheld there must be an effective remedy[12].

1 As to the meaning of 'governing body' see PARA 1117 note 1.
2 Ie the Education Act 1994 Pt II (ss 20–22).
3 As to the meaning of 'students' union' see PARA 1115.
4 As to the establishments in England and Wales to which the provisions relating to students' unions apply see PARA 1116.
5 Education Act 1994 s 22(2).
6 As to the meaning of 'all students' see PARA 1119 note 2.
7 Education Act 1994 s 22(2)(m)(i).
8 As to the meaning of 'members' see PARA 1119 note 1.
9 Ie the right referred to in the Education Act 1994 s 22(2)(c)(i) (see PARA 1119).
10 Education Act 1994 s 22(2)(m)(ii). The right not to be represented by a representative body is the right referred to in s 22(2)(c)(ii) (see PARA 1119).
11 Education Act 1994 s 22(2)(m).
12 Education Act 1994 s 22(2)(n).

1124. Duty to prepare codes of practice in relation to students' unions. The governing body[1] of every establishment to which the provisions of the Education Act 1994[2] relating to students' unions[3] apply[4] must prepare and issue, and when necessary revise, a code of practice as to the manner in which the requirements to be observed in relation to students' unions[5] are to be carried into effect in relation to any students' union for students at the establishment, setting out in relation to each of the requirements details of the arrangements made to secure its observance[6]. The governing body must, as regards any students' union for students at the establishment, bring the code of practice currently in force to the attention of all students[7], at least once a year[8].

1 As to the meaning of 'governing body' see PARA 1117 note 1.
2 Ie the Education Act 1994 Pt II (ss 20–22).
3 As to the meaning of 'students' union' see PARA 1115.
4 As to the establishments in England and Wales to which the provisions relating to students' unions apply see PARA 1116.
5 Ie the requirements set out in the Education Act 1994 s 22(1)–(2) (see PARAS 1117–1123).
6 Education Act 1994 s 22(3).
7 As to the meaning of 'all students' see PARA 1119 note 2.
8 Education Act 1994 s 22(4)(a).

1125. Duty to publicise provisions safeguarding freedom of speech. The governing body[1] of every establishment to which the provisions of the Education Act 1994[2] relating to students' unions[3] apply[4] and to which the provisions relating to freedom of speech in universities[5] apply must, as regards any students' union for students at the establishment, bring to the attention of all students[6], at least once a year, those provisions and any code of practice issued under them, relevant to the activities or conduct of the union[7].

1   As to the meaning of 'governing body' see PARA 1117 note 1.
2   Ie the Education Act 1994 Pt II (ss 20–22).
3   As to the meaning of 'students' union' see PARA 1115.
4   As to the establishments in England and Wales to which the provisions relating to students'
    unions apply see PARA 1116.
5   Ie the Education (No 2) Act 1986 s 43 (see PARA 6). See also a House of Commons briefing
    paper of 20 May 2015 entitled 'Freedom of speech and preventing extremism in UK higher
    education institutions'; and PARA 6.
6   As to the meaning of 'all students' see PARA 1119 note 2.
7   Education Act 1994 s 22(4)(c).

1126.   Duty to publicise restrictions on union activities arising under law of charities. The governing body[1] of every establishment to which the provisions of the Education Act 1994[2] relating to students' unions[3] apply[4] must, as regards any students' union for students at the establishment, bring to the attention of all students[5], at least once a year, any restrictions imposed on the activities of the union by the law relating to charities[6].

1   As to the meaning of 'governing body' see PARA 1117 note 1.
2   Ie the Education Act 1994 Pt II (ss 20–22).
3   As to the meaning of 'students' union' see PARA 1115.
4   As to the establishments in England and Wales to which the provisions relating to students'
    unions apply see PARA 1116.
5   As to the meaning of 'all students' see PARA 1119 note 2.
6   Education Act 1994 s 22(4)(b). See in particular CHARITIES vol 8 (2015) PARA 20.

10. INSPECTION AND INTERVENTION

(1) THE INSPECTION REGIME

1127.   General responsibility for inspections. The Office for Standards in Education, Children's Services and Skills ('Ofsted')[1] includes Her Majesty's Chief Inspector of Education, Children's Services and Skills[2] and his staff amongst whom are Her Majesty's Inspectors of Education, Children's Services and Skills[3]. The Office performs a strategic role[4] in relation to the performance by the Chief Inspector of his functions which, for the purposes of this title, relate to the quality and inspection of any form of education and training in England[5]. The Chief Inspector's remit extends to independent schools[6], and he may also inspect any local authority in England in relation to its education functions[7].

In relation to Wales, Her Majesty's Chief Inspector of Education and Training in Wales[8] has responsibility for the quality of the education in schools[9] and of education and training for persons aged 16 or over[10]. The Chief Inspector's remit extends to independent schools[11] and he may also inspect any local authority in Wales in relation to its education functions[12].

Quality assurance and inspections of higher education are carried out by the Quality Assurance Agency for Higher Education[13].

1   As to the Office for Standards in Education, Children's Services and Skills (Ofsted) see PARA 1128 et seq.
2   As to Her Majesty's Chief Inspector of Education, Children's Services and Skills see PARA 1133.
3   As to Her Majesty's Inspectors of Education, Children's Services and Skills see PARA 1146.
4   As to the functions of the Office for Standards in Education, Children's Services and Skills see PARA 1129 et seq.
5   As to the functions of Her Majesty's Chief Inspector of Education, Children's Services and Skills see PARA 1136 et seq. As to the inspection of schools in England see PARA 1162 et seq.
6   See PARA 396.
7   See PARA 1289 et seq.
8   As to Her Majesty's Chief Inspector of Education and Training in Wales see PARA 1148.
9   As to the functions of Her Majesty's Chief Inspector of Education and Training in Wales see PARA 1151 et seq. As to the inspection of schools in Wales see PARA 1182 et seq.
10 See PARA 1268 et seq.
11 See PARA 418.
12 See PARA 1293 et seq.
13 See PARA 690.

(2) INSPECTION BODIES

(i) The Office for Standards in Education, Children's Services and Skills

A. ESTABLISHMENT AND ADMINISTRATION

1128.   Establishment and administration. The Office for Standards in Education, Children's Services and Skills ('Ofsted')[1] is a body corporate[2] performing functions[3] on behalf of the Crown[4].

Ofsted has power[5] to appoint staff:

(1)   for the purposes of the performance of its own functions[6]; and

(2)   for the purposes of the performance of functions of the Her Majesty's Chief Inspector of Education, Children's Services and Skills[7].

Ofsted may establish committees, and any committee so established may establish sub-committees[8].

The application of the seal of Ofsted must be authenticated by the signature of any member of Ofsted[9], or some other person who has been authorised for that purpose by Ofsted, whether generally or specially[10].

The Documentary Evidence Act 1868 has effect in relation to Ofsted[11].

1 The Office for Standards in Education, Children's Services and Skills operates under the name 'Ofsted'. Information concerning Ofsted and its activities can found on its website.
2 See the Education and Inspections Act 2006 s 112(1). As to bodies corporate see COMPANIES vol 14 (2009) PARA 2; CORPORATIONS vol 24 (2010) PARA 301 et seq.
3 In the Education and Inspections Act 2006 Pt 8 (ss 112–159), 'functions' includes powers and duties: s 159(1).
4 Education and Inspections Act 2006 s 112(3). As to the constitution of Ofsted and remuneration of members see Sch 11 paras 1–5.
5 However, this power is exercisable only by Her Majesty's Chief Inspector of Education, Children's Services and Skills acting on behalf of Ofsted: see the Education and Inspections Act 2006 Sch 11 para 6(2). As to Her Majesty's Chief Inspector of Education, Children's Services and Skills see PARA 1133.
6 Education and Inspections Act 2006 Sch 11 para 6(1)(a). As to Ofsted's functions see PARA 1129 et seq.
7 Education and Inspections Act 2006 Sch 11 para 6(1)(b). As to the functions of Her Majesty's Chief Inspector of Education, Children's Services and Skills see PARA 1136 et seq. Her Majesty's Inspectors of Education, Children's Services and Skills serve as members of Ofsted's staff: see PARA 1146. As to the conditions of service and management of Ofsted staff see Sch 11 para 6(3), (4). Nothing in Sch 11 is to be read as preventing any delegation of the functions by the Chief Inspector under Sch 12 para 9 (see PARA 1138): Sch 11 para 6(5).
8 Education and Inspections Act 2006 Sch 11 para 7(1). As to the regulation of the procedure of committees and sub-committees see Sch 11 para 8. As to the delegation by Ofsted of functions to a committee or sub-committee see PARA 1130. As to the constitution and remuneration of the committee and sub-committee see Sch 11 para 7(2), (3).
9 Education and Inspections Act 2006 Sch 11 para 10(a).
10 Education and Inspections Act 2006 Sch 11 para 10(b).
11 The Documentary Evidence Act 1868 has effect in relation to Ofsted as if:
    (1) Ofsted were included in the first column of the Schedule to that Act;
    (2) any member or other person authorised to act on behalf of Ofsted were mentioned in the second column of that Schedule; and
    (3) the regulations referred to in that Act included any document issued by or under the authority of Ofsted: Education and Inspections Act 2006 Sch 11 para 11.
    As to the Documentary Evidence Act 1868 see CIVIL PROCEDURE vol 11 (2009) PARA 889 et seq. 'Document' means anything in which information of any description is recorded, including personal records as defined by the Police and Criminal Evidence Act 1984 s 12 (see POLICE AND INVESTIGATORY POWERS vol 84A (2013) PARA 454): Education and Inspections Act 2006 s 159(1).

B. FUNCTIONS

1129. Functions. The Office for Standards in Education, Children's Services and Skills ('Ofsted')[1] has the following functions[2]:
    (1) to determine strategic priorities for Her Majesty's Chief Inspector of Education, Children's Services and Skills[3] in connection with the performance of his functions[4];
    (2) to determine strategic objectives and targets relating to such priorities[5]; and
    (3) to secure that the Chief Inspector's functions are performed efficiently and effectively[6].
Ofsted is to have such other functions in connection with the performance of the Chief Inspector's functions as may be assigned to it by the Secretary of State[7].

1 As to the Office for Standards in Education, Children's Services and Skills see PARA 1128.
2 As to the meaning of 'functions' see PARA 1128 note 3.

3   As to Her Majesty's Chief Inspector of Education, Children's Services and Skills see PARA 1133.
4   Education and Inspections Act 2006 s 116(1)(a). As to the functions of Her Majesty's Chief
    Inspector of Education, Children's Services and Skills see PARA 1136 et seq.
5   Education and Inspections Act 2006 s 116(1)(b).
6   Education and Inspections Act 2006 s 116(1)(c).
7   Education and Inspections Act 2006 s 116(2). As to the Secretary of State see PARA 58.

1130. Performance of functions. The Office for Standards in Education, Children's Services and Skills ('Ofsted')[1] is to perform its functions[2] for the general purpose of encouraging:

(1)   the improvement of activities within the remit of Her Majesty's Chief Inspector of Education, Children's Services and Skills[3];

(2)   the carrying on of such activities as user-focused activities[4]; and

(3)   the efficient and effective use of resources in the carrying on of such activities[5].

In performing its functions Ofsted is to have regard to:

(a)   the need to safeguard and promote the rights and welfare of children[6];

(b)   any matters raised by the Children's Commissioner with the Office or the Chief Inspector[7];

(c)   views expressed by relevant persons[8] about activities within the Chief Inspector's remit[9];

(d)   levels of satisfaction with such activities on the part of relevant persons[10];

(e)   the need to promote the efficient and effective use of resources in the carrying on of such activities[11];

(f)   the need to ensure that action by the Chief Inspector in relation to such activities is proportionate to the risks against which it would afford safeguards[12];

(g)   any developments in approaches to inspection or regulatory action[13]; and

(h)   best practice amongst persons performing functions comparable to those of the Chief Inspector[14].

In performing its functions Ofsted must also have regard to such aspects of government policy as the Secretary of State[15] may direct[16].

Anything authorised or required to be done by Ofsted may be done by any member of Ofsted[17] who is authorised for the purpose by Ofsted (whether generally or specially)[18]; or any committee or sub-committee of Ofsted which has been so authorised[19].

Ofsted may do anything that it considers is necessary or expedient for the purposes of, or in connection with, its functions[20].

1   As to the Office for Standards in Education, Children's Services and Skills see PARA 1128.
2   As to the meaning of 'functions' see PARA 1128 note 3. As to Ofsted's functions see PARA 1129.
3   See the Education and Inspections Act 2006 s 117(1)(a). For the purposes of Pt 8 (ss 112–159):
    (1)   'activities' includes the provision of any form of education, training or care, the
          provision of any form of services or facilities and the performance of any function
          (s 117(5), (6)(a));
    (2)   activities are within the Chief Inspector's remit if he exercises any inspection function in
          relation to them (s 117(5), (6)(b)(i)), or if they are services of the kind provided by
          persons in respect of whom he is the registration authority by virtue of any enactment
          (s 117(5), (6)(b)(ii)); and
    (3)   references to persons for whose benefit activities are carried on are, in relation to
          activities within head (1)(a) or (b) above, references to persons for whom the education,
          training or care is provided, or (as the case may be) for whom the services or facilities
          are provided (s 117(5), (6)(c)).

As to Her Majesty's Chief Inspector of Education, Children's Services and Skills see PARA 1133. As to the functions of Her Majesty's Chief Inspector of Education, Children's Services and Skills see PARA 1136 et seq. As to the meaning of 'person' see PARA 7 note 6. 'The registration authority' means the person exercising functions relating to registration: s 159(1). As to the meaning of 'enactment' see PARA 26 note 15.

4   Education and Inspections Act 2006 s 117(1)(b). In Pt 8 (ss 112–159) any reference to the carrying on of activities as 'user-focused' activities is a reference to the carrying on of the activities in a way that focuses on the needs of those for whose benefit the activities are carried on: s 159(2).

5   Education and Inspections Act 2006 s 117(1)(c).

6   Education and Inspections Act 2006 s 117(2)(a). 'Children' means persons under the age of 18: s 117(4)(a). As to the time at which a person attains a particular age see PARA 7 note 6.

7   Education and Inspections Act 2006 s 17(2)(aa) (added by the Children and Families Act 2014 s 116(2)(a)). As to the Children's Commissioner see CHILDREN AND YOUNG PERSONS vol 9 (2012) PARA 180 et seq.

8   'Relevant persons', in relation to activities within the Chief Inspector's remit, means persons who have an interest in such activities, whether as persons for whose benefit they are carried on (Education and Inspections Act 2006 s 117(4)(b)(i)), or as parents (if they are carried on for the benefit of children) (s 117(4)(b)(ii)), or as employers (s 117(4)(b)(iii)). 'Parents' includes persons who are not parents of children but have parental responsibility for them (within the meaning of the Children Act 1989: see CHILDREN AND YOUNG PERSONS vol 9 (2012) PARA 151) (Education and Inspections Act 2006 s 117(4)(c)(i)), or who have care of children (s 117(4)(c)(ii)).

9   Education and Inspections Act 2006 s 117(2)(b).

10 Education and Inspections Act 2006 s 117(2)(c).

11 Education and Inspections Act 2006 s 117(2)(d).

12 Education and Inspections Act 2006 s 117(2)(e).

13 Education and Inspections Act 2006 s 117(2)(f).

14 Education and Inspections Act 2006 s 117(2)(g).

15 As to the Secretary of State see PARA 58.

16 Education and Inspections Act 2006 s 117(3).

17 As to the membership of Ofsted see PARA 1128.

18 Education and Inspections Act 2006 Sch 11 para 9(a).

19 Education and Inspections Act 2006 Sch 11 para 9(b). As to committees and sub-committees see PARA 1128.

20 Education and Inspections Act 2006 Sch 11 para 13(1). To the extent that Sch 11 para 6 (see PARA 1128) or Sch 11 para 12 (see PARA 1131) makes provision for restricting the exercise of any such power, the power is accordingly exercisable subject to any such restriction: Sch 11 para 13(2).

1131. Supplementary powers. The Office for Standards in Education, Children's Services and Skills ('Ofsted')[1], in connection with the performance of its own functions[2] or in connection with the performance of functions of Her Majesty's Chief Inspector of Education, Children's Services and Skills[3], has power:

(1)   to enter into contracts[4];

(2)   to acquire, and dispose of, land[5] or other property[6]; and

(3)   to arrange for the provision of accommodation[7].

However, these powers are exercisable only by the Chief Inspector acting on behalf of Ofsted[8], and the management of any property or accommodation held or used in connection with the performance of any of those functions is to be the responsibility of the Chief Inspector[9].

Nothing in these provisions is to be read as preventing any delegation[10] by the Chief Inspector[11].

1   As to the Office for Standards in Education, Children's Services and Skills see PARA 1128.

2   As to the meaning of 'functions' see PARA 1128 note 3. As to Ofsted's functions and their performance see PARAS 1129–1130.

3   As to Her Majesty's Chief Inspector of Education, Children's Services and Skills see PARA 1133. As to the functions of Her Majesty's Chief Inspector of Education, Children's Services and Skills see PARA 1136 et seq.

4   Education and Inspections Act 2006 Sch 11 para 12(1)(a).
5   In any Act, unless the contrary intention appears, 'land' includes buildings and other structures, land covered with water, and any estate, interest, easement, servitude or right in or over land: Interpretation Act 1978 s 5, Sch 1.
6   Education and Inspections Act 2006 Sch 11 para 12(1)(b).
7   Education and Inspections Act 2006 Sch 11 para 12(1)(c).
8   Education and Inspections Act 2006 Sch 11 para 12(2).
9   Education and Inspections Act 2006 Sch 11 para 12(3).
10   Ie under the Education and Inspections Act 2006 Sch 12 para 9: see PARA 1128.
11   Education and Inspections Act 2006 Sch 11 para 12(4).

1132. Common inspection framework. The Office for Standards in Education, Children's Services and Skills ('Ofsted')[1] has introduced changes to the way it inspects schools, further education and skills and early years provision[2]. Among other changes, a common inspection framework now applies which sets out the principles that apply to the inspections of maintained schools[3], academies[4], independent schools[5], further education and skills providers[6] and registered early years settings[7].

1   As to the Office for Standards in Education, Children's Services and Skills see PARA 1128.
2   The changes introduced took effect from September 2015: see the Guidance document '*Changes to education inspection from September 2015*' (15 June 2015), available at the date at which this volume states the law on the Government website.
3   As to maintained schools see PARA 99 et seq.
4   As to academies see PARA 345 et seq.
5   As to independent schools see PARA 369 et seq.
6   As to further education see PARA 555 et seq.
7   As to early years provision see PARA 95. See the handbook '*The common inspection framework: education, skills and early years*', available at the date at which this volume states the law on the Government website. The handbook applies to inspections carried out under the Education Act 2005 s 5 (schools: see PARA 1389), the Education and Skills Act 2008 s 109 (independent schools: see PARA 492), the Education and Inspections Act 2006 (further education and skills: see PARA 1498 et seq), and the Childcare Act 2006 (see CHILDREN AND YOUNG PERSONS). The framework is accompanied by an inspection handbook for each remit.

C. HER MAJESTY'S CHIEF INSPECTOR OF EDUCATION, CHILDREN'S SERVICES AND SKILLS

(A) Appointment and Administration

1133. Appointment. Her Majesty may by Order in Council[1] appoint a person to the office of Her Majesty's Chief Inspector of Education, Children's Services and Skills[2]. The Chief Inspector is to be a member of the Office for Standards in Education, Children's Services and Skills ('Ofsted')[3]. The Chief Inspector holds and vacates office in accordance with the terms of his appointment[4] which are to be determined by the Secretary of State[5]. However, the Chief Inspector must not be appointed for a term of more than five years[6], may at any time resign by giving written[7] notice to the Secretary of State[8], and may be removed from office by Her Majesty on the grounds that he is unable or unfit to carry out the duties of his office[9]. The previous appointment of a person as Chief Inspector does not affect his eligibility for appointment[10].

If there is a vacancy in the office of Chief Inspector, the Secretary of State may appoint a person to be Chief Inspector during such period (not exceeding one year) as he thinks fit[11]. Any such appointment is to be on such terms as the Secretary of State may determine[12], and those terms may include provision for the Secretary of State to terminate the appointment before the time when it would otherwise end[13].

Ofsted is to pay the Chief Inspector such remuneration, and such travelling and other allowances, as the Secretary of State may determine[14]. In the case of any Chief Inspector determined by the Secretary of State, Ofsted is to pay such pension, allowance or gratuity to or in respect of him[15], or such contributions or payments towards provision for such a pension, allowance or gratuity[16], as the Secretary of State may determine[17]. If, when any person ceases to hold office as Chief Inspector, the Secretary of State determines that there are special circumstances which make it right that he should receive compensation, Ofsted may pay to him such sum by way of compensation as the Secretary of State may determine[18].

1   Sir Michael Wilshaw was appointed the office of Her Majesty's Chief Inspector of Education, Children's Services and Skills on 1 January 2012: see the Chief Inspector of Education, Children's Services and Skills Order 2011, SI 2011/2720.
2   Education and Inspections Act 2006 s 113(1). The office of Her Majesty's Chief Inspector of Schools in England (ie the office created under the Education Act 2005 s 1 (repealed)) is abolished: Education and Inspections Act 2006 s 113(8). But any person holding that office immediately before the appointed day is to become, as from that day, Her Majesty's Chief Inspector of Education, Children's Services and Skills: s 113(9). As from the appointed day: the Order in Council by which such a person was appointed has effect as if it were an Order in Council under s 113(1) appointing him as Chief Inspector (s 113(10)(a)); and the terms of his appointment have effect as if determined under s 113(5) (see the text to note 5) (s 113(10)(b)). 'The appointed day' means the day appointed under s 188 for the coming into force of s 113: s 113(11). Section 113 was brought into force on 8 November 2006 in so far as it confers power to make subordinate legislation (see s 188(1)) and on 1 April 2007 for remaining purposes (see s 188(3); Education and Inspections Act 2006 (Commencement No 3 and Transitional Provisions and Savings) Order 2007, SI 2007/935, art 5(s)).
    The Chief Inspector is a person designated for the purposes of the Regulation of Investigatory Powers Act 2000 s 28 as having power to grant authorisations for the carrying out of directed surveillance: see Sch 1 Pt 2 para 27B (added by SI 2003/3171); and POLICE AND INVESTIGATORY POWERS vol 84A (2013) PARA 688.
3   Education and Inspections Act 2006 s 113(3). As to such membership see Sch 11 para 1; and PARA 1128.
4   Education and Inspections Act 2006 s 113(4).
5   See the Education and Inspections Act 2006 s 113(5). As to the Secretary of State see PARA 58.
6   Education and Inspections Act 2006 s 113(6)(a).
7   As to the meaning of 'written' see PARA 76 note 8.
8   Education and Inspections Act 2006 s 113(6)(b).
9   Education and Inspections Act 2006 s 113(6)(c).
10 Education and Inspections Act 2006 s 113(7).
11 Education and Inspections Act 2006 Sch 12 para 2(1).
12 Education and Inspections Act 2006 Sch 12 para 2(2).
13 Education and Inspections Act 2006 Sch 12 para 2(3).
14 Education and Inspections Act 2006 Sch 12 para 1(1).
15 Education and Inspections Act 2006 Sch 12 para 1(2)(a).
16 Education and Inspections Act 2006 Sch 12 para 1(2)(b).
17 Education and Inspections Act 2006 Sch 12 para 1(2). Service as Chief Inspector is one of the kinds of service to which a scheme under the Superannuation Act 1972 s 1 (see CONSTITUTIONAL AND ADMINISTRATIVE LAW vol 20 (2014) PARA 298) can apply: Education and Inspections Act 2006 Sch 12 para 1(4). Ofsted must pay to the Minister for the Civil Service, at such times as he may direct, such sums as he may determine in respect of any increase attributable to Sch 12 para 1(4) in the sums payable out of money provided by Parliament under the Superannuation Act 1972: Education and Inspections Act 2006 Sch 12 para 1(5). As to the Minister for the Civil Service see CONSTITUTIONAL AND ADMINISTRATIVE LAW vol 20 (2014) PARA 235.
18 Education and Inspections Act 2006 Sch 12 para 1(3).

1134.   Documents. The application of the seal of Her Majesty's Chief Inspector of Education, Children's Services and Skills[1] must be authenticated by the signature of the Chief Inspector[2], or some other person who has been authorised for that purpose by the Chief Inspector, whether generally or specially[3].

The Documentary Evidence Act 1868 has effect in relation to the Chief Inspector[4].

1   As to Her Majesty's Chief Inspector of Education, Children's Services and Skills see PARA 1133.
2   Education and Inspections Act 2006 Sch 12 para 4(a).
3   Education and Inspections Act 2006 Sch 12 para 4(b).
4   The Documentary Evidence Act 1868 (see CIVIL PROCEDURE vol 11 (2009) PARA 889 et seq) has effect in relation to the Chief Inspector as if he were mentioned in the first column of the Schedule to that Act, as if he and any person authorised to act on his behalf were mentioned in the second column of that Schedule and as if the regulations referred to in that Act included any document issued by him or any such person: Education and Inspections Act 2006 Sch 12 para 5. As to the meaning of 'document' see PARA 1128 note 11.

1135.   Relationship with Ofsted.   For all purposes relating to the government department constituted by the Office for Standards in Education, Children's Services and Skills ('Ofsted')[1], Her Majesty's Chief Inspector of Education, Children's Services and Skills[2] is to be regarded:

(1)   as part of that government department, whether acting in his capacity as holder of the office of Chief Inspector or in his capacity as a member of Ofsted[3]; and

(2)   as performing his functions[4] (in whatever capacity) on behalf of it[5].

However[6], the Secretary of State[7] may by order[8] make such provision as he considers appropriate for supplementing or modifying the effect of the above provisions[9], or prescribing other matters in connection with responsibilities of the Chief Inspector in relation to Ofsted or otherwise connected with the relationship between them[10]. Such an order may in particular provide:

(a)   for allocating functions, property, rights or liabilities as between Ofsted and the Chief Inspector[11];

(b)   for conferring on the Chief Inspector responsibilities in relation to property, rights or liabilities of Ofsted, including responsibilities as to the conduct of proceedings[12];

(c)   for the capacity in which the Chief Inspector is to discharge any such functions or responsibilities[13].

1   As to the Office for Standards in Education, Children's Services and Skills see PARA 1128.
2   As to Her Majesty's Chief Inspector of Education, Children's Services and Skills see PARA 1133.
3   Education and Inspections Act 2006 Sch 12 para 8(1)(a). As to the Chief Inspector as a member of Ofsted see PARAS 1128; 1133.
4   As to the meaning of 'functions' see PARA 1128 note 3. As to the functions of Her Majesty's Chief Inspector of Education, Children's Services and Skills see PARA 1136 et seq.
5   Education and Inspections Act 2006 Sch 12 para 8(1)(b).
6   The Education and Inspections Act 2006 Sch 12 para 8(1) (see the text to notes 1–5) applies subject to any provision made by virtue of Sch 12 para 8(3): Sch 12 para 8(2).
7   As to the Secretary of State see PARA 58.
8   The Office for Standards in Education, Children's Services and Skills and Her Majesty's Chief Inspector of Education, Children's Services and Skills (Allocation of Rights and Liabilities) Order 2007, SI 2007/600, has been made. Any responsibilities relating to rights and liabilities relating to functions, staff and property of Ofsted are the responsibilities of Ofsted, and Ofsted has responsibility for the conduct of any legal proceedings in relation to those rights and liabilities: see art 2(1). But any responsibilities in relation to rights and liabilities (including the conduct of legal proceedings) relating to powers of Ofsted exercisable only by the Chief Inspector acting on behalf of Ofsted are responsibilities of the Chief Inspector in his capacity as a member of Ofsted: see art 2(2). Any responsibilities in relation to the rights and liabilities (including the conduct of legal proceedings) relating to functions conferred on the Chief Inspector in his capacity as holder of the office of Chief Inspector are the responsibilities of the

Chief Inspector in that capacity: see art 3. As to Ofsted's functions see PARA 1129 et seq. As to the appointment of staff by Ofsted see PARA 1128. As to the powers of Ofsted exercisable only by the Chief Inspector acting on its behalf see PARAS 1128, 1131.

9   Education and Inspections Act 2006 Sch 12 para 8(3)(a).
10   Education and Inspections Act 2006 Sch 12 para 8(3)(b).
11   Education and Inspections Act 2006 Sch 12 para 8(4)(a).
12   Education and Inspections Act 2006 Sch 12 para 8(4)(b).
13   Education and Inspections Act 2006 Sch 12 para 8(4)(c).

(B) Functions

1136. Functions. Her Majesty's Chief Inspector of Education, Children's Services and Skills[1] has the general duty[2] of keeping the Secretary of State[3] informed about:

(1)   the quality of activities within the Chief Inspector's remit[4] and (where appropriate) the standards achieved by those for whose benefit such activities are carried on[5];

(2)   improvements in the quality of such activities and in any such standards[6];

(3)   the extent to which such activities are being carried on as user-focused activities[7]; and

(4)   the efficient and effective use of resources in the carrying on of such activities and services[8].

If requested to do so by the Secretary of State, the Chief Inspector must provide him with information or advice on such matters relating to activities within the Chief Inspector's remit as are specified in the request[9]. The Chief Inspector may at any time give advice to the Secretary of State on any matter connected with any activities within his remit, including advice relating to a particular establishment, institution or agency[10]. The Chief Inspector is to have such other functions in connection with activities within his remit as may be assigned to him by the Secretary of State[11].

Nothing in the above provisions prejudices the operation of any other enactment relating to functions of the Chief Inspector[12].

The Chief Inspector's functions in relation to education extend to the inspection of schools in England[13]; the inspection of further education and training in England[14]; the inspection and review of local authorities in England[15]; the inspection of registered independent educational institutions in England[16], certain functions in relation to the registration of such institutions[17], and the reporting on independent inspectorates in relation to such institutions[18].

The Chief Inspector also has certain other functions relating to matters other than education. These are the inspection of the Children and Family Court Advisory and Support Service functions[19]; the inspection of secure training centres and secure colleges[20]; and the inspection of premises in connection with adoption and fostering functions[21]. He is also the registration authority in relation to children's homes, residential family centres, fostering agencies, voluntary adoption agencies, and adoption support agencies[22].

1   As to Her Majesty's Chief Inspector of Education, Children's Services and Skills see PARA 1133. As to the performance by the Chief Inspector of his functions see PARA 1137. As to the functions of the Office for Standards in Education, Children's Services and Skills ('Ofsted') in the setting of strategic objectives and priorities for, and in securing the performance of, the Chief Inspector's functions see PARA 1129. In performing its functions Ofsted is to encourage the improvement of activities within the Chief Inspector's remit: see the Education and Inspections Act 2006 s 117; and PARA 1130.

2 Subject to the provisions of the Education and Inspections Act 2006 ss 123–159, the functions of Her Majesty's Chief Inspector of Schools in England under or by virtue of any enactment are transferred to Her Majesty's Chief Inspector of Education, Children's Services and Skills: see s 122(1), (2). The office of Her Majesty's Chief Inspector of Schools in England (ie the office created under the Education Act 2005 s 1 (repealed)) is abolished: see the Education and Inspections Act 2006 s 113(8); and PARA 1133. As to the meaning of 'functions' see PARA 1128 note 3. As to the meaning of 'enactment' see PARA 26 note 15.

Functions conferred on the Chief Inspector by virtue of Pt 8 (ss 112–159) or any other enactment are conferred on him in his capacity as holder of the office of Chief Inspector and not in his capacity as a member of the Ofsted: Sch 12 para 7(1). However, this does not apply to any function of the Chief Inspector under s 114(4) (see PARA 1146), Sch 11 para 6 (see PARA 1128), Sch 11 para 12 (see PARA 1131), or Sch 12 para 3 (see PARA 1138): Sch 12 para 7(2). Any proceedings brought in respect of any such function of the Chief Inspector are to be brought against the Chief Inspector in his capacity as holder of that office: Sch 12 para 7(4).

3 As to the Secretary of State see PARA 58.
4 As to the meaning of 'activities within the Chief Inspector's remit' see PARA 1130 note 3.
5 Education and Inspections Act 2006 s 118(1)(a). As to the meaning of references to persons for whose benefit activities are carried on see PARA 1130 note 3.
6 Education and Inspections Act 2006 s 118(1)(b).
7 Education and Inspections Act 2006 s 118(1)(c). As to the meaning of references to the carrying on of activities as user-focused activities see PARA 1130 note 4.
8 Education and Inspections Act 2006 s 118(1)(d).
9 Education and Inspections Act 2006 s 118(2). Where the Chief Inspector is so requested to provide the Secretary of State with information or advice on matters relating to activities within the Chief Inspector's remit (s 118(5)), any enactment by virtue of which an inspection may be conducted by the Chief Inspector in relation to the activities in question (whether or not in pursuance of any duty) or any power of entry is exercisable by him in relation to those activities, is to have effect, with any necessary modifications, so as to enable him to conduct an inspection, or exercise any such power, for the purpose of complying with the request (s 118(6)). Any such reference to a power of entry includes a reference to a power to inspect documents or a power conferred in connection with the inspection of documents: s 118(7). As to the meaning of 'document' see PARA 1128 note 11.
10 Education and Inspections Act 2006 s 118(3).
11 Education and Inspections Act 2006 s 118(4).
12 Education and Inspections Act 2006 s 118(8).
13 See the Education Act 2005 Pt 1 (s 1–63); and PARA 1162 et seq. As to the meaning of 'England' see PARA 7 note 3.
14 See the Education and Inspections Act 2006 Pt 8 Ch 3 (ss 123–134); and PARA 1260 et seq.
15 See the Education and Inspections Act 2006 Pt 8 Ch 4 (ss 135–142); and PARA 1289 et seq.
16 See the Education and Skills Act 2008 ss 108–113; and PARA 396 et seq.
17 See the Education and Skills Act 2008 ss 97, 99, 103; and PARAS 384, 386, 389.
18 See the Education and Skills Act 2008 s 107; and PARA 395.
19 See the Education and Inspections Act 2006 Pt 8 Ch 5 (ss 143–145); and CHILDREN AND YOUNG PERSONS vol 9 (2012) PARA 225.
20 See the Education and Inspections Act 2006 s 146; and PRISONS AND PRISONERS vol 85 (2012) PARA 409.
21 See the Education and Inspections Act 2006 s 147; and CHILDREN AND YOUNG PERSONS vol 9 (2012) PARA 228.
22 See the Education and Inspections Act 2006 s 148; Care Standards Act 2000 Pt 2 (ss 11–42); and CHILDREN AND YOUNG PERSONS vol 9 (2012) PARA 228.

1137. Performance of functions. Her Majesty's Chief Inspector of Education, Children's Services and Skills[1] is to perform his functions[2] for the general purpose of encouraging:

(1) the improvement of activities within the Chief Inspector's remit[3];
(2) the carrying on of such activities as user-focused activities[4]; and
(3) the efficient and effective use of resources in the carrying on of such activities[5].

The Chief Inspector must ensure that his functions are performed efficiently and effectively[6]; and that, so far as practicable, those functions are performed in a way that responds to the needs of persons for whose benefit activities within the Chief Inspector's remit are carried on[7], and the views expressed by other relevant persons[8] about such activities[9].

In performing his functions the Chief Inspector must have regard to:

(a) the need to safeguard and promote the rights and welfare of children[10];

(b) any matters raised by the Children's Commissioner with the Office or the Chief Inspector[11];

(c) views expressed by relevant persons about activities within the Chief Inspector's remit[12];

(d) levels of satisfaction with such activities on the part of relevant persons[13];

(e) the need to promote the efficient and effective use of resources in the carrying on of such activities[14];

(f) the need to ensure that action by the Chief Inspector in relation to such activities is proportionate to the risks against which it would afford safeguards[15];

(g) any developments in approaches to inspection or regulatory action[16];

(h) best practice amongst persons performing functions comparable to those of the Chief Inspector[17]; and

(i) such aspects of government policy as the Secretary of State[18] may direct[19].

Information obtained by the Chief Inspector in connection with any of his functions may be used by him in connection with any of his other functions[20].

The Chief Inspector may do anything that he considers necessary or expedient for the purposes of, or in connection with, his functions[21].

1   As to Her Majesty's Chief Inspector of Education, Children's Services and Skills see PARA 1133.
2   As to the meaning of 'functions' see PARA 1128 note 3. As to the functions of Her Majesty's Chief Inspector of Education, Children's Services and Skills see PARA 1136.
3   Education and Inspections Act 2006 s 119(1)(a). As to the meaning of 'activities within the Chief Inspector's remit' see PARA 1130 note 3.
4   Education and Inspections Act 2006 s 119(1)(b). As to the meaning of references to the carrying on of activities as user-focused activities see PARA 1130 note 4.
5   Education and Inspections Act 2006 s 119(1)(c).
6   Education and Inspections Act 2006 s 119(2)(a).
7   Education and Inspections Act 2006 s 119(1)(b)(i). As to the meaning of references to persons for whose benefit activities are carried on see PARA 1130 note 3.
8   'Relevant persons' has the same meaning as in the Education and Inspections Act 2006 s 117 (see PARA 1130 note 8): s 119(4). As to the meaning of 'person' see PARA 7 note 6.
9   Education and Inspections Act 2006 s 119(1)(b)(ii).
10   Education and Inspections Act 2006 ss 117(2)(a), 119(3)(a). As to the meaning of 'children' see PARA 1130 note 6.
11   Education and Inspections Act 2006 ss 117(2)(aa), 119(3)(aa) (added by the Children and Families Act 2014 s 116(2)). As to the Children's Commissioner see CHILDREN AND YOUNG PERSONS vol 9 (2012) PARA 180 et seq.
12   Education and Inspections Act 2006 ss 117(2)(b), 119(3)(a).
13   Education and Inspections Act 2006 ss 117(2)(c), 119(3)(a).
14   Education and Inspections Act 2006 ss 117(2)(d), 119(3)(a).
15   Education and Inspections Act 2006 ss 117(2)(e), 119(3)(a).
16   Education and Inspections Act 2006 ss 117(2)(f), 119(3)(a).
17   Education and Inspections Act 2006 ss 117(2)(g), 119(3)(a).
18   As to the Secretary of State see PARA 58.
19   Education and Inspections Act 2006 s 119(3)(b).
20   Education and Inspections Act 2006 s 153.
21   Education and Inspections Act 2006 Sch 12 para 6.

1138. Delegation of functions. Anything authorised or required by or under any enactment[1] to be done by Her Majesty's Chief Inspector of Education, Children's Services and Skills[2] may be done by:

(1)   any of Her Majesty's Inspectors of Education, Children's Services and Skills[3];

(2)   any other member of the staff of the Office for Standards in Education, Children's Services and Skills ('Ofsted')[4];

(3)   any additional inspector[5]; or

(4)   any inspection administrator[6],

who is authorised generally or specially for the purpose by the Chief Inspector[7]. However, the making of any report of an inspection of a school[8] which states the opinion that special measures are required to be taken in relation to the school must be personally authorised by the Chief Inspector[9], or an Inspector of Education, Children's Services and Skills who is authorised by the Chief Inspector for these purposes[10].

Where an inspector[11], a member of the staff of Ofsted[12], an additional inspector[13], or an inspection administrator[14], is authorised to act on behalf of the Chief Inspector in connection with the carrying out of any of the activities within his remit[15], the Chief Inspector must ensure that the person concerned has such qualifications, experience and skills as are necessary to secure that he is able to perform the function[16], or (as the case may be) assist with its performance, in an effective manner[17].

Any person exercising[18]:

(a)   any power of entry conferred on the Chief Inspector by virtue of any enactment[19];

(b)   any power to inspect documents so conferred[20]; or

(c)   any power so conferred in connection with the inspection of documents[21],

must, if so required, produce a duly authenticated document showing his authority to exercise the power concerned[22].

The Chief Inspector may delegate any of his inspection functions[23] (to such extent as he may determine) to another public authority[24]. If the carrying out of an inspection is so delegated it is nevertheless to be regarded for the purposes of any enactment as carried out by the Chief Inspector[25].

1   As to the meaning of 'enactment' see PARA 26 note 15.

2   As to Her Majesty's Chief Inspector of Education, Children's Services and Skills see PARA 1133. As to the functions of Her Majesty's Chief Inspector of Education, Children's Services and Skills see PARA 1136.

3   Education and Inspections Act 2006 Sch 12 para 9(1)(a). The Chief Inspector may designate one of Her Majesty's Inspectors of Education, Children's Services and Skills to perform his functions during any period when he is absent or unable to act: see Sch 12 para 3(1). If (at a time when no such designation is in force) it appears to the chairman of Ofsted that the Chief Inspector is, as a result of any incapacity unable to act, and unable to make such a designation, the chairman may designate one of Her Majesty's Inspectors of Education, Children's Services and Skills to perform the Chief Inspector's functions so long as he remains in office and is unable to act: see Sch 12 para 3(2). For these purposes the Chief Inspector's functions include his functions as a member of the Ofsted: Sch 12 para 3(3). As to Her Majesty's Inspectors of Education, Children's Services and Skills see PARA 1146.

4   Education and Inspections Act 2006 Sch 12 para 9(1)(b). As to the Office for Standards in Education, Children's Services and Skills see PARA 1128.

5   Education and Inspections Act 2006 Sch 12 para 9(1)(c). As to additional inspectors see PARA 1139.

6   Education and Inspections Act 2006 Sch 12 para 9(1)(d) (added by the Apprenticeships, Skills, Children and Learning Act 2009 s 226(1), (2)). As to inspection administrators see PARA 1139.

7   Education and Inspections Act 2006 Sch 12 para 9(1). However, Sch 12 para 9(1) has effect subject to Sch 12 paras 9(3), 10(2) (see the text to notes 8–10, 16–17), Sch 12 paras 11(4), 11A(3) (see PARA 1139), and any contrary provision made by any enactment: Sch 12 para 9(2) (amended by the Apprenticeships, Skills, Children and Learning Act 2009 s 226(1), (3)). Without prejudice to the generality of the Education and Inspections Act 2006 Sch 12 para 9(1), references to the Chief Inspector:

(1)   in the Education Act 2005 s 10 (power of entry for purposes of inspection under s 5 or 8: see PARA 1162) (Education and Inspections Act 2006 Sch 12 para 9(4)(a)); or

(2)   in any other enactment by virtue of which any power of entry is exercisable by the Chief Inspector, or otherwise having effect in connection with any such power of entry (Sch 12 para 9(4)(b)),

include references to any person authorised to act on his behalf under Sch 12 para 9(1) (Sch 12 para 9(4)). The reference to any power of entry includes a reference to a power to inspect documents or a power conferred in connection with the inspection of documents: Sch 12 para 9(5). As to the meaning of 'document' see PARA 1128 note 11.

8   Ie under the Education Act 2005 s 5: see PARA 1162.

9   Education and Inspections Act 2006 Sch 12 para 9(3)(a).

10   Education and Inspections Act 2006 Sch 12 para 9(3)(b).

11   Education and Inspections Act 2006 Sch 12 para 10(1)(a).

12   Education and Inspections Act 2006 Sch 12 para 10(1)(b).

13   Education and Inspections Act 2006 Sch 12 para 10(1)(c).

14   Education and Inspections Act 2006 Sch 12 para 10(1)(d) (added by the Apprenticeships, Skills, Children and Learning Act 2009 s 226(1), (4)).

15   Education and Inspections Act 2006 Sch 12 para 10(1). As to the meaning of 'activities within the Chief Inspector's remit' see PARA 1130 note 3.

16   As to the meaning of 'function' see PARA 1128 note 3.

17   Education and Inspections Act 2006 Sch 12 para 10(2).

18   Ie in accordance with the Education and Inspections Act 2006 Sch 12 para 9: see the text to notes 1–10.

19   Education and Inspections Act 2006 s 150(1)(a).

20   Education and Inspections Act 2006 s 150(1)(b).

21   Education and Inspections Act 2006 s 150(1)(c).

22   Education and Inspections Act 2006 s 150(2). Nothing in s 150 applies in relation to any exercise of the power conferred by s 141(1) (see PARA 1292): s 150(3).

23   'Inspection functions' means functions relating to, or connected with, inspections: Education and Inspections Act 2006 Sch 13 para 1(4).

24   Education and Inspections Act 2006 Sch 13 para 3(1). As to the meaning of 'public authority' see PARA 1141 note 11.

25   Education and Inspections Act 2006 Sch 13 para 3(2).

1139.   Arrangements for assistance in performance of functions.   Her Majesty's Chief Inspector of Education, Children's Services and Skills[1] may enter into arrangements with such persons[2] as he thinks fit for them to assist him in the performance of his functions[3] in a particular case or class of case[4]. The Chief Inspector may also enter into arrangements with persons ('inspection service providers') under which they provide the services of inspectors to carry out inspections on behalf of the Chief Inspector[5]. A person assisting the Chief Inspector in pursuance of such arrangements[6] is to be known as an 'additional inspector'[7].

The Chief Inspector may not authorise an additional inspector to conduct an inspection of a school[8] unless the inspection is to be supervised by one of Her Majesty's Inspectors of Education, Children's Services and Skills[9], or the additional inspector has previously conducted such an inspection under the supervision of one of Her Majesty's Inspectors of Education, Children's Services and Skills to the satisfaction of that inspector[10].

The Chief Inspector may enter into arrangements with inspection service providers under which they provide the services of persons to provide administrative support in connection with the carrying out of inspections[11]. A person providing administrative support in pursuance of such arrangements is to be known as an 'inspection administrator'[12]. The Chief Inspector may not authorise an inspection administrator to conduct an inspection[13].

1 As to Her Majesty's Chief Inspector of Education, Children's Services and Skills see PARA 1133.
2 As to the meaning of 'person' see PARA 7 note 6.
3 As to the meaning of 'functions' see PARA 1128 note 3. As to the functions of Her Majesty's Chief Inspector of Education, Children's Services and Skills see PARA 1136.
4 Education and Inspections Act 2006 Sch 12 para 11(1).
5 Education and Inspections Act 2006 Sch 12 para 11(2). In relation to arrangements made with inspection service providers under Sch 12 para 11(2) ('ISP arrangements') (see Sch 12 para 12(1)), in pursuance of his duty under Sch 12 para 10(2) (see PARA 1138), so far as applying to additional inspectors provided under ISP arrangements, the Chief Inspector must publish in such manner as he thinks fit (Sch 12 para 12(2)(a)), and may from time to time revise (Sch 12 para 12(2)(b)), a statement of the following matters:
   (1) the qualifications or experience (or both) that are to be required of additional inspectors provided under ISP arrangements (Sch 12 para 12(2), (3)(a)); and
   (2) the standards that such additional inspectors are to be required to meet in the exercise of their functions and the skills that they are to be required to demonstrate in the exercise of those functions (Sch 12 para 12(2), (3)(b)).
   ISP arrangements must be made on terms that require the inspection service provider to secure compliance with any requirements that are for the time being published under Sch 12 para 12(2): Sch 12 para 12(4). Where the Chief Inspector has entered into any ISP arrangements, he must publish, at intervals of not more than 12 months, a list of the names of the persons who are, at a specified date, currently notified to him by the inspection service provider as persons with whom the provider proposes to make arrangements for the carrying out of inspections on behalf of the Chief Inspector: Sch 12 para 12(5). As to the meaning of 'month' see PARA 54 note 26.
6 Ie arrangements under the Education and Inspections Act 2006 Sch 12 para 11(1) or (2): see the text to notes 1–5.
7 Education and Inspections Act 2006 Sch 12 para 11(3).
8 Ie under the Education Act 2005 s 5: see PARA 1162.
9 Education and Inspections Act 2006 Sch 12 para 11(4)(a). As to Her Majesty's Inspectors of Education, Children's Services and Skills see PARA 1146.
10 See the Education and Inspections Act 2006 Sch 12 para 11(4)(b). The reference in Sch 12 para 11(4)(b) to one of Her Majesty's Inspectors of Education, Children's Services and Skills is, in relation to an inspection conducted before 1 April 2007 (ie date of the commencement of Sch 12 para 11), to be read as a reference to one of Her Majesty's Inspectors of Schools in England: Sch 12 para 11(5). Her Majesty's Inspectors of Schools in England were appointed under the Education Act 2005 s 1(2) (repealed).
11 Education and Inspections Act 2006 Sch 12 para 11A(1) (Sch 12 para 11A added by the Apprenticeships, Skills, Children and Learning Act 2009 s 226(1), (5)).
12 Education and Inspections Act 2006 Sch 12 para 11A(2) (as added: see note 11).
13 Education and Inspections Act 2006 Sch 12 para 11A(3) (as added: see note 11).

1140. Inspection programmes and frameworks. Her Majesty's Chief Inspector of Education, Children's Services and Skills[1] must from time to time, or at such times as the Secretary of State[2] may specify by order[3], prepare a document setting out what inspections he proposes to carry out (an 'inspection programme')[4], and a document setting out the manner in which he proposes to carry out his functions[5] of inspecting and reporting (an 'inspection framework')[6]. The Secretary of State may by order specify the form that inspection programmes or inspection frameworks are to take[7].

Before preparing an inspection programme or an inspection framework the Chief Inspector must consult[8] the Secretary of State[9], the inspection authorities[10], and any other person[11] or body specified by an order made by the Secretary of State[12]; and he must send to each of those persons or bodies a copy of each programme or framework once it is prepared[13].

1 As to Her Majesty's Chief Inspector of Education, Children's Services and Skills see PARA 1133.

2   As to the Secretary of State see PARA 58.
3   At the date at which this volume states the law no such order had been made.
4   Education and Inspections Act 2006 Sch 13 para 4(1)(a).
5   As to the meaning of 'functions' see PARA 1128 note 3. As to the functions of Her Majesty's
    Chief Inspector of Education, Children's Services and Skills see PARA 1136 et seq.
6   Education and Inspections Act 2006 Sch 13 para 4(1)(b). The Chief Inspector may determine
    that any document or combination of documents prepared for the purposes of any other
    enactment or enactments is to be treated as a document prepared for the purposes of Sch 13
    para 4(1)(b) (so long as any requirements applying under or by virtue of Sch 13 para 4 are
    complied with in relation to the document or documents concerned): Sch 13 para 4(4). As to the
    meaning of 'enactment' see PARA 26 note 15.
7   Education and Inspections Act 2006 Sch 13 para 4(3). At the date at which this volume states
    the law no such order had been made.
8   As to the exercise of the duty to consult see JUDICIAL REVIEW vol 61 (2010) PARA 627.
9   Education and Inspections Act 2006 Sch 13 para 4(2)(a).
10 Education and Inspections Act 2006 Sch 13 para 4(2)(b). The 'inspection authorities' are Her
    Majesty's Chief Inspector of Prisons; Her Majesty's Chief Inspector of Constabulary; Her
    Majesty's Chief Inspector of the Crown Prosecution Service; Her Majesty's Chief Inspector of
    Probation for England and Wales; and the Care Quality Commission: Sch 13 para 1(1), (2)
    (amended by the Local Government and Public Involvement in Health Act 2007 ss 146(3), 241,
    Sch 9 para 1(1), (2)(y), Sch 18 Pt 9; the Health and Social Care Act 2008 ss 95, 166, Sch 5 Pt 3
    para 81(1), (2), Sch 15 Pt 1; SI 2008/912; SI 2012/2401; and the Local Audit and Accountability
    Act 2014 Sch 12 para 62(2)(a)(ii)). As to Her Majesty's Chief Inspector of Prisons see PRISONS
    AND PRISONERS vol 85 (2012) PARA 409. As to Her Majesty's Inspectors of Constabulary see
    POLICE AND INVESTIGATORY POWERS vol 84 (2013) PARAS 152–153. As to Her Majesty's Chief
    Inspector of the Crown Prosecution Service see CRIMINAL PROCEDURE vol 27 (2010) PARA 24.
    As to Her Majesty's Chief Inspector of Probation for England and Wales see SENTENCING AND
    DISPOSITION OF OFFENDERS vol 92 (2010) PARA 755. As to Her Majesty's Chief Inspector of
    Court Administration see COURTS AND TRIBUNALS vol 24 (2010) PARA 841.
11 As to the meaning of 'person' see PARA 7 note 6.
12 Education and Inspections Act 2006 Sch 13 para 4(2)(c). At the date at which this volume states
    the law no such order had been made.
13 Education and Inspections Act 2006 Sch 13 para 4(2).

1141. Interaction with other authorities. If an inspection authority[1] is
proposing to carry out an inspection that would involve inspecting a specified
institution[2], and Her Majesty's Chief Inspector of Education, Children's Services
and Skills considers that the proposed inspection would impose an unreasonable
burden on that institution, or would do so if carried out in a particular manner[3],
he must give a notice[4] to that authority requiring it not to carry out the proposed
inspection, or not to carry it out in that manner[5]. Where such a notice is given,
the proposed inspection is not to be carried out, or (as the case may be) is not to
be carried out in the manner mentioned in the notice[6]. However, the Secretary of
State, if satisfied that the proposed inspection would not impose an unreasonable
burden on the institution in question[7], or would not do so if carried out in a
particular manner[8], may give consent to the inspection being carried out, or
being carried out in that manner[9].

The Chief Inspector must co-operate with the inspection authorities[10], and
any other public authority[11] specified by order made by the Secretary of State[12],
where it is appropriate to do so for the efficient and effective exercise of his
functions[13]. The Chief Inspector may act jointly with another public authority
where it is appropriate to do so for the efficient and effective exercise of his
functions[14]. The Chief Inspector may, if he thinks it appropriate to do so, provide
advice or assistance to another public authority[15] for the purpose of the exercise
by that authority of its functions[16].

The Chief Inspector may make arrangements with a public authority for the
carrying out by him in England or Wales[17], or in Northern Ireland[18], of

inspections of any institution or matter which he is not required or authorised to carry out by virtue of any other enactment[19]. The Chief Inspector may make arrangements with a public authority or the relevant overseas authority[20] for the carrying out by him outside the United Kingdom of inspections of any institution or matter[21].

1 As to the meaning of 'inspection authority' see PARA 1140 note 10.
2 Education and Inspections Act 2006 Sch 13 para 5(1)(a). 'Specified institution' means a person or body specified by order made by the Secretary of State: Sch 13 para 5(2). A person or body may be so specified only if the person or body discharges functions or carries on other activities in relation to which Her Majesty's Chief Inspector of Education, Children's Services and Skills exercises inspection functions by virtue of any enactment (Sch 13 para 5(3)(a)) or is a person or body in respect of whom the Chief Inspector is the registration authority by virtue of any enactment (Sch 13 para 5(3)(b)). A person or body may be specified in relation to particular functions that it has; and in the case of a person or body so specified, Sch 13 para 5(1)(a) is to be read as referring to an inspection that would involve inspecting the discharge of any of its functions in relation to which it is specified: Sch 13 para 5(4). As to the meaning of 'person' see PARA 7 note 6. As to the Secretary of State see PARA 58. As to the meaning of 'functions' see PARA 1128 note 3. As to Her Majesty's Chief Inspector of Education, Children's Services and Skills see PARA 1133. As to the functions of Her Majesty's Chief Inspector of Education, Children's Services and Skills see PARA 1136 et seq. As to the meaning of 'inspection functions' see PARA 1138 note 23. As to the meaning of 'enactment' see PARA 26 note 15. As to the meaning of 'registration authority' see PARA 1130 note 3. At the date at which this volume states the law no order had been made under Sch 13 para 5(2).
3 Education and Inspections Act 2006 Sch 13 para 5(1)(b).
4 The Secretary of State may by order specify cases or circumstances in which a notice need not, or may not, be given: Education and Inspections Act 2006 Sch 13 para 5(5). The Secretary of State may by order make provision supplementing that made by Sch 13 para 5, including in particular provision about the form of notices, provision prescribing the period within which notices are to be given, provision prescribing circumstances in which notices are, or are not, to be made public, provision for revising or withdrawing notices, provision for setting aside notices not validly given: Sch 13 para 5(8)(a)–(e). At the date at which this volume states the law no such orders had been made.
5 Education and Inspections Act 2006 Sch 13 para 5(1).
6 Education and Inspections Act 2006 Sch 13 para 5(6).
7 Education and Inspections Act 2006 Sch 13 para 5(7)(a).
8 Education and Inspections Act 2006 Sch 13 para 5(7)(b).
9 Education and Inspections Act 2006 Sch 13 para 5(7).
10 Education and Inspections Act 2006 Sch 13 para 6(a). For these purposes the 'inspection authorities' are: Her Majesty's Chief Inspector of Prisons; Her Majesty's Inspectors of Constabulary; Her Majesty's Chief Inspector of the Crown Prosecution Service; Her Majesty's Inspectorate of Probation for England and Wales; and the Care Quality Commission: Education and Inspections Act 2006 Sch 13 para 1(1), (3) (amended by the Health and Social Care Act 2008 s 95, Sch 5 Pt 3 para 81(1), (3); by the Local Audit and Accountability Act 2014 Sch 12 para 69(2)(b); and by SI 2008/912; SI 2012/2401). As to Her Majesty's Chief Inspector of Prisons see PRISONS AND PRISONERS vol 85 (2012) PARA 409. As to Her Majesty's Inspectors of Constabulary see POLICE AND INVESTIGATORY POWERS vol 84 (2013) PARAS 152–153. As to Her Majesty's Inspectorate of Probation for England and Wales see SENTENCING AND DISPOSITION OF OFFENDERS vol 92 (2010) PARA 755.
11 'Public authority' includes any person certain of whose functions are functions of a public nature, but does not include either House of Parliament or a person exercising functions in connection with proceedings in Parliament: Education and Inspections Act 2006 Sch 13 para 2(1). Subject to Sch 13 para 8(3) (see the text to note 15), references to a public authority do not include a public authority outside the United Kingdom: Sch 13 para 2(2). As to the meaning of 'United Kingdom' see PARA 73 note 3.
12 Education and Inspections Act 2006 Sch 13 para 6(b). At the date at which this volume states the law no such order had been made.
13 Education and Inspections Act 2006 Sch 13 para 6.
14 Education and Inspections Act 2006 Sch 13 para 7.
15 For these purposes, the reference to another public authority includes a public authority in the Channel Islands or the Isle of Man: Education and Inspections Act 2006 Sch 13 para 8(3).

16 Education and Inspections Act 2006 Sch 13 para 8(1). The advice or assistance may be provided on such terms as the Chief Inspector thinks fit: see Sch 13 para 8(2) (substituted by the Local Audit and Accountability Act 2014 Sch 12 para 69(3)(b)). The Chief Inspector may, with the consent of the Secretary of State, enter into arrangements for charges to be made for providing such advice or assistance: see the Education and Inspections Act 2006 Sch 13 para 10(a).

17 Education and Inspections Act 2006 Sch 13 para 9(1)(a). As to the meanings of 'England' and 'Wales' see PARA 7 note 3.

18 Education and Inspections Act 2006 Sch 13 para 9(1)(b).

19 Education and Inspections Act 2006 Sch 13 para 9(1). Such inspections may be carried out on such terms as the Chief Inspector thinks fit: Sch 13 para 9(4). The Chief Inspector may, with the consent of the Secretary of State, enter into arrangements for charges to be made for carrying out such inspections: Sch 13 para 10(b).

20 'The relevant overseas authority' means the authority in the jurisdiction concerned that is responsible for the institution or other matter: Education and Inspections Act 2006 Sch 13 para 9(3).

21 Education and Inspections Act 2006 Sch 13 para 9(2). Such inspections may be carried out on such terms as the Chief Inspector thinks fit: Sch 13 para 9(4). The Chief Inspector may, with the consent of the Secretary of State, enter into arrangements for charges to be made for carrying out such inspections: Sch 13 para 10(b).

1142. Publication of inspection reports. For the purposes of the law of defamation, a report made by Her Majesty's Chief Inspector of Education, Children's Services and Skills[1] which is published under any enactment[2], or is not so published but is made in pursuance of his functions[3] under any enactment[4], is privileged[5] unless its publication is shown to have been made with malice[6]. Where by virtue of any enactment the Chief Inspector has power to arrange for a report made by him to be published in a manner determined by him, he may (if he considers it appropriate to do so) arrange for the report to be published by electronic means only[7].

1 As to Her Majesty's Chief Inspector of Education, Children's Services and Skills see PARA 1133.

2 Education and Inspections Act 2006 s 151(1)(a). As to the meaning of 'enactment' see PARA 26 note 15.

3 As to the meaning of 'functions' see PARA 1128 note 3. As to the functions of Her Majesty's Chief Inspector of Education, Children's Services and Skills see PARA 1136 et seq.

4 Education and Inspections Act 2006 s 151(1)(b).

5 As to privilege and malice in the law of defamation see DEFAMATION vol 32 (2012) PARAS 594 et seq, 651 et seq.

6 Education and Inspections Act 2006 s 151(1). Nothing in s 151 limits any privilege subsisting apart from s 151(1): s 151(3)(a).

7 Education and Inspections Act 2006 s 151(2). Nothing in s 151 prejudices the generality of any power of the Chief Inspector subsisting apart from s 151(2): s 151(3)(b).

1143. Combined reports. Nothing in any enactment[1] prevents Her Majesty's Chief Inspector of Education, Children's Services and Skills[2] from combining in a single document two or more reports which are required to be made by him under any enactment or enactments[3]; or from combining in a single document one or more such reports and one or more reports which are required to be made by one or more other persons[4] under any enactment or enactments[5]; and (in either case) combining the substantive reports to such extent as he considers appropriate[6].

The Chief Inspector may arrange for a combined report to be published in any manner he considers appropriate, but this does not limit any duty as to publication imposed by any enactment[7].

1 As to the meaning of 'enactment' see PARA 26 note 15.

2 As to Her Majesty's Chief Inspector of Education, Children's Services and Skills see PARA 1133. As to the functions of Her Majesty's Chief Inspector of Education, Children's Services and Skills see PARA 1136.

3   Education and Inspections Act 2006 s 152(1)(a).
4   As to the meaning of 'person' see PARA 7 note 6.
5   Education and Inspections Act 2006 s 152(1)(b).
6   Education and Inspections Act 2006 s 152(1). Such a document is referred to as a 'combined report': s 152(2). Where a combined report is made, any reference in any enactment to the publication of a report (s 152(3)(a)), or to the giving or making available to any person of a copy of a report (s 152(3)(b)), is to be read, so far as necessary, as a reference to the publication of the combined report, or to the giving or making available to that person of a copy of the combined report: s 152(3).
7   Education and Inspections Act 2006 s 152(4). The provisions of s 151 (see PARA 1142) apply to a combined report (whether or not they would otherwise so apply): s 152(5).

1144. Annual and other reports. Her Majesty's Chief Inspector of Education, Children's Services and Skills[1] must make an annual report to the Secretary of State[2]. The Chief Inspector may make to the Secretary of State such other reports relating to matters which fall within the scope of the Chief Inspector's functions[3] as he considers appropriate[4]. The Chief Inspector may arrange for any report made by him[5] to be published in such manner as he considers appropriate[6].

1   As to Her Majesty's Chief Inspector of Education, Children's Services and Skills see PARA 1133. As to the functions of Her Majesty's Chief Inspector of Education, Children's Services and Skills see PARA 1136.
2   Education and Inspections Act 2006 s 121(1).
3   As to the meaning of 'functions' see PARA 1128 note 3.
4   Education and Inspections Act 2006 s 121(3).
5   Ie under the Education and Inspections Act 2006 s 121.
6   Education and Inspections Act 2006 s 121(4).

1145. Payment of annual fee to the Chief Inspector by local authorities. Regulations[1] made by the Secretary of State[2] may require a local authority in England[3] to pay to Her Majesty's Chief Inspector of Education, Children's Services and Skills[4] an annual fee in respect of the discharge by the authority of any of its relevant functions[5] specified in the regulations[6]. The regulations must specify the amount of the fee[7], and the time at which it is to be paid[8]. The Chief Inspector may make a scheme that is to have effect at a time when no such regulations are in force[9].

A fee payable by virtue of these provisions may be recovered summarily as a civil debt[10], but this is not to be read as prejudicing any other method of recovery[11].

1   As to the regulations made see the Her Majesty's Chief Inspector of Education, Children's Services and Skills (Fees and Frequency of Inspections) (Children's Homes etc) Regulations 2015, SI 2015/551.
2   As to the Secretary of State see PARA 58.
3   'Local authority in England' means a county council in England; a metropolitan district council; a non-metropolitan district council for an area for which there is no county council; a London borough council; the Common Council of the City of London (in its capacity as a local authority); the Council of the Isles of Scilly: Education and Inspections Act 2006 s 159(1). As to the meaning of 'England' see PARA 7 note 3. As to local government areas and authorities in England see LOCAL GOVERNMENT vol 69 (2009) PARA 22 et seq.
4   As to Her Majesty's Chief Inspector of Education, Children's Services and Skills see PARA 1133.
5   'Relevant functions', in relation to a local authority, has the same meaning as in the Care Standards Act 2000 Pt III (ss 43–53) (see CHILDREN AND YOUNG PERSONS vol 10 (2012) PARA 999): Education and Inspections Act 2006 s 155(12).
6   Education and Inspections Act 2006 s 155(1).
7   Education and Inspections Act 2006 s 155(2)(a).
8   Education and Inspections Act 2006 s 155(2)(b).
9   Education and Inspections Act 2006 s 155(3). A scheme may provide for a local authority in England to be required to pay to the Chief Inspector an annual fee in respect of the discharge by

the authority of any of its relevant functions specified in the scheme: s 155(4). The amount of the fee payable by virtue of a scheme is to be such as may be specified in, or calculated or determined under, the scheme: s 155(5). A scheme may include provision:

(1) for different fees to be paid in different cases or classes of case (s 155(6)(a));
(2) for the amount of a fee to be determined by the Chief Inspector in accordance with specified factors (s 155(6)(b));
(3) for the time by which a fee must be paid (s 155(6)(c));
(4) for varying or revoking a previous scheme (s 155(6)(d)).

Before making a scheme the Chief Inspector must consult such persons as he considers appropriate: s 155(7). The Chief Inspector must arrange for a scheme to be published in such manner as he considers appropriate: s 155(8). A local authority in England must provide the Chief Inspector with such information as he requires for the purpose of determining the amount of a fee payable by the authority by virtue of a scheme: s 155(9). As to the meaning of 'person' see PARA 7 note 6. As to the exercise of the duty to consult see JUDICIAL REVIEW vol 61 (2010) PARA 627.

10 Education and Inspections Act 2006 s 155(10). As to the summary recovery of civil debts see MAGISTRATES vol 71 (2013) PARA 625.

11 Education and Inspections Act 2006 s 155(11).

D. HER MAJESTY'S INSPECTORS OF EDUCATION, CHILDREN'S SERVICES AND SKILLS

1146. Appointment. Her Majesty may by Order in Council[1] appoint persons as Her Majesty's Inspectors of Education, Children's Services and Skills[2]. An Inspector is to serve, in accordance with the terms of his appointment, as a member of the staff of the Office for Standards in Education, Children's Services and Skills ('Ofsted')[3]. Those terms are to be determined by Her Majesty's Chief Inspector of Education, Children's Services and Skills[4]. A person's appointment as an Inspector ends when he ceases to serve as a member of Ofsted's staff[5].

1 Such orders are considered to be of local effect and are not generally recorded in this work; however, see eg the Inspectors of Education, Children's Services and Skills (No 3) Order 2015, SI 2015/1525. As to Orders in Council see CONSTITUTIONAL AND ADMINISTRATIVE LAW vol 20 (2014) PARA 581.

2 Education and Inspections Act 2006 s 114(1). Any person who was one of Her Majesty's Inspectors of Schools in England immediately before the appointed day, and was then serving as member of the staff of Her Majesty's Chief Inspector of Schools in England or of the Adult Learning Inspectorate, was to become, as from that day, one of Her Majesty's Inspectors of Education, Children's Services and Skills: see s 114(6). As from the appointed day the Order in Council by which such a person was appointed has effect as if it were an Order in Council under s 114(1) appointing him as one of Her Majesty's Inspectors of Education, Children's Services and Skills (see s 114(7)(a)), and the terms of his appointment have effect as if determined under s 114(4) (see the text to note 4) (s 114(7)(b)). 'The appointed day' means the day appointed under s 188 for the coming into force of s 114: s 114(8). Section 114 came into force, in so far as it confers power to make subordinate legislation, on 8 November 2006 (see s 188(1)) and for remaining purposes on 1 April 2007 (see s 188(3); Education and Inspections Act 2006 (Commencement No 3 and Transitional Provisions and Savings) Order 2007, SI 2007/935, art 5(s)). Her Majesty's Inspectors of Schools in England were appointed under the Education Act 2005 s 1(2) (repealed). The Adult Learning Inspectorate was established under the Learning and Skills Act 2000 s 52 (repealed).

3 Education and Inspections Act 2006 s 114(3). As to the Office for Standards in Education, Children's Services and Skills see PARA 1128.

4 Education and Inspections Act 2006 s 114(4). As to Her Majesty's Chief Inspector of Education, Children's Services and Skills see PARA 1133. As to the delegation by the Chief Inspector of his functions to an Inspector see PARA 1138.

5 Education and Inspections Act 2006 s 114(5).

(ii) Her Majesty's Inspectorate of Education and Training in Wales

A. IN GENERAL

1147. Power of the Welsh Ministers to change the inspection framework. The Welsh Ministers[1] may by order[2]:

(1)   make provision[3] in relation to Wales[4] corresponding to that made in relation to England[5] by any English inspection provision[6], or that which could be made in relation to England by regulations under any English inspection provision[7];

(2)   repeal any Welsh inspection provision[8] which does not correspond to an English inspection provision[9]; and

(3)   make such provision as the Welsh Ministers think fit in connection with any provision made by virtue of head (1) or head (2) above[10].

1   As to the Welsh Ministers see PARA 59. The functions under the Education Act 2005 s 62 were originally vested in the National Assembly for Wales and are now exercisable by the Welsh Ministers by virtue of the Government of Wales Act 2006 s 162(1), Sch 11 paras 30, 32.
2   At the date at which this volume states the law no such order had been made.
3   The power conferred by the Education Act 2005 s 62(1)(a) includes power to amend or repeal any enactment (whenever passed or made), including any provision of the Education Act 2005: see s 62(3). 'Enactment' includes an enactment comprised in subordinate legislation, within the meaning of the Interpretation Act 1978 (see PARA 1 note 13): Education Act 2005 s 62(5).
4   As to the meaning of 'Wales' see PARA 7 note 3.
5   As to the meaning of 'England' see PARA 7 note 3.
6   Education Act 2005 s 62(1)(a)(i). 'English inspection provision' means:
       (1)   any provision of Pt 1 Chs 1, 2 (ss 1–18) (see PARA 1162 et seq);
       (2)   ss 48–49 (denominational education in England: see PARA 1178 et seq);
       (3)   the School Standards and Framework Act 1998 Sch 26 (nursery education: repealed) so far as relating to England; or
       (4)   the Education and Skills Act 2008 ss 106–113 (independent educational institutions in England: see PARA 395 et seq): Education Act 2005 s 62(4)(a)(i)–(iv) (amended by the Education and Skills Act 2008 s 169(1), Sch 1 Pt 1 paras 25, 29).
7   Education Act 2005 s 62(1)(a)(ii).
8   'Welsh inspection provision' means any provision of:
       (1)   the Education Act 2005 Pt 1 Chs 3–4 (ss 19–43) (see PARA 1148 et seq);
       (2)   s 50 and Sch 6 (denominational education in Wales: see PARA 1201 et seq);
       (3)   s 52 (provision of inspection services by local authorities in Wales: see PARA 1204);
       (4)   the School Standards and Framework Act 1998 Sch 26 (nursery education: see PARA 1253 et seq) so far as relating to Wales; or the Education Act 2002 ss 163–164 (independent schools in Wales: see PARA 418): Education Act 2005 s 62(4)(b)(i)–(v) (s 62(4)(b)(iii) amended by SI 2010/1158).
9   Education Act 2005 s 62(1)(b). In relation to s 39 (statement to be prepared by appropriate authority for maintained school: see PARA 1197), the power conferred by s 62(1)(b) includes power, instead of repealing the provision, to limit the cases in which it applies: s 62(2).
10   Education Act 2005 s 62(1)(c). The power conferred by s 62(1)(c) includes power to amend or repeal any enactment (whenever passed or made), including any provision of the Education Act 2005: see s 62(3). See also note 3.

B. ESTABLISHMENT AND ADMINISTRATION

1148. Appointment of Chief Inspector and other inspectors. Her Majesty may by Order in Council[1] appoint a person to the office of Her Majesty's Chief Inspector of Education and Training in Wales[2]. The Chief Inspector holds and vacates office in accordance with the terms of his appointment, but he must not be appointed for a term of more than five years[3]. The Chief Inspector may at any time resign by giving written notice[4] to the Welsh Ministers[5]. He may be removed from office by Her Majesty on the ground of incapacity or misconduct[6].

The previous appointment of a person as Chief Inspector does not affect his eligibility for re-appointment[7]. There are to be paid to the Chief Inspector such remuneration, and such travelling and other allowances, as the Welsh Ministers may determine[8].

Her Majesty may also by Order in Council appoint persons as Her Majesty's Inspectors of Education and Training in Wales[9]. The terms of a person's appointment are to be determined by the Chief Inspector with the approval of the Welsh Ministers[10]. Any person so appointed must serve, in accordance with the terms and conditions on which he is appointed, as a member of the staff of the Chief Inspector[11].

1 Such orders are considered to be of local effect and are not recorded in this work. As to Orders in Council see CONSTITUTIONAL AND ADMINISTRATIVE LAW vol 20 (2014) PARA 581.
2 Education Act 2005 s 19(1). As to the Welsh Ministers see PARA 59. As to the Secretary of State see PARA 58. The functions under s 19, Sch 2 were originally vested in the National Assembly for Wales and are now exercisable by the Welsh Ministers by virtue of the Government of Wales Act 2006 s 162(1), Sch 11 paras 30, 32. The office of Her Majesty's Chief Inspector of Education and Training in Wales is subject to investigation by the Public Services Ombudsman for Wales: see the Public Services Ombudsman (Wales) Act 2005 s 28, Sch 3; and LOCAL GOVERNMENT vol 69 (2009) PARA 854. Her Majesty's Chief Inspector of Education and Training in Wales is also subject to review by the Children's Commissioner for Wales: see the Care Standards Act 2000 s 72B, Sch 2A para 10; and CHILDREN AND YOUNG PERSONS vol 9 (2012) PARA 184. The Chief Inspector is disqualified for membership of the House of Commons: see the House of Commons Disqualification Act 1975 s 1, Sch 1 Pt III (amended by the Learning and Skills Act 2000 s 73(1), (3)(a)); and PARLIAMENT vol 78 (2010) PARA 908.
3 Education Act 2005 s 19(4)(a).
4 As to the meaning of 'written' see PARA 76 note 8. As to the service of notices see the Education Act 1996 s 572 (applied by the Education Act 2005 s 122(2), (3)); and PARA 76.
5 Education Act 2005 s 19(4)(b).
6 Education Act 2005 s 19(4)(c). If the Welsh Ministers consider that the power conferred by s 19(4)(c) ought to be exercised, they must advise the Secretary of State on any recommendation to be made to Her Majesty as to the exercise of the power: see s 19(6).
7 Education Act 2005 s 19(5). Further provision is made by Sch 2 (see the text to note 8; and PARAS 1149, 1150) with respect to the Chief Inspector and his staff: s 19(8).
8 Education Act 2005 Sch 2 para 3(1). In the case of any such Chief Inspector as may be determined by the Welsh Ministers, there is to be paid such pension, allowance or gratuity to or in respect of him (Sch 2 para 3(2)(a)), or such contributions or payments towards provision for such a pension, allowance or gratuity (Sch 2 para 3(2)(b)), as may be so determined (Sch 2 para 3(2)). If, when any person ceases to hold office as Chief Inspector, the Welsh Ministers determine that there are special circumstances which make it right that he should receive compensation, there may be paid to him such sum by way of compensation as may be determined by the Welsh Ministers: Sch 2 para 3(3).
9 Education Act 2005 s 19(2). If the Welsh Ministers considers that the power conferred by s 19(2) ought to be exercised, they must advise the Secretary of State on any recommendation to be made to Her Majesty as to the exercise of the power: see s 19(6). Several orders have been made under s 19(2). At the date at which this volume states the law the most recent was the Education (Inspectors of Education and Training in Wales) Order 2014, SI 2014/2922.
10 Education Act 2005 s 19(7).
11 Education Act 2005 s 19(3).

1149. Power of the Chief Inspector to appoint staff and additional inspectors.
Her Majesty's Chief Inspector of Education and Training in Wales[1] may, with the approval of the Welsh Ministers[2] as to numbers and terms and conditions of service, appoint such staff, in addition to inspectors who are members of his staff[3], as he thinks fit[4].

The Chief Inspector may arrange for such persons[5] as he thinks fit to assist him in the discharge of any of his functions[6] in relation to a particular case or class of case[7], such persons being known as 'additional inspectors'[8]. An additional inspector acting within the authority conferred on him by the Chief

Inspector has all the powers of one of Her Majesty's Inspectors of Education and Training in Wales[9]. Any arrangements which provide for assistance by persons who are not members of the Chief Inspector's staff must be made on terms agreed by him with the Welsh Ministers[10].

1   As to Her Majesty's Chief Inspector of Education and Training in Wales see PARA 1148.
2   As to the Welsh Ministers see PARA 59. The functions under the Education Act 2005 Sch 2 were originally vested in the National Assembly for Wales and are now exercisable by the Welsh Ministers by virtue of the Government of Wales Act 2006 s 162(1), Sch 11 paras 30, 32.
3   Ie by virtue of the Education Act 2005 s 19(3): see PARA 1148.
4   Education Act 2005 Sch 2 para 1.
5   As to the meaning of 'person' see PARA 7 note 6.
6   As to the meaning of 'functions' see PARA 18 note 5 (definition applied by the Education Act 2005 s 122(2), (3)). As to the functions of Her Majesty's Chief Inspector of Education and Training in Wales see PARA 1151 et seq.
7   Education Act 2005 Sch 2 para 2(1).
8   See the Education Act 2005 Sch 2 para 2(2).
9   Education Act 2005 Sch 2 para 2(4). As to Her Majesty's Inspectors of Education and Training in Wales see PARA 1148.
10 Education Act 2005 Sch 2 para 2(3).

1150. Official seal and documentary evidence. Her Majesty's Chief Inspector of Education and Training in Wales[1] has an official seal for the authentication of documents required for the purposes of his functions[2].

The Documentary Evidence Act 1868 has effect in relation to the Chief Inspector[3].

1   As to Her Majesty's Chief Inspector of Education and Training in Wales see PARA 1148.
2   See the Education Act 2005 Sch 2 para 4. As to the meaning of 'functions' see PARA 18 note 5 (definition applied by s 122(2), (3)). As to the functions of Her Majesty's Chief Inspector of Education and Training in Wales see PARA 1151 et seq.
3   The Documentary Evidence Act 1868 (see CIVIL PROCEDURE vol 11 (2009) PARA 889 et seq) has effect in relation to the Chief Inspector as if:
    (1)   he were included in the first column of the Schedule to that Act;
    (2)   he and any person authorised to act on his behalf were mentioned in the second column of that Schedule; and
    (3)   the regulations referred to in that Act included any document issued by him or any such person: Education Act 2005 Sch 2 para 6.

C. FUNCTIONS

1151. Functions of the Chief Inspector. Her Majesty's Chief Inspector of Education and Training in Wales[1] has the general duty of keeping the Welsh Ministers[2] informed about[3]:

(1)   the quality of the education provided by schools[4] in Wales[5];

(2)   how far that education meets the needs of the range of pupils[6] at those schools[7];

(3)   the educational standards achieved in those schools[8];

(4)   the quality of the leadership in and management of those schools, including whether the financial resources made available to those schools are managed efficiently[9];

(5)   the spiritual, moral, social and cultural development of pupils at those schools[10];

(6)   the contribution made by those schools to the well-being[11] of those pupils[12]; and

(7)   actions taken at maintained schools[13] to promote healthy eating and drinking[14].

When asked to do so by the Welsh Ministers, the Chief Inspector must give advice to them on such matters as may be specified in the request[15], and inspect and report on such school, or class of school, as may be so specified[16].

The Chief Inspector has, in addition, the following specific duties:

(a) establishing and maintaining the register of inspectors[17];

(b) giving guidance to inspectors registered in that register, and such other persons[18] as he considers appropriate, in connection with inspections of schools in Wales[19] and the making of reports of such inspections[20];

(c) keeping under review the system of inspecting schools[21] and, in particular, the standard of such inspections and of the reports made by registered inspectors[22];

(d) keeping under review the extent to which any requirement imposed by or under Education Act 2005[23], or any other enactment, on any registered inspector, local authority[24], proprietor[25] of a school or governing body[26] in relation to inspections of schools in Wales is complied with[27];

(e) promoting efficiency in the conduct and reporting of inspections of schools in Wales by encouraging competition in the provision of services by registered inspectors[28].

The Chief Inspector may at any time give advice to the Welsh Ministers on any matter connected with schools, or a particular school, in Wales[29]. The Chief Inspector has such other functions[30] in connection with schools in Wales, including functions with respect to the training of teachers[31] for such schools, as may be assigned to him by the Welsh Ministers[32]. In exercising his functions, the Chief Inspector must have regard to such aspects of policy adopted or formulated by the Welsh Ministers as they may direct[33].

Anything authorised or required by or under the Education Act 2005[34] or any other enactment to be done by the Chief Inspector may be done by any of Her Majesty's Inspectors of Education and Training in Wales[35], any other member of his staff[36], or any additional inspector[37], who is authorised generally or specially in that behalf by the Chief Inspector[38].

The Chief Inspector has additional functions in relation to education and training for persons aged 16 or over[39], independent schools[40], and the inspection of local authorities in Wales in relation to their education functions[41].

1   As to Her Majesty's Chief Inspector of Education and Training in Wales see PARA 1148.
2   As to the Welsh Ministers see PARA 59. The functions under the Education Act 2005 s 20 were originally vested in the National Assembly for Wales and are now exercisable by the Welsh Ministers by virtue of the Government of Wales Act 2006 s 162(1), Sch 11 paras 30, 32.
3   The Education Act 2005 s 20 does not apply in relation to education which is brought within the remit of the Chief Inspector by the Learning and Skills Act 2000 Pt IV (ss 73–88) (extended remit of the Chief Inspector: see PARA 1268 et seq): Education Act 2005 s 20(7).
4   As to the meaning of 'school' see PARA 91 (definition applied by the Education Act 2005 s 122(2), (3)).
5   Education Act 2005 s 20(1)(a). As to the meaning of 'Wales' see PARA 7 note 3.
6   As to the meaning of 'pupil' see PARA 20 note 4 (definition applied by the Education Act 2005 s 122(2), (3)).
7   Education Act 2005 s 20(1)(b).
8   Education Act 2005 s 20(1)(c).
9   Education Act 2005 s 20(1)(d).
10 Education Act 2005 s 20(1)(e).
11 'Well-being', in relation to pupils at a school, is a reference to their well-being having regard to the matters mentioned in the Children Act 2004 s 25(2) (see CHILDREN AND YOUNG PERSONS vol 9 (2012) PARA 209): Education Act 2005 s 31(1).
12 Education Act 2005 s 20(1)(f).

13 'Maintained school' means a community, foundation or voluntary school, a community special school, a maintained nursery school or a pupil referral unit in Wales: Education Act 2005 s 31(1) (definition added by the Healthy Eating in Schools (Wales) Measure 2009 s 3(1), (3); and amended by the School Standards and Organisation (Wales) Act 2013 Sch 5 para 22(3)). As to the meaning of references to a community, foundation or voluntary school or a community special school see PARA 106. As to the meaning of 'maintained nursery school' see PARA 99 note 4 (definition applied by the Education Act 2005 s 122(2), (3)). As to pupil referral units see PARA 427 et seq.

14 Education Act 2005 s 20(1)(g) (added by the Healthy Eating in Schools (Wales) Measure 2009 s 3(1), (2)).

15 Education Act 2005 s 20(2)(a).

16 Education Act 2005 s 20(2)(b). As to combined reports under the inspection enactments see PARA 1206.

17 Education Act 2005 s 20(3)(a). The register referred to is that established under s 25(1) (see PARA 1156): see s 20(3)(a). As to Her Majesty's Inspectors of Education and Training in Wales see PARA 1148. As to the power of the Chief Inspector to appoint additional inspectors see PARA 1149.

18 As to the meaning of 'person' see PARA 7 note 6.

19 Ie under the Education Act 2005 s 28: see PARA 1182.

20 Education Act 2005 s 20(3)(b).

21 Ie under the Education Act 2005 s 28: see PARA 1182.

22 Education Act 2005 s 20(3)(c).

23 Ie by or under the Education Act 2005 Pt 1 (ss 5–63).

24 As to the meaning of 'local authority' see PARA 25 (definition applied by the Education Act 2005 s 122(2), (3)).

25 As to the meaning of 'proprietor' see PARA 51 note 4 (definition applied by the Education Act 2005 s 122(2), (3)).

26 As to the governing bodies of maintained schools in Wales see PARA 195.

27 Education Act 2005 s 20(3)(d) (amended by SI 2010/1158).

28 Education Act 2005 s 20(3)(e).

29 Education Act 2005 s 20(4).

30 As to the meaning of 'functions' see PARA 18 note 5 (definition applied by the Education Act 2005 s 122(2), (3)).

31 As to the training of teachers see PARA 1054 et seq.

32 Education Act 2005 s 20(5).

33 Education Act 2005 s 20(6). As to directions under the Education Act 2005 see PARA 75.

34 Ie by or under the Education Act 2005 Pt 1 (ss 5–63).

35 Education Act 2005 Sch 2 para 5(1)(a).

36 Education Act 2005 Sch 2 para 5(1)(b). As to the appointment of staff see PARA 1149.

37 Education Act 2005 Sch 2 para 5(1)(c).

38 Education Act 2005 Sch 2 para 5(1).

39 See the Learning and Skills Act 2000 Pt IV (ss 73–88); and PARA 1268 et seq.

40 See the Education Act 2002 s 163; and PARA 418.

41 See the Education Act 1997 Pt VI Ch I (ss 38–41A); and PARA 1293 et seq.

1152. Powers of entry. For the purposes of the exercise of any function[1] conferred on him[2], Her Majesty's Chief Inspector of Education and Training in Wales[3] has at all reasonable times:

(1) a right of entry to the premises[4] of any school[5] in Wales[6]; and

(2) a right to inspect, and take copies of, any records kept by the school, and any other documents containing information relating to the school, which he requires for those purposes[7]; and

(3) a right of entry to any premises (other than school premises) on which, by virtue of arrangements made by a school in Wales, any pupils who are registered[8] at the school[9] and have attained the age of 15[10], or will attain that age in the current school year[11], but have not ceased to be of compulsory school age[12], are provided with part of their education by any person ('the provider')[13]; and

(4)   a right of entry to any premises of the provider used in connection with the provision by him of that education[14]; and

(5)   a right to inspect and take copies of any records kept by the provider relating to the provision of that education[15], and any other documents containing information so relating[16], which the Chief Inspector requires for those purposes[17].

It is an offence[18] wilfully to obstruct the Chief Inspector:

(a)   in the exercise of his functions[19] in relation to the inspection of a school[20]; or

(b)   in the exercise of any right under heads (1) to (5) above for the purposes of the exercise of any other function[21].

1   As to the meaning of 'function' see PARA 18 note 5 (definition applied by the Education Act 2005 s 122(2), (3)).
2   Ie under the Education Act 2005 s 20: see PARA 1151.
3   Without prejudice to the generality of the Education Act 2005 Sch 2 para 5(1) (see PARA 1151), the references to Her Majesty's Chief Inspector of Education and Training in Wales in s 23 include references to any person authorised to act on his behalf under Sch 2 para 5(1): Sch 2 para 5(2). As to Her Majesty's Chief Inspector of Education and Training in Wales see PARA 1148.
4   As to the meaning of 'premises' see PARA 62 note 19 (definition applied by the Education Act 2005 s 122(2), (3)).
5   As to the meaning of 'school' see PARA 91 (definition applied by the Education Act 2005 s 122(2), (3)).
6   See the Education Act 2005 s 23(1)(a). As to the meaning of 'Wales' see PARA 7 note 3.
7   Education Act 2005 s 23(1)(b). Any person authorised by any provision of Pt 1 (ss 5–63) to inspect records or other documents is entitled at any reasonable time to have access to, and inspect and check the operation of, any computer and any associated apparatus or material which is or has been in use in connection with the records or other documents in question: s 58(a). He may also require the person by whom or on whose behalf the computer is or has been so used or any person having charge of, or otherwise concerned with the operation of, the computer, apparatus or material, to afford him such assistance as he may reasonably require, including, in particular, the making of information available for inspection or copying in a legible form: s 58(b). As to the meaning of 'person' see PARA 7 note 6.
8   As to the meaning of 'registered pupil' see PARA 437 (definition applied by the Education Act 2005 s 122(2), (3)).
9   Education Act 2005 s 23(2)(a)(i).
10 As to the time at which a person attains a particular age see PARA 7 note 6.
11 As to the meaning of 'school year' see PARA 19 note 12 (definition applied by the Education Act 2005 s 122(2), (3)).
12 Education Act 2005 s 23(2)(a)(ii). As to the meaning of 'compulsory school age' see PARA 19.
13 Education Act 2005 s 23(2)(a).
14 Education Act 2005 s 23(2)(b).
15 Education Act 2005 s 23(2)(c)(i).
16 Education Act 2005 s 23(2)(c)(ii).
17 Education Act 2005 s 23(2)(c). See also note 7.
18 The penalty for such an offence is, on summary conviction, a fine not exceeding level 4 on the standard scale: see the Education Act 2005 s 23(4). As to the standard scale see SENTENCING AND DISPOSITION OF OFFENDERS vol 92 (2010) PARA 142.
19 Ie under the Education Act 2005 s 20(2)(b): see PARA 1151.
20 Education Act 2005 s 23(3)(a).
21 Education Act 2005 s 23(3)(b).

1153.   Power of Chief Inspector to arrange for inspections.   Her Majesty's Chief Inspector of Education and Training in Wales[1] may cause any school[2] in Wales[3] to be inspected by one or more of Her Majesty's Inspectors of Education and Training in Wales[4]. Where an inspection of a school in Wales is being conducted by a registered inspector[5], the Chief Inspector may arrange for that inspection to be monitored by one or more of Her Majesty's Inspectors of

Education and Training in Wales[6]. Any of Her Majesty's Inspectors of Education and Training in Wales inspecting a school or monitoring an inspection has at all reasonable times:

(1) a right of entry to the premises[7] of the school[8];

(2) a right of entry to any other premises on which, by virtue of arrangements made by the school, any pupils who are registered[9] at the school[10] and have attained the age of 15[11], or will attain that age in the current school year[12], but have not ceased to be of compulsory school age[13], are receiving part of their education from any person[14] ('the provider')[15];

(3) a right of entry to any premises of the provider used in connection with the provision by him of that education[16];

(4) a right to inspect, and take copies of, any records kept by the school, and any other documents containing information relating to the school, which he considers relevant to the discharge of his functions[17]; and

(5) a right to inspect and take copies of any records kept by the provider relating to the provision of education for pupils registered at the school, and any other documents containing information so relating, which the inspector considers relevant to the discharge of his functions[18].

It is an offence wilfully to obstruct any of Her Majesty's Inspectors of Education and Training in Wales in the exercise of any of these functions[19].

1 As to Her Majesty's Chief Inspector of Education and Training in Wales see PARA 1148.
2 As to the meaning of 'school' see PARA 91 (definition applied by the Education Act 2005 s 122(2), (3)).
3 As to the meaning of 'Wales' see PARA 7 note 3.
4 Education Act 2005 s 24(1). An inspection of a school conducted under s 24(1) may not extend to any education of a kind brought within the remit of the Chief Inspector by the Learning and Skills Act 2000 Pt IV (ss 73–88) (extended remit of the Chief Inspector: see PARA 1268 et seq) that is provided by the school: Education Act 2005 s 24(6). As to Her Majesty's Inspectors of Education and Training in Wales see PARA 1148. As to the publication of inspection reports see PARA 1190.
5 Ie under the Education Act 2005 s 28: see PARA 1182. As to the registration of inspectors under the Education Act 2005 see PARA 1156.
6 Education Act 2005 s 24(2).
7 As to the meaning of 'premises' see PARA 62 note 19 (definition applied by the Education Act 2005 s 122(2), (3)).
8 Education Act 2005 s 24(3)(a).
9 As to the meaning of 'registered pupil' see PARA 437 (definition applied by the Education Act 2005 s 122(2), (3)).
10 Education Act 2005 s 24(3)(b)(i).
11 As to the time at which a person attains a particular age see PARA 7 note 6.
12 As to the meaning of 'school year' see PARA 19 note 12 (definition applied by the Education Act 2005 s 122(2), (3)).
13 Education Act 2005 s 24(3)(b)(ii). As to the meaning of 'compulsory school age' see PARA 19.
14 As to the meaning of 'person' see PARA 7 note 6.
15 Education Act 2005 s 24(3)(b).
16 Education Act 2005 s 24(3)(c).
17 Education Act 2005 s 24(3)(d). As to the meaning of 'functions' see PARA 18 note 5 (definition applied by s 122(2), (3)). A person authorised to inspect records or other documents is entitled at any reasonable time to have access to, and inspect and check the operation of, any computer and any associated apparatus or material which is or has been in use in connection with the records or other documents in question: s 58(a)). He may also require the person by whom or on whose behalf the computer is or has been so used, or any person having charge of, or otherwise concerned with the operation of, the computer, apparatus or material, to afford him such assistance as he may reasonably require (including, in particular, the making of information available for inspection or copying in a legible form): s 58(b).
18 Education Act 2005 s 24(3)(e). See also note 17.

19 See the Education Act 2005 s 24(4). A person guilty of such an offence is liable on summary
    conviction to a fine not exceeding level 4 on the standard scale: s 24(5). As to the standard scale
    see SENTENCING AND DISPOSITION OF OFFENDERS vol 92 (2010) PARA 142.

1154.   Annual and other reports. Her Majesty's Chief Inspector of Education
and Training in Wales[1]:

(1)   must make an annual report to the Welsh Ministers[2], who must publish
      any report that is so made[3];

(2)   may make such other reports to the Welsh Ministers, with respect to
      matters which fall within the scope of his functions, as he considers
      appropriate[4]; and

(3)   may arrange for any report made by him under head (1) or (2) above to
      be published in such manner as he considers appropriate[5].

For the purposes of the law of defamation any report published by the Chief
Inspector under head (3) above is privileged unless the publication is shown to
have been made with malice[6].

1   As to Her Majesty's Chief Inspector of Education and Training in Wales see PARA 1148.
2   Education Act 2005 s 21(1)(a). As to the Welsh Ministers see PARA 59. The functions under s 21
    were originally vested in the National Assembly for Wales and are now exercisable by the Welsh
    Ministers by virtue of the Government of Wales Act 2006 s 162(1), Sch 11 paras 30, 32. The
    annual report of the Chief Inspector required by the Education Act 2005 s 21(1)(a) to be made
    to the Welsh Ministers must include an account of the exercise of the functions imposed or
    conferred on him by or under the School Standards and Framework Act 1998 Sch 26 (nursery
    education: see PARA 1253 et seq): see Sch 26 para 14(2); and PARA 1259. As to the meaning of
    'functions' see PARA 18 note 5 (definition applied by s 142(8); Education Act 2005 s 122(2), (3)).
    The annual report of the Chief Inspector required by the Education Act 2005 s 21(1)(a) must
    include an account of the exercise of functions of the Chief Inspector under the Learning and
    Skills Act 2000 Pt IV (ss 73–88): see s 86(1); and PARA 1277.
3   See the Education Act 2005 s 21(2).
4   Education Act 2005 s 21(1)(b). The power conferred by s 21(1)(b) to make other reports to the
    Welsh Ministers includes a power to make reports with respect to matters which fall within the
    scope of the Chief Inspector's functions by virtue of the School Standards and Framework
    Act 1998 Sch 26 (nursery education: see PARA 1253 et seq): see Sch 26 para 14(2); and PARA
    1259.
5   Education Act 2005 s 21(1)(c).
6   See the Education Act 2005 s 29(3). Section 29(3) does not limit any privilege subsisting apart
    therefrom: s 29(4). As to privilege and malice in the law of defamation see DEFAMATION vol 32
    (2012) PARAS 594 et seq, 651 et seq.

1155.   Advisory panel. The Welsh Ministers[1] may by regulations[2] establish a
panel for the purpose of providing advice to the Welsh Ministers on matters
relating to the functions[3] that are at any time exercisable by Her Majesty's Chief
Inspector of Education and Training in Wales[4] under the Education Act 2005[5] or
any other enactment[6], and make provision as to the functions of the panel[7].

1   As to the Welsh Ministers see PARA 59. The functions under the Education Act 2005 s 22 were
    originally vested in the National Assembly for Wales and are now exercisable by the Welsh
    Ministers by virtue of the Government of Wales Act 2006 s 162(1), Sch 11 paras 30, 32.
2   The regulations may in particular:
    (1)   make provision about the appointment of members of the panel (Education Act 2005
          s 22(2)(a));
    (2)   make provision for remuneration and allowances to be paid to members of the panel
          (s 22(2)(b));
    (3)   require the panel and the Chief Inspector to co-operate with each other (s 22(2)(c));
    (4)   require the panel to make reports to the Welsh Ministers (s 22(2)(d)).
    The regulations may, in particular, include provision for the designation by the Welsh
    Ministers, in accordance with the regulations, of particular schools or categories of school for
    the purposes of the application of particular provisions of the regulations in relation to such

schools: see s 120(3). As to the meaning of 'school' see PARA 91 (definition applied by
s 122(2), (3)). At the date at which this volume states the law no regulations had been made
under s 22.
3   As to the meaning of 'functions' see PARA 18 note 5 (definition applied by the Education
     Act 2005 s 122(2), (3)).
4   As to Her Majesty's Chief Inspector of Education and Training in Wales see PARA 1148. As to
     the functions of Her Majesty's Chief Inspector of Education and Training in Wales see PARA
     1151 et seq.
5   Ie under the Education Act 2005 Pt 1 (ss 5–63).
6   Education Act 2005 s 22(1)(a).
7   Education Act 2005 s 22(1)(b).

D. REGISTERED INSPECTORS

1156. Registration of inspectors. No one may conduct an inspection of any
school[1] in Wales[2] unless he is a member of the Inspectorate[3], or registered as an
inspector in a register kept[4] by Her Majesty's Chief Inspector of Education and
Training in Wales[5]. The Chief Inspector may not register a person unless, having
regard to any conditions that he proposes to impose[6], it appears to him that that
person is a fit and proper person for discharging the functions[7] of a registered
inspector[8]; and that that person will be capable of conducting inspections[9]
competently and effectively[10]. Furthermore, a person may not be registered if he
falls within a category of persons prescribed[11] for these purposes[12].

An application for registration must be made in such manner, and be
accompanied by such particulars, as the Chief Inspector may direct[13], and it must
be accompanied by the prescribed fee[14]. On an application duly made, the Chief
Inspector may register the applicant[15], refuse to register him[16] or register him
subject to such conditions as the Chief Inspector considers it appropriate to
impose[17]. The matters to which the Chief Inspector may have regard in deciding
whether to register the applicant include, in particular the extent to which the
Chief Inspector proposes to exercise his discretion[18] to secure that regular
inspections[19] are conducted by members of the Inspectorate rather than
registered inspectors[20]; and the extent to which there is a need for registered
inspectors in Wales[21]. Where a person is registered subject to conditions, he must
be taken to be authorised to act as a registered inspector only so far as those
conditions permit[22].

The period for which any registration has effect must be determined by the
Chief Inspector and must be entered in the register kept by him[23].

1   As to the meaning of 'school' see PARA 91 (definition applied by the Education Act 2005
     s 122(2), (3)).
2   Ie under the Education Act 2005 s 28: see PARA 1182. As to the meaning of 'Wales' see PARA 7
     note 3.
3   Education Act 2005 s 25(1)(a). 'Member of the Inspectorate' means Her Majesty's Chief
     Inspector of Education and Training in Wales, any of Her Majesty's Inspectors of Education and
     Training in Wales and any additional inspector appointed under Sch 2 para 2 (see PARA 1149):
     s 31(1). As to Her Majesty's Chief Inspector of Education and Training in Wales see PARA 1148.
4   Ie for the purposes of the Education Act 2005 Pt 1 Ch 3 (ss 19–31).
5   Education Act 2005 s 25(1)(b).
6   Ie under the Education Act 2005 s 25(4)(c): see the text to note 17.
7   As to the meaning of 'functions' see PARA 18 note 5 (definition applied by the Education
     Act 2005 s 122(2), (3)).
8   Education Act 2005 s 25(2)(a).
9   Ie the Education Act 2005 Pt 1 Ch 3 (ss 19–31).
10   Education Act 2005 s 25(2)(b).
11   'Prescribed' means prescribed by regulations; and 'regulations' means regulations made by the
     Welsh Ministers under the Education Act 2005 Pt 1 Ch 3 (ss 19–31): see s 31(1). At the date at

which this volume states the law no such regulations had been made. As to the Welsh Ministers see PARA 59. The functions under s 25 in relation to Wales were originally vested in the National Assembly for Wales and are now exercisable by the Welsh Ministers by virtue of the Government of Wales Act 2006 s 162(1), Sch 11 paras 30, 32.

12 See the Education Act 2005 s 25(2).
13 Education Act 2005 s 25(3)(a). As to directions under the Education Act 2005 see PARA 75.
14 Education Act 2005 s 25(3)(b). The prescribed fee is £150: see the Education (School Inspection) (Wales) Regulations 2006, SI 2006/1714, reg 5.
15 Education Act 2005 s 25(4)(a). As to removal from the register see PARA 1157.
16 Education Act 2005 s 25(4)(b). As to appeals against a refusal to register see PARA 1158.
17 Education Act 2005 s 25(4)(c). Conditions under s 25(4)(c) may be conditions applying generally in relation to all cases, or particular classes of case, or such conditions together with specific conditions applying in the particular case: s 25(6). For the purposes of Pt 1 Ch 3 (ss 19–31), any reference to a condition imposed under s 25(4)(c) includes a reference to a condition imposed under s 26(3) (see PARA 1157): s 31(2). As to the variation of conditions and the imposition of conditions subsequent to registration see PARA 1157. As to appeals against the imposition or variation of conditions see PARA 1158.
18 Ie under the Education Act 2005 s 28(1): see PARA 1182.
19 Ie inspections under the Education Act 2005 s 28: see PARA 1182.
20 Education Act 2005 s 25(5)(a).
21 Education Act 2005 s 25(5)(b).
22 Education Act 2005 s 25(7).
23 Education Act 2005 s 25(8). Nothing in s 25(8) is to be taken as preventing a registered inspector from applying for a fresh registration to take effect immediately on the expiry of his current registration: s 25(9).

1157. Removal from register and imposition or variation of conditions. If Her Majesty's Chief Inspector of Education and Training in Wales[1] is satisfied that any of the conditions mentioned in heads (1) to (4) below is satisfied with respect to an inspector registered in his register[2], he may remove the name of that inspector from that register[3]. The conditions are that:

(1) he is no longer a fit and proper person for discharging the functions[4] of a registered inspector[5];

(2) he is no longer capable of conducting inspections[6] competently and effectively[7];

(3) there has been a significant failure on his part to comply with any condition imposed by the Chief Inspector[8] and subject to which his registration has effect[9];

(4) he has, without reasonable explanation, produced a report of an inspection which is, in whole or in part, seriously misleading[10].

If the Chief Inspector is satisfied that he is authorised[11] to remove the name of an inspector from his register[12], or that it would otherwise be in the public interest to act[13], he may vary any condition subject to which the registration of that inspector has effect or vary that registration by imposing a condition subject to which it will have effect[14].

1 As to Her Majesty's Chief Inspector of Education and Training in Wales see PARA 1148.
2 As to the registration of inspectors see PARA 1156.
3 Education Act 2005 s 26(1). As to appeals against removal from the register see PARA 1158.
4 Ie under the Education Act 2005 Pt 1 Ch 3 (ss 19–31). As to the meaning of 'functions' see PARA 18 note 5 (definition applied by s 122(2), (3)).
5 Education Act 2005 s 26(2)(a).
6 Ie under the Education Act 2005 Pt 1 Ch 3 (ss 19–31).
7 Education Act 2005 s 26(2)(b).
8 Ie imposed under the Education Act 2005 s 25(4)(c): see PARA 1156. For these purposes, any reference to a condition imposed under s 25(4)(c) includes a reference to a condition imposed under s 26(3) (see the text to notes 11–14): s 31(2).
9 Education Act 2005 s 26(2)(c).
10 Education Act 2005 s 26(2)(d).

11 Ie by the Education Act 2005 s 26(2): see the text to notes 4–10.
12 Education Act 2005 s 26(3)(a).
13 Education Act 2005 s 26(3)(b).
14 Education Act 2005 s 26(3). As to appeals against the imposition or variation of conditions see PARA 1158.

1158. Appeals in relation to registration. Any person who is aggrieved[1] by:

(1)   the refusal of Her Majesty's Chief Inspector of Education and Training in Wales[2] to renew his registration[3];

(2)   the imposition or variation of any condition subject to which he is registered[4]; or

(3)   the removal of his name[5] from the register[6],

may appeal against the Chief Inspector's decision to a tribunal[7]. Where a decision to refuse to renew a person's registration is expressed to be based on the ground that there is a reduced need for registered inspectors in Wales[8], or that there is no longer any need for registered inspectors in Wales[9], and the tribunal is satisfied that the decision was based on one of those grounds[10], the tribunal must confirm the decision to refuse renewal[11].

No decision of the Chief Inspector falling within head (2) or head (3) above has effect until the disposal of any appeal against it[12], or the period within which an appeal may be made has expired without an appeal having been made[13], unless the Chief Inspector is satisfied that the circumstances of the case justify the decision in question taking effect immediately, or earlier than would otherwise be the case[14]; and he notifies the person concerned to that effect[15].

On determining any appeal under these provisions, the tribunal may confirm, reverse or vary the decision appealed against[16]; or it may remit the case to the Chief Inspector with directions as to the action to be taken by him[17].

1   As to persons aggrieved see JUDICIAL REVIEW vol 61 (2010) PARA 656.
2   As to Her Majesty's Chief Inspector of Education and Training in Wales see PARA 1148.
3   Education Act 2005 s 27(1)(a). The registration referred to is that under s 25 (see PARA 1156): see s 27(1)(a).
4   Education Act 2005 s 27(1)(b). As to the imposition and variation of conditions see PARAS 1156, 1384.
5   Ie under the Education Act 2005 s 26: see PARA 1157.
6   Education Act 2005 s 27(1)(c).
7   Education Act 2005 s 27(1). The tribunal is one constituted in accordance with Sch 3 (see PARAS 1159–1387): see s 27(1).
8   Education Act 2005 s 27(2)(a)(i). As to the meaning of 'Wales' see PARA 7 note 3.
9   Education Act 2005 s 27(2)(a)(ii).
10 Education Act 2005 s 27(2)(b).
11 Education Act 2005 s 27(2). As to appeals against decisions of a tribunal see PARA 1161.
12 See the Education Act 2005 s 27(3)(a).
13 Education Act 2005 s 27(3)(b).
14 Education Act 2005 s 27(4)(a).
15 Education Act 2005 s 27(4)(b). As to the service of notices and documents see the Education Act 1996 s 572 (applied by the Education Act 2005 s 122(2), (3)); and PARA 76.
16 Education Act 2005 s 27(5)(a).
17 Education Act 2005 s 27(5)(b).

1159. Constitution of tribunals. A tribunal constituted to hear an appeal in relation to registration[1] consists of a chairman appointed by the Lord Chief Justice[2] after consulting the Lord Chancellor[3], and two other members appointed by the Welsh Ministers[4].

The Welsh Ministers may make such provision as they think fit for the allocation of staff for any tribunal[5], the remuneration of members of tribunals and the reimbursement of their expenses[6], and defraying any reasonable expenses incurred by any tribunal[7].

1 Ie an appeal under the Education Act 2005 s 27: see PARA 1158.
2 The Lord Chief Justice may nominate a judicial office holder (as defined in the Constitutional Reform Act 2005 s 109(4): see COURTS AND TRIBUNALS vol 24 (2010) PARA 961) to exercise his functions under the Education Act 2005 Sch 3 para 1: Sch 3 para 1(4) (added by SI 2006/1016). As to the meaning of 'functions' see PARA 18 note 5 (definition applied by the Education Act 2005 s 122(2), (3)). As to the Lord Chief Justice see COURTS AND TRIBUNALS vol 24 (2010) PARA 604.
3 Education Act 2005 Sch 3 para 1(1)(a) (amended by SI 2006/1016). To be qualified for appointment as chairman of a tribunal, a person must satisfy the judicial-appointment eligibility condition on a five-year basis: Education Act 2005 Sch 3 para 1(2) (amended by the Tribunals, Courts and Enforcement Act 2007 s 50, Sch 10 Pt 1 para 42). A person may not be appointed after the day on which he attains the age of 70 to be the chairman of a tribunal: Education Act 2005 Sch 3 para 1(3). As to the time at which a person attains a particular age see PARA 7 note 6. As to the Lord Chancellor see CONSTITUTIONAL AND ADMINISTRATIVE LAW vol 20 (2014) PARA 255 et seq. As to the judicial-appointment eligibility condition on a five-year basis see COURTS AND TRIBUNALS vol 24 (2010) PARA 645.
4 Education Act 2005 Sch 3 para 1(1)(b). As to the Welsh Ministers see PARA 59. The functions under the Education Act 2005 Sch 3 were originally vested in the National Assembly for Wales and are now exercisable by the Welsh Ministers by virtue of the Government of Wales Act 2006 s 162(1), Sch 11 paras 30, 32.
5 Education Act 2005 Sch 3 para 3(a).
6 Education Act 2005 Sch 3 para 3(b).
7 Education Act 2005 Sch 3 para 3(c).

1160. Procedure of tribunals. The Welsh Ministers[1] may by regulations[2] make provision with respect to the making of appeals to, and the procedure to be followed by, tribunals[3]. The regulations may, in particular, make provision:

(1) as to the period within which, and manner in which, appeals must be brought[4];
(2) for the holding of hearings in private in prescribed[5] circumstances[6];
(3) as to the persons[7] who may appear on behalf of the parties[8];
(4) for enabling hearings to be conducted even though a member of the tribunal, other than the chairman, is absent[9];
(5) as to the disclosure by the appellant, and others, of documents and the inspection of documents[10];
(6) requiring persons to attend the proceedings and give evidence[11];
(7) as to the payment of expenses incurred by persons compelled to attend proceedings by regulations made by virtue of head (6) above[12];
(8) authorising the administration of oaths[13] to witnesses[14];
(9) as to the withdrawal of appeals[15];
(10) as to costs and expenses incurred by any party to the proceedings[16]; and
(11) authorising preliminary or incidental matters in relation to an appeal to be dealt with by the chairman of the tribunal hearing that appeal[17].

1 As to the Welsh Ministers see PARA 59. The functions under the Education Act 2005 Sch 3 were originally vested in the National Assembly for Wales and are now exercisable by the Welsh Ministers by virtue of the Government of Wales Act 2006 s 162(1), Sch 11 paras 30, 32.
2 At the date at which this volume states the law no such regulations had been made. However, until the date on which regulations made by the Welsh Ministers under the Education Act 2005 Sch 3 para 2 come into force, the following regulations made by the Secretary of State under the School Inspections Act 1996 Sch 2 para 2 (repealed) in force on 31 August 2006 continue to have effect in relation to Wales: see the Education Act 2005 (Commencement No 1 and Transitional Provisions) (Wales) Order 2006, SI 2006/1338, art 6, Sch 4 para 6. The regulations

in question are the Education (Registered Inspectors of Schools Appeal Tribunal and Registered Nursery Education Inspectors Appeal Tribunal) (Procedure) Regulations 1999, SI 1999/265 (amended by the Learning and Skills Act 2000, s 73(3); SI 2001/1149; SI 2008/2683; and SI 2011/2085).

3   Education Act 2005 Sch 3 para 2(1). The tribunals referred to are those constituted to hear appeals under s 27 (see PARA 1158): see Sch 3 paras 1, 2(1). As to the constitution of such tribunals see PARA 1159.

4   Education Act 2005 Sch 3 para 2(2)(a).

5   'Prescribed' means prescribed by the regulations: see the Education Act 2005 s 31(1).

6   Education Act 2005 Sch 3 para 2(2)(b).
7   As to the meaning of 'person' see PARA 7 note 6.

8   Education Act 2005 Sch 3 para 2(2)(c).

9   Education Act 2005 Sch 3 para 2(2)(d).

10   Education Act 2005 Sch 3 para 2(2)(e).

11   Education Act 2005 Sch 3 para 2(2)(f).

12   Education Act 2005 Sch 3 para 2(2)(g).
13   As to the meaning of 'oath' see PARA 1035 note 15.

14   Education Act 2005 Sch 3 para 2(2)(h).

15   Education Act 2005 Sch 3 para 2(2)(i).

16   Education Act 2005 Sch 3 para 2(2)(j).

17   Education Act 2005 Sch 3 para 2(2)(k).

1161. Appeals to the High Court. If any party to proceedings before a tribunal constituted to hear appeals in relation to registration[1] is dissatisfied in point of law with a decision[2] of the tribunal he may, according as rules of court may provide, either appeal from the tribunal to the High Court or require the tribunal to state and sign a case for the opinion of the High Court[3]. Rules of court may provide for authorising or requiring the tribunal, in the course of proceedings before it, to state a special case for the decision of the High Court on any question of law arising in the proceedings[4]. Appeal from the decision of the High Court lies to the Court of Appeal[5].

The Lord Chancellor[6] may by order provide for an appeal against a decision of the tribunal to be made to the Upper Tribunal[7], instead of to the High Court[8].

1   Ie a tribunal constituted in accordance with the Education Act 2002 Sch 3: see PARA 1159.

2   'Decision' includes any direction or order, and references to the giving of a decision must be construed accordingly: Tribunals and Inquiries Act 1992 s 11(10).

3   See the Tribunals and Inquiries Act 1992 s 11(1), Sch 1 para 15(d) (s 11(1), amended by the Special Educational Needs and Disability Act 2001 s 42(1), Sch 8 Pt 2 paras 19, 20(a); Tribunals and Inquiries Act 1992 Sch 1 para 15(d) amended by the School Inspections Act 1996 s 47(1), Sch 6 para 5; the School Standards and Framework Act 1998 s 140(1), Sch 30 para 47(b); and the Education Act 2005 s 61, Sch 9 para 6). As to the High Court of Justice in England and Wales see COURTS AND TRIBUNALS vol 24 (2010) PARA 695 et seq.

4   See the Tribunals and Inquiries Act 1992 s 11(3)–(5).

5   See note 4.
6   As to the Lord Chancellor see CONSTITUTIONAL AND ADMINISTRATIVE LAW vol 20 (2014) PARA 255 et seq.

7   As to the Upper Tribunal see COURTS AND TRIBUNALS vol 24 (2010) PARA 883 et seq.

8   See the Tribunals, Courts and Enforcement Act 2007 s 32(3), (4), Sch 6 Pt 7. At the date at which this volume states the law no such order had been made.

(3) INSPECTION OF SCHOOLS

(i) Inspection of Schools in England

1162. Duty to inspect certain schools at prescribed intervals. It is the duty of Her Majesty's Chief Inspector of Education, Children's Services and Skills[1] to inspect, at such intervals as may be prescribed[2], every school[3] in England[4] within the following categories[5], namely:

(1) community, foundation and voluntary schools[6];

(2) community and foundation special schools[7];

(3) maintained nursery schools[8];

(4) academy schools[9];

(5) alternative provision academies[10];

(6) city technology colleges[11];

(7) city colleges for the technology of the arts[12]; and

(8) special schools[13] which are not community or foundation special schools but are for the time being approved[14] by the Secretary of State[15].

However, this duty does not apply to any school which is a closing school[16], and in respect of which the Chief Inspector has decided, having regard to the date on which the closure is to take effect, that no useful purpose would be served by the school being so inspected[17]. Nor does it apply to prescribed categories of school in prescribed circumstances ('an exempt school')[18].

It is the general duty of the Chief Inspector when conducting an inspection under these provisions to report on the quality of education provided in the school[19]. The report must in particular cover the achievement of pupils[20] at the school[21], the quality of teaching in the school[22], the quality of the leadership in and management of the school[23] and the behaviour and safety of pupils at the school[24]. In reporting, the Chief Inspector must consider the spiritual, moral, social and cultural development of pupils at the school[25] and the extent to which the education provided at the school meets the needs of the range of pupils at the school, and in particular the needs of pupils who have a disability[26] and pupils who have special educational needs[27].

When the inspection has been completed, it is the duty of the Chief Inspector to make a report of the inspection in writing[28].

When inspecting a school, the Chief Inspector has at all reasonable times:

(a) a right of entry to the premises[29] of the school[30];

(b) a right of entry to any other premises on which, by virtue of arrangements made by the school, any pupils who are registered[31] at the school[32] and have attained the age of 15[33], or will attain that age in the current school year, but have not ceased to be of compulsory school age[34], are receiving part of their education from any person ('the provider')[35];

(c) a right of entry to any premises of the provider used in connection with the provision by him of that education[36];

(d) a right to inspect, and take copies of, any records kept by the school, and any other documents containing information relating to the school, which he considers relevant to the discharge of his functions[37]; and

(e) a right to inspect and take copies of any records kept by the provider relating to the provision of education for pupils registered at the school, and any other documents containing information so relating, which the Chief Inspector considers relevant to the discharge of his functions[38].

It is an offence intentionally to obstruct the Chief Inspector in relation to the inspection of a school[39].

1   As to Her Majesty's Chief Inspector of Education, Children's Services and Skills see PARA 1133. As to the delegation by the Chief Inspector of his functions see PARA 1138.

2   'Prescribed' means prescribed by regulations; and 'regulations' means regulations made by the Secretary of State under the Education Act 2005 Pt 1 Ch 1 (ss 1–12): see s 12. Regulations under Pt 1 (ss 1–63) may, in particular, include provision for the designation by the Secretary of State, in accordance with the regulations, of particular schools or categories of school for the purposes of the application of particular provisions of the regulations in relation to such schools: s 120(3). As to the Secretary of State see PARA 58. As to the meaning of 'school' see PARA 91 (definition applied by s 122(2), (3)). As to the regulations made see the Education (School Inspection) (England) Regulations 2005, SI 2005/2038 (amended by SI 2008/1723; SI 2009/1564; SI 2010/1172; SI 2012/956 and SI 2015/170). As to such intervals see further note 5.

3   As to the application of the Education Act 2005 Pt 1 (ss 1–63) in relation to pupil referral units in England see the Education (Pupil Referral Units) (Application of Enactments) (England) Regulations 2007, SI 2007/2979, regs 1(3), 3, Sch 1, Pt 1, para 21. As to pupil referral units see PARA 427 et seq.

4   As to the meaning of 'England' see PARA 7 note 3. As to the inspection of schools in Wales see PARA 1182 et seq.

5   See the Education Act 2005 s 5(1)(a). If the Chief Inspector so elects in the case of any inspection under s 8 (see PARA 1165) of a school to which s 5 applies, that inspection is to be treated for the purposes of s 5(1) and of Ch 2 (ss 13–18) (see PARA 1167 et seq) as if it were an inspection under s 5: ss 5(6), 9(1) (amended by the Education and Inspections Act 2006 ss 157, 184, Sch 14 paras 98, 101, Sch 18 Pt 5; and renumbered by the Education Act 2011 s 40(5)(a)). In the case of an inspection of an exempt school under the Education Act 2005 s 8, the Chief Inspector may elect to treat the inspection for the purposes of s 5(5), (5A), (5B), (7), ss 6, 7 and Ch 2 as if it were an inspection under s 5: s 9(2) (s 9(2)–(5) added by the Education Act 2011 s 40(5)(b)). In the case of an inspection of an exempt school under the Education Act 2005 s 8(1), the Secretary of State may require the Chief Inspector to treat the inspection for the purposes of s 5(5), (5A), (5B), (7), ss 6, 7 and Ch 2 as if it were an inspection under s 5: s 9(3) (as so added). In the case of an inspection of a school under s 8(2) which is carried out in response to a request from the appropriate authority for the school, the Chief Inspector must treat the inspection for the purposes of s 5(5), (5A), (5B), (7), ss 6, 7 and Ch 2 as if it were an inspection under s 5: s 9(4) (as so added). As to the meaning of 'appropriate authority' see s 6(3); and PARA 1163 note 1 (applied by s 9(6) (as so added)).

    The Education (School Inspection) (England) Regulations 2005, SI 2005/2038, reg 3 prescribes the interval between inspections of a school for the purposes of the Education Act 2005 s 5(1)(a): Education (School Inspection) (England) Regulations 2005, SI 2005/2038, reg 3(1) (reg 3 substituted by SI 2015/170). Where the school is not awarded a grade of 'good' or better in the earlier of the inspections mentioned in the Education (School Inspection) (England) Regulations 2005, SI 2005/2038, reg 3(1) for the quality of education it provides or where the school is awarded such a grade in that inspection and no relevant inspection under the Education Act 2005 s 8 is subsequently carried out, the interval is a period not exceeding 5 years after the end of the school year in which the earlier of the inspections mentioned in the Education (School Inspection) (England) Regulations 2005, SI 2005/2038, reg 3(1) was carried out: reg 3(2)–(4) (as so substituted). A relevant inspection made under the Education Act 2005 s 8 is an inspection of a school carried out under s 8(2) (see PARA 1165) in relation to which the following two conditions are met:

    (1)   that the inspection is carried out within the period of 5 years beginning with the end of the school year in which the inspection was carried out or, if one or more relevant inspections under s 8 have already been carried out, the end of the school year in which the most recent of those inspections was carried out (see the Education (School Inspection) (England) Regulations 2005, SI 2005/2038, reg 3(7), (9)(a) (as so substituted));

    (2)   that the Chief Inspector carries out the inspection for the purposes of determining whether the school would be likely to achieve a grade of 'good' or better for the quality of education it provides if an inspection under the Education Act 2005 s 5 were carried out and, having carried out the inspection, is satisfied that the evidence does not suggest

that the school would not achieve such a grade if an inspection under s 5 were carried out (see the Education (School Inspection) (England) Regulations 2005, SI 2005/2038, reg 3(7), (9)(b) (as so substituted)).

Where the school is awarded a grade of 'good' or better in the earlier of the inspections mentioned in reg 3(1) for the quality of education it provides, and one or more relevant inspections under the Education Act 2005 s 8 are subsequently carried out, the interval is a period not exceeding 5 years after the end of the school year in which the latest of the inspections was carried out: Education (School Inspection) (England) Regulations 2005, SI 2005/2038, reg 3(5), (6) (as so substituted).

As to the meaning of 'school year' see PARA 19 note 12 (definition applied by the Education Act 2005 s 122(2), (3)). As to the application of this regulation to pupil referral units in England see the Education (Pupil Referral Units) (Application of Enactments) (England) Regulations 2007, SI 2007/2979, regs 1(3), 3, Sch 1, Pt 1, para 27. As to the duty to notify parents of inspections see PARA 1163. As to the duty to have regard to certain views when conducting inspections see PARA 1164. As to the procedure for inspections see PARA 1167 et seq. As to interim statements between inspections see PARA 1172 et seq. As to inspections other than inspections at prescribed intervals see PARA 1165. As to the power of the Chief Inspector to investigate complaints against schools see PARA 1175.

6   Education Act 2005 s 5(2)(a). As to the meaning of references to a community, foundation or voluntary school see PARA 106.
7   Education Act 2005 s 5(2)(b). As to the meaning of references to a community special school see PARA 106.
8   Education Act 2005 s 5(2)(c). As to the meaning of 'maintained nursery school' see PARA 99 note 4 (definition applied by s 122(2), (3)).
9   Education Act 2005 s 5(2)(d) (s 5(2)(d) substituted and s 5(2)(da) added by the Education Act 2011 Sch 13 para 15(2)). As to the meaning of 'academy' see PARA 346 note 7 (definition applied by s 122(2), (3)).
10 Education Act 2005 s 5(2)(da) (as added: see note 9). As to the meaning of 'alternative provision academy' see PARA 346 note 14 (definition applied by s 122(2), (3)).
11 Education Act 2005 s 5(2)(e). As to city technology colleges see PARA 345.
12 Education Act 2005 s 5(2)(f). As to city colleges for the technology of the arts see PARA 345.
13 As to the meaning of 'special school' see PARA 1041 (definition applied by the Education Act 2005 s 122(2), (3)).
14 Ie under the Education Act 1996 s 342: see PARA 1042.
15 Education Act 2005 s 5(2)(g). As from a day to be appointed, s 5(2)(g) is substituted so as to refer to schools approved under the Education Act 1996 s 342 (non-maintained special schools): Education Act 2005 s 5(2)(g) (prospectively substituted by the Education and Skills Act 2008 s 169(1), Sch 1 Pt 1 paras 25, 26). At the date at which this volume states the law no such day had been appointed.
16 Education Act 2005 s 5(3)(a). For this purpose, a 'closing school' means:
   (1)   any community, foundation or voluntary school, community or foundation special school or maintained nursery school in respect of which proposals to discontinue the school have been approved, adopted or determined under any enactment (s 5(4)(a));
   (2)   a foundation or voluntary school in respect of which the governing body has given notice of discontinuance under the School Standards and Framework Act 1998 s 30 (see PARA 116) (Education Act 2005 s 5(4)(b));
   (3)   a community, foundation or voluntary or community or foundation special school in respect of which the Secretary of State has given a direction to discontinue the school under the Education and Inspections Act 2006 s 17 (see PARA 117) or s 68 (see PARA 1217) (Education Act 2005 s 5(4)(c) (amended by the Education and Inspections Act 2006 s 71, Sch 7 Pt 2 para 23));
   (4)   an academy in respect of which notice of termination of academy arrangements has been given (Education Act 2005 s 5(4)(d) (substituted by the Academies Act 2010 s 14, Sch 2 paras 16, 17)); or
   (5)   a special school which is not a community or foundation special school but is for the time being approved by the Secretary of State under the Education Act 1996 s 342 (approval of non-maintained special schools: see PARA 1042) and which the proprietor has decided to close (Education Act 2005 s 5(4)(e)).
   As to the meaning of 'academy arrangements' see PARA 346 note 4; and as to the meaning of 'proprietor' see PARA 51 note 4 (definitions applied by s 122(2), (3)).
17 Education Act 2005 s 5(3)(b).
18 Education Act 2005 s 5(4A), (4B) (s 5(4A), (4B) added by the Education Act 2011 s 82(1)(b)). The categories of school that are prescribed for these purposes are those falling within head (1),

head (4) (unless it is an educational institution as described in the Academies Act 2010 s 1A(2) (see PARA 346 note 12)), head (5) and head (7) in the text: Education (Exemption from School Inspection) (England) Regulations 2012, SI 2012/1293, reg 3. The circumstances prescribed for the purposes of the Education Act 2005 s 5(4A) are as follows:

(1) the school's overall effectiveness was awarded the highest grade in the school's most recent inspection under s 5;

(2) in the case of a school which is an academy school that has not previously been inspected under s 5 and has a predecessor school, either its predecessor school's overall effectiveness was awarded the highest grade in its inspection under s 5 or, if that academy school has two or more predecessor schools, each predecessor school's overall effectiveness was awarded the highest grade in its last inspection under s 5 (Education (Exemption from School Inspection) (England) Regulations 2012, SI 2012/1293, reg 4(1)–(3)).

For these purposes a reference to an inspection under the Education Act 2005 s 5 includes a reference to an inspection under s 8 (see PARA 1165) which has been treated by the Chief Inspector as an inspection under s 5; and a reference to an academy school's 'predecessor school' is a reference to the school that was discontinued and which that academy school replaced or the maintained school which converted into that academy school in accordance with the Education Act 2010 s 4 (see PARA 350): Education (Exemption from School Inspection) (England) Regulations 2012, SI 2012/1293, reg 4(4). As to the meaning of 'academy school' see PARA 346 note 12 (definition applied by the Education Act 2005 s 122(2), (3)).

19 Education Act 2005 s 5(5) (s 5(5) substituted and s 5(5A), (5B) added by the Education Act 2011 s 82(1)(b)).

20 As to the meaning of 'pupil' see PARA 20 note 4 (definition applied by the Education Act 2005 s 122(2), (3)).

21 Education Act 2005 s 5(5A)(a) (as added: see note 19).

22 Education Act 2005 s 5(5A)(b) (as added: see note 19).

23 Education Act 2005 s 5(5A)(c) (as added: see note 19).

24 Education Act 2005 s 5(5A)(d) (as added: see note 19).

25 Education Act 2005 s 5(5B)(a) (as added: see note 19). However, an inspection which is required under s 5 must not extend to denominational education, or to the content of collective worship which falls to be inspected under s 48 (inspection of religious education: see PARA 1178): s 5(7). As to the meaning of 'denominational education' see PARA 1178 note 6. Note should also be made of guidance published by the Department for Education on 27 November 2014 on promoting British values in schools to ensure young people leave school prepared for life in modern Britain. The guidance aims to help both independent and state-maintained schools understand their responsibilities in this area. According to the guidance, all have a duty to 'actively promote' the fundamental British values of democracy, the rule of law, individual liberty, and mutual respect and tolerance of those with different faiths and beliefs. These values were first set out by the government in the 'Prevent' strategy in 2011. See 'Protecting children from radicalisation: the prevent duty' (1 July 2015), under which the promotion of 'fundamental British values' is an important part. See also PARAS 8 note 4, 910 note 6.

26 Ie for the purposes of the Equality Act 2010 (see DISCRIMINATION vol 33 (2013) PARA 1 et seq).

27 Education Act 2005 s 5(5B)(b) (as added: see note 19).

28 See the Education Act 2005 s 5(1)(b). As to the meaning of 'writing' see PARA 76 note 8. As to the publication of inspection reports see PARA 1166.

29 As to the meaning of 'premises' see PARA 62 note 19 (definition applied by the Education Act 2005 s 122(2), (3)).

30 Education Act 2005 s 10(1)(a).

31 As to the meaning of 'registered pupil' see PARA 437 (definition applied by the Education Act 2005 s 122(2), (3)).

32 Education Act 2005 s 10(1)(b)(i).

33 As to the time at which a person attains a particular age see PARA 7 note 6.

34 Education Act 2005 s 10(1)(b)(ii). As to the meaning of 'compulsory school age' see PARA 19.

35 Education Act 2005 s 10(1)(b). As to the meaning of 'person' see PARA 7 note 6.

36 Education Act 2005 s 10(1)(c).

37 Education Act 2005 s 10(1)(d). As to the meaning of 'functions' see PARA 18 note 5 (definition applied by s 122(2), (3)). A person authorised by any provision of the Education Act 2005 Pt 1 (ss 1–63) to inspect records or other documents is entitled at any reasonable time to have access to, and inspect and check the operation of, any computer and any associated apparatus or material which is or has been in use in connection with the records or other documents in question (s 58(a)); and may require the person by whom or on whose behalf the computer is or has been so used, or any person having charge of, or otherwise concerned with the operation of,

the computer, apparatus or material, to afford him such assistance as he may reasonably require (including, in particular, the making of information available for inspection or copying in a legible form) (s 58(b)).

38 Education Act 2005 s 10(1)(e). See also note 37.

39 See the Education Act 2005 s 10(2). A person guilty of such an offence is liable on summary conviction to a fine not exceeding level 4 on the standard scale: s 10(3). As to the standard scale see SENTENCING AND DISPOSITION OF OFFENDERS vol 92 (2010) PARA 142.

1163. Duty to notify parents of inspections at prescribed intervals. If the appropriate authority for a school[1] is notified by, or under arrangements made by, Her Majesty's Chief Inspector of Education, Children's Services and Skills[2] that the Chief Inspector is proposing to inspect the school under his duty to inspect schools at prescribed intervals[3], the appropriate authority must take such steps as are reasonably practicable to notify the registered[4] parents[5] of registered pupils[6] at the school[7], and such other persons[8] as may be prescribed[9], of the time when the inspection is to take place[10].

1 'Appropriate authority' means:
    (1)   in relation to a community, foundation or voluntary school, a community or foundation special school or a maintained nursery school, the school's governing body or, if the school does not have a delegated budget, the local authority (Education Act 2005 s 6(3)(a) (amended by SI 2010/1158)); and
    (2)   in relation to an academy, city technology college, city college for the technology of the arts, or a special school approved under the Education Act 1996 s 342 (see PARA 1042), the proprietor of the school (see the Education Act 2005 s 6(3)(b)).
  As to the meaning of references to a community, foundation or voluntary school or a community or foundation special school see PARA 106. As to the meaning of 'maintained nursery school' see PARA 99 note 4; as to the meaning of 'local authority' see PARA 25; as to academies see PARA 345 et seq; as to the meaning of 'special school' see PARA 1041; and as to the meaning of 'proprietor' see PARA 51 note 4 (definitions applied by s 122(2), (3)). As to the meaning of 'delegated budget' see PARA 323 (definition applied by s 63(1)). As to the governing bodies of maintained schools in England see PARA 150 et seq. As to city technology colleges and city colleges for the technology of the arts see PARA 345. As to the inspection of schools in Wales see PARA 1182 et seq.
  As to the application of Pt 1 (ss 1–63) in relation to pupil referral units in England see the Education (Pupil Referral Units) (Application of Enactments) (England) Regulations 2007, SI 2007/2979, regs 1(3), 3, Sch 1 Pt 1 para 21. As to pupil referral units see PARA 427 et seq.
2 As to Her Majesty's Chief Inspector of Education, Children's Services and Skills see PARA 1133.
3 Ie under the Education Act 2005 s 5: see PARA 1162.
4 As to the meaning of 'registered' see PARA 437 (definition applied by the Education Act 2005 s 122(2), (3)).
5 As to the meaning of 'parent' see PARA 7 note 6 (definition applied by the Education Act 2005 s 122(2), (3)).
6 As to the meaning of 'registered pupil' see PARA 437 (definition applied by the Education Act 2005 s 122(2), (3)).
7 Education Act 2005 s 6(1)(a). Any notification given under s 6(1)(a) must include a statement, in a form approved by the Chief Inspector, inviting the registered parents of registered pupils to inform the Chief Inspector of their views on matters relating to the school: s 6(2).
8 As to the meaning of 'person' see PARA 7 note 6.
9 Education Act 2005 s 6(1)(b). 'Prescribed' means prescribed by regulations; and 'regulations' means regulations made by the Secretary of State under Pt 1 Ch 1 (ss 1–12): s 12. As to the Secretary of State see PARA 58. As to the persons prescribed under s 6(1)(b) see the Education (School Inspection) (England) Regulations 2005, SI 2005/2038, reg 4 (amended by SI 2010/1172; SI 2012/956; and SI 2015/170). As to the application of this regulation to pupil referral units in England see the Education (Pupil Referral Units) (Application of Enactments) (England) Regulations 2007, SI 2007/2979, regs 1(3), 3, Sch 1, Pt 1, para 27.
10 Education Act 2005 s 6(1) (amended by the Education Act 2011 s 40(3)). As to the duty of the Chief Inspector, when conducting a school inspection, to have regard to the views of certain persons see PARA 1164.

1164. Duty to have regard to views when conducting inspections at prescribed intervals. In conducting an inspection of a school in England[1], the matters to which Her Majesty's Chief Inspector of Education, Children's Services and Skills[2] must have regard include any views expressed to him by any of the following persons[3]:

(1) the head teacher[4];

(2) in the case of a maintained school, the governing body[5];

(3) in the case of any other school, the proprietor[6] of the school[7];

(4) any person notified of the inspections as prescribed[8];

(5) members of the staff of the school[9];

(6) registered pupils[10] at the school[11]; and

(7) the registered parents[12] of registered pupils[13].

1 Ie under the Education Act 2005 s 5: see PARA 1162. As to the meaning of 'school' see PARA 91 (definition applied by the Education Act 2005 s 122(2), (3)). As to the meaning of 'England' see PARA 7 note 3. As to the inspection of schools in Wales see PARA 1182 et seq.

2 As to Her Majesty's Chief Inspector of Education, Children's Services and Skills see PARA 1133. As to the delegation by the Chief Inspector of his functions see PARA 1138.

3 As to the meaning of 'person' see PARA 7 note 6.

4 Education Act 2005 s 7(a). As to the meaning of 'head teacher' see PARA 86 note 4 (definition applied by s 122(2), (3)). As to the application of Pt 1 (ss 1–63) in relation to pupil referral units in England see the Education (Pupil Referral Units) (Application of Enactments) (England) Regulations 2007, SI 2007/2979, regs 1(3), 3, Sch 1 Pt 1 para 21. As to pupil referral units see PARA 427 et seq.

5 Education Act 2005 s 7(b). As to the governing bodies of maintained schools in England see PARA 150 et seq.

6 As to the meaning of 'proprietor' see PARA 51 note 4 (definition applied by the Education Act 2005 s 122(2), (3)).

7 Education Act 2005 s 7(c).

8 Education Act 2005 s 7(d). The persons referred to are those prescribed for the purposes of s 6(1)(b) (see PARA 1163): see s 7(d).

9 Education Act 2005 s 7(e). As to the staffing of schools generally see PARA 268 et seq.

10 As to the meaning of 'registered pupil' see PARA 437 (definition applied by the Education Act 2005 s 122(2), (3)).

11 Education Act 2005 s 7(f).

12 As to the meaning of 'registered' see PARA 348; and as to the meaning of 'parent' see PARA 7 note 6 (definitions applied by the Education Act 2005 s 122(2), (3)).

13 Education Act 2005 s 7(g). As to the duty to notify parents of inspections see PARA 1163.

1165. Other inspections. If requested to do so by the Secretary of State[1], Her Majesty's Chief Inspector of Education, Children's Services and Skills[2] must inspect and report on such school[3], or class of school, in England[4] as is specified in the request[5].

The Chief Inspector may also inspect any school in England in circumstances where he is not required[6] to do so[7] and, where the inspection has been carried out at the request from the appropriate authority[8] for the school, he may charge the appropriate authority for the cost of the inspection[9].

When inspecting a school under the above provisions, the Chief Inspector has at all reasonable times[10]:

(1) a right of entry to the premises[11] of the school[12];

(2) a right of entry to any other premises on which, by virtue of arrangements made by the school, any pupils who are registered[13] at the school[14] and have attained the age of 15[15], or will attain that age in the current school year[16], but have not ceased to be of compulsory school age[17], are receiving part of their education from any person ('the provider')[18];

(3) a right of entry to any premises of the provider used in connection with the provision by him of that education[19];

(4) a right to inspect, and take copies of, any records kept by the school, and any other documents containing information relating to the school, which he considers relevant to the discharge of his functions[20]; and

(5) a right to inspect and take copies of any records kept by the provider relating to the provision of education for pupils registered at the school, and any other documents containing information so relating, which the Chief Inspector considers relevant to the discharge of his functions[21].

It is an offence intentionally to obstruct the Chief Inspector in relation to the inspection of a school[22].

1 As to the Secretary of State see PARA 58.
2 As to Her Majesty's Chief Inspector of Education, Children's Services and Skills see PARA 1133. As to the delegation by the Chief Inspector of his functions see PARA 1138.
3 As to the meaning of 'school' see PARA 91 (definition applied by the Education Act 2005 s 122(2), (3)).
4 As to the meaning of 'England' see PARA 7 note 3. As to the inspection of schools in Wales see PARA 1182 et seq.
5 Education Act 2005 s 8(1) (s 8 substituted by the Education and Inspections Act 2006 s 157, Sch 14 paras 98, 100). As to inspections at prescribed intervals see PARA 1162. As to the publication of inspection reports see PARA 1166. As to the application of the Education Act 2005 Pt 1 (ss 1–63) in relation to pupil referral units in England see the Education (Pupil Referral Units) (Application of Enactments) (England) Regulations 2007, SI 2007/2979, regs 1(3), 3, Sch 1 Pt 1 para 21. As to pupil referral units see PARA 427 et seq.
6 Ie by the Education Act 2005 s 5 (see PARA 1162) or s 8(1) (see the text to notes 1–5).
7 Education Act 2005 s 8(2) (as substituted: see note 5).
8 As to the meaning of 'appropriate authority' see the Education Act 2005 s 6(3); and PARA 1163 (definition applied by s 8(4) (s 8(3), (4) added by the Education Act 2011 s 40(4))).
9 Education Act 2005 s 8(3) (as added: see note 8).
10 See the Education Act 2005 s 10(1).
11 As to the meaning of 'premises' see PARA 62 note 19 (definition applied by the Education Act 2005 s 122(2), (3)).
12 Education Act 2005 s 10(1)(a).
13 As to the meaning of 'registered pupil' see PARA 437 (definition applied by the Education Act 2005 s 122(2), (3)).
14 Education Act 2005 s 10(1)(b)(i).
15 As to the time at which a person attains a particular age see PARA 7 note 6.
16 As to the meaning of 'school year' see PARA 19 note 12 (definition applied by the Education Act 2005 s 122(2), (3)).
17 Education Act 2005 s 10(1)(b)(ii). As to the meaning of 'compulsory school age' see PARA 19.
18 Education Act 2005 s 10(1)(b). As to the meaning of 'person' see PARA 7 note 6.
19 Education Act 2005 s 10(1)(c).
20 Education Act 2005 s 10(1)(d). As to the meaning of 'functions' see PARA 18 note 5 (definition applied by s 122(2), (3)). A person authorised by any provision of the Education Act 2005 Pt 1 (ss 1–63) to inspect records or other documents is entitled at any reasonable time to have access to, and inspect and check the operation of, any computer and any associated apparatus or material which is or has been in use in connection with the records or other documents in question (s 58(a)); and may require the person by whom or on whose behalf the computer is or has been so used, or any person having charge of, or otherwise concerned with the operation of, the computer, apparatus or material, to afford him such assistance as he may reasonably require (including, in particular, the making of information available for inspection or copying in a legible form) (s 58(b)).
21 Education Act 2005 s 10(1)(e). See also note 20.
22 See the Education Act 2005 s 10(2). A person guilty of such an offence is liable on summary conviction to a fine not exceeding level 4 on the standard scale: s 10(3). As to the standard scale see SENTENCING AND DISPOSITION OF OFFENDERS vol 92 (2010) PARA 142.

1166. Publication of inspection reports. Her Majesty's Chief Inspector of Education, Children's Services and Skills[1] may arrange for any report of an inspection carried out by him under any provision of the Education Act 2005[2] (whether the report is required by any such provision or is otherwise made in pursuance of his functions[3] under that provision) to be published in such manner as he considers appropriate[4].

1   As to Her Majesty's Chief Inspector of Education, Children's Services and Skills see PARA 1133. As to the delegation by the Chief Inspector of his functions see PARA 1138.
2   Ie under any provision of the Education Act 2005 Pt 1 Ch 1 (ss 1–12). As to inspections see PARAS 1162, 1165.
3   As to the meaning of 'functions' see PARA 18 note 5 (definition applied by the Education Act 2005 s 122(2), (3)).
4   Education Act 2005 s 11(1). As to combined reports under the inspection enactments see PARA 1143. As to the application of the law of defamation to inspection reports see PARA 1142.

B. PROCEDURE FOR SCHOOL INSPECTION

1167.   Duties of Chief Inspector where school causes or has caused concern. If, on the completion of any inspection of a school in England[1], Her Majesty's Chief Inspector of Education, Children's Services and Skills[2] is of the opinion that special measures are required to be taken in relation to the school[3] or that the school requires significant improvement[4], he must send a draft of the report of the inspection to the governing body[5] (in the case of a maintained school)[6], and to the proprietor[7] of the school (in the case of any other school)[8] and he must consider any comments on the draft that are made to him within the prescribed period[9] by the governing body or proprietor, as the case may be[10].

If, after complying with above requirements[11], the Chief Inspector is of the opinion that the case is one where special measures are required to be taken in relation to the school or that the school requires significant improvement[12], he must without delay give a notice in writing[13], to the Secretary of State[14], the local authority (in the case of a maintained school)[15], and to the proprietor of the school (in the case of any other school)[16], and he must state his opinion in the report of the inspection[17].

If a report of a school inspection[18] is made in circumstances where:

(1)   in the latest report of an inspection of the school, the Chief Inspector stated that in his opinion special measures were required to be taken in relation to the school[19]; but

(2)   he is of the opinion that special measures are not required to be taken in relation to the school[20],

he must state his opinion in the report[21].

If a report of a school inspection[22] is made in circumstances where:

(a)   in the latest report of an inspection of the school, the Chief Inspector stated that in his opinion the school required significant improvement[23]; but

(b)   he is of the opinion that the school does not require significant improvement and that special measures are not required to be taken in relation to the school[24],

he must state his opinion in the report[25].

1   Ie an inspection under the Education Act 2005 s 5: see PARA 1162. As to the meaning of 'England' see PARA 7 note 3. As to the inspection of schools in Wales see PARA 1182 et seq.
2   As to Her Majesty's Chief Inspector of Education, Children's Services and Skills see PARA 1133. As to the delegation by the Chief Inspector of his functions see PARA 1138.
3   Education Act 2005 s 13(1)(a). For the purposes of Pt 1 (ss 1–63), special measures are required to be taken in relation to a school if the school is failing to give its pupils an acceptable standard of education (s 44(1)(a)); and the persons responsible for leading, managing or governing the

school are not demonstrating the capacity to secure the necessary improvement in the school (s 44(1)(b)). As to the meaning of 'school' see PARA 91; and as to the meaning of 'pupil' see PARA 20 note 4 (definitions applied by s 122(2), (3)). See generally *R v Secretary of State for Education and Employment and the North East London Education Association, ex p M* [1996] ELR 162, CA (decided under previous legislation).

As to the application of the Education Act 2005 Pt 1 (ss 1–63) in relation to pupil referral units in England see the Education (Pupil Referral Units) (Application of Enactments) (England) Regulations 2007, SI 2007/2979, regs 1(3), 3, Sch 1 Pt 1 para 21. As to pupil referral units see PARA 427 et seq.

4   Education Act 2005 s 13(1)(b). For the purposes of Pt 1 (ss 1–63), a school requires significant improvement if, although not falling within s 44(1) (see note 3), it is performing significantly less well than it might in all the circumstances reasonably be expected to perform: s 44(2).

5   As to the governing bodies of maintained schools in England see PARA 150 et seq.

6   Education Act 2005 s 13(2)(a)(i). For the purposes of Pt 1 Ch 2 (ss 13–18), 'maintained school' means a community, foundation or voluntary school, a community or foundation special school or a maintained nursery school: see s 18. As to the meaning of references to a community, foundation or voluntary school or a community or foundation special school see PARA 106. As to the meaning of 'maintained nursery school' see PARA 99 note 4 (definition applied by s 122(2), (3)).

7   As to the meaning of 'proprietor' see PARA 51 note 4 (definition applied by the Education Act 2005 s 122(2), (3)).

8   Education Act 2005 s 13(2)(a)(ii).

9   'Prescribed' means prescribed by regulations; and 'regulations' means regulations made by the Secretary of State under the Education Act 2005 Pt 1 Ch 2 (ss 13–18): see s 18. As to the Secretary of State see PARA 58. A period of five working days from the date of receipt of the draft report has been prescribed for the purpose of s 13(2)(b): see the Education (School Inspection) (England) Regulations 2005, SI 2005/2038, reg 5. As to the application of this regulation to pupil referral units in England see the Education (Pupil Referral Units) (Application of Enactments) (England) Regulations 2007, SI 2007/2979, regs 1(3), 3, Sch 1 Pt 1 para 27.

10 Education Act 2005 s 13(2)(b).

11 Ie complying with the Education Act 2005 s 13(2).

12 Ie that the case falls within the Education Act 2005 s 13(1)(a) or (b).

13 Stating that the case falls within the Education Act 2005 s 13(1)(a) or (b). As to the service of notices and documents see the Education Act 1996 s 572 (applied by the Education Act 2005 s 122(2), (3)); and PARA 76. As to the meaning of 'writing' see PARA 76 note 8.

14 Education Act 2005 s 13(3)(a)(i).

15 Education Act 2005 s 13(3)(a)(ii) (amended by SI 2010/1158). As to the meaning of 'local authority' see PARA 25 (definition applied by the Education Act 2005 s 122(2), (3)).

16 Education Act 2005 s 13(3)(a)(iii).

17 Education Act 2005 s 13(3)(b). As to the publication of inspection reports see PARA 1166.

18 Ie an inspection under the Education Act 2005 s 5: see PARA 1162.

19 Education Act 2005 s 13(4)(a).

20 Education Act 2005 s 13(4)(b).

21 Education Act 2005 s 13(4). The Chief Inspector must state his opinion in the report as mentioned in the text whether or not he is required by s 13(3)(b) (see the text to note 17) also to state the opinion that the school requires significant improvement: see s 13(4).

22 Ie an inspection under the Education Act 2005 s 5: see PARA 1162.

23 Education Act 2005 s 13(5)(a).

24 Education Act 2005 s 13(5)(b).

25 Education Act 2005 s 13(5).

1168.   Destination of reports of inspections of maintained schools. Her Majesty's Chief Inspector of Education, Children's Services and Skills[1] must ensure that a copy of the report of any inspection in England[2] of a maintained school[3] is sent without delay to the appropriate authority[4] for the school[5]. The Chief Inspector must ensure that copies of the report are sent to the head teacher[6] of the school[7], to whichever of the local authority and the governing body is not the appropriate authority[8], in the case of a school having foundation governors[9], to the person[10] who appoints them and (if different) to the appropriate appointing authority[11]; and, in such circumstances as may be prescribed, to such other persons (if any) as may be prescribed[12].

The appropriate authority must:

(1)   make a copy of any report sent to it[13] available for inspection by members of the public at such times and at such place as may be reasonable[14];

(2)   provide a copy of the report, free of charge or in prescribed cases[15] on payment of such fee as it thinks fit, not exceeding the cost of supply, to any person who asks for one[16]; and

(3)   take such steps as are reasonably practicable to secure that every registered parent[17] of a registered pupil[18] at the school receives a copy of the report within such period following receipt of the report by the authority as may be prescribed[19].

1   As to Her Majesty's Chief Inspector of Education, Children's Services and Skills see PARA 1133. As to the delegation by the Chief Inspector of his functions see PARA 1138.

2   Ie any inspection carried out under the Education Act 2005 s 5: see PARA 1162. As to the meaning of 'England' see PARA 7 note 3.

3   As to the meaning of 'maintained school' see PARA 1167 note 6.

4   'The appropriate authority', in relation to a maintained school, means the school's governing body or, if the school does not have a delegated budget, the local authority: see the Education Act 2005 s 18 (definition amended by SI 2010/1158). As to the governing bodies of maintained schools in England see PARA 150 et seq. As to the meaning of 'delegated budget' see PARA 323 (definition applied by the Education Act 2005 s 63(1)). As to the meaning of 'local authority' see PARA 25 (definition applied by s 122(2), (3)).

5   Education Act 2005 s 14(1). As to the application of Pt 1 (ss 1–63) to pupil referral units in England see the Education (Pupil Referral Units) (Application of Enactments) (England) Regulations 2007, SI 2007/2979, regs 1(3), 3, Sch 1 Pt 1 para 21. As to pupil referral units see PARA 427 et seq.

6   As to the meaning of 'head teacher' see PARA 86 note 4 (definition applied by the Education Act 2005 s 122(2), (3)).

7   Education Act 2005 s 14(2)(a).

8   Education Act 2005 s 14(2)(b) (amended by SI 2010/1158).

9   As to schools having foundation governors see PARA 108.

10   As to the meaning of 'person' see PARA 7 note 6.

11   Education Act 2005 s 14(2)(c). 'The appropriate appointing authority', in relation to a voluntary aided school, means the appropriate diocesan authority, if it is a Church of England school or a Roman Catholic Church school or, in any other case, the person who appoints the foundation governors: s 18 (definition amended by the Education and Inspections Act 2006 ss 71, 184, Sch 7 Pt 2 para 24, Sch 18 Pt 4). As to the meanings of 'appropriate diocesan authority', 'Church of England school' and 'Roman Catholic Church school' see PARA 146 note 12 (definitions applied by the Education Act 2005 s 63(1)).

12   Education Act 2005 s 14(2)(d). 'Prescribed' means prescribed by regulations; and 'regulations' means regulations made by the Secretary of State under Pt 1 Ch 2 (ss 13–18): see s 18. As to the Secretary of State see PARA 58. At the date at which this volume states the law no such regulations had been made.

13   Ie under the Education Act 2005 s 14(1): see the text to notes 1–5.

14   Education Act 2005 s 14(4)(a). As from a day to be appointed, s 14(4) is amended so as to provide that the appropriate authority must take such steps as are reasonably practicable, within such period following the receipt by it of the report as may be prescribed, to secure that every registered parent of a registered pupil at the school is informed of the overall assessment contained in the report of the quality of education provided in the school: s 14(4) (prospectively substituted by the Deregulation Act 2015 Sch 16 para 6(1), (3)). At the date at which this volume states the law no such day had been appointed.

15   As to the prescribed cases see the Education (School Inspection) (England) Regulations 2005, SI 2005/2038, reg 8 (substituted by SI 2008/1723). As to the application of this regulation to pupil referral units in England see the Education (Pupil Referral Units) (Application of Enactments) (England) Regulations 2007, SI 2007/2979, regs 1(3), 3, Sch 1 Pt 1 para 27.

16   Education Act 2005 s 14(4)(b). See note 14.

17　As to the meaning of 'registered' see PARA 437; and as to the meaning of 'parent' see PARA 7 note 6 (definitions applied by the Education Act 2005 s 122(2), (3)).

18　As to the meaning of 'registered pupil' see PARA 437 (definition applied by the Education Act 2005 s 122(2), (3)). As to the meaning of 'pupil' see PARA 20 note 4.

19　Education Act 2005 s 14(4)(c). See note 14. A period of five working days from the date of receipt of the report by the authority is prescribed for these purposes: see the Education (School Inspection) (England) Regulations 2005, SI 2005/2038, reg 6 (amended by SI 2015/170). As to the application of this regulation to pupil referral units in England see the Education (Pupil Referral Units) (Application of Enactments) (England) Regulations 2007, SI 2007/2979, regs 1(3), 3, Sch 1 Pt 1 para 27.

1169. Measures to be taken by local authority. Where, in a report of an inspection in England[1] of a maintained school[2], Her Majesty's Chief Inspector of Education, Children's Services and Skills[3] stated either[4] that in his opinion special measures were required to be taken in relation to the school[5], or that in his opinion the school required significant improvement[6], the local authority[7] must:

(1)　consider what action to take in the light of the report[8];

(2)　consider what arrangements to make for the purpose of informing registered parents[9] of the proposed action, ascertaining their views on the proposed action and taking account of those views[10];

(3)　consider whether those arrangements are to include the appointment of a specified person[11] for that purpose[12];

(4)　prepare a written[13] statement of (a) the action it proposes to take, and the period within which it proposes to take that action, or, if it does not propose to take such action, of the reasons for not doing so[14], and (b) of the arrangements it proposes to make for the purpose mentioned in head (2) above[15]; and

(5)　send a copy of that statement to the Chief Inspector[16], in the case of a voluntary aided school, to the person who appoints the foundation governors[17] and (if different) the appropriate appointing authority[18], and to such other persons as the Secretary of State[19] may specify[20].

Where the local authority has prepared a statement[21] in relation to a school[22], and it appears to the Secretary of State, on the basis of a report of an interim inspection[23] of the school by the Chief Inspector, that the case has become urgent[24], and no subsequent inspection of the school[25] has been made[26], the Secretary of State may by notice[27] require the local authority to[28]:

(a)　consider the action to be taken in the light of the report of the interim inspection and the arrangements to be made for the purpose mentioned in head (2) above[29];

(b)　prepare a written statement of the action it proposes to take, and the period within which it proposes to take that action, or, if it does not propose to take such action, of the reasons for not doing so[30], and of the arrangements it proposes to make for the purpose mentioned in head (2) above[31]; and

(c)　send a copy of the statement to the Secretary of State and to the persons mentioned in head (5) above[32].

It is the duty of the local authority to prepare a statement[33] within the statutory period[34], but this provision does not relieve the local authority of any duty to prepare a statement which has not been performed within that period[35]. In performing its functions[36] in relation to the preparation of statements under these provisions[37], the local authority must have regard to any guidance given from time to time by the Secretary of State[38].

1   Ie an inspection under the Education Act 2005 s 5: see PARA 1162. As to the meaning of 'England' see PARA 7 note 3.
2   As to the meaning of 'maintained school' see PARA 1167 note 6.
3   As to Her Majesty's Chief Inspector of Education, Children's Services and Skills see PARA 1133.
4   Education Act 2005 s 15(1) (amended by the Education and Inspections Act 2006 s 71, Sch 7 Pt 1 para 1(1), (2)). As to the application of the Education Act 2005 Pt 1 (ss 1–63) to pupil referral units in England see the Education (Pupil Referral Units) (Application of Enactments) (England) Regulations 2007, SI 2007/2979, regs 1(3), 3, Sch 1 Pt 1 para 21. As to pupil referral units see PARA 427 et seq.
5   Education Act 2005 s 15(1)(a). As to the meaning of references to special measures being required to be taken in relation to a school see PARA 1167 note 3.
6   Education Act 2005 s 15(1)(b). As to the meaning of references to schools requiring significant improvement see PARA 1167 note 4.
7   As to the meaning of 'local authority' see PARA 25 (definition applied by the Education Act 2005 s 122(2), (3)).
8   Education Act 2005 s 15(2)(a) (s 15(2) substituted by the Education and Inspections Act 2006 s 71, Sch 7 Pt 1 para 1(1), (3); and amended by SI 2010/1158).
9   As to the meaning of 'registered' see PARA 437; and as to the meaning of 'parent' see PARA 7 note 6 (definitions applied by the Education Act 2005 s 122(2), (3)).
10 Education Act 2005 s 15(2)(b) (as substituted: see note 8).
11 As to the meaning of 'person' see PARA 7 note 6.
12 Education Act 2005 s 15(2)(c) (as substituted: see note 8).
13 As to the meaning of 'written' see PARA 76 note 8.
14 Education Act 2005 s 15(2)(d)(i) (as substituted: see note 8).
15 Education Act 2005 s 15(2)(d)(ii) (as substituted: see note 8).
16 Education Act 2005 s 15(2)(e)(i) (as substituted: see note 8).
17 As to foundation governors see PARA 108.
18 Education Act 2005 s 15(2)(e)(ii) (as substituted: see note 8). As to the meaning of 'appropriate appointing authority' see PARA 1168 note 11.
19 As to the Secretary of State see PARA 58.
20 Education Act 2005 s 15(2)(e)(iii) (as substituted: see note 8).
21 Ie under the Education Act 2005 s 15(2): see the text to notes 7–20.
22 Education Act 2005 s 15(2A)(a) (s 15(2A)–(2C) added by the Education and Inspections Act 2006 s 71, Sch 7 Pt 1 para 1(1), (3); and the Education Act 2005 s 15(2A)(a), (2B) amended by SI 2010/1158).
23 An 'interim inspection' is an inspection under the Education Act 2005 s 8 (see PARA 1165) which is not treated as an inspection under s 5 (see PARA 1162) by virtue of s 9 (see PARA 1162 note 5) is made: s 15(2C) (as added (see note 22); amended by the Education Act 2011 s 40(7)).
24 Education Act 2005 s 15(2A)(b) (as added: see note 22).
25 Ie under the Education Act 2005 s 5: see PARA 1162.
26 Education Act 2005 s 15(2A)(c) (as added: see note 22).
27 As to the service of notices and documents see the Education Act 1996 s 572 (applied by the Education Act 2005 s 122(2), (3)); and PARA 76.
28 Education Act 2005 s 15(2B) (as added and amended: see note 22).
29 Education Act 2005 s 15(2B)(a) (as added: see note 22).
30 Education Act 2005 s 15(2B)(b)(i) (as added: see note 22).
31 Education Act 2005 s 15(2B)(b)(ii) (as added: see note 22).
32 Education Act 2005 s 15(2B)(c) (as added: see note 22).
33 Ie under the Education Act 2005 s 15(2) or (2B): see the text to notes 7–20, 28–32.
34 Ie the period allowed by the Education Act 2005 s 15(3), that is such period as may be prescribed (s 15(3)(a)) or. if the report states that the Chief Inspector is of the opinion that special measures are required to be taken in relation to the school (s 15(3)(b)(i)), and the Secretary of State is of the opinion that the urgency of the case requires a shorter period (s 15(3)(b)(ii)), such shorter period as the Secretary of State may direct (s 15(3)(b)). 'Prescribed' means prescribed by regulations; and 'regulations' means regulations made by the Secretary of State under Pt 1 Ch 2 (ss 13–18): see s 18. The prescribed period is ten working days from the date of receipt of the report by the local authority: see the Education (School Inspection) (England) Regulations 2005, SI 2005/2038, reg 7 (amended by SI 2010/1172). As to the application of this regulation to pupil referral units in England see the Education (Pupil Referral Units) (Application of Enactments) (England) Regulations 2007, SI 2007/2979, regs 1(3), 3, Sch 1 Pt 1 para 27. As to directions see the Education Act 2005 s 120(4); and PARA 75.
35 See the Education Act 2005 s 15(3) (amended by the Education and Inspections Act 2006 s 71, Sch 7 Pt 1 para 1(1), (4); SI 2010/1158).

36 As to the meaning of 'functions' see PARA 18 note 5 (definition applied by the Education Act 2005 s 122(2), (3)).
37 Ie its functions under the Education Act 2005 s 15(2)(a)–(d) (see the text to notes 7–15) and s 15(2B)(a), (b) (see the text to notes 27–31).
38 Education Act 2005 s 15(4) (added by the Education and Inspections Act 2006 s 71, Sch 7 Pt 1 para 1(1), (5); and amended by SI 2010/1158). As to the publication of guidance see the Education Act 1996 s 571 (applied by the Education Act 2002 s 212(2), (3)); and PARA 60.

1170. Destination of reports of inspections of a school which is not a maintained school. Her Majesty's Chief Inspector of Education, Children's Services and Skills[1] must ensure that a copy of the report of any inspection of a school in England[2] other than a maintained school[3] is sent without delay to the proprietor[4] of the school[5]. In the case of a special school[6] which is not a community or foundation special school[7], the proprietor must without delay send a copy of any such report to any local authority[8] that is paying fees in respect of the attendance of a registered pupil[9] at the school[10].

The proprietor of the school must:

(1) make any report sent to him[11] available for inspection by members of the public at such times and at such place as may be reasonable[12];

(2) provide a copy of the report, free of charge or in prescribed[13] cases on payment of such fee as it thinks fit, not exceeding the cost of supply, to any person[14] who asks for one[15]; and

(3) take such steps as are reasonably practicable to secure that every registered parent[16] of a registered pupil at the school receives a copy of the report within such period following receipt of the report by the authority as may be prescribed[17].

1   As to Her Majesty's Chief Inspector of Education, Children's Services and Skills see PARA 1133. As to the delegation by the Chief Inspector of his functions see PARA 1138.
2   Ie an inspection under the Education Act 2005 s 5: see PARA 1162. As to the meaning of 'England' see PARA 7 note 3.
3   As to the meaning of 'maintained school' see PARA 1167 note 6. As to the schools to which the Education Act 2005 s 5 applies see PARA 1162.
4   As to the meaning of 'proprietor' see PARA 51 note 4 (definition applied by the Education Act 2005 s 122(2), (3)).
5   Education Act 2005 s 16(1). As to the application of Pt 1 (ss 1–63) to pupil referral units in England see the Education (Pupil Referral Units) (Application of Enactments) (England) Regulations 2007, SI 2007/2979, regs 1(3), 3, Sch 1 Pt 1 para 21. As to pupil referral units see PARA 427 et seq.
6   As to the meaning of 'special school' see PARA 1041 (definition applied by the Education Act 2005 s 122(2), (3)).
7   As to the meaning of references to a community or foundation special school see PARA 106.
8   As to the meaning of 'local authority' see PARA 25 (definition applied by the Education Act 2005 s 122(2), (3)).
9   As to the meaning of 'registered pupil' see PARA 437.
10 Education Act 2005 s 16(2) (amended by SI 2010/1158).
11 Ie under the Education Act 2005 s 16(1): see the text to notes 1–5.
12 Education Act 2005 s 16(3)(a).
13 'Prescribed' means prescribed by regulations; and 'regulations' means regulations made by the Secretary of State under the Education Act 2005 Pt 1 Ch 2 (ss 13–18): see s 18. As to the Secretary of State see PARA 58. As to the provision made see the Education (School Inspection) (England) Regulations 2005, SI 2005/2038, reg 8 (substituted by SI 2008/1723). As to the application of this regulation to pupil referral units in England see the Education (Pupil Referral Units) (Application of Enactments) (England) Regulations 2007, SI 2007/2979, regs 1(3), 3, Sch 1 Pt 1 para 27.
14 As to the meaning of 'person' see PARA 7 note 6.
15 Education Act 2005 s 16(3)(b).
16 As to the meaning of 'registered' see PARA 437; and as to the meaning of 'parent' see PARA 7 note 6 (definitions applied by the Education Act 2005 s 122(2), (3)).

17 Education Act 2005 s 16(3)(c). A period of five working days from the date of receipt of the
report by the proprietor of the school is prescribed for these purposes: see the Education (School
Inspection) (England) Regulations 2005, SI 2005/2038, reg 6 (amended by SI 2015/170). As to
the application of this regulation to pupil referral units in England see the Education (Pupil
Referral Units) (Application of Enactments) (England) Regulations 2007, SI 2007/2979,
regs 1(3), 3, Sch 1 Pt 1 para 27.

**1171.   Statement to be prepared by proprietor of a school which is not a
maintained school.**   Where there is sent to the proprietor[1] of a school in
England[2] other than a maintained school[3] a report of an inspection[4] in which
Her Majesty's Chief Inspector of Education, Children's Services and Skills[5] states
that he is of the opinion that special measures are required to be taken in relation
to the school[6], or that he is of the opinion that the school requires significant
improvement[7], the proprietor must:
(1)   consider what action to take in the light of the report[8];
(2)   consider what arrangements to make for the purpose of informing
       registered parents[9] of the proposed action, ascertaining their views on
       the proposed action and taking account of those views[10];
(3)   consider whether those arrangements are to include the appointment of
       a specified person[11] for that purpose[12]; and
(4)   prepare a written[13] statement of the arrangements the proprietor
       proposes to make for the purpose mentioned in head (2) above[14] and of
       the action he proposes to take, and the period within which he proposes
       to take that action, or, if he does not propose to take such action, of his
       reasons for not doing so[15].
Where the proprietor of a school has prepared a statement[16] in relation to the
school[17], it appears to the Secretary of State[18], on the basis of a report of an
interim inspection[19] of the school by the Chief Inspector, that the case has
become urgent[20], and no subsequent inspection of the school[21] has been made[22],
the Secretary of State may by notice[23] require the proprietor to: (i) consider the
action to be taken in the light of the report of the interim inspection and the
arrangements to be made for the purpose mentioned in head (2) above[24]; and (ii)
prepare a written statement of the action the proprietor proposes to take, and the
period within which he proposes to take that action, or, if he does not propose to
take such action, of his reasons for not doing so[25], and of the arrangements the
proprietor proposes to make for the purpose mentioned in head (2) above[26].
It is the duty of the proprietor of the school to prepare the statement within
the statutory period[27], but this does not relieve the proprietor of the school of
any duty to prepare a statement which has not been performed within that
period[28]. Where a statement[29] has been prepared by the proprietor of the school,
he must, before the end of the prescribed period, send copies of it to[30]: (A) the
Chief Inspector[31]; (B) in the case of a statement required by notice served by the
Secretary of State[32], to the Secretary of State[33]; and (C) in such circumstances as
may be prescribed, to such other persons (if any) as may be prescribed[34]. In the
case of a special school[35] which is not a community or foundation special
school[36], the proprietor of the school must, before the end of the prescribed
period, send a copy of any such statement prepared by him to any local authority
that is paying fees in respect of the attendance of a registered pupil at the
school[37].
In performing his functions[38] under heads (1) to (4) and heads (i) and (ii)
above, the proprietor must have regard to any guidance given from time to time
by the Secretary of State[39].

1   As to the meaning of 'proprietor' see PARA 51 note 4 (definition applied by the Education Act 2005 s 122(2), (3)).
2   As to the meaning of 'England' see PARA 7 note 3.
3   As to the meaning of 'maintained school' see PARA 1167 note 6. As to the schools to which the Education Act 2005 s 5 applies see PARA 1162.
4   Ie an inspection under the Education Act 2005 s 5: see PARA 1162.
5   As to Her Majesty's Chief Inspector of Education, Children's Services and Skills see PARA 1133.
6   Education Act 2005 s 17(1)(a) (s 17(1) amended by the Education and Inspections Act 2006 ss 71, 184, Sch 7 Pt 1 para 2(1), (2), Sch 18 Pt 4). As to the meaning of references to special measures being required to be taken in relation to a school see PARA 1167 note 3. As to the application of the Education Act 2005 Pt 1 (ss 1–63) to pupil referral units in England see the Education (Pupil Referral Units) (Application of Enactments) (England) Regulations 2007, SI 2007/2979, regs 1(3), 3, Sch 1 Pt 1 para 21. As to pupil referral units see PARA 427 et seq.
7   Education Act 2005 s 17(1)(b) (as amended: see note 6). As to the meaning of references to schools requiring significant improvement see PARA 1167 note 4.
8   Education Act 2005 s 17(1A)(a) (s 17(1A)–(1D) added by the Education and Inspections Act 2006 s 71, Sch 7 Pt 1 para 2(1), (3)).
9   As to the meaning of 'registered' see PARA 437; and as to the meaning of 'parent' see PARA 7 note 6 (definitions applied by the Education Act 2005 s 122(2), (3)).
10 Education Act 2005 a 17(1A)(b) (as added: see note 8).
11 As to the meaning of 'person' see PARA 7 note 6.
12 Education Act 2005 a 17(1A)(c) (as added: see note 8).
13 As to the meaning of 'written' see PARA 76 note 8.
14 Education Act 2005 a 17(1A)(d)(ii) (as added: see note 8).
15 Education Act 2005 a 17(1A)(d)(i) (as added: see note 8).
16 Ie under the Education Act 2005 s 17(1A): see the text to notes 8–15.
17 Education Act 2005 a 17(1B)(a) (as added: see note 8).
18 As to the Secretary of State see PARA 58.
19 An 'interim inspection' is an inspection under the Education Act 2005 s 8 (see PARA 1165) which is not treated as an inspection under s 5 (see PARA 1162) by virtue of s 9 (see PARA 1162 note 5): s 17(1D) (as added (see note 8); amended by the Education Act 2011 s 40(8)).
20 Education Act 2005 a 17(1B)(b) (as added: see note 8).
21 Ie under the Education Act 2005 s 5: see PARA 1162.
22 Education Act 2005 a 17(1B)(c) (as added: see note 8).
23 As to the service of notices and documents see the Education Act 1996 s 572 (applied by the Education Act 2005 s 122(2), (3)); and PARA 76.
24 Education Act 2005 a 17(1C)(a) (as added: see note 8).
25 Education Act 2005 a 17(1C)(b)(i) (as added: see note 8).
26 Education Act 2005 a 17(1C)(b)(ii) (as added: see note 8).
27 Ie the period allowed by the Education Act 2005 s 17(2), that is such period as may be prescribed (s 17(2)(a)); or, if the report states that the Chief Inspector is of the opinion that special measures are required to be taken in relation to the school (s 17(2)(b)(i)), and the Secretary of State is of the opinion that the urgency of the case requires a shorter period (s 17(2)(b)(ii)), such shorter period as the Secretary of State may direct (s 17(2)(b)). 'Prescribed' means prescribed by regulations; and 'regulations' means regulations made by the Secretary of State under Pt 1 Ch 2 (ss 13–18): see s 18. The prescribed period is ten working days from the date of receipt of the report by the proprietor: see the Education (School Inspection) (England) Regulations 2005, SI 2005/2038, reg 7. As to the application of this regulation to pupil referral units in England see the Education (Pupil Referral Units) (Application of Enactments) (England) Regulations 2007, SI 2007/2979, regs 1(3), 3, Sch 1 Pt 1 para 27. As to directions see the Education Act 2005 s 120(4); and PARA 75.
28 Education Act 2005 s 17(2).
29 Ie under the Education Act 2005 s 17(1A) or (1C): see the text to notes 8–15, 23–26.
30 Education Act 2005 s 17(3) (amended by the Education and Inspections Act 2006 s 71, Sch 7 Pt 1 para 2(1), (4)(a)).
31 Education Act 2005 s 17(3)(a).
32 Ie a statement under the Education Act 2005 s 17(1C): see the text to notes 23–26.
33 Education Act 2005 s 17(3)(aa) (added by the Education and Inspections Act 2006 s 71, Sch 7 Pt 1 para 2(1), (4)(b)).
34 Education Act 2005 s 17(3)(b). The proprietor of the school must take such steps as are reasonably practicable to secure that every registered parent of a registered pupil at the school receives a copy of the report of an inspection under s 5 (see PARA 1162), within the period of five working days from the date of receipt of the report by the proprietor: see the Education (School

Inspection) (England) Regulations 2005, SI 2005/2038, reg 6 (amended by SI 2015/170). As to the application of this regulation to pupil referral units in England see the Education (Pupil Referral Units) (Application of Enactments) (England) Regulations 2007, SI 2007/2979, regs 1(3), 3, Sch 1 Pt 1 para 27. As to the meaning of 'registered pupil' see PARA 437 (definition applied by the Education Act 2005 s 122(2), (3)).
35 As to the meaning of 'special school' see PARA 1041 (definition applied by the Education Act 2005 s 122(2), (3)).
36 As to the meaning of references to a community or foundation special school see PARA 106.
37 Education Act 2005 s 17(4) (amended by SI 2010/1158). At the date at which this volume states the law no regulations had been made for this purpose.
38 As to the meaning of 'functions' see PARA 18 note 5 (definition applied by the Education Act 2005 s 122(2), (3)).
39 Education Act 2005 s 17(5) (added by the Education and Inspections Act 2006 s 71, Sch 7 Pt 1 para 2(1), (5)). As to the publication of guidance see the Education Act 1996 s 571 (applied by the Education Act 2002 s 212(2), (3)); and PARA 60.

C. INTERIM STATEMENTS

1172. Interim statements between inspections. Her Majesty's Chief Inspector of Education, Children's Services and Skills[1] may make a statement (an 'interim statement') about a school in England[2] to which the provisions relating to school inspections[3] apply[4]. An interim statement is a statement:

(1)   that the Chief Inspector is of the opinion that it is not necessary for the school to be inspected[5] for at least a year after the date on which the statement is made[6];

(2)   setting out the Chief Inspector's reasons for forming that opinion[7]; and

(3)   containing such other information (if any) as the Chief Inspector considers appropriate[8].

The Chief Inspector may arrange for an interim statement to be published in such manner as he considers appropriate[9].

1 As to Her Majesty's Chief Inspector of Education, Children's Services and Skills see PARA 1133. As to the delegation by the Chief Inspector of his functions see PARA 1138.
2 As to the meaning of 'England' see PARA 7 note 3.
3 Ie the Education Act 2005 s 5: see PARA 1162.
4 Education Act 2005 s 10A(1) (s 10A added by the Apprenticeships, Skills, Children and Learning Act 2009 s 225(1), (2)). As to schools to which the Education Act 2005 s 5 applies see PARA 1162. As to the destination of interim statements see PARAS 1173, 1174.
5 Ie under the Education Act 2005 s 5: see PARA 1162.
6 Education Act 2005 s 10A(2)(a) (as added: see note 4).
7 Education Act 2005 s 10A(2)(b) (as added: see note 4).
8 Education Act 2005 s 10A(2)(c) (as added: see note 4).
9 Education Act 2005 s 10A(3) (as added: see note 4). The Education and Inspections Act 2006 s 151 (publication of inspection reports: privilege and electronic publication: see PARA 1142) applies in relation to an interim statement as it applies in relation to a report: Education Act 2005 s 10A(4) (as so added).

1173. Destination of interim statements: maintained schools. Her Majesty's Chief Inspector of Education, Children's Services and Skills[1] must ensure that a copy of any interim statement[2] about a maintained school[3] in England[4] is sent without delay to the appropriate authority[5] for the school[6]. The Chief Inspector must ensure that copies of the statement are sent to the head teacher[7] of the school[8], whichever of the local authority[9] and the governing body[10] are not the appropriate authority[11], and, in the case of a school having foundation governors[12], to the person[13] who appoints them and (if different) to the appropriate appointing authority[14].

Until a day to be appointed[15] the appropriate authority must:

(1) make a copy of any statement sent to the authority available for inspection by members of the public at such times and at such places as may be reasonable[16];

(2) provide one copy of the statement free of charge to any person who asks for one[17]; and

(3) take such steps as are reasonably practicable to secure that every registered parent[18] of a registered pupil[19] at the school receives a copy of the statement within such period following receipt of the statement by the authority as may be prescribed[20].

1 As to Her Majesty's Chief Inspector of Education, Children's Services and Skills see PARA 1133. As to the delegation by the Chief Inspector of his functions see PARA 1138.
2 As to interim statements see PARA 1172.
3 As to the meaning of 'maintained school' see PARA 1167 note 6.
4 As to the meaning of 'England' see PARA 7 note 3.
5 As to the meaning of 'appropriate authority' see PARA 1168 note 4.
6 Education Act 2005 s 14A(1) (s 14A added by the Apprenticeships, Skills, Children and Learning Act 2009 s 225(1), (4)).
7 As to the meaning of 'head teacher' see PARA 86 note 4 (definition applied by the Education Act 2005 s 122(2), (3)).
8 Education Act 2005 s 14A(2)(a) (as added: see note 6).
9 As to the meaning of 'local authority' see PARA 25 (definition applied by the Education Act 2005 s 122(2), (3)).
10 As to the governing bodies of maintained schools in England see PARA 150 et seq.
11 Education Act 2005 s 14A(2)(b) (as added (see note 6); and amended by SI 2010/1158).
12 As to schools having foundation governors see PARA 108.
13 As to the meaning of 'person' see PARA 7 note 6.
14 Education Act 2005 s 14A(2)(c) (as added: see note 6). As to the meaning of 'appropriate appointing authority' see PARA 1168 note 11.
15 As from a day to be appointed the Education Act 2005 s 14A(4) (see the text and notes 16–20) is repealed by the Deregulation Act 2015 Sch 16 para 6(1)(2)(b). At the date at which this volume states the law no such day had been appointed.
16 Education Act 2005 s 14A(4)(a) (as added and prospectively repealed: see notes 6, 15).
17 Education Act 2005 s 14A(4)(b) (as added and prospectively repealed: see notes 6, 15). See note 15.
18 As to the meaning of 'registered' see PARA 437; and as to the meaning of 'parent' see PARA 7 note 6 (definitions applied by the Education Act 2005 s 122(2), (3)).
19 As to the meaning of 'registered pupil' see PARA 437 (definition applied by the Education Act 2005 s 122(2), (3)).
20 Education Act 2005 s 14A(4)(c) (as added and prospectively repealed: see notes 6, 15). See note 15. 'Prescribed' means prescribed by regulations; and 'regulations' means regulations made by the Secretary of State under Pt 1 Ch 2 (ss 13–18): see s 18. As to the Secretary of State see PARA 58. At the date at which this volume states the law no regulations had been made for this purpose.

1174. Destination of interim statements: non-maintained schools. Her Majesty's Chief Inspector of Education, Children's Services and Skills[1] must ensure that a copy of any interim statement[2] about a school in England[3] other than a maintained school[4] is sent without delay to the proprietor[5] of the school[6]. In the case of a special school[7] which is not a community or foundation special school[8], the proprietor must without delay send a copy of any interim statement sent to him to any local authority[9] that is paying fees in respect of the attendance of a registered pupil[10] at the school[11].

The proprietor of the school must:

(1) make any statement sent to him available for inspection by members of the public at such times and at such place as may be reasonable[12];

(2) provide one copy of the statement free of charge to any person[13] who asks for one[14]; and

(3)   take such steps as are reasonably practicable to secure that every
registered parent[15] of a registered pupil at the school receives a copy of
the statement within such period following receipt of the statement by
the proprietor as may be prescribed[16].

1   As to Her Majesty's Chief Inspector of Education, Children's Services and Skills see PARA 1133.
As to the delegation by the Chief Inspector of his functions see PARA 1138.
2   As to interim statements see PARA 1172.
3   As to the meaning of 'England' see PARA 7 note 3. The schools in question are those to which the
Education Act 2005 s 5 applies: see PARA 1162.
4   As to the meaning of 'maintained school' see PARA 1167 note 6.
5   As to the meaning of 'proprietor' see PARA 51 note 4 (definition applied by the Education
Act 2005 s 122(2), (3)).
6   Education Act 2005 s 16A(1) (s 16A added by the Apprenticeships, Skills, Children and
Learning Act 2009 s 225(1), (6)).
7   As to the meaning of 'special school' see PARA 1041 (definition applied by the Education
Act 2005 s 122(2), (3)).
8   As to the meaning of references to a community or foundation special school see PARA 106.
9   As to the meaning of 'local authority' see PARA 25 (definition applied by the Education Act 2005
s 122(2), (3)).
10   As to the meaning of 'registered pupil' see PARA 437 (definition applied by the Education
Act 2005 s 122(2), (3)).
11   Education Act 2005 s 16A(2) (as added (see note 6); and amended by SI 2010/1158).
12   Education Act 2005 s 16A(3)(a) (as added: see note 6).
13   As to the meaning of 'person' see PARA 7 note 6.
14   Education Act 2005 s 16A(3)(b) (as added: see note 6).
15   As to the meaning of 'registered' see PARA 437; and as to the meaning of 'parent' see PARA 7
note 6 (definitions applied by the Education Act 2005 s 122(2), (3)).
16   Education Act 2005 s 16A(3)(b) (as added: see note 6). 'Prescribed' means prescribed by
regulations; and 'regulations' means regulations made by the Secretary of State under Pt 1 Ch 2
(ss 13–18): see s 18. As to the Secretary of State see PARA 58. At the date at which this volume
states the law no regulations had been made for this purpose.

D. INVESTIGATION OF COMPLAINTS

1175.   Power of the chief inspector to investigate complaints about schools.
Her Majesty's Chief Inspector of Education, Children's Services and Skills[1] may
investigate a qualifying complaint if he thinks it is appropriate to do so:
(1)   for the purpose of determining whether it is or may be appropriate to
have regard to the matters raised by the complaint in carrying out any
of his functions[2] in relation to schools[3] in England[4]; and
(2)   in particular, for the purpose of determining, in the light of the
complaint when to carry out a prescribed inspection of the school[5] (in
so far as the timing of such an inspection is within his discretion[6]), and
whether it would be appropriate to carry out a discretionary
inspection[7].
A complaint is a 'qualifying complaint' if it is about a matter relating to a
relevant school[8] and that matter falls within a prescribed[9] description[10] and does
not fall within any prescribed exception[11], it is made in writing[12] to the Chief
Inspector[13] and it is made by a person[14] who satisfies prescribed conditions[15].

1   As to Her Majesty's Chief Inspector of Education, Children's Services and Skills see PARA 1133.
As to the delegation by the Chief Inspector of his functions see PARA 1138.
2   As to the meaning of 'functions' see PARA 18 note 5 (definition applied by the Education
Act 2005 s 122(2), (3)). As to the functions of Her Majesty's Chief Inspector of Education,
Children's Services and Skills see PARA 1136 et seq.
3   As to the meaning of 'school' see PARA 91 (definition applied by the Education Act 2005
s 122(2), (3)).

4   Education Act 2005 s 11A(1)(a) (s 11A added by the Education and Inspections Act 2006 s 160). As to the meaning of 'England' see PARA 7 note 3. As to investigations see PARA 1176. As to reports of investigations see PARA 1177.
5   Ie an inspection under the Education Act 2005 s 5: see PARA 1162.
6   Education Act 2005 s 11A(1)(b)(i) (as added: see note 4).
7   Education Act 2005 s 11A(1)(b)(ii) (as added: see note 4). The discretionary inspection referred to is one under s 8(2) (see PARA 1165): see s 11A(1)(b)(ii) (as so added).
8   'Relevant school' means any of the schools mentioned in the Education Act 2005 s 5(2)(a)–(g) (see PARA 1162): s 11A(5) (as added: see note 4).
9   'Prescribed' means prescribed by regulations; and 'regulations' means regulations made by the Secretary of State under the Education Act 2005 Pt 1 Ch 2 (ss 13–18): see s 18. As to the Secretary of State see PARA 58.
10 Education Act 2005 s 11A(2)(a)(i) (as added: see note 4). A complaint is of a prescribed description if it is about one or more of the following areas:
    (1)   the quality of the education provided in the school;
    (2)   how far the education provided in the school meets the needs of the range of pupils at the school;
    (3)   the educational standards achieved in the school;
    (4)   the quality of the leadership in and management of the school, including whether the financial resources made available to the school are managed effectively;
    (5)   the spiritual, moral, social and cultural development of the pupils at the school;
    (6)   the contribution made by the school to the well-being of those pupils; and
    (7)   the contribution made by the school to community cohesion: Education (Investigation of Parents' Complaints) (England) Regulations 2007, SI 2007/1089, reg 3 (amended by SI 2008/1723).
    As to the meaning of 'pupil' see PARA 20 note 4 (definition applied by the Education Act 2005 s 122(2), (3)).
11 Education Act 2005 s 11A(2)(a)(ii) (as added: see note 4). A complaint is not a qualifying complaint if it is about a matter falling to be dealt with in accordance with any procedures established or required to be established in relation to the school by or under any enactment other than the Education Act 2002 s 29(1)(a) (additional functions of governing body: see PARA 175): Education (Investigation of Parents' Complaints) (England) Regulations 2007, SI 2007/1089, reg 4.
12 As to the meaning of 'writing' see PARA 76 note 8.
13 Education Act 2005 s 11A(2)(b) (as added: see note 4).
14 As to the meaning of 'person' see PARA 7 note 6.
15 Education Act 2005 s 11A(2)(c) (as added: see note 4). The conditions prescribed for the purposes of s 11A(2)(c) may, in particular, require that the person has, before making the complaint to the Chief Inspector, taken advantage of other procedures of a prescribed description for dealing with the complaint: s 11A(3) (as so added). Regulations may enable the Chief Inspector to determine that a condition prescribed for the purposes of s 11A(2)(c) by virtue of s 11A(3) is not to apply in relation to a person making a complaint: s 11A(4) (as so added).
    A person making a complaint satisfies the prescribed condition if, before making the complaint, that person has followed any complaints procedure where the school falls within s 5(2)(a), (b) or (c) (see PARA 1162), established by the governing body of the relevant school pursuant to the Education Act 2002 s 29(1)(a) (see PARA 175); or where the school falls within the Education Act 2005 s 5(2)(d), (e), (f) or (g) (see PARA 1162), established in relation to the school: Education (Investigation of Parents' Complaints) (England) Regulations 2007, SI 2007/1089, reg 5. The Chief Inspector may determine that the condition in reg 5 is not to apply in relation to a person making a complaint: reg 6.
    As to the Office for Standards in Education, Children's Services and Skills (Ofsted) generally see PARA 1128 et seq.

1176.   Investigations of complaints. Where a qualifying complaint[1] is made to Her Majesty's Chief Inspector of Education, Children's Services and Skills[2] by a person who is a registered parent[3] of a registered pupil[4] at the school[5] to which the complaint relates[6], if the Chief Inspector so requests for the purposes of an investigation of the complaint[7], the governing body[8] of the school to which the complaint relates must provide him with such information held by it as may be specified or described in the Chief Inspector's request[9], and such other information held by it as it considers may be relevant to the investigation[10]. If the complaint relates to a maintained school and the Chief Inspector so requests for the purposes of an investigation of the complaint, the local authority[11] which maintains[12] the school must provide him with[13] such information held by it as may be specified or described in the Chief Inspector's request[14], and such other information held by it as it considers may be relevant to the investigation[15].

If, for the purposes of an investigation of the complaint, it appears to the Chief Inspector to be appropriate to hold a meeting for registered parents of registered pupils at the school to which the complaint relates he must give notice[16] to that effect to the governing body of the school[17], or if the school is a maintained school which does not have a delegated budget[18], the local authority which maintains the school[19]; and on being so notified, the governing body or (as the case may be) the local authority must co-operate with the Chief Inspector in the making of arrangements for the meeting[20]. In particular, the governing body or (as the case may be) the local authority must if so requested by the Chief Inspector[21]:

(1)   allow the meeting to be held on the premises[22] of the school[23];

(2)   fix a date for the meeting which is consistent with any request made by the Chief Inspector for that purpose[24]; and

(3)   take such steps as are specified by the Chief Inspector to give the registered parents of registered pupils at the school[25], and, if the school is a maintained school which has a delegated budget, the local authority which maintains the school[26], such notice as the Chief Inspector may specify of the date, time and place of the meeting and of its purpose[27].

In addition to the registered parents of registered pupils at the school, a representative of the governing body of the school[28] and, if the school is a maintained school, a representative of the local authority which maintains the school[29], may attend the meeting[30].

1   As to the meaning of 'qualifying complaint' see PARA 1175.
2   As to Her Majesty's Chief Inspector of Education, Children's Services and Skills see PARA 1133. As to the delegation by the Chief Inspector of his functions see PARA 1138.
3   As to the meaning of 'registered' see PARA 437; and as to the meaning of 'parent' see PARA 7 note 6 (definitions applied by the Education Act 2005 s 122(2), (3)).
4   As to the meaning of 'registered pupil' see PARA 437 (definition applied by the Education Act 2005 s 122(2), (3)).
5   As to the meaning of 'school' see PARA 91 (definition applied by the Education Act 2005 s 122(2), (3)).
6   Education Act 2005 s 11B(1) (s 11B added by the Education and Inspections Act 2006 s 160).
7   As to the power of the Chief Inspector to investigate complaints see PARA 1175. As to reports of investigations see PARA 1177.
8   'Governing body', in relation to a relevant school which is not a maintained school, means the proprietor of the school: Education Act 2005 s 11B(7) (as added: see note 6). As to the meaning of 'relevant school' see PARA 1175 note 8 (definition applied by s 11B(7) (as so added)). 'Maintained school' means a community, foundation or voluntary school, a community or foundation special school or a maintained nursery school: s 11B(7) (as so added). As to the meaning of references to a community, foundation or voluntary school or a community or foundation special school see PARA 106. As to the meaning of 'maintained nursery school' see PARA 99 note 4; and as to the meaning of 'proprietor' see PARA 51 note 4 (definitions applied by s 122(2), (3)). As to the governing bodies of maintained schools in England see PARA 150 et seq.
9   Education Act 2005 s 11B(2)(a) (as added: see note 6).
10   Education Act 2005 s 11B(2)(b) (as added: see note 6).
11   As to the meaning of 'local authority' see PARA 25 (definition applied by the Education Act 2005 s 122(2), (3)).
12   'Maintain', in relation to school, has the same meaning as in the School Standards and Framework Act 1998 (see PARA 306 note 4): Education Act 2005 s 11B(7) (as added: see note 6).

13 Education Act 2005 s 11B(3) (as added (see note 6); and amended by SI 2010/1158).
14 Education Act 2005 s 11B(3)(a) (as added: see note 6).
15 Education Act 2005 s 11B(3)(b) (as added: see note 6).
16 As to the service of notices and documents see the Education Act 1996 s 572 (applied by the Education Act 2005 s 122(2), (3)); and PARA 76.
17 Education Act 2005 s 11B(4)(a)(i) (as added: see note 6). This provision applies unless the school falls within s 11B(4)(a)(ii) (see the text to notes 18–19): see s 11B(4)(a)(i) (as so added).
18 As to the meaning of 'delegated budget' see PARA 323 (definition applied by the Education Act 2005 s 63(1)).
19 Education Act 2005 s 11B(4)(a)(ii) (as added (see note 6); and amended by SI 2010/1158).
20 Education Act 2005 s 11B(4)(b) (as added (see note 6); and amended by SI 2010/1158).
21 Education Act 2005 s 11B(5) (as added (see note 6); and amended by SI 2010/1158).
22 As to the meaning of 'premises' see PARA 62 note 19 (definition applied by the Education Act 2005 s 122(2), (3)).
23 Education Act 2005 s 11B(5)(a) (as added: see note 6).
24 Education Act 2005 s 11B(5)(b) (as added: see note 6).
25 Education Act 2005 s 11B(5)(c)(i) (as added: see note 6).
26 Education Act 2005 s 11B(5)(c)(ii) (as added (see note 6); and amended by SI 2010/1158).
27 Education Act 2005 s 11B(5)(c) (as added: see note 6).
28 Education Act 2005 s 11B(6)(a) (as added: see note 6).
29 Education Act 2005 s 11B(6)(b) (as added (see note 6); and amended by SI 2010/1158).
30 See the Education Act 2005 s 11B(6) (as added: see note 6).

1177. Reports of investigations. Where, for the purposes of an investigation of a qualifying complaint[1] made by a person who is a registered parent[2] of a registered pupil[3] at the school[4] to which the complaint relates[5] Her Majesty's Chief Inspector of Education, Children's Services and Skills[6]:

(1)   requests information[7] for the purposes of the investigation[8]; or

(2)   gives notice[9] that he considers it appropriate to hold a meeting for registered parents of registered pupils at the school to which the complaint relates[10],

the Chief Inspector may, if he considers it appropriate to do so, prepare a report of the outcome of the investigation by him of the complaint[11].

If the Chief Inspector prepares such a report he must send a copy of the report to the governing body[12] of the school[13], or, if the school is a maintained school which does not have a delegated budget[14], the local authority[15] which maintains the school[16]. Until a day to be appointed[17] the body to whom a report is so sent must, if so requested by the Chief Inspector, provide a copy of the report to the registered parents of registered pupils at the school to which the complaint relates[18].

1 As to the meaning of 'qualifying complaint' see PARA 1175.
2 As to the meaning of 'registered' see PARA 437; and as to the meaning of 'parent' see PARA 7 note 6 (definitions applied by the Education Act 2005 s 122(2), (3)).
3 As to the meaning of 'registered pupil' see PARA 437 (definition applied by the Education Act 2005 s 122(2), (3)).
4 As to the meaning of 'school' see PARA 91 (definition applied by the Education Act 2005 s 122(2), (3)).
5 Ie a qualifying complaint to which the Education Act 2005 s 11B applies: see PARA 1176.
6 As to Her Majesty's Chief Inspector of Education, Children's Services and Skills see PARA 1133. As to the delegation by the Chief Inspector of his functions see PARA 1138.
7 Ie information as mentioned in the Education Act 2005 s 11B(2) or (3): see PARA 1176.
8 See the Education Act 2005 s 11C(1)(a) (s 11C added by the Education and Inspections Act 2006 s 160).
9 Ie in pursuance of the Education Act 2005 s 11B(4)(a): see PARA 1176.
10 Education Act 2005 s 11C(1)(b) (as added: see note 8).
11 Education Act 2005 s 11C(2) (as added: see note 8). As to combined reports see PARA 1181.
12 'Governing body' has the same meaning as in the Education Act 2005 s 11B (see PARA 1176 note 8): s 11C(5) (as added: see note 8).

13   Education Act 2005 s 11C(3)(a) (as added: see note 8). This provision applies unless the school falls within s 11C(3)(b) (see the text to notes 14–16): see s 11C(3)(a) (as so added).

14   As to the meaning of 'delegated budget' see PARA 323 (definition applied by the Education Act 2005 s 63(1)).

15   As to the meaning of 'local authority' see PARA 25 (definition applied by the Education Act 2005 s 122(2), (3)).

16   Education Act 2005 s 11C(3)(b) (as added (see note 8); and amended by SI 2010/1158).

17   As from a day to be appointed the Education Act 2005 s 11C(4) (see the text and note 18) is repealed by the Deregulation Act 2015 Sch 16 para 6(1)(2)(a). At the date at which this volume states the law no such day had been appointed.

18   Education Act 2005 s 11C(4) (as added and prospectively repealed: see notes 8, 17).

E.   OTHER INSPECTIONS

(A)   Inspection of Religious Education

1178.   Inspection of religious education. It is the duty of the governing body[1] of any voluntary or foundation school[2] in England[3], which has been designated[4] by the Secretary of State[5] as having a religious character, to secure that any denominational education[6] given to pupils[7], and the content of the school's collective worship[8], are inspected[9]. Such an inspection is to be conducted by a person[10] chosen:

(1)   in the case of a voluntary controlled school, by the foundation governors[11] after consultation with any person prescribed[12] for these purposes in relation to the religion or religious denomination that is specified[13] in relation to the school[14]; and

(2)   by the governing body after consultation with any person so prescribed, in any other case[15].

The inspections must be carried out at such intervals as may be prescribed[16].

It is the general duty of a person conducting an inspection to report on the quality of the denominational education provided by the school for pupils to whom denominational education is given by the school[17], and to report on the content of the school's collective worship[18]; and any such person may report on the spiritual, moral, social and cultural development of pupils at the school[19]. A person conducting an inspection may do so with the assistance of such other persons chosen by him as are in his opinion fit and proper persons for carrying out the inspection[20].

1   As to the governing bodies of maintained schools in England see PARA 150 et seq.

2   As to the meaning of references to a foundation or voluntary school see PARA 106.

3   As to the meaning of 'England' see PARA 7 note 3.

4   Ie designated under the School Standards and Framework Act 1998 s 69(3): see PARA 914.

5   As to the Secretary of State see PARA 58.

6   In the Education Act 2005 Pt 1 (ss 1–63), 'denominational education', in relation to a school, means religious education which is required by the Education Act 2002 s 80(1)(a) (see PARA 857) to be included in the school's basic curriculum (Education Act 2005 s 47(a)), but is not required by any enactment to be given in accordance with an agreed syllabus (s 47(b)). As to the meaning of 'school' see PARA 91; and as to the meaning of 'agreed syllabus' see PARA 910 note 2 (definitions applied by s 122(2), (3)). As to the curriculum in England see PARA 856 et seq.

7   Education Act 2005 s 48(1)(a). As to the meaning of 'pupil' see PARA 20 note 4 (definition applied by the Education Act 2005 s 122(2), (3)). As to the application of Pt 1 (ss 1–63) to pupil referral units in England see the Education (Pupil Referral Units) (Application of Enactments) (England) Regulations 2007, SI 2007/2979, regs 1(3), 3, Sch 1 Pt 1 para 21. As to pupil referral units see PARA 427 et seq.

8   Education Act 2005 s 48(1)(b). In s 48 and s 49 (see PARA 1179), 'collective worship' means collective worship required by the School Standards and Framework Act 1998 s 70 (see PARA 920): Education Act 2005 s 48(6).

9   Education Act 2005 s 48(1). As to the procedure for inspections see PARA 1179. See PARA 1162 note 25.
10 As to the meaning of 'person' see PARA 7 note 6.
11 As to foundation governors see PARA 108.
12 'Prescribed' means prescribed by regulations made by the Secretary of State: Education Act 2005 s 49(6). As to the persons prescribed for these purposes see the Education (School Inspection) (England) Regulations 2005, SI 2005/2038, reg 9.
13 Ie specified under the School Standards and Framework Act 1998 s 69(4): see PARA 914.
14 Education Act 2005 s 48(2)(a).
15 Education Act 2005 s 48(2)(b).
16 Education Act 2005 s 48(3). The governing body must secure that any inspection takes place within five school years from the end of the school year in which the last inspection took place: Education (School Inspection) (England) Regulations 2005, SI 2005/2038, reg 10 (substituted by SI 2009/1564). As to the meaning of 'school year' see PARA 19 note 12 (definition applied by the Education Act 2005 s 122(2), (3)).
17 Education Act 2005 s 48(4)(a).
18 Education Act 2005 s 48(4)(b).
19 Education Act 2005 s 48(4). As to combined reports see PARA 1181.
20 Education Act 2005 s 48(5).

1179. Procedure for inspection of religious education. An inspection[1] of denominational education[2] and collective worship[3] must be carried out within such period as may be prescribed[4]. When an inspection has been completed, the person conducting the inspection[5] must, before the end of the prescribed period[6], prepare in writing a report of the inspection[7]. The person conducting the inspection must, without delay, send the report to the governing body[8] for the school[9] concerned[10]. The governing body must:

(1)   make any such report available for inspection by members of the public, at such times and at such a place as may be reasonable[11];

(2)   take such steps as are reasonably practicable to secure that every parent[12] of a registered pupil[13] at the school for whom the school provides denominational education[14], or who takes part in acts of collective worship[15], as the case may be, receives a copy of the report as soon as is reasonably practicable[16]; and

(3)   provide a copy of the report, free of charge or in prescribed cases on payment of such fee as it thinks fit, not exceeding the cost of supply[17], to any other person who asks for one[18].

1   Ie carried out under the Education Act 2005 s 48: see PARA 1178.
2   As to the meaning of 'denominational education' see PARA 1178 note 6.
3   As to the meaning of 'collective worship' see PARA 1178 note 8.
4   See the Education Act 2005 s 49(1). 'Prescribed' means prescribed by regulations made by the Secretary of State: s 48(6). As to the Secretary of State see PARA 58. For the purpose of s 49(1), there is prescribed, as the period within which an inspection must be carried out, the period of ten working days: Education (School Inspection) (England) Regulations 2005, SI 2005/2038, reg 11(1). As to the application of the Education Act 2005 Pt 1 (ss 1–63) to pupil referral units in England see the Education (Pupil Referral Units) (Application of Enactments) (England) Regulations 2007, SI 2007/2979, regs 1(3), 3, Sch 1 Pt 1 para 21. As to pupil referral units see PARA 427 et seq. As to the meaning of 'England' see PARA 7 note 3.
5   As to the persons conducting such an inspection see PARA 1178. As to the meaning of 'person' see PARA 7 note 6.
6   For the purpose of the Education Act 2005 s 49(2), there is prescribed, as the period in which the person conducting the inspection must prepare a report in writing of the inspection, the period of 15 working days from completion of the inspection: Education (School Inspection) (England) Regulations 2005, SI 2005/2038, reg 11(2). As to the meaning of 'writing' see PARA 76 note 8.
7   Education Act 2005 s 49(2). As to combined reports see PARA 1181.
8   As to the governing bodies of maintained schools in England see PARA 150 et seq.

9   As to the meaning of 'school' see PARA 91 (definition applied by the Education Act 2005 s 122(2), (3)). As to the schools to which ss 48, 49 apply see PARA 1178.

10 Education Act 2005 s 49(3).

11 Education Act 2005 s 49(4)(a). As from a day to be appointed, the wording for s 49(4) is replaced (see below): s 49(4) (prospectively substituted by the Deregulation Act 2015 Sch 16 para 6(1), (4)). The new wording is as follows: 'The governing body must take such steps as are reasonably practicable, within such period following the receipt by it of the report as may be prescribed, to secure that every registered parent of a registered pupil at the school is informed of the overall assessment contained in the report of (a) the quality of the denominational education provided by the school, and (b) the content of the school's collective worship.' At the date at which this volume states the law no such day had been appointed.

12 As to the meaning of 'parent' see PARA 7 note 6 (definition applied by the Education Act 2005 s 122(2), (3)).

13 As to the meaning of 'registered pupil' see PARA 437 (definition applied by the Education Act 2005 s 122(2), (3)).

14 Education Act 2005 s 49(4)(b)(i). See note 11.

15 Ie the content of which falls to be inspected under the Education Act 2005 s 48 (see PARA 1178): see s 49(4)(b)(ii). See note 11.

16 Education Act 2005 s 49(4)(b). See note 11.

17 The governing body may require payment of a fee (not exceeding the cost of supply) in all cases where it provides a copy of the report under the Education Act 2005 s 49(4)(c): see the Education (School Inspection) (England) Regulations 2005, SI 2005/2038, reg 12.

18 Education Act 2005 s 49(4)(c). See note 11.

(B) Inspection by Local Authority

1180. Power of local authority to inspect maintained school for specific purpose. Where, for the purpose of enabling it to exercise any of its education functions[1], a local authority[2] requires information about any matter in connection with a school[3] which is maintained by it[4], and it is not reasonably practicable for it to obtain the information in any other manner[5], the authority may cause an inspection of the school to be made by one or more of its officers for the purpose of obtaining the information[6].

An officer of a local authority inspecting a school under this power has at all reasonable times a right of entry to the premises[7] of the school[8].

1 As to the meaning of 'education functions' see PARA 25 (definition applied by the Education Act 2005 s 122(2), (3)).

2 As to the meaning of 'local authority' see PARA 25 (definition applied by the Education Act 2005 s 122(2), (3)).

3 As to the meaning of 'school' see PARA 91 (definition applied by the Education Act 2005 s 122(2), (3)).

4 Education Act 2005 s 51(1)(a) (amended by SI 2010/1158). As to maintained schools see PARA 106.

5 Education Act 2005 s 51(1)(b).

6 Education Act 2005 s 51(1). As to the application of Pt 1 (ss 1–63) to pupil referral units in England see the Education (Pupil Referral Units) (Application of Enactments) (England) Regulations 2007, SI 2007/2979, regs 1(3), 3, Sch 1 Pt 1 para 21. As to pupil referral units see PARA 427 et seq. As to the meaning of 'England' see PARA 7 note 3.

7 As to the meaning of 'premises' see PARA 62 note 19 (definition applied by the Education Act 2005 s 122(2), (3)).

8 Education Act 2005 s 51(2) (amended by SI 2010/1158).

F. REPORTS UNDER THE INSPECTION ENACTMENTS

1181. Combined reports under the inspection enactments. Where, following inspections conducted under two or more inspection enactments[1] by one person[2] or two or more different persons, that person is, or those persons are, required to make a report under each of those enactments, nothing in any of those enactments is to be regarded as preventing him, or them, from:

(1)   including those reports in a single document ('a combined report')[3]; and

(2)   to such extent as he considers, or they consider, appropriate, combining the substantive reports required by those enactments[4];

but this does not apply so as to authorise the making of a combined report by Her Majesty's Chief Inspector of Education, Children's Services and Skills[5], in respect of whom alternative provision is made[6].

Where a combined report is made, any reference in the inspection enactments to the publication of a report, or to the giving, or making available, to any person of a copy of a report is to be read so far as necessary as a reference to the publication of the combined report, or to the giving or making available to that person of a copy of the combined report[7].

1   For these purposes 'the inspection enactments' are the Education Act 2005 Pt 1 (ss 1–63) (see PARA 1162 et seq), the Children and Families (Wales) Measure 2010 Pt 2 (ss 19–56) (child minding and day care for children: see CHILDREN AND YOUNG PERSONS vol 10 (2012) PARA 1126 et seq), the School Standards and Framework Act 1998 s 122 and Sch 26 (inspection of nursery education in Wales: see PARA 1253 et seq), the Education Act 2002 Pt 10 Ch 1 (ss 157–171) (regulation of independent schools in Wales: see PARA 418 et seq) and the Childcare Act 2006 Pt 3 Ch 2 (ss 33–51), Ch 3 (ss 52–61) (regulation of early years and later years provision in England: see CHILDREN AND YOUNG PERSONS vol 10 (2012) PARA 1090 et seq) and the Education and Skills Act 2008 Pt 4 Ch 1 (ss 92–141) (regulation of independent educational provision in England: see PARA 382 et seq): Education Act 2005 s 59(1) (amended by the Childcare Act 2006 s 103(1), Sch 2 para 44; the Children and Families (Wales) Measure 2010 s 72, Sch 1 paras 17, 18; and the Education and Skills Act 2008 s 169(1), Sch 1 Pt 1 paras 25, 28).
    As to the application of the Education Act 2005 Pt 1 (ss 1–63) to pupil referral units in England see the Education (Pupil Referral Units) (Application of Enactments) (England) Regulations 2007, SI 2007/2979, regs 1(3), 3, Sch 1 Pt 1 para 21. As to pupil referral units see PARA 427 et seq. As to the meanings of 'England' and 'Wales' see PARA 7 note 3.
2   As to the meaning of 'person' see PARA 7 note 6.
3   Education Act 2005 s 59(2)(a).
4   Education Act 2005 s 59(2)(b).
5   As to Her Majesty's Chief Inspector of Education, Children's Services and Skills see PARA 1133.
6   See the Education Act 2005 s 59(2A) (added by the Education and Inspections Act 2006 s 157, Sch 14 paras 98, 105(1), (2)). As to the alternative provision see the Education and Inspections Act 2006 s 152: see PARA 1143.
7   Education Act 2005 s 59(3).

(ii)   Inspection of Schools in Wales

A.   DUTY TO ARRANGE REGULAR INSPECTIONS

1182.   Inspection of certain schools by registered inspectors.   It is the duty of Her Majesty's Chief Inspector of Education and Training in Wales[1] to secure that every school in Wales of the types listed in heads (1) to (4) below is inspected[2], at such intervals as may be prescribed[3], by a registered inspector[4] or by a member of the Inspectorate[5]. The schools to be inspected are:

(1)   community, foundation and voluntary schools[6];

(2)   community special schools[7];

(3)   maintained nursery schools[8]; and

(4)   until a day to appointed, special schools[9] which are not community or foundation special schools but are for the time being approved[10] by the Welsh Ministers[11];

however, there is no requirement to inspect any school which is a closing school[12], and in respect of which the Chief Inspector has decided, having regard to the date on which the closure is to take effect, that no useful purpose would be served by the school being inspected[13].

It is the general duty of any inspector conducting such an inspection to report[14] on:

(a) the quality of the education provided by the school[15];

(b) how far that education meets the needs of the range of pupils at the school[16];

(c) the educational standards achieved in the school[17];

(d) the quality of the leadership in and management of the school, including whether the financial resources made available to the school are managed effectively[18];

(e) the spiritual, moral, social and cultural development of pupils at the school[19]; and

(f) the contribution made by the school to the well-being[20] of those pupils[21].

An inspection required under these provisions does not extend to denominational education[22]; to education which is brought[23] within the remit the Chief Inspector[24]; or to the content of collective worship[25].

1 As to Her Majesty's Chief Inspector of Education and Training in Wales see PARA 1148. As to the functions of Her Majesty's Chief Inspector of Education and Training in Wales see PARA 1151 et seq. As to the meaning of 'Wales' see PARA 7 note 3.

2 As to the procedure for inspection see PARA 1191 et seq. As to the inspection of independent schools see PARA 418. As to the power of the Welsh Ministers to change the inspection framework see PARA 1147. As to the Welsh Ministers see PARA 59.

3 'Prescribed' means prescribed by regulations; and 'regulations' means regulations made by the Welsh Ministers under the Education Act 2005 Pt 1 Ch 3 (ss 19–31): see s 31(1). The functions under the Education Act 2005 s 28 were originally vested in the National Assembly for Wales and are now exercisable by the Welsh Ministers by virtue of the Government of Wales Act 2006 s 162(1), Sch 11 paras 30, 32.

  The Chief Inspector must secure that every school is inspected, in the case of a school which has not been previously inspected, within six years of the date on which pupils were first admitted to the school and, in all other cases, at least once within a six year period beginning on 1 September 2014 and ending on 31 August 2020 and at least once within every subsequent six year period beginning on the expiry of the previous six year period: see the Education (School Inspection) (Wales) Regulations 2006, SI 2006/1714, reg 6(1) (substituted by SI 2010/1436; SI 2014/1212). As to the meaning of 'pupil' see PARA 20 note 4 (definition applied by the Education Act 2005 s 122(2), (3)). As to the admission of pupils to schools see PARA 224 et seq. As to the application of the Education (School Inspection) (Wales) Regulations 2006, SI 2006/1714, Pt 2 (regs 4–12) to pupil referral units in Wales see the Education (Pupil Referral Units) (Application of Enactments) (Wales) Regulations 2007, SI 2007/1069, reg 3, Sch 1 Pt 2 para 13. As to pupil referral units see PARA 427 et seq.

4 Ie an inspector registered under the Education Act 2005 s 25: see PARA 1156.

5 Education Act 2005 s 28(1). Section 28(1) has effect subject to s 32 (inspections by members of the Inspectorate: see PARA 1191): s 28(6). Further provision with respect to inspections under s 28 is made by Sch 4 (see PARA 1183 et seq): s 28(8). As to the meaning of 'member of the Inspectorate' see PARA 1156 note 3.

6 Education Act 2005 s 28(2)(a). As to the meaning of references to a community, foundation or voluntary school see PARA 106.

7 Education Act 2005 s 28(2)(b) (amended by the School Standards and Organisational (Wales) Act 2013 Sch 5 para 22(2)(a)). As to the meaning of references to a community special school see PARA 106.

8 Education Act 2005 s 28(2)(c). As to the meaning of 'maintained nursery school' see PARA 99 note 4 (definition applied by s 122(2), (3)).

9 As to the meaning of 'special school' see PARA 1041 (definition applied by the Education Act 2005 s 122(2), (3)).

10 Ie under the Education Act 1996 s 342: see PARA 1042.

11	Education Act 2005 s 28(2)(d). As from a day to be appointed s 28(2)(d) is substituted so as to refer to schools approved under the Education Act 1996 s 342 (non-maintained special schools): Education Act 2005 s 28(2)(d) (prospectively substituted by the Education and Skills Act 2008 s 169(1), Sch 1 Pt 1 paras 25, 27). At the date at which this volume states the law no such day had been appointed.

12	See the Education Act 2005 s 28(3)(a). A 'closing school' means:

   (1)	a community, foundation or voluntary school, community special school or maintained nursery school in respect of which proposals to discontinue the school have been approved, adopted, confirmed or determined under any enactment (s 28(4)(a) (amended by SI 2005/3238; and the School Standards and Organisation (Wales) Act 2013 Sch 5 para 22(2)(b)(i)));

   (2)	a foundation or voluntary school in respect of which the governing body has given notice of discontinuance under the School Standards and Organisation (Wales) Act 2013 s 80 (see PARA 140) (Education Act 2005 s 28(4)(b) (amended by the School Standards and Organisation (Wales) Act 2013 Sch 5 para 22(2)(b)(ii)));

   (3)	a community, foundation or voluntary or community special school in respect of which the Welsh Ministers have given a direction to discontinue the school under the School Standards and Organisation (Wales) Act 2013 s 16(2) (see PARA 1234) or s 81(1) (see PARA 140) (Education Act 2005 s 28(4)(c) (amended by the School Standards and Organisation (Wales) Act 2013 Sch 5 para 22(2)(b)(iii))); or

   (4)	a special school which is not a community special school but which is for the time being approved by the Welsh Ministers under the Education Act 1996 s 342 (approval of non-maintained special schools: see PARA 1042) and which the proprietor has decided to close (Education Act 2005s 28(4)(d); amended by the School Standards and Organisation (Wales) Act 2013 Sch 5 para 22(2)(b)(iv))).

   As to the governing bodies of maintained schools in Wales see PARA 195. As to the meaning of 'proprietor' see PARA 51 note 4 (definition applied by s 122(2), (3)).

13	Education Act 2005 s 28(3)(b).

14	As to the publication of inspection reports see PARA 1190. As to combined reports see PARA 1206.

15	Education Act 2005 s 28(5)(a).

16	Education Act 2005 s 28(5)(b).

17	Education Act 2005 s 28(5)(c).

18	Education Act 2005 s 28(5)(d).

19	Education Act 2005 s 28(5)(e).

20	As to the meaning of 'well-being', in relation to pupils at a school, see PARA 1151 note 11.

21	Education Act 2005 s 28(5)(f).

22	Education Act 2005 s 28(7)(a). As to the meaning of 'denominational education' see PARA 1178 note 6. As to the inspection of denominational education see PARA 1201.

23	Ie by the Learning and Skills Act 2000 Pt IV (ss 73–88): see PARA 1268 et seq.

24	Education Act 2005 s 28(7)(b).

25	Education Act 2005 s 28(7)(c). The content of collective worship referred to is that which falls to be inspected under s 50 (see PARA 1201): see s 28(7)(c).

**1183.	Selection of registered inspectors.** Before entering into any arrangement for an inspection[1] by a registered inspector[2], Her Majesty's Chief Inspector of Education and Training in Wales[3] must invite tenders from at least two persons[4] who can reasonably be expected to tender for the proposed inspection and to do so at arm's length from each other, and each of whom is either a registered inspector[5] or a person who the Chief Inspector is satisfied would, if his tender were successful, arrange with a registered inspector for the inspection to be carried out[6].

Before an inspection takes place the Chief Inspector must consult[7] the appropriate authority[8] about the inspection[9].

1	Ie an inspection under the Education Act 2005 s 28: see PARA 1182.

2	Ie an inspector registered under the Education Act 2005 s 25: see PARA 1156.

3	As to Her Majesty's Chief Inspector of Education and Training in Wales see PARA 1148. As to the meaning of 'Wales' see PARA 7 note 3.

4	As to the meaning of 'person' see PARA 7 note 6.

5   Education Act 2005 Sch 4 para 2(1)(a). As to the application of Sch 4 to pupil referral units in Wales see the Education (Pupil Referral Units) (Application of Enactments) (Wales) Regulations 2007, SI 2007/1069, reg 3, Sch 1 Pt 1 para 11. As to pupil referral units see PARA 427 et seq.
6   Education Act 2005 Sch 4 para 2(1)(b).
7   As to the exercise of the duty to consult see JUDICIAL REVIEW vol 61 (2010) PARA 627.
8   'Appropriate authority' means:
    (1)   in relation to a community, foundation or voluntary school, a community special school or a maintained nursery school, the school's governing body or, if the school does not have a delegated budget, the local authority (Education Act 2005 Sch 4 para 1(a) (amended by SI 2010/1158; and the School Standards and Organisation (Wales) Act 2013 Sch 5 para 22(8)));
    (2)   in the case of a special school approved by the Welsh Ministers (ie a school falling within the Education Act 2005 s 28(2)(d): see PARA 1182), the proprietor of the school (Sch 4 para 1(b)).
    As to the meaning of references to a community, foundation or voluntary school or a community special school see PARA 106. As to the meaning of 'maintained nursery school' see PARA 99 note 4; as to the meaning of 'local authority' see PARA 25; and as to the meaning of 'proprietor' see PARA 51 note 4 (definitions applied by s 122(2), (3)). As to the meaning of 'delegated budget' see PARA 323 (definition applied by s 63(1)). As to the governing bodies of maintained schools in Wales see PARA 195. As to the Welsh Ministers see PARA 59.
9   Education Act 2005 Sch 4 para 2(2).

1184.   Inspection teams. Every inspection[1] must be conducted by a registered inspector[2] or by a member of the Inspectorate[3] with the assistance of a team (an 'inspection team')[4]. No person[5] may act as a member of an inspection team unless he is enrolled in the list kept[6] by Her Majesty's Chief Inspector of Education and Training in Wales[7], or he is a member of the Inspectorate and, if he is not the Chief Inspector, is authorised so to act by the Chief Inspector[8]. It is the duty of the inspector conducting the inspection to ensure that:
    (1)   at least one member of the inspection team is a person without personal experience in the management of any school[9] or in the provision of education in any school (otherwise than as a governor or in any other voluntary capacity)[10], and whose primary function on the team is not that of providing financial or business expertise[11]; and
    (2)   no member of the inspection team falls within a category of person prescribed[12] for these purposes[13].
Otherwise, the composition of the inspection team must be determined by the inspector conducting the inspection, subject (in the case of a registered inspector) to his complying with any imposed conditions[14]. It is the duty of the inspector conducting the inspection to ensure that no person takes any part in an inspection if he has, or has at any time had, any connection with the school in question[15], any person who is employed at the school[16], any person who is a member of the school's governing body[17] or the proprietor[18] of the school[19], of a kind which might reasonably be taken to raise doubts about his ability to act impartially in relation to that school[20].

1   Ie under the Education Act 2005 s 28: see PARA 1182.
2   Ie an inspector registered under the Education Act 2005 s 25: see PARA 1156.
3   As to the meaning of 'member of the Inspectorate' see PARA 1156 note 3.
4   Education Act 2005 Sch 4 para 3(1). As to the replacement of inspectors see PARA 1189. As to the application of Sch 4 to pupil referral units in Wales see the Education (Pupil Referral Units) (Application of Enactments) (Wales) Regulations 2007, SI 2007/1069, reg 3, Sch 1 Pt 1 para 11. As to the meaning of 'Wales' see PARA 7 note 3. As to pupil referral units see PARA 427 et seq.
5   As to the meaning of 'person' see PARA 7 note 6.
6   Ie under the Education Act 2005 Sch 4 para 4: see PARA 1185.
7   Education Act 2005 Sch 4 para 3(1)(a). As to Her Majesty's Chief Inspector of Education and Training in Wales see PARA 1148.

8 Education Act 2005 Sch 4 para 3(1)(b).
9 As to the meaning of 'school' see PARA 91 (definition applied by the Education Act 2005 s 122(2), (3)).
10 Education Act 2005 Sch 4 para 3(2)(a)(i). Any experience of a kind mentioned in Sch 4 para 3(2)(a) which it is reasonable to regard as insignificant, having regard to the purposes of Sch 4 para 3(2), may be ignored by the inspector conducting the inspection: Sch 4 para 3(4). As to the governing bodies of maintained schools in Wales see PARA 195.
11 Education Act 2005 Sch 4 para 3(2)(a)(ii).
12 'Prescribed' means prescribed by regulations; and 'regulations' means regulations made by the Welsh Ministers under the Education Act 2005 Pt 1 Ch 3 (ss 19–31): see s 31(1). As to the Welsh Ministers see PARA 59. The functions under Sch 4 were originally vested in the National Assembly for Wales and are now exercisable by the Welsh Ministers by virtue of the Government of Wales Act 2006 s 162(1), Sch 11 paras 30, 32. At the date at which this volume states the law no such regulations had been made.
13 Education Act 2005 Sch 4 para 3(2)(b).
14 See the Education Act 2005 Sch 4 para 3(3). The conditions referred to are any imposed under s 25(4)(c) (see PARA 1156): see Sch 4 para 3(3). For the purposes of Pt 1 Ch 3 (ss 19–31), any reference to a condition imposed under s 25(4)(c) includes a reference to a condition imposed under s 26(3) (see PARA 1157): s 31(2).
15 Education Act 2005 Sch 4 para 3(5)(a). As to the schools subject to inspection see PARA 1182.
16 Education Act 2005 Sch 4 para 3(5)(b).
17 Education Act 2005 Sch 4 para 3(5)(c).
18 As to the meaning of 'proprietor' see PARA 51 note 4 (definition applied by the Education Act 2005 s 122(2), (3)).
19 Education Act 2005 Sch 4 para 3(5)(d).
20 Education Act 2005 Sch 4 para 3(5).

1185. Enrolment of persons to act as team members. Her Majesty's Chief Inspector of Education and Training in Wales[1] must keep a list of persons[2] who may[3] act as members of an inspection team[4]. The Chief Inspector may not enrol any person in the list unless, having regard to any conditions that he proposes to impose[5], it appears to him that that person is a fit and proper person for carrying out an inspection[6] and will be capable of assisting in an inspection competently and effectively[7]. An application for enrolment in the list must, except in such circumstances as may be prescribed[8], be accompanied by the prescribed fee[9].

1 As to Her Majesty's Chief Inspector of Education and Training in Wales see PARA 1148. As to the meaning of 'Wales' see PARA 7 note 3.
2 As to the meaning of 'person' see PARA 7 note 6.
3 Ie by virtue of the Education Act 2005 Sch 4 para 3(1)(a): see PARA 1184.
4 Education Act 2005 Sch 4 para 4(1). As to inspection teams see PARA 1184. The provisions of s 25(3)(a), (4), (5)(b), (6)–(9) (conditions imposed on registration, and the period for which registration is to have effect: see PARA 1156) apply in relation to the enrolment of a person in the list and acting as a member of an inspection team as they apply in relation to the registration of a person under s 25(1) (see PARA 1156) and to acting as a registered inspector, but as if the reference in s 25(5)(b) to the need for registered inspectors were a reference to the need for enrolled persons: Sch 4 para 4(4). Section 26 (removal from register and imposition or variation of conditions: see PARA 1157), s 27 (appeals in relation to registration: see PARA 1158) and Sch 3 (tribunals hearing appeals in relation to registration: see PARAS 1159–1387) apply in relation to enrolment on the list and to a person so enrolled as they apply in relation to registration under s 25(1) and to a person so registered, but with any necessary modifications: Sch 4 para 4(5). As to the meaning of 'modification' see PARA 21 note 15 (definition applied by s 122(2), (3)). In its application to an enrolled person in accordance with Sch 4 para 4(5), s 26 has effect as if conditions mentioned in s 26(2) (see PARA 1157) were that:
   (1) that person is no longer a fit and proper person to act as a member of an inspection team (Sch 4 para 4(6)(a));
   (2) he is no longer capable of assisting in an inspection competently and effectively (Sch 4 para 4(6)(b));
   (3) there has been a significant failure on his part to comply with any condition imposed under s 25(4)(c) (see PARA 1156) as it applies in accordance with Sch 4 para 4(4) (Sch 4 para 4(6)(c)).

For the purposes of Pt 1 Ch 3 (ss 19–31), any reference to a condition imposed under s 25(4)(c) includes a reference to a condition imposed under s 26(3) (see PARA 1157): s 31(2). Without prejudice to the generality of Sch 3 para 2(1) (regulations may make provision as to the period and manner for the making of appeals: see PARA 1160), regulations under that provision may provide that, where a person is appealing simultaneously against a decision of the Chief Inspector relating to that person's registration (Sch 4 para 4(7)(a)) and against a decision of the Chief Inspector relating to that person's enrolment in the list (Sch 4 para 4(7)(b)), both appeals are to be heard at the same time (Sch 4 para 4(7)). At the date at which this volume states the law no regulations had been made for such purposes.
As to the application of Sch 4 to pupil referral units in Wales see the Education (Pupil Referral Units) (Application of Enactments) (Wales) Regulations 2007, SI 2007/1069, reg 3, Sch 1 Pt 1 para 11. As to pupil referral units see PARA 427 et seq.

5　Ie any condition imposed under the Education Act 2005 s 25(4)(c) (see PARA 1156) as it applies in accordance with Sch 4 para 4(4): see note 4.
6　Education Act 2005 Sch 4 para 4(2)(a). 'Inspection' means an inspection under s 28 (see PARA 1182): Sch 4 para 1.
7　Education Act 2005 Sch 4 para 4(2)(b).
8　'Prescribed' means prescribed by regulations; and 'regulations' means regulations made by the Welsh Ministers under the Education Act 2005 Pt 1 Ch 3 (ss 19–31): see s 31(1). As to the Welsh Ministers see PARA 59. The functions under Sch 4 were originally vested in the National Assembly for Wales and are now exercisable by the Welsh Ministers by virtue of the Government of Wales Act 2006 s 162(1), Sch 11 paras 30, 32. At the date at which this volume states the law no regulations had been made for this purpose.
9　Education Act 2005 Sch 4 para 4(3). At the date at which this volume states the law no regulations had been made for this purpose.

1186.　Training for inspections. No person who is not a member of the Inspectorate[1] may conduct an inspection[2] of a school[3] in Wales[4], or act as a member of an inspection team[5] for such a school, unless he has, in the opinion of Her Majesty's Chief Inspector of Education and Training in Wales[6], satisfactorily completed a course of training provided by, or complying with arrangements approved by, the Chief Inspector[7]. Where the Chief Inspector provides such training, he may charge such fees as are reasonable for the purpose of recovering the whole, or part, of the cost of providing it[8].

1　As to the meaning of 'member of the Inspectorate' see PARA 1156 note 3.
2　Ie an inspection under the Education Act 2005 s 28: see PARA 1182.
3　As to the schools subject to inspection see PARA 1182.
4　As to the meaning of 'Wales' see PARA 7 note 3.
5　As to inspection teams see PARA 1184.
6　As to Her Majesty's Chief Inspector of Education and Training in Wales see PARA 1148.
7　Education Act 2005 Sch 4 para 5(1). Schedule 4 para 5(1) does not apply in such circumstances as may be specified, either generally or in relation to a particular case or class of case, by the Chief Inspector: Sch 4 para 5(3). As to the application of Sch 4 to pupil referral units in Wales see the Education (Pupil Referral Units) (Application of Enactments) (Wales) Regulations 2007, SI 2007/1069, reg 3, Sch 1 Pt 1 para 11. As to pupil referral units see PARA 427 et seq.
8　Education Act 2005 Sch 4 para 5(2).

1187.　Meeting with parents. Where an inspection[1] is arranged, the appropriate authority[2] for the school[3] concerned must take such steps as are reasonably practicable to notify[4] the parents[5] of registered pupils[6] at the school[7], and such other persons[8] as may be prescribed[9], of the time when the inspection is to take place[10]. The appropriate authority must also arrange a meeting, in accordance with such provisions as may be prescribed[11], between the inspector conducting the inspection[12] and those parents of registered pupils at the school who wish to attend[13].

1　Ie an inspection under the Education Act 2005 s 28: see PARA 1182.
2　As to the meaning of 'appropriate authority' see PARA 1183 note 8.

3   As to the schools subject to inspection see PARA 1182. As to the application of the Education
    Act 2005 Sch 4 to pupil referral units in Wales see the Education (Pupil Referral Units)
    (Application of Enactments) (Wales) Regulations 2007, SI 2007/1069, reg 3, Sch 1 Pt 1 para 11.
    As to the meaning of 'Wales' see PARA 7 note 3. As to pupil referral units see PARA 427 et seq.
4   As to the service of notices and documents see the Education Act 1996 s 572 (applied by the
    Education Act 2005 s 122(2), (3)); and PARA 76.
5   As to the meaning of 'parent' see PARA 7 note 6 (definition applied by the Education Act 2005
    s 122(2), (3)).
6   As to the meaning of 'registered pupil' see PARA 437 (definition applied by the Education
    Act 2005 s 122(2), (3)).
7   Education Act 2005 Sch 4 para 6(a)(i).
8   As to the meaning of 'person' see PARA 7 note 6.
9   Education Act 2005 Sch 4 para 6(a)(ii). 'Prescribed' means prescribed by regulations; and
    'regulations' means regulations made by the Welsh Ministers under Pt 1 Ch 3 (ss 19–31): see
    s 31(1). As to the Welsh Ministers see PARA 59. The functions under the Sch 4 were originally
    vested in the National Assembly for Wales and are now exercisable by the Welsh Ministers by
    virtue of the Government of Wales Act 2006 s 162(1), Sch 11 paras 30, 32. As to the prescribed
    persons see the Education (School Inspection) (Wales) Regulations 2006, SI 2006/1714, reg 7
    (amended by SI 2010/1142). As to the application of the Education (School Inspection) (Wales)
    Regulations 2006, SI 2006/1714, Pt 2 (regs 4–12) to pupil referral units in Wales see the
    Education (Pupil Referral Units) (Application of Enactments) (Wales) Regulations 2007,
    SI 2007/1069, reg 3, Sch 1 Pt 2 para 13.
10 Education Act 2005 Sch 4 para 6(a).
11 As to the prescribed provision see the Education (School Inspection) (Wales) Regulations 2006,
    SI 2006/1714, reg 8 (amended by SI 2010/1142; SI 2014/1212).
12 As to inspection teams see PARA 1184.
13 Education Act 2005 Sch 4 para 6(b).

1188.   Rights of entry and inspection. An inspector[1] conducting an
inspection[2], and the members of his inspection team[3], have at all reasonable
times:

(1)   a right of entry to the premises[4] of the school[5] concerned[6];

(2)   a right to inspect, and take copies of, any records kept by the school,
      and any other documents containing information relating to the school,
      which he requires for the purposes of the inspection[7];

(3)   a right of entry to any premises (other than school premises) on which,
      by virtue of arrangements made by the school, any pupils who are
      registered[8] at the school[9] and have attained the age of 15[10], or will
      attain that age in the current school year[11], but have not ceased to be of
      compulsory school age[12], are receiving part of their education from any
      person ('the provider')[13];

(4)   a right of entry to any premises of the provider used in connection with
      the provision by him of that education[14];

(5)   a right to inspect and take copies of any records kept by the provider
      relating to the provision of that education[15], and any other documents
      containing information so relating[16], which the inspector or (as the case
      may be) member of the team requires for the purposes of the
      inspection[17].

Where pupils registered at the school concerned are, by arrangement with
another school, receiving part of their education at the other school[18], and the
inspector is satisfied that he cannot properly discharge his duty[19] in relation to
the school concerned without inspecting the provision made for those pupils at
that other school[20], heads (1) and (2) above apply in relation to that other school
as they apply in relation to the school concerned[21].

It is an offence wilfully to obstruct the inspector conducting the inspection, or a member of an inspection team, in the exercise of his functions[22] in relation to an inspection of a school[23].

1   As to the appointment of inspectors see PARA 1148.
2   Ie an inspection under the Education Act 2005 s 28: see PARA 1182.
3   As to inspection teams see PARA 1184.
4   As to the meaning of 'premises' see PARA 62 note 19 (definition applied by the Education Act 2005 s 122(2), (3)).
5   As to the schools subject to inspection see PARA 1182. As to the application of the Education Act 2005 Sch 4 to pupil referral units in Wales see the Education (Pupil Referral Units) (Application of Enactments) (Wales) Regulations 2007, SI 2007/1069, reg 3, Sch 1 Pt 1 para 11. As to the meaning of 'Wales' see PARA 7 note 3. As to pupil referral units see PARA 427 et seq.
6   Education Act 2005 Sch 4 para 7(1)(a).
7   Education Act 2005 Sch 4 para 7(1)(b). A person authorised by any provision of Pt 1 (ss 1–63) to inspect records or other documents is entitled at any reasonable time to have access to, and inspect and check the operation of, any computer and any associated apparatus or material which is or has been in use in connection with the records or other documents in question: s 58(a). Such a person may require the person by whom or on whose behalf the computer is or has been so used, or any person having charge of, or otherwise concerned with the operation of, the computer, apparatus or material, to afford him such assistance as he may reasonably require (including, in particular, the making of information available for inspection or copying in a legible form): s 58(b). As to the meaning of 'person' see PARA 7 note 6.
8   As to the meaning of 'registered pupil' see PARA 437 (definition applied by the Education Act 2005 s 122(2), (3)).
9   Education Act 2005 Sch 4 para 7(3)(a)(i).
10 As to the time at which a person attains a particular age see PARA 7 note 6.
11 As to the meaning of 'school year' see PARA 19 note 12 (definition applied by the Education Act 2005 s 122(2), (3)).
12 Education Act 2005 Sch 4 para 7(3)(a)(ii). As to the meaning of 'compulsory school age' see PARA 19.
13 Education Act 2005 Sch 4 para 7(3)(a).
14 Education Act 2005 Sch 4 para 7(3)(b).
15 Education Act 2005 Sch 4 para 7(3)(c)(i).
16 Education Act 2005 Sch 4 para 7(3)(c)(ii).
17 Education Act 2005 Sch 4 para 7(3)(c). See also note 7.
18 Education Act 2005 Sch 4 para 7(2)(a).
19 Ie under the Education Act 2005 s 28(5): see PARA 1182.
20 Education Act 2005 Sch 4 para 7(2)(b).
21 Education Act 2005 Sch 4 para 7(2).
22 As to the meaning of 'functions' see PARA 18 note 5 (definition applied by the Education Act 2005 s 122(2), (3)).
23 Education Act 2005 Sch 4 para 8(1). A person guilty of such an offence is liable on summary conviction to a fine not exceeding level 4 on the standard scale: Sch 4 para 8(2). As to the standard scale see SENTENCING AND DISPOSITION OF OFFENDERS vol 92 (2010) PARA 142.

1189. Replacement of inspector during course of inspection. Where, during an inspection[1], at any time after the required meeting with parents[2] is held[3], but before the making of the report of the inspection is completed[4], the inspector conducting the inspection[5] becomes, for any reason, unable to continue to discharge his functions[6] as an inspector in relation to the inspection[7], and if the conditions set out below are satisfied[8]:

(1)   Her Majesty's Chief Inspector of Education and Training in Wales[9] may arrange for that person to be replaced as the inspector conducting the inspection by another person who is either a registered inspector[10] or a member of the Inspectorate[11]; and

(2)   if he does so, anything done by or in relation to that person in

connection with the inspection must, so far as necessary for his effectual replacement by that other inspector, be regarded as done by or in relation to that other inspector[12].

The conditions are that the appropriate authority[13] for the school[14] concerned has given the Chief Inspector notice[15] in writing[16] of its agreement to the inspector being replaced[17] and that the replacement inspector does not have, and has not at any time had, any connection[18] with the school in question or with any other person[19] mentioned there[20].

1 Ie an inspection under the Education Act 2005 s 28: see PARA 1182.
2 Ie the meeting required by the Education Act 2005 Sch 4 para 6: see PARA 1187.
3 Education Act 2005 Sch 4 para 9(1)(a).
4 Education Act 2005 Sch 4 para 9(1)(b). As to the duty to make reports see PARA 1192.
5 As to inspection teams see PARA 1184.
6 As to the meaning of 'functions' see PARA 18 note 5 (definition applied by the Education Act 2005 s 122(2), (3)).
7 Education Act 2005 Sch 4 para 9(1). As to the application of Sch 4 to pupil referral units in Wales see the Education (Pupil Referral Units) (Application of Enactments) (Wales) Regulations 2007, SI 2007/1069, reg 3, Sch 1 Pt 1 para 11. As to the meaning of 'Wales' see PARA 7 note 3. As to pupil referral units see PARA 427 et seq.
8 Education Act 2005 Sch 4 para 9(2).
9 As to Her Majesty's Chief Inspector of Education and Training in Wales see PARA 1148.
10 As to the registration of inspectors under the Education Act 2005 see PARA 1156.
11 Education Act 2005 Sch 4 para 9(2)(a). As to the meaning of 'member of the Inspectorate' see PARA 1156 note 3.
12 Education Act 2005 Sch 4 para 9(2)(b).
13 As to the meaning of 'appropriate authority' see PARA 1183 note 8.
14 As to the schools subject to inspection see PARA 1182.
15 As to the service of notices and documents see the Education Act 1996 s 572 (applied by the Education Act 2005 s 122(2), (3)); and PARA 76.
16 As to the meaning of 'writing' see PARA 76 note 8.
17 Education Act 2005 Sch 4 para 9(3)(a).
18 Ie any connection of the kind mentioned in the Education Act 2005 Sch 4 para 3(5): see PARA 1184.
19 As to the meaning of 'person' see PARA 7 note 6.
20 Education Act 2005 Sch 4 para 9(3)(b).

1190. Publication of inspection reports. Her Majesty's Chief Inspector of Education and Training in Wales[1] may arrange for:

(1) any report[2] by a member of the Inspectorate[3] of an inspection[4] carried out by him[5]; or

(2) any report of a regular inspection[6] made by a registered inspector[7],

to be published in such manner as the Chief Inspector considers appropriate[8], including by electronic means[9].

For the purposes of the law of defamation any report published by the Chief Inspector[10] is privileged unless the publication is shown to have been made with malice[11]; but this does not limit any privilege otherwise[12] subsisting[13].

1 As to Her Majesty's Chief Inspector of Education, Children's Services and Skills see PARA 1133.
2 As to reports see PARAS 1192, 1193.
3 As to the meaning of 'member of the Inspectorate' see PARA 1156 note 3.
4 Ie an inspection carried out under any provision of the Education Act 2005 Pt 1 Ch 3 (ss 19–31) (whether the report is required by any such provision or is otherwise made in pursuance of his functions under that provision): see s 29(1)(a). As to the meaning of 'functions' see PARA 18 note 5 (definition applied by s 122(2), (3)).
5 See the Education Act 2005 s 29(1)(a).
6 Ie an inspection under the Education Act 2005 s 28: see PARA 1182.
7 Education Act 2005 s 29(1)(b). As to the registration of inspectors see PARA 1156.
8 Education Act 2005 s 29(1). As to combined reports see PARA 1206.

9   See the Education Act 2005 s 29(2). Section 29(2) is expressed to be without prejudice to the
     generality of s 21(1)(c) (arrangements for publication of reports: see PARA 1154) or s 29(1) (see
     the text to notes 1–8): see s 29(2).
10   Ie under the Education Act 2005 s 21(1)(c) (arrangements for publication of reports: see PARA
     1154) or s 29(1) (see the text to notes 1–8).
11   Education Act 2005 s 29(3). As to privilege and malice in the law of defamation see
     DEFAMATION vol 32 (2012) PARAS 594 et seq, 651 et seq.
12   Ie apart from the Education Act 2005 s 29(3): see the text to notes 10–11.
13   Education Act 2005 s 29(4).

B. PROCEDURE FOR SCHOOL INSPECTION

1191.   Inspections by members of the Inspectorate. If Her Majesty's Chief
Inspector of Education and Training in Wales[1] so elects in the case of any
inspection of a school[2] by a member of the Inspectorate[3], that inspection is to be
treated for the purposes of the relevant provisions[4] as if it were a regular
inspection[5].

1   As to Her Majesty's Chief Inspector of Education and Training in Wales see PARA 1148. As to
     the meaning of 'Wales' see PARA 7 note 3.
2   Ie under the Education Act 2005 s 20(2)(b) (see PARA 1151) or s 24(1) (see PARA 1153). As to
     the meaning of 'school' see PARA 91 (definition applied by the Education Act 2005 s 122(2), (3)).
3   In the Education Act 2005 Pt 1 Ch 4 (ss 32–43), 'member of the Inspectorate' means the Chief
     Inspector, any of Her Majesty's Inspectors of Education and Training in Wales and any
     additional inspector appointed under Sch 2 para 2 (see PARA 1149): s 43. As to Her Majesty's
     Inspectors of Education and Training in Wales see PARA 1148.
4   'The relevant provisions' means the Education Act 2005 s 28(1), (5) (see PARA 1182) and s 35
     (see PARA 1193), and:
     (1)   (in the case of an inspection of a maintained school) ss 38–40 (see PARA 1196 et seq)
            (s 32(2)(a)); and
     (2)   (in the case of an inspection of a school other than a maintained school) ss 41–42 (see
            PARA 1199 et seq) (s 32(2)(b)).
     In Pt 1 Ch 4 (ss 32–43), 'maintained school' means a community, foundation or voluntary
     school, a community special school or a maintained nursery school: s 43 (amended by the
     School Standards and Organisation (Wales) Act 2013 Sch 5 para 22(6)). As to the meaning of
     references to a community, foundation or voluntary school or a community special school see
     PARA 106. As to the meaning of 'maintained nursery school' see PARA 99 note 4 (definition
     applied by s 122(2), (3)).
5   See the Education Act 2005 s 32(1). A regular inspection is an inspection under s 28 (see PARA
     1182): see s 32(1). As to the application of Pt 1 (ss 1–63) to pupil referral units in Wales see the
     Education (Pupil Referral Units) (Application of Enactments) (Wales) Regulations 2007,
     SI 2007/1069, reg 3, Sch 1 Pt 1 para 11. As to pupil referral units see PARA 427 et seq.

1192.   Reports of inspections by registered inspectors. Where a regular
inspection[1] by a registered inspector[2] or a member of the Inspectorate[3] has been
completed, the inspector must make in writing[4] a report of the inspection and a
summary of the report[5].
    Where the inspection was conducted by a registered inspector and he is of the
opinion that special measures are required to be taken in relation to the school[6],
or that the school requires significant improvement[7], he must submit a draft of
the report of the inspection to Her Majesty's Chief Inspector of Education and
Training in Wales[8]. If the Chief Inspector so requests, an inspector who has
submitted such a draft must provide the Chief Inspector with such further
information as he may specify[9]. The Chief Inspector must inform an inspector
who has submitted such a draft whether he agrees or disagrees with the
inspector's opinion[10].
    Where the Chief Inspector informs the inspector that he disagrees with the
inspector's opinion[11], but the inspector remains of the opinion that special

measures are required to be taken in relation to the school or that the school requires significant improvement[12], the inspector may not make a report stating that opinion unless the terms in which he makes the report are substantially the same[13] as the draft or as a subsequent draft submitted to the Chief Inspector[14]. Where a subsequent draft is so submitted, the Chief Inspector must inform the inspector whether he agrees or disagrees with the inspector's opinion[15]. A report made by a registered inspector who is of the opinion that special measures are required to be taken in relation to the school or that the school requires significant improvement must state his opinion[16], and state whether the Chief Inspector agrees or disagrees with his opinion[17].

If a report of an inspection of a school by a registered inspector is made in circumstances where:

(1)   he is of the opinion that special measures are not required to be taken in relation to the school[18]; but

(2)   in the latest report of an inspection of the school, the person making the report stated that in his opinion such measures were required to be taken and either that person was a member of the Inspectorate, or the report stated that the Chief Inspector agreed with his opinion[19],

the registered inspector must state his opinion in the report[20].

If a report of an inspection of a school by a registered inspector is made in circumstances where:

(a)   he is of the opinion that the school does not require significant improvement and that special measures are not required to be taken in relation to the school[21]; but

(b)   in the latest report of an inspection of the school, the person making the report stated that in his opinion the school did require significant improvement and either that person was a member of the Inspectorate or the report stated that the Chief Inspector agreed with his opinion[22],

the registered inspector must state his opinion in the report[23].

1   Ie an inspection under the Education Act 2005 s 28: see PARA 1182.
2   As to the registration of inspectors see PARA 1156.
3   As to the meaning of 'member of the Inspectorate' see PARA 1191 note 3.
4   As to the meaning of 'writing' see PARA 76 note 8.
5   Education Act 2005 s 33. As to combined reports see PARA 1206. As to the application of Pt 1 (ss 1–63) to pupil referral units in Wales see the Education (Pupil Referral Units) (Application of Enactments) (Wales) Regulations 2007, SI 2007/1069, reg 3, Sch 1 Pt 1 para 11. As to pupil referral units see PARA 427 et seq. As to the meaning of 'Wales' see PARA 7 note 3.
6   Education Act 2005 s 34(1)(a). As to the meaning of 'special measures are required to be taken in relation to a school' see PARA 1167 note 3. As to the schools subject to inspection under s 28 see PARA 1182.
7   Education Act 2005 s 34(1)(b). As to the meaning of 'a school requires significant improvement' see PARA 1167 note 4.
8   Education Act 2005 s 34(1). As to Her Majesty's Chief Inspector of Education and Training in Wales see PARA 1148.
9   Education Act 2005 s 34(2).
10   Education Act 2005 s 34(3).
11   Education Act 2005 s 34(4)(a).
12   Education Act 2005 s 34(4)(b).
13   Ie except as to the statement required by the Education Act 2005 s 34(6)(b): see the text to note 17.
14   Education Act 2005 s 34(4).
15   Education Act 2005 s 34(5).
16   Education Act 2005 s 34(6)(a).
17   Education Act 2005 s 34(6)(b).
18   Education Act 2005 s 34(7)(a).

19 Education Act 2005 s 34(7)(b).
20 Education Act 2005 s 34(7). The registered inspector must state his opinion in the report as mentioned in the text whether or not he is required by s 34(6) (see the text to notes 16–17) also to state his opinion that the school requires significant improvement: see s 34(7).
21 Education Act 2005 s 34(8)(a).
22 Education Act 2005 s 34(8)(b).
23 Education Act 2005 s 34(8).

1193. Reports of inspections by members of the Inspectorate. Where on the completion of any inspection of a school[1] by a member of the Inspectorate[2], that person is of the opinion that special measures are required to be taken in relation to the school[3] or that the school requires significant improvement[4], he must prepare in writing[5] a report of the inspection and a summary of the report[6], and he must state his opinion in the report[7]. If on the completion of any such inspection of a school by a member of the Inspectorate in circumstances where:

(1)   he is of the opinion that special measures are not required to be taken in relation to the school[8]; but

(2)   in the latest report of an inspection of the school, the person making the report stated that in his opinion such measures were required to be taken and either that person was a member of the Inspectorate, or the report stated that Her Majesty's Chief Inspector of Education and Training in Wales[9] agreed with his opinion[10],

the member of the Inspectorate must prepare a report of the inspection and a summary of the report and state his opinion in the report[11].

If on the completion of any such inspection of a school by a member of the Inspectorate in circumstances where:

(a)   he is of the opinion that the school does not require significant improvement and that special measures are not required to be taken in relation to the school[12]; but

(b)   in the latest report of an inspection of the school, the person making the report stated that in his opinion the school did require significant improvement and either that person was a member of the Inspectorate or the report stated that the Chief Inspector agreed with his opinion[13],

the member of the Inspectorate must prepare a report of the inspection and a summary of the report and state his opinion in the report[14].

A report of a regular inspection[15] of a school by a member of the Inspectorate must, if he is of the opinion that special measures are required to be taken in relation to the school or that the school requires significant improvement, state his opinion[16]. If a report of such an inspection of a school by a member of the Inspectorate is made in circumstances where:

(i)   he is of the opinion that special measures are not required to be taken in relation to the school[17]; but

(ii)   in the latest report of an inspection of the school, the person making the report stated that in his opinion such measures were required to be taken and either that person was a member of the Inspectorate, or the report stated that the Chief Inspector agreed with his opinion[18],

the member of the Inspectorate must state his opinion in the report[19]. If a report of such an inspection of a school by a member of the Inspectorate is made in circumstances where:

(A)   he is of the opinion that the school does not require significant improvement and that special measures are not required to be taken in relation to the school[20]; but

(B)   in the latest report of an inspection of the school, the person making the report stated that in his opinion the school did require significant improvement and either that person was a member of the Inspectorate or the report stated that the Chief Inspector agreed with his opinion[21], the member of the Inspectorate must state his opinion in the report[22].

1 Ie under the Education Act 2005 s 20(2)(b) (see PARA 1151) or s 24(1) (see PARA 1153). As to the meaning of 'school' see PARA 91 (definition applied by s 122(2), (3)).
2 As to the meaning of 'member of the Inspectorate' see PARA 1191 note 3.
3 As to the meaning of 'special measures are required to be taken in relation to a school' see PARA 1167 note 3.
4 Education Act 2005 s 35(1). As to the meaning of 'a school requires significant improvement' see PARA 1167 note 4.
5 As to the meaning of 'writing' see PARA 76 note 8.
6 Education Act 2005 s 35(1)(a). As to combined reports see PARA 1206.
7 Education Act 2005 s 35(1)(b). As to the application of Pt 1 (ss 1–63) to pupil referral units in Wales see the Education (Pupil Referral Units) (Application of Enactments) (Wales) Regulations 2007, SI 2007/1069, reg 3, Sch 1 Pt 1 para 11. As to pupil referral units see PARA 427 et seq. As to the meaning of 'Wales' see PARA 7 note 3.
8 Education Act 2005 s 35(2)(a).
9 As to Her Majesty's Chief Inspector of Education and Training in Wales see PARA 1148.
10 Education Act 2005 s 35(2)(b).
11 Education Act 2005 s 35(2). The member of the Inspectorate must state his opinion in the report whether or not he is required by s 35(1)(b) (see the text to note 7) also to state his opinion that the school requires significant improvement: see s 35(2).
12 Education Act 2005 s 35(3)(a).
13 Education Act 2005 s 35(3)(b).
14 Education Act 2005 s 35(3).
15 Ie an inspection under the Education Act 2005 s 28: see PARA 1182. As to reports of such inspections by registered inspectors see PARA 1192.
16 Education Act 2005 s 35(4).
17 Education Act 2005 s 35(5)(a).
18 Education Act 2005 s 35(5)(b).
19 Education Act 2005 s 35(5). The member of the Inspectorate must state his opinion in the report whether or not he is required by s 35(4) (see the text to notes 15–16) also to state his opinion that the school requires significant improvement: see s 35(5).
20 Education Act 2005 s 35(6)(a).
21 Education Act 2005 s 35(6)(b).
22 Education Act 2005 s 35(6).

1194. Timing of inspections by registered inspectors. The carrying out of a regular inspection[1] (not being one carried out by a member of the Inspectorate[2]) must be completed by the time allowed, and the making of the required report[3] must be completed within the period allowed[4]. The time, and the period, allowed are such as may be prescribed[5], subject to any such extension of the period as Her Majesty's Chief Inspector of Education and Training in Wales[6] may consider necessary to make, but the total period allowed must not exceed the prescribed period extended by three months[7].

In the case of an inspection (not being one carried out by a member of the Inspectorate[8]) of a maintained school[9], the Chief Inspector must give notice in writing[10] of any extension to the inspector[11], the local authority (in the case of a maintained school)[12], and the governing body[13]. In the case of an inspection (not being one carried out by a member of the Inspectorate[14]) of a special school approved by the Welsh Ministers[15], the Chief Inspector must give notice in writing of any such extension to the inspector[16], the proprietor of the school[17], and the Welsh Ministers[18].

1 Ie an inspection under the Education Act 2005 s 28: see PARA 1182.
2 See the Education Act 2005 s 36(5). As to the meaning of 'member of the Inspectorate' see PARA 1191 note 3.

3   Ie the report required under the Education Act 2005 s 33: see PARA 1192.
4   Education Act 2005 s 36(1). As to the application of Pt 1 (ss 1–63) to pupil referral units in
     Wales see the Education (Pupil Referral Units) (Application of Enactments) (Wales)
     Regulations 2007, SI 2007/1069, reg 3, Sch 1 Pt 1 para 11. As to pupil referral units see PARA
     427 et seq. As to the meaning of 'Wales' see PARA 7 note 3.
5   'Prescribed' means prescribed by regulations; and 'regulations' means regulations made by the
     Welsh Ministers under the Education Act 2005 Pt 1 Ch 4 (ss 32–43): s 43. As to the Welsh
     Ministers see PARA 59. The functions under s 36 were originally vested in the National Assembly
     for Wales and are now exercisable by the Welsh Ministers by virtue of the Government of Wales
     Act 2006 s 162(1), Sch 11 paras 30, 32.
          For the purposes of the Education Act 2005 s 36, the carrying out of an inspection under
     s 28 must be completed within the period of two weeks from the date on which the inspection
     began: Education (School Inspection) (Wales) Regulations 2006, SI 2006/1714, reg 9(1). For
     those purposes there is prescribed, as the period within which the making of the report of such
     an inspection is to be completed, the period of 35 working days from the date on which the
     inspection was completed: reg 9(2). As to the application of Pt 2 (regs 4–12) to pupil referral
     units in Wales see the Education (Pupil Referral Units) (Application of Enactments) (Wales)
     Regulations 2007, SI 2007/1069, reg 3, Sch 1 Pt 2 para 13.
6   As to Her Majesty's Chief Inspector of Education and Training in Wales see PARA 1148.
7   Education Act 2005 s 36(2). As to the meaning of 'month' see PARA 54 note 26.
8   See the Education Act 2005 s 36(5).
9   As to the meaning of 'maintained school' see PARA 1191 note 4.
10   As to the service of notices and documents see the Education Act 1996 s 572 (applied by the
     Education Act 2005 s 122(2), (3)); and PARA 76. As to the meaning of 'writing' see PARA 76 note
     8.
11   Education Act 2005 s 36(3)(a).
12   Education Act 2005 s 36(3)(b) (amended by SI 2010/1158). As to the meaning of 'local
     authority' see PARA 25 (definition applied by the Education Act 2005 s 122(2), (3)).
13   Education Act 2005 s 36(3)(c). As to the governing bodies of maintained schools in Wales see
     PARA 195.
14   See the Education Act 2005 s 36(5).
15   Ie a school falling within the Education Act 2005 s 28(2)(d): see PARA 1182.
16   Education Act 2005 s 36(4)(a).
17   Education Act 2005 s 36(4)(b). As to the meaning of 'proprietor' see PARA 51 note 4 (definition
     applied by s 122(2), (3)).
18   Education Act 2005 s 36(4)(c).

**1195.   Duty to notify where inspection shows maintained school causing
concern.**   Where:

(1)   following an inspection[1] of a maintained school[2] by a member of the
       Inspectorate[3], that member has informed Her Majesty's Chief Inspector
       of Education and Training in Wales[4] of his opinion that special
       measures are required to be taken in relation to the school[5], or that the
       school requires significant improvement[6]; or

(2)   the Chief Inspector agrees with the opinion of a registered inspector[7],
       expressed in a draft report submitted to the Chief Inspector[8] that special
       measures are required to be taken in relation to a maintained school[9], or
       that the school requires significant improvement[10],

the Chief Inspector must without delay give the Welsh Ministers[11] and the local
authority[12] notice in writing[13] stating that the case falls within head (1) or (2)
above[14].

1   Ie under the Education Act 2005 Pt 1 Ch 3 (ss 19–31): see PARA 1182 et seq.
2   As to the meaning of 'maintained school' see PARA 1191 note 4.
3   As to the meaning of 'member of the Inspectorate' see PARA 1191 note 3.
4   As to Her Majesty's Chief Inspector of Education and Training in Wales see PARA 1148.
5   See the Education Act 2005 s 37(1)(a)(i). As to the meaning of 'special measures are required to
     be taken in relation to a school' see PARA 1167 note 3.
6   See the Education Act 2005 s 37(1)(a)(ii). As to the meaning of 'a school requires significant
     improvement' see PARA 1167 note 4.

7 As to the registration of inspectors see PARA 1156.
8 Ie a draft report submitted under the Education Act 2005 s 34(1): see PARA 1192.
9 See the Education Act 2005 s 37(1)(b)(i).
10 See the Education Act 2005 s 37(1)(b)(ii).
11 As to the Welsh Ministers see PARA 59. The functions under the Education Act 2005 s 37 were
   originally vested in the National Assembly for Wales and are now exercisable by the Welsh
   Ministers by virtue of the Government of Wales Act 2006 s 162(1), Sch 11 paras 30, 32.
12 As to the meaning of 'local authority' see PARA 25 (definition applied by the Education Act 2005
   s 122(2), (3)).
13 As to the service of notices and documents see the Education Act 1996 s 572 (definition applied
   by the Education Act 2005 s 122(2), (3)); and PARA 76. As to the meaning of 'writing' see PARA
   76 note 8.
14 Education Act 2005 s 37(2) (amended by SI 2010/1158). As to the application of the Education
   Act 2005 Pt 1 (ss 1–63) to pupil referral units in Wales see the Education (Pupil Referral Units)
   (Application of Enactments) (Wales) Regulations 2007, SI 2007/1069, reg 3, Sch 1 Pt 1 para 11.
   As to pupil referral units see PARA 427 et seq. As to the meaning of 'Wales' see PARA 7 note 3.

1196. Destination of reports of inspections of maintained schools. In the case
of a report of a regular inspection[1] of a maintained school[2], the person making
the report must without delay send[3] a copy of the report together with the
summary of it to the appropriate authority[4] for the school[5]. In a case where a
report of an inspection of a maintained school is made by a member of the
Inspectorate[6], and he is required[7] to state in the report that he is of the opinion
that special measures are required to be taken in relation to the school[8] or that
the school requires significant improvement[9], the member of the Inspectorate
must send a copy of the report together with the summary of it to the
appropriate authority for the school[10].

In any case, copies of the report and summary must be sent by the person who
made the report to Her Majesty's Chief Inspector of Education and Training in
Wales[11], unless the report was made by a member of the Inspectorate[12], to the
head teacher[13] of the school[14], to whichever of the local authority and the
governing body is not the appropriate authority[15], in the case of a school having
foundation governors[16], to the person[17] who appoints them and, if different, to
the appropriate appointing authority[18]; and in such circumstances as may be
prescribed, to such other persons, if any, as may be prescribed[19].

The appropriate authority must:

(1)   make a copy of any report and summary sent to it[20] available for
      inspection by members of the public at such times and at such place as
      may be reasonable[21];

(2)   provide a copy of the report and summary, free of charge or in
      prescribed cases on payment of such fee as it thinks fit, not exceeding
      the cost of supply, to any person who asks for one[22]; and

(3)   take such steps as are reasonably practicable to secure that every
      registered[23] parent[24] of a registered pupil[25] at the school receives a copy
      of the summary within such period following receipt of the report by the
      authority as may be prescribed[26].

If the inspection was a regular inspection[27] or was carried out by a member of
the Inspectorate[28], and the school provides full-time education suitable to the
requirements of pupils over compulsory school age[29], the person making the
report must send a copy (together with a copy of the summary, if there is one) to
the Welsh Ministers[30].

1 Ie an inspection under the Education Act 2005 s 28: see PARA 1182.
2 As to the meaning of 'maintained school' see PARA 1191 note 4. As to the application of the
   Education Act 2005 Pt 1 (ss 1–63) to pupil referral units in Wales see the Education (Pupil

Referral Units) (Application of Enactments) (Wales) Regulations 2007, SI 2007/1069, reg 3, Sch 1 Pt 1 para 11. As to pupil referral units see PARA 427 et seq. As to the meaning of 'Wales' see PARA 7 note 3.

3   As to the service of notices and documents see the Education Act 1996 s 572 (definition applied by the Education Act 2005 s 122(2), (3)); and PARA 76.

4   In the Education Act 2005 Pt 1 Ch 4 (ss 32–43), 'appropriate authority', in relation to a maintained school, means the school's governing body or, if the school does not have a delegated budget, the local authority: s 43 (definition amended by SI 2010/1158). As to the governing bodies of maintained schools in Wales see PARA 195. As to the meaning of 'delegated budget' see PARA 323 (definition applied by the Education Act 2005 s 63(1)). As to the meaning of 'local authority' see PARA 25 (definition applied by s 122(2), (3)).

5   Education Act 2005 s 38(1).

6   Education Act 2005 s 38(2)(a). As to the meaning of 'member of the Inspectorate' see PARA 1191 note 3.

7   Ie required by the Education Act 2005 s 35: see PARA 1193.

8   As to the meaning of 'special measures are required to be taken in relation to a school' see PARA 1167 note 3.

9   Education Act 2005 s 38(2)(b). As to the meaning of 'a school requires significant improvement' see PARA 1167 note 4.

10 Education Act 2005 s 38(2).

11 As to Her Majesty's Chief Inspector of Education and Training in Wales see PARA 1148.

12 Education Act 2005 s 38(3)(a).

13 As to the meaning of 'head teacher' see PARA 86 note 4 (definition applied by the Education Act 2005 s 122(2), (3)).

14 Education Act 2005 s 38(3)(b).

15 Education Act 2005 s 38(3)(c) (amended by SI 2010/1158).

16 As to schools having foundation governors see PARA 108.

17 As to the meaning of 'person' see PARA 7 note 6.

18 Education Act 2005 s 38(3)(d). In Pt 1 Ch 4 (ss 32–43), 'appropriate appointing authority', in relation to a voluntary aided school, means the appropriate diocesan authority, if it is a Church in Wales school, a Church of England school or Roman Catholic Church school, or, in any other case, the person who appoints the foundation governor: s 43. As to the meanings of 'the appropriate diocesan authority', 'Church in Wales school', 'Church of England school', and 'Roman Catholic Church school' see PARA 146 note 12 (definitions applied by s 63(1)). As to the meaning of references to a voluntary school see PARA 106.

19 Education Act 2005 s 38(3)(e). 'Prescribed' means prescribed by regulations; and 'regulations' means regulations made by the Welsh Ministers under Pt 1 Ch 4 (ss 32–43): see s 43. As to the Welsh Ministers see PARA 59. The functions under the Education Act 2005 s 38 were originally vested in the National Assembly for Wales and are now exercisable by the Welsh Ministers by virtue of the Government of Wales Act 2006 s 162(1), Sch 11 paras 30, 32. At the date at which this volume states the law no regulations had been made for these purposes.

20 Ie under the Education Act 2005 s 38(1) or s 38(2): see the text to notes 1–10.

21 Education Act 2005 s 38(4)(a).

22 Education Act 2005 s 38(4)(b). An appropriate authority may require payment of a fee (not exceeding the cost of supply) where it provides under s 38(4)(b) a copy of a report to any person who is not otherwise entitled to receive a copy of that report and whose home or principal office is located outside a radius of 4.828032 kilometres (three miles) of the school; or a copy of a summary to any person to whom they have previously provided a copy of that summary: see the Education (School Inspection) (Wales) Regulations 2006, SI 2006/1714, reg 12(1). As to the application of Pt 2 (regs 4–12) to pupil referral units in Wales see the Education (Pupil Referral Units) (Application of Enactments) (Wales) Regulations 2007, SI 2007/1069, reg 3, Sch 1 Pt 2 para 13.

23 As to the meaning of 'registered' see PARA 437 (definition applied by the Education Act 2005 s 122(2), (3)).

24 As to the meaning of 'parent' see PARA 7 note 6 (definition applied by the Education Act 2005 s 122(2), (3)).

25 As to the meaning of 'registered pupil' see PARA 437 (definition applied by the Education Act 2005 s 122(2), (3)).

26 Education Act 2005 s 38(4)(c). For the purposes of s 38(4)(c), there is prescribed, as the period within which the appropriate authority must take such steps as are reasonably practicable to secure that every registered parent of a registered pupil at the school receives a copy of the summary of the report of an inspection, the period of ten working days following receipt of the report: Education (School Inspection) (Wales) Regulations 2006, SI 2006/1714, reg 9(3).

27 Ie an inspection under the Education Act 2005 s 28: see PARA 1182.
28 Education Act 2005 s 38(5)(a).
29 Education Act 2005 s 38(5)(b). As to the meaning of 'compulsory school age' see PARA 19.
30 Education Act 2005 s 38(6) (amended by SI 2005/3238).

1197. Statement by appropriate authority in relation to maintained schools.
Where there is sent to the appropriate authority[1] for a maintained school[2] either
a report of a regular inspection[3] of the school[4], or a report of an inspection of the
school by a member of the Inspectorate[5] in which that person is required[6] to
state that he is of the opinion that special measures are required to be taken in
relation to the school[7] or that the school requires significant improvement[8], the
appropriate authority must prepare a written[9] statement of the action which it
proposes to take in the light of the report and the period within which it
proposes to take it[10]. It is the duty of the appropriate authority to prepare the
statement within the period allowed, that is:

(1)   such period as may be prescribed[11]; or
(2)   if:
  (a)   the report states that the person making it is of the opinion that
        special measures are required to be taken in relation to the school
        or that the school requires significant improvement[12];
  (b)   either that person is a member of the Inspectorate or the report
        states that Her Majesty's Chief Inspector of Education and
        Training in Wales[13] agrees with his opinion[14]; and
  (c)   the Welsh Ministers are of the opinion that the urgency of the case
        requires a shorter period[15], such shorter period as the Welsh
        Ministers may direct[16].

However, this does not relieve the appropriate authority of any duty to prepare a
statement which has not been performed within that period[17].

Where such a statement has been prepared by the appropriate authority, that
authority must, before the end of the prescribed period[18], send copies of it to the
Chief Inspector[19], to whichever of the governing body[20] and the local authority[21]
is not the appropriate authority[22] and, in such circumstances as may be
prescribed, to such other persons[23], if any, as may be prescribed[24].

If in the case of a maintained school, the statement is prepared in response to
a report of an inspection of the school in which the person who made the report
states that in his opinion special measures are required to be taken in relation to
the school or that the school requires significant improvement[25], and either that
person is a member of the Inspectorate or the report states that the Chief
Inspector agrees with his opinion[26], the appropriate authority must, before the
end of the prescribed period[27], send a copy of the statement to the Welsh
Ministers[28]. The appropriate authority must also send a copy of the statement in
the case of a school having foundation governors[29], to the person who appoints
them and, if different, to the appropriate appointing authority[30].

The appropriate authority must:

(i)   make any statement prepared by it available for inspection by members
      of the public, at such times and at such place as may be reasonable[31];
(ii) provide a copy of the statement, free of charge or in prescribed cases on
      payment of such fee as it thinks fit, not exceeding the cost of supply, to
      any person who asks for one[32]; and
(iii) take such steps as are reasonably practicable to secure that every
      registered[33] parent[34] of a registered pupil[35] at the school receives a copy
      of the statement as soon as is reasonably practicable[36].

Where the governing body of a school has prepared such a statement, it must in the governors' report[37] state the extent to which the proposals set out in the statement (or if there is more than one, the most recent statement) have been carried into effect[38].

1 As to the meaning of 'appropriate authority' see PARA 1196 note 4.
2 As to the meaning of 'maintained school' see PARA 1191 note 4. As to the application of the Education Act 2005 Pt 1 (ss 1–63) to pupil referral units in Wales see the Education (Pupil Referral Units) (Application of Enactments) (Wales) Regulations 2007, SI 2007/1069, reg 3, Sch 1 Pt 1 para 11. As to pupil referral units see PARA 427 et seq. As to the meaning of 'Wales' see PARA 7 note 3.
3 Ie an inspection under the Education Act 2005 s 28: see PARA 1182.
4 Education Act 2005 s 39(1)(a).
5 As to the meaning of 'member of the Inspectorate' see PARA 1191 note 3.
6 Ie required by the Education Act 2005 s 35(1)(b): see PARA 1193.
7 As to the meaning of 'special measures are required to be taken in relation to a school' see PARA 1167 note 3.
8 Education Act 2005 s 39(1)(b). As to the meaning of 'a school requires significant improvement' see PARA 1167 note 4.
9 As to the meaning of 'written' see PARA 76 note 8.
10 Education Act 2005 s 39(1).
11 Education Act 2005 s 39(2)(a). 'Prescribed' means prescribed by regulations; and 'regulations' means regulations made by the Welsh Ministers under Pt 1 Ch 4 (ss 32–43): see s 43. As to the Welsh Ministers see PARA 59. The functions under the Education Act 2005 s 39 were originally vested in the National Assembly for Wales and are now exercisable by the Welsh Ministers by virtue of the Government of Wales Act 2006 s 162(1), Sch 11 paras 30, 32.
  For the purposes of the Education Act 2005 s 39(2)(a) there is prescribed, as the period within which a statement is to be prepared, the period of 20 working days from the date on which the appropriate authority received the report of the inspection: see the Education (School Inspection) (Wales) Regulations 2006, SI 2006/1714, reg 10(1) (amended by SI 2014/1212). As to the application of Pt 2 (regs 4–12) to pupil referral units in Wales see the Education (Pupil Referral Units) (Application of Enactments) (Wales) Regulations 2007, SI 2007/1069, reg 3, Sch 1 Pt 2 para 13.
12 Education Act 2005 s 39(2)(b)(i).
13 As to Her Majesty's Chief Inspector of Education, Children's Services and Skills see PARA 1133.
14 Education Act 2005 s 39(2)(b)(ii).
15 Education Act 2005 s 39(2)(b)(iii).
16 Education Act 2005 s 39(2)(b). As to directions see s 120(4); and PARA 75.
17 Education Act 2005 s 39(2).
18 There is prescribed, as the period within which the appropriate authority is to distribute, in accordance with the Education Act 2005 s 39(3), (5) (see the text to notes 25–28), copies of a statement prepared by it:
  (1) where the person making the report of the inspection does not state that he or she is of the opinion that special measures are required to be taken in relation to the school or that the school requires significant improvement, five working days from the date on which the appropriate authority completed the preparation of the statement (Education (School Inspection) (Wales) Regulations 2006, SI 2006/1714, reg 10(2)(a));
  (2) where (in the case of a report by a registered inspector) the registered inspector states that he or she is of that opinion but it is also stated that the Chief Inspector disagrees with that opinion, five working days from the date on which the appropriate authority completed the preparation of the statement (reg 10(2)(b)); and
  (3) where the person making the report states that he or she is of the opinion that special measures are required to be taken in relation to the school or that the school requires significant improvement, and either that person is a member of the Inspectorate or the report states that the Chief Inspector agrees with that opinion, two days from the date on which the appropriate authority completed the preparation of the statement (reg 10(2)(c)).
  For the purposes of calculating the period prescribed by head (3) above no account is to be taken of Saturday, Sunday, Good Friday and Christmas Day or any day which is a bank holiday: reg 10(4).
19 Education Act 2005 s 39(3)(a). Where the report in question is a report of an inspection of a school under s 28 (duty to arrange regular inspections of certain schools: see PARA 1182),

s 39(3)(a) does not require a copy of the statement to be sent to the Chief Inspector unless the report states that the person making it is of the opinion that special measures are required to be taken in relation to the school (s 39(4)(a)) or that the school requires significant improvement (s 39(4)(b)).

20 As to the governing bodies of maintained schools in Wales see PARA 195.

21 As to the meaning of 'local authority' see PARA 25 (definition applied by the Education Act 2005 s 122(2), (3)).

22 Education Act 2005 s 39(3)(b) (amended by SI 2010/1158).

23 As to the meaning of 'person' see PARA 7 note 6.

24 Education Act 2005 s 39(3)(c). For these purposes, the appropriate authority must send copies of the statement to the following (in addition to the persons mentioned in, as the case may be, s 39(3)–(6)):

    (1)   in all cases, to all persons who are employed at the school and who have requested a copy (see the Education (School Inspection) (Wales) Regulations 2006, SI 2006/1714, reg 10(3)(a)); and

    (2)   in the case of a secondary school, to the Welsh Ministers (if they are not otherwise entitled to a copy) (reg 10(3)(b)).

As to the meaning of 'secondary school' see PARA 91 (definition applied by the Education Act 2005 s 122(2), (3)).

25 Education Act 2005 s 39(5)(a).

26 Education Act 2005 s 39(5)(b).

27 See note 18.

28 Education Act 2005 s 39(5).

29 As to schools having foundation governors see PARA 108.

30 Education Act 2005 s 39(6). As to the meaning of 'appropriate appointing authority' see PARA 1196 note 18.

31 Education Act 2005 s 39(7)(a).

32 Education Act 2005 s 39(7)(b). An appropriate authority may require payment of a fee (not exceeding the cost of supply) where it provides under s 39(7)(b), a copy of a statement to any person who is not otherwise entitled to receive a copy of that statement and whose home or principal office is located outside a radius of 4.828032 kilometres (three miles) of the school or to whom they have previously provided a copy of that statement: see the Education (School Inspection) (Wales) Regulations 2006, SI 2006/1714, reg 12(1)(b).

33 As to the meaning of 'registered' see PARA 437 (definition applied by the Education Act 2005 s 122(2), (3)).

34 As to the meaning of 'parent' see PARA 7 note 6 (definition applied by the Education Act 2005 s 122(2), (3)).

35 As to the meaning of 'registered pupil' see PARA 437 (definition applied by the Education Act 2005 s 122(2), (3)).

36 Education Act 2005 s 39(7)(c). The duty under s 39(7)(c) must be taken to be satisfied by the appropriate authority if it:

    (1)   takes such steps as are reasonably practicable to secure that every registered parent of a registered pupil at the school receives, as soon as is reasonably practicable, a copy of a document prepared by it which: (a) summarises the statement (s 39(8)(a)(i)); and (b) contains a statement of the right to request a copy of it under s 39(8)(b) (see head (2) below) (s 39(8)(a)(ii)); and

    (2)   provides a copy of the statement to every registered parent of a registered pupil at the school who asks for one (s 39(8)(b)).

37 Ie under the Education Act 2002 s 30: see PARA 218.

38 Education Act 2005 s 39(9).

1198. Statement by local authority. In circumstances where:

    (1)   in a report of an inspection[1] of a maintained school[2], the governing body[3] of which has a delegated budget[4], the person who made the report stated that in his opinion special measures were required to be taken in relation to the school[5] or that the school required significant improvement[6]; and

    (2)   either that person was a member of the Inspectorate[7] or the report stated that Her Majesty's Chief Inspector of Education and Training in Wales[8] agreed with his opinion[9]; and

(3)   either the local authority[10] has received a copy of a statement[11] in response to the report, or the prescribed period[12] has expired[13], the local authority must:

     (a)   prepare a written[14] statement of any action it proposes to take in the light of the report, and the period within which it proposes to take such action, or, if it does not propose to take any such action, of its reasons for not doing so[15]; and

     (b)   send a copy of the statement prepared under head (a) above, together with its comments on any statement[16] of which it has received a copy, to the Welsh Ministers and the Chief Inspector and, in the case of a voluntary aided school[17] to the person[18] who appoints the foundation governors[19], and, if different, to the appropriate appointing authority[20].

It is the duty of the local authority to prepare the statement within the period allowed, that is such period as may be prescribed[21], or if the Welsh Ministers are of the opinion that the urgency of the case requires a shorter period, such shorter period as they may direct[22]. However, this does not relieve the local authority of any duty to prepare a statement which has not been performed within that period[23].

1   Ie an inspection under the Education Act 2005 s 28: see PARA 1182.
2   As to the meaning of 'maintained school' see PARA 1191 note 4. As to the application of the Education Act 2005 Pt 1 (ss 1–63) to pupil referral units in Wales see the Education (Pupil Referral Units) (Application of Enactments) (Wales) Regulations 2007, SI 2007/1069, reg 3, Sch 1 Pt 1 para 11. As to pupil referral units see PARA 427 et seq. As to the meaning of 'Wales' see PARA 7 note 3.
3   As to the governing bodies of maintained schools in Wales see PARA 195.
4   As to the meaning of 'delegated budget' see PARA 323 (definition applied by the Education Act 2005 s 63(1)).
5   As to the meaning of 'special measures are required to be taken in relation to a school' see PARA 1167 note 3.
6   Education Act 2005 s 40(1)(a). As to the meaning of 'a school requires significant improvement' see PARA 1167 note 4.
7   As to the meaning of 'member of the Inspectorate' see PARA 1191 note 3.
8   As to Her Majesty's Chief Inspector of Education and Training in Wales see PARA 1148.
9   Education Act 2005 s 40(1)(b).
10   As to the meaning of 'local authority' see PARA 25 (definition applied by the Education Act 2005 s 122(2), (3)).
11   Ie prepared under the Education Act 2005 s 39: see PARA 1197.
12   Ie the period prescribed for the purposes of the Education Act 2005 s 40(3): see note 21. 'Prescribed' means prescribed by regulations; and 'regulations' means regulations made by the Welsh Ministers under Pt 1 Ch 4 (ss 32–43): see s 43. As to the Welsh Ministers see PARA 59. The functions under the Education Act 2005 s 40 in relation to Wales were originally vested in the National Assembly for Wales and are now exercisable by the Welsh Ministers by virtue of the Government of Wales Act 2006 s 162(1), Sch 11 paras 30, 32.
13   Education Act 2005 s 40(1)(c) (amended by SI 2010/1158).
14   As to the meaning of 'written' see PARA 76 note 8.
15   Education Act 2005 s 40(2)(a) (s 40(2) amended by SI 2010/1158).
16   Ie prepared under the Education Act 2005 s 39: see PARA 1197.
17   As to the meaning of references to a voluntary school see PARA 106.
18   As to the meaning of 'person' see PARA 7 note 6.
19   As to foundation governors see PARA 108.
20   Education Act 2005 s 40(2)(b) (as amended: see note 15). As to the meaning of 'appropriate appointing authority' see PARA 1196 note 18.
21   Education Act 2005 s 40(3)(a). For the purposes of s 40(3)(a), the period prescribed is the period of ten days from the date on which the local authority receives a copy of the statement in respect of the maintained school in question or 12 days from the expiry of the period prescribed by the Education (School Inspection) (Wales) Regulations 2006, SI 2006/1714, reg 10(2) (see PARA 1197 note 18), whichever first occurs: see reg 11(1) (amended by SI 2010/1142). For the

purposes of calculating this period no account is to be taken of Saturday, Sunday, Good Friday and Christmas Day or any day which is a bank holiday: Education (School Inspection) (Wales) Regulations 2006, SI 2006/1714, reg 11(2). As to the application of Pt 2 (regs 4–12) to pupil referral units in Wales see the Education (Pupil Referral Units) (Application of Enactments) (Wales) Regulations 2007, SI 2007/1069, reg 3, Sch 1 Pt 2 para 13.

22 Education Act 2005 s 40(3)(b). As to directions see s 120(4); and PARA 75.
23 Education Act 2005 s 40(3) (amended by SI 2010/1158).

1199. Destination of reports of inspections of a school which is not a maintained school. In the case of a report of a regular inspection[1] of a school[2] which is other than a maintained school[3], the person making the report must without delay:

(1) send[4] a copy of the report together with the summary of it to the proprietor[5] of the school, and (unless the person making it is a member of the Inspectorate[6]) to Her Majesty's Chief Inspector of Education and Training in Wales[7]; and

(2) if the report states that the person making it is of the opinion that special measures are required to be taken in relation to the school[8] or that the school required significant improvement[9], and either that person is a member of the Inspectorate or the report states that the Chief Inspector agrees with his opinion, send a copy of the report and summary to the Welsh Ministers[10].

In a case where a report of an inspection of a school other than a maintained school is made by a member of the Inspectorate[11], and he is required[12] to state in the report that he is of the opinion that special measures are required to be taken in relation to the school or that the school requires significant improvement[13], the member of the Inspectorate must send a copy of the report together with the summary of it to the proprietor of the school and to the Welsh Ministers[14].

In the case of a special school[15] which is not a community special school[16], the proprietor of the school must without delay send a copy of any report and summary sent to him[17] to any local authority[18] that is paying fees in respect of the attendance of a registered pupil[19] at the school[20].

The proprietor of the school must:

(a) make any report and summary sent to him[21] available for inspection by members of the public at such times and at such place as may be reasonable[22];

(b) provide a copy of the report and summary, free of charge or in prescribed[23] cases on payment of such fee as it thinks fit, not exceeding the cost of supply, to any person who asks for one[24]; and

(c) take such steps as are reasonably practicable to secure that every registered[25] parent[26] of a registered pupil at the school receives a copy of the summary within such period following receipt of the report by the authority as may be prescribed[27].

1 Ie an inspection under the Education Act 2005 s 28: see PARA 1182.
2 As to the meaning of 'school' see PARA 91 (definition applied by the Education Act 2005 s 122(2), (3)).
3 As to the meaning of 'maintained school' see PARA 1191 note 4.
4 As to the service of notices and documents see the Education Act 1996 s 572 (applied by the Education Act 2005 s 122(2), (3)); and PARA 76.
5 As to the meaning of 'proprietor' see PARA 51 note 4 (definition applied by the Education Act 2005 s 122(2), (3)).
6 As to the meaning of 'member of the Inspectorate' see PARA 1191 note 3.
7 Education Act 2005 s 41(1)(a). As to Her Majesty's Chief Inspector of Education and Training in Wales see PARA 1148. As to the application of Pt 1 (ss 1–63) to pupil referral units in Wales

see the Education (Pupil Referral Units) (Application of Enactments) (Wales) Regulations 2007, SI 2007/1069, reg 3, Sch 1 Pt 1 para 11. As to pupil referral units see PARA 427 et seq. As to the meaning of 'Wales' see PARA 7 note 3.

8   As to the meaning of 'special measures are required to be taken in relation to a school' see PARA 1167 note 3.

9   As to the meaning of 'a school requires significant improvement' see PARA 1167 note 4.

10 Education Act 2005 s 41(1)(b). As to the Welsh Ministers see PARA 59. The functions under the Education Act 2005 s 41 were originally vested in the National Assembly for Wales and are now exercisable by the Welsh Ministers by virtue of the Government of Wales Act 2006 s 162(1), Sch 11 paras 30, 32.

11 Education Act 2005 s 41(2)(a).

12 Ie required by the Education Act 2005 s 35(1)(b): see PARA 1193.

13 Education Act 2005 s 41(2)(b).

14 Education Act 2005 s 41(2).

15 As to the meaning of 'special school' see PARA 1041 (definition applied by the Education Act 2005 s 122(2), (3)).

16 As to the meaning of references to a community special school see PARA 106.

17 Ie under the Education Act 2005 s 41(1) or (2): see the text to notes 1–14.

18 As to the meaning of 'local authority' see PARA 25 (definition applied by the Education Act 2005 s 122(2), (3)).

19 As to the meaning of 'registered pupil' see PARA 437 (definition applied by the Education Act 2005 s 122(2), (3)).

20 Education Act 2005 s 41(3) (amended by SI 2010/1158; and the School Standards and Organisation (Wales) Act 2013 Sch 5 para 22(4)).

21 Ie under the Education Act 2005 s 41(1) or (2): see the text to notes 1–14.

22 Education Act 2005 s 41(4)(a).

23 'Prescribed' means prescribed by regulations; and 'regulations' means regulations made by the Welsh Ministers under the Education Act 2005 Pt 1 Ch 4 (ss 32–43): see s 43. A proprietor of a non-maintained special school may require payment of a fee (not exceeding the cost of supply) where he provides under s 41(4)(b):

(1)   a copy of a report to any person who is not otherwise entitled to receive a copy of that report and whose home or principal office is located outside a radius of 4.828032 kilometres (three miles) of the school; or

(2)   a copy of a summary to any person to whom it has previously provided a copy of that summary: see the Education (School Inspection) (Wales) Regulations 2006, SI 2006/1714, reg 12(1)(a).

As to the meaning of 'person' see PARA 7 note 6. As to the application of Pt 2 (regs 4–12) to pupil referral units in Wales see the Education (Pupil Referral Units) (Application of Enactments) (Wales) Regulations 2007, SI 2007/1069, reg 3, Sch 1 Pt 2 para 13.

24 Education Act 2005 s 41(4)(b).

25 As to the meaning of 'registered' see PARA 437 (definition applied by the Education Act 2005 s 122(2), (3)).

26 As to the meaning of 'parent' see PARA 7 note 6 (definition applied by the Education Act 2005 s 122(2), (3)).

27 Education Act 2005 s 41(4)(c). The prescribed period is ten working days following receipt of the report: see the Education (School Inspection) (Wales) Regulations 2006, SI 2006/1714, reg 9(3).

1200.   Statement to be prepared by proprietor of a school which is not a maintained school.   Where there is sent to the proprietor[1] of a school[2] other than a maintained school[3] either:

(1)   a report of a regular inspection[4] of the school[5]; or

(2)   a report of an inspection of the school made by a member of the Inspectorate[6] in which that person is required[7] to state that he is of the opinion that special measures are required to be taken in relation to the school[8] or that the school required significant improvement[9],

the proprietor of the school must prepare a written[10] statement of the action which he proposes to take in the light of the report and the period within which he proposes to take it[11]. It is the duty of the proprietor to prepare the statement within the period allowed, that is:

(a)   such period as may be prescribed[12]; or

(b)   if the report states that the person making it is of the opinion that special measures are required to be taken in relation to the school or that the school required significant improvement, and either that person is a member of the Inspectorate or the report states that Her Majesty's Chief Inspector of Education and Training in Wales[13] agrees with his opinion, and the Welsh Ministers are of the opinion that the urgency of the case requires a shorter period, such shorter period as they may direct[14].

However, this does not relieve the proprietor of the school of any duty to prepare a statement which has not been performed within that period[15].

Where such a statement has been prepared by the proprietor of the school, he must, before the end of the prescribed period[16], send copies of it to the Chief Inspector[17], the Welsh Ministers[18] and, in such circumstances as may be prescribed, to such other persons, if any, as may be prescribed[19]. In the case of a special school[20] which is not a community special school[21], the proprietor of the school must, before the end of the prescribed period[22], send a copy of any such statement prepared by him to any local authority[23], if the authority is paying fees in respect of the attendance of a registered pupil[24] at the school[25].

The proprietor of the school must:

(i)   make any such statement prepared by him available for inspection by members of the public, at such times and at such place as may be reasonable[26];

(ii) provide a copy of the statement, free of charge or in prescribed cases on payment of such fee as he thinks fit, not exceeding the cost of supply, to any person who asks for one[27]; and

(iii) take such steps as are reasonably practicable to secure that every registered[28] parent[29] of a registered pupil at the school receives a copy of the statement as soon as is reasonably practicable[30].

1   As to the meaning of 'proprietor' see PARA 51 note 4 (definition applied by the Education Act 2005 s 122(2), (3)).
2   As to the meaning of 'school' see PARA 91 (definition applied by the Education Act 2005 s 122(2), (3)).
3   As to the meaning of 'maintained school' see PARA 1191 note 4.
4   Ie an inspection under the Education Act 2005 s 28: see PARA 1182.
5   Education Act 2005 s 42(1)(a).
6   As to the meaning of 'member of the Inspectorate' see PARA 1191 note 3.
7   Ie required by the Education Act 2005 s 35(1)(b): see PARA 1193.
8   As to the meaning of 'special measures are required to be taken in relation to a school' see PARA 1167 note 3.
9   Education Act 2005 s 42(1)(b). As to the meaning of 'a school requires significant improvement' see PARA 1167 note 4.
10 As to the meaning of 'written' see PARA 76 note 8.
11 Education Act 2005 s 42(1). As to the application of Pt 1 (ss 1–63) to pupil referral units in Wales see the Education (Pupil Referral Units) (Application of Enactments) (Wales) Regulations 2007, SI 2007/1069, reg 3, Sch 1 Pt 1 para 11. As to pupil referral units see PARA 427 et seq. As to the meaning of 'Wales' see PARA 7 note 3.
12 Education Act 2005 s 42(2)(a). 'Prescribed' means prescribed by regulations; and 'regulations' means regulations made by the Welsh Ministers under Pt 1 Ch 4 (ss 32–43): see s 43. As to the Welsh Ministers see PARA 59. The functions under the Education Act 2005 s 42 were originally vested in the National Assembly for Wales and are now exercisable by the Welsh Ministers by virtue of the Government of Wales Act 2006 s 162(1), Sch 11 paras 30, 32.
     For the purposes of the Education Act 2005 s 42(2)(a) the prescribed period is 20 working days from the date on which the proprietor of the school received the report of the inspection: see the Education (School Inspection) (Wales) Regulations 2006, SI 2006/1714, reg 10(1) (amended by SI 2014/1212). As to the application of Pt 2 (regs 4–12) to pupil referral units in

Wales see the Education (Pupil Referral Units) (Application of Enactments) (Wales) Regulations 2007, SI 2007/1069, reg 3, Sch 1 Pt 2 para 13.

13 As to Her Majesty's Chief Inspector of Education and Training in Wales see PARA 1148.

14 Education Act 2005 s 42(2)(b). As to directions see s 120(4); and PARA 75.

15 Education Act 2005 s 42(2).

16 For the purposes of the Education Act 2005 s 42(3) and (4) (see the text to notes 20–25) the prescribed period is:

    (1)   where the person making the report of the inspection does not state that he or she is of the opinion that special measures are required to be taken in relation to the school or that the school requires significant improvement, five working days from the date on which the proprietor completed the preparation of the statement (see the Education (School Inspection) (Wales) Regulations 2006, SI 2006/1714, reg 10(2)(a));

    (2)   where (in the case of a report by a registered inspector) the registered inspector states that he or she is of that opinion but it is also stated that the Chief Inspector disagrees with that opinion, five working days from the date on which the proprietor completed the preparation of the statement (reg 10(2)(b)); and

    (3)   where the person making the report states that he or she is of the opinion that special measures are required to be taken in relation to the school or that the school requires significant improvement, and either that person is a member of the Inspectorate or the report states that the Chief Inspector agrees with that opinion, two days from the date on which the proprietor completed the preparation of the statement (reg 10(2)(c)).

For the purposes of calculating the period prescribed by reg 10(2)(c) no account is to be taken of Saturday, Sunday, Good Friday and Christmas Day or any day which is a bank holiday: reg 10(4).

17 Education Act 2005 s 42(3)(a).

18 Education Act 2005 s 42(3)(b).

19 Education Act 2005 s 42(3)(c). For these purposes, the proprietor must send copies of the statement to (in addition to the persons mentioned in, as the case may be, s 42(3) and (4) (see the text to notes 20–25)), in all cases, all persons who are employed at the school and who have requested a copy (see the Education (School Inspection) (Wales) Regulations 2006, SI 2006/1714, reg 10(3)(a)) and, in the case of a secondary school, to the Welsh Ministers if they are not otherwise entitled to a copy (reg 10(3)(b)). As to the meaning of 'secondary school' see PARA 91 (definition applied by the Education Act 2005 s 122(2), (3)).

20 As to the meaning of 'special school' see PARA 1041 (definition applied by the Education Act 2005 s 122(2), (3)).

21 As to the meaning of references to a community special school see PARA 106.

22 See note 16.

23 As to the meaning of 'local authority' see PARA 25 (definition applied by the Education Act 2005 s 122(2), (3)).

24 As to the meaning of 'registered pupil' see PARA 437 (definition applied by the Education Act 2005 s 122(2), (3)).

25 Education Act 2005 s 42(4) (amended by SI 2010/1158; and the School Standards and Organisation (Wales) Act 2013 Sch 5 para 22(5)).

26 Education Act 2005 s 42(5)(a).

27 Education Act 2005 s 42(5)(b). A proprietor of a non-maintained special school may require payment of a fee (not exceeding the cost of supply) where he provides under s 42(5)(b), a copy of a statement to any person who is not otherwise entitled to receive a copy of that statement and whose home or principal office is located outside a radius of 4.828032 kilometres (three miles) of the school or to whom he has previously provided a copy of that statement: see the Education (School Inspection) (Wales) Regulations 2006, SI 2006/1714, reg 12(1)(b). As to the meaning of 'person' see PARA 7 note 6.

28 As to the meaning of 'registered' see PARA 437 (definition applied by the Education Act 2005 s 122(2), (3)).

29 As to the meaning of 'parent' see PARA 7 note 6 (definition applied by the Education Act 2005 s 122(2), (3)).

30 Education Act 2005 s 42(5)(c). The duty under s 42(5)(c) is taken to be satisfied by the proprietor of the school if he:

    (1)   takes such steps as are reasonably practicable to secure that every registered parent of a registered pupil at the school receives, as soon as is reasonably practicable, a copy of a document prepared by him which summarises the statement and contains a statement of the right to request a copy of it under s 42(6)(b) (s 42(6)(a)); and

    (2)   provides a copy of the statement to every registered parent of a registered pupil at the school who asks for one (s 42(6)(b)).

C. OTHER INSPECTIONS

(A) *Inspection of Religious Education*

1201. Inspection of religious education. It is the duty of the governing body[1] of any voluntary or foundation school[2] in Wales[3], which has been designated by the Welsh Ministers[4] as having a religious character[5], to secure that denominational education[6] given to pupils[7], and the content of the school's collective worship[8], are inspected[9]. Such an inspection must be conducted by a person[10] chosen:

(1)   in the case of a voluntary controlled school, by the foundation governors[11] after consultation with any person prescribed[12] for these purposes in relation to the religion or religious denomination that is specified[13] in relation to the school[14]; and

(2)   by the governing body after consultation with any person so prescribed, in any other case[15]. The person chosen need not be a registered inspector[16]. Such inspections must be carried out at such intervals as may be prescribed[17].

It is the general duty of a person conducting an inspection of religious education:

(a)   to report on the quality of the denominational education provided by the school for any pupils to whom denominational education is given by the school[18]; and

(b)   to report on the content of the school's collective worship[19]; and any such person may report on the spiritual, moral, social and cultural development of pupils at the school[20].

A person conducting such an inspection may do so with the assistance of such other persons chosen by him as are in his opinion fit and proper persons for carrying out the inspection[21].

1   As to the governing bodies of maintained schools in Wales see PARA 195.
2   As to the meaning of references to a foundation or voluntary school see PARA 106.
3   As to the meaning of 'Wales' see PARA 7 note 3.
4   As to the Welsh Ministers see PARA 59.
5   Ie designated under the School Standards and Framework Act 1998 s 69(3): see PARA 914.
6   As to the meaning of 'denominational education' see PARA 1178 note 6.
7   As to the meaning of 'pupil' see PARA 20 note 4 (definition applied by the Education Act 2005 s 122(2), (3)).
8   'Collective worship' means collective worship required by the School Standards and Framework Act 1998 s 70 (see PARA 920): Education Act 2005 s 50(8).
9   Education Act 2005 s 50(1). As to the application of Pt 1 (ss 1–63) to pupil referral units in Wales see the Education (Pupil Referral Units) (Application of Enactments) (Wales) Regulations 2007, SI 2007/1069, reg 3, Sch 1 Pt 1 para 11. As to pupil referral units see PARA 427 et seq.
10 As to the meaning of 'person' see PARA 7 note 6.
11 As to foundation governors see PARA 108.
12 'Prescribed' means prescribed by regulations made by the Welsh Ministers: see the Education Act 2005 s 50(8). The functions under s 50 were originally vested in the National Assembly for Wales and are now exercisable by the Welsh Ministers by virtue of the Government of Wales Act 2006 s 162(1), Sch 11 paras 30, 32.
    For the purposes of the Education Act 2005 s 50(2)(a), (b) (see the text to note 15), there is prescribed, as a person who the foundation governors or governing body (as the case may be) of a Church in Wales school, Church of England school or Roman Catholic school must consult before choosing a person to conduct an inspection, the appropriate diocesan authority: Education (School Inspection) (Wales) Regulations 2006, SI 2006/1714, reg 15. As to the meanings of 'Church in Wales school', 'Church of England school', 'Roman Catholic school', and 'appropriate diocesan authority' see PARA 146 note 12 (definitions applied by the Education Act 2005 s 63(1)).

13 Ie specified under the School Standards and Framework Act 1998 s 69(4): see PARA 914.
14 Education Act 2005 s 50(2)(a).
15 Education Act 2005 s 50(2)(b). See also note 12.
16 Education Act 2005 s 50(3). A registered inspector is an inspector registered under s 25 (see
    PARA 1156): see s 50(3).
17 Education Act 2005 s 50(4). Where the governing body of a voluntary or foundation school are
    required by s 50(1) to secure that denominational education given to any pupil and the content
    of the school's collective worship are inspected they must secure that the inspection takes place:
    (1)   in the case of a school which had no previous inspection, within six years of the date on
            which pupils were first admitted to the school (Education (School Inspection) (Wales)
            Regulations 2006, SI 2006/1714, reg 14(a) (substituted by SI 2014/1212)); and
    (2)   in all other cases, at least once within a six year period beginning on 1 September 2014
            and ending on 31 August 2020 and at least once within every subsequent six year
            period beginning on the expiry of the previous six year period (Education (School
            Inspection) (Wales) Regulations 2006, SI 2006/1714, reg 14(b) (as so substituted)).
        As to the admission of pupils see PARA 224 et seq.
18 Education Act 2005 s 50(5)(a). As to combined reports see PARA 1206.
19 Education Act 2005 s 50(5)(b).
20 Education Act 2005 s 50(5).
21 Education Act 2005 s 50(6). Further provision is made by Sch 6 (see PARA 1202 et seq) with
    respect to inspections under s 50: s 50(7).

1202.   Inspectors' reports of denominational education and collective worship.   An inspection[1] of denominational education[2] and collective worship[3] must be carried out within such period as may be prescribed[4]. When an inspection has been completed, the inspector[5] must, before the end of the prescribed period[6], prepare in writing[7] a report of the inspection and a summary of the report[8]. The inspector must, without delay, send the report and summary to the governing body[9] for the school concerned[10]; and the governing body must:

(1)   make any such report and its accompanying summary available for inspection by members of the public, at such times and at such a place as may be reasonable[11];

(2)   provide a copy of the report and summary, free of charge or in prescribed cases on payment of such fee as it thinks fit, not exceeding the cost of supply, to any person who asks for one[12]; and

(3)   take such steps as are reasonably practicable to secure that every parent[13] of a registered pupil[14] at the school for whom the school provides denominational education, or who takes part in acts of collective worship[15], as the case may be, receives a copy of the summary as soon as is reasonably practicable[16].

1   Ie an inspection of a school under the Education Act 2005 s 50 (see PARA 1201): see Sch 6
    para 1.
2   As to the meaning of 'denominational education' see PARA 1178 note 6.
3   As to the meaning of 'collective worship' see PARA 1201 note 8.
4   Education Act 2005 Sch 6 para 2(1). 'Prescribed' means prescribed by regulations made by the
    Welsh Ministers: s 50(8). As to the Welsh Ministers see PARA 59. The functions under the
    Education Act 2005 Sch 6 were originally vested in the National Assembly for Wales and are
    now exercisable by the Welsh Ministers by virtue of the Government of Wales Act 2006
    s 162(1), Sch 11 paras 30, 32. The prescribed period is two weeks from the date on which the
    inspection began: see the Education (School Inspection) (Wales) Regulations 2006,
    SI 2006/1714, reg 16(2).
5   'Inspector' means the person conducting the inspection: Education Act 2005 Sch 6 para 1.
6   The prescribed period is 35 working days from the date on which the inspection was completed:
    see the Education (School Inspection) (Wales) Regulations 2006, SI 2006/1714, reg 16(3).
7   As to the meaning of 'writing' see PARA 76 note 8.
8   Education Act 2005 Sch 6 para 2(2). As to combined reports see PARA 1206.
9   As to the governing bodies of maintained schools in Wales see PARA 195.
10 Education Act 2005 Sch 6 para 2(3).

11 Education Act 2005 Sch 6 para 2(4)(a).
12 Education Act 2005 Sch 6 para 2(4)(b). A governing body may require payment of a fee (not exceeding the cost of supply) where it provides a copy of a report to any person who asks for one and whose home or principal office is located outside a radius of 4.828032 kilometres (three miles) of the school; or where it provides a copy of a summary to any person to whom it has previously provided a copy of that summary: see the Education (School Inspection) (Wales) Regulations 2006, SI 2006/1714, reg 17(1)(a). However, a governing body may not require payment of a fee if the document containing the copy of the report or summary, as the case may be, forms part of or is otherwise bound with a document containing a copy of the report or summary referred to in reg 9 (see PARA 1196 note 26) and a fee has been paid under reg 12 (see PARA 1196 note 22): reg 17(2). As to the meaning of 'person' see PARA 7 note 6.
13 As to the meaning of 'parent' see PARA 7 note 6 (definition applied by the Education Act 2005 s 122(2), (3)).
14 As to the meaning of 'registered pupil' see PARA 437 (definition applied by the Education Act 2005 s 122(2), (3)).
15 Ie the content of which falls to be inspected under the Education Act 2005 s 50: see PARA 1201.
16 Education Act 2005 Sch 6 para 2(4)(c).

1203. Action plans following inspection of religious education. The governing body[1] to whom an inspector[2] has reported[3] must, before the end of the prescribed[4] period, prepare a written[5] statement (referred to as 'the action plan') of the action which it proposes to take in the light of his report and the period within which it proposes to take it[6]. Where an action plan has been prepared by a governing body, it must, before the end of the prescribed period, send copies of it to the person[7] who appoints the school's foundation governors[8], to the local authority[9] and to such other persons, if any, in such circumstances, as may be prescribed[10]. The governing body must:

(1) make any action plan prepared by it available for inspection by members of the public, at such times and at such a place as may be reasonable[11];
(2) provide a copy of the plan, free of charge or in prescribed cases on payment of such fee as it thinks fit, not exceeding the cost of supply, to any person who asks for one[12]; and
(3) take such steps as are reasonably practicable to secure that every parent[13] of a registered pupil[14] at the school for whom the school provides denominational education[15], or who takes part in acts of collective worship[16], as the case may be, receives a copy of the plan as soon as is reasonably practicable[17].

Where the governing body of a school has prepared an action plan, it must include in its governors' report[18] a statement of the extent to which the proposals set out in the plan have been carried into effect[19].

1 As to the governing bodies of maintained schools in Wales see PARA 195.
2 'Inspector' means the person conducting the inspection: Education Act 2005 Sch 6 para 1.
3 Ie under the Education Act 2005 Sch 6: see PARA 1202.
4 'Prescribed' means prescribed by regulations made by the Welsh Ministers: Education Act 2005 s 50(8). As to the Welsh Ministers see PARA 59. The functions under the Education Act 2005 Sch 6 were originally vested in the National Assembly for Wales and are now exercisable by the Welsh Ministers by virtue of the Government of Wales Act 2006 s 162(1), Sch 11 paras 30, 32. The prescribed period is five working days from the date on which the governing body completed the preparation of the action plan: see the Education (School Inspection) (Wales) Regulations 2006, SI 2006/1714, reg 16(5).
5 As to the meaning of 'written' see PARA 76 note 8.
6 Education Act 2005 Sch 6 para 3(1).
7 As to the meaning of 'person' see PARA 7 note 6.
8 As to foundation governors see PARA 108.
9 As to the meaning of 'local authority' see PARA 25 (definition applied by the Education Act 2005 s 122(2), (3)).

10 Education Act 2005 Sch 6 para 3(2) (amended by SI 2010/1158). The prescribed persons are all persons who are either persons employed as teachers at the school or persons (other than pupils) who, although not so employed, participate in the school's collective worship (Education (School Inspection) (Wales) Regulations 2006, SI 2006/1714, reg 16(6)); and the prescribed circumstances are that they have requested copies of the action plan (see reg 16(7)). As to the meaning of 'pupil' see PARA 20 note 4 (definition applied by the Education Act 2005 s 122(2), (3)). As to the meaning of 'collective worship' see PARA 1201 note 8.
11 Education Act 2005 Sch 6 para 3(3)(a).
12 Education Act 2005 Sch 6 para 3(3)(b). A governing body may require payment of a fee (not exceeding the cost of supply) where it provides a copy of an action plan to any person who is not otherwise entitled to receive a copy of that action plan and whose home or principal office is located outside a radius of 4.828032 kilometres (three miles) of the school; or to whom they have previously provided a copy of that action plan: see the Education (School Inspection) (Wales) Regulations 2006, SI 2006/1714, reg 17(1)(b). However, a governing body may not require payment of a fee if the document containing the copy of the report or summary, as the case may be, forms part of or is otherwise bound with a document containing a copy of the report or summary referred to in reg 9 (see PARA 1196 note 26) and a fee has been paid under reg 12 (see PARA 1196 note 22): reg 17(2).
13 As to the meaning of 'parent' see PARA 7 note 6 (definition applied by the Education Act 2005 s 122(2), (3)).
14 As to the meaning of 'registered pupil' see PARA 437 (definition applied by the Education Act 2005 s 122(2), (3)).
15 As to the meaning of 'denominational education' see PARA 1178 note 6.
16 Ie the content of which falls to be inspected under the Education Act 2005 s 50: see PARA 1201.
17 Education Act 2005 Sch 6 para 3(3)(c).
18 Ie the governors' report under the Education Act 2002 s 30: see PARA 218.
19 Education Act 2005 Sch 6 para 3(4). Schedule 6 para 3(4) applies only in relation to the most recent action plan for the school in question: Sch 6 para 3(5).

(B) Inspection by Local Authority

1204. Provision of inspection services by local authorities. Any local authority[1] in Wales[2] may provide a school inspection service[3] for schools within its area[4]. Any school inspection service provided by a local authority may, in addition to providing for the inspection of schools which are maintained[5] by it, provide for the inspection of schools which are not maintained by it[6]. Any school inspection service provided by a local authority must be operated by the authority in such a way as can reasonably be expected to secure that the full cost of providing the service is recovered by way of charges made by the authority to those using the service[7]. The Welsh Ministers[8] may by regulations:

(1)   make provision as to the making of tenders[9] by local authorities[10];

(2)   make provision with respect to the accounts to be kept by local authorities in connection with any school inspection services provided by them[11]; and

(3)   make such incidental and supplemental provision with respect to school inspection services provided by local authorities as the Welsh Ministers consider appropriate[12].

1 As to the meaning of 'local authority' see PARA 25 (definition applied by the Education Act 2005 s 122(2), (3)).
2 As to the meaning of 'Wales' see PARA 7 note 3.
3 'School inspection service', in relation to any local authority in Wales, means a service providing for the inspection of schools under the Education Act 2005 s 28 (see PARA 1182), or s 50 (see PARA 1201) by officers of the authority: s 52(2) (amended by SI 2010/1158).
4 Education Act 2005 s 52(1) (amended by SI 2010/1158). As to the application of Pt 1 (ss 1–63) to pupil referral units in Wales see the Education (Pupil Referral Units) (Application of Enactments) (Wales) Regulations 2007, SI 2007/1069, reg 3, Sch 1 Pt 1 para 11. As to pupil referral units see PARA 427 et seq.
5 As to maintained schools see PARA 99 et seq.

6   Education Act 2005 s 52(3) (amended by SI 2010/1158)
7   Education Act 2005 s 52(4) (amended by SI 2010/1158).
8   As to the Welsh Ministers see PARA 59. The functions under the Education Act 2005 s 52 were
    originally vested in the National Assembly for Wales and are now exercisable by the Welsh
    Ministers by virtue of the Government of Wales Act 2006 s 162(1), Sch 11 paras 30, 32.
9   Ie as required by the Education Act 2005 Sch 4 para 2: see PARA 1183.
10 Education Act 2005 s 52(5)(a) (amended by SI 2010/1158). At the date at which this volume
    states the law no regulations had been made for this purpose.
11 Education Act 2005 s 52(5)(b) (amended by SI 2010/1158). As to the provision made see the
    Education (School Inspection) (Wales) Regulations 2006, SI 2006/1714, reg 18 (amended by
    SI 2010/1142).
12 Education Act 2005 s 52(5)(c) (amended by SI 2010/1158). At the date at which this volume
    states the law no regulations had been made for this purpose.

1205.   Power of local authority to inspect maintained school for specific purpose. Where, for the purpose of enabling it to exercise any of its education functions[1], a local authority[2] requires information about any matter in connection with a school[3] which is maintained by it[4], and it is not reasonably practicable for it to obtain the information in any other manner[5], it may cause an inspection of the school to be made by one or more of its officers for the purpose of obtaining the information[6].

An officer of a local authority inspecting a school under this power has at all reasonable times a right of entry to the premises[7] of the school[8].

1   As to the meaning of 'education functions' see PARA 25 (definition applied by the Education
    Act 2002 s 212(2), (3)).
2   As to the meaning of 'local authority' see PARA 25 (definition applied by the Education Act 2005
    s 122(2), (3)).
3   As to the meaning of 'school' see PARA 91 (definition applied by the Education Act 2005
    s 122(2), (3)).
4   Education Act 2005 s 51(1)(a) (amended by SI 2010/1158). As to maintained schools see PARA
    106.
5   Education Act 2005 s 51(1)(b).
6   Education Act 2005 s 51(1). As to the provision of inspection services by local authorities see
    PARA 1204.
7   As to the meaning of 'premises' see PARA 62 note 19 (definition applied by the Education
    Act 2005 s 122(2), (3)).
8   Education Act 2005 s 51(2) (amended by SI 2010/1158).

D.   REPORTS UNDER THE INSPECTION ENACTMENTS

1206.   Combined reports under the inspection enactments. Where, following inspections conducted under two or more inspection enactments[1] by one person[2] or two or more different persons, that person is, or those persons are, required to make a report under each of those enactments, nothing in any of those enactments is to be regarded as preventing him, or them, from[3]:

(1)   including those reports in a single document ('a combined report')[4]; and

(2)   to such extent as he considers, or they consider, appropriate, combining the substantive reports required by those enactments[5].

Where a combined report is made, any reference in the inspection enactments to the publication of a report, or to the giving, or making available, to any person of a copy of a report is to be read so far as necessary as a reference to the publication of the combined report, or to the giving or making available to that person of a copy of the combined report[6].

Her Majesty's Chief Inspector of Education and Training in Wales[7] may arrange for a combined report to be published in any manner he considers appropriate, but this does not limit any duty as to publication imposed by any of the inspection enactments[8].

1   As to the meaning of 'the inspection enactments' see PARA 1181 note 1.
2   As to the meaning of 'person' see PARA 7 note 6.
3   Education Act 2005 s 59(2). As to the application of Pt 1 (ss 1–63) to pupil referral units in Wales see the Education (Pupil Referral Units) (Application of Enactments) (Wales) Regulations 2007, SI 2007/1069, reg 3, Sch 1 Pt 1 para 11. As to pupil referral units see PARA 427 et seq. As to the meaning of 'Wales' see PARA 7 note 3.
4   Education Act 2005 s 59(2)(a).
5   Education Act 2005 s 59(2)(b).
6   Education Act 2005 s 59(3).
7   As to Her Majesty's Chief Inspector of Education and Training in Wales see PARA 1148.
8   Education Act 2005 s 59(4) (amended by the Education and Inspections Act 2006 s 157, Sch 14 paras 98, 105(1), (3)).

(iii) Intervention in Schools in England

A. SCHOOLS ELIGIBLE FOR INTERVENTION

1207. Performance standards and safety warning notice. A maintained school[1] is eligible for intervention[2] if:

(1)   the local authority[3] has given[4] the governing body[5] a warning notice[6];

(2)   the period beginning with the day on which the warning notice is given and ending with the fifteenth working day[7] following that day ('the initial period') has expired[8];

(3)   either the governing body made no representations[9] to Her Majesty's Chief Inspector of Education, Children's Services and Skills[10] against the warning notice during the initial period or the Chief Inspector has confirmed[11] the warning notice[12];

(4)   the governing body has failed to comply, or secure compliance, with the notice to the authority's satisfaction by the end of the compliance period[13]; and

(5)   the authority has given reasonable notice[14] in writing[15] to the governing body that it proposes to exercise its powers of intervention[16].

A local authority may give a warning notice to the governing body of a maintained school where the authority is satisfied[17]:

(a)   that the standards of performance of pupils[18] at the school are unacceptably low[19], and are likely to remain so unless the authority exercise its powers[20]; or

(b)   that there has been a serious breakdown in the way the school is managed or governed which is prejudicing, or likely to prejudice, such standards of performance[21]; or

(c)   that the safety of pupils or staff of the school is threatened (whether by a breakdown of discipline or otherwise)[22].

A 'warning notice' is a notice in writing by the local authority setting out[23]:

(i)   the matters on which the conclusion[24] is based[25];

(ii)   the action which it requires the governing body to take in order to remedy those matters[26];

(iii)   the initial period applying under head (2) above[27]; and

(iv)   the action which the local authority are minded to take[28] if the governing body fails to take the required action[29].

The warning notice must also inform the governing body of its right to make representations[30] during the initial period[31].

Before the end of the initial period, the governing body may make representations in writing to the Chief Inspector against the warning notice, and must send a copy of any such representations to the local authority[32]. The Chief Inspector must consider any representations so made to him and may, if he thinks fit, confirm the warning notice[33]. The Chief Inspector must give notice in writing of his decision whether or not to confirm the warning notice to the local authority, the governing body and such other persons as the Secretary of State may require[34].

1 In the Education and Inspections Act 2006 Pt 4 (ss 59–73), 'maintained school' means any of the following schools in England: a community, foundation or voluntary school, a community or foundation special school, or a maintained nursery school: s 59(1). As to the meaning of references to a community, foundation or voluntary school or a community or foundation special school see PARA 106. As to the meaning of 'maintained nursery school' see PARA 99 note 4 (definition applied by the Education and Inspections Act 2006 s 187(2), (3)). As to the meaning of 'England' see PARA 7 note 3.

2 In the Education and Inspections Act 2006 Pt 4 (ss 59–73), references to a school being 'eligible for intervention' are to be read in accordance with: s 60, s 60A (teachers' pay and conditions warning notice: see PARA 1208), s 61 (school requiring significant improvement: see PARA 1209), and s 62 (school requiring special measures: see PARA 1210): s 59(2) (amended by the Apprenticeships, Skills, Children and Learning Act 2009 s 203, Sch 13 paras 1, 2).

3 As to the meaning of 'local authority' see PARA 25 (definition applied by the Education and Inspections Act 2006 s 187(2), (3)).

4 Ie in accordance with the Education and Inspections Act 2006 s 60(2): see the text to notes 17–22. As to the service of notices and documents see the Education Act 1996 s 572 (applied by the Education and Inspections Act 2006 s 187(2), (3)); and PARA 76.

5 As to the governing bodies of maintained schools in England see PARA 150 et seq.

6 Education and Inspections Act 2006 s 60(1)(a) (amended by SI 2010/1158). As to the power of the Secretary of State to direct a local authority to consider giving a warning notice see s 69A; and PARA 1219. As to the Secretary of State see PARA 58.

7 In the Education and Inspections Act 2006 Pt 4 (ss 59–73), 'working day' means a day other than a Saturday, a Sunday, Christmas Day, Good Friday or a day which is a bank holiday under the Banking and Financial Dealings Act 1971 (see TIME vol 97 (2015) PARAS 320–321) in England: Education and Inspections Act 2006 ss 60(10), 73 (definition added by the Apprenticeships, Skills, Children and Learning Act 2009 s 203, Sch 13 paras 1, 11).

8 Education and Inspections Act 2006 s 60(1)(b).

9 Ie under the Education and Inspections Act 2006 s 60(7): see the text to note 32.

10 As to Her Majesty's Chief Inspector of Education, Children's Services and Skills see PARA 1133.

11 Ie under the Education and Inspections Act 2006 s 60(8): see the text to note 33.

12 Education and Inspections Act 2006 s 60(1)(c).

13 Education and Inspections Act 2006 s 60(1)(d). 'The compliance period', in relation to a warning notice, means, in a case where the governing body does not make representations under s 60(7) (see the text to note 32), the initial period mentioned in s 60(1)(b) (see head (2) in the text) and, in a case where the Chief Inspector confirms the warning notice under s 60(8) (see the text to note 33), the period beginning with the day on which he does so and ending with the fifteenth working day following that day: s 60(10)(a), (b).

14 Ie whether or not the notice is combined with a notice under the School Standards and Framework Act 1998 s 62(2A)(c): see PARA 511.

15 As to the meaning of 'writing' see PARA 76 note 8.

16 Education and Inspections Act 2006 s 60(1)(e). The powers referred to are those under any one or more of ss 63–66 (see PARA 1211 et seq): see s 60(1)(e).

17 Education and Inspections Act 2006 s 60(2) (amended by SI 2010/1158). The local authority must, at the same time as giving the governing body the warning notice, give a copy of the notice to each of the following persons the Chief Inspector, the head teacher of the school, in the case of a Church of England school or a Roman Catholic Church school, the appropriate diocesan authority and, in the case of a foundation or voluntary school, the person who appoints the foundation governors: Education and Inspections Act 2006 s 60(6) (amended by SI 2010/1158). As to the meaning of 'person' see PARA 7 note 6. As to the meaning of 'head teacher' see PARA 86 note 4 (definition applied by s 187(2), (3)). As to the meanings of 'Church of England school',

'Roman Catholic Church school' and 'appropriate diocesan authority' see PARA 146 note 12 (definitions applied by s 73). As to foundation governors see PARA 108.

18　As to the meaning of 'pupil' see PARA 20 note 4 (definition applied by the Education and Inspections Act 2006 s 187(2), (3)).

19　For these purposes, the standards of performance of pupils at a school are low if they are low by reference to any one or more of the following:

(1)　the standards that the pupils might in all the circumstances reasonably be expected to attain (Education and Inspections Act 2006 s 60(3)(a));

(2)　where relevant, the standards previously attained by them (s 60(3)(b)); or

(3)　the standards attained by pupils at comparable schools (s 60(3)(c)).

20　Education and Inspections Act 2006 s 60(2)(a). The powers referred to are those under Pt 4 (ss 59–73): see s 60(2)(a).

21　Education and Inspections Act 2006 s 60(2)(b).

22　Education and Inspections Act 2006 s 60(2)(c).

23　Education and Inspections Act 2006 s 60(4) (amended by SI 2010/1158).

24　Ie the conclusion mentioned in the Education and Inspections Act 2006 s 60(2): see the text to notes 17–22.

25　Education and Inspections Act 2006 s 60(4)(a).

26　Education and Inspections Act 2006 s 60(4)(b).

27　Education and Inspections Act 2006 s 60(4)(c).

28　Ie under one or more of the Education and Inspections Act 2006 ss 63–66 (see PARA 1211 et seq) or otherwise.

29　Education and Inspections Act 2006 s 60(4)(d) (amended by SI 2010/1158).

30　Ie under the Education and Inspections Act 2006 s 60(7): see the text to note 32.

31　Education and Inspections Act 2006 s 60(5).

32　Education and Inspections Act 2006 s 60(7) (amended by SI 2010/1158).

33　Education and Inspections Act 2006 s 60(8).

34　Education and Inspections Act 2006 s 60(9) (amended by SI 2010/1158).

1208. Teachers' pay and conditions warning notice. A maintained school[1] is eligible for intervention[2] if:

(1)　the local authority[3] has given[4] the governing body[5] a warning notice[6];

(2)　the period beginning with the day on which the warning notice is given and ending with the fifteenth working day[7] following that day ('the initial period') has expired[8];

(3)　either the governing body made no representations[9] to the local authority against the warning notice during the initial period or the local authority has confirmed[10] the warning notice[11];

(4)　the governing body has failed to comply, or secure compliance, with the notice to the authority's satisfaction by the end of the compliance period[12]; and

(5)　the authority has given reasonable notice in writing[13] to the governing body that it proposes to exercise its intervention powers[14].

A local authority may give a warning notice to the governing body of a maintained school where the authority is satisfied that[15] the governing body has failed to comply with a provision of an order relating to the determination of teachers' pay and conditions[16] that applies to a teacher at the school[17], or the governing body has failed to secure that the head teacher of the school complies with such a provision[18]. A 'warning notice' is a notice in writing by the local authority setting out[19]:

(a)　the matters on which the conclusion mentioned above[20] is based[21];

(b)　the action which it requires the governing body to take in order to remedy those matters[22];

(c)　the initial period applying under head (2) above[23]; and

(d)　the action which the local authority is minded to take[24] if the governing body fails to take the required action[25].

The warning notice must also inform the governing body of its right to make representations[26] during the initial period[27].

Before the end of the initial period, the governing body may make representations in writing to the local authority against the warning notice[28]. The local authority must consider any such representations made to it and may, if it thinks fit, confirm the warning notice[29]. The local authority must give notice in writing of its decision whether or not to confirm the warning notice to the governing body and such other persons as the Secretary of State may require[30].

1   As to the meaning of 'maintained school' see PARA 1207 note 1.
2   As to the meaning of 'eligible for intervention' see PARA 1207 note 2.
3   As to the meaning of 'local authority' see PARA 25 (definition applied by the Education and Inspections Act 2006 s 187(2), (3)).
4   Ie in accordance with the Education and Inspections Act 2006 s 60A(2): see the text to notes 15–18. As to the service of notices and documents see the Education Act 1996 s 572 (applied by the Education and Inspections Act 2006 s 187(2), (3)); and PARA 76.
5   As to the governing bodies of maintained schools in England see PARA 150 et seq.
6   Education and Inspections Act 2006 s 60A(1)(a) (s 60A added by the Apprenticeships, Skills, Children and Learning Act 2009 s 203, Sch 13 paras 1, 4; Education and Inspections Act 2006 s 60A(1)(a) amended by SI 2010/1158). As to the power of the Secretary of State to direct a local authority to consider giving a warning notice see s 69B; and PARA 1220. As to the Secretary of State see PARA 58.
7   As to the meaning of 'working day' see PARA 1207 note 7.
8   Education and Inspections Act 2006 s 60A(1)(b) (as added: see note 6).
9   Ie under the Education and Inspections Act 2006 s 60A(7): see the text to note 28.
10 Ie under the Education and Inspections Act 2006 s 60A(8): see the text to note 29.
11 Education and Inspections Act 2006 s 60A(1)(c) (as added (see note 6); and amended by SI 2010/1158).
12 Education and Inspections Act 2006 s 60A(1)(d) (as added: see note 6). 'The compliance period', in relation to a warning notice, means, in a case where the governing body does not make representations under s 60A(7) (see the text to note 28), the initial period mentioned in s 60A(1)(b) (see head (2) in the text) (s 60A(10)(a) (as so added)) and, in a case where the local authority confirm the warning notice under s 60A(8) (see the text to note 29), the period beginning with the day on which it does so and ending with the fifteenth working day following that day (s 60A(10)(b) (as so added; and amended by SI 2010/1158)).
13 As to the meaning of 'writing' see PARA 76 note 8.
14 Education and Inspections Act 2006 s 60A(1)(e) (as added: see note 6). The intervention powers are those under any one or more of ss 64–66 (see PARA 1212–1441): see s 60A(1)(e) (as so added).
15 Education and Inspections Act 2006 s 60A(2) (as added (see note 6); and s 60A(2), (6) amended by SI 2010/1158). The local authority must, at the same time as giving the governing body the warning notice, give a copy of the notice to the head teacher of the school, in the case of a Church of England school or a Roman Catholic Church school, the appropriate diocesan authority and, in the case of a foundation or voluntary school, the person who appoints the foundation governors: Education and Inspections Act 2006 s 60A(6) (as so added and amended). As to the meaning of 'person' see PARA 7 note 6. As to the meaning of 'head teacher' see PARA 86 note 4 (definition applied by s 187(2), (3)). As to the meanings of 'Church of England school', 'Roman Catholic Church school' and 'appropriate diocesan authority' see PARA 146 note 12 (definitions applied by s 73). As to the meaning of references to a foundation or voluntary school see PARA 106. As to foundation governors see PARA 108.
16 Ie an order under the Education Act 2002 s 122: see PARA 1078. References in the Education and Inspections Act 2006 s 60A(2) to an order under the Education Act 2002 s 122 include a document by reference to which provision is made in such an order: Education and Inspections Act 2006 s 60A(3) (as added: see note 6).
17 Education and Inspections Act 2006 s 60A(2)(a) (as added: see note 6).
18 Education and Inspections Act 2006 s 60A(2)(b) (as added: see note 6).
19 Education and Inspections Act 2006 s 60A(4) (as added (see note 6); and amended by SI 2010/1158).
20 Ie in the Education and Inspections Act 2006 s 60A(2): see the text to notes 15–18.
21 Education and Inspections Act 2006 s 60A(4)(a) (as added: see note 6).
22 Education and Inspections Act 2006 s 60A(4)(b) (as added: see note 6).

23 Education and Inspections Act 2006 s 60A(4)(c) (as added: see note 6).
24 Ie under one or more of the Education and Inspections Act 2006 ss 64–66 (see PARAS 1212–1214) or otherwise.
25 Education and Inspections Act 2006 s 60A(4)(d) (as added (see note 6); and amended by SI 2010/1158).
26 Ie under the Education and Inspections Act 2006 s 60A(7): see the text to note 28.
27 Education and Inspections Act 2006 s 60A(5) (as added: see note 6).
28 Education and Inspections Act 2006 s 60A(7) (as added (see note 6); and amended by SI 2010/1158).
29 Education and Inspections Act 2006 s 60A(8) (as added (see note 6); and amended by SI 2010/1158).
30 Education and Inspections Act 2006 s 60A(9) (as added (see note 6); and amended by SI 2010/1158).

1209. School requiring significant improvement. A maintained school[1] is eligible for intervention[2] if:

(1) following an inspection of the school[3], Her Majesty's Chief Inspector of Education, Children's Services and Skills[4] has given notice[5] stating his opinion that the school requires significant improvement[6]; and

(2) where any subsequent inspection of the school has been made[7], the notice has not been superseded by the person making the subsequent inspection making a report stating that in his opinion the school no longer requires significant improvement[8], or by the Chief Inspector giving the Secretary of State[9] a notice[10] stating his opinion that special measures are required to be taken in relation to the school[11].

1 As to the meaning of 'maintained school' see PARA 1207 note 1.
2 As to the meaning of 'eligible for intervention' see PARA 1207 note 2. As to the powers of a local authority where a school is eligible for intervention see the Education and Inspections Act 2006 ss 63–66; and PARAS 1211–1214.
3 Ie under the Education Act 2005 Pt 1 Ch 1 (ss 1–12).
4 As to Her Majesty's Chief Inspector of Education, Children's Services and Skills see PARA 1133.
5 Ie under the Education Act 2005 s 13(3)(a) in a case falling within s 13(1)(b): see PARA 1167.
6 See the Education and Inspections Act 2006 s 61(a).
7 Ie under the Education Act 2005 Pt 1 Ch 1 (ss 1–12).
8 Education and Inspections Act 2006 s 61(b)(i).
9 As to the Secretary of State see PARA 58.
10 Ie under the Education Act 2005 s 13(3)(a) in a case falling within s 13(1)(a): see PARA 1167.
11 See the Education and Inspections Act 2006 s 61(b)(ii). As to eligibility for intervention in relation to schools requiring special measures see PARA 1210.

1210. School requiring special measures. A maintained school[1] is eligible for intervention[2] if:

(1) following an inspection of the school[3], Her Majesty's Chief Inspector of Education, Children's Services and Skills[4] has given notice[5] stating his opinion that special measures are required to be taken in relation to the school[6]; and

(2) where any subsequent inspection of the school has been made[7], the person making it did not state that in his opinion special measures were not required to be taken in relation to the school[8].

1 As to the meaning of 'maintained school' see PARA 1207 note 1.
2 As to the meaning of 'eligible for intervention' see PARA 1207 note 2. As to the powers of a local authority where a school is eligible for intervention see the Education and Inspections Act 2006 ss 63–66; and PARAS 1211–1214.
3 Ie under the Education Act 2005 Pt 1 Ch 1 (ss 1–12).
4 As to Her Majesty's Chief Inspector of Education, Children's Services and Skills see PARA 1133.
5 Ie under the Education Act 2005 s 13(3)(a) in a case falling within s 13(1)(a): see PARA 1167.
6 Education and Inspections Act 2006 s 62(a).

7   Ie under the Education Act 2005 Pt 1 Ch 1 (ss 1–12).
8   Education and Inspections Act 2006 s 62(b).

B. INTERVENTION BY LOCAL AUTHORITY

1211. Power of local authority to require governing body to enter into arrangements. If at any time a maintained school[1] is eligible for intervention[2], then[3] the local authority[4] may, with a view to improving the performance of the school, give the governing body[5] of the school a notice[6] requiring the governing body[7]:

(1)   to enter into a contract or other arrangement with a specified person[8] (who may be the governing body of another school[9]) for the provision to the governing body of specified services of an advisory nature[10];

(2)   to make specified arrangements[11] with the governing body of such other school as may be specified[12];

(3)   to make specified arrangements[13] with a further education body[14]; or

(4)   to take specified steps for the purpose of creating or joining a federation[15].

Before exercising this power, the local authority must consult[16]: (a) the governing body of the school[17]; (b) in the case of a foundation or voluntary school[18] which is a Church of England school or a Roman Catholic Church school, the appropriate diocesan authority[19]; and (c) in the case of any other foundation or voluntary school, the person or persons by whom the foundation governors are appointed[20].

1   As to the meaning of 'maintained school' see PARA 1207 note 1.
2   Ie other than by virtue of the Education and Inspections Act 2006 s 60A (see PARA 1208): see s 63(1) (amended by the Apprenticeships, Skills, Children and Learning Act 2009 s 203, Sch 13 paras 1, 5(1), (2)). As to the meaning of 'eligible for intervention' see PARA 1207 note 2.
3   Ie subject to the Education and Inspections Act 2006 s 63(3): see s 63(1). Where the school is eligible for intervention by virtue of s 60 (school subject to performance standards and safety warning: see PARA 1207), the power conferred by s 63(1) is only exercisable within the period of two months following the end of the compliance period (as defined by s 60(10): see PARA 1207 note 13): s 63(3) (amended by the Apprenticeships, Skills, Children and Learning Act 2009 s 203, Sch 13 paras 1, 5(1), (3)). As to the meaning of 'month' see PARA 54 note 26.
4   As to the meaning of 'local authority' see PARA 25 (definition applied by the Education and Inspections Act 2006 s 187(2), (3)). As to the duty of a local authority to have regard to guidance given by the Secretary of State see PARA 1215.
5   As to the governing bodies of maintained schools in England see PARA 150 et seq.
6   As to the service of notices and documents see the Education Act 1996 s 572 (applied by the Education and Inspections Act 2006 s 187(2), (3)); and PARA 76.
7   Education and Inspections Act 2006 s 63(1) (amended by SI 2010/1158).
8   As to the meaning of 'person' see PARA 7 note 6.
9   As to the meaning of 'school' see PARA 91 (definition applied by the Education and Inspections Act 2006 s 187(2), (3)).
10 Education and Inspections Act 2006 s 63(1)(a). The notice may require the contract or other arrangement to contain specified terms and conditions: s 63(4).
11 Ie authorised by the Education Act 2002 s 26 (collaboration between schools): see PARA 157.
12 Education and Inspections Act 2006 s 63(1)(b).
13 Ie authorised by regulations under the Education and Inspections Act 2006 s 166 (collaboration arrangements: maintained schools and further education bodies): see PARA 172.
14 Education and Inspections Act 2006 s 63(1)(c). As to the meaning of 'further education body' see PARA 172 note 4 (definition applied by s 63(1)(c)).
15 Education and Inspections Act 2006 s 63(1)(d). As to the meaning of 'federation' see PARA 156 note 4 (definition applied by s 63(1)(d)).
16 Education and Inspections Act 2006 s 63(2) (amended by SI 2010/1158). As to the exercise of the duty to consult see JUDICIAL REVIEW vol 61 (2010) PARA 627.
17 Education and Inspections Act 2006 s 63(2)(a).

18 As to the meaning of references to a foundation or voluntary school see PARA 106.
19 Education and Inspections Act 2006 s 63(2)(b). As to the meanings of 'Church of England school', 'Roman Catholic Church school' and 'appropriate diocesan authority' see PARA 146 note 12 (definitions applied by s 73).
20 Education and Inspections Act 2006 s 63(2)(c). As to foundation governors see PARA 108.

1212. Power of local authority to appoint additional governors. If at any time a maintained school[1] is eligible for intervention[2], then[3] the local authority[4] may appoint such number of additional governors as it thinks fit[5].

If at any time a voluntary aided school[6] is eligible for intervention in relation to a performance standards and safety warning[7] or a teachers' pay and conditions warning[8], and the local authority has exercised its power[9] to appoint additional governors[10], and the Secretary of State has not exercised his power to appoint additional governors[11] in connection with the same warning notice[12], the appropriate appointing authority[13] may appoint such number of additional foundation governors as is equal to the number of additional governors appointed by the authority[14]. If at any time a voluntary aided school is eligible for intervention as a school requiring significant improvement[15] or as a school requiring special measures[16], the Secretary of State has not exercised his power to appoint additional governors[17] in connection with the same inspection[18], the Secretary of State has not exercised his power[19] to direct closure of school[20], and the appropriate appointing authority has received a notice in writing[21] from the Secretary of State informing it that he has received a notice[22] from Her Majesty's Chief Inspector of Education, Children's Services and Skills[23], the appropriate appointing authority may appoint such number of additional foundation governors as it thinks fit[24]. In the case of any such appointment[25] to the governing body of a school, the instrument of government for the school has effect as if[26] the instrument provided for the appropriate appointing authority to appoint such number of additional foundation governors as they are so authorised[27] to appoint[28].

1 As to the meaning of 'maintained school' see PARA 1207 note 1.
2 As to the meaning of 'eligible for intervention' see PARA 1207 note 2.
3 Ie subject to the Education and Inspections Act 2006 s 64(1A), (2): see s 64(1) (amended by the Apprenticeships, Skills, Children and Learning Act 2009 s 203, Sch 13 paras 1, 6(1), (2)). The Education and Inspections Act 2006 s 64(1) does not apply if the Secretary of State has exercised the power under s 67 (power to appoint additional governors: see PARA 1216) in connection with:
    (1) the same warning notice, where the school is eligible for intervention by virtue of s 60 (school subject to performance standards and safety warning: see PARA 1207) or s 60A (school subject to teachers' pay and conditions warning: see PARA 1208); or
    (2) the same inspection falling within s 61(a) (see PARA 1209) or s 62(a) (see PARA 1210), where the school is eligible for intervention by virtue of s 61 (school requiring significant improvement) or 62 (school requiring special measures): s 64(1A) (added by the Apprenticeships, Skills, Children and Learning Act 2009 s 203, Sch 13 paras 1, 6(1), (3)).
    As to the Secretary of State see PARA 58. Where the school is eligible for intervention by virtue of the Education and Inspections Act 2006 s 60 or s 60A, the power conferred by s 64(1) is only exercisable within the period of two months following the end of the compliance period (as defined by s 60(10) (see PARA 1207 note 13) or as the case may be s 60A(10) (see PARA 1208 note 12)): s 64(2) (amended by the Apprenticeships, Skills, Children and Learning Act 2009 s 203, Sch 13 paras 1, 6(1), (4)). As to the meaning of 'month' see PARA 54 note 26.
4 As to the meaning of 'local authority' see PARA 25 (definition applied by the Education and Inspections Act 2006 s 187(2), (3)). As to the duty of a local authority to have regard to guidance given by the Secretary of State see PARA 1215.
5 Education and Inspections Act 2006 s 64(1) (amended by SI 2010/1158). In relation to any appointment made by the local authority by virtue of the Education and Inspections Act 2006 s 64(1) to the governing body of a school, the instrument of government for the school has effect

as if (despite anything in regulations under the Education Act 2002 s 19: see PARA 150) it provided for the local authority to appoint such number of additional governors as it thinks fit: Education and Inspections Act 2006 s 64(3) (amended by SI 2010/1158). As to the governing bodies of maintained schools in England see PARA 150 et seq. During the interim period the local authority may not exercise any power conferred by the Education and Inspections Act 2006 s 64: see Sch 6 para 14(a); and PARA 1222 note 9.

6 Ie other than one falling within the Education and Inspections Act 2006 s 61 (see PARA 1209) or s 62 (see PARA 1210). As to the meaning of references to a voluntary school see PARA 106.

7 Ie eligible for intervention by virtue of the Education and Inspections Act 2006 s 60: see PARA 1207.

8 See the Education and Inspections Act 2006 s 64(4)(a) (amended by the Apprenticeships, Skills, Children and Learning Act 2009 s 203, Sch 13 paras 1, 6(1), (5)(a)). Eligibility for intervention in relation to a teachers' pay and conditions warning is eligibility by virtue of the Education and Inspections Act 2006 s 60A (see PARA 1208): see s 64(4)(a) (as so amended).

9 Ie under the Education and Inspections Act 2006 s 64(1): see the text to notes 1–5.

10 Education and Inspections Act 2006 s 64(4)(b) (amended by SI 2010/1158).

11 Ie the power under the Education and Inspections Act 2006 s 67: see PARA 1216.

12 Education and Inspections Act 2006 s 64(4)(c) (added by the Apprenticeships, Skills, Children and Learning Act 2009 s 203, Sch 13 paras 1, 6(1), (5)(c)).

13 References in the Education and Inspections Act 2006 s 64 to 'the appropriate appointing authority' in relation to any voluntary aided school are references:
   (1) to the appropriate diocesan authority, if it is a Church of England school or a Roman Catholic Church school (s 64(8)(a)); or
   (2) in any other case, to the person or persons by whom the foundation governors are appointed (s 64(8)(b)).

   However, where, in the case of any voluntary aided school not falling within s 64(8)(a) (see head (1) above), there are different powers to appoint foundation governors, references in s 64 to the appropriate appointing authority are references:
   (a) to all those persons who have any such power acting jointly (s 64(9)(a)); or
   (b) if they are unable to agree, to such of them acting jointly, or such one of them, as the Secretary of State may, after consulting all those persons, determine (s 64(8)(b)).

   As to the meanings of 'Church of England school', 'Roman Catholic Church school' and 'appropriate diocesan authority' see PARA 146 note 12 (definitions applied by s 73). As to the meaning of 'person' see PARA 7 note 6.

14 Education and Inspections Act 2006 s 64(4). Any additional foundation governors appointed under s 64(4) cease to hold office at the time when the additional governors appointed by the authority cease to do so (s 64(5)(a)) and are not eligible for re-appointment except where, and to the extent that, those governors are re-appointed (s 64(5)(b)).

15 Ie eligible for intervention by virtue of the Education and Inspections Act 2006 s 61: see PARA 1209.

16 See the Education and Inspections Act 2006 s 64(6)(a). Eligibility for intervention as a school requiring special measures is eligibility for intervention by virtue of s 62 (see PARA 1210): see s 64(6)(a).

17 Ie his power under the Education and Inspections Act 2006 s 67: see PARA 1216.

18 Education and Inspections Act 2006 s 64(6)(b). The inspection referred to is one falling within s 61(a) (see PARA 1209) or s 62(a) (see PARA 1210): see s 64(6)(b).

19 Ie under the Education and Inspections Act 2006 s 68: see PARA 1217.

20 Education and Inspections Act 2006 s 64(6)(c).

21 As to the meaning of 'writing' see PARA 76 note 8. As to the service of notices and documents see the Education Act 1996 s 572 (applied by the Education and Inspections Act 2006 s 187(2), (3)); and PARA 76.

22 Ie under the Education Act 2005 s 13(3)(a): see PARA 1167.

23 Education and Inspections Act 2006 s 64(6)(d). As to Her Majesty's Chief Inspector of Education, Children's Services and Skills see PARA 1133.

24 Education and Inspections Act 2006 s 64(6).

25 Ie made by virtue of the Education and Inspections Act 2006 s 64(4) or (6): see the text to notes 6–24.

26 Ie despite anything in regulations under the Education Act 2002 s 19: see PARA 150.

27 Ie under the Education and Inspections Act 2006 s 64(4) or (6) (as the case may be): see the text to notes 6–24.

28 Education and Inspections Act 2006 s 64(7).

1213.   Power of local authority to provide for governing body to consist of interim executive members.   If at any time a maintained school[1] is eligible for intervention[2], the local authority[3] may, with the consent of the Secretary of State[4], give the governing body[5] a notice in writing[6] stating that, as from a date specified in the notice, the governing body is to be constituted[7] as a governing body consisting of interim executive members[8]. Before exercising this power, the local authority must consult[9] the governing body of the school[10], in the case of a foundation or voluntary school[11] which is a Church of England school or a Roman Catholic Church school, the appropriate diocesan authority[12] and, in the case of any other foundation or voluntary school, the person[13] or persons by whom the foundation governors are appointed[14].

1   As to the meaning of 'maintained school' see PARA 1207 note 1.
2   As to the meaning of 'eligible for intervention' see PARA 1207 note 2.
3   As to the meaning of 'local authority' see PARA 25 (definition applied by the Education and Inspections Act 2006 s 187(2), (3)). As to the duty of a local authority to have regard to guidance given by the Secretary of State see PARA 1215.
4   As to the Secretary of State see PARA 58.
5   As to the governing bodies of maintained schools in England see PARA 150 et seq.
6   As to the meaning of 'writing' see PARA 76 note 8. As to the service of notices and documents see the Education Act 1996 s 572 (applied by the Education and Inspections Act 2006 s 187(2), (3)); and PARA 76.
7   Ie under the Education and Inspections Act 2006 Sch 6 (see PARA 1222 et seq): see ss 65(1), 70(a).
8   Education and Inspections Act 2006 s 65(1) (amended by SI 2010/1158).
9   Education and Inspections Act 2006 s 65(2) (amended by SI 2010/1158). As to the exercise of the duty to consult see JUDICIAL REVIEW vol 61 (2010) PARA 627.
10 Education and Inspections Act 2006 s 65(2)(a).
11 As to the meaning of references to a foundation or voluntary school see PARA 106.
12 Education and Inspections Act 2006 s 65(2)(b). As to the meanings of 'Church of England school', 'Roman Catholic Church school' and 'appropriate diocesan authority' see PARA 146 note 12 (definitions applied by s 73).
13 As to the meaning of 'person' see PARA 7 note 6.
14 Education and Inspections Act 2006 s 65(2)(c). As to the constitution of governing bodies of foundation schools see PARA 152.

1214.   Power of local authority to suspend right to delegated budget.   If at any time a maintained school[1] is eligible for intervention[2] and has a delegated budget[3], then[4] the local authority[5] may, by giving the governing body[6] of the school notice in writing[7] of the suspension, suspend the governing body's right to a delegated budget with effect from the receipt of the notice by the governing body[8]. A copy of a notice must be given to the head teacher[9] of the school at the same time as the notice is given to the governing body[10].

1   As to the meaning of 'maintained school' see PARA 1207 note 1.
2   Education and Inspections Act 2006 s 66(1)(a). As to the meaning of 'eligible for intervention' see PARA 1207 note 2.
3   Education and Inspections Act 2006 s 66(1)(b). 'Delegated budget' has the meaning given in the School Standards and Framework Act 1998 Pt 2 (ss 20–83) (see PARA 323): see the Education and Inspections Act 2006 s 66(1)(b).
4   Ie subject to the Education and Inspections Act 2006 s 66(2): see s 66(1). Where the school is eligible for intervention by virtue of s 60 (school subject to performance standards and safety warning: see PARA 1207) or s 60A (school subject to teachers' pay and conditions warning: see PARA 1208), the power conferred by s 66(1) is only exercisable within the period of two months following the end of the compliance period (as defined by s 60(10) (see PARA 1207 note 13) or, as the case may be, s 60A(10) (see PARA 1208 note 12)): s 66(2) (amended by the Apprenticeships, Skills, Children and Learning Act 2009 s 203, Sch 13 paras 1, 7). As to the meaning of 'month' see PARA 54 note 26.

5   As to the meaning of 'local authority' see PARA 25 (definition applied by the Education and Inspections Act 2006 s 187(2), (3)). As to the duty of a local authority to have regard to guidance given by the Secretary of State see PARA 1215.
6   As to the governing bodies of maintained schools in England see PARA 150 et seq.
7   As to the meaning of 'writing' see PARA 76 note 8. As to the service of notices and documents see the Education Act 1996 s 572 (applied by the Education and Inspections Act 2006 s 187(2), (3)); and PARA 76.
8   Education and Inspections Act 2006 s 66(1) (amended by SI 2010/1158). A suspension imposed under the Education and Inspections Act 2006 s 66 has effect for the purposes of the School Standards and Framework Act 1998 Pt 2 Ch 4 (ss 45–53A) as if made under Sch 15 para 1 (see PARA 325): Education and Inspections Act 2006 s 66(4). A local authority may not exercise the power under s 66(1) or the School Standards and Framework Act 1998 Sch 15 para 1 where the Secretary of State has exercised his power to appoint additional governors under the Education and Inspections Act 2006 s 67: see s 67(6); and PARA 1216. While a governing body is constituted to include interim members under Sch 6, a local authority may not exercise any power conferred by s 66: see Sch 6 para 12(3); and PARA 1226.
9   As to the meaning of 'head teacher' see PARA 86 note 4 (definition applied by the Education and Inspections Act 2006 s 187(2), (3)).
10 Education and Inspections Act 2006 s 66(3).

1215. Duty of local authority to have regard to guidance. A local authority[1] must, in exercising its functions[2] in relation to maintained schools[3] that are eligible for intervention[4], have regard to any guidance[5] given from time to time by the Secretary of State[6].

1   As to the meaning of 'local authority' see PARA 25 (definition applied by the Education and Inspections Act 2006 s 187(2), (3)).
2   As to the meaning of 'functions' see PARA 18 note 5 (definition applied by the Education and Inspections Act 2006 s 187(2), (3)).
3   As to the meaning of 'maintained school' see PARA 1207 note 1.
4   Ie the functions under the Education and Inspections Act 2006 Pt 4 (ss 59–73). As to the meaning of 'eligible for intervention' see PARA 1207 note 2.
5   As to the publication of guidance see the Education Act 1996 s 571 (applied by the Education and Inspections Act 2006 s 187(2), (3)); and PARA 60. See in particular 'Schools causing concern: Statutory guidance for local authorities' (January 2015).
6   Education and Inspections Act 2006 s 72 (amended by SI 2010/1158). As to the Secretary of State see PARA 58.

C. INTERVENTION BY SECRETARY OF STATE

1216. Power of Secretary of State to appoint additional governors. If at any time a maintained school[1] is eligible for intervention[2], the Secretary of State[3] may appoint such number of additional governors[4] as he thinks fit; and he may nominate one of those governors to be the chairman of the governing body in place of any person who has been elected as chairman of that body[5]. A governor appointed under these provisions holds office as governor for such term[6], and, if nominated as chairman of the governing body, is chairman of that body for such period[7], as the Secretary of State may determine[8]. The Secretary of State may pay to any governor so appointed such remuneration and allowances as the Secretary of State may determine[9].

Where the Secretary of State has exercised his power under these provisions in relation to a school, then:

(1)   in any such case the local authority may not exercise its power[10] to suspend the governing body's right to a delegated budget[11], and if it has already exercised either of those powers, the Secretary of State must, if requested to do so by the governing body, revoke the suspension[12]; and

(2)   in the case of a voluntary aided school, nothing in regulations under the

Education Act 2002[13] is to be read as authorising the appointment of foundation governors for the purpose of outnumbering the other governors as augmented by those appointed by the Secretary of State under these provisions[14].

1 As to the meaning of 'maintained school' see PARA 1207 note 1.
2 As to the meaning of 'eligible for intervention' see PARA 1207 note 2.
3 As to the Secretary of State see PARA 58. While a governing body is constituted to include interim members under the Education and Inspections Act 2006 Sch 6, the Secretary of State may not exercise any power conferred by s 67: see Sch 6 para 14(b); and PARA 1222 note 9.
4 As to the governing bodies of maintained schools in England see PARA 150 et seq.
5 Education and Inspections Act 2006 s 67(1) (amended by the Apprenticeships, Skills, Children and Learning Act 2009 ss 203, 266, Sch 13 paras 1, 8, Sch 16 Pt 6). Before making any such appointment, the Secretary of State must consult:
  (1) the local authority (Education and Inspections Act 2006 s 67(2)(a) (amended by SI 2010/1158));
  (2) the governing body of the school (Education and Inspections Act 2006 s 67(2)(b));
  (3) in the case of a foundation or voluntary school which is a Church of England school or a Roman Catholic Church school, the appropriate diocesan authority (s 67(2)(c)); and
  (4) in the case of any other foundation or voluntary school, the person or persons by whom the foundation governors are appointed (s 67(2)(d)).
 As to the meaning of 'local authority' see PARA 25 (definition applied by the Education and Inspections Act 2006 s 187(2), (3)). As to the meaning of references to a foundation or voluntary school see PARA 106. As to the meanings of 'Church of England school', 'Roman Catholic Church school' and 'appropriate diocesan authority' see PARA 146 note 12 (definitions applied by s 73). As to the meaning of 'person' see PARA 7 note 6. As to the constitution of governing bodies of foundation and voluntary schools see PARA 152 et seq. As to the exercise of the duty to consult see JUDICIAL REVIEW vol 61 (2010) PARA 627.
 In relation to any appointment made by the Secretary of State by virtue of s 67(1) to the governing body of a school, the instrument of government for the school has effect as if (despite anything in regulations under the Education Act 2002 s 19: see PARA 150) it provided for the Secretary of State to appoint such number of additional governors as he thinks fit: s 67(5).
6 Education and Inspections Act 2006 s 67(3)(a).
7 Education and Inspections Act 2006 s 67(3)(b).
8 Education and Inspections Act 2006 s 67(3).
9 Education and Inspections Act 2006 s 67(4).
10 Ie under the Education and Inspections Act 2006 s 66(1) (see PARA 1214) or the School Standards and Framework Act 1998 Sch 15 para 1 (see PARA 325).
11 Education and Inspections Act 2006 s 67(6)(a)(i) (amended by SI 2010/1158).
12 Education and Inspections Act 2006 s 67(6)(a)(ii). The revocation of a suspension must be notified to the local authority in writing (s 67(7)(a) (amended by SI 2010/1158)), and takes effect from such date as is specified in that notification (Education and Inspections Act 2006 s 67(7)(b)). As to the meaning of 'writing' see PARA 76 note 8. As to the service of notices and documents see the Education Act 1996 s 572 (applied by the Education and Inspections Act 2006 s 187(2), (3)); and PARA 76.
13 Ie under the Education Act 2002 s 19: see PARA 150.
14 Education and Inspections Act 2006 s 67(6)(b).

1217. Power of Secretary of State to direct closure of school. If at any time a maintained school[1] is eligible for intervention as a school requiring special measures[2], the Secretary of State[3] may give a direction[4] to the local authority[5] requiring the school to be discontinued[6] on a date specified in the direction[7]. Before giving such a direction, the Secretary of State must consult[8]:
 (1) the local authority and the governing body[9] of the school[10];
 (2) in the case of a foundation or voluntary school[11] which is a Church of England school or a Roman Catholic Church school, the appropriate diocesan authority[12];
 (3) in the case of any other foundation or voluntary school, the person[13] or persons by whom the foundation governors are appointed[14]; and

(4)   such other persons as the Secretary of State considers appropriate[15].

On giving such a direction the Secretary of State must give notice in writing[16] of the direction to the governing body of the school and its head teacher[17].

Where the local authority is given such a direction, it must discontinue the school in question on the date specified in the direction[18].

1   As to the meaning of 'maintained school' see PARA 1207 note 1.
2   Ie eligible for intervention other than by virtue of the Education and Inspections Act 2006 s 60A: see PARA 1208. As to the meaning of 'eligible for intervention' see PARA 1207 note 2.
3   As to the Secretary of State see PARA 58.
4   As to directions see the Education Act 1996 s 570 (applied by the Education and Inspections Act 2006 s 187(2), (3)); and PARA 75.
5   As to the meaning of 'local authority' see PARA 25 (definition applied by the Education and Inspections Act 2006 s 187(2), (3)).
6   In the Education and Inspections Act 2006 s 68 any reference to the discontinuance of a maintained school is a reference to the local authority ceasing to maintain it: s 68(5) (amended by SI 2010/1158).
7   Education and Inspections Act 2006 s 68(1) (amended by SI 2010/1158; and the Education Act 2011 s 44(2)). As to the application of the Education and Inspections Act 2006 s 68 to pupil referral units in England see the Education (Pupil Referral Units) (Application of Enactments) (England) Regulations 2007, SI 2007/2979, regs 1(3), 3, Sch 1 Pt 1 para 23 (amended by SI 2012/1825). As to pupil referral units see PARA 427 et seq. As to the meaning of 'England' see PARA 7 note 3.
8   As to the exercise of the duty to consult see JUDICIAL REVIEW vol 61 (2010) PARA 627.
9   As to the governing bodies of maintained schools in England see PARA 150 et seq.
10 Education and Inspections Act 2006 s 68(2)(a) (amended by SI 2010/1158).
11 As to the meaning of references to a foundation or voluntary school see PARA 106.
12 Education and Inspections Act 2006 s 68(2)(b). As to the meanings of 'Church of England school', 'Roman Catholic Church school' and 'appropriate diocesan authority' see PARA 146 note 12 (definitions applied by s 73).
13 As to the meaning of 'person' see PARA 7 note 6.
14 Education and Inspections Act 2006 s 68(2)(c). As to the constitution of governing bodies of foundation and voluntary schools see PARA 152 et seq.
15 Education and Inspections Act 2006 s 68(2)(e).
16 As to the meaning of 'writing' see PARA 76 note 8. As to the service of notices and documents see the Education Act 1996 s 572 (applied by the Education and Inspections Act 2006 s 187(2), (3)); and PARA 76.
17 Education and Inspections Act 2006 s 68(3). As to the meaning of 'head teacher' see PARA 86 note 4 (definition applied by s 187(2), (3)).
18 Education and Inspections Act 2006 s 68(4) (amended by SI 2010/1158). Nothing in the Education and Inspections Act 2006 ss 15–17 (see PARAS 115–117) or in the School Standards and Framework Act 1998 s 30 (see PARA 116) applies to the authority's discontinuance of the school under the Education and Inspections Act 2006 s 68: see s 68(4). As to the duty of a local authority to have regard to guidance given by the Secretary of State see PARA 1215.

1218.   Power of Secretary of State to provide for governing body to consist of interim executive members.   If at any time a maintained school[1] is eligible for intervention[2], the Secretary of State[3] may give the governing body[4] a notice in writing[5] stating that, as from the date specified in the notice, the governing body is to be constituted[6] as a governing body consisting of interim executive members[7].

Before exercising this power, the Secretary of State must consult[8]:

(1)   the local authority[9];
(2)   the governing body of the school[10];
(3)   in the case of a foundation or voluntary school[11] which is a Church of England school or a Roman Catholic Church school, the appropriate diocesan authority[12]; and
(4)   in the case of any other foundation or voluntary school, the person[13] or persons by whom the foundation governors are appointed[14].

However, the Secretary of State need not consult the persons mentioned in heads (2), (3) and (4) if the local authority has already[15] consulted them[16].

1   As to the meaning of 'maintained school' see PARA 1207 note 1.
2   As to the meaning of 'eligible for intervention' see PARA 1207 note 2.
3   As to the Secretary of State see PARA 58.
4   As to the governing bodies of maintained schools in England see PARA 150 et seq.
5   As to the meaning of 'writing' see PARA 76 note 8. As to the service of notices and documents see the Education Act 1996 s 572 (applied by the Education and Inspections Act 2006 s 187(2), (3)); and PARA 76.
6   Ie in accordance with the Education and Inspections Act 2006 Sch 6 (see PARA 1222 et seq): see ss 69(1), 70(b).
7   See the Education and Inspections Act 2006 s 69(1) (amended by the Apprenticeships, Skills, Children and Learning Act 2009 ss 203, 266, Sch 13 paras 1, 9, Sch 16 Pt 6).
8   The Education and Inspections Act 2006 s 69(2) does not apply if an academy order has effect in respect of the school: s 69(4) (added by the Academies Act 2010 s 14, Sch 2 paras 19, 21). As to the meaning of 'academy order' see PARA 350 note 3 (definition applied by the Education and Inspections Act 2006 s 187(2), (3)). As to the exercise of the duty to consult see JUDICIAL REVIEW vol 61 (2010) PARA 627.
9   Education and Inspections Act 2006 s 69(2)(a) (amended by SI 2010/1158). As to the meaning of 'local authority' see PARA 25 (definition applied by the Education and Inspections Act 2006 s 187(2), (3)).
10 Education and Inspections Act 2006 s 69(2)(b).
11 As to the meaning of references to a foundation or voluntary school see PARA 106.
12 Education and Inspections Act 2006 s 69(2)(c). As to the meanings of 'Church of England school', 'Roman Catholic Church school' and 'appropriate diocesan authority' see PARA 146 note 12 (definitions applied by s 73).
13 As to the meaning of 'person' see PARA 7 note 6.
14 Education and Inspections Act 2006 s 69(2)(d). As to the constitution of governing bodies of foundation and voluntary schools see PARA 152 et seq.
15 Ie under the Education and Inspections Act 2006 s 65(2) in relation to a proposed notice under s 65(1): see PARA 1213.
16 See the Education and Inspections Act 2006 s 69(3) (amended by SI 2010/1158).

1219.   Power of Secretary of State to direct local authority to consider giving performance standards and safety warning notice. If the Secretary of State[1] thinks that the following conditions are met[2] he may direct[3] the local authority[4] to consider giving a warning notice in relation to performance standards and safety[5] to the governing body[6] of a maintained school[7] in the terms specified in the direction[8]. The conditions are:

(1)   that there are reasonable grounds for a local authority to give such a warning notice to the governing body[9]; and
(2)   that one of the following applies:
  (a)   the authority has not given a warning notice to the governing body[10] on those grounds[11];
  (b)   the authority has done so, but in inadequate terms[12];
  (c)   the authority has given a warning notice to the governing body[13] on those grounds, but Her Majesty's Chief Inspector of Education, Children's Services and Skills[14] has failed or declined to confirm it[15];
  (d)   the school has become eligible for intervention on those grounds[16], but the period of two months[17] following the end of the compliance period[18] has ended[19].

If the Secretary of State gives such a direction to a local authority in respect of a governing body, the authority must[20] give the Secretary of State a written response to the direction before the end of the period of ten working days[21] beginning with the day on which the direction is given[22], and on the same day as it does so, give the Chief Inspector a copy of the response[23]. The local authority's response to the direction must either[24] state that the authority has decided to give a warning notice to the governing body in the specified terms[25] or state that the authority has decided not to give a warning notice to the governing body in those terms[26]. If the response states that the authority has decided to give a warning notice to the governing body in the specified terms, the authority must give the warning notice to the governing body in those terms before the end of the period of five working days beginning with the day on which the response is given[27], and, on the same day as it does so, give the Secretary of State a copy of the notice[28]. If the response states that the authority has decided not to give a warning notice to the governing body in the specified terms, it must set out the authority's reasons for the decision and the Secretary of State may direct the authority to give the warning to the governing body in those terms and to withdraw any previous warning[29] given to the governing body[30]. If the Secretary of State directs the authority to give such a warning to the governing body in the specified terms, the authority must comply with the direction before the end of the period of five working days beginning with the day on which that direction was given and on the same day as it does so it much give the Secretary of State a copy of the notice[31].

1 As to the Secretary of State see PARA 58.
2 Education and Inspections Act 2006 s 69A(1) (s 69A added by the Apprenticeships, Skills, Children and Learning Act 2009 s 203, Sch 13 paras 1, 10).
3 Any direction under the Education and Inspections Act 2006 s 69A must be in writing: s 69A(11) (added by the Education Act 2011 s 44(3)(a), (d)). As to the meaning of 'writing' see PARA 76 note 8. As to directions generally see the Education Act 1996 s 570 (applied by the Education and Inspections Act 2006 s 187(2), (3)); and PARA 75.
4 As to the meaning of 'local authority' see PARA 25 (definition applied by the Education and Inspections Act 2006 s 187(2), (3)).
5 Ie under the Education and Inspections Act 2006 s 60: see PARA 1207.
6 As to the governing bodies of maintained schools in England see PARA 150 et seq.
7 As to the meaning of 'maintained school' see PARA 1207 note 1.
8 See the Education and Inspections Act 2006 s 69A(4) (as added (see note 2); and amended by SI 2010/1158).
9 See the Education and Inspections Act 2006 s 69A(2) (as added (see note 2); and amended by SI 2010/1158).
10 Ie under the Education and Inspections Act 2006 s 60: see PARA 1207.
11 Education and Inspections Act 2006 s 69A(3)(a) (as added: see note 2).
12 Education and Inspections Act 2006 s 69A(3)(b) (as added: see note 2).
13 Ie under the Education and Inspections Act 2006 s 60: see PARA 1207.
14 As to Her Majesty's Chief Inspector of Education, Children's Services and Skills see PARA 1133.
15 Education and Inspections Act 2006 s 69A(3)(c) (as added: see note 2).
16 Ie by virtue of the Education and Inspections Act 2006 s 60: see PARA 1207.
17 As to the meaning of 'month' see PARA 54 note 26.
18 Ie as defined by the Education and Inspections Act 2006 s 60(10): see PARA 1207 note 13.
19 Education and Inspections Act 2006 s 69A(3)(d) (as added: see note 2).
20 Education and Inspections Act 2006 s 69A(6) (as added (see note 2); and amended by SI 2010/1158).
21 As to the meaning of 'working day' see PARA 1207 note 7.
22 Education and Inspections Act 2006 s 69A(6)(a) (as added: see note 2).
23 Education and Inspections Act 2006 s 69A(6)(b) (as added: see note 2).
24 Education and Inspections Act 2006 s 69A(7) (as added (see note 2); and amended by SI 2010/1158).
25 Education and Inspections Act 2006 s 69A(7)(a) (as added: see note 2).
26 Education and Inspections Act 2006 s 69A(7)(b) (as added: see note 2).
27 Education and Inspections Act 2006 s 69A(8)(a) (as added: see note 2). The authority must also withdraw any previous warning notice given to the governing body under s 60 (see PARA 1207): see s 69A(8)(a) (as so added).

28 Education and Inspections Act 2006 s 69A(8)(b) (as added: see note 2). Section 69A(8)(b) applies in addition to s 60(6) (see PARA 1207): s 69A(10) (as so added).

29 Ie a warning given under the Education and Inspections Act 2006 s 60 (see PARA 1207).

30 Education and Inspections Act 2006 s 69A(9) (as added (see note 2); s 69A(9) substituted and s 69A(9A) added by the Education Act 2011 s 44(3)(b)).

31 Education and Inspections Act 2006 s 69A(9A) (as added: see note 30).

1220. Power of Secretary of State to direct local authority to give teachers' pay and conditions warning notice. If the Secretary of State[1] thinks that the following conditions are met[2], he may direct[3] the local authority[4] to consider giving a warning notice in relation to teachers' pay and conditions[5] to the governing body[6] of a maintained school[7] in the terms specified in the direction[8]. The conditions are:

(1) that there are reasonable grounds for a local authority to give a teachers' pay and conditions warning notice to the governing body[9]; and

(2) that one of the following applies:

    (a) the authority has not given such a warning notice to the governing body on those grounds[10];

    (b) the authority has done so, but in inadequate terms[11];

    (c) the authority has given such a warning notice to the governing body on those grounds, but have declined or failed to confirm it[12];

    (d) the school has become eligible for intervention on those grounds[13], but the period of two months[14] following the end of the compliance period[15] has ended[16].

If the Secretary of State gives such a direction to a local authority in respect of a governing body, the authority must[17]:

(i) give[18] a copy of the direction to the governing body before the end of the period of two working days[19] beginning with the day on which the direction is given[20];

(ii) when it does so, invite the governing body to give the authority a written response before the end of the period of seven working days beginning with the day on which the direction is given[21]; and

(iii) give the Secretary of State the authority's written response, and any response received from the governing body in accordance with head (ii), before the end of the period of ten working days beginning with the day on which the direction is given[22].

The local authority's response to the direction must do one of the following[23]: (A) state that the authority has decided to give a warning notice to the governing body in the specified terms[24]; (B) state that the authority has decided not to give a warning notice to the governing body in those terms[25].

If the response states that the authority has decided to give a warning notice to the governing body in the specified terms, the authority must give the warning notice to the governing body in those terms before the end of the period of five working days beginning with the day on which the response is given[26] and, on the same day as it does so, give the Secretary of State a copy of the notice[27]. If the response states that the authority has decided not to give a warning notice to the governing body in the specified terms the response must set out the authority's reasons for the decision[28], and the Secretary of State may direct the authority to give the warning notice to the governing body in those terms and to withdraw any previous warning notice given[29] to the governing body[30]. If the Secretary of

State so directs the authority to give a warning notice to the governing body in
the specified terms, the authority must comply with that direction before the end
of the period of five working days beginning with the day on which that
direction is given[31] and, on the same day as it does so, give the Secretary of State
a copy of the notice[32].

1 As to the Secretary of State see PARA 58.
2 See the Education and Inspections Act 2006 s 69B(1) (s 69B added by the Apprenticeships,
   Skills, Children and Learning Act 2009 s 203, Sch 13 paras 1, 10).
3 A direction must be in writing: Education and Inspections Act 2006 s 69B(11) (as added: see
   note 2). As to the meaning of 'writing' see PARA 76 note 8. As to directions generally see the
   Education Act 1996 s 570 (applied by the Education and Inspections Act 2006 s 187(2), (3));
   and PARA 75.
4 As to the meaning of 'local authority' see PARA 25 (definition applied by the Education and
   Inspections Act 2006 s 187(2), (3)).
5 Ie a warning notice under the Education and Inspections Act 2006 s 60A: see PARA 1208.
6 As to the governing bodies of maintained schools in England see PARA 150 et seq.
7 As to the meaning of 'maintained school' see PARA 1207 note 1.
8 See the Education and Inspections Act 2006 s 69B(4) (as added (see note 2); and amended by
   SI 2010/1158).
9 See the Education and Inspections Act 2006 s 69B(2) (as added (see note 2); and amended by
   SI 2010/1158).
10 Education and Inspections Act 2006 s 69B(3)(a) (as added: see note 2).
11 Education and Inspections Act 2006 s 69B(3)(b) (as added: see note 2).
12 Education and Inspections Act 2006 s 69B(3)(c) (as added: see note 2).
13 Ie by virtue of the Education and Inspections Act 2006 s 60A: see PARA 1208.
14 As to the meaning of 'month' see PARA 54 note 26.
15 Ie as defined by the Education and Inspections Act 2006 s 60A(10): see PARA 1208 note 12.
16 Education and Inspections Act 2006 s 69B(3)(d) (as added: see note 2).
17 Education and Inspections Act 2006 s 69B(5) (as added (see note 2); and amended by
   SI 2010/1158).
18 As to the service of notices and documents see the Education Act 1996 s 572 (applied by the
   Education and Inspections Act 2006 s 187(2), (3)); and PARA 76.
19 As to the meaning of 'working day' see PARA 1207 note 7.
20 Education and Inspections Act 2006 s 69B(5)(a) (as added: see note 2).
21 Education and Inspections Act 2006 s 69B(5)(b) (as added: see note 2).
22 Education and Inspections Act 2006 s 69B(5)(c) (as added: see note 2).
23 Education and Inspections Act 2006 s 69B(6) (as added (see note 2); and amended by
   SI 2010/1158).
24 Education and Inspections Act 2006 s 69B(6)(a) (as added: see note 2).
25 Education and Inspections Act 2006 s 69B(6)(b) (as added: see note 2).
26 Education and Inspections Act 2006 s 69B(7)(a) (as added: see note 2). The authority must also
   withdraw any previous warning notice given to the governing body under s 60A (see PARA
   1208): see s 69B(7)(a) (as so added).
27 Education and Inspections Act 2006 s 69B(7)(b) (as added: see note 2).
      Section 69B(7)(b) applies in addition to s 60A(6) (see PARA 1208): see s 69B(10) (as so
   added).
28 Education and Inspections Act 2006 s 69B(8)(a) (as added: see note 2).
29 Ie under the Education and Inspections Act 2006 s 60A: see PARA 1208.
30 Education and Inspections Act 2006 s 69B(8)(b) (as added: see note 2).
31 Education and Inspections Act 2006 s 69B(9)(a) (as added: see note 2).
32 Education and Inspections Act 2006 s 69B(9)(b) (as added: see note 2).
      Section 69B(9)(b) applies in addition to s 60A(6) (see PARA 1208): see s 69B(10) (as so
   added).

1221. Power to require local authority to obtain advisory services. Where:

(1) one or more schools[1] maintained by a local authority[2] in England[3] are[4]
     eligible for intervention[5] and it appears to the Secretary of State[6] that
     the local authority[7]:

(a) has not been effective or is unlikely to be effective in eliminating deficiencies in the conduct of that school or those schools[8];

(b) is unlikely to be effective in eliminating deficiencies in the conduct of other schools which may in the future fall within head (a)[9]; or

(c) maintains a disproportionate number of schools falling within that head[10]; or

(2) it appears to the Secretary of State that a local authority in England maintains a disproportionate number of low-performing schools[11], and the authority:

(a) has not been effective or is unlikely to be effective in securing an improvement in the standards of performance of pupils[12] at those schools[13]; or

(b) is unlikely to be effective in securing an improvement in the standards of performance of pupils at other schools which may in the future be low-performing schools[14],

the Secretary of State may direct the local authority to enter into a contract or other arrangement with a person[15] specified in the direction, or a person falling within a class so specified, for the provision to the authority or the governing body[16] of any school maintained by it (or both) of specified services of an advisory nature[17]. The direction may require the contract or other arrangement to contain specified terms and conditions[18]. Any such direction is enforceable, on an application made on behalf of the Secretary of State, by a mandatory order[19].

Where the Secretary of State has notified a local authority that he is contemplating the giving of a direction under these provisions[20], the authority must give the Secretary of State, and any person authorised by the Secretary of State for these purposes, such assistance, in connection with the proposed contract or other arrangement, as the authority is reasonably able to give[21]. Where a direction is given to a local authority, the relevant person[22] is entitled, for the purposes of providing the advisory services[23], to exercise the following powers[24]:

(i) a right of entry, at all reasonable times, to the premises of the authority[25] or a school maintained by the authority[26]; and

(ii) a right, at all reasonable times, to inspect, and take copies of, any records or other documents[27] kept by the authority or a school maintained by the authority[28], and any other documents containing information relating to the authority or school, which he considers relevant to the provision of the advisory services[29].

Without prejudice to these powers[30], the authority must give the relevant person all assistance in connection with the provision of the advisory services which it is reasonably able to give[31].

1 'School' means a community, foundation or voluntary school, a community or foundation special school or a maintained nursery school: Education Act 2002 s 62A(4) (s 62A added by the Education and Inspections Act 2006 s 71, Sch 7 Pt 2 para 20). As to the meaning of references to a community, foundation or voluntary school or a community or foundation special school see PARA 106. As to the application of the Education Act 2002 s 62A to pupil referral units in England see the Education (Pupil Referral Units) (Application of Enactments) (England) Regulations 2007, SI 2007/2979, regs 1(3), 3, Sch 1 Pt 1 para 18. As to pupil referral units see PARA 427 et seq.

2 As to the meaning of 'local authority' see PARA 25 (definition applied by the Education Act 2002 s 212(1)). As to maintained schools see PARA 106.

3 As to the meaning of 'England' see PARA 7 note 3.

4 Ie for the purposes of the Education and Inspections Act 2006 Pt 4 (ss 59–73) (schools causing concern: England).

5 Ie by virtue of either of the Education and Inspections Act 2006 s 61 (school requiring significant improvement: see PARA 1209), or s 62 (school requiring special measures: see PARA 1210): see the Education Act 2002 s 62A(1)(a) (as added (see note 1); and amended by SI 2010/1158).

6 As to the Secretary of State see PARA 58.

7 Education Act 2002 s 62A(1)(b) (as added (see note 1); and amended by SI 2010/1158).

8 Education Act 2002 s 62A(1)(b)(i) (as added: see note 1).

9 Education Act 2002 s 62A(1)(b)(ii) (as added: see note 1).

10 Education Act 2002 s 62A(1)(b)(iii) (as added: see note 1).

11 Education Act 2002 s 62A(1A)(a) (s 62A as added (see note 1); s 62A(1A)–(1C) added by the Apprenticeships, Skills, Children and Learning Act 2009 s 204(1), (2); Education Act 2002 s 62A(1A)(a) amended by SI 2010/1158). 'Low-performing school' means a school at which the standards of performance of pupils are unacceptably low: Education Act 2002 s 62A(1B) (as so added). For these purposes the standards of performance of pupils at a school are low if they are low by reference to any one or more of the following:

    (1)   the standards that the pupils might in all the circumstances reasonably be expected to attain (s 62A(1C)(a) (as so added));

    (2)   where relevant, the standards previously attained by them (s 62A(1C)(b) (as so added));

    (3)   the standards attained by pupils at comparable schools (s 62A(1C)(c) (as so added)).

12 As to the meaning of 'pupil' see PARA 20 note 4 (definition applied by the Education Act 2002 s 62A(4) (s 62A as added (see note 1); definition added by the Apprenticeships, Skills, Children and Learning Act 2009 s 204(1), (3))).

13 Education Act 2002 s 62A(1A)(b)(i) (as added: see note 11).

14 Education Act 2002 s 62A(1A)(b)(ii) (as added: see note 11).

15 As to the meaning of 'person' see PARA 7 note 6.

16 As to the governing bodies of maintained schools in England see PARA 150 et seq.

17 Education Act 2002 s 62A(2) (as added (see note 1); and amended by SI 2010/1158).

18 Education Act 2002 s 62A(3) (as added: see note 1).

19 Education Act 2002 s 62A(5) (as added: see note 1). As to mandatory orders see JUDICIAL REVIEW vol 61 (2010) PARA 703 et seq.

20 Ie under the Education Act 2002 s 62A: see the text to notes 1–19.

21 See the Education Act 2002 s 64(1) (amended by the Education and Inspections Act 2006 s 71, Sch 7 Pt 2 para 22(1), (2); SI 2010/1158).

22 'The relevant person' means the person specified under the Education Act 2002 s 62A(2) (see the text to notes 15–17) or, where the direction specifies a class of persons, the person with whom the local authority enters into the contract or other arrangement required by the direction, and includes any person assisting that person in the provision of the advisory services: s 64(7) (definition amended by the Education and Inspections Act 2006 s 71, Sch 7 Pt 2 para 22(1), (3)(b); SI 2010/1158).

23 'The advisory services' means the services to be provided in pursuance of the direction under the Education Act 2002 s 62A: see s 64(7) (definition amended by the Education and Inspections Act 2006 s 71, Sch 7 Pt 2 para 22(1), (3)(a)).

24 See the Education Act 2002 s 64(2) (amended by the Education and Inspections Act 2006 s 71, Sch 7 Pt 2 para 22(1), (2); SI 2010/1158).

25 See the Education Act 2002 s 64(3)(a).

26 The Education Act 2002 s 64(3) applies in relation to any school maintained by the authority as it applies in relation to the authority; and without prejudice to that provision (as it so applies):

    (1)   the governing body of any such school must give the relevant person all assistance in connection with the provision of the advisory services which it is reasonably able to give (s 64(6)(a)); and

    (2)   the governing body of any such school and the authority must secure that all such assistance is also given by persons who work at the school (s 64(6)(b)).

27 'Documents' and 'records' each include information recorded in any form: Education Act 2002 s 64(7).

28 See note 26.

29 See the Education Act 2002 s 64(3)(b). The Education Act 1996 s 497B(3) (right of access to computers etc: see PARA 62) applies in relation to the exercise by the relevant person of the right conferred by the Education Act 2002 s 64(3) as it applies to the exercise by the specified person (within the meaning of that section) of the right conferred by the Education Act 1996 s 497B(2): Education Act 2002 s 64(4).

30 Ie without prejudice to the Education Act 2002 s 64(3): see the text to notes 25–29.

31 Education Act 2002 s 64(5).

D. GOVERNING BODIES CONSISTING OF INTERIM EXECUTIVE MEMBERS

1222. Effect of notice that governing body to consist of interim executive members. On the date specified in the notice given by the local authority[1] or the Secretary of State[2] to the governing body[3] of a maintained school[4] that the governing body is to be constituted so as to consist of interim executive members[5], the existing governors[6] vacate office[7], and the governing body of the school is to consist[8] of members appointed by the appropriate authority[9]. However, this does not prevent the appointment of an existing governor as an interim executive member[10].

The appropriate authority may in the notice[11] specify the duration of the period during which the governing body is constituted so as to consist of interim executive members ('the interim period')[12].

1   As to the meaning of 'local authority' see PARA 25 (definition applied by the Education and Inspections Act 2006 s 187(2), (3)).
2   As to the Secretary of State see PARA 58.
3   As to the governing bodies of maintained schools in England see PARA 150 et seq.
4   As to the meaning of 'maintained school' see PARA 1207 note 1.
5   Ie the notice under the Education and Inspections Act 2006 s 65(1) (see PARA 1213) or s 69(1) (see PARA 1218).
6   'Existing governors', in relation to a school in respect of which a notice under the Education and Inspections Act 2006 s 65(1) or s 69(1) has been given, means the governors who hold office immediately before the governing body becomes constituted in accordance with Sch 6: Sch 6 para 1(1).
7   See the Education and Inspections Act 2006 Sch 6 para 3(1).
8   Ie instead of being constituted in accordance with regulations made by virtue of the Education Act 2002 s 19: see PARA 150.
9   See the Education and Inspections Act 2006 Sch 6 para 2(1). In Sch 6 the governing body as constituted in accordance with Sch 6 is referred to as 'the interim executive board', and the members of the governing body as so constituted are referred to as 'interim executive members': Sch 6 para 2(2). 'The appropriate authority' means: (1) where Sch 6 applies by virtue of a notice under s 65(1) (see PARA 1213), the local authority who gave the notice; and (2) where Sch 6 applies by virtue of a notice under s 69(1) (see PARA 1218), the Secretary of State: Sch 6 para 1(1) (definition amended by SI 2010/1158).
        Regulations made by virtue of the Education Act 2002 s 19(2) or (3) (see PARA 150) do not apply in relation to the interim executive board: Education and Inspections Act 2006 Sch 6 para 13(1). The instrument of government of the school does not, so far as it relates to the constitution of the governing body, have effect in relation to the interim executive board: Sch 6 para 13(2). During the interim period the local authority may not exercise any power conferred by s 64 (power to appoint additional governors: see PARA 1212), and the Secretary of State may not exercise any power conferred by s 67 (power to appoint additional governors: see PARA 1216): Sch 6 para 14(a), (b) (Sch 6 para 14(a) amended by SI 2010/1158).
10 See the Education and Inspections Act 2006 Sch 6 para 3(2).
11 Ie under the Education and Inspections Act 2006 s 65(1) (see PARA 1213) or s 69(1) (see PARA 1218).
12 See the Education and Inspections Act 2006 Sch 6 paras 1(1), 7. During the interim period, any reference in any provision contained in, or made under, the Education Acts to a governor or foundation governor of a school has effect, in relation to the school, as a reference to an interim executive member: Sch 6 para 3(3). During the interim period, the School Standards and Framework Act 1998 s 83 (modification of provisions making governors of foundation or voluntary school ex officio trustees: see PARA 194) has effect in relation to the school with the substitution for paras (a)–(c) of a reference to the interim executive members: Education and Inspections Act 2006 Sch 6 para 3(4). As to the meaning of 'the Education Acts' see PARA 1 note 13.

1223. Appointment of interim executive members. The number of interim executive members[1] must not be less than two[2]. The initial appointment of interim executive members must be made so as to take effect on the date specified in the relevant notice[3]. The appropriate authority[4] may appoint further interim executive members at any time during the interim period[5].

Every appointment of an interim executive member must be made by an instrument in writing[6] setting out the terms of his appointment[7]. An interim executive member holds office in accordance with the terms of his appointment[8] and may at any time be removed from office by the appropriate authority for incapacity or misbehaviour[9]. The terms of appointment of an interim executive member may provide for his appointment to be terminable by the appropriate authority by notice[10].

The appropriate authority may nominate one of the interim executive members to be chairman of the interim executive board[11].

1   As to the meaning of 'interim executive member' see PARA 1222 note 9.
2   Education and Inspections Act 2006 Sch 6 para 4(1).
3   Education and Inspections Act 2006 Sch 6 para 4(2). The relevant notice is one under s 65(1) (see PARA 1213) or s 69(1) (see PARA 1218).
4   As to the meaning of 'appropriate authority' see PARA 1222 note 9.
5   Education and Inspections Act 2006 Sch 6 para 4(3). As to the meaning of 'interim period' see PARA 1222.
6   As to the meaning of 'writing' see PARA 76 note 8.
7   Education and Inspections Act 2006 Sch 6 para 5(1). The appropriate authority may pay to any interim executive member such remuneration and allowances as the appropriate authority may determine: Sch 6 para 9.
8   Education and Inspections Act 2006 Sch 6 para 5(2)(a).
9   Education and Inspections Act 2006 Sch 6 para 5(2)(b). This provision is expressed to be subject to Sch 6 para 18 (see PARA 1228): see Sch 6 para 5(2)(a).
10 Education and Inspections Act 2006 Sch 6 para 5(3).
11 Education and Inspections Act 2006 Sch 6 para 8. As to the meaning of 'interim executive board' see PARA 1222 note 9.

1224. Duty to inform other persons. The appropriate authority[1] must give a copy of the notice[2] and of every instrument of appointment of an interim executive member[3]:

(1)   to every interim executive member[4];
(2)   to every existing governor of the school[5];
(3)   where the local authority[6] is the appropriate authority, to the Secretary of State[7];
(4)   where the Secretary of State is the appropriate authority, to the local authority[8];
(5)   in the case of a foundation or voluntary school[9] which is a Church of England school or a Roman Catholic Church school, to the appropriate diocesan authority[10]; and
(6)   in the case of any other foundation or voluntary school, to the person[11] or persons by whom the foundation governors are appointed[12].

A failure to comply with this duty does not invalidate the notice or appointment[13].

1   As to the meaning of 'appropriate authority' see PARA 1222 note 9.
2   Ie the notice under the Education and Inspections Act 2006 s 65(1) (see PARA 1213) or s 69(1) (see PARA 1218).
3   As to the meaning of 'interim executive member' see PARA 1222 note 9. As to the appointment of interim executive members see PARA 1222.
4   Education and Inspections Act 2006 Sch 6 para 6(1)(a).
5   Education and Inspections Act 2006 Sch 6 para 6(1)(b). As to the meaning of 'existing governor' see PARA 1222 note 6.
6   As to the meaning of 'local authority' see PARA 25 (definition applied by the Education and Inspections Act 2006 s 187(2), (3)).

7   Education and Inspections Act 2006 Sch 6 para 6(1)(c) (amended by SI 2010/1158). As to the Secretary of State see PARA 58.

8   Education and Inspections Act 2006 Sch 6 para 6(1)(d) (amended by SI 2010/1158).

9   As to the meaning of references to a foundation or voluntary school see PARA 106.

10   Education and Inspections Act 2006 Sch 6 para 6(1)(e). As to the meanings of 'Church of England school', 'Roman Catholic Church school' and 'appropriate diocesan authority' see PARA 146 note 12 (definitions applied by s 73).

11   As to the meaning of 'person' see PARA 7 note 6.

12   Education and Inspections Act 2006 Sch 6 para 6(1)(f). As to the constitution of governing bodies of foundation and voluntary schools see PARA 152 et seq.

13   Education and Inspections Act 2006 Sch 6 para 6(2).

1225.   Duty of interim executive board. During the interim period[1], the interim executive board[2] must conduct the school so as to secure, so far as is practicable to do so, the provision of a sound basis for future improvement in the conduct of the school[3].

The interim executive board may determine its own procedure[4], and may make such arrangements as it thinks fit for the discharge of its functions[5] by any other person[6].

1   As to the meaning of 'interim period' see PARA 1222.

2   As to the meaning of 'interim executive board' see PARA 1222 note 9.

3   Education and Inspections Act 2006 Sch 6 para 10(1). This provision is without prejudice to the other duties of the interim executive board as governing body: Sch 6 para 10(2).

4   Education and Inspections Act 2006 Sch 6 para 11(1).

5   As to the meaning of 'functions' see PARA 18 note 5 (definition applied by the Education and Inspections Act 2006 s 187(2), (3)).

6   Education and Inspections Act 2006 Sch 6 para 11(2). As to the meaning of 'person' see PARA 7 note 6.

1226.   Effect on suspension of delegated budget. If, immediately before the date specified in the notice[1], the school does not have a delegated budget, the suspension of the governing body's right to a delegated budget[2] is revoked[3] with effect from that date[4]. If a notice relating to the suspension of a delegated budget for mismanagement[5] has been given to the governing body before the date specified in a notice[6] but has not yet taken effect, the notice of suspension ceases to have effect on that date[7].

During the interim period[8], the local authority[9] may not exercise the power[10] to suspend the right to a delegated budget[11].

1   Ie the notice under the Education and Inspections Act 2006 s 65(1) (see PARA 1213) or s 69(1) (see PARA 1218).

2   As to the meanings of 'delegated budget' and 'right to a delegated budget' see PARA 323 (definitions applied by the Education and Inspections Act 2006 Sch 6 para 12(4)).

3   Ie by virtue of the Education and Inspections Act 2006 Sch 6 para 12(1).

4   Education and Inspections Act 2006 Sch 6 para 12(1).

5   Ie a notice under the School Standards and Framework Act 1998 Sch 15 para 1: see PARA 325.

6   Ie a notice under the Education and Inspections Act 2006 s 65(1) (see PARA 1213) or s 69(1) (see PARA 1218).

7   Education and Inspections Act 2006 Sch 6 para 12(2).

8   As to the meaning of 'interim period' see PARA 1222.

9   As to the meaning of 'local authority' see PARA 25 (definition applied by the Education and Inspections Act 2006 s 187(2), (3)).

10   Ie conferred by the Education and Inspections Act 2006 s 66: see PARA 1214.

11   See the Education and Inspections Act 2006 Sch 6 para 12(3) (amended by SI 2010/1158).

1227.   Closure of school. At any time during the interim period[1], the interim executive board[2] may, if it thinks fit, make a report to the local authority[3] and the Secretary of State[4] recommending that the school be discontinued[5], and stating the reasons for that recommendation[6].

Where during the interim period the Secretary of State gives a direction[7] in relation to the discontinuance of the school[8], or the local authority determines to discontinue the school[9], the interim period is to continue until the discontinuance date[10], even where it would otherwise end before that date[11].

1   As to the meaning of 'interim period' see PARA 1222.
2   As to the meaning of 'interim executive board' see PARA 1222 note 9.
3   As to the meaning of 'local authority' see PARA 25 (definition applied by the Education and Inspections Act 2006 s 187(2), (3)).
4   As to the Secretary of State see PARA 58.
5   In the Education and Inspections Act 2006 Sch 6 any reference to the discontinuance of a maintained school is a reference to the local authority ceasing to maintain it: Sch 6 para 1(2) (amended by SI 2010/1158). As to the meaning of 'maintained school' see PARA 1207 note 1.
6   Education and Inspections Act 2006 Sch 6 para 15(1) (amended by SI 2010/1158). The interim executive board may not publish under the Education and Inspections Act 2006 s 15(2) (see PARA 115) proposals to discontinue the school, or serve notice under the School Standards and Framework Act 1998 s 30 (see PARA 116): Education and Inspections Act 2006 Sch 6 para 15(2).
7   Ie under the Education and Inspections Act 2006 s 17(1) (see PARA 117) or s 68(1) (see PARA 1217).
8   See the Education and Inspections Act 2006 Sch 6 para 16(1)(a).
9   Education and Inspections Act 2006 Sch 6 para 16(1)(b) (amended by SI 2010/1158).
10 'The discontinuance date' means the date on which proposals for discontinuing the school are implemented under the Education and Inspections Act 2006 Sch 2 Pt 4 (paras 28–31) (see PARA 129 et seq), the date on which the school is discontinued under the School Standards and Framework Act 1998 s 30 (see PARA 116) or the date specified in the direction under the Education and Inspections Act 2006 s 17(1) (see PARA 117) or s 68(1) (see PARA 1217), as the case may be: Sch 6 para 16(2).
11 Education and Inspections Act 2006 Sch 6 para 16(1) (amended by SI 2010/1158).

1228.   Resumption of government by normally constituted board.   Where the notice[1] did not specify the duration of the interim period[2], and the provisions relating to discontinuance of the school[3] do not apply[4], the appropriate authority[5] may give notice to the specified persons[6] specifying a date on which the governing body is to become a normally constituted governing body[7].

The interim executive members vacate office:

(1)   in a case where the school is to be discontinued[8], on the discontinuance date[9];

(2)   in a case where head (1) does not apply and the notice[10] specified the duration of the interim period, at the end of the specified period[11]; and

(3)   in any case, on the date specified in the notice[12] given by the appropriate authority[13]. However, this does not prevent the termination of the appointment of an interim executive member at any earlier time for incapacity or misconduct[14] or in accordance with the terms of his appointment[15].

Where interim executive members are to vacate office on the date referred to in head (2) or (3) above, the local authority must make arrangements providing for the constitution of the governing body on and after that date[16]. The Secretary of State may by regulations[17] make provision with respect to the transition from an interim executive board to a normally constituted governing body[18], which provision may include, in particular, provision enabling governors to be elected or appointed, and to exercise functions[19], before the end of the interim period[20].

1   Ie the notice under the Education and Inspections Act 2006 s 65(1) (see PARA 1213) or s 69(1) (see PARA 1218).

2   Education and Inspections Act 2006 Sch 6 para 17(1)(a). As to the meaning of 'interim period' see PARA 1222.

3   Ie the Education and Inspections Act 2006 Sch 6 para 16: see PARA 1227.

4   Education and Inspections Act 2006 Sch 6 para 17(1)(b).

5   As to the meaning of 'appropriate authority' see PARA 1222 note 9.

6   The specified persons are every interim executive member, where the local authority is the appropriate authority, the Secretary of State, where the Secretary of State is the appropriate authority, the local authority, in the case of a foundation or voluntary school which is a Church of England school or a Roman Catholic Church school, the appropriate diocesan authority and, in the case of any other foundation or voluntary school, the person or persons by whom the foundation governors are appointed: Education and Inspections Act 2006 Sch 6 para 17(2)(a)–(e) (Sch 6 para 17(b), (c) amended by SI 2010/1158). As to the meaning of 'interim executive member' see PARA 1222 note 9. As to the meaning of 'local authority' see PARA 25 (definition applied by the Education and Inspections Act 2006 s 187(2), (3)). As to the Secretary of State see PARA 58. As to the meaning of references to a foundation or voluntary school see PARA 106. As to the meanings of 'Church of England school', 'Roman Catholic Church school' and 'appropriate diocesan authority' see PARA 146 note 12 (definitions applied by s 73). As to the meaning of 'person' see PARA 7 note 6. As to the constitution of governing bodies of foundation and voluntary schools see PARA 152 et seq.

7   Education and Inspections Act 2006 Sch 6 para 17(1). 'A normally constituted governing body' means a governing body constituted in accordance with regulations made by virtue of the Education Act 2002 s 19 (see PARA 150): Education and Inspections Act 2006 Sch 6 para 1(1).

8   Ie in a case where the Education and Inspections Act 2006 Sch 6 para 16 applies: see PARA 1227.

9   Education and Inspections Act 2006 Sch 6 para 18(1)(a). As to the meaning of 'the discontinuance date' see PARA 1227 note 10 (definition applied by Sch 6 para 18(1)(a)).

10   Ie the notice under the Education and Inspections Act 2006 s 65(1) (see PARA 1213) or s 69(1) (see PARA 1218).

11   Education and Inspections Act 2006 Sch 6 para 18(1)(b).

12   Ie specified under the Education and Inspections Act 2006 Sch 6 para 17(1): see the text to notes 1–7.

13   See the Education and Inspections Act 2006 Sch 6 para 18(1)(c).

14   Ie under the Education and Inspections Act 2006 Sch 6 para 5(2)(b): see PARA 1223.

15   Education and Inspections Act 2006 Sch 6 para 18(2). As to the appointment of interim executive members see PARA 1223.

16   Education and Inspections Act 2006 Sch 6 para 19(1) (amended by SI 2010/1158).

17   As to the regulations made see the School Governance (Transition from an Interim Executive Board) (England) Regulations 2010, SI 2010/1918 (amended by SI 2015/883).

18   Education and Inspections Act 2006 Sch 6 para 19(2). The Secretary of State may in connection with that transition: (1) modify any provision made under any of the Education Act 2002 s 19 (see PARA 150), s 20 (see PARA 184), s 23 (see PARA 167), Sch 1 (see PARAS 150, 200, 214) (Education and Inspections Act 2006 Sch 6 para 19(2)(a)); (2) apply any such provision with or without modifications (Sch 6 para 19(2)(b)); and (3) make provision corresponding to or similar to any such provision (Sch 6 para 19(2)(c)). As to the meanings of 'modify' and 'modifications' see PARA 21 note 15 (definitions applied by s 187(2), (3)).

19   As to the meaning of 'functions' see PARA 18 note 5 (definition applied by the Education and Inspections Act 2006 s 187(2), (3)).

20   Education and Inspections Act 2006 Sch 6 para 19(3).

(iv) Intervention in Schools in Wales

A. INTERVENTION IN REGARD TO CONDUCT OF MAINTAINED SCHOOLS

1229. Legislation and guidance governing intervention. The School Standards and Organisation (Wales) Act 2013 Chapter 1 of Part 2[1] sets out the grounds[2] for intervention by local authorities[3] and the Welsh Ministers[4] in the conduct of maintained schools[5] that are causing concern[6]. It also provides a range of intervention powers[7] to enable local authorities and the Welsh Ministers to deal with the causes of concern[8].

In exercising its functions[9], a local authority must have regard to guidance given by the Welsh Ministers[10].

1   Ie the School Standards and Organisation (Wales) Act 2013 Pt 2 Ch 1 (ss 2–20).
2   As to the grounds for intervention see PARA 1230.
3   A 'local authority' (except in the School Standards and Organisation (Wales) Act 2013 s 54(2)(b) (see PARA 143)) means a county or county borough council in Wales: s 98(1).
4   As to the Welsh Ministers see PARA 59.
5   'Maintained school' means a school in Wales which is a community, foundation or voluntary school, a community special school or a maintained nursery school: School Standards and Organisation (Wales) Act 2013 s 98(3). As to the meaning of 'maintained nursery school' see PARA 99 note 4; and as to the meaning of 'special school' see PARA 1041 (definitions applied by s 98(1)).
6   School Standards and Organisation (Wales) Act 2013 s 1(3)(a).
7   As to the powers of intervention see PARA 1231.
8   School Standards and Organisation (Wales) Act 2013 s 1(3)(b).
9   Ie its functions under the School Standards and Organisation (Wales) Act 2013 Pt 1 Ch 1 (ss 2–20).
10 School Standards and Organisation (Wales) Act 2013 s 20.

1230. Grounds for intervention. The grounds for intervention in the conduct of a maintained school[1] are as follows[2].

Ground one is that the standards of performance of pupils[3] at the school[4] are unacceptably low[5]. For this purpose, the standards of performance of pupils are low if they are low by reference to any one or more of the following:

(1)   the standards that the pupils might in all the circumstances reasonably be expected to attain;
(2)   where relevant, the standards previously attained by them;
(3)   the standards attained by pupils at comparable schools[6].

Ground two is that there has been a breakdown in the way the school is managed or governed[7].

Ground three is that the behaviour of pupils at the school or any action taken by those pupils or their parents is severely prejudicing, or is likely to severely prejudice, the education of any pupils at the school[8].

Ground four is that the safety of pupils or staff of the school is threatened (whether by a breakdown of discipline or otherwise)[9].

Ground five is that the governing body or head teacher[10] has failed, or is likely to fail, to comply with a duty under the Education Acts[11].

Ground six is that the governing body or head teacher has acted, or is proposing to act, unreasonably in the exercise of any of its or his or her functions under the Education Acts[12].

Ground seven is that Her Majesty's Chief Inspector of Education and Training in Wales ('the Chief Inspector')[13] has given a notice[14] that the school requires significant improvement and that notice has not been superseded by the Chief Inspector giving such notice[15] that special measures are required to be taken in relation to the school or by a person making a subsequent inspection making a report stating that in his opinion the school no longer requires significant improvement[16].

Ground eight is that the Chief Inspector has given a notice[17] that special measures are required to be taken in relation to the school and that notice has not been superseded by a person making a subsequent inspection making a report stating that in his or her opinion the school no longer requires special measures[18].

1   As to the meaning of 'maintained school' see PARA 1229 note 5.
2   Ie for the purposes of the School Standards and Organisation (Wales) Act 2013 Pt 2 Ch 1 (ss 2–20).
3   As to the meaning of 'pupils' see PARA 20 note 4 (definition applied by the School Standards and Organisation (Wales) Act 2013 s 98(1)).

4   As to the meaning of 'school' see PARA 91 (definition applied by the School Standards and Organisation (Wales) Act 2013 s 98(1)).
5   School Standards and Organisation (Wales) Act 2013 s 2.
6   School Standards and Organisation (Wales) Act 2013 s 2.
7   School Standards and Organisation (Wales) Act 2013 s 2.
8   School Standards and Organisation (Wales) Act 2013 s 2.
9   School Standards and Organisation (Wales) Act 2013 s 2.
10 As to the meaning of 'head teacher' see PARA 86 note 4 (definition applied by the School Standards and Organisation (Wales) Act 2013 s 98(1)).
11 School Standards and Organisation (Wales) Act 2013 s 2. As to the meaning of 'the Education Acts' see PARA 1 note 13 (definition applied by s 98(1)).
12 School Standards and Organisation (Wales) Act 2013 s 2.
13 As to Her Majesty's Chief Inspector of Education and Training in Wales see PARA 1148.
14 Ie notice under the Education Act 2005 s 37(2) (see PARA 1195).
15 Ie notice under the Education Act 2005 s 37 (see PARA 1195).
16 School Standards and Organisation (Wales) Act 2013 s 2.
17 See note 13.
18 School Standards and Organisation (Wales) Act 2013 s 2.

1231. Warning notice. If a local authority[1] is satisfied that one or more of grounds one to six[2] of the grounds for intervention exist in relation to one of its maintained schools[3], the authority may give a warning notice to the governing body of the school[4]. If the local authority has not given such a warning notice[5], or has given a warning notice in terms that are inadequate in the opinion of the Welsh Ministers[6], and the Welsh Ministers are satisfied that one or more of grounds one to six of the grounds for intervention exist in relation to the school, then the Welsh Ministers may give a warning notice to the governing body of a maintained school[7].

The local authority, or the Welsh Ministers, as appropriate, must specify each of the following in the warning notice:

(1)   the grounds for intervention[8];
(2)   the reasons why they are satisfied that the grounds exist[9];
(3)   the action they require the governing body to take in order to deal with the grounds for intervention[10];
(4)   the period within which the action is to be taken by the governing body ('the compliance period')[11];
(5)   the action they are minded to take if the governing body fails to take the required action[12].

A copy of the warning notice must be sent to the head teacher[13] and, if the school is a foundation or voluntary school, to the person who appoints the foundation governors[14] and, if the school has a religious character[15], the appropriate religious body[16].

If the local authority gives the warning notice it must also send a copy to the Welsh Ministers[17] and if the Welsh Ministers give the warning they must send a copy to the local authority[18].

1   As to the meaning of 'local authority' see PARA 1229 note 3.
2   As to the different grounds for intervention see PARA 1230.
3   As to the meaning of 'maintained school' see PARA 1229 note 5.
4   School Standards and Organisation (Wales) Act 2013 s 3(1).
5   Ie under the School Standards and Organisation (Wales) Act 2013 s 3.
6   As to the Welsh Ministers see PARA 59.
7   See the School Standards and Organisation (Wales) Act 2013 s 10(1).
8   See the School Standards and Organisation (Wales) Act 2013 ss 3(2)(a), 10(2)(a).
9   See the School Standards and Organisation (Wales) Act 2013 ss 3(2)(b), 10(2)(b).
10 See the School Standards and Organisation (Wales) Act 2013 ss 3(2)(c), 10(2)(c).
11 See the School Standards and Organisation (Wales) Act 2013 ss 3(2)(d), 10(2)(d).

12 See the School Standards and Organisation (Wales) Act 2013 ss 3(2)(e), 10(2)(e).

13 See the School Standards and Organisation (Wales) Act 2013 ss 3(3)(a), 10(3)(b). As to the meaning of 'head teacher' see PARA 86 note 4 (definition applied by the School Standards and Organisation (Wales) Act 2013 s 98(1)).

14 'Foundation governor', in relation to a foundation school or a voluntary school, means a person appointed as a foundation governor in accordance with regulations under the Education Act 2002 s 19 (see PARA 195): School Standards and Organisation (Wales) Act 2013 s 98(3)). 'Regulations' means regulations made by the Welsh Ministers: s 98(1).

15 A reference in the School Standards and Organisation (Wales) Act 2013 to a school which has a religious character is to a school which is designated as having such a character by an order under the School Standards and Framework Act 1998 s 69(3) (see PARA 914 note 10): School Standards and Organisation (Wales) Act 2013 s 98(5).

16 School Standards and Organisation (Wales) Act 2013 ss 3(3)(b), 10(3)(c). 'Appropriate religious body' means, in the case of a Church in Wales school or a Roman Catholic Church school or proposed such school, the appropriate diocesan authority and, in the case of other schools or proposed schools, the body representing the religion or religious denomination stated, or that it is intended to be stated, in relation to the school in an order under the School Standards and Framework Act 1998 s 69(3) (see PARA 914 note 10): School Standards and Organisation (Wales) Act 2013 s 98(3). As to the meanings of 'Church of Wales School', 'Roman Catholic Church school' and 'appropriate diocesan authority' see PARA 146 note 12 (definitions applied by the School Standards and Organisation (Wales) Act 2013 s 98(3).

17 See the School Standards and Organisation (Wales) Act 2013 s 3(3)(c).

18 See the School Standards and Organisation (Wales) Act 2013 s 10(3)(a).

1232. Power to intervene. A local authority[1] and the Welsh Ministers[2] have the power to intervene[3] in the conduct of a maintained school[4] if one of the following[5] applies[6]:

(1) the local authority has given a warning notice[7] to the governing body of the school, and the governing body has failed to comply, or secure compliance, with the notice to the authority's satisfaction within the compliance period[8];

(2) the local authority, or the Welsh Ministers, as appropriate, are satisfied that one or more of grounds one to six of the grounds of intervention[9] exist in relation to the school and it, or they, have reason to believe that there is a related risk to the health or safety of any person that calls for urgent intervention[10];

(3) ground seven (school requiring significant improvement) or ground eight (school requiring special measures)[11] exists in relation to the school[12]; and a period of not less than ten days[13] has elapsed since the date on which that Her Majesty's Chief Inspector of Education and Training in Wales ('the Chief Inspector')[14] gave notice[15] that the maintained school was showing cause for concern[16];

(4) in relation to the Welsh Ministers, the Welsh Ministers have given a warning[17] to the governing body of the school and the governing body has failed to comply, or secure compliance, with the notice to the Welsh Ministers' satisfaction within the compliance period[18].

Where a local authority or the Welsh Ministers have the power to intervene, it, or they, must keep the circumstances giving rise to the power under review[19].

If the authority, or the Welsh Ministers, conclude that the grounds for intervention have been dealt with to its, or their, satisfaction, or that exercise of its, or their,powers of intervention[20] would not be appropriate for any other reason, it,or they, must notify the governing body of its, or their, conclusion in writing[21].

This power to intervene is not limited to the action stated in a warning notice[22].

1   As to the meaning of 'local authority' see PARA 1231 note 1.
2   As to the Welsh Ministers see PARA 59.
3   Ie under the School Standards and Organisation (Wales) Act 2013 Pt 2 Ch 1 (ss 2–20). A local
    authority's power to intervene continues in effect until one of the following events takes place:
    (1)   the authority gives notice under s 4(7) (see note 18) (s 4(9)(a));
    (2)   the Welsh Ministers determine that the power to intervene is no longer in effect and give
           notice in writing to the local authority and the governing body of their determination
           (s 4(9)(b));
    (3)   the Welsh Ministers give a warning notice to the governing body of the school under
           s 10 (see PARA 1231) (s 4(9)(c)).
4   As to the meaning of 'maintained school' see PARA 1229 note 5.
5   Ie if the School Standards and Organisation (Wales) Act 2013 s 4(2), (3) or (4) applies or, in
    relation to the Welsh Ministers s 11(2), (3), (4) or (5) applies.
6   See the School Standards and Organisation (Wales) Act 2013 ss 4(1), 11(1).
7   Ie under the School Standards and Organisation (Wales) Act 2013 s 3 (see PARA 1231).
8   See the School Standards and Organisation (Wales) Act 2013 ss 4(2), 11(2).
9   As to the different grounds for intervention see PARA 1230.
10 Ie urgent intervention under the School Standards and Organisation (Wales) Act 2013 Pt 2 Ch 1
    (ss 2–20): see ss 4(3), 11(4).
11 See note 9.
12 See the School Standards and Organisation (Wales) Act 2013 ss 4(4)(a), 11(5)(a).
13 The Welsh Ministers may, in relation to a particular school, determine that head (3) in the text
    has effect as if the reference to 10 days were to a shorter period specified in the determination:
    School Standards and Organisation (Wales) Act 2013 ss 4(5), 11(6).
14 As to Her Majesty's Chief Inspector of Education and Training in Wales see PARA 1148.
15 Ie notice to the local authority, or Welsh Ministers as appropriate, under the Education
    Act 2005 s 37(2) (see PARA 1195).
16 See the School Standards and Organisation (Wales) Act 2013 ss 4(4)(b), 11(5)(b). This is subject
    to s 4(5) (see note 12): s 4(4).
17 Ie under the School Standards and Organisation (Wales) Act 2013 s 10.
18 School Standards and Organisation (Wales) Act 2013 s 11(3).
19 School Standards and Organisation (Wales) Act 2013 ss 4(6), 11(7).
20 Ie its powers under the School Standards and Organisation (Wales) Act 2013 Pt 2 Ch 1.
21 School Standards and Organisation (Wales) Act 2013 ss 4(7), 11(8). If a local authority or the
    Welsh Ministers give notice under s 4(7) or s 11(8), it or they must at the same time send a copy
    of the notice to, in the case of a foundation or voluntary school the person who appoints the
    foundation governors and, if the school has a religious character, the appropriate religious body
    and the Welsh Ministers: ss 4(8), 11(9). The Welsh Ministers' power to intervene continues in
    effect until they give notice under s 11(8): s 11(10). As to the meaning of 'foundation governor',
    'appropriate religious body' and references to a school which has a religious character see PARA
    1231.
22 See the School Standards and Organisation (Wales) Act 2013 ss 4(10), 11(11).

1233. Intervention powers. The following apply where a local authority[1], or
the Welsh Ministers[2], have the power to intervene in the conduct of a maintained
schools[3].

The local authority, or the Welsh Ministers, may, with a view to improving the
performance of the school, direct[4] the governing body of the school to do either
or both of the following:

(1)   enter into a contract or other arrangement with a specified person (who
       may be the governing body of another school) for the provision to the
       governing body of specified services of an advisory nature[5];
(2)   exercise such of the powers to collaborate[6] as are specified in the
       direction[7].

The local authority, or the Welsh Ministers, may appoint as many additional
governors[8] to the governing body of the school as it thinks fit; and the
instrument of government for the school has effect as if it provided for such
appointments[9]. The local authority, or the Welsh Ministers, may nominate one of

those governors to be the chair of the governing body in place of any person who has been elected as chair of that body[10].

The local authority, or the Welsh Ministers, may give the governing body of the school a notice in writing stating that, as from a date specified in the notice, the governing body is to consist of interim executive members[11] appointed by the local authority, or the Welsh Ministers[12].

If the school has a delegated budget[13] the local authority may suspend the governing body's right to it by giving the governing body notice of the suspension[14]. However, where the Welsh Ministers have exercised the power to appoint additional governors to the governing body of the school[15] the local authority may not suspend the governing body's right to a delegated budget[16] and, if the local authority has already exercised that power[17], the Welsh Ministers may revoke the suspension[18].

If the local authority, or the Welsh Ministers, think it is appropriate for the purposes of dealing with the grounds for intervention, the authority or the Ministers may give directions to the governing body or head teacher or take any other steps[19].

The Welsh Ministers may direct the local authority, a governing body of a maintained school or a governing body of a federation[20] to provide for one or more of the following arrangements[21]:

(a)   the federation of the school causing concern and one or more maintained schools[22];

(b)   the federation of the school causing concern and an existing federation[23];

(c)   the federation of the school causing concern and an existing federation and one or more maintained schools[24];

(d)   where the school causing concern is part of a federation, the federation of that federation and one or more maintained schools[25];

(e)   where the school causing concern is part of a federation, the federation of that federation and another existing federation[26];

(f)   where the school causing concern is part of a federation, the federation of that federation and an existing federation and one or more maintained schools[27];

(g)   where the school causing concern is part of a federation, for the school to leave that federation[28].

1   As to the meaning of 'local authority' see PARA 1231 note 1.
2   As to the Welsh Ministers see PARA 59.
3   See the School Standards and Organisation (Wales) Act 2013 ss 5(1), 6(1), 7(1). 8(1)(a), 9(1), 12(1), 13(1), 14(1), 15(1), 17(1). As to the meaning of 'maintained school' see PARA 1230 note 4. As to the meaning of 'school' see PARA 91 (definition applied by s 98(1)). As to the local authority power of intervention see PARA 1232.
4   Before giving a direction the local authority, or the Welsh Ministers, must consult the governing body of the school and, in the case of a foundation or voluntary school, the person who appoints the foundation governors and, if the school has a religious character, the appropriate religious body: School Standards and Organisation (Wales) Act 2013 ss 5(3), 12(3). As to the meaning of 'foundation governor', 'appropriate religious body' and references to a school which has a religious character see PARA 1231. A governing body of a maintained school or a head teacher subject to a direction under the School Standards and Organisation (Wales) Act 2013 Pt 2 Ch 1 (ss 2–20) must comply with it: s 19(1). This includes a direction to exercise a power or duty that is contingent upon the opinion of the governing body or head teacher: s 19(2). The direction must be in writing, may be varied or revoked by a later direction and is enforceable by mandatory order on application by, or on behalf of, the person who gave the direction: s 19(3). As to the meaning of 'head teacher' see PARA 86 note 4 (definition applied by s 98(1)). A local authority, or an officer of an authority, subject to a direction or instruction under Pt 2 Ch 2

(ss 21–31) must comply with it: s 29(1). This includes a direction or an instruction to exercise a power or duty that is contingent upon the opinion of the local authority or an officer of the authority: s 29(2). A direction under Pt 2 Ch 2 must be in writing, it may be varied or revoked by a later direction and it is enforceable by mandatory order on application by, or on behalf of, the Welsh Ministers: s 29(3).

5   School Standards and Organisation (Wales) Act 2013 ss 5(2)(a), 12(2)(a). A direction under head (1) in the text may require the contract or other arrangement to contain specified terms and conditions: ss 5(4), 12(4).

6   Ie the powers under the Education (Wales) Measure 2011 s 5(2) (powers to collaborate: see PARA 199). In relation to the Welsh Ministers, this is subject to provision made in regulations made under s 6.

7   School Standards and Organisation (Wales) Act 2013 ss 5(2)(b), 12(2)(b). This is subject to provision made in regulations under the Education (Wales) Measure 2011 s 6 (see PARA 199).

8   A governor so appointed is to hold office for a period determined by the local authority, or the Welsh Ministers, as appropriate: School Standards and Organisation (Wales) Act 2013 ss 6(5), 13(5).

9   School Standards and Organisation (Wales) Act 2013 ss 6(2), 11(2). This applies despite anything in regulations under the Education Act 2002 s 19: see PARAS 150, 195). Before making any such appointment or nomination in relation to a voluntary aided school, the local authority, or the Welsh Ministers, as appropriate, must consult the person who appoints the foundation governors and, if the school has a religious character, the appropriate religious body: ss 6(4), 13(4). The local authority, or the Welsh Ministers, as appropriate, may pay remuneration and allowances to governors appointed under s 6: ss 6(7), 13(7).

10   School Standards and Organisation (Wales) Act 2013 ss 6(3), 13(5). A governor nominated by the local authority to be the chair of the governing body is to be the chair for a period determined by the local authority: ss 6(6), 13(6).

11   Ie it is to be constituted in accordance with the School Standards and Organisation (Wales) Act 2013 s 18, Sch 1 (governing bodies consisting of interim executive members).

12   See the School Standards and Organisation (Wales) Act 2013 ss 7(2), 14(2), Sch 1 paras 1, 2. Before giving a notice under s 7 the local authority must consult the governing body of the school and, in the case of a foundation or voluntary school, consult the person who appoints the foundation governors and, if the school has a religious character, the appropriate religious body: see s 7(3)(a), (b). The local authority must also obtain the consent of the Welsh Ministers: s 7(3)(c). Before giving notice under s 14 the Welsh Ministers must similarly consult the local authority: see s 14(3)(a). They must also consult the governing body of the school and, in the case of a foundation or voluntary school, consult the person who appoints the foundation governors and, if the school has a religious character, the appropriate religious body: s 14(3)(b), (c). However, the Welsh Ministers are not obliged to consult the persons mentioned in s 14(3)(b), (c) if the local authority has consulted them about the constitution of a governing body under s 7 on the basis of a power to intervene brought to an end by effect of s 4(9)(b) or (c): s 14(4).

13   Ie within the meaning of the School Standards and Framework Act 1998 Pt 2 (ss 20–83).

14   School Standards and Organisation (Wales) Act 2013 s 8(1)(b), (2). The suspension of the right to a delegated budget takes effect on receipt of the notice by the governing body: s 8(3). If the local authority gives a notice suspending the right to a delegated budget, it must give a copy of the notice to the head teacher at the same time: s 8(4). A suspension imposed under s 8 has effect for the purposes of the School Standards and Framework Act 1998 Pt 2 Ch 4 (financing of maintained schools) as if made under Sch 15 para 1 (suspension of financial delegation): School Standards and Organisation (Wales) Act 2013 s 8(5).

15   Ie where they have exercised their power under the School Standards and Organisation (Wales) Act 2013 s 13.

16   Ie the right under the School Standards and Framework Act 1998 Sch 15 para 1.

17   Or the power under the School Standards and Organisation (Wales) Act 2013 s 8.

18   School Standards and Organisation (Wales) Act 2013 s 13(8). The revocation of a suspension must be notified in writing to the local authority and takes effect from the date specified in that notification: s 13(10).

19   School Standards and Organisation (Wales) Act 2013 ss 9(2), 17(2).

20   As to the meaning of 'federation' see PARA 198 note 3 (definition applied by the School Standards and Organisation (Wales) Act 2013 s 15(5).

21   School Standards and Organisation (Wales) Act 2013 s 15(2). Before giving the direction, the Welsh Ministers must consult the local authority, the governing bodies concerned and, in the case of a foundation or voluntary school, the person who appoints the foundation governors and, if the school has a religious character, the appropriate religious body: s 15(4).

22 School Standards and Organisation (Wales) Act 2013 s 15(a).
23 School Standards and Organisation (Wales) Act 2013 s 15(b).
24 School Standards and Organisation (Wales) Act 2013 s 15(c).
25 School Standards and Organisation (Wales) Act 2013 s 15(d).
26 School Standards and Organisation (Wales) Act 2013 s 15(e).
27 School Standards and Organisation (Wales) Act 2013 s 15(f).
28 School Standards and Organisation (Wales) Act 2013 s 15(g).

1234. Power to direct closure of school. If the Welsh Ministers[1] have the power to intervene in the conduct of a maintained school[2] on the basis of Ground eight[3], they may give a direction[4] to the local authority requiring the school to be discontinued on a date specified in the direction[5] and, where the local authority is given such a direction, it must discontinue the school in question on the date specified in the direction[6].

1 As to the Welsh Ministers see PARA 59.
2 As to the meaning of 'maintained school' see PARA 1229 note 5.
3 Ie that special measures are required in relation to the school: see PARA 1230.
4 As to directions see PARA 1233 note 3. Before giving such a direction the Welsh Ministers must consult the local authority that maintains the school, the governing body of the school, in the case of a foundation or voluntary school, the person who appoints the foundation governors and, if the school has a religious character, the appropriate religious body, and any other persons the Welsh Ministers consider appropriate: School Standards and Organisation (Wales) Act 2013 s 16(3). On giving a direction to discontinue the school, the Welsh Ministers must also give notice in writing of the direction to the governing body of the school and its head teacher: s 16(4). For the purposes of s 16 any reference to the discontinuance of a maintained school is to the local authority ceasing to maintain it: s 16(6). As to the meaning of 'local authority' see PARA 1231 note 1. As to the meaning of 'appropriate religious body' and references to the religious character of a school see PARA 1231 notes 15, 16. As to the meaning of 'head teacher' see PARA 86 note 4 (definition applied by s 98(1)).
5 School Standards and Organisation (Wales) Act 2013 s 16(1), (2).
6 School Standards and Organisation (Wales) Act 2013 s 16(5). Nothing in Pt 3 (ss 38–83) applies to the discontinuance of the school under s 16: s 16(5).

B. INTERVENTION IN REGARD TO EXERCISE OF LOCAL AUTHORITIES' EDUCATION FUNCTIONS

1235. Legislation governing intervention. The School Standards and Organisation (Wales) Act 2013 Chapter 2 of Part 2[1] sets out the grounds for intervention by the Welsh Ministers[2] in the exercise of education functions by local authorities[3] that are causing concern and provides a range of intervention powers to enable the Welsh Ministers to deal with the causes of concern[4].

1 Ie the School Standards and Organisation (Wales) Act 2013 Pt 2 Ch 2 (ss 21–31).
2 As to the Welsh Ministers see PARA 59.
3 As to the meaning of 'local authority' see PARA 1231 note 1.
4 School Standards and Organisation (Wales) Act 2013 s 1(4).

1236. Grounds for intervention. The grounds for intervention in the exercise by a local authority[1] of its education functions[2] are as follows[3].

Ground one is that the local authority has failed, or is likely to fail, to comply with a duty that is an education function[4].

Ground two is that the local authority has acted, or is proposing to act, unreasonably in the exercise of an education function[5].

Ground three is that the local authority is failing, or is likely to fail, to perform an education function to an adequate standard[6].

1 As to the meaning of 'local authority' see PARA 1231 note 1.
2 As to the meaning of 'education functions' see the Education Act 1996 s 579(1); and PARA 25 (definition applied by the School Standards and Organisation (Wales) Act 2013 s 98(1)).

3   School Standards and Organisation (Wales) Act 2013 s 21.
4   School Standards and Organisation (Wales) Act 2013 s 21.
5   School Standards and Organisation (Wales) Act 2013 s 21.
6   School Standards and Organisation (Wales) Act 2013 s 21.

1237. Warning notice. The Welsh Ministers[1] may give a warning notice to a local authority[2] if they are satisfied that one or more of grounds one to three[3] exist in relation to the local authority[4]. The Welsh Ministers must specify each of the following in the warning notice:

(1)   the grounds for intervention[5];
(2)   the reasons why they are satisfied that the grounds exist[6];
(3)   the action they require the local authority to take in order to deal with the grounds for intervention[7];
(4)   the period within which the action is to be taken by the local authority ('the compliance period')[8];
(5)   the action they are minded to take if the local authority fails to take the required action[9].

1   As to the Welsh Ministers see PARA 59.
2   As to the meaning of 'local authority' see PARA 1231 note 1.
3   See PARA 1236.
4   School Standards and Organisation (Wales) Act 2013 s 22(1).
5   School Standards and Organisation (Wales) Act 2013 s 22(2)(a).
6   School Standards and Organisation (Wales) Act 2013 s 22(2)(b).
7   School Standards and Organisation (Wales) Act 2013 s 22(2)(c).
8   School Standards and Organisation (Wales) Act 2013 s 22(2)(d).
9   School Standards and Organisation (Wales) Act 2013 s 22(2)(e).

1238. Powers of Welsh Ministers to intervene. The Welsh Ministers[1] have the power to intervene[2] in the exercise of education functions[3] by a local authority[4] if the following apply[5]:

(1)   if the Welsh Ministers have given a warning notice and the local authority has failed to comply, or secure compliance, with the notice to the Welsh Ministers' satisfaction within the compliance period[6];
(2)   if the Welsh Ministers are satisfied that one or more of grounds one to three of the intervention grounds[7] exist in relation to the local authority and they have reason to believe that there is a related risk to the health or safety of any person that calls for urgent intervention[8] or the local authority is unlikely to be able to comply, or secure compliance, with a warning notice[9].

Where the Welsh Ministers have the power to intervene, they must keep the circumstances giving rise to the power under review[10]. If the Welsh Ministers conclude that the grounds for intervention have been dealt with to their satisfaction or that exercise of their powers[11] would not be appropriate for any other reason, they must notify the local authority of their conclusion in writing[12]. Where the Welsh Ministers have the power to intervene, they are not limited to taking the action they said they were minded to take in a warning notice[13].

1   As to the Welsh Ministers see PARA 59.
2   Ie under the School Standards and Organisation (Wales) Act 2013 Pt 2 Ch 2 (ss 21–31).
3   As to the meaning of 'education functions' see PARA 25 (definition applied by the School Standards and Organisation (Wales) Act 2013 s 98(1)).
4   As to the meaning of 'local authority' see PARA 1231 note 1.
5   School Standards and Organisation (Wales) Act 2013 s 23(1).
6   School Standards and Organisation (Wales) Act 2013 s 23(2).
7   As to the intervention grounds see PARA 1236.

8 Ie under the School Standards and Organisation (Wales) Act 2013 Pt 2 Ch 2 (ss 21–31).
9 School Standards and Organisation (Wales) Act 2013 s 23(3).
10 School Standards and Organisation (Wales) Act 2013 s 23(4).
11 Ie their powers under the School Standards and Organisation (Wales) Act 2013 Pt 2 Ch 2 (ss 21–31).
12 School Standards and Organisation (Wales) Act 2013 s 23(5). The Welsh Ministers' power to intervene continues in effect until they give notice under s 23(5): s 23(6).
13 School Standards and Organisation (Wales) Act 2013 s 23(7).

1239. Powers of intervention.   The following apply where the Welsh Ministers[1] have the power to intervene in the exercise of education functions[2] by a local authority[3].

The Welsh Ministers may direct[4] the local authority to enter into a contract or other arrangement with a specified[5] person, or a person falling within a specified class for the provision to the authority or the governing body of a school maintained by it (or both), of specified services of an advisory nature[6].

The Welsh Ministers may give such directions to the local authority or any of its officers as they think are appropriate for securing that the functions to which the grounds for intervention relate are performed on behalf of the authority by a person specified in the direction[7].

The Welsh Ministers may direct that the functions to which the grounds for intervention relate are to be exercised by the Welsh Ministers or a person nominated by them[8].

If they think it is appropriate in order to deal with the grounds for intervention, the Welsh Ministers may give directions to the local authority or any of its officers, or take any other steps[9].

1 As to the Welsh Ministers see PARA 59.
2 As to the meaning of 'education functions' see PARA 25 (definition applied by the School Standards and Organisation (Wales) Act 2013 s 98(1)).
3 See the School Standards and Organisation (Wales) Act 2013 ss 24(1), 25(1), 26(1), 28(1). As to the meaning of 'local authority' see PARA 1231 note 1.
4 A local authority, or an officer of an authority, subject to a direction or instruction under the School Standards and Organisation (Wales) Act 2013 Pt 2 Ch 2 (ss 21–31) must comply with it: s 29(1). This includes a direction or an instruction to exercise a power or duty that is contingent upon the opinion of the local authority or an officer of the authority: s 29(2). The direction must be in writing, it may be varied or revoked by a later direction and it is enforceable by mandatory order on application by, or on behalf of, the Welsh Ministers: s 29(3).
5 For these purposes 'specified' means specified in a direction under the School Standards and Organisation (Wales) Act 2013 s 24. The direction may require the contract or other arrangement to contain specified terms and conditions: s 24(3).
6 School Standards and Organisation (Wales) Act 2013 s 24(2). A person specified under s 24 or, where the direction specified a class of persons, the person with whom the local authority enters into the contract or other arrangement required by the direction, has a power of entry and inspection: see PARA 1241.
7 School Standards and Organisation (Wales) Act 2013 s 25(2). Such a direction may require that any contract or other arrangement made by the authority with the specified person contains terms and conditions specified in the direction: s 25(3). If a direction under s 25(2) is in force, the functions of the local authority to which it relates are to be treated for all purposes as being exercisable by the specified person: s 25(4) (added by the Education (Wales) Act 2014 s 44(2)). If the Welsh Ministers think it is expedient, a direction under the School Standards and Organisation (Wales) Act 2013 s 25 or 26 may relate to the performance of education functions in addition to the functions to which the grounds for intervention relate: s 27(1). The Welsh Ministers may have regard (among other things) to financial considerations in deciding whether it is expedient that a direction should relate to education functions other than functions relating to the grounds for intervention: s 27(2). As to the meaning of 'functions' see PARA 18 note 5 (definition applied by the School Standards and Organisation (Wales) Act 2013 s 98(1)). A person specified in a direction under s 25 has a power of entry and inspection: see PARA 1241.

8   School Standards and Organisation (Wales) Act 2013 s 26(2). If such a direction is made the
    local authority must comply with the instructions of the Welsh Ministers or their nominee in
    relation to the exercise of the functions.: s 26(3). See note 7. If a direction under s 26(2) is in
    force, the functions of the local authority to which it relates are to be treated for all purposes as
    being exercisable by the Welsh Ministers or their nominee: s 26(4) (added by the Education
    (Wales) Act 2014 s 44(3)). The Welsh Ministers in pursuance of a direction under s 26 and a
    person nominated by a direction under s 26 have a power of entry and inspection: see PARA
    1241.
9   School Standards and Organisation (Wales) Act 2013 s 28(2).

1240.   Duty to co-operate.   A local authority[1] and the governing body of a
maintained school[2] must give the Welsh Ministers[3] and any person specified[4] as
much assistance in connection with the exercise of functions[5] under or by virtue
of provisions relating to the intervention in local authorities[6] as they are
reasonably able to give[7]. The governing body of a maintained school and the
local authority that maintains the school must also secure, so far as reasonably
practicable, that persons who work at the school do the same[8].

1   As to the meaning of 'local authority' see PARA 1231 note 1.
2   As to the meaning of 'maintained school' see PARA 1229 note 5.
3   As to the Welsh Ministers see PARA 59.
4   The specified persons are:
    (1)   any person authorised for the purposes of the School Standards and Organisation
          (Wales) Act 2013 s 30 by the Welsh Ministers (s 30(3)(a));
    (2)   any person acting under directions under Pt 2 Ch 2 (s 30(3)(b));
    (3)   any person assisting the Welsh Ministers or assisting a person mentioned in head (1) or
          (2) (s 30(3)(c)).
5   As to the meaning of 'functions' see PARA 18 note 5 (definition applied by the School Standards
    and Organisation (Wales) Act 2013 s 98(1)).
6   Ie under or by virtue of the School Standards and Organisation (Wales) Act 2013 Pt 2 Ch 2
    (ss 21–31).
7   School Standards and Organisation (Wales) Act 2013 s 30(1).
8   School Standards and Organisation (Wales) Act 2013 s 30(2).

1241.   Power of entry and inspection.   Certain persons[1] specified in directions
relating to powers of intervention in local authorities[2] have at all reasonable
times:
    (1)   a right of entry to the premises of the local authority in question and
          any school maintained by it[3];
    (2)   a right to inspect, and take copies of, any records or other documents[4]
          kept by the authority or any school maintained by it, and any other
          documents containing information relating to the authority or any such
          school, which the person considers relevant to the exercise by the person
          of functions under or by virtue of provisions[5] relating to the invention
          of local authorities[6].
In exercising the right under head (2) above to inspect records or other
documents, a person ('P'):
    (a)   is entitled to have access to, and inspect and check the operation of, any
          computer and any associated apparatus or material which is or has been
          in use in connection with the records or other documents in question[7];
          and
    (b)   may require the following persons to provide any assistance P may
          reasonably require (including, among other things, the making of
          information available for inspection or copying in a legible form);
          (i)   the person by whom or on whose behalf the computer is or has
                 been so used[8];

(ii)   any person having charge of, or otherwise concerned with the operation of, the computer, apparatus or material[9].

1   The following persons fall within the School Standards and Organisation (Wales) Act 2013 s 31:
    (1)   the person specified in a direction under s 24 (see PARA 1239) or, where the direction specifies a class of persons, the person with whom the local authority enter into the contract or other arrangement required by the direction (s 31(2)(a));
    (2)   the person specified in a direction under s 25 (see PARA 1239) (s 31(2)(b));
    (3)   the Welsh Ministers in pursuance of a direction under s 26 (see PARA 1239) (s 31(2)(c));
    (4)   the person nominated by direction under s 26 (s 31(2)(d)).
    Any reference in s 31 to a person falling within s 31(2) includes a reference to any person assisting that person: s 31(4).
2   As to the meaning of 'local authority' see PARA 1231 note 1.
3   School Standards and Organisation (Wales) Act 2013 s 31(1)(a).
4   For these purposes 'document' and 'records' each include information recorded in any form: School Standards and Organisation (Wales) Act 2013 s 31(5).
5   Ie under or by virtue of the School Standards and Organisation (Wales) Act 2013 Pt 2 Ch 2 (ss 21–31).
6   School Standards and Organisation (Wales) Act 2013 s 31(1)(b).
7   School Standards and Organisation (Wales) Act 2013 s 31(3)(a).
8   School Standards and Organisation (Wales) Act 2013 s 31(3)(b)(i).
9   School Standards and Organisation (Wales) Act 2013 s 31(3)(b)(ii).

C. SCHOOL IMPROVEMENT GUIDANCE

1242.   School improvement guidance. The School Standards and Organisation (Wales) Act 2013[1] makes provision for the Welsh Ministers[2] to give guidance to the governing bodies of maintained schools[3], the head teachers[4] of such schools[5] and local authorities[6] on how functions[7] should be exercised with a view to improving the standard of education provided in maintained schools[8].

1   Ie the School Standards and Organisation (Wales) Act 2013 Pt 2 Ch 3 (ss 32–37).
2   As to the Welsh Ministers see PARA 59.
3   As to the meaning of 'maintained school' see PARA 1229 note 5.
4   As to the meaning of 'head teacher' see PARA 86 note 4 (definition applied by the School Standards and Organisation (Wales) Act 2013 s 98(1)).
5   As to the meaning of 'school' see PARA 91 (definition applied by the School Standards and Organisation (Wales) Act 2013 s 98(1)).
6   As to the local authority power of intervention see PARA 1232.
7   As to the meaning of 'functions' see PARA 18 note 5 (definition applied by the School Standards and Organisation (Wales) Act 2013 s 98(1)).
8   School Standards and Organisation (Wales) Act 2013 s 1(5).

1243.   Power to issue school improvement guidance. The Welsh Ministers[1] may issue guidance to a school authority[2] on how the authority should exercise its functions[3] with a view to improving the standard of education provided by any maintained school in respect of which the authority exercises functions ('school improvement guidance')[4].

The Welsh Ministers:
    (1)   may issue school improvement guidance to school authorities generally or to one or more particular authorities[5];
    (2)   may issue different school improvement guidance to different school authorities[6];
    (3)   may revise or revoke school improvement guidance by further guidance[7];
    (4)   may revoke school improvement guidance by issuing a notice to the school authorities to which it is directed[8].

The Welsh Ministers must arrange for school improvement guidance, or a notice revoking such guidance, to be published[9].

1 As to the Welsh Ministers see PARA 59.
2 In the School Standards and Organisation (Wales) Act 2013 Pt 2 Ch 3 (ss 32–37) 'school authority' means:
    (1) a local authority in the exercise of its education functions (s 32(a));
    (2) the governing body of a maintained school (s 32(b));
    (3) the head teacher of a maintained school (s 32(c)).
    As to the meaning of 'maintained school' see PARA 1229 note 5. As to the meanings of 'education functions' and 'head teacher' see PARAS 25, 86 note 4 (definitions applied by s 98(1)). As to the meaning of 'local authority' see PARA 1231 note 1.
3 As to the meaning of 'functions' see the Education Act 1996 s 579(1); and PARA 18 note 5 (definition applied by the School Standards and Organisation (Wales) Act 2013 s 98(1)).
4 School Standards and Organisation (Wales) Act 2013 s 33(1). The Welsh Ministers must ensure that school improvement guidance, or a notice revoking such guidance, states that it is issued under s 33 and the date on which it is to take effect: s 33(3).
5 School Standards and Organisation (Wales) Act 2013 s 33(2)(a).
6 School Standards and Organisation (Wales) Act 2013 s 33(2)(b).
7 School Standards and Organisation (Wales) Act 2013 s 33(2)(c).
8 School Standards and Organisation (Wales) Act 2013 s 33(2)(d).
9 School Standards and Organisation (Wales) Act 2013 s 33(4).

1244. Consultation about school improvement guidance, and duty to lay draft guidance before the National Assembly for Wales. Before issuing or revising school improvement guidance[1], the Welsh Ministers[2] must consult the following persons on a draft of the guidance:
    (1) the school authorities[3] likely to be affected by the guidance[4],
    (2) Her Majesty's Chief Inspector of Education and Training in Wales[5]; and
    (3) any other person the Welsh Ministers consider appropriate[6].
If the Welsh Ministers wish to proceed with the draft (with or without modifications) they must lay a copy of the draft before the National Assembly for Wales[7].

1 As to issuing school improvement guidance see PARA 1243.
2 As to the Welsh Ministers see PARA 59.
3 As to the meaning of 'school authority' see PARA 1243 note 2.
4 School Standards and Organisation (Wales) Act 2013 s 34(1)(a).
5 School Standards and Organisation (Wales) Act 2013 34(1)(b). As to Her Majesty's Chief Inspector of Education and Training in Wales see PARA 1148.
6 School Standards and Organisation (Wales) Act 2013 s 34(1)(c).
7 School Standards and Organisation (Wales) Act 2013 s 34(2). If, before the end of the 40 day period, the National Assembly resolves not to approve the draft of the guidance, the Welsh Ministers must not issue it in the form of that draft: s 34(3). If no such resolution is made before the end of that period, the Welsh Ministers must issue the guidance (or revised guidance) in the form of the draft: s 34(4). The 40 day period begins on the day on which the draft is laid before the National Assembly and does not include any time during which the National Assembly is dissolved or is in recess for more than four days: s 34(5). Section 34(3) does not prevent a new draft of proposed guidance or proposed revised guidance from being laid before the National Assembly: s 34(6).

1245. Duty to follow school improvement guidance. A school authority[1] must follow the course set out in school improvement guidance issued to it[2] when exercising a power or duty (including a power or duty that is contingent upon the opinion of the school authority); but this is subject to the following[3].
    A school authority that is a local authority[4] is not subject to this duty[5] so far as:
    (1) the authority thinks there is good reason for it not to follow the guidance in particular categories of case or at all[6];

(2) it decides on an alternative policy for the exercise of its functions in respect of the subject matter of the guidance[7]; and

(3) a policy statement[8] issued by the authority is in effect[9].

A school authority that is the governing body of a maintained school[10] or its head teacher[11] is not subject to the above duty[12] so far as:

(a) the governing body thinks there is good reason for it or the head teacher not to follow the guidance in particular categories of case or at all[13];

(b) the governing body decides on an alternative policy for the exercise of its, or the head teacher's, functions in respect of the subject matter of the guidance[14]; and

(c) a policy statement issued[15] by the governing body is in effect[16].

Where head (1) to (3) or (a) to (c) above applies[17] in the case of a school authority, the authority must follow the course set out in the policy statement and is subject to the duty[18] only so far as the subject matter of the school improvement guidance is not displaced by the policy statement[19].

1 As to the meaning of 'school authority' see PARA 1243 note 2.
2 Ie issued in accordance with the School Standards and Organisation (Wales) Act 2013 Pt 2 Ch 3 (ss 32–37). As to issuing school improvement guidance see PARA 1243.
3 School Standards and Organisation (Wales) Act 2013 s 35(1).
4 As to the meaning of 'local authority' see PARA 1231 note 1.
5 Ie the duty under the School Standards and Organisation (Wales) Act 2013 s 35(1).
6 School Standards and Organisation (Wales) Act 2013 s 35(2)(a).
7 School Standards and Organisation (Wales) Act 2013 s 35(2)(b). If, in relation to a policy statement issued by a school authority, the Welsh Ministers consider that the authority's alternative policy for the exercise of functions (in whole or in part) is not likely to improve the standard of education provided at a school to which the policy statement relates, the Welsh Ministers may direct the school authority to take any action which the Welsh Ministers consider appropriate for the purpose of securing the exercise of functions by the authority in accordance with the school improvement guidance issued to the authority in accordance with Pt 2 Ch 3 (ss 32–37): see s 37.
8 Ie issued in accordance with the School Standards and Organisation (Wales) Act 2013 s 36 (see PARA 1246)
9 School Standards and Organisation (Wales) Act 2013 s 35(2)(c).
10 As to the meaning of 'maintained school' see PARA 1230 note 4.
11 As to the meaning of 'head teacher' see PARA 86 note 4 (definition applied by the School Standards and Organisation (Wales) Act 2013 s 98(1)).
12 See note 5.
13 School Standards and Organisation (Wales) Act 2013 s 35(3)(a).
14 School Standards and Organisation (Wales) Act 2013 s 35(3)(b).
15 See note 8.
16 School Standards and Organisation (Wales) Act 2013 s 35(3)(c).
17 Ie where the School Standards and Organisation (Wales) Act 2013 s 35(2) or (3) applies.
18 See note 5.
19 School Standards and Organisation (Wales) Act 2013 s 35(4). The duties in s 35(1) and (4) do not apply to a school authority so far as it would be unreasonable for the authority to follow the school improvement guidance or policy statement in a particular case or category of case: s 35(5).

1246. Policy statements: requirements and ancillary powers. A policy statement[1] must set out how the local authority[2] or governing body (as the case may be) proposes that functions[3] should be exercised differently from the course set out in the school improvement guidance[4], and the authority's or the body's reasons for proposing that different course[5].

An authority or body that has issued a policy statement:

(1) may issue a revised policy statement[6];

(2) give notice revoking a policy statement[7].

1   Ie issued under the School Standards and Organisation (Wales) Act 2013 s 35(2) or (3) (see PARA 1245).
2   As to the meaning of 'local authority' see PARA 1231 note 1.
3   As to the meaning of 'functions' see PARA 18 note 5 (definition applied by the School Standards and Organisation (Wales) Act 2013 s 98(1)).
4   As to the school improvement guidance see PARA 1243.
5   School Standards and Organisation (Wales) Act 2013 s 36(1). A policy statement (or revised statement) must state that it is issued under s 35(2) or (3) (as the case may be), and the date on which it is to take effect: s 36(3).
6   School Standards and Organisation (Wales) Act 2013 s 36(2)(a).
7   School Standards and Organisation (Wales) Act 2013 s 36(2)(b). The authority or body that issues a policy statement (or revised statement), or gives a notice under s 36(2)(b) must arrange for a statement or notice to be published and send a copy of any statement or notice to the Welsh Ministers: s 36(4). As to the Welsh Ministers see PARA 59.

(v) Intervention in relation to Sixth Form Colleges

A. INTERVENTION FOR MISMANAGEMENT OR BREACH OF DUTY IN ENGLAND

1247.   Intervention by Secretary of State. If the Secretary of State[1] is satisfied, whether or not a complaint is made by any person[2], as to one or more the matters listed below in relation to a sixth form college[3], namely:

(1)   that the sixth form college's affairs have been or are being mismanaged by its governing body[4];
(2)   that the sixth form college's governing body has failed to discharge any duty imposed on it by or for the purposes of any Act[5];
(3)   that the sixth form college's governing body has acted or is proposing to act unreasonably with respect to the exercise of any power conferred or the performance of any duty imposed by or under any Act[6];
(4)   that the sixth form college is performing significantly less well than it might in all the circumstances reasonably be expected to perform, or is failing or likely to fail to give an accepted standard of education or training[7],

the Secretary of State may do one or more of the following things[8]:

(a)   remove all or any of the members of the sixth form college's governing body[9];
(b)   appoint new members of that body if there are vacancies (however arising)[10];
(c)   give to that body such directions[11] as the Secretary of State thinks expedient as to the exercise of the body's powers and performance of the body's duties[12].

Before doing one or more of those things, the Secretary of State must consult the trustees of the sixth form college and each person or body with power under the college's instrument of government to appoint or nominate one or more of its foundation governors[13]. After carrying out the consultation the Secretary of State must give the persons and bodies consulted a notice stating what he has decided to do and the reasons for the decision[14].

If the Secretary of State does one or more of those things listed in heads (a) to (c), he must at the same time give the sixth form college's governing body a notice stating the matter or matters listed in heads (1) to (4) above as to which he is satisfied and the reasons why he has decided to do that thing or those things[15].

The directions that may be given to a governing body include a direction requiring a governing body to make collaboration arrangements[16] with such bodies and on such terms as may be specified in the direction and a direction requiring a governing body to make a resolution[17] for the body to be dissolved on a date specified in the direction[18].

Directions may be given to a governing body despite any enactment making the exercise of a power or performance of a duty contingent on the body's opinion[19]. However, the Secretary of State may not direct a governing body[20] to dismiss a member of staff[21].

A governing body must comply with any directions given to it under these provisions[22].

1 As to the Secretary of State see PARA 58.
2 As to the meaning of 'person' see PARA 7 note 6.
3 See the Further and Higher Education Act 1992 s 56E(1) (s 56E added by the Apprenticeships, Skills, Children and Learning Act 2009 s 125, Sch 8 paras 1, 8; Further and Higher Education Act 1992 s 56E(1) amended by SI 2010/1158; and the Education Act 2011 Sch 12 para 30(2)). As to the meaning of references to 'sixth form colleges' see PARA 555 note 5. As to sixth form colleges generally see PARA 577 et seq.
4 Further and Higher Education Act 1992 s 56E(2)(a) (as added see note 3). As to the meaning of 'governing body' see PARA 560 note 6.
5 Further and Higher Education Act 1992 s 56E(2)(b) (as added: see note 3).
6 Further and Higher Education Act 1992 s 56E(2)(c) (as added: see note 3).
7 Further and Higher Education Act 1992 s 56E(2)(d) (as added: see note 3).
8 See the Further and Higher Education Act 1992 s 56E(3) (as added (see note 3); amended by the Education Act 2011 Sch 12 para 30(6)(a)).
9 Further and Higher Education Act 1992 s 56E(6)(a) (as added: see note 3).
10 Further and Higher Education Act 1992 s 56E(6)(b) (as added: see note 3). An appointment of a member of a governing body under s 56E has effect as if made in accordance with the governing body's instrument of government and articles of government: s 56E(12) (as so added).
11 As to directions see the Education Act 1996 s 570 (applied by the Further and Higher Education Act 1992 s 89(5)); and PARA 75.
12 Further and Higher Education Act 1992 s 56E(6)(c) (as added (see note 3); amended by the Education Act 2011 Sch 12 para 30(6)(b)).
13 Further and Higher Education Act 1992 s 56E(4A) (s 56E, 4 substituted and s 56E(4A), (4B) added by the Education Act 2011 Sch 12 para 30(4)). The Further and Higher Education Act 1992 s 56E(4A), (4B) apply to a sixth form college which is specified, or falls within a class specified, in an order under s 33J(2) (see PARA 583): s 56E(4) (as so substituted).
14 Further and Higher Education Act 1992 s 56E(4B) (as added: see note 13).
15 Further and Higher Education Act 1992 s 56E(5) (as added (see note 3); and amended by the Education Act 2011 Sch 12 para 30(5)).
16 Ie within the meaning of the Education and Inspections Act 2006 s 166: see PARA 172.
17 Ie a resolution under the Further and Higher Education Act 1992 s 33O(1) (see PARA 586). A governing body to which a direction such as is mentioned in s 56E(7)(b) is given is to be taken for the purposes of s 33O(1) to have complied with s 33N (see PARA 586) before making the resolution required by the direction: s 56E(7A) (added by the Education Act 2011 Sch 12 para 30(7)).
18 Further and Higher Education Act 1992 s 56E(7) (as added (see note 3); amended by the Education Act 2011 Sch 12 para 30(7)).
19 Further and Higher Education Act 1992 s 56E(8) (as added: see note 3).
20 Ie under the Further and Higher Education Act 1992 s 56E(6)(c): see head (c) in the text.
21 Further and Higher Education Act 1992 s 56E(9) (as added (see note 3); substituted by the Education Act 2011 Sch 12 para 30(8)).
22 Further and Higher Education Act 1992 s 56E(11) (as added: see note 3).

B. INTERVENTION RELATING TO SIXTH FORM EDUCATION IN WALES

(A) Proposals for Restructuring Sixth Form Education

1248. Making and determining proposals. The Welsh Ministers[1] may make proposals[2] for:

(1)   the establishment by a local authority[3] of one or more new community

or community special schools to provide secondary education[4] suitable to the requirements of sixth formers[5] (and no other secondary education)[6];

(2)   an alteration[7] described to one or more maintained schools[8];

(3)   the discontinuance[9] of one or more maintained schools which provide secondary education suitable to the requirements of sixth formers (and no other secondary education)[10].

Before publishing such proposals[11], the Welsh Ministers must consult on the proposals in accordance with the school organisation code[12] for the time being in force[13] and publish the proposals in accordance with the code[14]. Objections must be sent in writing to the Welsh Ministers before the end of 28 days beginning with the day on which the proposals were published[15]. At the end of this 28 day period the Welsh Ministers must determine whether to adopt the proposals, with or without modifications, or whether to withdraw the proposals[16].

1   As to the Welsh Ministers see PARA 59.
2   Ie under the School Standards and Organisation (Wales) Act 2013 s 71.
3   As to the meaning of 'local authority' see PARA 1231 note 1.
4   As to the meaning of 'secondary education' see PARA 21 (definition applied by the School Standards and Organisation (Wales) Act 2013 s 98(1)). As to the meaning of 'special school' see PARA 1041 (definition applied by s 98(1)).
5   A 'sixth former' is a person who is above compulsory school age but below the age of 19: School Standards and Organisation (Wales) Act 2013 s 71(2). As to the meaning of 'compulsory school age' see PARA 19 (definition applied by s 98(1)).
6   School Standards and Organisation (Wales) Act 2013 s 71(1)(a).
7   As described in the School Standards and Organisation (Wales) Act 2013 Sch 2 para 6 (see PARA 140).
8   School Standards and Organisation (Wales) Act 2013 s 71(1)(b).
9   A reference in the School Standards and Organisation (Wales) Act 2013 Pt 3 (ss 38–83 and Schs 2–4) to the discontinuance of a maintained school is a reference to the local authority ceasing to maintain it: s 83(3).
10   School Standards and Organisation (Wales) Act 2013 s 71(1)(c).
11   Ie proposals under the School Standards and Organisation (Wales) Act 2013 s 71.
12   Ie the code issued under the School Standards and Organisation (Wales) Act 2013 s 38(1) (see PARA 139).
13   School Standards and Organisation (Wales) Act 2013 s 72(1).
14   See the School Standards and Organisation (Wales) Act 2013 s 72(3).
15   School Standards and Organisation (Wales) Act 2013 s 72(4).
16   See the School Standards and Organisation (Wales) Act 2013 s 73(1). In making a determination under s 73(1), the Welsh Ministers must have regard to any objections made in accordance with s 72(4) and not withdrawn: s 73(2). Before adopting proposals subject to modifications, the Welsh Ministers must consult such persons as they consider appropriate: s 73(3). The adoption of proposals may be expressed to take effect only if an event specified in the adoption occurs by a date so specified: s 73(4). If the event does not occur by the specified date the Welsh Ministers must reconsider their determination under s 73(1): s 73(5). The Welsh Ministers may withdraw their proposals at any time before they make a determination under s 73(1): s 73(6).

1249.   Implementation of proposals for restructuring sixth form education. The following[1] apply to proposals for restructuring sixth form education which have been adopted[2] by the Welsh Ministers[3].

The proposals must[4] be implemented in the form in which they were adopted[5].

At the request of a specified body[6], the Welsh Ministers may modify[7] the adopted proposals[8] after consulting the specified bodies and, where the adoption of proposals was expressed to take effect subject to the occurrence of a specified event, they may specify a later date by which that event must occur[9].

The Welsh Ministers may determine that the requirement to implement the proposals in the form in which they were adopted[10] does not apply to the proposals if they are satisfied, after consulting the specified bodies that implementation of the proposals would be unreasonably difficult, or that circumstances have so altered since the proposals were adopted that implementation of the proposals would be inappropriate[11].

Proposals to establish a school must be implemented by the local authority that it is proposed will maintain the school[12]. Proposals to make an alteration[13] must be implemented:

(1)   in the case of proposals relating to a community school, by the local authority that maintains the school[14];

(2)   in the case of proposals relating to a voluntary aided school so far as relating to the provision of any relevant premises[15], by the local authority that maintains the school[16] and, otherwise, by the local authority that maintains the school and the governing body of the school to the extent (if any) as the proposals provide for each of them to do so[17];

(3)   in the case of proposals relating to any other school, by the local authority that maintains the school and the governing body of the school to the extent (if any) as the proposals provide for each of them to do so[18].

Proposals to discontinue a school must be implemented, in the case of proposals relating to a community or community special school, by the local authority that maintains the school and, in any other case, by the local authority that maintains the school and the governing body of the school[19].

If a school changes category[20] from a community school after proposals have been published under[21] but before they have been implemented, the proposals (to the extent that they have not been implemented) must be implemented by the local authority that maintains the school[22].

1   Ie the School Standards and Organisation (Wales) Act 2013 s 74. Where a local authority is required by virtue of s 75 to provide a site for a foundation or voluntary controlled school, Sch 3 para 7 (provision of site and buildings for foundation or voluntary controlled school) applies as it applies in the circumstances mentioned in Sch 3 para 7(1): s 76(1). As to the meaning of 'local authority' see PARA 1231 note 1. As to the meaning of 'school' see PARA 91 (definition applied by s 98(1)).

2   Ie proposals adopted under the School Standards and Organisation (Wales) Act 2013 s 73 (see PARA 1248).

3   School Standards and Organisation (Wales) Act 2013 s 74(1). As to the Welsh Ministers see PARA 59.

4   This is subject to the School Standards and Organisation (Wales) Act 2013 s 74(3)–(5).

5   School Standards and Organisation (Wales) Act 2013 s 74(2).

6   Each of the following is a 'specified body' for the purposes of the School Standards and Organisation (Wales) Act 2013 s 74(3), (4):

(1)   the governing body of the school to which the proposals relate (s 74(5)(a));

(2)   in the case of a proposal to establish a new school, the temporary governing body constituted in accordance with arrangements made under the Education Act 2002 s 34 (see PARA 197) (School Standards and Organisation (Wales) Act 2013 s 74(5)(b));

(3)   the local authority that maintains, or that it is proposed will maintain, the school to which the proposals relate (s 74(5)(c));

(4)   where the school to which the proposals relate is a community special school each local authority which maintains a statement of special educational needs under the Education Act 1996 Pt 4 in respect of a registered pupil at the school (School Standards and Organisation (Wales) Act 2013 s 75(5)(d)).

As to the meaning of 'special school' see PARA 1041 (definition applied by s 98(1)). As to the meaning of 'special educational needs' see PARA 989 (definition applied by s 98(1)). As to the meaning of 'registered pupil' see PARA 437 (definition applied by s 98(1)).

7 As to the meaning of 'modify' see PARA 21 note 15 (definition applied by s 98(1)).

8 See note 2.

9 School Standards and Organisation (Wales) Act 2013 s 74(3).

10 Ie that the School Standards and Organisation (Wales) Act 2013 s 74(2).

11 School Standards and Organisation (Wales) Act 2013 s 74(4).

12 School Standards and Organisation (Wales) Act 2013 s 75(1).

13 Ie as described in the School Standards and Organisation (Wales) Act 2013 Sch 2 para 6 (see PARA 140).

14 School Standards and Organisation (Wales) Act 2013 s 75(2)(a).

15 For these purposes 'relevant premises' means playing fields or buildings which are to form part of the school premises but are not to be school buildings: School Standards and Organisation (Wales) Act 2013 s 75(3).

16 School Standards and Organisation (Wales) Act 2013 s 75(2)(b)(i).

17 School Standards and Organisation (Wales) Act 2013 s 75(2)(b)(ii). Schedule 3 para 8 (grants in respect of certain expenditure relating to voluntary aided schools) applies in relation to the obligation under s 75(2)(b)(ii) as it applies in relation to the obligations referred to in Sch 3 para 8(1)(a): s 76(2). Schedule 3 para 9 (assistance from local authority in respect of voluntary aided schools) applies in relation to obligations imposed on the governing body of a voluntary aided school under s 75(2)(b)(ii) as it applies in relation to the obligations referred to in Sch 9 paras 9, 11 (duty on local authority to transfer interest in premises provided under Sch 9 paras 9 or 10) applies accordingly: s 76(3).

18 School Standards and Organisation (Wales) Act 2013 s 75(2)(c).

19 School Standards and Organisation (Wales) Act 2013 s 75(4).

20 A reference in the School Standards and Organisation (Wales) Act 2013 Pt 3 (ss 38–83 and Schs 2–4) to a school's category means one of the categories set out in the School Standards and Framework Act 1998 s 20(1) (see PARA 106) (and references to a change of category are to be read accordingly): School Standards and Organisation (Wales) Act 2013 s 83(2).

21 Ie under the School Standards and Organisation (Wales) Act 2013 s 72 (see PARA 1248).

22 School Standards and Organisation (Wales) Act 2013 s 75(5). This is despite s 75(2) and (4).

(B) Sixth Forms Requiring Significant improvement in Wales

1250. Schools with sixth forms requiring significant improvement in Wales.
The following[1] apply to a maintained school[2] in Wales which provides full-time education suitable to the requirements of pupils[3] over compulsory school age[4] and provides full-time education suitable to the requirements of pupils of compulsory school age[5].

Where a person carrying out a regular inspection of a school[6] is of the opinion that the school requires significant improvement in relation to its sixth form[7], provisions relating to reports of inspections by registered inspectors[8] or, as the case requires, provisions relating to reports by members of the Inspectorate[9] apply (with the necessary modifications) as they apply where the person is of the opinion that special measures are required to be taken in relation to the school[10].

Where the report of a regular inspection[11] states an opinion that a school requires significant improvement in relation to its sixth form, and it is made by a member of the Inspectorate or states that Her Majesty's Chief Inspector of Education and Training in Wales (the 'Chief Inspector') agrees with the opinion, the person making the report must send a copy (together with a copy of the summary, if there is one)[12] to the Welsh Ministers[13] and, if the person making the report is a member of the Inspectorate, to the appropriate authority[14] for the school[15].

If, in the course of an area inspection[16], the Chief Inspector forms the opinion that a school requires significant improvement in relation to its sixth form he must make a report about the school stating that opinion[17].

1 Ie the Education Act 2005 ss 44B–44D.

2 'Maintained school' means a community, foundation or voluntary school or a community special school: Education Act 2005 s 44F (ss 44A–44D, 44F added by the School Standards and Organisation (Wales) Act 2013 s 77).

3 As to the meaning of 'pupil' see PARA 20 note 4 (definition applied by the Education Act 2005 s 122(2), (3)).

4 As to the meaning of 'compulsory school age' see PARA 19 (definition applied by s 122(2), (3)).

5 Education Act 2005 s 44A(1) (as added: see note 2).

6 Ie an inspection under the Education Act 2005 Pt 1 Ch 3 (ss 19–31).

7 For the purposes of the Education Act 2005 ss 44B–44D a school requires significant improvement in relation to its sixth form if it is failing to give its pupils over compulsory school age an acceptable standard of education, or if, in relation to its provision for pupils over compulsory school age, the school is performing significantly less well than it might in all the circumstances reasonably be expected to perform: s 44A(2) (as added: see note 2).

8 Ie the Education Act 2005 s 34(1)–(6) (registered inspectors) (see PARA 1192).

9 Ie the Education Act 2005 s 35(1) (members of the Inspectorate) (see PARA 1193). 'Member of the Inspectorate' means the Chief Inspector, any of Her Majesty's Inspectors of Education and Training in Wales and any additional inspector appointed under Sch 2 para 2 (see PARA 1149): s 44F (as added: see note 2).

10 See the Education Act 2005 s 44B(1) (as added: see note 2).

11 Ie under the Education Act 2005 Pt 1 Ch 3 (ss 19–31 and Schs 2–4).

12 In the application of the Education Act 2005 s 44D a reference to a report and summary is to be taken as a reference to a report and, if there is one, its summary, and a reference to a summary alone is to be taken, in a case where there is no summary, as a reference to the report: s 44D(4) (as added: see note 2).

13 As to the Welsh Ministers see PARA 59.

14 'The appropriate authority', in relation to a maintained school, means the school's governing body or, if the school does not have a delegated budget, the local authority: Education Act 2005 s 44F (as added: see note 2).

15 See the Education Act 2005 s 44D(1), (2) (as added: see note 2). Sections 38(2), (4) (see PARA 1196), 39 (see PARA 1197) and, where the local authority receives a copy of a report about a school the governing body of which have a delegated budget, s 40(2), (3) (see PARA 1198) apply (with the necessary modifications) in relation to a report to with s 44D applies: see s 44D(3) (as so added).

16 Ie under the Learning and Skills Act 2000 s 83 (see PARA 1275).

17 Education Act 2005 s 44B(2) (as added: see note 2). The report is to be treated for the purposes of Pt 1 (ss 1–63 and Schs 1–9 as if it were a report of an inspection of the school under s 28 (see PARA 1182): s 44C(3) (as added: see note 2).

1251. Sixth form schools requiring significant improvement in Wales. If in the course of an area inspection[1] Her Majesty's Chief Inspector of Education and Training in Wales (the 'Chief Inspector') forms the opinion that special measures[2] are required to be taken in relation to a sixth form school[3] or that a sixth form school requires significant improvement[4] he must make a report about the school stating that opinion[5].

1 Ie under the Learning and Skills Act 2000 s 83 (see PARA 1275).

2 As to the meaning of 'special measures' see PARA 1167 note 3.

3 A 'sixth form school' is a maintained school which provides full-time education suitable to the requirements of pupils over compulsory school age and does not provide full-time education suitable to the requirements of pupils of compulsory school age: Education Act 2005 s 44E(4) (added by the School Standards and Organisation (Wales) Act 2013 s 77).

4 As to the meaning of 'significant improvement' see PARA 1167 note 4.

5 See the Education Act 2005 s 44E(1), (2) (as added: see note 3). s 44E(2). The report is to be treated for the purpose of Pt 1 (ss 1–63 and Schs 1–9) as if it were a report of an inspection of the school under s 28 (see PARA 1182): s 44E(3) (as so added).

(4) INSPECTION OF CHILDCARE, EARLY YEARS PROVISION AND NURSERY EDUCATION

(i) Inspection of Childcare and Early Years Provision in England

1252. Inspection of childcare provision and children's centres in England. The inspection of childcare, whether early years provision or later years provision, in respect of which the provider is registered under the Childcare Act 2006 is a function of Her Majesty's Chief Inspector of Education, Children's Services and Skills[1]. The Chief Inspector also has the function of inspecting children's centres[2]. The relevant statutory provisions are covered in detail elsewhere in this work[3].

1   See the Childcare Act 2006 ss 49–50, 60–61; and CHILDREN AND YOUNG PERSONS vol 10 (2012) PARAS 1099, 1106. As to Her Majesty's Chief Inspector of Education, Children's Services and Skills see PARA 1133.
2   See the Childcare Act 2006 ss 98A–98G; and CHILDREN AND YOUNG PERSONS vol 10 (2012) PARA 1080.
3   See notes 1–2.

(ii) Inspection of Nursery Education in Wales

1253. General functions of Her Majesty's Chief Inspector of Education and Training in Wales. Her Majesty's Chief Inspector of Education and Training in Wales[1] has the general duty of keeping the Welsh Ministers[2] informed about[3]:
(1)   the quality and standards of relevant nursery education[4];
(2)   how far relevant nursery education meets the needs of the range of children for whom it is provided[5];
(3)   the quality of leadership and management in connection with the provision of relevant nursery education[6];
(4)   the contribution of relevant nursery education to the well-being[7] of the children for whom it is provided[8]; and
(5)   the spiritual, moral, social and cultural development of children for whom relevant nursery education is provided[9].
When asked to do so by the Welsh Ministers, the Chief Inspector must give advice to the Welsh Ministers on such matters relating to relevant nursery education as may be specified in the request[10]. The Chief Inspector may at any time give advice to the Welsh Ministers on any matter connected with[11]:
(a)   relevant nursery education generally[12]; or
(b)   relevant nursery education, or nursery education under consideration for funding, provided at particular premises[13].

1   As to Her Majesty's Chief Inspector of Education and Training in Wales see PARA 1148.
2   As to the Welsh Ministers see PARA 59. The functions under the School Standards and Framework Act 1998 Sch 26 were originally vested in the National Assembly for Wales and are now exercisable by the Welsh Ministers by virtue of the Government of Wales Act 2006 s 162(1), Sch 11 paras 30, 32.
3   School Standards and Framework Act 1998 Sch 26 para 3 (amended by the Childcare Act 2006 s 103(1), Sch 2 para 36(1), (8)).
4   School Standards and Framework Act 1998 Sch 26 para 3(a). 'Relevant nursery education' means:
   (1)   nursery education provided in a maintained school in Wales or a maintained nursery school in Wales (Sch 26 para 1(1)(za) (added by the Education Act 2005 s 53, Sch 7 Pt 2 paras 8, 9(1), (2)(a); and amended by the Childcare Act 2006 s 103(1), Sch 2 para 36(1), (3)(a)));
   (2)   nursery education not falling within head (1) which is provided by a local authority in Wales (School Standards and Framework Act 1998 Sch 26 para 1(1)(a) (amended by

the Education Act 2005 s 53, Sch 7 Pt 2 paras 8, 9(1), (2)(b); the Childcare Act 2006 s 103(1), Sch 2 para 36(1), (3)(b); and SI 2010/1158));

(3)   nursery education which is provided by any other person under arrangements made with that person by a local authority in Wales in pursuance of the duty imposed on the authority by the School Standards and Framework Act 1998 s 118 (see PARA 96) and in consideration of financial assistance provided by the authority under the arrangements (Sch 26 para 1(1)(b) (substituted by the Education Act 2005 s 53, Sch 7 Pt 2 paras 8, 9(1), (2)(c); and amended by the Childcare Act 2006 s 103(1), Sch 2 para 36(1), (3)(c); SI 2010/1158)).

'Nursery education under consideration for funding' means nursery education provided by a person with whom a local authority in Wales is considering making arrangements in pursuance of the duty imposed on the authority by the School Standards and Framework Act 1998 s 118 (see PARA 96) for the provision of nursery education in consideration of financial assistance provided by the authority under the arrangements: Sch 26 para 1(2) (amended by the Education Act 2005 s 53, Sch 7 Pt 2 paras 8, 9(1), (3); the Childcare Act 2006 s 103(1), Sch 2 para 36(1), (4); and SI 2010/1158). Where:

(a)   any education is for the time being provided at any premises for children who have not attained the age prescribed for the purposes of the School Standards and Framework Act 1998 s 118(1)(b) (see PARA 96) ('the prescribed age') (Sch 26 para 1(3)(a) (Sch 26 para 1(3) substituted by the Education Act 2005 s 53, Sch 7 Pt 2 paras 8, 9(1), (4))); and

(b)   that education is provided by a person who proposes to provide nursery education at those premises for children who have attained the prescribed age, and with whom a local authority in Wales is considering making arrangements of the kind mentioned in the School Standards and Framework Act 1998 Sch 26 para 1(2) (Sch 26 para 1(3)(b) (as so substituted; and amended by the Childcare Act 2006 s 103(1), Sch 2 para 36(1), (5); and SI 2010/1158)),

the education is to be treated for the purposes of the School Standards and Framework Act 1998 Sch 26 as nursery education under consideration for funding even though it is provided for children who have not attained the prescribed age (Sch 26(1)(3) (as so substituted)). As to the meaning of 'nursery education' see PARA 95. As to the meaning of 'maintained school' see PARA 99. As to the meaning of 'Wales' see PARA 7 note 3. As to the meaning of 'maintained nursery school' see PARA 99 note 4. As to the meaning of 'local authority in Wales' see PARA 25; as to the meaning of 'child' see PARA 7 note 6; as to the meaning of 'premises' see PARA 62 note 19 (definitions applied by s 142(8)). As to the meaning of 'person' see PARA 7 note 6. 'Prescribed' means prescribed by regulations; and 'regulations' means regulations made by the Welsh Ministers under the School Standards and Framework Act 1998: s 142(1).

5   School Standards and Framework Act 1998 Sch 26 para 3(aa) (Sch 26 para 3(aa)–(ac) added by the Education Act 2005 s 53, Sch 7 Pt 2 paras 8, 11).

6   School Standards and Framework Act 1998 Sch 26 para 3(ab) (as added: see note 5).

7   'Well-being' in relation to children for whom nursery education is provided in Wales, is a reference to their well-being having regard to the matters mentioned in the Children Act 2004 s 25(2) (see CHILDREN AND YOUNG PERSONS vol 9 (2012) PARA 209): School Standards and Framework Act 1998 Sch 26 para 2(5) (substituted by the Childcare Act 2006 s 103(1), Sch 2 para 36(1), (7)).

8   School Standards and Framework Act 1998 Sch 26 para 3(ac) (as added: see note 5).

9   School Standards and Framework Act 1998 Sch 26 para 3(b).

10   School Standards and Framework Act 1998 Sch 26 para 4 (amended by the Childcare Act 2006 s 103(1), Sch 2 para 36(1), (9)).

11   School Standards and Framework Act 1998 Sch 26 para 5 (amended by the Childcare Act 2006 s 103(1), Sch 2 para 36(1), (10)).

12   School Standards and Framework Act 1998 Sch 26 para 5(a).

13   School Standards and Framework Act 1998 Sch 26 para 5(b).

1254. Registration of nursery education inspectors. Her Majesty's Chief Inspector of Education and Training in Wales[1] must establish and maintain a register of nursery education inspectors for Wales[2]. The Chief Inspector must not register a person unless, having regard to any conditions that he proposes to impose[3], it appears to him that the person[4] is a fit and proper person for discharging the functions[5] of a registered Welsh nursery education inspector[6] who will be capable of conducting inspections[7] competently and effectively; and no person may be so registered if he falls within a category of persons prescribed[8] for these purposes[9]. Subject to that, the Chief Inspector must register such persons as he considers appropriate[10]; and the factors which the Chief Inspector may take into account for these purposes include the extent to which there is a need for registered inspectors in any part of Wales[11].

The Chief Inspector may require payment of a fee before registering a person[12]. Registration may be subject to such conditions as the Chief Inspector considers it appropriate to impose[13]; and any conditions so imposed may be conditions applying generally in relation to all cases, or to particular classes of case, or such conditions together with specific conditions applying in the particular case[14]. Where a person is registered subject to conditions so imposed, he must be taken to be authorised to act as a registered Welsh nursery education inspector only so far as those conditions permit[15]. The period for which any registration is to have effect must be determined by the Chief Inspector and must be entered in the register[16].

If the Chief Inspector is satisfied that any of the following conditions is satisfied with respect to a nursery education inspector registered in his register, he may remove the name of that inspector from that register[17]. The conditions are that:

(1)   he is no longer a fit and proper person for discharging the functions[18] of a registered Welsh nursery education inspector[19];

(2)   he is no longer capable of conducting inspections[20] competently and effectively[21];

(3)   there has been a significant failure on his part to comply with any condition[22] subject to which his registration has effect[23];

(4)   he has, without reasonable explanation, produced a report of an inspection[24] which is, in whole or in part, seriously misleading[25].

The Chief Inspector may vary any condition subject to which the registration of an inspector has effect, or vary the registration of an inspector by imposing a condition subject to which it will have effect, if he is satisfied[26] that he is authorised[27] to remove the name of the inspector from his register[28], or that it would otherwise be in the public interest for him to do so[29].

Any person who is aggrieved[30] by:

(a)   the refusal of the Chief Inspector to renew his registration[31];

(b)   the imposition or variation of any condition subject to which he is registered[32]; or

(c)   the removal of his name from the register[33],

may appeal against the Chief Inspector's decision[34] to a tribunal[35]. On determining any appeal, the tribunal may confirm, reverse or vary the decision appealed against[36], or remit the case to the Chief Inspector with directions as to the action to be taken by him[37].

No decision against which an appeal may be so made has effect until any appeal against it which is duly made is disposed of[38], or the period within which an appeal may be made expires without an appeal being made[39], unless the Chief Inspector[40] is satisfied that the circumstances of the case justify the decision in question taking effect immediately or earlier than would otherwise be the case[41], and notifies the person concerned to that effect[42].

1   As to Her Majesty's Chief Inspector of Education and Training in Wales see PARA 1148.

2   School Standards and Framework Act 1998 Sch 26 para 8(1) (amended by the Learning and Skills Act 2000, s 73(1), (3)(a); Education Act 2005 ss 53, 123, Sch 7 Pt 2 paras 8, 14(1), (2), Sch 19 Pt 1). As to the meaning of 'Wales' see PARA 7 note 3. Any register of nursery education inspectors established by the Chief Inspector under the Nursery Education and

Grant-Maintained Schools Act 1996 Sch 1 (repealed) is to be treated as established by him under the School Standards and Framework Act 1998 Sch 26; and accordingly anything done under the Nursery Education and Grant-Maintained Schools Act 1996 Sch 1 (repealed) in connection with the registration of (or any refusal to register) any person in that register, if effective immediately before 1 October 1998, continues to have effect as if done under the School Standards and Framework Act 1998 Sch 26: s 122(3) (amended by the Education Act 2005 s 53, Sch 7 Pt 2 para 7(1), (2)).

3 Ie under the School Standards and Framework Act 1998 Sch 26 para 8(5B): see the text to note 13. References in Sch 26 to a condition imposed under Sch 26 para 8(5B) include a condition imposed under Sch 26 para 9(3) (see the text to note 26): Sch 26 para 9(4) (amended by the Education Act 2002 s 155, Sch 14 para 3).

4 School Standards and Framework Act 1998 Sch 26 para 8(3) (amended by the Education Act 2002 Sch 14 para 2(1), (2); Education Act 2005 s 53, Sch 7 Pt 2 paras 8, 14(1), (3)).

5 As to the meaning of 'functions' see PARA 18 note 5 (definition applied by the School Standards and Framework Act 1998 s 142(8)).

6 School Standards and Framework Act 1998 Sch 26 para 8(3)(a) (amended by the Education Act 2005 Sch 7 Pt 2 paras 8, 14(1), (5)). As to the meaning of 'registered nursery education inspector' see PARA 1255 note 6.

7 Ie under the School Standards and Framework Act 1998 Sch 26 para 6B: see PARA 1255.

8 Ie prescribed by regulations made by the Welsh Ministers under the School Standards and Framework Act 1998: see s 142(1). At the date at which this volume states the law no such regulations had been made. As to the Welsh Ministers see PARA 59. The functions under Sch 26 were originally vested in the National Assembly for Wales and are now exercisable by the Welsh Ministers by virtue of the Government of Wales Act 2006 s 162(1), Sch 11 paras 30, 32.

9 School Standards and Framework Act 1998 Sch 26 para 8(3)(b) (amended by the Education Act 2005 s 53, Sch 7 Pt 2 paras 8, 14(1), (5)(b)).

10 School Standards and Framework Act 1998 Sch 26 para 8(4) (substituted by the Education Act 2002 Sch 14 para 2(1), (3); and amended by the Education Act 2005 s 53, Sch 7 Pt 2 paras 8, 14(1), (3)).

11 School Standards and Framework Act 1998 Sch 26 para 8(5) (substituted by the Education Act 2002 Sch 14 para 2(1), (3); and amended by the Education Act 2005 ss 53, 123, Sch 7 Pt 2 paras 8, 14(1), (3) (6), Sch 19 Pt 1).

12 School Standards and Framework Act 1998 Sch 26 para 8(5A) (added by the Education Act 2002 Sch 14 para 2(1), (3); and amended by the Education Act 2005 s 53, Sch 7 Pt 2 paras 8, 14(1), (3)).

13 School Standards and Framework Act 1998 Sch 26 para 8(5B) (added by the Education Act 2002 Sch 14 para 2(1), (3); and amended by the Education Act 2005 s 53, Sch 7 Pt 2 paras 8, 14(1), (3)).

14 School Standards and Framework Act 1998 Sch 26 para 8(6) (amended by the Education Act 2002 Sch 14 para 2(1), (4)).

15 School Standards and Framework Act 1998 Sch 26 para 8(7) (amended by the Education Act 2002 Sch 14 para 2(1), (4); Education Act 2005 s 53, Sch 7 Pt 2 paras 8, 14(1), (7)).

16 School Standards and Framework Act 1998 Sch 26 para 8(8) (amended by the Education Act 2005 s 53, Sch 7 Pt 2 paras 8, 14(1), (3)).

17 School Standards and Framework Act 1998 Sch 26 para 9(1) (amended by the Education Act 2005 s 53, Sch 7 Pt 2 paras 8, 15(1), (2)).

18 Ie under the School Standards and Framework Act 1998 Sch 26 para 6B: see PARA 1255.

19 School Standards and Framework Act 1998 Sch 26 para 9(2)(a) (amended by the Education Act 2005 s 53, Sch 7 Pt 2 paras 8, 15(1), (3)).

20 Ie under the School Standards and Framework Act 1998 Sch 26 para 6B: see PARA 1255.

21 School Standards and Framework Act 1998 Sch 26 para 9(2)(b).

22 Ie imposed under the School Standards and Framework Act 1998 Sch 26 para 8(5B): see the text to note 13.

23 School Standards and Framework Act 1998 Sch 26 para 9(2)(c) (amended by the Education Act 2002 Sch 14 para 3).

24 Ie under the School Standards and Framework Act 1998 Sch 26 para 6B: see PARA 1255.

25 School Standards and Framework Act 1998 Sch 26 para 9(2)(d) (amended by the Education Act 2005 s 53, Sch 7 Pt 2 paras 8, 15(1), (3)(b)). As to inspection reports see PARA 1259.

26 School Standards and Framework Act 1998 Sch 26 para 9(3) (amended by the Education Act 2005 s 53, Sch 7 Pt 2 paras 8, 15(1), (4)). See also note 3.

27 Ie by the School Standards and Framework Act 1998 Sch 26 para 9(1): see the text to note 17.

28 School Standards and Framework Act 1998 Sch 26 para 9(3)(a).

29 School Standards and Framework Act 1998 Sch 26 para 9(3)(b).

30 As to persons aggrieved see JUDICIAL REVIEW vol 61 (2010) PARA 656.
31 School Standards and Framework Act 1998 Sch 26 para 10(1)(a) (amended by the Education Act 2005 s 53, Sch 7 Pt 2 paras 8, 16(1), (2)).
32 School Standards and Framework Act 1998 Sch 26 para 10(1)(b).
33 School Standards and Framework Act 1998 Sch 26 para 10(1)(c).
34 School Standards and Framework Act 1998 Sch 26 para 10(1).
35 An appeal under the School Standards and Framework Act 1998 Sch 26 para 10(1) must be made to a tribunal with the same constitution as a tribunal to hear an appeal under the Education Act 2005 s 27 (see PARA 1158); and Sch 3 para 2 (procedure: see PARA 1160) and Sch 3 para 3 (staff: see PARA 1159) apply to tribunals to hear such appeals as they apply to tribunals to hear appeals under the Education Act 2005 s 27: School Standards and Framework Act 1998 Sch 26 para 10(2) (substituted by the Education Act 2005 Sch 7 Pt 2 paras 8, 16(1), (4)).
36 School Standards and Framework Act 1998 Sch 26 para 10(5)(a).
37 School Standards and Framework Act 1998 Sch 26 para 10(5)(b) (amended by the Education Act 2005 s 53, Sch 7 Pt 2 paras 1, 16(1), (5)).
38 School Standards and Framework Act 1998 Sch 26 para 10(3)(a).
39 School Standards and Framework Act 1998 Sch 26 para 10(3)(b).
40 See the School Standards and Framework Act 1998 Sch 26 para 10(4) (amended by the Education Act 2005 s 53, Sch 7 Pt 2 paras 8, 16(1), (5)).
41 School Standards and Framework Act 1998 Sch 26 para 10(4)(a).
42 School Standards and Framework Act 1998 Sch 26 para 10(4)(b). As to the service of notices and documents see the Education Act 1996 s 572 (applied by the School Standards and Framework Act 1998 s 142(8)); and PARA 76.

1255. Inspections. Her Majesty's Chief Inspector of Education and Training in Wales[1]:

(1) must secure that relevant nursery education[2] provided in Wales[3] at any premises[4] is inspected by a member of the Welsh Inspectorate[5] or a registered Welsh nursery education inspector[6] at such intervals as may be prescribed[7];

(2) must also secure that relevant nursery education, or nursery education under consideration for funding[8], provided in Wales is inspected by a member of the Welsh Inspectorate or a registered Welsh nursery education inspector at any time when the Welsh Ministers[9] require the Chief Inspector to secure its inspection[10];

(3) may secure that relevant nursery education, or nursery education under consideration for funding, provided in Wales is inspected by a member of the Welsh Inspectorate or a registered Welsh nursery education inspector at any other time when the Chief Inspector considers that it would be appropriate for it to be inspected[11].

The Chief Inspector may comply with the requirements of heads (1) to (3) above either by organising inspections or by making arrangements with others for them to organise inspections[12].

A person conducting an inspection must report on[13]:

(a) the quality and standards of the nursery education provided[14];

(b) how far that nursery education meets the needs of the range of children[15] for whom the education is provided[16];

(c) the quality of leadership and management in connection with the provision of the nursery education[17];

(d) the contribution made by that nursery education to the well-being[18] of those children[19]; and

(e) so far as it is reasonably practicable to do so, the spiritual, moral, social and cultural development of the children for whom the nursery education is provided[20].

A person must not undertake an inspection of nursery education provided by a person[21] at any premises, or accompany a person undertaking such an inspection, if he has, or has at any time had, any connection with[22] the person by whom the education is provided (or, where it is provided by a body, any member of the body)[23], or any person employed by that person (whether or not at the premises), of a kind which might reasonably be taken to raise doubts about his ability to act impartially[24].

The Chief Inspector must:

(i) give guidance to registered Welsh nursery education inspectors and such other persons as he considers appropriate in connection with inspections and the making of reports of such inspections[25]; and

(ii) keep under review the system of inspections[26] and, in particular, the standard of such inspections and of the reports made of them[27].

1 As to Her Majesty's Chief Inspector of Education and Training in Wales see PARA 1148.
2 As to the meaning of 'relevant nursery education' see PARA 1253 note 4.
3 As to the meaning of 'Wales' see PARA 7 note 3.
4 As to the meaning of 'premises' see PARA 62 note 19 (definition applied by the School Standards and Framework Act 1998 s 142(8)).
5 'Members of the Welsh Inspectorate' means Her Majesty's Chief Inspector of Education and Training in Wales, Her Majesty's Inspectors of Education and Training in Wales and additional inspectors with whom the Chief Inspector has made arrangements to give him assistance under the Education Act 2005 Sch 2 para 2 (see PARA 1149): School Standards and Framework Act 1998 Sch 26 para 2(3) (substituted by the Education Act 2005 s 53, Sch 7 Pt 2 paras 8, 10(1), (4)). As to Her Majesty's Inspectors of Education and Training in Wales see PARA 1148.
6 References to 'registered nursery education inspectors' are references to persons registered Welsh under the School Standards and Framework Act 1998 Sch 26 para 8 (see PARA 1254): Sch 26 para 2(2) (amended by the Education Act 2005 Sch 7 Pt 2 paras 8 10(1), (2)).
7 School Standards and Framework Act 1998 Sch 26 para 6B(1)(a) (Sch 26 para 6B added by the Education Act 2005 Sch 7 Pt 2 paras 8, 12). The School Standards and Framework Act 1998 Schedule 26 para 6B(1)(a) does not apply to nursery education provided at a school to which the Education Act 2005 s 28 (duty to arrange regular inspections of certain schools: see PARA 1182) applies: School Standards and Framework Act 1998 Sch 26 para 6B(2) (as so added). The Chief Inspector must secure that relevant nursery education is inspected, where there has been no previous inspection, within six years of the date on which relevant nursery education was first provided at the premises concerned and, in all other cases at least once within a six year period beginning on 1 September 2014 and ending on 31 August 2020 and at least once within every subsequent six year period beginning on the expiry of the previous six year period: Education (Inspection of Nursery Education) (Wales) Regulations 1999, SI 1999/1441, reg 4(1) (reg 4 substituted by SI 2010/1436; and amended by SI 2014/1212). For these purposes the date on which the last inspection was completed is the date of the report of the last inspection under the School Standards and Framework Act 1998 Sch 26 para 6B: Education (Inspection of Nursery Education) (Wales) Regulations 1999, SI 1999/1441, reg 4(2) (as so substituted). As to inspection reports see PARA 1259. As to the monitoring of inspections see PARA 1256. As to the requirement that inspectors be adequately trained see PARA 1257. As to rights of entry and other rights in connection with inspections see PARA 1258.
8 As to the meaning of 'nursery education under consideration for funding' see PARA 1253 note 4.
9 As to the Welsh Ministers see PARA 59. The functions under the School Standards and Framework Act 1998 Sch 26 were originally vested in the National Assembly for Wales and are now exercisable by the Welsh Ministers by virtue of the Government of Wales Act 2006 s 162(1), Sch 11 paras 30, 32.
10 School Standards and Framework Act 1998 Sch 26 para 6B(1)(b) (as added: see note 7). A requirement such as is mentioned in Sch 26 para 6B(1)(b) may relate to nursery education provided at particular premises or a class of premises: Sch 26 para 6B(4) (as so added). If the Chief Inspector elects in the case of an inspection within Sch 26 para 6B(1)(b) or (c) (see the text to note 11) that the inspection must be treated as if it were an inspection within Sch 26 para 6B(1)(a) (see the text to notes 2–7), the inspection must be so treated: Sch 26 para 16 (amended by the Education Act 2005 s 53, Sch 7 Pt 2 paras 8, 22; and the Childcare Act 2006 s 103, Sch 2 para 36(1), (11)(f), Sch 3 Pt 2).

11 School Standards and Framework Act 1998 Sch 26 para 6B(1)(c) (as added: see note 7). See also note 10.

12 School Standards and Framework Act 1998 Sch 26 para 6B(3) (as added: see note 7).

13 School Standards and Framework Act 1998 Sch 26 para 7 (Sch 26 para 7 substituted by the Education Act 2005 Sch 7 Pt 2 paras 8, 12; and amended by the Childcare Act 2006 s 103, Sch 2 para 36(1), (11)(c), Sch 3 Pt 2).

14 School Standards and Framework Act 1998 Sch 26 para 7(a) (as substituted: see note 13).

15 As to the meaning of 'child' see PARA 7 note 6 (definition applied by the School Standards and Framework Act 1998 s 142(8)).

16 School Standards and Framework Act 1998 Sch 26 para 7(b) (as substituted: see note 13).

17 School Standards and Framework Act 1998 Sch 26 para 7(c) (as substituted: see note 13).

18 As to the meaning of 'well-being' see PARA 1253 note 7.

19 School Standards and Framework Act 1998 Sch 26 para 7(d) (as substituted: see note 13).

20 School Standards and Framework Act 1998 Sch 26 para 7(e) (as substituted: see note 13).

21 As to the meaning of 'person' see PARA 7 note 6.

22 School Standards and Framework Act 1998 Sch 26 para 12 (amended by the Education Act 2005 s 53, Sch 7 Pt 2 paras 8, 19).

23 School Standards and Framework Act 1998 Sch 26 para 12(a).

24 School Standards and Framework Act 1998 Sch 26 para 12(b).

25 School Standards and Framework Act 1998 Sch 26 para 8(2)(a) (amended by the Education Act 2005 s 53, Sch 7 Pt 2 paras 8, 14(1), (4)).

26 Ie under the School Standards and Framework Act 1998 Sch 26 para 6B: see the text to notes 1–12.

27 School Standards and Framework Act 1998 Sch 26 para 8(2)(b) (amended by the Education Act 2005 s 53, Sch 7 Pt 2 paras 8, 14(1), (4)(a)).

1256.   Monitoring of inspections. Where an inspection in Wales[1] is being conducted[2] by a registered Welsh nursery education inspector[3], Her Majesty's Chief Inspector of Education and Training in Wales[4] may arrange for the inspection to be monitored by one or more members of the Welsh Inspectorate[5].

1 As to the meaning of 'Wales' see PARA 7 note 3.

2 Ie under the School Standards and Framework Act 1998 Sch 26 para 6B: see PARA 1255.

3 As to the meaning of 'registered nursery education inspector' see PARA 1255 note 6.

4 As to Her Majesty's Chief Inspector of Education and Training in Wales see PARA 1148.

5 School Standards and Framework Act 1998 Sch 26 para 17 (substituted by the Education Act 2005 Sch 7 Pt 2 paras 8, 23). As to the meaning of 'members of the Welsh Inspectorate' see PARA 1255 note 5.

1257.   Training for registered nursery education inspectors. A registered Welsh nursery education inspector[1] must not conduct an inspection[2] unless he has, in the opinion of Her Majesty's Chief Inspector of Education and Training in Wales[3], satisfactorily completed a course of training provided by the Chief Inspector or complying with arrangements approved by him[4]. However, this requirement does not apply in such circumstances as may be specified, either generally or in relation to a particular case or class of case, by the Chief Inspector[5]. Where the Chief Inspector provides such training he may charge such fees as are reasonable for the purpose of recovering the whole, or part, of the cost of providing it[6].

1 As to the meaning of 'registered nursery education inspector' see PARA 1255 note 6.

2 Ie under the School Standards and Framework Act 1998 Sch 26 para 6B: see PARA 1255.

3 As to Her Majesty's Chief Inspector of Education and Training in Wales see PARA 1148.

4 School Standards and Framework Act 1998 Sch 26 para 11(1) (amended by the Education Act 2005 s 53, Sch 7 Pt 2 paras 8, 18(1), (2)).

5 School Standards and Framework Act 1998 Sch 26 para 11(2) (amended by the Education Act 2005 s 53, Sch 7 Pt 2 paras 8, 18(1), (3)).

6 School Standards and Framework Act 1998 Sch 26 para 11(3) (amended by the Education Act 2005 s 53, Sch 7 Pt 2 paras 8, 18(1), (3)).

1258. Rights of entry etc in relation to inspections. A registered Welsh nursery education inspector[1] or member of the Welsh Inspectorate[2] conducting[3] an inspection[4], or a member of the Welsh Inspectorate monitoring[5] an inspection[6] has, at all reasonable times:

(1) a right of entry to the premises[7] at which the relevant nursery education[8] concerned is provided[9]; and

(2) a right to inspect, and take copies of any records[10] kept by the person[11] providing that education[12], and of any other documents[13] containing information relating to the provision of that education[14], which he requires for the purposes of conducting or (as the case may be) monitoring the inspection[15].

It is an offence intentionally to obstruct a member of the Welsh Inspectorate or a registered Welsh nursery education inspector in the exercise of his functions[16] in relation to an inspection[17].

1 As to the meaning of 'registered nursery education inspector' see PARA 1255 note 6.
2 As to the meaning of 'member of the Welsh Inspectorate' see PARA 1255 note 5.
3 Ie under the School Standards and Framework Act 1998 Sch 26 para 6B: see PARA 1255.
4 School Standards and Framework Act 1998 Sch 26 para 18(1)(b) (Sch 26 para 18(1) substituted by the Education Act 2005 s 53, Sch 7 Pt 2 paras 8, 24(1), (2)).
5 Ie under the School Standards and Framework Act 1998 Sch 26 para 17: see PARA 1256.
6 School Standards and Framework Act 1998 Sch 26 para 18(1)(c) (as substituted: see note 4). The inspection referred to is one under Sch 26 para 6B (see PARA 1255): see Sch 26 para 18(1)(c) (as so substituted).
7 As to the meaning of 'premises' see PARA 62 note 19 (definition applied by the School Standards and Framework Act 1998 s 142(8)).
8 As to the meaning of 'relevant nursery education' see PARA 1253 note 4.
9 School Standards and Framework Act 1998 Sch 26 para 18(2)(a).
10 'Records' includes information recorded in any form: see the School Standards and Framework Act 1998 Sch 26 para 18(6).
11 As to the meaning of 'person' see PARA 7 note 6.
12 School Standards and Framework Act 1998 Sch 26 para 18(2)(b)(i).
13 'Documents' includes information recorded in any form: see the School Standards and Framework Act 1998 Sch 26 para 18(6).
14 School Standards and Framework Act 1998 Sch 26 para 18(2)(b)(ii).
15 School Standards and Framework Act 1998 Sch 26 para 18(2)(b). The Education Act 2005 s 58 (inspection of computer records: see PARA 1152 note 7) applies for the purposes of the School Standards and Framework Act 1998 Sch 26 para 18 as it applies for the purposes of the Education Act 2005 Pt 1 Chs 3–4 (ss 19–43): School Standards and Framework Act 1998 Sch 26 para 18(3) (substituted by the Education Act 2005 Sch 7 Pt 2 paras 8, 24(1), (3)).
16 As to the meaning of 'functions' see PARA 18 note 5 (definition applied by the School Standards and Framework Act 1998 s 142(8)).
17 School Standards and Framework Act 1998 Sch 26 para 18(4)(b) (substituted by the Education Act 2005 s 53, Sch 7 Pt 2 paras 8, 24(1), (3)). Any person guilty of such an offence is liable on summary conviction to a fine not exceeding level 4 on the standard scale: School Standards and Framework Act 1998 Sch 26 para 18(5). As to the standard scale see SENTENCING AND DISPOSITION OF OFFENDERS vol 92 (2010) PARA 142.

1259. Reports of inspections. Where a person has conducted an inspection[1] he must make his report in writing[2] to Her Majesty's Chief Inspector of Education and Training in Wales[3] within such period as may be prescribed[4], subject to any extension not exceeding three months[5] which the Chief Inspector may consider necessary[6].

Once the report of an inspection has been made to the Chief Inspector, he must without delay send a copy of it to such authorities and persons[7] as may be prescribed[8]. Regulations may require any prescribed person to whom a copy of the report is sent to make a copy of the report available for inspection by prescribed persons[9]. The Chief Inspector may arrange for the report to be published by electronic means[10].

The annual report of the Chief Inspector required[11] to be made to the Welsh Ministers must include an account of the exercise of the functions[12] conferred or imposed on him[13] in relation to the inspection of nursery education; and the power conferred on him[14] to make other reports to the Welsh Ministers includes a power to make reports which fall within the scope of those functions[15].

1 Ie under the School Standards and Framework Act 1998 Sch 26 para 6B: see PARA 1255.
2 As to the meaning of 'writing' see PARA 76 note 8.
3 As to Her Majesty's Chief Inspector of Education and Training in Wales see PARA 1148.
4 'Prescribed' means prescribed by regulations; and 'regulations' means regulations made by the Welsh Ministers under the School Standards and Framework Act 1998: see s 142(1). As to the Welsh Ministers see PARA 59. The functions under Sch 26 were originally vested in the National Assembly for Wales and are now exercisable by the Welsh Ministers by virtue of the Government of Wales Act 2006 s 162(1), Sch 11 paras 30, 32.
   The prescribed period is 15 days beginning on the day following that on which the inspection is completed, or within a further five days where it is necessary to provide a translation of the report into Welsh or into English; and for the purposes of calculating this period, no account must be taken of Saturday, Sunday, Good Friday and Christmas Day or any day which is a bank holiday in England and Wales under the Banking and Financial Dealings Act 1971 (see TIME vol 97 (2015) PARAS 320–321): see the Education (Inspection of Nursery Education) (Wales) Regulations 1999, SI 1999/1441, reg 3(1), (2).
5 As to the meaning of 'month' see PARA 54 note 26.
6 School Standards and Framework Act 1998 Sch 26 para 13B(1) (Sch 26 para 13B added by the Education Act 2005 s 53, Sch 7 Pt 2 paras 8, 20).
7 As to the meaning of 'person' see PARA 7 note 6.
8 School Standards and Framework Act 1998 Sch 26 para 13B(2) (as added: see note 6). As to the prescribed persons see the Education (Inspection of Nursery Education) (Wales) Regulations 1999, SI 1999/1441, reg 3(3) (amended by SI 2005/2913; SI 2010/1142).
9 School Standards and Framework Act 1998 Sch 26 para 13B(3) (as added: see note 6). At the date at which this volume states the law no such regulations had been made.
10 See the Education Act 2005 s 29(2) (s 29(2)–(4) applied by the School Standards and Framework Act 1998 Sch 26 para 13B(4) (as added: see note 6)). For the purposes of the law of defamation any report so published by the Chief Inspector is privileged unless the publication is shown to have been made with malice (Education Act 2005 s 29(3) (as so applied)); but this does not limit any privilege subsisting apart therefrom (Education Act 2005 s 29(4) (as so applied)). As to privilege and malice in the law of defamation see DEFAMATION vol 32 (2012) PARAS 594 et seq, 651 et seq.
11 Ie by the Education Act 2005 s 21(1)(a): see PARA 1154.
12 As to the meaning of 'functions' see PARA 18 note 5 (definition applied by the School Standards and Framework Act 1998 s 142(8)).
13 Ie by or under the School Standards and Framework Act 1998 Sch 26.
14 Ie by the Education Act 2005 s 21(1)(b): see PARA 1154.
15 See the School Standards and Framework Act 1998 Sch 26 para 14(2) (Sch 26 para 14 substituted by the Education Act 2005 s 53, Sch 7 Pt 2 paras 8, 21).

(5) INSPECTION OF ADULT LEARNING AND FURTHER EDUCATION

(i) Inspections in England

1260. Framework for inspections. Her Majesty's Chief Inspector of Education, Children's Services and Skills[1] must devise a common set of principles applicable to all inspections[2] of further education and training[3], or two or more common sets of principles each of which is applicable to a particular description of such inspections[4]. A set of principles so devised is known as a 'framework'[5].

The Chief Inspector must publish a framework in such manner as he considers appropriate[6]. The Chief Inspector may at any time revise a framework[7]; and must publish a revised framework in such manner as he considers appropriate[8].

1 As to Her Majesty's Chief Inspector of Education, Children's Services and Skills see PARA 1133. The Adult Learning Inspectorate established under the Learning and Skills Act 2000 was abolished and the inspection of further education and training is now a function of Her Majesty's Chief Inspector of Education, Children's Services and Skills: see the Education and Inspections Act 2006 s 134.
2 Ie conducted under the Education and Inspections Act 2006 Pt 8 Ch 3 (ss 123–134).
3 Education and Inspections Act 2006 s 133(1)(a).
4 Education and Inspections Act 2006 s 133(1)(b). If the Chief Inspector devises two or more frameworks under s 133(1)(b), he must ensure that, taken together, they cover all inspections conducted under Pt 8 Ch 3: s 133(3).
5 See the Education and Inspections Act 2006 s 133(2).
6 Education and Inspections Act 2006 s 133(4).
7 Education and Inspections Act 2006 s 133(5).
8 Education and Inspections Act 2006 s 133(6).

1261. Inspection of further education and training. Her Majesty's Chief Inspector of Education, Children's Services and Skills[1] must conduct inspections of such education or training[2] as may be specified by the Secretary of State[3] and conduct inspections of such class of that education or training as may be so specified[4]. The inspections are to be conducted at such intervals as may be specified by the Secretary of State[5].

On completing an inspection, the Chief Inspector must make a written[6] report on it[7] which must state whether the Chief Inspector considers the education or training inspected to be of a quality adequate to meet the reasonable needs of those receiving it[8], and may deal with such other matters as he considers relevant[9]. The Chief Inspector must send copies of the report to the Secretary of State[10], any local authority in England[11] providing funds for the education or training inspected[12], and the provider of the education or training inspected[13]. Copies may also be sent to such other persons[14] as the Chief Inspector considers appropriate[15]. The Chief Inspector must arrange for the report to be published in such manner as he considers appropriate[16].

The following kinds of education and training are subject to such inspection[17]:

(1)   secondary education[18] provided in institutions which are in England and are within the further education sector[19];

(2)   further education[20] for persons aged 16 or over but under 19[21] which is provided in such institutions and wholly or partly funded by the Secretary of State[22];

(3)   education provided in 16 to 19 academies[23];

(4)   further education for persons aged 19 or over which is wholly or partly funded by the Secretary of State[24];

(5)   further education for persons aged under 19 which is provided by local authorities in England[25];

(6)   further education for persons aged 19 or over which is funded by such authorities[26];

(7)   training for persons aged 16 or over which is funded[27] by the Secretary of State[28];

(8)   training for persons aged 16 or over if it is training the whole or part of which takes place at the premises of an employer and which is wholly or partly funded by the Secretary of State[29];

(9)   such other education or training as may be prescribed by regulations
       made by the Secretary of State[30].

1   As to Her Majesty's Chief Inspector of Education, Children's Services and Skills see PARA 1133.
2   Ie education and training to which the Education and Inspections Act 2006 Pt 8 Ch 3
    (ss 123–134) applies. See further the text to notes 17–30.
3   Education and Inspections Act 2006 s 124(1)(a). As to the Secretary of State see PARA 58.
4   Education and Inspections Act 2006 s 124(1)(b) (s 124(1)(b), (c), (g) amended by the
    Deregulation Act 2015 Sch 14 Pt 2 paras 50, 51).
5   Education and Inspections Act 2006 s 124(2). As to the framework for inspections see PARA
    1260. As to powers of entry and related powers in relation to inspections see PARA 1267.
6   As to the meaning of 'written' see PARA 76 note 8.
7   Education and Inspections Act 2006 s 124(3). As to the publication of inspection reports see
    PARA 1142; and as to combined reports see PARA 1143.
8   Education and Inspections Act 2006 s 124(4)(a).
9   Education and Inspections Act 2006 s 124(4)(b).
10 Education and Inspections Act 2006 s 124(5)(a).
11 As to the meaning of 'local authority in England' see PARA 1145 note 3. As to the meaning of
    'England' see PARA 7 note 3.
12 Education and Inspections Act 2006 s 124(5)(c) (amended by SI 2010/1158).
13 Education and Inspections Act 2006 s 124(5)(d). As to the duty of a provider of education or
    training to prepare an action plan following an inspection see PARA 1264.
14 As to the meaning of 'person' see PARA 7 note 6.
15 Education and Inspections Act 2006 s 124(6).
16 Education and Inspections Act 2006 s 124(7).
17 Ie the Education and Inspections Act 2006 Pt 8 Ch 3 (ss 123–134) applies to the kinds of
    education listed in heads (1)–(8) in the text: see s 123(1). If regulations made by the Secretary of
    State so provide the provision of information, advice or guidance falling within the
    Apprenticeships, Skills, Children and Learning Act 2009 s 100(1)(j) (see PARA 783), or the
    provision of any description of such information, advice or guidance specified in the regulations,
    is to be treated for the purposes of the Education and Inspections Act 2006 Pt 8 Ch 3 as training
    to which it applies: s 123(3) (amended by SI 2010/1080; and the Education Act 2011, s 67(1),
    Sch 16, paras 29, 30(1), (3)). As to the regulations made see the Education and Inspections
    Act 2006 (Prescribed Education and Training etc) Regulations 2007, SI 2007/464, reg 5.
18 As to the meaning of 'secondary education' see PARA 21 (definition applied by the Education
    and Inspections Act 2006 s 123(4)(a)).
19 Education and Inspections Act 2006 s 123(1)(a). Any reference to institutions which are within
    the further education sector is to be read in accordance with the Further and Higher Education
    Act 1992 s 91(3) (see PARA 555): Education and Inspections Act 2006 s 123(4)(b).
20 As to the meaning of 'further education' see PARA 23 (definition applied by the Education and
    Inspections Act 2006 s 123(4)(a)).
21 As to the time at which a person attains a particular age see PARA 7 note 6.
22 Education and Inspections Act 2006 s 123(1)(b) (amended by SI 2010/1080; the Education
    Act 2011, s 67(1), Sch 16, paras 29, 30(1), (2); and the Deregulation Act 2015 Sch 14 Pt 2
    paras 50, 51).
23 Education and Inspections Act 2006 s 123(1)(ba) (added by the Education Act 2011 Sch 13
    para 16(6)). As to the meaning of '16 to 19 academy' see PARA 346 note 13 (definition applied
    by the Education and Inspections Act 2006 s 187(2), (3)).
24 Education and Inspections Act 2006 s 123(1)(c) (amended by SI 2010/1080; the Education
    Act 2011, s 67(1), Sch 16, paras 29, 30(1), (2) and the Deregulation Act 2015 Sch 14 Pt 2
    paras 50, 51).
25 Education and Inspections Act 2006 s 123(1)(d) (amended by SI 2010/1158).
26 Education and Inspections Act 2006 s 123(1)(e).
27 Ie under the Employment and Training Act 1973 s 2: see **EMPLOYMENT** vol 40 (2014) PARA 634.
28 Education and Inspections Act 2006 s 123(1)(f).
29 Education and Inspections Act 2006 s 123(1)(g) (amended by SI 2010/1080; the Education
    Act 2011, s 67(1), Sch 16, paras 29, 30(1), (2); and the Deregulation Act 2015 Sch 14 Pt 2
    paras 50, 51).
30 Education and Inspections Act 2006 s 123(1)(h). The training which may be prescribed by
    regulations under s 123(1)(h) includes training of or for teachers, lecturers, trainers or other
    persons engaged in the provision of education or training falling within s 123(1)(a)–(g) (see
    heads (1)–(9) in the text): s 123(2). As to the meaning of references to training in relation to

teachers see PARA 24 note 2. As to the regulations made see the Education and Inspections Act 2006 (Prescribed Education and Training etc) Regulations 2007, SI 2007/464, reg 3.

1262.   Inspection of further education institutions. Her Majesty's Chief Inspector of Education, Children's Services and Skills[1] must inspect all institutions within the further education sector[2]. The Secretary of State[3] may by regulations provide that this[4] duty does not apply to prescribed categories of institution ('an exempt institution') in prescribed circumstances[5].

The inspections are to be conducted at such intervals as may be specified by the Secretary of State[6].

On completing an inspection the Chief Inspector must make a written[7] report on it[8] which must state whether the Chief Inspector considers the education or training[9] inspected to be of a quality adequate to meet the reasonable needs of those receiving it[10], and may deal with such other matters as he considers relevant[11]. The Chief Inspector must send copies of the report to the Secretary of State[12], and the provider of the education or training inspected[13]. Copies may also be sent to such other persons[14] as the Chief Inspector considers appropriate[15]. The Chief Inspector must arrange for the report to be published in such manner as he considers appropriate[16].

1   As to Her Majesty's Chief Inspector of Education, Children's Services and Skills see PARA 1133.
2   Education and Inspections Act 2006 s 125(1). Any reference to institutions which are within the further education sector is to be read in accordance with the Further and Higher Education Act 1992 s 91(3) (see PARA 555): Education and Inspections Act 2006 s 123(4)(b). As to the framework for inspections see PARA 1260. As to powers of entry and related powers in relation to inspections see PARA 1267.
3   As to the Secretary of State see PARA 58.
4   Ie the duty under the Education and Inspections Act 2006 s 125(1).
5   See the Education and Inspections Act 2006 s 125(1A), (1B) (s 125(1A), (1B) added by the Education Act 2011 s 42(2)(b)). The categories of institution that are prescribed for the purposes of the Education and Inspections Act 2006 s 125(1A) are those falling within the Further and Higher Education Act 1992 s 91(3) (see PARA 555) and those falling within 16 to 19 academies (see PARA 346 note 13): Further Education Institutions (Exemption from Inspection) (England) Regulations 2012, SI 2012/2576, reg 3. The circumstance prescribed for the purposes of the Education and Inspections Act 2006 s 125(1A) is that the institution was awarded the highest grade for its overall effectiveness in the most recent inspection of that institution under s 125: Further Education Institutions (Exemption from Inspection) (England) Regulations 2012, SI 2012/2576 reg 4.
6   Education and Inspections Act 2006 s 125(2) (amended by the Education Act 2011 s 42(2)(c)).
7   As to the meaning of 'written' see PARA 76 note 8.
8   Education and Inspections Act 2006 s 125(3). As to the publication of inspection reports see PARA 1142; and as to combined reports see PARA 1143.
9   As to the education or training to which the Education and Inspections Act 2006 Pt 8 Ch 3 (ss 123–134) applies see s 123(1); and PARA 1261.
10 Education and Inspections Act 2006 s 125(4)(a).
11 Education and Inspections Act 2006 s 125(4)(b).
12 Education and Inspections Act 2006 s 125(5)(a).
13 Education and Inspections Act 2006 s 125(5)(c). As to the duty of a provider of education or training to prepare an action plan following an inspection see PARA 1264.
14 As to the meaning of 'person' see PARA 7 note 6.
15 Education and Inspections Act 2006 s 125(6).
16 Education and Inspections Act 2006 s 125(7).

1263.   Other inspections. Her Majesty's Chief Inspector of Education, Children's Services and Skills[1] may inspect any education or training[2] in a case where he is not otherwise[3] required to do so[4] and, must inspect an exempt institution[5] if requested to do so by the Secretary of State[6]. On completing any such inspection, the Chief Inspector must make a written[7] report on it[8], and arrange for the report to be published in such manner as he considers appropriate[9].

The Chief Inspector may also inspect any other education or training[10], whether provided in the United Kingdom or elsewhere[11], if it is further education[12] (whether for persons aged 16 or over but under 19, or for persons aged 19 or over) or training for persons aged 16 or over[13], and he is requested to conduct the inspection by the provider of the education or training[14]. On completing any such inspection[15], the Chief Inspector must make a written report on it[16], and arrange for the report to be published in such manner as he considers appropriate[17].

If the Chief Inspector makes a report of an inspection[18], he must send copies of the report to the Secretary of State[19], any local authority in England[20] providing funds for the education or training inspected[21], and the provider of the education or training inspected[22]. Copies may also be sent to such other persons[23] as the Chief Inspector considers appropriate[24].

1 As to Her Majesty's Chief Inspector of Education, Children's Services and Skills see PARA 1133.
2 Ie education or training to which the Education and Inspections Act 2006 Pt 8 Ch 3 (ss 123–134) applies: see s 126(1). As to such education and training see PARA 1261.
3 Ie by virtue of any provision of the Education and Inspections Act 2006 Pt 8 Ch 3 (ss 123–134). As to inspections of education and training see PARA 1261. As to inspections of further education institutions see PARA 1262.
4 Education and Inspections Act 2006 s 126(1). As to the framework for inspections see PARA 1260. As to powers of entry and related powers in relation to inspections see PARA 1267. In the case of an inspection conducted under s 126(1) in response to a request from the provider of the education or training concerned, the Chief Inspector may charge the provider for the cost of the inspection: s 126(5A) (added by the Education Act 2011, s 42(3), (8)).
5 As to the meaning of 'exempt institution' see PARA 1262 (definition applied by the Education and Inspections Act 2006 s 126(8) (added by the Education Act 2011 s 42(9)).
6 Education and Inspections Act 2006 s 126(1A) (s 125(1A), (2A) (added by the Education Act 2011 s 42(3)–(5)). As to the Secretary of State see PARA 58.
7 As to the meaning of 'written' see PARA 76 note 8.
8 Education and Inspections Act 2006 s 126(2A)(a) (added by the Education Act 2011 s 42(3), (5)).
9 Education and Inspections Act 2006 s 126(2A)(b) (as added: see note 8).
10 Ie any education or training to which the Education and Inspections Act 2006 Pt 8 Ch 3 (ss 123–134) does not apply.
11 For the purposes of the Education and Inspections Act 2006 s 126(2) it is immaterial whether the education or training concerned is provided in the United Kingdom or elsewhere: s 126(7). As to the meaning of 'United Kingdom' see PARA 73 note 3.
12 As to the meaning of 'further education' see PARA 23 (definition applied by the Education and Inspections Act 2006 s 123(4)(a)).
13 Education and Inspections Act 2006 s 126(2)(a). As to the time at which a person attains a particular age see PARA 7 note 6.
14 Education and Inspections Act 2006 s 126(2)(b). In the case of such an inspection the Chief Inspector may charge the provider of the education or training concerned for the cost of the inspection: s 126(6).
15 Ie on completing an inspection under the Education and Inspections Act 2006 s 126 conducted in any other case: s 126(3) (amended by the Education Act 2011 s 42(3), (6)).
16 Education and Inspections Act 2006 s 126(3)(a). As to the publication of inspection reports see PARA 1142; and as to combined reports see PARA 1143.
17 Education and Inspections Act 2006 s 126(3)(b).
18 Ie an inspection under the Education and Inspections Act 2006 s 126(1), (1A).
19 Education and Inspections Act 2006 s 126(4)(a).
20 As to the meaning of 'local authority in England' see PARA 1145 note 3. As to the meaning of 'England' see PARA 7 note 3.
21 Education and Inspections Act 2006 s 126(4)(c) (amended by SI 2010/1158).

22 Education and Inspections Act 2006 s 126(4)(d). As to the duty of a provider of education or training to prepare an action plan following an inspection see PARA 1264.
23 As to the meaning of 'person' see PARA 7 note 6.
24 Education and Inspections Act 2006 s 126(5).

1264.   Action plans. Where Her Majesty's Chief Inspector of Education, Children's Services and Skills[1] publishes a report of an inspection[2] of further education or training[3], the provider of the education or training which is the subject of the report must, unless the Chief Inspector waives the requirement[4], prepare a written[5] statement of the action which he proposes to take in the light of the report[6] and the period within which he proposes to take that action[7]. That person[8] must publish the statement within such period, and in such manner, as may be prescribed by regulations made by the Secretary of State[9], and send copies of it to such persons as may be so prescribed[10].

1   As to Her Majesty's Chief Inspector of Education, Children's Services and Skills see PARA 1133.
2   Ie an inspection conducted under the Education and Inspections Act 2006 s 124 (see PARA 1261), s 125 (see PARA 1262) or s 126(1) (see PARA 1263).
3   See the Education and Inspections Act 2006 s 127(1).
4   The requirements of the Education and Inspections Act 2006 s 127(2) may be waived by the Chief Inspector: s 127(4).
5   As to the meaning of 'written' see PARA 76 note 8.
6   Education and Inspections Act 2006 s 127(2)(a).
7   Education and Inspections Act 2006 s 127(2)(b).
8   As to the meaning of 'person' see PARA 7 note 6.
9   Education and Inspections Act 2006 s 127(3)(a). As to the Secretary of State see PARA 58. As to the regulations made see the Education and Inspections Act 2006 (Prescribed Education and Training etc) Regulations 2007, SI 2007/464, regs 6, 7.
10 Education and Inspections Act 2006 s 127(3)(b). See also note 9.

1265.   Area inspections. If requested to do so by the Secretary of State[1], Her Majesty's Chief Inspector of Education, Children's Services and Skills[2] must inspect:

(1)   the quality and availability of a specified description of education or training[3], in a specified area in England[4], for persons who are aged 15[5] or over but under 19[6];

(2)   the standards achieved by those receiving that education or training[7]; and

(3)   whether the financial resources made available to those providing that education and training are managed efficiently and used in a way which provides value for money[8].

Such an inspection is known as 'an area inspection'[9]. The Chief Inspector may also conduct such an inspection without being requested to do so[10].

A provider of education or training which is the subject of an area inspection must provide the Chief Inspector with any information reasonably requested by him in connection with the inspection[11]; and any local authority in England whose area is wholly or partly within the area which is the subject of an area inspection must provide the Chief Inspector with any information reasonably requested by him in connection with the inspection[12].

On completing an area inspection, the Chief Inspector must make a written[13] report on it[14]. The Chief Inspector must send copies of the report to the Secretary of State[15], and each local authority in England whose area is wholly or partly within the area subject to the inspection[16]. Copies may also be sent to such other persons[17] as the Chief Inspector considers appropriate[18]. The Chief Inspector must arrange for the report to be published in such manner as he considers appropriate[19].

1   As to the Secretary of State see PARA 58.
2   As to Her Majesty's Chief Inspector of Education, Children's Services and Skills see PARA 1133.
3   The education or training that may be made the subject of an inspection under the Education and Inspections Act 2006 s 128 is any education or training to which Pt 8 Ch 3 (ss 123–134) applies (s 128(5)(a)) or any other education or training within the scope of the Chief Inspector's functions (s 128(5)(b)). As to the education or training to which Pt 8 Ch 3 (ss 123–134) applies see s 123(1); and PARA 1261. As to the meaning of 'functions' see PARA 1128 note 3. As to the functions of the Chief Inspector see PARA 1136 et seq.
4   As to the meaning of 'England' see PARA 7 note 3.
5   In the Education and Inspections Act 2006 s 128(1)(a) the reference to persons who are aged 15 includes persons for whom education is being provided at a school (s 128(8)(a)) and who will attain that age in the current school year (s 128(8)(b)). As to the meaning of 'school' see PARA 91; and as to the meaning of 'school year' see PARA 19 note 12 (definitions applied by s 128(8)). As to the time at which a person attains a particular age see PARA 7 note 6.
6   Education and Inspections Act 2006 s 128(1)(a).
7   Education and Inspections Act 2006 s 128(1)(b).
8   Education and Inspections Act 2006 s 128(1)(c). If financial resources have been applied by the Secretary of State, or a local authority in England, in respect of education or training which is being inspected (see s 128(3) (amended by SI 2010/1080; SI 2010/1158; the Education Act 2011 Sch 16 para 14(7)); and the Deregulation Act 2015 Sch 14 Pt 2 paras 50, 55), the inspection may extend to considering whether the application of those resources in that way constituted an efficient and effective use of the resources for the purpose of meeting the needs of persons within the Education and Inspections Act 2006 s 128(1)(a) (see head (1) in the text) as regards education or training of the kind in question (s 128(4)(a)) and was appropriate to secure value for money (s 128(4)(b)). As to the meaning of 'local authority in England' see PARA 1145 note 3.
9   See the Education and Inspections Act 2006 s 128(5). As to the framework for inspections see PARA 1260. As to powers of entry and related powers in relation to inspections see PARA 1267.
10 Education and Inspections Act 2006 s 128(2).
11 Education and Inspections Act 2006 s 128(6).
12 Education and Inspections Act 2006 s 128(7).
13 As to the meaning of 'written' see PARA 76 note 8.
14 Education and Inspections Act 2006 s 129(1). As to the publication of inspection reports see PARA 1142; and as to combined reports see PARA 1143. As to the duty of a recipient of a report to prepare an action plan in respect of the report see PARA 1266.
15 Education and Inspections Act 2006 s 129(2)(a).
16 Education and Inspections Act 2006 s 129(2)(c) (substituted SI 2010/1158).
17 As to the meaning of 'person' see PARA 7 note 6.
18 Education and Inspections Act 2006 s 129(3).
19 Education and Inspections Act 2006 s 129(4).

1266. Action plans following area inspections. Where Her Majesty's Chief Inspector of Education, Children's Services and Skills[1] publishes a report of an area inspection[2] the Secretary of State[3] may direct a local authority in England[4] whose area is wholly or partly within the area covered by the report[5], to prepare a written[6] statement of the action which it proposes to take in the light of the report[7], and the period within which it proposes to take that action[8].

In preparing the statement the authority must consult[9] such persons[10] as the Secretary of State may direct[11]. The authority must publish the statement within such period, and in such manner, as may be prescribed by regulations made by the Secretary of State[12], and send copies of it to such persons as may be so prescribed[13].

1   As to Her Majesty's Chief Inspector of Education, Children's Services and Skills see PARA 1133.
2   Education and Inspections Act 2006 s 130(1). As to area inspections and reports see PARA 1265.
3   As to the Secretary of State see PARA 58.
4   As to the meaning of 'local authority in England' see PARA 1145 note 3.

5 See the Education and Inspections Act 2006 s 130(3) (amended by SI 2010/1158; and the Education Act 2011 Sch 16 para 36).
6 As to the meaning of 'written' see PARA 76 note 8.
7 Education and Inspections Act 2006 s 130(2)(a), (3)(a).
8 Education and Inspections Act 2006 s 130(2)(b), (3)(b).
9 As to the exercise of the duty to consult see JUDICIAL REVIEW vol 61 (2010) PARA 627.
10 As to the meaning of 'person' see PARA 7 note 6.
11 See the Education and Inspections Act 2006 s 130(4) (amended by SI 2010/1080; the Education Act 2011 Sch 16 para 36; and the Deregulation Act 2015 Sch 14 Pt 2 paras 50, 57(1), (3)).
12 See the Education and Inspections Act 2006 s 130(5)(a) (s 130(5) amended by SI 2010/1080; the Education Act 2011 Sch 16 para 36; and the Deregulation Act 2015 Sch 14 Pt 2 paras 50, 57(1), (4)). As to the regulations made see the Education and Inspections Act 2006 (Prescribed Education and Training etc) Regulations 2007, SI 2007/464, regs 8, 9.
13 Education and Inspections Act 2006 s 130(5)(b). See also note 14.

1267. Powers of entry and other powers. When conducting an inspection[1], Her Majesty's Chief Inspector of Education, Children's Services and Skills may, at any reasonable time, enter any premises on which the education or training[2] inspected is provided[3], and any premises of the provider of that education or training which are used in connection with its provision[4]. In respect of education or training provided by an employer in the workplace, this power of entry may be exercised only if the employer has been given reasonable notice in writing[5].

If the Chief Inspector considers it necessary or expedient for the purposes of the inspection, he may inspect, take copies of, or take away any documents[6] relating to the education or training inspected which are on any premises in relation to which he exercises his power of entry[7]. In connection with inspecting any such documents the Chief Inspector may obtain access to, and inspect and check the operation of, any computer and associated apparatus or material which he considers is or has been in use in connection with the documents[8], and may require a specified person[9] to afford him such reasonable assistance as he may require for that purpose[10]. These powers of inspection may be exercised by the Chief Inspector at reasonable times only; and a person may not be required to do anything in pursuance thereof otherwise than at a reasonable time[11].

Any person who without reasonable excuse;

(1) obstructs the exercise of any power conferred[12] by these provisions[13]; or

(2) fails to comply with any requirement imposed thereby[14] as to the inspection of documents[15],

is guilty of an offence[16].

1 The Education and Inspections Act 2006 ss 131, 132 apply to an inspection conducted by Her Majesty's Chief Inspector of Education, Children's Services and Skills under Pt 8 Ch 3 (ss 123–134), other than one conducted under s 126(2) (see PARA 1263): see ss 131(1), 132(1). As to Her Majesty's Chief Inspector of Education, Children's Services and Skills see PARA 1133. As to inspections under Pt 8 Ch 3 see PARAS 1261–1501, 1503.
2 As to the education or training to which the Education and Inspections Act 2006 Pt 8 Ch 3 (ss 123–134) applies see s 123(1); and PARA 1261.
3 Education and Inspections Act 2006 s 131(2)(a). As to the requirement that a person exercising any powers of entry or to inspect documents produce an authenticated document showing his authority to exercise that power see s 150; and PARA 1138. As to the use by the Chief Inspector of any information obtained by him in the exercise of his functions see s 153; and PARA 1137.
4 Education and Inspections Act 2006 s 131(2)(b).
5 Education and Inspections Act 2006 s 131(3). As to the meaning of 'writing' see PARA 76 note 8.
6 As to the meaning of 'document' see PARA 1128 note 11.
7 Education and Inspections Act 2006 s 132(2). See also note 3. The power in s 132(2) includes power to require any person holding or accountable for any documents kept on the premises to produce them (s 132(3)(a)) and, in relation to any such documents kept by means of a computer, power to require them to be produced in a form in which they are legible and can be taken away (s 132(3)(b)). As to the meaning of 'person' see PARA 7 note 6.

8 Education and Inspections Act 2006 s 132(4)(a).
9 Ie a person by whom or on whose behalf the computer is or has been used (Education and Inspections Act 2006 s 132(5)(a)), or a person having charge of, or otherwise concerned with the operation of, the computer, apparatus or material (s 132(5)(b)).
10 Education and Inspections Act 2006 s 132(4)(b).
11 Education and Inspections Act 2006 s 132(6).
12 Ie conferred by the Education and Inspections Act 2006 s 131 or s 132: see the text to notes 1–11.
13 Education and Inspections Act 2006 s 132(7)(a).
14 Ie by the Education and Inspections Act 2006 s 132: see the text to notes 6–11.
15 Education and Inspections Act 2006 s 132(7)(b).
16 Education and Inspections Act 2006 s 132(7). The penalty for such an offence is, on summary conviction, a fine not exceeding level 4 on the standard scale: see s 132(7). As to the standard scale see SENTENCING AND DISPOSITION OF OFFENDERS vol 92 (2010) PARA 142.

(ii) Inspections in Wales

1268. The extended remit of Her Majesty's Chief Inspector of Education and Training in Wales. The following kinds of education and training are within the remit of Her Majesty's Chief Inspector of Education and Training in Wales[1]:

(1) education or training for persons aged 16 or over[2] where the provider of the education or training is given financial support by the Welsh Ministers[3] in the discharge of their functions relating to further education in Wales[4] or by a local authority in Wales[5], either generally or for a specific purpose[6];

(2) education or training for persons aged 16 or over where the Welsh Ministers, in the discharge of their functions relating to further education in Wales[7], or a local authority in Wales is contemplating giving the provider of the education financial support, either generally or for a specific purpose[8];

(3) education or training provided for persons of compulsory school age[9] in an institution in Wales which is within the further education sector[10];

(4) further education provided[11] by a school[12];

(5) such other education or training in Wales as may be prescribed by regulations made by the Welsh Ministers[13].

1 As to Her Majesty's Chief Inspector of Education and Training in Wales see PARA 1148.
2 As to the time at which a person attains a particular age see PARA 7 note 6.
3 As to the Welsh Ministers see PARA 59. The functions under the Learning and Skills Act 2000 s 75 were originally vested in the National Assembly for Wales and are now exercisable by the Welsh Ministers by virtue of the Government of Wales Act 2006 s 162(1), Sch 11 paras 30, 32.
4 Ie their functions under the Learning and Skills Act 2000 Pt 2 (ss 31–41): see PARA 789 et seq. As to the meaning of 'Wales' see PARA 7 note 3.
5 As to the meaning of 'local authority in Wales' see PARA 25 (definition applied by the Learning and Skills Act 2000 s 74(1) (amended by SI 2010/1158)).
6 Learning and Skills Act 2000 s 75(1)(a) (amended by SI 2005/3238; SI 2010/1158). Neither the Learning and Skills Act 2000 s 75(1)(a) nor (b) (see head (2) in the text) applies to education of a kind that may be inspected under Education Act 2005 Pt 1 (ss 1–63) (see PARA 1182 et seq) (Learning and Skills Act 2000 s 75(2)(a) (amended by the Education Act 2005 s 61, Sch 9 para 24)) or, if the financial support mentioned therein is given for a specific purpose, to education or training at which that support is not directed (Learning and Skills Act 2000 s 75(2)(b)).
7 Ie their functions under the Learning and Skills Act 2000 Pt 2 (ss 31–41): see PARA 789 et seq.
8 Learning and Skills Act 2000 s 75(1)(b) (amended by SI 2005/3238; SI 2010/1158). See also note 6.
9 As to the meaning of 'compulsory school age' see PARA 19.
10 Learning and Skills Act 2000 s 75(1)(c). As to institutions within the further education sector see PARA 555.

11 Ie under the School Standards and Framework Act 1998 s 80: see PARA 588.
12 Learning and Skills Act 2000 s 75(1)(d).
13 Learning and Skills Act 2000 s 75(1)(e). As to the regulations made see the Youth and Community Work Education and Training (Inspection) (Wales) Regulations 2006, SI 2006/2804.

1269. Additional functions. Her Majesty's Chief Inspector of Education and Training in Wales[1] must keep the Welsh Ministers[2] informed about:

(1)   the quality of the education and training which is[3] within his remit[4];
(2)   the standards achieved by those receiving that education and training[5]; and
(3)   whether the financial resources made available to those providing it are managed efficiently and used so as to provide value for money[6].

When asked to do so by the Welsh Ministers, the Chief Inspector must:

(a)   give the Welsh Ministers advice on such matters relating to education and training which is[7] within his remit as the Welsh Ministers may specify[8];
(b)   inspect such education or training, or such class of education or training, within that remit as the Welsh Ministers may specify[9];
(c)   report on the result of such an inspection[10].

The Chief Inspector has such other functions in connection with education and training within his remit[11] as the Welsh Ministers may specify[12]. Such functions may include functions with respect to training of or for teachers[13], lecturers, trainers or other persons[14] engaged in the provision of such education or training[15].

In exercising functions in relation to the inspection of education and training within his remit[16], the Chief Inspector must have regard to advice given by the Welsh Ministers[17], and such aspects of the Welsh Ministers policy as they may specify[18].

1   As to Her Majesty's Chief Inspector of Education and Training in Wales see PARA 1148.
2   As to the Welsh Ministers see PARA 59. The functions under the Learning and Skills Act 2000 s 76 were originally vested in the National Assembly for Wales and are now exercisable by the Welsh Ministers by virtue of the Government of Wales Act 2006 s 162(1), Sch 11 paras 30, 32.
3   Ie by virtue of the Learning and Skills Act 2000 Pt IV (ss 73–88): see PARA 1268.
4   See the Learning and Skills Act 2000 s 76(1)(a).
5   Learning and Skills Act 2000 s 76(1)(b).
6   Learning and Skills Act 2000 s 76(1)(c).
7   Ie by virtue of the Learning and Skills Act 2000 Pt IV (ss 73–88): see PARA 1268.
8   Learning and Skills Act 2000 s 76(2)(a).
9   Learning and Skills Act 2000 s 76(2)(b).
10 Learning and Skills Act 2000 s 76(2)(c). As to reports see further s 88; and PARA 1279. As to the duty of a provider of education and training to prepare an action plan following a report of an inspection see PARA 1272.
11 Ie by virtue of the Learning and Skills Act 2000 Pt IV (ss 73–88): see PARA 1268.
12 Learning and Skills Act 2000 s 76(3).
13 As to the meaning of references to training of teachers see PARA 24 note 2.
14 As to the meaning of 'person' see PARA 7 note 6.
15 See the Learning and Skills Act 2000 s 76(4).
16 Ie functions under the Learning and Skills Act 2000 Pt IV (ss 73–88).
17 Learning and Skills Act 2000 s 76(5)(a).
18 Learning and Skills Act 2000 s 76(5)(b).

1270. Inspections. Her Majesty's Chief Inspector of Education and Training in Wales[1] must inspect education and training which is[2] within his remit[3]. Inspections are to be conducted at such intervals as may be prescribed in regulations made by the Welsh Ministers[4].

The Chief Inspector must report[5] in writing[6] on:

(1)   the quality of the education or training inspected[7];

(2)   the standards achieved by those receiving that education or training[8]; and

(3)   whether the financial resources made available to the provider of the education or training are managed efficiently and used in a way which provides value for money[9].

The report must be made within such period as may be prescribed[10]. The Chief Inspector must without delay send a copy of the report to the Welsh Ministers[11], any local authority in Wales[12] providing funds for the education or training inspected[13], and the provider of the inspected education or training[14]. Copies may also be sent to such other persons[15] as the Chief Inspector considers appropriate[16]. The Chief Inspector must arrange for the report to be published in such manner as he considers appropriate[17].

1   As to Her Majesty's Chief Inspector of Education and Training in Wales see PARA 1148.
2   Ie by virtue of the Learning and Skills Act 2000 Pt IV (ss 73–88): see PARA 1268.
3   See the Learning and Skills Act 2000 s 77(1). As to rights of entry in relation to inspections see PARA 1280.
4   See the Learning and Skills Act 2000 s 77(2), (9). As to the prescribed intervals see the Inspection of Education and Training (Wales) Regulations 2001, SI 2001/2501, reg 2 (substituted by SI 2010/1436). As to the Welsh Ministers see PARA 59. The functions under the Learning and Skills Act 2000 s 77 were originally vested in the National Assembly for Wales and are now exercisable by the Welsh Ministers by virtue of the Government of Wales Act 2006 s 162(1), Sch 11 paras 30, 32.
5   As to reports see further the Learning and Skills Act 2000 s 88; and PARA 1279. As to the duty of a provider of education and training to prepare an action plan following a report of an inspection see PARA 1272.
6   As to the meaning of 'writing' see PARA 76 note 8.
7   Learning and Skills Act 2000 s 77(3)(a).
8   Learning and Skills Act 2000 s 77(3)(b).
9   Learning and Skills Act 2000 s 77(3)(c).
10 Learning and Skills Act 2000 s 77(4). As to the timing for inspection reports see the Inspection of Education and Training (Wales) Regulations 2001, SI 2001/2501, reg 3 (amended by SI 2004/783).
11 Learning and Skills Act 2000 s 77(5)(a).
12 As to the meaning of 'local authority in Wales' see PARA 25 (definition applied by the Learning and Skills Act 2000 s 74(1) (amended by SI 2010/1158)).
13 Learning and Skills Act 2000 s 77(5)(c) (amended by SI 2010/1158).
14 Learning and Skills Act 2000 s 77(5)(d).
15 As to the meaning of 'person' see PARA 7 note 6.
16 Learning and Skills Act 2000 s 77(6). A copy may be supplied under s 77(6) free of charge or on payment of such fee, not exceeding the cost of supplying the copy, as the Chief Inspector may determine: s 77(7).
17 Learning and Skills Act 2000 s 77(8).

1271.   General powers.   Her Majesty's Chief Inspector of Education and Training in Wales[1] may give advice to the Welsh Ministers[2] on any matter relating to education or training which is[3] within his remit[4], and may inspect, and report[5] on, any education or training of that kind[6].

The Chief Inspector may also, if the provider of the education or training asks him to do so, inspect any education or training which is not of that kind[7], but which would be if it were funded in one of the ways[8] education and training of that kind is funded[9]. The Chief Inspector may arrange for a report of such an inspection to be published[10].

1   As to Her Majesty's Chief Inspector of Education and Training in Wales see PARA 1148.

2   As to the Welsh Ministers see PARA 59. The functions under the Learning and Skills Act 2000 s 78 were originally vested in the National Assembly for Wales and are now exercisable by the Welsh Ministers by virtue of the Government of Wales Act 2006 s 162(1), Sch 11 paras 30, 32.

3   Ie by virtue of the Learning and Skills Act 2000 Pt IV (ss 73–88): see PARA 1268.

4   Learning and Skills Act 2000 s 78(1).

5   As to reports see further the Learning and Skills Act 2000 s 88; and PARA 1279.

6   Learning and Skills Act 2000 s 78(2). The provisions of s 77(5)–(8) (supply of copies of reports of inspections: see PARA 1270) apply to a report under s 78(2) as they apply to a report under s 77: s 78(5). As to rights of entry in relation to inspections see PARA 1280. As to the duty of a provider of education and training to prepare an action plan following a report of an inspection see PARA 1272.

7   Learning and Skills Act 2000 s 78(3)(a).

8   Ie in one of the ways mentioned in the Learning and Skills Act 2000 s 75: see PARA 1268.

9   Learning and Skills Act 2000 s 78(3)(b). The Chief Inspector may charge for the cost of an inspection conducted under s 78(3): s 78(4).

10 Learning and Skills Act 2000 s 78(6).

1272. Action plans. If Her Majesty's Chief Inspector of Education and Training in Wales[1] publishes a report of an inspection[2], other than an inspection requested by a provider of education or training or an area inspection[3], the provider of the education or training which is the subject of the report must prepare a written[4] statement of the action which he proposes to take in the light of the report and the period within which he proposes to take it[5]. The person[6] making the statement must publish it within such period, and in such manner, as may be prescribed by regulations made by the Welsh Ministers[7], and send copies of it to such persons as may be so prescribed[8].

1   As to Her Majesty's Chief Inspector of Education and Training in Wales see PARA 1148.

2   Learning and Skills Act 2000 s 80(1). As to inspections see PARAS 1269–1509.

3   The Learning and Skills Act 2000 s 80 does not apply to a report of an inspection conducted as a result of a request under s 78(3) (see PARA 1271), or under s 83 (see PARA 1275): s 80(2).

4   As to the meaning of 'written' see PARA 76 note 8.

5   Learning and Skills Act 2000 s 80(3).

6   As to the meaning of 'person' see PARA 7 note 6.

7   Learning and Skills Act 2000 s 80(4)(a). As to the regulations made see the Inspection of Education and Training (Wales) Regulations 2001, SI 2001/2501, reg 4 (amended by SI 2004/783; SI 2005/3238; SI 2014/1212). As to the Welsh Ministers see PARA 59. The functions under the Learning and Skills Act 2000 s 80 were originally vested in the National Assembly for Wales and are now exercisable by the Welsh Ministers by virtue of the Government of Wales Act 2006 s 162(1), Sch 11 paras 30, 32.

8   Learning and Skills Act 2000 s 80(4)(b). As to the regulations made see note 7.

1273. Inspection of careers services. Her Majesty's Chief Inspector of Education and Training in Wales[1] has the general duty of keeping the Welsh Ministers[2] informed about the quality of the relevant services[3] provided in Wales[4] in pursuance of arrangements made or directions given[5] by the Welsh Ministers[6]. Any person[7] who provides, or arranges for the provision of, relevant services in accordance with such arrangements or directions (a 'service provider')[8] must be inspected by the Chief Inspector at prescribed intervals[9].

When asked to do so by the Welsh Ministers, the Chief Inspector must:

(1)   give advice to the Welsh Ministers on such matters relating to the provision of relevant services in Wales in pursuance of such arrangements or directions as may be specified in the request[10]; or

(2)   inspect any service provider[11].

The Chief Inspector may also at any time give advice to the Welsh Ministers relating to the provision of relevant services in Wales in pursuance of such arrangements or directions[12] or inspect any service provider[13]. An inspection of any service provider is to consist of a review of the way in which the person is discharging his responsibilities under or by virtue of the arrangements or directions in question, having regard to any guidance given by the Welsh Ministers with respect to the provision of relevant services[14].

If a person ('a relevant provider') who provides a relevant service also provides education, training or an advisory service in Wales in pursuance of arrangements[15] made by the Welsh Ministers[16], or with the assistance of a grant or loan[17], the Chief Inspector has the general duty of keeping the Welsh Ministers informed about the quality of any such education, training or advisory services provided by relevant providers in Wales[18]. The Chief Inspector must inspect any relevant provider at prescribed intervals[19].

When asked to do so by the Welsh Ministers, the Chief Inspector must either give advice to the Welsh Ministers on such matters relating to the provision of any such education, training or advisory services by relevant providers[20] or inspect any relevant provider[21]. The Chief Inspector may also at any time give advice to the Welsh Ministers relating to the provision of such education, training or advisory services by relevant providers[22] or inspect any service provider[23]. An inspection of any relevant provider is to consist of a review of the way in which the person is providing the education, training or advisory services[24].

Any inspection under the above provisions[25] must be conducted by one or more of any of Her Majesty's Inspectors of Education and Training in Wales[26] or any additional authorised[27] inspector[28]. However, such an inspector or inspectors may be assisted by such other persons, whether or not members of the Chief Inspector's staff, as the Chief Inspector thinks fit[29]. In conducting the inspection, the inspector or inspectors must act in accordance with any instructions or guidelines given from time to time by the Welsh Ministers[30]. The inspector conducting the inspection, and any person assisting him[31], has at all reasonable times a right of entry to any premises[32] where the relevant services or, as the case requires, the education, training or advisory services[33] are provided[34]; and a right to inspect, and take copies of, any records or other documents kept by the person being inspected, which he requires for the purposes of the inspection[35]. It is an offence intentionally to obstruct the inspector conducting the inspection[36], or any person assisting him[37], in the exercise of his functions[38] in relation to the inspection[39].

Where an inspection has been completed, the Chief Inspector must prepare a written[40] report on the inspection within a prescribed period[41], and send a copy of the report to the person inspected[42], the Welsh Ministers[43], any prescribed person[44], and any other person whom he considers appropriate[45]. The Chief Inspector must publish the report in the prescribed manner[46] or, if none is prescribed, in such manner as he considers appropriate[47]. Regulations may require the person inspected to prepare a written statement in response to the report of the inspection[48].

1   As to Her Majesty's Chief Inspector of Education and Training in Wales see PARA 1148.
2   As to the Welsh Ministers see PARA 59. The functions under the Education Act 2005 ss 55–57 were originally vested in the National Assembly for Wales and are now exercisable by the Welsh Ministers by virtue of the Government of Wales Act 2006 s 162(1), Sch 11 paras 30, 32.

3   'Relevant services' has the same meaning as in the Employment and Training Act 1973 ss 8, 9 (provision of careers services: see EMPLOYMENT vol 40 (2014) PARAS 638, 639): Education Act 2005 s 55(8).
4   As to the meaning of 'Wales' see PARA 7 note 3.

5   Ie under the Employment and Training Act 1973 s 10: see EMPLOYMENT vol 40 (2014) PARA 638.
6   See the Education Act 2005 s 55(1), (2). As to the application of Pt 1 (ss 1–63) to pupil referral units in Wales see the Education (Pupil Referral Units) (Application of Enactments) (Wales) Regulations 2007, SI 2007/1069, reg 3, Sch 1, Pt 1, para 11. As to pupil referral units see PARA 427 et seq.
7   As to the meaning of 'person' see PARA 7 note 6.
8   Education Act 2005 s 55(3).
9   Education Act 2005 s 55(4). 'Prescribed' means prescribed by regulations; and 'regulations' means regulations made by the Welsh Ministers: s 55(8). As to the regulations made see the Inspection of the Careers and Related Services (Wales) Regulations 2006, SI 2006/3103, regs 3, 4 (both substituted by SI 2010/1436; the Inspection of the Careers and Related Services (Wales) Regulations 2006, SI 2006/3103, reg 4 further amended by SI 2014/1212).
10 Education Act 2005 s 55(5)(a).
11 Education Act 2005 s 55(5)(b).
12 Education Act 2005 s 55(6)(a).
13 Education Act 2005 s 55(6)(b).
14 Education Act 2005 s 55(7). As to the publication of guidance see the Education Act 1996 s 571 (applied by the Education Act 2005 s 122(2), (3)); and PARA 60.
15 Ie made under the Employment and Training Act 1973 s 2: see EMPLOYMENT vol 40 (2014) PARA 634.
16 Education Act 2005 s 56(1)(a).
17 Education Act 2005 s 56(1)(b). The grant or loan referred to is one made under the Industrial Development Act 1982 s 12(1) (power to promote careers in industry: see TRADE AND INDUSTRY vol 97 (2015) PARA 1048): see the Education Act 2005 s 56(1)(b).
18 Education Act 2005 s 56(2).
19 Education Act 2005 s 56(3). As to the regulations made see the Inspection of the Careers and Related Services (Wales) Regulations 2006, SI 2006/3103, regs 3, 4 (both substituted by SI 2010/1436; the Inspection of the Careers and Related Services (Wales) Regulations 2006, SI 2006/3103, reg 4 further amended by SI 2014/1212).
20 Education Act 2005 s 56(4)(a).
21 Education Act 2005 s 56(4)(b).
22 Education Act 2005 s 56(5)(a).
23 Education Act 2005 s 56(5)(b).
24 See the Education Act 2005 s 56(6).
25 Ie under the Education Act 2005 s 55 or s 56 (see the text to notes 1–24): see s 57(1).
26 Education Act 2005 s 57(2)(a). As to Her Majesty's Inspectors of Education and Training in Wales see PARA 1148.
27 Ie authorised under the Education Act 2005 Sch 2 para 2: see PARA 1149.
28 Education Act 2005 s 57(2)(b).
29 Education Act 2005 s 57(2). As to the Chief Inspector's staff see PARA 1149.
30 Education Act 2005 s 57(3).
31 Ie assisting him by virtue of the Education Act 2005 s 57(2): see the text to note 29.
32 As to the meaning of 'premises' see PARA 62 note 19 (definition applied by the Education Act 2005 s 122(2), (3)).
33 Ie the education, training or advisory services falling within the Education Act 2005 s 56(1): see the text to notes 15–17.
34 Education Act 2005 s 57(4)(a).
35 Education Act 2005 s 57(4)(b).
36 Education Act 2005 s 57(5)(a).
37 Education Act 2005 s 57(5)(b).
38 As to the meaning of 'functions' see PARA 18 note 5 (definition applied by the Education Act 2005 s 122(2), (3)).
39 Education Act 2005 s 57(5). A person guilty of such an offence is liable on summary conviction to a fine not exceeding level 4 on the standard scale: s 57(6). As to the standard scale see SENTENCING AND DISPOSITION OF OFFENDERS vol 92 (2010) PARA 142.
40 As to the meaning of 'written' see PARA 76 note 8.
41 Education Act 2005 s 57(7)(a). As to the regulations made see the Inspection of the Careers and Related Services (Wales) Regulations 2006, SI 2006/3103, reg 5.
42 Education Act 2005 s 57(7)(b)(i).
43 Education Act 2005 s 57(7)(b)(ii).
44 Education Act 2005 s 57(7)(b)(iii). As to the regulations made see the Inspection of the Careers and Related Services (Wales) Regulations 2006, SI 2006/3103, reg 8.

45 Education Act 2005 s 57(7)(b)(iv).

46 As to the regulations made see the Inspection of the Careers and Related Services (Wales) Regulations 2006, SI 2006/3103, reg 9.

47 Education Act 2005 s 57(7)(c). Section 29(3), (4) (which relate to defamation: see PARA 1190) apply to the publication of such a report as they apply to the publication of a report under either of the provisions mentioned in s 29(2): s 57(8).

48 Education Act 2005 s 57(9). Such regulations may prescribe the matters to be dealt with in the statement (s 57(9)(a)) and the period within which it must be prepared (s 57(9)(b)) and may require the person who prepared it to send copies of the statement to prescribed persons and to publish it in the prescribed manner (s 57(9)(c)). As to the regulations made see the Inspection of the Careers and Related Services (Wales) Regulations 2006, SI 2006/3103, regs 6, 7 (reg 7 substituted by SI 2014/1212).

1274. Inspections of education and training provided under the Employment and Training Act 1973. Her Majesty's Chief Inspector of Education and Training in Wales[1] may, at the request of the Secretary of State[2] or Her Majesty's Chief Inspector of Education, Children's Services and Skills[3], inspect any education or training provided in Wales[4] by the Secretary of State in accordance with certain arrangements under the Employment and Training Act 1973[5].

A report of an inspection conducted at the request of the Secretary of State must be given to him[6]; and the Secretary of State may arrange for the report to be published in such manner as he considers appropriate[7]. A report of an inspection conducted at the request of Her Majesty's Chief Inspector of Education, Children's Services and Skills must be given to him[8]; and he may arrange for the report to be published in such manner as he considers appropriate[9]. Her Majesty's Chief Inspector of Education and Training in Wales must send a copy of any report[10] to the Welsh Ministers[11].

1 As to Her Majesty's Chief Inspector of Education and Training in Wales see PARA 1148.
2 As to the Secretary of State see PARA 58.
3 As to Her Majesty's Chief Inspector of Education, Children's Services and Skills see PARA 1133.
4 As to the meaning of 'Wales' see PARA 7 note 3.
5 Learning and Skills Act 2000 s 82(1), (7) (s 82(1) amended, s 82(7) added, by the Education and Inspections Act 2006 s 157, Sch 14, paras 55, 57(1), (5)). The arrangements referred to are any made under the Employment and Training Act 1973 s 2 (see EMPLOYMENT vol 40 (2014) PARA 634): see the Learning and Skills Act 2000 s 82(1) (as so amended).
6 Learning and Skills Act 2000 s 82(2). As to reports see further s 88; and PARA 1279.
7 Learning and Skills Act 2000 s 82(3).
8 Learning and Skills Act 2000 s 82(4) (amended by the Education and Inspections Act 2006 s 157, Sch 14 paras 55, 57(1), (3)).
9 Learning and Skills Act 2000 s 82(5) (amended by the Education and Inspections Act 2006 s 157, Sch 14 paras 55, 57(1), (4)).
10 Ie any report under the Learning and Skills Act 2000 s 82(2) or s 82(4): see the text to notes 6, 8.
11 Learning and Skills Act 2000 s 82(6). As to the Welsh Ministers see PARA 59. The functions under s 82 were originally vested in the National Assembly for Wales and are now exercisable by the Welsh Ministers by virtue of the Government of Wales Act 2006 s 162(1), Sch 11 paras 30, 32.

1275. Area inspections. If asked to do so by the Welsh Ministers[1], Her Majesty's Chief Inspector of Education and Training in Wales[2] must inspect:

(1)   the quality and availability of a specified description of education or training[3], in a specified area in Wales[4], for persons who are aged 15[5] or over[6];

(2)   the standards achieved by those receiving that education or training[7]; and

(3) whether the financial resources made available to those providing that education and training are managed efficiently and used in a way which provides value for money[8].

The Chief Inspector may also, without being asked to, conduct such an inspection[9]. An inspection under these provisions is known as an 'area inspection'[10].

A provider of education or training which is the subject of an area inspection must provide such information as the Chief Inspector may reasonably require in connection with the inspection[11]. The Welsh Ministers and any local authority in Wales within the area which is the subject of an area inspection must provide such information as the Chief Inspector may reasonably require in connection with the inspection[12]. The Welsh Ministers may by regulations[13] make further provision with respect to these obligations to provide information[14]. On completing an area inspection, the Chief Inspector for Wales must make a written[15] report[16].

If the Chief Inspector publishes a report of an area inspection[17], the Welsh Ministers may direct a local authority in Wales whose area is wholly or partly in the area covered by the report to prepare a written statement of the action which it proposes to take in the light of the report and the period within which it proposes to take it[18]. In preparing the statement the authority must consult such persons[19] as the Welsh Ministers may direct[20]. The authority must publish the statement within such period, and in such manner, as may be prescribed by regulations made by the Welsh Ministers[21], and send copies of it to such persons as may be so prescribed[22].

1　As to the Welsh Ministers see PARA 59. The functions under the Learning and Skills Act 2000 ss 83, 84 were originally vested in the National Assembly for Wales and are now exercisable by the Welsh Ministers by virtue of the Government of Wales Act 2006 s 162(1), Sch 11 paras 30, 32.
2　As to Her Majesty's Chief Inspector of Education and Training in Wales see PARA 1148.
3　The education or training that may be made the subject of an area inspection is any education or training within the remit of the Chief Inspector (whether as a result of the Learning and Skills Act 2000 Pt IV (ss 73–88) or of any other enactment): s 83(4). As to the education and training within the remit of the Chief Inspector by virtue of Pt IV see PARA 1268. As to the functions of the Chief Inspector generally see PARA 1151 et seq.
4　As to the meaning of 'Wales' see PARA 7 note 3.
5　'Persons who are aged 15' includes persons for whom education is being provided at a school who will attain that age in the current school year: Learning and Skills Act 2000 s 83(11) (added by the Education Act 2002 s 178(1), (4)(b)). As to the meaning of 'school' see PARA 91; and as to the meaning of 'school year' see PARA 19 note 12 (definitions applied by the Learning and Skills Act 2000 s 83(11) (as so added)). As to the time at which a person attains a particular age see PARA 7 note 6.
6　Learning and Skills Act 2000 s 83(1)(a) (amended by the Education Act 2002 s 178(1), (4)(a)).
7　Learning and Skills Act 2000 s 83(1)(b).
8　Learning and Skills Act 2000 s 83(1)(c). If financial resources have been applied by the Welsh Ministers or a local authority in Wales in respect of education or training which is being inspected, the inspection may extend to considering the manner in which those resources have been applied and whether they have been applied in a way which provides value for money: s 83(3) (amended by SI 2005/3238; SI 2010/1158). As to the meaning of 'local authority in Wales' see PARA 25 (definition applied by the Learning and Skills Act 2000 s 74(1) (amended by SI 2010/1158)).
9　Learning and Skills Act 2000 s 83(2).
10　See the Learning and Skills Act 2000 s 83(10). As to rights of entry in relation to inspections see PARA 1280.
11　Learning and Skills Act 2000 s 83(5).
12　Learning and Skills Act 2000 83(6) (amended by SI 2005/3238; SI 2010/1158).
13　At the date at which this volume states the law no such regulations had been made.
14　See the Learning and Skills Act 2000 s 83(7).

15 As to the meaning of 'written' see PARA 76 note 8.
16 Learning and Skills Act 2000 s 83(8). The provisions of s 77(4), (5)(a)–(c), (6)–(9) (see PARA 1270) apply to such a report as they apply to a report under s 77: s 83(9). As to reports see further s 88; and PARA 1279.
17 Learning and Skills Act 2000 s 84(1).
18 Learning and Skills Act 2000 s 84(3) (amended by SI 2010/1158).
19 As to the meaning of 'person' see PARA 7 note 6. As to the exercise of the duty to consult see JUDICIAL REVIEW vol 61 (2010) PARA 627. For provision on reporting on sixth forms found to be causing concern in an area inspection, see the Education Act 2005 ss 44C, 44E (see PARA 1251): Learning and Skills Act 2000 s 84(9A) (added by the School Standards and Organisation (Wales) Act 2013 Sch 5 para 20(3)).
20 Learning and Skills Act 2000 s 84(4) (amended by SI 2005/3238).
21 See the Learning and Skills Act 2000 s 84(5)(a). As to the regulations made see the Inspection of Education and Training (Wales) Regulations 2001, SI 2001/2501, reg 4 (amended by SI 2004/783; SI 2005/3238; SI 2014/1212).
22 Learning and Skills Act 2000 s 84(5)(b). As to the regulations made see note 21.

1276. Surveys and comparative studies. The Welsh Ministers[1] may direct Her Majesty's Chief Inspector of Education and Training in Wales[2] to carry out:

(1) a survey of Wales[3], or of a specified area within Wales, in respect of specified matters relating to policy concerned with education or training for persons aged 16 or over[4]; or

(2) a comparative study of the provision made outside Wales in respect of specified matters relating to such education or training[5].

The Chief Inspector may also, without being directed to, carry out a survey or study of that kind[6].

1 As to the Welsh Ministers see PARA 59. The functions under the Learning and Skills Act 2000 s 85 were originally vested in the National Assembly for Wales and are now exercisable by the Welsh Ministers by virtue of the Government of Wales Act 2006 s 162(1), Sch 11 paras 30, 32.
2 As to Her Majesty's Chief Inspector of Education and Training in Wales see PARA 1148.
3 As to the meaning of 'Wales' see PARA 7 note 3.
4 Learning and Skills Act 2000 s 85(1)(a). As to the time at which a person attains a particular age see PARA 7 note 6.
5 Learning and Skills Act 2000 s 85(1)(b).
6 Learning and Skills Act 2000 s 85(2).

1277. Annual reports. The annual report[1] of Her Majesty's Chief Inspector of Education and Training in Wales[2] must include an account of the exercise of his functions[3] in relation to the inspection of education or training in Wales[4]. The Chief Inspector's power to make other reports[5] includes a power to make reports with respect to matters relating to education or training which is[6] within his remit[7].

1 Ie the annual report required by the Education Act 2005 s 21(1)(a): see PARA 1154.
2 As to Her Majesty's Chief Inspector of Education and Training in Wales see PARA 1148.
3 Ie under the Learning and Skills Act 2000 Pt IV (ss 73–88).
4 Learning and Skills Act 2000 s 86(1). As to the meaning of 'Wales' see PARA 7 note 3.
5 Ie the power conferred by the Education Act 2005 s 21: see PARA 1154.
6 Ie by virtue of the Learning and Skills Act 2000 Pt IV (ss 73–88): see PARA 1268.
7 See the Learning and Skills Act 2000 s 86(2).

1278. Annual plan. Her Majesty's Chief Inspector of Education and Training in Wales[1] must[2] prepare a plan for each financial year[3]. The plan must contain estimates of:

(1) the expenditure necessary, in the financial year to which the plan relates, in order to secure that the functions of the Chief Inspector are discharged effectively[4]; and

(2)   the income which the Chief Inspector will receive in that financial year
and which may be applied towards meeting his expenses[5].

The plan must also contain proposals for the management of any funds which
may be provided by the Welsh Ministers[6] for that financial year[7].

The plan must be submitted to the Welsh Ministers by such time before the
beginning of the financial year to which it relates as they may direct[8]. The Chief
Inspector may, after the plan has been approved[9], publish it in such manner and
at such time as appears to him to be appropriate[10].

1   As to Her Majesty's Chief Inspector of Education and Training in Wales see PARA 1148.
2   Ie for the purposes of the consultation required under the Government of Wales Act 1998
    s 104(4) (funding of Her Majesty's Chief Inspector of Education and Training for Wales: see
    CONSTITUTIONAL AND ADMINISTRATIVE LAW vol 20 (2014) PARA 381): see the Learning and
    Skills Act 2000 s 87(1), (6).
3   Learning and Skills Act 2000 s 87(1).
4   Learning and Skills Act 2000 s 87(3)(a).
5   Learning and Skills Act 2000 s 87(3)(b).
6   As to the Welsh Ministers see PARA 59. The functions under the Learning and Skills Act 2000
    s 87 were originally vested in the National Assembly for Wales and are now exercisable by the
    Welsh Ministers by virtue of the Government of Wales Act 2006 s 162(1), Sch 11 paras 30, 32.
7   Learning and Skills Act 2000 s 87(4).
8   Learning and Skills Act 2000 s 87(2).
9   Ie under the Government of Wales Act 1998 s 104(4A): see CONSTITUTIONAL AND
    ADMINISTRATIVE LAW vol 20 (2014) PARA 381.
10 Learning and Skills Act 2000 s 87(5), (6).

1279. Reports and the law of defamation. For the purposes of the law of
defamation, any report made[1] by Her Majesty's Chief Inspector of Education
and Training in Wales[2] is privileged unless its publication is shown to have been
made with malice[3]. However, this does not limit any privilege otherwise[4]
subsisting[5].

1   Ie under the Learning and Skills Act 2000 Pt IV (ss 73–88).
2   As to Her Majesty's Chief Inspector of Education and Training in Wales see PARA 1148.
3   See the Learning and Skills Act 2000 s 88(1). As to privilege and malice in the law of defamation
    see DEFAMATION vol 32 (2012) PARAS 594 et seq, 651 et seq.
4   Ie apart from the Learning and Skills Act 2000 s 88(1): see the text to notes 1–3.
5   Learning and Skills Act 2000 s 88(2).

1280. Right of entry. When conducting an inspection[1], Her Majesty's Chief
Inspector of Education and Training in Wales[2] has, at all reasonable times:
(1)   a right of entry to premises on which the education or training being
       inspected is provided[3];
(2)   a right of entry to premises of the provider of that education or training
       which are used in connection with that provision[4];
(3)   a right to inspect, and take copies of, any records kept by that person[5],
       and any other documents containing information relating to the
       education or training, which the inspector requires for the purposes of
       the inspection[6].

In respect of education or training provided by an employer in the workplace,
the right of entry conferred by heads (1) to (3) above may be exercised only if the
employer has been given reasonable notice in writing[7].

It is an offence wilfully to obstruct the Chief Inspector in the exercise of
functions in relation to an inspection[8].

1   Ie under the Learning and Skills Act 2000 Pt IV (ss 73–88). As to inspections see PARAS
    1269–1271, 1274, 1275.

2   As to Her Majesty's Chief Inspector of Education and Training in Wales see PARA 1148.
3   Learning and Skills Act 2000 s 79(1)(a).
4   Learning and Skills Act 2000 s 79(1)(b).
5   As to the meaning of 'person' see PARA 7 note 6.
6   Learning and Skills Act 2000 s 79(1)(c). The right to inspect records conferred by s 79(1)(c) includes the right to have access to, and to inspect and check the operation of, any computer and any associated apparatus or material which is or has been in use in connection with the records in question: s 79(3). That right also includes the right to such assistance from the person by whom or on whose behalf the computer is or has been so used (s 79(4)(a)), or any person having charge of, or otherwise concerned with the operation of, the computer, apparatus or material (s 79(4)(b)), as the Chief Inspector may reasonably require (s 79(4)).
7   Learning and Skills Act 2000 s 79(2). As to the meaning of 'writing' see PARA 76 note 8.
8   Learning and Skills Act 2000 s 79(5). A person guilty of such an offence is liable on summary conviction to a fine not exceeding level 4 on the standard scale: s 79(6). As to the standard scale see SENTENCING AND DISPOSITION OF OFFENDERS vol 92 (2010) PARA 142.

(iii) Intervention

A. INTERVENTION IN ENGLAND

1281. Intervention by the Secretary of State. If the Secretary of State[1] is satisfied, whether or not a complaint is made by any person[2], as to one or more of the matters listed in heads (a) to (d) below in the case of an institution in England within the further education sector, other than a sixth form college[3], he may do one or more of the following[4]:

(1)   remove all or any of the members of the institution's governing body[5];

(2)   appoint new members of that body if there are vacancies (however arising)[6];

(3)   give to that body such directions he thinks expedient as to the exercise of its powers and performance of its duties[7].

The matters are:

(a)   that the institution's affairs have been or are being mismanaged by the institution's governing body[8];

(b)   that the institution's governing body has failed to discharge any duty imposed on it by or for the purposes of any Act[9];

(c)   that the institution's governing body has acted or is proposing to act unreasonably with respect to the exercise of any power conferred or the performance of any duty imposed by or under any Act[10];

(d)   that the institution is performing significantly less well than it might in all the circumstances reasonably be expected to perform, or is failing or likely to fail to give an acceptable standard of education or training[11].

At the same time as doing one or more of those things, the Secretary of State must give the institution's governing body a notice stating the matter or matters listed in heads (a) to (d) above as to which he is satisfied[12], the reasons why he is so satisfied[13], and the reasons why he has decided to do that thing or those things[14].

The directions that may be given to a governing body include a direction requiring a governing body to make collaboration arrangements[15] with such bodies and on such terms as may be specified in the direction[16] and a direction requiring a governing body[17] to make a resolution[18] for the body to be dissolved on a date specified in the direction[19].

Directions may be given to a governing body despite any enactment making the exercise of a power or performance of a duty contingent on the body's opinion[20]. The Secretary of State may not, however, direct a governing body[21] to dismiss a member of staff[22].

A governing body must comply with any directions given to it under these provisions[23].

1 As to the Secretary of State see PARA 58.
2 The Further and Higher Education Act 1992 s 56A if the Secretary of State is satisfied as to one or more of the matters listed in s 56A(2) (see heads (a)–(d) in the text) in the case of (1) an institution in England within the further education sector, other than a sixth form college; or (2) an institution in England which is maintained by a local authority and provides further education, other than an institution within the higher education sector, and, in either case, it is immaterial whether or not a complaint is made by any person: s 56A(1) (s 56A added by the Further Education and Training Act 2007 s 17; and amended by the Education Act 2011 Sch 12 para 25(2); and the Further and Higher Education Act 1992 s 56A(1) substituted by the Deregulation Act 2015 Sch 15 para 7). As to the meaning of 'person' see PARA 7 note 6. As to the meaning of 'England' see PARA 7 note 3. As to the meaning of 'institution within the further education sector' see PARA 555. As to the meaning of references to 'sixth form colleges' see PARA 555 note 5.
3 Further and Higher Education Act 1992 s 56A(1) (as added (see note 2); and amended by the Apprenticeships, Skills, Children and Learning Act 2009 ss 123(2), 125, Sch 6 paras 2, 7(1), (2), Sch 8, paras 1, 6; amended by the Education Act 2011 Sch 12 para 25(2)).
4 See the Further and Higher Education Act 1992 s 56A(3) (as added (see note 2); and amended by the Apprenticeships, Skills, Children and Learning Act 2009 s 123(2), Sch 6 paras 2, 7(1), (3); and the Education Act 2011 Sch 12 para 25(3)).
5 Further and Higher Education Act 1992 s 56A(6)(a) (as added: see note 2). As to the meaning of 'governing body' see PARA 560 note 6.
6 Further and Higher Education Act 1992 s 56A(6)(b) (as added: see note 2). An appointment of a member of a governing body under s 56A has effect as if made in accordance with the instrument of government and articles of government of the institution concerned: s 56A(12) (as so added).
7 Further and Higher Education Act 1992 s 56A(6)(c) (as added (see note 2; and amended by the Apprenticeships, Skills, Children and Learning Act 2009 s 123(2), Sch 6 paras 2, 7(1), (5)(b)). As to directions see the Education Act 1996 s 570 (applied by the Further and Higher Education Act 1992 s 89(5)); and PARA 75.
8 Further and Higher Education Act 1992 s 56A(2)(a) (as added: see note 2).
9 Further and Higher Education Act 1992 s 56A(2)(b) (as added: see note 2).
10 Further and Higher Education Act 1992 s 56A(2)(c) (as added: see note 2).
11 Further and Higher Education Act 1992 s 56A(2)(d) (as added: see note 2).
12 Further and Higher Education Act 1992 s 56A(5)(a) (as added (see note 2); and amended by the Apprenticeships, Skills, Children and Learning Act 2009 s 123(2), Sch 6, paras 2, 7(1), (4); and the Education Act 2011 Sch 12 para 25).
13 Further and Higher Education Act 1992 s 56A(5)(b) (as added (see note 2); and amended by the Apprenticeships, Skills, Children and Learning Act 2009 s 123(2), Sch 6, paras 2, 7(1), (4); and the Education Act 2011 Sch 12 para 25).
14 Further and Higher Education Act 1992 s 56A(5)(c) (as added (see note 2); and amended by the Apprenticeships, Skills, Children and Learning Act 2009 s 123(2), Sch 6, paras 2, 7(1), (4); and the Education Act 2011 Sch 12 para 25).
15 Ie within the meaning of the Education and Inspections Act 2006 s 166: see PARA 172.
16 Further and Higher Education Act 1992 s 56A(7) (as added (see note 2); amended by the Education Act 2011 Sch 12, para 25(6)).
17 A governing body to which such a direction is given is to be taken for the purposes of the Education and Inspections Act 2006 s 27A(1) to have complied with s 27 (see PARA 571) before making the resolution required by the direction: s 56A(7A) (added by the Education Act 2011 Sch 12 para 25(6)).
18 Ie under the Further and Higher Education Act 1992 s 27A(1) (see PARA 571).
19 Further and Higher Education Act 1992 s 56A(7) (amended by the Education Act 2011 Sch 12 para 25(6)).
20 Further and Higher Education Act 1992 s 56A(8) (as added: see note 2).
21 Ie under the Further and Higher Education Act 1992 s 56A(6)(c): see head (3) in the text.

22 See the Further and Higher Education Act 1992 s 56A(9) (as added (see note 2); and substituted by the Education Act 2011 Sch 12 para 25(7)).
23 Further and Higher Education Act 1992 s 56A(11) (as added: see note 2).

B. INTERVENTION IN WALES

1282. Intervention by the Welsh Ministers. If one or more of the conditions listed in heads (a) to (d) below is satisfied regarding an institution in Wales[1] within the further education sector[2] (whether or not a complaint is made by any person)[3], the Welsh Ministers[4] may by order[5] declare which of the conditions is (or are) satisfied[6], and do one or more of the following things[7]:

(1)   remove all or any of the members of the institution's governing body[8];
(2)   appoint new members of that body if there are vacancies (however arising)[9];
(3)   give to that body such directions[10] as they think expedient as to the exercise of its powers and performance of its duties[11].

The conditions are that the Welsh Ministers are satisfied:

(a)   that the institution's affairs have been or are being mismanaged by its governing body[12];
(b)   that the institution's governing body has failed to discharge any duty imposed on it by or for the purposes of any Act or any Measure of the National Assembly for Wales[13];
(c)   that the institution's governing body has acted or is proposing to act unreasonably with respect to the exercise of any power conferred or the performance of any duty imposed by or under any Act or any Measure of the National Assembly for Wales[14];
(d)   that the institution is performing significantly less well than it might in all the circumstances reasonably be expected to perform, or is failing or likely to fail to give an acceptable standard of education or training[15].

The directions that may be given to a governing body include a direction requiring a governing body to make collaboration arrangements[16] with such bodies and on such terms as may be specified in the direction[17] and a direction requiring a governing body to make a resolution[18] for the body to be dissolved on a date specified in the direction[19]. However, the Welsh Ministers may not direct a governing body[20] to dismiss a member of staff[21].

A governing body must comply with any such directions given to it[22].

1   As to the meaning of 'Wales' see PARA 7 note 3.
2   As to the meaning of 'institution within the further education sector' see PARA 555.
3   See the Further and Higher Education Act 1992 s 57(1) (s 57 substituted by the Learning and Skills Act 2000 s 149, Sch 9 paras 1, 34; Further and Higher Education Act 1992 s 57(1) amended by the Further Education and Training Act 2007 s 29, Sch 1 paras 6, 9(1), (2)). As to the meaning of 'person' see PARA 7 note 6.
4   As to the Welsh Ministers see PARA 59.
5   Such orders are not made by statutory instrument (see the Further and Higher Education Act 1992 s 89(2)) and are not recorded in this work.
6   Further and Higher Education Act 1992 s 57(4)(a) (as substituted (see note 3); s 57(4) amended by the Further Education and Training Act 2007 s 29, Sch 1 paras 6, 9(5)).
7   Further and Higher Education Act 1992 s 57(4)(b) (as substituted: see note 3).
8   Further and Higher Education Act 1992 s 57(5)(a) (s 57 as substituted (see note 3); s 57(5) amended by the Further Education and Training Act 2007 s 29, Sch 1 paras 6, 9(6)). As to the meaning of 'governing body' see PARA 560 note 6.
9   Further and Higher Education Act 1992 s 57(5)(b) (as substituted: see note 3). An appointment of a member of a governing body under the Further and Higher Education Act 1992 s 57 has effect as if made in accordance with the instrument of government and articles of government of the institution concerned: s 57(8) (as so substituted).

10 As to directions see the Education Act 1996 s 570 (applied by the Further and Higher Education Act 1992 s 89(5)); and PARA 75.
11 Further and Higher Education Act 1992 s 57(5)(c) (as substituted and amended: see note 8). Directions may be given to a body under s 57 despite any enactment making the exercise of a power or performance of a duty contingent on the body's opinion: s 57(6) (as so substituted).
12 Further and Higher Education Act 1992 s 57(2)(a) (as substituted (see note 3); and amended by the Further Education and Training Act 2007 s 29, Sch 1 paras 6, 9(1), (3)(a)).
13 Further and Higher Education Act 1992 s 57(2)(b) (as substituted (see note 3); and amended by the Further Education and Training Act 2007 s 29, Sch 1 paras 6, 9(1), (3)(b); Learner Travel (Wales) Measure 2008 s 25, Sch 1 para 3(1), (2)). As to the National Assembly for Wales see CONSTITUTIONAL AND ADMINISTRATIVE LAW vol 20 (2014) PARA 351 et seq.
14 Further and Higher Education Act 1992 s 57(2)(c) (as substituted (see note 3); and amended by the Further Education and Training Act 2007 s 29, Sch 1 paras 6, 9(1), (3)(b); Learner Travel (Wales) Measure 2008 s 25, Sch 1 para 3(1), (3)).
15 Further and Higher Education Act 1992 s 57(2)(d) (s 57 as substituted (see note 3); s 57(2)(d) further substituted by the Further Education and Training Act 2007 s 18(1), (2)).
16 Ie to exercise powers under Education (Wales) Measure 2011 s 5(2)(b)–(f), (h) to collaborate with such persons.
17 Further and Higher Education Act 1992 s 57(5A)(a) (s 57 as substituted (see note 3); s 57(5A) added by the Further Education and Training Act 2007 s 18(1), (3); the Further and Higher Education Act 1992 s 57(5A)(a) numbered as such the Further and Higher Education (Governance and Information) (Wales) Act 2014 s 5(2)(a) and amended by the Education (Wales) Measure 2011 s 9(1)).
18 Ie under the Further and Higher Education Act 1992 s 27A(1) (see PARA 571).
19 Further and Higher Education Act 1992 s 57(5A)(b) (added by the Further and Higher Education (Governance and Information) (Wales) Act 2014 s 5(2)(b)). A governing body to which a direction such as is mentioned in the Further and Higher Education Act 1992 s (5A)(b) is given is to be taken for the purposes of s 27A(1) to have complied with s 27 before making the resolution required by the direction: s 57(5B) (added by the Further and Higher Education (Governance and Information) (Wales) Act 2014 s 5(3)).
20 Ie under the Further and Higher Education Act 1992 s 57(5)(c): see head (3) in the text.
21 Further and Higher Education Act 1992 s 57(6A) (s 57 as substituted (see note 3); s 57(6A), (6B) added by the Further Education and Training Act 2007 s 18(1), (4)). The Further and Higher Education Act 1992 s 57(6A) does not prevent the Welsh Ministers, where they consider that it may be appropriate to dismiss a member of staff whom the governing body has power under its institution's articles of government to dismiss, from giving the governing body such directions as are necessary to secure that the procedures applicable to the consideration of the case for dismissal of that member of staff are given effect to in relation to that member of staff: s 57(6B) (as so substituted and added).
22 Further and Higher Education Act 1992 s 57(7) (as substituted: see note 3).

(iv) Inspection of Accounts

1283. Inspection of accounts. The accounts of any further education corporation[1], any sixth form college corporation[2], and any designated institution[3], are open to the inspection of the Comptroller and Auditor General[4]. In the case of any such corporation or institution this power[5], and the powers[6] relating to examinations into the economy, efficiency and effectiveness of certain bodies and access to documents and information conferred[7] on the Comptroller and Auditor General[8], are exercisable only in, or in relation to accounts or other documents which relate to, any financial year in which expenditure is incurred by the corporation, or by the governing body[9] of the institution in question, in respect of which grants, loans or other payments are made[10] to it[11].

1 Further and Higher Education Act 1992 s 53(1)(a). As to the meaning of 'further education corporation' see PARA 555 note 3.
2 Further and Higher Education Act 1992 s 53(1)(aa) (added by SI 2010/1080). As to the meaning of 'sixth form college corporation' see PARA 577 note 7.
3 Further and Higher Education Act 1992 s 53(1)(b). As to the meaning of 'designated institution' see PARA 572.

4 Further and Higher Education Act 1992 s 53(1). As to the Comptroller and Auditor General see CONSTITUTIONAL AND ADMINISTRATIVE LAW vol 20 (2014) PARAS 494–496. As to the power of the Secretary of State by order to provide for functions of the Comptroller and Auditor General to be transferred to, or become functions also of, the Auditor General for Wales, see the Government of Wales Act 1998 s 146; and CONSTITUTIONAL AND ADMINISTRATIVE LAW vol 20 (2014) PARA 402.

5 Further and Higher Education Act 1992 s 53(2)(a).

6 Ie under the National Audit Act 1983 ss 6, 8: see CONSTITUTIONAL AND ADMINISTRATIVE LAW vol 20 (2014) PARA 489.

7 Ie by virtue of the National Audit Act 1983 s 6(3)(c): see CONSTITUTIONAL AND ADMINISTRATIVE LAW vol 20 (2014) PARA 489.

8 Further and Higher Education Act 1992 s 53(2)(b).

9 As to the meaning of 'governing body' see PARA 560 note 6.

10 Ie under the Education Act 1996 s 15ZA (see PARA 32) or 18A (see PARA 38), the Education Act 2002 s 14 (see PARA 615), or the Apprenticeships, Skills, Children and Learning Act 2009 s 100 (see PARA 783).

11 Further and Higher Education Act 1992 s 53(2) (amended by SI 2010/1080; and the Education Act 2011 Sch 12 para 24).

(6) INSPECTION OF HIGHER EDUCATION

1284. Quality assessment in the higher education sector. The Higher Education Funding Council for England[1] and the Higher Education Funding Council for Wales[2] have statutory responsibilities for assessing the quality of education provided in institutions within the higher education sector[3]. In practice it is the Quality Assurance Agency for Higher Education that carries out quality assessment reviews in this sector[4].

1 As to the Higher Education Funding Council for England see PARA 691.

2 As to the Higher Education Funding Council for Wales see PARA 691 et seq.

3 See PARAS 688, 689. As to the meaning of 'higher education' see PARA 24. As to the meaning of 'institution within the higher education sector' see PARA 619.

4 As to the Agency and its role see PARA 690.

(7) INSPECTION OF TEACHER TRAINING INSTITUTIONS

1285. Inspection of teacher training in England. Her Majesty's Chief Inspector of Education, Children's Services and Skills[1] may inspect and report on:

(1) any initial training of teachers[2], or of specialist teaching assistants, for schools[3]; or

(2) any in-service training[4] of such teachers or assistants[5],

which is provided by a training provider[6]. If requested to do so by the Secretary of State[7], the Chief Inspector must inspect and report on such one or more relevant training providers[8] in England[9] as may be specified in the request[10]. The Chief Inspector may at any time give advice to the Secretary of State[11] on any matter connected with training falling within head (1) or (2) above[12].

When inspecting a training provider, the Chief Inspector has at all reasonable times a right of entry to the premises[13] of the training provider[14] and a right to inspect, and take copies of, any records[15] kept by the training provider, and any other documents[16] containing information relating to the training provider, which he considers relevant to the exercise of his functions[17] under these provisions[18]. Without prejudice to these rights, a training provider to which an inspection relates must give the Chief Inspector all assistance in connection with the exercise of his functions which he is reasonably able to give[19], and must secure that all such assistance is also given by persons who work for the training provider[20].

The Chief Inspector may not carry out any inspection of training provided by a training provider in Wales[21] unless:

(a)   at least eight weeks previously, he has given notice[22] of his intention to carry out the inspection to the training provider concerned[23], or where the training is provided by a partnership or association of training providers, to one of those training providers[24]; or

(b)   with the agreement of that training provider or (as the case may be) one of those training providers, he has given it shorter notice of that intention[25].

The Chief Inspector may make such reports of inspections carried out by him under these provisions as he considers appropriate[26], and arrange for any such report to be published in such manner as he considers appropriate[27].

1   As to Her Majesty's Chief Inspector of Education, Children's Services and Skills see PARA 1133. Any reference in the Education Act 1994 s 18B to the Chief Inspector is to be read, in relation to any inspection which he is authorised or required to carry out under s 18B, as including a reference to any person authorised to act on his behalf under the Education and Inspections Act 2006 Sch 12 para 9(1) (see PARA 1138): Education Act 1994 s 18B(10) (s 18B added by the Education Act 2005 s 98, Sch 14 para 13; Education Act 1994 s 18B(10) amended by the Education and Inspections Act 2006 s 157, Sch 14 para 19(1), (6)). Nothing in the Education Act 1994 s 18B is to be taken as prejudicing the generality of the Education and Inspections Act 2006 Sch 12 para 9(1): Education Act 1994 s 18B(11) (as so added; and amended by the Education and Inspections Act 2006, s 157, Sch 14, para 19(1), (7)).
2   As to the meaning of references to training of teachers see PARA 24 note 2.
3   Education Act 1994 s 18B(1)(a) (as added: see note 1). As to the meaning of 'school' see PARA 91 (definition applied by s 19(5) (amended by the Education Act 1996 s 582(1), Sch 37 para 128; Education Act 2005 Sch 14 para 14(b))).
4   'In-service training' includes any training provided to a teacher serving an induction period (within the meaning of the Teaching and Higher Education Act 1998 s 19 (repealed)): Education Act 1994 s 18B(12)(d) (as added: see note 1).
5   Education Act 1994 s 18B(1)(b) (as added: see note 1).
6   Education Act 1994 s 18B(1) (as added (see note 1); and amended by the Education and Inspections Act 2006 s 157, Sch 14 para 19(1), (2)). As to the meaning of 'training provider' see PARA 1059 note 3 (definition applied by the Education Act 1994 s 18B(12)(b) (as so added)). Nothing in the Education Act 1994 s 18B confers any right or imposes any duty, whether as regards the carrying out of any inspection or otherwise, in relation to any course which consists of instruction given wholly or mainly for purposes other than training falling within s 18B(1)(a) or (b) (see heads (1) and (2) in the text): s 18B(9) (as so added).
7   As to the Secretary of State see PARA 58.
8   'Relevant training provider' means any training provider who provides training falling within the Education Act 1994 s 18B(1)(a) or (b) (see heads (1) and (2) in the text): s 18B(12)(c) (as added: see note 1).
9   As to the meaning of 'England' see PARA 7 note 3.
10   Education Act 1994 s 18B(2) (as added (see note 1); and substituted by the Education and Inspections Act 2006 s 157, Sch 14 para 19(1), (3)).
11   Education Act 1994 s 18B(3)(b) (as added (see note 1); amended by the Education Act 2011 Sch 5 para 8). As to the Secretary of State see PARA 58.
12   Education Act 1994 s 18B(3) (as added (see note 1); and amended by the Education and Inspections Act 2006 ss 157, 184, Sch 14 para 19(1), (4), Sch 18 Pt 5; and the Education Act 2011 Sch 2 para 18).
13   As to the meaning of 'premises' see PARA 62 note 19 (definition applied by s 19(5) (amended by the Education Act 1996 s 582(1), Sch 37 para 128; Education Act 2005 Sch 14 para 14(b))).
14   Education Act 1994 s 18B(5)(a) (as added: see note 1).
15   'Records' include information recorded in any form: Education Act 1994 s 18B(12)(e) (as added: see note 1).
16   'Documents' include information recorded in any form: Education Act 1994 s 18B(12)(e) (as added: see note 1).

17 As to the meaning of 'functions' see PARA 18 note 5 (definition applied by s 19(5) (amended by the Education Act 1996 s 582(1), Sch 37 para 128; Education Act 2005 Sch 14 para 14(b))).
18 Education Act 1994 s 18B(5)(b) (as added: see note 1). The Education Act 2005 s 58 (inspection of computer records: see PARA 1152 note 7) applies for these purposes as it applies for the purposes of the Education Act 2005 Pt 1 (ss 1–63): Education Act 1994 s 18B(5)(b) (as so added).
19 Education Act 1994 s 18B(6)(a) (as added: see note 1).
20 Education Act 1994 s 18B(6)(b) (as added: see note 1).
21 As to the meaning of 'Wales' see PARA 7 note 3. As to the inspection of teacher training in Wales generally see PARA 1286.
22 Any such notice must be given in writing (Education Act 1994 s 18B(8)(a) (as added: see note 1)), and may be sent by post (s 18B(8)(b) (as so added)); and any such notice may (without prejudice to any other lawful method of giving it) be addressed to a training provider at any address which the training provider has notified to the Secretary of State as its address (s 18B(8) (as so added); amended by the Education Act 2011 Sch 5 para 8). As to the meaning of 'writing' see PARA 76 note 8. As to the service of documents by post generally see PARA 76 note 5.
23 Education Act 1994 s 18B(7)(a)(i) (as added: see note 1).
24 Education Act 1994 s 18B(7)(a)(ii) (as added: see note 1).
25 Education Act 1994 s 18B(7)(b) (as added: see note 1).
26 Education Act 1994 s 18B(4)(a) (as added: see note 1).
27 Education Act 1994 s 18B(4)(b) (as added: see note 1).

1286. Inspection of teacher training in Wales. Her Majesty's Chief Inspector of Education and Training in Wales[1] may inspect and report on:

(1) any initial training of teachers[2], or of specialist teaching assistants, for schools[3]; or

(2) any in-service training[4] of such teachers or assistants[5],

which is provided by a training provider[6] in Wales[7]. When asked to do so by the Welsh Ministers[8], the Chief Inspector must give advice to the Welsh Ministers on such matters connected with training falling within head (1) or (2) above as may be specified in the request[9] and inspect and report on such one or more relevant training providers[10] as may be so specified[11]. The Chief Inspector may at any time give advice to the Welsh Ministers[12], a funding agency[13], or the Education Workforce Council (formerly the General Teaching Council for Wales) [14] on any matter connected with training falling within head (1) or (2) above[15].

When inspecting a training provider, the Chief Inspector has at all reasonable times a right of entry to the premises[16] of the training provider[17] and a right to inspect, and take copies of, any records[18] kept by the training provider, and any other documents[19] containing information relating to the training provider, which he considers relevant to the exercise of his functions[20] under these provisions[21]. Without prejudice to these rights, a training provider to which an inspection relates must give the Chief Inspector all assistance in connection with the exercise of his functions which it is reasonably able to give[22], and must secure that all such assistance is also given by persons who work for the training provider[23]. The Chief Inspector may not carry out any inspection[24] unless:

(i) at least eight weeks previously, he has given notice[25] of his intention to carry out the inspection to the training provider concerned[26], or where the training is provided by a partnership or association of training providers, to one of those training providers[27]; or

(ii) with the agreement of that training provider or (as the case may be) one of those training providers, he has given it shorter notice of that intention[28].

The Chief Inspector may make such reports of inspections carried out by him under these provisions as he considers appropriate[29], and arrange for any such report to be published in such manner as he considers appropriate[30].

1   As to Her Majesty's Chief Inspector of Education and Training in Wales see PARA 1148. Any
     reference in the Education Act 1994 s 18C to the Chief Inspector must be read, in relation to
     any inspection which he is authorised or required to carry out under s 18C, as including a
     reference to any person authorised to act on his behalf under the Education Act 2005 Sch 2
     para 5(1) or (2) (see PARA 1150): Education Act 1994 s 18C(10) (s 18C added by the Education
     Act 2005 s 98, Sch 14 para 13). Nothing in the Education Act 1994 s 18C is to be taken as
     prejudicing the generality of the Education Act 2005 ss 20–23 or Sch 2 para 5(1) or (2) (see
     PARA 1151): Education Act 1994 s 18C(11) (as so added).
2   As to the meaning of references to training of teachers see PARA 24 note 2.
3   Education Act 1994 s 18C(1)(a) (as added: see note 1). As to the meaning of 'school' see PARA
     91 (definition applied by s 19(5) (amended by the Education Act 1996 s 582(1), Sch 37
     para 128; Education Act 2005 Sch 14 para 14(b))).
4   'In-service training' includes any training provided to a teacher serving an induction period
     (within the meaning of the Teaching and Higher Education Act 1998 s 19 (repealed)): Education
     Act 1994 s 18C(12)(e) (as added: see note 1).
5   Education Act 1994 s 18C(1)(b) (as added: see note 1).
6   As to the meaning of 'training provider' see PARA 1059 note 3 (definition applied by the
     Education Act 1994 s 18C(12)(c) (as added: see note 1)).
7   Education Act 1994 s 18C(1) (as added: see note 1). As to the meaning of 'Wales' see PARA 7
     note 3. Nothing in s 18C confers any right or imposes any duty, whether as regards the carrying
     out of any inspection or otherwise, in relation to any course which consists of instruction given
     wholly or mainly for purposes other than training falling within s 18C(1)(a) or (b) (see heads (1)
     and (2) in the text): s 18C(9) (as so added).
8   As to the Welsh Ministers see PARA 59. The functions under the Education Act 1994 s 18C were
     originally vested in the National Assembly for Wales and are now exercisable by the Welsh
     Ministers by virtue of the Government of Wales Act 2006 s 162(1), Sch 11 paras 30, 32.
9   Education Act 1994 s 18C(2)(a) (as added: see note 1).
10   'Relevant training provider' means any training provider who provides training falling within
     the Education Act 1994 s 18C(1)(a) or (b) (see heads (1) and (2) in the text): s 18C(12)(d) (as
     added: see note 1).
11   Education Act 1994 s 18C(2)(b) (as added: see note 1).
12   Education Act 1994 s 18C(3)(a) (as added: see note 1).
13   Education Act 1994 s 18C(3)(b) (as added: see note 1). 'Funding agency' means the Higher
     Education Funding Council for Wales: s 18C(12)(b) (as so added; amended by the Education
     Act 2011 Sch 5 para 9). As to the Higher Education Funding Council for Wales see PARA 691 et
     seq.
14   Education Act 1994 s 18C(3)(c) (as added: see note 1). As to the Education Workforce Council
     (formerly the General Teaching Council for Wales) see PARA 1066, 1075.
15   Education Act 1994 s 18C(3) (as added: see note 1).
16   As to the meaning of 'premises' see PARA 62 note 19 (definition applied by the Education
     Act 1994 s 19(5) (amended by the Education Act 1996 s 582(1), Sch 37 para 128; Education
     Act 2005 Sch 14 para 14(b))).
17   Education Act 1994 s 18C(5)(a) (as added: see note 1).
18   'Records' includes information recorded in any form: Education Act 1994 s 18C(12)(f) (as
     added: see note 1).
19   'Document' includes information recorded in any form: Education Act 1994 s 18C(12)(f) (as
     added: see note 1).
20   As to the meaning of 'functions' see PARA 18 note 5 (definition applied by the Education
     Act 1994 s 19(5) (amended by the Education Act 1996 s 582(1), Sch 37 para 128; Education
     Act 2005 Sch 14 para 14(b))).
21   Education Act 1994 s 18C(5)(b) (as added: see note 1). The Education Act 2005 s 58 (inspection
     of computer records: see PARA 1152 note 7) applies for these purposes as it applies for the
     purposes of the Education Act 2005 Pt 1 (ss 1–63): Education Act 1994 s 18C(5)(b) (as so
     added).
22   Education Act 1994 s 18C(6)(a) (as added: see note 1).
23   Education Act 1994 s 18C(6)(b) (as added: see note 1).
24   Ie under the Education Act 1994 s 18C(1): see the text to notes 1–7.
25   Any such notice must be given in writing (Education Act 1994 s 18C(8)(a) (as added: see
     note 1)), and may be sent by post (s 18C(8)(b) (as so added)); and any such notice may (without
     prejudice to any other lawful method of giving it) be addressed to a training provider at any
     address which the training provider has notified to a funding agency as its address (s 18C(8) (as
     so added)). As to the meaning of 'writing' see PARA 76 note 8. As to the service of documents by
     post generally see PARA 76 note 5.

26 Education Act 1994 s 18C(7)(a)(i) (as added: see note 1).
27 Education Act 1994 s 18C(7)(a)(ii) (as added: see note 1).
28 Education Act 1994 s 18C(7)(b) (as added: see note 1).
29 Education Act 1994 s 18C(4)(a) (as added: see note 1).
30 Education Act 1994 s 18C(4)(b) (as added: see note 1). The provisions of the Education
    Act 2005 s 29(2)–(4) (publication of inspection reports: see PARA 1190) apply in relation to the
    publication of any such report as they apply in relation to the publication of a report under any
    of the provisions mentioned in s 29(2): Education Act 1994 s 18C(4) (as so added).

(8) INSPECTION OF SUPPORT AND SERVICES FOR YOUNG PEOPLE

1287. Inspection in England. Her Majesty's Chief Inspector of Education, Children's Services and Skills[1] must, when requested[2] to do so by the Secretary of State[3], inspect and report on the provision of support services[4] for young persons[5], and may undertake such other inspections of the provision of those services as the Chief Inspector thinks fit[6].

A person carrying out or participating in the inspection has the same powers of entry to premises and to inspect records and documents[7], including inspection of computer records[8], as the Chief Inspector has when inspecting a school[9]. The Chief Inspector may arrange for any report of an inspection to be published in such manner as he considers appropriate[10].

A person who wilfully obstructs a person in carrying out or participating in the inspection is guilty of an offence[11].

1   As to Her Majesty's Chief Inspector of Education, Children's Services and Skills see PARA 1133.
2   A request may be in general terms or in relation to specific matters (Education and Skills
    Act 2008 s 75(2)(a)), may relate to a specific person providing services, or to a specific class of
    person (s 75(2)(b)), and may relate to a specific area (s 75(2)(c)). As to the meaning of 'person'
    see PARA 7 note 6.
3   As to the Secretary of State see PARA 58.
4   Ie in pursuance of the Education and Skills Act 2008 s 68 (see PARA 802) or s 74 (see PARA 805).
    A reference in s 75(1) to the provision of services includes a reference to the management and
    use of resources in providing services: s 75(3).
5   See the Education and Skills Act 2008 s 75(1)(a).
6   Education and Skills Act 2008 s 75(1)(b). See also note 4.
7   Ie equivalent powers to those under the Education Act 2005 s 10(1)(a), (d) (see PARAS 1162,
    1392): see the Education and Skills Act 2008 s 75(4), (5)(a).
8   Ie equivalent powers to those under the Education Act 2005 s 58 (see PARA 1152 note 7): see the
    Education and Skills Act 2008 s 75(4), (5)(b).
9   See the Education and Skills Act 2008 s 75(4), (5).
10 Ie the Education Act 2005 s 11 (publication of inspection reports: see PARA 1166) applies: see
    the Education and Skills Act 2008 s 75(4), (6).
11 See the Education and Skills Act 2008 s 75(4), (7)(a). The penalty for such an offence is, on
    summary conviction, a fine not exceeding level 4 on the standard scale: see s 75(4), (7)(b). As to
    the standard scale see SENTENCING AND DISPOSITION OF OFFENDERS vol 92 (2010) PARA 142.

1288. Inspection in Wales. Her Majesty's Chief Inspector of Education and Training in Wales[1]:

(1)   must advise the Welsh Ministers[2] on request about matters relating to the provision[3] of youth support services[4];

(2)   may give the Welsh Ministers other advice about those matters[5];

(3)   must, when requested to do so by the Welsh Ministers, inspect and report on the provision of those services[6]; and

(4)   may undertake such other inspections of the provision of those services as he thinks fit[7].

The Welsh Ministers must consult the Chief Inspector before making a request under head (1) or (3) above[8].

Where a service is inspected pursuant to a request under head (3) or in accordance with head (4) above[9], a person carrying out or participating in the inspection has the same powers of entry to premises and to inspect records and documents[10], including computer records[11], as an inspector has when inspecting a school[12]. The Chief Inspector may arrange for any report of an inspection to be published in such manner as he considers appropriate[13]. Where the Chief Inspector arranges for the publication of a report of an inspection, the person[14] who provides the inspected service must prepare a written[15] statement of the action which he proposes to take in the light of the report and the period within which he proposes to take it[16], publish the statement within such period, and in such manner, as may be prescribed by regulations made by the Welsh Ministers[17], and send copies of the statement to such persons as may be prescribed by regulations made by the Welsh Ministers[18]. Where a local authority[19] provides an inspected service, or secures or participates in the provision of an inspected service, the authority must ensure that the action specified in any such statement is sufficient to remedy any weakness mentioned in the report[20], and take all reasonable steps to ensure that the action specified in the statement is taken within the period specified[21]. If the Welsh Ministers consider that a local authority is failing to comply with those duties they may give directions to the local authority about the performance of those duties[22], and the authority must comply with the directions[23].

1   As to Her Majesty's Chief Inspector of Education and Training in Wales see PARA 1148.
2   As to the Welsh Ministers see PARA 59. The functions under the Learning and Skills Act 2000 ss 127, 128 were originally vested in the National Assembly for Wales and are now exercisable by the Welsh Ministers by virtue of the Government of Wales Act 2006 s 162(1), Sch 11 paras 30, 32.
3   Ie in pursuance of the Learning and Skills Act 2000 s 123(1) (see PARA 813) or the Learning and Skills (Wales) Measure 2009 s 40(1) (see PARA 812).
4   See the Learning and Skills Act 2000 s 127(1)(a) (amended by the Learning and Skills (Wales) Measure 2009 s 42(1), (3)). The reference in the Learning and Skills Act 2000 s 127(1) to the provision of services includes a reference to the management and use of resources in providing services: s 127(4).
5   Learning and Skills Act 2000 s 127(1)(b).
6   Learning and Skills Act 2000 s 127(1)(c). A request under s 127(1)(c) may: (1) be general or in relation to specific matters (s 127(3)(a)); (2) relate to a specific person or institution providing services, or to a specific class of person or institution (s 127(3)(b)); and (3) may relate to a specific area (s 127(3)(c)).
7   Learning and Skills Act 2000 s 127(1)(d).
8   Learning and Skills Act 2000 s 127(2).
9   See the Learning and Skills Act 2000 s 128(1).
10 Ie equivalent powers to those under the Education Act 2005 s 24(3)(a) and (d) (see PARA 1153): see the Learning and Skills Act 2000 s 128(2)(a) (s 128(2) substituted by the Education Act 2005 s 61, Sch 9 para 27(1), (2)).
11 Ie equivalent powers to those under the Education Act 2005 s 58 (see PARA 1152 note 7): see the Learning and Skills Act 2000 s 128(2)(b) (as substituted: see note 10).
12 See the Learning and Skills Act 2000 s 128(2) (as substituted: see note 10).
13 Ie the Education Act 2005 s 29 (publication of reports: see PARA 1190) applies: see the Learning and Skills Act 2000 s 128(3) (amended by the Education Act 2005 s 61, Sch 9 para 27(1), (3)).
14 As to the meaning of 'person' see PARA 7 note 6.
15 As to the meaning of 'written' see PARA 76 note 8.
16 Learning and Skills Act 2000 s 128(4)(a).
17 Learning and Skills Act 2000 s 128(4)(b). As to the regulations made see the Inspection of Youth Support Services in Wales Regulations 2004, SI 2004/679, reg 2(1), (2).

18 Learning and Skills Act 2000 s 128(4)(c). As to the regulations made see the Inspection of Youth Support Services in Wales Regulations 2004, SI 2004/679, reg 2(3), (4) (reg 2(3) amended by SI 2005/3238).

19 'Local authority' means a county borough council: see the Learning and Skills Act 2000 s 129(1). As to local government areas and authorities in Wales see LOCAL GOVERNMENT vol 69 (2009) PARA 37 et seq.

20 Learning and Skills Act 2000 s 128(5)(a).

21 Learning and Skills Act 2000 s 128(5)(b).

22 Learning and Skills Act 2000 s 128(6)(a).

23 Learning and Skills Act 2000 s 128(6)(b).

(9) INSPECTION OF LOCAL AUTHORITIES

(i) Inspection of Local Authorities in England

1289.   Inspection of local authorities. Her Majesty's Chief Inspector of Education, Children's Services and Skills[1] may inspect:

(1)   the overall performance[2] by any local authority in England of the education functions[3] of the authority[4]; or

(2)   the performance by any such authority of any particular function or functions comprised in the education functions of the authority[5].

An inspection of the performance by an authority of any function must include an inspection of any related activity[6].

When requested to do so by the Secretary of State, the Chief Inspector must conduct an inspection under these provisions in relation to the local authority specified in the request[7]. Such a request may specify particular matters which the Chief Inspector must inspect[8].

The functions of the Chief Inspector under these provisions extend to other matters within his remit which are not related to the education functions of a local authority in England. Those matters are:

(a)   the functions conferred on the authority under Part 1 of the Childcare Act 2006[9];

(b)   the functions conferred on the authority under certain provisions of the Children Act 2004[10];

(c)   the social services functions[11] of the authority, so far as relating to persons aged under 18[12];

(d)   (whether or not within head (c)) functions conferred on or exercisable by the authority under the Children Act 1989, the Adoption (Intercountry Aspects) Act 1999 or the Adoption and Children Act 2002 and functions continuing to be exercisable by the authority under the Adoption Act 1976[13]; and

(e)   such other functions of the authority as may be prescribed by regulations made by the Secretary of State[14].

1 As to Her Majesty's Chief Inspector of Education, Children's Services and Skills see PARA 1133.

2 For the purposes of the Education and Inspections Act 2006 Pt 8 Ch 4 (ss 135–142), references to the performance by a local authority in England of any function include references to anything done in any place by the authority in the performance of the function and anything done in any place by another person pursuant to arrangements made by the authority in the performance of the function: s 142(2). As to the meaning of 'local authority in England' see PARA 1145 note 3. As to the meaning of 'functions' see PARA 1128 note 3. As to the meaning of 'person' see PARA 7 note 6.

    The Education and Inspections Act 2006 Pt 8 Ch 4 (ss 135–142) applies in relation to the Isles of Scilly subject to such modifications as may be specified by order made by the Secretary of State: s 142(3). As to the Secretary of State see PARA 58. At the date at which this volume states the law no such order had been made. As to the Council of the Isles of Scilly see LOCAL GOVERNMENT vol 69 (2009) PARA 36.

3   As to the meaning of 'education functions' see PARA 25 (definition applied by the Education and Inspections Act 2006 s 135(1)(b) (substituted by SI 2010/1158)).

4   See the Education and Inspections Act 2006 ss 135(1)(b), 136(1)(a) (s 135(1)(b) as substituted: see note 3).

5   See the Education and Inspections Act 2006 ss 135(1)(b), 136(1)(b) (s 135(1)(b) as substituted: see note 3). As to powers of entry and inspection of documents in relation to an inspection see PARA 1291. As to the power to require information see PARA 1292.

6   Education and Inspections Act 2006 s 136(2). In Pt 8 Ch 4 (ss 135–142) 'related activity', in relation to a function, means anything done in any place by, or pursuant to arrangements made by, the authority under the Local Government Act 2000 s 2(1)(a) or (b) (promotion of economic and social well-being: see LOCAL GOVERNMENT vol 69 (2009) PARA 463) or the Localism Act 2011 s 1 (local authority's general power of competence: see LOCAL GOVERNMENT vol 69 (2009) PARA 462A) which is similar in nature to anything which could be done by the authority in the performance of the function in question: see the Education and Inspections Act 2006 s 135(2) (amended by SI 2012/961).

7   Education and Inspections Act 2006 s 136(3).

8   Education and Inspections Act 2006 s 136(4).

9   Education and Inspections Act 2006 s 135(1)(a). As to the Childcare Act 2006 Pt 1 (ss 1–21) see CHILDREN AND YOUNG PERSONS vol 10 (2012) PARA 1077 et seq).

10 See the Education and Inspections Act 2006 s 135(1)(c). The provisions in question are the Children Act 2004 ss 10, 12 and 17–19: see CHILDREN AND YOUNG PERSONS vol 9 (2012) PARAS 203, 204, 207. In relation to a function within the Education and Inspections Act 2006 s 135(1)(c), (d) or (e) (see the text to notes 11–13), anything done as mentioned in s 135(2) (see note 6) is a 'related activity' only if it is done in relation to or for the benefit of persons aged under 18, persons aged 18 or over in relation to whom the authority has functions under any of the Children Act 1989 ss 23C–24D (see CHILDREN AND YOUNG PERSONS vol 10 (2012) PARA 925 et seq) or persons not within head (1) or (2) above in connection with adoption or special guardianship: Education and Inspections Act 2006 s 135(3)(a)–(c). 'Special guardianship' means special guardianship under the Children Act 1989 ss 14A–14G (see CHILDREN AND YOUNG PERSONS vol 9 (2012) PARA 305 et seq): Education and Inspections Act 2006 s 135(3).

11 Ie within the meaning of the Local Authority Social Services Act 1970: see SOCIAL SERVICES AND COMMUNITY CARE vol 95 (2013) PARA 1.

12 Education and Inspections Act 2006 s 135(1)(d). See also note 10.

13 Education and Inspections Act 2006 s 135(1)(e). See also note 10. As to the Adoption (Intercountry Aspects) Act 1999, the Adoption and Children Act 2002, the Adoption Act 1976 and related functions under the Children Act 1989 see CHILDREN AND YOUNG PERSONS vol 9 (2012) PARA 360 et seq.

14 Education and Inspections Act 2006 s 135(1)(f). In relation to a function prescribed by regulations under s 135(1)(f), anything done as mentioned in s 135(2) (see note 6) is a 'related activity' only if it is prescribed as such by the regulations: s 135(4). At the date at which this volume states the law no such regulations had been made.

1290. Reports of inspections. On completing an inspection of a local authority in England[1], Her Majesty's Chief Inspector of Education, Children's Services and Skills[2] must make a written[3] report on the matters which were the subject of the inspection[4]. The Chief Inspector must send copies of the report to the local authority which was inspected[5] and the Secretary of State[6]; and may arrange for any such report to be published in such manner as he considers appropriate[7].

Where an authority receives a copy of such a report, it must prepare a written statement of the action which it proposes to take in the light of the report[8], and the period within which it proposes to take that action[9]. The authority must publish the report[10], and the statement prepared by it[11], within such period, and in such manner, as may be prescribed by regulations made by the Secretary of State[12].

1   Ie an inspection under the Education and Inspections Act 2006 s 136: see PARA 1289. As to the meaning of 'local authority in England' see PARA 1145 note 3.
2   As to Her Majesty's Chief Inspector of Education, Children's Services and Skills see PARA 1133.
3   As to the meaning of 'written' see PARA 76 note 8.
4   Education and Inspections Act 2006 s 137(1). As to combined reports see s 152; and PARA 1143. As to the use by the Chief Inspector of information obtained by him in connection with any of his functions see s 153; and PARA 1137.
5   Education and Inspections Act 2006 s 137(2)(a).
6   Education and Inspections Act 2006 s 137(2)(b). As to the Secretary of State see PARA 58.
7   Education and Inspections Act 2006 s 137(6). As to the publication of inspection reports see s 151; and PARA 1142.
8   Education and Inspections Act 2006 s 137(3)(a).
9   Education and Inspections Act 2006 s 137(3)(b).
10   Education and Inspections Act 2006 s 137(4)(a).
11   Education and Inspections Act 2006 s 137(4)(b).
12   Education and Inspections Act 2006 s 137(4). Such regulations may provide for the authority to charge a reasonable fee for providing a person with a copy of a document published under s 137(4): s 137(5). As to the regulations made see the Education and Inspections Act 2006 (Inspection of Local Authorities) Regulations 2007, SI 2007/462.

1291. Powers of entry and inspection of documents. Her Majesty's Chief Inspector of Education, Children's Services and Skills[1] may, at any reasonable time, enter any premises for the purposes of any inspection[2] other than[3] any premises that are domestic premises[4] that are not a school[5].

If the Chief Inspector considers it necessary or expedient for the purposes of any such inspection he may do any of the following:

(1)   inspect, take copies of, or take away any documents[6] which relate to the performance by the local authority being inspected of its education functions, or to any related activity[7], and are on any premises in relation to which he exercises his power of entry[8];

(2)   inspect or take away any other item which is on the premises[9];

(3)   interview in private any person working on the premises[10];

(4)   interview in private any person accommodated or cared for there, provided consent to the interview is given by or on behalf of the person concerned[11]; and

(5)   make any other examination into the state and management of the premises and treatment of persons accommodated or cared for there[12].

In connection with inspecting any such documents, the Chief Inspector may obtain access to, and inspect and check the operation of, any computer and associated apparatus or material which he considers is or has been in use in connection with the documents[13]. He may also require a person by whom or on whose behalf the computer is or has been used[14], or a person having charge of, or otherwise concerned with the operation of, the computer, apparatus or material[15], to afford him such reasonable assistance as he may require for that purpose[16].

The Chief Inspector may require any person to afford him such facilities and assistance with respect to matters within the person's control as are necessary to enable him to exercise his powers[17] of entry or inspection[18], and may take such measurements and photographs and make such recordings as he considers necessary to enable him to exercise those powers[19]. However, the powers of inspection[20] may be exercised by the Chief Inspector at reasonable times only; and a person may not be required to do anything in pursuance of those powers otherwise than at a reasonable time[21].

Any person exercising these powers of entry and inspection must, if so required, produce a duly authenticated document showing his authority to exercise the power concerned[22].

Any person who without reasonable excuse:

(a) obstructs the exercise of any power conferred by the above powers[23] of entry or inspection[24]; or

(b) fails to comply with any requirement imposed[25] in respect of the above powers of inspection[26],

is guilty of an offence[27].

1 As to Her Majesty's Chief Inspector of Education, Children's Services and Skills see PARA 1133.
2 Ie any inspection conducted by the Chief Inspector under the Education and Inspections Act 2006 s 136 (see PARA 1289): see ss 139(1)(a), 140(1)(a).
3 See the Education and Inspections Act 2006 s 139(2). As to the meaning of 'education functions' see PARA 25 (definition applied by s 135(1)(b) (substituted by SI 2010/1158)). As to the application of the Education and Inspections Act 2006 Pt 8 Ch 4 (ss 135–142) to local authority functions other than education functions see PARA 1289.
4 'Domestic premises' means premises which are used wholly or mainly as a private dwelling: Education and Inspections Act 2006 s 159(1).
5 See the Education and Inspections Act 2006 s 139(3). As to the meaning of 'school' see PARA 91 (definition applied by s 139(3)). As to the use by the Chief Inspector of information obtained by him in connection with any of his functions see s 153; and PARA 1137. As to the power to require information see PARA 1292.
6 The power in the Education and Inspections Act 2006 s 140(2)(a) includes power to require any person holding or accountable for any documents kept on the premises to produce them (s 140(4)(a)) and, in relation to documents kept by means of a computer, power to require them to be produced in a form in which they are legible and can be taken away (s 140(4)(b)). As to the meaning of 'document' see PARA 1128 note 11. As to the meaning of 'person' see PARA 7 note 6.
7 Education and Inspections Act 2006 s 140(2)(a)(i) (amended by SI 2012/1879). As to the meaning of 'related activity' see PARA 1289 note 6.
8 Education and Inspections Act 2006 s 140(2)(a)(ii).
9 Education and Inspections Act 2006 s 140(2)(b).
10 Education and Inspections Act 2006 s 140(2)(c)(i).
11 See the Education and Inspections Act 2006 s 140(2)(c)(ii), (3).
12 Education and Inspections Act 2006 s 140(2)(d).
13 Education and Inspections Act 2006 s 140(5)(a).
14 See the Education and Inspections Act 2006 s 140(6)(a).
15 See the Education and Inspections Act 2006 s 140(6)(b).
16 Education and Inspections Act 2006 s 140(5)(b).
17 Ie under the Education and Inspections Act 2006 s 139 or 140: see the text to notes 1–18.
18 Education and Inspections Act 2006 s 140(7)(a).
19 Education and Inspections Act 2006 s 140(7)(b).
20 Ie the powers under the Education and Inspections Act 2006 s 140: see the text to notes 8–21.
21 See the Education and Inspections Act 2006 s 140(8).
22 See the Education and Inspections Act 2006 s 150(2); and PARA 1138.
23 Ie by the Education and Inspections Act 2006 s 139 or s 140: see the text to notes 1–23.
24 See the Education and Inspections Act 2006 s 140(9)(a).
25 Ie by the Education and Inspections Act 2006 s 140: see the text to notes 8–23.
26 See the Education and Inspections Act 2006 s 140(9)(b).
27 Education and Inspections Act 2006 s 140(9). The penalty for such an offence is, on summary conviction, a fine not exceeding level 4 on the standard scale: see s 140(9). As to the standard scale see SENTENCING AND DISPOSITION OF OFFENDERS vol 92 (2010) PARA 142.

1292. Power to require information. Her Majesty's Chief Inspector of Education, Children's Services and Skills[1] may at any time require a local authority in England[2], or any person[3] with whom the authority has entered into arrangements in the performance of any of its education functions[4] or in connection with any related activity[5], to provide him with any information, documents[6] or other items which relates or relate to the performance by the local authority of any of those functions or any related activity[7], and which the Chief Inspector considers it necessary or expedient to have for the purposes of, or in connection with, the performance by him of any function[8] in relation to the inspection and review of local authorities in England[9]. This power includes, in relation to documents kept by means of a computer, power to require them to be produced in a form in which they are legible and can be taken away[10].

Any person who without reasonable excuse fails to comply with any requirement imposed by virtue of the above provisions is guilty of an offence[11].

1   As to Her Majesty's Chief Inspector of Education, Children's Services and Skills see PARA 1133.
2   See the Education and Inspections Act 2006 s 141(2)(a). As to the meaning of 'local authority in England' see PARA 1145 note 3.
3   As to the meaning of 'person' see PARA 7 note 6.
4   See the Education and Inspections Act 2006 s 141(2)(b)(i). As to the meaning of 'education functions' see PARA 25 (definition applied by s 135(1)(b) (substituted by SI 2010/1158)). As to the application of the Education and Inspections Act 2006 Pt 8 Ch 4 (ss 135–142) to local authority functions other than education functions see PARA 1289.
5   Education and Inspections Act 2006 s 141(2)(b)(ii). As to the meaning of 'related activity' see PARA 1289 note 6.
6   As to the meaning of 'document' see PARA 1128 note 11.
7   Education and Inspections Act 2006 s 141(1)(a).
8   Ie under the Education and Inspections Act 2006 Pt 8 Ch 4 (ss 135–142). As to the meaning of 'function' see PARA 1128 note 3.
9   See the Education and Inspections Act 2006 s 141(1)(b). As to the use by the Chief Inspector of information obtained by him in connection with any of his functions see s 153; and PARA 1137. As to rights of entry and inspection of documents see PARA 1291.
10 Education and Inspections Act 2006 s 141(3).
11 Education and Inspections Act 2006 s 141(4). The penalty for such an offence is, on summary conviction, a fine not exceeding level 4 on the standard scale: see s 141(4). As to the standard scale see SENTENCING AND DISPOSITION OF OFFENDERS vol 92 (2010) PARA 142.

(ii) Inspection of Local Authorities in Wales

1293. Inspection of local authorities. Her Majesty's Chief Inspector of Education and Training in Wales may[1], and if requested to do so by the Welsh Ministers[2], must, arrange for the inspection of any local authority in Wales[3]. Such an inspection consists of a review of the way in which the authority is performing[4] any of its education functions[5], and the functions conferred on it under the Children Act 2004[6] so far as relating to education, training or youth support services[7]. Any such inspection must be conducted by one of Her Majesty's Inspectors of Schools in Wales[8], or by any additional inspector authorised[9] by the Chief Inspector[10]; but he may be assisted by such other persons (whether or not members of the Chief Inspector's staff) as the Chief Inspector thinks fit[11].

For the purposes of such an inspection a local authority in Wales must provide the Chief Inspector with such information as may be prescribed[12], and must do so in such form and within such period following a request made by the Chief Inspector in any prescribed circumstances[13], or at such other times[14], as regulations may provide[15].

Where an inspection has been completed, the inspector[16] must make a written[17] report on the matters reviewed in the course of the inspection, and must send copies of the report to any local authority in Wales to which the inspection relates[18] and the Welsh Ministers[19]. The Chief Inspector may arrange for any such report to be published in such manner as he considers appropriate[20]. Where a local authority in Wales receives a copy of such a report, it must prepare a written statement of the action which it proposes to take in the light of the report and the period within which it proposes to take it[21]. The authority must publish the report[22] and the statement[23]within such period, and in such manner, as may be prescribed[24].

If requested to do so by the Chief Inspector, the Auditor General for Wales[25] may assist with any inspection of a local authority in Wales[26]. The Auditor General for Wales must not provide such assistance unless, before he does so, the Chief Inspector has agreed to pay the Wales Audit Office a fee[27] (which may not exceed the full cost incurred by the Auditor General in providing the assistance)[28].

1   Education Act 1997 s 38(1)(a). As to Her Majesty's Chief Inspector of Education and Training in Wales see PARA 1148.
2   A request by the Welsh Ministers under the Education Act 1997 s 38 may relate to one or more local authorities, and must specify the local authority or authorities concerned (s 38(3)(a) (amended by SI 2010/1158)), and the functions to which the inspection is to relate (Education Act 1997 s 38(3)(b)). Before making any such request the Welsh Ministers must consult the Chief Inspector as to the matters to be specified in the request in accordance with s 38(3): s 38(4). As to the meaning of 'functions' see PARA 18 note 5. (definition applied by s 56(2)). As to the Welsh Ministers see PARA 59. The functions under ss 38, 39 in relation to Wales were formerly vested in the National Assembly for Wales by virtue of the National Assembly for Wales (Transfer of Functions) Order 1999, SI 1999/672, art 2, Sch 1, and are now exercisable by the Welsh Ministers by virtue of the Government of Wales Act 2006 s 162(1), Sch 11 paras 30, 32.
3   See the Education Act 1997 s 38(1) (amended by SI 2010/1158). As to the meaning of 'local authority in Wales' see PARA 25 (definition applied by the Education Act 1997 s 56(2)). As to rights of entry and other rights in relation to an inspection see PARA 1294.
4   Education Act 1997 s 38(2A) (added by the Children Act 2004 s 51; and amended by SI 2010/1158).
5   See the Education Act 1997 s 38(2A)(a) (as added (see note 4); and substituted SI 2010/1158). As to the meaning of 'education functions' see PARA 25 (definition applied by the Education Act 1997 s 56(2)).
6   Ie under the Children Act 2004 ss 25 and 26: see CHILDREN AND YOUNG PERSONS vol 9 (2012) PARA 209.
7   Education Act 1997 s 38(2A)(b) (as added (see note 4); and amended by the Childcare Act 2006 s 103(1), Sch 2 para 28). As to the meaning of 'youth support services' see PARA 813 note 3 (definition applied by the Education Act 1997 s 38(2A)(b) (as so added and amended)).
8   Education Act 1997 s 38(5)(a) (amended by the Education and Inspections Act 2006 ss 157, 184, Sch 14 para 22(1), (3)(a), Sch 18 Pt 5). As to Her Majesty's Inspectors of Education and Training in Wales see PARA 1148.
9   Ie under the Education Act 2005 Sch 2 para 2: see PARA 1149.
10 Education Act 1997 s 38(5)(b) (amended by the Education Act 2005 s 61, Sch 9 para 11; Education and Inspections Act 2006 ss 157, 184, Sch 14 paras 20, 22(1), (3)(b), Sch 18 Pt 5).
11 Education Act 1997 s 38(5). As to the Chief Inspector's staff see PARA 1149.
12 'Prescribed' means prescribed by regulations; and 'regulations' means regulations made by the Welsh Ministers under the Education Act 1997: see s 56(1). At the date at which this volume states the law no regulations had been made under s 38(6).
13 Education Act 1997 s 38(6)(a).
14 Education Act 1997 s 38(6)(b).
15 Education Act 1997 s 38(6) (amended by SI 2010/1158).
16 References to 'the inspector' in relation to an inspection under the Education Act 1997 s 38 are references to the person conducting the inspection: s 38(7).
17 As to the meaning of 'written' see PARA 76 note 8.
18 Education Act 1997 s 39(1)(a) (amended by SI 2010/1158).
19 Education Act 1997 s 39(1)(b).
20 Education Act 1997 s 39(4). The Education Act 2005 s 29(2)–(4) (see PARA 1190) applies in relation to the publication of any such report as it applies in relation to the publication of a report under any of the provisions mentioned in s 29(2): Education Act 1997 s 39(4) (amended by the School Standards and Framework Act 1998 s 134(3); the Education Act 2005 s 61, Sch 9 para 12; and the Education and Inspections Act 2006 ss 157, 184, Sch 14 paras 20, 23, Sch 18 Pt 5).
21 Education Act 1997 s 39(2) (amended by SI 2010/1158).

22 Education Act 1997 s 39(3)(a).

23 Education Act 1997 s 39(3)(b).

24 Education Act 1997 s 39(3). As to the regulations made see the Education (Publication of Local Authority Inspection Reports) Regulations 1998, SI 1998/880 (amended by SI 2001/783; SI 2001/3710; SI 2002/2469; SI 2005/761; SI 2005/3238; SI 2010/1142; SI 2010/1172; SI 2013/235).

25 As to the Auditor General for Wales see LOCAL GOVERNMENT vol 69 (2009) PARA 796 et seq.

26 Education Act 1997 s 41A(1) (s 41A added by the Public Audit (Wales) Act 2004 s 66, Sch 2 paras 17, 19; Education Act 1997 s 41A(1) amended by SI 2010/1158). Where the Auditor General for Wales assists with any such inspection (see the Education Act 1997 s 41A(1) (as so added)), s 40 (see PARA 1294) applies to the Auditor General for Wales and to any authorised person as it applies to the inspector (s 41A(2) (as so added)). 'Authorised person' means a person authorised by the Auditor General for Wales for the purposes of s 41A: s 41A(7) (as so added). Any information obtained by virtue of s 40 by a person falling within one of the categories mentioned below may be disclosed for the purposes of the inspection, or the preparation or making of the report under s 39(1) (see the text to notes 17–19), to a person falling within the other category: s 41A(3) (as so added). Those categories are: (1) the Auditor General for Wales and any authorised person (s 41A(4)(a) (as so added)); and (2) the inspector and any person assisting him (s 41A(4)(b) (as so added)). Any report prepared under s 39(1) must be prepared by the inspector acting in conjunction with the Auditor General for Wales: s 41A(5) (as so added).

27 Ie a fee in accordance with a scheme for charging fees prepared under the Public Audit (Wales) Act 2013 s 24 (see CONSTITUTIONAL AND ADMINISTRATIVE LAW vol 20 (2014) PARA 405).

28 Education Act 1997 s 41A(6) (as added (see note 26); amended by the Public Audit (Wales) Act 2013 Sch 4 para 4).

1294. Inspector's rights of entry etc. Where a local authority in Wales[1] is inspected[2], the inspector[3], and any person assisting him, has at all reasonable times a right of entry to:

(1) the premises of the local authority[4];

(2) the premises[5] of any school maintained by the authority[6]; and

(3) any other premises at which exceptional provision of education at schools or otherwise[7] is provided, other than premises which are or form part of a private dwelling house but are not a school[8].

The inspector, and any person assisting him, also has at all reasonable times a right to inspect and take copies of any records[9] kept by, and any other documents[10] containing information relating to, the local authority or any school maintained by the authority[11] and any records kept by a person[12] who provides exceptional provision of education at schools or otherwise[13] that relate to the provision of that education, and any other documents containing information that so relates[14], which he considers relevant to the exercise of his functions[15].

The local authority and the governing body of any school maintained by the authority[16] must give the inspector and any person assisting him, all assistance in connection with the exercise of his functions which they are reasonably able to give[17]. Furthermore they must secure that all such assistance is also given by persons who work at the school[18].

It is an offence wilfully to obstruct the inspector or any person assisting him in the exercise of his functions in relation to the inspection[19].

1 As to the meaning of 'local authority in Wales' see PARA 25 (definition applied by the Education Act 1997 s 56(2)).

2 Ie inspected under the Education Act 1997 s 38 (see PARA 1293): s 40(1) (s 40 substituted by the Education Act 2002 s 180; and the Education Act 1997 s 40(1) amended by SI 2010/1158). As to the application of the Education Act 1997 s 40 to the Auditor General for Wales where he assists with any inspection, see s 41A; and PARA 1293.

3 As to the meaning of 'the inspector' see PARA 1293 note 16.

4 Education Act 1997 s 40(2)(a) (as substituted(see note 2); and amended by SI 2010/1158).

5 As to the meaning of 'premises' in relation to a school see PARA 62 note 19 (definition applied by the Education Act 1997 s 56(2)). As to the meaning of 'school' see PARA 91 (definition as so applied).

6 Education Act 1997 s 40(2)(b) (as substituted: see note 2). As to maintained schools see PARA 99 et seq.

7 Ie 'relevant section 19 education', being education provided to a child by virtue of arrangements made by the local authority under the Education Act 1996 s 19 (exceptional provision of education at schools or otherwise: see PARA 427): see the Education Act 1997 s 40(2)(c), (8) (as substituted (see note 2); s 40(8) amended by SI 2010/1158).

8 Education Act 1997 s 40(2)(c) (as substituted: see note 2).

9 'Records' includes information recorded in any form: see the Education Act 1997 s 40(8) (as substituted: see note 2).

10 'Document' includes information recorded in any form: see the Education Act 1997 s 40(8) (as substituted: see note 2).

11 Education Act 1997 s 40(3)(a) (as substituted (see note 2); and amended by SI 2010/1158).

12 As to the meaning of 'person' see PARA 7 note 6.

13 Ie 'relevant section 19 education': see note 7.

14 Education Act 1997 s 40(3)(b) (as substituted: see note 2).

15 Education Act 1997 s 40(3) (as substituted: see note 2). As to the meaning of 'functions' see PARA 18 note 5 (definition applied by s 56(2)). The Education Act 2005 s 58 (inspection of computer records: see PARA 1152 note 7) applies for the purposes of the Education Act 1997 s 40(3) as it applies for the purposes of the Education Act 2005 Pt 1 (ss 1–63): Education Act 1997 s 40(4) (as so substituted; and amended by the Education Act 2005 s 61, Sch 9 para 13).

16 Education Act 1997 s 40(5) (as substituted (see note 2); amended by SI 2010/1158). The Education Act 1997 s 40(5) is without prejudice to s 40(2)–(3) (see the text to notes 1–15): see s 40(5) (as so substituted). As to the governing bodies of maintained schools in Wales see PARA 195.

17 Education Act 1997 s 40(5)(a) (as substituted: see note 2).

18 Education Act 1997 s 40(5)(b) (as substituted: see note 2).

19 Education Act 1997 s 40(6) (as substituted: see note 2). A person guilty of such an offence is liable on summary conviction to a fine not exceeding level 4 on the standard scale: s 40(7) (as so substituted). As to the standard scale see SENTENCING AND DISPOSITION OF OFFENDERS vol 92 (2010) PARA 142.

11. LAND AND PREMISES

(1) PROVISION OF SITES AND PREMISES FOR CERTAIN SCHOOLS

1295. Provision of sites and buildings for foundation, voluntary controlled and foundation special schools. In the case of a foundation, voluntary controlled or foundation special school[1], the local authority[2] must provide any new site[3] which is to be provided in addition to, or instead of, the school's existing site or part of its existing site[4], and provide any buildings which are to form part of the school premises[5]. However, this does not apply in relation to the provision of any site or buildings which the authority or the person by whom any proposals were made is required[6] to provide[7], or require the local authority to finance the acquisition by the governing body[8] of any site or buildings provided otherwise than by the authority[9].

Where a site is provided for a school under these provisions, the local authority must transfer its interest[10] in the site, and in any buildings on the site which are to form part of the school premises: (1) to the trustees of the school to be held by them on trust for the purposes of the school[11]; or (2) if the school has no trustees, to the school's foundation body[12] or, in the absence of such a body, to the governing body, to be held by that body for the relevant purposes[13]. Where: (a) such a transfer is made[14]; and (b) the transfer is made to persons who possess, or are or may become entitled to, any sum representing proceeds of the sale of other premises which have been used for the purposes of the school[15], those persons must notify the local authority that head (b) above applies to them and they or their successors must pay to the local authority so much of that sum as, having regard to the value of the interest transferred, may be determined to be just, either by agreement between them and the authority or, in default of agreement, by the appropriate national authority[16].

1   As to foundation, voluntary controlled and foundation special schools see PARA 106 et seq; and as to special schools generally see PARA 1041 et seq.

2   As to the meaning of 'local authority' see PARA 25 (definition applied by the School Standards and Framework Act 1998 s 142(8)).

3   For these purposes, 'site' does not include playing fields but otherwise includes any site which is to form part of the premises of the school in question: School Standards and Framework Act 1998 Sch 3 para 2(11). As to the meanings of 'premises' and 'school' see PARA 62 note 19 and PARA 91 respectively (both definitions applied by virtue of the School Standards and Framework Act 1998 s 142(8)).

4   School Standards and Framework Act 1998 Sch 3 para 2(1)(a) (Sch 3 para 2(1), (2)(b), (3), (6) amended by SI 2010/1158).

5   School Standards and Framework Act 1998 Sch 3 para 2(1)(b).

6   Ie in the case of a school in England by virtue of the Education and Inspections Act 2006 Sch 2 Pt 3 (paras 21–26) (provision of premises in connection with proposals for establishment of school: see PARA 124 et seq) or by virtue of regulations under s 24 (implementation of proposals for alteration of school: see PARA 136), and in the case of a school in Wales by virtue of the School Standards and Organisation (Wales) Act 2013 Sch 3 Pt 2 (paras 7–11) (provision of premises and other assistance).

7   School Standards and Framework Act 1998 Sch 3 para 2(2)(a) (Sch 3 para 2(2)(a) substituted by the Education and Inspections Act 2006 Sch 3 para 31; and amended by the School Standards and Organisation (Wales) Act 2013 Sch 5 Pt 2 para 19(1), (12)(a)).

8   As to the governing body of a maintained school, in relation to England, see PARA 150 et seq; and as to the governing body of a maintained school, in relation to Wales, see PARA 195.

9   School Standards and Framework Act 1998 Sch 3 para 2(2)(b) (as amended: see note 4).

10   As to references to 'land' and to an 'interest' in land see PARA 116 note 18 (both definitions applied by virtue of the School Standards and Framework Act 1998 s 142(8)).

11 School Standards and Framework Act 1998 Sch 3 para 2(3)(a) (as amended: see note 4). References to land or other property held on trust, or by trustees, for the purposes of a school include references to land or other property which: (1) is held on trust for purposes which (whether the trust deed expressly so provides or not) include the purposes of the school; and (2) is used for the purposes of the school: s 21(3)(c).

12 As to the meaning of 'foundation body' see PARA 108 note 6.

13 School Standards and Framework Act 1998 Sch 3 para 2(3)(b). For these purposes, 'the relevant purposes' means: (1) in relation to a transfer to a school's foundation body, the purposes of the schools comprising the group for which that body acts; and (2) in relation to a transfer to a school's governing body, the purposes of the school: Sch 3 para 2(11). As to the meaning of 'the group' see PARA 108 note 6.

Where any doubt or dispute arises as to the persons to whom the authority is required to make the transfer, it is to be made to such persons as the appropriate national authority (ie the Secretary of State or, in relation to Wales, the Welsh Ministers) thinks proper: Sch 3 para 2(4). The authority must pay to the persons to whom the transfer is made their reasonable costs in connection with the transfer: Sch 3 para 2(5).

The functions of the Secretary of State under Sch 3, so far as exercisable in relation to Wales, were transferred to the National Assembly for Wales (see the National Assembly for Wales (Transfer of Functions) Order 1999, SI 1999/672, art 2, Sch 1) and are now vested in the Welsh Ministers (see the Government of Wales Act 2006 s 162(1), Sch 11 para 30). As to the Secretary of State see PARA 58. As to the Welsh Ministers see PARA 59. As to the meaning of 'Wales' see PARA 7 note 3.

14 School Standards and Framework Act 1998 Sch 3 para 2(6)(a).

15 School Standards and Framework Act 1998 Sch 3 para 2(6)(b). The reference in Sch 3 para 2(6)(b) to proceeds of the sale of other premises includes a reference to: (1) consideration for the creation or disposition of any kind of interest in other premises, including rent; and (2) interest which has accrued in respect of any such consideration: Sch 3 para 2(7).

16 School Standards and Framework Act 1998 Sch 3 para 2(6) (as amended: see note 4). For the purposes of any agreed determination under Sch 3 para 2(6), regard must be had to any guidance given from time to time by the appropriate national authority: Sch 3 para 2(7). Any sum paid under Sch 3 para 2(6) must be treated for the purposes of the Schools Sites Act 1841 s 14 (sale or exchange of land held on trust for the purposes of a school: see PARA 1297) as a sum applied in the purchase of a site for the school: School Standards and Framework Act 1998 Sch 3 para 2(8).

A determination may be made under Sch 3 para 2(6) in respect of any property subject to a trust which has arisen under the Reverter of Sites Act 1987 s 1 (right of reverter replaced by trust for sale: see CHARITIES vol 8 (2015) PARA 70) if, and only if: (1) the determination is made by the appropriate national authority; and (2) the appropriate national authority is satisfied that steps have been taken to protect the interests of the beneficiaries under the trust: School Standards and Framework Act 1998 Sch 3 para 2(9).

Schedule 3 para 2(6) applies for the purpose of compensating the authority notified thereunder only in relation to such part of the sum mentioned in Sch 3 para 2(6)(b) (see head (b) in the text), if any, as remains after the application of Sch 22 paras A1–A16 (see PARAS 1305–1307) or Sch 22 paras 1–3 (see PARAS 1313–1318) to that sum: Sch 3 para 2(10) (amended, by the Education and Inspections Act 2006 Sch 4 Pt 3 para 22).

1296. Provision of sites for voluntary aided schools. In the case of a voluntary aided school[1], the local authority[2] must provide any new site[3] which is to be provided in addition to, or instead of, the school's existing site, or part of its existing site[4]. However, this does not apply in relation to the provision of any site which persons other than the authority are required to provide by virtue of any enactment[5], nor does this require the local authority to finance the acquisition by the governing body[6] of any site or buildings provided otherwise than by the authority[7].

Where a site is provided for a school under these provisions, the local authority must transfer its interest in the site, and in any buildings on the site which are to form part of the school premises: (1) to the trustees of the school to be held by them on trust for the purposes of the school[8]; or (2) if the school has no trustees, to the school's foundation body[9], to be held by that body for the relevant purposes[10].

Where a site is provided for a school under these provisions[11] and work is required to be done to the site to clear it or make it suitable for building purposes[12], the local authority and the governing body of the school may make an agreement providing for the making of such payments, or of such other adjustments of their respective rights and liabilities[13], as will secure that the cost of the work is borne by the local authority[14]. Where a site is provided for a school under these provisions[15] and there are buildings on the site which are of value for the purposes of the school[16], the local authority and the governing body of the school may make an agreement providing for the making of such payments, or of such other adjustments of their respective rights and liabilities, as appear to be desirable having regard to the governing body's duties[17] with respect to the school premises (or, in Wales, the school buildings)[18].

1   As to voluntary schools see PARA 106 et seq.
2   As to the meaning of 'local authority' see PARA 25.
3   For these purposes, 'site' does not include playing fields but otherwise includes any site which is to form part of the premises of the school in question: School Standards and Framework Act 1998 Sch 3 para 4(9). As to the meanings of 'premises' and 'school' see PARAS 62 note 19 and 91 respectively (both definitions applied by virtue of s 142(8)).
4   School Standards and Framework Act 1998 Sch 3 para 4(1) (Sch 3 para 4(1), (2)(b), (3), (6), (7) amended by SI 2010/1158).
5   School Standards and Framework Act 1998 Sch 3 para 4(2)(a) (amended by the Education Act 2002 Sch 21 para 114).
6   As to the governing body of a maintained school, in relation to England, see PARA 150 et seq; and as to the governing body of a maintained school, in relation to Wales, see PARA 195.
7   School Standards and Framework Act 1998 Sch 3 para 4(2)(b) (as amended: see note 4).
8   School Standards and Framework Act 1998 Sch 3 para 4(3)(a) (as amended: see note 4). As to the meaning of 'land or other property held on trust, or by trustees, for the purposes of a school' see PARA 108 note 6/1295 note 11.
9   As to the meaning of 'foundation body' see PARA 108 note 6.
10   School Standards and Framework Act 1998 Sch 3 para 4(3)(b). For these purposes, 'the relevant purposes' means, in relation to a transfer to a school's foundation body, the purposes of the schools comprising the group for which that body acts: Sch 3 para 4(9). As to the meaning of 'the group' see PARA 108 note 6.
     Where any doubt or dispute arises as to the persons to whom the local authority is required to make the transfer, it is to be made to such persons as the appropriate national authority (ie the Secretary of State or, in relation to Wales, the Welsh Ministers) thinks proper: Sch 3 para 4(4). The local authority must pay to the persons to whom the transfer is made their reasonable costs in connection with the transfer: Sch 3 para 4(5).
     The functions of the Secretary of State under Sch 3, so far as exercisable in relation to Wales, were transferred to the National Assembly for Wales (see the National Assembly for Wales (Transfer of Functions) Order 1999, SI 1999/672, art 2, Sch 1) and are now vested in the Welsh Ministers (see the Government of Wales Act 2006 s 162(1), Sch 11 para 30). As to the Secretary of State see PARA 58. As to the Welsh Ministers see PARA 59. As to the meaning of 'Wales' see PARA 7 note 3.
11   School Standards and Framework Act 1998 Sch 3 para 4(6)(a).
12   School Standards and Framework Act 1998 Sch 3 para 4(6)(b).
13   As to the meaning of 'liability' see PARA 108 note 22 (definition applied by virtue of the School Standards and Framework Act 1998 s 142(8)).
14   School Standards and Framework Act 1998 Sch 3 para 4(6) (as amended: see note 4). Where it appears to the appropriate national authority that provision for any payment or other adjustment ought to have been made under Sch 3 para 4(6) but has not been made, the appropriate national authority may give directions providing for the making of such payment or other adjustment as it thinks proper: Sch 3 para 4(8).
15   School Standards and Framework Act 1998 Sch 3 para 4(7)(a).
16   School Standards and Framework Act 1998 Sch 3 para 4(7)(b).
17   Ie under the School Standards and Framework Act 1998 Sch 3 para 3 (see PARA 311).

18 School Standards and Framework Act 1998 Sch 3 para 4(7) (as amended (see note 4); and
amended in relation to England by SI 2002/906). 'School buildings', in relation to a school,
means any building or part of a building forming part of the school premises, other than a
building or part required only: (1) as a caretaker's dwelling; (2) for use in connection with
playing fields; (3) to afford facilities for the carrying out of functions under the National Health
Service Act 2006 under Sch 1 para 1 or 8 (which relate to the provision of medical services for
pupils: see HEALTH SERVICES vol 54 (2008) PARAS 33, 34); or (4) to afford facilities for providing
milk, meals or other refreshment for pupils in attendance at the school: Education Act 1996
s 579(1) (amended by the National Health Service (Consequential Provisions) Act 2006 Sch 1
para 185; and the Health and Social Care Act 2012 Sch 5 paras 77, 80) (definition applied by
virtue of the School Standards and Framework Act 1998 s 142(8)).

Where it appears to the appropriate national authority that provision for any payment or
other adjustment ought to have been made under Sch 3 para 4(7) but has not been made, the
appropriate national authority may give directions providing for the making of such payment or
other adjustment as it thinks proper: Sch 3 para 4(8).

1297. Provision of school premises under the School Sites Acts. The School
Sites Acts[1] afforded facilities for persons and bodies who might otherwise be
under disabilities to convey land for certain purposes connected with education[2].

The School Sites Act 1841 enabled a donor with a beneficial interest in land to
convey up to one acre of the land as a site for a school for the education of poor
persons or for a teacher's residence, subject to provisos, one of which was that
the land should revert to him or his successors if at any time in the future the
land ceased to be used for the purposes mentioned in the Act[3].

Difficulties arose where reverter occurred but the donor or his successors
could not be traced[4]. The Reverter of Sites Act 1987 substituted a trust for sale[5]
for the right of reverter[6] and provided for the making of Charity Commission
schemes, enabling an alternative use to be made of school sites if and when the
school closed[7].

The Charity Commission is empowered to establish a scheme extinguishing
the rights of beneficiaries under the trust and requiring the property to be held
on trust for specified charitable purposes, such purposes to be as similar as
possible to those obtaining before the reverter and be capable of having a
significant social or economic effect; and must also provide for enabling a
beneficiary who has not consented to the scheme to claim compensation within
five years[8]. Before a scheme is made, notice of the application for a scheme must
be published in two national newspapers and a local one[9]. An appeal against the
making of a scheme may be brought[10].

It is also provided that the power of sale of land or buildings[11] is exercisable
at any time in relation to land in relation to which (but for the exercise of the
power) a trust may subsequently arise[12], and that the exercise of that power in
respect of any land prevents any such trust arising in relation to that land or any
land representing the proceeds of sale of that land[13].

1 Ie the School Sites Act 1841, the School Sites Act 1844, the School Sites Act 1849, the School
Sites Act 1851 and the School Sites Act 1852: see the text and notes 2–3.
2 Such disabilities existed under the Mortmain and Charitable Uses Act 1888 (repealed by the
Charities Act 1960 s 38, Sch 7 Pt II). The powers are therefore no longer necessary but much
land was conveyed under the School Sites Acts and their provisions continue to apply to the land
so conveyed. As to the School Sites Act 1841 see the text and note 3.

The School Sites Act 1844 was concerned with parliamentary grants for the education of the
poor: see s 1 (modified, in relation to the references to 'managers', by the Education Act 1996
Sch 39, para 4) (terms and conditions upon which parliamentary aid is given towards the
building of schools); the School Sites Act 1844 s 2 (amended by the Statute Law Revision
Act 1891) (applications by trustees of ancient endowed schools for parliamentary aid for
rebuilding schools); the School Sites Act 1844 s 4 (grant of sites to ministers and churchwardens
and their successors); and s 5 (grant of part of glebe). Where any parliamentary grant was made

towards the provision, repair or furnishing of any school premises with the consent of the trustees or holders of the legal estate, no sale, exchange or mortgage can validly be made of the premises, subject to certain exceptions, without the consent of the Secretary of State unless the grant is repaid to the Treasury: see the School Grants Act 1855 s 1 (amended by the Statute Law Revision 1892; the Statute Law (Repeals) Act 1978; and the Statute Law (Repeals) Act 1981; and modified, in relation to the references to 'managers', by the Education Act 1996 Sch 39, para 4). As to savings in relation to purchasers for value without notice see the School Grants Act 1855 s 2. As to the Treasury see CONSTITUTIONAL AND ADMINISTRATIVE LAW vol 20 (2014) PARA 262 et seq.

The School Sites Act 1849 extended and explained the provisions of the School Sites Acts: see the School Sites Act 1849 s 1 (amended by the Statute Law Revision Act 1891) (apportionment of rents and fines); the School Sites Act 1849 s 2 (amended by the Statute Law Revision Act 1891) (liabilities of tenants and remedies of landlords); the School Sites Act 1849 s 3 (amended by the Statute Law Revision Act 1891) (limitation of land to be granted in same parish); the School Sites Act 1849 s 4 (amended by the Statute Law Revision Act 1891; and the Charities Act 1960 Sch 7 Pt II; and modified, in relation to the reference to 'elementary schools', by the Education Act 1996 Sch 39, para 4) (sites for schools for instruction of masters of elementary schools); and the School Sites Act 1849 s 5 (power to convey to corporations as trustees).

The School Sites Act 1851 amended the School Sites Act 1841 and the School Sites Act 1849: see the School Sites Act 1851 ss 1, 2.

The School Sites Act 1852 concerned conveyances and endowments: see the School Sites Act 1852 s 1 (amended by the Irish Church Act 1869 s 69; the School Sites Act 1841; the School Sites Act 1844; the School Sites Act 1849; the School Sites Act 1851; and the Trustee Appointment Act 1850).

3   See the School Sites Act 1841 s 2 (amended by the Statute Law Revision (No 2) Act 1888; the Education (Scotland) Act 1945 Sch 5; and the Commons Act 2006 s 48(2)(b), Sch 6 Pt 3). The words in the School Sites Act 1841 s 2 regarding 'the purposes in this Act mentioned' relate to education in general: *Fraser v Canterbury Diocesan Board of Finance (No 2)* [2005] UKHL 65, [2006] 1 AC 377, [2006] 1 All ER 315 (revsg [2004] EWCA Civ 15, 148 Sol Jo LB 149, [2004] All ER (D) 261 (Jan), (2004) Independent, 6 February; and disapproving *Fraser v Canterbury Diocesan Board of Finance* [2001] Ch 669, [2001] 2 WLR 1103, CA). See also *Marchant v Onslow* [1995] Ch 1, [1994] 2 All ER 707, [1994] ELR 451; *Bath and Wells Diocesan Board of Finance v Jenkinson* [2002] EWHC 218 (Ch), [2003] Ch 89, [2002] 4 All ER 245. There is no reference in the School Sites Act 1841 s 2 to 'the purposes in the deed of grant mentioned', so that a breach of any restrictions in the deed would not have the drastic consequence of causing a reverter, although those restrictions could be enforced in the same way as those in any other charitable trust: *Fraser v Canterbury Diocesan Board of Finance (No 2)*. See also CHARITIES vol 8 (2015) PARA 70.

The School Sites Act 1841 made provision in relation to: the grant of land by the Chancellor and Council of the Duchy of Lancaster (see s 3 (amended by the Statute Law Revision (No 2) Act 1888; and the Statute Law (Revision) (No 2) Act 1890)); persons entitled to convey lands (see the School Sites Act 1841 s 5 (amended by the Mental Treatment Act 1930 s 20(5); the Law Reform (Married Women and Tortfeasors) Act 1935 Sch 2; and the Mental Health Act 1959 s 149(4))); the conveyance of land by corporations, justices and trustees (see the School Sites Act 1841 s 6 (amended by the Local Government Act 1929 Sch 12 Pt VII; the Local Government Act 1933 Sch 11 Pt IV; and the London Government Act 1939 Sch 8)); grants of land to corporations or trustees to be held by them for school purposes (see the School Sites Act 1841 s 7 (amended by the Statute Law Revision (No 2) Act 1888)); estates vested in trustees which may be conveyed to the minister and churchwardens (see the School Sites Act 1841 s 8 (amended by the Statute Law Revision (No 2) Act 1888)); the number of sites which may be granted by one person for separate schools (see the School Sites Act 1841 s 9 (amended by the Statute Law Revision (No 2) Act 1888)); forms of grants (see the School Sites Act 1841 s 10 (amended by the Statute Law Revision (No 2) Act 1888; and the Education (Scotland) Act 1945 Sch 5)); application of purchase money for land sold by any ecclesiastical corporation sole (see the School Sites Act 1841 s 11 (amended by the Statute Law Revision (No 2) Act 1888)); form of certificate required by ecclesiastical corporations sole (see the School Sites Act 1841 s 13 (amended by the Statute Law Revision (No 2) Act 1888)); sale or exchange land or buildings by trustees (see the School Sites Act 1841 s 14 (amended by the Statute Law Revision (No 2) Act 1888; and the Statute Law (Repeals) Act 1978)); and the prohibition of schoolmasters acquiring life interest by virtue of appointment (see the School Sites Act 1841 s 17 (amended by the Statute Law Revision (No 2) Act 1888)).

As to the Chancellor and Council of the Duchy of Lancaster see CROWN AND CROWN PROCEEDINGS vol 29 (2014) PARA 219. As to ecclesiastical corporations sole see ECCLESIASTICAL LAW vol 34 (2011) PARA 1013.

4 See eg *Re Clayton's Deed Poll, Williams Deacon's Bank Ltd v Kennedy* [1980] Ch 99, [1979] 2 All ER 1133; *Re Rowhook Mission Hall, Horsham* [1985] Ch 62, [1984] 3 All ER 179.

5 Trusts for sale have now been subsumed under trusts of land: see the Trusts of Land and Appointment of Trustees Act 1996 ss 1, 4, 5; and REAL PROPERTY AND REGISTRATION vol 87 (2012) PARA 105.

6 See the Reverter of Sites Act 1987 s 1; and CHARITIES vol 8 (2015) PARA 70.
7 See the Reverter of Sites Act 1987 ss 2, 3; and CHARITIES vol 8 (2015) PARAS 71, 72.
8 See the Reverter of Sites Act 1987 s 2; and CHARITIES vol 8 (2015) PARA 71.
9 See the Reverter of Sites Act 1987 s 3(1); and CHARITIES vol 8 (2015) PARA 72.
10 See the Reverter of Sites Act 1987 s 4(2), (4); and CHARITIES vol 8 (2015) PARA 73.

11 Ie the power of sale conferred by the School Sites Act 1841 s 14: see note 3.
12 Ie under the Reverter of Sites Act 1987 s 1: see CHARITIES vol 8 (2015) PARA 70.
13 See the Reverter of Sites Act 1987 s 6(2); and CHARITIES vol 8 (2015) PARA 70.

(2) ACQUISITION, APPROPRIATION AND DISPOSAL OF LAND

(i) Acquisition of Land by Agreement

1298. Acquisition of land by agreement. For the removal of doubt, it has been declared that making land[1] available for the purposes of a school[2] or institution which is, or is to be, maintained by a local authority[3] or which such an authority has power to assist[4], is a function of the authority[5], even though the land will not be held by the authority[6]. A local authority must not acquire by agreement any land required for the purposes of a foundation, voluntary or foundation special school[7] unless it is satisfied that the arrangements made[8]:

(1)   as to the vesting of the land to be acquired[9]; and

(2)   as to the appropriation of that land for the purposes of the school[10],

are such as to secure that the expenditure ultimately borne by it will not include any expenditure which, if the land had been acquired by the governing body[11] of the school, would have fallen to be borne by the governing body[12].

1 As to the meaning of 'land' see PARA 116 note 18.
2 As to the meaning of 'school' see PARA 91.

3 Education Act 1996 s 531(1)(a) (s 531(1)(a), (2) amended by SI 2010/1158). As to the meaning of 'local authority' see PARA 25; and as to maintained schools generally see PARA 99 et seq.
4 Education Act 1996 s 531(1)(b). As to assisted schools see PARA 51.

5 Ie a function within the meaning of the Local Government Act 1972 s 120 (which relates to the acquisition by a local authority by agreement of land for the purpose of any of their functions: see LOCAL GOVERNMENT vol 69 (2009) PARA 509).

6 Education Act 1996 s 531(1).
7 As to foundation, voluntary and foundation special schools see PARA 106 et seq; and as to special schools generally see PARA 1041 et seq.

8 Education Act 1996 s 531(2) (as amended (see note 3); and further amended by the School Standards and Framework Act 1998 Sch 30 para 147).

9 Education Act 1996 s 531(2)(a).
10 Education Act 1996 s 531(2)(b).
11 As to the governing body of a maintained school, in relation to England, see PARA 150 et seq; and as to the governing body of a maintained school, in relation to Wales, see PARA 195.
12 Education Act 1996 s 531(2).

(ii) Compulsory Purchase of Land

1299. Compulsory purchase of land. The appropriate national authority[1] may authorise a local authority[2] to purchase compulsorily any land[3], whether within or outside its area, which:

(1)   is required for the purposes of any school[4] or institution which is, or is to be, maintained by it or which it has power to assist[5];

(2)   is otherwise required for the purposes of its functions[6] under the Education Act 1996[7]; or

(3)   is required for the purposes of an academy[8] (whether established or to be established)[9].

The appropriate national authority must not authorise the compulsory purchase of any land required for the purposes of a foundation, voluntary or foundation special school[10] unless satisfied that the arrangements made[11]:

(a)   as to the vesting of the land to be purchased[12]; and

(b)   as to the appropriation of that land for the purposes of the school[13],

are such as to secure that the expenditure ultimately borne by the local authority will not include any expenditure which, if the land had been purchased by the governing body[14] of the school, would have fallen to be borne by the governing body[15].

1   Ie the Secretary of State or, in relation to Wales, the Welsh Ministers. As to the Secretary of State see PARA 58. As to the Welsh Ministers see PARA 59. As to the meaning of 'Wales' see PARA 7 note 3. The functions of the Secretary of State under the Education Act 1996 s 530, so far as exercisable in relation to Wales, were transferred to the National Assembly for Wales (see the National Assembly for Wales (Transfer of Functions) Order 1999, SI 1999/672, art 2, Sch 1) and are now vested in the Welsh Ministers (see the Government of Wales Act 2006 s 162(1), Sch 11 para 30).

2   As to the meaning of 'local authority' see PARA 25.

3   As to the meaning of 'land' see PARA 116 note 18. In the Education Act 1996 s 530 'land' includes buildings and other structures and land covered with water: s 530(4).

4   As to the meaning of 'school' see PARA 91.

5   Education Act 1996 s 530(1)(a) (s 530(1)–(3) amended by SI 2010/1158). As to maintained schools generally see PARA 99 et seq. As to assisted schools see PARA 51.

6   As to the meaning of 'functions' see PARA 18 note 5.

7   Education Act 1996 s 530(1)(b).

8   As to the meaning of 'academy' see PARA 346. As to academies see PARA 345 et seq.

9   Education Act 1996 s 530(1)(c) (added by the Education Act 2002 Sch 8 para 9(2); Education Act 1996 s 530(1)(c), (3)(a), (b) substituted by the Education and Inspections Act 2006 Sch 3 para 11(1)–(3)).

10   As to foundation, voluntary and foundation special schools see PARA 106 et seq; and as to special schools generally see PARA 1041 et seq.

11   Education Act 1996 s 530(2) (amended by the School Standards and Framework Act 1998 Sch 30 para 146(a)).

12   Education Act 1996 s 530(2)(a).

13   Education Act 1996 s 530(2)(b).

14   As to the governing body of a maintained school, in relation to England, see PARA 150 et seq; and as to the governing body of a maintained school, in relation to Wales, see PARA 195.

15   Education Act 1996 s 530(2) (as amended: see note 5). However, s 530(2) does not apply where the local authority proposes that expenditure to be incurred in connection with the purchase should ultimately be borne by it:

    (1)   in the case of an authority in England, under any provision of regulations under the Education and Inspections Act 2006 s 24 (implementation of proposals under s 19: see PARA 136) which by virtue of s 24(7) authorises a local authority to provide assistance to the governing body of a voluntary aided school in connection with the implementation of the obligations of the governing body under the regulations (Education Act 1996 s 530(3)(a) (as substituted and amended (see notes 5, 9); further amended by SI 2010/1080));

    (2)   in the case of an authority in Wales, under the School Standards and Organisation

(Wales) Act 2013 Sch 3 para 9 (assistance in respect of maintenance and other obligations relating to voluntary aided schools) (including Sch 3 para 9 as applied by s 76(3)) (Education Act 1996 s 530(3)(b) (as so substituted; amended by the School Standards and Organisation (Wales) Act 2013 Sch 5 para 17(6)).

(iii) Appropriation of Land

1300.   Appropriation of land by local authority. A local authority[1] may appropriate[2] for any purpose for which it is authorised by statute to acquire land[3] by agreement[4] any land which belongs to it and is no longer required[5] for the purpose for which it is held immediately before the appropriation[6]. The appropriation is, however, also subject to the rights of other persons in, over or in respect of the land concerned[7].

1   Ie a 'principal council', which includes a local authority (see LOCAL GOVERNMENT vol 69 (2009) PARA 23).
2   Ie subject to the Local Government Act 1972 s 122(2), (2A), (2B), (4): see LOCAL GOVERNMENT vol 69 (2009) PARA 513. As to restrictions on the change in use of school playing fields see PARA 1326; and as to restrictions on the appropriation of land formerly used as a school see PARA 1326.
3   'Land' includes any interest in land and any easement or right in, to or over land: Local Government Act 1972 s 270(1).
4   Ie under the Local Government Act 1972 or under any other enactment (see PARA 1298); and LOCAL GOVERNMENT vol 69 (2009) PARA 509.
5   The authority is the sole judge of whether or not the land is still required for the purpose for which it is held immediately before the appropriation, and its decision cannot be challenged in the absence of bad faith: *Dowty Boulton Paul Ltd v Wolverhampton Corpn (No 2)* [1973] Ch 94, [1972] 2 All ER 1073; affd [1976] Ch 13, [1973] 2 All ER 491, CA.
6   See the Local Government Act 1972 s 122(1); and LOCAL GOVERNMENT vol 69 (2009) PARA 513.
7   See the Local Government Act 1972 s 122(1); and LOCAL GOVERNMENT vol 69 (2009) PARA 513.

1301.   Appropriation of land held by local authority for the purposes of a school or 16 to 19 academy. Where a freehold or leasehold interest in land[1] is held by a local authority[2] and the authority proposes to make an appropriation of the land under the Local Government Act 1972[3] and at any time in the period of eight years ending with the day on which the appropriation is proposed to be made the land was used wholly or mainly for the purposes of a school or a 16 to 19 academy[4], the authority must not make the appropriation unless the Secretary of State consents[5].

Where a local authority has made an appropriation in contravention of these provisions[6] the Secretary of State may purchase the land concerned compulsorily[7].

1   Where a freehold or leasehold interest in land is held by a local authority, the authority proposes to change the use of the land in such a way that (were the change made) the land would cease to be capable of use wholly or mainly for the purposes of a school or a 16 to 19 academy, and at any time in the period of eight years ending with the date of the proposed change of use the land was used wholly or mainly for the purposes of a school or a 16 to 19 academy, the authority must inform the Secretary of State of the proposal: Academies Act 2010 Sch 1 para 9(1), (2) (Sch 1 substituted by the Education Act 2011 Sch 14 para 1). As to the meaning of 'school' see PARA 91 (definition applied by the Academies Act 2010 s 17(4)); and as to the meaning of '16 to 19 academy' see PARA 346 note 13. As to the treatment of a dwelling-house used for occupation by a person employed to work at an educational institution as used for the purposes of a school see PARA 1341 note 4. As to the meaning of 'local authority' see PARA 25 and (in the context of the Academies Act 2010) PARA 351 note 3. As to the Secretary of State see PARA 58.
2   Academies Act 2010 Sch 1 para 6(1)(a) (as substituted: see note 1).

3	Academies Act 2010 Sch 1 para 6(1)(b) (as substituted: see note 1). The reference in the text to an appropriation of land under the Local Government Act 1972 is to one under s 122 (see **LOCAL GOVERNMENT** vol 69 (2009) PARA 513).

4	Academies Act 2010 Sch 1 para 6(1)(c) (as substituted: see note 1).

5	Academies Act 2010 Sch 1 para 6(2) (as substituted: see note 1). For the purposes of Sch 1 para 6(2), the consent of the Secretary of State may be given in relation to a particular case or class of case, and may be given subject to conditions: Sch 1 para 8 (as so substituted).

As to guidance see in particular 'Disposal or change of use of playing field and school land: Departmental advice for local authorities, maintained schools, special schools, academies and free schools' (May 2015).

6	Academies Act 2010 Sch 1 para 7(1) (as substituted: see note 1). The reference in the text to provisions is to those under Sch 1 para 6(2) (see the text and note 5).

7	Academies Act 2010 Sch 1 para 7(2) (as substituted: see note 1). Schedule 1 para 5(6)–(9) (see PARA 1304) apply to a compulsory purchase of land under Sch 1 para 7(2) as they apply to a compulsory purchase of land under Sch 1 para 5(5) (see PARA 1304): Sch 1 para 7(3) (as so substituted).

(iv) Disposal of Land

A. DISPOSAL OF LAND BY LOCAL AUTHORITIES

1302. Disposal of land under the Local Government Act 1972 by a local authority. The Local Government Act 1972 provides that a local authority[1] may, subject to certain conditions[2], dispose of land in any manner it wishes[3]. Except with the consent of the appropriate national authority[4], a local authority must not dispose of land under these provisions, otherwise than by way of a short tenancy[5] for a consideration less than the best that can reasonably be obtained[6]. A local authority may not dispose of any land consisting or forming part of an open space unless, before disposing of the land, it causes notice of its intention to do so, specifying the land in question, to be advertised in two consecutive weeks in a newspaper circulating in the area in which the land is situated, and considers any objections to the proposed disposal which may be made to it[7].

1	Ie a 'principal council', which includes a local authority (see **LOCAL GOVERNMENT** vol 69 (2009) PARA 23).

2	Ie subject to the Local Government Act 1972 s 123(2), (2A), (2AA), (2B) (see the text and notes 3–7; and **LOCAL GOVERNMENT** vol 69 (2009) PARA 515) and to the Playing Fields (Community Involvement in Disposal Decisions) (Wales) Measure 2010 (see **LOCAL GOVERNMENT** vol 69 (2009) PARA 515A): see the Local Government Act 1972 s 123(1) (amended by the Playing Fields (Community Involvement in Disposal Decisions) (Wales) Measure 2010 s 2(1), (2)(a)). As to restrictions on the disposal of school playing fields see PARA 1326; and as to the restriction on the disposal of land formerly used as a school see PARA 1326.

3	See the Local Government Act 1972 s 123(1); and **LOCAL GOVERNMENT** vol 69 (2009) PARA 515. In *R v Barnet London Borough Council, ex p Pardes House School Ltd* [1989] COD 512, [1989] EGCS 64, Farquharson J held that, when disposing of land used for educational purposes, the local authority (then the local education authority), in fulfilling its duty to act fairly, must consider its own policy with regard to the use of land for educational purposes.

4	Ie the Secretary of State or, in relation to Wales, the Welsh Ministers. As to the Secretary of State see PARA 58. As to the Welsh Ministers see PARA 59. As to the meaning of 'Wales' see PARA 7 note 3. The functions of the Secretary of State under the Local Government Act 1972 s 123, so far as exercisable in relation to Wales, were transferred to the National Assembly for Wales (see the National Assembly for Wales (Transfer of Functions) Order 1999, SI 1999/672, art 2, Sch 1) and are now vested in the Welsh Ministers (see the Government of Wales Act 2006 s 162(1), Sch 11 para 30).

5	For these purposes, a disposal of land is a disposal by way of a short tenancy if it consists: (1) of the grant of a term not exceeding seven years; or (2) of the assignment of a term which at the date of the assignment has not more than seven years to run: see the Local Government Act 1972 s 123(7); and **LOCAL GOVERNMENT** vol 69 (2009) PARA 515.

6   See the Local Government Act 1972 s 123(2); and LOCAL GOVERNMENT vol 69 (2009) PARA
    515. Section 123(2) (prohibition on disposal of land below market value without consent of the
    Secretary of State: see LOCAL GOVERNMENT vol 69 (2009) PARA 515) does not apply in the case
    of a disposal: (1) to the governing body of a foundation, voluntary or foundation special school;
    or (2) to persons proposing to establish such a school: School Standards and Framework
    Act 1998 Sch 3 para 12. As to the disapplication of restrictions on local authority disposals see
    also PARA 309. As to foundation, voluntary and foundation special schools see PARA 106 et seq;
    and as to special schools generally see PARA 1041 et seq.
7   See the Local Government Act 1972 s 123(2A); and LOCAL GOVERNMENT vol 69 (2009) PARA
    515. Section 123(2A) does not apply to a disposal to which the provisions of regulations made
    under the Playing Fields (Community Involvement in Disposal Decisions) (Wales) Measure 2010
    s 1 (see LOCAL GOVERNMENT vol 69 (2009) PARA 515A) apply: Local Government Act 1972
    s 123(2AA) (added by the Playing Fields (Community Involvement in Disposal Decisions)
    (Wales) Measure 2010 s 2(1), (2)(b)). Where by virtue of the Local Government Act 1972
    s 123(2A), or in accordance with the provisions of regulations made under of the Playing Fields
    (Community Involvement in Disposal Decisions) (Wales) Measure 2010 s 1 (see LOCAL
    GOVERNMENT vol 69 (2009) PARA 515A), a local authority disposes of land which is held for the
    purposes of the Public Health Act 1875 s 164 (pleasure grounds: see OPEN SPACES AND
    COUNTRYSIDE vol 78 (2010) PARA 556) or held in accordance with the Open Spaces Act 1906
    s 10 (duty to maintain open spaces and burial grounds: see OPEN SPACES AND COUNTRYSIDE
    vol 78 (2010) PARA 577), the land is by virtue of the disposal to be freed from any trust arising
    solely by virtue of its being land held in trust for enjoyment by the public in accordance with
    those statutory provisions: see the Local Government Act 1972 s 123(2B) (added by the Local
    Government, Planning and Land Act 1980 Sch 23 para 14; and amended by the Playing Fields
    (Community Involvement in Disposal Decisions) (Wales) Measure 2010 s 2(1), (2)(c)); and
    LOCAL GOVERNMENT vol 69 (2009) PARA 515.

**1303.   Disposal of land of a voluntary aided school by a local authority in
England.**   Where a local authority in England[1] disposes[2] of relevant land[3]
enhanced in value wholly or partly by means of capital expenditure[4] incurred by
the governing body of a voluntary aided school after 1 April 2002[5], the authority
must notify the relevant body[6] that these provisions apply to them and must pay
to the relevant body so much of the proceeds of disposal[7] as may be determined
to be just by agreement between the authority and the relevant body[8] or by the
adjudicator where the authority or the relevant body refer the matter to him for
determination and by the time of his determination, the matter has not been
determined by agreement between the authority and the relevant body[9].
However, these provisions do not apply unless the relevant body gives to the
local authority no later than 12 months after the expenditure is incurred a
statement setting out the amount of expenditure[10], and stating that it is capital
expenditure[11].

If the local authority permits relevant land to be used for purposes not
connected with the school, it must be treated for these purposes as having
disposed of the land[12], and must pay to the relevant body so much of the value of
the land as may be determined to be just by agreement between the authority and
the relevant body[13] or by the adjudicator where the authority or the relevant
body refer the matter to him for determination and by the time of his
determination, the matter has not been determined by agreement between the
authority and the relevant body[14].

1   The School Standards and Framework Act 1998 Sch 22 para 11 was added by SI 2002/906,
    which applies only in relation to England (see art 2). As to the meaning of 'England' see PARA 7
    note 3. As to the meaning of 'local authority' see PARA 25.
2   For the purposes of the School Standards and Framework Act 1998 Sch 22 'disposal' includes:
    (1) a compulsory disposal (School Standards and Framework Act 1998 Sch 22 para 10(1)(b)(i));
    and (2) in the case of any premises held under a tenancy to which the Landlord and Tenant
    Act 1954 Pt II (ss 23–46) (see LANDLORD AND TENANT vol 63 (2012) PARA 817 et seq) applies,
    the termination of that tenancy under Pt II (School Standards and Framework Act 1998 Sch 22

para 10(1)(b)(ii)). For the purposes of Sch 22 para 10(1)(b)(ii), expressions to which a meaning is given for the purposes of the Landlord and Tenant Act 1954 have the same meaning as in the Landlord and Tenant Act 1954: School Standards and Framework Act 1998 Sch 22 para 10(2).

3   For these purposes, 'relevant land' means any caretaker's dwelling, or other buildings which are not school buildings, which form part of the premises of a voluntary aided school: School Standards and Framework Act 1998 Sch 22 para 11(1)(d) (as added: see note 1). As to references to 'land' see PARA 84 note 9 (definition applied by virtue of s 142(8)). As to the meaning of 'school building' for these purposes see PARA 1296 note 18. As to the meanings of 'premises' and 'school' see PARAS 62 note 19 and 91 respectively (both definitions applied by virtue of the School Standards and Framework Act 1998 s 142(8)). As to voluntary schools see PARA 106 et seq.

4   For these purposes, 'capital expenditure' means expenditure of the governing body in question which falls to be capitalised in accordance with proper accounting practices: School Standards and Framework Act 1998 Sch 22 para 11(1)(a) (as added (see note 1); Sch 22 para 11(1)(a), (4)(a), (b) substituted by, Sch 22 para 11(1)(b), (5) amended by, and Sch 22 paras 11(4A), (4B), (5A)–(5C), (7), (8), 12 added by, the Education and Inspections Act 2006 Sch 4 paras 1, 16, 17).
    For the purposes of the School Standards and Framework Act 1998 Sch 22 para 11(1)(a) 'proper accounting practices', in relation to a governing body, means those accounting practices:
    (1)   which, whether by virtue of any enactment or by reference to any generally recognised published code or otherwise, are regarded as proper accounting practices to be followed in the keeping of accounts by the governing body (Sch 22 para 12(1)(a) (as so added)); or
    (2)   which, whether by virtue of any enactment or by reference to any generally recognised published code or otherwise, are regarded as proper accounting practices to be followed in the keeping of accounts by the local authority (Sch 22 para 12(1)(b) (as so added; and amended by SI 2010/1158)).
    In the event of conflict between the accounting practices falling within the School Standards and Framework Act 1998 Sch 22 para 12(1)(a) and those falling within Sch 22 para 12(1)(b), only those falling within Sch 22 para 12(1)(a) are to be regarded as proper accounting practices: Sch 22 para 12(2) (as so added).
    The Secretary of State may by regulations prescribe classes or descriptions of expenditure which are to be treated for the purposes of the School Standards and Framework Act 1998 Sch 22 para 11 as being, or as not being, capital expenditure of any governing body or of any prescribed class or description of governing body (Sch 22 para 11(7)(a) (as so added)) and may by direction provide that expenditure of a particular governing body which is expenditure of a particular class or description is to be treated for the purposes of Sch 22 para 11 as being, or as not being, capital expenditure of that body (Sch 22 para 11(7)(b) (as so added)). Directions under Sch 22 para 11(7)(b) may be expressed to have effect in specified circumstances or subject to specified conditions: Sch 22 para 11(8) (as so added). At the date at which this volume states the law no regulations had been made under Sch 22 para 11(7)(a). As to the Secretary of State see PARA 58. As to the governing body of a maintained school see PARA 150 et seq.

5   School Standards and Framework Act 1998 Sch 22 para 11(2) (as added (see note 1); and amended by SI 2010/1158). The 'commencement date' is 1 April 2002, being the date on which the Regulatory Reform (Voluntary Aided Schools Liabilities and Funding) (England) Order 2002, SI 2002/906, came into force (see reg 1(1)): see the School Standards and Framework Act 1998 Sch 22 para 11(1)(b) (as so added; and as amended (see note 4).

6   For these purposes, 'relevant body' means the governing body of a voluntary aided school, or, if the school has been discontinued and the governing body dissolved, the trustees: School Standards and Framework Act 1998 Sch 22 para 11(1)(c) (as added: see note 1). As to proposals to discontinue a voluntary school see PARAS 116 et seq. For the purposes of Sch 22, 'the trustees' in relation to a school, means any person (other than the governing body) holding property on trust for the purposes of the school: Sch 22 para 10(1)(a).

7   For the purposes of the School Standards and Framework Act 1998 Sch 22, references to 'proceeds of disposal' in relation to a disposal of land, are references to: (1) any consideration for the disposal, including rent (Sch 22 para 10(1)(c)(i)); (2) any compensation for the disposal, including any compensation paid by the landlord on the quitting of any premises within Sch 22 para 10(1)(b)(ii) (see note 2) by the governing body, foundation body or trustees, whether or not the compensation is required to be paid by the Landlord and Tenant Act 1954 s 37 (compensation where order for new tenancy precluded on certain grounds: see LANDLORD AND TENANT vol 63 (2012) PARAS 875–877) (School Standards and Framework Act 1998 Sch 22 para 10(1)(c)(ii)); and (3) interest which has accrued in respect of any such consideration or compensation (Sch 22 para 10(1)(c)(iii)). For the purposes of Sch 22 para 10(1)(c)(ii),

expressions to which a meaning is given for the purposes of the Landlord and Tenant Act 1954 have the same meaning as in the Landlord and Tenant Act 1954: School Standards and Framework Act 1998 Sch 22 para 10(2).

8   School Standards and Framework Act 1998 Sch 22 para 11(4)(a) (as added and substituted (see notes 1, 4); and amended by SI 2010/1158).

9   School Standards and Framework Act 1998 Sch 22 para 11(4)(b) (as added and substituted (see notes 1, 4); and amended by SI 2010/1158). In determining whether to make a reference to the adjudicator under Sch 22 para 11(4)(b) the authority or, as the case may be, the relevant body, must have regard, in particular, to any guidance given from time to time by the Secretary of State: Sch 22 para 11(4A) (as added: see notes 1, 4). Before making a reference to the adjudicator under Sch 22 para 11(4)(b), the authority or, as the case may be, the relevant body, must give the other notice of its intention to make the reference: Sch 22 para 11(4B) (as added: see notes 1, 4).

In making the determination under Sch 22 para 11(4), the relevant body and the local authority, or the adjudicator, as the case may be, must have regard in particular to any guidance given from time to time by the Secretary of State and to any enhancement in value of the relevant land attributable to expenditure by or on behalf of the governing body: Sch 22 para 11(5) (as so added; as amended (see note 4); further amended by SI 2010/1158).

A determination made by the adjudicator on a reference made to him under Sch 22 para 11(4)(b) may be varied or revoked by a further determination made by him if the matter is referred to him by the local authority or the relevant body (Sch 22 para 11(5A)(a) (as added (see notes 1, 4); and amended by SI 2010/1158) and before making the further determination, the adjudicator consults such persons as he considers appropriate (Sch 22 para 11(5A)(b) (as so added)). In determining whether to make a reference to the adjudicator under Sch 22 para 11(5A)(a), the local authority or the relevant body must have regard, in particular, to any guidance given from time to time by the Secretary of State: Sch 22 para 11(5B) (as added (see notes 1, 4); and amended by SI 2010/1158). School Standards and Framework Act 1998 Sch 22 para 11(1)(a) Sch 22 para 11(5) (see above) applies in relation to the further determination of any matter by the adjudicator, by virtue of Sch 22 para 11(5A), as it applies in relation to the original determination of the matter: Sch 22 para 11(5C) (as added: see notes 1, 4).

10 School Standards and Framework Act 1998 Sch 22 para 11(3)(a) (as added (see note 1); and amended by SI 2010/1158).

11 School Standards and Framework Act 1998 Sch 22 para 11(3)(b) (as added: see note 1).

12 School Standards and Framework Act 1998 Sch 22 para 11(6)(a) (as added (see note 1); and amended by SI 2010/1158).

13 School Standards and Framework Act 1998 Sch 22 para 11(4)(a), (6)(b) (Sch 22 para 11 as added (see note 1); Sch 22 para 11(4)(a) as substituted (see note 4); and amended by SI 2010/1158).

14 School Standards and Framework Act 1998 Sch 22 para 11(4)(b) (as added and substituted: see notes 1, 4).

1304. Disposal of land held for purposes of a school or 16 to 19 academy.

Where:

(1)   a freehold or leasehold interest[1] in land is held by a local authority[2];

(2)   the authority proposes to make a disposal[3] in respect of the land[4]; and

(3)   at any time in the period of eight years ending with the day on which the disposal is proposed to be made, the land was used wholly or mainly for the purposes of a school or a 16 to 19 academy[5],

the authority must not make the disposal unless the Secretary of State consents[6]. However, a disposal is not invalid only because it is made in contravention of this requirement[7] and a person acquiring land, or entering into a contract to acquire it[8], is not to be concerned to enquire whether the consent so required has been given[9].

Where a local authority has made a disposal in contravention[10] of the above provisions[11]:

(a)   in a case where the authority has made a disposal[12] because it has granted an option[13], the Secretary of State may by notice served on the option holder repudiate the option at any time before it is exercised[14];

(b)   in a case where the authority has made such a disposal because it has entered into a contract to dispose of land[15], the Secretary of State may by notice served on the other party to the contract repudiate it at any time before a conveyance of the land is executed[16];

(c)   in a case where the land has been transferred (whether or not in pursuance of an option or contract falling within head (a) or head (b) above, the Secretary of State may purchase the land compulsorily[17] and on completion of a compulsory purchase of land[18] the Secretary of State must transfer it to a person concerned with the running of an academy[19].

If the Secretary of State so acquires land by compulsory purchase, he is entitled to recover from the authority an amount equal to the aggregate of:

(i)   the compensation agreed or awarded in respect of the purchase[20];

(ii)   any interest payable by the Secretary of State in respect of the compensation[21]; and

(iii)   the costs and expenses incurred by the Secretary of State in connection with the making of the compulsory purchase order[22].

1   Where a freehold or leasehold interest in land is held by a local authority, the authority proposes to change the use of the land in such a way that (were the change made) the land would cease to be capable of use wholly or mainly for the purposes of a school or a 16 to 19 academy, and at any time in the period of eight years ending with the date of the proposed change of use the land was used wholly or mainly for the purposes of a school or a 16 to 19 academy, the authority must inform the Secretary of State of the proposal: Academies Act 2010 Sch 1 para 9(1), (2) (Sch 1 substituted by the Education Act 2011 Sch 14 para 1). As to the meaning of 'school' see PARA 91 (definition applied by the Academies Act 2010 s 17(4)); and as to the meaning of '16 to 19 academy' see PARA 346 note 13. As to the treatment of a dwelling-house used for occupation by a person employed to work at an educational institution as used for the purposes of a school see PARA 1341 note 4. As to the meaning of 'local authority' see PARA 25 and (in the context of the Academies Act 2010) PARA 351 note 3. As to the Secretary of State see PARA 58.
2   Academies Act 2010 Sch 1 para 4(1)(a) (as substituted: see note 1).
3   References in the Academies Act 2010 Sch 1 to a disposal of land are to the disposal of a freehold or leasehold interest in the land or to the grant of a lease in respect of the land: Sch 1 para 22(4) (as so substituted). References in Sch 1 to a disposal of land include references to a compulsory disposal, in the case of any premises held under a tenancy to which the Landlord and Tenant Act 1954 Pt 2 (ss 23–46) applies (see LANDLORD AND TENANT vol 63 (2012) PARA 817), the termination of the tenancy under Pt 2, entering into a contract to dispose of land, and granting an option to acquire a freehold or leasehold interest in land: Sch 1 para 22(5)(a)–(d) (as so substituted).
4   Academies Act 2010 Sch 1 para 4(1)(b) (as substituted: see note 1).
5   Academies Act 2010 Sch 1 para 4(1)(c) (as substituted: see note 1).
6   Academies Act 2010 Sch 1 para 4(2) (as substituted: see note 1). Sch 1 para 4(2) does not apply to a disposal made in pursuance of a contract made, or option granted, before 26 July 2002: Sch 1 para 4(3) (as so substituted). For the purposes of Sch 1 para 4(2) the consent of the Secretary of State may be given in relation to a particular case or class of case, and may be given subject to conditions: Sch 1 para 8 (as so substituted).
7   Ie in contravention of the Academies Act 2010 Sch 1 para 4(2) (see the text and note 6).
8   Academies Act 2010 Sch 1 para 4(4) (as substituted: see note 1).
9   Academies Act 2010 Sch 1 para 4(5) (as substituted: see note 1).
10 See note 7.
11 Academies Act 2010 Sch 1 para 5(1) (as substituted: see note 1).
12 Ie within the meaning of the Academies Act 2010 Sch 1 (see note 3).
13 See the Academies Act 2010 Sch 1 para 22(5)(d) (see note 3).
14 Academies Act 2010 Sch 1 para 5(2) (as substituted: see note 1). A repudiation under Sch 1 para 5(2) or 5(3) has effect when the notice is served, and as if the repudiation were made by the authority: Sch 1 para 5(4) (as so substituted).
15 Ie under the Academies Act 2010 Sch 1 para 22(5)(c) (see note 3).
16 Academies Act 2010 Sch 1 para 5(2) (as substituted: see note 1). See note 14.
17 Academies Act 2010 Sch 1 para 5(5) (as substituted: see note 1). The Acquisition of Land Act 1981 (see COMPULSORY ACQUISITION OF LAND vol 18 (2009) PARA 556) applies in relation

to the compulsory purchase of land under the Academies Act 2010 Sch 1 para 5(5): Sch 1
para 5(6) (as so substituted). The authority must provide the Secretary of State with such
information as the Secretary of State may require it to provide in connection with a compulsory
purchase under Sch 1 para 5(5): Sch 1 para 5(9) (as so substituted).
18 Ie under the Academies Act 2010 Sch 1 para 5(5) (see the text and note 17).
19 Academies Act 2010 Sch 1 para 5(7) (as substituted: see note 1).
20 Academies Act 2010 Sch 1 para 5(8)(a) (as substituted: see note 1).
21 Academies Act 2010 Sch 1 para 5(8)(b) (as substituted: see note 1).
22 Academies Act 2010 Sch 1 para 5(8)(c) (as substituted: see note 1).

B. DISPOSAL OF LAND BY FOUNDATION, VOLUNTARY OR FOUNDATION SPECIAL SCHOOLS

(A) Foundation, Voluntary or Foundation Special Schools in England

**1305.   Disposal of land by governing bodies of foundation, voluntary or
foundation special schools.** The governing body of a foundation, voluntary or
foundation special school[1] in England must give the Secretary of State[2] notice[3] of
its intention to dispose of any non-playing field land[4]:

(1)   acquired or transferred via specified statutory procedures[5];
(2)   acquired from a foundation body[6];
(3)   acquired from the Funding Agency for Schools[7];
(4)   acquired, or enhanced in value, wholly or partly by means of any
      maintenance, special purpose or capital grant[8];
(5)   acquired, or enhanced in value, wholly or partly by means of any grant
      made[9] on or after 1 April 2007 by the Secretary of State in relation to
      which the appropriate notice is given[10];
(6)   acquired, or enhanced in value, wholly or partly by means of
      expenditure incurred for the purposes of the school and treated by the
      local authority as expenditure of a capital nature[11]; or
(7)   acquired, or enhanced in value, wholly or partly with the proceeds of
      disposal of any land acquired or enhanced in value as mentioned in any
      of heads (1) to (6) above[12],

and upon receipt of the notice, the Secretary of State must decide whether to
make a direction[13] in respect of the land, and notify the governing body of that
decision[14]. The governing body may not dispose of the land until it has been
notified of the Secretary of State's decision[15] and if the Secretary of State decides
to make a direction in respect of the land, the governing body may not dispose of
the land except in accordance with the direction[16].

   Where the governing body receives a notification that the Secretary of State
has decided not to make a direction in respect of non-playing field land[17] it must
give the local authority[18] notice[19] of its intention to dispose of the land[20] and the
authority may, within the requisite period[21] (during which the disposal may not
in general be made[22]) give the governing body any or all of the following
notices[23]:

(a)   notice of its objection to the disposal, giving reasons for its objection[24];
(b)   notice of its objection to the proposed use of the publicly funded
      proceeds of disposal, giving reasons for its objection[25]; and
(c)   notice of its claim to the whole or a part of the publicly funded proceeds
      of disposal[26],

upon the giving of each of which the matter in question will be referred for
resolution[27] or determination[28] and disposal will be prevented or delayed until
specified requirements have been met[29]. If the disposal is ultimately made the
governing body must notify the authority that the disposal has been made and of

the amount of the proceeds of disposal[30], whereupon those proceeds of the disposal must be distributed in accordance with statute[31]. If the authority gave notice of its objection to the disposal[32] and the adjudicator has determined that he does not approve the disposal[33], the governing body may apply to the adjudicator for an order to be made by him requiring the land or any part of the land to be transferred to such local authority as he may specify[34].

1　As to foundation, voluntary and foundation special schools see PARA 106 et seq; and as to special schools generally see PARA 1041 et seq. As to the governing body of a maintained school see PARA 150 et seq.

2　As to the Secretary of State see PARA 58. As to the meaning of 'England' see PARA 7 note 3.

3　As to the giving of notice to the Secretary of State under the School Standards and Framework Act 1998 Sch 22 para A1A see Sch 22 para A19(A1); and PARA 1309 text to note 29.

4　See the School Standards and Framework Act 1998 Sch 22 para A1A(1), (3), (4) (Sch 22 Pt A1 (paras A1–A27) added by the Education and Inspections Act 2006 Sch 4 paras 1, 2; School Standards and Framework Act 1998 Sch 22 para A1A further added by the Education Act 2011 Sch 14 paras 2, 4). 'Non-playing field land' means land which does not include playing fields within the meaning of the School Standards and Framework Act 1998 s 77 (see PARA 1326): Sch 22 para A1A(2) (as so added). However these requirements (ie the provisions of Sch 22 para A1: see the text and notes 5–12) do not apply in the case of any disposal which is made by the governing body of a foundation or foundation special school after 25 May 2007 (ie the date on which these provisions were brought into force by the Education and Inspections Act 2006 (Commencement No 3 and Transitional Provisions and Savings) Order 2007, SI 2007/935, art 7(p)) and is a disposal to the trustees of the school made on the school becoming a school with a foundation established otherwise than under the School Standards and Framework Act 1998: Sch 22 para A1(2) (as so added). As to the meaning of 'the trustees' see PARA 1303 note 6.

5　School Standards and Framework Act 1998 Sch 22 paras A1(1)(a)–(c) (as added (see note 4); Sch 22 para A1(1)(b) amended by the Education Act 2011 Sch 14 paras 2, 3). The statutory procedures referred to are: transfers under the Education Act 1996 s 201(1)(a) (repealed); acquisitions under the School Standards and Framework Act 1998 Sch 3 para 2 (see PARA 1295), Sch 6 para 16 (repealed) (including that provision as applied by any enactment), Sch 22 para 5(4)(c), (4B)(d) (see PARAS 1320–1321) or Sch 22 para 8A (see PARA 1312); acquisitions under the Education and Inspections Act 2006 Sch 2 para 28(2) (including that provision as applied by any enactment) (see PARA 129); acquisitions under the Academies Act 2010 Sch 1 paras 15(3)(d) or Sch 1 para 16(6)(d) (see PARA 1343); and acquisitions under regulations made under the School Standards and Framework Act 1998 Sch 8 para 5 (repealed), the Education and Inspections Act 2006 s 24 by virtue of s 24(3)(b) (see PARA 136), or s 27 by virtue of s 27(2)(b) (see PARA 138): School Standards and Framework Act 1998 Sch 22 para A1(1)(a)–(c) (as so added and amended).

　　In Sch 22 paras A1(1), A13(1), (2), (3)(a), A24–A26, 1(1), 3(1), 4(3), references, in relation to the governing body or trustees of a foundation, voluntary or foundation special school and in relation to a time before 1 September 1999 (ie the appointed day: see PARA 106 note 3) to any land being acquired in a particular way are references to the land being acquired in that way by the governing body or trustees of that school at a time when it was a voluntary, grant-maintained or grant-maintained special school within the meaning of the Education Act 1996; and in the School Standards and Framework Act 1998 Sch 22 paras A1(1), 1(1), references, in relation to the governing body of a foundation, voluntary or foundation special school, to any land being acquired in a particular way, include references to the land being acquired in that way by the temporary governing body for the school: Sch 22 para 10(3)(a), (5) (Sch 22 para 10(3), (5) amended by the Education and Inspections Act 2006 Sch 4 paras 1, 15).

6　School Standards and Framework Act 1998 Sch 22 para A1(1)(d) (as added: see note 4). As to foundation bodies see PARA 108 note 6.

7　School Standards and Framework Act 1998 Sch 22 para A1(1)(e) (as added: see note 4). The Funding Agency for Schools was dissolved on 1 November 1999: see s 132(1); and the Funding Agency for Schools Dissolution Order 1999, SI 1999/2767.

8　School Standards and Framework Act 1998 Sch 22 para A1(1)(f) (as added: see note 4). The reference in the text to a maintenance, special purpose or capital grant is a reference to a maintenance, special purpose or capital grant within the meaning of the Education Act 1996 Pt III Ch 6 (ss 244–258) (repealed).

　　In the School Standards and Framework Act 1998 Sch 22 paras A1(1), A13(1), (2), (3)(a), A24–A26, 1(1), 3(1), 4(3) references, in relation to the governing body or trustees of a foundation, voluntary or foundation special school and in relation to a time before the appointed day, to any grant being provided in a particular way, are references to the grant being provided in that way to, the governing body or trustees of that school at a time when it was a voluntary, grant-maintained or grant-maintained special school within the meaning of the Education Act 1996: School Standards and Framework Act 1998 Sch 22 para 10(3)(b) (as amended: see note 5).

9 Ie made under the School Standards and Framework Act 1998 Sch 3 para 5 (including that provision as applied by any enactment) (see PARA 312).

10 School Standards and Framework Act 1998 Sch 22 para A1(1)(g) (as added: see note 4). The appropriate notice is notice under Sch 22 para A27 (as so added), which provides that where a grant is made on or after 1 April 2007 by the Secretary of State under Sch 3 para 5 (including that provision as applied by any enactment), the Secretary of State may within the period of six months beginning with the date upon which the grant is made give the body or other persons to whom the grant is made notice that any land acquired or enhanced in value, wholly or partly by means of the grant, is land falling within Sch 22 paras A1(1)(g), A7(1)(f) (see PARAS 1305–1306), Sch 22 para A13(1)(j) (see PARA 1307), and any land acquired wholly or partly by means of the grant is land falling within Sch 22 paras A24(1)(g), A25(1)(f), A26(1)(h) (see PARA 1311).

11 School Standards and Framework Act 1998 Sch 22 para A1(1)(h) (as added (see note 4); Sch 22 para A1(1)(h) amended by SI 2010/1158). The School Standards and Framework Act 1998 Sch 22 para A1(1)(h) does not apply in the case of any expenditure incurred on or after the appointed day unless the authority prepared an appropriate statement in relation to the expenditure and sent a copy of the statement to the governing body either before, or no later than 12 months after, the expenditure was incurred: Sch 22 para A1(3) (as so added). An 'appropriate statement' in relation to expenditure is a statement in writing which contains details of the amount of the expenditure, the acquisition or works funded (or to be funded) by such expenditure, and the total cost (or estimated total cost) of that acquisition or those works and indicates that the expenditure was being treated by the authority as expenditure of a capital nature: Sch 22 para A1(4) (as so added).

References in Sch 22 paras A1(1), A13(1), 1(1), 3(1), in relation to the governing body or trustees of a foundation, voluntary or foundation special school and in relation to a time before 1 September 1999 (ie the appointed day: see PARA 106 note 3), to any expenditure being incurred for the purposes of the school are references to such expenditure being incurred for the purposes of that school at a time when it was a voluntary, grant-maintained or grant-maintained special school within the meaning of the Education Act 1996: School Standards and Framework Act 1998 Sch 22 para 10(4) (amended by the Education and Inspections Act 2006 Sch 4 paras 1, 15).

12 School Standards and Framework Act 1998 Sch 22 para A1(1)(i) (as added: see note 4).

13 School Standards and Framework Act 1998 Sch 22 para A1A(5)(a) (as added: see note 4). The reference in the text to a direction is to one under the Academies Act 2010 Sch 1 para 12 (transfer to academy) (see PARA 1341).

14 School Standards and Framework Act 1998 Sch 22 para A1A(5)(b) (as added: see note 4).

15 School Standards and Framework Act 1998 Sch 22 para A1A(6) (as added: see note 4).

16 School Standards and Framework Act 1998 Sch 22 para A1A(7) (as added: see note 4).

17 School Standards and Framework Act 1998 Sch 22 para A2(1) (as added (see note 4); and substituted by the Education Act 2011 Sch 14 paras 2, 5). The reference in the text to a direction is to one under the School Standards and Framework Act 1998 Sch 22 para A1A(5)(b) (see the text and note 14).

18 As to the meaning of 'local authority' see PARA 25. See also note 34.

19 Such notification must specify the relevant capital expenditure upon which it is proposed the publicly funded proceeds of disposal are to be used (School Standards and Framework Act 1998 Sch 22 para A2(5)(a) (as added: see note 4)) and the estimated amount of the proceeds of disposal (Sch 22 para A2(5)(b) (as so added)). For the purposes of Sch 22 paras A2–A4, the 'publicly funded proceeds of disposal' means the proceeds of disposal which are attributable to the land having been acquired or enhanced in value, or both, as the case may be, as mentioned in the relevant provision of Sch 22 para A1(1) (see the text and notes 5–12): Sch 22 para A2(6) (as so added). As to the meanings of 'disposal' and 'proceeds of disposal' see PARA 1303 notes 2, 7. As to references to 'land' see PARA 116 note 18 (definition applied by virtue of s 142(8)).

For the purposes of Sch 22 paras A2–A4, 'relevant capital expenditure', in relation to a disposal of land by the governing body of a foundation, voluntary or foundation special school, means capital expenditure in relation to: the premises of the school (Sch 22 para A6(1)(a) (as so added)), any existing foundation, voluntary or foundation special school, city technology college, city college for the technology of the arts, or academy (Sch 22 para A6(1)(b) (as so added))); or any proposed foundation, voluntary or foundation special school, or academy (Sch 22 para A6(1)(c) (as so added)). For the purposes of Sch 22 para A6(1)(c) it is irrelevant whether proposals have yet been published under any enactment in respect of the proposed school or academy in question: Sch 22 para A6(2) (as so added). As to the meaning of 'academy' see PARA 346 note 7 (definition applied by virtue of s 142(8)).

The reference to 'capital expenditure' in the definition of 'relevant capital expenditure' in Sch 22 para A6 is a reference to expenditure which, if it were to be incurred by the governing body, would fall to be capitalised in accordance with proper accounting practices: Sch 22 para A21(1), (2)(a) (as so added). The Secretary of State may by regulations prescribe classes or descriptions of expenditure which are to be treated for the purposes of Sch 22 para A6 as being, or as not being, capital expenditure of any governing body, or any prescribed class or description of governing body (Sch 22 para A21(3)(a) (as so added)); and may by direction provide that expenditure of a particular governing body, which is expenditure of a particular class or description, is to be treated for the purposes of Sch 22 para A6 as being, or as not being, capital expenditure of that body (Sch 22 para A21(4)(a) (as so added)). At the date at which this volume states the law no such regulations had been made. Directions may be expressed to have effect in specified circumstances or subject to specified conditions: Sch 22 para A21(5) (as so added).

For the purposes of Sch 22 para A21 'proper accounting practices', in relation to a governing or foundation body, or to trustees, means those accounting practices which, whether by virtue of any enactment or by reference to any generally recognised published code or otherwise, are regarded as proper accounting practices to be followed in the keeping of accounts by that body, or as the case may be, those persons (Sch 22 para A22(1)(a) (as so added)), or which, whether by virtue of any enactment or by reference to any generally recognised published code or otherwise, are regarded as proper accounting practices to be followed in the keeping of accounts by the local authority to whom notice of the disposal in question is required to be given under Sch 22 para A2, Sch 22 para A8 (see PARA 1306) or Sch 22 para A14 (see PARA 1307) (Sch 22 para A22(1)(b), (2) (as so added; Sch 22 para A22(1)(b), (2) amended by SI 2010/1158)). In the event of conflict between the accounting practices falling within the School Standards and Framework Act 1998 Sch 22 para A22(1)(a) and those falling within Sch 22 para A22(1)(b), only those falling within Sch 22 para A22(1)(a) are to be regarded as proper accounting practices: Sch 22 para A22(3) (as so added).

20 School Standards and Framework Act 1998 Sch 22 para A2(4) (as added (see note 4); and amended by SI 2010/1158).
21 Ie the period of six weeks beginning with the date upon which the governing body gave notification of the disposal to the authority under the School Standards and Framework Act 1998 Sch 22 para A2(4) (see the text and note 4): Sch 22 para A2(8) (as added: see note 4).
22 The governing body may not make the disposal within the requisite period unless within that period the authority gives the governing body notice that it relinquishes any right to give notice under the School Standards and Framework Act 1998 Sch 22 para A2(7)(a) (see the text and note 16) in relation to the disposal or, in a case where the authority gives notice of its objection to the disposal in accordance with Sch 22 para A2(7)(a), the relevant requirements in relation to such a notice are met: Sch 22 para A2(10) (as added: see note 4).
23 School Standards and Framework Act 1998 Sch 22 para A2(7) (as added: see note 4). A notice given under Sch 22 para A2(7) may be withdrawn at any time by the authority giving the governing body notice to that effect: Sch 22 para A2(9) (as so added). As to the duty to have regard to guidance and other factors in the matter of giving notices see Sch 22 para A19; and PARA 1309.
24 School Standards and Framework Act 1998 Sch 22 para A2(7)(a) (as added: see note 4).
25 School Standards and Framework Act 1998 Sch 22 para A2(7)(b) (as added: see note 4).
26 School Standards and Framework Act 1998 Sch 22 para A2(7)(c) (as added: see note 4).
27 Where the authority gives the governing body notice of its objection to the disposal in accordance with the School Standards and Framework Act 1998 Sch 22 para A2(7)(a) (see the text and note 16), the governing body or the authority may refer the matter to the adjudicator for a determination by him as to whether he approves the disposal: Sch 22 para A3(1) (as added: see note 3). Before making a reference to the adjudicator under Sch 22 para A3(1), the governing body or, as the case may be, the authority, must give the other notice of its intention to make the reference (Sch 22 para A3(4) (as so added)), and on such a reference the adjudicator may determine the proportion (if any) of the proceeds of disposal that are or will be the publicly funded proceeds of disposal (Sch 22 para A3(5) (as so added)). As to the duty to have regard to guidance and other factors in the matter of references and applications to the adjudicator, the making of determinations by the adjudicator and the determination of the publicly funded

proceeds of disposal see Sch 22 para A19; and PARA 1309. As to the variation or revocation of determinations made by the adjudicator see Sch 22 para A20(1)–(3), (7); and PARA 1310.

28 Where the authority gives the governing body notice of its objection to the proposed use of the publicly funded proceeds of disposal in accordance with the School Standards and Framework Act 1998 Sch 22 para A2(7)(b) (see the text and note 25), or where the authority gives the governing body notice of its claim to the whole or a part of the publicly funded proceeds of disposal in accordance with Sch 22 para A2(7)(c) (see the text and note 26), the relevant capital expenditure upon which those proceeds are to be used (in the former case), and the amount of those proceeds which it is appropriate for the governing body to pay to the authority (the 'appropriate amount') (in the latter case), is to be determined: (1) by agreement between the governing body and the authority (Sch 22 para A3(2)(a), (3)(a) (as added: see note 4)); or (2) by the adjudicator where the governing body or the authority refers the matter to him for determination (Sch 22 para A3(2)(b)(i), (3)(b)(i) (as so added)) and by the time of his determination the matter has not been determined by agreement between the governing body and the authority (Sch 22 para A3(2)(b)(ii), (3)(b)(ii) (as so added)). As to the duty to have regard to guidance and other factors in the matter of the determination of the appropriate amount see Sch 22 para A19; and PARA 1309. Before making a reference to the adjudicator under Sch 22 para A3(2)(b) or (3)(b), the governing body or, as the case may be, the authority, must give the other notice of its intention to make the reference (Sch 22 para A3(4) (as so added)), and on such a reference the adjudicator may determine the proportion (if any) of the proceeds of disposal that are or will be the publicly funded proceeds of disposal (Sch 22 para A3(5) (as so added)).

29 If the authority gives notice of its objection to the disposal in accordance with the School Standards and Framework Act 1998 Sch 22 para A2(7)(a) (see the text and note 24), the governing body may not make the disposal on or after the expiry of the requisite period until the relevant requirements in relation to such a notice (ie that the adjudicator has approved the disposal on a reference made under Sch 22 para A3(1) (see note 27) or that the authority has withdrawn notice of its objection to the disposal in accordance with Sch 22 para A2(9) (see note 23)) are met: Sch 22 para A2(11), (12) (as added: see note 3). If the authority gives, in relation to the disposal in accordance with Sch 22 para A2(7), either or both of: (1) notice of its objection to the proposed use of the publicly funded proceeds of disposal under Sch 22 para A2(7)(b) (see the text and note 25); or (2) notice of its claim to the whole or a part of the publicly funded proceeds of disposal under Sch 22 para A2(7)(c) (see the text and note 26), the governing body may not use the publicly funded proceeds of disposal until the relevant requirements in relation to each notice so given are met: Sch 22 para A2(13) (as so added). The relevant requirements in relation to a notice given under Sch 22 para A2(7)(b) are met if the relevant capital expenditure upon which the publicly funded proceeds of disposal are to be used has been determined in accordance with Sch 22 para A3(2) (see the text and note 28), or the authority has withdrawn notice of its objection to the proposed use of the publicly funded proceeds of disposal in accordance with Sch 22 para A2(9) (see the text and note 23) (Sch 22 para A2(14) (as so added)), and the relevant requirements in relation to a notice given under Sch 22 para A2(7)(c) are met if the 'appropriate amount' has been determined in accordance with Sch 22 para A3(3) (see the text and note 28) or the authority has withdrawn notice of its claim in accordance with Sch 22 para A2(9) (Sch 22 para A2(15) (as so added)).

30 School Standards and Framework Act 1998 Sch 22 para A4(1), (2) (as added: see note 4).

31 Where the authority gave notice of its claim to the whole or a part of the publicly funded proceeds of disposal in accordance with the School Standards and Framework Act 1998 Sch 22 para A2(7)(c) (see the text and note 26), and the 'appropriate amount' has been determined in accordance with Sch 22 para A3(3) (see note 28) to be an amount greater than zero, the governing body must pay the 'appropriate amount' to the authority: Sch 22 para A4(3) (as added: see note 3). The governing body must ensure that the remaining publicly funded proceeds of disposal are used on the agreed relevant capital expenditure: Sch 22 para A4(4) (as so added). If the amount of the remaining publicly funded proceeds of disposal exceeds the amount of the agreed relevant capital expenditure, then the governing body must ensure that the surplus amount is used on relevant capital expenditure: Sch 22 para A4(5) (as so added). The 'agreed relevant capital expenditure' means: (1) in a case where no notice of objection to the proposed use of the publicly funded proceeds of disposal was given by the authority in accordance with Sch 22 para A2(7)(b) (see the text and note 25), or such a notice was so given and was then withdrawn in accordance with Sch 22 para A2(9) (see note 23), the relevant capital expenditure specified in the notification of the disposal given to the authority under Sch 22 para A2(4) (see the text and note 20) (Sch 22 para A4(6)(a) (as so added)); and (2) in a case where such notice of objection was so given and was not withdrawn, the relevant capital expenditure upon which the publicly funded proceeds of disposal are to be used as determined in accordance with Sch 22

para A3(2) (see the text and note 28) (Sch 22 para A4(6)(b) (as so added)). The 'remaining publicly funded proceeds of disposal' means the amount of the publicly funded proceeds of disposal which remains after deducting the 'appropriate amount' (if any) determined in accordance with Sch 22 para A3(3) (see note 28): Sch 22 para A4(7) (as so added). Schedule 22 para A4(3)–(5) are subject to Sch 22 para A2(13) (restriction on use of publicly funded proceeds of disposal where notices given under Sch 22 para A2(7)(b) or (c): see the text and notes 25–26): Sch 22 para A4(8) (as so added).

32 School Standards and Framework Act 1998 Sch 22 para A5(1)(a) (as added: see note 4). The reference in the text to the notice of objection to the disposal is to such notice given in accordance with the School Standards and Framework Act 1998 Sch 22 para A2(7)(a) (see the text and note 24).

33 School Standards and Framework Act 1998 Sch 22 para A5(1)(b) (as added: see note 4).

34 School Standards and Framework Act 1998 Sch 22 para A5(2) (as added: see note 4). The making of such an order will be subject to the payment by the transferee authority of such sum by way of consideration (if any) as the adjudicator determines to be appropriate: Sch 22 para A5(2) (as so added). Before making an application under Sch 22 para A5(2), the governing body must give notice of its intention to do so to the authority mentioned in Sch 22 para A5(1)(a) (see the text and note 32): Sch 22 para A5(3) (as so added; and amended by SI 2010/1158). For these purposes, 'local authority' includes a non-metropolitan district council for an area for which there is a county council: School Standards and Framework Act 1998 Sch 22 para A5(4) (as so added; Sch 22 para A5(4) further added by SI 2010/1158). As to the duty to have regard to guidance and other factors in determining the amount of the consideration to be paid under School Standards and Framework Act 1998 Sch 22 para A5 see Sch 22 para A19; and PARA 1309. As to the variation or revocation of orders made by an adjudicator under Sch 22 para A5 see Sch 22 para A20(4)–(7); and PARA 1310.

Where a transfer under Sch 22 paras A5, A11, A17, A23, 1(3)(a), 2(3)(a), 4(2), 5(4)(a), (4)(c), 6(2)(b), 8(2)(b) or Sch 22 para 8A relates to registered land it is the duty of the transferor to execute any such instrument under the Land Registration Act 2002, to deliver any such certificate under that Act, and to do such other things under that Act, as he would be required to execute, deliver or do in the case of a transfer by agreement between the transferor and the transferee: School Standards and Framework Act 1998 Sch 22 para 9(1) (amended by the Land Registration Act 2002 Sch 11 para 37; and the Education and Inspections Act 2006 Sch 4 paras 1, 14). As to registerable dispositions under the Land Registration Act 2002 see REAL PROPERTY AND REGISTRATION vol 87 (2010) PARA 427 et seq.

1306. Disposal of land by foundation bodies. A foundation body in England[1] must give the Secretary of State[2] notice[3] of its intention to dispose of any non-playing field land[4]:

(1) acquired via specified statutory procedures[5];

(2) acquired from the governing body of a maintained school[6];

(3) acquired from another foundation body[7];

(4) acquired, or enhanced in value, wholly or partly by means of any grant[8] provided by the Secretary of State on or after 25 May 2007[9];

(5) acquired, or enhanced in value, wholly or partly by means of any grant made[10] on or after 1 April 2007 by the Secretary of State in relation to which the appropriate notice is given[11];

(6) acquired, or enhanced in value, wholly or partly by means of expenditure incurred for the purposes of any of the schools comprising the group for which the body acts and treated by the local authority as expenditure of a capital nature[12]; or

(7) acquired, or enhanced in value, wholly or partly with the proceeds of disposal of any land acquired or enhanced in value as mentioned in any of heads (1) to (6) above[13],

and upon receipt of the notice, the Secretary of State must decide whether to make a direction[14] in respect of the land, and notify the foundation body of that decision[15]. The foundation body may not dispose of the land until it has been notified of the Secretary of State's decision[16] and if the Secretary of State decides to make a direction in respect of the land, the foundation body may not dispose of the land except in accordance with the direction[17].

Where a foundation body receives a notification that the Secretary of State has decided not to make a direction in respect of non-playing field land[18], the foundation body must give the local authority notice[19] of its intention to dispose of the land[20] and the authority may, within the requisite period[21] (during which the disposal may not in general be made[22]) give the foundation body any or all of the following notices[23]:

(a)   notice of its objection to the disposal, giving reasons for its objection[24];

(b)   notice of its objection to the proposed use of the publicly funded proceeds of disposal, giving reasons for its objection[25]; and

(c)   notice of its claim to the whole or a part of the publicly funded proceeds of disposal[26],

upon the giving of each of which the matter in question will be referred for resolution[27] or determination[28] and disposal will be prevented or delayed until specified requirements have been met[29]. If the disposal is ultimately made the foundation body must notify the authority that the disposal has been made and of the amount of the proceeds of disposal[30], whereupon those proceeds of the disposal must be distributed in accordance with statute[31]. If the authority gave notice of its objection to the disposal[32] and the adjudicator has determined that he does not approve the disposal[33], the foundation body may apply to the adjudicator for an order to be made by him requiring the land or any part of the land to be transferred to such local authority as he may specify[34].

1   As to the meaning of 'foundation body' see PARA 108 note 6. In these provisions a 'foundation body in England' means a foundation body where each of the schools comprising the group of schools for which the foundation body acts is maintained by a local authority in England: School Standards and Framework Act 1998 Sch 22 para A7(2) (Sch 22 Pt A1 (paras A1–A27) added by the Education and Inspections Act 2006 Sch 4 paras 1, 2). As to the meaning of 'England' see PARA 7 note 3. As to the meaning of 'local authority' see PARA 25. See also note 34.

2   As to the Secretary of State see PARA 58.

3   As to the giving of notice to the Secretary of State under the School Standards and Framework Act 1998 Sch 22 para A7A see Sch 22 para A19(A1); and PARA 1309 note 28.

4   See the School Standards and Framework Act 1998 Sch 22 paras A7(1), A7A(1), (3), (4) (as added (see note 1); Sch 22 para A7A further added by the Education Act 2011 Sch 14 para 7). 'Non-playing field land' means land which does not include playing fields within the meaning of the School Standards and Framework Act 1998 s 77 (see PARA 1326): Sch 22 para A7A(2) (as so added). However these requirements (ie the provisions of Sch 22 para A7) do not apply in the case of any disposal which is made by a foundation body after 25 May 2007 (ie the date on which these provisions were brought into force by the Education and Inspections Act 2006 (Commencement No 3 and Transitional Provisions and Savings) Order 2007, SI 2007/935, art 7(p)) and is a disposal to the trustees of a foundation or a foundation special school made on the school leaving the group for which the foundation body acts and becoming a school with a foundation established otherwise than under the School Standards and Framework Act 1998: Sch 22 para A7(3) (as so added). As to the meaning of 'the trustees' see PARA 1303 note 6.

5   School Standards and Framework Act 1998 Sch 22 paras A7(1)(a), (b) (as added: see note 1; Sch 22 para A7(1)(b) amended by the Education Act 2011 Sch 14 para 6). The statutory procedures referred to are: acquisitions under the School Standards and Framework Act 1998 Sch 3 paras 2, 4 (see PARAS 1295, 1296), Sch 3 para 9 (see PARA 311), Sch 6 paras 16, 20 (repealed) (including those provisions as applied by any enactment), Sch 21 paras 5, 6 (see PARA 1340), Sch 22 para 5(4B)(d) (see PARA 1321) and any regulations made under Sch 8 para 5 (repealed); acquisitions under the Education Act 2002 Sch 8 para 8(5) (repealed); acquisitions under the Education Act 2005 Sch 10 para 14(5) (repealed); acquisitions under the Education and Inspections Act 2006 Sch 2 paras 28(2), 31(1) (see PARAS 129, 131); acquisitions under the Academies Act 2010 Sch 1 paras 15(3)(d), 16(6)(d) (see PARAS 1343); and acquisitions under regulations made under the Education and Inspections Act 2006 s 24 by virtue of s 24(3)(b) (see PARA 136), or s 27 by virtue of s 27(2)(b) (see PARA 138): School Standards and Framework Act 1998 Sch 22 paras A7(1)(a), (b) (as so added and amended).

6   School Standards and Framework Act 1998 Sch 22 para A7(1)(c) (as added: see note 1). As to the governing body of a maintained school, in relation to England, see PARA 150 et seq.

7   School Standards and Framework Act 1998 Sch 22 para A7(1)(d) (as added: see note 1).

8   Ie other than a grant made on or after 1 April 2007 under the School Standards and Framework Act 1998 Sch 3 para 5 (including that provision as applied by any enactment) (see PARA 312).

9   School Standards and Framework Act 1998 Sch 22 para A7(1)(e) (as added: see note 1); Education and Inspections Act 2006 (Commencement No 3 and Transitional Provisions and Savings) Order 2007, SI 2007/935.

10   Ie made under the School Standards and Framework Act 1998 Sch 3 para 5 (including that provision as applied by any enactment (see PARA 312)).

11   School Standards and Framework Act 1998 Sch 22 para A7(1)(f) (as added: see note 1). The appropriate notice is notice under Sch 22 para A27 (as so added); as to which see PARA 1305 note 10.

12   School Standards and Framework Act 1998 Sch 22 para A7(1)(g) (as added: see note 1). As to the meaning of 'the group' see PARA 108 note 6. Schedule 22 para A7(1)(g) does not apply in the case of any expenditure incurred on or after 1 September 1999 (ie the appointed day: see PARA 106 note 3) unless the authority prepared an appropriate statement in relation to the expenditure and sent a copy of the statement to the foundation body either before, or no later than 12 months after, the expenditure was incurred: Sch 22 para A7(3) (as so added). An 'appropriate statement' in relation to expenditure is a statement in writing which contains details of the amount of the expenditure, the acquisition or works funded (or to be funded) by such expenditure, and the total cost (or estimated total cost) of that acquisition or those works and indicates that the expenditure was being treated by the authority as expenditure of a capital nature: Sch 22 para A7(5) (as so added).

13   School Standards and Framework Act 1998 Sch 22 para A7(1)(h) (as added: see note 1).

14   School Standards and Framework Act 1998 Sch 22 para A7A(5)(a) (as added: see notes 1, 3). The reference in the text to a direction is to one under the Academies Act 2010 Sch 1 para 12 (transfer to academy) (see PARAS 1341–1342).

15   School Standards and Framework Act 1998 Sch 22 para A7A(5)(b) (as added: see notes 1, 3).

16   School Standards and Framework Act 1998 Sch 22 para A7A(6) (as added: see notes 1, 3).

17   School Standards and Framework Act 1998 Sch 22 para A7A(7) (as added: see notes 1, 3).

18   School Standards and Framework Act 1998 Sch 22 para A8(1) (as added (see note 1); and substituted by the Education Act 2011 Sch 14 para 8). The reference in the text to a direction is to one under the School Standards and Framework Act 1998 Sch 22 para A7A(5)(b) (see the text and note 15).

19   Such notification must specify the relevant capital expenditure upon which it is proposed the publicly funded proceeds of disposal are to be used (School Standards and Framework Act 1998 Sch 22 para A8(5)(a) (as added: see note 1)) and the estimated amount of the proceeds of disposal (Sch 22 para A8(5)(b) (as so added)). For the purposes of Sch 22 paras A8–A10, the 'publicly funded proceeds of disposal' means the proceeds of disposal which are attributable to the land having been acquired or enhanced in value, or both, as the case may be, as mentioned in the relevant provision: Sch 22 para A8(6) (as so added). As to the meanings of 'disposal' and 'proceeds of disposal' see PARA 1303 notes 2, 7. As to references to 'land' see PARA 84 note 9 (definition applied by virtue of s 142(8)).

     For the purposes of Sch 22 paras A8–A10, 'relevant capital expenditure', in relation to a disposal of land by a foundation body, means capital expenditure in relation to the premises of any of the schools comprising the group for which the body acts (Sch 22 para A12(1)(a) (as so added)), any existing foundation, voluntary or foundation special school, city technology college, city college for the technology of the arts, or academy (Sch 22 para A12(1)(b) (as so added)), or any proposed foundation, voluntary or foundation special school, or academy (Sch 22 para A12(1)(c) (as so added)). For the purposes of Sch 22 para A12(1)(c) it is irrelevant whether proposals have yet been published under any enactment in respect of the proposed school or academy in question: Sch 22 para A12(2) (as so added). As to foundation, voluntary and foundation special schools see PARA 106 et seq; and as to special schools generally see PARA 1041 et seq. As to the meaning of 'academy' see PARA 346 note 7 (definition applied by virtue of s 142(8)).

     The reference to 'capital expenditure' in the definition of 'relevant capital expenditure' in Sch 22 para A12 is a reference to expenditure which, if it were to be incurred by the foundation body, would fall to be capitalised in accordance with proper accounting practices: Sch 22 para A21(1), (2)(b) (as so added). The Secretary of State may by regulations prescribe classes or descriptions of expenditure which are to be treated for the purposes of Sch 22 para A12 as being, or as not being, capital expenditure of any foundation body, or any prescribed class or description of foundation body (Sch 22 para A21(3)(b) (as so added)); and may by direction provide that expenditure of a particular foundation body, which is expenditure of a particular class or description, is to be treated for the purposes of Sch 22 para A12 as being, or as not being, capital expenditure of that body (Sch 22 para A21(4)(b) (as so added)). At the date at which this volume states the law no such regulations had been made. Directions may be expressed to have effect in specified circumstances or subject to specified conditions: Sch 22 para A21(5) (as so added). As to the meaning of 'proper accounting practices' see PARA 1305 note 3.

20 School Standards and Framework Act 1998 Sch 22 para A8(4) (as added (see notes 1, 3); and amended by SI 2010/1158).

21 Ie the period of six weeks beginning with the date upon which the foundation body gave notification of the disposal to the authority under the School Standards and Framework Act 1998 Sch 22 para A8(4) (see the text and note 3): Sch 22 para A8(8) (as added: see note 1).

22 The foundation body may not make the disposal within the requisite period unless within that period the authority gives the foundation body notice that it relinquishes any right to give notice under the School Standards and Framework Act 1998 Sch 22 para A8(7)(a) (see the text and note 16) in relation to the disposal or, in a case where the authority gives notice of its objection to the disposal in accordance with Sch 22 para A8(7)(a), the relevant requirements in relation to such a notice are met: Sch 22 para A8(10) (as added: see note 1).

23 School Standards and Framework Act 1998 Sch 22 para A8(7) (as added: see note 1). A notice given under the School Standards and Framework Act 1998 Sch 22 para A8(7) may be withdrawn at any time by the authority giving the foundation body notice to that effect: Sch 22 para A8(9) (as so added). As to the duty to have regard to guidance and other factors in the matter of giving notices see Sch 22 para A19; and PARA 1309.

24 School Standards and Framework Act 1998 Sch 22 para A8(7)(a) (as added: see note 1).

25 School Standards and Framework Act 1998 Sch 22 para A8(7)(b) (as added: see note 1).

26 School Standards and Framework Act 1998 Sch 22 para A8(7)(c) (as added: see note 1).

27 Where the authority gives the foundation body notice of its objection to the disposal in accordance with the School Standards and Framework Act 1998 Sch 22 para A8(7)(a) (see the text and note 24), the foundation body or the authority may refer the matter to the adjudicator for a determination by him as to whether he approves the disposal: Sch 22 para A9(1) (as added: see note 1). Before making a reference to the adjudicator under Sch 22 para A9(1), the foundation body or, as the case may be, the authority, must give the other notice of its intention to make the reference (Sch 22 para A9(4) (as so added)), and on such a reference the adjudicator may determine the proportion (if any) of the proceeds of disposal that are or will be the publicly funded proceeds of disposal (Sch 22 para A9(5) (as so added)). As to the duty to have regard to guidance and other factors in the matter of references and applications to the adjudicator, the making of determinations by the adjudicator and the determination of the publicly funded proceeds of disposal see Sch 22 para A19; and PARA 1309. As to the variation or revocation of determinations made by the adjudicator see Sch 22 para A20(1)–(3), (7); and PARA 1310.

28 Where the authority gives the foundation body notice of its objection to the proposed use of the publicly funded proceeds of disposal in accordance with the School Standards and Framework Act 1998 Sch 22 para A8(7)(b) (see the text and note 25), or where the authority gives the foundation body notice of its claim to the whole or a part of the publicly funded proceeds of disposal in accordance with Sch 22 para A8(7)(c) (see the text and note 26), the relevant capital expenditure upon which those proceeds are to be used (in the former case), and the amount of those proceeds which it is appropriate for the foundation body to pay to the authority (the 'appropriate amount') (in the latter case), is to be determined: (1) by agreement between the foundation body and the authority (Sch 22 para A9(2)(a), (3)(a) (as added: see note 1)); or (2) by the adjudicator where the foundation body or the authority refers the matter to him for determination (Sch 22 para A9(2)(b)(i), (3)(b)(i) (as so added)) and by the time of his determination the matter has not been determined by agreement between the foundation body and the authority (Sch 22 para A9(2)(b)(ii), (3)(b)(ii) (as so added)). As to the duty to have regard to guidance and other factors in the matter of the determination of the appropriate amount see Sch 22 para A19; and PARA 1309. Before making a reference to the adjudicator under Sch 22 para A9(2)(b) or (3)(b), the foundation body or, as the case may be, the authority, must give the other notice of its intention to make the reference (Sch 22 para A9(4) (as so added)), and on such a reference the adjudicator may determine the proportion (if any) of the proceeds of disposal that are or will be the publicly funded proceeds of disposal (Sch 22 para A9(5) (as so added)).

29 If the authority gives notice of its objection to the disposal in accordance with the School Standards and Framework Act 1998 Sch 22 para A8(7)(a) (see the text and note 24), the foundation body may not make the disposal on or after the expiry of the requisite period until the relevant requirements in relation to such a notice (ie that the adjudicator has approved the disposal on a reference made under Sch 22 para A9(1) (see the text and note 27)) or that the

authority has withdrawn notice of its objection to the disposal in accordance with Sch 22 para A8(9) (see note 23)) are met: Sch 22 para A8(11), (12) (as added: see note 1). If the authority gives, in relation to the disposal in accordance with Sch 22 para A8(7), either or both of: (1) notice of its objection to the proposed use of the publicly funded proceeds of disposal under Sch 22 para A8(7)(b) (see the text and note 25); or (2) notice of its claim to the whole or a part of the publicly funded proceeds of disposal under Sch 22 para A8(7)(c) (see the text and note 26), the foundation body may not use the publicly funded proceeds of disposal until the relevant requirements in relation to each notice so given are met: Sch 22 para A8(13) (as so added). The relevant requirements in relation to a notice given under Sch 22 para A8(7)(b) are met if the relevant capital expenditure upon which the publicly funded proceeds of disposal are to be used has been determined in accordance with Sch 22 para A9(2) (see the text and note 28), or the authority has withdrawn notice of its objection to the proposed use of the publicly funded proceeds of disposal in accordance with Sch 22 para A8(9) (see note 23) (Sch 22 para A8(14) (as so added)), and the relevant requirements in relation to a notice given under Sch 22 para A8(7)(c) are met if the 'appropriate amount' has been determined in accordance with Sch 22 para A9(3) (see the text and note 28) or the authority has withdrawn notice of its claim in accordance with Sch 22 para A8(9) (Sch 22 para A8(15) (as so added)).

30 School Standards and Framework Act 1998 Sch 22 para A10(1), (2) (as added: see note 1).

31 Where the authority gave notice of its claim to the whole or a part of the publicly funded proceeds of disposal in accordance with the School Standards and Framework Act 1998 Sch 22 para A8(7)(c) (see the text and note 26), and the 'appropriate amount' has been determined in accordance with Sch 22 para A9(3) (see the text and note 28) to be an amount greater than zero, the foundation body must pay the 'appropriate amount' to the authority: Sch 22 para A10(3) (as added: see note 1). The foundation body must ensure that the remaining publicly funded proceeds of disposal are used on the agreed relevant capital expenditure: Sch 22 para A10(4) (as so added). If the amount of the remaining publicly funded proceeds of disposal exceeds the amount of the agreed relevant capital expenditure, then the foundation body must ensure that the surplus amount is used on relevant capital expenditure: Sch 22 para A10(5) (as so added). The 'agreed relevant capital expenditure' means: (1) in a case where no notice of objection to the proposed use of the publicly funded proceeds of disposal was given by the authority in accordance with Sch 22 para A8(7)(b) (see the text and note 25), or such a notice was so given and was then withdrawn in accordance with Sch 22 para A8(9) (see note 23), the relevant capital expenditure specified in the notification of the disposal given to the authority under Sch 22 para A8(4) (see the text and note 20) (Sch 22 para A10(6)(a) (as so added)); and (2) in a case where such notice of objection was so given and was not withdrawn, the relevant capital expenditure upon which the publicly funded proceeds of disposal are to be used as determined in accordance with Sch 22 para A9(2) (see the text and note 28) (Sch 22 para A10(6)(b) (as so added)). The 'remaining publicly funded proceeds of disposal' means the amount of the publicly funded proceeds of disposal which remains after deducting the 'appropriate amount' (if any) determined in accordance with Sch 22 para A9(3) (see the text and note 28): Sch 22 para A10(7) (as so added). The provisions of Sch 22 para A10(3)–(5) are subject to Sch 22 para A8(13) (restriction on use of publicly funded proceeds of disposal where notices given under Sch 22 para A8(7)(b) or (c): see note 29): Sch 22 para A10(8) (as so added).

32 School Standards and Framework Act 1998 Sch 22 para A11(1)(a) (as added: see note 1). The reference in the text to the notice of objection to the disposal is to such notice given in accordance with Sch 22 para A8(7)(a) (see the text and note 24).

33 School Standards and Framework Act 1998 Sch 22 para A11(1)(b) (as added: see note 1).

34 School Standards and Framework Act 1998 Sch 22 para A11(2) (as added: see note 1). The making of such an order will be subject to the payment by the transferee authority of such sum by way of consideration (if any) as the adjudicator determines to be appropriate: Sch 22 para A11(2) (as so added). Before making an application under Sch 22 para A11(2), the foundation body must give notice of its intention to do so to the authority mentioned in Sch 22 para A11(1)(a) (see the text and note 32): Sch 22 para A11(3) (as so added; and amended by SI 2010/1158). For these purposes, 'local authority' includes a non-metropolitan district council for an area for which there is a county council: School Standards and Framework Act 1998 Sch 22 para A11(4) (as so added; Sch 22 para A11(4) further added by SI 2010/1158).As to the duty to have regard to guidance and other factors in determining the amount of the consideration to be paid under the School Standards and Framework Act 1998 Sch 22 para A11 see Sch 22 para A19; and PARA 1309. As to the variation or revocation of orders made by an adjudicator under Sch 22 para A11 see Sch 22 para A20(4)–(7); and PARA 1310. As to the duties of the transferor in connection with transfers of registered land under this provision see PARA 1305 note 26.

1307. Disposal of land by trustees of foundation, voluntary or foundation special schools. The trustees of a foundation, voluntary or foundation special school in England[1] must give the Secretary of State[2] notice[3] of their intention to dispose of any non-playing field land[4]:

(1)   acquired via specified statutory procedures[5];

(2)   acquired, or enhanced in value, wholly or partly by means of expenditure incurred on or after the appointed day[6] for the purposes of the school and treated by the local authority as expenditure of a capital nature[7];

(3)   acquired from the Funding Agency for Schools[8];

(4)   acquired, or enhanced in value, wholly or partly by means of any maintenance, special purpose or capital grant[9] or any other grant paid[10] in respect of the provision of premises for the school[11];

(5)   acquired wholly or partly with the proceeds of disposal of any land acquired or enhanced in value as mentioned in head (3) or head (4) above[12];

(6)   acquired, or enhanced in value, wholly or partly by means of any grant made in pursuance of a special agreement[13];

(7)   acquired, or enhanced in value, wholly or partly by means of any grant made[14] on or after 1 April 2007 by the Secretary of State in relation to which the appropriate notice is given[15];

(8)   acquired, or enhanced in value, wholly or partly with the proceeds of disposal of any land acquired or enhanced in value as mentioned in head (7) above[16];

(9)   (in the case of a proposed disposal by the trustees of a foundation or foundation special school only) acquired by the trustees from the governing body[17] of the school or of another foundation or foundation special school which was land acquired by the governing body under specified statutory procedures[18], or acquired or enhanced in value wholly or partly with the proceeds of disposal of any land acquired under specified statutory procedures[19];

(10) (in the case of a proposed disposal by the trustees of a voluntary school only) acquired by the trustees from the governing body of the school which was land acquired by the governing body under a statutory transfer[20] or wholly or partly with the proceeds of disposal of any land so acquired[21], and transferred by the governing body to be held on trust by the trustees[22]; or

(11) (in the case of a proposed disposal by the trustees of a voluntary aided school which was, immediately before the appointed day[23], a controlled school[24] only) acquired, or enhanced in value, wholly or partly by means of expenditure incurred[25] pursuant to the establishment of such a school[26],

and on receipt of the notice, the Secretary of State must decide whether to make a direction[27] in respect of the land, and notify the trustees of that decision[28]. The trustees may not dispose of the land until they have been notified of the Secretary of State's decision[29] and if the Secretary of State decides to make a direction in respect of the land, the trustees may not dispose of the land except in accordance with the direction[30].

Where trustees receive a notification[31] that the Secretary of State has decided not to make a direction in respect of the land[32] they must give the local authority[33] notice[34] of their intention to dispose of the land[35] and the authority may, within the requisite period[36] (during which the disposal may not in general be made[37]) give the trustees any or all of the following notices[38]:

(a)   notice of its objection to the disposal, giving reasons for its objection[39];

(b)   notice of its objection to the proposed use of the publicly funded proceeds of disposal, giving reasons for its objection[40]; and

(c)   notice of its claim to the whole or a part of the publicly funded proceeds of disposal[41],

upon the giving of each of which the matter in question will be referred for resolution[42] or determination[43] and disposal will be prevented or delayed until specified requirements have been met[44]. If the disposal is ultimately made the trustees must notify the authority that the disposal has been made and of the amount of the proceeds of disposal[45], whereupon those proceeds of the disposal must be distributed in accordance with statute[46]. If the authority gave notice of its objection to the disposal[47] and the adjudicator has determined that he does not approve the disposal[48], the trustees may apply to the adjudicator for an order to be made by him requiring the land or any part of the land to be transferred to such local authority as he may specify[49].

1   As to foundation, voluntary and foundation special schools see PARA 106 et seq; and as to special schools generally see PARA 1041 et seq. As to the meaning of 'the trustees' see PARA 1303 note 6. As to the meaning of 'England' see PARA 7 note 3.

2   As to the Secretary of State see PARA 58.

3   As to the giving of notice to the Secretary of State under the School Standards and Framework Act 1998 Sch 22 para A13A see Sch 22 para A19(A1); and PARA 1309 note 28.

4   See the School Standards and Framework Act 1998 Sch 22 para A13A(6) (Sch 22 Pt A1 (paras A1–A27) added by the Education and Inspections Act 2006 Sch 4 paras 1, 2; School Standards and Framework Act 1998 Sch 22 para A13A added by the Education Act 2011 Sch 14 para 10). The School Standards and Framework Act 1998 Sch 22 para A13A (see the text and notes 27–30) applies to a disposal of land to which Sch 22 para A13(1), (2) or (3) (see the text and notes 5–26) applies if, or to the extent that, it comprises a disposal of non-playing field land which is not land acquired under the Education Act 1996 s 60 or s 61 (both repealed) or under the School Standards and Framework Act 1998 Sch 3 para 2 or para 4 (see PARAS 1295, 1296) by the trustees of an institution which is, or has at any time been, within the further education sector (as defined by the Education Act 1996 s 4(3): see PARA 555) (School Standards and Framework Act 1998 Sch 22 para A13A(1), (2), (5) (as so added). In Sch 22 paras A14–A17 (see the text and notes 44–49), A19 (see PARA 1309) references to the disposal are to the disposal by the trustees of the non-playing field land and references to the land are to that non-playing field land: Sch 22 para A13A(4) (as so added). 'Non-playing field land' means land which does not include playing fields within the meaning of s 77 (see PARA 1326): Sch 22 para A13A(3) (as so added). As to references to 'land' see PARA 84 note 9 (definition applied by virtue of s 142(8)).

5   School Standards and Framework Act 1998 Sch 22 paras A13(1)(a)–(d) (as added: see note 4; Sch 22 para 13(1)(d) amended by the Education Act 2011 Sch 14 para 9). The statutory procedures are: acquisitions under the Education Act 1996 ss 60, 61 (both repealed) or s 70 (repealed) (School Standards and Framework Act 1998 Sch 22 para A13(1)(a) (as so added)); acquisitions under the School Standards and Framework Act 1998 Sch 3 para 2 (see PARA 1295), Sch 6 para 16 (repealed) (including that provision as applied by any enactment), Sch 22 para 5(4B)(d) (see PARA 1321) or any regulations made under Sch 8 para 5 (repealed) (Sch 22 para A13(1)(b) (as so added)); acquisitions under Sch 3 para 4 (see PARA 1296) or Sch 3 para 9 (see PARA 311) or Sch 6 para 20 (repealed) (including that provision as applied by any enactment) (Sch 22 para A13(1)(c) (as so added)); acquisitions under the Education Act 2002 Sch 8 para 8(5) (repealed), the Education Act 2005 Sch 10 para 14(5) (repealed), the Education and Inspections Act 2006 Sch 2 para 28(2) or Sch 2 para 31(1) (including that provision as applied by any enactment) (see PARAS 129, 131); acquisitions under the Academies Act 2010 Sch 1 paras 15(3)(d), 16(6)(d) (see PARAS 1343); or acquisition under any regulations made under the Education and Inspections Act 2006 s 24 by virtue of s 24(3)(b) (see PARA 136) (School Standards and Framework Act 1998 Sch 22 para A13(1)(d) (as so added and amended)). As to references to land being acquired in a particular way for these purposes see PARA 1305 note 5.

6   Ie 1 September 1999 (see PARA 106 note 3).

7 School Standards and Framework Act 1998 Sch 22 para A13(1)(e) (as added: see note 4; and amended by SI 2010/1158). School Standards and Framework Act 1998 Sch 22 para A13(1)(e) does not apply in the case of any expenditure unless the authority prepared an appropriate statement in relation to the expenditure and sent a copy of the statement to the trustees either before, or no later than 12 months after, the expenditure was incurred: Sch 22 para A13(5) (as so added). An 'appropriate statement' in relation to expenditure is a statement in writing which contains details of the amount of the expenditure, the acquisition or works funded (or to be funded) by such expenditure, and the total cost (or estimated total cost) of that acquisition or those works and indicates that the expenditure was being treated by the authority as expenditure of a capital nature: Sch 22 para A13(6) (as so added). As to references to expenditure being incurred for the purposes of the school see PARA 1305 note 11.

8 School Standards and Framework Act 1998 Sch 22 para A13(1)(f) (as added: see note 4). The Funding Agency for Schools was dissolved on 1 November 1999: see s 132(1); and the Funding Agency for Schools Dissolution Order 1999, SI 1999/2767.

9 The reference in the text to a maintenance, special purpose or capital grant is a reference to a maintenance, special purpose or capital grant within the meaning of the Education Act 1996 Pt III Ch 6 (ss 244–258) (repealed). As to references to grants being provided in a particular way for these purposes see PARA 1305 note 8.

10 Ie under the Education Act 1996 s 216(2) (repealed).

11 School Standards and Framework Act 1998 Sch 22 para A13(1)(g) (as added: see note 4).

12 School Standards and Framework Act 1998 Sch 22 para A13(1)(h) (as added: see note 4).

13 School Standards and Framework Act 1998 Sch 22 para A13(1)(i) (as added: see note 4). 'Special agreement' was defined by the Education Act 1996 s 32(5) (repealed).

14 Ie made under the School Standards and Framework Act 1998 Sch 3 para 5 (including that provision as applied by any enactment) (see PARA 312).

15 School Standards and Framework Act 1998 Sch 22 para A13(1)(j) (as added: see note 4). The appropriate notice is notice under Sch 22 para A27 (as so added); as to which see PARA 1305 note 10.

16 School Standards and Framework Act 1998 Sch 22 para A13(1)(k) (as added: see note 4).

17 As to the governing body of a maintained school, in relation to England, see PARA 150 et seq.

18 School Standards and Framework Act 1998 Sch 22 para A13(2)(a) (as added: see note 4). The specified statutory procedures are: acquisition by transfer under the Education Act 1996 s 201(1)(a) (repealed); acquisition under any of the provisions mentioned in the School Standards and Framework Act 1998 Sch 22 para A13(1)(b) (see note 5) or under Sch 22 para 8A (see PARA 1312); or acquisition or enhancement in value, wholly or partly with the proceeds of disposal of land so acquired (Sch 22 para A13(2)(a)(i)–(iii) (as so added)). As to references to land being acquired in a particular way for these purposes see PARA 1305 note 5.

19 School Standards and Framework Act 1998 Sch 22 para A13(2)(b) (as added: see note 4). The specified statutory procedures are any of the provisions mentioned in Sch 22 para A13(1)(b) (see note 5): Sch 22 para A13(2)(b) (as so added).

20 School Standards and Framework Act 1998 Sch 22 para A13(3)(a)(i) (as added: see note 4). The transfer referred to is a transfer under the Education Act 1996 s 201(1)(a) (repealed). As to references to land being acquired in a particular way for these purposes see PARA 1305 note 5.

21 School Standards and Framework Act 1998 Sch 22 para A13(3)(a)(ii) (as added: see note 4).

22 School Standards and Framework Act 1998 Sch 22 para A13(3)(a) (as added: see note 4).

23 See note 6.

24 Ie a controlled school within the meaning of the Education Act 1996: see s 32 (repealed).

25 Ie under the Education Act 1996 s 63 or s 64 (both repealed).

26 School Standards and Framework Act 1998 Sch 22 para A13(3)(b), (4) (as added: see note 4).

27 School Standards and Framework Act 1998 Sch 22 para A13A(7)(a) (as added: see note 4). The reference in the text to a direction is to one under the Academies Act 2010 Sch 1 para 12 (transfer to academy) (see PARAS 1341–1342).

28 School Standards and Framework Act 1998 Sch 22 para A13A(7)(b) (as added: see note 4).

29 School Standards and Framework Act 1998 Sch 22 para A13A(8) (as added: see note 4).

30 School Standards and Framework Act 1998 Sch 22 para A13A(9) (as added: see note 4).

31 Ie under the School Standards and Framework Act 1998 Sch 22 para 13A(7)(b) (see the text and note 28).

32 School Standards and Framework Act 1998 Sch 22 para A14(1) (as added: see note 4; substituted by the Education Act 2011 Sch 14 paras 2, 11).

33 As to the meaning of 'local authority' see PARA 25. See also note 49.

34 Such notification must specify the relevant capital expenditure upon which it is proposed the publicly funded proceeds of disposal are to be used (School Standards and Framework Act 1998 Sch 22 para A14(7)(a) (as added: see note 4) and the estimated amount of the proceeds of

disposal (School Standards and Framework Act 1998 Sch 22 para A14(7)(b) (as so added)). For the purposes of Sch 22 paras A14–A16, the 'publicly funded proceeds of disposal' means the proceeds of disposal which are attributable to the land having been acquired or enhanced in value, or both, as the case may be, as mentioned in the relevant provision: Sch 22 para A14(8) (as so added). As to the meanings of 'disposal' and 'proceeds of disposal' see PARA 1303 notes 2, 7.

For the purposes of Sch 22 paras A14–A16, 'relevant capital expenditure', in relation to a disposal of land by the trustees of a foundation, voluntary or foundation special school, means capital expenditure in relation to the premises of the school (Sch 22 para A18(1)(a) (as so added)), any existing foundation, voluntary or foundation special school, city technology college, city college for the technology of the arts, or academy (Sch 22 para A18(1)(b) (as so added)), or any proposed foundation, voluntary or foundation special school, or academy (Sch 22 para A18(1)(c) (as so added)). For the purposes of Sch 22 para A18(1)(c) it is irrelevant whether proposals have yet been published under any enactment in respect of the proposed school or academy in question: Sch 22 para A18(2) (as so added). As to the meaning of 'academy' see PARA 346 note 7 (definition applied by virtue of s 142(8)).

The reference to 'capital expenditure' in the definition of 'relevant capital expenditure' in Sch 22 para A18 is a reference to expenditure which, if it were to be incurred by the trustees, would fall to be capitalised in accordance with proper accounting practices: Sch 22 para A21(1), (2)(c) (as so added). The Secretary of State may by regulations prescribe classes or descriptions of expenditure which are to be treated for the purposes of Sch 22 para A18 as being, or as not being, capital expenditure of any trustees, or any prescribed class or description of trustee (Sch 22 para A21(3)(c) (as so added)); and may by direction provide that expenditure of particular trustees, which is expenditure of a particular class or description, is to be treated for the purposes of Sch 22 para A18 as being, or as not being, capital expenditure of those persons (Sch 22 para A21(4)(c) (as so added)). At the date at which this volume states the law no such regulations had been made. Directions may be expressed to have effect in specified circumstances or subject to specified conditions: Sch 22 para A21(5) (as so added). As to the meaning of 'proper accounting practices' see PARA 1305 note 3.

35 School Standards and Framework Act 1998 Sch 22 para A14(6) (as added: see note 4).

36 Ie the period of six weeks beginning with the date upon which the trustees gave notification of the disposal to the authority under the School Standards and Framework Act 1998 Sch 22 para A14(6) (see the text and note 35): Sch 22 para A14(10) (as added: see note 4).

37 The trustees may not make the disposal within the requisite period unless within that period the authority gives the trustees notice that it relinquishes any right to give notice under the School Standards and Framework Act 1998 Sch 22 para A14(9)(a) (see the text and note 39) in relation to the disposal or, in a case where the authority gives notice of its objection to the disposal in accordance with Sch 22 para A14(9)(a), the relevant requirements in relation to such a notice are met: Sch 22 para A14(12) (as added: see note 4).

38 A notice given under the School Standards and Framework Act 1998 Sch 22 para A14(9) may be withdrawn at any time by the authority giving the trustees notice to that effect: Sch 22 para A14(11) (as added: see note 4). As to the duty to have regard to guidance and other factors in the matter of giving notices see Sch 22 para A19; and PARA 1309.

39 School Standards and Framework Act 1998 Sch 22 para A14(9)(a) (as added: see note 4).

40 School Standards and Framework Act 1998 Sch 22 para A14(9)(b) (as added: see note 4).

41 School Standards and Framework Act 1998 Sch 22 para A14(9)(c) (as added: see note 4).

42 Where the authority gives the trustees notice of its objection to the disposal in accordance with the School Standards and Framework Act 1998 Sch 22 para A14(9)(a) (see the text and note 39), the trustees or the authority may refer the matter to the adjudicator for a determination by him as to whether he approves the disposal: Sch 22 para A15(1) (as added: see note 4). Before making a reference to the adjudicator under Sch 22 para A15(1), the trustees or, as the case may be, the authority, must give the other notice of its intention to make the reference (Sch 22 para A15(4) (as so added)), and on such a reference the adjudicator may determine the proportion (if any) of the proceeds of disposal that are or will be the publicly funded proceeds of disposal (Sch 22 para A15(5) (as so added)). As to the duty to have regard to guidance and other factors in the matter of references and applications to the adjudicator, the making of determinations by the adjudicator and the determination of the publicly funded proceeds of disposal see Sch 22 para A19; and PARA 1309. As to the variation or revocation of determinations made by the adjudicator see Sch 22 para A20(1)–(3), (7); and PARA 1310.

43 Where the authority gives the trustees notice of its objection to the proposed use of the publicly funded proceeds of disposal in accordance with the School Standards and Framework Act 1998 Sch 22 para A14(9)(b) (see the text and note 40), or where the authority gives the trustees notice of its claim to the whole or a part of the publicly funded proceeds of disposal in accordance with

Sch 22 para A14(9)(c) (see the text and note 41), the relevant capital expenditure upon which those proceeds are to be used (in the former case), and the amount of those proceeds which it is appropriate for the trustees or their successors to pay to the authority (the 'appropriate amount') (in the latter case), is to be determined: (1) by agreement between the trustees and the authority (Sch 22 para A15(2)(a), (3)(a) (as added: see note 4)); or (2) by the adjudicator where the trustees or the authority refer the matter to him for determination (Sch 22 para A15(2)(b)(i), (3)(b)(i) (as so added)) and by the time of his determination the matter has not been determined by agreement between the trustees and the authority (Sch 22 para A15(2)(b)(ii), (3)(b)(ii) (as so added)). As to the duty to have regard to guidance and other factors in the matter of the determination of the appropriate amount see Sch 22 para A19; and PARA 1309. Before making a reference to the adjudicator under Sch 22 para A15(2)(b) or (3)(b), the trustees or, as the case may be, the authority, must give the other notice of its intention to make the reference (Sch 22 para A15(4) (as so added)), and on such a reference the adjudicator may determine the proportion (if any) of the proceeds of disposal that are or will be the publicly funded proceeds of disposal (Sch 22 para A15(5) (as so added)).

44 If the authority gives notice of its objection to the disposal in accordance with the School Standards and Framework Act 1998 Sch 22 para A14(9)(a) (see the text and note 39), the trustees may not make the disposal on or after the expiry of the requisite period until the relevant requirements in relation to such a notice (ie that the adjudicator has approved the disposal on a reference made under Sch 22 para A15(1) (see the text and note 42)) or that the authority has withdrawn notice of its objection to the disposal in accordance with Sch 22 para A14(11) (see note 38)) are met: Sch 22 para A14(13), (14) (as added: see note 4). If the authority gives, in relation to the disposal in accordance with Sch 22 para A14(9), either or both of: (1) notice of its objection to the proposed use of the publicly funded proceeds of disposal under Sch 22 para A14(9)(b) (see the text and note 40); or (2) notice of its claim to the whole or a part of the publicly funded proceeds of disposal under Sch 22 para A14(9)(c) (see the text and note 41), the trustees may not use the publicly funded proceeds of disposal until the relevant requirements in relation to each notice so given are met: Sch 22 para A14(15) (as so added). The relevant requirements in relation to a notice given under Sch 22 para A14(9)(b) are met if the relevant capital expenditure upon which the publicly funded proceeds of disposal are to be used has been determined in accordance with Sch 22 para A15(2) (see note 43), or the authority has withdrawn notice of its objection to the proposed use of the publicly funded proceeds of disposal in accordance with Sch 22 para A14(11) (see note 38) (Sch 22 para A14(16) (as so added)), and the relevant requirements in relation to a notice given under Sch 22 para A14(9)(c) are met if the 'appropriate amount' has been determined in accordance with Sch 22 para A15(3) (see note 43) or the authority has withdrawn notice of its claim in accordance with Sch 22 para A14(11) (Sch 22 para A14(17) (as so added)).

45 School Standards and Framework Act 1998 Sch 22 para A16(1), (2) (as added: see note 4).

46 Where the authority gave notice of its claim to the whole or a part of the publicly funded proceeds of disposal in accordance with the School Standards and Framework Act 1998 Sch 22 para A14(9)(c) (see the text and note 41), and the 'appropriate amount' has been determined in accordance with Sch 22 para A15(3) (see note 43) to be an amount greater than zero, the trustees or their successors must pay the 'appropriate amount' to the authority: Sch 22 para A16(3) (as added: see note 4). The trustees and their successors must ensure that the remaining publicly funded proceeds of disposal are used on the agreed relevant capital expenditure: Sch 22 para A16(4) (as so added). If the amount of the remaining publicly funded proceeds of disposal exceeds the amount of the agreed relevant capital expenditure, then the trustees and their successors must each ensure that the surplus amount is used on relevant capital expenditure: Sch 22 para A16(5) (as so added). The 'agreed relevant capital expenditure' means: (1) in a case where no notice of objection to the proposed use of the publicly funded proceeds of disposal was given by the authority in accordance with Sch 22 para A14(9)(b) (see the text and note 40), or such a notice was so given and was then withdrawn in accordance with Sch 22 para A14(11) (see note 38), the relevant capital expenditure specified in the notification of the disposal given to the authority under Sch 22 para A14(6) (see the text and notes 33–35) (Sch 22 para A16(6)(a) (as so added)); and (2) in a case where such notice of objection was so given and was not withdrawn, the relevant capital expenditure upon which the publicly funded proceeds of disposal are to be used as determined in accordance with Sch 22 para A15(2) (see note 43) (Sch 22 para A16(6)(b) (as so added)). The 'remaining publicly funded proceeds of disposal' means the amount of the publicly funded proceeds of disposal which remains after deducting the 'appropriate amount' (if any) determined in accordance with Sch 22 para A15(3) (see note 43): Sch 22 para A16(7) (as so added). Schedule 22 para A16(3)–(5) are subject to Sch 22 para A14(15) (restriction on use of publicly funded proceeds of disposal where notices given under Sch 22 para A14(9)(b) or (c): see the text and notes 40–41): Sch 22 para A16(8) (as so added).

47 Ie in accordance with the School Standards and Framework Act 1998 Sch 22 para A14(9)(a) (see the text and note 39).

48 School Standards and Framework Act 1998 Sch 22 para A17(1) (as added: see note 4).

49 School Standards and Framework Act 1998 Sch 22 para A17(2) (as added: see note 4). The making of such an order will be subject to the payment by the transferee authority of such sum by way of consideration (if any) as the adjudicator determines to be appropriate: Sch 22 para A17(2) (as so added). Before making an application under Sch 22 para A17(2), the trustees must give notice of their intention to do so to the local authority mentioned in Sch 22 para A17(1)(a) (see the text and note 48): Sch 22 para A17(3) (as so added; and amended by SI 2010/1158). For these purposes, 'local authority' includes a non-metropolitan district council for an area for which there is a country council: School Standards and Framework Act 1998 Sch 22 para A17(4) (as so added; further added by SI 2010/1158). As to the duty to have regard to guidance and other factors in determining the amount of the consideration to be paid under the School Standards and Framework Act 1998 Sch 22 para A17 see Sch 22 para A19; and PARA 1309. As to the variation or revocation of orders made by an adjudicator under Sch 22 para A17 see Sch 22 para A20(4)–(7); and PARA 1310. As to the duties of the transferor in connection with transfers of registered land under this provision see PARA 1305 note 26.

1308. Change of use of land by trustees of foundation, voluntary or foundation special schools. Where the trustees of a foundation, voluntary or foundation special school in England[1] wish, in the case of any non-playing field land[2] held by them for the purposes of the school, to use the land for purposes not connected with the provision of education in maintained schools or academies, they must give the Secretary of State[3] notice[4] of their intention to change the use of the land if it is land:

   (1)   acquired via specified statutory procedures[5];

   (2)   acquired, or enhanced in value, wholly or partly by means of expenditure incurred on or after the appointed day[6] for the purposes of the school and treated by the local authority as expenditure of a capital nature[7];

   (3)   acquired from the Funding Agency for Schools[8];

   (4)   acquired, or enhanced in value, wholly or partly by means of any maintenance, special purpose or capital grant[9] or any other grant paid[10] in respect of the provision of premises for the school[11];

   (5)   acquired wholly or partly with the proceeds of disposal of any land acquired or enhanced in value as mentioned in head (3) or (4) above[12];

   (6)   acquired, or enhanced in value, wholly or partly by means of any grant made in pursuance of a special agreement[13];

   (7)   acquired, or enhanced in value, wholly or partly by means of any grant made[14] on or after 1 April 2007 by the Secretary of State in relation to which the appropriate notice is given[15];

   (8)   acquired, or enhanced in value, wholly or partly with the proceeds of disposal of any land acquired or enhanced in value as mentioned in head (7) above[16];

   (9)   (in the case of a proposed change of use by the trustees of a foundation or foundation special school only) acquired by the trustees from the governing body[17] of the school or of another foundation or foundation special school which was land acquired by the governing body under specified statutory procedures[18], or acquired or enhanced in value wholly or partly with the proceeds of disposal of any land acquired under specified statutory procedures[19];

  (10)   (in the case of a proposed change of use by the trustees of a voluntary school only) acquired by the trustees from the governing body of the school which was land acquired by the governing body under a

statutory transfer[20] or wholly or partly with the proceeds of disposal of any land so acquired[21], and transferred by the governing body to be held on trust by the trustees[22]; or

(11) (in the case of a proposed change of use by the trustees of a voluntary aided school which was, immediately before the appointed day[23], a controlled school[24] only) acquired, or enhanced in value, wholly or partly by means of expenditure incurred[25] pursuant to the establishment of such a school[26],

and on receipt of the notice, the Secretary of State must decide whether to make a direction[27] in respect of the land, and notify the trustees of that decision[28]. The trustees may not change the use of the land until they have been notified of the Secretary of State's decision[29] and if the Secretary of State decides to make a direction in respect of the land, the trustees may not change the use of the land except in accordance with the direction[30].

Where trustees receive a notification[31] that the Secretary of State has decided not to make a direction in respect of the land[32] they must give the local authority[33] notice[34] of their intention to change the use of the land[35] and the authority may, within the requisite period[36] (during which the change of use may not in general be effected[37]) give the trustees notice[38] of its objection to the proposed purposes for which the land is to be used[39], giving reasons for its objection. Upon the giving of such notice the proposed change of use will be referred for determination[40] and the change of use will be prevented or delayed until specified requirements have been met[41]. If the change of use is ultimately effected the trustees must notify the authority[42], whereupon the land may only be used for the agreed purposes[43].

1 As to foundation, voluntary and foundation special schools see PARA 106 et seq; and as to special schools generally see PARA 1041 et seq. As to the meaning of 'the trustees' see PARA 1303 note 6. As to the meaning of 'England' see PARA 7 note 3.

2 School Standards and Framework Act 1998 Sch 22 para A13A (see the text and notes 4, 27–30) applies to a change of use of land to which Sch 22 para A13(1), (2) or (3) (see the text and notes 5–26) applies if, or to the extent that, it comprises a change of use of non-playing field land which is not land acquired under the Education Act 1996 s 60 or s 61 (both repealed) or under the School Standards and Framework Act 1998 Sch 3 para 2 or para 4 (see PARAS 1295, 1296) by the trustees of an institution which is, or has at any time been, within the further education sector (as defined by the Education Act 1996 s 4(3): see PARA 555) (School Standards and Framework Act 1998 Sch 22 paras A13(7) (amended by the Education Act 2011 Sch 14 paras 2, 9(1), (3)), School Standards and Framework Act 1998 A13A(1), (2), (5) (Sch 22 Pt A1 (paras A1–A27) added and Sch 22 para A13A further added by the Education and Inspections Act 2006 Sch 4 paras 1, 2 and the Education Act 2011 Sch 14 paras 2, 10 respectively). In the School Standards and Framework Act 1998 Sch 22 paras A14–A16 (see the text and notes 44–49), A17 (see PARA 1307), A19 (see PARA 1309) references to the change of use are to the change of use by the trustees of the non-playing field land and references to the land are to that non-playing field land: Sch 22 paras A13(7), A13A(4) (as so added and amended). As to the meaning of 'non-playing field land' see PARA 1307 note 4. As to references to 'land' see PARA 84 note 9 (definition applied by virtue of s 142(8)).

3 As to the Secretary of State see PARA 58. As to the meaning of 'academy' see PARA 346 note 7 (definition applied by s 142(8)). As to academies see PARA 345 et seq.

4 See the School Standards and Framework Act 1998 Sch 22 para A13A(6) (as added: see note 2). As to the giving of notice to the Secretary of State under the Sch 22 para A13A see Sch 22 para A19(A1); and PARA 1309 note 28.

5 School Standards and Framework Act 1998 Sch 22 paras A13(1)(a)–(d) (as added: see note 2; Sch 22 para 13(1)(d) amended by the Education Act 2011 Sch 14 para 9). The statutory procedures are: acquisitions under the Education Act 1996 ss 60, 61 (both repealed) or s 70 (repealed) (School Standards and Framework Act 1998 Sch 22 para A13(1)(a) (as so added)); acquisitions under the School Standards and Framework Act 1998 Sch 3 para 2 (see PARA 1295), Sch 6 para 16 (repealed) (including that provision as applied by any enactment), Sch 22

para 5(4B)(d) (see PARA 1321) or any regulations made under Sch 8 para 5 (repealed) (Sch 22 para A13(1)(b) (as so added)); acquisitions under Sch 3 para 4 (see PARA 1296) or Sch 3 para 9 (see PARA 311) or Sch 6 para 20 (repealed) (including that provision as applied by any enactment) (Sch 22 para A13(1)(c) (as so added)); acquisitions under the Education Act 2002 Sch 8 para 8(5) (repealed), the Education Act 2005 Sch 10 para 14(5) (repealed), the Education and Inspections Act 2006 Sch 2 para 28(2) or Sch 2 para 31(1) (including that provision as applied by any enactment) (see PARAS 129, 131); acquisitions under the Academies Act 2010 Sch 1 paras 15(3)(d), 16(6)(d) (see PARAS 1343); or acquisition under any regulations made under the Education and Inspections Act 2006 s 24 by virtue of s 24(3)(b) (see PARA 136) (School Standards and Framework Act 1998 Sch 22 para A13(1)(d) (as so added and amended)). As to references to land being acquired in a particular way for these purposes see PARA 1305 note 5.

6   Ie 1 September 1999 (see PARA 106 note 3).

7   School Standards and Framework Act 1998 Sch 22 para A13(1)(e) (as added: see note 2; and amended by SI 2010/1158). School Standards and Framework Act 1998 Sch 22 para A13(1)(e) does not apply in the case of any expenditure unless the authority prepared an appropriate statement in relation to the expenditure and sent a copy of the statement to the trustees either before, or no later than 12 months after, the expenditure was incurred: Sch 22 para A13(5) (as so added). As to the meaning of 'appropriate statement' in relation to expenditure see PARA 1307 note 7. As to references to expenditure being incurred for the purposes of the school see PARA 1305 note 11.

8   School Standards and Framework Act 1998 Sch 22 para A13(1)(f) (as added: see note 2). The Funding Agency for Schools was dissolved on 1 November 1999: see s 132(1); and the Funding Agency for Schools Dissolution Order 1999, SI 1999/2767.

9   The reference in the text to a maintenance, special purpose or capital grant is a reference to a maintenance, special purpose or capital grant within the meaning of the Education Act 1996 Pt III Ch 6 (ss 244–258) (repealed). As to references to grants being provided in a particular way for these purposes see PARA 1305 note 8.

10 Ie under the Education Act 1996 s 216(2) (repealed).

11 School Standards and Framework Act 1998 Sch 22 para A13(1)(g) (as added: see note 2).

12 School Standards and Framework Act 1998 Sch 22 para A13(1)(h) (as added: see note 2). As to the meanings of 'disposal' and 'proceeds of disposal' see PARA 1303 notes 2, 7.

13 School Standards and Framework Act 1998 Sch 22 para A13(1)(i) (as added: see note 2). 'Special agreement' was defined by the Education Act 1996 s 32(5) (repealed).

14 Ie made under the School Standards and Framework Act 1998 Sch 3 para 5 (including that provision as applied by any enactment (see PARA 312)).

15 School Standards and Framework Act 1998 Sch 22 para A13(1)(j) (as added: see note 2). The appropriate notice is notice under Sch 22 para A27 (as so added); as to which see PARA 1305 note 10.

16 School Standards and Framework Act 1998 Sch 22 para A13(1)(k) (as added: see note 2).

17 As to the governing body of a maintained school, in relation to England, see PARA 150 et seq.

18 School Standards and Framework Act 1998 Sch 22 para A13(2)(a) (as added: see note 2). The specified statutory procedures are: acquisition by transfer under the Education Act 1996 s 201(1)(a) (repealed); acquisition under any of the provisions mentioned in the School Standards and Framework Act 1998 Sch 22 para A13(1)(b) (see note 5) or under Sch 22 para 8A (see PARA 1312); or acquisition or enhancement in value, wholly or partly with the proceeds of disposal of land so acquired (Sch 22 para A13(2)(a)(i)–(iii) (as so added)). As to references to land being acquired in a particular way for these purposes see PARA 1305 note 5.

19 School Standards and Framework Act 1998 Sch 22 para A13(2)(b) (as added: see note 2). The specified statutory procedures are any of the provisions mentioned in Sch 22 para A13(1)(b) (see note 5): Sch 22 para A13(2)(b) (as so added).

20 School Standards and Framework Act 1998 Sch 22 para A13(3)(a)(i) (as added: see note 2). The transfer referred to is a transfer under the Education Act 1996 s 201(1)(a) (repealed). As to references to land being acquired in a particular way for these purposes see PARA 1305 note 5.

21 School Standards and Framework Act 1998 Sch 22 para A13(3)(a)(ii) (as added: see note 2).

22 School Standards and Framework Act 1998 Sch 22 para A13(3)(a) (as added: see note 2).

23 See note 6.

24 Ie a controlled school within the meaning of the Education Act 1996: see s 32 (repealed).

25 Ie under the Education Act 1996 s 63 (repealed) or s 64 (repealed).

26 School Standards and Framework Act 1998 Sch 22 para A13(3)(b), (4) (as added: see note 2).

27 School Standards and Framework Act 1998 Sch 22 para A13A(7)(a) (as added: see note 2). The reference in the text to a direction is to one under the Academies Act 2010 Sch 1 para 12 (transfer to academy) (see PARAS 1341–1342).

28 School Standards and Framework Act 1998 Sch 22 para A13A(7)(b) (as added: see note 2).
29 School Standards and Framework Act 1998 Sch 22 paras A13(7), A13A(8) (as added and amended: see note 2).
30 School Standards and Framework Act 1998 Sch 22 paras A13(7), A13A(9) (as added and amended: see note 2).
31 Ie under the School Standards and Framework Act 1998 Sch 22 para 13A(7)(b) (see the text and note 28).
32 School Standards and Framework Act 1998 Sch 22 para A14(1) (as added: see note 3; substituted by the Education Act 2011 Sch 14 paras 2, 11).
33 As to the meaning of 'local authority' see PARA 25. See also note 49.
34 Such notification must specify the purposes for which it is proposed the land is to be used: School Standards and Framework Act 1998 Sch 22 para A14(7) (as so added; and modified by Sch 22 para A14(18)(a)).
35 School Standards and Framework Act 1998 Sch 22 paras A13(7), A14(6) (as added and amended: see note 2).
36 Ie the period of six weeks beginning with the date upon which the trustees gave notification of the change of use to the authority under the School Standards and Framework Act 1998 Sch 22 para A14(6) (see the text and note 35): Sch 22 paras A13(7), A14(10) (as added and amended: see note 2).
37 The trustees may not effect the change of use within the requisite period unless within that period the authority gives the trustees notice that it relinquishes any right to give notice under Sch 22 para A14(9)(a) (see the text and note 39) in relation to the change of use or, in a case where the authority gives notice of its objection to the change of use in accordance with Sch 22 para A14(9)(a), the relevant requirements in relation to such a notice are met: Sch 22 para A14(12) (as added: see note 2).
38 A notice given under the School Standards and Framework Act 1998 Sch 22 para A14(9) may be withdrawn at any time by the authority giving the trustees notice to that effect: Sch 22 para A14(11) (as added: see note 3). As to the duty to have regard to guidance and other factors in the matter of giving notices see Sch 22 para A19; and PARA 1309.
39 School Standards and Framework Act 1998 Sch 22 para A14(9)(b) (as added (see note 3); Sch 22 para A14(9) modified by Sch 22 para 14(18)(b)).
40 Where the authority gives the trustees notice of its objection to the proposed purposes for which the land is to be used in accordance with Sch 22 para A14(9)(b) (see the text and note 39), the purposes for which the land is to be used are to be determined: (1) by agreement between the trustees and the authority (Sch 22 para A15(2)(a) (as added (see note 2); and modified by Sch 22 para A15(6)); or (2) by the adjudicator where the trustees or the authority refer the matter to him for determination (Sch 22 para A15(2)(b)(i) (as so added; and modified by Sch 22 para A15(6)) and by the time of his determination the matter has not been determined by agreement between the trustees and the authority (Sch 22 para A15(2)(b)(ii) (as so added; and modified by Sch 22 para A15(6)). Before making a reference to the adjudicator under Sch 22 para A15(2)(b), the trustees or, as the case may be, the authority, must give the other notice of its intention to make the reference: Sch 22 para A15(4) (as so added). As to the duty to have regard to guidance and other factors in the matter of references and applications to the adjudicator and the making of determinations by the adjudicator see Sch 22 para A19; and PARA 1309. As to the variation or revocation of determinations made by the adjudicator see Sch 22 para A20(1)–(3), (7); and PARA 1310.
41 If the authority gives notice of its objection to the proposed purposes for which the land is to be used under the School Standards and Framework Act 1998 Sch 22 para A14(9)(b) (see the text and notes 27–29), the trustees may not use the land for purposes not connected with the provision of education in maintained schools until the relevant requirements in relation to each notice so given are met: Sch 22 para A14(15)(a) (as added (see note 2); and modified by Sch 22 para A14(18)(c)). The relevant requirements in relation to a notice given under Sch 22 para A14(9)(b) are met if the purposes for which the land is to be used have been determined in accordance with Sch 22 para A15(2) (see the text and note 30), or the authority has withdrawn notice of its objection to the proposed purposes for which the land is to be used in accordance with Sch 22 para A14(11) (see the text and note 29): Sch 22 para A14(16) (as so added; and modified by Sch 22 para A14(18)(d)).
42 School Standards and Framework Act 1998 Sch 22 para A16(1), (2) (as added (see note 2); and modified by Sch 22 para A16(9)(a)).
43 The trustees and their successors must ensure that the land is used for the agreed purposes: School Standards and Framework Act 1998 Sch 22 para A16(4) (as added (see note 2); and modified by Sch 22 para A16(9)(b)). The 'agreed purposes' means: (1) in a case where no notice of objection to the proposed purposes for which the land is to be used was given by the

authority in accordance with Sch 22 para A14(9)(b) (see the text and note 31), or such a notice was so given and was then withdrawn in accordance with Sch 22 para A14(11) (see the text and note 29), the proposed purposes specified in the notification of the change of use given to the authority under Sch 22 para A14(6) (see the text and notes 1–5) (Sch 22 para A16(6)(a) (as so added; and modified by Sch 22 para A16(9)(d)(i)–(iii))); and (2) in a case where such notice of objection was so given and was not withdrawn, the purposes for which the land is to be used as determined in accordance with Sch 22 para A15(2) (see the text and note 34) (Sch 22 para A16(6)(b) (as so added; and modified by Sch 22 para A16(9)(d)(iv))).

1309. Duty to have regard to guidance in making and consideration of disposals. A local authority[1], a governing body[2], a foundation body[3] and trustees[4] must have regard, in particular, to any guidance given from time to time by the Secretary of State[5] in determining[6] whether to give a notice, or make a reference or application to the adjudicator[7], or in determining[8] the publicly funded proceeds of disposal[9] or the 'appropriate amount'[10], and the adjudicator must also have regard, in particular, to any such guidance in determining[11] any such matter[12]. In addition to having regard to the applicable guidance[13], a local authority, a governing body, a foundation body, trustees and the adjudicator, must also, in determining[14] the publicly funded proceeds of disposal[15], the 'appropriate amount'[16] and the amount of the consideration (if any) to be[17] paid[18], have regard, in particular, to:

(1) in the case of any disposal, the value of the land as at the date of the determination[19];

(2) in the case of any disposal, any enhancement in value of the land attributable to expenditure on the land by the local authority or a relevant person[20];

(3) in the case of any disposal, any expenditure on the land by a relevant person[21];

(4) in the case of any disposal, any relevant payments[22] made by a relevant person to the local authority or the Secretary of State[23];

(5) in the case of any disposal, to the extent that they do not fall within head (3) or (4) above, any payments in respect of the acquisition of the land[24]; and

(6) in the case of certain specified disposals[25], the extent to which the proceeds of disposal mentioned in the provision in question were[26] publicly funded proceeds of disposal[27].

A governing body must have regard to any guidance given from time to time by the Secretary of State in determining whether, and how, to give notice[28] to the Secretary of State[29].

1   As to the meaning of 'local authority' see PARA 25.
2   As to the governing body of a maintained school, in relation to England, see PARA 150 et seq. As to the disposal of land by governing bodies of foundation, voluntary or foundation special schools see PARA 1305. As to references to 'land' see PARA 84 note 9 (definition applied by virtue of the School Standards and Framework Act 1998 s 142(8)). As to the meaning of 'England' see PARA 7 note 3.
3   As to the meaning of 'foundation body' see PARA 108 note 6. As to the disposal of land by foundation bodies see PARA 1306.
4   As to the disposal of land by trustees of foundation, voluntary or foundation special schools see PARA 1307; as to changes of use of such land see PARA 1308.
5   As to the Secretary of State see PARA 58.
6   Ie under any of the School Standards and Framework Act 1998 Sch 22 paras A2–A17 (see PARAS 1305–1308).
7   School Standards and Framework Act 1998 Sch 22 para A19(1)(a) (Sch 22 Pt A1 (paras A1–A27) added by the Education and Inspections Act 2006 Sch 4 paras 1, 2; and School Standards and Framework Act 1998 Sch 22 para A19(1), (3), (4), (7), (8) amended by SI 2010/1158).

8   Ie for the purposes of any of the School Standards and Framework Act 1998 Sch 22 paras A2–A17 (see PARAS 1305–1308).

9   As to the publicly funded proceeds of disposal see PARAS 1305 note 3, 1306 note 2, 1307 note 3. As to the meanings of 'disposal' and 'proceeds of disposal' see PARA 1303 notes 2, 7; and as to references to 'disposal' for these particular purposes see the School Standards and Framework Act 1998 Sch 22 paras A2(3), A8(3), A14(4); and PARAS 1305 note 14, 1306 note 14, 1307 note 28.

10 School Standards and Framework Act 1998 Sch 22 para A19(1)(b) (as added: see note 7). As to the 'appropriate amount' see PARAS 1305 note 20, 1306 note 20, 1307 note 34.

11 See note 8.

12 School Standards and Framework Act 1998 Sch 22 para A19(2) (as added: see note 7).

13 Ie guidance as required under the School Standards and Framework Act 1998 Sch 22 para A19(1)(b), (2) (see the text and notes 8–12).

14 See note 8.

15 School Standards and Framework Act 1998 Sch 22 para A19(3)(a) (as added and amended: see note 7).

16 School Standards and Framework Act 1998 Sch 22 para A19(3)(b) (as added: see note 7).

17 Ie under School Standards and Framework Act 1998 Sch 22 para A5 (see PARA 1305), para A11 (see PARA 1306) or para A17 (see PARA 1307).

18 School Standards and Framework Act 1998 Sch 22 para A19(3)(c) (as added: see note 7).

19 School Standards and Framework Act 1998 Sch 22 para A19(4)(a) (as added and amended: see note 7).

20 School Standards and Framework Act 1998 Sch 22 para A19(4)(b) (as added: see note 7). A 'relevant person' means: (1) in the case of a disposal to which Sch 22 para A2 (see PARA 1305) or Sch 22 para A14 (see PARA 1307) applies, the governing body or the trustees of the school in question (Sch 22 para A19(5)(a) (as so added)); and (2) in the case of a disposal to which Sch 22 para A8 (see PARA 1306) applies, the foundation body in question (Sch 22 para A19(5)(b) (as so added)). As to the meaning of 'the trustees' see PARA 1303 note 6.

    The reference in Sch 22 para A19(5)(a) to the governing body or the trustees of the school in question includes: (a) where the school was established in pursuance of proposals published under s 28(2) (repealed) or s 28A(2) (repealed), the persons who published the proposals (Sch 22 para A19(7)(a) (as so added)); (b) where the school was established in pursuance of proposals published under the Education Act 2002 s 70 (repealed) or the Education Act 2005 s 66 (repealed) which were made by persons other than a local authority, the persons by whom the proposals were made (School Standards and Framework Act 1998 Sch 22 para A19(7)(b) (as so added; and as amended (see note 7))); and (c) where the school was established in pursuance of proposals published under the Education and Inspections Act 2006 s 7 (see PARA 111), s 10 (see PARA 112) or s 11 (see PARA 113), any persons, other than a local authority, by whom the proposals were treated for the purposes of Sch 2 (see PARA 118 et seq) as having been made (School Standards and Framework Act 1998 Sch 22 para A19(7)(c) (as so added and amended)).

    The reference in Sch 22 para A19(5)(b) to the foundation body in question includes: (i) where the school or any of the schools to which the land in question relates was established in pursuance of proposals published under s 28(2) or s 28A(2), the persons who published the proposals (Sch 22 para A19(8)(a) (as so added)); (ii) where the school or any of the schools to which the land in question relates was established in pursuance of proposals published under the Education Act 2002 s 70 or the Education Act 2005 s 66 which were made by persons other than a local authority, the persons by whom the proposals were made (School Standards and Framework Act 1998 Sch 22 para A19(8)(b) (as so added; and as amended (see note 7))); and (iii) where the school or any of the schools to which the land in question relates was established in pursuance of proposals published under the Education and Inspections Act 2006 s 7, s 10 or s 11, any persons, other than a local authority, by whom the proposals were treated for the purposes of Sch 2 as having been made (School Standards and Framework Act 1998 Sch 22 para A19(8)(c) (as so added and amended)).

21 School Standards and Framework Act 1998 Sch 22 para A19(4)(c) (as added: see note 7).

22 A 'relevant payment' means:
    (1)   in the case of any disposal, a payment in respect of the current school site or sites to which the land relates (School Standards and Framework Act 1998 Sch 22 para A19(6)(a) (as added: see note 7));
    (2)   in the case of any disposal, a payment under Sch 3 para 2(6) (see PARA 1295), Sch 6 para 16(5) (repealed) (including that provision as applied by any enactment), the Education Act 1996 s 60(4) (repealed) or the Education and Inspections Act 2006 Sch 2 para 28(5) (see PARA 129) (including that provision as applied by any enactment) (School Standards and Framework Act 1998 Sch 22 para A19(6)(b) (as so added)); and

(3)   in the case of a disposal of land falling within Sch 22 para A1(1)(f) or (1)(g) (see PARA
        1305), Sch 22 para A7(1)(e) or (1)(f) (see PARA 1306), or Sch 22 para A13(1)(g), (1)(i)
        or (1)(j) (see PARA 1307), a payment in respect of the grant mentioned in the provision
        in question (Sch 22 para A19(6)(c) (as so added)).

23 School Standards and Framework Act 1998 Sch 22 para A19(4)(d) (as added and amended: see
      note 7).
24 School Standards and Framework Act 1998 Sch 22 para A19(4)(e) (as added: see note 7).
25 Ie disposal falling within the School Standards and Framework Act 1998 Sch 22 para A1(1)(i)
      (see PARA 1305), Sch 22 para A7(1)(h) (see PARA 1306) or Sch 22 para A13(1)(h) or (1)(k),
      (2)(a)(iii) or (b), or (3)(a)(ii) (see PARA 1307).
26 Ie as defined by the School Standards and Framework Act 1998 Sch 22 para A2 (see PARA
      1305), Sch 22 para A8 (see PARA 1306) or Sch 22 para A14 (see PARA 1307).
27 School Standards and Framework Act 1998 Sch 22 para A19(4)(f) (as added: see note 7).
28 Ie under the School Standards and Framework Act 1998 Sch 22 paras A1A (see PARA 1305),
      A7A (see PARA 1306), A13A (see PARAS 1307, 1308).
29 School Standards and Framework Act 1998 Sch 22 para A19(A1) (as added (see note 7); further
      added by the Education Act 2011 Sch 14 paras 2, 12).

1310. Power to revoke determinations and orders. A determination made by
the adjudicator on a reference made to him[1] pursuant to a proposed disposal of
land may be varied or revoked by a further determination made by him if the
matter is referred to him by a relevant person[2] in relation to the determination[3]
and before making the further determination, the adjudicator consults such
persons as he considers appropriate[4].

An order made by the adjudicator on an application for the transfer of land to
another local authority where the existing local authority has objected to its
disposal[5] may be varied or revoked by a further order made by him if an
application for its variation or revocation is made to him by an appropriate
person[6] in relation to the order[7] and before making the further order, the
adjudicator consults such persons as he considers appropriate[8].

The duty to have regard to guidance and other factors[9] applies in relation to
any further determination by the adjudicator[10] of a relevant matter[11] as it applies
in relation to the original determination of the matter[12].

1   Ie under any of the School Standards and Framework Act 1998 Sch 22 paras A3–A15 (see PARAS
      1305–1307).
2   A 'relevant person' in relation to a determination means the local authority, governing body,
      foundation body or trustees who made the reference to the adjudicator in relation to which the
      determination was made (School Standards and Framework Act 1998 Sch 22 para A20(2)(a)
      (Sch 22 Pt A1 (paras A1–A27) added by the Education and Inspections Act 2006 Sch 4
      paras 1, 2; and School Standards and Framework Act 1998 Sch 22 para A20(2), (5) amended by
      SI 2010/1158)) or any other of those persons who could have made that reference (School
      Standards and Framework Act 1998 Sch 22 para A20(2)(b) (as so added)). As to the meaning of
      'local authority' see PARA 25; as to the governing body of a maintained school, in relation to
      England, see PARA 150 et seq (and as to the disposal of land by governing bodies of foundation,
      voluntary or foundation special schools see PARA 1305); as to the meaning of 'foundation body'
      see PARA 108 note 6 (and as to the disposal of land by foundation bodies see PARA 1306); as to
      the meaning of 'disposal' see PARA 1303 note 2; and as to the disposal of land by trustees of
      foundation, voluntary or foundation special schools see PARA 1307. As to references to 'land' see
      PARA 84 note 9 (definition applied by virtue of s 142(8)).
3   School Standards and Framework Act 1998 Sch 22 para A20(1)(a) (as added: see note 2). In
      determining whether to make a reference to the adjudicator under Sch 22 para A20(1)(a), a
      relevant person must have regard, in particular, to any guidance given from time to time by the
      Secretary of State: Sch 22 para A20(3) (as so added). As to the Secretary of State see PARA 58.
4   School Standards and Framework Act 1998 Sch 22 para A20(1)(b) (as added: see note 2).
5   Ie an order made by the adjudicator on an application under School Standards and Framework
      Act 1998 Sch 22 para A5 (see PARA 1305), para A11 (see PARA 1306) or para A17 (see PARA
      1307).
6   An 'appropriate person' in relation to an order made under the School Standards and
      Framework Act 1998 Sch 22 paras A5, A11 or A17 means: the governing body, the foundation

body or the trustees, as the case may be, who applied for the order, the local authority, or, if different from that authority, the local authority (within the meaning of Sch 22 paras A5 (see PARA 1305), A11 (see PARA 1306) or A17) (see PARA 1307) to whom land is required to be transferred under the order: Sch 22 para A20(5) (as added and amended: see note 2). As to the meaning of 'the trustees' see PARA 1303 note 6.

7 School Standards and Framework Act 1998 Sch 22 para A20(4)(a) (as added: see note 2). In determining whether to make an application to the adjudicator under Sch 22 para A20(4)(a), an appropriate person must have regard, in particular, to any guidance given from time to time by the Secretary of State: Sch 22 para A20(6) (as so added).
8 School Standards and Framework Act 1998 Sch 22 para A20(4)(b) (as added: see note 2).
9 Ie the School Standards and Framework Act 1998 Sch 22 para A19 (see PARA 1309).
10 Ie by virtue of the School Standards and Framework Act 1998 Sch 22 para A20(1) (see the text and notes 1–4) or Sch 22 para A20(4) (see the text and notes 5–8).
11 Ie any matter for the purposes of any of the School Standards and Framework Act 1998 Sch 22 paras A2–A17 (see PARAS 1305–1307).
12 School Standards and Framework Act 1998 Sch 22 para A20(7) (as added: see note 2).

1311. Land required by local authorities for certain purposes. A local authority[1] in England may apply to the adjudicator[2] for a transfer order in relation to publicly funded land[3] which:

(1) is held for the purposes of a foundation, voluntary or foundation special school by the governing body of the school[4];

(2) is held by a foundation body for the purposes of the group of schools for which it acts[5]; or

(3) is held, or held on trust, for the purposes of a foundation, voluntary or foundation special school by the trustees of the school[6].

A transfer order is an order requiring the land in relation to which it is made to be transferred by the body or trustees holding it to the authority, subject to the payment by the authority of such sum by way of consideration (if any) as the adjudicator determines to be appropriate[7], and where an application is made for a transfer order in relation to publicly funded land the adjudicator may make a transfer order[8] if he is satisfied that:

(a) the land is not required for the purposes of the school or, as the case may be, the schools in the group[9];

(b) the land is required by the authority for the stated purpose[10];

(c) the stated purpose is a qualifying purpose[11]; and

(d) it is appropriate for the land to be used for that purpose[12].

Where a transfer order is made, the authority must use the land to which it relates for the stated purpose[13]. Provision is made for the variation and revocation of transfer orders[14].

1 As to the meaning of 'local authority' see PARA 25.
2 Ie under the School Standards and Framework Act 1998 Sch 22 para A23 (see the text and notes 1, 3–14).
3 For the purposes of School Standards and Framework Act 1998 Sch 22 para A23, land held for the purposes of a foundation, voluntary or foundation special school by the governing body of the school is 'publicly funded land' if it is:
    (1) land acquired under a transfer under the Education Act 1996 s 201(1)(a) (repealed) (School Standards and Framework Act 1998 Sch 22 para A24(1)(a) (Sch 22 Pt A1 (paras A1–A27) added by the Education and Inspections Act 2006 Sch 4 paras 1, 2));
    (2) land acquired under any of: the School Standards and Framework Act 1998 Sch 3 para 2 (see PARA 1295); Sch 6 para 16 (repealed) (including that provision as applied by any enactment); Sch 22 paras 5(4)(c), (4B)(d) (see PARAS 1320, 1321) or Sch 22 para 8A (see PARA 1312); regulations made under Sch 8 para 5 (repealed); or the Education and Inspections Act 2006 Sch 2 para 28(2) (including that provision as applied by any enactment) (see PARA 129) (School Standards and Framework Act 1998 Sch 22 para A24(1)(b) (as so added));
    (3) land acquired under any regulations made under the Education and Inspections

Act 2006 s 24 by virtue of s 24(3)(b) (see PARA 136) or s 27 by virtue of s 27(2)(b) (see PARA 138) (School Standards and Framework Act 1998 Sch 22 para A24(1)(c) (as so added));

(4)   land acquired from a foundation body (Sch 22 para A24(1)(d) (as so added));

(5)   land acquired from the Funding Agency for Schools (Sch 22 para A24(1)(e) (as so added));

(6)   land acquired wholly by means of any maintenance, special purpose or capital grant within the meaning of the Education Act 1996 Pt III Ch 6 (ss 244–258) (repealed) or any grant paid under any regulations made under the School Standards and Framework Act 1998 Sch 32 para 4 (transitional provisions and savings) other than a grant paid under such regulations to the governing body of a voluntary aided school (Sch 22 para A24(1)(f) (as so added));

(7)   land acquired wholly or partly by means of any grant made under Sch 3 para 5 (including that provision as applied by any enactment) (see PARA 312) on or after 1 April 2007 by the Secretary of State in relation to which notice is given under Sch 22 para A27 (see PARA 1305 note 10) (Sch 22 para A24(1)(g) (as so added));

(8)   land acquired wholly by means of expenditure incurred for the purposes of the school and treated by the local authority as expenditure of a capital nature (Sch 22 para A24(1)(h) (as so added; and amended by SI 2010/1158)); or

(9)   land acquired wholly with the proceeds of disposal of any land acquired as mentioned in any of heads (1) to (8) above (School Standards and Framework Act 1998 Sch 22 para A24(1)(i) (as so added)).

Schedule 22 para A24(1)(h) (see head (8) above) does not apply in the case of any expenditure incurred on or after 1 September 1999 (ie the appointed day: see PARA 106 note 3) unless the authority prepared an appropriate statement in relation to the expenditure and sent a copy of the statement to the foundation body either before, or no later than 12 months after, the expenditure was incurred: Sch 22 para A24(2) (as so added). An 'appropriate statement' in relation to expenditure is a statement in writing which contains details of the amount of the expenditure, the acquisition or works funded (or to be funded) by such expenditure, and the total cost (or estimated total cost) of that acquisition or those works and indicates that the expenditure was being treated by the authority as expenditure of a capital nature: Sch 22 para A24(3) (as so added).

For the purposes of Sch 22 para A23, land held by a foundation body for the purposes of the group of schools for which it acts is 'publicly funded land' if it is:

(a)   land acquired under any of: the School Standards and Framework Act 1998 Sch 3 para 2 or 4 (see PARAS 1295, 1296) or Sch 3 para 9 (see PARA 311); Sch 6 para 16 or 20 (repealed) (including those provisions as applied by any enactment); Sch 21 para 5 or 6 (see PARA 1340); Sch 22 para 5(4B)(d) (see PARA 1321); and regulations made under Sch 8 para 5 (repealed) (Sch 22 para A25(1)(a) (as so added));

(b)   land acquired under any of: the Education Act 2002 Sch 8 para 8(5) (repealed); the Education Act 2005 Sch 10 para 14(5) (repealed); the Education and Inspections Act 2006 Sch 2 para 28(2) or 31(1) (see PARAS 129, 131); any regulations made under s 24 by virtue of s 24(3)(b) (see PARA 136); and any regulations made under s 27 by virtue of s 27(2)(b) (see PARA 138) (School Standards and Framework Act 1998 Sch 22 para A25(1)(b) (as so added));

(c)   land acquired from the governing body of a maintained school (Sch 22 para A25(1)(c) (as so added));

(d)   land acquired from another foundation body (Sch 22 para A25(1)(d) (as so added));

(e)   land acquired wholly by means of any grant provided by the Secretary of State on or after 1 September 1999 (ie the appointed day: see PARA 106 note 3) other than a grant made on or after 1 April 2007 under Sch 3 para 5 (including that provision as applied by any enactment) (see PARA 312), or any grant paid under any regulations made under Sch 32 para 4 (transitional provisions and savings) other than a grant paid under such regulations to the governing body of a voluntary aided school) (Sch 22 para A25(1)(e) (as so added));

(f)   land acquired wholly or partly by means of any grant made on or after 1 April 2007 by the Secretary of State under Sch 3 para 5 (including that provision as applied by any enactment) (see PARA 312) in relation to which notice is given in accordance with Sch 22 para A27 (see PARA 1305 note 10) (Sch 22 para A25(1)(f) (as so added));

(g)   land acquired wholly by means of expenditure incurred for the purposes of any of the schools comprising the group for which the body acts and treated by the local authority as expenditure of a capital nature (Sch 22 para A25(1)(g) (as so added; and amended by SI 2010/1158)); or

(h)   land acquired wholly with the proceeds of disposal of any land acquired as mentioned in any of heads (a) to (g) above (School Standards and Framework Act 1998 Sch 22 para A25(1)(h) (as so added)).

Schedule 22 para A25(1)(g) (see head (g) above) does not apply in the case of any expenditure incurred on or after the appointed day unless the authority prepared an appropriate statement in relation to the expenditure and sent a copy of the statement to the foundation body either before, or no later than 12 months after, the expenditure was incurred: Sch 22 para A25(2) (as so added). An 'appropriate statement' in relation to expenditure is a statement in writing which contains details of the amount of the expenditure, the acquisition or works funded (or to be funded) by such expenditure, and the total cost (or estimated total cost) of that acquisition or those works and indicates that the expenditure was being treated by the authority as expenditure of a capital nature: Sch 22 para A25(3) (as so added).

For the purposes of Sch 22 para A23, land held, or held on trust, for the purposes of a foundation, voluntary or foundation special school by the trustees of the school is 'publicly funded land' if it is:

(i)   land acquired under the Education Act 1996 ss 60, 61 (both repealed) or s 70 (repealed) (School Standards and Framework Act 1998 Sch 22 para A26(1)(a) (as so added));

(ii)   land acquired under any of Sch 3 para 2 (see PARA 1295), Sch 6 para 16 (repealed) (including that provision as applied by any enactment), Sch 22 para 5(4B)(d) (see PARA 1321) or any regulations made under Sch 8 para 5 (repealed) (Sch 22 para A26(1)(b) (as so added));

(iii)   land acquired under any of Sch 3 para 4 (see PARA 1296) or Sch 3 para 9 (see PARA 311) or Sch 6 para 20 (repealed) (including that provision as applied by any enactment) (Sch 22 para A26(1)(c) (as so added));

(iv)   land acquired under any of: the Education Act 2002 Sch 8 para 8(5) (repealed); the Education Act 2005 Sch 10 para 14(5) (repealed); the Education and Inspections Act 2006 Sch 2 para 28(2) or 31(1) (including that provision as applied by any enactment) (see PARAS 129, 131); or any regulations made under s 24 by virtue of s 24(3)(b) (see PARA 136) (School Standards and Framework Act 1998 Sch 22 para A26(1)(d) (as so added));

(v)   land acquired wholly by means of expenditure incurred on or after the appointed day for the purposes of the school and treated by the local authority as expenditure of a capital nature (Sch 22 para A26(1)(e) (as so added; and amended by SI 2010/1158));

(vi)   land acquired from the Funding Agency for Schools (School Standards and Framework Act 1998 Sch 22 para A26(1)(f) (as so added));

(vii)   land acquired wholly by means of any maintenance, special purpose or capital grant within the meaning of the Education Act 1996 Pt III Ch 6 (ss 244–258) (repealed), any grant paid under s 216(2) (repealed) or any grant paid under any regulations made under the School Standards and Framework Act 1998 Sch 32 para 4 (transitional provisions and savings) other than a grant paid under such regulations to the governing body of a voluntary aided school (Sch 22 para A26(1)(g) (as so added));

(viii)   land acquired wholly or partly by means of any grant made on or after 1 April 2007 by the Secretary of State under Sch 3 para 5 (including that provision as applied by any enactment) in relation to which notice is given in accordance with Sch 22 para A27 (as so added) (see PARA 1305) (Sch 22 para A26(1)(h) (as so added));

(ix)   land acquired wholly with the proceeds of disposal of any land acquired as mentioned in any of heads (vi) to (viii) above (Sch 22 para A26(1)(i) (as so added)); or

(x)   land acquired wholly by means of any grant made in pursuance of a special agreement (as defined by the Education Act 1996 s 32(5) (repealed)) (School Standards and Framework Act 1998 Sch 22 para A26(1)(j) (as so added)).

Schedule 22 para A26(1)(e) (see head (v) above) does not apply in the case of any expenditure unless the authority prepared an appropriate statement in relation to the expenditure and sent a copy of the statement to the trustees either before, or no later than 12 months after, the expenditure was incurred: Sch 22 para A26(6) (as so added). An 'appropriate statement' in relation to expenditure is a statement in writing which contains details of the amount of the expenditure, the acquisition or works funded (or to be funded) by such expenditure, and the total cost (or estimated total cost) of that acquisition or those works and indicates that the expenditure was being treated by the authority as expenditure of a capital nature: Sch 22 para A26(7) (as so added).

For the purposes of Sch 22 para A23, land held, or held on trust, for the purposes of a foundation or foundation special school by the trustees of the school is also 'publicly funded land' if it is:

(A)   land acquired by the trustees from the governing body of the school or of another foundation or foundation special school which was land acquired by the governing body under a transfer under the Education Act 1996 s 201(1)(a) (repealed), acquired by the governing body under any of the School Standards and Framework Act 1998 Sch 3 para 2 (see PARA 1295), Sch 6 para 16 (repealed) (including that provision as applied by any enactment), Sch 22 para 5(4B)(d) (see PARA 1321) or any regulations made under Sch 8 para 5 (repealed), or acquired by the governing body wholly with the proceeds of disposal of land so acquired (Sch 22 para A26(2)(a) (as so added)); or

(B) land acquired wholly with the proceeds of disposal of any land acquired under any of Sch 3 para 2 (see PARA 1295), Sch 6 para 16 (repealed) (including that provision as applied by any enactment), Sch 22 para 5(4B)(d) (see PARA 1321) or any regulations made under Sch 8 para 5 (repealed) (Sch 22 para A26(2)(b) (as so added)).

For the purposes of Sch 22 para A23, land held, or held on trust, for the purposes of a voluntary school by the trustees of the school is also 'publicly funded land' if it is:

(aa) land acquired by the governing body of the school under a transfer under the Education Act 1996 s 201(1)(a) (repealed) or wholly with the proceeds of disposal of any land so acquired, and transferred by the governing body to be held on trust by the trustees (Sch 22 para A26(3)(a) (as so added)); or

(bb) in the case of a voluntary aided school which was, immediately before the appointed day, a controlled school within the meaning of the Education Act 1996 (see s 32 (repealed)), land acquired wholly by means of expenditure incurred under s 63 (repealed) or s 64 (repealed) (Sch 22 para A26(3)(b), (4) (as so added)).

Land held, or held on trust, for the purposes of a foundation, voluntary or foundation special school by the trustees of the school is not 'publicly funded land' for the purposes of the School Standards and Framework Act 1998 Sch 22 para A23 if it is land acquired under the Education Act 1996 s 60 or s 61 (both repealed) or land acquired under the School Standards and Framework Act 1998 Sch 3 para 2 or 4 (see PARAS 1295, 1296), by the trustees of an institution which is, or has at any time been, within the further education sector (as defined by the Education Act 1996 s 4(3) (see PARA 555): School Standards and Framework Act 1998 Sch 22 para A26(5) (as so added).

As to references to 'land' see PARA 84 note 9 (definition applied by virtue of s 142(8)). As to the meanings of 'disposal' and 'proceeds of disposal' see PARA 1303 notes 2, 7. As to references to land being acquired in a particular way for these purposes see PARA 1305 note 5. As to references to grants being provided in a particular way for these purposes see PARA 1305 note 8. As to foundation, voluntary and foundation special schools see PARA 106 et seq; and as to special schools generally see PARA 1041 et seq. As to the governing body of a maintained school see PARA 150 et seq. As to the meaning of 'foundation body' see PARA 108 note 6. As to the meaning of 'the trustees' see PARA 1303 note 6. As to the Secretary of State see PARA 58.The Funding Agency for Schools was dissolved on 1 November 1999: see s 132(1); and the Funding Agency for Schools Dissolution Order 1999, SI 1999/2767.

4　School Standards and Framework Act 1998 Sch 22 para A23(1)(a) (as added: see note 3; and amended by SI 2010/1158).

5　School Standards and Framework Act 1998 Sch 22 para A23(1)(b) (as added: see note 3). As to the meaning of 'the group' see PARA 108 note 6.

6　School Standards and Framework Act 1998 Sch 22 para A23(1)(c) (as added: see note 3).

7　School Standards and Framework Act 1998 Sch 22 para A23(2) (as added: see note 3). In determining whether to make an application under Sch 22 para A23(1) for a transfer order, a local authority must have regard, in particular, to any guidance given from time to time by the Secretary of State (Sch 22 para A23(3) (as so added; and amended by SI 2010/1158)), and before making such an application in relation to publicly funded land the authority must give the body or trustees holding the land and the Secretary of State notice of the authority's intention to make the application (School Standards and Framework Act 1998 Sch 22 para A23(4)(a), (b) (as so added; and substituted by the Education Act 2011 Sch 14 paras 2, 13(1), (2))). An application must state the purpose for which the land to which it relates is required by the authority ('the stated purpose') (School Standards and Framework Act 1998 Sch 22 para A23(5) (as so added)), and in relation to the content of such an application or such notice, a local authority must have regard, in particular, to any guidance given from time to time by the Secretary of State (Sch 22 para A23(6) (as so added; and amended by the Education Act 2011 Sch 14 paras 2, 13(1), (3); and SI 2010/1158)). On receipt of a notice under the School Standards and Framework Act 1998 Sch 22 para A23(4)(b), the Secretary of State must decide whether to make a direction under the Academies Act 2010 Sch 1 para 12 (transfer to academy) (see PARAS 1341–1342) in respect of the land, and notify the local authority of that decision (School Standards and Framework Act 1998 Sch 22 para A23(6A) (as so added; Sch 22 para A23(6A), (6B) further added by the Education Act 2011 Sch 14 paras 2, 13(1), (4))) and if the Secretary of State decides to make such a direction in respect of the land, the local authority may not make an application under the School Standards and Framework Act 1998 Sch 22 para A23(1) (see the text and notes 1–6) for a transfer order in relation to the land (Sch 22 para A23(6B) (as so added)). As to the duties of the transferor in connection with transfers of registered land under this provision see PARA 1305 note 26.

8   Before making a transfer order the adjudicator must consult the body or trustees holding the land in relation to which the application for the transfer order is made (School Standards and Framework Act 1998 Sch 22 para A23(10) (as added: see note 3)), and in determining whether to make a transfer order, the adjudicator must have regard, in particular, to any guidance given from time to time by the Secretary of State (Sch 22 para A23(11) (as so added)).

9   School Standards and Framework Act 1998 Sch 22 para A23(7)(a) (as added: see note 3).

10   School Standards and Framework Act 1998 Sch 22 para A23(7)(b) (as added: see note 3).

11   School Standards and Framework Act 1998 Sch 22 para A23(7)(c) (as added: see note 3). For the purposes of Sch 22 para A23(7)(c) the stated purpose is a qualifying purpose if it falls within one or more of the following descriptions of purpose:

(1)   the land is required for the purposes of any school or institution which is, or is to be, maintained by the authority, or which they have power to assist (Sch 22 para A23(8)(a) (as so added));

(2)   the land is otherwise required for the purposes of the exercise of any of the education functions of the authority (Sch 22 para A23(8)(b) (as so added; and amended by SI 2010/1158));

(3)   the land is required for the provision of children's services by or on behalf of the authority in the exercise of any of its relevant functions (School Standards and Framework Act 1998 Sch 22 para A23(8)(c) (as so added; and amended by SI 2010/1158)).

For the purposes of the School Standards and Framework Act 1998 Sch 22 para A23(8)(c), by virtue of Sch 22 para A23(9) (as so added; amended by the Children and Families Act 2014 Sch 3 paras 67, 70; and SI 2010/1080), 'children's services' are services provided for or in relation to any of the following persons (whether or not they are also provided for or in relation to any other persons):

(a)   children;

(b)   persons aged 18 or 19;

(c)   persons over the age of 19 who are receiving services under the Children Act 1989 ss 23C–24D (see CHILDREN AND YOUNG PERSONS vol 10 (2012) PARAS 925–935); and

(d)   persons over the age of 19 but under the age of 25 who have a learning difficulty or disability, within the meaning of the Education Act 1996 s 15ZA(6), (7) (see PARA 32 note 11), and are receiving services under s 15ZA or the Apprenticeships, Skills, Children and Learning Act 2009 s 86 (see PARA 778) or s 87 (see PARA 779),

and 'relevant functions' means the functions described in the Education and Inspections Act 2006 s 135(1)(a), (c), (d) or (e) (see PARA 1289) (School Standards and Framework Act 1998 Sch 22 para A23(9) (as so added and amended)).

12   School Standards and Framework Act 1998 Sch 22 para A23(7)(d) (as added: see note 3).

13   School Standards and Framework Act 1998 Sch 22 para A23(12) (as added: see note 3).

14   A transfer order made by the adjudicator may be varied or revoked by a further order made by the adjudicator if an application for its variation or revocation is made to him by a relevant person in relation to the order (School Standards and Framework Act 1998 Sch 22 para A23(13)(a) (as added: see note 3)) and before making the further order, the adjudicator consults such persons as he considers appropriate (Sch 22 para A23(13)(b) (as so added)). A 'relevant person' in relation to a transfer order means the local authority who applied for the transfer order (Sch 22 para A23(14)(a) (as so added; and amended by SI 2010/1158)) or the body or trustees who held the land to which the order relates (School Standards and Framework Act 1998 Sch 22 para A23(14)(b) (as so added)). In determining whether to make an application to the adjudicator under Sch 22 para 23(13)(a), a relevant person must have regard, in particular, to any guidance given from time to time by the Secretary of State (Sch 22 para A23(15) (as so added)), and in determining whether to make a further order by virtue of Sch 22 para A23(13), the adjudicator must have regard, in particular, to any guidance given from time to time by the Secretary of State (Sch 22 para A23(11), (16) (as so added)).

1312. Transfer of land from trustee to governing body. Where the trustee of one or more foundation or foundation special schools[1] to which the requirements as to foundations[2] apply is a body corporate and:

(1)   the body corporate has under any enactment passed a resolution for its winding up[3];

(2)   a court has made an order for the winding up of the body corporate[4];

(3)   the body corporate has been removed[5] from the register of charities[6]; or

(4)   prescribed conditions relating to the ability of the body corporate to pay its debts or to its continued existence as a body corporate or as a charity are met[7],

the Secretary of State may make an order directing that any land acquired under specified statutory provisions[8] held by the body corporate on trust for one or more foundation or foundation special schools to which the requirements as to foundations[9] apply is to be transferred to[10], and by virtue of the order vest in:

(a)   the governing body of the school[11]; or

(b)   where the land is held on trust for two or more schools, such of the governing bodies of the schools as the Secretary of State thinks proper[12].

1   As to foundation and foundation special schools see PARA 106 et seq; and as to special schools generally see PARA 1041 et seq. As to the governing body of a maintained school see PARA 150 et seq.
     In a case where:
     (1)   proposals to establish a new foundation or foundation special school fall to be implemented under the Education and Inspections Act 2006 Sch 2 (see PARA 118 et seq) (School Standards and Framework Act 1998 Sch 22 para 8A(5)(a) (Sch 22 para 8A added by the Education and Inspections Act 2006 Sch 4 paras 1, 13)); and
     (2)   the local authority has before the school opening date transferred land to be held on trust for the school (School Standards and Framework Act 1998 Sch 22 para 8A(5)(b) (as so added; amended by SI 2010/1018); and SI 2010/1158),
     references in the School Standards and Framework Act 1998 Sch 22 para 8A to a foundation or foundation special school include references to a proposed such school, references to a governing body include references to a proposed governing body and for the purpose of Sch 22 para 8A(1), s 23A (see PARA 109) is to be taken to apply to the proposed school if it would apply to the school when it is established (Sch 22 para 8A(5) (as so added)). In Sch 22 para 8A 'foundation' means a foundation established otherwise than under the School Standards and Framework Act 1998: Sch 22 para 8A(6) (as so added). As to the meaning of 'local authority' see PARA 25. As to references to 'land' see PARA 84 note 9 (definition applied by virtue of s 142(8)).
2   Ie the requirements of the School Standards and Framework Act 1998 s 23A (see PARA 109).
3   School Standards and Framework Act 1998 Sch 22 para 8A(1), (2)(a) (as added: see note 1).
4   School Standards and Framework Act 1998 Sch 22 para 8A(2)(b) (as added: see note 1).
5   Ie under the Charities Act 2011 s 34 (see CHARITIES vol 8 (2015) PARA 307).
6   School Standards and Framework Act 1998 Sch 22 para 8A(2)(c) (as added (see note 1); and amended by the Charities Act 2011 Sch 7 para 79). The register of charities is kept under the Charities Act 2011 s 29 (see CHARITIES vol 8 (2015) PARA 307).
7   School Standards and Framework Act 1998 Sch 22 para 8A(2)(d) (as added: see note 1). Conditions may be prescribed under Sch 22 para 8A(2)(d) by reference to the opinion of the Secretary of State as to any prescribed matter: Sch 22 para 8A(3) (as so added). For the prescribed conditions see the School Organisation (Removal of Foundation, Reduction in Number of Foundation Governors and Ability of Foundation to Pay Debts) (England) Regulations 2007, SI 2007/3475, regs 20, 21.
8   Ie:
     (1)   any land acquired under the School Standards and Framework Act 1998 Sch 3 para 2 (see PARA 1295), Sch 6 para 16 (repealed) (including that provision as applied by any enactment), Sch 22 para 5(4B)(d) (see PARA 1321) or any regulations made under Sch 8 para 5 (repealed) (Sch 22 paras A13(1)(b), 8A(4) (Sch 22 para A13 added by the Education and Inspections Act 2006 Sch 4 paras 1, 2; School Standards and Framework Act 1998 Sch 22 para 8A(4) as added (see note 1).
     (2)   any land acquired by the trustees from the governing body of the school or of another foundation or foundation special school which was land acquired by the governing body by transfer under the Education Act 1996 s 201(1)(a) (repealed), land acquired by the governing body under any of the provisions referred to in head (1) above or under the School Standards and Framework Act 1998 Sch 22 para 8A, or land acquired or

enhanced in value, wholly or partly with the proceeds of disposal of land so acquired, or any land acquired or enhanced in value wholly or partly with the proceeds of disposal of any land acquired as mentioned in head (1) above (Sch 22 paras A13(2), 8A(4) (as so added)).

As to the meaning of 'the trustees' see PARA 1303 note 6. As to the meanings of 'disposal' and 'proceeds of disposal' see PARA 1303 notes 2, 7.

9 See note 2.
10 As to the duties of the transferor in connection with transfers of registered land under this provision see PARA 1305 note 26.
11 School Standards and Framework Act 1998 Sch 22 para 8A(2), (4)(a) (as added: see note 1).
12 School Standards and Framework Act 1998 Sch 22 para 8A(2), (4)(b) (as added: see note 1).

(B) Foundation or Voluntary Schools in Wales

1313. Disposal of land by governing bodies of foundation or voluntary schools. Where the governing body[1] of a foundation or voluntary school in Wales[2] proposes to make a disposal[3] of any land[4]:

(1) acquired via specified statutory procedures[5];
(2) acquired from a foundation body[6];
(3) acquired, or enhanced in value, wholly or partly by means of any maintenance, special purpose or capital grant[7];
(4) acquired, or enhanced in value, wholly or partly by means of expenditure incurred for the purposes of the school and treated by the local authority[8] as expenditure of a capital nature[9]; or
(5) acquired, or enhanced in value, wholly or partly with the proceeds of disposal of any land acquired or enhanced in value as mentioned in any of heads (1) to (4) above[10],

the governing body may not make any such disposal without the written consent of the Welsh Ministers[11], and where the governing body apply to the Welsh Ministers for their consent to any such disposal and the Ministers decide to give that consent, the Ministers may do one or more of the following, namely:

(a) require the land or any part of the land to be transferred to such local authority as the Ministers may specify, subject to the payment by that authority of such sum by way of consideration (if any) as the Ministers determine to be appropriate[12]; and
(b) give the governing body, when the land or any part of the land is disposed of, a direction to pay, either to the Ministers or to such local authority as the Ministers may specify, the whole or any part of the proceeds of disposal[13] and a direction as to the use to which the whole or any part of the proceeds of disposal should be put[14].

1 As to the governing body of a maintained school, in relation to Wales, see PARA 195.
2 As to foundation and voluntary schools see PARA 106 et seq. As to the meaning of 'Wales' see PARA 7 note 3.
3 Ie other than a disposal which is made by the governing body of a foundation or foundation special school after 7 June 2005 (School Standards and Framework Act 1998 Sch 22 para 1(1A)(a) (Sch 22 para 1(1)–(3) amended, and Sch 22 para 1(1A) added, by the Education Act 2005 Sch 17 paras 1, 2)) and is a disposal to the trustees of the school made on the school becoming a school with a foundation established otherwise than under the School Standards and Framework Act 1998 (Sch 22 para 1(1A)(b) (as so added; Sch 22 para 1(1), (1A)(b), (2), (3) amended by the Education and Inspections Act 2006 Sch 4 paras 1, 4)). 7 June 2005 is the date on which the Education Act 2005 Sch 17 paras 1, 2 were brought into force by s 125(2). As to the meanings of 'disposal' and 'the trustees' see PARA 1303 notes 2, 6.
4 School Standards and Framework Act 1998 Sch 22 para 1(1) (as amended (see note 3); and further amended by the School Standards and Organisation (Wales) Act 2013 Sch 5 para 19(1), (14)(a)(i)). As to references to 'land' see PARA 84 note 9 (definition applied by virtue of the School Standards and Framework Act 1998 s 142(8)).

5 School Standards and Framework Act 1998 Sch 22 para 1(1)(a) (as amended: see note 3). The specified statutory procedures are: acquisition by transfer under the Education Act 1996 s 201(1)(a) (repealed); acquisitions under the School Standards and Framework Act 1998 Sch 3 para 2 (see PARA 1295), Sch 6 para 16 (repealed) (including that provision as applied by any enactment), Sch 22 paras 5(4)(c), (4B)(d) (see PARAS 1320, 1321) or Sch 8 para 5 (repealed); acquisitions under the School Standards and Organisation (Wales) Act 2013 Sch 3 para 7 (provision of site and buildings for foundation or voluntary controlled school) (see PARA 143) as applied by s 76(1), or Sch 4 Pt 3 (transfer of land) (see PARA 143): School Standards and Framework Act 1998 Sch 22 para 1(1)(a) (as so amended; and further amended by the Education Act 2002 Sch 21 para 118), School Standards and Framework Act 1998 Sch 22 para 1(1)(aa) (added by the School Standards and Organisation (Wales) Act 2013 Sch 5 para 19(1), (14)(a)(ii)). As to references to land being acquired in a particular way for these purposes see PARA 1305 note 5.

6 School Standards and Framework Act 1998 Sch 22 para 1(1)(b). As to the meaning of 'foundation body' see PARA 108 note 6.

7 School Standards and Framework Act 1998 Sch 22 para 1(1)(d). The reference in the text to a maintenance, special purpose or capital grant is a reference to a maintenance, special purpose or capital grant within the meaning of the Education Act 1996 Pt III Ch 6 (ss 244–258) (repealed). As to references to grants being provided in a particular way for these purposes see PARA 1305 note 8.

8 As to the meaning of 'local authority' see PARA 25.

9 School Standards and Framework Act 1998 Sch 22 para 1(1)(e) (amended by SI 2010/1158). As to references to expenditure being incurred for the purposes of the school see PARA 1305 note 11. School Standards and Framework Act 1998 Sch 22 para 1(1)(e) does not apply in the case of any expenditure incurred on or after 1 September 1999 (ie the appointed day: see PARA 106 note 3) unless the authority prepared a statement in writing containing details of the amount of the expenditure, the acquisition or works funded (or to be funded) by such expenditure and the total cost (or estimated total cost) of that acquisition or those works and indicating that the expenditure was being treated by it as expenditure of a capital nature (Sch 22 para 1(5)(a)) and sent a copy of the statement to the governing body either before, or no later than 12 months after, the expenditure was incurred (Sch 22 para 1(5)(b)).

10 School Standards and Framework Act 1998 Sch 22 para 1(1)(f).

11 School Standards and Framework Act 1998 Sch 22 para 1(2) (as amended: see note 3). As to the Welsh Ministers see PARA 59.

12 School Standards and Framework Act 1998 Sch 22 para 1(3)(a) (as amended: see note 3). As to the duties of the transferor in connection with transfers of registered land under this provision see PARA 1305 note 26.

13 School Standards and Framework Act 1998 Sch 22 para 1(3)(b)(i) (as amended: see note 3). As to the meaning of 'proceeds of disposal' see PARA 1303 note 7. More than one direction may be given under Sch 22 para 1(3)(b)(i) in relation to a disposal of land within Sch 22 para 1(1) (see the text and notes 1–10) where it is just to do so, in particular where the disposal involves the creation of a lease: Sch 22 para 1(4).

14 School Standards and Framework Act 1998 Sch 22 para 1(3)(b)(ii).

1314. Disposal of land by foundation bodies. Where a foundation body in Wales[1] proposes to make a disposal[2] of any land[3]:

(1)   acquired via specified statutory procedures[4];

(2)   acquired from the governing body of a maintained school[5];

(3)   acquired from another foundation body[6];

(4)   acquired, or enhanced in value, wholly or partly by means of any grant provided by the Welsh Ministers on or after 1 September 1999[7];

(5)   acquired, or enhanced in value, wholly or partly by means of expenditure incurred for the purposes of any of the schools comprising the group for which the body acts and treated by the local authority as expenditure of a capital nature[8]; or

(6)   acquired, or enhanced in value, wholly or partly with the proceeds of disposal of any land acquired or enhanced in value as mentioned in any of heads (1) to (5) above[9],

it may not make any such disposal without the written consent of the Welsh Ministers[10], and where the governing body apply to the Welsh Ministers for their consent to any such disposal and the Ministers decide to give that consent, the Ministers may do either or both of the following, namely:

(a) require the land or any part of the land to be transferred to such local authority as the Ministers may specify, subject to the payment by that authority of such sum by way of consideration (if any) as the Ministers determine to be appropriate[11]; and

(b) give the foundation body, when the land or any part of the land is disposed of, a direction to pay, either to the Ministers or to such local authority as the Ministers may specify, the whole or any part of the proceeds of disposal[12] and a direction as to the use to which the whole or any part of the proceeds of disposal should be put[13].

1 As to the meaning of 'foundation body' see PARA 108 note 6. A 'foundation body in Wales' means a foundation body where each of the schools comprising the group of schools for which the foundation body acts is maintained by a local authority in Wales: School Standards and Framework Act 1998 Sch 22 para 2(1A) (Sch 22 para 2(1)–(3) amended, and Sch 22 para 2(1A) added, by the Education and Inspections Act 2006 Sch 4 paras 1, 5; and amended by SI 2010/1158). As to the meaning of 'local authority' see PARA 25. As to the meaning of 'Wales' see PARA 7 note 3.

2 School Standards and Framework Act 1998 Sch 22 para 2(1) (as amended: see note 1). As to the meaning of 'disposal' see PARA 1303 note 2.

3 As to references to 'land' see PARA 84 note 9 (definition applied by virtue of the School Standards and Framework Act 1998 s 142(8)).

4 School Standards and Framework Act 1998 Sch 22 para 2(1)(a) (Sch 22 para 2(1) as amended (see note 1); and further amended by the Education Act 2002 Sch 21 para 118). The statutory procedures referred to are: acquisitions under the School Standards and Framework Act 1998 Sch 3 para 2 or 4 (see PARAS 1295, 1296), Sch 3 para 9 (see PARA 311), Sch 6 para 16 or 20 (repealed) (including those provisions as applied by any enactment), Sch 21 para 5 or 6 (see PARA 1340), regulations made under Sch 8 para 5 (repealed); and acquisitions under the School Standards and Organisation (Wales) Act 2013 Sch 3 para 7 or 11, under either of those paragraphs as applied by s 76(1) or s 76(3), or under Sch 4 Pt 3: School Standards and Framework Act 1998 Sch 22 para 2(1)(a), (1)(aa) (Sch 22 para 2(1)(a) as so amended; Sch 22 para 2(1)(aa) added by the School Standards and Organisation (Wales) Act 2013 Sch 5 para 19(1), (14)(b)). As to references to land being acquired in a particular way for these purposes see PARA 1305 note 5.

5 School Standards and Framework Act 1998 Sch 22 para 2(1)(b). As to the governing body of a maintained school, in relation to Wales, see PARA 195. As to maintained schools generally see PARA 99 et seq.

6 School Standards and Framework Act 1998 Sch 22 para 2(1)(c).

7 School Standards and Framework Act 1998 Sch 22 para 2(1)(d) (as amended: see note 1). 1 September 1999 is the appointed day (see PARA 106 note 3). As to references to grants being provided in a particular way for these purposes see PARA 1305 note 8.

8 School Standards and Framework Act 1998 Sch 22 para 2(1)(e) (amended by SI 2010/1158). As to references to expenditure being incurred for the purposes of the school see PARA 1305 note 11. As to the meaning of 'the group' see PARA 108 note 6. School Standards and Framework Act 1998 Sch 22 para 2(1)(e) does not apply in the case of any expenditure incurred on or after 1 September 1999 unless the authority prepared a statement in writing containing details of the amount of the expenditure, the acquisition or works funded (or to be funded) by such expenditure and the total cost (or estimated total cost) of that acquisition or those works and indicating that the expenditure was being treated by it as expenditure of a capital nature (Sch 22 para 2(5)(a)) and sent a copy of the statement to the foundation body either before, or no later than 12 months after, the expenditure was incurred (Sch 22 para 2(5)(b)).

9 School Standards and Framework Act 1998 Sch 22 para 2(1)(f).

10 School Standards and Framework Act 1998 Sch 22 para 2(2) (as amended: see note 1). As to the Welsh Ministers see PARA 59.

11 School Standards and Framework Act 1998 Sch 22 para 2(3)(a) (as amended (see note 1); and further amended by the Education Act 2005 Sch 17 paras 1, 3). As to the duties of the transferor in connection with transfers of registered land under this provision see PARA 1305 note 26.

12 School Standards and Framework Act 1998 Sch 22 para 2(3)(b) (as amended (see note 1); and further amended by the Education Act 2005 Sch 17 paras 1, 3). As to the meaning of 'proceeds of disposal' see PARA 1303 note 7. More than one direction may be given under the School Standards and Framework Act 1998 Sch 22 para 2(3)(b) in relation to a disposal of land within Sch 22 para 2(1) (see the text and notes 1–9) where it is just to do so, in particular where the disposal involves the creation of a lease: Sch 22 para 2(4).

13 School Standards and Framework Act 1998 Sch 22 para 2(3)(b) (as amended: see note 1). See also note 12.

1315. Consent of the Welsh Ministers required for disposal of land by trustees of foundation schools. Where the trustees of a foundation school in Wales[1] propose to make a disposal[2] of any land[3]:

(1)   acquired via specified statutory procedures[4];

(2)   acquired, or enhanced in value, wholly or partly with the proceeds of disposal[5] of any land so acquired under head (1)[6]; or

(3)   any land which had been acquired by the governing body[7] via specified statutory procedures[8], or which had been acquired by the governing body, or enhanced in value, wholly or partly with the proceeds of disposal of land so acquired under head (1)[9], which was acquired by the trustees[10] from the governing body of the school or of another foundation school[11],

the trustees may not make any such disposal without the written consent of the Welsh Ministers[12], and where the trustees apply to the Ministers for their consent to any such disposal and the Ministers decide to give that consent, the Ministers may do one or more of the following, namely:

(a)   require the land or any part of the land to be transferred to such local authority[13] as the Ministers may specify, subject to the payment by that authority of such sum by way of consideration (if any) as the Ministers determine to be appropriate[14]; and

(b)   give the trustees, when the land or any part of the land is disposed of a direction to pay to such local authority as the Ministers may specify the whole or any part of the proceeds of the disposal[15], and a direction as to the use to which the whole or any part of the proceeds of disposal should be put[16].

1   As to foundation schools see PARA 106 et seq. As to the meaning of 'Wales' see PARA 7 note 3.

2   School Standards and Framework Act 1998 Sch 22 para 2A(1) (Sch 22 para 2A added by the Education Act 2005 Sch 17 paras 1, 4; School Standards and Framework Act 1998 Sch 22 para 2A(1), (3), (4) amended by the Education and Inspections Act 2006 Sch 4 paras 1, 6; School Standards and Framework Act 1998 Sch 22 para 2A(1)(aa) added by, and Sch 22 para 2A(1), (2) amended by, the School Standards and Organisation (Wales) Act 2013 Sch 5 para 19(1), (14)(c)). As to the meaning of 'disposal' see PARA 1303 note 2.

3   As to references to 'land' see PARA 84 note 9 (definition applied by virtue of the School Standards and Framework Act 1998 s 142(8)).

4   School Standards and Framework Act 1998 Sch 22 para 2A(1)(a) (as added and amended: see note 2). The specified statutory procedures are: acquisitions under the School Standards and Framework Act 1998 Sch 3 para 2 (see PARA 1295), Sch 6 para 16 (repealed) (including that provision as applied by any enactment), Sch 22 para 5(4B)(d) (see PARA 1321), regulations made under Sch 8 para 5 (repealed); or acquisitions under the School Standards and Organisation (Wales) Act 2013 Sch 3 para 7 (provision of site and buildings for foundation or voluntary controlled school) (see PARA 143), as applied by s 76(1), or Sch 4 Pt 3 (transfer of land) (see PARA 143): School Standards and Framework Act 1998 Sch 22 para 2A(1)(a), (1)(aa) (as so added and amended). As to references to land being acquired in a particular way for these purposes see PARA 1305 note 5.

5   As to the meaning of 'proceeds of disposal' see PARA 1303 note 7.

6   School Standards and Framework Act 1998 Sch 22 para 2A(1)(b) (as added and amended: see note 2).

7 As to the governing body of a maintained school, in relation to Wales, see PARA 195 et seq.
8 School Standards and Framework Act 1998 Sch 22 para 2A(1)(c), (2)(a) (as added and amended: see note 2). The specified statutory procedures are those mentioned in Sch 22 para 2A(1)(a), (1)(aa): see note 4.
9 School Standards and Framework Act 1998 Sch 22 para 2A(1)(c), (2)(b) (as added and amended: see note 2).
10 As to the meaning of 'the trustees' see PARA 1303 note 6.
11 School Standards and Framework Act 1998 Sch 22 para 2A(1)(c) (as added and amended: see note 2).
12 School Standards and Framework Act 1998 Sch 22 para 2A(3) (as added and amended: see note 2). As to the Welsh Ministers see PARA 59.
13 As to the meaning of 'local authority' see PARA 25.
14 School Standards and Framework Act 1998 Sch 22 para 2A(4)(a) (as added and amended: see note 2).
15 School Standards and Framework Act 1998 Sch 22 para 2A(4)(b)(i) (as added and amended: see note 2). More than one direction may be given under Sch 22 para 2A(4)(b)(i) in relation to a disposal of land within Sch 22 para 2A(1) (see the text and notes 1–11) where it is just to do so, in particular where the disposal involves the creation of a lease: Sch 22 para 2A(5) (as so added).
16 School Standards and Framework Act 1998 Sch 22 para 2A(4)(b)(ii) (as added: see note 2).

1316. Consent of the Welsh Ministers required for change of use of land by trustees of foundation schools. Where the trustees of a foundation school in Wales[1] wish, in the case of any land held[2] by them for the purposes of the school, to use the land for purposes not connected with the provision of education in maintained schools, they may not effect such a change of use without the written consent of the Welsh Ministers[3] if the land was:

(1) acquired via specified statutory procedures[4];
(2) acquired, or enhanced in value, wholly or partly with the proceeds of disposal[5] of any land so acquired under head (1)[6]; or
(3) any land which had been acquired by the governing body[7] via specified statutory procedures[8], or which had been acquired by the governing body, or enhanced in value, wholly or partly with the proceeds of disposal of land so acquired under head (1)[9], which was acquired by the trustees[10] from the governing body of the school or of another foundation[11],

and where the trustees apply to the Ministers for their consent to any such change of use and the Ministers decide to give that consent, the Ministers may do one or more of the following, namely:

(a) require the land or any part of the land to be transferred to such local authority[12] as the Ministers may specify, subject to the payment by that authority of such sum by way of consideration (if any) as the Ministers determine to be appropriate[13]; and
(b) give the trustees, when the change of use is effected, a direction to pay to such local authority as the Ministers may specify the whole or any part of the value of the land as at the date of such direction[14], and a direction as to the use to which the whole or any part of such a payment should be put[15].

1 As to foundation schools see PARA 106 et seq. As to the meaning of 'Wales' see PARA 7 note 3.
2 As to references to 'land' see PARA 84 note 9 (definition applied by virtue of the School Standards and Framework Act 1998 s 142(8)).
3 School Standards and Framework Act 1998 Sch 22 para 2A(3), (6)(a) (Sch 22 para 2A added by the Education Act 2005 Sch 17 paras 1, 4; School Standards and Framework Act 1998 Sch 22 para 2A(1), (3), (4), (6) amended by the Education and Inspections Act 2006 Sch 4 paras 1, 6; School Standards and Framework Act 1998 Sch 22 para 2A(1)(aa) added by, and Sch 22 para 2A(1), (2), (6) amended by, the School Standards and Organisation (Wales) Act 2013 Sch 5 para 19(1), (14)(c)). As to the Welsh Ministers see PARA 59.

4 School Standards and Framework Act 1998 Sch 22 para 2A(1)(a) (as added and amended: see note 3). The specified statutory procedures are: acquisitions under the School Standards and Framework Act 1998 Sch 3 para 2 (see PARA 1295), Sch 6 para 16 (repealed) (including that provision as applied by any enactment), Sch 22 para 5(4B)(d) (see PARA 1321), regulations made under Sch 8 para 5 (repealed); or acquisitions under the School Standards and Organisation (Wales) Act 2013 Sch 3 para 7 (provision of site and buildings for foundation or voluntary controlled school) (see PARA 143), as applied by s 76(1), or Sch 4 Pt 3 (transfer of land) (see PARA 143): School Standards and Framework Act 1998 Sch 22 para 2A(1)(a), (1)(aa) (as so added and amended). As to references to land being acquired in a particular way for these purposes see PARA 1305 note 5.

5 As to the meanings of 'disposal' and 'proceeds of disposal' see PARA 1303 notes 2, 7.

6 School Standards and Framework Act 1998 Sch 22 para 2A(1)(b) (as added and amended: see note 3).

7 As to the governing body of a maintained school, in relation to Wales, see PARA 195.

8 School Standards and Framework Act 1998 Sch 22 para 2A(1)(c),(2)(a) (as added and amended: see note 3). The specified statutory procedures are those mentioned in Sch 22 para 2A(1)(a), (1)(aa): see note 4.

9 School Standards and Framework Act 1998 Sch 22 para 2A(1)(c), (2)(b) (as added and amended: see note 3).

10 As to the meaning of 'the trustees' see PARA 1303 note 6.

11 School Standards and Framework Act 1998 Sch 22 para 2A(1)(c) (as added and amended: see note 3).

12 As to the meaning of 'local authority' see PARA 25.

13 School Standards and Framework Act 1998 Sch 22 para 2A(4)(a), (6)(a) (as added and amended: see note 3).

14 School Standards and Framework Act 1998 Sch 22 para 2A(4)(b)(i), (6)(b) (as added and amended: see note 3). More than one direction may be given under Sch 22 para 2A(4)(b)(i) in relation to a change of use within Sch 22 para 2A(1) (see the text and notes 1–11) where it is just to do so, in particular where the disposal involves the creation of a lease: Sch 22 para 2A(5) (as so added).

15 School Standards and Framework Act 1998 Sch 22 para 2A(4)(b)(ii), (6)(b) (as added and amended: see note 3).

1317. Disposal of land by trustees of foundation or voluntary schools: payment and use of proceeds. Where the trustees[1] of a foundation or voluntary school in Wales[2] propose to make a disposal[3] of any land[4]:

(1) acquired via specified statutory procedures[5];

(2) acquired, or enhanced in value, wholly or partly by means of expenditure incurred on or after 1 September 1999[6] for the purposes of the school and treated by the local authority[7] as expenditure of a capital nature[8];

(3) any land acquired by the governing body[9] of the school via specified statutory procedures[10] or wholly or partly with the proceeds of disposal[11] of any land so acquired[12], and transferred by the governing body to be held on trust by the trustees[13]; or

(4) (where a voluntary aided school in Wales was, immediately before 1 September 1999, a controlled school[14] only), acquired, or enhanced in value, wholly or partly by means of expenditure incurred via specified statutory procedures[15],

the trustees must notify the local authority that the relevant provisions apply to them and they or their successors must pay to the authority so much of the proceeds of disposal as may be determined to be just, either by agreement between them and the authority or, in default of agreement, by the Welsh Ministers[16].

Where the trustees of a foundation or voluntary school in Wales propose to make a disposal of any land:

(a) acquired, or enhanced in value, wholly or partly by means of any maintenance, special purpose or capital grant[17] or any other grant paid[18] in respect of the provision of premises for the school[19]; or

(b) any land acquired wholly or partly with the proceeds of disposal of any land so acquired or enhanced in value under head (a)[20],

the trustees must notify the local authority that the relevant provisions[21] apply to them and they and their successors must[22] undertake to the authority to use the proceeds of disposal for the purposes of the school[23] or for the purposes of any other existing foundation or voluntary school[24] or of any other proposed voluntary school, whether or not proposals have yet been published under any enactment in respect of that proposed school[25], and where it appears to the Welsh Ministers that the trustees have not given a suitable undertaking the Ministers may direct the trustees to pay to the authority either the whole or any part of the proceeds of disposal as the Ministers determine to be just[26].

Where the trustees of a foundation or voluntary school in Wales propose to make a disposal of any land acquired, or enhanced in value, wholly or partly by means of any grant made in pursuance of a special agreement[27], the governing body of the school must repay the grant[28] to the local authority by whom the school is maintained, unless the governing body and the authority otherwise agree[29].

1   As to the meaning of 'the trustees' see PARA 1303 note 6.
2   As to foundation and voluntary schools see PARA 106 et seq. As to the meaning of 'Wales' see PARA 7 note 3.
3   As to the meaning of 'disposal' see PARA 1303 note 2. Nothing in the School Standards and Framework Act 1998 Sch 22 para 3(1) applies in relation to any disposal to the extent that it is a disposal to which Sch 22 para 2A (see PARA 1315) applies: Sch 22 para 3(1), (2A) (Sch 22 para 3(1), (8)(b)(ii) amended by the Education Act 2002 Sch 21 para 118; School Standards and Framework Act 1998 Sch 22 para 3(1) amended, Sch 22 para 3(2A) added, by the Education Act 2005 Sch 17 paras 1, 5; School Standards and Framework Act 1998 Sch 22 para 3(1)–(4), (8), (9) amended by the Education and Inspections Act 2006 Sch 4 paras 1, 7; School Standards and Framework Act 1998 Sch 22 para 3(1)(aa) added by, and Sch 22 para 3(1), (3)–(4), (8) amended by, the School Standards and Organisation (Wales) Act 2013 Sch 5 para 19(1), (14)(d); School Standards and Framework Act 1998 Sch 22 para 3(1)(b), (3), (4)(b), (8), (11) amended by SI 2010/1158).
4   As to references to 'land' see PARA 84 note 9 (definition applied by virtue of the School Standards and Framework Act 1998 s 142(8)).
5   School Standards and Framework Act 1998 Sch 22 para 3(1)(a) (as amended: see note 3). The statutory procedures referred to are: acquisitions under any of the Education Act 1996 ss 60, 61 (both repealed) or s 70 (repealed), or under the School Standards and Framework Act 1998 Sch 3 para 2 or 4 (see PARAS 1295, 1296), Sch 3 para 9 (see PARA 311), Sch 6 para 16 or 20 (repealed) (including those provisions as applied by any enactment), Sch 22 para 5(4B)(d) (see PARA 1321), regulations made under Sch 8 para 5 (repealed); or acquisitions under the School Standards and Organisation (Wales) Act 2013 Sch 3 para 7 (provision of site and buildings for foundation or voluntary controlled school) (see PARA 143) or para 11 (duty to transfer interest in premises) (see PARA 143), under either of those paragraphs as applied by s 76(1), or Sch 4 Pt 3 (transfer of land) (see PARA 143): School Standards and Framework Act 1998 Sch 22 para A3(1)(a), (1)(aa) (as so added and amended). As to references to land being acquired in a particular way for these purposes see PARA 1305 note 5.
6   Ie the appointed day (see PARA 106 note 3).
7   As to the meaning of 'local authority' see PARA 25.
8   School Standards and Framework Act 1998 Sch 22 para 3(1)(b) (as amended: see note 3). Schedule 22 para 3(1)(b) does not apply in the case of any expenditure unless the authority prepared a statement in writing containing details of the amount of the expenditure, the acquisition or works funded (or to be funded) by such expenditure and the total cost (or estimated total cost) of that acquisition or those works and indicating that the expenditure was being treated by it as expenditure of a capital nature (Sch 22 para 3(6)(a)) and sent a copy of the statement to the trustees either before, or no later than 12 months after, the expenditure was incurred (Sch 22 para 3(6)(b)). As to references to expenditure being incurred for the purposes of the school see PARA 1305 note 11.

9   As to the governing body of a maintained school, in relation to Wales, see PARA 195.
10 School Standards and Framework Act 1998 Sch 22 para 3(1)(c)(i). The specified statutory procedures are acquisition by transfer under the Education Act 1996 s 201(1)(a) (repealed).
11 As to the meaning of 'proceeds of disposal' see PARA 1303 note 7.
12 School Standards and Framework Act 1998 Sch 22 para 3(1)(c)(ii).
13 School Standards and Framework Act 1998 Sch 22 para 3(1)(c).
14 Ie a controlled school within the meaning of the Education Act 1996: see s 32 (repealed).
15 School Standards and Framework Act 1998 Sch 22 para 3(2) (as amended: see note 3). The specified statutory procedures are acquisitions under the Education Act 1996 s 63 (repealed) or s 64 (repealed).
16 School Standards and Framework Act 1998 Sch 22 para 3(3) (as amended (see note 3)). As to the Welsh Ministers see PARA 59. In making any such determination the trustees and the authority, or the Welsh Ministers, as the case may be, must have regard in particular to: (1) the value, as at the date of the determination, of the land acquired from the authority (Sch 22 para 3(4)(a) (as so amended)); (2) any enhancement in value of the land attributable to expenditure by the local authority, the trustees or the governing body of the school on school buildings on the land (Sch 22 para 3(4)(b) (as so amended)); and (3) any payments already made by the trustees to the authority in respect of the current school site or under the Education Act 1996 s 60(4) (repealed) or the School Standards and Framework Act 1998 Sch 3 para 2(6) (see PARA 1295) or Sch 6 para 16(5) (repealed) or under the School Standards and Organisation (Wales) Act 2013 Sch 3 (Sch 22 para 3(4)(c) (as so amended)). More than one determination may be made under Sch 22 para 3(3) in relation to a disposal of land within Sch 22 para 3(1) or (2) (see the text and notes 1–15) where it is just to do so, in particular where the disposal involves the creation of a lease: Sch 22 para 3(5).
    Schedule 22 para 3(3) does not apply in the case of land acquired under the Education Act 1996 ss 60, 61 (both repealed) or under the School Standards and Framework Act 1998 Sch 3 para 2 or 4 (see PARAS 1295, 1296) by the trustees of an institution which is, or has at any time been, within the further education sector (as defined by the Education Act 1996 s 4(3): see PARA 555): School Standards and Framework Act 1998 Sch 22 para 3(7).
17 Ie within the meaning of the Education Act 1996 Pt III Ch 6 (ss 244–258) (repealed). As to references to grants being provided in a particular way for these purposes see PARA 1305 note 8.
18 Ie under the Education Act 1996 s 216(2) (repealed).
19 School Standards and Framework Act 1998 Sch 22 para 3(1)(e).
20 School Standards and Framework Act 1998 Sch 22 para 3(1)(f) (as amended: see note 3).
21 Ie the School Standards and Framework Act 1998 Sch 22 para 3(1)(e) or (1)(f) (see the text and notes 17–20).
22 Ie subject to the School Standards and Framework Act 1998 Sch 22 para 3(9) (see the text and note 26).
23 School Standards and Framework Act 1998 Sch 22 para 3(8)(a) (as amended: see note 3).
24 School Standards and Framework Act 1998 Sch 22 para 3(8)(b)(i) (as amended: see note 3).
25 School Standards and Framework Act 1998 Sch 22 para 3(8)(b)(ii) (as amended: see note 3).
26 School Standards and Framework Act 1998 Sch 22 para 3(9) (as amended: see note 3). More than one direction may be given under Sch 22 para 3(9) in relation to a disposal of land within Sch 22 para 3(1) (see the text and notes 17–20) where it is just to do so, in particular where the disposal involves the creation of a lease: Sch 22 para 3(10).
27 School Standards and Framework Act 1998 Sch 22 para 3(1)(g). 'Special agreement' was defined by the Education Act 1996 s 32(5) (repealed).
28 Ie the grant referred to in the School Standards and Framework Act 1998 Sch 22 para 3(1)(g).
29 School Standards and Framework Act 1998 Sch 22 para 3(11) (as amended: see note 3).

1318.   Change of use of land by trustees of foundation or voluntary schools: payment and application of the value of the land.   Where the trustees[1] of a foundation or voluntary school in Wales[2] wish to use for purposes not connected with the provision of education in maintained schools any land[3] held by them for the purposes of the school which was:

(1)   acquired via specified statutory procedures[4];
(2)   acquired, or enhanced in value, wholly or partly by means of expenditure incurred on or after 1 September 1999[5] for the purposes of the school and treated by the local authority[6] as expenditure of a capital nature[7];

(3)   any land acquired by the governing body[8] of the school via specified statutory procedures[9] or wholly or partly with the proceeds of disposal[10] of any land so acquired[11], and transferred by the governing body to be held on trust by the trustees[12]; or

(4)   (where a voluntary aided school in Wales was, immediately before 1 September 1999, a controlled school[13] only), acquired, or enhanced in value, wholly or partly by means of expenditure incurred via specified statutory procedures[14],

the trustees must notify the local authority that the relevant provisions apply to them and they or their successors must pay to the authority so much of the value of the land as may be determined to be just, either by agreement between them and the authority or, in default of agreement, by the Welsh Ministers[15].

Where the trustees of a foundation or voluntary school in Wales wish to use for purposes not connected with the provision of education in maintained schools any land held by them for the purposes of the school which was:

(a)   acquired, or enhanced in value, wholly or partly by means of any maintenance, special purpose or capital grant[16] or any other grant paid[17] in respect of the provision of premises for the school[18]; or

(b)   any land acquired wholly or partly with the proceeds of disposal of any land so acquired or enhanced in value under head (a)[19],

the trustees must notify the local authority that the relevant provisions[20] apply to them and they and their successors must[21] undertake to the authority to apply the value of the land for the purposes of the school[22] or for the purposes of any other existing foundation or voluntary school[23] or of any other proposed foundation or voluntary school, whether or not proposals have yet been published under any enactment in respect of that proposed school[24], and where it appears to the Welsh Ministers that the trustees have not given a suitable undertaking the Ministers may direct the trustees to pay to the authority either the whole or any part of the value of the land (at the date of any such direction) as the Ministers determine to be just[25].

Where the trustees of a foundation or voluntary school in Wales wish to use for purposes not connected with the provision of education in maintained schools any land held by them for the purposes of the school which was land acquired, or enhanced in value, wholly or partly by means of any grant made in pursuance of a special agreement[26], the governing body of the school must repay the grant[27] to the local authority by whom the school is maintained, unless the governing body and the authority otherwise agree[28].

1   As to the meaning of 'the trustees' see PARA 1303 note 6.
2   As to foundation and voluntary schools see PARA 106 et seq. As to the meaning of 'Wales' see PARA 7 note 3.
3   As to references to 'land' see PARA 84 note 9 (definition applied by virtue of the School Standards and Framework Act 1998 s 142(8)). Nothing in Sch 22 para 3(1) applies in relation to any change of use to the extent that it is a change of use to which Sch 22 para 2A (see PARA 1316) applies: Sch 22 para 3(1), (2A), (12)(a) (Sch 22 para 3(1), (8)(b)(ii) amended by the Education Act 2002 Sch 21 para 118; School Standards and Framework Act 1998 Sch 22 para 3(1) amended, Sch 22 para 3(2A) added, by the Education Act 2005 Sch 17 paras 1, 5; School Standards and Framework Act 1998 Sch 22 para 3(1)–(4), (8), (9), (12) amended by the Education and Inspections Act 2006 Sch 4 paras 1, 7; School Standards and Framework Act 1998 Sch 22 para 3(1)(aa) added by, and Sch 22 para 3(1), (3)–(4), (8), (12) amended by, the School Standards and Organisation (Wales) Act 2013 Sch 5 para 19(1), (14)(d); School Standards and Framework Act 1998 Sch 22 para 3(1)(b), (3), (4)(b), (8), (11) amended by SI 2010/1158).
4   School Standards and Framework Act 1998 Sch 22 para 3(1)(a) (as amended: see note 3). The statutory procedures referred to are: acquisitions under any of the Education Act 1996 ss 60, 61

(both repealed) or s 70 (repealed), or under the School Standards and Framework Act 1998 Sch 3 para 2 or 4 (see PARAS 1295, 1296), Sch 3 para 9 (see PARA 311), Sch 6 para 16 or 20 (repealed) (including those provisions as applied by any enactment), Sch 22 para 5(4B)(d) (see PARA 1321), regulations made under Sch 8 para 5 (repealed); or acquisitions under the School Standards and Organisation (Wales) Act 2013 Sch 3 para 7 (provision of site and buildings for foundation or voluntary controlled school) (see PARA 143) or para 11 (duty to transfer interest in premises) (see PARA 143), under either of those paragraphs as applied by s 76(1), or Sch 4 Pt 3 (transfer of land) (see PARA 143): School Standards and Framework Act 1998 Sch 22 para A3(1)(a), (1)(aa) (as so added and amended). As to references to land being acquired in a particular way for these purposes see PARA 1305 note 5.

5 Ie the appointed day (see PARA 106 note 3).
6 As to the meaning of 'local authority' see PARA 25.
7 School Standards and Framework Act 1998 Sch 22 para 3(1)(b) (as amended (see note 3)). Schedule 22 para 3(1)(b) does not apply in the case of any expenditure unless the authority prepared a statement in writing containing details of the amount of the expenditure, the acquisition or works funded (or to be funded) by such expenditure and the total cost (or estimated total cost) of that acquisition or those works and indicating that the expenditure was being treated by it as expenditure of a capital nature (Sch 22 para 3(6)(a)) and sent a copy of the statement to the trustees either before, or no later than 12 months after, the expenditure was incurred (Sch 22 para 3(6)(b)). As to references to expenditure being incurred for the purposes of the school see PARA 1305 note 11.
8 As to the governing body of a maintained school, in relation to Wales, see PARA 195.
9 School Standards and Framework Act 1998 Sch 22 para 3(1)(c)(i). The specified statutory procedures are acquisition by transfer under the Education Act 1996 s 201(1)(a) (repealed).
10 As to the meanings of 'disposal' and 'proceeds of disposal' see PARA 1303 notes 2, 7.
11 School Standards and Framework Act 1998 Sch 22 para 3(1)(c)(ii).
12 School Standards and Framework Act 1998 Sch 22 para 3(1)(c).
13 Ie a controlled school within the meaning of the Education Act 1996: see s 32 (repealed).
14 School Standards and Framework Act 1998 Sch 22 para 3(2) (as amended: see note 3). The specified statutory procedures are acquisitions under the Education Act 1996 s 63 (repealed) or s 64 (repealed).
15 School Standards and Framework Act 1998 Sch 22 para 3(3), (12)(b) (as amended: see note 3). As to the Welsh Ministers see PARA 59. In making any such determination the trustees and the authority, or the Welsh Ministers, as the case may be, must have regard in particular to: (1) the value, as at the date of the determination, of the land acquired from the authority (Sch 22 para 3(4)(a) (as so amended)); (2) any enhancement in value of the land attributable to expenditure by the local authority, the trustees or the governing body of the school on school buildings on the land (Sch 22 para 3(4)(b) (as so amended)); and (3) any payments already made by the trustees to the authority in respect of the current school site or under the Education Act 1996 s 60(4) (repealed) or the School Standards and Framework Act 1998 Sch 3 para 2(6) (see PARA 1295) or Sch 6 para 16(5) (repealed) (Sch 22 para 3(4)(c) (as so amended)). More than one determination may be made under Sch 22 para 3(3) in relation to a disposal of land within Sch 22 para 3(1) or (2) (see the text and notes 1–14) where it is just to do so, in particular where the disposal involves the creation of a lease: Sch 22 para 3(5).
   Schedule 22 para 3(3) does not apply in the case of land acquired under the Education Act 1996 ss 60, 61 (both repealed) or under the School Standards and Framework Act 1998 Sch 3 para 2 or 4 (see PARAS 1295, 1296) by the trustees of an institution which is, or has at any time been, within the further education sector (as defined by the Education Act 1996 s 4(3): see PARA 555): School Standards and Framework Act 1998 Sch 22 para 3(7).
16 Ie within the meaning of the Education Act 1996 Pt III Ch 6 (ss 244–258) (repealed). As to references to grants being provided in a particular way for these purposes see PARA 1305 note 8.
17 Ie under the Education Act 1996 s 216(2) (repealed).
18 School Standards and Framework Act 1998 Sch 22 para 3(1)(e).
19 School Standards and Framework Act 1998 Sch 22 para 3(1)(f) (as amended: see note 3).
20 Ie the School Standards and Framework Act 1998 Sch 22 para 3(1)(e) or (1)(f), (12) (see the text and notes 16–19).
21 Ie subject to the School Standards and Framework Act 1998 Sch 22 para 3(9) (see the text and note 25).
22 School Standards and Framework Act 1998 Sch 22 para 3(8)(a) (as amended: see note 3).
23 School Standards and Framework Act 1998 Sch 22 para 3(8)(b)(i) (as amended: see note 3).
24 School Standards and Framework Act 1998 Sch 22 para 3(8)(b)(ii) (as amended: see note 3).
25 School Standards and Framework Act 1998 Sch 22 para 3(9), (12)(b) (as amended: see note 3). More than one direction may be given under Sch 22 para 3(9) in relation to a change of use

within Sch 22 para 3(1), (12) (see the text and notes 16–19) where it is just to do so, in particular where the change of use involves the creation of a lease: Sch 22 para 3(10).

26 School Standards and Framework Act 1998 Sch 22 para 3(1)(g). 'Special agreement' was defined by the Education Act 1996 s 32(5) (repealed).

27 Ie the grant referred to in the School Standards and Framework Act 1998 Sch 22 para 3(1)(g).

28 School Standards and Framework Act 1998 Sch 22 para 3(11) (as amended: see note 3).

1319. Land required by local authority for new school. Where, on an application made by a local authority[1] in Wales[2], the Welsh Ministers[3] are satisfied:

(1) that any relevant land[4] held, or held on trust, for the purposes of a foundation or voluntary school[5] by the governing body[6] or the trustees[7] of the school[8], or held by a foundation body for the purposes of the group of schools for which it acts[9], is not required for the purposes of the school or (as the case may be) those schools[10]; and

(2) that that land is required by the authority as the site for a new maintained school or as the site to which a maintained school is to be transferred[11],

the Ministers may by order require the relevant land to be transferred to the authority by the body or trustees holding the land, subject to the payment by the authority of such sum by way of consideration (if any) as the Ministers determine to be appropriate[12].

1 As to the meaning of 'local authority' see PARA 25.
2 As to the meaning of 'Wales' see PARA 7 note 3.
3 As to the Welsh Ministers see PARA 59.
4 Ie land which was acquired by the governing body of the school, or (as the case may be) one of the schools, mentioned in the School Standards and Framework Act 1998 Sch 22 para 4(1)(a) under a transfer under the Education Act 1996 s 201(1)(a) (repealed): School Standards and Framework Act 1998 Sch 22 para 4(3). As to references to land being acquired in a particular way for these purposes see PARA 1305 note 5. As to references to 'land' see PARA 84 note 7 (definition applied by virtue of s 142(8)).
5 As to foundation and voluntary schools see PARA 106 et seq.
6 As to the governing body of a maintained school, in relation to Wales, see PARA 195.
7 As to the meaning of 'the trustees' see PARA 1303 note 6.
8 School Standards and Framework Act 1998 Sch 22 para 4(1)(a)(i) (Sch 22 para 4(1) amended by the Education and Inspections Act 2006 Sch 4 paras 1, 8; the School Standards and Organisation (Wales) Act 2013 Sch 5 para 19(1), (14)(e); and SI 2010/1158).
9 School Standards and Framework Act 1998 Sch 22 para 4(1)(a)(ii) (as amended: see note 8). As to the meaning of 'the group' see PARA 108 note 6.
10 School Standards and Framework Act 1998 Sch 22 para 4(1)(a) (as amended: see note 8).
11 School Standards and Framework Act 1998 Sch 22 para 4(1)(b) (as amended: see note 8).
12 School Standards and Framework Act 1998 Sch 22 para 4(2) (Sch 22 para 4(2) amended by the Education and Inspections Act 2006 Sch 4 paras 1, 8). As to the duties of the transferor in connection with transfers of registered land under this provision see PARA 1305 note 26.

C. DISPOSAL OF LAND AND PREMISES ON DISCONTINUANCE OF FOUNDATION, VOLUNTARY OR FOUNDATION SPECIAL SCHOOLS

1320. Disposal of land by governing bodies and foundation bodies on discontinuance of foundation, voluntary or foundation special schools. Provision is made for the disposal by governing[1] or foundation[2] bodies of land[3] the disposal of which is restricted by statute[4] where:

(1) proposals to discontinue a foundation, voluntary or foundation special school[5] have been approved, adopted, confirmed or determined to be implemented under any enactment[6]; or

(2)	the appropriate authority[7] has given a direction[8] requiring a foundation, voluntary or foundation special school to be discontinued[9].

The governing body of the school or, where the school is a member of the group for which a foundation body acts, that body, must, in the case of any such land[10], apply to the appropriate authority for it to exercise one or more of the following powers:

(a)	to require the land or any part of the land to be transferred to such local authority[11] as the appropriate authority may specify, subject to the payment by that local authority of such sum by way of consideration (if any) as the appropriate authority determines to be appropriate[12];

(b)	in the case of a school in England, to make a direction that the land be transferred to an academy[13];

(c)	to direct the governing body or the foundation body, as the case may be, to pay, either to the appropriate authority or to such local authority as the appropriate authority may specify, the whole or any part of the value, as at the date of the direction, of the whole or any part of the land[14]; and

(d)	in a case where the discontinuance of the school is connected with proposals under any enactment to establish, or to make a prescribed alteration or regulated alteration to, any other school or schools, to require the land or any part of the land to be transferred to the governing body of such maintained school or the temporary governing body of such new school as the appropriate authority may specify[15].

Where the governing or foundation body fails to make such an application[16] the appropriate authority may nevertheless make or give any applicable[17] requirement or direction[18].

1	As to the governing body of a maintained school, in relation to England, see PARA 150 et seq; and as to the governing body of a maintained school, in relation to Wales, see PARA 195.
2	As to the meaning of 'foundation body' see PARA 108 note 6.
3	As to references to 'land' and to an 'interest' in land see PARA 84 note 9 (definitions applied by virtue of the School Standards and Framework Act 1998 s 142(8)).
4	Ie restricted as specified in note 10.
5	As to foundation, voluntary and foundation special schools see PARA 106 et seq; and as to special schools generally see PARA 1041 et seq.
6	School Standards and Framework Act 1998 Sch 22 para 5(1)(a) (Sch 22 para 5(1)(a) substituted by, and Sch 22 para 5(4)(c) amended by, the Education Act 2002 Sch 21 para 118; School Standards and Framework Act 1998 Sch 22 para 5(1)(a) amended by SI 2005/3238). However, School Standards and Framework Act 1998 Sch 22 para 5 does not apply where proposals mentioned in Sch 22 para 5(1)(a) have been approved, adopted, confirmed or determined to be implemented in consequence of an academy order made in respect of the school: Sch 22 para 5(1A) (added by the Education Act 2011 Sch 14 para 14(2), (3)). As to academy orders see PARAS 350–351.
7	Ie the Secretary of State (in relation to England) or the Welsh Ministers (in relation to Wales): see the School Standards and Framework Act 1998 Sch 22 para 10(1)(e) (added by the Education and Inspections Act 2006 Sch 4 paras 1, 15). As to the meanings of 'England' and 'Wales' see PARA 7 note 3. As to the Secretary of State see PARA 58. As to the Welsh Ministers see PARA 59.
8	Ie in relation to a school in England, under the Education and Inspections Act 2006 s 17(1) (see PARA 117) or s 68(1) (see PARA 1217), as the case may be, or, in relation to a school in Wales, under the School Standards and Organisation (Wales) Act 2013 s 16 (see PARA 1234).
9	School Standards and Framework Act 1998 Sch 22 para 5(1)(b)(i), (iii)–(iv) (Sch 22 para 5(1)(b), (2)–(4), (5) amended by, Sch 22 paras 5(1)(b)(i)–(iv), (4)(a) substituted by and Sch 22 paras 5(2A), (2B), (3A), (3B) added, by the Education and Inspections Act 2006 Sch 4 paras 1, 9, 15; School Standards and Framework Act 1998 Sch 22 para 5(1)(b) further amended by the School Standards and Organisation (Wales) Act 2013 Sch 5 para 4(1), (9)). See note 6.
10	Ie any land held by the governing body for the purposes of the school or held by the foundation body for the purposes of the schools comprising the group which:

(1)   if the school is in England and the application is being made by the governing body, falls within the School Standards and Framework Act 1998 Sch 22 para A1(1)(a)–(i) (see PARA 1305) (Sch 22 para 5(2)(a) (as amended: see note 9)), other than land which falls within Sch 22 para A1(1)(g) by virtue of being land enhanced in value as mentioned therein or land falling within Sch 22 para A1(1)(i) by virtue of being land acquired, or enhanced in value, wholly or partly with the proceeds of disposal of any such land (Sch 22 para 5(2A) (as added: see note 9));

(2)   if the school is in Wales and the application is being made by the governing body, falls within Sch 22 para 1(1)(a)–(f) (see PARA 1313) (Sch 22 para 5(2)(b) (as so amended));

(3)   if the school is in England and is a member of the group for which a foundation body acts, falls within Sch 22 para A7(1)(a)–(h) (see PARA 1306) (Sch 22 para 5(3)(a) (as amended: see note 9)), other than land which falls within Sch 22 para A7(1)(f) by virtue of being land enhanced in value as mentioned therein or land falling within Sch 22 para A7(1)(h) by virtue of being land acquired, or enhanced in value, wholly or partly with the proceeds of disposal of any such land (Sch 22 para 5(3A) (as added: see note 9)); and

(4)   if the school is in Wales, falls within Sch 22 para 2(1)(a)–(f) (see PARA 1314) (Sch 22 para 5(3)(b) (as so amended).

As to the meaning of 'the group' see PARA 108 note 6. If the school is in England and the governing body disposes of any land falling within Sch 22 para 5(2A) (see above) which is held by it for the purposes of the school, Sch 22 para A1 (see PARA 1305) applies to it (Sch 22 para 5(2B) (as added: see note 9)); and if the school is in England and the foundation body disposes of any land falling within Sch 22 para 5(3A) which is held by it for the purposes of the schools comprising the group, Sch 22 para A7 (see PARA 1306) applies to it (Sch 22 para 5(3B) (as added: see note 9)). See note 6.

11 As to the meaning of 'local authority' see PARA 25. In the School Standards and Framework Act 1998 Sch 22 para 5 'local authority' includes a non-metropolitan district council for an area for which there is a county council: Sch 22 para 5(7) (added by SI 2010/1158). As to the local authorities in England and Wales generally see LOCAL GOVERNMENT vol 69 (2009) PARA 22 et seq.

12 School Standards and Framework Act 1998 Sch 22 para 5(4)(a) (as amended and substituted: see note 9). As to the duties of the transferor in connection with transfers of registered land under this provision see PARA 1305 note 26. See note 6.

13 School Standards and Framework Act 1998 Sch 22 para 5(4)(aa) (Sch 22 para 5(4) as amended (see note 9); Sch 22 para 5(4)(aa) added by the Education Act 2011 Sch 14 paras 2 14). The reference in the text to a direction in respect of the land is to a direction under the Academies Act 2010 Sch 1 para 11 (transfer to academy) (see PARA 1341 et seq). See note 6. As to the meaning of 'academy' see PARA 346 note 7 (definition applied by the School Standards and Framework Act 1998 s 142(8)). As to academies see PARA 345 et seq.

14 School Standards and Framework Act 1998 Sch 22 para 5(4)(b) (as amended: see note 9). See note 6. 'The land' refers to the land referred to in Sch 22 para 5(2) or (3) (see note 10), as the case may be.

15 School Standards and Framework Act 1998 Sch 22 para 5(4)(c) (as amended: see notes 6, 9; further amended by the School Standards and Organisation (Wales) Act 2013 Sch 5 para 19(1), (14)). See note 6. As to the duties of the transferor in connection with transfers of registered land under this provision see PARA 1305 note 26.

16 Ie any application as required by the School Standards and Framework Act 1998 Sch 22 para 5(2), (3), as the case may be (see the text and notes 10–14): Sch 22 para 5(5) (as amended (see note 9); further amended by the Education Act 2005 Sch 17 paras 1, 6). See note 6.

17 Ie make any requirement or give any such direction as is mentioned in the School Standards and Framework Act 1998 Sch 22 para 5(4) (see the text and notes 11–14): Sch 22 para 5(5) (as amended: see notes 9, 15).

18 School Standards and Framework Act 1998 Sch 22 para 5(5) (as amended: see notes 9, 15). See note 6.

1321. Disposal of land by trustees on discontinuance of foundation, voluntary or foundation special schools.

Provision is made for the disposal by trustees[1] of land[2] the disposal of which is restricted by statute[3] where:

(1)   proposals to discontinue a foundation, voluntary or foundation special school[4] have been approved, adopted, confirmed or determined to be implemented under any enactment[5]; or

(2)   the appropriate authority[6] has given a direction[7] requiring a foundation, voluntary or foundation special school to be discontinued[8].

Where the school is in England, or where the school is in Wales and is a foundation school which has a foundation, the trustees of the school must, in relation to any such land[9], apply to the appropriate authority for it to exercise its powers:

(a)   to require the land or any part of the land to be transferred to such local authority as the appropriate authority may specify, subject to the payment by that local authority[10] of such sum by way of consideration (if any) as the appropriate authority determines to be appropriate[11];

(b)   in the case of a school in England, to make a direction that the land be transferred to an academy[12];

(c)   where the trustees have power to use the land for the purposes of another foundation, voluntary or foundation special school[13] or for the purposes of another foundation or voluntary school[14], to direct the trustees to exercise that power in such manner as the appropriate authority may specify[15];

(d)   to direct the trustees to pay to such local authority as the appropriate authority may specify the whole or any part of the value, as at the date of the direction, of the whole or any part of the land[16]; and

(e)   in a case where the discontinuance of the school is connected with proposals under any enactment to establish, or to make a prescribed alteration or regulated alteration to, any other school or schools, to require the land or any part of the land to be transferred to the trustees, foundation body or governing body of such maintained school as the appropriate authority may specify or to the trustees, foundation body or temporary governing body of such new school as the appropriate authority may specify[17].

Where the trustees fail to make such an application[18] the appropriate authority may nevertheless make or give any applicable[19] requirement or direction[20].

1   As to the meaning of 'the trustees' see PARA 1303 note 6.
2   As to references to 'land' and to an 'interest' in land see PARA 116 note 18 (definitions applied by virtue of the School Standards and Framework Act 1998 s 142(8)).
3   Ie restricted as specified in note 9.
4   As to foundation, voluntary and foundation special schools see PARA 106 et seq; and as to special schools generally see PARA 1041 et seq.
5   School Standards and Framework Act 1998 Sch 22 para 5(1)(a) (Sch 22 para 5(1)(a) substituted by the Education Act 2002 Sch 21 para 118; and amended by SI 2005/3238). However, School Standards and Framework Act 1998 Sch 22 para 5 does not apply where proposals mentioned in Sch 22 para 5(1)(a) have been approved, adopted, confirmed or determined to be implemented in consequence of an academy order made in respect of the school: Sch 22 para 5(1A) (added by the Education Act 2011 Sch 14 para 14(2), (3)). As to academy orders see PARAS 350–351.
6   Ie the Secretary of State (in relation to England) or the Welsh Ministers (in relation to Wales) (see PARA 1320 note 7). As to the meanings of 'England' and 'Wales' see PARA 7 note 3. As to the Secretary of State see PARA 58. As to the Welsh Ministers see PARA 59.
7   Ie in relation to a school in England, under the Education and Inspections Act 2006 s 17(1) (see PARA 117) or s 68(1) (see PARA 1217), as the case may be, or in relation to a school in Wales under the School Standards and Organisation (Wales) Act 2013 s 16 (see PARA 1234).
8   School Standards and Framework Act 1998 Sch 22 para 5(1)(b)(i), (iii)–(iv) (Sch 22 para 5(1)(b), (4A), (4B), (5), (6) amended by, Sch 22 para 5(1)(b)(i)–(iv), (4B)(a) substituted by and Sch 22 para 5(4ZA), (4ZB), (5A) added by, the Education and Inspections Act 2006 Sch 4

paras 1, 9, 15; School Standards and Framework Act 1998 Sch 22 para 5(1)(b) further amended by the School Standards and Organisation (Wales) Act 2013 Sch 5 para 4(1), (9)).

9 Ie any land which is held by the trustees for the purposes of the school which:

(1) in relation to a school in England, falls within the School Standards and Framework Act 1998 Sch 22 para A13(1), (2) or (3) (see PARA 1307) (Sch 22 para 5(4ZA) (as added: see note 8)), other than land which falls within Sch 22 para A13(1)(j) by virtue of being land enhanced in value as mentioned therein or land which falls within Sch 22 para A13(1)(k) by virtue of being land acquired, or enhanced in value, wholly or partly with the proceeds of disposal of any such land (Sch 22 para 5(4ZB) (as added: see note 8)); and

(2) in relation to a foundation school in Wales which has a foundation, falls within Sch 22 para 2A(1)(a), (aa), (b) or (c) (see PARA 1315) (Sch 22 para 5(4A) (Sch 22 para 5(4A), (4B) added by and Sch 22 para 5(5), (6) amended by, the Education Act 2005 Sch 17 paras 1, 6; School Standards and Framework Act 1998 Sch 22 para 5(4A) as amended (see note 8); further amended by the School Standards and Organisation (Wales) Act 2013 Sch 5 para 19(1), (14)).

If the school is in England and the trustees of the school dispose of any land falling within Sch 22 para 5(4ZB) or wish to use any such land for purposes not connected with the provision of education in maintained schools or academies, Sch 22 para A13 (see PARAS 1307, 1308) applies to them (Sch 22 para 5(5A) (as so added (see note 8); and amended by the Education Act 2011 Sch 14 paras 2, 14)), and where the school is in Wales and the trustees of the school dispose of any land falling within Sch 22 para 3(1) or (2) (see PARAS 1317, 1318) but not within Sch 22 para 2A(1)(a), (aa), (b) or (c) (see PARAS 1315, 1316), or wish to use any such land for purposes not connected with the provision of education in maintained schools, Sch 22 para 3 applies to them (Sch 22 para 5(6) (as so amended and amended (see note 8); further amended by the School Standards and Organisation (Wales) Act 2013 Sch 5 para 19(1), (14))). See note 5. As to the meaning of 'academy' see PARA 346 note 7 (definition applied by the School Standards and Framework Act 1998 s 142(8)). As to academies see PARA 345 et seq.

10 As to the meaning of 'local authority' see PARA 25. As to the meaning of 'local authority' in the School Standards and Framework Act 1998 Sch 22 para 5 see PARA 1320 note 7. As to the local authorities in England and Wales generally see LOCAL GOVERNMENT vol 69 (2009) PARA 22 et seq.

11 School Standards and Framework Act 1998 Sch 22 para 5(4B)(a) (as added, substituted and amended: see notes 8, 9). See note 5.

12 School Standards and Framework Act 1998 Sch 22 para 5(4B)(aa) (Sch 22 para 5(4B) as added and amended (see notes 8, 9); Sch 22 para 5(4)(aa) added by the Education Act 2011 Sch 14 paras 2, 14). See note 5. The reference in the text to a direction in respect of the land is to a direction under the Academies Act 2010 Sch 1 para 11 (transfer to academy) (see PARA 1341 et seq).

13 Ie in England.

14 Ie in Wales.

15 School Standards and Framework Act 1998 Sch 22 para 5(4B)(b) (as added and amended: see notes 8, 9; and further amended by the School Standards and Organisation (Wales) Act 2013 Sch 5 para 19(1), (14)). See note 5.

16 School Standards and Framework Act 1998 Sch 22 para 5(4B)(c) (as added and amended: see notes 8, 9). See note 5. 'The land' refers to the land referred to in Sch 22 para 5(4ZA) or (4A) (see note 9), as the case may be.

17 School Standards and Framework Act 1998 Sch 22 para 5(4B)(d) (as added and amended: see notes 8, 9; and further amended by the School Standards and Organisation (Wales) Act 2013 Sch 5 para 19(1), (14)). See note 5.

18 Ie any application as required by the School Standards and Framework Act 1998 Sch 22 para 5(4ZA) or (4A) (see the text and notes 9–16): Sch 22 para 5(5) (as amended: see notes 8, 9). See note 5.

19 Ie make any requirement or give any such direction as is mentioned in the School Standards and Framework Act 1998 Sch 22 para 5(4B) (see the text and notes 10–16): Sch 22 para 5(5) (as amended: see notes 8, 9).

20 School Standards and Framework Act 1998 Sch 22 para 5(5) (as amended: see notes 8, 9). See note 5.

1322. Disposal of land and premises by governing bodies or foundation bodies on discontinuance of foundation or voluntary schools by notice. Where the governing body[1] of a foundation or voluntary school[2] applies for the appropriate authority's[3] consent to serve a notice of its intention to discontinue the school[4] and the appropriate authority gives such consent, the appropriate authority may impose any requirements in relation to the governing body or, where the school is a member of the group[5] for which a foundation body[6] acts, the foundation body that the appropriate authority thinks just:

(1)   in respect of the repayment of all or part of any expenditure incurred[7] by the appropriate authority[8];

(2)   in respect of the transfer to the local authority[9] of any premises[10] used for the purposes of the school which the appropriate authority is satisfied the local authority will need for any purpose connected with education[11];

(3)   (where any premises are to be so transferred) in respect of the payment by the local authority of so much of the value of those premises as is just having regard to the extent to which the premises were provided otherwise than at public expense[12]; and

(4)   (where any premises used for the purposes of the school are not to be so transferred) in respect of the payment by the governing body or the foundation body, as the case may be, to the local authority of so much of the value of those premises as is just having regard to the extent to which they were provided at public expense[13].

1   As to the governing body of a maintained school, in relation to England, see PARA 150 et seq; and as to the governing body of a maintained school, in relation to Wales, see PARA 195 et seq.
2   As to foundation and voluntary schools see PARA 106 et seq.
3   Ie the Secretary of State (in relation to England) or the Welsh Ministers (in relation to Wales) (see PARA 1320 note 7). As to the meanings of 'England' and 'Wales' see PARA 7 note 3. As to the Secretary of State see PARA 58. As to the Welsh Ministers see PARA 59.
4   School Standards and Framework Act 1998 Sch 22 para 6(1) (amended by the Education and Inspections Act 2006 Sch 4 paras 1, 10; and the School Standards and Organisation (Wales) Act 2013 Sch 5 para 19(1), (14). The reference in the text to a notice is to one under the School Standards and Framework Act 1998 s 30(1) (see PARA 116) or the School Standards and Organisation (Wales) Act 2013 s 80 (notice by governing body to discontinue foundation or voluntary school) (see PARA 140).
5   As to the meaning of 'the group' see PARA 108 note 6.
6   As to the meaning of 'foundation body' see PARA 108 note 6.
7   Ie as mentioned in the School Standards and Framework Act 1998 s 30(2) (see PARA 116) or the School Standards and Organisation (Wales) Act 2013 s 80(2) (notice by governing body to discontinue foundation or voluntary school) (see PARA 140).
8   School Standards and Framework Act 1998 Sch 22 para 6(2)(a) (Sch 22 para 6(2) amended by the Education and Inspections Act 2006 Sch 4 paras 1, 10; the School Standards and Organisation (Wales) Act 2013 Sch 5 para 19(1), (14); and SI 2010/1158).
9   As to the meaning of 'local authority' see PARA 25.
10   As to the meaning of 'premises' see PARA 62 note 19 (definition applied by virtue of the School Standards and Framework Act 1998 s 142(8)).
11   School Standards and Framework Act 1998 Sch 22 para 6(2)(b) (as amended: see note 8). As to the duties of the transferor in connection with transfers of registered land under this provision see PARA 1305 note 26.
12   School Standards and Framework Act 1998 Sch 22 para 6(2)(c) (as amended: see note 8). In the School Standards and Framework Act 1998 Sch 22 para 6(2) 'at public expense' means at the expense of the Funding Agency for Schools or any local authority or an authority within s 30(2)(d) (see PARA 116): Sch 22 para 6(3) (amended by SI 2010/1158). The Funding Agency for Schools was dissolved on 1 November 1999: see the School Standards and Framework Act 1998 s 132(1); and the Funding Agency for Schools Dissolution Order 1999, SI 1999/2767.
13   School Standards and Framework Act 1998 Sch 22 para 6(2)(d) (as amended: see note 8). See *R v Secretary of State for Education and Science, ex p Inner London Education Authority* [1990] COD 412, (1990) Times, 17 May, CA.

1323. Disposal of land and premises by trustees on discontinuance of foundation or voluntary schools by notice. Where the governing body[1] of a foundation or voluntary school[2] applies for the appropriate authority's[3] consent to serve a notice of its intention to discontinue the school[4], and the trustees[5] of the school either dispose of any land[6] acquired or enhanced in value via specified statutory procedures[7] or wish to use any such land for purposes not connected with the provision of education in maintained schools[8], the provisions relating to the disposal of land by the trustees of foundation, voluntary and foundation special schools[9] apply to them[10].

1 As to the governing body of a maintained school, in relation to England, see PARA 150 et seq; and as to the governing body of a maintained school, in relation to Wales, see PARA 195 et seq.
2 As to foundation and voluntary schools see PARA 106 et seq.
3 Ie the Secretary of State (in relation to England) or the Welsh Ministers (in relation to Wales) (see PARA 1320 note 7). As to the meanings of 'England' and 'Wales' see PARA 7 note 3. As to the Secretary of State see PARA 58. As to the Welsh Ministers see PARA 59.
4 School Standards and Framework Act 1998 Sch 22 para 6(1) (amended by the Education and Inspections Act 2006 Sch 4 paras 1, 10; and the School Standards and Organisation (Wales) Act 2013 Sch 5 para 19(1), (14). The reference in the text to a notice is to one under the School Standards and Framework Act 1998 s 30(1) (see PARA 116) or the School Standards and Organisation (Wales) Act 2013 s 80 (see PARA 116).
5 As to the meaning of 'the trustees' see PARA 1303 note 6.
6 As to references to 'land' and to an 'interest' in land see PARA 116 note 18 (definitions applied by virtue of the School Standards and Framework Act 1998 s 142(8)).
7 School Standards and Framework Act 1998 Sch 22 para 6(3A)(a), (4)(a) (Sch 22 para 6(4) amended, Sch 22 para 6(3A) added, by the Education and Inspections Act 2006 Sch 4 paras 1, 10). The specified statutory procedures referred to are: (1) where the school is in England, those referred to in the School Standards and Framework Act 1998 Sch 22 para A13(1), (2) or (3) (see PARA 1307); and (2) where the school is in Wales, those referred to in the School Standards and Framework Act 1998 Sch 22 para 3(1) or (2) (see PARA 1317): Sch 22 para 6(3A)(a), (4)(a) (as so added and amended).
8 School Standards and Framework Act 1998 Sch 22 para 6(3A)(b), (4)(b) (as added and amended: see note 7). As to the meaning of 'maintained school' see PARA 99.
9 Ie the School Standards and Framework Act 1998 Sch 22 para A13 (where the school is in England) (see PARA 1307), or Sch 22 para 3 (where the school is in Wales) (see PARA 1317).
10 School Standards and Framework Act 1998 Sch 22 para 6(3A), (4) (as added and amended: see note 7).

1324. Disposal of property held by, and rights and liabilities of, governing bodies of maintained schools on dissolution. Where the governing body[1] of a maintained school[2] is dissolved under statute[3] all land or other property[4] of the governing body which is used or held for the purposes of the school[5], and all rights and liabilities (including rights and liabilities in relation to staff) of the governing body subsisting immediately before the date of dissolution which were acquired or incurred for the purposes of the school[6], must on the date of dissolution be transferred to and[7] vest in the local authority[8] or one or more of the governing body of a maintained school, the temporary governing body of a new school and in the case of the dissolution of a governing body of a maintained school in England, a person concerned with the running of an academy[9], if the appropriate authority so directs before the date of dissolution[10].

A governing body which is to be dissolved under statute[11] may transfer any land or other property which is held by it on trust for the purposes of the school to any person to hold such land or other property on trust for purposes connected with the provision of education in maintained schools[12].

1 As to the governing body of a maintained school, in relation to England, see PARA 150 et seq; and as to the governing body of a maintained school, in relation to Wales, see PARA 195 et seq.
2 As to the meaning of 'maintained school' see PARA 99.

3   Ie by virtue of the Education Act 2002 Sch 1 para 5 (see PARAS 150, 195) other than a dissolution by virtue of Sch 1 para 5(2)(a)(iv) (dissolution following academy order) (see PARA 1342): School Standards and Framework Act 1998 Sch 22 para 7(1) (amended by the Education Act 2002 Sch 21 para 118; and the Education Act 2011 Sch 14 paras 2, 15). As to academy orders see PARAS 350–351.

4   As to references to 'land' and to an 'interest' in land see PARA 116 note 18 (definitions applied by virtue of the School Standards and Framework Act 1998 s 142(8)). Schedule 22 para 7(2) does not apply to any land or other property for which provision has been made for transfer or payment under Sch 22 para 5(4) (see PARAS 1320–1321) or Sch 22 para 6(2) (see PARA 1322) (Sch 22 para 7(3)(a)), any property of whatever nature which is held by the governing body on trust for the purposes of the school (Sch 22 para 7(3)(b)), or, unless the appropriate authority otherwise directs by order made before the date of dissolution, any liabilities of the governing body in respect of any loan made to the governing body (Sch 22 para 7(3)(c) (Sch 22 para 7(2)(b)(ii), (3)(c), (6) amended by the Education and Inspections Act 2006 Sch 4 paras 1, 11)). The 'appropriate authority' is the Secretary of State (in relation to England) or the Welsh Ministers (in relation to Wales) (see PARA 1320 note 7). As to the meanings of 'England' and 'Wales' see PARA 7 note 3. As to the Secretary of State see PARA 58. As to the Welsh Ministers see PARA 59.

5   School Standards and Framework Act 1998 Sch 22 para 7(2)(a).

6   School Standards and Framework Act 1998 Sch 22 para 7(2)(b).

7   Ie by virtue of the School Standards and Framework Act 1998.

8   School Standards and Framework Act 1998 Sch 22 para 7(2)(b)(i) (amended by SI 2010/1158). As to the meaning of 'local authority' see PARA 25.

9   School Standards and Framework Act 1998 Sch 22 para 7(2A) (added by the Education Act 2011 Sch 14 paras 2, 15). As to the meaning of 'new school' see the School Standards and Framework Act 1998 s 72(3); and PARA 155 (definition applied by virtue of the School Standards and Framework Act 1998 para 10(1)(d)). As to the meaning of 'academy' see PARA 346 note 7 (definition applied by s 142(8)). As to academies see PARA 345 et seq.

10   School Standards and Framework Act 1998 Sch 22 para 7(2)(b)(ii) (as amended (see note 4); further amended by the Education Act 2011 Sch 14 paras 2, 15). This is the general situation. Where an academy is established under the Academies Act 2010 the situation is different (see PARA 1341).

11   See note 3.

12   School Standards and Framework Act 1998 Sch 22 para 7(4). Schedule 22 para 7(4) does not apply to any land or other property so held by the governing body of a foundation, voluntary or foundation special school where any other persons also hold any property on trust for the purposes of the school; and any such land or other property must on the date of dissolution be transferred to, and by virtue of the School Standards and Framework Act 1998, vest in, those persons: Sch 22 para 7(5). If any doubt or dispute arises as to the persons to whom any land or other property within Sch 22 para 7(5) falls to be transferred thereunder, it must be treated as falling to be so transferred to such persons as the appropriate authority thinks proper: Sch 22 para 7(6) (as amended: see note 4).

1325.   Notice by trustees terminating foundation or voluntary school's occupation of existing site.   Where trustees[1] have given a notice[2] which is effective to terminate a foundation or voluntary school's[3] occupation of any land ('the relevant premises')[4] and any expenditure has been incurred[5] on the relevant premises, the appropriate authority[6] may impose any requirements that it thinks just:

(1)   in respect of the repayment by the trustees of all or part of any such expenditure which was incurred by the appropriate authority[7];

(2)   in respect of the transfer by the trustees to the local authority[8] of the whole or part of the relevant premises where the appropriate authority is satisfied the local authority will need them for any purpose connected with education[9];

(3)   (to the extent that the relevant premises are to be so transferred) in respect of the payment by the local authority to the trustees of so much of the value of those premises as is just having regard to the extent to which the premises were provided otherwise than at public expense[10];

(4)   (to the extent that the relevant premises are not to be so transferred) in respect of the payment by the trustees to the local authority of so much of the value of those premises as is just having regard to the extent to which they were provided at public expense[11].

1   As to the meaning of 'the trustees' see PARA 1303 note 6.
2   Ie a notice falling within the School Standards and Framework Act 1998 s 30(10) (see PARA 116) or the School Standards and Organisation (Wales) Act 2013 s 80(11) (see PARA 116).
3   As to foundation and voluntary schools see PARA 106 et seq.
4   School Standards and Framework Act 1998 Sch 22 para 8(1) (amended by the School Standards and Organisation (Wales) Act 2013 Sch 5 para 19(1), (14)). As to references to 'land' and to an 'interest' in land see PARA 116 note 18 (definitions applied by virtue of the School Standards and Framework Act 1998 s 142(8)).
5   Ie as mentioned in the School Standards and Framework Act 1998 s 30(2)(a)–(d) (see PARA 116) or the School Standards and Organisation (Wales) Act 2013 s 80(2) (see PARA 116).
6   Ie the Secretary of State (in relation to England) or the Welsh Ministers (in relation to Wales) (see PARA 1320 note 7). As to the meanings of 'England' and 'Wales' see PARA 7 note 3. As to the Secretary of State see PARA 58. As to the Welsh Ministers see PARA 59.
7   School Standards and Framework Act 1998 Sch 22 para 8(2)(a) (Sch 22 para 8(2) amended by the Education and Inspections Act 2006 Sch 4 paras 1, 12; the School Standards and Organisation (Wales) Act 2013 Sch 5 para 19(1), (14); and SI 2010/1158).
8   As to the meaning of 'local authority' see PARA 25.
9   School Standards and Framework Act 1998 Sch 22 para 8(2)(b) (as amended: see note 7). As to the duties of the transferor in connection with transfers of registered land under this provision see PARA 1305 note 26.
10 School Standards and Framework Act 1998 Sch 22 para 8(2)(c) (as amended: see note 7). In Sch 22 para 8(2) 'at public expense' means at the expense of the Funding Agency for Schools or any local authority or an authority within s 30(2)(d) (see PARA 116): Sch 22 para 8(3) (amended by SI 2010/1158). The Funding Agency for Schools was dissolved on 1 November 1999: see the School Standards and Framework Act 1998 s 132(1); and the Funding Agency for Schools Dissolution Order 1999, SI 1999/2767.
11 School Standards and Framework Act 1998 Sch 22 para 8(2)(d) (as amended: see note 7).

D. SCHOOL PLAYING FIELDS IN ENGLAND

1326. Control of disposals or changes in use of school playing fields in England. In respect of any playing fields[1]:
(1)   which are used[2] by a maintained school[3] for the purposes of the school[4]; or
(2)   which are not then so used but have been so used at any time within the preceding period of ten years[5],

a local authority[6], the governing body of a maintained school[7], a foundation body[8] or the trustees of a foundation, voluntary or foundation special school[9] may not, except with the consent of the Secretary of State[10], dispose of such playing fields[11] (other than pursuant to a transfer order[12] or on discontinuance[13] or in pursuance of a transfer scheme[14] or direction[15]) or take any action[16] which is intended or likely to result in a change of use of any such playing fields whereby the playing fields will be used for purposes which do not consist of or include their use as playing fields by such a school for the purposes of the school or by an academy school for the purposes of the academy school[17].

1   Ie land in the open air which is provided for the purposes of physical education or recreation, other than any prescribed description of such land: School Standards and Framework Act 1998 s 77(7).
2   Ie immediately before the date of the disposal or action referred to in the School Standards and Framework Act 1998 s 77(1), (3).
3   In the School Standards and Framework Act 1998 s 77 'maintained school' includes a maintained nursery school: s 77(7) (s 77(1), (3), (7) amended, s 77(2) substituted, s 77(2A),

(2B), (4A) added, by the Education and Inspections Act 2006 Sch 4 para 18). For the purposes of the School Standards and Framework Act 1998 s 77 any reference to a maintained school includes, in relation to any time falling before 1 September 1999 (ie the appointed day: see PARA 106 note 3), a reference to the school as a county, voluntary or maintained special school or a grant-maintained or grant-maintained special school, within the meaning of the Education Act 1996: School Standards and Framework Act 1998 s 77(8).

4   School Standards and Framework Act 1998 s 77(1)(a), (3)(a) (as amended (see note 3); s 77(3) further amended by the Education Act 2011 Sch 13 para 10(2)(b), Sch 14 para 18(3)).

5   School Standards and Framework Act 1998 s 77(1)(b), (3)(b) (as amended: see notes 3, 4). The reference to 'the preceding period of ten years' is a reference to the period of ten years ending with the date of the disposal or action referred to in the School Standards and Framework Act 1998 s 77(1), (3).

6   School Standards and Framework Act 1998 s 77(2)(a) (as substituted: see note 3). As to the meaning of 'local authority' see PARA 25; in the School Standards and Framework Act 1998 s 77 'local authority' includes a non-metropolitan district council for an area for which there is a county council and a parish council: s 77(7) (definition substituted by SI 2010/1158). As to the local authorities in England generally see LOCAL GOVERNMENT vol 69 (2009) PARA 22 et seq.

7   School Standards and Framework Act 1998 s 77(2)(b) (as substituted: see note 3). As to the governing body of a maintained school, in relation to England, see PARA 150 et seq.

8   School Standards and Framework Act 1998 s 77(2)(c) (as substituted: see note 3). As to the meaning of 'foundation body' see PARA 108 note 6.

9   School Standards and Framework Act 1998 s 77(2)(d) (as substituted: see note 3). As to foundation, voluntary and foundation special schools see PARA 106 et seq; and as to special schools generally see PARA 1041 et seq. The School Standards and Framework Act 1998 s 77(1), (3)) applies in the case of a disposal by the trustees of a foundation, voluntary or foundation special school, only if the disposal is of land falling within Sch 22 para A13(1), (2) or (3) (see PARA 1307) (s 77(2A) (as added: see note 3)), and s 77(3) applies in relation to the trustees of a foundation, voluntary or foundation special school only if the playing fields in question are land falling within those provisions (s 77(4A) (as added: see note 3)).

10   As to the Secretary of State see PARA 58. Nothing in the School Standards and Framework Act 1998 s 77 applies in relation to Wales: s 77(9). As to the meanings of 'England' and 'Wales' see PARA 7 note 3. For the purposes of s 77 the Secretary of State's consent may be given in relation to a particular disposal or change of use or generally in relation to disposals or changes of use of a particular description, and in either case may be given subject to conditions: s 77(5). Any consent which a local authority is required to obtain by virtue of s 77 is in addition to any consent required by virtue of the Local Government Act 1972 s 123 or s 127 (general power to dispose of land: see LOCAL GOVERNMENT vol 69 (2009) PARAS 515, 520): see the School Standards and Framework Act 1998 s 77(6).

    On receiving an application for consent under s 77(1) or (3), the Secretary of State may direct that the playing fields, or any part of them, be transferred to a person concerned with the running of an academy school, subject to the payment by that person or the Secretary of State of such sum by way of consideration, if any, as the Secretary of State determines to be appropriate: s 77(4B) (added by the Education Act 2011 Sch 14 para 18(5); and amended by Sch 13 para 10(2)(c)). As to the meaning of 'academy school' see PARA 346 note 12 (definition applied by the School Standards and Framework Act 1998 s 142(8)).

11   School Standards and Framework Act 1998 s 77(1) (as amended: see note 3). These provisions have effect despite anything in the Local Government Act 1972 s 123 or s 127 (general power to dispose of land: see LOCAL GOVERNMENT vol 69 (2009) PARAS 515, 520) or in any other enactment: School Standards and Framework Act 1998 s 77(6).

12   These provisions (ie the School Standards and Framework Act 1998 s 77(1) (see the text and notes 1–11)) do not apply to a disposal in pursuance of a transfer order under Sch 22 para A23 (see PARA 1311): s 77(2B)(a) (as added (see note 3); and amended by the Education Act 2011 Sch 14 para 18).

13   These provisions (ie the School Standards and Framework Act 1998 s 77(1) (see the text and notes 1–11)) do not apply to a disposal to which Sch 22 para 5 or 6 (disposals on discontinuance: see PARAS 1321, 1322) apply: s 77(2B)(b) (as added: see note 3).

14   These provisions (ie the School Standards and Framework Act 1998 s 77(1) (see the text and notes 1–11)) do not apply to a disposal in pursuance of a transfer scheme under the Academies Act 2010 Sch 1 para 1 or 2 (transfer to person concerned with running of academy: see PARAS 1341–1342): s 77(2B)(c)(i) (s 77(2B)(c) added by the Education Act 2011 Sch 14 para 18(2); and amended by Sch 13 para 10(2)(a)). As to academies see PARA 345 et seq.

15   These provisions (ie the School Standards and Framework Act 1998 s 77(1) (see the text and notes 1–11)) do not apply to a disposal in pursuance of a direction under the Academies

Act 2010 Sch 1 para 10 (direction to transfer to local authority or person concerned with running of academy school, where academy order made: see PARAS 1341–1342): s 77(2B)(c)(ii) (as added and amended: see note 14). As to academy orders see PARAS 350–351.

16 Ie other than the making of a disposal which falls within the School Standards and Framework Act 1998 s 77(1) (see the text and notes 1–11) or is excluded from that provision by s 77(2B)(a), (b) or (c) (see the text and notes 12–15): s 77(3) (as amended: see notes 3, 4).

17 School Standards and Framework Act 1998 s 77(3) (as amended: see notes 3, 4). As to guidance see in particular 'Disposal or change of use of playing field and school land: Departmental advice for local authorities, maintained schools, special schools, academies and free schools' (May 2015).

E. DISPOSAL OF LAND USED AND HELD BY FURTHER EDUCATION INSTITUTIONS

1327. Disposal of land in the case of designated institutions. Where trustees dispose of land[1]:

(1) which is transferred[2] to trustees[3] under the provisions concerning the transfer of property on designation of a further education institution[4];

(2) which is held by trustees for the purposes of an institution which became[5] a designated institution[6]; and

(3) which was acquired or enhanced in value wholly or partly by means of certain grants paid under the Education Act 1996 or the School Standards and Framework Act 1998[7],

they must notify the Secretary of State, in respect of land in England held[8], or[9] the Welsh Ministers[10], as the case may be, and pay to the Secretary of State or Welsh Ministers so much of the proceeds of disposal as may be determined[11] to be just[12].

Where trustees permit land to be used for purposes not connected with the designated institution they are treated for the purposes of these provisions as having disposed of the land[13], and must pay to the Secretary of State or Welsh Ministers, as the case may be, so much of the value of the land as may be determined[14] to be just[15].

Where a designated institution has ceased to exist, these provisions apply to land which satisfied the conditions of heads (1) to (3) above immediately before the institution ceased to exist[16]. Where trustees permit such land to be used for purposes not connected with an institution within the further education sector[17] they are treated as having disposed of the land[18], and must pay to the Secretary of State or Welsh Ministers, as the case may be, so much of the value of the land as may be determined[19] to be just[20].

1 Learning and Skills Act 2000 s 144(3) (s 144(3), (4), (9) amended by, and s 144(4)(b)(i), (ii) substituted by, SI 2005/3238).

2 Ie after 1 October 2000 (in relation to England) or after 1 April 2001 (in relation to Wales): Learning and Skills Act 2000 s 144(1); Learning and Skills Act 2000 (Commencement No 2 and Savings) Order 2000, SI 2000/2559; Learning and Skills Act 2000 (Commencement No 3 and Transitional Provisions) (Wales) Order 2001, SI 2001/1274. As to the meanings of 'England' and 'Wales' see PARA 7 note 3.

3 Ie the 'appropriate transferees' under the Further and Higher Education Act 1992 s 32(3)(b) (repealed) (ie in relation to an institution not conducted by a company).

4 Learning and Skills Act 2000 s 144(1).

5 Ie after 1 October 2000 (in relation to England) or after 1 April 2001 (in relation to Wales): Learning and Skills Act 2000 s 144(2)(a); Learning and Skills Act 2000 (Commencement No 2 and Savings) Order 2000, SI 2000/2559; Learning and Skills Act 2000 (Commencement No 3 and Transitional Provisions) (Wales) Order 2001, SI 2001/1274.

6 Learning and Skills Act 2000 s 144(2)(a).

7 Learning and Skills Act 2000 s 144(2)(b). This provision applies to grants under the Education Act 1996 s 65 (repealed) or the School Standards and Framework Act 1998 s 22, Sch 3 para 5 (grants: see PARA 312).

8 Learning and Skills Act 2000 s 144(3), (9)(a) (s 144(3) as amended (see note 1); s 144(9)(a) substituted by SI 2010/1080; and amended by the Education Act 2011 Sch 16 para 15(4); and the Deregulation Act 2015 Sch 14 Pt 2 par 45(a)). As to the Secretary of State see PARA 58.
9 Ie in respect of land in Wales: Learning and Skills Act 2000 s 144(9)(b) (as amended: see note 1).
10 Learning and Skills Act 2000 s 144(9)(b) (as amended: see note 1). As to the Welsh Ministers see PARA 59.
11 Ie by agreement between the trustees and the Secretary of State or Welsh Ministers (Learning and Skills Act 2000 s 144(4)(a) (as amended: see note 1)), or in default of agreement: (1) in the case of land in England held for the purposes of a sixth form college or land in Wales, by an arbitrator to be appointed in default of agreement by the President of the Chartered Institute of Arbitrators (s 144(4)(b)(i) (s 144(b)(i), (b)(ii) substituted by the Education Act 2011 Sch 16 paras 13, 15(1), (2))); or (2) in the case of any other land in England, by the Secretary of State (Learning and Skills Act 2000 s 144(4)(b)(ii) (as so substituted)). The expense of an arbitrator appointed under s 144(4)(b)(i) is to be borne equally by: (a) the trustees and the Secretary of State, in the case of land in England; or (b) the trustees and the Welsh Ministers, in the case of land in Wales: see s 144(4A) (added by the Education Act 2011 Sch 16 paras 13, 15(2), (3)). In making a determination under the Learning and Skills Act 2000 s 144(4) regard must be had, in particular, to: (i) the value of the land at the date of the determination (s 144(5)(a)); and (ii) any enhancement of the land's value which is attributable to expenditure by the trustees or the governing body of the designated institution (s 144(5)(b)). More than one determination may be made under s 144(4) in relation to a particular disposal where it is just to do so, in particular where the disposal involves the creation of a lease: s 144(6).
12 Learning and Skills Act 2000 s 144(4) (as amended: see note 1).
13 Learning and Skills Act 2000 s 144(7)(a).
14 See note 11.
15 Learning and Skills Act 2000 s 144(4), (7)(b) (s 144(4) as amended: see note 1).
16 Learning and Skills Act 2000 s 144(8)(a).
17 Ie within the meaning given by the Further and Higher Education Act 1992 s 91(3) (see PARA 555).
18 Learning and Skills Act 2000 s 144(7)(a), (8)(b).
19 See note 11.
20 Learning and Skills Act 2000 s 144(4), (7)(b), (8)(b) (s 144(4) as amended: see note 1).

1328. Disposal of land held by further education corporations. Where a further education corporation[1] resolves[2] that the corporation should be dissolved on a specified date[3] ('the dissolution date')[4] it must notify the appropriate authority[5] of the resolution and the dissolution date as soon as reasonably practicable[6]. At any time before the dissolution date, the corporation may transfer any of its property, rights or liabilities[7] to such person or body, or a person or body of such description, as may be prescribed[8]. Any such transfer requires the consent of the person or body concerned[9] and takes effect on the dissolution date[10].

Where a person or body prescribed, or of a description prescribed[11] is not a charity[12] established for charitable purposes which are exclusively educational purposes[13] any property transferred to the person or body must be transferred on trust to be used for charitable purposes which are exclusively educational purposes[14].

1 As to the meaning of 'further education corporation' see PARA 555 note 3.
2 Ie after complying with the Further and Higher Education Act 1992 s 27 (see PARA 571).
3 Further and Higher Education Act 1992 s 27A(1) (s 27A added by the Education Act 2011 Sch 12 paras 1, 7; and substituted, together with ss 27, 27B, 27C, by new ss 27, 27A, 27B, by the Further and Higher Education (Governance and Information) (Wales) Act 2014 s 3). As to the dissolution of further education corporations see PARA 571.
4 See the Further and Higher Education Act 1992 s 27A(2); and PARA 571 note 10.
5 Ie, in relation to a further education corporation in England, the Secretary of State and in relation to a further education corporation in Wales, the Welsh Ministers: see the Further and Higher Education Act 1992 s 27(5); and PARA 571 note 5 (definition applied by the Further and Higher Education Act 1992 s 27A(5) (as added and substituted: see note 3). As to the meanings of 'England' and 'Wales' see PARA 7 note 3. As to the Secretary of State see PARA 58; and as to

the Welsh Ministers see PARA 59. The functions of the Secretary of State under the Further and Higher Education Act 1992 ss 27A, 27B so far as exercisable in relation to Wales, were transferred to the National Assembly for Wales (see the National Assembly for Wales (Transfer of Functions) Order 1999, SI 1999/672, art 2, Sch 1) and are now vested in the Welsh Ministers (see the Government of Wales Act 2006 s 162(1), Sch 11 para 30).

6   Further and Higher Education Act 1992 s 27A(3) (as added and substituted: see note 3).

7   As to the transfer of rights and liabilities see PARA 568 note 9. As to the meaning of 'liability' see PARA 568 note 15. Stamp duty is not chargeable in respect of any transfer effected under or by virtue of the Further and Higher Education Act 1992 s 27B: s 88(1) (amended by the Education Act 2011 Sch 12 paras 1, 38). This is subject to the requirement that no instrument (other than a statutory instrument) made or executed under or in pursuance of the Further and Higher Education Act 1992 s 27B may be treated as duly stamped unless it is stamped with the duty to which it would, but for s 88 (and, if applicable, the Finance Act 1982 s 129 (see STAMP TAXES vol 96 (2012) PARA 363)), be liable or it has, in accordance with the Stamp Act 1891 s 12 (see STAMP TAXES vol 96 (2012) PARA 384), been stamped with a particular stamp denoting that it is not chargeable with any duty or that it has been duly stamped: Further and Higher Education Act 1992 s 88(2). A land transaction effected under or by virtue of s 27B is also exempt from charge for the purposes of stamp duty land tax: s 88A(1) (s 88A added by SI 2003/2867; and amended by the Education Act 2011 Sch 12 paras 1, 39). Relief under the Further and Higher Education Act 1992 s 88A must be claimed in a land transaction return or an amendment of such a return: s 88A(2) (as so added). As to the meanings of 'land transaction' and 'land transaction return' see PARA 571 note 16.

8   Ie prescribed by regulations made by the appropriate authority: see note 5 (definition applied by the Further and Higher Education Act 1992 s 27B(6) (as added and substituted: see note 3)). As to the meaning of 'person' see PARA 7 note 6. As to the descriptions of persons or bodies which have been prescribed see the Dissolution of Further Education Corporations and Sixth Form College Corporations (Prescribed Bodies) Regulations 2012, SI 2012/1167; and the Dissolution of Further Education Corporations (Publication of Proposals and Prescribed Bodies) (Wales) Regulations 2014, SI 2014/2126.

9   Further and Higher Education Act 1992 s 27B(1), (2) (as added and substituted: see note 3).

10 Further and Higher Education Act 1992 s 27B(3) (as added and substituted: see note 3).

11 Ie under the Further and Higher Education Act 1992 s 27B(1): see the text and note 9.

12 As to charities generally see CHARITIES.

13 Further and Higher Education Act 1992 s 27B(4) (as added and substituted: see note 3). As to the charitable status of further education corporations see PARA 566.

14 Further and Higher Education Act 1992 s 27B(5) (as added and substituted: see note 3).

F. DISPOSAL OF LAND USED AND HELD BY HIGHER EDUCATION INSTITUTIONS

1329.   Disposal of land under the Universities and College Estates Acts.   The universities and colleges to which the Universities and College Estates Acts 1925 and 1964 apply[1] have statutory powers, exercisable in accordance with their statutes[2] and additional to any pre-existing powers[3], to dispose of their land[4], including land held upon any trusts or for purposes connected with the university or college[5]. These powers include powers of sale and exchange[6], leasing powers[7], and powers to accept surrenders of leases and regrants in fee simple[8], to grant water rights[9], to grant land for public and charitable purposes[10], to dedicate streets and open spaces[11], to enter into forestry dedication covenants[12], to compromise claims and release restrictions[13], to vary leases and grants[14], to apportion rents[15], to deal separately with the surface and minerals[16], to grant options[17], to enter into contracts[18], and to do and execute all necessary acts and deeds[19]. There are prescribed modes of investing or applying capital money[20]. There is power to raise money and a general power to effect other transactions concerning land[21].

Changes were made under the Universities and Colleges Estates Act 1964 in the law relating to property held by universities or their colleges, the most important of which are: (1) to release land transactions by colleges and halls in universities in England and Wales from restrictions imposed by the Ecclesiastical

Leases Acts of 1571, 1572, 1575 and 1836[22]; (2) to enable the universities of Oxford, Cambridge and Durham and their colleges to execute most transactions relating to land themselves[23]; and (3) to make provision for the transfer to those universities and their colleges and halls of all capital money held on their behalf and to enable them to receive and apply capital money derived from their land transactions[24].

1   The Universities and College Estates Acts 1925 and 1964 apply to the universities (and their colleges and halls) of Oxford (including the Cathedral or House of Christ Church in Oxford), Cambridge and Durham (but not Newcastle) and the Colleges of St Mary of Winchester and of King Henry VI at Eton: Universities and College Estates Act 1925 s 1; Universities and College Estates Act 1964 s 2(1); Universities of Durham and Newcastle upon Tyne Act 1963 s 19.

2   See the Universities and College Estates Act 1925 s 41(2).

3   See the Universities and College Estates Act 1925 s 42 (amended by the Universities and College Estates Act 1964 Sch 1 Pt II para 14).

4   'Land' includes land of any tenure, and mines and minerals whether or not held apart from the surface, buildings or parts of buildings (whether the division is horizontal, vertical or otherwise) and all other corporeal hereditaments; also a manor, an advowson, and a rent and all other incorporeal hereditaments, and an easement, right, privilege, or benefit in, over, or derived from land: Universities and College Estates Act 1925 s 43(iv) (amended by the Trusts of Land and Appointment of Trustees Act 1996 s 25(2)). 'Mines and minerals' mean mines and minerals whether already opened or in work or not, and include all minerals and substances in, on, or under the land, obtainable by underground or by surface working: see the Universities and College Estates Act 1925 s 43(vii) (amended by the Universities and College Estates Act 1964 s 4(1)). 'Hereditaments' means real property which on an intestacy might before the commencement of the Law of Property Act 1922 (see REAL PROPERTY AND REGISTRATION vol 87 (2012) PARA 10) have devolved on an heir: University and College Estates Act 1925 s 43(iii). 'Manor' includes lordship, and reputed manor or lordship: see s 43(vi). 'Rent' includes yearly or other rent, and toll, duty, royalty, or other reservation, by the acre, or the ton, or otherwise: see s 43(ix).

5   See the University and College Estates Act 1925 s 41(1). As to the power to transfer to the university or college lands vested in individual members see s 40 (amended by the Universities and College Estates Act 1964 Sch 1 Pt I para 9).

6   See the Universities and College Estates Act 1925 s 2 (amended by the Statute Law (Repeals) Act 1969; and the Universities and College Estates Act 1964 Sch 1 Pt I para 1); the University and Colleges Estates Act 1925 s 3 (amended by the Universities and College Estates Act 1964 Sch 1 Pt II para 1; and the Law of Property (Amendment) Act 1926 s 7, Schedule); and the University and Colleges Estates Act 1925 ss 4, 5 (amended by the Universities and College Estates Act 1964 Sch 1 Pt II para 2). See also the Settled Land Act 1925 ss 38–40; and SETTLEMENTS vol 91 (2012) PARAS 728–737.

7   See the Universities and College Estates Act 1925 ss 6, 7 (amended by the Universities and College Estates Act 1964 Sch 1 Pt II para 3); the University and Colleges Estates Act 1925 ss 8, 9 (amended by virtue of the Decimal Currency Act 1969 s 10(1)); the Universities and College Estates Act 1925 s 10 (amended by SI 1978/443); and the Universities and College Estates Act 1925 ss 11–12. See also the Settled Land Act 1925 ss 41–48; and SETTLEMENTS vol 91 (2012) PARAS 738–748.
    As to the effect of the Ecclesiastical Leases Act 1571 see *Eton College v Minister of Agriculture, Fisheries and Food* [1964] Ch 274, [1962] 3 All ER 290; and ECCLESIASTICAL LAW vol 34 (2011) PARA 926.

8   See the Universities and College Estates Act 1925 s 13 (amended by the Universities and College Estates Act 1964 Sch 1 Pt II para 4). See also the Settled Land Act 1925 s 52; and SETTLEMENTS vol 91 (2012) PARA 760.

9   See the Universities and College Estates Act 1925 s 14 (amended by the Universities and College Estates Act 1964 Sch 1 Pt II para 5). See also the Settled Land Act 1925 s 54; and SETTLEMENTS vol 91 (2012) PARA 769.

10 See the Universities and College Estates Act 1925 s 15 (amended by the Universities and College Estates Act 1964 Sch 1 Pt I para 2, Sch 1 Pt II para 6; and SI 1978/443). See also the Settled Land Act 1925 s 55; and SETTLEMENTS vol 91 (2012) PARA 765.

11 See the Universities and College Estates Act 1925 s 16 (amended by the Highways Act 1959 Sch 22; the London Government Act 1963 Sch 6 para 70, Sch 18 Pt II; the Universities and College Estates Act 1964 Sch 1 Pt II para 7; the Highways Act 1980 Sch 24 para 3; and the

Constitutional Reform Act 2005 Sch 11 Pt 2 para 4(1), (3)). See also the Settled Land Act 1925 s 56; and SETTLEMENTS vol 91 (2012) PARA 766.

12 See the Forestry Act 1967 Sch 2 para 2; and FORESTRY vol 52 (2014) PARA 120.

13 See the Universities and College Estates Act 1925 s 17 (amended by the Universities and College Estates Act 1964 Sch 1 Pt I para 3); the Universities and College Estates Act 1925 s 20 (amended by the Universities and College Estates Act 1964 Sch 1 Pt II para 8). See also the Settled Land Act 1925 ss 58, 61; and SETTLEMENTS vol 91 (2012) PARAS 764, 773.

14 See the Universities and College Estates Act 1925 ss 18, 20 (as amended: see note 13). See also the Settled Land Act 1925 ss 59(1), 61; and SETTLEMENTS vol 91 (2012) PARAS 761, 764.

15 See the Universities and College Estates Act 1925 ss 19, 20 (as amended: see note 13). See also the Settled Land Act 1925 ss 60, 61; and SETTLEMENTS vol 91 (2012) PARAS 763–764.

16 See the Universities and College Estates Act 1925 s 22. See also the Settled Land Act 1925 s 50; and SETTLEMENTS vol 91 (2012) PARA 757.

17 See the Universities and College Estates Act 1925 s 23 (amended by the Universities and College Estates Act 1964 Sch 1 Pt I para 4, Sch 1 Pt II para 9). See also the Settled Land Act 1925 s 51; and SETTLEMENTS vol 91 (2012) PARA 772.

18 See the Universities and College Estates Act 1925 s 24 (amended by the Universities and College Estates Act 1964 Sch 1 Pt II para 10). See also the Settled Land Act 1925 s 90; and SETTLEMENTS vol 91 (2012) PARAS 770–771.

19 See the Universities and College Estates Act 1925 s 25. See also the Settled Land Act 1925 s 112; and SETTLEMENTS vol 91 (2012) PARAS 603, 776.

20 See the Universities and College Estates Act 1925 s 26 (amended by the Finance Act 1963 Sch 14 Pt VI; the Universities and College Estates Act 1964 Sch 1 Pt I para 5, Sch 1 Pt II para 11; the Statute Law (Repeals) Act 1969; the Agricultural Holdings Act 1986 Sch 14 para 13; the Statute Law (Repeals) Act 1998; and the Trustee Act 2000 Sch 2 Pt II para 29). See also the Settled Land Act 1925 s 73; and SETTLEMENTS vol 91 (2012) PARA 709. As to further provisions in relation to application of moneys see the Universities and College Estates Act 1925 s 27 (amended by the Constitutional Reform Act 2005 Sch 11 Pt 2 para 4(1), (3)); the Universities and College Estates Act 1925 s 28 (amended by the Universities and College Estates Act 1964 Sch 1 Pt II para 12); and the Universities and College Estates Act 1925 s 29 (amended by the Universities and College Estates Act 1964 Sch 1 Pt II para 13, Sch 3 Pt II). See also the Settled Land Act 1925 s 79; and SETTLEMENTS vol 91 (2012) PARA 708.

21 See the Universities and College Estates Act 1925 ss 21, 30 (s 30 amended by the Universities and College Estates Act 1964 Sch 1 Pt I para 6); the Universities and College Estates Act 1925 s 31 (amended by the Universities and College Estates Act 1964 Sch 1 Pt I para 7); the Universities and College Estates Act 1925 s 32 (amended by the Universities and College Estates Act 1964 Sch 1 Pt I para 8; and the Statute Law (Repeals) Act 2004); the Universities and College Estates Act 1925 s 38 (amended by the Universities and College Estates Act 1964 Sch 1 Pt I para 9); and the Universities and College Estates Act 1925 Sch 1 (amended by the Universities and College Estates Act 1964 Sch 3 Pt II, Sch 4). In relation to capital money see the Universities and College Estates Act 1964 s 3.

22 Universities and College Estates Act 1964 s 1(1) (amended by the Statute Law (Repeals) Act 1998). As to the Ecclesiastical Leases Act 1571 see ECCLESIASTICAL LAW vol 34 (2011) PARA 926.

23 See the Universities and College Estates Act 1964 s 2, Sch 1.

24 See the Universities and College Estates Act 1964 s 3, Sch 2.

(3) LAND AND PROPERTY TRANSFERS

(i) Procedures for Property Transfers

A. PROCEDURE FOR PROPERTY TRANSFERS IN GENERAL

1330. Land and property transfers in relation to educational establishments.
The procedures for land and property transfers in relation to educational establishments were originally performed by the Education Transfer Council[1]. On the dissolution of the Education Transfer Council some of its functions became the responsibility of the Secretary of State in relation to England or the National Assembly for Wales (now the Welsh Ministers) in relation to Wales[2].

The provisions relating to the Education Transfer Council have not been repealed, so that it is possible that a successor body to the Education Transfer Council might be established or that the Education Transfer Council might be re-established[3].

The procedures which became the responsibility of the Secretary of State and the Welsh Ministers concern land transfers in relation to schools changing category or joining or leaving foundation bodies[4], property transfers to former grant-maintained schools[5] (both of which are effected under the Education Reform Act 1988) and property transfers under the Further and Higher Education Act 1992[6]. Other functions which were not transferred to the Secretary of State or the Welsh Ministers may be exercisable where a successor body to the Education Transfer Council is established or the Education Transfer Council is re-established[7].

1 As to the establishment and operation of the Education Transfer Council see the Education Reform Act 1988 s 197, Sch 8 (both amended by the School Standards and Framework Act 1998 ss 136(2), 140, Schs 30, 31). The Council was formerly known as the 'Education Assets Board': see the School Standards and Framework Act 1998 s 136. The Council was dissolved on 31 December 2000: see s 137(3)(a); the Education Transfer Council (Winding up) Regulations 2000, SI 2000/2729, reg 3; and the Education Transfer Council (Dissolution) Order 2000 (dated 13 December 2000).

2 See the Education Reform Act 1988 s 198, Sch 10; and PARAS 1331–1338. As to the Secretary of State see PARA 58. As to the Welsh Ministers see PARA 59.

3 See note 1.

4 The Education (New Procedures for Property Transfers) Regulations 2000, SI 2000/3209, modify the Education Reform Act 1988 s 198, Sch 10 so that the appropriate national authority (ie the Secretary of State or the Welsh Ministers) may exercise powers in relation to transfers of land on schools changing category or joining or leaving foundation bodies under any regulations made or to be made under the School Standards and Framework Act 1998 s 21(5) (see PARA 108) or Sch 8 para 5 (repealed): see the Education (New Procedures for Property Transfers) Regulations 2000, SI 2000/3209, regs 5–7 (revoked in relation to England by SI 2007/1289); and PARAS 1332–1338.

5 The provisions of the Education Reform Act 1988 s 198, Sch 10, as they are applied to transfers under the Education Act 1996 s 201 (repealed) by the School Standards and Framework Act 1998 (Commencement No 5 and Saving and Transitional Provisions) Order 1999, SI 1999/120, art 4 and the School Standards and Framework Act 1998 (Commencement No 7 and Saving and Transitional Provisions) Order 1999, SI 1999/2323, art 8, are modified by the Education (New Procedures for Property Transfers) Regulations 2000, SI 2000/3209, regs 16–19: see reg 15; and PARAS 1332–1338. As to grant-maintained schools see PARA 106 note 15.

6 As to the procedures in relation to property transfers under the Further and Higher Education Act 1992 see the Education (New Procedures for Property Transfers) Regulations 2000, SI 2000/3209, regs 8–14; and PARAS 1332–1338.

7 Where a successor body to the Education Transfer Council is established or the Education Transfer Council is re-established, the Education Reform Act 1988 s 198 (see PARA 1331) applies to any transfer under any of the following provisions: (1) s 126 (see PARA 649) (higher education corporations) or s 130 (see PARA 672) (designated institutions); (2) the School Standards and Framework Act 1998 Sch 21 (see PARA 1340); (3) any regulations made under s 21(5), (9) (see PARA 108) or under Sch 2 para 10 (see PARA 106) or Sch 8 para 5 (repealed); or (4) the School Standards and Organisation (Wales) Act 2013 Sch 4 Pt 3 (transfer of land) (see PARA 143): Education Reform Act 1988 s 198(1) (substituted by the School Standards and Framework Act 1998 s 137, Sch 29 para 2(2); and amended by the School Standards and Organisation (Wales) Act 2013 Sch 5 para 14).

    The provisions described in heads (1)–(4) above, so far as they relate to transfers, have in each case effect subject to the Education Reform Act 1988 Sch 10 (see PARAS 1332–1338): see s 198(1) (as so substituted and amended). However, nothing in the provisions of Sch 10 other than Sch 10 para 2(4) (see PARA 1333) or s 198(3) (see PARA 1331) applies in relation to any transfer agreement falling to be made under the School Standards and Framework Act 1998 Sch 21 para 4 or 7 (see PARA 1340) or any corresponding provision of regulations under the

School Standards and Framework Act 1998: Education Reform Act 1988 s 198(1A) (added by the School Standards and Framework Act 1998 Sch 29 para 2(2)).

B. PROCEDURES UNDER THE EDUCATION REFORM ACT 1988

1331. Procedures for property transfers. The powers described below are exercisable by the appropriate national authority[1] until such time as a successor body to the Education Transfer Council is established or the Education Transfer Council is re-established[2].

The procedures under the Education Reform Act 1988 for transfers[3] have effect for the purpose of:

(1) dividing and apportioning property, rights and liabilities[4] which fall to be transferred by a transferor authority or body where that property has been used or held, or the rights or liabilities have been acquired or incurred, for the purposes of more than one school[5] or other educational institution[6];

(2) excluding from transfer certain property, rights and liabilities which would otherwise fall to be transferred[7];

(3) providing for identifying and defining the property, rights and liabilities which fall to be transferred[8]; and

(4) making supplementary and consequential provision in relation to such transfers[9].

In carrying out the functions conferred or imposed under the procedure for transfers, the appropriate national authority must not act on behalf of the transferor, the transferee or any other interested person, but must seek to ensure that all such persons' interests are protected[10].

If a successor body to the Education Transfer Council is established or the Education Transfer Council is re-established, then further provision is made as to its powers[11].

1 Ie the Secretary of State or, in relation to Wales, the Welsh Ministers, the functions of the Secretary of State under the Education Reform Act 1988 s 198, so far as exercisable in relation to Wales, were transferred to the National Assembly for Wales (see the National Assembly for Wales (Transfer of Functions) Order 1999, SI 1999/672, art 2, Sch 1) and are now vested in the Welsh Ministers (see the Government of Wales Act 2006 s 162(1), Sch 11 para 30). As to the Secretary of State see PARA 58. As to the Welsh Ministers see PARA 59. As to the meaning of 'Wales' see PARA 7 note 3.

2 As to the Education Transfer Council and its dissolution see PARA 1330.

3 Ie the Education Reform Act 1988 s 198(2), Sch 10 (see PARAS 1332–1338). As to the transfers to which Sch 10 applies see PARA 1330.

4 As to the meaning of 'liability' see PARA 84 note 11.

5 As to the meaning of 'school' see PARA 91 (definition applied by virtue of the Education Reform Act 1988 s 235(7) (amended by the Education Act 1996 Sch 37 para 81(4))).

6 Education Reform Act 1988 s 198(2)(a) (s 198(2)–(4) substituted by the School Standards and Framework Act 1998 Sch 29 para 2(2)). As to the modification of the Education Reform Act 1988 s 198 in relation to property transfers to former grant-maintained schools in England see the Education (New Procedures for Property Transfers) Regulations 2000, SI 2000/3209, reg 16. As to the division and apportionment of property see PARA 1332. As to grant-maintained schools see PARA 106 note 15.

7 Education Reform Act 1988 s 198(2)(b) (as substituted: see note 6).

8 Education Reform Act 1988 s 198(2)(c) (as substituted: see note 6). As to the identification of property rights and liabilities see PARA 1333.

9 Education Reform Act 1988 s 198(2)(d) (as substituted: see note 6). As to the supplementary and consequential provisions that have been made see PARAS 1334–1338.

10 Education Reform Act 1988 s 198(3)(a) (as substituted: see note 6); Education (New Procedures for Property Transfers) Regulations 2000, SI 2000/3209, reg 6(a) (revoked in relation to England by SI 2007/1289).

Where a successor body to the Education Transfer Council is established or the Education Transfer Council is re-established, in carrying out the functions conferred or imposed on it by the Education Reform Act 1988 Sch 10 (see PARAS 1332–1338): (1) it must, subject to s 198(4), not act on behalf of the transferor, the transferee or any other interested person, but must seek to ensure that all such persons' interests are protected; and (2) it is its duty, so far as it is reasonably practicable for it to do so, to secure that each transfer to which s 198 applies is, so far as possible, fully effective on the date on which it takes effect under the Education Reform Act 1988 or under or by virtue of the School Standards and Framework Act 1998: Education Reform Act 1988 s 198(3) (as so substituted). As to the functions conferred or imposed on the Education Transfer Council by Sch 10 see PARA 1330. See also *R v Secretary of State for Education, ex p Southwark London Borough Council* [1995] ELR 308, [1994] COD 298.

11 As to the provisions that apply where a successor body to the Education Transfer Council is established or the Education Transfer Council is re-established see the Education (New Procedures for Property Transfers) Regulations 2000, SI 2000/3209, regs 6(b), 16 (reg 6(b) revoked in relation to England by SI 2007/1289). Where the transferor under any transfer to which the Education Reform Act 1988 s 198 applies is a local authority and in accordance with Sch 10 (see PARAS 1332–1338) anything falls to be or may be done by the Education Transfer Council for the purposes of or in connection with that transfer: (1) it may not be done by the transferee; and (2) in doing it the Education Transfer Council must be regarded as acting on behalf and in the name of the transferee: s 198(4)(a), (b) (as substituted: see note 6). In a case where the transferee is a body corporate established under the Education Reform Act 1988 or the School Standards and Framework Act 1998, head (2) above applies both in relation to things done before and in relation to things done after that body is established: Education Reform Act 1988 s 198(4) (as so substituted). As to the meaning of 'local authority' see PARA 25.

Not later than the end of the period of six months beginning with the transfer date applicable in relation to any transfer to a higher education corporation under the Education Reform Act 1988 s 126 (see PARA 649), the Education Transfer Council must provide the higher education funding council with a written statement giving such particulars of all property, rights and liabilities transferred to that corporation as are then available to the Education Transfer Council: s 198(5) (amended by the Further and Higher Education Act 1992 Sch 8 para 44; and the School Standards and Framework Act 1998 Sch 29 para 2(3)). If in any case within the Education Reform Act 1988 s 198(5) full particulars of all property, rights and liabilities transferred to the corporation concerned are not given in the statement required under s 198(5), the Education Transfer Council must provide the higher education funding council with a further written statement giving any such particulars omitted from the earlier statement as soon as it is possible for it to do so: s 198(6) (amended by the School Standards and Framework Act 1998 Sch 29 para 2(3)). As to the meaning of 'transfer date' in relation to higher education corporations see PARA 647 note 7. In relation to a designated institution, 'transfer date' means the designation date in relation to that institution: see the Education Reform Act 1988 ss 130(8), 228(10). As to the designation dates see PARAS 84, 672. As to the Higher Education Funding Councils see PARA 691 et seq.

1332. Division and apportionment of property. The provisions described below are exercisable by the appropriate national authority[1] until such time as a successor body to the Education Transfer Council is established or the Education Transfer Council is re-established[2].

Any property, rights and liabilities[3] of a transferor authority[4] held or used or subsisting:

(1) for the purposes of more than one relevant institution[5]; or

(2) partly for the purposes of one or more relevant institutions and partly for other purposes of the transferor authority[6],

must, where the nature of the property, right or liability permits, be divided or apportioned between the transferees, or, as the case may be, between the transferor authority and the transferee or transferees, in such proportions as may be appropriate[7]. Similarly, any property, rights or liabilities of a transferor body must, where the nature of the property, rights or liability permits, be divided or apportioned between the transferees or, as the case may be, between the transferor body and the transferee or transferees, in such proportions as may be appropriate[8].

Where any estate or interest in land falls to be divided in accordance with the provisions described above[9] any rent payable under a lease in respect of that estate or interest[10] and any rent charged on that estate or interest[11] must correspondingly be divided or apportioned so that each part is payable in respect of, or charged on, only one part of the estate or interest and the other part or parts are payable in respect of, or charged on, only the other part or parts of the estate or interest[12].

1　Ie the Secretary of State or, in relation to Wales, the Welsh Ministers. As to the Secretary of State see PARA 58. As to the Welsh Ministers see PARA 59. As to the meaning of 'Wales' see PARA 7 note 3. The functions of the Secretary of State under the Education Reform Act 1988 Sch 10, so far as exercisable in relation to Wales, were transferred to the National Assembly for Wales (see the National Assembly for Wales (Transfer of Functions) Order 1999, SI 1999/672, art 2, Sch 1) and are now vested in the Welsh Ministers (see the Government of Wales Act 2006 s 162(1), Sch 11 para 30).

2　As to the Education Transfer Council and its dissolution see PARA 1330.

3　As to the meaning of 'liability' see PARA 84 note 11.

4　For these purposes, references to a transferor authority are references to a local authority which is the transferor for the purposes of any transfer to which the Education Reform Act 1988 s 198(2), Sch 10 applies: Sch 10 para 1(5)(c) (Sch 10 paras 1, 2 substituted by the School Standards and Framework Act 1998 Sch 29 paras 3, 4). As to the meaning of 'local authority' see PARA 25; for the purposes of the Education Reform Act 1988 Sch 10 para 1(5) 'local authority' includes a non-metropolitan district council for an area for which there is a county council: Sch 10 para 1(6)(b) (added by SI 2010/1158). As to the local authorities in England and Wales generally see LOCAL GOVERNMENT vol 69 (2009) PARA 22 et seq.

5　Education Reform Act 1988 Sch 10 para 1(1)(a) (as substituted: see note 4). As to the transfers to which Sch 10 applies see PARA 1330. For these purposes, 'relevant institution' means: (1) any institution which a body corporate is established under the Education Reform Act 1988 to conduct; (2) any institution to which s 130 (see PARA 672) applies; and (3) any maintained school: Sch 10 para 1(5)(a) (as so substituted). For the purposes of Sch 10 para 1(5) references to a maintained school have the same meanings as in the School Standards and Framework Act 1998 (see PARA 99 et seq): Education Reform Act 1988 Sch 10 para 1(6)(a) (added by SI 2010/1158).

6　Education Reform Act 1988 Sch 10 para 1(1)(b) (as substituted: see note 4).

7　Education Reform Act 1988 Sch 10 para 1(1) (as substituted: see note 4). Any such property, right or liability as is mentioned in Sch 10 para 1(1) the nature of which does not permit its division or apportionment must be transferred to the transferee (or to one or other of the transferees) or retained by the transferor authority or body according to: (1) in the case of an estate or interest in land, whether on the transfer date the transferor authority or body or the transferee (or one or other of the transferees) appears to be in greater need of the security afforded by that estate or interest or, where none of them appears to be in greater need of that security, which of them appears on that date to be likely to make use of the land to the greater extent; or (2) in the case of any other property or any right or liability, which of them appears on the transfer date to be likely to make use of the property or (as the case may be) to be affected by the right or liability to the greater extent: Sch 10 para 1(4) (as so substituted). For these purposes, references to a transferor body are references to any foundation body which is the transferor for the purposes of any transfer to which Sch 10 applies: Sch 10 para 1(5)(d) (as so substituted). For the purposes of Sch 10 para 1(5) references to a foundation body have the same meaning as in the School Standards and Framework Act 1998 (see PARA 108 note 6): Education Reform Act 1988 Sch 10 para 1(6)(a) (added by SI 2010/1158). As to the meanings of 'interest in land', and 'land', see PARA 84 note 9.

　　However, where these provisions apply to land transfers in relation to schools changing category or joining or leaving foundation bodies, the cases described in heads (1) and (2) above are subject to such arrangements for the protection of the other person or persons concerned as may be agreed between the transferor authority or body and the relevant person (in relation to England) or the transferee (in relation to Wales) or determined by the Welsh Ministers under the Education Reform Act 1988 Sch 10 para 3 (see PARA 1334): Sch 10 para 1(4) (as so substituted);

Education (New Procedures for Property Transfers) Regulations 2000, SI 2000/3209, reg 7(a) (revoked in relation to England by SI 2007/1289).

Where a successor body to the Education Transfer Council is established or the Education Transfer Council is re-established, the cases described in heads (1) and (2) above are subject to such arrangements for the protection of the other person or persons concerned as may be agreed between the transferor authority or body and the relevant person or determined by the appropriate national authority under the Education Reform Act 1988 Sch 10 para 3 (see PARA 1334): Sch 10 para 1(4) (as so substituted). For these purposes, 'the relevant person' means: (a) in a case where the transferor is a transferor authority, the successor body or the Education Transfer Council; (b) in a case where the transferor is a transferor body, the transferee: Sch 10 para 1(5)(b) (as so substituted). As to the transfer date see PARA 1331 note 11. As to schools changing categories see PARAS 132, 141; and as to schools joining or leaving foundation bodies see PARA 108. As to the modification of Sch 10 para 1(5)(b) in relation to schools in Wales changing category or joining or leaving foundation bodies see the Education (New Procedures for Property Transfers) Regulations 2000, SI 2000/3209 reg 7(b) (revoked in relation to England by SI 2007/1289).

Any transfer of any estate or interest in land under the Education Reform Act 1988 Sch 10 para 1 whether by virtue of an agreement or instrument entered into before or after the transfer date, is regarded as having taken place on the transfer date: Sch 10 para 2(5) (as so substituted).

8 Education Reform Act 1988 Sch 10 para 1(2) (as substituted: see note 4). Any such property, right or liability as is mentioned in Sch 10 para 1(2) the nature of which does not permit its division or apportionment must be transferred to the transferee (or to one or other of the transferees) or retained by the transferor authority or body according to: (1) in the case of an estate or interest in land, whether on the transfer date the transferor authority or body or the transferee (or one or other of the transferees) appears to be in greater need of the security afforded by that estate or interest or, where none of them appears to be in greater need of that security, which of them appears on that date to be likely to make use of the land to the greater extent; or (2) in the case of any other property or any right or liability, which of them appears on the transfer date to be likely to make use of the property or (as the case may be) to be affected by the right or liability to the greater extent: Sch 10 para 1(4) (as so substituted). However, where these provisions apply to land transfers in relation to schools in Wales changing category or joining or leaving foundation bodies, the cases described in heads (1) and (2) above are subject to such arrangements for the protection of the other person or persons concerned as may be agreed between the transferor authority or body and the transferee or determined by the Welsh Ministers under Sch 10 para 3 (see PARA 1334): Sch 10 para 1(4) (as so substituted); Education (New Procedures for Property Transfers) Regulations 2000, SI 2000/3209, reg 7(a) (revoked in relation to England by SI 2007/1289). Where a successor body to the Education Transfer Council is established or the Education Transfer Council is re-established, the cases described in heads (1) and (2) above are subject to such arrangements for the protection of the other person or persons concerned as may be agreed between the transferor authority or body and the relevant person or determined by the appropriate national authority under the Education Reform Act 1988 Sch 10 para 3 (see PARA 1334): Sch 10 para 1(4) (as so substituted).

9 Ie through the Education Reform Act 1988 Sch 10 para 1(1) or Sch 10 para 1(2): see the text and notes 1–8.

10 Education Reform Act 1988 Sch 10 para 1(3)(a) (as substituted: see note 4).

11 Education Reform Act 1988 Sch 10 para 1(3)(b) (as substituted: see note 4).

12 Education Reform Act 1988 Sch 10 para 1(3) (as substituted: see note 4). As to the modification of Sch 10 para 1(3) in relation to property transfers to former grant-maintained schools see the Education (New Procedures for Property Transfers) Regulations 2000, SI 2000/3209 reg 17(a). As to grant-maintained schools see PARA 106 note 15.

1333. Identification of property, rights and liabilities. The functions described below are exercisable by the appropriate national authority[1] until such time as a successor body to the Education Transfer Council is established or the Education Transfer Council is re-established[2].

The transferor and the transferee[3] must, whether before or after the transfer date[4], so far as practicable arrive at such written agreements and execute such other instruments as are necessary or expedient to identify or define the property, rights and liabilities[5] transferred to the transferee or retained by the transferor or for making any arrangements relating to the division and apportionment of property[6] and as will[7]:

(1)	afford to the transferor and the transferee as against one another such rights and safeguards as they may require for the proper discharge of their respective functions[8]; and

(2)	make as from such date, not being earlier than the transfer date, as may be specified in the agreement or instrument such clarifications and modifications of the effect of the provision of the Education Reform Act 1988 or of the School Standards and Framework Act 1998 (or any regulations made under it) under which the transfer is required on the property, rights and liabilities of the transferor as will best serve the proper discharge of the respective functions of the transferor and the transferee[9].

Any such agreement must provide so far as it is expedient: (a) for the granting of leases and for the creation of other liabilities and rights over land whether amounting in law to interests in land or not, and whether involving the surrender of any existing interest or the creation of a new interest or not[10]; (b) for the granting of indemnities in connection with the severance of leases and other matters[11]; (c) for responsibility for registration of any matter in any description of statutory register[12].

If and to the extent that it is requested to do so by the transferor or the transferee, the appropriate national authority must[13]:

(i)	assist the transferor, the transferee and any other interested person in identifying or defining the property, rights and liabilities transferred to the transferee or retained by the transferor[14];

(ii)	advise such persons as to the terms of any agreement or instrument falling to be made under the provisions described above[15];

(iii)	prepare drafts of any such agreement or instrument[16]; and

(iv)	assist the parties in executing and giving effect to any such agreement or instrument[17].

Within six months after the transfer date the transferor must send the appropriate national authority a copy of an executed transfer agreement or, if no agreement has been executed, so notify him or it[18].

1	Ie the Secretary of State or, in relation to Wales, the Welsh Ministers. As to the Secretary of State see PARA 58. As to the Welsh Ministers see PARA 59. As to the meaning of 'Wales' see PARA 7 note 3. The functions of the Secretary of State under the Education Reform Act 1988 Sch 10, so far as exercisable in relation to Wales, were transferred to the National Assembly for Wales (see the National Assembly for Wales (Transfer of Functions) Order 1999, SI 1999/672, art 2, Sch 1) and are now vested in the Welsh Ministers (see the Government of Wales Act 2006 s 162(1), Sch 11 para 30).

2	As to the Education Transfer Council and its dissolution see PARA 1330.

3	Where a successor body to the Education Transfer Council is established or the Education Transfer Council is re-established, the Education Reform Act 1988 s 198(2), Sch 10 para 2(1) applies to the transferor and the relevant person: see Sch 10 para 2(1) (Sch 10 para 2 substituted by the School Standards and Framework Act 1998 Sch 29 para 4). As to the transfers to which the Education Reform Act 1988 Sch 10 applies see PARA 1330. As to the modification of Sch 10 para 2(1) in relation to property transfers to former grant-maintained schools in England see the Education (New Procedures for Property Transfers) Regulations 2000, SI 2000/3209, reg 17(b). As to grant-maintained schools see PARA 106 note 15. For these purposes, 'the relevant person' means: (1) in a case where the transferor is a local authority, the Education Transfer Council; (2) in a case where the transferor is not a local authority, the transferee: Education Reform Act 1988 Sch 10 para 2(6) (as so substituted). As to the meaning of 'local authority' see PARA 25. As to the modification of Sch 10 para 2(6) in relation to schools in Wales changing category or joining or leaving foundation bodies see the Education (New Procedures for Property Transfers) Regulations 2000, SI 2000/3209 reg 7(g) (revoked in relation to England by SI 2007/1289).

4　As to the transfer date see PARA 1331 note 11.

5　As to the meaning of 'liability' see PARA 84 note 11.

6　Ie such arrangements as are mentioned in the Education Reform Act 1988 Sch 10 para 1(4) (see PARA 1332).

7　Education Reform Act 1988 Sch 10 para 2(1) (as substituted: see note 3); Education (New Procedures for Property Transfers) Regulations 2000, SI 2000/3209, reg 7(c) (revoked in relation to England by SI 2007/1289).

8　Education Reform Act 1988 Sch 10 para 2(1)(a) (as substituted: see note 3).

9　Education Reform Act 1988 Sch 10 para 2(1)(b) (as substituted: see note 3). This provision also applies to any regulations made under the School Standards and Framework Act 1998.

Where a successor body to the Education Transfer Council is established or the Education Transfer Council is re-established and it appears to the successor body or the Education Transfer Council, in the case of any transfer under which the transferor is a local authority, that any agreements and instruments required to be made or executed in pursuance of the Education Reform Act 1988 Sch 10 para 2(1) have been made or executed, it must deliver those agreements and instruments, if any, to the transferee: Sch 10 para 10 (amended by the School Standards and Framework Act 1998 Sch 29 paras 9, 10). Where land is transferred in relation to schools changing category or joining or leaving foundation bodies, the Education Reform Act 1988 Sch 10 para 10 does not apply: see the Education (New Procedures for Property Transfers) Regulations 2000, SI 2000/3209, reg 7(o) (revoked in relation to England by SI 2007/1289). The Education Reform Act 1988 Sch 10 para 10 does not apply in relation to property transfers to former grant-maintained schools in England: see the Education (New Procedures for Property Transfers) Regulations 2000, SI 2000/3209, reg 17(h). As to the meaning of 'local authority' see PARA 25. As to schools changing categories see PARAS 132, 141; and as to schools joining or leaving foundation bodies see PARA 108.

Any transfer of any estate or interest in land under the Education Reform Act 1988 Sch 10 para 2, whether by virtue of an agreement or instrument entered into before or after the transfer date, is regarded as having taken place on the transfer date: Sch 10 para 2(5) (as substituted: see note 3). As to the meanings of 'interest in land' and 'land' see PARA 84 note 9.

10　Education Reform Act 1988 Sch 10 para 2(2)(a) (as substituted: see note 3).

11　Education Reform Act 1988 Sch 10 para 2(2)(b) (as substituted: see note 3).

12　Education Reform Act 1988 Sch 10 para 2(2)(c) (as substituted: see note 3).

13　Education Reform Act 1988 Sch 10 para 2(3) (as substituted: see note 3); Education (New Procedures for Property Transfers) Regulations 2000, SI 2000/3209, reg 7(d)(i) (revoked in relation to England by SI 2007/1289). Where a successor body to the Education Transfer Council is established or the Education Transfer Council is re-established, it must carry out the duties conferred by the Education Reform Act 1988 Sch 10 para 2(3), except in a case where the transferor is a local authority: Sch 10 para 2(3) (as so substituted). As to the modification of Sch 10 para 2(3) in relation to property transfers to former grant-maintained schools in England see the Education (New Procedures for Property Transfers) Regulations 2000, SI 2000/3209, reg 17(c).

14　Education Reform Act 1988 Sch 10 para 2(3)(a) (as substituted: see note 3).

15　Education Reform Act 1988 Sch 10 para 2(3)(b) (as substituted: see note 3). The reference in the text to the provisions described above is a reference to Sch 10 para 2(1): see the text and notes 3–9.

16　Education Reform Act 1988 Sch 10 para 2(3)(d) (as substituted: see note 3).

17　Education Reform Act 1988 Sch 10 para 2(3)(e) (as substituted: see note 3). Where a successor body to the Education Transfer Council is established or the Education Transfer Council is re-established, it must, except in a case where the transferee is a local authority, assist the transferor, the transferee and any other interested person to negotiate any agreement or instrument made under Sch 10 para 2(1) (see the text and notes 3–9) and mediate in any such negotiations: see Sch 10 para 2(3)(c) (as so substituted). Where land is transferred in relation to schools changing category or joining or leaving foundation bodies, Sch 10 para 2(3)(c) does not apply: see the Education (New Procedures for Property Transfers) Regulations 2000, SI 2000/3209, reg 7(d)(ii) (revoked in relation to England by SI 2007/1289).

If and to the extent that it is requested to do so by any person falling to make a transfer agreement under the School Standards and Framework Act 1998 Sch 21 para 4 or 7 (see PARA 1340) or any corresponding provision of regulations under the School Standards and Framework Act 1998, the appropriate national authority must exercise any one or more functions falling within the Education Reform Act 1988 Sch 10 para 2(3) in relation to such an agreement, or an instrument made pursuant to such an agreement, as if it were an agreement or instrument falling to be made under Sch 10 para 2(1) (see the text and notes 3–9): Sch 10 para 2(4) (as so substituted); Education (New Procedures for Property Transfers) Regulations 2000, SI 2000/3209, reg 7(f) (revoked in relation to England by SI 2007/1289).

Where a successor body to the Education Transfer Council is established or where the Education Transfer Council is re-established, if and to the extent that it is requested to do so by any person falling to make a transfer agreement under the School Standards and Framework Act 1998 Sch 21 para 4 or 7 (see PARA 1340) or any corresponding provision of regulations under the School Standards and Framework Act 1998, it must exercise any one or more functions falling within the Education Reform Act 1988 Sch 10 para 2(3) in relation to such an agreement, or an instrument made pursuant to such an agreement, as if it were an agreement or instrument falling to be made under Sch 10 para 2(1) (see the text and notes 3–9): Sch 10 para 2(4) (as so substituted).

As to the modification of Sch 10 para 2(4) in relation to property transfers to former grant-maintained schools in England see the Education (New Procedures for Property Transfers) Regulations 2000, SI 2000/3209, reg 17(c).

18 Education Reform Act 1988 Sch 10 para 2(3A); Education (New Procedures for Property Transfers) Regulations 2000, SI 2000/3209, reg 7(e) (revoked in relation to England by SI 2007/1289). However, where a successor body to the Education Transfer Council is established or where the Education Transfer Council is re-established, the Education Reform Act 1988 Sch 10 para 2(3A) does not apply: see the Education (New Procedures for Property Transfers) Regulations 2000, SI 2000/3209, reg 7(e) (revoked).

1334. Resolution of disputes regarding the identification of property, rights and liabilities. The powers described below are exercisable by the appropriate national authority[1] until such time as a successor body to the Education Transfer Council is established or the Education Transfer Council is re-established[2].

In the case of any matter on which agreement is required to be reached under the statutory provisions relating to the identification of property, rights and liabilities[3], if such an agreement has not been reached within a period of six months from the transfer date[4], the appropriate national authority may give a direction determining that matter, and may include in the direction any provision which might have been included in an agreement under the provisions relating to the identification of property, rights and liabilities[5].

Any property, rights or liabilities required by such a direction to be transferred to the transferee are regarded as having been transferred to, and vested[6] in, the transferee on the transfer date[7]. The appropriate national authority must consult the transferor, the transferee and any other interested person before giving a direction[8].

Any reference in a determination of the Education Transfer Council to a matter being referred to the Education Transfer Council for determination in the event of the parties failing to reach agreement is to be read as requiring the matter to be referred to the appropriate national authority in such event[9].

1 Ie the Secretary of State or, in relation to Wales, the Welsh Ministers. As to the Secretary of State see PARA 58. As to the Welsh Ministers see PARA 59. As to the meaning of 'Wales' see PARA 7 note 3. The functions of the Secretary of State under the Education Reform Act 1988 Sch 10, so far as exercisable in relation to Wales, were transferred to the National Assembly for Wales (see the National Assembly for Wales (Transfer of Functions) Order 1999, SI 1999/672, art 2, Sch 1) and are now vested in the Welsh Ministers (see the Government of Wales Act 2006 s 162(1), Sch 11 para 30).

2 As to the Education Transfer Council and its dissolution see PARA 1330.

3 Ie the Education Reform Act 1988 s 198(2), Sch 10 para 2(1) (see PARA 1333). As to the meaning of 'liability' see PARA 84 note 11.

4 As to the transfer date see PARA 1331 note 11.

5 Education Reform Act 1988 Sch 10 para 3(2) (Sch 10 para 3 substituted by the School Standards and Framework Act 1998 Sch 29 para 5); Education (New Procedures for Property

Transfers) Regulations 2000, SI 2000/3209, reg 7(i) (revoked in relation to England by SI 2007/1289). As to the transfers to which the Education Reform Act 1988 Sch 10 applies see PARA 1330.

Where a successor body to the Education Transfer Council is established or the Education Transfer Council is re-established, it must notify the appropriate national authority if it appears to it that it is unlikely in the case of any matter on which agreement is required to be reached under Sch 10 para 2(1) (see PARA 1333) that such an agreement will be reached: Sch 10 para 3(1) (as so substituted). Where the appropriate national authority has received such a notification under Sch 10 para 3(1), it may, whether before or after the transfer date, give a direction determining that matter, and may include in the direction any provision which might have been included in an agreement under Sch 10 para 2(1): Sch 10 para 3(2) (as so substituted). Where land is transferred in relation to schools changing category or joining or leaving foundation bodies Sch 10 para 3(1) does not apply: see the Education (New Procedures for Property Transfers) Regulations 2000, SI 2000/3209, reg 7(h) (revoked in relation to England by SI 2007/1289). As to the meaning of 'land' see PARA 84 note 9. As to schools changing categories see PARAS 132, 141; and as to schools joining or leaving foundation bodies see PARA 108.

As to the modification of the Education Reform Act 1988 Sch 10 para 3 in relation to property transfers to former grant-maintained schools in England see the Education (New Procedures for Property Transfers) Regulations 2000, SI 2000/3209, reg 17(d). See also regs 18, 19. As to grant-maintained schools see PARA 106 note 15.

Where a successor body to the Education Transfer Council is established or the Education Transfer Council is re-established and it appears, in the case of any transfer under which the transferor is a local authority, that any agreements and instruments required to be made or executed in pursuance of a direction under the Education Reform Act 1988 Sch 10 para 3 have been made or executed, it must deliver those agreements and instruments, if any, to the transferee: Sch 10 para 10 (amended by the School Standards and Framework Act 1998 Sch 29 paras 9, 10). Where land is transferred in relation to schools changing category or joining or leaving foundation bodies, the Education Reform Act 1988 Sch 10 para 10 does not apply: see the Education (New Procedures for Property Transfers) Regulations 2000, SI 2000/3209, reg 7(o) (revoked in relation to England by SI 2007/1289). The Education Reform Act 1988 Sch 10 para 10 does not apply in relation to property transfers to former grant-maintained schools in England: see the Education (New Procedures for Property Transfers) Regulations 2000, SI 2000/3209, reg 17(h). As to the meaning of 'local authority' see PARA 25.

6   Ie by virtue of the Education Reform Act 1988.
7   Education Reform Act 1988 Sch 10 para 3(3) (as substituted: see note 5).
8   Education Reform Act 1988 Sch 10 para 3(4) (as substituted: see note 5); Education (New Procedures for Property Transfers) Regulations 2000, SI 2000/3209, reg 7(j) (revoked in relation to England by SI 2007/1289). Where a successor body to the Education Transfer Council is established or the Education Transfer Council is re-established, the appropriate national authority must consult the transferor, the transferee and any other interested person before giving a direction under the Education Reform Act 1988 Sch 10 para 3: Sch 10 para 3(4) (as so substituted). The successor body or the Education Transfer Council must give the appropriate national authority such assistance and advice as it may require for the purpose of determining any matter under Sch 10 para 3: Sch 10 para 3(5) (as so substituted). Where land is transferred in relation to schools changing category or joining or leaving foundation bodies Sch 10 para 3(5) does not apply: see the Education (New Procedures for Property Transfers) Regulations 2000, SI 2000/3209, reg 7(k) (revoked in relation to England by SI 2007/1289).
9   Education (New Procedures for Property Transfers) Regulations 2000, SI 2000/3209, reg 4. Where a successor body to the Education Transfer Council is established or the Education Transfer Council is re-established, reg 4 will not apply (see PARA 1330).

1335.   Right to production of documents of title. Where a transfer to which these provisions apply[1] relates to registered land[2], it is the duty of the transferor to execute any such instrument under the Land Registration Acts 1925 to 1986[3], to deliver any such certificate under those Acts and to do such other things under those Acts as he would be required to execute, deliver or do in the case of a transfer by agreement between the transferor and the transferee[4]. Where on any such transfer the transferor is entitled to retain possession of any documents relating in part to the title to any land or other property transferred to the transferee, the transferor is treated as having given to the transferee an acknowledgment in writing of the right of the transferee to production of that document and to delivery of copies of it[5].

1 Ie a transfer to which the Education Reform Act 1988 s 198(2), Sch 10 applies (see PARA 1330).
2 As to the meaning of 'land' see PARA 84 note 9.
3 As to the Land Registration Acts 1925 to 1986 see REAL PROPERTY AND REGISTRATION vol 87 (2012) PARAS 232–234.
4 Education Reform Act 1988 Sch 10 para 4(1) (added by the Further and Higher Education Act 1992 Sch 8 para 65; and amended by the Education Act 1993 s 47(8); and the Education Act 1996 Sch 37 para 82(1)(a), (2)(b)).
5 Education Reform Act 1988 Sch 10 para 4(2) (renumbered by the Further and Higher Education Act 1992 Sch 8 para 65). The Law of Property Act 1925 s 64 (production and safe custody of documents: see CONVEYANCING vol 23 (2013) PARA 105) has effect accordingly, and on the basis that the acknowledgment did not contain any such expression of contrary intention as is mentioned in s 64 (see CONVEYANCING vol 23 (2013) PARA 105): Education Reform Act 1988 Sch 10 para 4(2) (as so renumbered).

1336. Proof of title by certificate. The powers described below are exercisable by the appropriate national authority[1] until such time as a successor body to the Education Transfer Council is established or the Education Transfer Council is re-established[2].

The appropriate national authority may issue[3] a certificate stating that any property specified in the certificate, or any such interest in or right over any such property as may be so specified, or any right or liability[4] so specified, was or was not transferred by virtue of the Education Reform Act 1988 or the School Standards and Framework Act 1998 to any body corporate or persons so specified, and any such certificate is conclusive evidence for all purposes of that fact[5].

1 Ie the Secretary of State or, in relation to Wales, the Welsh Ministers. As to the Secretary of State see PARA 58. As to the Welsh Ministers see PARA 59. As to the meaning of 'Wales' see PARA 7 note 3. The functions of the Secretary of State under the Education Reform Act 1988 Sch 10, so far as exercisable in relation to Wales, were transferred to the National Assembly for Wales (see the National Assembly for Wales (Transfer of Functions) Order 1999, SI 1999/672, art 2, Sch 1) and are now vested in the Welsh Ministers (see the Government of Wales Act 2006 s 162(1), Sch 11 para 30).
2 As to the Education Transfer Council and its dissolution see PARA 1330.
3 Where a successor body to the Education Transfer Council is established or the Education Transfer Council is re-established, it may issue a certificate: see the Education Reform Act 1988 Sch 10 para 5 (amended by the School Standards and Framework Act 1998 Sch 29 paras 6, 10).
4 As to the meaning of 'liability' see PARA 84 note 11.
5 Education Reform Act 1988 Sch 10 para 5 (as amended: see note 3); Education (New Procedures for Property Transfers) Regulations 2000, SI 2000/3209, reg 7(l) (revoked in relation to England by SI 2007/1289). As to the transfers to which the Education Reform Act 1988 Sch 10 applies see PARA 1330. As to the modification of Sch 10 para 5 in relation to property transfers to former grant-maintained schools in England see the Education (New Procedures for Property Transfers) Regulations 2000, SI 2000/3209, reg 17(e). As to grant-maintained schools see PARA 106 note 15.

1337. Construction of agreements. Where in the case of any transfer to which these provisions apply[1] any rights or liabilities[2] transferred are rights or liabilities under an agreement[3] to which the transferor was a party immediately before the transfer date[4], the agreement, unless the context otherwise requires, has effect on and after the transfer date as if:

(1)   the transferee had been a party to the agreement[5];
(2)   for any reference[6] to the transferor there were substituted, as respects anything falling to be done on or after the transfer date, a reference to the transferee[7];

(3)   any reference[8] to a specified officer of the transferor or a person employed by the transferor in a specified capacity were, as respects anything falling to be done on or after the transfer date, a reference to such person as the transferee may appoint or, in default of appointment, to an officer or employee of the transferee who corresponds as closely as possible to the person referred to in the agreement[9]; and

(4)   where the agreement refers to property, rights or liabilities which fall to be apportioned or divided between the transferor and the transferee, the agreement constituted two separate agreements separately enforceable by and against the transferor and the transferee as regards the part of the property, rights or liabilities retained by the transferor or, as the case may be, the part vesting in the transferee, and not as regards the other part[10].

The transferee under a transfer to which these provisions apply and any other person has[11], as from the transfer date, the same rights, powers and remedies, and in particular the same rights and powers as to the taking or resisting of legal proceedings or the making or resisting of applications to any authority, for ascertaining, perfecting or enforcing any right or liability transferred to and vested in the transferee[12] as he would have had if that right or liability had at all times been a right or liability of the transferee[13].

Any legal proceedings or applications to any authority pending on the transfer date by or against the transferor, in so far as they relate to any property, right or liability transferred to the transferee[14], or to any agreement relating to any such property, right or liability, is continued by or against the transferee to the exclusion of the transferor[15].

1   Ie a transfer to which the Education Reform Act 1988 Sch 10 applies (see PARA 1330).
2   As to the meaning of 'liability' see PARA 84 note 11.
3   The Education Reform Act 1988 Sch 10 para 6(1) (see the text and notes 5–10) applies to any agreement whether in writing or not and whether or not of such a nature that rights and liabilities under it could be assigned by the transferor: Sch 10 para 6(2).
4   As to the transfer date see PARA 1331 note 11.
5   Education Reform Act 1988 Sch 10 para 6(1)(a). Schedule 10 para 6 has effect for the interpretation of agreements subject to the context, and does not apply where the context otherwise requires: Sch 10 para 8.
6   Ie any reference whether express or implied and, if express, however worded: Education Reform Act 1988 Sch 10 para 6(1)(b).
7   Education Reform Act 1988 Sch 10 para 6(1)(b). See also note 5.
8   Ie any reference whether express or implied and, if express, however worded: Education Reform Act 1988 Sch 10 para 6(1)(c).
9   Education Reform Act 1988 Sch 10 para 6(1)(c). See also note 5.
10   Education Reform Act 1988 Sch 10 para 6(1)(d). Schedule 10 para 6(1)(d) applies in particular to the covenants, stipulations and conditions of any lease by or to the transferor: Sch 10 para 6(1). See also note 5.
11   Ie without prejudice to the generality of the Education Reform Act 1988 Sch 10 para 6: see the text and notes 1–10.
12   Ie by virtue of the Education Reform Act 1988 or the School Standards and Framework Act 1998.
13   Education Reform Act 1988 Sch 10 para 7(1) (amended by the School Standards and Framework Act 1998 Sch 29 para 7). The Education Reform Act 1988 Sch 10 para 7 has effect for the interpretation of agreements subject to the context, and does not apply where the context otherwise requires: Sch 10 para 8.
14   Ie by virtue of the Education Reform Act 1988 or the School Standards and Framework Act 1998.
15   Education Reform Act 1988 Sch 10 para 7(2) (amended by the School Standards and Framework Act 1998 Sch 29 para 7). See also note 13.

1338. Third parties affected by vesting provisions. The provisions described below are exercisable by the appropriate national authority[1] until such time as a successor body to the Education Transfer Council is established or the Education Transfer Council is re-established[2].

Any transaction effected between a transferor and a transferee[3] is binding[4] on all other persons, and notwithstanding that it would otherwise have required the consent or concurrence of any person other than the transferor and the transferee[5]. Where as a result of any such transaction any person's rights or liabilities[6] become enforceable as to part by or against the transferor and as to part by or against the transferee, the transferee[7] must give that person written notification of that fact[8].

Where in consequence of a transfer to which these provisions apply[9] or of anything done in pursuance of these provisions:

(1)   the rights or liabilities of any person other than the transferor or the transferee which were enforceable against or by the transferor become enforceable as to part against or by the transferor and as to part against or by the transferee[10]; and

(2)   the value of any property or interest of that person is thereby diminished[11],

such compensation as may be just must be paid to that person by the transferor, the transferee or both[12].

Where the transferor or the transferee purports by any conveyance or transfer to transfer to some person other than the transferor or the transferee for consideration any land[13] or other property which before the transfer date[14] belonged to the transferor, or which is an interest in property which before that date belonged to the transferor, the conveyance or transfer is as effective as if both the transferor and the transferee had been parties to it and had thereby conveyed or transferred all their interest in the property conveyed or transferred[15].

A court has the power described below[16] if at any stage in proceedings before it to which the transferor or transferee and a person other than the transferor or the transferee are parties it appears that the issues in the proceedings: (a) depend on the identification or definition of any of the property, rights or liabilities transferred which the transferor and the transferee have not yet effected[17]; or (b) raise a question of construction on the relevant statutory provisions[18] which would not arise if the transferor and the transferee constituted a single person[19]. In any such case the court has power, if it thinks fit on the application of a party to the proceedings other than the transferor or the transferee, to hear and determine the proceedings on the footing that such one of the transferor and the transferee as is a party to the proceedings represents and is answerable for the other of them, and that the transferor and the transferee constitute a single person[20].

1   Ie the Secretary of State or, in relation to Wales, the Welsh Ministers. As to the Secretary of State see PARA 58. As to the Welsh Ministers see PARA 59. As to the meaning of 'Wales' see PARA 7 note 3. The functions of the Secretary of State under the Education Reform Act 1988 Sch 10, so far as exercisable in relation to Wales, were transferred to the National Assembly for Wales (see the National Assembly for Wales (Transfer of Functions) Order 1999, SI 1999/672, art 2, Sch 1) and are now vested in the Welsh Ministers (see the Government of Wales Act 2006 s 162(1), Sch 11 para 30).

2   As to the Education Transfer Council and its dissolution see PARA 1330.

3   Ie in pursuance of the Education Reform Act 1988 Sch 10 para 2(1) (see PARA 1333) or of a direction under Sch 10 para 3 (see PARA 1334).

4   Ie without prejudice to the generality of the Education Reform Act 1988 Sch 10 paras 6–8 (see PARA 1337).
5   Education Reform Act 1988 Sch 10 para 9(1). As to the transfers to which Sch 10 applies see PARA 1330.
6   As to the meaning of 'liability' see PARA 84 note 11.
7   Where a successor body to the Education Transfer Council is established or the Education Transfer Council is re-established, it must give the written notification: see the Education Reform Act 1988 Sch 10 para 9(2) (amended by the School Standards and Framework Act 1998 Sch 29 para 10).
8   Education Reform Act 1988 Sch 10 para 9(2) (as amended: see note 7); Education (New Procedures for Property Transfers) Regulations 2000, SI 2000/3209, reg 7(m) (revoked in relation to England by SI 2007/1289). As to the modification of the Education Reform Act 1988 Sch 10 para 9(2) in relation to property transfers to former grant-maintained schools in England see the Education (New Procedures for Property Transfers) Regulations 2000, SI 2000/3209, reg 17(f). As to grant-maintained schools see PARA 106 note 15.
9   Ie a transfer to which the Education Reform Act 1988 Sch 10 applies (see PARA 1330).
10 Education Reform Act 1988 Sch 10 para 9(3)(a).
11 Education Reform Act 1988 Sch 10 para 9(3)(b).
12 Education Reform Act 1988 Sch 10 para 9(3). Any dispute as to whether and if so how much compensation is payable under Sch 10 para 9(3), or as to the person to whom it is to be paid, must be referred to and determined by an arbitrator: see Sch 10 para 9(4).
    As to appointments to the office of arbitrator in exercise of the function under Sch 10 para 9(4) see COURTS AND TRIBUNALS vol 24 (2010) PARA 944. Any function of the Lord Chancellor under the Education Reform Act 1988 Sch 10 para 9(4) is a 'protected function' within the meaning of the Constitutional Reform Act 2005 and may not be transferred, modified or abolished by an order under s 19(1): see Sch 7 para 4; and CONSTITUTIONAL AND ADMINISTRATIVE LAW vol 20 (2014) PARA 261. As to the Lord Chancellor see CONSTITUTIONAL AND ADMINISTRATIVE LAW vol 20 (2014) PARA 255 et seq.
13 As to the meaning of 'land' see PARA 84 note 9.
14 As to the transfer date see PARA 1331 note 11.
15 Education Reform Act 1988 Sch 10 para 9(5).
16 Ie the power set out in the Education Reform Act 1988 Sch 10 para 9(7): see the text to note 20.
17 Education Reform Act 1988 Sch 10 para 9(6)(a) (amended by the School Standards and Framework Act 1998 Sch 29 paras 8(c)); Education (New Procedures for Property Transfers) Regulations 2000, SI 2000/3209, reg 7(n) (revoked in relation to England by SI 2007/1289). Where a successor body to the Education Transfer Council is established or the Education Transfer Council is re-established, the Education Reform Act 1988 Sch 10 para 9(6)(a) also applies to the successor body or the Education Transfer Council: see Sch 10 para 9(6)(a) (amended by the School Standards and Framework Act 1998 Sch 29 paras 8(a), (c), 10). As to the modification of the Education Reform Act 1988 Sch 10 para 9(6) in relation to property transfers to former grant-maintained schools in England see the Education (New Procedures for Property Transfers) Regulations 2000, SI 2000/3209, reg 17(g).
18 Ie the relevant provisions of the Education Reform Act 1988 or the School Standards and Framework Act 1998, or any regulations made under the School Standards and Framework Act 1998.
19 Education Reform Act 1988 Sch 10 para 9(6)(b) (amended by the School Standards and Framework Act 1998 Sch 29 para 8(b)).
20 Education Reform Act 1988 Sch 10 para 9(7). Any judgment or order given by a court in proceedings determined on that footing bind both the transferor and the transferee accordingly: Sch 10 para 9(8). It is the duty of the transferor and of the transferee to keep one another informed of any case where the transferor or the transferee under a transfer to which Sch 10 applies may be prejudiced by Sch 10 para 9(5) (see the text and notes 13–15) or any judgment or order given by virtue of Sch 10 para 9(8): Sch 10 para 9(9) (amended by the School Standards and Framework Act 1998 Sch 29 para 8(c)); Education (New Procedures for Property Transfers) Regulations 2000, SI 2000/3209, reg 7(n) (revoked in relation to England by SI 2007/1289). Where a successor body to the Education Transfer Council is established or the Education Transfer Council is re-established, the Education Reform Act 1988 Sch 10 para 9(9) applies to the successor body or the Education Transfer Council: see Sch 10 para 9(9) (amended by the School Standards and Framework Act 1998 Sch 29 para 8(c), 10). As to the modification of the Education Reform Act 1988 Sch 10 para 9(9) in relation to property transfers to former grant-maintained schools in England see the Education (New Procedures for Property Transfers) Regulations 2000, SI 2000/3209, reg 17(g).

If either the transferor or the transferee claims that he has been prejudiced under the Education Reform Act 1988 Sch 10 para 9(9) and that the other of them ought to indemnify or make a payment to him on that account and has unreasonably failed to meet that claim, he may refer the matter to the appropriate national authority for determination by that authority: Sch 10 para 9(10).

1339. Provision of information. Any local authority[1], governing body[2] of a maintained school and institution within the further education sector[3] must give the appropriate national authority[4] such information as the authority may require for the purposes of the exercise of its functions in relation to certain property transfers[5].

1   As to the meaning of 'local authority' see PARA 25.
2   As to the governing body of a maintained school, in relation to England, see PARA 150 et seq; and as to the governing body of a maintained school, in relation to Wales, see PARA 195 et seq. As to maintained schools generally see PARA 99 et seq.
3   Ie within the meaning of the Further and Higher Education Act 1992 s 91 (see PARA 555).
4   Ie the Secretary of State or, in relation to Wales, the Welsh Ministers. As to the Secretary of State see PARA 58. As to the Welsh Ministers see PARA 59. As to the meaning of 'Wales' see PARA 7 note 3. The functions of the Secretary of State under the Education (New Procedures for Property Transfers) Regulations 2000, SI 2000/3209, so far as exercisable in relation to Wales, are now vested in the Welsh Ministers (see the Government of Wales Act 2006 s 162(1), Sch 11 para 30).
5   Education (New Procedures for Property Transfers) Regulations 2000, SI 2000/3209, reg 3 (amended by SI 2010/1172). This provision applies to property transfers under the Education Acts as modified by the Education (New Procedures for Property Transfers) Regulations 2000, SI 2000/3209. As to the meaning of 'the Education Acts' see PARA 1 note 13 (definition applied by virtue of the School Standards and Framework Act 1998 s 142(8)). As to the transfers to which the Education (New Procedures for Property Transfers) Regulations 2000, SI 2000/3209, apply see PARA 1330. Where a successor body to the Education Transfer Council is established or the Education Transfer Council is re-established, reg 3 will not apply (see PARA 1330). As to the Education Transfer Council and its dissolution see PARA 1330.

(ii) Transfer of Land from Grant-maintained Schools on 1 September 1999

1340. Rules relating to transfers. Provision was made for the transfer of land[1] from grant-maintained or grant-maintained special schools[2] to community, foundation, voluntary or community special schools[3] on 1 September 1999[4]. Where any land was transferred to and vested in any body on 1 September 1999, any rights or liabilities[5] enjoyed or incurred by the transferor in connection with the land, and subsisting immediately before 1 September 1999, were also transferred to, and vested[6] in, that body[7].

1   As to references to 'land' see PARA 116 note 18 (definition applied by virtue of the School Standards and Framework Act 1998 s 142(8)).
2   As to the meanings of 'grant-maintained school' and 'grant-maintained special school' see PARA 106 notes 15, 16 (definitions applied by virtue of the School Standards and Framework Act 1998 Sch 21 para 1).
3   As to community, foundation, voluntary and community special schools see PARA 106 et seq; and as to special schools generally see PARA 1041 et seq.
4   See the School Standards and Framework Act 1998 Sch 21 paras 4–10 (amended by SI 2010/1158). The reference in the text to 1 September 1999 is a reference to the appointed day (see PARA 106 note 3). The provisions of the School Standards and Framework Act 1998 Sch 21 Pt II paras 3–9 applied to schools which, in accordance with s 20, Sch 2 became community, foundation, voluntary or community special schools on 1 September 1999: Sch 21 para 3(1). Schedule 21 Pt II has effect subject to Sch 21 Pt III para 10 (property excluded from transfers): Sch 21 para 3(2).
5   As to the meaning of 'liability' see PARA 108 note 22 (definition applied by virtue of the School Standards and Framework Act 1998 s 142(8)).

6 Ie by virtue of the School Standards and Framework Act 1998.
7 See the School Standards and Framework Act 1998 Sch 21 para 2(1).

(iii) Transfer of Land in relation to Academies

1341. Transfer schemes in relation to land held by local authority. The Secretary of State[1] may make a transfer scheme in relation to land[2] which either:

(1) was formerly used[3] for the purposes of a school or 16 to 19 academy[4] but[5] is no longer so used or is thought by the Secretary of State to be about to be no longer so used[6]; or

(2) forms the whole or part of a site specified[7] as a possible site for a new school[8],

and when such a scheme comes into force[9] it has effect to transfer (in accordance with its provisions) the land, rights and liabilities to which it applies[10]. The scheme must meet the following requirements[11]:

(a) the scheme must provide for a transfer of the land or such part of it as is specified in the scheme[12];

(b) the scheme must specify whether the transfer is the transfer of a freehold or leasehold interest in the land or the grant of a lease in respect of the land[13];

(c) the transfer must be to a person who is specified in the scheme and is concerned with the running of an academy[14];

(d) the transfer must be made to the transferee for the purposes of the academy[15]; and

(e) in the case of a scheme made pursuant to proposals for the establishment of a new school[16], the academy must have been the subject of proposals[17] for the establishment of a new school[18]; and

(f) the scheme must make provision about the transfer to the transferee of any right or liability held by the local authority as holder of the land or specified part concerned[19].

Further provision in connection with transfer schemes may be made by regulations[20].

1 As to the Secretary of State see PARA 58.
2 Ie land in which a local authority holds a freehold or leasehold interest when the transfer scheme is made: Academies Act 2010 Sch 1 paras 1(1), (2)(a), 2(1), (2)(a) (Sch 1 substituted by the Education Act 2011 Sch 14 para 1). As to the meaning of 'local authority' see PARA 25 and (in the context of the Academies Act 2010), PARA 351 note 3.
3 Ie at any time in the period of eight years ending with the day on which the scheme is made: Academies Act 2010 Sch 1 para 1(2)(b) (as substituted: see note 2).
4 Academies Act 2010 Sch 1 para 1(2)(b) (as substituted: see note 2). As to the meaning of 'school' see PARA 91 (definition applied by s 17(4)); and as to the meaning of '16 to 19 academy' see PARA 346 note 13. A dwelling-house used for occupation by a person employed to work at an educational institution is to be treated for the purposes of Sch 1 as used for the purposes of the school: Sch 1 para 22(1) (as so substituted).
5 Ie at the time the scheme is made: Academies Act 2010 Sch 1 para 1(2)(c) (as substituted: see note 2).
6 Academies Act 2010 Sch 1 para 1(2)(c) (as substituted: see note 2).
7 Ie specified in a notice published under the Education and Inspections Act 2006 s 6A (requirement to seek proposals for establishment of new academies: see PARA 111) or s 7 (invitation for proposals for establishment of new schools: see PARA 111).
8 Academies Act 2010 Sch 1 para 2(2)(b) (as substituted: see note 2). Before making a scheme in respect of such land the Secretary of State must consult the authority: Sch 1 para 2(2)(c) (as so substituted).
9 A scheme comes into force on the day it specifies for it to come into force or on the day it otherwise identifies as the day for it to come into force: Academies Act 2010 Sch 1 para 3(5) (as

substituted: see note 2). The scheme must be so expressed that it does not come into force while the land concerned is used for the purposes of the school or 16 to 19 academy mentioned in Sch 1 para 1(2)(b) (see the text and note 3): Sch 1 para 3(4).

10 Academies Act 2010 Sch 1 para 3(6) (as substituted: see note 2). A transfer made by virtue of a scheme is binding on all persons even if, apart from this provision, it would have required the consent or concurrence of any person: Sch 1 para 3(7) (as so substituted). A scheme may include incidental, consequential, supplemental and transitional provision: Sch 1 para 3(3) (as so substituted).

References in Sch 1 to a transfer of land are to the transfer of a freehold or leasehold interest in the land or to the grant of a lease in respect of the land: Sch 1 para 22(4) (as so substituted). References in Sch 1 to a lease include references to a sub-lease: Sch 1 para 22(7) (as so substituted).

Where land is transferred for no consideration for the purposes of an academy (whether or not by virtue of a scheme under Sch 1 para 1 (see the text and notes 1–6) or Sch 1 para 2 (see the text and notes 1–8) or pursuant to a direction under Sch 1 para 4 (see PARA 1342)) and the person who transferred the land is granted an option (other than an option granted before 26 July 2002) to make a re-acquisition of the land (subject to whatever conditions), the rule against perpetuities (see PERPETUITIES AND ACCUMULATIONS vol 80 (2013) PARA 9 et seq) does not apply to the option: Sch 1 para 19(1), (2) (as so substituted). Where a lease is granted or transferred to a person for the purposes of an academy on or after 26 July 2002, the Law of Property Act 1925 s 153 (enlargement of leases granted for no rent etc: see REAL PROPERTY AND REGISTRATION vol 87 (2012) PARAS 83–86) does not apply to permit that person to enlarge the term under the lease: Academies Act 2010 Sch 1 para 20(1) (as so substituted). As to the meaning of 'academy' see PARA 346.

The Local Government Act 1972 s 123 (disposals of land by principal councils: see LOCAL GOVERNMENT vol 69 (2009) PARA 515) do not apply to a disposal of land to a person for the purposes of an academy: Sch 1 para 20(2) (as so substituted).

11 Academies Act 2010 Sch 1 paras 1(3), 2(3) (as substituted: see note 2).

12 Academies Act 2010 Sch 1 para 3(1)(a) (as substituted: see note 2).

13 Academies Act 2010 Sch 1 para 3(1)(b) (as substituted: see note 2). See note 10.

14 Academies Act 2010 Sch 1 para 3(1)(c) (as substituted: see note 2).

15 Academies Act 2010 Sch 1 para 3(1)(d) (as substituted: see note 2).

16 Ie a scheme made under the Academies Act 2010 Sch 1 para 2 (see the text and notes 1–8).

17 Ie proposals published under the Education and Inspections Act 2006 s 6A (requirement to seek proposals for establishment of new academies: see PARA 111 note 5) or s 7 (invitation for proposals for establishment of new schools: see PARA 111).

18 Academies Act 2010 Sch 1 para 3(1)(e) (as substituted: see note 2).

19 Academies Act 2010 Sch 1 para 3(1)(f) (as substituted: see note 2). In this provision the reference to a right or liability includes a reference to a right or liability as a trustee but excludes a reference to a liability in respect of the principal of or interest on a loan: Sch 1 para 3(2) (as so substituted).

20 The Secretary of State may make regulations containing such incidental, consequential, supplemental and transitional provisions as the Secretary of State thinks are appropriate in consequence of the Academies Act 2010 Sch 1 or for giving it full effect: Sch 1 para 21(1) (as substituted: see note 2). Such regulations may in particular include provision:

(1)　requiring a person to be appointed by the Secretary of State in connection with the proposed making of a scheme (Sch 1 para 21(2)(a) (as so substituted));

(2)　requiring the appointed person to identify the land, rights and liabilities to be transferred by or under a scheme (Sch 1 para 21(2)(b) (as so substituted));

(3)　requiring a transferor under a scheme to provide the appointed person with such documents as may be required in order to identify the land, rights and liabilities to be transferred by or under the scheme (Sch 1 para 21(2)(c) (as so substituted));

(4)　requiring a transferor under a scheme to execute such instruments, deliver such certificates and do any other such things as are required by the Land Registration Act 2002 (see REAL PROPERTY AND REGISTRATION vol 87 (2012) PARA 232 et seq) in order to transfer the land (Academies Act 2010 Sch 1 para 21(2)(d) (as so substituted)); and

(5)　treating a transferor under a scheme as having given acknowledgement in writing of the rights to production of documents (Sch 1 para 21(2)(e) (as so substituted)).

The following regulations have been made under Sch 1 para 21 in relation to England only: Academies (Land Transfer Schemes) Regulations 2012, SI 2012/1829.

As to guidance see in particular (including in regard to the Academies Act 2010 Sch 1) 'Disposal or change of use of playing field and school land: Departmental advice for local authorities, maintained schools, special schools, academies and free schools' (May 2015).

1342. Transfers of land held by a governing body, a foundation body or trustees. Where an academy order[1] has effect in respect of a foundation, voluntary or foundation special school[2] and the school is to be converted into an academy school[3] the Secretary of State[4] may, in respect of publicly funded land[5] which is held for the purposes of the school by the governing or foundation body or trustees of the school, direct[6]:

(1)	that the land or any part of the land be transferred[7] to such local authority[8] as the Secretary of State may specify, subject to the payment by that local authority of such sum by way of consideration (if any) as the Secretary of State determines to be appropriate[9];

(2)	that the governing body, the foundation body or the trustees, as the case may be, pay, either to the Secretary of State or to such local authority as the Secretary of State may specify, the whole or any part of the value, as at the date of the direction, of the whole or any part of the land[10]; or

(3)	that the land or any part of the land be transferred to a person concerned with the running of the academy school, subject to the payment by that person or the Secretary of State of such sum by way of consideration (if any) as the Secretary of State determines to be appropriate[11].

Where the Secretary of State has received an application[12] in respect of land held by a governing body, foundation body or trustees on the discontinuance of a school[13], he may direct that the land or any part of the land to which the application relates be transferred to a person concerned with the running of an academy, subject to the payment by that person or the Secretary of State of such sum by way of consideration (if any) as the Secretary of State determines to be appropriate[14].

Where the Secretary of State has received a notice by:

(a)	a governing body of its intention to dispose of publicly funded land[15];

(b)	a foundation body of its intention to dispose of publicly funded land[16];

(c)	trustees of their intention to dispose of publicly funded land[17];

(d)	a local authority of its intention to apply for a transfer order in respect of publicly funded land[18],

he may direct that the land or any part of the land to which the notice relates be transferred to a person concerned with the running of an academy, subject to the payment by that person or the Secretary of State of such sum by way of consideration (if any) as the Secretary of State determines to be appropriate[19].

Where the governing body of a school is[20] to be dissolved, and holds[21] publicly funded land for the purposes of the school[22] which is not[23] to be transferred[24], then when that governing body is so dissolved all publicly funded land which is held by it for the purposes of the school[25], all other property of the governing body which is used or held for the purposes of the school[26] and all its rights and liabilities (including rights and liabilities in relation to staff) which were acquired or incurred for the purposes of the school[27], are[28] transferred to and vest[29] in either the local authority that maintained the school[30] or such person concerned with the running of an academy school as the Secretary of State directs[31].

A governing body which is to be dissolved[32] may transfer any land or other property which is held by them on trust for the purposes of the school to any person to hold such land or other property on trust for purposes connected with the provision of education in schools[33].

Further provision in connection with transfers may be made by regulations[34].

1   As to the meaning of 'academy order' see PARA 350.
2   As to foundation, voluntary and foundation special schools see PARA 106 et seq; and as to special schools generally see PARA 1041 et seq.
3   As to the meaning of 'academy school' see PARA 346 note 12.
4   As to the Secretary of State see PARA 58.
5   In the Academies Act 2010 Sch 1 'publicly funded land' means:
    (1)   in relation to land held by a governing body, land falling within the School Standards and Framework Act 1998 Sch 22 para A1(1)(a)–(i) (disposals of school land on discontinuance etc: see PARA 1305) (Academies Act 2010 Sch 1 para 22(3)(a) (Sch 1 substituted by the Education Act 2011 Sch 14 para 1);
    (2)   in relation to land held by a foundation body, land falling within the School Standards and Framework Act 1998 Sch 22 para A7(1)(a)–(h) (see PARA 1306) (Academies Act 2010 Sch 1 para 22(3)(b) (as so substituted));
    (3)   in relation to land held by trustees, other than land held for the purposes of an academy, land falling within the School Standards and Framework Act 1998 Sch 22 para A13(1), (2) or Sch 22 para A13(3) (see PARA 1307) (Academies Act 2010 Sch 1 para 22(3)(c) (as so substituted));
    (4)   in relation to land held for the purposes of an academy: (a) land acquired from a governing body, foundation body or trustees that was, at the time of the acquisition, publicly funded land within the meaning of head (1), head (2) or head (3) above (Sch 1 para 22(3)(d)(i) (as so substituted)); (b) land held by trustees for the purposes of an academy which was previously held by the trustees for the purposes of a maintained school and which, at the time it was held for the purposes of a maintained school, was publicly funded land within the meaning of head (3) above (Sch 1 para 22(3)(d)(ii) (as so substituted)); (c) land acquired from a local authority (Sch 1 para 22(3)(d)(iii) (as so substituted)); (d) land in relation to which a notice has been served under Sch 1 para 14 (Sch 1 para 22(3)(d)(iv) (as so substituted)); (e) land acquired from a person concerned with the running of an academy that was, at the time of the acquisition, publicly funded land within the meaning of heads (a) to (d) or this head (e) (Sch 1 para 22(3)(d)(v) (as so substituted)).
    Where land is held for the purposes of an academy and has been acquired or enhanced in value wholly or partly by payments made by or on behalf of a local authority, or the Secretary of State, a notice that the land is publicly funded land for the purposes of Sch 1 may be served: (i) in the case of land acquired or enhanced in value wholly or partly by payments made by or on behalf of a local authority, to the authority; and (ii) in the case of land acquired or enhanced in value wholly or partly by payments made by or on behalf of the Secretary of State, to the Secretary of State: see Sch 1 para 14(1), (4)–(6) (as so substituted). However, if a leasehold interest in land is held for the purposes of a new academy, Sch 1 para 14 does not apply to that or any other leasehold interest in the land, or a freehold interest in the land: Sch 1 para 14(2) (as so substituted). An academy is a 'new academy' for these purposes if, by virtue of s 9(1)(a) (new educational institutions: see PARA 347), the duty in s 9(2) (impact on other schools etc: see PARA 347) applied when the Secretary of State was deciding whether to enter into academy arrangements in relation to it: Sch 1 para 14(3) (as so substituted).
    Where a person (A) holds a freehold or leasehold interest in land from which a leasehold interest has been granted to another person (B), and that other person is concerned with the running of an academy, for the purposes of this Schedule both A and B are to be treated as holding land for the purposes of an academy: Sch 1 para 22(6) (as so substituted).
    As to the meaning of the 'foundation body', in relation to a school see PARA 108 note 6 (definition applied by Sch 1 para 22(2) (as so substituted)).For the purposes of Sch 1, the 'trustees', in relation to a school, means any person (other than the governing body) holding property on trust for the purposes of the school: Academies Act 2010 Sch 1 para 22(2) (as so substituted). As to the meaning of 'academy' see PARA 346. As to the governing body of a maintained school, in relation to England, see PARA 150 et seq; and as to the governing body of a maintained school, in relation to Wales, see PARA 195 et seq. As to maintained schools generally see PARA 99 et seq.

6   Academies Act 2010 Sch 1 para 10(1), (2) (as substituted (see note 5); and amended by the Education Act 2011 Sch 13 paras 1, 5, Sch 14 para 1). One or more of the directions referred to in heads (1)–(3) in the text may be made: Academies Act 2010 Sch 1 para 10(2) (as so substituted). A direction under this Schedule may include such incidental, consequential, supplemental and transitional provision as the Secretary of State thinks is appropriate for giving it full effect: Sch 1 para 18(2) (as so substituted).

7   Unless otherwise specified in the direction, any transfer of land pursuant to the Academies Act 2010 Sch 1 para 10(3) is to take place on the conversion date (see PARA 351): Sch 1 para 10(4) (as substituted: see note 5). As to references to transfers of land under these provisions, and as to the disapplication of the rules against perpetuities and other legislation in respect of such transfers, see Sch 1 paras 19, 20, 22(4); and PARA 1341 note 10. Where a transfer pursuant to a direction under Sch 1 relates to registered land, it is the duty of the transferor to execute any such instrument under the Land Registration Act 2002 (see REAL PROPERTY AND REGISTRATION vol 87 (2012) PARA 232 et seq), to deliver any such certificate under that Act and to do such other things under that Act, as the transferor would be required to execute, deliver or do in the case of a transfer by agreement between the transferor and the transferee: Academies Act 2010 Sch 1 para 18(2) (as so substituted).

8   As to the meaning of 'local authority' see PARA 25 and (in the context of the Academies Act 2010), PARA 351 note 3.

9   Academies Act 2010 Sch 1 para 10(3)(a) (as substituted: see note 5).

10   Academies Act 2010 Sch 1 para 10(3)(b) (as substituted: see note 5).

11   Academies Act 2010 Sch 1 para 10(3)(c) (as substituted: see note 5).

12   Ie under the School Standards and Framework Act 1998 Sch 22 para 5(2), (3) or (4ZA) (see PARA 1321).

13   Academies Act 2010 Sch 1 para 11(1) (as substituted: see note 5).

14   Academies Act 2010 Sch 1 para 11(2) (as substituted: see note 5).

15   Academies Act 2010 Sch 1 para 12(1)(a) (as substituted: see note 5). The notice referred to in the text is one under the School Standards and Framework Act 1998 Sch 22 para A1A(4) (see para 1305).

16   Academies Act 2010 Sch 1 para 12(1)(b) (as substituted: see note 5). The notice referred to in the text is one under the School Standards and Framework Act 1998 Sch 22 para A7A(4) (see para 1306).

17   Academies Act 2010 Sch 1 para 12(1)(c) (as substituted: see note 5). The notice referred to in the text is one under the School Standards and Framework Act 1998 Sch 22 para A13A(6) (see para 1308).

18   Academies Act 2010 Sch 1 para 12(1)(d) (as substituted: see note 5). The notice referred to in the text is one under the School Standards and Framework Act 1998 Sch 22 para A23(4)(b) (see PARA 1311).

19   Academies Act 2010 Sch 1 para 12(2) (as substituted: see note 5).

20   Ie by virtue of the Education Act 2002 Sch 1 para 5(2)(a)(iv) (dissolution of governing body on conversion date following academy order: see PARA 150).

21   Ie on the conversion date (see PARA 351).

22   As to land held for the purposes of the school see PARA 1341 note 4.

23   See note 21.

24   Ie pursuant to a direction under the Academies Act 2010 Sch 1 para 10 (see the text and notes 6–11) or otherwise.

25   Academies Act 2010 Sch 1 para 13(1), (2)(a) (as substituted: see note 5). Schedule 1 para 13(2) does not apply to any land for which provision has been made for payment under Sch 1 para 10(3)(b) (see the text and note 10) (Sch 1 para 13(4)(a) (as so substituted)) or any land or other property which is held by the governing body on trust for the purposes of the school (Sch 1 para 13(4)(b) (as so substituted)).

26   Academies Act 2010 Sch 1 para 13(2)(c) (as substituted: see note 5). Schedule 1 para 13(2) does not apply to any property or rights to which s 7 (transfer of school surpluses: see PARA 351) applies (Sch 1 para 13(4)(c) (as so substituted)).

27   Academies Act 2010 Sch 1 para 13(2)(c) (as substituted: see note 5). See note 26. Sch 1 para 13(2) does not, unless the Secretary of State otherwise directs before the conversion date, apply to any liabilities of the governing body in respect of a loan made to the governing body: Sch 1 para 13(4)(d) (as so substituted).

28   See note 21.

29   Ie by virtue of the Academies Act 2010.

30   Academies Act 2010 Sch 1 para 13(3)(a) (as substituted: see note 5).

31   Academies Act 2010 Sch 1 para 13(3)(b) (as substituted: see note 5; and amended by the Education Act 2011 Sch 13 paras 1, 5). The Secretary of State must give such a direction before

the conversion date: Academies Act 2010 Sch 1 para 13(3)(b) (as so substituted). A direction under Sch 1 may include such incidental, consequential, supplemental and transitional provision as the Secretary of State thinks is appropriate for giving it full effect: Sch 1 para 18(2) (as so substituted).

32 Ie as mentioned in the Academies Act 2010 Sch 1 para 13(1) (see the text and note 25).

33 Academies Act 2010 Sch 1 para 13(5) (as substituted: see note 5). This does not apply to land in respect of which a direction has been made under Sch 1 para 10(3)(a) or Sch 1 para 10 (3)(c) (see the text and notes 9, 11) (Sch 1 para 13(6) (as so substituted)) or to land or other property held by a governing body on trust for the purposes of the school in a case where any other persons ('other trustees') also hold land or other property on trust for the purposes of the school (Sch 1 para 13(7) (as so substituted)). In a case mentioned in Sch 1 para 13(7), the land or other property held on trust by the governing body is, on the conversion date, transferred to, and by virtue of the Academies Act 2010 vests in, the other trustees: Sch 1 para 13(8) (as so substituted). If any doubt or dispute arises as to the persons to whom land or other property is transferred under Sch 1 para 13(8), it is to be treated as so transferred to such persons as the Secretary of State directs: Sch 1 para 13(9) (as so substituted).

34 See the Academies Act 2010 Sch 1 para 21(1); and PARA 1341 note 20.

1343. Transfers of land held for the purposes of an academy. Where an educational institution ceases to be an academy[1]; and immediately before it does so, publicly funded land[2] is held by a person for the purposes of the academy[3], the Secretary of State[4] may direct[5]:

(1) that the land or any part of the land be transferred to such local authority[6] as the Secretary of State may specify, subject to the payment by that authority of such sum by way of consideration (if any) as the Secretary of State determines to be appropriate[7];

(2) that the person holding the land pay, either to the Secretary of State or to such local authority as the Secretary of State may specify, the whole or any part of the value, as at the date of the direction, of the whole or any part of the land[8];

(3) that the land or any part of the land be transferred to a person concerned with the running of an academy, subject to the payment by that person or the Secretary of State of such sum by way of consideration (if any) as the Secretary of State determines to be appropriate[9];

(4) that the land or any part of the land be transferred to the governing body, foundation body or trustees[10] of a school, subject to the payment by that body or trustees (as the case may be) or the Secretary of State of such sum by way of consideration (if any) as the Secretary of State determines to be appropriate[11].

Where:

(a) land has been held for the purposes of a maintained school by the trustees of the school[12];

(b) such land is held by the trustees for the purposes of an academy[13];

(c) the termination of the academy's occupation of the land would have the result that it was not reasonably practicable for the academy to continue to be conducted at its existing site[14],

and a notice that is effective to terminate an academy's occupation of land[15] relates to such land[16], the Secretary of State may direct[17]:

(i) that the land or any part of the land be transferred to such local authority as the Secretary of State may specify, subject to the payment by that authority of such sum by way of consideration (if any) as the Secretary of State determines to be appropriate[18];

(ii) that the trustees pay, either to the Secretary of State or to such local authority as the Secretary of State may specify, the whole or any part of the value, as at the date of the direction, of the whole or any part of the land[19];

(iii) that the land or any part of the land be transferred to a person concerned with the running of an academy, subject to the payment by that person or the Secretary of State of such sum by way of consideration (if any) as the Secretary of State determines to be appropriate[20];

(iv) that the land or any part of the land be transferred to the governing body, foundation body or trustees of a school, subject to the payment by that body or trustees, as the case may be, or the Secretary of State of such sum by way of consideration (if any) as the Secretary of State determines to be appropriate[21].

Further provision in connection with directions may be made by regulations[22].

1   Academies Act 2010 Sch 1 para 15(1)(a) (Sch 1 substituted by the Education Act 2011 Sch 14 para 1). Academies Act 2010 Sch 1 para 15(1)(a) applies whether or not, on the educational institution ceasing to be an academy, it simultaneously ceases to function as an educational institution: Sch 1 para 15(2) (as so substituted). See also note 3. As to the meaning of 'academy' see PARA 346.
2   As to the meaning of 'publicly funded land' see PARA 1342 note 5.
3   Academies Act 2010 Sch 1 para 15(1)(b) (as substituted: see note 1). One or more of the directions referred to in heads (1)–(4) in the text may be made: Sch 1 para 15(3) (as so substituted). A direction under Sch 1 may include such incidental, consequential, supplemental and transitional provision as the Secretary of State thinks is appropriate for giving it full effect: Sch 1 para 18(2) (as so substituted).
4   As to the Secretary of State see PARA 58.
5   Academies Act 2010 Sch 1 para 15(3) (as substituted: see note 1).
6   As to references to transfers of land under these provisions, and as to the disapplication of the rules against perpetuities and other legislation in respect of such transfers, see Sch 1 paras 19, 20, 22(4); and PARA 1341 note 10. As to transfers of registered land see PARA 1342 note 7. As to the meaning of 'local authority' see PARA 25.
7   Academies Act 2010 Sch 1 para 15(3)(a) (as substituted: see note 1).
8   Academies Act 2010 Sch 1 para 15(3)(b) (as substituted: see note 1).
9   Academies Act 2010 Sch 1 para 15(3)(c) (as substituted: see note 1).
10 As to the meaning of 'foundation body' see PARA 1342 note 5. As to the meaning of 'trustees' see PARA 1342 note 5. As to the governing body of a maintained school, in relation to England, see PARA 150 et seq; and as to the governing body of a maintained school, in relation to Wales, see PARA 195 et seq. As to maintained schools generally see PARA 99 et seq.
11 Academies Act 2010 Sch 1 para 15(3)(d) (as substituted: see note 1).
12 Academies Act 2010 Sch 1 para 16(1)(a) (Sch 1 substituted by the Education Act 2011 Sch 14 para 1).
13 Academies Act 2010 Sch 1 para 16(1)(b) (as substituted: see note 3).
14 Academies Act 2010 Sch 1 para 16(1)(c) (as substituted: see note 3).
15 A notice given by the trustees to the academy proprietor that purports to terminate the academy's occupation of the land is not effective unless the period of notice is reasonable, having regard to the length of time that it would take to terminate the academy arrangements, and in any event is not less than two years and a copy of the notice is given to the Secretary of State and the local authority by which the school was maintained at the same time as the notice is given to the proprietor: Academies Act 2010 Sch 1 para 16(2) (as so substituted). Where the trustees give, at the same (or substantially the same) time, notices purporting to terminate an academy's occupation of two or more pieces of land held by the trustees for the purposes of the academy, then for the purpose of determining whether Sch 1 para 16(1)(c) (see the text and note 14) applies in relation to any of those pieces of land, regard may be had to the combined effect of terminating the academy's occupation of both or all of them: Academies Act 2010 Sch 1 para 16(3) (as so substituted). If a question arises as to whether the termination of an academy's occupation of any land would have the result mentioned in Sch 1 para 16(1)(c) (including a question as to whether Sch 1 para 16(3) applies in any particular circumstances), it is to be determined by the Secretary of State: Sch 1 para 16(4) (as so substituted).
16 Academies Act 2010 Sch 1 para 16(5) (as substituted: see note 3).

17 Academies Act 2010 Sch 1 para 16(6) (as substituted: see note 3). One or more of the directions referred to in heads (a)–(d) in the text may be made: Sch 1 para 16(6) (as so substituted). A notice under Sch 1 para 16(6) must be served on the person holding the land, within the period of six months beginning with the date on which the payments were made, or, if there is more than one such date, the latest of those dates (Sch 1 para 14(7) (as so substituted)) save where the land is vested in the official custodian for charities in trust for a charity, in which case the notice must be served on the charity, if the charity is a corporate charity, or on the persons having the general control and management of the administration of the charity, in any other case (Sch 1 para 14(8) (as so substituted)). As to the official custodian for charities see CHARITIES vol 8 (2015) PARA 300 et seq. A direction under Sch 1 may include such incidental, consequential, supplemental and transitional provision as the Secretary of State thinks is appropriate for giving it full effect: Sch 1 para 18(2) (as so substituted).
18 Academies Act 2010 Sch 1 para 16(6)(a) (as substituted: see note 3).
19 Academies Act 2010 Sch 1 para 16(6)(b) (as substituted: see note 3).
20 Academies Act 2010 Sch 1 para 16(6)(c) (as substituted: see note 3).
21 Academies Act 2010 Sch 1 para 16(6)(d) (as substituted: see note 3).
22 See the Academies Act 2010 Sch 1 para 21(1); and PARA 1341 note 20.

(4) EDUCATIONAL PREMISES

(i) Required Standards for School Premises

1344. **Prescribed standards for school premises.** The standards to which the premises[1] of schools maintained[2] by local authorities[3] must conform are prescribed by regulations[4]. Different standards may be prescribed[5] for such descriptions of schools as are specified in the regulations[6]. Where a school is maintained by a local authority, the authority must secure that the school premises conform to the prescribed standards[7].

Any function of a local authority in England which is conferred by or under these provisions[8] may be exercised by, or by employees of, such person as may be authorised in that behalf by the local authority whose function it is[9].

1 As to the meaning of 'premises' see PARA 62 note 19.
2 As to maintained schools generally see PARA 99 et seq.
3 As to the meaning of 'local authority' see PARA 25.
4 Education Act 1996 s 542(1) (s 542(1), (4) amended by the School Standards and Framework Act 1998 Sch 30 para 158, Sch 31; Education Act 1996 s 542(1), (2), (4) amended by SI 2010/1158). 'Regulations' means regulations made by the appropriate national authority under the Education Act 1996: s 579(1) (definition amended by the Apprenticeships, Skills, Children and Learning Act 2009 Sch 2, paras 1, 12(b)). The appropriate national authority for the purposes of the Education Act 1996 is the Secretary of State or, in relation to Wales, the Welsh Ministers, the functions of the Secretary of State, so far as exercisable in relation to Wales, having been transferred to the National Assembly for Wales (see the National Assembly for Wales (Transfer of Functions) Order 1999, SI 1999/672, art 2, Sch 1) and subsequently vested in the Welsh Ministers (see the Government of Wales Act 2006 s 162(1), Sch 11 para 30). As to the Secretary of State see PARA 58. As to the Welsh Ministers see PARA 59. As to the meaning of 'Wales' see PARA 7 note 3.

As to the regulations that have been made under s 542(1), in relation to maintained schools in England (including pupil referral units (see PARA 427 et seq)), see the School Premises (England) Regulations 2012, SI 2012/1943, regs 4–10, which prescribe the standard for all schools to which the regulations apply, including toilet and washing facilities (reg 4), medical accommodation (reg 5), health, safety and welfare (reg 6), acoustics (reg 7), lighting (reg 8), water supplies (reg 9), and outdoor space (reg 10). As to the regulations which have been made under s 542(1), in relation to maintained schools in Wales, see the Education (School Premises) Regulations 1999, SI 1999/2, Pt II (regs 1A, 3–7) (reg 1A added by SI 2012/1943), which prescribes the standard for school facilities, including washrooms for pupils and staff (Education (School Premises) Regulations 1999, SI 1999/2, regs 3, 4), medical accommodation (reg 5), staff accommodation (reg 6), and ancillary facilities (reg 7); Pt III (regs 8–14), which prescribes standards applying only to boarding schools including sleeping (reg 8), washroom (reg 9), and living accommodation (reg 10), accommodation for the preparation and consumption of meals (reg 11), sick rooms (reg 12), staff accommodation (reg 13) and storage facilities (reg 14); Pt IV (regs 15–23), which prescribes the structural requirements of schools, including load bearing structures (reg 15), weather protection (reg 16), health, safety and welfare (reg 17), acoustics (reg 18), lighting (reg 19), heating (reg 20), ventilation (reg 21), water supplies (reg 22) and drainage (reg 23); and Pt V (reg 24, Sch 2), which specifies the standard and size of team playing fields. As to the determination of numbers of pupils for the purposes of the Education (School Premises) Regulations 1999, SI 1999/2, see reg 2, Sch 1.

As to the application of regulations made prior to the Education Act 1996 see *Reffell v Surrey County Council* [1964] 1 All ER 743, [1964] 1 WLR 358; *Ward v Hertfordshire County Council* [1970] 1 All ER 535, [1970] 1 WLR 356, CA. See also *Ching v Surrey County Council* [1910] 1 KB 736, 8 LGR 369, CA; *Morris v Carnarvon County Council* [1910] 1 KB 840, 8 LGR 485, CA.

5 Ie without prejudice to the generality of the Education Act 1996 s 569(4) (regulations may make different provision for different cases, etc).
6 Education Act 1996 s 542(1) (as amended: see note 4).
7 Education Act 1996 s 542(2) (as amended: see note 4). Section 542(2) has effect subject to s 543 (see PARA 1345): s 542(4) (as so amended). In relation to Wales, any expenses incurred in making to the school buildings of a voluntary aided school such alterations as may be required by the local authority for the purpose of securing that the school premises conform to the standards prescribed under the Education Act 1996 s 542 are payable by the governing body of the school: School Standards and Framework Act 1998 Sch 3 para 3(2)(a) (amended by SI 2010/1158). As to the meaning of 'school building' see PARA 1296 note 18 (definition applied by virtue of the School Standards and Framework Act 1998 s 142(8)). As to voluntary schools see PARA 106 et seq. As to the governing body of a maintained school, in relation to England, see PARA 150 et seq; and as to the governing body of a maintained school, in relation to Wales, see PARA 195 et seq.
8 Ie conferred by or under the Education Act 1996 s 542: see the text and notes 1–7.
9 Contracting Out (Local Education Authority Functions) (England) Order 2002, SI 2002/928, art 3, Sch 1 para (aaa) (art 3 amended by SI 2010/1172).

1345. Relaxation of prescribed standards for school premises in special cases.
Where the appropriate national authority[1] is satisfied, having regard to the nature of the school's[2] existing site[3], to any existing buildings on the site[4], or to other special circumstances affecting the school premises[5], that it would be unreasonable to require conformity with any prescribed requirement[6] as to any matter[7], the authority may direct that despite the fact that the prescribed requirement is not satisfied the school premises are to be taken, as respects the matters specified in the direction, to conform to the prescribed standards so long as[8] the direction remains in force[9] and any conditions specified in the direction as respects those matters are observed[10].

Where the school is to have an additional or new site[11], and the appropriate national authority is satisfied, having regard to the shortage of suitable sites, that it would be unreasonable to require conformity with any prescribed requirement relating to sites[12], the authority may direct that, despite the fact that the prescribed requirement is not satisfied, the school premises are to be taken, as respects the matters specified in the direction, to conform to the prescribed standards so long as[13] the direction remains in force[14] and any conditions specified in the direction as respects those matters are observed[15].

Where the school is to have additional buildings, or is to be transferred to a new site[16], where existing buildings not previously part of the school premises or where temporary buildings are to be used for that purpose[17], and where the appropriate national authority is satisfied, having regard to the need to control public expenditure in the interests of the national economy, that it would be unreasonable to require conformity with any prescribed requirement relating to buildings[18], the authority may direct that, despite the fact that the prescribed requirement is not satisfied, the school premises are to be taken, as respects the matters specified in the direction, to conform to the prescribed standards so long as[19] the direction remains in force[20] and any conditions specified in the direction as respects those matters are observed[21].

Where in relation to any playing fields[22] used by the school for the purposes of the school, if the appropriate national authority is satisfied that, having regard to other facilities for physical education available to the school, it would be unreasonable to require conformity with any prescribed requirement relating to playing fields[23], the authority may direct that, despite the fact that the prescribed requirement is not satisfied, the school premises are to be taken, as respects the matters specified in the direction, to conform to the prescribed standards so long as[24] the direction remains in force[25] and any conditions specified in the direction as respects those matters are observed[26].

1 Ie the Secretary of State or, in relation to Wales, the Welsh Ministers, the functions of the Secretary of State under the Education Act 1996 s 543, so far as exercisable in relation to Wales, having been transferred to the National Assembly for Wales (see the National Assembly for Wales (Transfer of Functions) Order 1999, SI 1999/672, art 2, Sch 1) and subsequently vested in the Welsh Ministers (see the Government of Wales Act 2006 s 162(1), Sch 11 para 30). As to the Secretary of State see PARA 58. As to the Welsh Ministers see PARA 59. As to the meaning of 'Wales' see PARA 7 note 3.
2 As to the meaning of 'school' see PARA 91.
3 Education Act 1996 s 543(2)(a).
4 Education Act 1996 s 543(2)(b).
5 Education Act 1996 s 543(2)(c). As to the meaning of 'premises' see PARA 62 note 19.
6 For these purposes 'prescribed requirement' means a requirement of regulations under the Education Act 1996 s 542 (see PARA 1344): s 543(5).
7 Education Act 1996 s 543(2).
8 Education Act 1996 s 543(1) (s 543(1) amended by, and s 543(4A) added by, the School Standards and Framework Act 1998 s 140(1), Sch 30 para 159).
9 Education Act 1996 s 543(1)(a).
10 Education Act 1996 s 543(1)(b).
11 Education Act 1996 s 543(3)(a).
12 Education Act 1996 s 543(3)(b).
13 Education Act 1996 s 543(1) (as amended: see note 8).
14 Education Act 1996 s 543(1)(a).
15 Education Act 1996 s 543(1)(b).
16 Education Act 1996 s 543(4)(a).
17 Education Act 1996 s 543(4)(b).
18 Education Act 1996 s 543(4)(c).
19 Education Act 1996 s 543(1) (as amended: see note 8).
20 Education Act 1996 s 543(1)(a).
21 Education Act 1996 s 543(1)(b).
22 As to the meaning of 'playing fields' see PARA 1326 note 1 (definition applied by virtue of the Education Act 1996 s 543(4A) (as added: see note 8)). As to the meaning of 'land' see PARA 116 note 18.
23 Education Act 1996 s 543(4A) (as added: see note 8).
24 Education Act 1996 s 543(1) (as amended: see note 8).
25 Education Act 1996 s 543(1)(a).
26 Education Act 1996 s 543(1)(b).

1346. Approval of school premises and boarding hostels. The appropriate national authority[1] may by regulation[2] make provision requiring the authority's approval to be obtained for the provision of new premises[3] for, or the alteration[4] of the premises[5]: (1) of any school maintained by a local authority[6] and of any special school[7] not maintained by a local authority[8]; or (2) of any boarding hostel provided by a local authority for persons receiving education at any such school[9]. Provision may also be made by regulation for the inspection of any such hostel[10].

1 Ie the Secretary of State or, in relation to Wales, the Welsh Ministers, the functions of the Secretary of State under the Education Act 1996 s 544, so far as exercisable in relation to Wales, having been transferred to the National Assembly for Wales (see the National Assembly for Wales (Transfer of Functions) Order 1999, SI 1999/672, art 2, Sch 1) and subsequently vested in the Welsh Ministers (see the Government of Wales Act 2006 s 162(1), Sch 11 para 30). As to the Secretary of State see PARA 58. As to the Welsh Ministers see PARA 59. As to the meaning of 'Wales' see PARA 7 note 3.

2 'Regulations' means regulations made by the Secretary of State or, in relation to Wales, the Welsh Ministers: see Education Act 1996 s 579(1). At the date at which this volume states the law no regulations had been made under s 544 but, by virtue of Sch 39 para 1, the Education (Schools and Further and Higher Education) Regulations 1989, SI 1989/351 (amended by SI 2001/3708; and SI 2010/1142) have effect in relation to Wales as if so made (having been revoked in relation to England by SI 2001/692; SI 2004/571; and SI 2008/1701). See further note 10.

3 As to the meaning of 'premises' see PARA 62 note 19.

4 As to the meaning of 'alteration' see PARA 311 note 25.

5 Education Act 1996 s 544(1) (s 544(1), (3) amended by the School Standards and Framework Act 1998 Sch 30 para 160, Sch 31; and by SI 2010/1158).

6 Education Act 1996 s 544(1)(a), (3)(a) (as amended: see note 5). As to the meaning of 'local authority' see PARA 25. As to maintained schools see PARA 99.

7 As to special schools see PARA 1041 et seq.

8 Education Act 1996 s 544(1)(a), (3)(c) (as amended: see note 5).

9 Education Act 1996 s 544(1)(b) (as amended: see note 5).

10 Education Act 1996 s 544(2). As to the inspection of hostels in Wales for pupils with special educational needs see the Education (Schools and Further and Higher Education) Regulations 1989, SI 1989/351, reg 9 (revoked, in relation to England: see note 2).

1347. Exemption from building byelaws of approved buildings. Where plans for, or particulars in respect of, a building required for the purposes of any school[1] or other educational institution are approved by the appropriate national authority[2], the authority may by order direct that any provision of a local Act or of a byelaw made under a local Act[3]: (1) does not apply in relation to the building[4]; or (2) does apply in relation to it with such modifications as may be specified in the order[5].

1 As to the meaning of 'school' see PARA 91.

2 Ie the Secretary of State or, in relation to Wales, the Welsh Ministers, the functions of the Secretary of State under the Education Act 1996 s 545, so far as exercisable in relation to Wales, having been transferred to the National Assembly for Wales (see the National Assembly for Wales (Transfer of Functions) Order 1999, SI 1999/672, art 2, Sch 1) and subsequently vested in the Welsh Ministers (see the Government of Wales Act 2006 s 162(1), Sch 11 para 30). As to the Secretary of State see PARA 58. As to the Welsh Ministers see PARA 59. As to the meaning of 'Wales' see PARA 7 note 3.

  The reference in the text to plans or particulars approved by the appropriate national authority includes a reference to particulars submitted to and approved by the authority under regulations under the Education Act 1996 s 544 (see PARA 1346): Education Act 1996 s 545(2)(a) (amended by the Education Act 2002 Sch 21, para 55, Sch 22 Pt 3).

3 Education Act 1996 s 545(1). Orders under s 545 are not statutory instruments (see s 568(2)) and are not recorded in this work.

4 Education Act 1996 s 545(1)(a).

5 Education Act 1996 s 545(1)(b).

1348. Access and facilities for the disabled in educational institutions. Any person undertaking the provision of a building intended for purposes of any of the following[1]:

(1)   universities, university colleges and colleges, schools and halls of universities[2];

(2)   institutions within the higher education sector[3];

(3) schools and institutions which provide higher education or further education (or both) and are maintained or assisted by local authorities[4];

(4) institutions within the further education sector[5],

must, in the means of access both to and within the building and in the parking facilities and sanitary conveniences, make provision, in so far as it is in the circumstances both practicable and reasonable, for the needs of persons using the building who are disabled[6].

The Equality Act 2010 places a duty upon education providers to make reasonable adjustments to facilities to prevent discrimination[7].

1 Chronically Sick and Disabled Persons Act 1970 s 8(1).

2 Chronically Sick and Disabled Persons Act 1970 s 8(2)(a).

3 Chronically Sick and Disabled Persons Act 1970 s 8(2)(aa) (s 8(2)(aa) added by, and s 8(2)(b) substituted by, the Education Reform Act 1988 Sch 12 para 69; Chronically Sick and Disabled Persons Act 1970 s 8(2)(aa) substituted by, and s 8(2)(ba) added by, the Further and Higher Education Act 1992 Sch 8 Pt II para 72). The reference in the text to institutions within the higher education sector is a reference to institutions within the higher education sector within the meaning of the Further and Higher Education Act 1992 s 91(5) (see PARA 619).

4 Chronically Sick and Disabled Persons Act 1970 s 8(2)(b) (as substituted (see note 3); and amended by SI 2010/1158). As to the meanings of 'further education', 'higher education' and 'school' see PARAS 23, 24, 91 (definitions applied by virtue of the Chronically Sick and Disabled Persons Act 1970 s 8(2) (amended by the Education Act 1996 Sch 37 para 19)).

5 Chronically Sick and Disabled Persons Act 1970 s 8(2)(ba) (as added: see note 3). The reference in the text to institutions within the further education sector is a reference to institutions within the further education sector within the meaning of the Further and Higher Education Act 1992 s 91(3) (see PARA 555).

6 Chronically Sick and Disabled Persons Act 1970 s 8(1). As to the power of the Secretary of State to define the expression 'disabled' for the purposes of the Chronically Sick and Disabled Persons Act 1970 see s 28; and HEALTH SERVICES vol 54 (2008) PARA 36.

7 See the Equality Act 2010 ss 20–22, Pt 6 (ss 84–99); and DISCRIMINATION vol 33 (2013) PARAS 187, 250–254.

(ii) Control of Harmful Materials

1349. Control of potentially harmful materials and apparatus in schools. In relation to any school[1] maintained by a local authority[2], and any special school[3] not maintained by a local authority[4], regulations[5] may make provision for requiring the appropriate national authority's approval to be obtained for the use in such schools of such materials or apparatus as may be specified in the regulations, being materials or apparatus which could or might involve a serious risk to health[6].

1 As to the meaning of 'school' see PARA 91.

2 Education Act 1996 s 546(2)(a) (amended by the School Standards and Framework Act 1998 Sch 30 para 162; and by SI 2010/1158). As to the meaning of 'local authority' see PARA 25. As to maintained schools generally see PARA 99 et seq.

3 As to special schools see PARA 1041 et seq.

4 Education Act 1996 s 546(2)(c).

5 'Regulations' means regulations made by the appropriate national authority under the Education Act 1996: s 579(1).

The appropriate national authority is the Secretary of State or, in relation to Wales, the Welsh Ministers, the functions of the Secretary of State under the Education Act 1996 s 546, so far as exercisable in relation to Wales, having been transferred to the National Assembly for Wales (see the National Assembly for Wales (Transfer of Functions) Order 1999, SI 1999/672, art 2, Sch 1) and subsequently vested in the Welsh Ministers (see the Government of Wales Act 2006 s 162(1), Sch 11 para 30). As to the Secretary of State see PARA 58. As to the Welsh Ministers see PARA 59. As to the meaning of 'Wales' see PARA 7 note 3.

At the date at which this volume states the law, the Education (Schools and Further and Higher Education) Regulations 1989, SI 1989/351 (amended by SI 2001/3708; and

SI 2010/1142) have effect in relation to Wales as if so made (having been revoked in relation to England by SI 2001/692; SI 2004/571; and SI 2008/1701). No regulations are in force in relation to England. As to substances and apparatus involving health hazards in Wales see the Education (Schools and Further and Higher Education) Regulations 1989, SI 1989/351, reg 7 (amended by SI 2004/571; and revoked in relation to England by SI 2008/1701). As to the control of hazardous equipment and materials in further education institutions see PARA 1350.

6   Education Act 1996 s 546(1).

1350.   Control of hazardous equipment and materials in further education institutions. The Secretary of State[1] may by regulations[2] require the governing body[3] of a further education institution[4] in England or the proprietor of a 16 to 19 academy[5] to prevent the use in the institution or academy of specified equipment or specified materials without the approval of the Secretary of State[6]. The Secretary of State may specify equipment or materials in this way only if he thinks the equipment or materials might endanger a person's health or safety[7].

The Welsh Ministers[8] may by regulations[9] require the governing body of a further education institution in Wales to prevent the use in the institution of specified equipment or specified materials without the approval of the Ministers[10]. The Ministers may specify equipment or materials in this way only if they think the equipment or materials might endanger a person's health or safety[11].

1   As to the Secretary of State see PARA 58.
2   'Regulations' means regulations made under the Education Act 2002 by the appropriate national authority: s 212(1). The appropriate national authority is the Secretary of State or, in relation to Wales, the Welsh Ministers, the functions of the National Assembly for Wales under the Education Act 1996 s 203, so far as exercisable in relation to Wales, having been transferred to the Welsh Ministers (see the Government of Wales Act 2006 s 162(1), Sch 11 para 30). As to the Welsh Ministers see PARA 59. As to the meaning of 'Wales' see PARA 7 note 3. As to the regulations made under s 203 in relation to England see the Education (Hazardous Equipment and Materials) (England) Regulations 2004, SI 2004/571.
3   As to the meaning of 'governing body' in relation to an educational institution under the Further and Higher Education Act 1992 see PARA 560 note 6.
4   For the purposes of the Education Act 2002 s 203, 'further education institution' means an institution within the further education sector: s 203(5). As to references to institutions within the further education sector see PARA 555.
5   As to the meaning of 'proprietor' see PARA 51 note 4 (definition applied by the Education Act 1992 s 203(5) (definition added by the Education Act 2011 Sch 13 para 13(1), (5)(b))). As to the meaning of '16 to 19 academy' see PARA 346 note 13 (definition applied by the Education Act 2002 s 212(2), (3)).
6   Education Act 2002 s 203(1), (1A) (s 203(1A) added by the Education Act 2011 Sch 13 para 13(1), (5)(a)). As to academies see PARA 345 et seq.
7   Education Act 2002 s 203(2).
8   See note 2.
9   By virtue of the Interpretation Act 1978 s 17(2)(b), the Education (Schools and Further and Higher Education) Regulations 1989, SI 1989/351, reg 7 (amended by SI 2004/571), which was made under the Education Reform Act 1988 s 218(1)(e) (repealed), has effect as if made under the Education Act 2002 s 203 in relation to Wales.
10   Education Act 2002 s 203(3).
11   Education Act 2002 s 203(4).

(iii) Nuisance or Disturbance

1351.   Nuisance or disturbance on school premises. The Education Act 1996 makes provision in relation to nuisance and disturbance on:

(1)   premises[1] including playgrounds, playing fields and other premises for outdoor recreation of any school maintained by a local authority[2], any

special school not so maintained[3], any independent school[4], and any alternative provision academy that is not an independent school[5]; or

(2)   premises which are provided by a local authority pursuant to its functions in respect of the provision of: (a) in England, facilities for recreation and training for children and leisure time activities for young persons[6]; or (b) in Wales, facilities for recreation and social and physical training[7], and used wholly or mainly in connection with the provision of instruction or leadership in sporting, recreational or outdoor activities[8].

Any person who without lawful authority is present on such premises and causes or permits nuisance or disturbance to the annoyance of persons who lawfully use those premises, whether or not any such persons are present at the time, is guilty of an offence[9]. Where a police constable, or a person whom the appropriate authority[10] has authorised to exercise this power, has reasonable cause to suspect that any person is committing or has committed such an offence, he may remove him from the premises in question[11].

Proceedings for such an offence may not be brought by any person other than a police constable or an authorised person[12]; and proceedings for such an offence committed on premises of a foundation, voluntary aided or foundation special school may not be brought by a local authority without first obtaining the consent of the governing body[13].

1   As to the meaning of 'premises' see PARA 62 note 19.
2   Education Act 1996 s 547(2)(a) (amended by SI 2010/1158). As to the meaning of 'local authority' see PARA 25. As to maintained schools generally see PARA 99 et seq. As to licence generally to enter school premises see *Wandsworth London Borough Council v A* [2000] 1 WLR 1246, [2000] LGR 81, [2000] ELR 257, CA.
3   Education Act 1996 s 547(2)(aa) (s 547(2)(aa), (ab), (2A) added by, s 547(3) amended by, and s 547(4), (6), (7) substituted by, the Education Act 2002 Sch 20 para 1). As to special schools see PARA 1041 et seq.
4   Education Act 1996 s 547(2)(ab) (as added: see note 3). As to the meaning of 'independent school' see PARA 369.
5   Education Act 1996 s 547(2)(ac) (s 547(2)(ac) added by, and s 547(4), (7) amended by, SI 2012/976). As to the meaning of 'alternative provision academy' see PARA 346 note 14.
6   Ie under the Education Act 1996 s 507A or s 507B (see PARAS 503, 504).
7   Ie under the Education Act 1996 s 508 (see PARA 505).
8   Education Act 1996 s 547(2A) (as added (see note 3); and amended by the Education and Inspections Act 2006 Sch 1 paras 2, 6; SI 2010/1158).
9   Education Act 1996 s 547(1). A person guilty of an offence under s 547(1) is liable on summary conviction to a fine not exceeding level 2 on the standard scales: s 547(1). As to the standard scale see SENTENCING AND DISPOSITION OF OFFENDERS vol 92 (2010) PARA 142.
10 For these purposes, 'the appropriate authority' means: (1) in relation to premises of a foundation, voluntary aided or foundation special school, a local authority or the governing body; (2) in relation to premises of any other school maintained by a local authority, and premises provided by a local authority under the Education Act 1996 s 507A, s 507B or s 508 (see notes 6, 7), a local authority; and (3) in relation to premises of a special school which is not so maintained or of an independent school or (in relation to England only) of an alternative provision academy that is not an independent school, the proprietor of the school: s 547(4) (as substituted and amended (see notes 3, 5); further amended by SI 2010/1158). As to the meaning of 'proprietor' see PARA 51 note 4. As to foundation, voluntary and foundation special schools see PARA 106 et seq. As to the governing body of a maintained school, in relation to England, see PARA 150 et seq; and as to the governing body of a maintained school, in relation to Wales, see PARA 195 et seq.
11 Education Act 1996 s 547(3) (as amended: see note 3). A local authority may not authorise a person to exercise the power conferred by the Education Act 1996 s 547(3) in relation to premises of a foundation, voluntary or foundation special school without first obtaining the consent of the governing body: s 547(5) (s 547(5), (8) amended by the School Standards and Framework Act 1998 Sch 30 para 163).
12 Education Act 1996 s 547(6) (as substituted: see note 3). For these purposes, 'authorised person' means: (1) in relation to an offence committed on premises of a foundation, voluntary aided or

foundation special school, a local authority or a person whom the governing body has authorised to bring such proceedings; (2) in relation to an offence committed on premises of any other school maintained by a local authority, or on premises provided by a local authority under the Education Act 1996 s 507A, s 507B or s 508 (see notes 6, 7), a local authority; and (3) in relation to an offence committed on premises of a special school which is not so maintained or of an independent school or (in relation to England only) of an alternative provision academy that is not an independent school, a person whom the proprietor of the school has authorised to bring such proceedings: s 547(7) (as substituted and amended: see notes 3, 5).

13 Education Act 1996 s 547(8) (as amended (see note 11); further amended by SI 2010/1158).

1352.   Nuisance or disturbance on premises of further or higher education institutions. The Further and Higher Education Act 1992[1] makes provision in relation to nuisance and disturbance on premises[2], including playing fields and other premises for outdoor recreation, of: (1) any institution other than a school[3] which is maintained by a local authority[4] and which provides further education[5] or higher education[6] or both[7]; (2) any institution within the further education sector[8]; and (3) any 16 to 19 academy[9].

Any person who without lawful authority is present on such premises and causes or permits nuisance or disturbance to the annoyance of persons who lawfully use those premises, whether or not any such persons are present at the time, is guilty of an offence[10]. Where a police constable, or a person whom the appropriate authority[11] has authorised to exercise this power, has reasonable cause to suspect that any person is committing or has committed such an offence, he may remove him from the premises in question[12].

Proceedings for such an offence may not be brought by any person other than a police constable or an authorised person[13].

1   Ie the Further and Higher Education Act 1992 s 85A (added by the Education Act 2002 Sch 20 para 2).
2   As to the meaning of 'premises' see PARA 62 note 19 (definition applied by virtue of the Further and Higher Education Act 1992 s 90(5) (amended by the Education Act 1996 Sch 37 para 115(3); and the School Standards and Framework Act 1998 Sch 30 para 46(b))).
3   As to the meaning of 'school' see PARA 91 (definition applied by virtue of the Further and Higher Education Act 1992 s 90(5) (as amended: see note 2)).
4   As to the meaning of 'local authority' see PARA 25.
5   As to the meaning of 'further education' see PARA 23 (definition applied by the Further and Higher Education Act 1992 s 90(1) (definition added by the Education Act 1996 Sch 37 para 115(2))).
6   As to the meaning of 'higher education' see PARA 24 (definition applied by the Further and Higher Education Act 1992 s 90(1)).
7   Further and Higher Education Act 1992 s 85A(2)(a) (as added (see note 1); and amended by SI 2010/1158).
8   Further and Higher Education Act 1992 s 85A(2)(b) (as added: see note 1). As to the meaning of 'institution within the further education sector' see PARA 555.
9   Further and Higher Education Act 1992 s 85A(2)(c) (s 85A as added (see note 1); s 85A(2)(c), (4)(c), (6)(c) further added by the Education Act 2011 Sch 13 para 8). As to the meaning of '16 to 19 academy' see PARA 346 note 13 (definition applied by the Further and Higher Education Act 1992 s 90(5) (as amended: see note 2)).
10 Further and Higher Education Act 1992 s 85A(1) (as added: see note 1). A person guilty of an offence under s 85A(1) is liable on summary conviction to a fine not exceeding level 2 on the standard scale: s 85A(1) (as so added). As to the standard scale see SENTENCING AND DISPOSITION OF OFFENDERS vol 92 (2010) PARA 142.
11 For these purposes 'the appropriate authority' means: (1) in relation to premises of any institution (other than a school) which is maintained by a local authority and provides further education or higher education (or both), a local authority (Further and Higher Education Act 1992 s 85A(2)(a), (4)(a) (as added (see note 1); and amended by SI 2010/1158)); or (2) in relation to premises of an institution within the further education sector, the governing body (Further and Higher Education Act 1992 s 85A(4)(b) (as so added)); and (3) in relation to

premises of a 16 to 19 academy, the proprietor (s 85A(4)(c) (as added: see notes 1, 9)). As to the meaning of 'governing body' in relation to an educational institution see PARA 560 note 6.

12 Further and Higher Education Act 1992 s 85A(3) (as added: see note 1).

13 Further and Higher Education Act 1992 s 85A(5) (as added: see note 1). For these purposes, 'authorised person' means: (1) in relation to an offence committed on premises of any institution (other than a school) which is maintained by a local authority and provides further education or higher education (or both), a local authority (s 85A(2)(a), (6)(a) (as added (see note 1); and amended by SI 2010/1158)); (2) in relation to an offence committed on premises of an institution within the further education sector, a person whom the governing body has authorised to bring such proceedings (Further and Higher Education Act 1992 s 85A(6)(b) (as so added)); and (3) in relation to an offence committed on premises of a 16 to 19 academy, a person whom the proprietor has authorised to bring such proceedings (s 85A(6)(c) (as added: see notes 1, 9)).

(iv) Health and Safety

1353. Health and safety in relation to schools and further and higher education institutions. The statutory duties imposed by the Health and Safety at Work etc Act 1974 on employers are applicable in relation to schools and further and higher education institutions[1]. The duties owed are not just to employees[2], but also to other persons[3]. An employer has the duty to ensure, so far as is reasonably practicable, the health, safety and welfare at work of all his employees[4]. The duty to ensure the health, safety and welfare at work extends to include in particular[5]:

(1) the provision and maintenance of plant and systems of work that are, so far as is reasonably practicable, safe and without risks to health[6];

(2) arrangements for ensuring, so far as is reasonably practicable, safety and absence of risks to health in connection with the use, handling, storage and transport of articles and substances[7];

(3) the provision of such information, instruction, training and supervision as is necessary to ensure, so far as is reasonably practicable, the health and safety at work of his employees[8];

(4) so far as is reasonably practicable as regards any place of work under the employer's control, the maintenance of it in a condition that is safe and without risks to health and the provision and maintenance of means of access to and egress from it that are safe and without such risks[9];

(5) the provision and maintenance of a working environment for his employees that is, so far as is reasonably practicable, safe, without risks to health, and adequate as regards facilities and arrangements for their welfare at work[10].

It is the duty of every employee while at work[11] to take reasonable care for the health and safety of himself and of other persons who may be affected by his acts or omissions at work[12] and, as regards any duty or requirement imposed on his employer or any other person by or under any of the relevant statutory provisions, to co-operate with him so far as is necessary to enable that duty or requirement to be performed or complied with[13].

1 See the Health and Safety at Work etc Act 1974 s 2(1); and HEALTH AND SAFETY AT WORK vol 52 (2014) PARA 385.

2 See the Health and Safety at Work etc Act 1974 s 2; and HEALTH AND SAFETY AT WORK vol 52 (2014) PARA 385.

3 See the Health and Safety at Work etc Act 1974 s 3 (conduct of employer's undertaking: see HEALTH AND SAFETY AT WORK vol 52 (2014) PARA 386) and s 4 (duties of persons concerned with premises: see HEALTH AND SAFETY AT WORK vol 52 (2014) PARA 387). As to the duties imposed by s 4 in relation to commercially operated play centres see *Moualem v Carlisle City Council* [1995] ELR 22, (1994) 158 JP 1110.

4   See the Health and Safety at Work etc Act 1974 s 2(1); and HEALTH AND SAFETY AT WORK vol 52 (2014) PARA 385.
5   See the Health and Safety at Work etc Act 1974 s 2(2); and HEALTH AND SAFETY AT WORK vol 52 (2014) PARA 385.
6   See the Health and Safety at Work etc Act 1974 s 2(2)(a); and HEALTH AND SAFETY AT WORK vol 52 (2014) PARA 385.
7   See the Health and Safety at Work etc Act 1974 s 2(2)(b); and HEALTH AND SAFETY AT WORK vol 52 (2014) PARA 385.
8   See the Health and Safety at Work etc Act 1974 s 2(2)(c); and HEALTH AND SAFETY AT WORK vol 52 (2014) PARA 385. See *Vaile v Havering LBC* [2011] EWCA Civ 246, [2011] ELR 274, [2011] All ER (D) 124 (Mar) (system for protecting teachers from pupils with autistic spectrum disorder was inadequate).
9   See the Health and Safety at Work etc Act 1974 s 2(2)(d); and HEALTH AND SAFETY AT WORK vol 52 (2014) PARA 385.
10   See the Health and Safety at Work etc Act 1974 s 2(2)(e); and HEALTH AND SAFETY AT WORK vol 52 (2014) PARA 385.
11   As to the general duties of employees at work see HEALTH AND SAFETY AT WORK vol 52 (2014) PARA 410 et seq.
12   See the Health and Safety at Work etc Act 1974 s 7(a); and HEALTH AND SAFETY AT WORK vol 52 (2014) PARA 410.
13   See the Health and Safety at Work etc Act 1974 s 7(b); and HEALTH AND SAFETY AT WORK vol 52 (2014) PARA 410.

(v) Occupiers' Liability

1354. Occupiers' liability in relation to educational premises. In relation to the duty owed to visitors in respect of dangers due to the state of the premises or things done or omitted to be done on them, occupiers of educational premises have the same statutory liability as occupiers of other premises[1]. This is also true of the duty owed to persons other than visitors[2]. There is a common law duty of care to ensure that young children are not permitted to stray from school premises[3].

1   See the Occupiers' Liability Act 1957 s 1(1); and NEGLIGENCE vol 78 (2010) PARAS 29, 31. In general an occupier owes the same common duty of care to all his visitors: see s 2(1); and NEGLIGENCE vol 78 (2010) PARA 38. See also *Griffiths v Smith* [1941] AC 170, [1941] 1 All ER 66, HL. He must be prepared for children to be less careful than adults: see the Occupiers' Liability Act 1957 s 2(3)(a); and NEGLIGENCE vol 78 (2010) PARA 32. The duty of care extends to the state and condition of the school premises: *Lyes v Middlesex County Council* (1962) 61 LGR 443. Cases in which specific defects of premises were considered include: *Morris v Carnarvon County Council* [1910] 1 KB 840, CA (unsuitable heavy swing door); *Jackson v LCC* (1912) 76 JP 217, CA (dangerous materials left in playground); *Smerkinich v Newport Corpn* (1912) 76 JP 454 (unguarded machine); *Fryer v Salford Corpn* [1937] 1 All ER 617, CA (unguarded gas cooker); *Gillmore v LCC* [1938] 4 All ER 331 (slippery floor); *Ralph v LCC* (1947) 111 JP 548, CA (fragile glass partitions); *Rich v LCC* [1953] 2 All ER 376, [1953] 1 WLR 895, CA (coke in playground); *Jefferey v LCC* (1954) 119 JP 45 (fragile glass roof accessible by way of drainpipe); *Lyes v Middlesex County Council* (dangerous door); *Reffell v Surrey County Council* [1964] 1 All ER 743, [1964] 1 WLR 358 (dangerous door); *Martin v Middlesbrough Corpn* (1965) 63 LGR 385, 109 Sol Jo 576, CA (broken glass in playground); *Butt v Inner London Education Authority* (1968) 66 LGR 379, CA (unguarded machine); *Ward v Hertfordshire County Council* [1970] 1 All ER 535, [1970] 1 WLR 356, CA (playground wall with jagged flints); *Mays v Essex County Council* (1975) Times, 11 October (ice slide in playground); *Smart v Gwent County Council* (25 April 1991, unreported), CA (thumb in a door); *G v Upshire Primary School* [2002] ELR 169, QBD (stair rail used as a slide). As to occupiers' liability in relation to children and holiday camps see *Perry v Butlins Holiday World (t/a Butlins Ltd)* [1997] EGCS 171, CA. However, the Occupiers' Liability Act 1957 has been held not to apply to gymnastics on a mat in a youth house sports room as the accident did not arise out of the unsafe condition of the premises themselves: see *Fowles v Bedfordshire County Council* [1996] ELR 51, [1995] PIQR P389, CA.
2   See the Occupiers' Liability Act 1984 s 1; and NEGLIGENCE vol 78 (2010) PARA 40. See also *Ratcliff v Harper Adams Agricultural College* [1999] Ed CR 523.

3　See *Carmarthenshire County Council v Lewis* [1955] AC 549, [1955] 1 All ER 565, HL;
　　Nwabudike v Southwark London Borough Council [1997] ELR 35, (1996) 140 Sol Jo LB 128;
　　Wilson v Governors of Sacred Heart Roman Catholic School [1998] 1 FLR 663, [1998] ELR
　　637, CA; *Jenney (A Minor) v North Lincolnshire County Council* [2000] LGR 269, sub nom
　　J v North Lincolnshire County Council [2000] ELR 245, CA.

(5)　CONTROL OF USE OF SCHOOL PREMISES BY GOVERNING BODIES

(i)　Use of School Premises in England

1355.　Occupation and use of premises of community and community special schools. Until a day to be appointed[1] the occupation and use of the premises[2] of a community or community special school[3] in England[4], both during and outside school hours[5], is under the control of the governing body[6]. This is subject to:

(1)　any directions given by the local authority[7];

(2)　any transfer of control agreement entered into by the governing body[8]; and

(3)　any requirements of an enactment other than the School Standards and Framework Act 1998 or regulations made under it[9].

The local authority may give such directions as to the occupation and use of the premises of a community or community special school as it thinks fit[10]. In exercising control of the occupation and use of the premises of the school outside school hours, the governing body must have regard to the desirability of those premises being made available for community use[11].

1　The School Standards and Framework Act 1998 Sch 13 (see the text and notes 2–11; and PARAS
　　1356–1361) is repealed by the Education Act 2002 Sch 22 Pt 3. At the date at which this volume
　　states the law this repeal had been brought into force only in relation to Wales (see the
　　Education Act 2002 (Commencement No 11 and Transitional and Savings Provisions) (Wales)
　　Order 2007, SI 2007/3611), and accordingly the School Standards and Framework Act 1998
　　Sch 13 continues to have effect in relation to England until a day to be appointed. Provision for
　　the control and use of school premises in Wales is now made under the Education Act 2002 s 31
　　(see PARA 1362 et seq), which will also apply in relation to England as from a day to be
　　appointed. As to the meanings of 'England' and 'Wales' see PARA 7 note 3.
2　As to the meanings of 'premises' and 'school' see PARAS 62 note 19, 91 respectively (definitions
　　applied by virtue of the School Standards and Framework Act 1998 s 142(8)).
3　School Standards and Framework Act 1998 Sch 13 para 1(1) (prospectively repealed: see
　　note 1). As to community and community special schools see PARA 106 et seq; and as to special
　　schools generally see PARA 1041 et seq.
4　The School Standards and Framework Act 1998 Sch 13 applies only in relation to schools in
　　England: see note 1.
5　For these purposes 'school hours' means any time during a school session or during a break
　　between sessions on the same day; and 'school session', in relation to any school, means a school
　　session beginning and ending at such times as may from time to time be determined for that
　　school in accordance with s 41 (repealed) (see now PARA 458): School Standards and
　　Framework Act 1998 Sch 13 para 9 (prospectively repealed: see note 1).
6　School Standards and Framework Act 1998 Sch 13 para 1(2) (prospectively repealed: see
　　note 1). As to the governing body of a maintained school, in relation to England, see PARA 150
　　et seq. The power of the governing body of a maintained school to control the occupation and
　　use of the premises of the school is subject to any arrangements made under or by virtue of: (1)
　　an agreement made under the Education Reform Act 1988 Sch 10 para 1 (see PARA 1332) or
　　Sch 10 para 2 (see PARA 1333) or a determination made in accordance with the Further and
　　Higher Education Act 1992 Sch 8 paras 62, 63; or (2) an agreement made under Sch 5 paras 1,
　　2 (repealed) or a determination made in accordance with Sch 5 paras 3, 4 (repealed): School
　　Standards and Framework Act 1998 Sch 13 para 8 (as so prospectively repealed). See also, in
　　connection with the control and use of pupil referral units, the Education (Pupil Referral Units)
　　(Application of Enactments) (England) Regulations 2007, SI 2007/2979, Sch 1 para 10.

7   School Standards and Framework Act 1998 Sch 13 para 1(2)(a) (prospectively repealed (see note 1); and amended by SI 2010/1158). The reference in the text to directions is a reference to directions under Sch 13 para 1(3) (see the text and note 10). As to the meaning of 'local authority' see PARA 25.
8   School Standards and Framework Act 1998 Sch 13 para 1(2)(b) (prospectively repealed: see note 1). The reference in the text to an agreement is a reference to an agreement entered into under Sch 13 para 2 (see PARA 1356).
9   School Standards and Framework Act 1998 Sch 13 para 1(2)(c) (prospectively repealed: see note 1).
10 School Standards and Framework Act 1998 Sch 13 para 1(3) (prospectively repealed (see note 1); and amended by SI 2010/1158).
11 School Standards and Framework Act 1998 Sch 13 para 1(4) (prospectively repealed: see note 1). For these purposes 'community use' means the use of school premises (when not required by or in connection with the school) by members of the local community: Sch 13 para 9 (as so prospectively repealed).

1356.   Transfer of control agreements for community or community special schools.   Until a day to be appointed[1] the governing body[2] of a community or community special school[3] in England[4] may enter into a transfer of control agreement[5] with any body or person if its purpose, or one of its purposes, in doing so is to promote community use[6] of the whole or any part of the school premises[7]. However, the governing body must not enter into any transfer of control agreement which makes or includes provision for the use of the whole or any part of the school premises during school hours[8] unless it has first obtained the local authority's[9] consent to the agreement in so far as it makes such provision[10]. A transfer of control agreement is taken to include the following terms, namely:

(1)   that the governing body must notify the controlling body[11] of any directions given to the governing body[12];

(2)   that the controlling body, in exercising control of the use of any premises subject to the agreement:
   (a)   must do so in accordance with any directions from time to time notified to that body in pursuance of head (1) above[13]; and
   (b)   must have regard to the desirability of the premises being made available for community use[14]; and

(3)   that, if reasonable notice is given in writing by the governing body to the controlling body that such of the premises subject to the agreement as may be specified in the notice are reasonably required for use by or in connection with the school at such times as may be so specified, then:
   (a)   the use of the specified premises at those times must be under the control of the governing body[15]; and
   (b)   accordingly, those premises may be used at those times by or in connection with the school for such purposes as may be specified in the notice[16],

even though their use at those times would otherwise be under the control of the controlling body[17].

1   The School Standards and Framework Act 1998 Sch 13 (see the text and notes 2–17; and PARAS 1355, 1357–1361) is repealed by the Education Act 2002 Sch 22 Pt 3. At the date at which this volume states the law this repeal had been brought into force only in so far as relating to Wales (see the Education Act 2002 (Commencement No 11 and Transitional and Savings Provisions) (Wales) Order 2007, SI 2007/3611), and accordingly the School Standards and Framework Act 1998 Sch 13 continues to have effect in relation to England until a day to be appointed. Provision for the control and use of school premises in Wales is now made under the Education Act 2002 s 31 (see PARA 1362 et seq), which will also apply in relation to England as from a day to be appointed. As to the meanings of 'England' and 'Wales' see PARA 7 note 3.

2   As to the governing body of a maintained school, in relation to England, see PARA 150 et seq.
3   As to community and community special schools see PARA 106 et seq; and as to special schools generally see PARA 1041 et seq.
4   The School Standards and Framework Act 1998 Sch 13 applies only in relation to schools in England: see note 1.
5   For these purposes 'transfer of control agreement' means an agreement which (subject to the School Standards and Framework Act 1998 Sch 13 para 2(3) (see the text and notes 11–17)) provides for the use of so much of the school premises as may be specified in the agreement to be under the control, at such times as may be so specified, of such body or person as may be so specified: Sch 13 para 2(7) (prospectively repealed: see note 1). As to the meanings of 'premises' and 'school' see PARAS 62 note 19, 91 respectively (definitions applied by virtue of s 142(8)).
6   As to the meaning of 'community use' see PARA 1355 note 11.
7   School Standards and Framework Act 1998 Sch 13 para 2(1) (prospectively repealed: see note 1). As to the use of school premises for community purposes see *Islwyn Borough Council and Gwent County Council v Newport Borough Council* [1994] ELR 141, 6 Admin LR 386, CA.
8   As to the meaning of 'school hours' see PARA 1355 note 5.
9   As to the meaning of 'local authority' see PARA 25.
10 School Standards and Framework Act 1998 Sch 13 para 2(2) (prospectively repealed (see note 1); and amended by SI 2010/1158).
11 For these purposes 'the controlling body' means the body or person (other than the governing body) which has control of the use of the whole or any part of the school premises under the transfer of control agreement in question: School Standards and Framework Act 1998 Sch 13 para 2(7) (prospectively repealed: see note 1).
12 School Standards and Framework Act 1998 Sch 13 para 2(3)(a) (prospectively repealed: see note 1). The reference in the text to directions is a reference to directions given under Sch 13 para 1(3) (see PARA 1355).
    Where the governing body enters into a transfer of control agreement, it must, so far as reasonably practicable, secure that the controlling body exercises control in accordance with any such directions as are notified to that body in pursuance of Sch 13 para 2(3)(a): Sch 13 para 2(6) (prospectively repealed: see note 1).
13 School Standards and Framework Act 1998 Sch 13 para 2(3)(b)(i) (prospectively repealed: see note 1).
14 School Standards and Framework Act 1998 Sch 13 para 2(3)(b)(ii) (prospectively repealed: see note 1).
15 School Standards and Framework Act 1998 Sch 13 para 2(3)(c)(i) (prospectively repealed: see note 1).
16 School Standards and Framework Act 1998 Sch 13 para 2(3)(c)(ii) (prospectively repealed: see note 1).
17 School Standards and Framework Act 1998 Sch 13 para 2(3)(c) (prospectively repealed: see note 1). Where a transfer of control agreement makes express provision for the use of any school premises which are subject to the agreement to be occasionally under the control of the governing body, instead of the controlling body, in such circumstances, at such times or for such purposes as may be provided by or under the agreement, Sch 13 para 2(3)(c) does not have effect in relation to the transfer of control agreement if, at the time of entering into it, the governing body was of the opinion that the express provision would be more favourable to the interests of the school than the term that would otherwise be included by virtue of Sch 13 para 2(3)(c): Sch 13 para 2(4), (5) (as so prospectively repealed).

1357. Occupation and use of foundation and foundation special schools.
Until a day to be appointed[1] the occupation and use of the premises[2] of a foundation or foundation special school[3] in England[4], both during and outside school hours[5], is under the control of the governing body[6], subject to:

(1)   any transfer of control agreement[7] entered into by the governing body[8]; and

(2)   any requirements of an enactment other than the School Standards and Framework Act 1998 or regulations made under it[9].

In exercising control of the occupation and use of the premises of the school outside school hours, the governing body must have regard to the desirability of those premises being made available for community use[10].

1   The School Standards and Framework Act 1998 Sch 13 (see the text and notes 2–10; and PARAS 1355–1356, 1358–1361) is repealed by the Education Act 2002 Sch 22 Pt 3. At the date at which this volume states the law this repeal had been brought into force only in so far as relating to Wales (see the Education Act 2002 (Commencement No 11 and Transitional and Savings Provisions) (Wales) Order 2007, SI 2007/3611), and accordingly the School Standards and Framework Act 1998 Sch 13 continues to have effect in relation to England until a day to be appointed. Provision for the control and use of school premises in Wales is now made under the Education Act 2002 s 31 (see PARA 1362 et seq), which will also apply in relation to England as from a day to be appointed. As to the meanings of 'England' and 'Wales' see PARA 7 note 3.

2   As to the meanings of 'premises' and 'school' see PARAS 62 note 19, 91 respectively (definitions applied by virtue of the School Standards and Framework Act 1998 s 142(8)).

3   School Standards and Framework Act 1998 Sch 13 para 3(1) (prospectively repealed: see note 1). As to foundation and foundation special schools see PARA 106 et seq; and as to special schools generally see PARA 1041 et seq.

4   The School Standards and Framework Act 1998 Sch 13 applies only in relation to schools in England: see note 1.

5   As to the meaning of 'school hours' see PARA 1355 note 5.

6   As to the governing body of a maintained school, in relation to England, see PARA 150 et seq. Where the school has a trust deed which provides for any person other than the governing body to be entitled to control the occupation and use of the school premises to any extent, then, if and to the extent that, disregarding any transfer of control agreement made under the School Standards and Framework Act 1998 Sch 13 para 4 (see PARA 1358), the use of those premises is or would be under the control of such a person, Sch 13 para 3 and Sch 13 para 4 have effect in relation to the school with the substitution of references to that person for references to the governing body: Sch 13 para 3(4) (prospectively repealed: see note 1). As to the meaning of 'trust deed' see PARA 108 note 6 (definition applied by virtue of s 142(8)).

7   As to the meaning of 'transfer of control agreement' see PARA 1358 note 5.

8   School Standards and Framework Act 1998 Sch 13 para 3(2)(a) (prospectively repealed: see note 1).

9   School Standards and Framework Act 1998 Sch 13 para 3(2)(b) (prospectively repealed: see note 1).

10 School Standards and Framework Act 1998 Sch 13 para 3(3) (prospectively repealed: see note 1). As to the meaning of 'community use' see PARA 1355 note 11.

1358. Transfer of control agreements for foundation or foundation special schools. Until a day to be appointed[1] the governing body[2] of any foundation or foundation special school[3] in England[4] has power to enter into a transfer of control agreement[5] with any body or person if its purpose, or one of its purposes, in doing so is to promote community use[6] of the whole or any part of the school premises[7]. It may do so even though the school has a trust deed[8] that would otherwise expressly or impliedly preclude it from entering into such an agreement with that body or person or from conferring control on the controlling body[9] in question[10], but it must not enter into a transfer of control agreement unless the use to which the premises may be put under the agreement is in all other respects in conformity with any such requirements, prohibitions or restrictions imposed by any such trust deed as would apply if control were being exercised by the governing body[11]. However, the governing body must not enter into any transfer of control agreement which makes or includes provision for the use of the whole or any part of the school premises during school hours[12] unless it has first obtained the Secretary of State's[13] consent to the agreement in so far as it makes such provision[14]. A transfer of control agreement is taken to include the following terms, namely:

(1)   that the controlling body, in exercising control of the use of any premises subject to the agreement, must have regard to the desirability of the premises being made available for community use[15]; and

(2)   that, if reasonable notice is given in writing by the governing body to the controlling body that such of the premises subject to the agreement

as may be specified in the notice are reasonably required for use by or in connection with the school at such times as may be so specified, then:

(a) the use of the specified premises at those times must be under the control of the governing body[16]; and

(b) accordingly, those premises may be used at those times by or in connection with the school for such purposes as may be specified in the notice[17],

even though their use at those times would otherwise be under the control of the controlling body[18].

1 The School Standards and Framework Act 1998 Sch 13 (see the text and notes 2–18; and PARAS 1355–1357, 1359–1361) is repealed by the Education Act 2002 Sch 22 Pt 3. At the date at which this volume states the law this repeal had been brought into force only in so far as relating to Wales (see the Education Act 2002 (Commencement No 11 and Transitional and Savings Provisions) (Wales) Order 2007, SI 2007/3611), and accordingly the School Standards and Framework Act 1998 Sch 13 continues to have effect in relation to England until a day to be appointed. Provision for the control and use of school premises in Wales is now made under the Education Act 2002 s 31 (see PARA 1362 et seq), which will also apply in relation to England as from a day to be appointed. As to the meanings of 'England' and 'Wales' see PARA 7 note 3.

2 As to the governing body of a maintained school, in relation to England, see PARA 150 et seq.

3 As to foundation and foundation special schools see PARA 106 et seq; and as to special schools generally see PARA 1041 et seq.

4 The School Standards and Framework Act 1998 Sch 13 applies only in relation to schools in England: see note 1.

5 For these purposes 'transfer of control agreement' means an agreement which (subject to the School Standards and Framework Act 1998 Sch 13 para 4(3) (see the text and notes 15–18)) provides for the use of so much of the school premises as may be specified in the agreement to be under the control, at such times as may be so specified, of such body or person as may be so specified: Sch 13 para 4(6) (prospectively repealed: see note 1). As to the meanings of 'premises' and 'school' see PARAS 62 note 19, 91 respectively (definitions applied by virtue of s 142(8)).

6 As to the meaning of 'community use' see PARA 1355 note 11.

7 School Standards and Framework Act 1998 Sch 13 para 4(1) (prospectively repealed: see note 1).

8 As to the meaning of 'trust deed' see PARA 108 note 6 (definition applied by virtue of the School Standards and Framework Act 1998 s 142(8)).

9 For these purposes 'the controlling body' means the body or person (other than the governing body) which has control of the use of the whole or any part of the school premises under the transfer of control agreement in question: School Standards and Framework Act 1998 Sch 13 para 4(6) (prospectively repealed: see note 1).

10 School Standards and Framework Act 1998 Sch 13 para 4(1)(a) (prospectively repealed: see note 1).

11 School Standards and Framework Act 1998 Sch 13 para 4(1)(b) (prospectively repealed: see note 1).

12 As to the meaning of 'school hours' see PARA 1355 note 5.

13 As to the Secretary of State see PARA 58.

14 School Standards and Framework Act 1998 Sch 13 para 4(2) (prospectively repealed: see note 1).

15 School Standards and Framework Act 1998 Sch 13 para 4(3)(a) (prospectively repealed: see note 1).

16 School Standards and Framework Act 1998 Sch 13 para 4(3)(b)(i) (prospectively repealed: see note 1).

17 School Standards and Framework Act 1998 Sch 13 para 4(3)(b)(ii) (prospectively repealed: see note 1).

18 School Standards and Framework Act 1998 Sch 13 para 4(3)(b) (prospectively repealed: see note 1). Where a transfer of control agreement makes express provision for the use of any school premises which are subject to the agreement to be occasionally under the control of the governing body, instead of the controlling body, in such circumstances, at such times or for such purposes as may be provided by or under the agreement, Sch 13 para 4(3)(b) does not have effect in relation to the transfer of control agreement if, at the time of entering into it, the governing body was of the opinion that the express provision would be more favourable to the

interests of the school than the term that would otherwise be included by virtue of Sch 13 para 4(3)(b): Sch 13 para 4(4), (5) (as so prospectively repealed).

1359. Occupation and use of premises of voluntary schools. Until a day to be appointed[1] the occupation and use of the premises[2] of a voluntary school[3] in England[4], both during and outside school hours[5], is under the control of the governing body[6], subject to:

(1) any directions given by the local authority[7];

(2) any transfer of control agreement entered into by the governing body[8]; and

(3) any requirements of an enactment other than the School Standards and Framework Act 1998 or regulations made under it[9].

However, the local authority may[10] give such directions as to the occupation and use of the premises of a voluntary controlled school as it thinks fit[11].

1 The School Standards and Framework Act 1998 Sch 13 (see the text and notes 2–11; and PARAS 1355–1358, 1360–1361) is repealed by the Education Act 2002 Sch 22 Pt 3. At the date at which this volume states the law this repeal had been brought into force only in so far as relating to Wales (see the Education Act 2002 (Commencement No 11 and Transitional and Savings Provisions) (Wales) Order 2007, SI 2007/3611), and accordingly the School Standards and Framework Act 1998 Sch 13 continues to have effect in relation to England until a day to be appointed. Provision for the control and use of school premises in Wales is now made under the Education Act 2002 s 31 (see PARA 1362 et seq), which will also apply in relation to England as from a day to be appointed. As to the meanings of 'England' and 'Wales' see PARA 7 note 3.

2 As to the meanings of 'premises' and 'school' see PARAS 62 note 19, 91 respectively (definitions applied by virtue of the School Standards and Framework Act 1998 s 142(8)).

3 School Standards and Framework Act 1998 Sch 13 para 5(1) (prospectively repealed: see note 1). As to voluntary schools see PARA 106 et seq.

4 The School Standards and Framework Act 1998 Sch 13 applies only in relation to schools in England: see note 1.

5 As to the meaning of 'school hours' see PARA 1355 note 5.

6 As to the governing body of a maintained school, in relation to England, see PARA 150 et seq. Where the trust deed for a voluntary school provides for any person other than the governing body to be entitled to control the occupation and use of the school premises to any extent, then, if and to the extent that, disregarding any transfer of control agreement made under the School Standards and Framework Act 1998 Sch 13 para 6 (see PARA 1360), the use of those premises is or would be under the control of such a person, Sch 13 paras 5–7 (see PARAS 1360–1361) have effect in relation to the school with the substitution of references to that person for references to the governing body: Sch 13 para 5(4) (prospectively repealed: see note 1). As to the meaning of 'trust deed' see PARA 108 note 6 (definition applied by virtue of s 142(8)).

7 School Standards and Framework Act 1998 Sch 13 para 5(2)(a) (prospectively repealed (see note 1); and amended by SI 2010/1158). The reference in the text to directions is a reference, in the case of a voluntary controlled school, to directions under Sch 13 para 5(3) (see the text and notes 10–11), or, in the case of a voluntary aided school, to directions under Sch 13 para 7(3) (see PARA 1361): Sch 13 para 5(2)(a) (as so prospectively repealed). As to the meaning of 'local authority' see PARA 25.

8 School Standards and Framework Act 1998 Sch 13 para 5(2)(b) (prospectively repealed: see note 1). The reference in the text to an agreement is a reference to an agreement under Sch 13 para 6 (see PARA 1360).

9 School Standards and Framework Act 1998 Sch 13 para 5(2)(c) (prospectively repealed: see note 1).

10 Ie subject to the School Standards and Framework Act 1998 Sch 13 para 7(1), (2) (see PARA 1361).

11 School Standards and Framework Act 1998 Sch 13 para 5(3) (prospectively repealed (see note 1); and amended by SI 2010/1158).

1360. Transfer of control agreements for voluntary schools. Until a day to be appointed[1] the governing body[2] of any voluntary school[3] in England[4] has power to enter into a transfer of control agreement[5] with any body or person if the governing body's purpose, or one of its purposes, in doing so is to promote community use[6] of the whole or any part of the school premises[7]. It may do so even though the trust deed[8] for the school would otherwise expressly or impliedly preclude it from entering into such an agreement with that body or person or from conferring control on the controlling body[9] in question[10], but it must not enter into a transfer of control agreement unless the use to which the premises may be put under the agreement is in all other respects in conformity with any such requirements, prohibitions or restrictions imposed by the trust deed as would apply if control were being exercised by the governing body[11]. However, the governing body must not enter into any transfer of control agreement which makes or includes provision for the use of the whole or any part of the school premises during school hours[12] unless it has first obtained the consent of the local authority[13] to the agreement in so far as it makes such provision[14]. A transfer of control agreement is taken to include the following terms, namely:

(1)   that the governing body must notify the controlling body of any directions given to the governing body[15] and any determination made by the foundation governors[16];

(2)   that the controlling body, in exercising control of the use of any premises subject to the agreement, must do so in accordance with any directions or determinations from time to time notified to that body in pursuance of head (1) above[17], and must have regard to the desirability of the premises being made available for community use[18]; and

(3)   that, if reasonable notice is given in writing by the governing body to the controlling body that such of the premises subject to the agreement as may be specified in the notice are reasonably required for use by or in connection with the school at such times as may be so specified, then:

    (a)   the use of the specified premises at those times must be under the control of the governing body[19]; and

    (b)   accordingly, those premises may be used at those times by or in connection with the school for such purposes as may be specified in the notice[20],

even though their use at those times would otherwise be under the control of the controlling body[21].

1   The School Standards and Framework Act 1998 Sch 13 (see the text and notes 2–21; and PARAS 1355–1359, 1361) is repealed by the Education Act 2002 Sch 22 Pt 3. At the date at which this volume states the law this repeal had been brought into force only in so far as relating to Wales (see the Education Act 2002 (Commencement No 11 and Transitional and Savings Provisions) (Wales) Order 2007, SI 2007/3611), and accordingly the School Standards and Framework Act 1998 Sch 13 continues to have effect in relation to England until a day to be appointed. Provision for the control and use of school premises in Wales is now made under the Education Act 2002 s 31 (see PARA 1362 et seq), which will also apply in relation to England as from a day to be appointed. As to the meanings of 'England' and 'Wales' see PARA 7 note 3.

2   As to the governing body of a maintained school, in relation to England, see PARA 150 et seq.

3   As to voluntary schools see PARA 106 et seq.

4   The School Standards and Framework Act 1998 Sch 13 applies only in relation to schools in England: see note 1.

5   For these purposes, 'transfer of control agreement' means an agreement which (subject to the School Standards and Framework Act 1998 Sch 13 para 6(3) (see the text and notes 15–21)) provides for the use of so much of the school premises as may be specified in the agreement to be under the control, at such times as may be so specified, of such body or person as may be so specified: Sch 13 para 6(7) (prospectively repealed: see note 1). As to the meanings of 'premises' and 'school' see PARAS 62 note 19, 91 respectively (definitions applied by virtue of s 142(8)).

6   As to the meaning of 'community use' see PARA 1355 note 11.

7 School Standards and Framework Act 1998 Sch 13 para 6(1) (prospectively repealed: see note 1).

8 As to the meaning of 'trust deed' see PARA 108 note 6 (definition applied by virtue of the School Standards and Framework Act 1998 s 142(8)).

9 For these purposes 'the controlling body' means the body or person (other than the governing body) who has control of the use of the whole or any part of the school premises under the transfer of control agreement in question: School Standards and Framework Act 1998 Sch 13 para 6(7) (prospectively repealed: see note 1).

10 School Standards and Framework Act 1998 Sch 13 para 6(1)(a) (prospectively repealed: see note 1).

11 School Standards and Framework Act 1998 Sch 13 para 6(1)(b) (prospectively repealed: see note 1).

12 As to the meaning of 'school hours' see PARA 1355 note 5.

13 As to the meaning of 'local authority' see PARA 25.

14 School Standards and Framework Act 1998 Sch 13 para 6(2) (prospectively repealed (see note 1); and amended by SI 2010/1158).

15 School Standards and Framework Act 1998 Sch 13 para 6(3)(a)(i) (prospectively repealed: see note 1). The reference in the text to directions is a reference, in the case of a voluntary controlled school, to directions under Sch 13 para 5(3) (see PARA 1359), or, in the case of a voluntary aided school, to directions under Sch 13 para 7(3) (see PARA 1361).

16 School Standards and Framework Act 1998 Sch 13 para 6(3)(a)(ii) (prospectively repealed: see note 1). The reference in the text to a determination is a reference, in the case of a voluntary controlled school, to a determination made under Sch 13 para 7(2) (see PARA 1361). As to the meaning of 'foundation governor' see PARA 108 note 6.

Where the governing body enters into a transfer of control agreement, it must, so far as reasonably practicable, secure that the controlling body exercises control in accordance with any such directions or determinations as are notified to that body in pursuance of Sch 13 para 6(3)(a): Sch 13 para 6(6) (as so prospectively repealed).

17 School Standards and Framework Act 1998 Sch 13 para 6(3)(b)(i) (prospectively repealed: see note 1).

18 School Standards and Framework Act 1998 Sch 13 para 6(3)(b)(ii) (prospectively repealed: see note 1).

19 School Standards and Framework Act 1998 Sch 13 para 6(3)(c)(i) (prospectively repealed: see note 1).

20 School Standards and Framework Act 1998 Sch 13 para 6(3)(c)(ii) (prospectively repealed: see note 1).

21 School Standards and Framework Act 1998 Sch 13 para 6(3)(c) (prospectively repealed: see note 1). Where a transfer of control agreement makes express provision for the use of any school premises which are subject to the agreement to be occasionally under the control of the governing body, instead of the controlling body, in such circumstances, at such times or for such purposes as may be provided by or under the agreement, Sch 13 para 6(3)(c) does not have effect in relation to the transfer of control agreement if, at the time of entering into it, the governing body was of the opinion that the express provision would be more favourable to the interests of the school than the term that would otherwise be included by virtue of Sch 13 para 6(3)(c): Sch 13 para 6(4), (5) (as so prospectively repealed).

1361. Control of use of premises of voluntary school outside school hours.

Until a day to be appointed[1] the governing body[2] may determine the use to which the premises[3] of a voluntary controlled school[4] in England[5], or any part of them, are put on Saturdays when not required[6] for the purposes of the school[7], or for any purpose connected with education or with the welfare of the young for which the local authority[8] desires to provide accommodation on the premises, or on the part in question[9].

The foundation governors[10] may determine the use to which the premises of a voluntary controlled school, or any part of them, are put on Sundays[11].

Where the local authority desires to provide accommodation for any purpose connected with education or with the welfare of the young[12], and is satisfied that there is no suitable alternative accommodation in its area for that purpose[13], it may direct the governing body of a voluntary aided school to provide accommodation free of charge for that purpose on the school premises, or any part of them, on any weekday when not needed for the purposes of the school[14].

In exercising control of the occupation and use of the premises of a voluntary school outside school hours[15] the governing body must have regard to the desirability of those premises being made available for community use[16].

1   The School Standards and Framework Act 1998 Sch 13 (see the text and notes 2–16; and PARAS 1355–1360) is repealed by the Education Act 2002 Sch 22 Pt 3. At the date at which this volume states the law this repeal had been brought into force only in so far as relating to Wales (see the Education Act 2002 (Commencement No 11 and Transitional and Savings Provisions) (Wales) Order 2007, SI 2007/3611), and accordingly the School Standards and Framework Act 1998 Sch 13 continues to have effect in relation to England until a day to be appointed. Provision for the control and use of school premises in Wales is now made under the Education Act 2002 s 31 (see PARA 1362 et seq), which will also apply in relation to England as from a day to be appointed. As to the meanings of 'England' and 'Wales' see PARA 7 note 3.
2   As to the governing body of a maintained school, in relation to England, see PARA 150 et seq.
3   As to the meanings of 'premises' and 'school' see PARAS 62 note 19, 91 respectively (definitions applied by virtue of the School Standards and Framework Act 1998 s 142(8)).
4   As to voluntary schools see PARA 106 et seq.
5   The School Standards and Framework Act 1998 Sch 13 applies only in relation to schools in England: see note 1.
6   School Standards and Framework Act 1998 Sch 13 para 7(1) (prospectively repealed: see note 1).
7   School Standards and Framework Act 1998 Sch 13 para 7(1)(a) (prospectively repealed: see note 1).
8   As to the meaning of 'local authority' see PARA 25.
9   School Standards and Framework Act 1998 Sch 13 para 7(1)(b) (prospectively repealed (see note 1); and amended by SI 2010/1158).
10 As to the meaning of 'foundation governor' see PARA 108 note 6.
11 School Standards and Framework Act 1998 Sch 13 para 7(2) (prospectively repealed: see note 1).
12 School Standards and Framework Act 1998 Sch 13 para 7(3)(a) (prospectively repealed: see note 1).
13 School Standards and Framework Act 1998 Sch 13 para 7(3)(b) (prospectively repealed: see note 1).
14 School Standards and Framework Act 1998 Sch 13 para 7(3) (prospectively repealed (see note 1); and amended by SI 2010/1158). The local authority must not exercise its power under Sch 13 para 7(3) so as to direct the governing body to provide accommodation on more than three days in any week: Sch 13 para 7(4) (as so prospectively repealed; and amended by SI 2010/1158).
15 As to the meaning of 'school hours' see PARA 1355 note 5.
16 School Standards and Framework Act 1998 Sch 13 para 7(5) (prospectively repealed: see note 1). As to the meaning of 'community use' see PARA 1355 note 11.

(ii) Use of School Premises in Wales

1362. Occupation and use of premises of community and community special schools and maintained nursery schools. The occupation and use of the premises[1] of a community or community special school[2] or maintained nursery school[3] in Wales[4] (both during and outside school hours[5]) are under the control of the governing body[6], subject to:

(1)   any directions given by the local authority[7];
(2)   any transfer of control agreement entered into[8] by the governing body[9]; and
(3)   any statutory[10] requirements[11].

In exercising control of the occupation and use of the premises of the school outside school hours the governing body must have regard to the desirability of those premises being made available for community use[12].

1   As to the meanings of 'premises' and 'school' see PARAS 62 note 19, 91 respectively (definitions applied by virtue of the Education Act 2002 s 212(2), (3)(a)).
2   As to community and community special schools see PARA 106 et seq; and as to special schools generally see PARA 1041 et seq.
3   As to the meaning of 'maintained nursery school' see PARA 103 note 3.
4   The Control of School Premises (Wales) Regulations 2008, SI 2008/136 (see the text and notes 5–12; and PARA 1363 et seq), apply only in relation to schools in Wales: see reg 1(2). The regulations were made under the Education Act 2002 s 31, which provides that regulations may make provision relating to the control by the governing body of a maintained school of the occupation and use of school premises, and which at the date at which this volume states the law had been brought into force only in so far as relating to Wales (see the Education Act 2002 (Commencement No 11 and Transitional and Savings Provisions) (Wales) Order 2007, SI 2007/3611). As to the meaning of 'Wales' see PARA 7 note 3.
5   'School hours' means any time during a school session or during a break between school sessions on the same day; and 'school session', in relation to any school, means a school session beginning and ending at such times as may from time to time be determined in that school in accordance with the Education Act 2002 s 32 (see PARA 458): Control of School Premises (Wales) Regulations 2008, SI 2008/136, reg 2.
6   As to the governing body of a maintained school, in relation to Wales, see PARA 195 et seq.
7   Control of School Premises (Wales) Regulations 2008, SI 2008/136, reg 3(1)(a). The local authority may give such directions as to the occupation and use of the premises of a community or community special school or maintained nursery school as it thinks fit: reg 3(2). As to the meaning of 'local authority' see PARA 25.
8   Ie under the Control of School Premises (Wales) Regulations 2008, SI 2008/136, reg 4 (see PARA 1363).
9   Control of School Premises (Wales) Regulations 2008, SI 2008/136, reg 3(1)(b).
10 Ie any requirements of an enactment other than the Education Act 2002 or regulations made thereunder: Control of School Premises (Wales) Regulations 2008, SI 2008/136, reg 3(1)(c).
11 Control of School Premises (Wales) Regulations 2008, SI 2008/136, reg 3(1)(c).
12 Control of School Premises (Wales) Regulations 2008, SI 2008/136, reg 3(3). 'Community use' means the use of school premises (when not required by or in connection with the school) for charitable purposes by pupils at the school or their families, or people who live or work in the locality in which the school is situated: reg 2.

1363.   Transfer of control agreements for community and community special schools and maintained nursery schools.   The governing body[1] of any community or community special school[2] or maintained nursery school[3] in Wales[4] may enter into a transfer of control agreement[5] with any body or person if its purpose (or one of its purposes) in doing so is to promote community use[6] of the whole or any part of the school premises[7], provided that the governing body may not enter into any transfer of control agreement which makes or includes provision for the use of the whole or any part of the school premises during school hours[8] unless it has first obtained the local authority's[9] consent to the agreement in so far as it makes such provision[10]. A transfer of control agreement is taken to include the following terms, namely:

(1)   that the governing body must notify the controlling body[11] of any directions given[12] to the governing body[13];

(2)   that the controlling body, in exercising control of the use of any premises subject to the agreement must do so in accordance with any directions from time to time so notified to that body[14] and must have regard to the desirability of the premises being made available for community use[15]; and

(3)   that, if reasonable notice is given in writing by the governing body to the controlling body that such of the premises subject to the agreement as may be specified in the notice are reasonably required for use by or in connection with the school at such times as may be so specified, then the use of the specified premises at those times is to be under the control of

the governing body[16] and, accordingly, those premises may be used at those times by or in connection with the school for such purposes as may be specified in the notice[17], even though their use at those times would otherwise[18] be under the control of the controlling body[19].

1 As to the governing body of a maintained school, in relation to Wales, see PARA 195 et seq.
2 As to community and community special schools see PARA 106 et seq; and as to special schools generally see PARA 1041 et seq.
3 As to the meaning of 'maintained nursery school' see PARA 103 note 3.
4 The Control of School Premises (Wales) Regulations 2008, SI 2008/136 (see the text and notes 5–19; and PARA 1362 et seq), apply only in relation to schools in Wales: see reg 1(2); and PARA 1362 note 4.
5 'Transfer of control agreement' means an agreement which (subject to the Control of School Premises (Wales) Regulations 2008, SI 2008/136, reg 4(3) (see the text and notes 11–19)) provides for the use of so much of the school premises as may be specified in the agreement to be under the control, at such times as may be so specified, of such body or person as may be so specified: reg 4(7). As to the meanings of 'premises' and 'school' see PARAS 62 note 19, 91 respectively (definitions applied by virtue of the Education Act 2002 s 212(2), (3)(a)).
6 As to the meaning of 'community use' see PARA 1362 note 12.
7 Control of School Premises (Wales) Regulations 2008, SI 2008/136, reg 4(1).
8 As to the meaning of 'school hours' see PARA 1362 note 5.
9 As to the meaning of 'local authority' see PARA 25.
10 Control of School Premises (Wales) Regulations 2008, SI 2008/136, reg 4(2).
11 'The controlling body' means the body or persons (other than the governing body) which has or have control of the use of the whole or any part of the school premises under the transfer of control agreement in question: Control of School Premises (Wales) Regulations 2008, SI 2008/136, reg 4(7).
12 Ie under the Control of School Premises (Wales) Regulations 2008, SI 2008/136, reg 3(2) (see PARA 1362).
13 Control of School Premises (Wales) Regulations 2008, SI 2008/136, reg 4(3)(a). Where the governing body enters into a transfer of control agreement, the governing body must so far as reasonably practicable secure that the controlling body exercises control in accordance with any such directions as are notified to that body in pursuance of reg 4(3)(a): reg 4(6).
14 Control of School Premises (Wales) Regulations 2008, SI 2008/136, reg 4(3)(b)(i).
15 Control of School Premises (Wales) Regulations 2008, SI 2008/136, reg 4(3)(b)(ii).
16 Control of School Premises (Wales) Regulations 2008, SI 2008/136, reg 4(3)(c)(i).
17 Control of School Premises (Wales) Regulations 2008, SI 2008/136, reg 4(3)(c)(ii).
18 Ie apart from the Control of School Premises (Wales) Regulations 2008, SI 2008/136, reg 4(3).
19 Control of School Premises (Wales) Regulations 2008, SI 2008/136, reg 4(3)(c). Where a transfer of control agreement makes express provision for the use of any school premises which are subject to the agreement to be occasionally under the control of the governing body, instead of the controlling body, in such circumstances, at such times or for such purposes as may be provided by or under the agreement, reg 4(3)(c) does not have effect in relation to the transfer of control agreement if, at the time of entering into it, the governing body was of the opinion that the express provision would be more favourable to the interests of the school than the term that would otherwise be included by virtue of reg 4(3)(c): reg 4(4), (5).

1364. Occupation and use of foundation and foundation special schools. The occupation and use of the premises[1] of a foundation or foundation special school[2] in Wales[3], both during and outside school hours[4], is under the control of the governing body[5], subject to:

(1) any transfer of control agreement[6] entered into by the governing body[7]; and

(2) any requirements of an enactment other than the Education Act 2002 or regulations made under it[8].

In exercising control of the occupation and use of the premises of the school outside school hours, the governing body must have regard to the desirability of those premises being made available for community use[9].

1   As to the meanings of 'premises' and 'school' see PARAS 62 note 19, 91 respectively (definitions applied by virtue of the Education Act 2002 s 212(2), (3)(a)).
2   As to foundation and foundation special schools see PARA 106 et seq; and as to special schools generally see PARA 1041 et seq.
3   The Control of School Premises (Wales) Regulations 2008, SI 2008/136 (see the text and notes 5–9; and PARA 1362 et seq), apply only in relation to schools in Wales: see reg 1(2); and PARA 1362 note 4.
4   As to the meaning of 'school hours' see PARA 1362 note 5.
5   Control of School Premises (Wales) Regulations 2008, SI 2008/136, reg 5(1). As to the governing body of a maintained school, in relation to Wales, see PARA 195 et seq. Where the school has a trust deed which provides for any person other than the governing body to be entitled to control the occupation and use of the school premises to any extent, then, if and to the extent that, disregarding any transfer of control agreement made under the Control of School Premises (Wales) Regulations 2008, SI 2008/136, reg 6 (see PARA 1365), the use of those premises is or would be under the control of such a person, regs 5, 6 have effect in relation to the school with the substitution of references to that person for references to the governing body: reg 5(3). As to the meaning of 'trust deed' see PARA 108 note 6 (definition applied by virtue of the Education Act 2002 s 212(2), (3)(a)).
6   As to the meaning of 'transfer of control agreement' see PARA 1365 note 4.
7   Control of School Premises (Wales) Regulations 2008, SI 2008/136, reg 5(1)(a).
8   Control of School Premises (Wales) Regulations 2008, SI 2008/136, reg 5(1)(b).
9   Control of School Premises (Wales) Regulations 2008, SI 2008/136, reg 5(2). As to the meaning of 'community use' see PARA 1362 note 12.

1365. Transfer of control agreements for foundation or foundation special schools. The governing body[1] of any foundation or foundation special school[2] in Wales[3] has power to enter into a transfer of control agreement[4] with any body or person if its purpose, or one of its purposes, in doing so is to promote community use[5] of the whole or any part of the school premises[6]. It may do so even though the school has a trust deed[7] that would otherwise expressly or impliedly preclude it from entering into such an agreement with that body or person or from conferring control on the controlling body[8] in question[9], but it must not enter into a transfer of control agreement unless the use to which the premises may be put under the agreement is in all other respects in conformity with any such requirements, prohibitions or restrictions imposed by any such trust deed as would apply if control were being exercised by the governing body[10]. However, the governing body must not enter into any transfer of control agreement which makes or includes provision for the use of the whole or any part of the school premises during school hours[11] unless it has first obtained the Welsh Ministers'[12] consent to the agreement in so far as it makes such provision[13]. A transfer of control agreement is taken to include the following terms, namely:

(1)   that the controlling body, in exercising control of the use of any premises subject to the agreement, must have regard to the desirability of the premises being made available for community use[14]; and

(2)   that, if reasonable notice is given in writing by the governing body to the controlling body that such of the premises subject to the agreement as may be specified in the notice are reasonably required for use by or in connection with the school at such times as may be so specified, then:

   (a)   the use of the specified premises at those times must be under the control of the governing body[15]; and

   (b)   accordingly, those premises may be used at those times by or in connection with the school for such purposes as may be specified in the notice[16],

   even though their use at those times would otherwise be under the control of the controlling body[17].

1   As to the governing body of a maintained school, in relation to Wales, see PARA 195 et seq.
2   As to foundation and foundation special schools see PARA 106 et seq; and as to special schools generally see PARA 1041 et seq.
3   The Control of School Premises (Wales) Regulations 2008, SI 2008/136 (see the text and notes 4–17; and PARA 1362 et seq), apply only in relation to schools in Wales: see reg 1(2); and PARA 1362 note 4.
4   For these purposes 'transfer of control agreement' means an agreement which (subject to the Control of School Premises (Wales) Regulations 2008, SI 2008/136, reg 6(5) (see the text and notes 14–17)) provides for the use of so much of the school premises as may be specified in the agreement to be under the control, at such times as may be so specified, of such body or person as may be so specified: reg 6(8). As to the meanings of 'premises' and 'school' see PARAS 62 note 19, 91 respectively (definitions applied by virtue of the Education Act 2002 s 212(2), (3)(a)).
5   As to the meaning of 'community use' see PARA 1362 note 12.
6   Control of School Premises (Wales) Regulations 2008, SI 2008/136, reg 6(1).
7   As to the meaning of 'trust deed' see PARA 108 note 6 (definition applied by virtue of the Education Act 2002 s 212(2), (3)(a)).
8   For these purposes 'the controlling body' means the body or person (other than the governing body) which has control of the use of the whole or any part of the school premises under the transfer of control agreement in question: Control of School Premises (Wales) Regulations 2008, SI 2008/136, reg 6(8).
9   Control of School Premises (Wales) Regulations 2008, SI 2008/136, reg 6(2).
10 Control of School Premises (Wales) Regulations 2008, SI 2008/136, reg 6(3).
11 As to the meaning of 'school hours' see PARA 1362 note 5.
12 As to the Welsh Ministers see PARA 59.
13 Control of School Premises (Wales) Regulations 2008, SI 2008/136, reg 6(4).
14 Control of School Premises (Wales) Regulations 2008, SI 2008/136, reg 6(5)(a).
15 Control of School Premises (Wales) Regulations 2008, SI 2008/136, reg 6(5)(b)(i).
16 Control of School Premises (Wales) Regulations 2008, SI 2008/136, reg 6(5)(b)(ii).
17 Control of School Premises (Wales) Regulations 2008, SI 2008/136, reg 6(5)(b). Where a transfer of control agreement makes express provision for the use of any school premises which are subject to the agreement to be occasionally under the control of the governing body, instead of the controlling body, in such circumstances, at such times or for such purposes as may be provided by or under the agreement, reg 6(5)(b) does not have effect in relation to the transfer of control agreement if, at the time of entering into it, the governing body was of the opinion that the express provision would be more favourable to the interests of the school than the term that would otherwise be included by virtue of reg 6(5)(b): reg 6(6), (7).

1366. Occupation and use of premises of voluntary schools. The occupation and use of the premises[1] of a voluntary school[2] in Wales[3], both during and outside school hours[4], is under the control of the governing body[5], subject to:

(1)   any directions given by the local authority[6];
(2)   any transfer of control agreement entered into by the governing body[7]; and
(3)   any requirements of an enactment other than the Education Act 2002 or regulations made under it[8].

However, the local authority may[9] give such directions as to the occupation and use of the premises of a voluntary controlled school as it thinks fit[10].

1   As to the meanings of 'premises' and 'school' see PARAS 62 note 19, 91 respectively (definitions applied by virtue of the Education Act 2002 s 212(2), (3)(a)).
2   As to voluntary schools see PARA 106 et seq.
3   The Control of School Premises (Wales) Regulations 2008, SI 2008/136 (see the text and notes 4–10; and PARA 1362 et seq), apply only in relation to schools in Wales: see reg 1(2); and PARA 1362 note 4.
4   As to the meaning of 'school hours' see PARA 1362 note 5.
5   Control of School Premises (Wales) Regulations 2008, SI 2008/136, reg 7(1). As to the governing body of a maintained school, in relation to Wales, see PARA 195 et seq. Where the trust deed for a voluntary school provides for any person other than the governing body to be entitled to control the occupation and use of the school premises to any extent, then, if and to the extent that, disregarding any transfer of control agreement made under the Control of School Premises (Wales) Regulations 2008, SI 2008/136, reg 8 (see PARA 1367), the use of those

premises is or would be under the control of such a person, regs 7–9 (see PARAS 1366–1368) have effect in relation to the school with the substitution of references to that person for references to the governing body: reg 7(3). As to the meaning of 'trust deed' see PARA 108 note 6 (definition applied by virtue of the Education Act 2002 s 212(2), (3)(a)).

6 Control of School Premises (Wales) Regulations 2008, SI 2008/136, reg 7(1)(a). The reference in the text to directions is a reference, in the case of a voluntary controlled school, to directions under reg 7(2) (see the text and notes 9–10), or, in the case of a voluntary aided school, to directions under reg 9(3) (see PARA 1368). As to the meaning of 'local authority' see PARA 25.

7 Control of School Premises (Wales) Regulations 2008, SI 2008/136, reg 7(1)(b). The reference in the text to an agreement is a reference to an agreement under reg 8 (see PARA 1367).

8 Control of School Premises (Wales) Regulations 2008, SI 2008/136, reg 7(1)(c).

9 Ie subject to the Control of School Premises (Wales) Regulations 2008, SI 2008/136, reg 9(1), (2) (see PARA 1368).

10 Control of School Premises (Wales) Regulations 2008, SI 2008/136, reg 7(2).

1367. Transfer of control agreements for voluntary schools. The governing body[1] of any voluntary school[2] in Wales[3] has power to enter into a transfer of control agreement[4] with any body or person if the governing body's purpose, or one of its purposes, in doing so is to promote community use[5] of the whole or any part of the school premises[6]. It may do so even though the trust deed[7] for the school would otherwise expressly or impliedly preclude it from entering into such an agreement with that body or person or from conferring control on the controlling body[8] in question[9], but it must not enter into a transfer of control agreement unless the use to which the premises may be put under the agreement is in all other respects in conformity with any such requirements, prohibitions or restrictions imposed by the trust deed as would apply if control were being exercised by the governing body[10]. However, the governing body must not enter into any transfer of control agreement which makes or includes provision for the use of the whole or any part of the school premises during school hours[11] unless it has first obtained the consent of the local authority[12] to the agreement in so far as it makes such provision[13]. A transfer of control agreement is taken to include the following terms, namely:

(1) that the governing body must notify the controlling body of any directions given to the governing body[14] and any determination made by the foundation governors[15];

(2) that the controlling body, in exercising control of the use of any premises subject to the agreement, must do so in accordance with any directions or determinations from time to time notified to that body in pursuance of head (1) above[16], and must have regard to the desirability of the premises being made available for community use[17]; and

(3) that, if reasonable notice is given in writing by the governing body to the controlling body that such of the premises subject to the agreement as may be specified in the notice are reasonably required for use by or in connection with the school at such times as may be so specified, then:

(a) the use of the specified premises at those times must be under the control of the governing body[18]; and

(b) accordingly, those premises may be used at those times by or in connection with the school for such purposes as may be specified in the notice[19],

even though their use at those times would otherwise be under the control of the controlling body[20].

1 As to the governing body of a maintained school, in relation to Wales, see PARA 195 et seq.
2 As to voluntary schools see PARA 106 et seq.

3 The Control of School Premises (Wales) Regulations 2008, SI 2008/136 (see the text and notes 4–20; and PARAS 1362–1368), apply only in relation to schools in Wales: see reg 1(2); and PARA 1362 note 4.

4 For these purposes, 'transfer of control agreement' means an agreement which (subject to the Control of School Premises (Wales) Regulations 2008, SI 2008/136, reg 8(5) (see the text and notes 14–20)) provides for the use of so much of the school premises as may be specified in the agreement to be under the control, at such times as may be so specified, of such body or person as may be so specified: reg 8(9). As to the meanings of 'premises' and 'school' see PARAS 62 note 19, 91 respectively (definitions applied by virtue of the Education Act 2002 s 212(2), (3)(a)).

5 As to the meaning of 'community use' see PARA 1362 note 12.

6 Control of School Premises (Wales) Regulations 2008, SI 2008/136, reg 8(1).

7 As to the meaning of 'trust deed' see PARA 108 note 6 (definition applied by virtue of the Education Act 2002 s 212(2), (3)(a)).

8 For these purposes 'the controlling body' means the body or person (other than the governing body) who has control of the use of the whole or any part of the school premises under the transfer of control agreement in question: Control of School Premises (Wales) Regulations 2008, SI 2008/136, reg 8(9).

9 Control of School Premises (Wales) Regulations 2008, SI 2008/136, reg 8(2).

10 Control of School Premises (Wales) Regulations 2008, SI 2008/136, reg 8(3).

11 As to the meaning of 'school hours' see PARA 1362 note 5.

12 As to the meaning of 'local authority' see PARA 25.

13 Control of School Premises (Wales) Regulations 2008, SI 2008/136, reg 8(4).

14 Control of School Premises (Wales) Regulations 2008, SI 2008/136, reg 8(5)(a)(i). The reference in the text to directions is a reference, in the case of a voluntary controlled school, to directions under reg 7(2) (see PARA 1366), or, in the case of a voluntary aided school, to directions under reg 9(3) (see PARA 1368).

15 Control of School Premises (Wales) Regulations 2008, SI 2008/136, reg 8(5)(a)(ii). The reference in the text to a determination is a reference, in the case of a voluntary controlled school, to a determination made under reg 9(2) (see PARA 1368). As to the meaning of 'foundation governor' see PARA 108 note 6 (definition applied by virtue of the Education Act 2002 s 212(2), (3)(a)).

Where the governing body enters into a transfer of control agreement, it must, so far as reasonably practicable, secure that the controlling body exercises control in accordance with any such directions or determinations as are notified to that body in pursuance of reg 8(5)(a): reg 8(8).

16 Control of School Premises (Wales) Regulations 2008, SI 2008/136, reg 8(5)(b)(i).

17 Control of School Premises (Wales) Regulations 2008, SI 2008/136, reg 8(5)(b)(ii).

18 Control of School Premises (Wales) Regulations 2008, SI 2008/136, reg 8(5)(c)(i).

19 Control of School Premises (Wales) Regulations 2008, SI 2008/136, reg 8(5)(c)(ii).

20 Control of School Premises (Wales) Regulations 2008, SI 2008/136, reg 8(5)(c). Where a transfer of control agreement makes express provision for the use of any school premises which are subject to the agreement to be occasionally under the control of the governing body, instead of the controlling body, in such circumstances, at such times or for such purposes as may be provided by or under the agreement, reg 8(5)(c) does not have effect in relation to the transfer of control agreement if, at the time of entering into it, the governing body was of the opinion that the express provision would be more favourable to the interests of the school than the term that would otherwise be included by virtue of reg 8(5)(c): reg 8(6), (7).

1368. Control of use of premises of voluntary school outside school hours. The governing body[1] may determine the use to which the premises[2] of a voluntary controlled school[3] in Wales[4], or any part of them, are put on Saturdays when not required[5] for the purposes of the school[6], or for any purpose connected with education or with the welfare of the young for which the local authority[7] desires to provide accommodation on the premises, or on the part in question[8].

The foundation governors[9] may determine the use to which the premises of a voluntary controlled school, or any part of them, are put on Sundays[10].

Where the local authority desires to provide accommodation for any purpose connected with education or with the welfare of the young[11], and is satisfied that there is no suitable alternative accommodation in its area for that purpose[12], it may direct the governing body of a voluntary aided school to provide accommodation free of charge for that purpose on the school premises, or any part of them, on any weekday when not needed for the purposes of the school[13].

In exercising control of the occupation and use of the premises of a voluntary school outside school hours[14] the governing body must have regard to the desirability of those premises being made available for community use[15].

1 As to the governing body of a maintained school, in relation to Wales, see PARA 195 et seq.
2 As to the meanings of 'premises' and 'school' see PARAS 62 note 19, 91 respectively (definitions applied by virtue of the Education Act 2002 s 212(2), (3)(a)).
3 As to voluntary schools see PARA 106 et seq.
4 The Control of School Premises (Wales) Regulations 2008, SI 2008/136 (see the text and notes 5–15; and PARAS 1362–1368), apply only in relation to schools in Wales: see reg 1(2); and PARA 1362 note 4.
5 Control of School Premises (Wales) Regulations 2008, SI 2008/136, reg 9(1).
6 Control of School Premises (Wales) Regulations 2008, SI 2008/136, reg 9(1)(a).
7 As to the meaning of 'local authority' see PARA 25.
8 Control of School Premises (Wales) Regulations 2008, SI 2008/136, reg 9(1)(b).
9 As to the meaning of 'foundation governor' see PARA 108 note 6 (definition applied by virtue of the Education Act 2002 s 212(2), (3)(a)).
10 Control of School Premises (Wales) Regulations 2008, SI 2008/136, reg 9(2).
11 Control of School Premises (Wales) Regulations 2008, SI 2008/136, reg 9(3)(a).
12 Control of School Premises (Wales) Regulations 2008, SI 2008/136, reg 9(3)(b).
13 Control of School Premises (Wales) Regulations 2008, SI 2008/136, reg 9(3). The local authority must not exercise its power under reg 9(3) so as to direct the governing body to provide accommodation on more than three days in any week: reg 9(4).
14 As to the meaning of 'school hours' see PARA 1362 note 5.
15 Control of School Premises (Wales) Regulations 2008, SI 2008/136, reg 9(5). As to the meaning of 'community use' see PARA 1362 note 12.

(6) RATING OF EDUCATIONAL PREMISES

1369. Rating of educational premises generally. Educational premises are classified as non-domestic hereditaments for the purposes of rating[1], and, therefore, a local authority is rateable for its schools[2].

Where an employee of an educational institution is required to occupy a hereditament in order to carry out the purposes of his employer's business, or to secure the better performance of his duties, the occupation for rating purposes is that of the employer[3].

1 See the Local Government Finance Act 1988 Pt III (ss 41–67); and LOCAL GOVERNMENT FINANCE vol 70 (2012) PARA 109 et seq. However, a building used by university students of a particular religious denomination for recreation or social purposes has been held to be exempted from non-domestic rates: see *Mageean v Valuation Comr* [1960] NI 141, NI CA; and LOCAL GOVERNMENT FINANCE vol 70 (2012) PARA 90.
2 See *West Bromwich School Board v West Bromwich Overseers* (1884) 13 QBD 929, CA; *R v London School Board* (1886) 17 QBD 738, CA; *Laughlin v Saffron-Hill Overseers* (1865) 12 LT 542; *London School Board v Wandsworth and Clapham Unions Assessment Committee* (1900) 16 TLR 137, DC; and LOCAL GOVERNMENT FINANCE vol 70 (2012) PARA 72. As to the rating of maintained schools see PARA 1370.
3 See *Northern Ireland Comr of Valuation v Fermanagh Protestant Board of Education* [1969] 3 All ER 352, [1969] 1 WLR 1708, HL (house owned by school and used as schoolmasters' residences); *Hirst v Sargent* (1966) 65 LGR 127, [1966] RA 605, DC (house owned by school and occupied by school groundsman who was able to prevent trespass and damage to playing fields from the hereditament); and LOCAL GOVERNMENT FINANCE vol 70 (2012) PARA 67.

1370. Rating of maintained schools. For the purposes of the statutory provisions relating to non-domestic rating[1], the occupier of any hereditament so far as consisting of the premises[2] of a maintained school[3] is taken to be the local authority[4], where it is a community, voluntary controlled or community special school[5], or the governing body[6], where it is a foundation, voluntary aided or foundation special school[7].

1   Ie the Local Government Finance Act 1988 Pt III (ss 41–67) (see LOCAL GOVERNMENT FINANCE vol 70 (2012) PARA 109 et seq). As to the rating of educational premises see generally PARA 1369.
2   As to the meanings of 'premises' and 'school' see PARAS 62 note 19, 91 respectively (definitions applied by virtue of the School Standards and Framework Act 1998 s 142(8)).
3   As to the meaning of 'maintained school' see PARA 99.
4   As to the meaning of 'local authority' see PARA 25.
5   School Standards and Framework Act 1998 s 78(a) (amended by SI 2010/1158). As to community and voluntary schools and community special schools see PARA 106 et seq; and as to special schools generally see PARA 1041 et seq.
6   As to the governing body of a maintained school, in relation to England, see PARA 150 et seq; and as to the governing body of a maintained school, in relation to Wales, see PARA 195 et seq.
7   School Standards and Framework Act 1998 s 78(b). As to foundation schools and foundation special schools see PARA 106 et seq.

12. EDUCATIONAL TRUSTS

1371. Trusts for the advancement of education. For the purposes of the law of England and Wales, a charity is an institution which is established for charitable purposes only, and falls to be subject to the control of the High Court in the exercise of its jurisdiction with respect to charities[1]. A charitable purpose is a purpose which falls within any one of the statutory descriptions of purposes and is for the public benefit[2]. The advancement of education is one of the statutory descriptions of purpose[3]. Many purposes which fall to be considered under this description of charitable purpose may also be considered charitable as being for the advancement of the arts, culture, heritable or science[4], and may be accepted as falling under either or both of these descriptions[5].

In addition, it is charitable to provide, or assist in the provision of, facilities for recreation, or other leisure-time occupation, if the facilities are provided in the interests of social welfare[6].

1 See the Charities Act 2011 s 1; and CHARITIES vol 8 (2015) PARA 1.
2 See the Charities Act 2011 s 2; and CHARITIES vol 8 (2015) PARA 2.
3 See the Charities Act 2011 s 3(1)(b); and CHARITIES vol 8 (2015) PARAS 2, 20 et seq.
4 Ie under the Charities Act 2011 s 3(1)(f); see CHARITIES vol 8 (2015) PARAS 2, 36.
5 See eg *Re Shakespeare Memorial Trust, Earl of Lytton v A-G* [1923] 2 Ch 398; *Re Hopkins' Will Trusts, Naish v Francis Bacon Society Inc* [1965] Ch 669, [1964] 3 All ER 46; *Construction Industry Training Board v A-G* [1971] 3 All ER 449, [1971] 1 WLR 1303 (affd without dealing with this point [1973] Ch 173, [1972] 2 All ER 1339, CA); *Incorporated Council of Law Reporting for England and Wales v A-G* [1972] Ch 73, [1971] 3 All ER 1029, CA.
6 See the Charities Act 2011 s 5 (consolidating the provisions of the Recreational Charities Act 1958 (repealed)); and CHARITIES vol 8 (2015) PARA 52 et seq.

1372. Extent of local authorities' powers relating to trusts for charitable purposes. A local authority has no standing to institute legal proceedings for the construction of a will purporting to create a charitable trust[1]. However, a local authority which does not have education functions[2] may help with education matters by establishing a trust fund to provide free or assisted places at independent schools[3].

1 *Re Belling, Enfield London Borough Council v Public Trustee* [1967] Ch 425, [1967] 1 All ER 105.
2 As to local authorities and their education functions see PARA 25.
3 *Manchester City Council v Greater Manchester Metropolitan County Council* (1980) 78 LGR 560, HL. As to independent schools see PARA 369 et seq.

1373. Local authorities' powers to accept gifts for educational purposes. A local authority[1] may accept, hold and administer any property on trust for purposes connected with education[2].

Any intention on the part of a local authority in England that a school[3] should be vested in the authority as trustees must be treated[4] as an intention to establish a new community school[5], community special school[6] or maintained nursery school[7], so that proposals for that purpose must be published[8] and the statutory provisions in relation to proposals for establishment or discontinuance of schools in England[9] apply accordingly[10].

Any intention on the part of a local authority in Wales that a school should be vested in the authority as trustees must be treated[11] as an intention to establish a new community school, community special school or maintained nursery school and the statutory provisions relating to the procedure and implementation for proposals concerning schools in Wales[12] apply accordingly[13].

Any school which in accordance with the above provisions[14] is vested in a local authority as trustees must be a community school, a community special school or a maintained nursery school[15].

1 As to the meaning of 'local authority' see PARA 25.
2 Education Act 1996 s 529(1) (amended by SI 2010/1158). As to the application of an endowment of an existing school transferred to the local authority see *Re Poplar and Blackwall Free School* (1878) 8 ChD 543.
3 As to the meaning of 'school' see PARA 91.
4 Ie for the purposes of the Education and Inspections Act 2006 s 7 (see PARA 111), s 10 (see PARA 112) and s 11 (see PARA 113).
5 As to community schools see PARA 107.
6 As to the meaning of 'special school' see PARA 1041.
7 As to the meaning of 'maintained nursery school' see PARA 99 note 4.
8 Ie in accordance with the Education and Inspections Act 2006 s 7 (see PARA 111), s 10 (see PARA 112) or s 11 (see PARA 113).
9 Ie the Education and Inspections Act 2006 Sch 2 (see PARA 118 et seq).
10 Education Act 1996 s 529(1A) (added by the Education and Inspections Act 2006 Sch 3 para 10(1), (2); and amended by SI 2010/1158).
11 Ie for the purposes of the School Standards and Organisation (Wales) Act 2013 s 41 (proposals to establish mainstream schools: see PARA 140) and s 44 (proposals to establish, alter or discontinue community special schools: see PARA 140).
12 Ie the School Standards and Organisation (Wales) Act 2013 ss 48–55, Sch 3 (proposals: publication, consultation and objections) (see PARA 143).
13 Education Act 1996 s 529(2) (amended by the Education and Inspections Act 2006 Sch 3 para 10(1), (3), Sch 18 Pt 3; and the School Standards and Organisation (Wales) Act 2013 Sch 5 para 17(1), (5)(a)).
14 Ie the Education Act 1996 s 529(1A) or s 529(2) (see the text to notes 3–13).
15 Education Act 1996 s 529(3) (amended by the School Standards and Framework Act 1998 Sch 30 para 145(b); and the Education and Inspections Act 2006 Sch 3 para 10(1), (4)).

1374. Modification of educational trust deeds and instruments. The appropriate national authority[1] may by order make such modifications of any trust deed or other instrument relating to: (1) a school which is a foundation, voluntary or foundation special school; or (2) property held on trust for the purposes of such a school, as appear to it to be necessary or expedient in connection with the operation of any provision of the School Standards and Framework Act 1998, the Learning and Skills Act 2000, the Education Act 2002, the Education and Inspections Act 2006, the Academies Act 2010 or the School Standards and Organisation (Wales) Act 2013 or anything done under or for the purposes of any such provision[2].

The appropriate national authority may also by order make such modifications of any trust deed or other instrument relating to or regulating any institution that provides or is concerned in the provision of educational services, or is concerned in educational research, as, after consultation with the persons responsible for the management of the institution, appear to it to be requisite to enable them to fulfil any condition or meet any requirement imposed by regulations[3].

Any modification made by any such order may be made to have permanent effect or to have effect for such period as may be specified in the order[4].

1 Ie the Secretary of State or, in relation to Wales, the Welsh Ministers. As to the Secretary of State see PARA 58. As to the Welsh Ministers see PARA 59. As to the meaning of 'Wales' see PARA 7 note 3. The functions of the Secretary of State under the School Standards and Framework Act 1998 s 82 and the Education Act 1996 s 489, so far as exercisable in relation to Wales, were transferred to the National Assembly for Wales (see the National Assembly for Wales (Transfer of Functions) Order 1999, SI 1999/672, art 2, Sch 1) and are now vested in the Welsh Ministers (see the Government of Wales Act 2006 s 162(1), Sch 11 para 30).

<caption>727 | Educational Trusts | Para 1376.</caption>

2 See the School Standards and Framework Act 1998 s 82(1); and PARA 146.
3 See the Education Act 1996 s 489(3); and PARA 83.
4 See the School Standards and Framework Act 1998 s 82(3) (see PARA 146); Education Act 1996 s 489(4) (see PARA 83).

1375. Schemes under the Endowed Schools Acts. Where under any provision, however expressed, of a scheme made under the Endowed Schools Acts 1869 to 1948[1] the power of the trustees under the scheme to apply any property to which the scheme relates for purposes authorised by the scheme is subject to the approval or order of any other person[2], the scheme has effect as if no such approval or order was required[3]. The appropriate national authority[4] may, on the application of any person whose approval or order would otherwise be required under such a scheme, direct[5] that the requirement is to continue to have effect[6], but no liability[7] is to be taken to have been incurred in respect of any failure before the making of such a direction to obtain any such approval or order[8].

1 Ie the Endowed Schools Act 1869; the Endowed Schools Act 1873; and the Education (Miscellaneous Provisions) Act 1948 s 2, Sch 1 Pt II (all repealed).
2 As to the meaning of 'person' see PARA 7 note 6.
3 Education Act 1996 s 553(1). Where, under any scheme made before 18 August 1918 (ie the date on which the Education Act 1918 was passed) relating to an educational charity, the approval of the Board of Education was required for the exercise by the trustees under the scheme of a power of appointing new trustees, the scheme has effect as if no such approval were required: s 47 (amended by the Education Act 1973 s 1(4), Sch 2 Pt I). As to the Board of Education see PARA 58.
4 Ie the Secretary of State or, in relation to Wales, the Welsh Ministers. As to the Secretary of State see PARA 58. As to the Welsh Ministers see PARA 59. As to the meaning of 'Wales' see PARA 7 note 3. The functions of the Education Act 1996 s 553, so far as exercisable in relation to Wales, were transferred to the National Assembly for Wales (see the National Assembly for Wales (Transfer of Functions) Order 1999, SI 1999/672, art 2, Sch 1) and are now vested in the Welsh Ministers (see the Government of Wales Act 2006 s 162(1), Sch 11 para 30).
5 As to directions see the Education Act 1996 s 570; and PARA 75.
6 Ie despite the Education Act 1996 s 553(1): see the text to notes 1–3.
7 As to the meaning of 'liability' see PARA 108 note 22.
8 Education Act 1996 s 553(2).

1376. Powers in relation to trusts for religious education. Where in relation to any time before 1 September 1999[1], the premises[2] of a voluntary or grant-maintained school[3] have ceased to be used for such a school[4], or in relation to any time on or after 1 September 1999: (1) the premises of a foundation[5] or voluntary school have ceased to be used for such a school[6]; or (2) in the opinion of the appropriate national authority[7] it is likely such premises will cease to be so used[8], the appropriate national authority may by order[9] made by statutory instrument make new provision as to the use of any endowment if it is shown[10] either[11]:

 (a) that the endowment is or has been held wholly or partly for or in connection with the provision at the school of religious education in accordance with the tenets of a particular religion or religious denomination[12]; or

 (b) that the endowment is or has been used wholly or partly for or in connection with the provision at the school of such religious education and that the following requirements are fulfilled[13], namely:

  (i) that the school was or has been maintained as a voluntary or grant-maintained school or as a foundation or voluntary school since 1 April 1945[14]; and

(ii) that religious education in accordance with the tenets of the religion or denomination concerned is, and from that date has been, provided at the school or, where the premises have ceased to be used for the purposes of the school, was provided at the school from that date until immediately before the premises ceased to be so used[15].

Such an order may require or authorise the disposal by sale or otherwise of any land[16] or other property forming part of an endowment affected by the order, including the premises of the school and any teacher's dwelling-house[17], and may consolidate any endowments to be dealt with by the scheme[18]. Subject to this, and to any statutory provision affecting the endowments, such an order must establish and give effect, with a view to enabling the religion or denomination concerned to participate more effectively in the administration of the statutory system of public education, to a scheme or schemes[19] for the endowments dealt with by the order to be used[20] for appropriate educational purposes[21].

Where a scheme so given effect[22] provides for the endowments dealt with by the order or any part of them to be used for the purposes specified in the provision relating to uniform statutory trusts for educational endowments[23], any such scheme may provide for the endowments thereby dealt with or any part of them to be added to any existing endowment applicable for those purposes (whether it is so applicable by virtue of a scheme so given effect or otherwise)[24]. Any such order has effect despite any Act of Parliament (other than a public general Act), letters patent or other instrument relating to, or trust affecting, the endowments dealt with by the order[25].

1 Ie the appointed day (see PARA 106 note 3) (definition applied by the Education Act 1996 s 554(1) (substituted by the School Standards and Framework Act 1998 s 140(1), Sch 30 para 168(1), (2))).
2 As to the meaning of 'premises' see PARA 62 note 19.
3 As to voluntary schools see PARA 108; and as to grant-maintained schools see PARA 106.
4 Education Act 1996 s 554(1)(a) (as substituted: see note 1). Section 554 applies where the premises of a non-provided public elementary school ceased before 1 April 1945 to be used for such a school as it applies where the premises of a voluntary school have ceased to be used for such a school: s 554(6).
5 As to foundation schools see PARA 108.
6 Education Act 1996 s 554(1)(b)(i) (as substituted: see note 1).
7 Ie the Secretary of State or, in relation to Wales, the Welsh Ministers. As to the Secretary of State see PARA 58. As to the Welsh Ministers see PARA 59. As to the meaning of 'Wales' see PARA 7 note 3. The functions of the Secretary of State under the Education Act 1996 ss 554–556, so far as exercisable in relation to Wales, were transferred to the National Assembly for Wales (see the National Assembly for Wales (Transfer of Functions) Order 1999, SI 1999/672, art 2, Sch 1) and are now vested in the Welsh Ministers (see the Government of Wales Act 2006 s 162(1), Sch 11 para 30).
8 Education Act 1996 s 554(1)(b)(ii) (as substituted: see note 1).
9 The order may be made only on the application of the persons appearing to the appropriate national authority to be the appropriate authority of the denomination concerned: Education Act 1996 s 555(1). The appropriate national authority must, not less than one month before making the order give notice of the proposed order and of the right of persons interested to make representations on it: s 555(2). The notice must be given: (1) by giving to any persons appearing to the appropriate national authority to be trustees of an endowment affected by the proposed order a notice of the proposal to make it, together with a draft or summary of the provisions proposed to be included (s 555(3)(a)); and (2) by publishing, in such manner as the appropriate national authority thinks sufficient for informing any other persons interested, a notice of the proposal to make the order and of the place where any person interested may, during a period of not less than a month, inspect such a draft or summary, and by keeping a draft or summary available for inspection in accordance with the notice (s 555(3)(b)). The

appropriate national authority must take into account any representations that may be made to it by any person interested in it before the order is made: s 555(4). As to the meaning of 'person' see PARA 7 note 6. As to the meaning of 'month' see PARA 54 note 26. 'Endowment' includes property not subject to any restriction on the expenditure of capital: Education Act 1996 ss 554(5), 555(5), 556(8). As to the service of notices and documents see s 572; and PARA 76. Orders made under s 554, being local in nature, are not recorded in this work.

10 'Shown' means shown to the satisfaction of the appropriate national authority: Education Act 1996 s 554(5).

11 Education Act 1996 s 554(2). This provision is expressed to be subject to s 555 (see note 9) and s 556(1), (2) (see the text to notes 16–21): see s 554(2).

12 Education Act 1996 s 554(2)(a).

13 Education Act 1996 s 554(2)(b). This provision is expressed to be subject to s 554(4) (see note 15): see s 554(2)(b).

14 Education Act 1996 s 554(3)(a) (substituted by the School Standards and Framework Act 1998 Sch 30 para 168(3)(a)). 1 April 1945 is the date on which the Education Act 1944 Pt II (ss 6–69) (repealed) came into force: see the Education Act 1996 s 554(3)(a) (as so substituted).

15 Education Act 1996 s 554(3)(b). 'Used' in this context means used in pursuance of ss 377–378, 380–381 (all repealed) (or any corresponding earlier enactment), or the School Standards and Framework Act 1998 Sch 19 para 3 (see PARA 916) or Sch 19 para 4 (see PARA 917): see the Education Act 1996 s 554(3)(b) (amended by the School Standards and Framework Act 1998 Sch 30 para 168(3)(b)). Where in the case of any school falling within the Education Act 1996 s 554(3)(a) (see head (b)(i) in the text) it is shown that religious education in accordance with the tenets of a particular religion or denomination is provided at the school, or if the premises have ceased to be used for the purposes of the school, such religious education was so provided immediately before the premises ceased to be so used, such religious education is taken to have been provided at the school from 1 April 1945, unless the contrary is shown: s 554(4)(a). Where religious education in accordance with such tenets is shown to have been given to any pupils at: (1) a controlled school; (2) a grant-maintained school which was a controlled school immediately before it became a grant-maintained school; or (3) a foundation or voluntary controlled school with a religious character, the religious education is taken to have been given to them at the request of their parents, unless the contrary is shown: s 554(4)(b) (substituted by the School Standards and Framework Act 1998 Sch 30 para 168(4)). As to the meaning of 'pupil' see PARA 20 note 4. As to the meaning of 'parent' see PARA 7 note 6.

As to the adoption of uniform statutory trusts as the trusts on which endowments regulated by an order under the Education Act 1996 s 554 are to be held see s 557, Sch 36; and PARA 1377.

16 As to the meaning of 'land' see PARA 118 note 18.

17 Education Act 1996 s 556(1)(a).

18 Education Act 1996 s 556(1)(b). Section 568(5) (general provision as to orders) does not apply to an order under s 554, but such an order may include such incidental or supplementary provisions as appear to the appropriate national authority to be necessary or expedient either for the bringing into force or for the operation of any scheme established by it, including in particular provisions: (1) for the appointment and powers of trustees of the property comprised in the scheme or, if the property is not all applicable for the same purposes, of any part of that property (s 556(6)(a)); and (2) for the property or any part of it to vest by virtue of the scheme in the first trustees under the scheme or trustees of any endowment to which it is to be added or, if not so vested, to be transferred to them (s 556(6)(b)).

19 Such a scheme: (1) may provide for the retention of the capital of any endowment and the application of the accruing income (Education Act 1996 s 556(4)(a)); or (2) may authorise the application or expenditure of capital to such extent and subject to such conditions as may be determined by or in accordance with the scheme, and any such scheme may provide for the endowments dealt with by the scheme or any part of them to be added to any existing endowment applicable for any such purpose as is authorised for the scheme by s 556(2) (see the text to notes 20–21) (s 556(4)(b)).

20 Ie either in connection with schools which are foundation schools or voluntary schools or partly in connection with such schools (or either description of such schools) and partly in other ways related to the locality served by the school at the premises referred to in the Education Act 1996 s 554(1) (see the text to notes 1–8): s 556(2) (amended by the School Standards and Framework Act 1998 Sch 30 para 169(a), (b)).

21 Education Act 1996 s 556(2). 'Use for appropriate educational purposes' means use for educational purposes in connection with the provision of religious education in accordance with the tenets of the religion or denomination concerned (including use for any purpose specified in Sch 36 (uniform statutory trusts for educational endowments: see PARA 1377)): s 556(3).

22 Ie given effect under the Education Act 1996 s 554: see the text to notes 1–15.
23 Ie for purposes specified in the Education Act 1996 Sch 36: see PARA 1377.
24 Education Act 1996 s 556(5).
25 Education Act 1996 s 556(7).

1377. Adoption of statutory trusts. The trustees of any endowments[1] may by resolution[2] adopt the uniform statutory trusts[3] as the trusts on which those endowments are to be held[4]. On the adoption by trustees of the uniform statutory trusts in respect of any endowments the scheme or order which regulates the endowments has effect as if the uniform statutory trusts were incorporated in the scheme or order to the exclusion of the corresponding provisions of the scheme or order[5]. The trustees of two or more endowments which are held on the uniform statutory trusts may, by resolution[6], consolidate all or any of those endowments and, where they do so, the endowments must be treated, for all purposes, as held for the purposes of a single charity[7].

The trustees may, after payment of any expenses incurred in connection with the administration of the trust, apply the capital and income of the relevant trust assets[8] for any of the following purposes:

(1)   in or towards the purchase of a site for, or the erection, improvement or enlargement of, the premises of any relevant school[9] in the area[10];

(2)   for the maintenance of any relevant school in the area[11];

(3)   in or towards the purchase of a site for, or the erection, improvement or enlargement of, the premises of a teacher's house for use in connection with any relevant school in the area[12]; and

(4)   for the maintenance of a teacher's house for use in connection with any relevant school in the area[13].

The trustees may also, after payment of any expenses incurred in connection with the administration of the trust, apply the income of the relevant trust assets for any of the following purposes:

(a)   in or towards the provision of advice, guidance and resources (including materials) in connection with any matter related to the management of, or education provided at, any relevant school in the area[14];

(b)   the provision of services for the carrying out of any inspection of any relevant school in the area required by the Education Act 2005[15]; and

(c)   to defraying the cost of employing or engaging staff in connection with[16]:

(i)   the application of income of the relevant trust assets for either of the purposes referred to in heads (a) and (b) above[17]; or

(ii)   the application of capital or income of the relevant trust assets for any of the purposes referred to in heads (1) to (4) above[18].

1   As to the meaning of 'endowment' see PARA 1376 note 9 (definition applied by the Education Act 1996 s 557(9)). Section 557 applies to endowments which are:

(1)   regulated by a qualifying scheme under the Endowed Schools Acts 1869 to 1948 (repealed) as applied by the Education Act 1944 s 86(1) (repealed) or by an order under the Education Act 1996 s 554 (see PARA 1376) or the Education Act 1973 s 2 (repealed) (Education Act 1996 s 557(1)(a)); and

(2)   held under any such scheme or order on trusts which provide for capital or income or both to be applicable for or in connection with:

(a)   the provision of religious education at relevant schools, or relevant schools of any description (but not only at a particular school or schools) in a diocese or other geographical area (s 557(1)(b)(i)); or

(b)   the provision of premises for relevant schools, or relevant schools of any description (but not only at a particular school or schools) at which religious education is or is to be provided in a diocese or other geographical area (s 557(1)(b)(ii)), but s 557 does not apply to an endowment if or in so far as it constitutes a religious education fund: s 557(1)(b).

'Qualifying scheme' means a scheme in force on 1 January 1994 (the date when the Education Act 1993 s 287 (repealed) came into force): Education Act 1996 s 557(9). 'Religious education' means religious education in accordance with the tenets of a particular religion or religious denomination: s 557(9). 'Relevant school' means a foundation or voluntary school: s 557(9) (amended by the School Standards and Framework Act 1998 s 140(1), Sch 30 para 170). As to foundation and voluntary schools see PARA 108. 'Provision', in relation to premises, means provision by the purchase of a site, the erection of premises or the maintenance, improvement or enlargement of premises: Education Act 1996 s 557(9). As to the meaning of 'premises' see PARA 62 note 19. 'Religious education fund' includes a Sunday school fund: s 557(9).

2   The resolution must be passed by a simple majority of the trustees or, if the trustees are a body corporate or a company, by a simple majority of the members of the body corporate or an ordinary resolution of the company, and it must be recorded in the records of the decisions of the trustees affecting the endowments of the trust: Education Act 1996 s 557(6). 'Company' means a company as defined in the Companies Act 2006 s 1(1) (see COMPANIES vol 14 (2009) PARA 1): Education Act 1996 s 557(9) (definition substituted by SI 2009/1941).

3   The uniform statutory trusts are those set out in the Education Act 1996 Sch 36 (see the text to notes 8–18): s 557(3).

4   Education Act 1996 s 557(2). Where trustees pass a resolution under s 557(2), it is their duty to send a copy of the resolution to the Secretary of State or, in relation to Wales, the Welsh Ministers: see s 577(7). As to the Secretary of State see PARA 58. As to the Welsh Ministers see PARA 59. As to the meaning of 'Wales' see PARA 7 note 3. The functions of the Secretary of State under s 577, so far as exercisable in relation to Wales, were transferred to the National Assembly for Wales (see the National Assembly for Wales (Transfer of Functions) Order 1999, SI 1999/672, art 2, Sch 1) and are now vested in the Welsh Ministers (see the Government of Wales Act 2006 s 162(1), Sch 11 para 30).

The uniform statutory trusts applicable to endowments to which the Education Act 1996 s 577 applies do not affect:

   (1)   the rights of any person under the School Sites Act 1841 s 2 proviso 3 (see PARA 1297), under the Education Act 1944 s 86(3) (repealed) or under the Reverter of Sites Act 1987 s 1 (rights replacing certain reversionary interests in land: see PARA 1297) (Education Act 1996 s 557(8)(a)); or

   (2)   the rights of any local authority which have arisen under the Education Act 1946 Sch 1 para 7 (repealed) or Sch 1 para 8 (repealed) (rights in relation to school sites provided by such authorities) or which may arise under the Education Act 1996 s 60(4) (repealed) or s 62(2) (repealed) (s 557(8)(b) (amended by SI 2010/1158)),

except in so far as any right falling within s 557(8)(a) is or has been extinguished by an order under s 554 (see PARA 1376) or the Education Act 1973 s 2 (repealed) made by virtue of the Reverter of Sites Act 1987 s 5: Education Act 1996 s 557(8). As to the meaning of 'person' see PARA 7 note 6. As to the meaning of 'local authority' see PARA 25. See *R v Secretary of State for Education and Employment, ex p Rochdale Metropolitan Borough Council* [2000] ELR 709.

5   Education Act 1996 s 557(4).

6   Ie complying with the Education Act 1996 s 557(6): see note 2.

7   Education Act 1996 s 557(5).

8   For the purposes of the Education Act 1996 Sch 36, as incorporated in any scheme or order, 'the relevant trust assets' means the endowments in respect of which the trustees have adopted the uniform statutory trusts, including the income derived from them: s 557(10).

9   For the purposes of the Education Act 1996 Sch 36, as incorporated in any scheme or order, 'relevant school' means a relevant school, academy school, alternative provision academy, city technology college or city college for the technology of the arts, at which the religious education provided for in the scheme or order, as the case may be, is or is to be provided: s 557(10) (amended by the Education Act 2002 s 69; and the Education Act 2011 Sch 13 para 9(1), (16)). As to the meaning of 'academy school' see PARA 346 note 12. As to city technology colleges and city colleges for the technology of the arts see PARA 345. As to academies see PARA 345 et seq.

10   Education Act 1996 Sch 36 para 1(a). In Sch 36, as incorporated in any scheme or order, 'the area' means the diocese or other geographical area within which the trust assets may be applied under the scheme or order, as the case may be: s 557(10).

11   Education Act 1996 Sch 36 para 1(b).

12   Education Act 1996 Sch 36 para 1(c).

13   Education Act 1996 Sch 36 para 1(d).

14   Education Act 1996 Sch 36 para 2(a).

15 Education Act 1996 Sch 36 para 2(b) (amended by the Education Act 2005 s 61, Sch 9 para 10).
    The relevant provisions of the Education Act 2005 are Pt I (ss 1–63) (repealed): see the
    Education Act 1996 Sch 36 para 2(b).
16 Education Act 1996 Sch 36 para 2(c).
17 Education Act 1996 Sch 36 para 2(c)(i).
18 Education Act 1996 Sch 36 para 2(c)(ii).

1378.   Sex discrimination: application by trustees to remove or modify restriction. In relation to a trust deed or other instrument which:

(1)   concerns property applicable for or in connection with the provision of education in an establishment[1] in England and Wales[2]; and

(2)   in any way restricts the benefits available under the instrument to persons of one sex[3],

if, on the application of the trustees or the responsible body[4], a minister of the Crown[5] is satisfied that the removal or modification of the restriction would be conducive to the advancement of education without sex discrimination[6], the minister may by order[7] make such modifications of the instrument as appear to the minister expedient for removing or modifying the restriction[8].

The minister must require the applicant to publish a notice containing particulars of the proposed order[9], and stating that representations may be made to the minister within a period specified in the notice[10]. The applicant must publish the notice in the manner specified by the minister[11]. Before making the order, the minister must take account of representations made in accordance with the notice[12].

1   Ie an establishment to which the Equality Act 2010 s 85 (see PARA 9 note 1) or s 91 (see PARA 13) applies.
2   Equality Act 2010 Sch 14 para 1(1)(a). As to the meanings of 'England' and 'Wales' see PARA 7 note 3.
3   Equality Act 2010 Sch 14 para 1(1)(b).
4   Ie within the meaning of the Equality Act 2010 s 85 (see PARA 9 note 1) or s 91 (see PARA 13 note 1).
5   As to ministers of the Crown see CONSTITUTIONAL AND ADMINISTRATIVE LAW vol 20 (2014) PARA 151.
6   Equality Act 2010 Sch 14 para 1(2). As to the meaning of 'sex discrimination' see DISCRIMINATION vol 33 (2013) PARA 70.
7   Such orders, being of local effect, are not recorded in this work.
8   Equality Act 2010 Sch 14 para 1(3). If the trust was created by a gift or bequest, an order must not be made until the end of the period of 25 years after the date when the gift or bequest took effect: Sch 14 para 1(4). However, this does not apply if the donor or the personal representatives of the donor or testator consent in writing to making the application for the order: Sch 14 para 1(5). As to the meaning of 'writing' see PARA 76 note 8.
9   Equality Act 2010 Sch 14 para 1(6)(a).
10 Equality Act 2010 Sch 14 para 1(6)(b). The period must be not less than one month beginning with the day after the date of the notice: Sch 14 para 1(7). As to the meaning of 'month' see PARA 54 note 26.
11 Equality Act 2010 Sch 14 para 1(8). The cost of publication may be paid out of the property of the trust: Sch 14 para 1(9).
12 Equality Act 2010 Sch 14 para 1(10).

INDEX

Education

ADULT LEARNING—*continued*
  Wales, inspection in—*continued*
    general powers of Chief Inspector
      1271
    information for Welsh Ministers,
      provision of 1269
    privileged nature of reports 1279
    report—
      defamation, and 1279
      duty to make 1270
      power to make 1271
      privileged nature of 1279
      publication 1270, 1271
    survey, power to carry out 1276

AGE
  school, compulsory 19

ANNUAL REPORT
  Commonwealth Scholarship
    Commission, by 1113
  Her Majesty's Chief Inspector of
    Education and Training in Wales,
    by 1154
  Marshall Aid Commemoration
    Commission, by 1114
  Ofqual, by 852

APPRENTICESHIP
  meaning 820n[15]
  England, in—
    apprenticeship certificate—
    meaning 763
      application for, regulations as to
        763
      fee for 763
      power to issue 763
    approved apprenticeship standards
      762
    approved English apprenticeship—
    meaning 760
      alternative English apprenticeship
        760n[2]
      completion 760
    approved English apprenticeship
      agreement 761
    delegation of Secretary of State's
      functions 764
    facilities for training, provision of—
      adult detention, persons subject
        to—
        education and training for 778
        encouragement of education and
          training for 781
        needs of, consideration to be
          given to 782
      apprenticeship offer 777
      apprenticeship opportunity 777

APPRENTICESHIP—*continued*
  England, in—*continued*
    facilities for training, provision
      of—*continued*
      apprenticeship training: meaning
        776n[2]
      learning aims for persons aged 19
        or over—
        facilities, provision of 779
        tuition fees, payment of 780
      persons aged 16 to 18 776
      persons aged 19 or over without
        EHC plan—
        education and training for 778
        encouragement of education and
          training for 781
      persons aged 19 to 25 with EHC
        plan, training for 776
      proper facilities: meaning 777
      Secretary of State's duty 777
      special educational needs of,
        consideration to be given to
        persons with 782
  Wales, in—
    apprenticeship agreement—
    meaning 766
      application of statutory provisions
        to 766
      conditions to be satisfied 766
      nature of 766
      variation to 766
    apprenticeship framework—
      draft, submission of 772
      issue 771
      recognised Welsh framework 771n[4]
      Welsh issuing authority 770
    apprenticeship standards, specification
      of—
      draft, preparation 773
      generally 773
      modification—
        effect on recognised Welsh
          framework 775
        power to order 774
      on-the-job training 773n[15]
      relevant occupational
        competencies 773n[18]
      relevant technical knowledge
        773n[19]
      replacement, effect on recognised
        Welsh framework 775
      requirements to be met 773
    certificate—
      contents 769
      issue 768

References are to paragraph numbers; superior figures refer to notes

EDUCATION AND TRAINING FOR
    YOUNG PERSONS—*continued*
England, participation in—*continued*
    support services—*continued*
        guidance as to provision of 802
        information about student,
            provision of 804
        internet and telephone, by 805
        person providing services, supply of
            information by 807
        provision by local authority 802
        public bodies, supply of
            information by 808
        relevant information, provision of
            804n[1]
        relevant young adult 802n[3]
        restricted information, offence of
            disclosing 806n[23]
        Secretary of State, supply of
            information by 807
        social security information, supply
            of 806
        support: meaning 803n[3]
        young person: meaning 802n[2]
    training: meaning 32n[4]
    transport services—
        adult learners, for 810
        guidance as to 810
        relevant young adult: meaning
            810n[9]
        transport policy statement—
            guidance as to 810
            preparation of 810
            revision following complaint 811
    grants for—
        parties to whom payable 818
        payment and terms etc 818
        power to authorise 818
        qualifying account, conditions as to
            818n[3]
        qualifying arrangements, conditions as
            to 818n[4]
        regulations 818
    information, use for assessment
        functions 801
Wales, participation in—
    16 to 18-year-olds—
        core entitlement 724
        facilities for 789, 791
        powers as to 34
    efficiency studies 798
    facilities, provision of—
        encouragement of education and
            training 790
        learning difficulties, persons with
            791

EDUCATION AND TRAINING FOR
    YOUNG PERSONS—*continued*
Wales, participation in—*continued*
    facilities, provision of—*continued*
        persons aged 16 to 19 789
        persons over 19 789
    financial resources, provision of—
        conditions attached to 793
        manner of 792
        means tests 795
        performance assessments for
            providers 795
        power to secure 792
        qualifying accounts, promotion of
            796
        qualifying arrangements, making
            of 796
        relevant persons 792
        sixth forms, funding of 794
    functions—
        joint exercise of 800
        services in connection with exercise
            of, provision of 799
    governing body, provision of services
        by. *See* learner support services
        below
    information about 797
    learner support services—
        meaning 812n[4]
        direction from Welsh Ministers 812
        information, access and facilities,
            provision of 812, 816
        inspection of 812
        provision of 812
    local authority, provision of services
        by. *See* youth support services
        below
    post-16 education: meaning 790n[2]
    post-16 training: meaning 790n[2]
    youth support services—
        meaning 813n[3]
        consultation and co-ordination by
            local authority 814
        direction from Welsh Ministers 813
        information, access and facilities,
            provision of 812, 816
        information, supply by public
            bodies 817
        inspection of 813
        local authority—
            meaning 813n[2]
            duties and powers 815
        provision of 813
    young person: meaning 802n[2]

References are to paragraph numbers; superior figures refer to notes

References are to paragraph numbers; superior figures refer to notes

GOVERNING BODY (MAINTAINED
   SCHOOL)—*continued*
membership—*continued*
   foundation school 152
   generally 150, 151
   interim executive members 158
   voluntary school 152
new school—
   meaning 155n[4]
   arrangements for 155
   school opening date: meaning 155n[9]
no properly constituted body, powers
   where 154
parent council—
   establishment 178
   parent member: meaning 178n[14]
   qualifying school 178n[2]
parent governor—
   meaning 151n[5]
   appointment 159
   election 159
   removal 164
partnership governor—
   meaning 152n[4]
   appointment 161
   nomination 161
   removal 164
powers—
   borrowing 169n[12]
   community facilities, provision of 174
   companies providing services, forming
      or investing in 173
   further education, provision of 171
   generally 169
   higher education, provision of 170,
      679
   security, grant of 169n[12]
public authority for purposes of Human
   Rights Act 150n[3]
reports on discharge of functions 189
requirement to have 150
school premises, control of 180
seal, use of 183
Secretary of State—
   participation in international surveys,
      power to direct 193
   provision of information to 190
special educational needs, duties as to
   pupils with—
   England, in 969
   Wales, in 1020
staff governor—
   meaning 151n[8]
   election 160
substitute governor—
   meaning 152n[6]

GOVERNING BODY (MAINTAINED
   SCHOOL)—*continued*
substitute governor—*continued*
   tenure of office 163
terms, fixing dates of 458
title 150
Wales, in—
   clerk, appointment etc 202
   collaboration between schools—
      collaboration objective: meaning
         199n[3]
      exercise of power 199
      powers of collaboration: meaning
         199n[2]
   conduct of school, responsibility for
      203
   constitution of—
      federation of schools, for 198
      regulations as to 195
      temporary governing body 197
   consultation with pupils 212
   duties—
      annual report, preparation of 218
      complaints procedure 209
      consultation with pupils 212
      health and safety, in relation to 210
      information, provision of 218
      meeting after petition by parents,
         holding of 219
      welfare of children, as to 211
   ex officio trustees 223
   federation of schools, proposals for
      198
   governors—
      allowances 200
      appointment 200
      disqualification 200
      election 200
      qualifications 200
      removal 200
      tenure 200
      training and support 201
   guidance from Welsh Ministers—
      consultation with pupils, as to 212
      generally 195
   information—
      distribution of—
         further education institutions,
            about 222
         secondary education, about
            schools providing 221
      provision of—
         annual report 218
         generally 218
         Welsh Ministers, to 220

HER MAJESTY'S CHIEF INSPECTOR
OF EDUCATION AND TRAINING
IN WALES—*continued*
inspection of schools—*continued*
See further SCHOOL INSPECTION
(WALES)
Inspectorate. *See* HER MAJESTY'S
INSPECTORATE OF EDUCATION AND
TRAINING IN WALES
learner support services, inspection of
812
local authority, inspection of—
assistance, duty to provide 1294
Auditor General of Wales, assistance
from 1293
conduct of 1293
documents and other records, right to
inspect, take away etc 1294
duty to inspect 1293
entry etc rights 1294
information, right to 1293
obstruction, offence 1294
power to inspect 1293
report 1293
response to report 1293
written statement in response to 1293
nursery education, inspection of—
annual report to include details of
1259
conduct of 1255
documents etc, right to inspect etc
1258
duty to carry out 1255
entry and seizure rights in relation to
1258
frequency 1255
general functions of Chief Inspector
1253
guidance as to 1255
inspectors—
appeals by inspectors 1254
registration of 1254
removal from register 1254
training for 1257
variation of registration conditions
1254
monitoring 1256
relevant nursery education: meaning
$1253n^4$
report, duty to make 1255, 1259
restrictions on person carrying out
1255
obstruction, offence of 1152
official seal, use of 1150
reports by 1154
resignation 1148

HER MAJESTY'S CHIEF INSPECTOR
OF EDUCATION AND TRAINING
IN WALES—*continued*
staff, power to appoint 1149
teacher training, inspection of 1286
youth support services, inspection of
813, 1288

HER MAJESTY'S CHIEF INSPECTOR
OF EDUCATION, CHILDREN'S
SERVICES AND SKILLS
academies, inspection of 365
adult learning. *See* ADULT LEARNING
(England, inspection in)
appointment 1133
children's centres, inspection of 1252
compensation on ceasing to hold office
1133
documentary evidence, application of
legislation 1134
early years provision, inspection of
1252
entry powers 1165
functions—
assistance in performance,
arrangements for 1139
delegation of 1138
generally 1136
information obtained, use of 1137
information or advice, providing
Secretary of State with 1136
matters to be considered 1137
non-education matters 1136
purpose 1137
performance 1137
independent schools—
independent inspectorate, report on
395
inspection of 384, 396, 1127
inspection authorities—
meaning $1140n^{10}$, $1141n^{10}$
interaction with 1141
inspection of schools. *See* SCHOOL
INSPECTION (ENGLAND)
inspection programmes and
frameworks 1140
inspection report, publication of 1166
later years provision, inspection of 1252
local authority—
meaning $1145n^3$
annual fee payable by 1145
inspection of—
authority, duty to supply proof of
1291
entry etc powers 1291
extended remit 1289

HIGHER EDUCATION—*continued*
institution—
  generally. *See* HIGHER EDUCATION
    INSTITUTION
  local authority, maintained by—
    ceasing to be maintained 683
    government 680
    physical training, provision of
      clothing for 682
    transport, provision of 681
  local authority functions 39, 678
  maintained school, provision by
    governing body of—
    generally 170, 679
    Wales, in 679n^6
  quality assessment. *See* HIGHER
    EDUCATION FUNDING COUNCIL FOR
    ENGLAND; HIGHER EDUCATION
    FUNDING COUNCIL FOR WALES;
    QUALITY ASSURANCE AGENCY FOR
    HIGHER EDUCATION
  university. *See* UNIVERSITY

HIGHER EDUCATION CORPORATION
meaning 645
accounts—
  audit 666n^8
  duty to maintain 666
  inspection 667
articles of government, conduct of
  institution in accordance with 664
block release: meaning 651n^4
charitable status 668
day release: meaning 651n^4
dissolution 670
established after 6 May 1992—
  change of name, power to provide
    for 658
  committees, establishment 662
  instrument of government, need for
    657
  membership—
    allowances 662
    appointing authority 661
    appointment 659, 660
    determination with respect to
      numbers 660
    disqualified from 659
    minimum and maximum numbers
      659
    procedural requirements 662
    provisions as to 659
    term of office etc 662
  proof of documents 663
  validity of proceedings 663
established before 6 May 1992—
  committees and proceedings 655

HIGHER EDUCATION
CORPORATION—*continued*
established before 6 May
  1992—*continued*
  initial constitution 652
  membership—
    appointing authority 654
    determination with respect to
      numbers 653
    independent members 652n^8
  proof of instruments 656
  seal, application of 656
first financial year: meaning 666n^3
full-time equivalent enrolment
  numbers—
  appropriate multipliers 651n^4
  determination of 651
  total full-time equivalent enrolment
    number 647n^5
full-time student: meaning 651n^1
incorporation—
  further 647
  property, rights and liabilities, transfer
    of—
    generally 649
    loan liabilities excepted from 650
    stamp duty, whether chargeable
      649n^4
    transfer date 649n^6
    transferred institution: meaning
      649n^7
  specified institutions, of 646
  staff, transfer of 648
instrument of government, established
  by. *See* established after 6 May
  1992 *above*
open or distance learning: meaning
  651n^4
powers 665
sandwich course: meaning 651n^4
trust deed, modification 669

HIGHER EDUCATION FUNDING
COUNCIL FOR ENGLAND
accounts 697
chief officer 692
committees 694
constitution 691
Crown, and 691
directions, compliance with 700
documents, proof of 696
efficiency studies 709
establishment 691
functions—
  additional, power to impose 699
  directions, need to comply with 700

INDEPENDENT SCHOOL—*continued*
Education and Skills Act 2008,
　regulation and inspection
　under—*continued*
independent educational institution
　standards—
　meaning 394
　action plan. *See* action plan *above*
　regulations 394
independent inspectorate—
　powers of 395
　report on 395
independent post-16 college—
　meaning 383n[4]
　application of provisions 383
inspection—
　direction of Secretary of State, on
　　397
　entry powers 398
　fees 399
　independent inspectorate, by 395
　prescribed intervals, at 396
　publication of report of 400
　records, of 398
　right of 398
　Secretary of State's powers 395
material change—
　meaning 388
　application for approval of—
　　determination 390
　　inspection and report 389
　　requirement 388
　unapproved, deregistration where
　　391
notice and other documents, service
　of 415
offences—
　body corporate, by 413
　proceedings for 412
　unincorporated body, by 414
participation in management,
　prohibition on—
　appeals 411
　appropriate authority, direction by
　　409
　information, provision of 410
part-time education, provision of
　382n[6]
registration—
　application for—
　　determination of 386
　　procedure 385
　　proprietor, by 385
　deregistration 387
　information, proprietor's duty to
　　provide 393

INDEPENDENT SCHOOL—*continued*
Education and Skills Act 2008,
　regulation and inspection
　under—*continued*
registration—*continued*
　material change. *See* material
　　change *above*
　register, duty to keep 384
　unsuitable person, removal from
　　register 392
relevant restriction—
　imposition of—
　　meaning 403
　　emergency, in 404
　　Secretary of State, by 403
　　Tribunal, by 408
　variation or revocation 403
fees 381
individual pupil information, provision
　of 374
National Curriculum, adoption of—
　England, for 859
　Wales, for 873
powers—
　non-maintained schools, provision of
　　education at 371
　Secretary of State—
　　general powers 373
　　performance information, to
　　　require 371
　Welsh Ministers—
　　general powers 373
　　performance information, to
　　　require 371
religious education, preferment of
　teachers willing to give 378
special educational needs in 376
staff at—
　employment of 377
　preferment of teachers willing to give
　　religious education 378
　religious character, certain schools
　　with 379
　suitability etc 377
travelling and subsistence allowances for
　governors 380
Wales, in—
　meaning 9n[1]
　regulation and inspection. *See*
　　Education Act 2002, regulation
　　and inspection under *above*
special educational needs, and 376
welfare of child accommodated in 375

INSPECTION
schools, of—
England, in. *See* SCHOOL INSPECTION
(ENGLAND)
Wales, in. *See* SCHOOL INSPECTION
(WALES)

INTERNATIONAL COVENANT ON
ECONOMIC, SOCIAL AND
POLITICAL RIGHTS
education, right to 5

INTERVENTION IN SCHOOLS
(ENGLAND)
eligible schools—
low performance standards etc—
meaning 1207n[19]
notice of unacceptability 1207
See also warning notice as to
standards and safety *below*
safety warning notice, issue of. *See*
warning notice as to standards
and safety *below*
significant improvement, school
requiring 1209
special measures, school requiring
1210
teachers' pay and conditions warning
notice, issue of. *See* teachers' pay
and conditions warning notice
below
governing body to consist of interim
executive members—
appointment of members 1223
chairman, nomination of 1223
closure of school 1227
conduct of 1225
delegated budget, effect on suspension
of 1226
delegation of functions 1225
duration of period for 1222
duty to inform other persons 1224
existing governors: meaning 1222n[6]
local authority, provision by 1213
minimum number 1223
notice—
copies, on whom served 1224
effect 1222
procedure, determining 1225
removal of members 1223
resumption of government by
normally constituted board 1228
Secretary of State, provision by 1218
terms of appointment 1223
local authority, by—
additional inspectors, appointment
of 1212

INTERVENTION IN SCHOOLS
(ENGLAND)—*continued*
local authority, by—*continued*
delegated budget, suspension of right
to 1214
governing body to enter into
arrangements, power to require
1211
guidance, duty to have regard to
1215
interim executive members, power to
provide for governing body to
consist of 1213
schools eligible for. *See* eligible schools
above
Secretary of State, by—
additional governors, power to
appoint 1216
advisory services, power to require
local authority to obtain 1221
closure of school, power to direct
1217
interim executive members, power to
provide for governing body to
consist of 1218
performance standards and safety
warning notice, power to direct
issue of 1219
teachers' pay and conditions warning
notice, power to direct issue of
1220
sixth form college, Secretary of State's
powers 1247
teachers' pay and conditions warning
notice—
meaning 1208
compliance period for 1208n[12]
copies, service of 1208n[15]
decision as to whether to confirm
1208
issue of 1208
representations against 1208
Secretary of State's power to direct
issue of 1220
warning notice as to standards and
safety—
meaning 1207
compliance period for 1207n[13]
copies, service of 1207n[17]
decision as to whether to confirm
1207
issue of 1207
representations against 1207
Secretary of State's power to direct
issue of 1220

LOCAL AUTHORITY—*continued*
accessibility strategies and plans, duty to
  implement 11
admission to school. *See* SCHOOL
  ADMISSION
assistance to school by 51
chief education officer, appointment 57
clothing, power to provide 482
compulsory school age, persons over—
  apprenticeship training $32n^4$
  education and training for 32
  work experience for 33
conferences, organisation etc 53
director of children's services,
  appointment 57
education—
  detention order, persons subject to
    $27n^6$
  functions. *See* education functions
    below
  general responsibility for 27
  primary schools, as to 31
  provision of. *See* education functions
    below
  secondary schools, as to 31
education committee—
  appointment of members, power to
    direct 56
  regulations as to 56
education functions—
  meaning 25
  appropriate education, provision of
    $31n^8$
  childcare, provision of 30
  Education Act 1996, persons not
    covered by 46
  enforcement by Secretary of State 45,
    62
  generally 37
  higher education, provision of 39,
    678
  nursery schools, provision of 29
  persons over compulsory school age,
    education and training for 32
  persons over 19, as to 36
  pupil referral units, provision of
    education in 37
  statutory list of $25n^6$
  transfer of local education authority
    functions 26
  welfare of children, and 28
  youth detention, persons subject to
    38
educational research, powers as to 53
England, in—
  meaning 25

LOCAL AUTHORITY—*continued*
England, in—*continued*
  annual performance targets 49
  core entitlement, duties as to 35
  director of children's services,
    appointment 57
  education and training for 16 to
    18-year-olds, powers as to 34
  high standards and fulfilment of
    potential, promotion of 43
  inspection of. *See under* HER
    MAJESTY'S CHIEF INSPECTOR OF
    EDUCATION, CHILDREN'S SERVICES
    AND SKILLS
  persons over compulsory school age
    32
  relevant education function: meaning
    $43n^2$
  travel arrangements. *See under*
    SCHOOL ATTENDANCE (travel
    arrangements)
  travel functions $466n^3$
  See also education functions *above*
English: meaning $26n^7$
financial statement 329
goods and services, powers as to supply
  of 54
governors, travelling and subsistence
  allowances to 52
grant to school or other institution by
  51
high standards, duty to promote 43
holidays, fixing dates of 458
information, provision of 48, 605, 940
inspection of—
  England, in. *See under* HER MAJESTY'S
    CHIEF INSPECTOR OF EDUCATION,
    CHILDREN'S SERVICES AND SKILLS
  Wales, in. *See under* HER MAJESTY'S
    CHIEF INSPECTOR OF EDUCATION
    AND TRAINING IN WALES
legal proceedings, documentary evidence
  in 50
loan of money, powers as to 54
maintained school, inspection for
  specific purpose 1180
medical officer: meaning $50n^5$
non-maintained schools, provision of
  education at 40
overview and scrutiny committees—
  appointment 55
  discharge of functions by 55
  members' voting powers 55
  procedure etc 55
  Secretary of State's powers as to 55
  Welsh Ministers' powers as to 55

PUPIL—*continued*
  exclusion—*continued*
    review of—*continued*
      review panel—*continued*
        facts, approach to establishing 539
        majority vote 539
        representations, right to make 539
        SEN expert's functions etc 539
      time limits 537
    temporarily excluded pupil: meaning $521n^6$
    unlawful, claim for damages $517n^4$
  good behaviour—
    governing body's duty to promote 509
    guidance $509n^{12}$
    head teacher's duty to determine policy 510
    mental health, and $509n^{12}$
    parenting contract in case of misbehaviour 516
    See also discipline *above*
  junior: meaning $20n^4$
  medical condition, duty to support pupil with 501
  medical examination, power to require 498
  medical inspection and treatment 499
  negligent supervision of 1088
  parenting contract—
    excluded pupil, in case of 525
    misbehaviour, in case of 516
    pupil's failure to attend school regularly, where 450
  performance targets 939
  possessions $514n^{21}$, $543n^3$, $544n^4$
  recreation and physical training—
    appropriate national authority's powers 502
    children under 13, for 503
    grants for 502
    knowledge as to value of, dissemination of 502
    leisure time activities for young people 504
    Wales, in 505
  registration—
    offence as to 437
    prescribed particulars 437
    proprietor of school, by 437
    registered pupil: meaning 437
    regulations, provisions in 437
  restraint of, use of force for—
    powers of 541

PUPIL—*continued*
  restraint of, use of force for—*continued*
    recording and reporting of use of 542
  scholarships, grant of 483
  school expenses, payment of 483
  school meals. *See* SCHOOL MEALS
  school-based counselling in Wales 500
  search powers—
    guidance $544n^{18}$
    prohibited items 544
    weapons 543
  senior: meaning $21n^4$
  Wales, in—
    recreation and social and physical training, facilities for 505
    school-based counselling 500
    withdrawal from primary school for secondary education 438
PUPIL REFERRAL UNIT
  meaning 91, 427
  curriculum 430
  exclusion of pupil—
    duty to inform parents 519
    management committee, functions of 529
    power to exclude 431, 517
    reconsideration by managing committee 534
    review of—
      generally 533
      See also under PUPIL (exclusion)
  information to parents, provision of 432
  legislation, adaptation and modification of 428
  litter 428
  local authority duties—
    information to parents, provision of 432
    management committee, establishment 434
    provision of education, as to 427
  management committee 434
  political indoctrination etc 428
  provision of education in 427
  registration 429
  school attendance order, named in 433
  special educational provision in Wales, duty to inform parents 1019
  suitable education: meaning $427n^3$
QUALIFICATIONS AND CURRICULUM DEVELOPMENT AGENCY
  abolition 824
  Secretary of State, replacement by 824
QUALIFICATIONS BODY
  meaning $17n^1$

QUALIFICATIONS BODY—*continued*
  duty not to discriminate 17

QUALIFICATIONS WALES
  establishment 853
  Qualifications Wales Act 2015,
    empowering provisions in 855
  role 853
  transfer of powers from Welsh
    Ministers 853

QUALITY ASSURANCE AGENCY FOR
  HIGHER EDUCATION
  meaning 690
  establishment 690
  generally 1284
  role 690, 1127

REGIONAL SCHOOLS
  COMMISSIONER
  responsibilities 366
  role 366

RELIGIOUS EDUCATION
  agreed syllabus—
    meaning 910n^2
    conference to reconsider—
      committees 912
      constitution 912
      duty to convene 911
    in force before 1 November 1996,
      where 910
    new, preparation by appointed body
      913
    reconsideration 913
    requirements 910
    school without religious character
      915
  approved special school, in 919
  British values, guidance on promoting
    910n^6
  community school, in 915
  court's role in identifying religious
    belief 3n^{22}
  duty to secure provision of 914
  exclusion from, parent's right to insist
    on 7
  foundation school—
    with religious character 916
    without religious character 915
  human rights legislation, and 3
  inspection of—
    England, schools in—
      conduct of 1178
      duty to carry out 1178
      frequency of 1178
      procedure 1179
      report on 1178, 1179

RELIGIOUS EDUCATION—*continued*
  inspection of—*continued*
    Wales, schools in—
      action plan following inspection
        1203
      conduct of 1201
      denominational education and
        collective worship, reports of
        1202
      duty to carry out 1201
      frequency of 1201
  place of religious worship, no
    requirement of attendance at 931
  secondary school without religious
    character 915
  standing advisory council—
    appointment of members 925
    collective worship, determination as
      to whether applicable—
      application for 927
      discharge of duty, direction on
        failure as to 929
      documents, inspection or access to
        930
      matters for council to consider 927
      meetings, access to 930
      notification of decision 927
      representations, head teacher's right
        to make 928
      review 928
      revocation, direction for 929
    constitution 925
    functions 926
    membership 925
    regulation of proceedings 925
    representative groups 925
    validity of proceedings 925
  Sunday school, no requirement of
    attendance at 931
  trust deed, whether in accordance with
    918
  trusts for, appropriate national
    authority's powers 1376
  voluntary aided school with religious
    character 917
  voluntary controlled school with
    religious character 916
  voluntary school without religious
    character 915

RELIGIOUS WORSHIP
  collective. *See* COLLECTIVE WORSHIP

RETRAINING CENTRE
  access to, under EU law 4

ROYAL ACADEMY OF ENGINEERING
  grant to 85

SCHOLARSHIP
　Commonwealth Scholarship
　　Commission. *See* COMMONWEALTH
　　SCHOLARSHIP COMMISSION
　industrial 1112
　Marshall Aid Commemoration
　　Commission. *See* MARSHALL AID
　　COMMEMORATION COMMISSION

SCHOOL
　meaning 91
　absence from, regulations as to 459
　accessibility strategies and plans 11
　adjudicator. *See* SCHOOLS ADJUDICATOR
　admission of pupils. *See* SCHOOL
　　ADMISSION
　choice of, dispute between parents as
　　to $7n^6$
　complaints against—
　　exclusion, as to $546n^{24}$
　　generally 546
　　investigation of, in England. *See*
　　　SCHOOL INSPECTION (ENGLAND)
　　　(complaints, investigation of)
　　Ofqual. *See* OFQUAL
　　Ofsted. *See* OFSTED
　　procedure 546
　　special educational needs, in case of
　　　546
　　type of school, relevance 546
　　useful information, availability of 546
　compulsory school age 19
　day, regulations as to duration of 459
　discrimination in—
　　accessibility strategies and plans 11
　　application of legislation $9n^1$
　　detriment: meaning $9n^{11}$
　　disability, contravention of duty as
　　　to 12
　　duty not to discriminate in provision
　　　of education 9
　　single-sex schools turning
　　　co-educational 10
　equality duties. *See* EQUALITY (schools,
　　in)
　governors, travelling and subsistence
　　allowances to 52
　independent. *See* INDEPENDENT SCHOOL
　inspection—
　　England, in. *See* SCHOOL INSPECTION
　　　(ENGLAND)
　　Wales, in. *See* SCHOOL INSPECTION
　　　(WALES)
　intervention. *See* INTERVENTION IN
　　SCHOOLS (ENGLAND);
　　　INTERVENTION IN SCHOOLS (WALES)
　maintained. *See* MAINTAINED SCHOOL

SCHOOL—*continued*
　nursery. *See* NURSERY SCHOOL
　primary. *See* PRIMARY SCHOOL
　proprietor: meaning $51n^4$
　responsible body: meaning $9n^1$
　secondary. *See* SECONDARY SCHOOL
　staffing of. *See* SCHOOL STAFF
　trustees of $1303n^7$
　types 91
　year, regulations as to duration of 459

SCHOOL ADMISSION
　appeals—
　　excluded children, in relation to 252
　　governing body's right to appeal 252
　　parents, arrangements for 251
　　sixth form children, arrangements
　　　for 251
　charges for—
　　allowed, where 334
　　prohibition on 334
　circumstances preventing 224
　code for—
　　approval 226
　　issue 225
　　making of 226
　　revision 225
　compulsory school age, children under
　　257
　direction to admit child to specified
　　school—
　　local authority, by—
　　　conditions to be satisfied 253
　　　generally 253
　　　governing body's response 254
　　　looked after child—
　　　　England, in 255
　　　　Wales, in 256
　　　power to give 253
　　　procedure for giving 254
　　　suitable education: meaning $253n^7$
　discrimination in relation to 233
　England, arrangements in—
　　adjudicator—
　　　decisions of—
　　　　binding nature of 242
　　　　matters relating to 242
　　　　regulations as to 242
　　　functions 241
　　　objections referred to 240
　　　reports by local authorities to 245
　　　variations referred to 238
　　co-ordination of 243
　　establishment or expansion,
　　　restriction or alteration
　　　following 239

SCHOOL INSPECTION
(ENGLAND)—*continued*
inspection enactments—
    meaning 1181n[1]
    combined reports under 1181
inspection report, publication of 1166
inspectors—
    appointment 1146
    to whom sent—
        maintained school 1173
        non-maintained school 1174
interim inspection: meaning 1169n[23]
interim statement between inspections—
    meaning 1172
    power to make 1172
local authority, by 1180
maintained schools, report on—
    copies, availability of 1168
    inspection of 1168
    local authority, measures to be taken
        by 1169
    opinion stated in 1167
    to whom sent 1168
non-maintained schools, report on—
    inspection and availability of 1170
    proprietor's statement in response to
        1171
    to whom sent 1170
obstruction, offence 1162, 1165
Ofsted. *See* OFSTED
parents, duty to notify 1163
prescribed intervals—
    duty to inspect at 1162
    duty to notify parents 1163
    views, duty to have regard to 1164
religious education, of. *See under*
    RELIGIOUS EDUCATION (inspection
    of)
reports—
    combined 1143, 1181
    contents 1162
    duty to compile 1162
    maintained school, on. *See* maintained
        schools, report on *above*
    opinion stated in 1167
    significant improvement, whether
        required 1167n[4]
    special measures, whether required
        1167
school causing or having caused
    concern, where 1167
Secretary of State requesting 1165
significant improvement required,
    circumstances for 1167n[4]
special measures required, circumstances
    for 1167n[3]

SCHOOL INSPECTION
(ENGLAND)—*continued*
views to be regarded 1164

SCHOOL INSPECTION (WALES)
Chief Inspector. *See* HER MAJESTY'S
    CHIEF INSPECTOR OF EDUCATION
    AND TRAINING IN WALES
closing school—
    meaning 1162n[16]
    exemption for
combined report 1206
consultation with appropriate authority
    prior to 1183
entry rights 1188
exclusion from provisions 1182
frequency 1182n[3]
inspection of documents etc 1188
inspection report. *See* report *below*
inspection team—
    meaning 1184
    composition, determining 1184
    enrolment of persons to act as 1185
    generally 1184
    inspector's duties as to 1184
    obstruction, offence 1188
    qualification for membership of 1184
Inspectorate—
    inspection by member of 1191
    report by member of 1193
inspectors—
    appointment 1148, 1149
    entry and inspection rights 1188
    obstruction, offence 1153, 1188
    registration, need for. *See* registered
        inspector *below*
    replacement during course of
        inspection 1189
    rights 1153
    terms and conditions, service in
        accordance with 1148
    See also inspection team *above*
length of 1194
local authority, by—
    maintained school, power to inspect
        for specific purpose 1205
    provision of inspection services by
        1204
    school inspection service: meaning
        1204n[3]
maintained school—
    causing concern, duty to notify 1195
    statement by appropriate authority in
        relation to 1197
    statement by local authority 1198
    to whom report sent 1196

SCHOOL LAND—*continued*
  disposal—*continued*
    foundation, voluntary or foundation
      special schools, of—
      England, in. *See* England,
        foundation, voluntary or
        foundation special schools in
        above
      Wales, in. *See* Wales, foundation or
        voluntary schools in *below*
    local authority, by—
      Local Government Act 1972,
        under 1302
      restrictions on 1302
      short tenancy, by way of 1302n[5]
      voluntary aided school, belonging
        to 1303
    playing fields in England, control of
      disposal 1326
    proceeds of disposal: meaning 1303n[7]
    voluntary aided school, belonging to
      1303
    Wales, foundation or voluntary
      schools in—
      foundation body, by 1314
      governing body, by 1313
      new school, local authority
        requiring land for 1319
      trustees of foundation schools—
        change of use of land by 1316,
          1318
        disposal by 1315, 1317
      trustees of voluntary schools—
        change of use of land by 1318
        disposal by 1317
  playing fields in England, control of
    disposal or change in use 1326
  property transfers, procedure for—
    Education Reform Act 1988, under—
      construction of agreements 1337
      division or apportionment 1332
      documents of title, right to
        production of 1335
      information to appropriate
        authority, provision of 1339
      powers, exercise of 1331
      property, rights and liabilities,
        identification of—
        agreement as to 1333
        duty as to 1333
        executed transfer agreement,
          provision of 1333
        procedure 1333
        proof of title by certificate 1336
        resolution of disputes as to 1334

SCHOOL LAND—*continued*
  property transfers, procedure
    for—*continued*
    Education Reform Act 1988,
      under—*continued*
      transferor authority: meaning
        1332n[4]
      vesting provisions, third parties
        affected by 1338
    from grant-maintained schools,
      transfer on 1 September 1999
      1340
    generally 1330
    Secretary of State's responsibility for
      1330, 1331
    Welsh Ministers' responsibility for
      1330, 1331
SCHOOL MEAL
  charges for 486
  drinking water, provision of 492
  free—
    determining eligibility for 491
    duty to provide 486
    eligibility, statutory provisions 491n[12]
    universal infant 78, 352
  governing body—
    duties 487
    provision of meals, functions as to
      490
    transfer of functions to 487
  local authority functions 486
  milk, provision of 486
  non-maintained schools, at 489
  nutritional standards or requirements
    492
  provision of 486
  requirements as to 492
  school lunch: meaning 486n[10]
  school lunches obligations: meaning
    486n[46]
  tax and social security matters, supply
    of information relating to 491
  Wales, in—
    free breakfasts 493
    healthy eating and drinking,
      promotion of 488
SCHOOL PLAYING FIELD
  meaning 1326n[1]
  disposal or change in use, control of
    1326
  prescribed standards, relaxation 1345
SCHOOL PREMISES. *See also* SCHOOL
    LAND; SCHOOL SITE
  additional buildings, relaxation of
    prescribed standards 1345
  alteration, approval 1346

SPECIAL EDUCATIONAL NEEDS AND
   DISABILITY TRIBUNAL—*continued*
establishment 979
SPECIAL EDUCATIONAL NEEDS
   TRIBUNAL FOR WALES
  chairman's panel—
    eligibility for appointment to 1034n[5]
    generally 1034
    holding and vacating office 1034n[5]
    reappointment 1034n[5]
  constitution 1034
  generally 1034
  jurisdiction 1037
  lay panel 1024
  proceedings, regulations as to 1035
  regulations as to 1034, 1035
  remuneration and allowances 1034
  Upper Tribunal, appeal to 1036
SPECIAL SCHOOL
  meaning 91
  absence from, regulations as to 459
  admission arrangements 257
  regulations as to duration of school day,
    year etc 459
  special educational provision by. *See*
    under SPECIAL EDUCATIONAL NEEDS
    AND DISABILITIES (England, in;
    Wales, in)
SPECIALIST SCHOOLS PROGRAMME
  functions of 100
STUDENT
  meaning 67n[8]
  block release, on 651n[4]
  complaints by—
    judicial review 1089
    statutory scheme. *See* statutory
      complaints scheme *below*
  contractual relationship with university
    1089
  day release, on 651n[4]
  financial support—
    awards—
      discretionary 1110
      eligibility rules, power to make
        1110
      students not connected with UK,
        power to charge higher fees
        1111
    former legislation, continuing effect
      1095
    functions relating to—
      appeals as to transfer or delegation
        of 1100
      delegation 1099
      transfer 1098
    information in connection with 1102

STUDENT—*continued*
  financial support—*continued*
    loan. *See* STUDENT LOAN
    provision of 1096
    regulations as to provision of 1096
    Scottish institutions, parity of
      provision as to 1103
    statutory framework 1095
    students not connected with UK,
      power to charge higher fees 1111
  full-time: meaning 651n[1]
  higher education institution, legal
    relationship with 1089
  learning difficulty, with 568n[6]
  legal relationship with university 1089
  loan. *See* STUDENT LOAN
  open or distance learning: meaning
    651n[4]
  sandwich course, on 651n[4]
  scholarship. *See* SCHOLARSHIP
  status 723
  statutory complaints scheme—
    academic judgment, matters of
      1090n[7]
    conditions to be met by 1092
    court proceedings, treatment as 1090
    eligibility 1089
    interested parties: meaning 1091n[13]
    introduction 1089
    operator—
      conditions to be met by 1092
      designated—
        meaning 1091n[4]
        duties 1093
      designation—
        duration of 1094
        power to designate 1091
        procedure for designating 1091
        termination, procedure on 1094
    qualifying complaint—
      meaning 1090
      parties to 1092n[12]
      reviewer 1092n[14]
    review of complaint under 1090
    visitor's jurisdiction, restriction on
      1090
  union. *See* STUDENTS' UNION
STUDENT FEES
  England, in—
    conditions, Secretary of State's duty to
      impose 717
    Director of Fair Access to Education,
      functions of 715
    plan—
      approval 719
      basic amount in 717n[14]

STUDENT FEES—*continued*
England, in—*continued*
plan—*continued*
content 718
duration 719
enforcement 720
higher amount in 717n^{14}
variation 719
qualifying course 717n^{10}
qualifying fees 717n^{11}
Wales, in—
fee and access plans, code for
institutions with 722
generally 721
statutory authority 721

STUDENT INFORMATION
meaning 72n^4
duty to provide 72

STUDENT LOAN
meaning 1105n^2, 1109n^2
information in connection with 1101
interest on 1096n^{18}
recovery of—
adjustment of arrangements for 1104
arrangements for 1097
Secretary of State's powers 1104n^{11}
regulations as to 1096
requirements attached to 1096n^{18}
sale of—
onward 1106
repayment to loan purchaser 1108
transfer arrangements. *See* transfer
arrangements *below*
Secretary of State's power to repay or
extinguish 1095
student loans scheme: meaning 1101n^5
transfer arrangements—
further: meaning 1106n^3
power to make 1105
report about 1107
Welsh Ministers, by 1109

STUDENTS' UNION
meaning 1115
accountability of union for finances
1117
applicable establishments 1116
associations of 1115
fair and democratic manner, union to
operate in 1117
freedom of speech 6
governing bodies, duties of—
affiliations of unions, as to 1122
appointment, election and tenure of
officers, as to 1120

STUDENTS' UNION—*continued*
governing bodies, duties of—*continued*
charities, publication of restrictions
on union activities arising under
law of 1126
codes of practice, duty to prepare
1124
complaints, as to 1123
constitution, as to 1118
financial affairs, as to 1121
freedom of speech, publication of
provisions safeguarding 1125
general duty 1117
right not to join, as to 1119
statutory authority for 1115

STUDIO SCHOOL
complaint against 546
generally 368

SUNDAY SCHOOL
maintained school, pupil at, no
requirement to attend 931

SUPPORT SERVICES
inspection of—
England, for young people in 1287
Wales, for young people in 1288

TEACHER. *See also* SCHOOL STAFF
alleged sexual misconduct, disclosure of
information 3n^{13}
benefits. *See* pensions and benefits
below
certificated—
meaning 1084n^2
deferred annuity 1084
disablement allowance 1084
pension scheme for 1084
statutory pension provisions
applicable to 1084
superannuation allowance 1084
conduct, regulation of—
England, in. *See* NATIONAL COLLEGE
FOR TEACHING AND LEADERSHIP
Wales, in 1075
Disclosure and Barring Service 1053
duties towards pupils—
bullying, to prevent 1087
common law 1087
negligent supervision of pupils 1088
standard of care—
generally 1087
gradual raising of, case-law
demonstrating 1087n^3
supervision, in case of 1088n^2
statutory 1087
supervision—
age of child, relevance 1088n^5
judicial consideration of 1088n^1

Words and Phrases

Words in parentheses indicate the context in which the word or phrase is used

ability 258n[3]
academic year—
  (Academies Act 2010) 348n[1]
  (Education Act 1996) 460n[3], 464n[3]
  (Education Act 2002) 88n[3]
  (Education and Skills Act 2008) 382n[6]
  (Learner Travel (Wales) Measure 2008)
    468n[1]
  (Learning and Skills Act 2000) 896n[15]
  (School Standards and Framework
    Act 1998) 248n[3]
academy 91, 345, 346
academy agreement 346
academy arrangements 346
academy financial assistance 346
academy order 350
accessibility plan 11n[6]
accessibility strategy 11n[3]
accountable resources 63n[6]
accreditation condition 831n[11]
Act 1n[13]
act of collective worship 920n[5]
action plan—
  (Education Act 2002) 418n[29]
  (Education and Skills Act 2008) 401
actual guided learning 727n[5], 728n[4],
  838n[7]
adjudicator 147
admission authority 227n[6]
admission forum 227n[3]
admissions decision 12n[13]
adult 810n[5]
advisory services 1221n[23]
agreed syllabus 910n[2]
alternative English apprenticeship 760n[2]
alternative Welsh completion conditions
  767
amendment notice 1006n[10]
appeal arrangements 12n[12, 17]
appeal panel 225n[6]
apprenticeship 820n[15]
apprenticeship agreement 766
apprenticeship certificate 763
apprenticeship offer 777
apprenticeship opportunity 777
apprenticeship training 32n[4], 776n[2]
appropriate education 31n[8]
appropriate national authority 56n[4]
appropriate full-time education or
  training 726

appropriate special educational provision
  549n[7]
approved apprenticeship standards 762
approved English apprenticeship 760
approved English apprenticeship
  agreement 761
area inspection 1265
army school 146n[15]
arranging authority 537n[3]
assess 859n[3]
assessment—
  (Education Act 1996) 335n[6], 995n[3]
  (Further and Higher Education
    Act 1992) 685n[5]
  (Learning and Skills Act 2000) 998n[2]
assessment arrangements—
  (England) 859
  (Wales) 873
assessment function 801n[9]
assessment standards objective 826
assist (Education Act 1996) 51n[5]
assistance 80n[4]
associate member 162n[9]
attainment targets—
  (England) 859
  (Wales) 873
attendance notice 748
authorised officer 523n[1]
authorised staff member 523n[1]
award 685n[4]
awarding body 831n[2]
awareness objective 826
ballot regulations 264n[6]
beginning of the detention 548n[3], 993n[7]
belief 466n[7]
biometric information 69n[4]
biometric recognition system 69n[4]
block release 651n[4]
boarder 31n[19]
budget share 315
bus 471n[2]
capital expenditure—
  (foundation body) 1306n[19]
  (foundation school) 1305n[19], 1307n[34]
  (foundation special school) 1305n[19],
    1307n[34]
  (voluntary aided school) 311n[9], 1303n[4]
  (voluntary school) 1305n[19], 1307n[34]
career 820n[11, 23]
careers adviser 822n[1]
careers education 820n[23]